CONSTITUTIONAL RIGHTS OF PRISONERS

John W. Palmer, J.D.

Stephen E. Palmer, J.D.

Seventh Edition

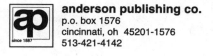
anderson publishing co.
p.o. box 1576
cincinnati, oh 45201-1576
513-421-4142

Constitutional Rights of Prisoners, Seventh Edition

Copyright © 1973, 1977 The W.H. Anderson Company
© 1985, 1991, 1997, 1999, 2004
Anderson Publishing Co.
a member of the LexisNexis Group
2035 Reading Rd.
Cincinnati, OH 45202

Phone 877-374-2919
Web Site www.andersonpublishing.com

Palmer, John W., 1933-
    Constitutional rights of prisoners / John W. Palmer, Stephen E. Palmer. -- 7th ed.
        p. cm.
    Includes index.
    ISBN 1-58360-555-X (pbk.)

Cover design by Tin Box Studio, Inc.

EDITOR Elisabeth Roszmann Ebben
ACQUISITIONS EDITOR Michael C. Braswell

To my family

Preface

Despite the restrictions of the Prison Litigation Reform Act, federal litigation concerning the constitutional rights of prisoners continues unabated. The 2001 case of *Booth v. Churner* and the 2002 case of *Porter v. Nussle* now make it clear that prison inmates, jail inmates, and certain juveniles confined in correctional or detention facilities must exhaust any available administrative remedies before filing a lawsuit in federal court.

The number of confined persons in the United States grows daily. According to numbers released by the Bureau of Justice Statistics during the summer of 2002, the number of adults in the correctional population is increasing. At year-end 2001, nearly 6.6 million people were on probation, in jail or prison, or on parole. This amounts to approximately 3.1 percent of all U.S. adult residents or one in every 32 adults, or a total of 1,406,031, with 1,249,038 under state jurisdiction and 156,933 under federal jurisdiction.

Local jails held or supervised 702,044 persons awaiting trial or serving a sentence at midyear 2001. Approximately 70,800 of these were persons serving their sentence in the community.

Between 1995 and year-end 2001, the incarcerated population grew an average of 3.6 percent annually. Population growth during the 12-month period ending December 31, 2001, was significantly lower in state prisons (up 0.4%) and local jails (up 1.6%) than in previous years, but the federal prison population grew by seven percent.

As indicated by *Hope v. Pelzer*, decided by the Supreme Court in 2002, cruel and unusual punishment through the unjustified use of force remains a constitutional concern.

Religious issues continue to make headlines. According to an Associated Press article, during the summer of 2002 the Kentucky Department of Corrections suspended formal satanic worship services at the Green River Correctional Complex while officials worked to shape a statewide policy on the practice. The inmates had been allowed to hold weekly satanic services as part of the official religious services calendar.

Green River is not alone. Inmates of at least two of Kentucky's other 14 prisons practice satanism. Kentucky did not suspend Wiccan services, which are held at Green River and three other prisons. Wicca practices witchcraft, but sees the divine in every element of nature. Prison authorities do not believe that Wicca compromises the safety of the institutions. The warden at Green

River thought that it was safer to give inmates a specific time and place to worship where they would be monitored, rather than letting them practice among themselves on the prison yard.

Texas, where 150 inmates say they practice satanism, prohibits the services, believing that what satanic doctrine advocates would put Texas prisons at risk, safety-wise, because one of their tenets is revenge—if somebody hurts you, you hurt them back.

The death penalty as practiced in the United States continues to conflict with world opinion. European nations oppose the death penalty and will not cooperate with the United States when the death penalty is involved. Germany also objects to furnishing information about terrorists when they face possible death sentences if prosecuted in the United States. Added to the Appendix in this edition is a decision of the International Court of Justice holding that the United States was in violation of international law when Arizona executed a German national. The U.S. Supreme Court refused to stop the execution. Only time will tell how this will play out.

On June 16, 2003, after this book was sent to the publisher, the U.S. Supreme Court held that Michigan prison regulations placing severe restrictions on visitation were constitutional. The fact that the regulations bear a rational relation to legitimate penological interests was sufficient to sustain them regardless of whether prisoners have a constitutional right of association that has survived incarceration. The restrictions concerned children and prisoners with substance abuse problems (*Overton v. Bazzetta*, 123 S. Ct. 2162 (June 16, 2003)).

Columbus, Ohio
July 1, 2003

John W. Palmer
Stephen E. Palmer

Contents

Chapter 3
Prisoners' Rights to Visitation/Association; Searches   **35**

Chapter 4
Prisoners' Rights to Use of the Mail and Telephone   **51**

Chapter 5
Isolated Confinement—"The Hole" and
Administrative Segregation   **77**

Chapter 6
Religion in Prison   **91**

Chapter 7
Legal Services   **131**

Chapter 10
Right to Rehabilitation Programs, Right to Medical Aid, and Right to Life   **227**

Chapter 11
Civil and Criminal Liabilities of Prison Officials   **263**

An Overview
of the Judicial System 1

Chapter Outline

§ 1.1 Introduction

Law is the set of rules that governs the conduct of individuals and entities in our society. The rules are applied in cases or controversies by the judicial branch of government in the United States. There are three principal sources of laws: federal and state constitutions, federal and state statutes, and the common law, or judge-made law. Taken collectively, these sources establish what is known as the law.

The federal Constitution is the product of a balance of power between the sovereign states in the late eighteenth century. It established the basic form of the federal government of the United States as we know it today.

It divided federal power among three branches of government: the legislative, the executive, and the judicial. Only limited power is granted by the sovereign states to the federal government. All power not expressly or implicitly granted to the federal government is reserved to the states. Congress is given the duty of legislating in areas of national interest, the executive branch carries out the execution of federal laws, and the judicial branch is entrusted with the administration of federal laws and justice. Each branch of government has specifically enumerated functions and powers under the Constitution. Thus, the Constitution is the supreme law of the land, because it provides the basic rules for the functioning of the national government. It also governs the relationships between the states and the federal government, between the sovereign states themselves, and between states and foreign governments.

State constitutions, on the other hand, are limitations on the power of the states. Whereas the federal government can act only in the areas in which the Constitution specifically or implicitly so provides, state governments can legislate in any area, except where state or federal constitutions limit their power. State constitutions also provide for the organization of the state government and for the duties and powers of the members of government that they create.

Federal and state statutes are other sources of law. Congress is entrusted with enacting laws for the national good, while state legislatures provide for the welfare of the citizens of the respective states. The statutes enacted for these purposes become the law, subject only to the limitations of state and federal constitutions. Statutes are enacted to specifically guide the conduct of affected individuals or entities. The courts, both federal and state, apply the rules thus established, which are then enforced by the executive branch of government.

State authorities have increasingly turned to administrative law as a source of prison law. Administrative law is part executive, judicial, and legislative, and has been sometimes referred to as the "headless fourth Branch" of government.[1]

The other major source of law in the United States is a body of rules called the *common law*. Common law, in the sense used here,[2] is the rule of law that has its origins in the courts rather than in the legislatures.

§ 1.2 The American Common Law

The common law is so called because originally it was the law common to all of England. It was the law that the English courts used in deciding cases when there was no legislative enactment.

The common law has never been regarded as static. It is "the wisdom, counsel, experience, and observation of many ages of wise and observing men."[3]

The common law for many centuries was oral and there were no written reports of judicial decisions. Thus, it was often known as the "unwritten law." With the practice of reporting decisions,[4] the written opinions of the judges in deciding actual cases provided a starting point in determining the legal principles applicable to new factual situations that faced the courts. The "old" law was applied when the facts of a "new" case were the same as the facts of the "old" case. If the facts were different, a new rule often developed.

The English common law was transplanted to America through English colonization. The charters of colonies provided for the protection of the rights of free men according to the laws of England.[5] Several state constitutions, such as those of Massachusetts, New York, New Jersey, and Maryland specifically adopted the English common law as the law in that state except as changed by the state statutes.[6] Other state statutes and court decisions adopted the English common law as the law of the land.[7] Once transplanted, however, American common law was adapted to meet the needs of the American economic and social systems.

---

[1]   *See* Freytag v. Internal Revenue Comm'r, 501 U.S. 868 (1991).

[2]   The term *common law* has many meanings, usually depending upon the context. In its broadest sense, common law refers to the entire Anglo-American system of law, in contrast to the civil law (entirely code-based) systems of most non-English speaking nations. It also can refer to the body of law originating in the courts of common law, as opposed to the law of the courts of equity.

[3]   1 KENT'S COMMENTARIES 472 (12th ed. 1873).

[4]   Some of the first reports were made during the reign of Henry III (1216-1272), with the first volume of reports, called the Year Books, which began in the latter part of the reign of Edward II (1307-1326) and continued until Henry VIII (1509-1547). However, the Year Books were first printed during the reign of James I (1603-1625) and reprinted in 1679. Parts of the Year Books were incorporated into the treatises of the legal scholars of the times, such as Statham, Fitzherbert and Brooke. When the practice of reporting cases for the Year Books was discontinued by the Crown, English lawyers made reports for their own uses. Legal scholars then began to make their commentaries serve the function of the reporter of the common law.

[5]   *The Law in the Massachusetts Bay Colony,* READINGS IN AMERICAN LEGAL HISTORY 101-102 (M. Howe, ed. 1949).

[6]   1 KENT'S COMMENTARIES 472-473 (12th ed. 1873).

[7]   *Id.*

§ 1.2.1 —Equity as Part of the Common Law

At the end of the thirteenth century in England, there were three main court systems: The King's courts (including King's Bench, Common Pleas, and Exchequer), the communal courts of the counties and hundreds, and the ecclesiastical courts. The King's courts administered the King's justice common to all of England (common law); the communal courts and ecclesiastical courts administered specialized justice that was not within the jurisdiction of the King's courts.

To secure access to the King's courts, a person had to procure a "writ" from the King's Chancellor, who was the King's "Secretary of State for all departments whose office was responsible for any writing done in the King's name."[8] A writ was a command from the King to a named person to appear in one of the King's courts to answer a claim. There were certain standardized claims, or forms of action, that could be issued by the Chancellor, although the Chancellor had the authority to frame new writs when the case was similar to cases in which existing writs were issued as a matter of right. For a writ to be valid, it had to follow the rigid patterns set by the common law principles that the King's courts administered. As a result of the rigid rules applied by the King's judges in the common law courts, which had to conform to the writ issued, many people who were wronged were denied adequate relief. It was essentially "no writ, no remedy."

The King, as the source of all justice in England, naturally could fill the void left by the rigidity of the common law. Thus, people could petition the King and his council for redress as a matter of favor, if no relief was available in the common law courts.

The Chancellor, as the King's chief minister and secretary, and keeper of the Great Seal, was delegated the power and authority to grant redress in such cases in the King's name. The Chancellor was generally a cleric, often a bishop. He dispensed the King's justice, also called *equity,* and was strongly influenced by moral and ethical considerations and the justice of the conflict rather than by previous court decisions. The Chancellor became the conscience of the legal system.

The granting of a special favor in a particular case in which no adequate remedy existed at common law became an accepted practice. The relief granted by the Chancellor was popular and much sought after. Once established, relief given by the Chancellor, known as *equitable relief,* became an integral part of the law, standing side by side with the common law, rather than something granted as a favor of the King. It became more than one man could manage, and this led to the establishment of a Court of Chancery (or court of equity). The body of principles of moral justice applied to individual cases developed into rules of equity by subsequent repetition. Thus, a body of court-made law separate from the traditional common law developed—administered by a separate court of equity. The separation of common law courts and courts

---

8   W. GELDART, ELEMENTS OF ENGLISH LAW 23 (6th ed. 1959).

of equity remained until fairly recent times, *e.g.*, 1848 in New York, 1873-1875 in Great Britain. Now, in most states, a single court administers both "law," in the sense of common law, as well as "equity."

Distinctions still remain, however, depending upon whether the relief sought was traditionally administered by common law courts or courts of equity. For example, the right to a jury trial attached only when the claim was recognized by the "law" courts, because a claim in the court of equity was decided by the Chancellor without the aid of a jury. Also, the traditional remedy granted by equity was an order against a person (*i.e.*, an injunction) while the traditional remedy of the common law courts was an order involving property (*i.e.*, damages).

Equity has the power of contempt of court to enforce its orders, because equity relief is directed against the person and not against the person's property. Contempt of court occurs when a person willfully disobeys an order of the court of equity, either in the presence of the court (direct contempt) or when a person obstructs the justice of the court out of the presence of the court (indirect contempt). Thus, one cannot be held in contempt of court for failing to pay a monetary judgment, because that is a judgment at "law." The court can only execute judgment and levy on the property of the defendant.

Equitable relief is discretionary and can only be granted when the remedy at law, or in damages, is inadequate. If monetary damages will adequately compensate a wrong, equitable relief, such as an injunction against future conduct, cannot be obtained.

§ 1.2.2 —The Role of Case Law

As the previous sections indicated, the legal principles applied in a particular case before a court become part of the common law. It takes its place as a part of the body of court-made rules that will form the basis of future decisions.

With the publication of reports of cases contemporaneous with the decisions in England, published cases were at first merely instructive and informative. However, courts began to cite previously decided cases to support their own conclusions, and ever-increasing weight was placed on reported cases. For the past three centuries, the decisions of judges of higher courts have been precedent for later cases.[9] *Precedent* is the decision of a court that furnishes authority for an identical or similar case that arises subsequently. The practice of using past case law as the basis for current decisions is called *stare decisis,* which means "let the decision stand." The use of a case as precedent or authority requires that the exact rule or principle of law, known as the *holding*, be determined from the language of the reported decision. Any reasoning or principle of law in a decision that is not part of the holding, or not essential to the determination of the case, is termed *obiter dictum*, or simply *dictum*, meaning words "spoken by the way."

---

[9]   *Id.* at 6-7.

The precise effect of precedent, or the doctrine of *stare decisis*, depends upon the factual similarity between a prior case and a subsequent controversy. The principle of *stare decisis* rests upon the presumption that a previous court determined the law applicable to a factual situation after reasonable consideration and that it provides authority for later decisions made in similar cases.

The reasons for applying the doctrine of *stare decisis* include: (1) certainty and predictability of the law, which is necessary for the regulation of personal conduct and commerce; (2) growth when new issues arise; (3) equality of application; and (4) respect for the prior judgments of an esteemed legal mind.

As an exposition of the applicable law, the prior decision of a court is binding on that court and the inferior courts (courts lower in the hierarchical judicial structure) of that judicial system. Thus, a decision of the Supreme Court of the United States on questions of federal law is binding on all lower federal courts (courts of appeals and district courts). Likewise, the decisions of the highest court of each state are binding on the inferior state courts. However, a decision of the Supreme Court of Ohio is not precedent for a New York court. The New York court may follow the Ohio precedent voluntarily, due to its persuasiveness, but it is not bound to do so.

However, certain handicaps are present in the doctrine of *stare decisis*, such as hardships resulting from rigidity, illogical distinctions on the facts of a case, and the sheer numbers of reported cases that establish law. Also, the American social and economic systems change with the passage of time. As has been said:

> The life of the law has not been logic: it has been experience. The felt necessities of the time, the prevalent moral and political theories, institutions of public policy, avowed or unconscious, even the prejudices which judges share with their fellow-men, have had a good deal more to do than the syllogism in determining the rules by which men should be governed.[10]

The methods for changing case-made law to meet new demands on the law are *distinguishing* or *overruling* previous cases.

Distinguishing previous cases occurs when later courts confine prior decisions strictly to their facts, and apply a new rule to the facts of the controversy at issue. The effect is to give very limited application to an earlier case.

A court overrules a prior rule of law by finding that it was improperly decided or that the social and economic conditions have changed from the time the prior decision was made. Hence, a new rule of law should apply.

---

[10]   O. HOLMES, THE COMMON LAW 1 (1881).

§ 1.3 The American Court Structure

The court system of the United States is composed of 51 independent court systems. The federal court system and each of the 50 state systems operate within their own judicial spheres.

The states operate their court systems as one of the powers reserved to them by the Tenth Amendment to the United States Constitution. Each state has its own system, with the structure and jurisdiction of the courts established by the state constitution and statutes. However, all court structures include two types of courts: *trial courts* and *appellate courts*.

State trial courts generally include courts of *limited jurisdiction* and courts of *general jurisdiction*. The limited jurisdictional courts are the numerous local courts that have the power to hear civil cases involving limited monetary amounts and minor criminal offenses, such as traffic violations. Above the limited jurisdictional courts in the hierarchical structure are the trial courts of general jurisdiction. They generally have the power to hear all civil cases involving any monetary amount greater than that handled by the limited jurisdiction courts.

The functions of the trial court are receiving proper evidence, compiling a record of the evidence introduced, finding disputed facts from the evidence introduced, applying the appropriate law to the facts, and granting appropriate relief. The fact-finding function of a trial can be exercised either by the jury, if the right to jury trial exists and is exercised, or by the judge, who then has two separate and distinct duties: fact-finding and applying the proper law.

Every state has at least one level of appellate courts. The highest appellate court is generally called the *supreme court*, with some states calling it the *court of appeals* (*e.g.*, New York). The supreme court of a state is the "court of last resort" because it is the final, authoritative source of judicial relief in the state court system. In the more populous states, such as California, Florida, Illinois, Ohio, or Texas, there is an intermediate appellate court in the state court system, generally called a *court of appeals*. These courts handle appeals from the trial courts and their decisions, in turn, are reviewable by the supreme court of the state. The function of the appellate courts is to review the decisions of trial courts, or lower-level appellate courts, for errors that might have prejudiced the rights of a party, such as errors in procedure or errors in applying the proper rule of law to the facts established by the evidence. The factual findings of the trial court are generally final and, therefore, the appellate courts do not receive any evidence when reviewing a case, but use the record of the trial court. Whenever there was a dispute at the trial level as to the existence of a particular fact, the decision of the trier of fact (either the judge or jury) is binding upon the appellate court, and the appellate court cannot overturn the trial court's factual findings unless they are clearly erroneous.

The federal court system was created by the Constitution, which expressly provided for the Supreme Court and authorized Congress to create inferior federal courts. As a result of this grant of power to Congress, federal statutes provide for 94 federal trial courts (district courts) and 13 intermediate appellate courts (courts of appeals).

The types of cases that a federal court can adjudicate are limited; that is, the federal courts have *limited jurisdiction*. The limited jurisdiction of the federal courts is a result of the structure of our federal government. The sovereign states have granted (to the federal government through the Constitution) certain powers to be exercised for the common good, among them the judicial power as specified. The federal judicial power extends to cases arising under the Constitution, federal laws or treaties, all cases affecting ambassadors, public ministers and consuls, admiralty and maritime cases, controversies in which the United States is a party, controversies between states, between a state and a citizen of another state, between citizens of the same state claiming lands under grants from different states, and in cases between a state or citizen of a state and foreign countries, their citizens, or subjects.[11]

In order for a case to be heard in a federal court, it must fall under one of these categories. The greatest number of federal cases are those arising under the Constitution, cases based upon federal statutory rights, and cases between citizens of different states, referred to as "diversity of citizenship" cases. Cases arising under the Constitution are those that enforce the provisions of the Constitution; that is, a right created by the Constitution itself, such as the First Amendment freedom of speech provisions. Controversies arising under federal laws are cases in which a federal statute has specifically provided a procedure for judicial relief, such as the various Civil Rights Acts.

Diversity of citizenship cases are those in which the cause of action, or right to seek judicial relief, arises under state law, either statutory or common, but is between citizens of different states. In a diversity case, the federal court applies state law. The federal court merely provides a neutral forum for resolving the dispute. Congress has placed a statutory limit on diversity cases by requiring that the controversy involve an amount in excess of $75,000. This was done to limit the number of cases using the federal court system at the expense of the state court systems, and the amount has increased over the years. In 1972, the amount was $10,000.

The federal district courts' jurisdictional areas (in a geographical sense) are the result of a division of the nation into 94 judicial districts by population. For example, New York is divided into four districts, while in less populated states, such as Maine or Arizona, the district encompasses the entire state.

The federal district court is a trial court for federal criminal prosecutions and civil actions, with its function being the same as a state trial court. It also has the power to review the decisions of certain federal administrative agencies.

Federal statutes have also created several specialty courts that have the same functions as a district court, but limit the type of cases heard to one subject, such as tax, patents, or military appeals. These courts are created to handle a highly specialized subject so that the judges of the courts will have exceptional knowledge of the complex subject involved.

---

[11] U.S. CONST. art. III, § 2.

The federal courts of appeals are the intermediate appellate courts. There are 13 circuits, dividing the country geographically according to the volume of the judicial caseload. One circuit is provided exclusively for the District of Columbia, due to the heavy volume of appeals from federal administrative agencies. The Federal Court of Appeals hears cases involving patents, copyrights, trademarks, and cases from the Court of Claims and Court of International Trade. The function of the federal courts of appeals is similar to that of a state court of appeals. These courts review the decisions of the federal district courts and some federal administrative agencies.

The United States Supreme Court serves as the court of last resort for cases from the federal system. The Supreme Court is the ultimate interpreter of the Constitution and federal statutes. It reviews the decisions of the courts of appeals, and some direct appeals from district courts. The Supreme Court also reviews the decisions of state courts involving matters of federal constitutional rights when the case has been finally adjudicated in the state court system. Besides its appellate function, the Court has original jurisdiction in suits in which a state is a party and in controversies involving ambassadors, ministers, and consuls.[12]

Cases are brought to the Supreme Court for consideration by two methods: (1) appeal as of right, and (2) discretion of the court. The appeals of right are appeals that are expressly provided for by statute. The court grants discretionary review by issuing a *writ of certiorari,* which is an order to review the action of an inferior court. The court grants few petitions for the writ of certiorari. Less than five percent of the petitions submitted are granted.[13]

§ 1.3.1   The Trial

In the federal system, the parties to a lawsuit for damages are entitled to a jury trial under the Seventh Amendment.[14] The Seventh Amendment applies to all civil rights actions for damages.

However, if the lawsuit is in *equity,* asking for injunctive and similar relief, the Seventh Amendment does not apply and the judge decides all factual issues. There is no trial by jury in equity.

A civil suit begins by the filing of a **complaint**. The defendant then files an **answer** or a **motion to dismiss** on the grounds that the complaint filed by the plaintiff does not constitute a legal wrong or that the defendant is protected by a privilege.

After an answer is filed, the parties begin the **discovery** process. Discovery may take the form of **depositions**, in which parties and witnesses are examined under oath in a somewhat informal setting; **interrogatories**, in which parties are asked to provide statements under oath or provide docu-

---

[12]   *Id.*
[13]   D. Karlen, The Citizen in Court 23 (1964).
[14]   In criminal cases, an accused is entitled to trial by jury under the Sixth Amendment.

ments; or **requests for admissions**, in which parties are asked to admit to certain facts or to the genuineness of documents. Interrogatories and requests for admissions can only be used against parties to the lawsuit. They may not be used with witnesses who are not parties to the suit.

At any time during the proceedings, but generally before the trial begins, either party can file a **motion for summary judgment,** alleging that there are no substantive facts in dispute and that the party filing the motion is entitled to judgment as a matter of law. Motions for summary judgment are supported by the pleadings, written statements under oath called **affidavits**, and other evidence obtained through the discovery process

After all pretrial motions and procedures are finished, the jury phase of the trial begins. After selecting a jury through *voir dire* of a jury panel and the opening statements by the parties, evidence is presented. Prior to the admission of any evidence, the opposing party has the right to object to particular methods of proof. These questions concerning the admissibility of evidence are for the judge alone to decide, because they involve matters of *law* as distinguished from matters of *fact,* which are for the jury to decide.

Evidence may take several forms:

> **Testimony**: A person, called a *witness*, tells the court what he or she saw, heard, did, or experienced in relation to the incident in question.

> **Documents**: Letters, notes, deeds, bills, receipts, etc. that provide information about the case.

> **Physical Evidence**: Tangible items, such as weapons, drugs, and clothing, that can provide clues to the facts.

> **Expert Testimony**: A professional person, someone not involved in the incident, gives medical, scientific, or similar expert instruction to help the trier of fact understand the evidence presented.

At the end of the plaintiff's case, the defendant will normally make a **motion for a directed verdict**. The judge will then determine whether the plaintiff has presented sufficient evidence to support each and every element of his or her claim. The judge does not weigh the evidence; that is for the jury. However, if there is a total failure of proof on a substantive issue in the case, the motion will be granted and the lawsuit is over. If the judge overrules the motion, the case proceeds and the defense begins its case.

When all of the evidence has been presented, both sides make motions for a directed verdict. If there are any substantive facts in dispute, the judge will overrule the motion and the case will then be submitted to the jury.

Prior to jury deliberations, lawyers for the parties make final arguments, summarizing the evidence that is most favorable to their side. The judge then instructs the jury on the law to be applied to the facts they find to be true and the jury retires to deliberate. When the jury returns, it may return a verdict for either side, decide the amount of damages, if applicable, or be "hung" and unable to reach a verdict. In this event, the trial begins anew with a different jury at a later date.

The Burden of Proof

In every lawsuit, one or more parties have what is known as the **burden of proof**.

In a civil case, the plaintiff has the burden of proof. Plaintiffs must convince the factfinder that they have proved their case **by a preponderance of the evidence**. This means that their proof is slightly more convincing than the defendant's. Some refer to this as meaning that 51 percent or more of the evidence supports the plaintiff's side, or that the plaintiff's theory is "more probable than not."

In a criminal case, the burden of proof is much more strict, because the defendant will be punished if the prosecutor proves the state's case. Therefore, the prosecutor must convince the judge or jury **beyond a reasonable doubt** that the accused committed the crime.

In an equity case, the facts are decided by the judge alone. In such cases, the burden of proof is **clear and convincing**, a standard that falls approximately halfway between the civil and criminal standards.

In civil and criminal trials, when the jury decides who wins, the judge then enters a verdict.

§ 1.3.2   The Appeal

Parties may appeal on questions of law, not questions of fact. Appeals might involve issues concerning the admission of evidence, instructions of the judge to the jury, or whether motions made by either of the parties were properly decided.

In principle, an appeal can be made only from a final judgment. However, in certain circumstances, during the trial process itself, a party who loses a motion may file an **interlocutory appeal** with an appellate court. The trial process stops when there is an interlocutory appeal and resumes when the court of appeals has ruled on the motion.

Generally, there is an automatic right to one appeal. After that, appeals to higher courts are discretionary.

§ 1.4 Anatomy of a Case

Case law is a major source of law in a common law system of jurisprudence. A great amount of a lawyer's time is spent reading and studying cases to determine the rule of law on a particular point. It is appropriate, then, to briefly describe the anatomy of a decision.

A *case* is the published report of an opinion indicating the decision of a court on a controversy heard by the reporting court. Generally, only appellate court decisions are published on a national basis, except for decisions of the federal district courts. The report contains the *opinion of the court,* which is the decision of the court as decided by a numerical majority of the tribunal (court) making the decision. The report is written by a judge of the court who expresses the opinion for the court. If any judge of the court (when more than one judge hears the controversy) disagrees with the majority decision, he or she may write a separate opinion, called a *dissenting opinion,* explaining his or her reasons for holding a view that is different from the majority opinion of the court. A judge may also agree with the results of the decision of the court, but for different or additional reasons not shared by the majority of the court. This opinion is called a *concurring opinion.*

When the opinion, or opinions, are made public, they are kept by the clerk of the court and accumulated along with other opinions until published in a volume. The volumes are numbered consecutively by the clerk; they are called *state reports* when they involve state court decisions. West Publishing Company also publishes the appellate decisions in a series of reports (called the National Reporter System) that contain the decisions of all state and federal courts. West groups the state jurisdictions geographically.

§ 1.4.1 —Citations

In order to find a particular opinion among the staggering number of reported decisions, a reference system has developed, called *citations.* The following is an example of a citation, or *cite,* to a state court opinion: *Ford Motor Co. v. London,* 217 Tenn. 400, 398 S.W.2d 240 (1966). The citation indicates the following information: (1) The names of the parties, generally with the plaintiff first **(Ford Motor Co.)** and the defendant second **(London)**; (2) the volume of the state reporter where the opinion is found **(217)**; (3) the state reporter system **(Tenn.)**; (4) the page in the state reporter system volume where the opinion begins **(400)**. Then listed is the exact same case in the West National Reporter system: (5) the volume of the West Reporter system **(398)**; (6) the West Reporter where the opinion is found **(S.W.2d)**; (7) the page in the West Reporter where the opinion begins **(240)**; and (8) the date that the court decided the case **(1966)**. In California and New York, the decisions of the state courts may appear in two West Reporters, the regional reporter (Pacific and North Eastern, respectively) and a special supplement reporter that deals exclusively with the cases of that particular state (California Reporter and New York Supplement). An example of a citation of a case from New York is: *Greenburg v. Lorenz*, 9 N.Y.2d 195, 196 N.E.2d 430, 213 N.Y.S.2d 39 (1966).

A citation to a case from a federal district court appears as: *Landman v. Royster*, 333 F. Supp. 621 (E.D. Va. 1971). The citation gives the following information about the case: (1) The parties, plaintiff first and defendant second (**Landman v. Royster**); (2) the volume of the West Federal Reporter where the opinion appears (**333**); (3) the West Reporter that publishes the case (**F. Supp.**); (4) the page in the reporter where the opinion begins (**621**); (5) the court that decided the case (**E.D. Va.**), the federal district court for the Eastern District of Virginia; and (6) the date of the decision (**1971**). A citation to a federal court of appeals, for example, *Jackson v. Bishop*, 404 F.2d 571 (8th Cir. 1968), gives the same information—parties, volume, reporter, page, court, and date.

The symbol "2d" or "3d" appearing in many citations indicates that the reporter system has begun a second or third series.

The citation may also give a history of the case. Such history is only included in the citation if it is significant to the point of law for which the case is cited. The signals of citation used to indicate history are:

> *aff'd*—the decision of the court was upheld on appeal.

> *rev'd*—the decision of the court was overruled on appeal.

> *aff'd (or rev 'd) on other grounds*—the rule of law cited from the case was unaffected by a subsequent affirmation (or overruling) of the court's decision.

> *cert. denied (or granted)*—petition for writ of certiorari, or grant of discretionary review of an inferior court's decision, was denied (or granted).

> *modified*—the decision of a case was modified by a reviewing court.

> *sub nom.*—the names of the parties of the appellate decision differ from the names of the lower court decisions.

The reader may also find several citations that read [44 U.S.L.W. 1000] or [19 Cr. L. 2133]. These represent publications that provide judicial decisions to the public before they are printed in the publications mentioned earlier. These publications serve to keep the public current on the most recent decisions from the judiciary. U.S.L.W. stands for *United States Law Week* and Cr. L. is an abbreviation for *Criminal Law Reporter.*

Citations increasingly include Internet citations. Numerous databases that contain cases, statutes, administrative regulations, and articles, both domestic and foreign, are available via the World Wide Web.[1]

---

[1]   For example, a district court decision may also be included in the citation as: "2002 U.S. Dist. LEXIS ____."

§ 1.5 Conclusion

The first chapter has provided an overview of the American judicial system, including common law, equity, the role of case law, the American court structure, and an illustrative case anatomy. To derive the most benefit from this chapter, the reader should review key concepts, giving special attention to the significant terms used by courts. All are essential to understanding the legal system in which we function.

THE WEST NATIONAL REPORTER SYSTEM
AND RESPECTIVE JURISDICTIONS

Atlantic (A.)

Connecticut	New Jersey
Delaware	Pennsylvania
Maine	Rhode Island
Maryland	Vermont
New Hampshire	
District of Columbia	
(Municipal Court of Appeals)	

North Eastern (N.E.)

Illinois	New York
Indiana	Ohio
Massachusetts	

Southern (So.)

Alabama	Louisiana
Florida	Mississippi

West's California Reporter (Cal.)

California Supreme Court
District Courts of Appeal
Superior Court, Appellate Department

Pacific (P.)

Alaska	Montana
Arizona	Nevada
California	New Mexico
(Sup. Ct. only)	Oklahoma
Colorado	Oregon
Hawaii	Utah
Idaho	Washington
Kansas	Wyoming

South Eastern (S.E.)

Georgia	Virginia
North Carolina	West Virginia
South Carolina	

South Western (S.W.)

Arkansas	Tennessee
Kentucky	Texas
Missouri	

New York Supplement (N.Y.S.)

Court of Appeals
Appellate Division
Miscellaneous

North Western (N.W.)

Iowa	Nebraska	Wisconsin
Michigan	North Dakota	
Minnesota	South Dakota	

Federal Supplement (F. Supp.)

U S. District Courts
U.S. Customs Courts

Federal Rules Decisions (F.R.D.)

U.S. District Courts

Federal (F.)

U.S. Court of Appeals
Federal Court of Appeals

U.S. Supreme Court* (S. Ct.)

*Supreme Court decisions are also reported by the government, cited as U.S., and reported by Lawyers Co-Operative Publishing Co., cited as L. Ed.

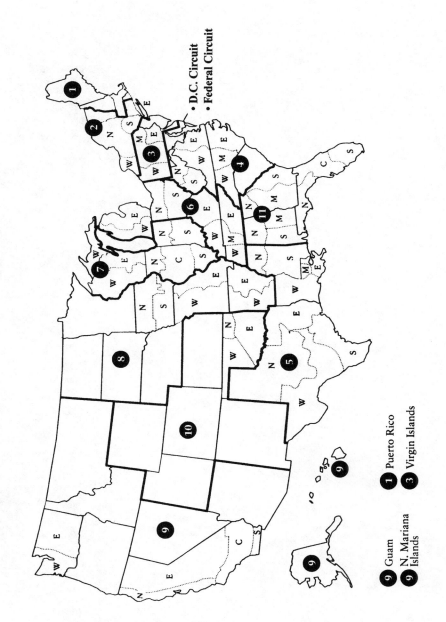

Geographical Boundaries of U.S. Courts of Appeals and District Courts

Use of Force; Use of Corporal Punishment to Enforce Prison Discipline 2

Chapter Outline

§ 2.1 Introduction

As the legal custodians of large numbers of men, including many who are being confined for crimes of violence, prison staffs are often confronted with situations in which it is necessary to use force against an inmate or a group of inmates. Force, in this connection, means any physical force directed toward another, either by direct physical contact or by the use of a weapon such as tear gas, chemical mace, a billy club, or a firearm.

Earlier in our jurisprudential history, all excessive force claims were analyzed under a single substantive due process standard. Quite apart from any specific provision of the Bill of Rights, application of excessive force was viewed in any context as a deprivation of substantive due process when the government official's conduct "shocked the conscience."[1]

These principles were changed by *Graham v. Connor*.[2] In *Graham*, the Supreme Court turned away from the use of the "shocks the conscience" standard applicable to all excessive force claims brought under the Civil Rights Act.[3] It ruled instead that excessive force claims must be examined under the standard applicable to the specific constitutional right allegedly violated, which in most instances will be the Fourth or Eighth Amendment—the main sources of individual protection under the Constitution against physically abusive official conduct. *Graham* arose in the context of a person's seizure by police officers. The excessive force claim was governed by Fourth Amendment objective reasonableness standards.

Graham called into question whether Fourteenth Amendment substantive due process survived as a source of a federal right to be free from excessive force. One reading of *Graham* suggested that such protection did not survive, and that the relatively unusual excessive force cases falling beyond the ambit of the Fourth and Eighth Amendments are redressable only by recourse to state

---

[1]   Johnson v. Glick, 481 F.2d 1028, 1032-1033 (2d Cir.), *cert. denied,* 414 U.S. 1033 (1973).
[2]   490 U.S. 386 (1989).
[3]   42 U.S.C. § 1983; *See* Chapter 11.

tort law. Other readings suggest that *Graham* leaves the law untouched in that narrow area, and in the non-seizure, non-prisoner context, the substantive due process right to be free from excessive force is alive and well.[4]

Every person, including an incarcerated felon, has the right to be free from the fear of offensive bodily contact and to be free from actual offensive bodily contact. Any person who violates either of these rights can be held liable, both civilly and criminally, unless such conduct is privileged. It is merely a question of finding the right theory and the right court.

It has generally been recognized that prison officials are privileged to use force against inmates in five situations. These situations are: (1) self-defense; (2) defense of third persons; (3) enforcement of prison rules and regulations; (4) prevention of escape; and (5) prevention of crime.

§ 2.2 Degree of Force Permitted

The situations (listed above) in which a prison official is justified in using force are relatively easy to recognize. However, the degree of force that may be used in these situations is not as clear. The courts speak of the justification of using "reasonable" force in a given situation to control the inmate. The factual elements in each case determine whether the force used was excessive, and thus not privileged.

The controlling factual elements are the degree of force used by the inmate, the inmate's possession or nonpossession of a deadly weapon, the reasonable perception on the part of the correctional officer that he or a third person is in danger of death or serious bodily harm, and the means of force available to the officer.

When discussing the amount of force that is legally permissible, it is helpful to distinguish deadly force and nondeadly force. "Deadly force" may be defined as force that will likely cause death or serious bodily harm. Knives and firearms are always considered instruments of deadly force. "Nondeadly" force is force that will normally cause neither death nor serious bodily harm. The use of fists, judo holds, chemical mace, and tear gas are examples of nondeadly force.

---

4   *See* Bella v. Chamberlain, 24 F.3d 1251, 1257 (10th Cir. 1994) ("Without deciding the issue, we assume that excessive force claims arising outside the context of a seizure still may be analyzed under substantive due process principles."), *cert. denied*, 513 U.S. 1109 (1995); Wilson v. Northcutt, 987 F.2d 719, 722 (11th Cir. 1993) (holding, as a matter of first impression in the circuit, that a Fourteenth Amendment excessive force claim survives *Graham* when there is no seizure); Landol-Rivera v. Cruz Cosme, 906 F.2d 791, 796 (1st Cir. 1990) ("We assume that claims of excessive force outside the context of a seizure still may be analyzed under substantive due process principles."); Braley v. City of Pontiac, 906 F.2d 220, 225 n.5 (6th Cir. 1990) (noting that *Graham* "calls into question the continued existence of this 'species' of substantive due process, at least insofar as it exists apart from any specific of the Bill of Rights"); Pleasant v. Zamieski, 895 F.2d 272, 276 n.2 (6th Cir.) (despite *Graham's* broad phasing, presumably substantive due process analysis is preserved for non-seizure excessive force claims), *cert. denied*, 498 U.S. 851 (1990).

Employing certain methods of applying force cannot, in the abstract, be categorized as either the use of deadly or nondeadly force. Certain factual elements of the case, primarily the area of the body struck, must be considered. For example, a blow to the head from a billy club is likely to cause death or serious bodily harm, and thus must be regarded as the use of deadly force. However, a blow to the knees would probably constitute nondeadly force.

Our society places great value on human life and on the right of every person to be free from offensive physical contact by another. Consequently, the use of force by one individual against another is frowned upon. For this reason, force is permissible only when all non-force alternatives have failed.

Uncertainties in the law were put to rest in *Hudson v. McMillian.*[5] A prison inmate testified that the minor bruises, facial swelling, loosened teeth, and cracked dental plate he suffered were the result of a beating by correctional officers. He testified that the beating took place while he was handcuffed and shackled following an argument with one of the officers, and that a supervisor on duty watched the beating, but merely told the officers "not to have too much fun." The district court found that the officers used force when there was no need to do so, and that the supervisor expressly condoned their actions. The court ruled that they had violated the Eighth Amendment's prohibition of cruel and unusual punishments, and awarded damages to the inmate. The Court of Appeals reversed, holding, among other things, that inmates alleging the use of excessive force in violation of the Eighth Amendment must prove "significant injury" and that the inmate in *Hudson* could not prevail because his injuries were "minor" and required no medical attention.

The United States Supreme Court reversed. It held that the use of excessive physical force against a prisoner may constitute cruel and unusual punishment even though the inmate does not suffer serious injury.

Whenever prison officials are accused of using excessive physical force constituting "the unnecessary and wanton infliction of pain" that violates the cruel and unusual punishments clause, the core judicial inquiry is that set out in *Whitley v. Albers*—whether the force used was applied in a good faith effort to maintain or restore discipline, or maliciously and sadistically to cause harm. The extension of *Whitley*'s application of the "unnecessary and wanton infliction of pain" standard to all allegations of force, whether the prison disturbance is a riot or a lesser disruption, worked no innovation.

Under the *Whitley* approach, the extent of injury suffered by an inmate is one of the factors to be considered in determining whether the use of force is wanton and unnecessary. The absence of serious injury is relevant to, but does not end, the Eighth Amendment inquiry. There was no merit to the assertion that a significant injury requirement is mandated by what the Supreme Court termed, in *Wilson v. Seiter,*[6] as the "objective component" of Eighth Amendment analysis: namely, whether the alleged wrongdoing was objectively

---

[5]   Hudson v. McMillian, 503 U.S. 1 (1992). *See* §12.6, which specifically addresses conditions-of-confinement issues.

[6]   475 U.S. 312 (1986).

"harmful enough" to establish a constitutional violation. That component is contextual and responsive to the "contemporary standards of decency" test of *Estelle v. Gamble.*[7] In the excessive force context, such standards are always violated when prison officials maliciously and sadistically use force to cause harm, whether or not significant injury is evident. Moreover, although the Eighth Amendment does not reach *de minimis* uses of physical force, provided that such use is not of a sort repugnant to the conscience of mankind, the blows directed at the prisoner were not *de minimis*, and the extent of his injuries provided no basis for dismissal of his claim.

It should be noted that the Supreme Court in *Graham* took no position on the legal argument of the prison officials that the conduct of the guards was isolated, unauthorized, and against prison policy, and therefore beyond the scope of "punishment" prohibited by the Eighth Amendment. This argument was not supported by the record, as the Court of Appeals left intact the lower court's determination that the violence at issue was not an isolated assault. The argument also ignored the finding that a supervisor expressly condoned the use of force.

Overall, the Court in *Graham* made clear that a distinction will be made between Eighth Amendment excessive force cases, Eighth Amendment conditions-of-confinement cases, and Eighth Amendment medical needs cases. A different standard must be applied in each type of case.[8]

In *Al-Jundi v. Mancusi,*[9] the Second Circuit Court of Appeals determined that the *Graham* standard applied to allegations concerning decisions by officials of Attica Prison as to whether, and to what extent, force could be used to recapture portions of the prison that were taken over by prisoners. Thus, if the force used in response to the prisoner takeover did not amount to wanton infliction of pain, then it did not violate the Constitution. However, the court refused to extend the standard to claims that the prison officials failed to make adequate provisions for prisoners' medical needs after the recapture. The court stated that the medical needs issue was one of fact and therefore precluded summary judgment on grounds of qualified immunity.

With respect to pretrial detainees, it is the due process clause that provides the appropriate constitutional basis for determining whether a detention official's use of deliberate force on such a detainee is excessive. According to a Fifth Circuit case,[10] neither the search and seizure clause of the Fourth Amendment, nor the cruel and unusual punishments clause of the Eighth Amendment applies. Both *Bell*[11] and *Graham*[12] reason that the appropriate question under the due process clause is whether the detention official applied force with the

---

[7]   Estelle v. Gamble, 429 U.S. 97 (1976). *See* §10.3 for further discussion of the "deliberate indifference" standard.

[8]   *See* §§ 10.3 and 12.6.

[9]   Al-Jundi v. Mancusi, 926 F.2d 235 (2d Cir.), *cert. denied*, 502 U.S. 861 (1991).

[10]   Valencia v. Wiggins, 981 F.2d 1440 (5th Cir. 1993).

[11]   Bell v. Wolfish, 441 U.S. 520 (1979).

[12]   Graham v. Connor, 490 U.S. 386 (1989).

intent to punish the pretrial detainee. Guided by *Whitley*[13] and *Hudson*[14] with respect to excessive force claims in the context of prison disturbances, the court held that the question is whether force was applied in a good faith effort to maintain or restore discipline, or maliciously and sadistically to cause harm. The focus of this standard is on the detention facility official's subjective intent to punish. In determining such intent, it was pointed out that the trier of fact must include such objective factors as the extent of injuries suffered, the apparent need for the application of force, the degree of force exerted, the threat reasonably perceived by the detention facility official, and the need to act quickly and decisively.

Hudson v. McMillian[15] clarified the standards for determining whether Eighth Amendment violations have occurred. Whenever prison officials are accused of using excessive physical force in violation of the cruel and unusual punishments clause, the core judicial inquiry is whether force was applied in a good faith effort to maintain or restore discipline, or maliciously and sadistically to cause harm. In *Davidson v. Flynn,*[16] correctional officers, who needed to handcuff an inmate being transported to another prison, deliberately applied the handcuffs too tightly in retaliation for his litigiousness. It was held that the inmate's constitutional rights were violated.

See § 11.6 for civil rights cases involving the use of excessive force.

§ 2.3 Self-Defense

Every person has the right to protect him- or herself against an assault by another. Prison officials may use force against an inmate in their own self-defense.[17] Correctional officers may use the degree of force reasonably necessary under the circumstances to protect themselves from the assault and to subdue the inmates.[18] While prison officials are afforded broad discretion in maintaining order, they are not justified in using any amount of force when the threat of disorder has subsided.[19] The extent of such force depends upon the degree of force being used by the inmate, the officers' reasonable perception of injury, and the means of resisting the assault. The test of reasonable force is whether the degree of force used is necessary under the facts and circumstances of the particular case,[20] as illustrated by the two following cases.

In a Maryland case, a fight erupted between five inmates and a number of correctional officers. The inmates received numerous injuries, including severe cuts and bruises and broken bones. One of the officers was hurt so

---

[13]   Whitley v. Albers, 475 U.S. 312 (1986).
[14]   Hudson v. Palmer, 468 U.S. 517 (1984).
[15]   503 U.S. 1 (1992).
[16]   32 F.3d 27 (2d Cir. 1994).
[17]   Tate v. Kassulke, 409 F. Supp. 651 (W.D. Ky. 1976).
[18]   Suits v. Lynch, 437 F. Supp. 38 (D. Kan. 1977).
[19]   Ridley v. Leavitt, 631 F.2d 358 (4th Cir. 1980); Spain v. Procunier, 600 F.2d 189 (9th Cir. 1979).
[20]   Jackson v. Allen, 376 F. Supp. 1393 (E.D. Ark. 1974).

severely that he had to be hospitalized in the intensive care unit. After hearing the evidence, the court found that the inmates were resisting prison authority and that the force used was reasonable and necessary under the circumstances.[21]

The use of excessive force by correctional officers is again illustrated in the case of *Inmates of Attica Correctional Facility v. Rockefeller.*[22] The case arose out of the bloody rioting that occurred at the Attica (New York) Correctional Facility in September of 1971. The inmates alleged that, after the prison was retaken by force on September 13, state officials constantly subjected the inmates to unprovoked acts of brutality, including the following:

> Injured prisoners, some on stretchers, were struck, prodded or beaten with sticks, belts, bats or other weapons. Others were forced to strip and run naked through gauntlets of guards armed with clubs which they used to strike the bodies of the inmates as they passed. Some were dragged on the ground, some marked with an "X" on their backs, some spat upon or burned with matches, and others poked in the genitals or arms with sticks. According to the testimony of the inmates, bloody or wounded inmates were apparently not spared in this orgy of brutality.[23]

The federal appellate court approved of the injunction against state officials from future acts of brutality and torture, and authorized the district court to station federal monitors in the institution if necessary.

Deadly force as a means of self-defense is never justified unless the prison official is in reasonable apprehension of death or serious injury and the use of deadly force is a last resort.

It is obduracy and wantonness, not inadvertence or error in good faith, that characterize the conduct prohibited by the cruel and unusual punishments clause, whether that conduct occurs in connection with establishing conditions of confinement, supplying medical needs, or restoring control over a tumultuous cell block.

The infliction of pain in the course of a prison security measure does not amount to cruel and unusual punishment simply because it may appear in retrospect that the degree of force authorized or used for security purposes was unreasonable, and unnecessary in the strict sense. The general requirement that an Eighth Amendment claimant establish the unnecessary and wanton infliction of pain should also be applied with due regard for differences in the kind of conduct involved. Consequently, when a prison security measure is undertaken to resolve a disturbance that poses significant risks to the safety of

---

[21]   Green v. Hawkins (Unreported, D. Md. 1977).

[22]   Inmates of Attica Correctional Facility v. Rockefeller, 453 F.2d 12 (2d Cir. 1971); *see also* George v. Evans, 633 F.2d 413 (5th Cir. 1980) (use of undue force by a prison guard against a prisoner is actionable as a deprivation of due process).

[23]   Inmates of Attica Correctional Facility v. Rockefeller, *supra,* at 18-19.

inmates and prison staff, the question of whether the measure taken inflicted unnecessary and wanton pain and suffering ultimately turns on whether force was applied in a good faith effort to maintain or restore discipline, or maliciously and sadistically for the purpose of causing harm.

An error in judgment when prison officials decide on a plan that employs potentially deadly force falls far short of a showing that there was no plausible basis for their belief that this degree of force was necessary. Shooting may be part and parcel of a good faith effort to restore prison security. Further, the due process clause of the Fourteenth Amendment is not an alternative basis for finding prison officials guilty of using excessive force, independently of the Eighth Amendment. In the prison security context, the due process clause affords a prisoner no greater protection than does the cruel and unusual punishments clause.[24]

§ 2.4 Defense of Third Persons

Force may be used against an inmate[25] in defense of third persons, such as another inmate, prison staff, or visitors. The law regarding the use of force to prevent injury to third persons is similar to the rules regarding self-defense. A person is justified in using the degree of force reasonably necessary under the circumstances to protect the third party and to control the attacker. Prison officials may find themselves under a duty to provide inmates with reasonable protection from constant threats of violence.[26] What is reasonable under the circumstances again depends upon the degree of force being used by the attacker, the person's reasonable estimate of injury to the third party, and the means available to the person to control the attacker. Deadly force may be used against the attacker only if the third party reasonably appears to be in danger of death or serious injury and the use of deadly force is the last resort.

§ 2.5 Enforcement of Prison Rules and Regulations

Courts have long recognized that penal authorities have the right and duty to prescribe rules and regulations for the internal discipline and control of inmates. The necessary corollary to this authority is the privilege of using reasonable force to see that the rules are enforced. A distinction must be drawn between the use of force as punishment for the violation of a prison rule and the use of force as a means of ensuring that the inmate is brought under control. For example, in the case of *Johnson v. Glick,*[27] the court stated "the man-

---

[24]   Whitley v. Albers, 475 U.S. 312 (1986).

[25]   Harrah v. Leverette, 271 S.W.2d 322 (W. Va. 1980).

[26]   O'Neal v. Evans, 496 F. Supp. 867 (S.D. Ga. 1980); Barnard v. State, 265 N.W.2d 620 (Iowa 1978); Woodhous v. Virginia, 487 F.2d 889 (4th Cir. 1973); Wilson v. City of Kotzebue, 627 P.2d 623 (Alaska 1981); Leonardo v. Moran, 611 F.2d 397 (1st Cir. 1979).

[27]   481 F.2d 1028 (2d Cir. 1973).

agement by a few guards of large numbers of prisoners, not usually the most gentle or tractable of men and women, may require and justify the use of a degree of intentional force."[28]

If a prisoner resists an officer's reasonable order, additional officers should be summoned to control the prisoner. Even when the order is based on a prison rule that is later found to be unconstitutional, guards may use reasonable force to obtain inmate compliance.[29] It is difficult to imagine any justification for using force sufficient to kill or maim in order to compel compliance with a disciplinary rule. If the inmate's resistance amounts to an assault upon an officer, that officer has the privilege of self-defense, and other officers have the privilege of defending third persons. The rules pertaining to self-defense and defense of third persons would then be controlling, because the situation would no longer be one of using force solely to maintain discipline.

§ 2.6 Prevention of Crime

Prison officials have the duty, sometimes imposed by statute,[30] to prevent inmates from committing crimes within a detention facility. Therefore, these officials have the privilege of using reasonable force to prevent either a misdemeanor or a felony. However, the degree of force permissible will depend on whether the attempted crime is a misdemeanor or a felony. Generally, deadly force can be employed to prevent the commission of a felony,[31] but only after all other means reasonably available have failed.[32] Examples of common felonies committed within a prison are rioting and assault with a weapon upon another inmate.

Deadly force is never justified to prevent the commission of a misdemeanor.[33] If, however, an inmate physically resists nondeadly force employed by a correctional officer to prevent the commission of a misdemeanor and becomes an aggressor, the rules pertaining to self-defense apply.

---

[28]   *Id.* at 1033.

[29]   Jackson v. Allen, 376 F. Supp. 1393 (E.D. Ark. 1974).

[30]   *See* Ohio Rev. Code § 5145.04 (Anderson 1996).

[31]   *See* State v. Taylor, 9 Ariz. App. 290, 451 P.2d 648 (1969). The use of deadly force to prevent the escape of all felony suspects, whatever the circumstances, is constitutionally unreasonable. The broad common law rule has been rejected. Where a law enforcement officer has probable cause to believe that the suspect poses a threat of serious physical harm, either to the officer or to others, it is not constitutionally unreasonable to prevent an escape by the use of deadly force. If the suspect threatens the officer with a weapon or there is probable cause to believe that the suspect has committed a crime involving the infliction or threatened infliction of serious physical harm, deadly force may be used as necessary to prevent escape and, where feasible, some warning has been given. Because this case involved a fleeing burglary suspect, it is not directly applicable to prisoners going "over the wall." The law remains unclear. Tennessee v. Garner, 471 U.S. 1 (1985).

[32]   6 C.J.S. *Arrest,* 13b (1937).

[33]   *See* State v. Jones, 211 S.C. 300, 44 S.E.2d 841 (1947).

§ 2.7 Prevention of Escape

Almost every state has, by statute, made escape or attempted escape by a convicted felon a felony.[34] Thus, the rules regarding use of force to prevent a felony apply to preventing an escape; that is, force, including deadly force as a last resort, may be employed. In *Henry v. Perry*,[35] a correctional officer shot an escaping prisoner. Handcuffed, the prisoner had climbed a gate beside the bus in which he was being returned to prison and was running away. Using deadly force appeared to be the only means of preventing the escape. The officer gave a verbal warning and fired warning shots in an effort to halt the escape before shooting the prisoner. Although it was acknowledged that the use of deadly force by correctional officers may be cruel and unusual punishment within the meaning of the Eighth Amendment, when the escapee has committed a crime involving the infliction of serious bodily harm, deadly force may be used if necessary to prevent escape and if, where feasible, some warning has been given.[36]

§ 2.8 The Use of Corporal Punishment to Enforce Prison Discipline

The term "corporal punishment," as used in this book, means the infliction of physical pain upon an inmate as a punishment for the violation of a prison rule or regulation. Such forms of conduct include, but are not limited to, whipping, cold showers, electrical shocking devices, and suspension from cell bars by handcuffs. The use of solitary confinement as a method for punishing violations of prison discipline is not included within the definition of corporal punishment. Many states have no statutes that specifically forbid the use of corporal punishment. Other states, however, prohibit corporal punishment in detention facilities by statute.[37]

§ 2.8.1 —Brief History of Corporal Punishment

Corporal punishment has a long history of use in prisons, as was stated in *United States v. Jones*:[38]

> From time immemorial prison officials were vested with the power and authority of imposing corporal punishment upon prisoners as a part of the discipline and restraint . . . [F]or centuries whipping or corporal punishment has been a recognized method of discipline of convicts.

---

[34] *See* Pa. Stat. Ann. tit. 18 § 4309 (Supp. 1972); Wash. Rev. Code Cpt. 9.31.010 (1961); Model Penal Code § 242.6 (Proposed Official Draft, 1962).

[35] 866 F.2d 657 (3d Cir. 1989).

[36] *See* Tennessee v. Garner, 471 U.S. 1 (1985).

[37] *See, e.g.,* Cal. Penal Code Title 16 § 673.

[38] 108 F. Supp. 266, 270 (S.D. Fla. 1952), *rev'd on other grounds*, 207 F.2d 785 (5th Cir. 1953).

The use of corporal punishment to enforce prison discipline continued into the early parts of the twentieth century. In 1927, a North Carolina statute authorizing the whipping of convicts was upheld.[39] In 1963, in *State v. Cannon*,[40] the Delaware Supreme Court held that the use of whipping to punish certain crimes did not violate either the state or federal constitutional bans on cruel and unusual punishment. In *Talley v. Stevens*,[41] the court refused to declare whipping unconstitutional as such, but held that whipping must not be excessive and must be inflicted as dispassionately as possible. A 1949 case involving handcuffing a prisoner to a cell door for 60 hours without food also discusses the use and misuse of corporal punishment.[42] Corporal punishment, including the use of electrical shocking devices, was used openly by the state of Arkansas until the 1960s. In a 1976 Minnesota case, electric shock treatments that served a legitimate purpose were not considered cruel and unusual punishment.[43]

§ 2.8.2 —Is Corporal Punishment Rational?

Advocates of corporal punishment maintain that, in order to enforce prison discipline, it is necessary to punish past offenders, hopefully deterring future rule infractions. However, the harmful effects of such treatment may well outweigh any of its supposed benefits. The possible psychological effects of inhumane punishment have been described as follows:[44]

> [M]ethods of discipline have a profound effect on the offender in regard to his mental and social attitudes both within the prison and after release. This is particularly evident in the case of first offenders, in whom permanent attitudes are often established which make for later social success or for a continued life of crime. The consequences of discipline are also grave in their effect on the mental conditions of offenders, leading them often into the so-called "prison neurosis" if unfavorable, or leading to constructive modification of personality if constructively administered.

---

39   State v. Revis, 193 N.C. 192, 136 S.E. 346 (1927). In 1955, however, North Carolina enacted a statute forbidding the use of corporal punishment on any prisoner. Cpt. 48, Art. 2, N.C. Gen. Stat. § 148-20 (1964).

40   55 Del. 587, 190 A.2d 514 (1963).

41   247 F. Supp. 683 (E.D. Ark. 1965).

42   State v. Carpenter, 231 N.C. 229, 56 S.E.2d 713 (1949).

43   Price v. Sheppard, 239 N.W.2d 905 (Minn. 1976).

44   J. Wilson and M. Pescor, Problems in Prison Psychiatry 226 (1939).

Prison authorities have also recognized the futility of corporal punishment. The American Correctional Association has stated unequivocally that "corporal punishment should never be used under any circumstances."[45] In justifying this position, the Association commented:

> Punishments out of all proportion to the offense, employing inhumane and archaic methods and dictated by brutality coupled with ignorance, incompetence, fear and weakness, are demoralizing both to inmates and staff. Staff punishments substantially increase the chances that the inmates will continue to be disciplinary problems in the institution and will return to crime after release.[46]

James V. Bennett, Director of Federal Prisons from 1937 to 1964, testified during the trial of *Jackson v. Bishop* that whipping and other forms of corporal punishment were "brutal and medieval and did no real good.[47]

§ 2.8.3 —Judicial Treatment of Corporal Punishment

Until the late 1960s, cases could be found which held that corporal punishment was not cruel and unusual punishment. In *United States v. Jones,*[48] the director of a Florida convict camp was charged with deprivation of the civil rights of several inmates, whom he allegedly assaulted and whipped. The district court, relying strongly on the proposition that the administration of state penal institutions was a matter of exclusive state jurisdiction, held that an inmate has no constitutional right to be free from corporal punishment. The court further stated that, although Florida law prohibited the use of corporal punishment, the law was based "on principles of Christianity and humanity" and not on the federal Constitution, thereby intimating that the use of corporal punishment could be reestablished by the Florida legislature at any time.

State v. Cannon[49] involved the constitutionality of a Delaware law that prescribed whipping as a form of punishment for specified crimes. Discussing the validity of whipping in light of the state constitution's ban on cruel and unusual punishment, the court reasoned that because whipping had been permitted in the state since 1719, while other forms of punishment that had formerly been used, such as burning at the stake, had been eliminated by the state legislature, it must be presumed that whipping was not considered cruel by the people of Delaware. Any change, the court declared, must come from the state legislature. As for the Eighth Amendment to the United States Constitution,

---

[45] AMERICAN CORRECTIONAL ASSOCIATION, A MANUAL OF CORRECTIONAL STANDARDS 417 (3d ed. 1966). *See also* NATIONAL ADVISORY COMMISSION ON CRIMINAL JUSTICE STANDARDS AND GOALS, STANDARD 2.4 (1973), in Appendix.

[46] *Id.*

[47] Jackson v. Bishop, 268 F. Supp. 804, 813 (E.D. Ark. 1967), *aff'd,* 404 F.2d 571 (8th Cir. 1968).

[48] 108 F. Supp. 266 (S.D. Fla. 1952), *rev'd on other grounds,* 207 F.2d 785 (5th Cir. 1953).

[49] 55 Del. 587, 190 A.2d 514 (1963).

the court said that it could not find a single case as of that time in which a court had held, as a matter of federal constitutional law, that whipping violates the Eighth Amendment.

State v. Cannon was decided in 1963; in 1968, however, the United States Court of Appeals for the Eight Circuit held, in the case of *Jackson v. Bishop,*[50] that whipping as a means of enforcing prison discipline *did* violate the Eighth and Fourteenth Amendments. The court stated that the prohibition against cruel and unusual punishment could not be defined exactly, but that "the applicable standards are flexible . . . and that broad and idealistic concepts of dignity, civilized standards, humanity, and decency are useful and usable."[51] Using these criteria, the court held whipping to be cruel and unusual punishment for the following reasons:

> (1) We are not convinced that any rule or regulation as to the use of the strap, however seriously or sincerely conceived and drawn, will successfully prevent abuse . . . (2) Rules in this area often seem to go unobserved . . . (3) Regulations are easily circumvented . . . (4) Corporal punishment is easily subject to abuse in the hands of the sadistic and unscrupulous. (5) Where power to punish is granted to persons in lower levels of administrative authority, there is an inherent and natural difficulty in enforcing the limitations of that power. (6) There can be no argument that excessive whipping or an inappropriate manner of whipping or too great frequency of whipping or the use of studded or overlong straps all constitute cruel and unusual punishment. But if whipping were to be authorized, how does one, or any court, ascertain the point which would distinguish the permissible from that which is cruel and unusual? (7) Corporal punishment generates hate toward the keepers who punish and toward the system which permits it. It is degrading to the punisher and to the punished alike. It frustrates correctional and rehabilitative goals . . . (8) Whipping creates other penological problems and makes adjustment to society more difficult. (9) Public opinion is obviously adverse. Counsel concede that only two states still permit the use of the strap.[52]

The reasoning of *Jackson v. Bishop* in eliminating corporal punishment has been consistently followed in judicial decisions, statutes, and administrative rulings in this country. Any attempt to revive the practice, at this time, would face serious, if not insurmountable, constitutional challenges. Also significant is the fact that the opinion in *Jackson v. Bishop* was written by then-Judge Blackmun, who later became a member of the United States Supreme Court.

---

[50]   404 F.2d 571 (8th Cir. 1968).
[51]   *Id.* at 579.
[52]   *Id.* at 579-580.

The Supreme Court continues to find state systems violating the most basic standards of decency. An Alabama prison inmate was twice handcuffed to a hitching post for disruptive conduct. During a two-hour period, he was offered drinking water and a bathroom break every 15 minutes, and his responses were recorded on an activity log. He was handcuffed above shoulder height, and when he tried moving his arms to improve circulation, the handcuffs cut into his wrists, causing pain and discomfort. After an altercation with a guard at his chain gang's worksite, the inmate was subdued, handcuffed, placed in leg irons, and transported back to the prison, where he was ordered to take off his shirt, and spent seven hours in the sun handcuffed to the hitching post. During this seven-hour period, he was given one or two water breaks, but no bathroom breaks, and a guard taunted him about his thirst.

These facts established Eighth Amendment violations. Among the unnecessary and wanton inflictions of pain constituting cruel and unusual punishment are those that are totally without penological justification. This determination is made in the prison context by ascertaining whether an official acted with deliberate indifference to the inmate's health or safety, a state of mind that can be inferred from the fact that the risk of harm is obvious. Here, the Eighth Amendment violation was obvious. Any safety concerns had long since abated by the time the inmate was handcuffed to the hitching post because he had already been subdued, handcuffed, placed in leg irons, and transported back to prison. He was separated from his work squad and not given the opportunity to return. Despite the clear lack of an emergency, prison officials knowingly subjected him to a substantial risk of physical harm, unnecessary pain, unnecessary exposure to the sun, prolonged thirst, and taunting, and a deprivation of bathroom breaks that created a risk of particular discomfort and humiliation.[53]

In another case, an inmate was beaten when he refused to leave his cell for a cell search. This violated the Eighth Amendment. The inmate claimed that after he was incapacitated by the shock of an electronic shield used by officers to conduct the cell extraction, he was kicked, stomped on, and punched. He suffered injuries that required a nine-day hospital stay and long recuperation.[54]

Cruel and unusual punishment was shown where an inmate sustained bruising, swelling, and scarring injuries as a result of an unprovoked assault and choking by a sheriff's deputy. The Supreme Court recognizes no per se non-de minimis injury requirement. The Eighth Amendment does not afford guards in a detention center a cloak of insulation so long as an assault is not too severe.[55]

In another Virginia case, the equal protection clause was violated when an inmate was restrained with a five-point restraint for 48 hours because of his race and his complaints about previous expressions of racism. He was shown a drawing of person in a noose, apparently implying that he would be lynched.[56]

---

[53]   Hope v. Pelzer, 536 U.S. 730 (2002).
[54]   Skrtich v. Thornton, 280 F.3d 1295 (11th Cir. 2002).
[55]   Watford v. Bruce, 126 F. Supp. 2d 425 (E.D. Va. 2001).
[56]   Davis v. Lester, 156 F. Supp. 2d 588 (W.D. Va. 2001).

§ 2.8.4 —Alternatives to Corporal Punishment

Prison officials must have methods of punishing violations of prison rules and regulations. As previously stated, some prison administrators would like to include the use of corporal punishment among their possible methods of enforcing discipline. However, there are numerous other punishments that may be employed, none of which involves the infliction of physical pain, and thus these punishments may be more effective both in maintaining discipline and in rehabilitating the inmate.

§ 2.9   Conclusion

In recognizing that prisons do not house the most docile or easily governed persons, courts will allow the use of reasonable force by prison officials in five situations: self-defense, defense of third persons, enforcement of prison rules and regulations, prevention of escape, and prevention of crime. The test of reasonableness is whether the force is reasonable and necessary under the facts and circumstances of the particular case.

Unreasonable corporal punishment to enforce prison discipline is considered cruel and unusual punishment, prohibited by the Eighth Amendment. Prison officials who attempt to revive the use of corporal punishment may find themselves facing criminal and civil actions. To avoid criminal and civil liability, prison officials should refrain from corporal punishment and seek alternative methods of inmate control.

Prisoners' Rights to Visitation/Association; Searches

3

Chapter Outline

§ 3.1 Introduction

Traditionally, the right of inmates to have visitors while incarcerated has been strictly limited by prison officials. Many states permit an inmate to see only those persons who have been approved by the prison administrators. Cases concerning inmates' rights to have visitors generally hold that controlling this activity is within the prison officials' discretion and that such control is not subject to judicial reversal unless a clear abuse of discretion is shown.[1] Further, any restrictions imposed by prison visitation policies must merely be reasonably related to a legitimate government interest.[2]

Although visitation privileges are considered matters within the scope of internal prison administration, this fact does not permit discriminatory application of visiting regulations.[3] For example, refusal to permit visitation privileges because the visitor and inmate are of different races constitutes racial discrimination under the Fourteenth Amendment.[4]

Visiting regulations that set forth procedures under which visitors "may" be refused admittance and have visitation privileges suspended does not give state inmates a liberty interest in receiving visitors that is entitled to the protection of the due process clause. In order to create a protected liberty interest in the prison context, state regulations must use "explicitly mandatory language," in connection with the establishment of "specific substantive predicates" to limit official discretion, and thereby require that a particular outcome be reached upon a finding that the relevant criteria have been met.

Although regulations provide certain "substantive predicates" to guide prison decisionmakers in determining whether to allow visitation, regulations have no protected federal constitutional interest unless they are worded in such a way that an inmate could reasonably form an objective expectation that a visit would necessarily be allowed, absent the occurrence of one of the listed conditions, or could reasonably expect to enforce the regulations against prison officials should that visit not be allowed.[5]

---

[1] Walker v. Pate, 356 F.2d 502 (7th Cir. 1966), *cert. denied,* 384 U.S. 966 (1966).

[2] James v. Wallace, 406 F. Supp. 318 (M.D. Ala. 1976).

[3] Underwood v. Loving, 391 F. Supp. 1214 (W.D. Va. 1975) was reversed in part on appeal with no published opinion. Underwood v. Loving, 538 F.2d 325 (4th Cir. 1976).

[4] Martin v. Wainwright, 525 F.2d 983 (5th Cir. 1976).

[5] Kentucky v. Thompson, 490 U.S. 454 (1989). Due to the 1995 decision of the Supreme Court in *Sandin v. Conner,* state regulations may not necessarily create constitutionally protected liberty interests. *See* §§ 5.3.2 and 8.1.

The question has been raised as to whether the right to visitation may be restricted for disciplinary reasons. In *Agron v. Montanye*,[6] inmates challenged the practice of barring visits from family and friends to inmates who refused to shave. The court granted a preliminary injunction because there was a New York policy not to bar visitation to inmates as punishment. The court, in its analysis, drew attention to the constitutional dimensions of an inmate's right to visitation with reference to rights of association as well as the interests of family members who need and want to visit with the inmate, citing *Pell v. Procunier*.[7] Because most courts defer to the authority of prison officials, it is doubtful that the case would have been decided similarly, absent the preexisting state policy.

In *Ribideau v. Stoneman*,[8] it was held that the transfer of inmates and its effects on visitation rights did not raise a federal constitutional issue.

In *Block v. Rutherford*, Michigan prison inmates and prospective prison visitors challenged regulations that restricted prison visitation rights. The visits at issue were "contact visits," which customarily take place in a "visitation room" or other area set aside for this purpose and permit "innocent-only" physical contact between prisoner and visitor. Non-contact visits, on the other hand, take place in small booths or cubicles, and no physical contact is permitted.

Prisoners were graded on the basis of their dangerous propensities. The grades were numbered I through VI. The most dangerous inmates were placed in either grade V or grade VI. With rare exceptions, contact visits were not permitted in either of these two grades. This restriction was not at issue.[9] The issue for decision was whether the no-contact rule could be applied broadly to all classification grades.

Michigan officials attempted to accommodate, to some extent, the visitation desires of prisoners in the lower grades, but security problems developed. The liberal visitation policy opened institutions to drugs, weapons, and other contraband. Visitors could easily conceal contraband and pass it to an inmate. Aside from these security considerations, there were also additional expenses associated with the allowance of contact visitation. As a result of these concerns, contact visits were prohibited.

A Michigan District Court upheld the revised prison regulations. The court reasoned that the benefits of the blanket prohibition outweighed the costs—financial and otherwise—of any alternative method. Otherwise, jail personnel who were free from the complicated, expensive, and time-consuming processes of interviewing, searching, and processing visitors, would have to be reassigned to perform these tasks. The hiring of additional personnel would be required. Intrusive strip searches after contact visits would be necessary. Finally, as the District Court noted, at the very least, "modest" improvements of existing facilities would be required to accommodate a con-

---

6   392 F. Supp. 454 (W.D.N.Y. 1975).
7   417 U.S. 817 (1974).
8   398 F. Supp. 805 (D. Vt. 1975).
9   *See* Block v. Rutherford, 468 U.S. 576 (1984).

tact visitation program if the prison authorities did not purchase or build a new facility elsewhere. The Sixth Circuit Court of Appeals affirmed the District Court's decision.[10]

In reaching these conclusions, the Sixth Circuit also approved an Administrative Code promulgated by the Michigan Department of Corrections. Briefly summarized, the Code provided that a visitor younger than 18 had to be a prisoner's child, stepchild, or grandchild and had to be accompanied by an immediate family member or legal guardian. Prisoners could not visit with their natural children if their parental rights had been terminated. Prisoners could have only 10 nonfamily individuals on their approved visitors list. Members of the general public could be on only one prisoner's visitation list. A former prisoner could visit a current prisoner only if the former prisoner was an immediate family member or a person with special qualifications such as a lawyer, clergy member, or government representative.

In upholding the regulations, the Sixth Circuit cited numerous decisions of the Supreme Court that stressed that problems of prison administration were best resolved by prison authorities and that their resolution should be accorded deference by the courts. Moreover, when a federal court reviews the constitutionality of a state penal system, federal courts should, wherever possible, defer to the appropriate prison authorities. The important word, one that appears specifically or by implication in all the pertinent Supreme Court opinions, is "deference."

The court further held that when prison regulations were reasonably related to and supportive of legitimate penological interests, there should be no federal intervention. The decision in *Bazzetta* follows the well-established principle that there is no inherent, absolute constitutional right to contact visits with prisoners. The restrictions in this case did not constitute cruel and unusual punishment under the Eighth Amendment, because the rules applied only to contact visits. Moreover, to the extent that they could be construed as "punishments," they were punishments that were imposed upon every prisoner at the time of sentencing. They were the "rules of the game," pursuant to which the Michigan penal system operated.[11]

§ 3.2 Pretrial Detainees

Pretrial detainees constitute a special category of inmates. It has been generally held that pretrial detainees are entitled to the same rights as other citizens except to the extent necessary to assure their appearance at trial and the

---

[10] Bazzetta v. McGinnis, 124 F.3d 774 (6th Cir. 1997).

[11] Subsequent to the *Bazzetta* decision, the Michigan Department of Corrections applied the opinion to non-contact visitations. The Sixth Circuit then issued a Supplementary Opinion solely for the purpose of clarification. The opinion emphasized that the Court's earlier decision only concerned limitations on contact visitation and did not apply to non-contact visitation. Bazzetta v. McGinnis, 133 F.3d 382 (6th Cir. 1998).

security of the institution.[12] Although a pretrial detainee may be subject to some of the same restrictions as convicted prisoners, the restrictions are not unconstitutional unless they amount to punishment.[13] Some courts have held that, for pretrial detainees, restrictions on visitor access must be justified by a compelling interest.[14]

In a strip-search case, a department of corrections was enjoined from continuing an unconstitutional strip-search policy. A department cannot constitutionally conduct strip and visual body cavity searches of prearraignment detainees that are not based upon reasonable suspicion that a particular detainee is concealing weapons or contraband.

There have been a number of cases that have dealt with the particular rights of visitation for pretrial detainees. One such case is *Rhem v. Malcolm*,[15] in which pretrial detainees demanded a minimum number of visitors per visit (three), as well as a minimum number and length of visits per week (two hours daily). The court reasoned that the detainees did not have a constitutional right to receive a minimum number of visitors at any one time. Another is *Jordan v. Wolke*,[16] in which the Seventh Circuit Court of Appeals ruled that if jail officials' blanket refusal to allow contact visits for pretrial detainees is not intended as punishment, is rationally related to the goal of maintaining order and security in the jail, and is not excessive in relation to that goal, it does not constitute "punishment" forbidden by the Fourteenth Amendment due process clause. Further, under a standard of reasonableness, the number of visitors allowed at any one time was a function of the capacity of the facility. The court also ruled that pretrial detainees had no constitutional right to the minimum number and length of visits.

See § 4.13 concerning the use of telephones.

§ 3.3 Communication Among Prisoners and Union Formation

In terms of "visitation" or communication among prisoners, it has been held that rules against communication at certain times and places between prisoners are not unreasonable. This view was explained in *United States v. Dawson*,[17] in which the court reasoned that increased prison violence makes the need to regulate prison life more compelling.

---

[12]   Bell v. Wolfish, 441 U.S. 520 (1979); Rhem v. Malcolm, 396 F. Supp. 1195 (S.D.N.Y.), *aff'd*, 527 F.2d 1041 (2d Cir. 1975).

[13]   Occhino v. United States, 686 F.2d 1302 (8th Cir. 1982).

[14]   Inmates of Allegheny County Jail v. Pierce, 612 F.2d 754 (3d Cir. 1979); Cooper v. Morin, 49 N.Y.2d 69, 399 N.E.2d 1188, *cert. denied*, 466 U.S. 983 (1979); Epps v. Levine, 480 F. Supp. 50 (D. Md. 1979).

[15]   *Supra* n. 9.

[16]   615 F.2d 749 (7th Cir. 1980); In re Smith, 169 Cal. Rptr. 564 (Cal. App. 1980) (a jail policy that prohibited the visitation of minor children with their incarcerated parents was a denial of the incarcerated parents' rights); Valentine v. Englehardt, 492 F. Supp. 1039 (D.N.J. 1980).

[17]   516 F.2d 796 (9th Cir. 1975).

Jail officials may have a blanket prohibition on any pretrial detainee's contact visits with outsiders. This includes even low-risk detainees. The prohibition is a reasonable, nonpunitive response to legitimate security concerns. The dispositive inquiry is whether the challenged practice or policy constitutes punishment or is reasonably related to a legitimate government objective. Courts should play a very limited role in this inquiry. Such considerations are uniquely within the province and professional expertise of corrections officials. It was recognized that contact visits invite a host of security problems. They expose a detention facility to drugs, weapons, and other contraband. Also, to expose the detainees, who are awaiting trial for serious, violent offenses or have prior convictions, to others carries with it the risk that the safety of innocent individuals will be jeopardized. Therefore, totally disallowing contact visits is not excessive in relation to security and other interests.[18]

In *Brooks v. Wainwright,*[19] the court dismissed an inmate's complaint that he was deprived of his First Amendment freedoms and his right to equal protection when his custody classification was changed after he had attempted to organize a prisoner's union. The court felt that the opposition by prison officials to the formation of this union was not a deprivation of the inmate's constitutional rights. The court stated:

> Prisons are not motels or resorts where inmates can check in or out at their liberty. Neither is a prison a public forum providing open access to citizens to freely express their beliefs. The full range of constitutional freedoms that ordinary members of society enjoy must be curtailed in order to achieve the legitimate purposes of imprisonment. So long as the restrictions and limitations are not patently unreasonable, the discretionary decisions of prison officials will be given deference by the courts.[20]

In this case, the court found that the prison officials' argument—that organizing a prisoners' union carried with it inherent dangers and threats to the security of the prison—was reasonable.

The California courts, however, have not gone so far in some respects. They have held that, while inmates have no constitutional right to participate in a prisoners' union meeting,[21] their right to freedom of speech was unlawfully restricted by prison officials' denial of permission for the prisoners to wear prisoner union lapel buttons.[22]

The Supreme Court has denied the rights of inmates to solicit membership for a "union." In *North Carolina Prisoners' Union v. Jones,*[23] the prison administration permitted membership in a "union" that was actually a prison

---

[18]   Block v. Rutherford, 468 U.S. 576 (1984).
[19]   439 F. Supp. 1335 (M.D. Fla. 1977).
[20]   *Id.* at 1340.
[21]   In re Price, 158 Cal. Rptr. 873, 600 P.2d 1330 (Cal. 1979).
[22]   In re Reynolds, 157 Cal. Rptr. 892 (Cal. 1979).
[23]   433 U.S. 119 (1977).

reform organization. At issue was the prison rule forbidding members from soliciting other inmates to join the organization. The lower court saw little sense and even less legality in this rule and held that because membership was already permitted, solicitation for membership was also to be permitted. The Supreme Court disagreed. The lower court also held that, although outsiders may urge prisoners to join the union, the prison administrator may prohibit entry of those whose proposed mission is one of union proselytism. The Supreme Court, however, reversed the District Court and held that prisoners do not have the right to organize prison unions. The Supreme Court also held that prison regulations prohibiting unions did not violate the First Amendment.

Rights of prisoners were further limited in *Rowland v. California Men's Colony*, 506 U.S. 194 (1993). A representative association of inmates in a California prison sought leave to proceed *in forma pauperis* under 28 U.S.C. § 1915(a), which permits litigation without prepayment of fees, costs, or security "by a person who makes affidavit that he is unable to pay." The Supreme Court held that only a natural person may qualify for treatment *in forma pauperis* under § 1915.

§ 3.4 Conjugal Visitation

Many foreign countries and several states have provided facilities in their penal institutions for conjugal visits; that is, visits by an inmate's spouse with an opportunity for intimate sexual relations.[24] However, a federal appellate court has held, in *Payne v. District of Columbia*,[25] that such visits are not constitutionally required. The holding in *Payne* was buttressed in the case of *Tarlton v. Clark*,[26] in which a different federal appellate court said that an inmate's claim to a right to conjugal visitation "would not come up to the level of a federal constitutional right so as to be cognizable as a basis for relief in the federal court."[27] The cases of *Polakoff v. Henderson*[28] and *Lyons v. Gilligan*[29] indicate the continuing refusal of the federal courts to recognize conjugal visitation as a constitutional right of prison inmates. *Polakoff* declared that the denial of conjugal visitation did not constitute cruel and unusual punishment prohibited by the Eighth Amendment. In *Lyons*, the court denied the inmate's assertion that failure to provide conjugal visits violated a married couple's right to privacy. Even assuming that such a right of privacy could be implied from the Supreme Court's decision in *Griswold v. Connecticut*[30] to apply to a

---

[24] *See* Kent, *The Legal and Sociological Dimensions of Conjugal Visitations in Prisons*, 2 NEW ENG. J. ON PRISON L. 47 (1975).

[25] 253 F.2d 867 (D.C. Cir. 1958).

[26] 441 F.2d 384 (5th Cir.), *cert. denied*, 403 U.S. 934 (1971).

[27] *Id.* at 385.

[28] 370 F. Supp. 690 (N.D. Ga. 1973), *aff'd*, 488 F.2d 977 (5th Cir. 1974).

[29] 382 F. Supp. 198 (N.D. Ohio 1974).

[30] 381 U.S. 479 (1965).

prison setting, the Court explained: "The rub of *Griswold* was restraint on governmental intrusion. It cannot be extended to impose an affirmative duty on the government."[31]

Conjugal visits are inconsistent with the principles of incarceration and isolation from society. The Circuit Courts of Appeals have long held that prisoners do not retain the right to contact visits.[32]

State prison regulations authorizing conjugal visits create no enforceable rights. In *Champion v. Artuz,*[33] a prisoner's conjugal visits were revoked after prison guards found that the wife, herself an ex-offender, was carrying various items that they viewed as potential instrumentalities for escape, including a wig, a camouflage handkerchief, and a man's identification card. It was held that, following *Sandin,* the state regulations permitting correctional facilities to allow conjugal visits to prisoners did not give the prisoner a liberty interest in such visits.

The same federal appellate court that decided *Tarlton* indicated the firmness of its position in a subsequent case, *McCray v. Sullivan,*[34] when it said: "Failure to permit conjugal visits does not deny an inmate a federal constitutional right."[35] However, the visiting rights of a wife cannot be summarily suspended after she and her prisoner husband were caught together in an unauthorized area of the prison during visiting hours.[36]

§ 3.5   News Media Interviews

In *Seattle-Tacoma Newspaper Guild v. Parker,*[37] a federal appellate court held that a regulation of the Federal Bureau of Prisons that completely denied press interviews with individual inmates did not violate the inmates' First Amendment freedom of speech. The regulation was also seen as not unduly restricting the flow of information to the public through the news media. Recognizing that the Director of the Bureau of Prisons and the warden at the fed-

---

[31]   Lyons v. Gilligan, 382 F. Supp. 198, 200 (N.D. Ohio 1974).

[32]   *See* Toussaint v. McCarthy, 801 F.2d 1080 (9th Cir. 1986), *cert. denied,* 481 U.S. 1069 (1987) (prisoners have no right to contact visits); Hernandez v. Coughlin, 18 F.3d 133 (2d Cir. 1994) (prisoners have no right to conjugal visits because "rights of marital privacy . . . are necessarily and substantially abridged in the prison setting"); Bellamy v. Bradley, 729 F.2d 416, 420 (6th Cir. 1984), *cert. denied,* 469 U.S. 845 (1984) ("prison inmates have no absolute constitutional right to visitation"); Ramos v. Lamm, 639 F.2d 559, 580 n. 26 (10th Cir. 1980), *cert. denied,* 450 U.S. 1041 (1981) ("weight of present authority clearly establishes that there is no constitutional right to contact visitation . . . we agree with this view."); Lynott v. Henderson, 610 F.2d 340, 342 (5th Cir. 1980) ("convicted prisoners have no absolute constitutional right to visitation"); Peterkin v. Jeffes, 661 F. Supp. 895, 913-914 (E.D. Pa. 1987) ("the weight of authority concludes that a ban on contact visits for convicted persons does not run afoul of the Eighth Amendment"), *modified,* 855 F.2d 1021 (3d Cir. 1988). *Cf.,* Block v. Rutherford, 468 U.S. 576 (1984) ("That there is a valid rational connection between a ban on contact visits and internal security of a detention facility is too obvious to warrant discussion.").

[33]   76 F.3d 483 (2d Cir. 1996).

[34]   509 F.2d 1332 (5th Cir.), *cert. denied,* 423 U.S. 859 (1975).

[35]   *Id.* at 1334.

[36]   McKinnis v. Mosley, 693 F.2d 1054 (11th Cir. 1982).

[37]   480 F.2d 1062 (9th Cir. 1973).

eral prison must be given wide discretion in formulating rules to govern prison life, the court observed that there were sufficient alternative means of communication that would ensure that "any real complaint about the treatment of the inmate or the administration of the prison"[38] would not go unredressed. The court noted that the challenged regulation would not affect an inmate's right to confer freely with his or her counsel, to conduct unlimited confidential correspondence, to visit with relatives and friends, to counsel with the clergy of his or her faith, and to have free access to the courts. In view of the damaging consequences of a policy permitting press-inmate interviews, such as increased disciplinary problems and the creation of "big wheel" status for certain inmates, who often become less subject to constructive rehabilitation, the court said it was convinced that any burden imposed on the media's ability to report occasioned by the interview ban was more than justified.[39]

The companion cases of *Pell v. Procunier*[40] and *Saxbe v. Washington Post Company*[41] presented the United States Supreme Court with the question of the constitutionality of the same federal regulation at issue in *Seattle-Tacoma,* along with a similar provision from the *California Department of Corrections Manual.* In *Pell,* the court answered the claim of four inmates and three professional journalists that the state prison regulation violated their First Amendment freedom of speech by declaring that neither the prisoners nor the press had a freedom of speech right to specific personal interviews. Alternative channels of communication were seen to be open to inmates, and would be protected by the court's ruling in *Procunier v. Martinez,*[42] which established standards for the review of inmate correspondence by prison officials.[43] So long as the restriction on interviews operated in a neutral fashion, without regard to the content of expression, it was seen as falling within the appropriate rules and regulations to which inmates are necessarily subject.[44] As to members of the press, the courts said that because such interviews were not available to members of the general public, they need not be made available to the media on a privileged basis.

In *Saxbe,* the challenge to the federal prison regulation prohibiting personal interviews by the news media and individually designated inmates was made only by news media representatives. Referring to its decision in *Pell,* the court declared that the regulation did not violate any First Amendment guarantees, because it "does not deny the press access to sources of information available to members of the general public," but is merely a particularized application of the general rule that nobody may enter the prison and designate an inmate whom he would like to visit, unless the prospective visitor is a lawyer, clergy, relative, or friend of that inmate.[45]

---

38   *Id.* at 1066.
39   *Id.* at 1067.
40   417 U.S. 817 (1974).
41   417 U.S. 843 (1974).
42   416 U.S. 396 (1974).
43   Pell v. Procunier, 417 U.S. 817, 824 (1974).
44   *Id.* at 828.
45   Saxbe v. Washington Post Co., 417 U.S. 843, 849 (1974).

In the case of *Main Road v. Aytch*,[46] a federal district court and a federal appellate court had occasion to apply the holdings of *Pell* and *Saxbe* in a suit brought by pretrial detainees of the Philadelphia prison system. Inmates of the Philadelphia prisons had, on two separate occasions, sought permission from the superintendent to hold press conferences in which they desired to express to the public their concern about problems encountered by them in dealings with a defenders' association that represented many of the inmates in their criminal cases, and to allege improprieties in probation procedures. Both requests were denied, although the district court found that the superintendent had authorized other large gatherings of inmates and outsiders, particularly other group press conferences.[47] The decisions in *Pell* and *Saxbe* were announced while *Main Road* was under consideration by the district court, and although the evidence presented indicated that permission to hold the press conferences had been denied on the basis of their expected content, contrary to the neutral approach mandated by *Pell*, the trial judge denied injunctive or declaratory relief, on the ground that he believed such censorship was unlikely to recur.[48]

On appeal, the appellate court also observed that the ban had not been applied in a neutral fashion without regard to the content of the expression, and declared that the criteria the superintendent applied in determining whether to permit a news conference provided too much occasion for subjective evaluation, thus enabling him to act as a censor.[49] Whether subjects were "explosive" or "sensitive" were said to be standards lacking the constitutionally indispensable "narrowly drawn limitations" on administrative discretion, which therefore ran afoul of the tests of valid prison regulations prescribed in *Procunier v. Martinez*.[50] The case was remanded, and the district court was directed to determine whether the superintendent intended to continue to grant some, but not all, prisoner requests for interviews and press conferences. If such were the case, the superintendent was to develop proposed regulations governing the issuance of such permission, which delineated precise and objective tests, on the basis of which permission may be denied. Additionally, the district court was directed to implement a review process that would assure a fair determination of the facts upon which a prison administrator denied permission to hold a news conference.[51]

The case of *KQED v. Houchins*[52] dealt further with the issue of the standards followed by prison authorities in denying media access to prisons and prisoners. A sheriff refused to allow the anchors of an educational radio-television station to inspect the grounds of a county jail after a program by the station reported the suicide of an inmate there, together with certain allegations

---

[46]   385 F. Supp. 105 (E.D. Pa. 1974), *vacated and remanded,* 522 F.2d 1080 (3d Cir. 1975).
[47]   *Id.* at 1084.
[48]   *Id.* at 1090.
[49]   *Id.* at 1089.
[50]   *Id.* at 1090.
[51]   *Id.*
[52]   438 U.S. 1 (1978).

made by a staff psychiatrist as to jail conditions. The exclusion was justified as a matter of "policy," but subsequently a limited program of monthly public tours of the facility was implemented. The federal district court read *Pell* as standing for the proposition that a prison or jail administrator may curtail media access upon a showing of past resultant disruption or present institutional tension, but found that the sheriff had not made such a showing in this case.[53] The inadequacy of the policy in question was more apparent in view of the fact that officials at two neighboring facilities testified that media interviews of inmates had proved neither unduly disruptive nor dangerous to prison security. A preliminary injunction was issued prohibiting the sheriff from excluding, as a matter of general policy, responsible representatives of the news media from the jail facilities.

The decision was appealed to the United States Supreme Court in *Houchins v. KQED*. The Court reversed the lower court's decision and held that the news media has no constitutional right of access to a county jail, over and above that of other persons, to interview inmates and make sound recordings, films, and photographs for publication and broadcasting by newspapers, radio, and television. There is no requirement that prison officials provide the press with information. The Supreme Court saw the issue as involving the question of whether the news media has a constitutional right of access to a county jail, over and above that of other persons, to interview inmates and gather other information. It held that the degree of openness of a penal institution is a question of policy that a legislature, and not a court, must resolve.[54]

§ 3.6 Attorney Representatives

It is impermissible for prison officials to arbitrarily limit an inmate's right to an attorney's assistance in perfecting appeals of conviction or protesting prison conditions. However, what about the legal paraprofessional, investigator, or law student working for an attorney or legal clinic? Does the inmate have a constitutional right to meet with these people?

In *Souza v. Travisono*,[55] the court recognized that a corollary to the right of access to the courts was the right of access to reasonably available, competent legal assistance. The warden's arbitrary decision to exclude a student legal assistant was held unconstitutional. Although prison officials may not arbitrarily limit access to non-attorney legal assistance, they may place reasonable regulations on such visits. The time, place, and manner of visits may be regulated to further the governmental interests of security, order, or rehabilitation.[56]

---

[53]   *Id.*

[54]   *Id.* at 12.

[55]   368 F. Supp. 459 (D.R.I. 1973), *aff'd,* 498 F.2d 1120 (1st Cir. 1974); *see also* Dreher v. Sielaff, 636 F.2d 1141 (7th Cir. 1980); United States v. Blue Thunder, 604 F.2d 550 (8th Cir. 1979).

[56]   *See* Shakur v. Malcolm, 525 F.2d 1144 (2d Cir. 1975); Reed v. Evans, 455 F. Supp. 1339 (S.D. Ga. 1978), *aff'd,* 592 F.2d 1189 (5th Cir. 1979).

The Court of Appeals affirmed the District Court ruling, but refused to decide whether inmates must be given reasonable access to law students for the resolution of such issues as divorce, bankruptcy, or probate. Resolution of these issues lies in future litigation.[57]

§ 3.7   Searches of Visitors

Visits may be conditioned on the willingness of the visitors to submit to reasonable searches of their property and person. Visiting pursuant to reasonable regulations would trigger the "consent exception" to the search warrant requirement. However, without an adequate basis to believe that contraband is being smuggled into the facility, no forcible search may be made. The sanction would be to immediately terminate visiting rights, subject to appropriate due process hearings.[58]

Strip searches raise different issues.[59] Strip searches of prison visitors were considered unreasonable when they were based solely on anonymous tips that were not investigated to confirm their validity. To justify a strip search of a visitor, prison officials must point to specific objective facts and rational inferences drawn from those facts, which indicate that the visitor will attempt to smuggle contraband into the prison on his or her person. Individualized suspicion is essential.[60]

Searches of prisoners following visits are more easily justified. Strip searches, including visual rectal searches, of segregation unit inmates following interviews with visitors, including attorneys, and after visits to the prison law library, do not violate the Fourth and Eighth Amendments, any right of privacy, or any denial of free access to the courts.[61]

Several Sixth Circuit Court of Appeals decisions concern such searches. In *Long v. Norris*,[62] it was held that a Tennessee prison regulation created a constitutionally protected liberty interest in visitation.[63] Thus, an official's threats to remove visitation rights in retaliation for visitors' refusal to submit to strip and body cavity searches in the absence of probable cause was contrary to the prison regulation. The relevant provisions of the Tennessee prison regulation stated that inmates "shall" have visitation rights, and that visits "shall be limited only by the institution's space and personnel resources," and that visitation rights may not be suspended absent a showing of good cause.

In another case, a woman wanted to visit a Kentucky prison inmate, but the prison staff refused to allow her to visit unless she submitted to a strip and body cavity search. They also refused to allow her to leave without a similar

---

[57]   *See* § 7.8.

[58]   *See* § 12.4 concerning searches of prisoners.

[59]   Cf. Bell v. Wolfish, 441 U.S. 520 (1979).

[60]   Hunter v. Auger, 672 F.2d 668 (8th Cir. 1982).

[61]   Arruda v. Fair, 547 F. Supp. 1324 (D. Mass. 1982).

[62]   Long v. Norris, 929 F.2d 1111 (6th Cir.), *cert. denied*, 502 U.S. 863 (1991).

[63]   Any decision prior to the 1995 case of *Sandin v. Conner* must be reevaluated as to whether a state law or regulation has created a constitutionally protected liberty interest. *See* §§ 5.3.1 and 8.1.

search. The Sixth Circuit[64] recognized the search to be "an embarrassing and humiliating experience." However, the Fourth Amendment does not afford a person seeking to enter a penal institution the same rights that a person would have on public streets or in a home. A prisoner does not have a due process right to unfettered visitation.[65] A citizen simply does not have the right to unfettered visitation of a prisoner that rises to a constitutional dimension. In seeking entry to such a controlled environment, a visitor simultaneously acknowledges a lesser expectation of privacy.[66] The unauthorized use of narcotics is a problem that plagues virtually every penal and detention center in the country[67] and a detention facility is a unique place, fraught with serious security dangers. The smuggling of money, drugs, weapons, and other contraband is an all-too-common occurrence.

The Sixth Circuit recognized that prison authorities have greater leeway in conducting searches of visitors, such as a pat-down or a metal detector sweep, merely as a condition of visitation, absent any suspicion. However, because a strip and body cavity search is the most intrusive type of search, courts have attempted to balance the need for institutional security against the remaining privacy interests of visitors. Even for strip and body cavity searches, prison authorities need not secure a warrant or have probable cause. However, the residual privacy interests of visitors in being free from such an invasive search requires prison authorities to have at least a reasonable suspicion that the visitor is carrying contraband before conducting such a search.

In another circuit,[68] a woman sued prison authorities because of a strip search to which she was subjected before being permitted to visit her father. She had been a regular visitor since she was very young. She had never violated a prison visitation rule or presented any threat to institutional security. Prior to a visit, the woman was informed that she would not be allowed to visit her father that day, or ever again, until she submitted to a strip search. She was presented with a form containing a consent to search, which she signed. Two female correctional officers then led her into a bathroom, where she was told to remove her clothing. A correctional officer checked her hair and her ears. She was instructed to squat, hold her head to her chest and cough, while two female correction officers stood behind her. No contraband was discovered and the appellant was permitted to visit her father. The woman was emotionally shaken by the experience. The First Circuit recognized that a prison visitor retains the Fourth Amendment right to be free from unreasonable searches and seizures. It was also recognized that a strip search, by its very nature, constitutes an extreme intrusion upon personal privacy, as well as an offense to the dignity of the individual.[69]

---

64   Spear v. Sowders, 71 F.3d 626 (6th Cir. 1995).

65   Kentucky v. Thompson, 490 U.S. 454 (1989).

66   Blackburn v. Snow, 771 F.2d 556, 565 (1st Cir. 1985).

67   Block v. Rutherford, 468 U.S. 576 (1984).

68   Cochrane v. Quattrocchi, 949 F.2d 11 (1st Cir. 1991).

69   *See* Burns v. Loranger, 907 F.2d 233 (1st Cir. 1990); Arruda v. Fair, 710 F.2d 886 (1st Cir. 1983); Hunter v. Auger, 672 F.2d 668, 674 (8th Cir. 1982).

The court rejected the argument that the daughter's signing of the consent form rendered moot any question as to whether there was a reasonable basis for the strip search. A prison visitor confronted with the choice between submitting to a strip search or foregoing a visit cannot provide a legally cognizable consent.[70] A directed verdict for the prison authorities was reversed.

The Sixth Circuit[71] discussed the rights of visitors. Because prison officials may properly limit the visitation rights of the prisoners on the grounds that limitations are reasonably related to legitimate penological interests, the effect of these limitations upon persons outside the prison are considered to be largely irrelevant.[72] The Sixth Circuit cited an Eighth Circuit case,[73] which stated that a court could not subject prison regulations to the "strict scrutiny" test[74] every time a family member was affected by a prison regulation. Incarceration necessarily deprives an individual of the freedom to be with family and friends and to form the other enduring attachments of normal life. Consequently, by its very nature, incarceration necessarily affects the prisoner's family.[75]

§ 3.8 Searches of Prisoners

In a Sixth Circuit case,[76] a prisoner was strip-searched following a prison uprising. It was recognized that a convicted prisoner maintains some reasonable expectations of privacy while in prison, particularly when those claims are related to forced exposure to strangers of the opposite sex, and that the prisoner raised a valid privacy claim under the Fourth Amendment.

---

[70] Blackburn v. Snow, 771 F.2d 556, 563 (1st Cir. 1985). Pretermitting the question of whether a visitor possessed a constitutional right, or merely a privilege, to visit the prison, *Blackburn* concluded that conditioning "access to the Jail upon sacrifice of [the visitor's] right to be free of an otherwise unreasonable strip search" was "dispositive of the consent issue." *Id.* at 568. *Blackburn* rejected the argument that the visitor's right to leave rather than submit to search, or to decline to return after the first strip search, in any way affected the issue; "for it is the very choice to which she was put that is constitutionally intolerable . . ."

[71] Bazzetta v. McGinnis, 124 F.3d 774 (6th Cir. 1997).

[72] *See* Thornburgh v. Abbott, 490 U.S. 401 (1989), in which the Supreme Court held that it was insufficient to focus solely on the identity of the individuals whose rights allegedly have been infringed. Although the Court took special note in *Procunier v. Martinez,* 416 U.S. 396 (1974), of the fact that the rights of nonprisoners were at issue, and stated a rule in *Turner v. Safley,* 482 U.S. 78 (1987), for the circumstances in which a prison regulation impinges on inmates' constitutional rights, any attempt to forge separate standards for cases implicating the rights of outsiders was inconsistent with the intervening decisions in *Pell v. Procunier,* 417 U.S. 817 (1974), *Jones v. North Carolina Prisoners' Labor Union, Inc.,* 433 U.S. 119 (1977), and *Bell v. Wolfish,* 441 U.S. 520 (1979). These cases, on which the Court expressly relied in *Turner* when it announced the reasonableness standard for "inmates' constitutional rights" cases, all involved regulations that affected rights of prisoners and outsiders.

[73] Goodwin v. Turner, 908 F.2d 1395 (8th Cir. 1990).

[74] As distinguished from the "rational basis" test.

[75] Subsequent to the *Bazzetta* decision, the Michigan Department of Corrections applied the opinion to noncontact visitations. The Sixth Circuit then issued a Supplementary Opinion solely for the purpose of clarification. The opinion emphasized that the court's earlier decision only concerned limitations on contact visitation and did not apply to noncontact visitations. Bazzetta v. McGinnis, 133 F.3d 382 (6th Cir. 1998).

[76] Cornwell v. Dahlberg, 963 F.2d 912 (6th Cir. 1992).

Despite the fact that the prisoner's Fourth Amendment privacy claim was properly submitted to the jury, the trial court improperly charged the jury on the Fourth Amendment privacy claim arising from the strip search. In its charge, the court instructed the jury to determine whether, under the Fourth Amendment, defendants acted in an "objectively reasonable manner" during the detention and the strip search. In doing so, the court encouraged the jury to consider, among other factors, the "availability of alternate locations" for the strip search.

In charging the jury regarding the prisoner's Fourth Amendment privacy claim, the court failed to adequately instruct the jury to find a valid, rational connection between the prison policy and a legitimate penological interest. Also, the trial court failed to inform the jury of the necessity of deference to prison officials in establishing these policies. As a result, the Sixth Circuit held that the charge as a whole did not adequately inform the jury of the applicable law regarding invasion of privacy under the Fourth Amendment. Further, the charge as a whole failed to instruct the jury to determine whether the prison policy of strip searching was reasonably related to a legitimate penological objective. The case was reversed on these issues.

In a state case, *Gadson v. Maryland*,[77] the question presented was the constitutional right of a state to detain a prospective visitor long enough to conduct a canine "sniff" inspection of the visitor's motor vehicle after the visitor, upon being told of the procedure, objected and expressed a desire to leave without entering the prison. While it is proper to require the visitor to submit to such a detention as a condition of entry, the court held that absent some reasonable, articulable suspicion of criminal activity, it was unreasonable under the Fourth Amendment to the United States Constitution to detain visitors who, prior to entering the prison, indicated a preference to leave rather than submit to the detention.

Employees are also subject to search. A visual body cavity search of a prison employee was constitutionally permissible where the search was within the scope of a warden's authority. The warden had a particularized and individualized tip from an informant that the employee was bringing contraband into the prison hidden in a tampon on a specific occasion.[78]

See also § 11.6.2, for a discussion of qualified immunity and other immunity defenses.

§ 3.9 Conclusion

The liberalizing trend of judicial decisions over the years regarding visitors and associations have been drastically curtailed by such cases as *Sandin v. Conner*. However, limits on the right of prison authorities to search visitors remain viable, either on Fourth Amendment grounds or privacy grounds.

---

[77] 341 Md. 1 (Md. Ct. App. 1995).
[78] Leverette v. Bell, 247 F.3d 160 (4th Cir. 2001).

Prisoners' Rights to Use of the Mail and Telephone

4

Chapter Outline

§ 4.1 Introduction

Detention in a penal institution necessitates a withdrawal of full enjoyment of constitutional rights. But exactly which rights are completely terminated and which are retained is usually unclear. Even rights not forfeited by incarceration are often retained in a diminished form. These general statements are illustrated by an analysis of the inmate's specific right to use the mail system to send and receive various items such as letters, legal materials, books, and magazines.

Article I, § 8 of the Constitution vests power in Congress to establish post offices; this power has been interpreted by the Supreme Court as granting to Congress and the U.S. Postal Service the exclusive right to regulate the postal system of the country.[1] That an inmate has at least a qualified federal right to use the mail system would thus seem clear. However, a long line of cases has established the principle that prison officials may place reasonable restrictions on this right.[2] Restrictions include limiting the number of persons with whom an inmate can correspond, opening and reading incoming and outgoing material, deleting sections from both incoming and outgoing mail, and refusing to mail material for an inmate or to forward correspondence to an inmate subject to important exceptions discussed below. For purposes of this chapter, the phrase "mail censorship" will be used to denote deletion of material from inmate mail.

Two general reasons have been advanced by both prison administrators and the judiciary to justify placing restrictions on an inmate's right to use the mail system.

First, prison security requires such restrictions. Contraband must be kept out of the prisons; escape plans must be detected; material that might incite the prison population must be excluded.

The second rationale for mail restrictions—that the orderly administration of a prison requires them—is closely related to the first. The correctional systems do not have unlimited funds that can be used to hire employees to enforce the restrictions placed on sending and receiving mail. However, because prison

---

[1] Public Clearing House v. Coyne, 194 U.S. 497 (1904).
[2] Adams v. Ellis, 197 F.2d 483 (5th Cir. 1952); Numer v. Miller, 165 F.2d 986 (9th Cir. 1948); Medlock v. Burke, 285 F. Supp. 67 (E.D. Wis. 1968); Sherman v. MacDougatt, 656 F.2d 527 (9th Cir. 1981); Parnell v. Waldrep, 511 F. Supp. 764 (D.N.C. 1981).

security may reasonably demand that inmate mail be opened, inspected for contraband, read, and some sections deleted, some limit on the amount of mail to be checked must be established. Thus, prison officials have justified rules limiting the quantity of mail that an individual can send and receive.

A third reason, rehabilitation of inmates, is infrequently either implicitly or explicitly used to justify mail restrictions. Thus, although the requirements of security and administration may justify limiting the amount of mail each inmate may send or receive, neither requirement will justify the establishment of a mail list whereby an inmate can send or receive mail only from sources approved by the prison authorities. However, the goal of rehabilitation has been advanced by penal administrators to justify such action.[3]

Several topics that could logically have been included in this chapter are covered elsewhere. They are: the right to buy and receive legal material;[4] the right to correspond with religious leaders;[5] and the right to receive religious literature.[6]

§ 4.2   The General Right to Control an Inmate's Use of the Mail System—The Traditional Approach

This section, together with the following sections, will discuss the general right of prison authorities to regulate inmate mail, and several of the specific procedures they use to accomplish this regulation.

As a starting point, it may be stated that a myriad of previous cases have established and maintained the proposition that control of inmate mail is an administrative matter in which the courts will not interfere, unless it is shown that an independent constitutional right is being infringed.[7] This may, for lack of a better phrase, be called the "traditional view" of the courts on inmate mail regulation. The reason most often advanced to support the traditional view is that courts will not become involved in the normal management of a prison system.

In retrospect, we can see that in cases in which the courts did interfere with prison mail rules, another constitutional right was involved. Thus, communication between an inmate and a court involved the right of access to the court system. Communication between an inmate and his or her attorney involved both the right of access to courts and the Sixth Amendment's guarantee of counsel for criminals. The First Amendment right to petition government for redress of grievances justified court intervention in correspondence to and from nonjudicial public officials and agencies. The cherished American

---

3   Carothers v. Follette, 314 F. Supp. 1014 (S.D.N.Y. 1970); Milburn v. McNiff, 437 N.Y.S.2d 445 (N.Y. App. Div. 1981).

4   *See* Chapter 7.

5   *See* Chapter 6.

6   *Id.*

7   *E.g.,* Brown v. Wainwright, 419 F.2d 1308 (5th Cir. 1969); Ortega v. Ragen, 216 F.2d 561 (7th Cir. 1954); Medlock v. Burke, 285 F. Supp. 67 (E.D. Wis. 1968); Zaczek v. Hutto, 642 F.2d 74 (4th Cir. 1981).

freedoms of speech and press were involved in regulations concerning access to news media. These rights also were involved in attempts by prison officials to exclude newspapers, magazines, and books from an institution. Inclusion of white-oriented periodicals on approved mailing lists that excluded black-oriented materials raised an equal protection argument.

If, however, an inmate could not couple his or her complaint of undue restriction on use of the mail with an allegation that a separate constitutional right was thereby infringed, he or she was, under the "traditional view," doomed to failure in the courts. Thus, in *Dayton v. McGranery*,[8] an inmate's allegation that he was prevented from writing to a young woman was dismissed because he did not state a cause of action. *Stroud v. Swope*[9] affirmed the dismissal of an inmate's complaint that sought to restrain a federal prison warden from refusing to mail the inmate's manuscript to a publisher. Such allegations, the court held, did not constitute a deprivation of any of the petitioner's rights. Several federal appellate courts also refused to inquire into the reasons for not allowing an inmate to take a correspondence course. Such decisions are "simply an exercise of administrative discretion."[10]

§ 4.2.1 —The New Approach

Reading and inspection of inmate mail serves two purposes: (1) it prevents contraband from being smuggled into or out of an institution; and (2) it enables the prison authorities to detect plans for illegal activity—namely escape. Thus, such action, at least for incoming mail, has uniformly been upheld by the courts.[11] However, the administrators' refusal to mail correspondence that does not contain contraband or details of illegal schemes has been subject to judicial criticism. Under the traditional view, described in the preceding section, such a refusal is normally considered unreviewable. Under what we call the "new approach," prison officials are judicially required to justify such actions. Thus, in *McNamara v. Moody*,[12] prison officials were held to have violated a prisoner's constitutional rights by refusing to mail a letter to the inmate's girlfriend. The court held that censorship must be limited to concrete violations such as escape plans, plans for disruption of the prison system or work routine, or plans for importing contraband.[13]

---

[8]   201 F.2d 711 (D.C. Cir. 1953); Carwile v. Ray, 481 F. Supp. 33 (E.D. Wa. 1979).

[9]   187 F.2d 850 (9th Cir. 1951), *cert. denied,* 342 U.S. 829 (1951).

[10]   Diehl v. Wainwright, 419 F.2d 1309 (5th Cir. 1970); Carey v. Settle, 351 F.2d 483 (8th Cir. 1965); Numer v. Miller, 165 F.2d 986 (9th Cir. 1948); Cook v. Brockway, 424 F. Supp. 1046 (N.D. Tex. 1977), *aff'd,* 559 F.2d 1214 (5th Cir. 1977).

[11]   Sostre v. McGinnis, 442 F.2d 178 (2d Cir. 1971), *cert. denied,* 405 U.S. 978 (1972); Jones v. Wittenberg, 330 F. Supp. 707 (N.D. Ohio 1971) (incoming parcels or letters addressed to inmates awaiting trial can be inspected for contraband, but letters cannot be read); Palmigiano v. Travisono, 317 F. Supp. 776 (D.R.I. 1970) (all incoming mail may be read and inspected, but no outgoing mail may be read without a search warrant); Smith v. Shimp, 562 F.2d 423 (7th Cir. 1977).

[12]   606 F.2d 621 (5th Cir. 1979); Carothers v. Follette, 314 F. Supp. 1014 (S.D.N.Y. 1970).

[13]   McNamara v. Moody, *supra* n. 12.

The new approach to regulation of inmate mail is best illustrated by contrasting *Procunier v. Martinez*[14] with *Turner v. Safley*[15] and *Thornburgh v. Abbott*.[16] The inmate-plaintiffs attacked the validity of a California prison mail regulation that authorized prison officials to refuse to send inmate mail, and to refuse to distribute mail to inmates. The United States Supreme Court held the regulation void due to vagueness and overbreadth. In doing so, the Court recognized that the First Amendment rights of the "free world" correspondent were at issue. Guidelines for regulating prison mail were established.

Censorship of prison mail is justified if the following criteria are met. First, the regulation must further a substantial governmental interest that is *unrelated to the suppression of expression*. Prison officials may not censor inmate correspondence simply to eliminate unflattering or unwelcome opinions or factually inaccurate statements. Rather, they must show that the regulation authorizing censorship furthers one or more of the substantial government interests of security, order, and rehabilitation. Second, the limitation of First Amendment freedoms must be no greater than is necessary or incidental to the protection of the particular government interest involved.[17]

In addition to providing the criteria for censorship, *Procunier* enunciated the minimum procedure that must be followed when prison officials censor or withhold mail. The inmate must be notified of the rejection of his or her letter, the letter's author must be allowed to protest the refusal and the complaint must be decided by an official other than the one who made the original decision to refuse delivery.[18]

Thirteen years later, in *Turner v. Safley*, a different standard was used. The United States Supreme Court held that lower courts had been in error in holding that *Martinez* required the application of a strict scrutiny standard of review for resolving prisoners' constitutional complaints. Rather, a lesser standard is appropriate when an inquiry is made into whether a prison regulation that impinges on inmates' constitutional rights is "reasonably related" to legitimate penological interests. In determining reasonableness, relevant factors include: (1) whether there is a "valid, rational connection" between the regulation and a legitimate and neutral governmental interest put forward to justify it, and the connection cannot be so remote as to render the regulation arbitrary or irrational; (2) whether there are alternative means of exercising the asserted constitutional rights that remain open to inmates, and the alternatives, if they exist, will require a measure of judicial deference to the corrections officials' expertise; (3) whether and the extent to which accommodation of the asserted right will have an impact on prison staff, on inmates' liberty, and on the allocation of limited prison resources, and whether the impact, if substantial, will require particular deference to corrections officials; and (4) whether the regu-

---

14   416 U.S. 396 (1974).
15   482 U.S. 78 (1987).
16   490 U.S. 401 (1989).
17   *Id.* at 413.
18   *See* Padgett v. Stein, 406 F. Supp. 287 (M.D. Pa. 1975); Gates v. Collier, 525 F.2d 965 (5th Cir. 1976).

lation represents an "exaggerated response" to prison concerns, the existence of a ready alternative that fully accommodates the prisoner's rights at *de minimis* costs to valid penological interests being evidence of unreasonableness.

Inmate correspondence regulations that permitted correspondence between immediate family members who were inmates at different institutions within a jurisdiction, and between inmates "concerning legal matters," but allowed other inmate correspondence only if each inmate's classification was reasonable and factually valid, passed constitutional review. The regulations were logically related to the legitimate security concerns of prison officials. It was felt that mail between prisons could be used to communicate escape plans, to arrange violent acts, and to foster prison gang activity. The regulation did not deprive prisoners of all means of expression, but simply barred communication with a limited class of people—other inmates—with whom authorities have particular cause to be concerned. The regulation was entitled to deference on the basis of the significant impact of prison correspondence on the liberty and safety of other prisoners and prison personnel. Such correspondence facilitates the development of informal organizations that threaten safety and security at penal institutions. Nor was there an obvious, easy alternative to the regulation, because monitoring inmate correspondence imposed more than a *de minimis* cost in terms of the burden on staff resources required to conduct item-by-item censorship. It also created an appreciable risk of missing dangerous communications. The regulation was content-neutral and did not unconstitutionally abridge the First Amendment rights of prison inmates.

Two years later, in *Thornburgh v. Abbott*, the Supreme Court reviewed Federal Bureau of Prisons regulations that generally permitted prisoners to receive publications from the "outside," but authorized wardens, pursuant to specified criteria, to reject an incoming publication if it is found "to be detrimental to the security, good order, or discipline of the institution or if it might facilitate criminal activity." Wardens could not reject a publication solely because of its religious, philosophical, political, social, sexual, unpopular, or repugnant content, or establish an excluded list of publications, but were required to review each issue of a subscription separately.

The Court held that mail regulations that affect sending publications to prisoners must be analyzed under the standard set forth in *Turner v. Safley* and are valid if they are reasonably related to legitimate penological interests. Prison officials are due considerable deference in regulating the delicate balance between prison order and security and the legitimate demands of "outsiders" who seek to enter the prison environment. The less deferential standard of *Martinez*—whereby prison regulations authorizing mail censorship must be "generally necessary" to protect one or more legitimate government interests—was limited to regulations concerning outgoing personal correspondence from prisoners, *i.e.*, regulations that are not centrally concerned with the maintenance of prison order and security. In addition, *Martinez* was overruled to the extent that it might support the drawing of a categorical distinction between incoming correspondence from prisoners (to which *Turner* applied its reasonableness standard) and incoming correspondence from non-prisoners.

The regulations under review were factually valid under the *Turner* standard. Their underlying objective of protecting prison security was legitimate, and was neutral with regard to the content of the expression regulated. The broad discretion that the regulations accorded wardens was rationally related to security interests. Further, alternative means of expression remained open to the inmates, because the regulations permitted a broad range of publications to be sent, received, and read, even though specific publications were prohibited. Finally, the prisoners established no alternative to the regulations that would accommodate their constitutional rights at a *de minimis* cost to valid penological interests.

The "new approach" to inmate mail advanced by *Martinez, Turner, and Abbott* did not eliminate mail censorship, but only regulated it. When the screening of mail is done pursuant to regulations that are reasonably related to legitimate government interests, the prison official's right to read, inspect, and stop inmate correspondence remains intact.

Mail issues are subject to the exhaustion requirement. The return of documents mailed to an inmate by his mother in a torn and mutilated condition would not support a civil rights claim where the inmate failed to pursue an adequate state post-deprivation remedy in a court of claims action.[19]

§ 4.3 Communication with the Courts

It has been the law of the land since 1941 that a state and its officers may not abridge or impair an inmate's right to apply to a federal court for a writ of habeas corpus.[20] In *Ex parte Hull*,[21] the inmate-plaintiff was confined in the Michigan State Prison. He had prepared a petition for a writ of habeas corpus to be filed in the United States Supreme Court, but a prison official refused to mail it, pursuant to a prison regulation requiring legal papers to go through the institutional welfare officer. The regulation provided that if the writ were favorably acted upon, it would be referred to the legal section of the parole board, and then if found to be properly drawn, it would be directed to the appropriate court. The Supreme Court of the United States held this regulation invalid, declaring that a state and its officers may not abridge or impair an inmate's right to apply to a federal court for a writ of habeas corpus. Whether the writ is properly drawn is a question for the court to determine, not prison officials.

Since the decision in *Ex parte Hull*, federal courts have closely scrutinized any prison regulation that allows prison administrators to refuse to forward inmate mail. For example, in *Bryan v. Werner*,[22] a federal court struck down a prison regulation that permitted officials to refuse to mail legal matters for inmates if the officials felt the form used was improper.

---

[19]   Jackson v. Burke, 256 F.3d 93 (2d Cir. 2001).

[20]   *See* § 12.9, *ex post facto*.

[21]   Ex parte Hull, 312 U.S. 546 (1941).

[22]   516 F.2d 233 (3d Cir. 1975).

Although there would seem to be no rational basis for distinguishing between legal material that pertains to the inmate's conviction and legal material that involves other matters, at least one federal appellate court has sustained such a distinction. *Kirby v. Thomas*[23] involved a regulation of the Kentucky Department of Corrections that forbade the mailing of legal papers unless they pertained to the validity of the inmate's conviction. The court stated only one reason for upholding the regulation: the state prison administrator's need for discretion in maintaining discipline.

However, the vast majority of courts now recognize that an inmate has the right to petition the courts concerning not only his or her conviction, but also the constitutionality of the conditions of his or her confinement. Access to the courts is a fundamental right and "all other rights of an inmate are illusory without it . . ."[24]

§ 4.3.1   —Censorship of Communication with the Courts

Several decisions have dealt with the right of prison officials to censor mail sent to and received from a court by an inmate. In *Smith v. Shimp*[25] the court stated that privileged mail, i.e., mail between an inmate and attorneys, government officials, or news media personnel, can be opened only in the presence of the inmate and only to verify the addressee. Emphasizing the inmate's right of access to the courts, the Eighth Circuit Court of Appeals held that legal mail that is identified as such cannot be opened for inspection for contraband except in the presence of the prisoner.[26]

The clear state of the case law is to allow incoming mail from the courts to be inspected for contraband, but with prohibitions against reading the correspondence.

§ 4.4   Communication with Attorneys

A basic corollary to the right of access to the courts is the inmate's right to communicate with an attorney concerning the validity of his or her conviction or the constitutionality of conditions within the detention facility.[27] If the

---

[23]   336 F.2d 462 (6th Cir. 1964).

[24]   McCray v. Sullivan, 509 F.2d 1332, 1337 (5th Cir.), *cert. denied*, 423 U.S. 859 (1975); *cf.*, Coleman v. Crisp, 444 F. Supp. 31 (W.D. Okla. 1977). *See* Johnson v. Texas Department of Corrections in § 9.2, in which the parole board was enjoined from discriminating against prison writ writers.

[25]   562 F.2d 423 (7th Cir. 1977); Frazier v. Donelon, 381 F. Supp. 911 (E.D. La. 1974), *aff'd*, 520 F.2d 941 (5th Cir. 1975).

[26]   Jensen v. Klecker, 648 F.2d 1179 (8th Cir. 1981); Ramos v. Lamm, 639 F.2d 559 (10th Cir. 1980); Jones v. Diamond, 594 F.2d 997 (5th Cir. 1979); Taylor v. Sterrett, 532 F.2d 462 (5th Cir. 1976).

[27]   Sostre v. McGinnis, 442 F.2d 178 (2d Cir. 1971), *cert. denied*, 405 U.S. 978 (1972); Blanks v. Cunningham, 409 F.2d 220 (4th Cir. 1969); Marsh v. Moore, 325 F. Supp. 392 (D. Mass. 1971); Thibadoux v. LaVallee, 411 F. Supp. 862 (W.D.N.Y. 1976).

inmate is not represented by counsel, he or she has the right to correspond with an attorney in an attempt to secure legal representation, and this communication may set forth factual elements of his or her claim, even though critical of the prison administration.[28] The right to seek legal representation extends not only to the right to communicate with individual members of the bar, but also to the right to seek advice and possible representation from legal organizations such as the American Civil Liberties Union.[29]

The right to communicate with an attorney has been limited to communication involving legal matters. In *Rhinehart v. Rhay,*[30] for example, Washington state prison officials refused to mail several letters from the plaintiff to his attorney. The officials claimed, and the court agreed, that the purpose of the letters in question was to express the plaintiff's belief that homosexual acts among consenting prisoners ought to be legalized. There was no evidence that the plaintiff was denied access to his attorney for the purpose of perfecting an appeal of his conviction.

§ 4.4.1 —Censorship of Communication with Attorneys

The right of an inmate to communicate with his or her attorney concerning pending or contemplated legal action is recognized by all courts today. Of more importance, however, is the right of prison authorities to open, read, and censor such communications. Inmates often complain that such conduct interferes with their right to counsel as guaranteed by the Sixth Amendment.

Generally, the cases concerning censorship of inmate letters to their attorneys fall into three groups. In the first group are cases that recognize that the censoring of inmate mail, including correspondence to attorneys, is a matter of internal prison administration with which the courts hesitate to interfere.[31] These cases hold that inspection of inmate mail is necessary to detect contraband or to discover escape plans, and as long as the contents of the communications are not disclosed to the prosecuting attorney, and the inmate is afforded ample time to confer privately with his or her attorney in the institution, there is no infringement on the inmate's Sixth Amendment right to counsel.[32] An extreme application of this reasoning is found in *Cox v. Crouse.*[33] In that case, the inmate was being tried on a criminal charge, and the warden systematically opened and read the inmate's correspondence with his attorney, and

---

[28]   Bounds v. Smith, 430 U.S. 817 (1977).

[29]   Burns v. Swenson, 430 F.2d 771 (8th Cir. 1970), *cert. denied,* 404 U.S. 1062 (1971), *reh'g denied,* 405 U.S. 969 (1971); Nolan v. Scafati, 430 F.2d 548 (1st Cir. 1970).

[30]   314 F. Supp. 81 (W.D. Wash. 1970).

[31]   Brabson v. Wilkins, 19 N.Y.2d 433, 280 N.Y.S.2d 561 (1967); Frazier v. Donelon, 381 F. Supp. 911 (E.D. La. 1974), *aff'd,* 520 F.2d 941 (5th Cir. 1975).

[32]   Ramer v. United States, 411 F.2d 30 (9th Cir. 1969), *cert. denied,* 396 U.S. 965 (1969); Haas v. United States, 344 F.2d 56 (8th Cir. 1965).

[33]   367 F.2d 824 (10th Cir. 1967).

then communicated the contents to the state attorney general. The inmate argued that prejudice could be presumed from such disclosure; the court rejected this claim, stating that the inmate must show actual prejudice in order to be entitled to relief.

In the second group, *Sostre v. McGinnis*[34] represents a compromise between the position of no censorship of correspondence between an inmate and an attorney and the position of treating such correspondence like any other type of mail, and allowing it to be censored. In *Sostre*, the court held that officials could open and read such letters, but could not delete anything from them or refuse to forward them unless the inmate was clearly abusing the privilege. Two examples of clear abuse of the privilege, the court stated, would be mailing or receiving contraband and mailing plans for an illegal activity.

Smith v. Robbins,[35] another federal appellate decision, sought to give even more protection to inmate-attorney correspondence than did *Sostre*. In *Smith*, the warden was enjoined from reading the correspondence, and he could open such material to inspect for contraband only in the presence of the inmate involved.

The third group of cases represents the current view, which is a significant break with the past. These cases hold that prison officials are permitted to open attorney correspondence in the presence of the inmate to check for contraband, but the contents may not be read. This procedure of checking for contraband neither constitutes censorship, nor does it have a chilling effect on the correspondence.[36] However, reasonable regulations of the correspondence are permitted. Such regulations may require that the attorney first identify himself or herself in a signed letter or that the inmate supply prison officials with the name and business address of his or her attorney.[37]

Inmates who are serving sentences need the assistance of counsel to perfect appeals of their convictions and to initiate and litigate civil actions. Many inmates of detention facilities, however, are not convicted of any crime, but are being held pending trial on charges filed against them. The pretrial detainee's need for counsel is crucial. Therefore, it is not surprising that cases recognize the right to uncensored correspondence between pretrial detainees and their legal counsel.[38]

§ 4.5 Communication with Nonjudicial Public Officials and Agencies

One of the rights specified in the First Amendment is the right to petition the government for the redress of alleged grievances. This right is especially important to prisoners when they complain of conditions of confinement.

---

[34] 442 F.2d 178 (2d Cir. 1971), *cert. denied,* 405 U.S. 978 (1972).
[35] 454 F.2d 696 (1st Cir. 1972).
[36] Wolff v. McDonnell, 418 U.S. 539 (1974); Jensen v. Klecker, 648 F.2d 1179 (8th Cir. 1981).
[37] Taylor v. Sterrett, 532 F.2d 462 (5th Cir. 1976).
[38] *Id.*

Quite often, however, an administrative complaint to the department of government ultimately responsible for the management of the prison is both faster and more effective than seeking judicial review. Hence, the courts have generally protected the right of inmates to utilize the mail system to communicate with nonjudicial public officials and agencies. *LeVier v. Woodson*[39] prevented state prison officials from stopping letters (complaining of prison conditions) to the state governor, attorney general, and the attorney working for the state's pardon agency.

Reading and censoring inmate correspondence became more restricted after the *Procunier* and *Wolff* decisions. The rationale of these two cases was relied upon in *Taylor v. Sterrett,*[40] and applied to inmate correspondence with government agencies. Emphasizing the inmate's First Amendment right to petition the government for redress of grievances, and finding the reading of government agency correspondence not substantially related to jail security, the court enjoined prison officials from reading the correspondence. The decision, however, allowed prison officials to continue opening incoming mail to check for contraband.

Punishing an inmate for communicating his or her complaints to higher administrative levels is as much a denial of the right to petition government as is the outright refusal to mail such letters. This principle is exemplified by *Cavey v. Williams,*[41] in which a warden was ordered to pay compensatory and punitive damages to the inmate plaintiff because the warden violated the inmate's First Amendment rights by punishing him for a letter he wrote criticizing prison policies.

The few cases that are cited in support of the proposition (that inmates do not have the right to use the mails to voice complaints to government officials) either are devoid of legal reasoning or simply do not involve a petition seeking redress of prison grievances. For example, the inmate-plaintiff in *McCloskey v. Maryland*[42] sought to enjoin state penal officials from refusing to mail letters from him to his elected state and federal legislators. However, the letters did not complain of conditions of confinement, but were expressions of the inmate's anti-Semitic views. In such a case, the court held, refusal to mail the letters was not an abuse of the prison officials' control over inmates' mailing privileges. *McCloskey*, therefore, is not authority for the view that prison administrators may arbitrarily refuse to forward a letter from an inmate to the state director of corrections, complaining of conditions within the prison, even though it has been cited as such.[43] A case similar to *McCloskey* is *United States ex rel. Thompson v. Fay,*[44] in which the court held that a state prisoner had no right to mail a letter, seeking legal advice, to a fed-

---

[39]   443 F.2d 360 (10th Cir. 1971).

[40]   532 F.2d 462 (5th Cir. 1976).

[41]   435 F. Supp. 475 (D. Md. 1977), *aff'd,* 580 F.2d 1047 (4th Cir. 1978); Fulwood v. Clemmer, 206 F. Supp. 370 (D.C. Cir. 1962).

[42]   337 F.2d 72 (4th Cir. 1964).

[43]   Belk v. Mitchell, 294 F. Supp. 800 (W.D.N.C. 1968).

[44]   197 F. Supp. 855 (S.D.N.Y. 1961).

eral committee that was investigating the problems of indigent defendants accused of federal crimes. The committee was not rendering legal aid to indigents and furthermore, the inmate had not been charged or convicted of a federal crime. Thus, not only did the correspondence fail to complain of conditions of confinement, but was entirely frivolous.

Prison rules for mailing non-privileged matter required mailing a form to the addressee with whom the prisoner wanted to correspond. The form had to be mailed back by the addressee. The prisoner then requested permission to mail his "correspondence request" mail sealed. The rules did not permit the prisoner to state on the form his reasons for requesting permission to correspond. The rule was held to be irrational and unconstitutional as applied to three letters to public officials or agencies and one to the American Civil Liberties Union.[45]

Reasonable prison regulations will be enforced. An action to have prison officials have checks issued to a county court clerk and law library so that an inmate could obtain legal materials was properly dismissed, notwithstanding that this prevented an inmate from filing pretrial motions on his criminal charges. The inmate did not detail sufficiently the legal materials he was seeking, did not clarify that the library at the prison and its resources were inadequate for his needs, and did not explain that his legal claim was nonfrivolous.[46]

§ 4.6 Communication with News Media—Inmates' Right to Use the Mail to Contact News Media

The First Amendment prohibits governmental interference with freedom of speech and freedom of the press. Although the judiciary has construed the amendment to allow reasonable restraints on these freedoms, it is still true that these rights occupy a preferred position in the American system of government. Hence, the courts generally require that any restriction on First Amendment rights be based upon a "substantial and controlling" state interest that requires such restriction,[47] and requires that the restriction be the least drastic method of accomplishing the state goal.[48]

A prison ban on inmates sending letters that complain of internal conditions in the institution to the news media—radio, television, and the press—restricts First Amendment freedoms in two ways. First, the inmate's right to free speech is curtailed. Second, the public's right to know what is happening within the prison system, a right that can only be fulfilled through an informed press, is restricted.

---

[45] Davidson v. Skully, 694 F.2d 50 (2d Cir. 1982).
[46] McBride v. Deer, 240 F.3d 1287 (10th Cir. 2001).
[47] Jackson v. Godwin, 400 F.2d 529, 541 (5th Cir. 1968).
[48] Shelton v. Tucker, 364 U.S. 479 (1960); Vienneau v. Shanks, 425 F. Supp. 676 (W.D. Wis. 1977).

Regardless of the degree of restriction on the actual flow of information between inmate and reporter, however, prisoners would seem to have an interest in communication with the public through the press that is distinctive from and in addition to their interest in simply communicating with the news media.[49]

In *Nolan v. Fitzpatrick*,[50] inmates contested the legality of a Massachusetts state prison regulation that totally banned letters from inmates to the news media. The right of prison officials to read such letters and to inspect them for contraband or for escape plans was not challenged. The prison officials advanced various reasons in support of the rule: that such communications would inflame the inmates and, thus, endanger prison security; that complaint letters would create administrative problems because they would encourage the news media to seek personal interviews with inmates; and that complaint letters would inhibit the rehabilitation of both the writer and other inmates. The district court found these reasons to be either unsupported by evidence or insufficient to require a total ban on letters to the press.

The rationale of *Procunier v. Martinez* and its applicability to all classes of inmate correspondence becomes evident. Applying the *Procunier* rationale to inmate contact with the media, a federal court invalidated prison regulations on the grounds that they ". . . provide too much occasion for subjective evaluation, thus enabling the licensing official to act as a censor."[51] Similarly, in *Taylor v. Sterrett*,[52] the court recognized the inmate's right to communicate with the press under *Procunier* guidelines:

> . . . the interest of jail security necessitates that incoming mail from the press be inspected for contraband. . . . And the distinctive ethical standards attorneys are held to cannot apply to the press. We cannot say, therefore, that the reading of outgoing inmate correspondence to the press does not further a substantial governmental interest. Transmitting unread mail to supposed members of the press could be used as a subterfuge for discussing illegal activities.

> . . . Since the free expression and petition interests of the inmate-plaintiffs are operative in this case, the practice of reading this mail must be essential to jail security.

The decision further stated that the inmate-press correspondence should be treated under procedures similar to those applying to inmate-attorney mail.[53]

---

49   *The Supreme Court, 1973 Term,* 88 HARV. L. REV. 165-173 (1974).
50   451 F.2d 545 (1st Cir. 1971), *rev'g,* 326 F. Supp. 209 (D. Mass. 1971).
51   Main Road v. Aytch, 522 F.2d 1080 (3d Cir. 1975).
52   532 F.2d 462 (5th Cir. 1976).
53   *See* § 4.4.1.

§ 4.7   Communication with Inmates in Other Institutions

The courts have generally given prison administrators unfettered discretion in refusing to allow one inmate to correspond with another inmate. The reason most often given to justify such action is that the control of inmate mail is an administrative function in which the courts refuse to intervene. Thus, in *Schlobohm v. United States Attorney General*,[54] a federal district court held that a prison policy of prohibiting correspondence between inmates of different institutions was permissible. The court stated that indefinite mail restriction imposed as a punishment was a legitimate exercise of disciplinary power when a prisoner had violated existing prison mail regulations.[55]

Johnson v. Avery[56] held that prison officials who fail to provide adequate legal assistance cannot forbid a jailhouse lawyer from rendering legal assistance to a fellow inmate. The case left open the interesting question concerning correspondence between inmates. Even though prison officials might have the general power to prevent such correspondence, would the *Johnson* rationale prevent the refusal to allow an inmate to engage in legal correspondence with an inmate in another institution? The Ninth Circuit Court of Appeals held that the complete prohibition of an inmate's correspondence with his jailhouse lawyer in another institution was a violation of that inmate's rights.[57]

In the Eighth Circuit, a prison policy prohibiting correspondence between inmates housed in different units of the same institution is valid.[58]

While an inmate was incarcerated in state prison, he learned that a fellow inmate had been charged with assaulting a correctional officer. He decided to assist the inmate with his defense and sent him a letter, which was intercepted in accordance with prison policy. Based on the letter's content, the prison sanctioned the inmate for violating prison rules prohibiting insolence and interfering with due process hearings.

In *Shaw v. Murphy*,[59] the Supreme Court held that inmates do not possess a special First Amendment right to provide legal assistance to fellow inmates that enhances the protections otherwise available under *Turner v. Safley*.[60] Prisoners' constitutional rights are more limited in scope than the constitutional rights held by individuals in society at large. The Supreme Court commented that some First Amendment rights are simply inconsistent with the correctional system's legitimate penological objectives. Moreover, because courts are ill-equipped to deal with the complex and intractable problems of prisons, the Supreme Court has generally deferred to prison officials' judg-

---

54   Schlobohm v. United States Attorney General, 479 F. Supp. 401 (M.D. Pa. 1979); Lawrence v. Davis, 401 F. Supp. 1203 (W.D. Pa. 1979).
55   *Id.*
56   393 U.S. 483 (1969).
57   Storseth v. Spellman, 654 F.2d 1349 (9th Cir. 1981).
58   Goff v. Nix, 113 F.3d 887 (8th Cir. 1997).
59   532 U.S. 223 (2001).
60   *See* 4.2.1 *supra.*

ment in upholding regulations against constitutional challenge. *Turner* reflects this understanding, setting a unitary, deferential standard for reviewing prisoners' claims that does not permit an increase in the constitutional protection whenever a prisoner's communication includes legal advice. To increase the constitutional protection based upon a communication's content first requires an assessment of that content's value. But the *Turner* test simply does not accommodate valuations of content. On the contrary, it concerns only the relationship between the asserted penological interests and the prison regulation. Moreover, prison officials are to remain the primary arbiters of the problems that arise in prison management. Seeking to avoid unnecessary federal courts involvement in prison administration affairs, the Supreme Court rejected an alteration of the *Turner* analysis that would involve additional federal court oversight. Even if the Supreme Court were to consider giving special protection to particular kinds of speech based on content, it would not do so for speech that includes legal advice. Augmenting First Amendment protection for such advice would undermine prison officials' ability to address the complex and intractable problems of prison administration. The legal text could be an excuse for making clearly inappropriate comments, which may circulate among prisoners despite prison measures to screen individual inmates or officers from the remarks. Further, there is a presumption that prison officials act within their broad discretion.

§ 4.8 Receipt of Inflammatory Material

The Supreme Court has held that the First Amendment freedoms of speech and press encompass the "right to receive information and ideas."[61] These rights are not absolute, however, but are subject to two important qualifications: (1) pornographic material is not protected by the First Amendment, and (2) the First Amendment does not protect activity that involves a clear and present danger of inciting or producing imminent lawless action.[62] This section will discuss the authority of prison administrators to exclude material, mainly magazines and books, from the institution because they constitute a clear and present danger of disrupting prison security.

Although the "clear and present danger" test did not originate in prison litigation, it applies as a general principle of law to that specific environment. In fact, due to the tense atmosphere that often exists in such institutions, prison officials may be able to exclude material using this test, even though such material is clearly protected by the First Amendment outside of the prison walls. The application of the clear and present danger test in a prison setting was explained in the case of *Sostre v. Otis*:

---

[61] Stanley v. Georgia, 394 U.S. 557, 564 (1969).
[62] Brandenburg v. Ohio, 395 U.S. 444 (1969).

We accept the premise that certain literature may pose such a clear and present danger to the security of a prison, or to the rehabilitation of prisoners, that it should be censored. To take an extreme example, if there were mailed to a prisoner a brochure demonstrating in detail how to saw prison bars with utensils used in the mess hall, or how to provoke a prison riot, it would properly be screened. A magazine detailing for incarcerated drug addicts how they might obtain an euphoric "high," comparable to that experienced from heroin, by sniffing aerosol or glue available for other purposes within the prison walls, would likewise be censorable as restraining effective rehabilitation. Furthermore, it is undoubtedly true that in the volatile atmosphere of a prison, where a large number of men, many with criminal tendencies, live in close proximity to each other, violence can be fomented by the printed word much more easily than in the outside world. Some censorship or prior restraint on inflammatory literature sent into prisons is, therefore, necessary to prevent such literature from being used to cause disruption or violence within the prison. It may well be that in some prisons where the prisoners' flash-point is low, articles regarding bombing, prison riots, or the like, which would be harmless when sold on the corner newsstand, would be too dangerous for release to the prison population.[63]

Even though all courts previously accepted the proposition that prison officials can exclude literature that presents a clear and present danger to prison security, the judiciary was often called upon to review the procedure that administrators use to make the determination that a certain book or newspaper is a clear and present danger to the institution's security. This aspect of judicial review is crucial; if the courts routinely sanction the officials' decision, with little or no analysis of the process and standards used to reach that decision, the First Amendment rights of the inmates are likely to be lost. This loss can be illustrated by two cases decided by the federal courts. In the first case, *Abernathy v. Cunningham,*[64] the prisoner-plaintiff sought court permission to obtain a book titled *The Message to the Black Man in America* and to subscribe to the newspaper, *Elijah Muhammad Speaks.* Both publications pertained to the Black Muslim religion. The appellate court upheld the prison officials' refusal to comply with the requests, stating that the evaluation of the literature by the officials as to its probable effects on the prison population must be given great weight.

In the later case of *Battle v. Anderson,*[65] the court recognized that an inmate retains some of his or her First Amendment rights even while incarcerated, and the prison officials had the burden of proving to the court that the publications *Elijah Muhammad Speaks* and *The Message to the Black Man in America,* present a threat to security, discipline, and order within the institution.

---

[63]   Sostre v. Otis, 330 F. Supp. 941, 944-945 (S.D.N.Y. 1971).
[64]   393 F.2d 775 (4th Cir. 1968).
[65]   376 F. Supp. 402 (E.D. Okla. 1974).

Battle was written to conform to *Procunier* standards for protecting the inmate's right to receive literature, delineating the restrictions and procedures under which mail may be censored. Accordingly, "censorship of these publications is permissible only if it furthers the prison's substantial interest in security, order, or rehabilitation, and no less restrictive means would suffice to protect the prison's interest."[66] Recognizing the significant contributions of *Procunier* to prison mail regulation, later decisions have refined the holding to fashion the law concerning inflammatory material.[67] Publications containing enlarged views of the inner mechanisms of guns may be withheld.[68]

§ 4.9 Receipt of Obscene Material

In 1957, the United States Supreme Court held that obscene literature is not within the ambit of constitutionally protected freedoms of speech or press.[69] Therefore, obscene material can be regulated by both federal and state governments. Federal regulation is usually effected by prohibiting the mailing of obscene material. State regulation is accomplished by confiscating such material and by criminally punishing those who sell it. In a prison environment, however, pornography is controlled by refusing to forward such literature to the inmate. Because pornographic material is not protected by the First Amendment, such refusal by prison administrators is not unconstitutional.[70] At least one case has stated that obscene material can also be excluded from a prison because of its tendency to incite homosexual activity, which in turn often leads to violence.[71]

Sexually explicit material may be kept from inmates on the grounds that the material is detrimental to rehabilitation and leads to deviate sexual behavior by some inmates.[72] Regulations excluding such material must not be overbroad so that "nudes," not designed primarily to arouse sexual desires, are unconstitutionally excluded.[73] However, the Court of Appeals for the District of Columbia held that a law banning sexually explicit materials in federal prisons violated the First Amendment.[74]

The problem in excluding pornography from the prisons is similar to the problem encountered in excluding allegedly inflammatory literature: Is the decision to exclude made under safeguards that protect the inmates' rights to

---

[66] Carpenter v. South Dakota, 536 F.2d 759 (8th Cir. 1976).

[67] *E.g.,* Chiarello v. Bohlinger, 391 F. Supp. 1153 (S.D.N.Y. 1975) (refusal to mail inmate's manuscript); Morgan v. LaVallee, 526 F.2d 221 (2d Cir. 1975) (refusal to allow inmate to receive specific publication); Aikens v. Jenkins, 534 F.2d 751 (7th Cir. 1976) (regulations concerning publications must not be overbroad); Blue v. Hogan, 553 F.2d 960 (5th Cir. 1977) (regulations must be governed by the test in *Procunier*).

[68] Sherman v. MacDougatt, 656 F.2d 527 (9th Cir. 1981).

[69] Roth v. United States, 354 U.S. 476 (1957).

[70] In re Van Geldern, 14 Cal. App. 3d 838, 92 Cal. Rptr. 592 (1971).

[71] *Ibid.*

[72] Carpenter v. South Dakota, 536 F.2d 759 (8th Cir. 1976).

[73] Aikens v. Jenkins, 534 F.2d 751 (7th Cir. 1976).

[74] Amatel v. Reno, 156 F.3d 192 (D.C. Cir. 1997).

receive constitutionally protected material? If the decision to exclude literature as obscene is left to a prison censor, without meaningful administrative or judicial review, the inmates' rights will often depend on highly subjective decisions. This is not necessarily the fault of the censor; although he or she may be judicially ordered to exclude only those "books or periodicals which would come clearly within the definition of pornography established by the decisions of the Supreme Court . . ."[75] The definition of "pornographic" is nebulous at best.

The Supreme Court first sanctioned the following test: material is obscene if "to the average person, applying contemporary community standards, the dominant theme of the material taken as a whole appeals to the prurient interest."[76] Subsequent cases, however, led to various interpretations of this definition by different members of the Court. Two justices believed "community standards" meant varying local standards;[77] others felt it meant a uniform national standard.[78] Another justice found it impossible to define obscenity, but stated "I know it when I see it . . ."[79]

In 1973, the Supreme Court of the United States decided *Miller v. California*[80] and held that contemporary community standards were not necessarily a national standard. However, no case has held, or could reasonably be expected to hold, that the "community" is the prison itself!

With this variety of definitions, a prison censor must be fully informed as to the current legal definition of pornography. Memoranda from the institution's legal advisor could accomplish this need. One court, however, decided to relieve the censor of such worries by allowing him to use the *Roth* guidelines, without regard to post-*Roth* decisions.[81] In any event, minimum due process and opportunity to appeal the censor's decision would seem to be required.

A prison director's refusal to deliver to an inmate copies of adult magazines on obscenity grounds was not in reckless or callous disregard of the inmate's First Amendment rights, even though the director had tools at his disposal to satisfy himself that his policies were not being appropriately applied and had the ability to change misapplication of his policies. The director was not liable for punitive damages as the director took steps to correct an improper application of the constitutional standard of obscenity upon receipt of a court order.[82]

---

[75]   Jones v. Wittenberg, 330 F. Supp. 707, 720 (N.D. Ohio 1971), *aff'd,* 456 F.2d 854 (6th Cir. 1972).
[76]   Roth v. United States, 354 U.S. 476 (1957).
[77]   Jacobellis v. Ohio, 378 U.S. 184 (1964) (Warren, C.J. and Clark, J., dissenting).
[78]   *Id.* at 192-195 (Brennan and Goldberg, JJ.).
[79]   *Id.* at 197 (Stewart, J. concurring).
[80]   413 U.S. 15 (1973).
[81]   Palmigiano v. Travisono, 317 F. Supp. 776, 790 (D.R.I. 1970).
[82]   Broulette v. Starns, 161 F. Supp. 2d 1021 (D.C. Ariz. 2001).

§ 4.10 Receipt of Racially Oriented Newspapers and Magazines

The Fourteenth Amendment to the Constitution forbids the states to deny any person "equal protection of the laws;" that is, the state must treat all similarly situated persons in an identical manner. Black inmates at several institutions have successfully used the equal protection clause to contest the refusal of prison officials to allow them to subscribe to non-subversive periodicals published primarily for blacks (for example, national magazines such as *Ebony* and *Sepia*). *Jackson v. Godwin*[83] is illustrative of such cases. Petitioner Jackson, an inmate in the Florida State Prison, alleged that although one-half of the institution's population was black, non-subversive newspapers and magazines written primarily for blacks were systematically kept off the approved list of periodicals, while numerous white-oriented publications were approved for receipt. The administrators claimed that the establishment of an approved periodicals list was a function of prison management that was not reviewable by the courts, and that the literature in question would harm prison security.

The court held that an inmate retains his or her Fourteenth Amendment right to equal protection even while he or she is incarcerated, and that the exclusion of all black-oriented periodicals from a prison in which the receipt of many white-oriented publications is permitted, violated the equal protection clause. The penal officials were ordered to allow blacks to subscribe to non-subversive black newspapers and magazines.

The case of *Aikens v. Lash*,[84] relying on *Procunier* standards, held that prison officials must afford inmates minimal due process when publications are prohibited. The "liberty interest" required the following form of review: (1) written notice to the inmate of the denial and reason for denial of the publication; (2) opportunity to object to the denial; and (3) prompt review by a prison official other than the one who made the original denial to forward the publication.

§ 4.11 Use of Mail Lists

One method commonly used by prison authorities to control correspondence between an inmate and the outside world is the requirement that an inmate send mail to and receive mail from only those persons approved by the prison authorities. Names can be added to and deleted from the mail list at any time. Administrators justify the use of mail lists on two grounds: (1) that the time-consuming task of reading and inspecting inmate mail requires a limit on the number of persons with whom an inmate can correspond; and (2) that the rehabilitation of inmates requires controls upon the people with whom an inmate corresponds.

---

[83] 400 F.2d 529 (5th Cir. 1968); *accord,* Owens v. Brierley, 452 F.2d 640 (3d Cir. 1971); *see also* Martin v. Wainwright, 525 F.2d 983 (5th Cir. 1976).

[84] 390 F. Supp. 663 (N.D. Ind. 1975), *modified in,* 514 F.2d 55 (7th Cir. 1975); Hopkins v. Collins, 548 F.2d 503 (4th Cir. 1977).

Generally, the few cases that have considered the legality of mail lists have held that the establishment and maintenance of such lists is a necessary incident of prison administration that does not violate any federal right.[85] *Jones v. Wittenberg*[86] prohibited county jail officials from placing limitations on the persons to whom inmates awaiting trial could write. However, in another case involving inmates who were awaiting trial, a federal district court sanctioned the use of an approved addressee list of seven persons to whom an inmate could write.[87] Such a regulation, the court stated, "is a reasonable method of maintaining prison security without undue restriction on the First Amendment rights of prisoners . . ."[88]

The use of mail lists has been closely scrutinized by the courts. Prison officials have been required to justify mail list regulations with evidence that such rules are "necessary to protect a substantial government interest unrelated to the suppression of expression and the limitations imposed were no greater than necessary to accomplish that objective."[89] Hence, *Finney v. Arkansas Board of Corrections*[90] enjoined prison officials from enforcing a broad regulation concerning mail lists until the tests of *Procunier* had been met. Prohibiting prisoners from corresponding with minors to whom they were not related by blood or marriage, without the prior consent of the minor's parents, violates the First Amendment.[91]

§ 4.12   Receipt of Books and Packages from Outside Sources

The United States Supreme Court approved special institutional regulations regarding the receipt of books and packages in *Bell v. Wolfish*.[92] The Court recognized that prisons have a legitimate government purpose to provide security and order. This permits placing restrictions on an inmate's receipt of books and packages. The institution's regulations prohibited the inmates and pretrial detainees from receiving any books that did not come directly from a publisher. The Court held that the regulation was a rational response by officials to the contraband smuggling problem.[93]

Likewise, the Court upheld a regulation prohibiting the receipt of packages from the outside. The fact that packages are easily used for smuggling contraband justified the prohibition and served the government interest of

---

[85]   Lee v. Tahash, 352 F.2d 970 (8th Cir. 1965) (number of persons with whom inmate could correspond limited to 12); Labat v. McKeithen, 243 F. Supp. 662 (E.D. La. 1965) (Louisiana statute limiting death row inmate's correspondence to specific persons).

[86]   330 F. Supp. 707 (N.D. Ohio 1971).

[87]   Palmigiano v. Travisono, 317 F. Supp. 776 (D.R.I. 1970).

[88]   *Id.* at 791.

[89]   Finney v. Arkansas Board of Corrections, 505 F.2d 194, at 210-211 (8th Cir. 1974).

[90]   *Ibid.*

[91]   Hearn v. Morris, 526 F. Supp. 267 (E.D. Cal. 1981).

[92]   441 U.S. 520 (1979).

[93]   *Id.* at 550, 551; Rich v. Luther, 514 F. Supp. 481 (W.D.N.C. 1981).

maintaining institutional security and order. Therefore, under this decision, prisoners, including pretrial detainees, have no constitutional right to receive packages from outside sources. Institutions may restrict or completely prohibit the flow of incoming packages to prisoners because of their overriding interest in protecting the security and order of the institution.[94]

In *Parratt v. Taylor*,[95] mailed materials were lost when the normal procedure for receipt of mail packages was not followed. It was held that there was no deprivation of a right, privilege, or immunity secured by the Constitution or laws of the United States. The case for relief under the Civil Rights Act[96] was dismissed.

Prison mail regulations prohibited prisoners from receiving bulk rate, third and fourth class mail. This was unconstitutional as applied to for-profit, prepaid, subscription publications, where prison officials failed to demonstrate that banning the incoming mail based on postage rates was rationally related to legitimate government objectives. However, a rule requiring the complete return address was justified as necessary for facilitating investigations in prison.[97]

However, corrections officials were entitled to qualified immunity in a claim by inmates challenging under the First Amendment a Department of Corrections policy of prohibiting the receipt of standard rate mail, as applied to subscription mail from a non-profit organization. The contours of the publisher's right to send and the inmates' right to receive subscription non-profit organization standard mail were not clearly established, and Department officials may have relied upon unpublished decisions upholding the departmental regulation at issue.[98]

§ 4.13   Use of the Telephone

Prison walls do not form a barrier that separates prison inmates from the protections of the Constitution,[99] nor do they bar free citizens from exercising their own constitutional rights by reaching out to those on the "inside."[100] Prisoners retain their First Amendment rights to communicate with family and friends.[101] Courts have determined that there is no legitimate governmental purpose to be achieved by not allowing reasonable access to the telephone, and such use is protected by the First Amendment.[102]

---

[94]   *Id.* at 554, 555; Jones v. Diamond, 594 F.2d 997 (5th Cir. 1979).
[95]   451 U.S. 527 (1981).
[96]   42 U.S.C. § 1983.
[97]   Morrison v. Hall, 261 F.3d 896 (9th Cir. 2001).
[98]   Prison Legal News v. Cook, 238 F.3d 1145 (9th Cir. 2001).
[99]   Turner v. Safley, 482 U.S. 78 (1987).
[100]   *Id.;* Thornburgh v. Abbott, 490 U.S. 401 (1989).
[101]   Morgan v. LaVallee, 526 F.2d 221 (2d Cir. 1975).
[102]   Johnson v. Galli, 596 F. Supp. 135 (D. Nev. 1984).

However, a prisoner does not have the right to unlimited telephone use.[103] A prisoner's right to telephone access is subject to rational limitations in the face of legitimate security interests of the penal institution.[104] The exact nature of telephone service to be provided to inmates is generally to be determined by prison administrators, subject to court scrutiny for unreasonable restrictions.[105]

Washington v. Reno[106] involved replacing the collect-call telephone system available to federal prison inmates with a direct-dial system monitored by correctional facility employees.

On April 4, 1994, the Bureau of Prisons promulgated a final rule concerning telephone use by inmates in federal correctional institutions.[107] That final rule altered the previously existing inmate telephone system (ITS) procedures and requirements in response to many prisoner concerns. Specifically, the final rule amended the phone-list requirement that accompanied the advent of the ITS system. Under the final rule, an inmate may ordinarily place up to 30 numbers on the call list—a 50 percent increase from the former total of 20 numbers. In addition, "the Associate Warden may authorize the placement of additional numbers on an inmate's telephone list based on the inmate's individual situation, *e.g.,* size of family."[108]

The rule abandoned the controversial Request for Telephone Privilege Form that required private information from potential call recipients outside the prison system. In place of the form, the rule provides that the inmate must acknowledge "to the best of the inmate's knowledge, the person or persons on the list are agreeable to receiving the inmate's telephone call and that the proposed calls are to be made for a purpose allowable under Bureau policy or institution guidelines."[109] Ordinarily, all such numbers listed by the prisoner will then be placed on the call list. When numbers of individuals other than the prisoner's immediate family and prison visitors are listed, however, the Bureau of Prisons sends a notice to the additional individuals informing them that they have been designated as telephone call recipients of the prisoner. If a recipient desires to be deleted from the call list, a written request to the Bureau will suffice.

In response to concerns raised regarding potential discrimination against indigent prisoners in the operation of the direct-dial system, the rule also provided that a minimum of one collect call per month (exclusive of legal calls to an attorney) may be made by inmates without funds.[110] Additionally, the war-

---

[103] Benzel v. Grammer, 869 F.2d 1105, 1108 (8th Cir.), *cert. denied,* 493 U.S. 895 (1989), citing Lopez v. Reyes, 692 F.2d 15 (5th Cir. 1982).

[104] Strandberg v. City of Helena, 791 F.2d 744 (9th Cir. 1986)

[105] Fillmore v. Ordonez, 829 F. Supp. 1544, 1563-1564 (D. Kan. 1993), *aff'd,* 17 F.3d 1436 (10th Cir. 1994), and citing Feeley v. Sampson, 570 F.2d 364, 374 (1st Cir. 1978), and Jeffries v. Reed, 631 F. Supp. 1212, 1219 (E.D. Wash. 1986).

[106] 35 F.3d 1093 (6th Cir. 1994).

[107] 59 Fed. Reg. 15812-15825 (Apr. 4, 1994).

[108] 59 Fed. Reg. 15824 (Apr. 4, 1994); 28 C.F.R. § 540.101(a).

[109] 59 Fed. Reg. 15824 (Apr. 4, 1994); 28 C.F.R. § 540.101(a)(1).

[110] 59 Fed. Reg. 15824 (Apr. 4, 1994); 28 C.F.R. § 540.105(b).

dens of the federal institutions are authorized by the rule to increase the number of collect calls available to such indigent inmates "based upon local institution conditions (*e.g.,* institution population, staff resources, and usage demand)."[111]

In response to concerns that the ITS tie-in with the inmate financial responsibility program would place an undue hardship on inmates and their families because additional funds sent to the inmates for phone calls would be used for increased program payments, the rule created a limited exemption for such outside funds. Prison officials developing an inmate's financial responsibility plan "shall exclude from its assessment $50 a month deposited into the inmate's trust fund account. . . . This $50 is excluded to allow the inmate the opportunity to better maintain telephone communication under the Inmate Telephone System (ITS)."[112] The regulation also increased the number of calls allowed to an inmate who refuses to participate in the financial responsibility program. Whereas the previous policy of the Bureau of Prisons was to limit such non-participants to one telephone call every three months, the regulation[113] provided that, effective January 3, 1995, the inmate "will be allowed to place no more than one telephone call every month . . ."

Prison authorities argued that inmate use of a telephone is not a right at all, but merely a privilege extended by the correctional facility to foster continued communication with family and friends outside the prison walls. They further argued that implementation of a direct-dialing system did not violate a right of free expression and association because any restrictions imposed are "reasonably related" to legitimate penological interests, because the restrictions are content-neutral and are unrelated to the purpose of suppressing expression, and because inmates may still communicate with family and friends through alternate means of expression such as prison visits and letters.

The Bureau regulation concerning inmate use of the prison telephone system addressed and remedied the prior restraint concerns identified by the district judge when he issued an injunction. According to the *Washington* court, the amendment of applicable prison regulations by the Bureau substantially lessened the likelihood that the prisoners could succeed on the merits of their existing First Amendment claims.

The Sixth Circuit felt that any perceived harm to the prisoners' First Amendment, due process, or administrative statutory rights had been cured by the final promulgation of amendments to 28 C.F.R. §§ 540 and 545. Those amendments so altered the existing ITS guidelines in response to proper rule-making procedures that the prisoners' concerns regarding alleged constitutional and statutory violations were adequately addressed or rendered moot.

It should be remembered that regulations of the Federal Bureau of Prisons have no direct effect on state prison systems. They only apply to the federal prison system.

---

[111] 59 Fed. Reg. 15824 (Apr. 4, 1994); 28 C.F.R. § 540.105(b).

[112] 28 C.F.R. § 545.11(b); 59 Fed. Reg. 15825 (Apr. 4, 1994).

[113] 28 C.F.R. § 545.11(d)(10).

§ 4.14 Conclusion

Prison administrators may place reasonable restrictions on mail, subject to the inmate's qualified right to use the mail system. Formerly, many federal courts refused to intervene in inmate suits that alleged undue restriction on mail rights unless the inmate alleged that restrictions infringed upon another federal right, such as the rights of free speech and press, the right to petition the government for the redress of grievances, the right to communicate with an attorney, and the right to receive information.

Following *Turner* and *Abbott*, prison officials have great discretion in allowing inmates to send and receive mail and publications. As long as they act "reasonably," their actions will not be reviewed by the federal courts. The standards to determine "reasonableness" include whether there is a "valid, rational connection" between the regulation and a legitimate and neutral governmental interest put forward to justify it; the existence of alternative means of exercising the asserted constitutional rights that remain open to inmates; the extent to which accommodation of the asserted right will have an impact on prison staff, on inmates' liberty, and on the allocation of limited prison resources; and whether the regulation represents an "exaggerated response" to prison concerns.

The extent to which state prisoners may use telephones is unsettled. The federal prison system controls the use of telephones through administrative regulations that are not of constitutional significance.

Isolated Confinement—
"The Hole" and
Administrative Segregation 5

Chapter Outline

§ 5.1 Introduction

Prison administrators have always faced the task of maintaining order and discipline in a prison. Some means of dealing with inmates who violate instructional rules and regulations are required.

One such means is the use of punitive isolation, which is isolation from the general prison population imposed as a penalty for violating institutional rules.

> Almost every correctional institution includes a special confinement unit for those who misbehave seriously after they are incarcerated. This "prison within a prison" usually is a place of solitary confinement . . . accompanied by a reduced diet and limited access to reading materials and other diversions, and occasionally without any kind of light.[1]

Another means is administrative isolation, which is isolation from the general population for any reason other than punishment, such as protective isolation or isolation during investigation of an alleged institutional rule violation or a felony.

§ 5.2 Intervention by the Courts

Prior to the mid-1960s, the federal courts applied the traditional "hands-off" doctrine and refused to grant relief to state prisoners who challenged the use or conditions of isolated confinement. The rule of law that was applied to cases of prison policies or affairs was that these were matters of internal prison concern, beyond the power of the courts to supervise. This doctrine, with regard to federal prisons, was based on the separation of powers, because federal prisons were part of the executive branch of government. As for state prisons, the courts held that their administration was within the power reserved to the states under the Tenth Amendment to the U.S. Constitution, and that any

---

[1] PRESIDENT'S COMMISSION ON LAW ENFORCEMENT AND ADMINISTRATION OF JUSTICE. TASK FORCE REPORT: CORRECTIONS, 50-51 (1967).

federal judicial review would interfere with prison administrators' performance of their duties. It was also held that the courts had only limited power to supervise the rules and regulations of prisons.

§ 5.3   Application of the Eighth Amendment

Even when a federal court is willing to review an inmate's complaint concerning isolated confinement, a federally protected right must be involved. The right involved is created by the Eighth Amendment to the U.S. Constitution, which prohibits "cruel and unusual punishments." The Supreme Court has interpreted this clause to prohibit punishments that indicate torture, unnecessary cruelty, or something inhuman and barbarous,[2] when the punishment is disproportionate to the offense,[3] and when a punishment is unnecessarily cruel in view of the purpose for which it is used.[4]

In order for the Eighth Amendment's prohibition to apply, a punishment must be involved. In a criminal law sense, punishment is "Any fine, penalty, or confinement inflicted upon a person by the authority of the law and the judgment and sentence of a court, for some crime . . . or for his omission of a duty enjoined by law."[5]

As applied to correctional law, a punishment consists of four elements: (1) Action by an administrative body, (2) which constitutes the imposition of a sanction, (3) for the purpose of penalizing the affected person, and (4) as the result of the commission of an offense.

One court has suggested that "any treatment to which a prisoner is exposed is a form of punishment,"[6] because it is an additional punishment above that imposed by the sentencing criminal court. As the result of being a punishment, it is subject to the Eighth Amendment standards.[7]

§ 5.3.1   —Constitutionality of the Use of Isolated Confinement

During the past 20 years, many actions by state and federal inmates have challenged the validity of the use of isolated confinement, claiming that the practice is *per se* unconstitutional; that is, unconstitutional without the need for any proof other than the fact that the petitioner (inmate) is held in isolated

---

[2]   In re Kemmler, 136 U.S. 436 (1890); Wilkerson v. Utah, 99 U.S. 130 (1878).

[3]   Trop v. Dulles, 356 U.S. 86 (1958); Weems v. United States, 217 U.S. 349 (1910).

[4]   Robinson v. California, 370 U.S. 660 (1962) (Douglas, J., concurring opinion); Weems v. United States, 217 U.S. 349 (1910).

[5]   BLACK'S LAW DICTIONARY (6th ed. 1990).

[6]   Landman v. Royster, 333 F. Supp. 621, 645 (E.D. Va. 1971).

[7]   *See* the *Graham* analysis in § 2.1, dealing with use of force.

confinement. This contention has been rejected by the federal courts.[8] The use of isolated confinement is seen as a valid means of protecting the general prison population and for preventing disobedience, disorder, or escapes. However, the conditions of isolated confinement can be disproportionate to the offense involved or used for an improper means and thus run afoul of the Eighth Amendment. Furthermore, the procedure by which isolation is enforced can be fundamentally unfair, thus violating due process of law.[9]

Segregation alone is not a constitutional issue. An inmate could not use the Civil Rights Act to contest his segregation, as an inmate has neither liberty nor property interests in remaining in a prison's general population.[10]

Segregation as a result of the exercise of constitutional rights raises a different issue. A disciplinary proceeding led to the ultimate acquittal of an inmate on charges of stabbing a fellow inmate. However, the charges resulted in his spending 93 days in a special housing unit, where the restrictions included loss of telephone privileges, one hour of exercise per day, and three showers per week. As a matter of law, the inmate did not suffer atypical or significant hardship, so due process was not violated.[11]

Violation of constitutional rights may result in monetary damages. An inmate's $660,000 verdict for wrongful confinement to administrative segregation for four years was reduced to $237,500. The damages awarded by the jury were excessive.[12]

§ 5.3.2   —Constitutionality of the Conditions of Isolated Confinement

A federal remedy exists when the conditions of isolated confinement violate the Eighth Amendment's ban on cruel and unusual punishments. Proof of the existence of the unconstitutional conditions is the initial burden on the inmate bringing an action. Failure to sufficiently establish the existence of the alleged conditions as a fact is a major basis for denying relief in complaints involving isolated confinement.[13] When the facts of the allegation are estab-

---

[8]   Sostre v. McGinnis, 442 F.2d 178 (2d Cir. 1971), *cert. denied,* 405 U.S. 978 (1972); Burns v. Swenson, 430 F.2d 771 (8th Cir. 1970); Ford v. Board of Managers of New Jersey State Prison, 407 F.2d 937 (3d Cir. 1969); Graham v. Willingham, 384 F.2d 367 (10th Cir. 1967); Krist v. Smith, 309 F. Supp. 497 (S.D. Ga. 1970), *aff'd,* 439 F.2d 146 (5th Cir. 1971); Roberts v. Barbosa, 227 F. Supp. 20 (S.D. Cal. 1964); Bauer v. Sielaff, 372 F. Supp. 1104 (E.D. Pa. 1974); Villanueva v. George, 632 F.2d 707 (8th Cir. 1980); Nadeau v. Helgemoe, 423 F. Supp. 1250 (D.N.H. 1976), *modified in* 561 F.2d 411 (1st Cir. 1977); Morris v. Travisono, 549 F. Supp. 291 (D.D.C. 1982), *aff'd,* 707 F.2d 28 (1st Cir. 1983) (segregated confinement for 8½ years was unjustified and violates the Eighth Amendment); Gibson v. Lynch, 652 F.2d 348 (3d Cir. 1981) (there is no state-created "liberty interest" that entitles a prisoner to get out of solitary confinement and enter the general population after his or her first 30 days in prison).

[9]   *See* Chapter 8 for a discussion on procedures for disciplining inmates.

[10] Montgomery v. Anderson, 262 F.3d 641 (7th Cir. 2001).

[11] Alvarado v. Kerrigan, 152 F. Supp. 2d 350 (S.D.N.Y 2001).

[12] McClary v. Coughlin, 87 F. Supp. 2d 205 (W.D.N.Y 2000), sub. app. 237 F.3d 185 (2d Cir. 2001).

[13] Courtney v. Bishop, 409 F.2d 1185 (8th Cir.), *cert. denied,* 396 U.S. 915 (1969); Landman v. Peyton, 370 F.2d 135 (4th Cir. 1966), *cert. denied,* 388 U.S. 920 (1967).

lished, it is then a matter of law (as opposed to fact) as to whether the factual conditions are such that a violation of the prohibition on cruel and unusual punishments exists. At this stage, it is then a matter for the court, not a jury, to decide whether the Eighth Amendment has been violated. Each court must look at the facts as proved and determine in its judgment whether the conditions amount to the infliction of cruel and unusual punishment.

Conditions that have been scrutinized include the personal hygienic conditions of the inmate, physical conditions of the cell, exercise allowed, diet, and duration of the isolated confinement.

Where an inmate is deprived of the means of maintaining personal hygiene, such as soap, water, towels, toilet paper, toothbrush, or clothing, the conditions become constitutionally intolerable.[14] However, where the inmate is provided with water, soap, towels, and periodic bathing, the conditions have been held to be constitutionally acceptable.[15] One court has found that lack of water and a shower provided every fifth day did not constitute unhygienic conditions.[16] However, another court[17] held that the deprivation of a comb, pillow, toothbrush, and toothpaste for seven to 10 days in a maximum-security cell with continuous lighting, a few roaches and mice in the cell, and no reading material, did not constitute cruel and unusual punishment where the inmate was not denied the minimum necessities of food, water, sleep, exercise, toilet facilities, and human contact. Contrast that with *Griffin v. Smith*,[18] in which the court held that conditions that might constitute infringements of civil rights of prisoners in a special housing unit included excessive and unnecessary use of force by guards, grossly inadequate provision for exercise, denial of access to psychological specialists, unsanitary food utensils, including cigarette burns and hair on food trays, portions smaller than those provided to the general inmate population, or loss of mail sent to the superintendent.

The physical state of the cell is another aspect of the conditions of isolated confinement. The existence of certain conditions in cells has led to varying results. Confinement of more than two men in a single cell in punitive isolation or administrative segregation is not unconstitutional *per se*.

In *Hutto v. Finney*, the Supreme Court refused to overturn the district court's series of detailed remedial orders holding that punitive isolation in sections of the Arkansas penal system violated the Eighth Amendment. These orders included limits placed on the number of men that could be confined to one cell, required that each man have a bunk, discontinued the "gruel" diet, and set 30 days as the maximum isolation sentence.[19]

---

14   Wright v. McMann, 387 F.2d 519 (2d Cir. 1967); Knuckles v. Prasse, 302 F. Supp. 1036 (E.D. Pa. 1969), *aff'd*, 435 F.2d 1255 (3d Cir. 1970); Hancock v. Avery, 301 F. Supp. 786 (M.D. Tenn. 1969); Jordan v. Fitzharris, 257 F. Supp. 674 (N.D. Cal. 1966); Kimbrough v. O'Neil, 523 F.2d 1057 (7th Cir. 1975); Brown v. State, 391 So. 2d 13 (La. Ct. App. 1980).

15   Sostre v. McGinnis, 442 F.2d 178 (2d Cir. 1971), *cert. denied*, 405 U.S. 978 (1972); Gibson v. Lynch, 652 F.2d 348 (3d Cir. 1981).

16   Ford v. Board of Managers of New Jersey State Prison, 407 F.2d 937 (3d Cir. 1969).

17   Bauer v. Sielaff, 372 F. Supp. 1104 (E.D. Pa. 1974).

18   493 F. Supp. 129 (W.D.N.Y. 1980).

19   Hutto v. Finney, 437 U.S. 678 (1978); cf. Rhodes v. Chapman, 452 U.S. 337 (1981).

The rationale the Court expressed in *Hutto* was that if the state had fully complied with the district court's earlier orders, the present limits may not have been necessary. However, when a system refuses to comply with orders to remedy cruel and unusual conditions in isolation cells, a federal court is fully justified in substituting its judgment by entering a comprehensive order to ensure against the risk of inadequate compliance.

From this decision, it is clear that there is not yet a minimum standard set on the number of days or other conditions that will constitute cruel and unusual punishment in punitive isolation in every situation. The Supreme Court stated that the length of confinement was only one factor in the decision, and short durations of oppressive conditions may not rise to the level of a constitutional deprivation.

Courts have found that the lack of lighting or windows in the cells and lack of mattresses are not impermissible.[20] These same conditions, however, when coupled with overcrowding in the cells, unclean cells, or lack of heat, have been held to violate the Eighth Amendment.[21]

The personal hygiene of the inmate, the physical condition of the inmate, and the physical condition of the isolation cell have been the focal points of most judicial attention in the area of isolated confinement. However, other aspects have received judicial consideration as well. Exercise outside the cell that an inmate is allowed during isolated confinement has been noted by several courts. Conditions have been upheld when there is an opportunity for exercise[22] even though it is for only one hour every 11 days[23] or when the allotted exercise time does not meet the requirements of the Bureau of Prisons policy.[24] It has been held that inmates on death row may not be confined in their cells for long periods without outdoor exercise.[25] This reasoning also applies to isolated confinement. The prisoner could also be deprived of contact visits, library privileges, and radio and television, so long as nutritional and hygienic needs are met.[26]

---

[20] Novak v. Beto, 453 F.2d 661 (5th Cir. 1971); Ford v. Board of Managers of New Jersey State Prison, 407 F.2d 937 (3d Cir. 1969); Knuckles v. Prasse, 302 F. Supp. 1036 (E.D. Pa. 1969), *aff'd,* 435 F.2d 1255 (3d Cir. 1970).

[21] Anderson v. Nosser, 438 F.2d 183 (5th Cir. 1971); Wright v. McMann, 387 F.2d 519 (2d Cir. 1967); Landman v. Royster, 333 F. Supp. 621 (E.D. Va. 1971); Hancock v. Avery, 301 F. Supp. 786 (M.D. Tenn. 1969); Knuckles v. Prasse, 302 F. Supp. 1036 (E.D. Pa. 1969), *aff'd,* 435 F.2d 1255 (3d Cir. 1979); Holt v. Sarver, 300 F. Supp. 825 (E.D. Ark. 1969); Jordan v. Fitzharris, 257 F. Supp. 674 (N.D. Cal. 1966); Newson v. Sielaff, 375 F. Supp. 1189 (E.D. Pa. 1974).

[22] Sostre v. McGinnis, 442 F.2d 178 (2d Cir. 1971), *cert. denied,* 405 U.S. 978 (1972); Knuckles v. Prasse, 302 F. Supp. 1036 (E.D. Pa. 1969), *aff'd,* 435 F.2d 1255 (3d Cir. 1970).

[23] Lake v. Lee, 329 F. Supp. 196 (S.D. Ala. 1971).

[24] Jordan v. Arnold, 408 F. Supp. 869 (M.D. Pa. 1976).

[25] Sinclair v. Henderson, 331 F. Supp. 1123 (E.D. La. 1971).

[26] Gibson v. Lynch, 652 F.2d 348 (3d Cir. 1981).

The diet that an inmate receives while in isolated confinement has been a factor in several cases. Where the diet is basically the same as the general prison population, no problem is presented.[27] A "reduced" diet has been approved,[28] and so has a diet of bread and water supplemented with a full meal every third day.[29] However, a bread and water diet has been termed "generally disapproved and obsolescent"[30] and has been strongly disapproved by the American Correctional Association as constituting the imposition of physical (corporal) punishment.[31] Similarly, at least one court has ruled that broadly prohibiting prisoners in isolation or segregated confinement from attending prison chapel is unconstitutional.[32]

The length of isolated confinement has been considered by several courts. A distinction exists between administrative and punitive isolation, in that the reason for isolating inmates is either for punishment for specific actions (punitive isolation) or for more severe behavioral problems for longer periods (administrative isolation). It is a distinction of form rather than of substance, because the basic difference is the length of time. One court held that punitive isolation for a period of more than 15 days was cruel and unusual punishment;[33] but this judgment was subsequently overturned.[34] While periods of 36 days[35] and 15 days[36] have been held by some courts to be constitutionally permissible, other courts have found shorter periods, for example 48 hours, to violate an inmate's right to be free from cruel and unusual punishment.[37] Administrative isolation lasting 12 months[38] and 187 consecutive days[39] has been upheld. Placement in disciplinary segregation for an indeterminate amount of time did not violate the inmate's rights as long as the inmate was given a hearing to comply with due process safeguards at the earliest reasonable time.[40]

Confinement for five years in the maximum-security section of a prison where an inmate is allowed out of his or her cell for one hour daily to exercise, and is not permitted any outdoor exercise, does not violate the Eighth Amendment's prohibition against cruel and unusual punishment. The court found that where a prisoner had participated in a riot, assaulted correctional officers, and

---

[27] Sostre v. McGinnis, 442 F.2d 178 (2d Cir. 1971), *cert. denied,* 405 U.S. 978 (1972); Royal v. Clark, 447 F.2d 501 (5th Cir. 1971).

[28] Knuckles v. Prasse, 302 F. Supp. 1036 (E.D. Pa. 1969), *aff'd,* 435 F.2d 1255 (3d Cir. 1970).

[29] Novak v. Beto, 453 F.2d 661 (5th Cir. 1972); Ford v. Board of Managers of New Jersey State Prison, 407 F.2d 937 (3d Cir. 1969).

[30] Landman v. Royster, 333 F. Supp. 621, 647 (E.D. Va. 1971).

[31] AMERICAN CORRECTIONAL ASSOCIATION, A MANUAL OF CORRECTIONAL STANDARDS 417 (1966).

[32] St. Claire v. Cuyler, 634 F.2d 109 (3d Cir. 1980).

[33] Sostre v. Rockefeller, 312 F. Supp. 863 (S.D.N.Y. 1970), *aff'd, rev'd,* and *modified sub nom.,* Sostre v. McGinnis, 442 F.2d 178 (2d Cir. 1971), *cert. denied,* 405 U.S. 978 (1972).

[34] Sostre v. McGinnis, 442 F.2d 178 (2d Cir. 1971), *cert. denied,* 405 U.S. 978 (1972).

[35] Stiltner v. Rhay, 322 F.2d 314 (9th Cir. 1963), *cert. denied,* 376 U.S. 920 (1964). *See also* Bloeth v. Montanye, 514 F.2d 1192 (2d Cir. 1975).

[36] Novak v. Beto, 453 F.2d 661 (5th Cir. 1971); Jackson v. Werner, 394 F. Supp. 805 (W.D. Pa. 1975).

[37] O'Connor v. Keller, 510 F. Supp. 1359 (D. Md. 1981).

[38] Sostre v. McGinnis, 442 F.2d 178 (2d Cir. 1971), *cert. denied,* 405 U.S. 978 (1972).

[39] Knuckles v. Prasse, 302 F. Supp. 1036 (E.D. Pa. 1969), *aff'd,* 435 F.2d 1255 (3d Cir. 1970).

[40] Adams v. Carlson, 376 F. Supp. 1228 (E.D. Ill. 1974).

was convicted of murdering another inmate while in the maximum-security section of the prison, this past prison conduct justified the reclassification board's decision to keep the prisoner in maximum security.[41]

Appointed counsel must be provided to inmates who are in administrative detention pending investigation and trial on felonies committed in prison. Counsel must be appointed prior to indictment. Solitary confinement effectively curtails an inmate's ability to investigate evidence and interview witnesses. This is particularly meaningful, considering the transient nature of prison society. In order for the right to counsel to attach, the inmate must ask for an attorney, establish indigence, and make a *prima facie* showing that the reason for his or her continued detention is the investigation of a felony. Once this is done, the prison administration must either refute the showing, appoint counsel, or return the prisoner to the general population. A decision that when these steps are not followed, there is a presumption of prejudice, was reversed by the Supreme Court.[42] For example, an inmate in maximum security has no right to unlimited use of the telephone.[43]

An inmate's claim that he was placed in solitary confinement without any notice of charges or any hearing, that he was threatened with violence when he asked what the charges were, and that he was still in "the hole" a week later, states a cause of action. The claim may not be dismissed summarily on the ground that the case was moot because the prisoner had been transferred to another facility. Further, the inmate's inartful pleading must be construed liberally.[44]

Until 1995, as a general rule, state prisoners had no liberty interest protected by the United States Constitution in continued confinement in the general prison population. However, states could create such interests by the repeated use, in the state prison regulations governing administrative segregation, of explicit mandatory language about procedures and by requirements that administrative segregation not occur absent specified substantive predicates. When such interests are created, a due process hearing is required. The hearing should be an informal, nonadversarial evidentiary review that is preceded by notice to the prisoner. This notice must offer the prisoner an opportunity to submit his or her views in writing, and must occur within a reasonable period after the prisoner's transfer to administrative segregation. The prison officials must then decide whether the prisoner represents a security threat, requiring confinement in administrative segregation pending completion of an investigation into misconduct charges against him or her. In one case, the inmate was placed in segregation pending an investigation into his role in a riot. The next day he received notice of a misconduct charge against him. Five days after his transfer, a hearing committee reviewed the evidence. The inmate acknowledged that he had an opportunity to have his version of the events reported, but no finding of guilt was made. Criminal charges were filed, but later dropped. A

---

[41]   Wilkerson v. Maggio, 703 F.2d 909 (5th Cir. 1983).
[42]   United States v. Gouveia, 704 F.2d 1116 (9th Cir. 1983), *rev'd*, 467 U.S. 180 (1984).
[43]   Lopez v. Reyes, 692 F.2d 15 (5th Cir. 1982).
[44]   Boag v. MacDougall, 454 U.S. 364 (1982).

review committee concluded that the inmate should remain in administrative segregation because he posed a threat to the safety of other inmates, prison officials, and the security of the prison. Ultimately, the hearing committee, based on a second misconduct report, found the inmate guilty of the second charge and ordered him confined in disciplinary segregation for six months, while dropping the first charge. This procedure satisfied due process.[45]

However, in June of 1995, the United States Supreme Court severely reconfigured the analysis for determining whether a prisoner subjected to disciplinary or administrative confinement has a protected liberty interest that entitles him or her to the procedural protections afforded under the due process clause.[46] In so doing, the Court rejected the analysis established by *Hewitt v. Helms* and its progeny, returning to the due process principles established in *Wolff v. McDonnell*,[47] and *Meachum v. Fano*.[48] Prior to *Sandin*, analysis of whether a liberty interest was protected would contain an examination of the text of prison guidelines or regulations to determine whether mandatory language that limited prison officials' discretion created an enforceable expectation that the state would produce a particular outcome with respect to the prisoner's conditions of confinement. The *Sandin* majority rejected this test because it created disincentives for states to codify prison management procedures in the interest of uniform treatment and because the approach led to the involvement of the federal courts in the day-to-day management of prisons, often squandering judicial resources with little offsetting benefit to anyone.

Insisting that protected liberty interests be of "real substance," *Sandin* limited state-created liberties to freedom from restraint which, while not exceeding the sentence in such an unexpected manner as to give rise to protection by the due process clause of its own force, nonetheless imposes atypical and significant hardship on the inmate in relation to the ordinary incidents of prison life.

Courts have difficulty applying *Sandin*. Before *Sandin*, the deprivation of any right containing some vestige or modicum of freedom within the prison that the state conferred on a prisoner was actionable. When a prisoner's status within the prison system changed, the question was not how great the change was, but whether it infringed upon a right that the state had conferred. *Sandin* shifted the focus from whether there was an entitlement to whether the entitlement related to some meaningful amount of liberty.

In a Seventh Circuit case, *Wagner v. Hanks*,[49] a state prisoner filed for federal *habeas corpus*, claiming to have been deprived of liberty within the meaning of the due process clause of the Fourteenth Amendment, by being placed in disciplinary segregation. The Court recognized that, in deciding whether such a deprivation had occurred, a federal court after *Sandin* must compare

---

[45]   Hewitt v. Helms, 459 U.S. 460 (1983).
[46]   Sandin v. Conner, 515 U.S. 472 (1995). See § 8.1 for a more detailed explanation of the new doctrine of protected liberty interests.
[47]   418 U.S. 539 (1974).
[48]   427 U.S. 215 (1976).
[49]   Wagner v. Hanks, 128 F.3d 1173 (7th Cir. 1997).

conditions in disciplinary segregation with conditions in which the general population of the prison is confined or with those in which the general population of any prison in the state is confined.

The prisoner was ordered to serve one year in disciplinary segregation. Confinement in disciplinary segregation constituted a substantial incremental deprivation of his liberty. Because the prison was likely to provide facilities for and create conditions of administrative segregation and protective custody that are virtually identical to the facilities for and conditions of disciplinary segregation, this was sufficient under *Sandin* to deny the prisoner's claim. The manual of policies and procedures issued by the Indiana Department of Corrections indicated that the facilities and conditions were indeed the same in disciplinary and non-disciplinary segregation, except that prisoners in administrative segregation or protective custody were permitted "contact" visits and were entitled to make phone calls to persons other than lawyers. The denial of so limited an increment of privileges did not create a significant deprivation of liberty. However, the Court hesitated to base its decision on a procedure manual that may not have been accurate or up-to-date.

The Court commented that if the prison were a "country club" in which the prisoners enjoyed a great deal of freedom, spending little time in their cells or even in the prison buildings, confinement for a protracted period in what amounts to solitary confinement would work an atypical and significant deprivation of their liberty. This was not the situation in *Wagner*.

The Court was bothered by the assumption that the proper comparison group was the population of the prisoner's own prison. This is not necessarily so. In the Court's view, the comparison group may be any prison population in the state or perhaps in the entire country. In that event, Wagner would lose unless the conditions of disciplinary segregation in his facility were substantially more restrictive than even those in the state's other Level V prisons. Under *Sandin,* the key comparison is between disciplinary segregation and non-disciplinary segregation rather than between disciplinary segregation and the general prison population.

The Seventh Circuit did not think that comparison could be limited to conditions in the same prison, unless it was the state's most secure prison. To distinguish between the different parts of the same prison and the different prisons in the same system would be arbitrary. The decision to create high-security segregation units in each prison or to concentrate them in one or a few special prisons bears no relation to any interest protected by the Constitution.

The Court felt that when *Sandin* is interpreted in light of the transfer cases,[50] it is apparent that the right to litigate disciplinary confinements has

---

[50] The transfer of a prisoner from one prison to another is not actionable as a deprivation of constitutionally protected liberty even if the conditions of confinement are much more restrictive in the prison to which the prisoner is being transferred. Meachum v. Fano, 427 U.S. 215 (1976); Montanye v. Haymes, 427 U.S. 236 (1976); and Olim v. Wakinekona, 461 U.S. 238 (1983). To have held otherwise would require the courts to adjudicate transfers within a prison—to determine, for example, whether the petitioner had been deprived of liberty by being transferred from a large cell to a small one. Federal judges would then be plunged into the minutiae of prison administration, much as if they were managing a hotel chain.

become small. Prison discipline cases can, however, be actionable in the federal courts when discipline takes the form of prolonging the prisoner's incarceration or otherwise depriving him of what has been held to be liberty or property within the meaning of the due process clauses.[51] But when the entire sanction is confinement in disciplinary segregation for a period that does not exceed the remaining term of the prisoner's incarceration, the Court found it difficult to see how it could form the basis of a suit complaining about a deprivation of liberty after *Sandin*.

The Court recognized that every state had somewhere in its prison system single-person cells in which prisoners were sometimes confined not because they misbehaved, but simply because the prison had no other space, wanted to protect some prisoners from others, wished to keep prisoners isolated from one another in order to minimize the risk of riots or other disturbances, or hoped to prevent the spread of disease.[52] Under *Sandin,* this possibility was enough to prevent any deprivation of liberty if a prisoner were transferred into segregation for a disciplinary infraction.[53]

Another issue the Court considered still open was whether the comparison group could be confined to a single state. Indiana frequently swapped prisoners with other states pursuant to an interstate compact. The Seventh Circuit felt that it would make a good deal of sense to view the entire federal and state jail and prison systems as a single system in order to balance the total prisoner load, which was in excess of one million people. By this reasoning, a prisoner in Indiana could serve a portion of his sentence in another state, and that state might have even more restrictive conditions than Indiana. The logic of *Sandin* implies that the conditions of Wagner's disciplinary segregation were atypical only if no prison in the United States to which he might be transferred for non-disciplinary reasons is more restrictive.

However, *Sandin* does not mean that a prisoner can always be placed in segregated confinement without the observance of due process standards. In the Second Circuit, a prisoner received 180 days in segregation and loss of good time, but was not allowed to be present for the testimony of some witnesses or even to read transcripts of their testimony. In this case, *Sandin* did not apply.[54]

In the Seventh Circuit, an allegation that a correctional officer falsely accused a prisoner of misconduct and caused him to be brought up on disciplinary charges and confined in administrative segregation did not violate the prisoner's civil rights.[55]

---

[51]   *See, e.g.,* Wolff v. McDonnell, 418 U.S. 539 (1974), Vitek v. Jones, 445 U.S. 480 (1980), and Washington v. Harper, 494 U.S. 210 (1990).

[52]   Almost six percent of the nation's prison inmates are in segregation. CRIMINAL JUSTICE INSTITUTE, INC., CORRECTIONS YEARBOOK 22 (1997). The great majority of these are not in disciplinary segregation. *See* CRIMINAL JUSTICE INSTITUTE, INC., CORRECTIONS YEARBOOK: ADULT CORRECTIONS 27 (1995). In 1995, almost five percent of all prison inmates were in nondisciplinary segregation.

[53]   The question whether the comparison group includes other prisons did not have to be answered in *Sandin,* and was not discussed in either the majority opinion or any of the separate opinions.

[54]   Miller v. Selsky, 111 F.3d 7 (2d Cir. 1997).

[55]   Leslie v. Doyle, 125 F.3d 1132 (7th Cir. 1997).

§ 5.3.3   —The Purpose of Isolated Confinement

In addition to granting relief on the basis of isolated confinement conditions, federal courts have also found a violation of the Eighth Amendment when the punishment is imposed for an improper purpose. The courts view the proper purpose of isolated confinement to be the maintenance of order within the institution.[56] Therefore, any punishment that is not necessary to maintain order is cruel and unusual and prohibited by the Eighth Amendment. Thus, unsanitary conditions in confinement are unnecessarily punitive in nature and violate the Eighth Amendment.[57]

An inmate cannot be placed in isolated confinement because of his or her militant political ideas or his past or threatened litigation.[58] Nor can he or she be denied access to paper for use in petitioning courts or communicating with his or her attorney.[59] Also, denying food for a 50-hour period was held to go beyond what was necessary to achieve a legitimate correctional aim.[60] A trial court's order that prison officials place a defendant in solitary confinement and feed him only bread and water on the anniversary of his offense was impermissible.[61]

§ 5.3.4   —Punishment Proportional to the Offense

A further basis for granting relief is when the punishment is disproportionate to the infraction committed by the inmate. Thus, again, the unsanitary conditions of a cell can make the punishment disproportionate to the offense.[62] Another example of a disproportionate punishment was found when isolation was imposed for five months for failure to sign a safety sheet.[63] The unconstitutionality of disproportionate punishment also applies to other areas of correctional law. It was the basis for one court to prohibit whipping[64] and for another court to find that the entire prison system as administered in Arkansas was disproportionate punishment for any offense[65] and, thus unconstitutional.

---

[56] River v. Fogg, 371 F. Supp. 938 (W.D.N.Y. 1974); Kelly v. Brewer, 239 N.W.2d 109 (Iowa Sup. Ct.); Daughtery v. Carlson, 372 F. Supp. 1320 (E.D. Ill. 1974); Clifton v. Robinson, 500 F. Supp. 30 (E.D. Pa. 1980).

[57] Hancock v. Avery, 301 F. Supp. 786 (M.D. Tenn. 1969); Jordan v. Fitzharris, 257 F. Supp. 674 (N.D. Cal. 1966); Attorney General v. Sheriff of Worcester Cty, 413 N.E.2d 772 (Mass. 1980); West v. Lamb, 497 F. Supp. 989 (D. Nev. 1980); Milhouse v. Carlson, 652 F.2d 371 (3d Cir. 1981).

[58] Wojtczak v. Cuyler, 480 F. Supp. 1288 (E.D. Pa. 1979); Morgan v. LaVallee, 526 F.2d 221 (2d Cir. 1975).

[59] Dearman v. Woods, 429 F.2d 1288 (10th Cir. 1970); McCray v. Sullivan, 399 F. Supp. 271 (S.D. Ala. 1975).

[60] Dearman v. Woods, 429 F.2d 1288 (10th Cir. 1970).

[61] People v. Joseph, 434 N.E.2d 453 (Ill. Ct. App. 1982).

[62] Jordan v. Fitzharris, 257 F. Supp. 674, 679 (N.D. Cal. 1966).

[63] Wright v. McMann, 321 F. Supp. 127 (N.D.N.Y. 1970).

[64] Jackson v. Bishop, 404 F.2d 571 (8th Cir. 1968).

[65] Holt v. Sarver, 309 F. Supp. 362 (E.D. Ark. 1970), aff'd, 442 F.2d 304 (8th Cir. 1971).

§ 5.4 Conclusion

Courts have found that the use of isolated confinement is a valid method of penal administration. However, federal courts will provide relief for deprivation of an inmate's constitutional right to be free of cruel and unusual punishment during his or her stay in isolated confinement. When the conditions of the confinement become such that an inmate is deprived of personal hygiene and the facility or his or her diet are inadequate, the Eighth Amendment is violated. Also, punishment that is imposed for an improper purpose or is disproportionate to the offense committed can violate the Eighth Amendment.

However, the procedure used in placing a prisoner in administrative or disciplinary segregation depends on the existence of a protected liberty interest. Whether such a protected liberty interest exists remains an open question, depending upon the nature of the system for isolated confinement created under state law. Cases prior to *Sandin* that find protected liberty interests are now of questionable authority.

Religion in Prison 6

Chapter Outline

§ 6.1 Introduction: Effect of Imprisonment on Religious Rights

The First Amendment to the United States Constitution states in part that "Congress shall make no law respecting an establishment of religion, or prohibiting the free exercise thereof. . . ."[1] An obvious contradiction exists within the two clauses of this Amendment. This contradiction is particularly apparent when the amendment is applied to the inmates of correctional systems. In *Gittlemacker v. Prasse,*[2] the inherent difficulty in applying First Amendment religious freedom to inmates is pointed out:

> The requirement that a state interpose no unreasonable barriers to the free exercise of an inmate's religion cannot be equated with the suggestion that the state has an affirmative duty to provide, furnish, or supply every inmate with a clergyman or religious services of his choice. It is one thing to provide facilities for worship and the opportunity for any clergy to visit the institution. This may be rationalized on the basis that since society has removed the prisoner from the community where he could freely exercise his religion, it has an obligation to furnish or supply him with the opportunity to practice his faith during confinement. Thus, the Free Exercise Clause is satisfied.

But to go further and suggest that the free exercise clause demands that the state not only furnish the opportunity to practice, but also supply the clergy, is a concept that dangerously approaches the jealously guarded frontiers of the establishment clause.

The existence of this conflict between the free exercise clause and the establishment clause provides one explanation for the recognition by the courts of a need to balance the interests of the state with the interests of the inmate. Although the state interest in avoiding the establishment of religion is a problem of constitutional proportions, this interest has not negated the equally significant right of the inmate to the free exercise of his or her religious beliefs.

---

[1]   U.S. CONST. amend. I; *see* Appendix I.
[2]   428 F.2d 1 (3d Cir. 1970).

In spite of the difficulty in balancing these two fundamental and conflicting rights, courts have given increasing attention to the needs of inmates in this area. The traditional reluctance of the judiciary to interfere in the management of the prison[3] is no longer apparent. Rather than simply dismissing an action, as in the past, the courts are now giving recognition to the existence of First Amendment rights behind prison walls. Furthermore, they have required prison officials to provide a reasonable explanation for any attempt to limit such rights.

The requirement for prison officials to explain their rationale for impeding the free exercise of religion was pointed out in *Barnett v. Rodgers,*[4] where the court stated:

> To say that religious freedom may undergo modification in a prison environment is not to say that it can be suppressed or ignored without adequate reason. And although "within the prison society as well as without, the practice of religious beliefs is subject to reasonable regulation necessary for the protection and welfare of the community involved," the mere fact that government, as a practical matter, stands a better chance of justifying curtailment of fundamental liberties where prisoners are involved does not eliminate the need for reasons imperatively justifying the particular retraction of rights challenged at bar. Nor does it lessen governmental responsibility to reduce the resulting impact upon those rights to the fullest extent consistent with the justified objective.[5]

Although a state would impede the free exercise of religion if it sought to ban the performance of, or abstention from, physical acts *solely* because of their religious motivation, the Constitution does not relieve the obligation to comply with a law that *incidentally* forbids, or requires, the performance of an act that his or her religious belief requires, or forbids, if the law is not specifically directed to religious practice and is otherwise constitutional as applied to those who engage in the specified act for nonreligious reasons.

In *Employment Division, Department of Human Resources of Oregon v. Smith,*[6] two Native Americans were fired by a private drug rehabilitation organization because they ingested peyote, a hallucinogenic drug, for sacramental purposes at a ceremony of their Native American Church. The Supreme Court held that the free exercise clause permitted the state to prohibit sacramental peyote use and to deny unemployment benefits to persons discharged for such use. Although it is constitutionally *permissible* to exempt sacramental peyote use from the operation of drug laws, it is not constitutionally *required.*

---

[3]   Wright v. McMann, 257 F. Supp. 739 (N.D.N.Y. 1966), *rev'd on other grounds,* 387 F.2d 519 (2d Cir. 1967).

[4]   410 F.2d 995 (D.C. Cir. 1969).

[5]   *Id.* at 1000-1001.

[6]   494 U.S. 872 (1990).

Several significant cases involve the conflict between religious practices and institutional concerns and the application of the Religious Freedom Restoration Act (RFRA) of 1993.[7]

§ 6.2 Restrictions on the Free Exercise of Religion

In response to demands of the courts, prison officials have provided a number of explanations for the restrictions they have placed upon the inmate's free exercise of religion. Among these are the maintenance of discipline or security, proper exercise of authority and official discretion, the fact that the regulation is reasonable, as well as economic considerations. Frequently, these explanations are used interchangeably by the courts, and it is sometimes difficult to determine which justification was the basis of the decision. However, in most cases, if prison officials are able to show that restrictions on religious practices are actually based upon one or more of these enumerated reasons, the courts will allow the restrictions to continue. In addition to providing explanations for the restrictions placed upon the inmate's free exercise of religion, prison officials and the courts have attempted to define what a "religion" is, and what "religious practices" are, for purposes of First Amendment protection. Unfortunately, few precise guidelines have emerged.[8]

A prison chaplain who engages in inherently ecclesiastical functions, even if a full-time state employee, is not a 'state actor' for purposes of the Civil Rights Act.[9]

---

[7] See § 6.4.9 below.

[8] Theriault v. Sibler, 391 F. Supp. 578 (W.D. Tex. 1975), *vacated and remanded,* 547 F.2d 1279 (5th Cir. 1977). The court of appeals held that the requirement of a belief in a supreme being as a criterion to determine whether a practice constitutes a religion within the protection of the First Amendment is too narrow. The court stated: "When reconsidering what constitutes a religion, a thorough study of the existing case law should be accompanied by appropriate evidentiary exploration of philosophical, theological, and other related literature and resources on this issue." *Id.* at 1281. In a subsequent case, Theriault v. Sibler, 453 F. Supp. 254 (W.D. Tex. 1978), a Texas federal court ruled that an inmate-created religion was not entitled to First Amendment protection, because it was not a true "religion" for purposes of federal law. After reviewing the facts in the case, the court concluded: "The professed views of Mr. Theriault that he 'would have established a New World order' with Harry W. Theriault as the head of the Order . . . are, in the opinion of the Court more closely akin to the megalomania of Adolph Hitler and the Nazis or Charles Manson and his 'family' than any 'belief . . . that occupies a place parallel to that filled by the orthodox belief in God.'); Remmers v. Brewer, 396 F. Supp. 145 (S.D. Iowa 1975), *rev'd on other grounds,* 529 F.2d 656 (8th Cir. 1976); *cf.* Ron v. Lennane, 445 F. Supp. 98 (D. Conn. 1977); *cf.* Loney v. Scurr, 474 F. Supp. 1186 (S.D. Iowa 1979) (the Church of the New Song was a religion entitled to the protection of the First Amendment); Africa v. Commonwealth of Pennsylvania, 662 F.2d 1025 (3d Cir. 1981) (On the facts of the case, an inmate's belief was not a religion within the purview of the First Amendment. His organization did not address fundamental and ultimate questions. It was not comprehensive in nature and did not have the defining structural characteristics of a traditional religion.)

[9] Montano v. Hedgepeth, 120 F.3d 844 (8th Cir. 1997). *See* Chapter 11.

§ 6.2.1 —Restrictions Based on the Maintenance of Discipline or Security

The duty of prison officials to maintain security within an institution is the most frequently cited justification for limiting an inmate's religious freedom. In *Jones v. Willingham*,[10] the court, concerned with: (1) the trouble allegedly caused by Black Muslims in the early 1960s, and (2) the fact that the petitioner was confined at Leavenworth, Kansas, a maximum-security institution, held that the warden had a duty to prevent disruptions and thus concluded that there was no religious discrimination under the facts of the case. In *St. Claire v. Cuyler*,[11] the court held that a reasonable relationship to security interests justified the denial of a prisoner's request to attend religious services. The prisoner had the burden to prove by substantial evidence that the security concerns were unreasonable or exaggerated. In *Wojtczak v. Cuyler*,[12] a Pennsylvania court held that inmates confined in segregation for their own safety may not be unduly restricted in the rights held by prisoners in the general population; however, the inmate bears the heavy burden of disproving a claim that different treatment is based upon genuine security considerations.

This rationale likewise was applied in *McDonald v. Hall*.[13] The appellate court took notice of an affidavit, filed by prison officials, which indicated that allowing segregated inmates to attend services outside of their unit would pose a safety threat. The court upheld the officials' decision because it was neither arbitrary nor capricious.

In *Cooper v. Pate*,[14] the court allowed prison officials to restrict the religious freedom of certain individuals where the officials showed that such free exercise had been abused at a prior time. It held that, although a complete ban on religious services was discrimination, precautions that were necessary for security would be sanctioned. Inmates with records of prior misconduct "which reasonably demonstrates a high degree of probability that the individual would seriously misuse the opportunity for participation with the group"[15] could be excluded from religious services at the authorities' discretion.

The use of the "clear and present danger" test enunciated by the United States Supreme Court[16] as a valid reason for limiting First Amendment freedom of speech was utilized by analogy by the court in *Knuckles v. Prasse*.[17] The court permitted certain infringements of religious freedoms on the basis that they presented a "clear and present danger of a breach of prison security or discipline or some other substantial interference with the orderly function-

---

[10]   248 F. Supp. 791 (D. Kan. 1965).
[11]   634 F.2d 109 (3d Cir. 1980); Montoya v. Tanksley, 446 F. Supp. 226 (D. Colo. 1978).
[12]   480 F. Supp. 1288 (E.D. Pa. 1979).
[13]   McDonald v. Hall, 576 F.2d 120 (1st Cir. 1978).
[14]   382 F.2d 518 (7th Cir. 1967).
[15]   *Id.* at 523.
[16]   Brandenburg v. Ohio, 395 U.S. 444 (1969).
[17]   302 F. Supp. 1036 (E.D. Pa. 1969), *aff'd*, 435 F.2d 1255 (3d Cir. 1970).

ing of the institution."[18] The court further stated that prison officials had the right to be present and to monitor religious services and if the services became nonreligious, the authorities could cancel them. Prisons must not be forced to "experience a catastrophic riot . . ."[19] The court further found that its ". . . task is not to evaluate plaintiffs' religious wisdom but rather to determine whether regulations of that religion in a prison context are reasonable."[20]

Prison officials are under an obligation to maintain security and discipline within the institution. For this reason, the courts analyze restrictions of religious freedom within the prison setting in the framework of that obligation. A proper justification by prison officials of the need for such restrictions will frequently result in its approval by the courts.

Female inmates unsuccessfully contended that a Washington State prison policy subjecting fully clothed female inmates to random "pat searches" by male as well as female correctional officers infringed their religious freedom.[21] The female inmates' beliefs prohibited them from being touched by men other than their husbands. The majority of the court concluded, however, that the policy was reasonably related to prison officials' legitimate interests in institutional security, and that it therefore passed muster under *Turner v. Safley*.[22] The majority relied on the testimony of prison officials that the same-sex searches would conflict with the officers' collective bargaining agreement, create security problems by requiring female guards to leave their posts to conduct the searches, and make the searches more predictable.[23] In *Schreiber v. Ault*, a free exercise of religion claim failed. An inmate believed for religious reasons that after his blood was used for routine medical tests it should have been poured on the ground and covered with dust. The routine decontamination and disposal of inmates' blood after medical testing was reasonably related to public health and safety concerns.[24]

A case involving religious practices of Native Americans was *Hamilton v. Schriro*,[25] in which a Native American inmate was denied access to a "sweat lodge."

The correctional facility provides cross-denominational religious facilities inside prison buildings. Native Americans are allowed to pray, to gather together for regularly scheduled services, to meet with outside spiritual leaders, and to obtain religious reading material from the library. They are also allowed to carry medicine bags containing ceremonial items and have access to a ceremonial pipe and kinnikinnik (a ceremonial "tobacco" consisting of willow, sweet grass, sage, and cedar). Authorities do not allow a sweat lodge, sweat lodge ceremony, or fires on the premises.

---

[18]   *Id.* at 1049, citing Long v. Parker, 390 F.2d 816, 822 (3d Cir. 1968).
[19]   *Id.* at 1058.
[20]   *Ibid.*
[21]   Jordan v. Gardner, 986 F.2d 1521 (9th Cir. 1993).
[22]   Turner v. Safley, 482 U.S. 78 (1987).
[23]   *See* § 12.4, Search and Seizure.
[24]   Schreiber v. Ault, 280 F.3d 891 (8th Cir. 2002).
[25]   74 F.3d 1545 (8th Cir. 1996).

The sweat lodge ceremony primarily takes place inside a dome-shaped structure constructed of bent willow poles and covered with hides, blankets, or tarps. Rocks heated in a separate fire are placed in the center of the lodge. During the ceremony, several tools are used, including an axe (to split the firewood), a shovel (to transfer the hot rocks from the fire to the sweat lodge), and deer antlers. Participants, who are nude, pour water on the hot rocks to create steam, which causes them to sweat. Throughout the ceremony, the lodge remains covered to retain the steam and to keep out the light. The ceremony lasts between one and three hours. When the lodge is not in use, the covers are removed but the willow poles remain intact.

The sweat lodge ceremony is instrumental to the practice of a Native American's religion because it purifies the participant. Purity is a prerequisite to participating in other religious ceremonies, such as offering prayers and smoking the sacred pipe. Participants in these ceremonies must be seated outdoors on the ground. There was testimony that if a Native American could not have access to a sweat lodge ceremony, he would not and could not practice any aspect of his religion. There was also testimony that other states permit sweat lodge ceremonies to be conducted in their prison facilities without any major problems.

The Eighth Circuit Court of Appeals held that the prisoner failed to establish a deprivation under either his constitutional or statutory right to free exercise of religion.

Native Americans have no constitutional or statutory right to sweat lodges. The court concluded that the prison officials' denial of access to a sweat lodge was rationally related to the legitimate penological interests of safety and security at the institution.

First, prohibiting prisoners from meeting in a completely enclosed area is rationally connected to preventing the type of harm prison officials fear would occur in the sweat lodge. Second, alternative means remain open to prisoners for exercising their religion, including carrying a medicine bag containing ceremonial items, having access to a ceremonial pipe and kinnikinnik, and praying with other Native American inmates. Third, accommodating the request for a sweat lodge would have an adverse impact on prison staff, other inmates, and prison resources, due to the risk of assaulting participants in the ceremony, as well as possible resentment resulting from the construction of an exclusive religious facility. Finally, the prisoner failed to point to an alternative that fully accommodates the prisoner's rights at *de minimis* cost to valid penological interests.

On the basis of the record below, the court applied the same reasoning to sweat lodges. However, the decision did not foreclose the possibility of a successful sweat lodge claim under different circumstances, such as under the Religious Freedom Restoration Act (RFRA) of 1993.[26]

A Native American complained about prison policy not allowing him the use of herbs for ceremonial "smudging." The prison provided him with the opportunity for substitute smudging with nonaddictive tobacco. He was given

---

[26]   See § 6.4.9.

alternative means of exercising his religious beliefs, and the policy was justified by institutional security because the fragrance from herbs could mask the smell of illicit drugs. Prison personnel could not visually distinguish between "sacred herbs" and marijuana.[27] There was no constitutional violation.

§ 6.2.2 —Restrictions Based on the Exercise of Authority and Official Discretion

The argument that control over religious freedom in prison is a proper subject for the exercise of authority and official discretion is a carryover from the historical approach of non-interference by the judiciary. Although this argument is now subject to closer court scrutiny, it has not been completely abandoned. *Knuckles v. Prasse* again pointed out that constitutional standards for the practice of religion in prison must be analyzed in the realistic context of the prison situation. The process requires a balancing of broad discretionary powers vested in prison officials with the right of inmates to practice religion in a prison.[28]

The non-interference approach was further evidenced in *Kennedy v. Meacham,*[29] a case involving the free exercise of the "satanic religion." The court recognized that matters of inmate regulation and discipline are to be left to the discretion of prison authorities as long as the officials' conduct does not involve the deprivation of constitutional rights and is not clearly capricious or arbitrary.

Assuming for the sake of argument that "Satanism" is a religion, the state's interest in the proper administration of its penal system outweighs a prisoner's right to organize a branch of his or her sect within the prison. The prisoner's request to hold meetings was properly denied in view of his inability to provide the name of a sponsor or information relating to the proposed activities of the group. Safety considerations also justified the denial of the use of candles or incense in a cell. Denial of the right to borrow library books for group use was consistent with general prison policies and, in any event, the prisoner was not prejudiced because he owned many of the books himself.[30]

Another case in which the significance of unlimited discretion exercised by prison officials was reviewed is *Belk v. Mitchell.*[31] The prisoner was placed in solitary confinement for 30 days, and his request to attend Sunday services was denied. The court held:

---

[27] Tart v. Young, 168 F. Supp. 2d 590 (W.D. Va. 2001).

[28] 302 F. Supp. 1036 at 1048 (E.D. Pa. 1969), *aff'd,* 435 F.2d 1255 (3d Cir. 1970).

[29] Kennedy v. Meacham, 382 F. Supp. 996 (D. Wyo. 1974), vacated and remanded on appeal, Kennedy v. Meacham, 540 F.2d 1057 (10th Cir. 1976). The court of appeals ruled that the district court improperly dismissed the complaint and the case would be remanded to determine whether the practice of a religious belief was involved, whether there were restrictions imposed upon it, and whether such restrictions were justified.

[30] Childs v. Duckworth, 705 F.2d 915 (7th Cir. 1983).

[31] Belk v. Mitchell, 294 F. Supp. 800 (W.D.N.C. 1968).

> If the solitary confinement itself is justifiable, then it would seem
> entirely reasonable to allow some discretion to the prison authorities
> whether to allow or not allow the Sunday morning commingling of
> solitary prisoners with the others. Prison authorities of course have
> no right to restrict the prisoner's freedom of religious beliefs and
> convictions. However, absent a showing of prolonged and unjustifi-
> able discrimination, his "public" exercise of his religious beliefs and
> his access to publicly provided chaplains during temporary punitive
> solitary confinement would seem to be matters within the reason-
> able discretion of the prison authorities.[32]

In *Mims v. Shapp*,[33] the denial of congregational prayer to inmates in a
segregation unit was held not to have been an improper denial of the right to
practice religion, but rather a proper exercise of official discretion.

In this connection, contrast the *Mims* case with the case of *Collins v.
Vitek*,[34] in which the court held that all inmates, regardless of status, were entitled to attend religious services of their choice. Although this case reflects a
departure from the holdings in the *Belk* and *Mims* decisions, it does not necessarily reflect a basic change in the courts' traditional view of approving
broad official discretion.

Sweet v. Department of Corrections[35] recognized the need for broad official
discretion in light of the peculiar problems necessary to the maintenance of a
prison. Because prison society is both sensitive and explosive, it is necessary for
those with experience to make decisions in light of their particular knowledge.
For this reason, prison authorities may adopt any regulation dealing with the
inmates' exercise of religion that may be reasonable and substantially justified
by consideration of prison administrative requirements. The court's rationale in
the *Sweet* decision is significant in that, like most courts, it demonstrates a certain hesitancy to interfere with the internal management of a prison.

Another case in which the significance of unlimited discretion exercised
by prison officials was reviewed was *Wojtczak v. Cuyler*.[36] The court held:

> Prisoners confined for their own safety in segregation may not be
> unduly restricted in the rights held by prisoners in the general pop-
> ulation. However, the prisoner bears a heavy burden to disprove a
> claim that different treatment is based upon genuine security con-
> siderations. . . . The state must permit the prisoner in segregation to
> receive both a chaplain and communion in his cell . . . but need not
> escort him to the prison chapel . . . .[37]

---

[32] *Id.* at 802.
[33] Mims v. Shapp, 399 F. Supp. 818 (W.D. Pa. 1975), vacated and remanded on appeal, Mims v. Shapp, 541 F.2d 415 (2d Cir. 1976). The court of appeals held that the inmates' affidavits sufficiently alleged personal bias of the judge and that the district judge erred in denying the inmates' refusal motion.
[34] 375 F. Supp. 856 (D.N.H. 1974).
[35] Sweet v. Department of Corrections, 529 F.2d 854 (4th Cir. 1974).
[36] 480 F. Supp. 1288 (E.D. Pa. 1979); Nadeau v. Helgemoe, 423 F. Supp. 1250 (D.N.H. 1976), *modified*, 561 F.2d 411 (1st Cir. 1977); 581 F.2d 275 (1st Cir. 1978).
[37] Wojtczak v. Cuyler, 480 F. Supp. 1288 (E.D. Pa. 1979).

In *Jones v. Bradley,*[38] the Ninth Circuit Court of Appeals held that the right to the free exercise of religion was not absolute, but could be restricted by the legitimate policies of correctional institutions. In this connection, contrast the case of *Montoya v. Tanksley,*[39] in which the court held that religious freedom was of such importance that it could only be overridden by compelling state interests of the highest order.

In *McDonald v. Hall,*[40] corrections officials decided not to provide Catholic group religious services to the departmental segregation unit due to safety concerns and also because non-Catholic inmates would have been compelled to listen to the services. Agreeing with the Fourth Circuit in the *Sweet* case, the First Circuit Court of Appeals ruled in favor of the prison officials, holding that their decision was "neither arbitrary nor without reason."

Another relevant and closely related issue in discussing official discretion arises when arguments are made that prison rules and regulations are capricious and arbitrary. This was pointed out in *In re Ferguson,*[41] in which the court discussed the reasonableness of a regulation restricting the activities of Black Muslims. The court stated:

> [I]n the instant circumstances, the refusal to allow these petitioners to pursue their requested religious [activities] does not appear to amount to such extreme mistreatment, so as to warrant the application of whatever federal constitutional guarantees which may exist for the protection of inmates in state prisons. * * * We are . . . reluctant to apply federal constitutional doctrines to state prison rules reasonably necessary to the orderly conduct of the state institution.
>
> * * * Even conceding the Muslims to be a religious group it cannot be said under the circumstances here presented that the Director of Corrections has made an unreasonable determination in refusing to allow petitioners the opportunity to pursue their claimed religious activities while in prison.[42]

The court then determined that in view of the inflammatory nature of the Koran, the officials were under no obligation to retract a restriction on its use.

While the courts have upheld the suppression of inflammatory religious literature, in at least one case, *Mukmuk v. Commissioner,*[43] it was held that an inmate cannot be punished for the mere possession of religious literature.

---

[38]   590 F.2d 294 (9th Cir. 1979).
[39]   446 F. Supp. 226 (D. Colo. 1978).
[40]   576 F.2d 120 (1st Cir. 1978), citing Sweet v. Department of Corrections, 529 F.2d 854 (4th Cir. 1974).
[41]   361 P.2d 417 (Cal. 1961).
[42]   *Id.* at 421.
[43]   529 F.2d 272 (2d Cir. 1976).

§ 6.2.3 —Restrictions Based on Economic Considerations

Although carefully circumscribed, economic considerations are another factor cited by prison administrators as a justification for controlling the inmate's free exercise of religion. In *Gittlemacker v. Prasse,*[44] a Jewish prisoner alleged a violation of the First Amendment because the state did not provide him with a rabbi. The court stated that the requirement that a state interpose no unreasonable barriers to the free exercise of a prisoner's religion could not be equated with the suggestion that the state had the affirmative duty to provide, furnish, or supply every prisoner with clergy or with religious services of his or her choice. The court pointed out that it was no great burden on the institution or on prison officials to provide facilities of worship and the opportunity for clergy to visit the institution. This requirement could be rationalized on the basis that, because society had removed the prisoner from the community where he could freely exercise his religion, the state had an obligation to furnish or supply the prisoner with the opportunity to practice his faith.

But to go further and suggest that the free exercise clause demands that the state not only furnish the opportunity to practice, but also supply the clergyman, is a concept that dangerously approaches the jealously guarded frontiers of the establishment clause.[45]

The court pointed out that the sheer number of religious sects was a practical consideration. It suggested that there were perhaps 120 distinct established religious denominations in the state. To the court, it became readily apparent that to accept the inmate's contention was to suggest that each state prison have an extravagant number of clergy available. Although the court did not reach this question, it did recognize that explicit in the First Amendment were two separate and distinct concepts designed to guarantee religious liberties: (1) the establishment clause, and (2) the free exercise clause. The court also recognized that under the circumstances of the case, a slavish insistence upon a maximum interpretation of rights vested in one clause would collide with the restrictions of the other clause. Using the analogy of the school prayer cases, the court approved the language:

> It is no defense to urge that the religious practices here may be relatively minor encroachments on the First Amendment. The breach of neutrality that is today a trickling stream may all too soon become a raging torrent, and, in the words of Madison, "it is proper to take alarm at the first experiment on our liberties."[46]

---

[44] 428 F.2d 1 (3d Cir. 1970).

[45] *Id.* at 4.

[46] *Id.* at 5.

In *Gittlemacker*, the inmate alleged that the officials denied Jewish inmates a rabbi in regular attendance, although they provided Catholic and Protestant chaplains. The response of the prison superintendent was: "The small number of Jewish inmates at Dallas, usually two or three, makes the use of a full-time rabbi economically unfeasible and unwarranted."[47] The court also found that the superintendent had, on numerous occasions, attempted to secure the services of a rabbi for Jewish inmates. It was asserted that the official intended to have him come to the institution on a fee basis. The court concluded that the inmate's claim of religious discrimination was effectively and conclusively refuted.

In *Walker v. Blackwell*,[48] Muslim inmates proposed that they be provided with a special meal during Ramadan, their religious period, and that it be served after the normal dinner time, but at a time that would not interfere with their work schedules. Inmates asserted that the cost of purchasing the special foods would not be prohibitive, and that, under present conditions, they could not make adequate selections from the menus prepared because pork was included. The prison officials' argument was that they could not afford to buy the various special items within the limits of the existing budget. They further pointed out that while once-a-year special purchases were made for Passover, the Muslims were requesting 30 days of special menus.

With respect to the after-sunset meals, the court felt that supplying such meals could only be done at a prohibitive cost. It held further that there were problems of security and additional staff involved in serving Muslims after all other prisoners had eaten. In the court's opinion, considerations of expense and security outweighed "whatever constitutional deprivation petitioners may claim. In this regard . . . the government has demonstrated a substantial compelling interest. . . ."[49]

The same analysis has been applied to the Jewish kosher food cases. Represented by the holding in *Kahane v. Carlson*,[50] the attitude of the courts appears to be that there is no obligation to provide all Jewish inmates with kosher food on a full-time basis.[51]

In a significant United States Supreme Court case concerning prison inmates who were members of the Islamic faith, it was contended that prison policies prevented them from attending Jumu'ah, a congregational service held on Friday afternoons, and thereby violated their rights under the free exercise clause of the First Amendment. The first policy required inmates in the plaintiff's custody classifications to work outside the buildings in which they were housed and in which Jumu'ah was held, while the second prohibited inmates assigned to outside work from returning to those buildings during the day.

---

[47]   *Ibid.*
[48]   411 F.2d 23 (5th Cir. 1969).
[49]   *Id.* at 26.
[50]   527 F.2d 492 (2d Cir. 1975).
[51]   *See* § 6.4.6.

However, the Ninth Circuit held that a policy of serving only one kosher meal per day to Orthodox Jewish inmates imposes an impermissible burden on the free exercise of religion. In place of expensive frozen dinners, prison authorities could supply foods such as whole fruits, tinned fish, and kosher cereals that met kosher standards.[52]

The United States Supreme Court held that there was no burden on prison officials to disprove the availability of alternative methods of accommodating prisoners' religious rights. The Constitution allows respect for and deference to the judgment of prison administrators. The policies were reasonably related to legitimate penological interests, and therefore did not offend the free exercise clause of the First Amendment. Both policies had a rational connection to the legitimate governmental interests in institutional order and security invoked to justify them. One was a response to critical overcrowding and was designed to ease tension and drain on the facilities during the part of the day when the inmates were outside. The policy was necessary because returns from outside work details generated congestion and delays at the main gate, a high-risk area. Decisions involving return requests placed pressure on officers supervising outside work details. Rehabilitative concerns also supported the policy as corrections officials sought to simulate working conditions and responsibilities in society. Although the policies may have prevented some Muslim prisoners from attending Jumu'ah, they did not deprive the Muslims of all forms of religious exercise but instead allowed participation in a number of Muslim religious ceremonies. There were no obvious, easy alternatives to the policies because both of the suggested accommodations would, in the judgment of prison officials, have adverse effects on the prison institution. Placing all Muslim inmates in inside work details would be inconsistent with the legitimate prison concerns, while providing weekend labor for Muslims would require extra supervision that would be a drain on scarce human resources. Both proposed accommodations would also threaten prison security by fostering "affinity groups" likely to challenge institutional authority, while any special arrangements for one group would create a perception of favoritism on the part of other inmates.

Even when claims are made under the First Amendment, the Supreme Court will not substitute its judgment on difficult and sensitive matters of institutional administration for the determinations of those charged with the formidable task of running a prison.[53]

---

[52]   Ashelman v. Wawrzaszek, 111 F.3d 674 (9th Cir. 1997).

[53]   O'Lone v. Estate of Shabazz, 482 U.S. 342 (1987).

§ 6.3   Religious Discrimination: The Equal Protection Clause

The cases dealing with religious freedom frequently refer to the equal protection clause of the Fourteenth Amendment. Section I of that amendment provides, in part, that "Nor shall any state . . . deny to any person within its jurisdiction the equal protection of the laws."[54]

The application of the equal protection clause is particularly relevant in cases dealing with minority religions. This was apparent in *Newton v. Cupp,*[55] in which the court stated: "If members of one faith can practice their religious beliefs and possess religious materials, equivalent opportunity must be available to members of another faith."[56]

The soundness of this decision is apparent from the Supreme Court's subsequent decision in *Cruz v. Beto,*[57] holding that Texas prison officials had discriminated against an inmate by denying him a reasonable opportunity to pursue his Buddhist faith comparable to that offered other inmates adhering to conventional religious precepts. Similarly, in *People ex rel. Rockey v. Krueger,*[58] the court found that because an orthodox Jew would be allowed to retain his beard without being placed in solitary confinement, a Muslim who had been placed in solitary confinement for not shaving his beard was entitled to be released. Thus, because prison policy permitted orthodox Jews to wear beards, other religious beliefs requiring beards could not be suppressed even in the face of a Commissioner of Correction's Regulation, which required that prisoners be "clean-shaven."

In *Konigsberg v. Ciccone,*[59] an inmate alleged the denial of exercise of his religious rights. He claimed that while he was confined in close custodial supervision, he was not permitted to attend any religious services. Further, when he was transferred from such custody, his attendance at Jewish religious services was conditioned upon a pass, issued specifically for that purpose. On the other hand, Protestant and Catholic prisoners in close custody confinement were allowed to attend services. The prison officials established that the Protestants and Catholics did not need passes to attend services because those services were held at a time when no other activity was in progress. Thus, the destination of people moving through the corridors could be easily identified. Also, it was proved that sufficient staff were available to guarantee security at that time. However, prison officials stated that inmates who attended services at times other than Sunday needed passes to move through the corridors just as any other inmate would at the same time.

---

[54]   U.S. CONST., amend. XIV, § 1. *See* Appendix III.
[55]   474 P.2d 532 (Or. App. 1970).
[56]   *Id.* at 536.
[57]   405 U.S. 319 (1972). *See* § 6.4.1.
[58]   306 N.Y.S.2d 359 (Sup. Ct. 1969); *see also* Maguire v. Wilkinson, 405 F. Supp. 637 (D. Conn. 1975).
[59]   285 F. Supp. 585 (W.D. Mo. 1968), *aff'd,* 417 F.2d 161 (8th Cir. 1969), *cert. denied,* 397 U.S. 963 (1970).

The court would not accept as reasonable the prison officials' basis for denying minority religions the right to attend services while at the same time permitting Protestants and Catholics to do so. The court said that it was unrealistic to take the position that sufficient escorts were not available to conduct them to services "in view of the high importance the law places on the right to worship and [on] the right to be free of religious discrimination."[60] The court then directed that such an inmate be allowed to attend religious services unless: (1) his physician certified medical reasons; (2) there was proof that the inmate was a dangerous security risk; or (3) his attendance would substantially and adversely affect security.

In *Cooper v. Pate,*[61] the court stopped prison officials from preventing an inmate's communication (by mail and visitation) with ministers of his faith, subject to usual prison regulations. The court felt that such communication did not present a clear and present danger to prison security, and to grant it to one faith, but deny it to another, was religious discrimination. However, note in this case that the inmate also wished to purchase Swahili grammar books. He pointed out that prisoners were allowed to purchase foreign language books. The lower court held that these books were not necessary for the practice of the prisoner's religion and that the denial was based on staff and facility limitations. The court of appeals affirmed the holding that this involved no impairment of a constitutional right.

State v. Cubbage[62] also expressed the importance of equal protection of minority religions. Of primary concern to the petitioning inmates were the general discriminatory practices against the Black Muslim religion. The court concluded that in fact there had been no discrimination as to religious beliefs, but that the inmates had been denied equal protection of the laws because they were not given an opportunity to practice their beliefs or to wear religious symbols. The state asserted that this denial of equal protection should be weighed against the "clear and present danger" test. The court, however, held that this test was inapplicable when it stated that "the right to equal protection of law is almost an absolute right, always to be respected."[63] Furthermore, the court found "no reason to deny the relators the equal protection of the laws, even if it is feared they might hereafter abuse the rights herein recognized."[64]

§ 6.4 Specific Areas of Constitutional Concern

While the right of Black Muslims to practice their religious beliefs has dominated the litigated cases in the past, controversy over this right has declined. Issues such as the right to attend services, to obtain literature, and to wear religious medals were usually raised by Black Muslims because, unlike

---

[60]   *Id.* at 595.
[61]   382 F.2d 518 (7th Cir. 1967).
[62]   210 A.2d 555 (Del. Super. Ct. 1965).
[63]   *Id.* at 567.
[64]   *Id.* at 568.

Protestant or Catholic inmates, the Black Muslims had been denied the right to engage in such practices. The threshold question was the recognition of the Black Muslim faith as a "religion." It has been recognized as a religion in several cases[65] and, for this reason, it can now be asserted—at least in theory—that a Black Muslim retains the same constitutional protection offered to other members of recognized religions.

In spite of the general recognition of the Black Muslim faith as a religion, certain specific problems remain relative to the free exercise of its beliefs. Those problems, although usually presented by Black Muslim petitioners, are common among all inmates seeking to exercise religious freedoms. For this reason, it must be assumed that the rights accorded by the judiciary to the Black Muslim inmate must also be rendered to all recognized religions. The general applicability of these decisions to all recognized religions practiced within penal institutions is consistent with the constitutional mandate of the First Amendment and the equal protection clause.

Later cases shifted the focus to Native Americans.

§ 6.4.1 —The Right to Hold Religious Services

Numerous cases have recognized the Black Muslims' right to hold some sort of religious service.[66] However, the cases in which this right was not extended were usually based upon the belief that a congregation of Black Muslim inmates would result in some security risk. This was apparent in the decisions of *Jones v. Willingham*[67] and *Cooke v. Tramburg.*[68] In the first of these decisions, *Jones*, the court refused to grant the Black Muslims the right to assemble for worship. The court based its decision on the duty of the warden to prevent breaches of security. It asserted that, in view of the possibility of disruptions resulting from a congregation of Black Muslims, the restriction was a valid exercise of the warden's duty. In *Cooke*, the court also denied the right to hold religious services because of the danger it believed was inherent in such assemblage. It was found that freedom to exercise religious beliefs is not absolute, but is subject to restriction for the protection of the society as a whole.

However, *Banks v. Havener*[69] held that a prison could not prohibit the practice of an established religion unless it could prove (by satisfactory evidence) that the teaching and practice of the act created a clear and present danger to the orderly functioning of the institution. Absent such evidence, the court in *Battle v. Anderson*[70] found that the policy of prison officials of deny-

---

[65]   *See* Howard v. Smyth, 365 F.2d 428 (4th Cir. 1966); Lee v. Crouse, 284 F. Supp. 541 (D. Kan. 1968), *aff'd,* 396 F.2d 952 (10th Cir. 1968); Fulwood v. Clemmer, 206 F. Supp. 370 (D.C. Cir. 1962); State v. Cubbage, 210 A.2d 555 (Del. Super. Ct. 1965).

[66]   *See* Knuckles v. Prasse, 435 F.2d 1255 (3d Cir. 1970); Sewell v. Pegelow, 304 F.2d 670 (4th Cir. 1962); Banks v. Havener, 234 F. Supp. 27 (E.D. Va. 1964).

[67]   248 F. Supp. 791 (D. Kan. 1965).

[68]   43 N.J. 514, 205 A.2d 889 (1964).

[69]   234 F. Supp. 27 (E.D. Va. 1964).

[70]   376 F. Supp. 402 (E.D. Okla. 1974).

ing to all inmates, including Muslims, the opportunity to gather together for corporate religious services, was unjustified.

Cases concerning the right of nontraditional religious groups to hold services are *Theriault v. Carlson*[71] and *Remmers v. Brewer,*[72] both dealing with an inmate-devised religion based on the Eclatarian faith and organized around The Church of the New Song of Universal Life. In *Theriault*, the inmate who devised the religion and who was head of the newly developed church was confined in punitive segregation for attempting to hold religious services to promote the new belief. Although the district court ordered his restoration to the general prison population and directed prison officials to permit the inmate to hold religious services, this ruling was overturned on appeal and remanded for an evidentiary hearing.[73] On remand, a different district court concluded that the Eclatarian faith was not a "religion" entitled to First Amendment protection, but was rather "a masquerade designed to obtain protection for acts which otherwise would have been unlawful and/or reasonably disallowed by various prison authorities."[74]

While failing to provide a precise definition of what a "religion" is for purposes of First Amendment protection, the court declared that such protection does not extend to so-called religions "which tend to mock established institutions and are obviously shams and absurdities and whose members are patently devoid of religious sincerity."[75]

Essentially the same issue was present in *Remmers,* but the court in that case, while aware of the holdings in the *Theriault* case, nevertheless decided that the Eclatarian faith was a "religion" and that members of such religion were entitled to protection under the free exercise clause. However, the court declared that if it were subsequently proved that the Eclatarian faith, as practiced at the prison, was in fact a sham, then the prison administrators and the court could deal with the eventuality. These two decisions highlight the continuing legal problem facing prison administrators when apparently inconsistent decisions are rendered by different federal courts, and the United States Supreme Court is either unwilling or unable to resolve the conflict.

A number of courts have adjudicated petitions that have alleged that religious liberties were denied when authorities prohibited attendance at general services while the petitioner was confined in a correctional cell.[76] A majority of these courts dismissed the complaint and distinguished between one's free-

---

[71]   339 F. Supp. 375 (N.D. Ga. 1972), *vacated and remanded,* 495 F.2d 390 (5th Cir.), *cert. denied,* 419 U.S. 1003 (1974).

[72]   361 F. Supp. 537 (S.D. Iowa 1973), *aff'd,* 494 F.2d 1277 (8th Cir. 1974), *cert. denied,* 419 U.S. 1012 (1974).

[73]   Theriault v. Carlson, 495 F.2d 390 (5th Cir. 1974).

[74]   Theriault v. Sibler, 391 F. Supp. 578 (W.D. Tex. 1975), *vacated and remanded,* 547 F.2d 1279 (5th Cir. 1977).

[75]   *Ibid.*

[76]   *See* Sharp v. Sigler, 408 F.2d 966 (8th Cir. 1969); Belk v. Mitchell, 294 F. Supp. 800 (W.D.N.C. 1968); Konigsberg v. Ciccone, 285 F. Supp. 585 (W.D. Mo. 1968), *aff'd,* 417 F.2d 161 (8th Cir. 1969), *cert. denied,* 397 U.S. 963 (1970); Morgan v. Cook, 236 So. 2d 749 (Miss. 1970).

dom to believe and one's freedom to exercise one's belief. Such a restriction on the free exercise of beliefs is justified on the basis of maintaining both security and institutional internal correctional discipline.[77] However, in *Konigsberg v. Ciccone*, the Jewish petitioner established that Protestant and Catholic inmates confined in close custodial supervision were permitted to attend services although he was not. The court refused to accept as reasonable the administration's contention that they could not find sufficient escorts to conduct him to services. The court held that he should be allowed to attend services unless: (1) a physician certified medical reasons; (2) an officer certified that the prisoner was a security risk; or (3) his attendance would substantially and adversely affect security.

A Mississippi court[78] indicated that full access to a minister of one's denomination while confined in a maximum-security unit (correctional cells) satisfies the constitutional right to free exercise of religion. This case could be cited for two propositions: (1) that it is not necessary to release prisoners from maximum-security cells to attend services with the general population, or (2) that it is not necessary to conduct formal services for prisoners confined in correctional custody. Note, however, that this court held that full access to a minister of one's denomination satisfied the constitutional requirements. Another court[79] ruled, however, that the petitioner who was being held on death row be permitted to attend midweek services in the chapel instead of having to receive communion and services in a shower room.

Prison rules and policies prohibiting inmates from leading religious services and requiring that all services be conducted in an interfaith chapel do not violate the equal protection clause.[80] Further, a prison regulation prohibiting inmates from leading religious groups is valid under the First Amendment if it is reasonably related to legitimate penological interests.[81] However, a prison rule prohibiting unauthorized religious services is vague and is in violation of the Fourteenth Amendment as applied to a prisoner for engaging in solitary, silent, but "demonstrative" prayer. A New York rule neither provided notice that such conduct was prohibited nor gave adequate guidance to those who must enforce it.[82]

---

[77]   *See* Sharp v. Sigler, 408 F.2d 966 (8th Cir. 1969); Belk v. Mitchell, 294 F. Supp. 800 (W.D.N.C. 1968); McBride v. McCorkle, 44 N.J. Super. 468, 130 A.2d 881 (App. Div. 1957).

[78]   Morgan v. Cook, 236 So. 2d 749 (Miss. 1970).

[79]   Gunn v. Wilkinson, 309 F. Supp. 411 (W.D. Mo. 1970).

[80]   Samad v. Ridge, U.S. Dist. LEXIS 6348 (E.D. Pa. 1998).

[81]   Anderson v. Angelone, 123 F.3d 1197 (9th Cir. 1997).

[82]   Chatin v. New York, 1998 U.S. Dist. LEXIS 8351 (S.D.N.Y 1998), *aff'd sub nom* Chatin v. Coomb, 186 F.3d 82 (2d Cir. 1999).

§ 6.4.2 —The Wearing of Religious Medals

In general, the courts have recognized that Black Muslims have a right to possess and wear religious medals.[83] This recognition has, in at least two cases,[84] been based upon the fact that inmates practicing other religions had been given such a right by prison officials. However, the issue of internal security has been asserted in this area as well as in the other areas concerning religious freedoms. In *Rowland v. Sigler,*[85] the court felt that, in view of the possibility of a prisoner using a medallion as a weapon, prison officials could justifiably prohibit the prisoner from wearing the medallion. Any possible infringement of First Amendment rights was justified by the state interest in regulating the non-speech aspect, *i.e.,* the use of a medallion as a weapon. This case would not, of course, support the denial (by prison officials) of medallions to Black Muslims where officials permitted medallions to be worn by Catholics.

Prisoners contended that the state's requirement that they give up their cross necklaces substantially burdened their religious exercise.[86] Rejecting a constitutional attack, the court also concluded that the Religious Freedom Restoration Act did not violate the principle of federalism embodied in the Tenth and Eleventh Amendments and was within the power of Congress to enact.[87]

§ 6.4.3 —The Right to Correspond with Religious Leaders

Numerous prisoners have petitioned the court for the right to correspond with Elijah Muhammad, a Black Muslim leader. Some institutions have a general restriction pertaining to correspondence with heads of religious groups. This regulation is based on the theory that such communications are not "meaningful contacts."[88] Occasionally, courts have accepted this rationale and have held that because the policy applies to all religions, it does not result in religious discrimination. However, in *Walker v. Blackwell,*[89] when prison officials gave as their reasons for not allowing such correspondence the fact that Elijah Muhammad had a prison record, and that the prison had a general policy not to allow Catholics to correspond with the Pope, the court held that Elijah Muhammad's confinement had occurred more than 25 years earlier, that a criminal record was only one factor to be considered in approving a corre-

---

[83] *See* Knuckles v. Prasse, 302 F. Supp. 1036 (E.D. Pa. 1969), *aff'd,* 435 F.2d 1255 (3d Cir. 1970).

[84] *See* Coleman v. District of Columbia Commissioners, 234 F. Supp. 408 (E.D. Va. 1964) and State v. Cubbage, 210 A.2d 555 (Del. Super. Ct. 1965).

[85] 327 F. Supp. 821 (D.C. Neb. 1971).

[86] Sasnett v. Department of Corrections, 891 F. Supp. 1305 (W.D. Wis. 1995).

[87] *See* § 6.4.9.

[88] *See* Knuckles v. Prasse, 302 F. Supp. 1036 (E.D. Pa. 1969), *aff'd,* 435 F.2d 1255 (3d Cir. 1970); Long v. Katzenbach, 258 F. Supp. 89 (M.D. Pa. 1966); Desmond v. Blackwell, 235 F. Supp. 246 (M.D. Pa. 1964).

[89] 411 F.2d 23 (5th Cir. 1969).

spondence according to the Bureau of Prisons, and that "[t]he prohibition against Catholics' correspondence with the Pope is of questionable constitutional merit."[90] Nevertheless, both *Theriault* and *Remmers* expressly declare that prison authorities may ascertain the contents of such correspondence with religious leaders in order to make certain that what is sought is spiritual guidance and advice, and that such correspondence is not used for other than religious purposes.[91]

§ 6.4.4   —The Right to Proselytize

Although there is no case that recognized an absolute right of a prisoner to proselytize, we could say that Black Muslims have the same right to proselytize in the prison as do other prisoners. This right does not extend, however, to such activity that would create a disturbance or interfere with the privacy rights of other inmates.[92] Furthermore, when the purpose of proselytizing is "to cause or encourage disruption of established prison discipline for the sake of disruption," such activity enjoys no First Amendment protection because it is not based on an underlying "religion."[93] In *Fulwood v. Clemmer,*[94] prison authorities presented evidence to show that the prisoner's "field preaching" had resulted in a disturbance among the other prisoners. As a result, he had been placed in solitary confinement for six months, excluded from the prison population for two years, and denied the use of rehabilitation and recreational facilities. The court held that this punishment was not reasonably related to the infraction.

Proselytizing can also be done by prison employees. In the Ninth Circuit, a guard's unauthorized religious proselytizing while on the job did not violate a county jail inmate's rights under the First Amendment.[95]

---

[90]   *Id.* at 29.

[91]   Theriault v. Carlson, 339 F. Supp. 375 (N.D. Ga. 1972), *vacated and remanded,* 495 F.2d 390 (5th Cir. 1974), *cert. denied,* 419 U.S. 1003 (1974); Remmers v. Brewer, 361 F. Supp. 537 (S.D. Iowa 1973), *aff'd,* 494 F.2d 1277 (8th Cir. 1974), *cert. denied,* 419 U.S. 1012 (1974).

[92]   *See* Evans v. Ciccone, 377 F.2d 4 (8th Cir. 1967); Sewell v. Pegelow, 304 F.2d 670 (4th Cir. 1962); Long v. Katzenbach, 258 F. Supp. 89 (M.D. Pa. 1966).

[93]   Theriault v. Sibler, 391 F. Supp. 578 (W.D. Tex. 1975), *vacated and remanded,* 547 F.2d 1279 (5th Cir. 1977). The court of appeals held that the requirement of a belief in a supreme being as a criterion to determine whether a practice constitutes a religion within the protection of the First Amendment is too narrow. The court stated that: "When reconsidering what constitutes a religion, a thorough study of the existing case law should be accompanied by appropriate evidentiary exploration of philosophical, theological, and other related literature and resources on this issue." *Id.* at 1281.

[94]   206 F. Supp. 370 (D.D.C. 1962).

[95]   Canell v. Lighter, 143 F.3d 1210 (9th Cir. 1998).

§ 6.4.5 —Free Access to Ministers

The cases dealing with the right of an inmate, particularly a Black Muslim, to have access to a minister have been inconsistent. In two of these cases, *Jones v. Willingham*[96] and *Coleman v. Commissioner,*[97] the courts held that the prison officials could exclude Muslim ministers for protection or for security in the institution. In *Cooper v. Pate,*[98] however, the court enjoined the administration from refusing to permit an inmate to communicate through the mail or personal visitation with the ministers of their faith. It was found that because such communication did not constitute a clear and present danger to prison security and because such communication was permitted for other religious denominations, the restriction against the Black Muslims was discriminatory.

There can be little doubt, irrespective of the controversy regarding security within the institution, that Black Muslim ministers, once admitted to the institution, must be permitted to wear such religious robes and raiment as they desire.[99] Furthermore, they must be paid at an hourly rate comparable to that paid to chaplains of other faiths.[100]

§ 6.4.6 —Restrictions of Diet

As a general rule, the courts have refused to order prisons to provide Black Muslims with pork-free meals, in spite of the fact that such dietary restraint is an essential doctrine found in that faith. The rationales for such refusal have been diverse. For example, in *Northern v. Nelson,*[101] in which the petitioner sought special meals during the period of Ramadan, the court asserted that budgetary restrictions constituted a justifiable reason for refusing to serve pork-free meals. The court found that, despite the constitutional deprivations claimed, the government had demonstrated a substantial compelling interest and, for that reason, dismissed relief.

Another court[102] justified the failure to provide pork-free meals by finding that a prisoner could acquire adequate nourishment by avoiding pork foods. In view of this fact, the prison was under no obligation to provide specified meals. In a third case, *Childs v. Pegelow,*[103] the court simply found that there was no constitutional issue involved and that, essentially, the Muslims were demanding special privileges rather than constitutional rights.

---

[96]   248 F. Supp. 791 (D. Kan. 1965).

[97]   234 F. Supp. 408 (E.D. Va. 1964).

[98]   382 F.2d 518 (7th Cir. 1967).

[99]   *See* Samarion v. McGinnis, 314 N.Y.S.2d 715 (N.Y.A.D. 1970).

[100]   *See* Northern v. Nelson, 315 F. Supp. 687 (N.D. Cal. 1970).

[101]   *Ibid.; See also* Young v. Robinson, 29 Cr. L. 2587 (M.D. Pa. 1981). (Muslim inmates are not required to be furnished with diets that conform to their religious beliefs.)

[102]   Childs v. Pegelow, 321 F.2d 487 (4th Cir. 1963), *cert. denied,* 376 U.S. 932 (1964); *cf.* Muhammad-D.C.C. v. Keve, 479 F. Supp. 1311 (D. Del. 1979) (Muslim inmates have a constitutional right to a pork-free diet.)

[103]   *Id.* at 100.

A unique approach to the issue of pork-free meals is found in *Barnett v. Rodgers.*[104] The District of Columbia Circuit Court held that the lower court erred in dismissing the inmate's complaint without determining whether the government had compelling justification and purposes for denying their request. The court felt that the prison officials had not adequately demonstrated a budgetary constraint that would prevent the use of pork, and had not shown why they could not post a menu or why they could not distribute pork meals more evenly throughout the week. "To say that religious freedom may undergo modification in a prison environment is not to say that it can be suppressed or ignored without adequate reason."[105] On remand, judgment was entered in favor of the prison superintendent.[106]

A District Court injunction obtained by Muslim inmates in Iowa was reversed. Several parts of the injunction dealing with congregational prayer sessions, pork-free diets, and prayer classes were not based on findings of constitutional or statutory violations. Also reversed were requirements that Muslim inmates be allowed to wear prayer caps and robes outside their prayer services, and that Muslim religious leaders be allowed to visit with Muslim inmates after the initial five-day period of an emergency lockdown. The Appeals Court held that prison officials had cited security reasons for opposing these measures, and the District Court should have deferred to their judgment.[107]

Generally, the analysis employed in the Black Muslim food cases had been echoed in the Jewish kosher food cases. Cases out of New York have added much to the discussion of the kosher food question. Within two days of one another, two federal district courts in New York came to apparently opposite conclusions. Both cases involved Jewish prisoners who had applied to the court for orders directing the Bureau of Prisons to make kosher foods—meeting the requirements of Jewish orthodox dietary laws—available to them during their incarceration.

In the first case, *United States v. Huss,*[108] the court ruled that the prison was not obligated to provide kosher food. In arriving at this conclusion, the court relied on four primary considerations: (1) the extra cost of providing kosher foods to Jewish prisoners on a regular basis; (2) the obvious problems that would arise from special treatment given to such prisoners; (3) the security risk involved, given the relative ease of smuggling contraband to a prisoner when it is known that the food is for a designated prisoner; and (4) the availability of substitute foods to ensure a sufficient diet. On appeal, this judgment was vacated on procedural grounds.[109] The second case, *United States v. Kahane,*[110] involved the kosher food requests of an orthodox rabbi. In this case, the court decided that the inmate was entitled to receive kosher meals. It

---

[104]   410 F.2d 995 (D.C. Cir. 1969).

[105]   *Id.* at 100

[106]   Unreported decisions HC 174-66 and HC 66-66 (S.D.N.Y. 1975).

[107]   Rogers v. Scurr, 676 F.2d 1211 (8th Cir. 1982).

[108]   United States v. Huss, 394 F. Supp. 752 (S.D.N.Y.), *vacated,* 520 F.2d 598 (2d Cir. 1975).

[109]   United States v. Huss, 520 F.2d 598 (2d Cir. 1975).

[110]   396 F. Supp. 687 (E.D.N.Y.), *modified sub nom.,* Kahane v. Carlson, 527 F.2d 492 (2d Cir. 1975).

was reasoned that comparatively simple administrative procedures—*i.e.*, a combination of pre-prepared frozen kosher meals and suitable dietary alternatives—would result in a nutritionally sound diet consistent with kosher requirements. In the court's opinion, the government had shown no serious reasons why providing a kosher diet for the inmate would affect prison security or discipline.

The conflict arising from these two cases is somewhat settled by *Kahane v. Carlson*.[111] In this decision, the Second Circuit Court of Appeals affirmed and modified *United States v. Kahane*. The court agreed that the finding of deep religious significance for a practicing orthodox Jew was justified and was entitled to constitutional protection. It was explained that the difficulties encountered by the prisons were surmountable in view of the small number of practicing orthodox Jews in federal prisons (approximately 12).[112] The court clarified and modified the district court's decision by explaining that the use of frozen prepared kosher foods, while helpful, was not constitutionally required. Rather, the prison was required to provide the incarcerated orthodox rabbi with a diet sufficient to sustain his good health without violating Jewish dietary laws. However, the court did not mandate specific items of diet.

While the court ordered the provision of a kosher diet in this instance, it should be noted that this does not necessarily apply to all Jewish inmates. The application of this decision seems to require a situation involving a practicing orthodox Jew before a prison is required to provide a kosher diet.

Where the Jewish prison population was small, it was within the official's discretion whether to provide a rabbi and other Jewish services upon request.[113]

A lawsuit against a maximum-security chaplain was based on the claim that food service provided inadequate nutrition and was handled under conditions so unsanitary as to violate the Eighth Amendment. The chaplain only had the authority to authorize medical or religious diets. As he was not involved in food preparation or delivery, the suit was dismissed.[114]

Finally, with respect to dietary restrictions and isolated confinement, it was held in *Jones v. Gallahan*[115] that prison officials must provide an inmate in isolation with a diet containing a daily minimum caloric requirement that will not be rejected on religious grounds. The court noted that this requirement may be met by providing acceptable food alternatives.

---

[111]   527 F.2d 492 (2d Cir. 1975).
[112]   *Id.* at 495.
[113]   Garza v. Miller, 688 F.2d 480 (7th Cir. 1982).
[114]   Caldwell v. Caesar, 150 F. Supp. 2d 50 (D.D.C. 2001).
[115]   370 F. Supp. 488 (W.D. Va. 1974).

§ 6.4.7 —Access to Religious Literature

Inmate access to religious literature is a controversial issue. The justification for suppressing religious literature that prison administrators frequently advance is that the material is inflammatory and will cause disruptions and breaches in security. Consequently, the decisions usually turn on when the court believes that the material requested is of a nature tending to incite disruptions or security problems. A case finding no such tendency is *Northern v. Nelson*.[116] Here, the court held that the prison library was under an obligation to make available copies of the Koran. Further, the court ordered that prisoners be allowed to receive the publication *Muhammad Speaks,* unless it could be clearly demonstrated that a specific issue would substantially disrupt prison discipline.

In *Walker v. Blackwell,*[117] although the district court held that issues of *Muhammad Speaks* were inflammatory, the Fifth Circuit Court of Appeals reached a conclusion similar to *Northern*, and reversed the district court. The basis of its decision is found in the following:

> First, taken as a whole, the newspapers are filled with news and editorial comment, a substantial portion of which generally encourages the Black Muslim to improve his material and spiritual condition of life by labor and study. Nowhere, including the supposedly inflammatory portions described by the court below, does there appear any direct incitement to the Black Muslims to engage in any physical violence.

> This court thus concluded that *Muhammad Speaks* was not inflammatory and ordered that Black Muslims be allowed to receive the newspaper. The court qualified this, however, by saying that they were not holding that exclusion of the newspaper could not take place, if it became inflammatory. The order was merely to direct that the warden not arbitrarily deny Black Muslims the right to read *Muhammad Speaks.*[118]

While *Northern* and *Walker* have found that, taken as a whole, the Muslim publications presented no threat to prison security, other courts have come to the opposite conclusion. In *Knuckles v. Prasse,*[119] the district court found that it was not mandatory that prison officials make available Muslim books and periodicals. The court found that, without proper guidance and interpretation by trained Muslim ministers, these materials might be misinterpreted by an inmate. An uninformed inmate could read the material as an encouragement to defy whites generally and prison authorities specifically. Thus, the lit-

---

[116]   315 F. Supp. 687 (N.D. Cal. 1970).
[117]   411 F.2d 23 (5th Cir. 1969).
[118]   *Id*. at 28-29.
[119]   302 F. Supp. 1036 (E.D. Pa. 1969).

erature could constitute "a clear and present danger of a breach of prison security or discipline or some other substantial interference with the orderly functioning of the institution."[120] Another decision following this basic rationale is *Abernathy v. Cunningham.*[121] In that case, an inmate desired to obtain a copy of "Muhammad's Message to the Black Man in America," and to subscribe to *Muhammad Speaks.* The Fourth Circuit held that the prison's decision denying access to this literature, so far as the record disclosed, was not motivated by religious prejudice, and that the particular materials in question contained recurring themes of black superiority and hatred for the white race. It was the prison authorities' opinion that such materials would be inflammatory and subversive to discipline. The court felt that it should not attempt to substitute its judgment on the nature of the publication for that of the prison authorities. For this reason, the court denied relief. In his dissent, Judge Craven stated that he failed to understand why the prisoner could not be granted access to the materials on the condition that he could not circulate them throughout the prison. Because this alternative was available, exclusion was not the only remedy to prevent danger to internal discipline.

In spite of the courts' determination as to whether material is inflammatory, most courts place the burden of proving that the deprivation of constitutional rights is justified upon the prison. In *Burns v. Swenson,*[122] prison officials were ordered to return the plaintiff's Koran. The court felt that deprivation of his holy book would interfere with his right to freely practice his religion, particularly because the prison officials had given no explanation of why this book should not be returned to the prisoner. Similarly, in *Long v. Parker,*[123] the Third Circuit Court of Appeals placed the burden on prison authorities who wished to suppress *Muhammad Speaks.* The court found that the administration must show that "[t]he literature creates a clear and present danger of a breach of prison security or discipline or some other substantial interference with the orderly functioning of the institution."[124] However, it also required the Muslims to establish that it was basic religious literature essential to their belief and understanding of their religion.

As indicated above, the courts have been fairly uniform in supporting administrative decisions to exclude various Black Muslim publications. With the primary emphasis placed on maintaining security, the courts have given the following reasons for excluding such publications: (1) without proper guidance by trained Muslims, the reader could interpret them as condoning disruption within institutions; (2) such publications may advocate and encourage conduct that the officials may lawfully suppress; (3) they advocate themes of black superiority and hatred of the white race and are thus inflammatory and subversive to discipline; and (4) publications that are not necessary to the practice of religion may be excluded.

---

[120] *Id.* at 1049.
[121] 393 F.2d 775 (4th Cir. 1968).
[122] 288 F. Supp. 4 (W.D. Mo. 1968), *modified,* 300 F. Supp. 759 (W.D. Mo. 1969).
[123] 390 F.2d 816 (3d Cir. 1968).
[124] *Id.* at 822.

It must be noted that although inflammatory religious material may be suppressed, at least one case, *Mukmuk v. Commissioner*,[125] has held that an inmate may not be punished for possession of religious literature.

In *Sasnett v. Department of Corrections*, Wisconsin state prisoners challenged several internal management procedures, emergency rules, and permanent administrative rules regulating the types and amounts of personal property they may possess while in prison. They contended that the enforcement of these procedures and rules violated their constitutional rights to the free exercise of their religions under the Constitution and the Religious Freedom Restoration Act of 1993.[126]

Rules regulating inmate personal property and clothing procedures, which included limiting the amount of personal and state-issued property an inmate may possess, were issued. As a result, a prisoner was forced to relinquish approximately 11 religious books, including The Amplified Bible, volumes one through three of the Jamison, Fauset Brown Commentary, the Inductive Study Bible, the NIV Interliner Greek-English New Testament and the NIV Interliner Hebrew-English Old Testament. These religious books were sent out of the prison to or with Sasnett's pastor. Because of the new rules, one prisoner was forced to dispose of several Jehovah's Witnesses pamphlets.

After holding that the prisoners had no property interest that was protected under the due process clause, it granted the prisoners relief. Unlike property interests, liberty interests can arise from the Constitution. The right to "liberty" guaranteed by the Fourteenth Amendment denoted a freedom to worship God according to the dictates of one's own conscience, as well as the right to petition the courts for redress.[127] Also applicable was the Religious Freedom Restoration Act, which, according to the court, manifested a congressional intent to protect the liberty of free religious exercise embodied in the First Amendment.[128]

§ 6.4.8 —Classification on Religious Grounds

It is a frequent practice in various correctional institutions to require that an inmate specify his or her religious preference upon entering the prison. The inmate is then forbidden to alter this choice during his period of confinement. For the most part, such practices have been upheld by courts.

In *Long v. Katzenbach*,[129] the court sustained the classification procedure as a valid means of controlling the proselytizing that had been a source of disruption within the institution. A similar finding was handed down in *Peek v. Ciccone*,[130] in which prison officials had refused to permit a non-Jewish

---

[125]   529 F.2d 272 (2d Cir. 1976).

[126]   Sasnett v. Department of Corrections, 891 F. Supp. 1305 (W.D. Wis. 1995). *See* § 6.4.9.

[127]   Williams v. Lane, 851 F.2d 867, 881 (7th Cir. 1988), *cert. denied*, 488 U.S. 1047 (1989).

[128]   42 U.S.C. § 2000bb(a) and (b). *See* § 6.4.10 below.

[129]   258 F. Supp. 89 (M.D. Pa. 1966).

[130]   288 F. Supp. 329 (W.D. Mo. 1968).

inmate to attend Jewish services. The prison allowed inmates to attend any service connected with their specified religious affiliation. The court found that such a restriction was not unreasonable in that it did not curtail religious belief. This was especially true in light of the fact that the rabbi in the institution had a policy of refusing conversion of inmates to the Jewish faith. The court found that religious practices, as distinguished from religious beliefs, may properly be the subject of administrative control.

A law which stated that legal recognition of religious names adopted by prisoners could be withheld was held unconstitutional. Further, corrections officials may maintain inmate records in the names that inmates used when convicted. There is no right to force prison officials to put inmate-adopted religious names on their official records.[131]

A prisoner commenced suit against the superintendent of the institution, alleging that the superintendent had violated his statutory and constitutional rights to freely exercise his religion. Where the prisoner could not specifically state how the restrictive institutional policies were violating his rights, and which of his religious rights were specifically being violated, the superintendent had qualified immunity from a § 1983 civil suit.[132]

A pat-down search of a prisoner conducted by a female officer does not violate the constitutional right to free exercise of religion of a prisoner whose faith teaches that a man is forbidden to be touched by a woman not of his family.[133]

Although the issue is not entirely clear, religious classification would appear to be supportable so long as equal treatment is afforded to all religious groups and there is a rational basis for such classification.

§ 6.4.9 —Beards and Haircuts

Both *Brown v. Wainwright*[134] and *Brooks v. Wainwright*[135] held that regulations requiring shaves and haircuts were proper and were not a source of religious discrimination. However, the court in *People ex rel. Rockey v. Krueger*[136] heard evidence from the prisoner that he was being held in solitary confinement because he had refused to shave his beard. The prison administration justified the regulation as one for the protection of health. The jail supervisor also testified that there was no formal regulation about hair, but that the order to the staff was that inmates were only permitted to wear neatly trimmed mustaches. He said that an orthodox Jew would not be required to shave his beard. The court held that, on the basis of the treatment afforded orthodox Jews, the prisoner was the subject of religious discrimination.

---

[131] Barrett v. Commonwealth of Virginia, 689 F.2d 498 (4th Cir. 1982).
[132] Green v. White, 693 F.2d 45 (8th Cir. 1982).
[133] Sam'l v. Mintzes, 554 Supp. 416 (E.D. Mich. 1983).
[134] 419 F.2d 1376 (5th Cir. 1970).
[135] 428 F.2d 652 (5th Cir. 1970).
[136] People ex rel. Rockey v. Krueger, 306 N.Y.S.2d 359 (Sup. Ct. 1969).

In cases concerning prison haircut regulations as applied to Native Americans, at least three courts have held that where a long hairstyle is motivated by indisputably sincere religious beliefs, then such regulations impermissibly infringe on the inmate's right under the First Amendment to the free exercise of his religion.[137] However, in *Proffitt v. Ciccone*,[138] the court upheld prison haircut regulations, despite the inmate's contention that he was thereby forced to violate religious vows he had taken. In this area, in order to restrict inmate conduct based upon religious motivations, prison authorities face a heavy burden.

A one-half-blooded Cherokee Indian may not be required to cut his hair if the prison regulation infringes on his religious beliefs.[139]

In *Benjamin v. Coughlin*,[140] the Second Circuit Court of Appeals held that prison authorities' legitimate interest in obtaining accurate photos for identification purposes must be accommodated with inmates' religious rights. Requiring inmates to tie back their hair was preferable to requiring all inmates to have their hair cut. Rastafarian inmates, who were required to cut their dreadlocks, successfully raised a First Amendment claim. The regulation requiring haircuts was held unconstitutional as applied.

In *Cleveland v. Garner*,[141] a prisoner alleged that the prison's grooming regulations interfered with the free exercise of his religion in violation of both the First Amendment and the Religious Freedom Restoration Act (RFRA) of 1993. 42 U.S.C. § 2000bb-1(b).[142]

The prisoner professed the Rastafari religion. Based on the Biblical vow of the Nazarite, Rastafari practices include never cutting or combing one's hair, instead allowing it to grow in dreadlocks.[143] Diametrically opposed to that tenet of the Rastafari religion is the aspect of the prison grooming regulations that prohibits long hair and beards.

The rule is well established that inmates retain their First Amendment right to the free exercise of religion.[144] The right, however, is subject to reasonable restrictions and limitations necessitated by penological goals.[145]

It was conceded that, as a general proposition, the prisoner's religious practices conflicted with penological interests, such as prison security and ease of inmate identification. However, it was contended that an exception

---

[137] Teterud v. Gillman, 371 F. Supp. 282 (W.D. Mo. 1973), *aff'd* 506 F.2d 1020 (8th Cir. 1974); Teterud v. Gillman, 385 F. Supp. 153 (S.D. Iowa 1974), *aff'd*, 522 F.2d 357 (8th Cir. 1975), and Crowe v. Erickson, 17 Cr. L. 2093 (D.S.D. 1975); Gallahan v. Hollyfield, 516 F. Supp. 1004 (E.D. Va. 1981), *aff'd*, 670 F.2d 1345 (4th Cir. 1982).

[138] Proffitt v. Ciccone, 371 F. Supp. 282 (W.D. Mo. 1973), *aff'd*, 506 F.2d 1020 (8th Cir. 1974).

[139] *Ibid.*

[140] Benjamin v. Coughlin, 708 F. Supp. 570 (S.D.N.Y. 1989), *aff'd*, 905 F.2d 571 (2d Cir. 1990), *cert. denied*, 498 U.S. 951 (1990).

[141] 69 F.3d 22 (5th Cir. 1995).

[142] *See* § 6.4.10 below.

[143] Numbers 6:6-1. Verse five of that vow reads: "All the days of the vow of his separation there shall no razor come upon his head: until the days be fulfilled, in the which he separateth himself unto the Lord, he shall be holy, and shall let the locks of the hair of his head grow."

[144] Powell v. Estelle, 959 F.2d 22 (5th Cir.) (per curiam), *cert. denied sub nom.*, Harrison v. McKaskle, 506 U.S. 1025 (1992).

[145] *Id.* (citing Turner v. Safley, 482 U.S. 78 (1987)).

should be made on the basis that confinement in administrative segregation and segregation from the general prison population so significantly reduce the importance of these penological interests that they serve no valid purpose. The prisoner had no desire to return to the general prison population and, in his unique confinement situation, being forced to comply with the grooming regulations both interfered with his religious beliefs and served no actual penological interests.

The court held that, as a general principle, prison grooming regulations, including specifically the requirement that a prisoner cut his hair and beard, are rationally related to the achievement of valid penological goals, such as security and inmate identification.[146] Consequently, the prisoner's First Amendment claim was denied.

A prisoner who adheres to a minority religion must be given a reasonable opportunity to pursue his or her faith, comparable to the opportunity afforded fellow prisoners who adhere to conventional religious precepts.[147] It has long been the law that the religious needs of the inmate must be balanced against the reasonable penological goals of the prison.[148]

However, the Fifth Circuit concluded that the district court abuses its discretion by dismissing the claim under the RFRA, passed by Congress in 1993.

§ 6.4.10 Religious Freedom Restoration Act

The Religious Freedom Restoration Act states in pertinent part:

§ 2000bb-1. Free exercise of religion protected

(a) In general. Government shall not substantially burden a person's exercise of religion even if the burden results from a rule of general applicability, except as provided in subsection (b).

(b) Exception. Government may substantially burden a person's exercise of religion only if it demonstrates that application of the burden to the person—

(1) is in furtherance of a compelling governmental interest; and

(2) is the least restrictive means of furthering that compelling governmental interest.

---

[146] *See Powell*, 959 F.2d at 25 (holding that the prohibition on long hair and beards is rationally related to legitimate state objectives); Scott v. Mississippi Dep't of Corrections, 961 F.2d 77 (1992) (hair-grooming regulation that required short hair was reasonably related to legitimate penological concerns of identification and security).

[147] Cruz v. Beto, 405 U.S. 319 (1972).

[148] O'Lone v. Estate of Shabazz, 482 U.S. 342 (1987).

The purpose of the RFRA was to restore the compelling interest test in all cases in which the free exercise of religion is substantially burdened. Given this broad statement of purpose, the Fifth Circuit joined every other circuit that has addressed this issue in concluding that the RFRA clearly applies to prisoners' claims.[149] As a result of the RFRA, courts are required to analyze prisoners' religious rights using the "substantial burden" test rather than the less stringent "reasonable opportunity" test previously employed in prison litigation of religious issues.

Because the RFRA was new, its statutory contours vague, and its legal limits and standards yet to be defined, the Fifth Circuit decided to give the prisoner a "fighting chance" to develop the law. The Fifth Circuit held that the district court abused its discretion when it summarily dismissed the RFRA claim as frivolous.

To guide the lower court on remand, it was pointed out that the threshold inquiry under RFRA is whether the statute or conduct in question substantially burdens a person's religious practice. If there is no substantial burden, RFRA does not apply.[150]

As far as the standard of proof, a "substantial burden" has been defined in several different ways. The religious adherent has the obligation to prove that a government action burdens the adherent's practice of his or her religion by preventing him or her from engaging in conduct or having a religious experience that the faith mandates. This interference must be more than an inconvenience; the burden must be substantial and must interfere with a tenet or belief that is central to religious doctrine.[151]

To exceed the "substantial burden" threshold, government regulation must significantly inhibit or constrain conduct or expression that manifests some central tenet of a prisoner's individual beliefs, must meaningfully curtail a prisoner's ability to express adherence to his or her faith, or must deny a prisoner reasonable opportunities to engage in activities that are fundamental to a prisoner's religion.[152]

To be a "substantial burden," the government must either compel a person to do something in contravention of his or her religious beliefs or require him or her to refrain from doing something required by his or her religious beliefs.[153] A "substantial burden" occurs when the state conditions receipt of an important benefit upon conduct proscribed by a religious faith, or where it denies

---

149   *See* Bryant v. Gomez, 46 F.3d 948 (9th Cir. 1995) (per curiam); Brown-El v. Harris, 26 F.3d 68, 69 (8th Cir. 1994); Werner v. McCotter, 49 F.3d 1476 (10th Cir. 1995), *cert. denied,* 515 U.S. 1165, 115 S. Ct. 2625 (1995). These holdings were based on the fact that Congress debated and rejected an amendment that would have excluded prisons from the RFRA. *See* S. Rep. No. 111, 103rd Cong., 1st Sess. §§ V(d) and XI (1993); H.R. Rep. No. 88, 103rd Cong., 1st Sess. (1993).

150   Hicks v. Garner, 69 F.2d 22 (5th Cir. 1995); *See* Morris v. Midway Southern Baptist Church, 183 Bankr. 239, 251 (D. Kan. 1995).

151   Bryant v. Gomez, 46 F.3d 948, 949 (9th Cir. 1995); *see also* Morris, 183 Bankr. at 251.

152   Werner, 49 F.3d at 1480.

153   Morris, 183 Bankr. at 251.

such a benefit because of conduct mandated by religious belief, thereby putting substantial pressure on an adherent to modify his or her behavior and to violate his or her beliefs.[154]

Using similar arguments, Wisconsin state prisoners challenged several internal management procedures, emergency rules, and permanent administrative rules regulating the types and amounts of personal property they may possess while in prison. They contended that the enforcement of these procedures and rules violated their constitutional rights to the free exercise of their religions under the Constitution and the Religious Freedom Restoration Act.[155]

After holding that the prisoners had no property interest that was protected under the due process clause, it granted the prisoners relief. Unlike property interests, liberty interests can arise from the Constitution. The right to "liberty" guaranteed by the Fourteenth Amendment denoted a freedom to worship God according to the dictates of one's own conscience, as well as the right to petition the courts for redress.[156] Also applicable was the Religious Freedom Restoration Act, which, according to the court, manifested a congressional intent to protect the liberty of free religious exercise embodied in the First Amendment.[157]

The *Sasnett* court felt that *Employment Division, Department of Human Resources of Oregon v. Smith* was a historic decision involving governmental burdens on the First Amendment right to free religious exercise. Later views about *Smith* varied greatly. On the one hand, it was argued that it accurately depicted prior case law, resolving seeming inconsistencies into a coherent and consistent formula.[158] Others characterized it as judicial retrenchment.[159]

Congress saw the case as retrenchment and responded in 1993 with the Religious Freedom Restoration Act. Finding that *Smith* virtually eliminated the requirement that the government justify burdens on religious exercise imposed by laws neutral toward religion, Congress attempted to restore what it perceived to be prior law regarding governmental interference with the free exercise of religion. Borrowing language from Supreme Court precedent on free exercise doctrine,[160] Congress provided that "government shall not substantially burden a person's exercise of religion" unless it demonstrates first that "application of the burden to the person" is the "least restrictive means" available to further a "compelling state interest."[161] This is the doctrine rejected by the Supreme Court as the outer boundary of the free exercise clause.

---

[154]   Woods v. Evatt, 876 F. Supp. 756, 762 (D.S.C. 1995).

[155]   Sasnett v. Department of Corrections, 891 F. Supp. 1305 (W.D. Wis. 1995).

[156]   Williams v. Lane, 851 F.2d 867, 881 (7th Cir. 1988), *cert. denied,* 488 U.S. 1047 (1989).

[157]   42 U.S.C. § 2000bb(a) and (b).

[158]   *See e.g.,* Philip A. Hamburger, *A Constitutional Right of Religious Exemption: An Historical Perspective,* 60 GEO. WASH. L. REV. 915 (1992).

[159]   *See, e.g.,* Smith, 494 U.S. 872 (1990) (O'Connor, J., concurring in the judgment); and *id.* at 907 (Brennan, Marshall, Blackmun, JJ., dissenting); Matt Pawa, Note, *When the Supreme Court Restricts Constitutional Rights, Can Congress Save Us? An Examination of Section 5 of the Fourteenth Amendment,* 141 U. PA. L. REV. 1029, 1034-1037 (1993).

[160]   Sherbert v. Verner, 374 U.S. 398 (1963); Wisconsin v. Yoder, 406 U.S. 205 (1972).

[161]   42 U.S.C. § 2000bb-1(b).

Rejecting a constitutional attack, the court concluded that the Religious Freedom Restoration Act did not violate the principle of federalism embodied in the Tenth and Eleventh Amendments and was within the power of Congress to enact.

Another case involving religious practices of Native Americans was *Hamilton v. Schriro*.[162] Prison authorities required a prisoner to cut his hair by enforcing a regulation that prohibited hair length beyond the collar for male inmates.

Native American males believe that their hair is a gift from the Creator and is to be cut only when someone close to them dies. At one time the prisoner's hair was four feet long. According to prison officials, long hair poses a threat to prison safety and security. Prisoners could conceal contraband, including dangerous materials, in their long hair. Without the hair length regulation, prison staff would be required to perform more frequent searches of inmates, which could cause conflicts between staff and inmates. Searching an inmate's long hair would be difficult, especially if the hair was braided. Prison officials had also tried to control gangs by not allowing them to identify themselves through colors, clothes, or hair carvings. Exempting Native Americans from the hair length regulation could cause resentment on the part of other inmates. There was no alternative to the hair length policy because only short hair can easily be searched and remain free of contraband. Finally, long hair causes problems with inmate identification.

The district court found that the regulations and policies at issue in this lawsuit with regard to the plaintiff's practice of his religion substantially burdened the free exercise of religion.[163]

Although the case began as a § 1983 action alleging violation of the First Amendment, after this action was initiated, Congress enacted the Religious Freedom Restoration Act of 1993 (RFRA), which was to be applied retroactively.[164]

The Eighth Circuit Court of Appeals reversed the district court and held that the prisoner failed to establish a deprivation under either his constitutional or statutory right to the free exercise of religion.

The Eighth Circuit recognized that prison inmates do not forfeit all constitutional protections by reason of their conviction and confinement in prison,[165] that federal courts must take cognizance of the valid constitutional claims of prison inmates,[166] which include actions based on free exercise rights protected by the First Amendment.[167] The court also recognized that the lawful incarceration of prisoners brings about the necessary withdrawal or limitation of many privileges and rights, a retraction justified by the considerations underlying our penal system.[168] The fact of confinement and the needs of the penal institution

---

[162] 74 F.3d 1545 (8th Cir. 1996).

[163] Hamilton v. Schriro, 863 F. Supp. 1019, 1024 (W.D. Mo. 1994).

[164] *See* Brown-El v. Harris, 26 F.3d 68, 69 (8th Cir. 1994).

[165] Bell v. Wolfish, 441 U.S. 520 (1979).

[166] Turner v. Safley, 482 U.S. 78 (1987).

[167] *See* Pell v. Procunier, 417 U.S. 817 (1974).

[168] Jones v. North Carolina Prisoners' Labor Union, Inc., 433 U.S. 119 (1977); Price v. Johnston, 334 U.S. 266 (1948).

impose limitations on constitutional rights, including those derived from the First Amendment, which are implicit in incarceration. It was stressed that issues of prison management are, both by reason of separation of powers and highly practical considerations of judicial competence, peculiarly ill-suited to judicial resolution and, accordingly, courts should be loath to substitute their judgment for that of prison officials and administrators.[169] Prior decisions of the Eighth Circuit had rejected Native American claims regarding long hair.[170]

With respect to the application of RFRA, prison officials bear the burden of demonstrating that the regulation is the least restrictive means of achieving a compelling interest.[171] The primary question before the Court of Appeals is whether the district court erred in holding that the prison policies and regulations at issue were not the least restrictive means of achieving the compelling interest of prison safety and security.

The RFRA's legislative history indicates that the applicable test must be construed in the prison setting, giving due deference to the expert judgment of prison administrators. The legislative history of RFRA also shows that, while Congress intended for the same compelling interest test in the statute to apply to prisoners as well as non-prisoners, the outcome of the analysis would depend upon the context. Because the court was faced with a prison case in which the maintenance of institutional security was at issue, it gave the prison officials wide latitude within which to make appropriate limitations, which the court felt was the correct interpretation and application of the least restrictive means prong of the RFRA.

The court held that the prison officials demonstrated that the prison regulation and policy at issue were the least restrictive means of maintaining the prison's compelling interest in institutional safety and security.

Although no circuit other than the Eighth has yet decided whether the RFRA precludes prison hair length regulations, several district courts have upheld such regulations against RFRA challenges.[172]

The Religious Freedom Restoration Act requires the "strict scrutiny" and not the "reasonable basis" standard. This heightened standard was satisfied when a Rastafarian prisoner was required to undo his dreadlocks for a pre-transfer search because there was no reasonable alternative.[173]

---

[169] Iron Eyes v. Henry, 907 F.2d 810, 812 (8th Cir. 1990); Pitts v. Thornburgh, 866 F.2d 1450, 1453 (D.C. Cir. 1989).

[170] Iron Eyes, 907 F.2d at 813-816; *see also* Sours v. Long, 978 F.2d 1086 (8th Cir. 1992) (per curiam); Kemp v. Moore, 946 F.2d 588 (8th Cir. 1991) (per curiam), *cert. denied,* 504 U.S. 917 (1992).

[171] 42 U.S.C. § 2000bb-1(b).

[172] *See* Phipps v. Parker, 879 F. Supp. 734, 736 (W.D. Ky. 1995), holding that cutting inmates' hair short appeared to be the only plausible way to meet safety concerns, and thus satisfied the requirement that the least restrictive means available be used to achieve the compelling interests, and Diaz v. Collins, 872 F. Supp. 353, 359 (E.D. Tex. 1994), noting that the potential of hiding contraband in long hair cannot be vitiated except through a regulation that hair be kept short. In *Phipps*, the district court recognized that while other methods might be used, such as constantly searching inmates for contraband, such means would be impractical and just as likely to burden constitutional interests.

[173] May v. Baldwin, 109 F.3d 557 (9th Cir. 1997).

Congress enacted the RFRA in direct response to *Employment Div., Dept. of Human Resources of Ore. v. Smith,* 494 U.S. 872 (1990), in which the Supreme Court upheld against a free exercise challenge a state law of general applicability criminalizing peyote use, as applied to deny unemployment benefits to Native American Church members who lost their jobs because of such use. In so ruling, the Court declined to apply the balancing test of *Sherbert* v. *Verner,* 374 U.S. 398 (1963) which asks whether the law at issue substantially burdens a religious practice and, if so, whether the burden is justified by a compelling government interest. RFRA prohibits "government" from "substantially burdening" a person's exercise of religion even if the burden results from a rule of general applicability unless the government can demonstrate the burden (1) is in furtherance of a compelling governmental interest; and (2) is the least restrictive means of furthering that interest. RFRA's mandate applies to any branch of federal or state government, to all officials, and to other persons acting under color of law. Its universal coverage includes all federal and state law, and the implementation of that law, whether statutory or otherwise, and whether adopted before or after RFRA's enactment.

In imposing RFRA's requirements on the States, Congress relied on the Fourteenth Amendment, which, *inter alia,* guarantees that no State shall make or enforce any law depriving any person of "life, liberty, or property, without due process of law," or denying any person the "equal protection of the laws," and empowers Congress "to enforce" those guarantees by "appropriate legislation," Although Congress certainly can enact legislation enforcing the constitutional right to the free exercise of religion, its §5 power "to enforce" is only preventive or "remedial."

The Amendment's design and §5's text were held by the Supreme Court to be inconsistent with any suggestion that Congress has the power to decree the substance of the Amendment's restrictions on the states. Legislation that alters the free exercise clause's meaning cannot be said to be enforcing the clause. Congress does not enforce a constitutional right by changing what the right is. While the line between measures that remedy or prevent unconstitutional actions and measures that make a substantive change in the governing law is not easy to discern, and Congress must have wide latitude in determining where it lies, the distinction exists and must be observed. There must be a congruence and proportionality between the injury to be prevented or remedied and the means adopted to that end. Lacking such a connection, legislation may become substantive in operation and effect. The need to distinguish between remedy and substance is supported by the Fourteenth Amendment's history and the Supreme Court's case law. The Amendment's design had proved significant also in maintaining the traditional separation of powers between Congress and the Judiciary, depriving Congress of any power to interpret and elaborate on its meaning by conferring self-executing substantive rights against the States and thereby leaving the interpretive power with the Judiciary.

In *City of Boerne v. Flores*,[174] the Supreme Court held that RFRA was not a proper exercise of Congress' §5 enforcement power because it contradicts vital principles necessary to maintain separation of powers and the federal-state balance. RFRA's most serious shortcoming was in the fact that it was so out of proportion to a supposed remedial or preventive object that it cannot be understood as responsive to, or designed to prevent, unconstitutional behavior. It attempted a substantive change in constitutional protections, proscribing state conduct that the Fourteenth Amendment itself does not prohibit. Its sweeping coverage ensures its intrusion at every level of government, displacing laws and prohibiting official actions of almost every description and regardless of subject matter. Its restrictions applied to every government agency and official, and to all statutory or other law, whether adopted before or after its enactment. It had no termination date or termination mechanism. Any law is subject to challenge at any time by any individual who claimed a substantial burden on his or her free exercise of religion. Requiring a state to demonstrate a compelling interest and show that it has adopted the least restrictive means of achieving that interest is the most demanding test known to constitutional law. RFRA was a considerable congressional intrusion into the states' traditional prerogatives and general authority to regulate for the health and welfare of their citizens, and was not designed to identify and counteract state laws likely to be unconstitutional because of their treatment of religion. *Boerne* was limited to the impact of the RFRA on state systems, and had no effect on the federal system.

§ 6.4.11   Religious Land Use and Institutionalized Persons Act

In 2000, Congress enacted the Religious Land Use and Institutionalized Persons Act (RLUIPA)[175] in response to the Supreme Court's holding in *City of Boerne v. Flores*. The statute provides:

> No government shall impose a substantial burden on the religious exercise of a person residing in or confined to an institution . . . even if the burden results from a rule of general applicability, unless the government demonstrates that imposition of the burden on that person—
>
> (1)   is in furtherance of a compelling governmental interest; and
>
> (2)   is the least restrictive means of furthering that compelling governmental interest.

---

[174]   521 U.S. 507 (1997).
[175]   42 U.S.C. 2000cc-1(a).

Under the RLUIPA, once a plaintiff produces *prima facie* evidence to support a free exercise violation, the plaintiff bears the burden of persuasion on whether the regulation substantially burdens the plaintiff's exercise of religion and the state bears the burden of persuasion on all other elements.[176]

By its terms, RLUIPA is to be construed to broadly favor protection of religious exercise.[177] The statute defines religious exercise as "any exercise of religion, whether or not compelled by, or central to, a system of religious belief."[178] This reflects an extension of the definition provided for in RFRA, which defined exercise of religion as "the exercise of religion under the First Amendment to the Constitution."[179]

Like its predecessor RFRA, the RLUIPA requires a plaintiff to demonstrate that his right to free exercise of religion has been substantially burdened.[180]

As of August 2002, the constitutionality of the RLUIPA has been upheld at the District Court level. A Wisconsin inmate and practicing Muslim brought an action under the Religious Land Use and Institutionalized Persons Act. The inmate argued that enforcement of a prison Internal Management Procedure restricting his access to Islamic prayer oil and preventing him from celebrating more than one annual religious feast violates his rights under both the free exercise clause of the First Amendment and the Religious Land Use and Institutionalized Persons Act. The state challenged the Act's constitutionality. Pursuant to 28 U.S. §2403, the District Court certified to the Attorney General of the United States the fact that defendants had called into question the Act's constitutionality and gave the United States an opportunity to intervene on that question. After briefing, the court held that the Religious Land Use and Institutionalized Persons Act is a constitutionally valid exercise of Congress's spending power, does not violate the Tenth Amendment to the Constitution, and does not violate the First Amendment's establishment clause.[181]

According to a Michigan district court,[182] the Religious Land Use and Institutionalized Persons Act (RLUIPA), 42 U.S.C. §2000cc-1, as it applies to institutionalized persons, is constitutional. The defendants conceded that there is no indication that Congress relied upon §5 of the Fourteenth Amendment in enacting the RLUIPA. According to the court, it was clear that Congress enacted 42 U.S.C. §2000cc-1 under the alternative powers found in the Spending Clause and the Commerce Clause.

In another Michigan case, the district court rejected the argument that Congress exceeded its power under the commerce clause in enacting the RLUIPA, as the Constitution specifically grants to Congress the power to regulate commerce. 42 U.S.C. §2000cc-1(b)(2) provides that the protections

---

[176]   42 U.S.C. 2000cc-2(b). See Appendix II for the full Act.

[177]   42 U.S.C. 2000cc-3(g).

[178]   42 U.S.C. 2000cc-5(7)(A).

[179]   42 U.S.C. 2000bb-2(4).

[180]   *See Marria v. Broaddus*, 200 F. Supp. 2d 280 (S.D.N.Y 2002).

[181]   Charles v. Verhagen, 2002 U.S. Dist. LEXIS 16571 (W.D. Wisc. 2002).

[182]   Johnson v. Martin, 2002 U.S. Dist. LEXIS 12573 (W.D. Mich. 2002).

under(a)(1) apply when "the substantial burden affects, or removal of the substantial burden would affect, commerce with foreign nations, among the several States, or with Indian tribes." The clear language of the statute provides that congressional power under the commerce clause is only exercised when a regulation directly affects interstate commerce. In other words, as applied to the RLUIPA, if a governmental regulation imposing a substantial burden on religion has no effect on interstate commerce, the protections under 2000cc-1(a) could not apply under the scope of (b)(2). Accordingly, the commerce clause power would not be implicated. The power under the commerce clause is only implicated when the regulation substantially affects interstate commerce. The Supreme Court has clearly indicated that a statute that contains a jurisdictional element that ensures, on a case-by-case basis, that the regulation in question has a sufficient connection with interstate commerce withstands a challenge under the commerce clause (*Lopez*, 514 U.S. 549 (1995)). According to this court, the RLUIPA satisfied this concern.

Only time will tell how the higher appellate courts will rule on this issue, as it will take some time for these 2002 district court cases to weave their way to a final decision by the Supreme Court.

§ 6.5   Conclusion

The primary emphasis of decisions concerning an inmate's religious freedom has been on the fact that the prison is a closed environment. It is because of this fact that courts frequently invoke the "noninterference" logic so prevalent in early cases dealing with prisons. The state interest in maintaining security within the institution, together with the need for administrative discretion in handling disciplinary problems, has been held sufficient reason for limiting an inmate's First Amendment rights.

One of the few restrictions placed upon the prison administrator in his or her dealings with the First Amendment rights of inmates has been that of equal protection—that is, treating all classes of inmates equally. Courts have consistently held that when one religious group is permitted to engage in a particular activity, the same right must be accorded all other religious groups within the institution. Thus, it would appear that although prison officials have a right to regulate religious activity in order to promote valid institutional interests, the regulation must, in all cases, be equally applied to all groups. Likewise, where one group is permitted to manifest its religious beliefs in a certain manner, all other religious groups must be accorded the same privilege.

The Religious Freedom Restoration Act of 1993 has had a substantial impact on institution management.

Federal inmates may amend a complaint to set forth a claim under the Religious Freedom Restoration Act where they allege that federal prison officials refused to allow them to participate in Ramadan fast and that all Muslims must participate in that fast, because refusal constrains expression by inmates that manifests a central tenet of their religious beliefs, and inmates have substantial interference with free exercise sufficient to justify amending a complaint. Further, RFRA is a statute in which Congress has unequivocally waived sovereign immunity for the United States.[183]

However, a federal parolee failed to demonstrate any likelihood of success on the merits of a claim that parole conditions violated the RFRA where the underlying conviction established that the parolee/leader used religion as means of exhorting his followers to commit racketeering acts, and that the leader ordered followers to commit numerous murders. Conditions prohibiting the leader from worshiping, meeting, or communicating with followers without prior written consent of his parole officer advanced a compelling government interest by the least restrictive means of protecting such interest.[184]

---

[183] Crocker v. Durkin, 159 F. Supp. 2d 1258 (D.C. Kan. 2001).
[184] Yahweh v. United States Parole Comm'n, 158 F. Supp. 2d 1332 (S.D. Fla. 2001).

Legal Services 7

Chapter Outline

§ 7.1 Introduction: Access to the Courts as a Constitutional Right

The United States Supreme Court has repeatedly affirmed that one of the fundamental rights within the due process clause of the Fourteenth Amendment is the right of access to the courts. Essential to the concept of due process of law is the right of an individual to have "an opportunity . . . granted at a meaningful time and in a meaningful manner,"[1] "for [a] hearing appropriate to the nature of the case."[2]

The right of an inmate to exercise this basic constitutional right was established in the 1940 case of *Ex parte Hull*.[3] In *Hull*, a state prison regulation required that all legal documents in an inmate's court proceedings be submitted to a prison official for examination and censorship before they are filed with the court. The United States Supreme Court found this regulation invalid on the ground that "the state and its officers may not abridge or impair petitioner's right to apply to a federal court for a writ of habeas corpus."[4]

In spite of the rule of law established in *Hull*, courts have hesitated to interfere with the exercise of discretion by prison administrators in matters concerning institutional control. The courts have frequently stated that prison administration was a function relegated to the executive branch of government, and for this reason the judiciary would interfere only where the wrongs committed by institution officials were of monumental proportions.[5] This judicial reluctance offers insight as to why various prison practices (although they may violate the inmates' constitutional rights) have gone uncontested for the past several decades.

Neither the Eighth Amendment nor the due process clause requires states to appoint counsel for indigent death row inmates seeking state post-conviction relief. State collateral proceedings are not constitutionally required as an adjunct to the state criminal proceeding and serve a different and more limited purpose than either the trial or appeal. Eighth Amendment safeguards

---

[1] Armstrong v. Manzo, 380 U.S. 545, 552 (1965).
[2] Mullane v. Central Hanover Tr. Corp., 339 U.S. 306, 313 (1950).
[3] 312 U.S. 546 (1941); *See also* Webb v. State, 412 N.E.2d 790 (Ind. 1980).
[4] Ex parte Hull, 312 U.S. 546 (1941).
[5] *See* Lee v. Tahash, 352 F.2d 970 (8th Cir. 1965); United States v. Marchese, 341 F.2d 782 (9th Cir. 1965); *See also* Webb v. State, 412 N.E.2d 790 (Ind. 1980); Johnson v. Teasdale, 456 F. Supp. 1083 (W.D. Mo. 1978); Miller v. Stanmore, 636 F.2d 986 (5th Cir. 1981).

imposed at the trial stage—where the court and jury hear testimony, receive evidence, and decide the questions of guilt and punishment—are sufficient to assure the reliability of the process by which the death penalty is imposed.

The meaningful access requirement of *Bounds v. Smith*[6] can be satisfied in various ways, and state legislatures and prison administrators must be given "wide discretion" to select appropriate solutions from a range of complex options.[7]

The access of prisoners to the courts was somewhat clarified but cut back in *Lewis v. Casey*[8] by a 5-4 decision. Inmates of various prisons operated by the Arizona Department of Corrections brought a class action lawsuit alleging that state prison officials were furnishing them with inadequate legal research facilities and thereby depriving them of their right of access to the courts, in violation of *Bounds v. Smith*.[9] A broad, system-wide injunction was issued by the District Court, which found the restrictions to be unconstitutional.

The Supreme Court reversed, holding that any systemic challenge to the Arizona system was conditioned on the prisoner's ability to show widespread actual injury. The District Court failed to identify anything more than isolated instances of any actual injury. This made its finding of a systemic *Bounds* violation invalid.

Bounds did not create an abstract, free-standing right to a law library or legal assistance program. The right that *Bounds* acknowledged was the right of access to the courts. To establish a *Bounds* violation, the "actual injury" that an inmate must demonstrate is that the alleged shortcomings in the prison library or legal assistance program have hindered, or are presently hindering, his or her efforts to pursue a non-frivolous legal claim. The doctrine of "standing"[10] is a constitutional requirement for a federal court to exercise jurisdiction and decide a case. Thus, an actual injury was required. Although *Bounds* made no mention of an actual injury requirement, it did not eliminate that constitutional prerequisite.

The Supreme Court held in *Lewis* that any statements in *Bounds* suggesting that prison authorities must also enable the prisoner to discover grievances or to litigate effectively once in court find no precedent in the Court's pre-*Bounds* cases, and were rejected. Moreover, *Bounds* did not guarantee inmates the right to file any and every type of legal claim, but required only that they be provided with the tools to attack their sentences, directly or collaterally, and to challenge the conditions of their confinement.

The findings of the Arizona District Court as to actual injury did not support a system-wide injunction. A remedy must be limited to the inadequacy that produced the injury-in-fact that the plaintiff had established. Only one

---

6   430 U.S. 817 (1977).
7   Murray v. Giarratano, 492 U.S. 1 (1989).
8   518 U.S. 343 (1996).
9   430 U.S. 817 (1977).
10   Federal courts may only decide cases that involve actual cases or controversies and may not issue abstract advisory opinions.

named plaintiff was found to have suffered actual injury. This was a result of the failure to provide the special services he would have needed, in light of his particular disability of illiteracy. Eliminated from the proper scope of the injunction, therefore, were any provisions directed at special services or facilities required by non-English speakers, by prisoners in lockdown, or by the inmate population at large. Furthermore, the Supreme Court held that the inadequacy that caused any actual injury to illiterate inmates was not sufficiently widespread to justify system-wide relief.

The Supreme Court also criticized the District Court's restrictions on lockdown inmates as unjustified. The District Court failed to give the judgment of prison authorities the substantial deference required by cases such as *Turner v. Safley*.[11] The lower court also failed to leave the primary responsibility for devising a remedy with prison officials. The result of this improper procedure was an inordinately intrusive and invalid order.

In a typical access to the courts claim, the inmate must show that the officials actually prevented him or her from taking some meritorious legal action. The District Court decision holding that this standard does not apply to retaliation cases was vacated.[12] In the Sixth Circuit, in order to support a civil rights action based on a claim that prison officials retaliated against the filing of a lawsuit by interfering with an inmate's access to the courts, the inmate does not have to show any injury beyond that which results from the retaliation.

§ 7.2 The Nature of Legal Services in Prison— Prevailing Practices

Many of the practices that prevailed in prisons throughout the country until recent years have amounted to impairments of the inmates' right of access to the courts. Disciplinary actions for inmates pursuing legal remedies, censorship, or wholesale confiscation of a prisoner's legal documents, and other such practices were common in many of America's prison systems.

Further restriction on access to the courts was seen in the fact that prison officials seldom provided inmates with any services related to legal needs. In most cases, only a few outdated law books and, occasionally, the services of a notary public were supplied. As a result of this lack of legal assistance, inmates were frequently forced to accept the aid of a self-proclaimed "jailhouse lawyer" or "writ writer." A jailhouse lawyer is an inmate who, through self-education, has acquired minimum legal skills and, notwithstanding prison restriction, offers legal advice and counseling to fellow inmates, either with or without compensation. These individuals have been subject to a great deal of restriction and regulation by prison officials. It is on the restriction of the jail-

---

[11] 482 U.S. 78 (1987).
[12] Thaddeus-X v. Blatter, 175 F.3d 378 (6th Cir. 1997). See § 11.6 below.

house lawyer and alternatives to him or her that judicial concern has focused in the modern cases.

Restrictions on the legal practice of jailhouse lawyers, in light of the unique position of an incarcerated individual, place an impossible burden on the inmate seeking legal relief. These restrictions, coupled with the unavailability of legal assistance in the outside world, had resulted in the complete loss of a basic constitutional right. This loss and difficulty was finally acknowledged and partially resolved by the United States Supreme Court in 1969.

§ 7.3 The Rule of *Johnson v. Avery*

The United States Supreme Court case of *Johnson v. Avery*[13] has had a profound effect upon the power of prison officials to regulate or prohibit an inmate's right of access to the courts. The case involved the constitutionality of a Tennessee prison regulation that provided: "No inmate will advise, assist or otherwise contract to aid another, either with or without a fee, to prepare Writs or other legal matters. Inmates are forbidden to set themselves up as practitioners for the purpose of promoting a business of writing Writs."[14]

In analyzing this prison rule, the Supreme Court emphasized the fact that inmates, a great percentage of whom are illiterate, were frequently unable to obtain assistance in preparing requests for post-conviction relief from any source other than one available within the prison walls. Therefore, because the necessary legal assistance was usually available only in the form of a jailhouse lawyer or inmate writ-writer, the Supreme Court reasoned that a regulation that effectively cut off this assistance amounted to a denial of access to the courts. For this reason, together with the "fundamental importance of the writ of habeas corpus in our constitutional scheme . . . ,"[15] the Supreme Court declared the Tennessee regulation invalid.

Although *Johnson v. Avery* has played a prominent role in bringing about prison reform, the ruling itself was very narrow in scope. Essentially, the only "right" guaranteed by this decision was that of an illiterate prisoner to receive legal aid from a fellow prisoner in the preparation of petitions for writs of habeas corpus. This right was not absolute, but was restricted to inmates incarcerated in a prison system that had failed to provide a "reasonable alternative" by which access to the courts (i.e., competent legal assistance) could be gained. The Supreme Court further limited this right by allowing prison authorities to: (1) place reasonable restrictions upon the time and place where the inmates' legal counseling could be given, and (2) impose punishment or discipline for any exchange of consideration or payment for the services rendered. Thus, a prison rule that provided for the discipline of a jailhouse lawyer

---

[13]   393 U.S. 483 (1969).
[14]   *Id.* at 484.
[15]   *Id.* at 485.

who charges for his or her services or receives anything of value in return for such services is authorized under *Johnson v. Avery*.

§ 7.3.1 —Judicial Interpretation of *Johnson v. Avery*

Johnson v. Avery recognized the existence of two competing interests in the area of corrections: (1) the legitimate exercise of control by prison officials, and (2) the constitutionally protected rights retained by inmates. As a result of these dual concerns, lower courts applying the rule of *Johnson v. Avery* have attempted to balance the proper state concern with the concern of the inmate in obtaining the legal assistance necessary to gain access to the courts. The state has the choice of providing inmates with access to the courts by making available either adequate law libraries or persons trained in the law.[16] A clear test is found in a decision of the Supreme Court of California,[17] in which the court established three governing principles to guide future decisions. First, the court must determine the extent to which the institutional regulations impede or discourage mutual inmate legal assistance. Second, the court is to decide, from the standpoint of legitimate custodial objectives, how undesirable the conduct is that the particular regulation sought to avoid. Third, the court must determine whether there are alternative means of dealing with the undesirable conduct—means that do not result in significant restrictions on mutual inmate aid.[18] However, it should be noted that, consistent with the ruling of *Johnson*, emphasis is placed upon the needs of the inmate rather than on those of the institution. In effect, the court stated that where an irreconcilable conflict exists, the prison officials, rather than the inmate, must alter their practices.

Although other courts have not enumerated so specific a test as California, they have nevertheless maintained the same theoretical approach in dealing with the conflict existing in a prison setting.[19] There is a tendency for the courts to retain the same noninterference rhetoric used by the pre-*Johnson* cases, but an obvious change in attitude has occurred.

In *Cruz v. Hauck*,[20] the court held that a broad rule that prohibited inmates from giving or receiving legal assistance on habeas corpus or other general civil legal matters in jail was invalid. It approved, however, reasonable rules governing the time and place for inmates to obtain legal assistance. The court said that the officials have a duty to maintain security in the jail cellblock and can restrict the storage of law books in inmates' cells for security purposes. If inmates cannot safely store legal materials in their cells, arrangements for

---

[16]   Carter v. Kamka, 515 F. Supp. 825 (D. Md. 1980).

[17]   In re Harrell, 470 P.2d 640 (Cal. 1970).

[18]   *Id.*

[19]   *See* Gittlemacker v. Prasse, 428 F.2d 1 (3d Cir. 1970); Gilmore v. Lynch, 319 F. Supp. 105 (N.D. Cal. 1970), *aff'd sub nom.,* Younger v. Gilmore, 404 U.S. 15 (1971); Jordan v. Johnson, 381 F. Supp. 600 (E.D. Mich. 1974), *aff'd,* 513 F.2d 631, *cert. denied,* 423 U.S. 851 (1975); McKinney v. DeBord, 507 F.2d 501 (9th Cir. 1974).

[20]   515 F.2d 322 (5th Cir. 1975).

storage of these materials in a readily available area with reasonable procedures for their use are required. To maintain a proper balance between competing interests of prison control and prisoner rights, the court held that an inmate should be permitted to obtain legal materials from sources other than attorneys or publishing houses, subject to screening only for security purposes. Courts would no longer defer to administrative discretion, but would more closely scrutinize the fact situation in order to prevent possible violation of constitutional rights.

The *Johnson* case opened a new area of concern for the judiciary in its recognition of the necessity for mutual inmate legal assistance in the preparation of writs. Five primary concerns of the courts deal with the issue of mutual inmate legal assistance:

1. Which inmates are permitted to receive legal assistance from a jailhouse lawyer?
2. Who may act as a jailhouse lawyer?
3. How may prison authorities reasonably restrict the jailhouse lawyer?
4. What type of legal assistance may be received from the jailhouse lawyer?
5. What is a reasonable alternative to the jailhouse lawyer?

§ 7.4 Which Inmates Are Permitted to Receive Legal Assistance from the Jailhouse Lawyer?

The emphasis in *Johnson* was on recognition of the need for an illiterate or functionally illiterate inmate to receive legal assistance in the preparation of legal documents to be filed with the courts. The federal courts that have dealt with this issue, however, have refused to restrict the *Johnson* doctrine to its narrow confines.

Jailhouse lawyers may also play a role in internal prison matters. In *Kirby v. Blackledge,*[21] prison officials were required to allow the assistance of a fellow inmate, or some designated staff member, to be part of proceedings to transfer an illiterate and disadvantaged inmate to maximum security.

In *Clutchette v. Enomoto,*[22] the court held that prison discipline procedures must permit an inmate who is illiterate or who faces complex issues to have adequate assistance in lieu of counsel. The reason for counsel substitute was that the inmate might not have the capacity to collect and present necessary evidence for an adequate presentation of the case.

---

[21]   530 F.2d 583 (4th Cir. 1976).
[22]   471 F. Supp. 1113 (N.D. Cal. 1979); Moore v. Smith, 390 N.E.2d 1052 (Ind. Ct. App. 1979); *cf.* Lamb v. Hutto, 467 F. Supp. 562 (E.D. Va. 1979) (a prisoner does not have a right to counsel at a prison transfer hearing).

Restrictions that forbid the receipt of legal assistance by anyone but illiterate prisoners have been invalidated as contrary to the Supreme Court ruling. Where there is no "reasonable alternative," all inmates in the institution must be permitted to seek legal counsel from the jailhouse lawyer.[23] However, a paroled state inmate was found to be in the same situation as any other *pro se* plaintiff who had the choice of representing him or herself or finding an attorney. The parolee was not entitled to be represented by the jailhouse lawyer who had initially prepared the pleadings in the inmate's civil rights action against a prison physician.[24] The uncontrolled discretion of a prison official as to who may or may not receive legal counseling has been invalidated when official approval is not subject to established standards.[25]

An exception to the broad statement that all inmates must be permitted assistance from the jailhouse lawyer occurs when inmates have been temporarily confined in isolation. So long as the confinement is not for an extended period—thereby hindering access to the courts—isolated inmates need not be afforded assistance from the jailhouse lawyer.[26]

§ 7.5 Who May Act as the Jailhouse Lawyer?

Related to the issue of who may receive legal assistance from a jailhouse lawyer is the problem of who among the inmate population may function as the jailhouse lawyer. The courts have stressed that the right asserted in *Johnson* was not the privilege of the jailhouse lawyer to practice law. Rather, it was the right of an inmate to receive legal assistance from a fellow inmate.[27] This principle is most clearly expressed in cases in which jailhouse lawyers have attempted to send legal material to an inmate in another prison and, as a result, have been subjected to disciplinary action. The rule that has emerged from these cases has been that the "client" inmate could receive legal assistance from inmates in his or her own prison. Because his or her rights could be protected there, there was no necessity that legal assistance be furnished to him or her by an inmate confined in another prison. Therefore, because no inmate

---

[23] Wolff v. McDonnell, 418 U.S. 539 (1974); *See* Wainwright v. Coonts, 409 F.2d 1337 (5th Cir. 1969); United States ex rel. Stevenson v. Mancusi, 325 F. Supp. 1028 (W.D.N.Y. 1971); State v. Williams, 595 P.2d 1104 (Kan. 1979); Carter v. Kamka, 515 F. Supp. 825 (D. Md. 1980); Storseth v. Spellman, 654 F.2d 1349 (9th Cir. 1981).

[24] Rizzo v. Zubrik, 391 F. Supp. 1058 (S.D.N.Y. 1975).

[25] *See* Sostre v. McGinnis, 442 F.2d 178 (2d Cir. 1971), *cert. denied,* 405 U.S. 978 (1972); Williams v. Department of Justice, 433 F.2d 958 (5th Cir. 1970); Carothers v. Follette, 314 F. Supp. 1014 (S.D.N.Y. 1970); Prewitt v. State ex rel. Eyman, 315 F. Supp. 793 (D. Ariz. 1969).

[26] *See* In re Harrell, 470 P.2d 640 (Cal. 1970).

[27] *See* Guajardo v. Luna, 432 F.2d 1324 (5th Cir. 1970); In re Harrell, 470 P.2d 640 (Cal. 1970); Bounds v. Smith, 430 U.S. 817 (1977); Delgado v. Sheriff of Milwaukee County, 487 F. Supp. 649 (E.D. Wis. 1980); Rhodes v. Robinson, 612 F.2d 766 (3d Cir. 1979); State v. Williams, 595 P.2d 1104 (Kan. 1979).

needed legal assistance from a particular inmate in another prison, the jail-house lawyer could be restricted accordingly,[28] in the absence of evidence that alternative means of obtaining legal assistance were unavailable.[29]

§ 7.6 How May Prison Officials Restrict the Jailhouse Lawyer?

In *Johnson v. Avery,* the Supreme Court stated that the activities of the jail-house lawyer could be restricted as to time and place. Furthermore, an absolute prohibition on the jailhouse lawyer receiving fees was also enunciat-ed. As a result of the "reasonableness" requirement, the interpretation given this rule by the lower courts has been varied.

One of the most litigated issues involving restrictions upon mutual inmate legal assistance has concerned the proper exercise of discretion by prison offi-cials. Courts have asserted that the uncontrolled discretion of prison officials in restricting the practice of the jailhouse lawyer is unconstitutional under *Johnson.* This discretion, according to these courts, must be subject to estab-lished guidelines or standards in order to assure that they are reasonable.[30]

Another related issue is the validity of a rule that required all legal work to be conducted in a special writ room. The courts, both before and after the *Johnson* ruling, have approved such a rule, as long as prison officials were not unduly restrictive[31] in the hours of use they permitted.

The right of a jailhouse lawyer to have the legal papers of another inmate in his or her possession is unclear. In one case, in order for jailhouse lawyers to function effectively, the court held that they must be able to have in their possession papers that pertain to their "client's" case.[32]

Another court interpreted a prison regulation as authorizing the papers to be kept by the jailhouse lawyer only until such time as the petition was com-plete, after which the papers had to be returned to the "client."[33]

At a minimum, it would appear that a prison regulation could not forbid the jailhouse lawyer from having the papers of another inmate in his or her possession on that ground alone.

---

[28] *See* McKinney v. DeBord, 324 F. Supp. 928 (E.D. Cal. 1970); Putt v. Clark, 297 F. Supp. 27 (N.D. Ga. 1969); In re Harrell, 470 P.2d 640 (Cal. 1970); Storseth v. Spellman, 654 F.2d 1349 (9th Cir. 1981).

[29] Boehme v. Smith, 378 N.Y.S.2d 170 (N.Y. App. Div. 1976); Webb v. State, 412 N.E.2d 790 (Ind. 1980).

[30] *See* Sostre v. McGinnis, 442 F.2d 178 (2d Cir. 1971), *cert. denied,* 405 U.S. 978 (1972); Carothers v. Follette, 314 F. Supp. 1014 (S.D.N.Y. 1970); Prewitt v. State ex rel. Eyman, 315 F. Supp. 793 (D. Ariz. 1969); Wolff v. McDonnell, 418 U.S. 539, 71 Ohio Op. 2d 336 (1974).

[31] *See* Novak v. Beto, 320 F. Supp. 1206 (S.D. Tex. 1970), *rev'd on other grounds,* 453 F.2d 661 (5th Cir. 1972); Brown v. South Carolina, 286 F. Supp. 998 (D.S.C. 1968); Ex parte Wilson, 235 F. Supp. 988 (E.D.S.C. 1964); Corpus v. Estelle, 409 F. Supp. 1090 (S.D. Tex. 1975); Ford v. LaVallee, 390 N.Y.S.2d 269 (1976); Cruz v. Androd, 15998B Opinion (5th Cir. 1980); *cf.* Jensen v. Satran, 303 N.W.2d 568 (N.D. 1981).

[32] *See* In re Harrell, 470 P.2d 640 (Cal. 1970).

[33] Gilmore v. Lynch, 319 F. Supp. 105 (N.D. Cal. 1970), *aff'd sub nom.,* Younger v. Gilmore, 404 U.S. 15 (1971).

The Supreme Court of California, in the case of *In re Harrell*,[34] dealt extensively with the type of restrictions permissible under the *Johnson* ruling. The regulations discussed were typical of many institutions.

One regulation invalidated by the court forbade the jailhouse lawyer to file with a court an application for relief on behalf of, or as "next friend" of, his client. The court held that the *Johnson* rule authorized legal assistance in writ writing, not in representation before the courts. Although an application submitted by a "next friend" will not generally be accepted by a court unless there are exceptional circumstances, this judicial policy did not, according to *Harrell*, give prison officials the right to examine such applications to determine whether the request for relief had merit. This determination is a decision for the courts, not prison officials. Therefore, prison officials may not refuse to forward a document to the courts on the grounds that it is improperly prepared.[35]

Another disputed restriction dealt with the right of an inmate to correspond on legal matters with inmates in other institutions. The prisoner in *Harrell* sought to give legal advice through use of the mail. The court found that the prison rule restricting this practice was valid under *Johnson*. The *Johnson* rule, stated the court, guaranteed the right to be assisted, but did not give the "client" the right to be assisted by a particular jailhouse lawyer. No infringement upon that right necessarily resulted from a restriction on the activities of a particular inmate "lawyer." The restriction placed on the jailhouse lawyer in this area is valid because the inmates of another prison can seek assistance from jailhouse lawyers at their own prison.[36]

A third regulation attacked by the prisoner involved the number of books that could be retained by the jailhouse lawyer in his own cell. The court found that such restrictions on the jailhouse lawyer:

> [I]mpinge upon the rights enumerated in *Johnson* only to the extent it is shown that the ability of other inmates seeking legal assistance to gain such assistance is affected. Unless and until it is demonstrated that other sources of legal assistance—e.g., other inmates who use the library—cannot provide assistance to disadvantaged inmates, the state of any inmate's personal library is of no significance.[37]

Under the facts, the California regulation was upheld.

In 2001, the Supreme Court held[38] that inmates do not possess a special First Amendment right to provide legal assistance to fellow inmates that enhances the protections otherwise available under *Turner v. Safley*.

---

[34] 470 P.2d 640 (Cal. 1970).

[35] In re Harrell, 470 P.2d 640, 649.

[36] *Id.;* Boehme v. Smith, 378 N.Y.S.2d 170 (N.Y. App. Div. 1976).

[37] *Id.* See Storseth v. Spellman, 654 F.2d 1349 (9th Cir. 1981).

[38] Shaw v. Murphy, 532 U.S. 223 (2001). *See also* §4.7 *supra*.

§ 7.7 What Type of Legal Assistance May an Inmate Receive from the Jailhouse Lawyer?

The issue before the United States Supreme Court in *Johnson v. Avery* was concerned with habeas corpus petitions. It was because of the vital necessity to protect the right of an inmate to file this writ that the Supreme Court heard the case. The lower federal courts, however, have again refused to restrict themselves to such narrow applications of constitutional rights. They have, on the contrary, expanded the right to include other legal petitions besides habeas corpus petitions. Two cases have held that the theoretical basis of *Johnson* was protection of the inmate's right of access to the courts and, for this reason, the *Johnson* ruling must be extended beyond habeas corpus petitions. Similarly protected, the court said, was the right of a jailhouse lawyer to aid in preparing a specific type of petition outside of habeas corpus, such as a civil rights action under § 1983 of Title 42 of the United States Code.[39] In *Nolan v. Scafati*,[40] a prisoner alleged that his constitutional right of access to the courts was violated when prison officials refused to mail his letter to the American Civil Liberties Union. This letter sought advice and assistance on his constitutional rights in a prison disciplinary hearing. The court found that the rule of *Johnson v. Avery* stood for "the general proposition that an inmate's right of access to the courts involves a corollary right to obtain some assistance in preparing his communication with the court."[41] In view of this "general proposition," the court refused to confine the *Johnson* rule exclusively to inmates seeking post-conviction relief. The court felt that to so limit that rule would allow prison officials to silence—and perhaps to punish—inmates seeking vindication of constitutional rights clearly held by prison inmates.[42] The findings of the *Nolan* case were cited with approval by the court in *Cross v. Powers*.[43] The result of these two cases was to extend to all inmates the right to assistance in their preparation of civil rights actions against prison officials.

Subsequent cases have expanded the type of aid that may be given. In *Williams v. Department of Justice*,[44] the court went one step beyond the *Nolan* and *Cross* cases. Williams held that *Johnson* stood for the proposition that a prison regulation prohibiting inmate assistance in the drafting of *pro se* legal papers constituted a "deprivation of due process of law, where no 'reasonable alternative' was available to furnish legal advice."[45] This would appear to be an assertion that, at least to this court, inmates must be permitted the assistance of a jailhouse lawyer in the preparation of all of their legal petitions.

---

[39] *See* Nolan v. Scafati, 430 F.2d 548 (1st Cir. 1970); Cross v. Powers, 328 F. Supp. 899 (W.D. Wis. 1971).
[40] 430 F.2d 548 (1st Cir. 1970).
[41] *Id.* at 551.
[42] *Ibid.*
[43] 328 F. Supp. 899 (W.D. Wis. 1971).
[44] 433 F.2d 958 (5th Cir. 1970).
[45] *Id.* at 959. The term *pro se* is used to mean any petition filed by an individual for him or herself; Corpus v. Estelle, 409 F. Supp. 1090 (S.D. Tex. 1975).

Finally, in *Wolff v. McDonnell*,[46] the Supreme Court held that the doctrine of *Johnson v. Avery* was not limited to cases involving the preparation of habeas corpus petitions, but also applied to civil rights actions.

Therefore, unless the state provides a reasonable alternative to the "jailhouse lawyer" in the preparation of civil rights actions, prisoners cannot be barred from furnishing such assistance to one another. In compliance with *Wolff v. McDonnell*, *Graham v. State Dept. of Corrections*[47] held that a counsel substitute must be available whenever the inmate is unable to competently handle his or her case in a prison reclassification proceeding. If a counsel substitute is requested by an inmate on such grounds, and the request is denied, the record of the reclassification proceeding should contain findings to support the denial.

§ 7.8　What Is the Reasonable Alternative to the Jailhouse Lawyer?

The main thrust of *Johnson v. Avery* was that a state may not restrict the practices of the jailhouse lawyer unless a "reasonable alternative" to legal services is available to the inmates.

In the cases relating to this issue, it is clear that some measure of professional assistance must be made available if prison officials wish to suppress the activities of the jailhouse lawyer. In reality, this "professional assistance" means the services of an attorney or a law school assistance program. It should be noted, however, that the courts have differed as to the adequacy of legal assistance programs. Courts dealing with this issue have expressed little concern over the adequacy of the reasonable alternative provided by a prison.[48]

In *Ayers v. Ciccone*,[49] a single attorney working 12 hours per week was held to be a reasonable alternative to the jailhouse lawyer. It should be apparent, however, that an attorney working for such a limited period could not effectively meet the legal needs of many inmates. A similar decision was *Novak v. Beto*.[50] In that case, a Texas district court upheld an absolute restriction against a jailhouse lawyer because the state had provided the services of two full-time attorneys to assist the 13,000 inmates in the Texas correctional system. The failure of the district court to question the effectiveness of such a program in assuring the availability of assistance resulted in a reversal on appeal.[51] That this court found it necessary to inquire into the adequacy of the existing program is not unusual. This is evidenced by other cases dealing with the issue.

---

[46]　418 U.S. 539 (1974).

[47]　392 F. Supp. 1262 (W.D.N.C. 1975).

[48]　*See* Novak v. Beto, 320 F. Supp. 1206 (S.D. Tex. 1970); Ayers v. Ciccone, 303 F. Supp. 637 (W.D. Mo. 1969); Collins v. Haga, 373 F. Supp. 923 (W.D. Va. 1974). *But see* Bounds v. Smith, 430 U.S. 817 (1977).

[49]　303 F. Supp. 637 (W.D. Mo. 1969).

[50]　320 F. Supp. 1206 (S.D. Tex. 1970).

[51]　Novak v. Beto, 453 F.2d 661 (5th Cir. 1969).

Beard v. Alabama[52] held that an absolute restriction against jailhouse lawyers "might well be sustained if the state were to make available a sufficient number of qualified attorneys or other persons capable and willing to render voluntary assistance in the preparation of petitions for habeas corpus relief."[53] This court asserted that the state must provide a "sufficient" legal services system, implying that the courts have the obligation to inquire into the effectiveness of the legal services provided.

In *Noorlander v. Ciccone,*[54] the court of appeals remanded the case to the trial court to determine the adequacy of the prison law library and to see whether adequate alternatives to legal publications for inmates existed. The court rejected the inmate's claim that his right to self-representation required a law library at the institution. The reasoning of the court was that the public defender program was sufficient, and the inmate was provided reasonable opportunity for access to the courts. However, he was not entitled to access by all available means.

Two other cases that have given careful scrutiny to the legal services provided to inmates are *Williams v. Department of Justice*[55] and *Cross v. Powers.*[56] Both cases dealt with the use of a law school clinic program in prisons. It should also be noted that, as mentioned above, both cases expanded *Johnson* to legal actions beyond habeas corpus petitions. *Williams* included all *pro se* petitions and *Cross* allowed inmates filing civil rights actions to receive the assistance of a jailhouse lawyer. The crucial similarity between these cases is the fact that both courts found the clinic programs inadequate to meet the reasonable alternative requirements of *Johnson v. Avery.* The petitioner in *Williams* claimed that there was an 18-month delay between the time an inmate requested aid and the time he received it from the student clinic.[57] The court held that such a delay was inconsistent with the goals of the Supreme Court ruling.

Cross v. Powers[58] invalidated an absolute restriction against jailhouse lawyers because the law school clinic did not assist inmates who wished to file civil rights actions against prison officials. The effect of this decision is to require legal services programs to provide inmates with assistance not only in habeas corpus actions but also in cases in which an inmate seeks civil rights relief, if the prison officials wish to suppress jailhouse lawyers.

Prison officials act on questionable grounds if they attempt to restrict a law clinic from conducting full legal services. In *Bryan v. Werner*[59] the court held that restrictions preventing a law clinic from assisting inmates in suits against the prison were valid only if there were reasonable alternatives to the

---

[52] 413 F.2d 455 (5th Cir. 1969).

[53] *Id.* at 457.

[54] 489 F.2d 642 (8th Cir. 1973).

[55] 433 F.2d 958 (5th Cir. 1970).

[56] 328 F. Supp. 899 (W.D. Wis. 1971).

[57] *But see* Ramsey v. Ciccone, 310 F. Supp. 600 (W.D. Mo. 1970), in which the court asserted that some delay must necessarily accompany any new program and for this reason found a three-month delay acceptable.

[58] 328 F. Supp. 899 (W.D. Wis. 1971).

[59] 516 F.2d 233 (3d Cir. 1975).

clinic for obtaining assistance in such suits. The prison could prohibit the clinic from using its title in suits that were not authorized under clinic rules, but it could not prevent the clinic from notarizing or mailing legal papers relevant to such suits. Such practice would be invalid as impeding access to the courts.

A prison policy denying inmates access to law students who assisted attorneys in post-conviction or civil rights hearings was held invalid, although the court found that inmate access to law students as such is not always a matter of constitutional right.[60]

Although few prison officials will voluntarily open their prisons to law school clinics so that legal services will be provided to inmates suing them for monetary damages, it seems clear that such legal services must be provided if the jailhouse lawyer is prohibited. To not provide these legal services has been held a violation of the prisoner's rights to legal representation and access to the courts. In *Cruz v. Beto*[61] the former director of the Texas Department of Corrections was held personally liable in money damages to a group of indigent prisoners for depriving them of the opportunity to continue consultations with their attorney. The director alleged that the attorney was causing trouble and consequently prohibited her from visiting the state prisons. At trial, the allegations were never substantiated. The court noted that no criminal charges were ever filed against the attorney, nor was any complaint ever made to the state bar association.

In *Procunier v. Martinez,*[62] the United States Supreme Court considered a California prison regulation, which provided in part:

> Investigators for an attorney-of-record will be confined to not more than two. Such investigators must be licensed by the State or must be members of the State Bar. Designation must be made in writing by the Attorney.[63]

This regulation restricted access by the prisoners to members of the bar and licensed private investigators, and imposed an absolute ban on the use of law students and legal paraprofessionals by attorneys to interview prisoner clients. Attorneys were also prohibited from delegating to such persons the task of obtaining prisoners' signatures on legal documents. However, law school clinical programs were permitted in the prison.

Citing *Johnson v. Avery*, the Supreme Court held the regulation void because it created an artificial distinction between law students employed by practicing attorneys and those associated with law school programs providing legal assistance to the prisoners. Further, the regulation was overbroad.

---

[60] Souza v. Travisono, 498 F.2d 1120 (1st Cir. 1974).

[61] 19 Cr. L. 2094 (S.D. Tex. 1976); *See* Cruz v. Beto, 453 F. Supp. 905 (S.D. Tex. 1977) for the issue of attorney's fees in the earlier case.

[62] 416 U.S. 396 (1974).

[63] *Id.* at 419.

Its prohibition was not limited to prospective interviewers who posed some colorable threat to security or to inmates thought to be especially dangerous. Nor was it shown that a less restrictive regulation would unduly burden the administrative task of screening and monitoring visitors.[64]

Thus, it is clear that carefully drawn regulations placing reasonable limitations on lawyers' assistants will be held valid, and yet will not deny the prisoners "access to the courts."

§ 7.9 Access to Legal Materials

Prior to *Johnson v. Avery,* the courts, with few exceptions, staunchly deferred to official discretion as to what legal materials could be kept by an inmate in his or her own cell. Their rationale was the right of a state to impose reasonable restrictions upon the times and places where an inmate could engage in legal work.[65] It was felt that there was in fact no interference with access to the courts as a result of these types of reasonable restrictions.[66] Restrictions as to the possession of any law books or limitations on numbers were treated in much the same manner. It was felt that the inmate had no constitutional right to possess law books where no one had alleged a lack of access to the courts.[67] Therefore, where a limitation upon the number of books prisoners could possess was not found to be arbitrary, unreasonable, or discriminatory, discretion of the officials was valid and controlling.[68]

Although a majority of the courts took the conservative approach, later decisions have taken a contrary view. For example, a California court concluded that the constitutional right of an inmate of access to the courts:

> [I]ncludes not only the right to place a petition for relief in the mails, . . . but also the right to possess in his cell the legal materials which the inmate desires to include in such a document while they are being collated into mailable form.[69]

This right, however, was not interpreted to mean that inmates could collect in their cells all-purpose compendiums that could substitute for law books from the library. This decision did not prevent prison officials from restricting legal research to a certain area, and from forbidding the storage of legal notes in a prisoner's cell.

---

64   *Id.* at 420.

65   *See* Hatfield v. Bailleaux, 290 F.2d 632 (9th Cir. 1961); Edmundson v. Harris, 239 F. Supp. 359 (W.D. Mo. 1965); Austin v. Harris, 226 F. Supp. 304 (W.D. Mo. 1964).

66   *See* Taylor v. Burke, 278 F. Supp. 868 (E.D. Wis. 1968).

67   Williams v. Wilkins, 315 F.2d 396 (2d Cir. 1963), *cert. denied,* 375 U.S. 852 (1963); *See* Roberts v. Pepersack, 256 F. Supp. 415 (D. Md. 1966), *cert. denied,* 389 U.S. 877 (1967).

68   *See* Walker v. Pate, 356 F.2d 502 (7th Cir. 1966), *cert. denied,* 384 U.S. 966 (1966); People v. Matthewes, 46 Misc. 2d 1054, 261 N.Y.S.2d 654 (Sup. Ct. Crim. Term, 1965); Cruz v. Hauck, 515 F.2d 322 (5th Cir. 1975).

69   In re Schoingarth, 425 P.2d 200, 207 (Cal. 1967).

A county jail rule prohibiting storage of hardcover law books in inmates' cells and restricting storage of non-hardcover materials so as not to limit the "floor or wall space dimensional of the jail cell block" was held to be reasonable, in light of the duty of jail authorities to maintain security and to protect against dangers of fire.[70]

In *United States ex rel. Mayberry v. Prasse,*[71] the court found that the right of access to the courts included "the right of a prisoner to prepare, serve, and file legal papers and prosecute legal actions affecting his personal liberty."[72] The court held that, although there was no constitutional right to be supplied with a law library, the inmate could not be restrained from effectively prosecuting his appeal. Based upon the facts of that case, and in view of the absence of effective counsel to assist him in prosecuting his legal action, the inmate was permitted, through court order, to acquire the rules of procedure of Pennsylvania. Without these rules, access to the courts would be unconstitutionally restrained.

Another court ruled that, although prison officials may regulate the manner in which an inmate conducts his or her research, they may not engage in wholesale confiscation of significant legal documents. The court further suggested that the prison officials should consult the inmate about the relevance of legal materials in his or her possession before any action is taken to remove them.[73]

Johnson v. Avery did not substantially affect the law in this area. Courts have permitted prison officials to restrict the number of books kept by an inmate. Regulations forbidding the accumulation of a law library within the confines of an inmate's cell have been held valid for two reasons. First, the state has the right to reasonably restrict the time and manner in which legal research may be done, as long as no unconstitutional impediment of access to the courts arises,[74] and second, the condition of an inmate's personal law library carries no constitutional significance, so long as the inmates of the prison have other sources of assistance available, such as other jailhouse lawyers who use the prison law library. A prison regulation that does not impede access to the courts will be held valid.[75]

---

[70] Cruz v. Hauck, 515 F.2d 322 (5th Cir. 1975).

[71] 225 F. Supp. 752 (E.D. Pa. 1963).

[72] *Id.* at 754.

[73] *See* Konigsburg v. Ciccone, 285 F. Supp. 585, *aff'd,* 417 F.2d 161 (8th Cir. 1969), *cert. denied,* 397 U.S. 963 (1970); *See* Hiney v. Wilson, 520 F.2d 589 (2d Cir. 1975), in which the confiscation of inmates' legal papers may constitute a denial of access to the courts.

[74] *See* Gittlemacker v. Prasse, 428 F.2d 1 (3d Cir. 1970); McKinney v. DeBord, 324 F. Supp. 928 (E.D. Cal. 1970).

[75] *See* In re Harrell, 470 P.2d 640 (Cal. 1970). *But see* Sigafus v. Brown, 416 F.2d 105 (7th Cir. 1969), in which the court found that confiscation of legal materials necessary to afford reasonable access to the courts results in denial of due process for which damages may be claimed.

Thus, an inmate was not prejudiced by the inability to do his own research to supplement that of his legal counsel. A warden's policy of returning ordered law books to the publisher was upheld under such circumstances. The prison had a procedure for receiving books by mail, and the inmate failed to follow the procedure.[76]

On the other hand, in *Sigafus v. Brown,*[77] the court held that confiscation of materials necessary to afford reasonable access to the courts resulted in a denial of constitutional rights. Prison officials may not prevent an inmate from possessing his or her own legal material while permitting him or her to possess other articles, on the grounds that the legal material might serve as incendiary matter during future, although unanticipated, disturbances.[78]

It would thus appear that in cases both before and after *Johnson,* the majority of courts have allowed the state to have the discretion of determining where legal research may take place. As a result, prison officials may enforce a rule forbidding the possession of personal legal materials and books in an inmate's cell.

The application of this rule, however, led to inconsistent results. The confusion arises in cases in which a jailhouse lawyer has in his possession papers pertaining to another inmate's case. *In re Harrell*[79] held that a rule permitting confiscation of those papers prevented meaningful aid in the preparation of legal documents by the jailhouse lawyer. It was there asserted that the chief purpose of the rule of *Johnson v. Avery* was to permit inmates to assist one other in the drafting of legal documents. In view of this purpose, the court felt that prison officials were forbidden to impose a rule that prohibited inmates from possessing legal documents that pertained to another inmate's case. Similarly, *Gilmore v. Lynch*[80] considered the identical prison regulation found in *Harrell.* It stated: "One inmate may assist another inmate in the preparation of legal documents, but . . . all briefs, petitions, and other legal papers must be and remain in the possession of the inmate to whom they pertain."[81] This court applied a somewhat different rule to this regulation than that found in the *Harrell* decision. The court held that if the rules were applied only to completed documents, that application would be valid. Thus, the jailhouse lawyer may retain possession of another inmate's papers while preparing a brief or petition. However, upon their completion, he or she must deliver them to his or her client without accepting payment.

---

[76]   Russell v. Hendrick, 376 F. Supp. 158 (E.D. Pa. 1974); United States v. Wilson, 690 F.2d 1267 (9th Cir. 1982). There is no absolute right for an inmate to conduct his or her own legal research when he or she has appointed counsel to assist in preparing his or her defense. The services of a lawyer cannot be rejected as a means of achieving access to a law library.

[77]   416 F.2d 105 (7th Cir. 1969).

[78]   Adams v. Carlson, 352 F. Supp. 882 (E.D. Ill. 1973), *rev'd and rem'd on other grounds,* 488 F.2d 619 (7th Cir. 1973).

[79]   470 P.2d 640 (Cal. 1970).

[80]   319 F. Supp. 105 (N.D. Ca. 1970), *aff'd sub nom.,* Younger v. Gilmore, 404 U.S. 15 (1971).

[81]   *Id.* at 112.

The inconsistent results of these cases leave a double standard. An inmate may be restricted from having in his or her possession legal documents pertaining to his or her own case, while at the same time an inmate doing legal work for a fellow prisoner may keep with him or her legal materials pertaining to the other inmate's case.

Fortunately, the source from which personal legal materials may be obtained is better defined. Prison officials may restrict an inmate from ordering law books from any source other than that which is approved by them,[82] so long as this does not amount to a restriction of the type of book that may be ordered.[83]

A delay in delivery of books to an inmate does not necessarily infringe upon his or her access to the courts.[84] Requiring an inmate to wait, on one occasion for 10 days, to have a document notarized does not unconstitutionally deprive the inmate of access to the courts.[85] The justification for such a decision has been that prison officials have a legitimate right to prevent introduction of contraband through the prisoners' mail.[86]

§ 7.10 Legal Materials That Must Be Supplied by Prison Officials

The traditional view as to what legal materials prison officials must supply to inmates was expressed in the 1961 case of *Hatfield v. Bailleax*,[87] in which the court stated:

> State authorities have no obligation under the federal Constitution to provide library facilities and an opportunity for their use to enable an inmate to search for legal loopholes in the judgment and sentence under which he is held, or to perform services which only a lawyer is trained to perform. All inmates are presumed to be confined under valid judgments and sentences. If an inmate believes he has a meritorious reason for attacking his, he must be given an opportunity to do so. But he has no due process right to spend his prison time or utilize prison facilities in an effort to discover a ground for overturning a presumptively valid judgment.

Inmates have the constitutional right to waive counsel and act as their own lawyers, but this does not mean that a non-lawyer must be given the opportunity to acquire a legal education.[88]

---

[82] *See* McKinney v. DeBord, 324 F. Supp. 928 (E.D. Cal. 1970); Wakely v. Pennsylvania, 247 F. Supp. 7 (E.D. Pa. 1965).

[83] *See* In re Harrell, 470 P.2d 640 (Cal. 1970).

[84] Russell v. Hendrick, 376 F. Supp. 158 (E.D. Pa. 1974).

[85] Hudson v. Robinson, 678 F.2d 462 (3d Cir. 1982).

[86] *See* Lockhart v. Prasse, 250 F. Supp. 529 (E.D. Pa. 1965).

[87] 290 F.2d 632 (9th Cir. 1961).

[88] *Id.* at 640-641.

The view expressed by the *Hatfield* decision, however, was repudiated by the United States Supreme Court in the 1971 case of *Gilmore v. Lynch*.[89] *Gilmore* was decided by a three-judge panel in California and subsequently affirmed by the United States Supreme Court.[90] The district court stated that access to the courts is a right that encompasses "all the means a defendant or petitioner might require to get a fair hearing from the judiciary on all charges brought against him or grievances alleged by him."[91] In affirming, the Supreme Court, citing *Johnson v. Avery*, approved the invalidation of a regulation that had established, as a standard for prison libraries, a highly restrictive list of law books. The decision has set a new precedent by asserting that prison officials have a duty to take affirmative action in assuring inmates the right of access to the courts. The state must make available, notwithstanding economic difficulties, sufficient legal materials to assure that the prisoner is able to file petitions that contain at least some legal proficiency.

In *Bounds v. Smith*,[92] the Supreme Court took an affirmative view toward the responsibility of prison authorities to provide prisoners with adequate law libraries or some other viable source of legal knowledge. The Court did not mandate the use of law libraries if a sufficient alternative program for legal services is in operation. Law libraries were held to be one constitutionally acceptable method to ensure prisoners meaningful access to the courts. Other alternatives mentioned in the decision included the training of inmates as paralegal assistants to work under lawyers' supervision, the use of paraprofessionals and law students either as volunteers or in formal clinical programs, the organization of volunteer attorneys through bar associations or other groups, the hiring of lawyers on a part-time consultant basis, and the use of full-time staff attorneys working either in new prison legal assistance programs or as a part of a public defender or legal services office.

Several decisions have stressed the necessity of supplying inmates with sufficient material for legal research by listing exactly what state statutes and volumes of the court reporters the prison law library must contain.[93]

A plan for Georgia prison law libraries was approved, with the following mandatory revisions: The library must be kept open for a minimum of nine hours per week, and for such additional hours as may be needed to afford each inmate wishing to use the facility the equivalent of one full day (eight hours) of research time every three weeks; the library must contain certain reference materials; prisoners must be permitted to receive and use appropriate volumes

---

[89]   319 F. Supp. 105 (N.D. Cal. 1970), *aff'd,* 404 U.S. 15 (1971).

[90]   Gilmore v. Lynch, 404 U.S. 15 (1971).

[91]   Gilmore v. Lynch, 319 F. Supp. 105, 110 (N.D. Cal. 1970).

[92]   430 U.S. 817 (1977); *See* Morales v. Schmidt, 340 F. Supp. 544, 548 (W.D. Wis. 1972), in which Judge Doyle recognized that access by inmates "to a certain minimum of legal books and materials" was a constitutionally protected right; United States v. West, 557 F.2d 151 (8th Cir. 1977); Dreher v. Sielaff, 636 F.2d 1141 (7th Cir. 1980); State v. Simon, 297 N.W.2d 206 (Iowa 1980); State v. Ahearn, 403 A.2d 696 (Vt. 1979); Wojtczak v. Cuyler, 480 F. Supp. 1288 (E.D. Pa. 1979).

[93]   *See* Gaglie v. Ulibarri, 507 F.2d 721 (9th Cir. 1974); White v. Sullivan, 368 F. Supp. 292 (S.D. Ala. 1973); Craig v. Hocker, 405 F. Supp. 656 (D. Nev. 1975).

from the county library, subject only to a requirement that these materials be returned in good order within reasonable periods. The use of paralegals was not required.[94]

The limited resources of a law library do not violate the prisoner's right when he could obtain the materials needed by directing his appointed counsel to obtain such materials from a more complete law library.[95]

A state prisoner maintained that the denial of his request for free photocopies of legal precedents to use in preparation for a hearing on his motion for post-conviction relief had deprived him of his right of free access to the courts. The court held that because he had access to the law library at the county jail and had made no allegations of inadequacy of the facility, his complaint failed to state a cause of action.[96]

Casey v. Lewis[97] has had a substantial impact on all aspects of legal services as well as on the legal materials that must be made available to prisoners.

§ 7.11 The Inmate's Right to Counsel

An individual accused of a crime has a fundamental right to counsel and the right to be represented by an attorney of his or her choice, if the attorney indicates a willingness to represent him or her. If the individual is indigent and unable to afford counsel when he or she has a right to counsel, the state must appoint an attorney.[98] This right is protected by the Fifth and Sixth Amendments and may not be unreasonably limited by state officials.[99] This right is not altered when the individual is incarcerated. Prison officials may not unreasonably prevent legal counsel from meeting with their prisoner clients as long as the attorney observes all of the rules of the institution.[100] Nor may officials infringe upon an inmate's right to communicate with his or her attorney by placing undue restrictions on his or her correspondence[101] or visitation rights.[102] However, a prisoner who has exercised his or her right to proceed without counsel in pursuing his or her appeal does not have the right to receive for his or her use an adequate law library, where the state has offered to appoint counsel.[103]

Inmates in a federal prison were placed in administrative detention in individual cells during the investigation of the murder of a fellow inmate. They were held in administrative detention for 19 months before they were indicted

---

[94] Mercer v. Griffin, 29 Cr. L. 2058 (D.C. Ga. 1981).
[95] United States v. Garza, 664 F.2d 135 (7th Cir. 1981).
[96] Wanninger v. Davenport, 697 F.2d 992 (11th Cir. 1983); Johnson v. Parke, 642 F.2d 337 (10th Cir. 1981).
[97] 518 U.S. 343 (1996). *See* Part II for the *Casey* decision.
[98] Argersinger v. Hamlin, 407 U.S. 25 (1972).
[99] Sander v. Russell, 401 F.2d 241, 247 (5th Cir. 1968); State ex rel. McCamie v. McCoy, 276 S.E.2d 534 (W. Va. 1981).
[100] Lynott v. Henderson, 610 F.2d 340 (5th Cir. 1980).
[101] Jones v. Diamond, 594 F.2d 997 (5th Cir. 1979); *See* § 4.5.
[102] *See* § 3.6.
[103] Bell v. Hooper, 511 F. Supp. 452 (S.D. Ga. 1981).

and counsel was appointed. The court held that the inmates had no constitutional right to counsel while in administrative segregation and before any adversary proceedings had been initiated against them. The right to counsel attaches only at or after the initiation of adversary judicial proceedings. Further, providing a defendant with a pre-indictment private investigator is not a purpose of the right to counsel.[104]

Associated with the right to counsel is the right to call expert witnesses. In *McKinney v. Anderson,*[105] the Ninth Circuit Court of Appeals held that a federal district court has the discretion to appoint expert witnesses and to assess the cost of an expert's services entirely to one party within the meaning of Federal Rule of Evidence 706. In this case, an inmate claimed that compelled exposure to environmental tobacco smoke amounted to cruel and unusual punishment. *See* § 12.6, which deals with conditions of confinement as an Eighth Amendment claim. The district court was directed on remand to consider appointing an expert witness who could provide scientific information on health effects of environmental tobacco smoke and on concentration levels of the smoke in the prison in which the inmate was incarcerated.

§ 7.12 Retaliation for Exercising Constitutional Rights

A corrections officer warned a prisoner that if he did not become an informant, bad things would happen to him, including transfer to a less desirable part of the prison. The prisoner reported the alleged threat by a letter addressed to a United States District Judge who was presiding over pending prison litigation. As a result, the prisoner was issued a disciplinary charge for defiance. The constitutional right of access to the courts was violated by this retaliation.[106]

The necessary elements of a retaliation claim are: (1) a prison official acting under color of state law; and (2) intentional retaliation for the exercise of a constitutionally protected activity. The law is clearly established that a prison official may not retaliate against or harass an inmate for exercising the right of access to the courts.[107] Even the prison officials candidly conceded that this was a claim of constitutional proportions that is actionable. Further, the court determined that there was no immunity defense.

To state a claim of retaliation, an inmate must allege the violation of a specific constitutional right and be prepared to establish that but for the retaliatory motive, the incident would not have occurred.[108] This places a significant

---

[104] United States v. Gouveia, 467 U.S. 180 (1984).

[105] McKinney v. Anderson, 924 F.2d 1500 (9th Cir.), vacated *sub nom.,* Helling v. McKinney, 502 U.S. 903 (1991).

[106] Woods v. Smith, 60 F.3d 1161 (5th Cir. 1995).

[107] *See* Ruiz v. Estelle, 679 F.2d 1115 (5th Cir.), *opinion amended in part and vacated in part,* 688 F.2d 266 (5th Cir. 1982), *cert. denied,* 460 U.S. 1042 (1983); Gibbs v. King, 779 F.2d 1040 (5th Cir.), *cert. denied,* 476 U.S. 1117 (1986); Andrade v. Hauck, 452 F.2d 1071 (5th Cir. 1971).

[108] *See* McDonald v. Hall, 610 F.2d 16 (1st Cir. 1979).

burden on the inmate. Mere conclusory allegations of retaliation will not with-stand a summary judgment challenge.[109] The inmate must produce direct evidence of motivation or, the more probable scenario, allege a chronology of events from which retaliation may plausibly be inferred.

The court in *Woods* remained fully supportive of the proposition that although prison officials must have wide latitude in the control and discipline of inmates, such latitude does not encompass conduct that infringes on an inmate's substantive constitutional rights. However, the court agreed with the Fourth Circuit Court of Appeals when it cautioned that the prospect of endless claims of retaliation on the part of inmates would disrupt prison officials in the discharge of their most basic duties and that claims of retaliation must therefore be regarded with skepticism, lest the federal courts embroil themselves in every disciplinary act that occurs in state penal institutions.[110]

See also § 9.2, *Parole is Not a Right,* in which cases holding that discrimination against writ-writers in the granting of parole is unconstitutional are discussed.

§ 7.13 Restrictions on Access to the Courts

A prisoner appealed an order that dismissed his *in forma pauperis* complaint as "frivolous or malicious" within the meaning of 28 U.S.C. § 1915(d) (1988).[111] The relief sought was considered by the court to be a "trifle" and not worthy of adjudication. A court may dismiss an *in forma pauperis* claim as frivolous if, after considering the contending equities, the court determines that the claim is: (1) of little or no weight, value, or importance; (2) not worthy of serious attention; or (3) trivial.[112]

In *Deutsch v. United States,* the allegation requested $4.20 for loss of his pens, plus litigation costs, attorney's fees, and interest. The lower court was unable to conclude that the case was legally or factually frivolous, or that it was brought for a malicious purpose, but instead determined that under the doctrine of *de minimis non curat lex,*[113] the prisoner's claim, which was limited solely to monetary damages in the amount of $4.20, was encompassed by the phrase "frivolous or malicious" as used in § 1915(d). The Third Circuit affirmed the lower court, but on other grounds.

---

[109] *Id.*

[110] *See* Adams v. Rice, 40 F.3d 72, 74 (4th Cir. 1994), *cert. denied*, 514 U.S. 1022 (1995).

[111] § 1915(a) provides, in pertinent part, that any court of the United States may authorize the commencement, prosecution or defense of any suit, action, or proceeding, civil or criminal, or appeal therein, without prepayment of fees and costs or security therefor, by a person who makes affidavit that he is unable to pay such costs or give security therefor. This section was extensively amended by the Prison Litigation Reform Act. *See* Chapter 13.

[112] Deutsch v. United States, 67 F.3d 1080 (3d Cir. 1995). On the facts of the case, the prisoner, Deutsch, had filed 20 civil actions since 1992.

[113] The law does not care for, or take notice of, very small or trifling matters. The law does not concern itself about trifles. The venerable maxim *de minimis non curat lex* is part of the established background of legal principles against which all enactments are adopted, and which all enactments (absent contrary indication) are deemed to accept. Wisconsin Dep't of Revenue v. Wrigley, 505 U.S. 214 (1992).

Deutsch concluded that the plain meaning of the term "frivolous" authorized the dismissal of *in forma pauperis* claims that were of little or no weight, value, or importance, not worthy of serious consideration, or trivial.

The *in forma pauperis* statute, 28 U.S.C. § 1915, is designed to ensure that indigent litigants have meaningful access to the federal courts.[114] However, Congress was also concerned that indigent persons could abuse this cost-free access to the federal courts. As a result, Congress empowered the courts with the right to dismiss the abusive filings that could result from the absence of a cost barrier by including § 1915(d), which authorizes a court to dismiss an *in forma pauperis* complaint if satisfied that the action is frivolous or malicious.

According to *Deutsch,* to find that an *in forma pauperis* litigant's claim is trivial, a court must be satisfied that the record supports a finding that a reasonable paying litigant would not have filed the same claim after considering the costs of suit. A court must first find the actual amount in controversy under the claim presented and determine whether the amount in controversy is less than the expense of the court costs and filing fees. If the court so determines, then the claim may be dismissed as frivolous under § 1915(d).

A court must next determine whether the litigant has a meaningful non-monetary interest at stake under the claim, such that service of the complaint and an allocation of the court's resources for its adjudication is warranted, despite the fact that the claim is economically trivial. If, in addition to finding that the amount of damages in controversy is less than the court costs and filing fees, and the court is satisfied that there is no other meaningful interest at stake, then the suit is frivolous within the meaning of § 1915(d).

Deutsch recognized that emotions are intensified in the insular life of a correctional facility and that prisoners often must rely on the courts as the only available forum to redress their grievances, even when those grievances seem insignificant to one who is not so confined. A court is obligated to take into account the unique nature of each claim presented and the extent to which the claim is "meaningful" to one in the litigant's situation. Thus, in determining whether a claim is meaningful, a court must protect the right of indigent persons to have access to the courts.[115]

A court must also consider whether the prisoner is filing the suit to pursue a nonmeaningful activity, such as harassment or entertainment, or merely to hone litigation skills.[116] A court must balance the equities and dismiss the

---

[114] Neitzke v. Williams, 490 U.S. 319 (1989). Specifically, Congress enacted the *in forma pauperis* statute to ensure that administrative court costs and filing fees, both of which must be paid by everyone else who files a lawsuit, would not prevent indigent persons from pursuing meaningful litigation.

[115] *See* In re Oliver, 682 F.2d 443, 446 (3d Cir. 1982).

[116] *See* Cruz v. Beto, 405 U.S. 319 (1972) (per curiam) (Rehnquist, J., dissenting) ("[Inmates are] in a different litigating posture than persons who are unconfined. The inmate stands to gain something and lose nothing from a complaint stating facts that he is ultimately unable to prove. Though he may be denied legal relief, he will nonetheless have obtained a short sabbatical in the nearest federal courthouse."); Lumbert v. Illinois Dep't of Corrections, 827 F.2d 257, 259 (7th Cir. 1987) ("the problem of [frivolous litigation] is even more acute when the indigent plaintiff is a prison inmate, because the costs of a prisoner's time are very low."); Savage v. Central Intelligence Agency, 826 F.2d 561, 563-564 (7th Cir. 1987) ("No rational system of government burdens its highest courts with a class of litigation dominated by petty cases typically brought for their nuisance value by persons on whose hands time hangs heavy.").

claim only if it is satisfied that the claim is of little or no weight, worth, or importance; not worthy of serious attention; or trivial.

An *in forma pauperis* petition under 28 U.S.C. § 1915(d) may be dismissed if the district court is "satisfied that the action is frivolous or malicious."[117] However, a court may dismiss a claim as factually frivolous only if the facts are clearly baseless, a category encompassing allegations that are "fanciful," "fantastic," and "delusional."[118]

The Supreme Court has barred abusive prisoners from relief at the Supreme Court level from receiving *in forma pauperis* status.[119]

§ 7.14 Conclusion

In view of the very liberal interpretation given the *Johnson* decision by many lower courts, the prison administration is confronted with an extremely difficult task. In order to comply with constitutional standards, and to avoid possible court action, prison officials must either allow the jailhouse lawyer to practice or to implement an effective legal services program. Whichever alternative is selected will inevitably result in numerous difficulties. To allow the virtually unrestricted practice of inmate writ-writers would result in the continuation of long-recognized abuses. The alternative, to provide a judicially acceptable legal service program, presents equally difficult problems. The program must provide professional assistance sufficient to meet the needs of the inmate population without undue delay. Furthermore, it must provide assistance to any inmate wishing to file habeas corpus, civil rights, or *pro se* petitions. Only by providing such complete legal services can the prison administration protect itself against court action. The fact that this burden could be overwhelming in most states is irrelevant to the courts.

Casey v. Lewis has clarified many of the issues involving legal services for prisoners. It represents a conservative retrenchment of what legal services and materials must be provided to inmates in their quest for access to the courts.

---

[117] Neitzke v. Williams, 490 U.S. 319 (1989); Denton v. Hernandez, 504 U.S. 25 (1992).

[118] Cleveland v. Garner, 69 F.3d 22 (5th Cir. 1995).

[119] *See, e.g.,* In re Whitaker, 513 U.S.1 (1994) (per curiam) (barring abusive petitioner from proceeding *in forma pauperis* when seeking extraordinary relief); In re Anderson, 511 U.S. 364 (1994) (per curiam) (same); In re Sassower, 510 U.S. 4 (1993) (per curiam) (barring abusive petitioner from proceeding *in forma pauperis* in non-criminal matters when seeking extraordinary relief and certiorari review); Martin v. District of Columbia Court of Appeals, 506 U.S. 1 (1992) (per curiam) (barring abusive petitioner from receiving *in forma pauperis* status to file petitions for writs of certiorari); Zatko v. California, 502 U.S. at 18 (1991) (denying *in forma pauperis* status to two abusive petitioners); In re Demos, 500 U.S. 16 (1991) (per curiam) (barring abusive petitioner from proceeding *in forma pauperis* when seeking extraordinary relief); In re Sindram, 498 U.S. 177 (1991) (per curiam) (same).

Prison Disciplinary
Proceedings   8

Chapter Outline

§ 8.1 Introduction

Discipline, order, and control are major concerns of the administrative staffs of correctional institutions. These issues relate to the security of the institution, the safety of institutional staff and inmates, and the rehabilitation of the inmates.

The body or individual generally responsible for administering discipline for the violation of institutional rules and regulations has varying names in correctional institutions, ranging from a rules infraction board or committee, behavior committee, summary court, or simply "court." In recent years, great emphasis has been given by the courts to the disciplinary procedures and practices of prison administrators.

Before there can be federal court intervention in the management of state prison systems, there must first be a violation of a constitutional right. In the context of disciplinary proceedings, cases have arisen over the issue of a prisoner having a federally protected liberty interest that was violated by state prison officials.

In June of 1995, the United States Supreme Court completely changed the nature of protected liberty interests under the Fourteenth Amendment. In *Sandin v. Conner,*[1] a prisoner alleged that Hawaii prison officials deprived him of procedural due process when an adjustment committee refused to allow him to present witnesses during a disciplinary hearing and then sentenced him to segregation for misconduct. The District Court granted the officials summary judgment, but the Court of Appeals reversed, concluding that the prisoner had a liberty interest in remaining free of disciplinary segregation and that there was a disputed question of fact whether he had received all of the process due under *Wolff v. McDonnell.*[2] The Court of Appeals based its conclusion on a prison regulation instructing the committee to find guilt when a misconduct charge was supported by substantial evidence. The court reasoned that the committee's duty to find guilt was nondiscretionary. From that regulation, it drew a negative inference that the committee could not impose segregation if it did not find substantial evidence of misconduct. This was a state-created liberty interest. Therefore, *Wolff* entitled the prisoner to call witnesses.

---

[1]   515 U.S. 472 (1995).
[2]   418 U.S. 539 (1974). *See* § 8.3.

The Supreme Court reversed, holding that neither the Hawaii prison regulation nor the due process clause itself afforded the prisoner a protected liberty interest that would entitle him to the procedural protections set forth in *Wolff*.

Under *Wolff*, states in certain circumstances could create liberty interests that are protected by the due process clause. However, these interests are limited to freedom from restraint that, while not exceeding the sentence in such an unexpected manner as to give rise to protection by the due process clause of its own force, nonetheless imposes atypical and significant hardship on the inmate in relation to the ordinary incidents of prison life.[3]

The Supreme Court backed off from the methodology used in *Hewitt v. Helms*[4] and later cases, holding that these cases have impermissibly shifted the focus of the liberty interest inquiry from one based on the nature of the deprivation to one based on language of a particular regulation. Under *Hewitt's* methodology, prison regulations, such as the one in *Sandin*, have been examined to see whether mandatory language and substantive predicates create an enforceable expectation that the state would produce a particular outcome with respect to the prisoner's confinement conditions. *Hewitt* encouraged prisoners to comb through regulations in search of mandatory language on which to base entitlements to various state-conferred privileges. Courts have, in response, drawn negative inferences from that language. *Hewitt*, it was felt, created disincentives for states to codify prison management procedures in the interest of uniform treatment in order to avoid the creation of "liberty" interests. This led to the impermissible involvement of federal courts in the day-to-day management of prisons. The Supreme Court in *Sandin* felt that the time had come to return to due process principles that were correctly established and applied in *Wolff* and *Meachum*.

The Supreme Court rejected the assertion that any state action taken for a punitive reason encroaches upon a liberty interest under the due process clause, even in the absence of any state regulation.[5] In *Sandin*, the prisoner's discipline in segregated confinement did not present the type of atypical, significant deprivation in which a state might conceivably create a liberty interest. At the time of his punishment, disciplinary segregation mirrored conditions imposed upon inmates in administrative segregation and protective custody. Moreover, the state later expunged his disciplinary record with respect to the more serious of the charges against him. Further, his confinement did not exceed similar but totally discretionary confinement in either duration or degree of restriction. The situation in *Sandin* did not present a case in which the state's action would inevitably affect the duration of his sentence, because the chance that the misconduct finding would affect his parole status was simply too attenuated to invoke the due process clause's procedural guarantees.

---

3   *See* Meachum v. Fano, 427 U.S. 215 (1976).
4   459 U.S. 460 (1983).
5   *See* Bell v. Wolfish, 441 U.S. 520 (1979) and Ingraham v. Wright, 430 U.S. 651 (1977).

Lower courts have been forced by *Sandin* to reconsider earlier holdings involving liberty interests. For example, in *Delaney v. Selsky*,[6] the court stated that because the due process issues raised in the case were on their way to trial when the Supreme Court decided *Sandin,* and because *Sandin* profoundly altered the standards for determining when prisoners suffer a deprivation of constitutionally protected liberty interests, a motion for reconsideration was granted.

According to *Delaney,* the Supreme Court in *Sandin* reversed the judicial trend toward expanding prisoners' constitutionally protected liberty interests. The Supreme Court instructed federal courts to focus their liberty interest inquiries on the nature of alleged deprivations, rather than on negative inferences from the "shalls" that dot prison regulations designed mainly to guide the conduct of correctional officers. More specifically, *Sandin* held that where disciplinary segregation is substantially similar to the conditions imposed upon inmates in administrative segregation and protective custody, disciplinary segregation does not present the type of atypical, significant deprivation in which a state might conceivably create a liberty interest.

The dilemma faced within the courts of the Second Circuit is typical. In the months following *Sandin,* courts had opportunities to consider its impact on the due process rights of prisoners confined to administrative or disciplinary segregation. In *Eastman v. Walker,*[7] a district court held that where a prison regulation stated that a prisoner's keeplock status "shall" be changed within 72 hours, the decision to keep an inmate in keeplock for 96 hours instead to ensure institutional security and safety is not "atypical" and does not impose a "significant hardship" and does not violate an inmate's liberty interest.

A similar conclusion was reached in *Carter v. Carriero.*[8] *Carter* noted that New York prison regulations allow inmates to be placed in the segregated housing unit for disciplinary confinement, detention, administrative segregation, protective custody, keeplock confinement, and for any other reason, with the approval of the deputy commissioner for facility operations. *Carter* went on to hold that, given the similarities among segregated housing, disciplinary segregation, and administrative confinement in New York prisons, a penalty of 270 days in disciplinary segregation did not impose atypical and significant hardship on the inmate in relation to the ordinary incidents of prison life. Therefore, no constitutionally protected liberty interest entitled the prisoner to the procedural protection that he claimed he was due.

The same result was reached in the Southern District of New York. In *Uzzell v. Scully,*[9] the prisoner claimed that his due process rights were violated when a correctional officer placed him in keeplock, an administrative segregation unit, where he remained for 23 days, without the 24-hour notice of charges against him that the Supreme Court set forth in *Wolff v. McDonnell* as a requirement of procedural due process. Applying *Sandin,* the Court held that

---

[6]   899 F. Supp. 923 (N.D.N.Y. 1995).
[7]   895 F. Supp. 31 (N.D.N.Y 1995).
[8]   905 F. Supp. 99 (W.D.N.Y. 1995).
[9]   893 F. Supp. 259 (S.D.N.Y. 1995).

because prisoners do not have a protected liberty interest in remaining free from keeplock, the state can confine prisoners there without giving them 24 hours prior notice of the charges against them.

In *Delaney*, prison officials ignored the fact that even when the conditions of disciplinary confinement mirrored the conditions imposed upon inmates in administrative segregation and protective custody, an inappropriate duration of disciplinary confinement still raises due process concerns. The prisoner's original sentence was 168 days in disciplinary segregation after he completed the 197 days remaining on his keeplock sentence. He received this sentence after an administrative hearing whose procedural adequacy was not questioned. In *Carter*, the court held that 270 days' confinement in the segregated housing unit did not impose an atypical and significant hardship on the inmate in relation to the ordinary incidents of prison life. The *Delaney* court was not prepared to say that, as a matter of law, 365 days' confinement in the segregated housing unit was a sufficiently typical and insignificant hardship on the prisoner relative to the ordinary incidents of life in the correctional facility, to permit the state to deprive him of procedural protections before imposing that sanction. The *Delaney* court felt that *Sandin* did not compel a different conclusion.

The court felt that the 197 days that the prisoner spent in disciplinary confinement at the correctional facility were different in degree, if not duration, from similar administrative confinement. Because of his unusual height—almost seven feet—his confinement to the segregated housing unit for one year caused "back problems." The bed in his segregated housing unit cell was too small for him and as a segregated housing unit resident, he received only one hour of recreation per day. For most of his time in segregated housing, the prisoner was forced to stand or lie in an uncomfortable and compromising position.

According to *Delaney*, *Sandin* renders both the duration and the conditions of disciplinary confinement relevant to the issue of whether the nature of a prisoner's disciplinary sanction raises a liberty interest concern.

A prisoner contended that his detention in administrative segregation for three days without an opportunity to be heard violated his right to procedural due process. *Rodriguez v. Phillips*[10] held that discipline by prison officials in response to a wide range of misconduct falls within the expected parameters of the sentence imposed by a court of law. The discipline in *Rodriguez*, although concededly punitive, did not present a dramatic departure from the basic conditions of the prisoner's indeterminate sentence. Consequently, discipline in segregated confinement did not present the type of atypical, significant deprivation in which a state might conceivably create a liberty interest. Under *Hewitt*, the holding would have been otherwise.

Sandin may be read as calling into question the continuing viability of all cases holding that regulations afford inmates a state-created liberty interest in remaining free from administrative segregation.

---

[10]   66 F.3d 470 (2d Cir. 1995).

The director of inmate disciplinary programs, as a judge, has absolute immunity for his actions on administrative appeals arising out of determinations of disciplinary hearings held in New York State prisons. He performs a quasi-judicial role as a professional civilian hearing officer.[11]

Once a prisoner demonstrates that his exercise of a constitutional right was a substantial or motivating factor in a disciplinary action against him, prison officials may still prevail by proving that they would have made the same decision absent the protected conduct for reasons reasonably related to a legitimate penological interest.[12]

§ 8.2 Due Process of Law

The phrase *due process of law* is found in both the Fifth[13] and Fourteenth[14] Amendments to the Constitution. The Fifth Amendment applies to federal action, the Fourteenth Amendment to state action. The phrase means little on its own; it depends completely on court interpretation to give it relevant meaning. The Supreme Court has indicated that there are two aspects of due process: substantive and procedural.

The substantive aspect involves the fundamental rights of the individual (such as life, liberty, and property) that are protected from government action. It is a question of whether an individual's interest can be protected by the federal courts as a constitutional right. The individual rights or interests protected by substantive due process vary, depending on whether a particular court regards the interest as "fundamental." The first eight amendments to the United States Constitution specifically enumerate fundamental rights of citizens that are protected from federal government action, such as freedom of religion, speech, press, and right of assembly. The same fundamental rights are protected against state action by the Fourteenth Amendment. Substantive due process requires government to treat the people with "fundamental fairness."

The procedural aspect of due process deals with the procedures or means by which government action can affect the fundamental rights of the individual; it is the guarantee that only after certain fair procedures are followed can the government affect an individual's fundamental rights. The exact procedural rights guaranteed depend upon what procedural rights a particular court regards as required by "justice and liberty."[15]

---

[11] Gaston v. Coughlin, 861 F. Supp. 199 (W.D.N.Y. 1994), *remanded*, 249 F.3d 156 (2d Cir. 2001). *See also* §9.4 *infra*.

[12] Rauser v. Horn, 241 F.3d 330 (3d Cir. 2001).

[13] U.S. CONST. amend. V states in part, "no person shall . . . be deprived of life, liberty, or property, without due process of law . . ." This amendment is a prohibition on the federal government, and not the states. Barron v. Baltimore, 32 U.S. (7 Pet.) 243 (1833).

[14] U.S. CONST. amend. XIV states in part, "[N]or shall any state deprive any person of life, liberty, or property, without due process of law . . ." The language in the amendment indicates a specific prohibition on the states.

[15] Palko v. Connecticut, 302 U.S. 319 (1937); Snyder v. Massachusetts, 291 U.S. 97 (1934); Hurtado v. California, 110 U.S. 516 (1884).

A consideration of what procedures due process may require varies with the circumstances. The precise nature of the government function involved must be ascertained, as well as the private interest that has been affected by the government action.[16]

A planned series of disciplinary actions as retaliation for initiating a civil rights suit against prison officials has been determined to have violated the prisoner's rights.[17] Prison officials may not retaliate against an inmate for exercising his or her constitutional rights. An inmate accused prison officials of pursuing a widespread conspiracy to retaliate against him for filing a private criminal complaint. The inmate stated that after he attempted to seek redress through the courts, defendants increased his custody level, transferred him to a prison that had been documented as a place of danger, and denied him parole. Relief was denied. In retaliation cases, a prisoner must prove that he was engaged in a constitutionally protected activity. Second, a prisoner must demonstrate that he suffered some adverse action at the hands of the prison officials. This requirement is satisfied upon a showing that the action was sufficient to deter a person of ordinary firmness from exercising his constitutional rights. Third, a prisoner must prove that his constitutionally protected conduct was a substantial or motivating factor in the decision to discipline him. The burden then shifts to the defendant who must prove by a preponderance of the evidence that it would have taken the same disciplinary action even in the absence of the protected activity.[18]

A correctional officer violated an inmate's constitutional rights by writing false disciplinary reports against the inmate in retaliation for grievances filed against him. The inmate was transferred 250 miles from his home after he questioned the correctional officer regarding prisoners' rights to legal assistance.[19]

An inmate's allegation that he had been placed in solitary confinement without any notice of charges or any hearing for one week and that he was threatened with violence when he asked what the charges were, stated a cause of action under the Civil Rights Act.[20]

Inmates were deprived of procedural due process at a disciplinary hearing in which: (1) no independent evaluation of the reliability of a confidential informant was made, (2) the hearing officer merely accepted conclusions of the investigating officer who in turn merely accepted the conclusions of the warden, and (3) the investigating officer had no direct knowledge of what the informant told the warden about an inmate's plans for escape, who the informant was, or how he got information. The hearing officer had no evidence before him from anyone with direct contact with the informant.[21]

---

[16]   Cafeteria & Restaurant Workers Union v. McElroy, 367 U.S. 886 (1961).
[17]   Milhouse v. Carlson, 652 F.2d 371 (3d Cir. 1981).
[18]   McGrath v. Johnson, 155 F. Supp. 2d 294 (E.D. Pa. 2001).
[19]   Farver v. Schwartz, 255 F.3d 473 (8th Cir. 2001).
[20]   Boag v. MacDougall, 454 U.S. 364 (1982).
[21]   Broussard v. Johnson, 918 F. Supp. 1040 (E.D. Texas 1996), *sub. app* 253 F.3d 874 (5th Cir. 2001).

However, the imposition of four consecutive disciplinary sanctions of 90 days each in disciplinary segregation for four serious disciplinary infractions, which resulted in denial of out-of-cell exercise for one year, was not cruel and unusual punishment.[22]

§ 8.3 Due Process Requirements in a Prison Disciplinary Hearing

The "due process of law" involved in prison disciplinary proceedings is the procedural aspect of the due process requirement of the Fifth and Fourteenth Amendments. When federal courts initially considered inmates' due process rights, the courts that were willing to grant relief held that due process prevented only "capricious" or "arbitrary" actions by prison administrators. One court found that placing an inmate in solitary confinement, without a hearing, for activities associated with requests for Black Muslim services, was a violation of due process.[23] The same court, in another opinion, noted:

> Where the lack of effective supervisory procedures exposes men to the capricious imposition of added punishment, due process and Eighth Amendment questions inevitably arise.[24]

Another court found that reclassification that resulted in a loss of "merit" or "good" time was arbitrary action.[25] The court found that the reclassification was unreasonable due to lack of factual basis for the classification.

In the early 1970s the federal courts began to focus their attention on the specific procedures used in prison disciplinary proceedings. The courts have provided a forum for the protection of the right of an inmate to procedural due process. They have sought to balance the interest of the institution in maintaining order, discipline, and control, and a recognition of the need for prompt and individual treatment with the knowledge that the process can further burden an inmate's sentence or that the disciplinary action noted on his or her institutional record may affect his or her parole eligibility.

In deciding what procedures are constitutionally required by due process at prison disciplinary hearings, federal courts have been influenced by the due process requirements of administrative law. Administrative agencies, as a branch of government whose actions directly affect individuals, must ensure that indi-

---

[22] Pearson v. Ramos, 237 F.3d 881 (7th Cir. 2001).

[23] Howard v. Smyth, 365 F.2d 428 (4th Cir. 1966); *See also* Drayton v. Robinson, 519 F. Supp. 545 (M.D. Pa. 1981); In re Davis, 599 P.2d 690, 158 Cal. Rptr. 384 (Cal. 1979); McAlister v. Robinson, 488 F. Supp. 545 (D.C. Conn. 1978), *aff'd*, 607 F.2d 1058 (2d Cir. 1979).

[24] Landman v. Peyton, 370 F.2d 135, 141 (4th Cir. 1966), *cert. denied*, 388 U.S. 920 (1967).

[25] United States ex rel. Campbell v. Pate, 401 F.2d 55 (7th Cir. 1968); In re Westfall, 162 Cal. Rptr. 462 (Cal. Ct. App. 1980); South v. Franzen, 413 N.E.2d 523 (Ill. Ct. App. 1980); Bartholomew v. Reed, 477 F. Supp. 223 (D.C. Or. 1979); Taylor v. Franzen, 417 N.E.2d 242 (Ill. Ct. App. 1981); *cf.* People ex rel. Stringer v. Rowe, 414 N.E.2d 466 (Ill. Ct. App. 1980); McGhee v. Belisle, 501 F. Supp. 189 (E.D. La. 1980).

vidual procedural due process rights are guaranteed. In general terms, administrative agencies are required by due process to act only after adequate notice and only after an opportunity for a fair hearing.[26] In a case involving a state welfare department's procedure for terminating welfare benefits,[27] the Supreme Court found that adequate notice and an opportunity to be heard required: (1) that the affected welfare recipient receive timely and adequate notice of the proposed action, including the reasons for termination; (2) an opportunity to defend, which also meant: (a) the right to confront adverse witnesses, (b) the right to present arguments and evidence orally, and (c) the right to be represented at the hearing by retained counsel; and (3) an impartial decisionmaker who must state his or her reasons and indicate the evidence relied on, if welfare is terminated.[28]

Wolff v. McDonnell

Federal courts took all or part of the requirements imposed on administrative agencies and held that due process in the prison disciplinary setting required basically the same safeguards.[29] In 1974, the United States Supreme Court decided *Wolff v. McDonnell*,[30] which involved a state prisoner in Nebraska who had filed a civil rights action[31] in federal court, alleging that he had been denied due process during a prison disciplinary proceeding.

Considering the nature of prison disciplinary proceedings, the Court held that the full range of procedures mandated by *Morrissey*[32] and *Scarpelli*[33] for parole revocation did not apply. The Court felt that the unique environment of a prison demanded a more flexible approach in accommodating the interests of the prisoners and the needs of the prison. Specifically, the Court held that due process in a prison disciplinary setting requires:

1. Advance written notice of the charges against the prisoner, to be given at least 24 hours before the appearance before the prison disciplinary board;

2. A written statement by the fact finders as to the evidence relied upon and reasons for the disciplinary action;

3. That the prisoner be allowed to call witnesses and present documentary evidence in his or her defense, providing there is no undue hazard to institutional safety or correctional goals.

---

26   W. GELLHORN AND C. BYSE, ADMINISTRATIVE LAW 486 (3d ed. 1970).
27   Goldberg v. Kelly, 397 U.S. 254 (1970).
28   *Id.* at 267-268, 270, 271.
29   Landman v. Royster, 333 F. Supp. 621 (E.D. Va. 1971); Clutchette v. Procunier, 328 F. Supp. 767 (N.D. Cal. 1971); Clutchette v. Enomoto, 471 F. Supp. 1113 (N.D. Cal. 1979); Chavis v. Rowe, 643 F.2d 1281 (7th Cir. 1981); Wright v. Enomoto, 462 F. Supp. 397 (N.D. Cal. 1980), *summary aff'd,* 434 U.S. 1052 (1978); Powell v. Ward, 487 F. Supp. 917 (S.D.N.Y. 1980).
30   418 U.S. 539 (1974).
31   42 U.S.C. § 1983.
32   Morrissey v. Brewer, 408 U.S. 471 (1972).
33   Gagnon v. Scarpelli, 411 U.S. 778 (1973).

4. Counsel substitute (either a fellow prisoner, if permitted, or staff) should be allowed when the prisoner is illiterate or when the complexity of the issues makes it unlikely that the prisoner will be able to collect and present the evidence necessary for an adequate comprehension of the case.

5. The prison disciplinary board must be impartial.

Equally important is what the Court decided was *not* constitutionally required:

1. The prisoner has no constitutional right to confrontation and cross-examination. Whether to permit confrontation and cross-examination is left to the discretion of the prison disciplinary board.

2. The prisoner has no constitutional right to retained or appointed counsel.

Further, the *Wolff* decision is not to be applied retroactively; there is no right of a prisoner to have his or her prison record of prior disciplinary proceedings expunged.

It should also be noted that *Wolff* arose in the context of discipline for "serious misconduct." The Court stated: "We do not suggest, however, that the procedures required by today's decision for the deprivation of good-time would also be required for the imposition of lesser penalties such as the loss of privileges."[34]

Therefore, the Supreme Court has severely restricted the law that had been emerging from the Circuit Courts of Appeals, and recognizes that more flexibility and experimentation in the prison setting is needed before further review by the Court. As Mr. Justice White stated:

> Our conclusion that some, but not all, of the procedures specified in *Morrissey* and *Scarpelli* must accompany the deprivation of good-time by state prison authorities is not graven in stone. As the nature of the prison disciplinary process changes in future years, circumstances may then exist which will require further consideration and reflection of this Court.[35]

The decision in *Wolff* laid down constitutional guidelines, but left flexibility in the conduct of disciplinary hearings. This aspect of the case has been severely criticized. One court expressed regret that the Supreme Court failed to deal more precisely with the "profound federal constitutional issues implicated in the prison system." It was noted that *Wolff* "failed to make the constitution a living document for many human beings,"[36] by not requiring additional procedural rights in the prison context.

---

34   Wolff v. McDonnell, 418 U.S. at 571 (1974).
35   *Id.*
36   Taylor v. Schmidt, 380 F. Supp. 1222 (W.D. Wis. 1974).

Baxter v. Palmigiano

After the *Wolff* decision, the federal courts filled in some of the gaps, a task that *Wolff* had expressly left to the discretion of prison officials, *not* federal courts. One Circuit Court of Appeals held that:

1. Minimum notice and a right to respond are due an inmate faced with even a temporary suspension of privileges;

2. An inmate at a disciplinary hearing who is denied the privilege of confronting and cross-examining witnesses must receive written reasons or the denial will be deemed *prima facie* evidence of an abuse of discretion;

3. An inmate facing prison discipline for a violation that might also be punishable in state criminal proceedings has a right to legal counsel (not just counsel substitute) at the prison hearing.[37]

Another Circuit Court of Appeals held that where an inmate brought before a prison disciplinary committee faces possible prosecution for a violation of state law:

1. He must be advised of his right to remain silent and must not be questioned further once he exercises that right;

2. Such silence may not be used against him at that time or in future proceedings;

3. When criminal charges are a realistic possibility, prison authorities should consider whether legal counsel (not just counsel substitute), if requested, should be permitted at the proceeding.[38]

In 1976, the United States Supreme Court reversed both decisions. It held in *Baxter v. Palmigiano*[39] that the procedures set forth above were inconsistent with the "reasonable accommodation," reached in *Wolff v. McDonnell,* between institutional needs and objectives and the constitutional provisions of general application.

Specifically, the Court held that:

1. Prison inmates do not "have a right to either retained or appointed legal counsel in disciplinary hearings"; (citing *Wolff*)

2. An adverse inference may be drawn from an inmate's silence at his or her disciplinary proceeding;

3. Federal courts have no authority to expand the *Wolff* requirements, which leave the extent of cross-examination and confrontation of witnesses to the sound discretion of prison officials;

37　Clutchette v. Procunier, 497 F.2d 809 (9th Cir. 1974), *reh'g,* 510 F.2d 613 (9th Cir. 1975) in light of *Wolff.*

38　Palmigiano v. Baxter, 510 F.2d 534 (1st Cir. 1974).

39　Baxter v. Palmigiano, 425 U.S. 308 (1976); Enomoto v. Clutchette, 425 U.S. 308 (1976).

4. The Court of Appeals acted prematurely when it required procedures such as notice and an opportunity to respond even when an inmate is faced with a temporary suspension of privileges, as distinguished from a serious penalty.

Thus, the Supreme Court severely restricted the judicially imposed procedural requirements that had emerged in the wake of *Wolff* and added no new constitutional requirements to those set forth in *Wolff*. Thus, *Wolff* established maximum constitutional requirements, and not bare minimum requirements.

§ 8.3.1   —Notice of the Hearing

A prison disciplinary proceeding in which the inmate is not informed of the nature of the accusation against him or her, nor of the evidence to be used against him or her, does not comply with due process requirements.

Notice is required because it enables the inmate to prepare information to explain the alleged offense or defend him- or herself against the accusation. It gives the inmate information about the nature of the proceeding. The notice must adequately inform the inmate of the offense of which he or she is accused.[40]

Wolff requires that there be a minimum of 24 hours between receipt by the inmate of written notice of the charges and the inmate's appearance before the prison disciplinary board. However, when an inmate desires to expedite the hearing, he or she may waive his or her right to 24-hour notice, thereby appearing at the earliest hearing scheduled after he or she receives a conduct ticket or "write-up." The use of waivers may create legal difficulties due to the inherently coercive atmosphere of a prison. If waivers are used, it is submitted that the waiver should be in writing and signed by the inmate under such circumstances that the inmate is made fully aware of his or her right to the 24-hour notice and voluntarily waives it. However, the Supreme Court has said that a "knowing and intelligent" waiver is not demanded in every situation in which a person has relinquished a constitutional protection. Generally, the requirement of a "knowing and intelligent" waiver has been applied only to the rights that the constitution guarantees to a criminal defendant in order to preserve a fair trial.[41] Wherever waivers are used, the written waiver should be witnessed. Oral waivers may also be used, but care should be taken to document the waiver, because a question of proof may arise at a later date.

Inmates in disciplinary hearings are entitled to disclosure of the details concerning the charges against them, except when prison officials have made

---

[40]   Landman v. Royster, 333 F. Supp. 621 (E.D. Va. 1971); Clutchette v. Procunier, 328 F. Supp. 767 (N.D. Cal. 1971); Bundy v. Cannon, 328 F. Supp. 165 (D. Md. 1971); Carter v. McGinnis, 320 F. Supp. 1092 (W.D.N.Y. 1970); Nolan v. Scafati, 306 F. Supp. 1 (D. Mass. 1969) (dictum), *rev'd on other grounds,* 430 F.2d 548 (1st Cir. 1970); Chavis v. Rowe, 643 F.2d 1281 (7th Cir. 1981); Rinehard v. Brewer, 483 F. Supp. 165 (S.D. Iowa 1980); Flaherty v. Fogg, 421 N.Y.S.2d 736 (N.Y. App. Div. 1979).

[41]   Schneckloth v. Bustamonte, 412 U.S. 218 (1973).

a specific and independent finding that: (1) retaliation against an informant will result from his or her identification; (2) disclosure of the information will identify the informant; and (3) the identity of the informant would not otherwise be known to the accused. Further, the accused must be notified that he or she has not been provided with the specific details of the incidents charged because the prison officials have determined that the information would reveal the identity of informants and present a serious risk to their safety.[42]

§ 8.3.2   —An Opportunity to Be Heard

The right to notice and an opportunity to be heard are a part of the basic concept of procedural due process of law. As such, a hearing is required in the disciplinary process.

In administrative law, a hearing is an oral proceeding before a tribunal.[43] Professor Kenneth C. Davis, a leading authority in administrative law, points out two forms of hearings: trial and argument. The trial is a proceeding for presenting evidence, with cross-examination and rebuttal, and ends with a decision based on the record made at the proceeding. The trial is designed to resolve disputes of fact. Argument, on the other hand, is a process for the presentation of ideas, as distinguished from evidence. It is the process for resolving nonfactual issues, such as policy or discretion.

The courts have generally recognized that a hearing is fundamental to the concept of due process, and thus have required a hearing in some form. It is one of the procedural safeguards to which an inmate is entitled when action is taken against him or her.[44] As one court has said, "The right to be heard before being condemned to suffer grievous loss of any kind is a principle basic to our society."[45]

The Supreme Court in *Wolff* did not attempt to set forth comprehensive guidelines for the conduct of disciplinary hearings, but only the elements that are constitutionally required. The national body of prison administrators—the American Correctional Association—recognized that a hearing is a "common . . . concept" of the disciplinary procedure.[46] The Association's manual describes the function of the hearing as "an orderly attempt to arrive at the truth and is not a formal court proceeding."[47] The problem in defining the exact procedures required of the disciplinary hearing is that it combines two functions in the proceeding: (1) the fact-finding process and (2) the correctional process.

---

[42]   Franklin v. Israel, 537 F. Supp. 1112 (W.D. Wis. 1982).

[43]   KENNETH C. DAVIS, ADMINISTRATIVE LAW 157 (3d ed. 1972).

[44]   Meola v. Fitzpatrick, 322 F. Supp. 878 (D. Mass. 1971); Tyree v. Fitzpatrick, 325 F. Supp. 554 (D. Mass. 1971); Carothers v. Follette, 314 F. Supp. 1014 (S.D.N.Y. 1970), *appeal dismissed,* 631 F.2d 725 (3d Cir. 1980); Jordan v. Arnold, 472 F. Supp. 265 (M.D. Pa. 1979); Deane v. Coughlin, 439 N.Y.S.2d 792 (N.Y. App. Div. 1981); Hayes v. Walker, 555 F.2d 625 (7th Cir. 1977).

[45]   Kristsky v. McGinnis, 313 F. Supp. 1247, 1250 (N.D.N.Y. 1970); *See also* Mack v. Johnson, 430 F. Supp. 1139 (E.D. Pa. 1977) ($765.00 awarded to inmate placed in punitive segregation without opportunity to present evidence at disciplinary hearing), *aff'd,* 582 F.2d 1275 (3d Cir. 1978).

[46]   AMERICAN CORRECTIONAL ASSOCIATION, MANUAL OF CORRECTIONAL STANDARDS 408 (1966).

[47]   *Id.* at 410.

The fact-finding process involves a determination of the truth of the allegation that a specified institutional rule has been violated; that is, did the inmate in fact violate the rule? This function under administrative law has traditionally been handled in a trial-type hearing. The correctional process is a policy or judgment decision by a prison administrator or board of administrators who view every action taken in terms of its correctional or rehabilitative effects on the individual involved, on the inmates, and on the staff of the institution as a whole. The correctional process must be concerned with the best interests of the inmate involved (as determined by the prison administrators) and not be solely geared to the facts of a particular incident.

Combining these two functions in a single proceeding caused the courts to require, prior to *Wolff,* varying and often inconsistent procedures in the hearing itself. Some courts found that certain aspects of a trial-type hearing, such as the right to call witnesses and to have counsel, were required by due process in prison disciplinary hearings. Other courts found that the same features were not required for a "fair hearing" in accordance with due process. The precise features required of the hearing depended upon the definition of a "fair" hearing as interpreted by the individual court involved.

The procedures required by *Wolff* center around the effectiveness of an inmate's opportunity to be heard. However, a disciplinary board might be faced with an inmate who chooses not to take advantage of that opportunity and does not speak in his or her own defense. The Supreme Court in *Baxter*[48] held that the board was permitted to draw an "adverse inference" from such silence. Thus, it would be proper for the board to consider the fact that an inmate chose not to defend him- or herself in deciding whether he or she was guilty of the conduct charged. An inmate may be advised, in effect: "You have the right to remain silent. However, if you choose to remain silent, your silence can and will be used against you."

Care should be taken, however, to use silence to corroborate other evidence presented at the hearing. If the silence of the inmate is the only evidence presented, a finding of guilt would be constitutional error.

In *Baxter,* the Supreme Court was very careful to point out that a disciplinary proceeding was not a criminal proceeding, but a civil proceeding. Perhaps an analogy could be to a revocation of welfare benefits, even if the grounds for revocation would constitute criminal fraud.

Although a hearing-impaired inmate's complaint that he was not provided with interpreter services was denied, where he twice was subjected to 30 days' disciplinary segregation, and his classification was changed, it was held that neither of these deprivations was "atypical and significant," and he was not treated differently from similarly situated inmates.[49]

---

[48]　*Supra* note 35.

[49]　Randolph v. Rodgers, 980 F. Supp. 1051 (E.D. Mo. 1997) , *revd in part on other grounds, remanded* 170 F.3d 850 (8th Cir. 1999), *appeal after remand, remanded* 253 F.3d 342 (8th Cir. 2001).

§ 8.3.3   —Right to Counsel

In *Wolff,* the Supreme Court held that an inmate had no constitutional right to either retained or appointed legal counsel at a disciplinary proceeding. In *Baxter* this was reiterated, even when the inmate may be subject to outside criminal prosecution for the misconduct that is the subject of the prison proceeding.

However, *Wolff* does require "counsel substitute" (either a fellow prisoner, if permitted, or a staff member) if the prisoner is illiterate or if the complexity of the issues makes it unlikely that the prisoner will be able to collect and present the evidence necessary for an adequate comprehension of the case.

In cases in which inmates have complained that they were denied the right to "counsel substitute," the courts have relied on the record of the disciplinary proceeding to determine the literacy of the inmate, or whether the factual issues involved were complex.[50] The counsel substitute should be someone who is capable of offering helpful advice, but does not have to be a witness or someone connected with the incident in question.[51] It is essential for prison officials to make careful inquiry, and place such inquiries in the record, in order to avoid a later legal attack based on the failure to appoint counsel substitute.

§ 8.3.4   —Witnesses; Confrontation; Cross-Examination

Wolff v. McDonnell provided that the inmate should be allowed to call witnesses and present documentary evidence in his or her defense when there is no undue hazard to institutional safety or correctional goals. The right to call witnesses and present documentary evidence, thought advisable in *Wolff,* has been required by lower courts.[52] Under the *Wolff* standard, prison officials are permitted some discretion based on the "undue hazard" criterion. Care must be taken to avoid a later judicial finding of an "abuse of discretion." The disciplinary committee, or some official prior to the hearing, should review the inmate's requests for witnesses and act on each one using the "undue hazard" standard. It is also implicit in *Wolff* that discretion may also be used to avoid redundant and irrelevant testimony. Thus, when an inmate requests 100 fellow inmates as witnesses to an incident in a dining hall, to allow all those inmates to appear, one by one, before the disciplinary board, could create a major security problem, as well as being unduly repetitive. Calling one or a representative number of the 100 would probably be sufficient, if it was determined that

---

50 Daigle v. Helgemoe, 399 F. Supp. 416 (D.N.H. 1975); Grever v. Oregon State Correctional Institution, Corrections Division, 561 P.2d 669 (Or. App. 1977).

51 Mills v. Oliver, 367 F. Supp. 77 (E.D. Va. 1973); Clutchette v. Enomoto, 471 F. Supp. 1113 (N.D. Cal. 1979).

52 United States ex rel. Miller v. Twomey, 479 F.2d 701 (7th Cir. 1973), *cert. denied,* 414 U.S. 1146 (1974); Workman v. Mitchell, 502 F.2d 1201 (9th Cir. 1974); Murphy v. Wheaton, 318 F. Supp. 1252 (N.D. Ill. 1974); Adargo v. Barr, 482 F. Supp. 283 (D. Colo. 1980); Pollard v. Baskerville, 481 F. Supp. 1157 (E.D. Va. 1979), *aff'd,* 620 F.2d 294 (4th Cir. 1980); Pace v. Oliver, 634 F.2d 302 (5th Cir. 1981); Bekins v. Oregon State Penitentiary, 617 P.2d 653 (Or. Ct. App. 1980); Cruz v. Oregon State Penitentiary, 617 P.2d 650 (Or. Ct. App. 1980).

all the inmates would be offering identical testimony. To this end, it is suggested that the charged inmate be required to state, in a written request for witnesses prior to the hearing, what he or she expects them to say if they are called. The importance and relevance of their testimony can then be better balanced against the problems that may result if they are called as witnesses.

If the requested witness is in another institution, it has also been suggested that a written statement can be taken, and that "live" testimony of the inmate's witnesses is not constitutionally required. It should be recognized, however, that if written statements of a witness are used against the inmate, the issues of confrontation and cross-examination will arise.

The decision to grant or not grant a witness request should be made in the record, and should be supported by an explanation if the request is denied. The lack of such an explanation has led one court to label the refusal to call witnesses an "arbitrary" decision:[53] a label that can lead to civil liability.

Wolff left the issues of confrontation and cross-examination to the sound discretion of prison officials. By not requiring confrontation, disciplinary boards often must rely on written conduct reports as the only evidence on which to base a decision. The inmate may, of course, deny the allegations of such reports and call witnesses or present documents to dispute them, but may not directly face and question his or her accuser, except as prison officials deem wise. This exercise of discretion was reinforced by the decision in *Baxter*. It is not required that the board state reasons for denying cross-examination or confrontation. If the inmate pleads "guilty" and thereby waives his or her rights under *Wolff*, prison officials should carefully document the factual basis for the plea, and make certain that the plea was knowingly made.[54]

---

53   Murphy v. Wheaton, *supra* note 52; Devaney v. Hall, 509 F. Supp. 497 (D.C. Mass. 1981).

54   Cases deal with such diverse topics as: Smith v. Rabalais, 659 F.2d 539 (5th Cir. 1981) (In a disciplinary proceeding, it was not an abuse of discretion to refuse to provide an inmate with the identity of a confidential informant when there were possible fatal consequences to the informant and when the inmate would be given an opportunity to establish an alibi for the time, place, and date of the alleged sale of narcotics.); Kyle v. Hanberry, 677 F.2d 1386 (11th Cir. 1982) (A prison disciplinary finding based upon the affidavit of a prison chaplain, who was merely passing on the statements of a "reliable inmate source," was reversed. Minimum due process requires that the disciplinary committee undertake in good faith to establish the informant's reliability. There must be some information on the record from which a court can reasonably conclude that the committee undertook such an inquiry, and upon such inquiry, concluded that the informant was reliable. The committee should describe the nature of its inquiry to the extent that the committee is satisfied that such disclosure would not identify an informant.); Chavis v. Rowe, 643 F.2d 1281 (7th Cir. 1981) (A disciplinary committee must disclose to an inmate any exculpatory report as well as a written statement as to the evidence relied upon and reasons for the disciplinary action taken. It must also provide him or her with a written statement as to the evidence relied upon and reasons for the disciplinary action taken against him.); Bartholomew v. Watson, 665 F.2d 915 (9th Cir. 1981) (A prison procedure that prevented an inmate from calling an inmate or staff member as a witness in a disciplinary hearing violated due process.); Langton v. Berman, 667 F.2d 231 (1st Cir. 1981) (A state prisoner in a disciplinary hearing had no right to cross-examine witnesses. His right to confront his accusers and to have full access to all evidence should be left to the discretion of state prison officials.); Ward v. Johnson, 667 F.2d 1126 (4th Cir. 1981) (An inmate was denied due process when he was not permitted to call witnesses at a disciplinary hearing. Due process was involved even though the punishment was the loss of recreational time.); Segarra v. McDade, 706 F.2d 1301 (4th Cir. 1981) (Due process is not violated by a prison official's decision to prohibit an inmate from calling witnesses at a prison disciplinary hearing concerning the loss of good-time credits. Such is not required by *Wolff v. McDonnell*. In this case, the request was denied when he made his request during the hearing, after earlier refusing to compile a witness list or to allow statements to be taken.)

In *Ponte v. Real,* a state prisoner was charged with violating a prison regulation as the result of a fight that occurred in the prison office. At the disciplinary board hearing, the prisoner asked that certain witnesses be called, but the board refused to call the witnesses. No explanation was given at the time, nor as part of the written record of the disciplinary hearing. The prisoner was found guilty and 150 days of "good time" were forfeited. Due process does not require that the disciplinary board's reasons for denying the prisoner's witness request appear as part of the administrative record of the disciplinary hearing. Due process does require the board, at some time, to state its reason for refusing to call witnesses, but may do so either by making the explanations a part of the administrative record or by later presenting evidence in court if the deprivation of a "liberty" interest, such as that afforded by "good-time" credits, is challenged because of the refusal to call the requested witnesses. The arguments that the burden of proving noncompliance with *Wolff v. McDonnell* is on the prisoner, and that a prisoner may not challenge disciplinary procedures unless a "pattern of practice" was shown, were rejected. The Supreme Court stressed that explaining the decision at the disciplinary hearing will not immunize prison officials from later court challenges to their decision. However, so long as the reason for denying prisoner witness requests are logically related to preventing undue hazards to institutional safety or correctional goals, the explanation should satisfy due process requirements. It was also suggested that if prison security or similar paramount interests appear to require it, a court should allow, at least in the first instance, a prison official's justification for refusal to call witnesses to be presented to the court *in camera,* or outside the presence of the prisoner.[55]

In *Walker v. Bates,* a prisoner alleged that his procedural due process rights were violated in the course of a disciplinary hearing that resulted in a decision to confine him to a Special Housing Unit. He was charged with violation of an institutional rule prohibiting the possession of contraband in the form of a weapon and violation of another institutional rule prohibiting the possession of state bedding in excess of authorized issue.[56] The procedures established by New York in disciplinary proceedings comported with the procedural due process rights in disciplinary proceedings to which prison inmates are entitled under *Wolff v. McDonnell.* However, the Second Circuit held that the denial of an inmate's right to call witnesses constituted a compensable constitutional due process violation.[57]

It must be remembered that all such cases must be reevaluated in light of *Sandin.*

In *Johnson v. Coombe,* prison officials who violated an inmate's right to call witnesses at a disciplinary proceeding were not entitled to qualified immunity. The inmate's right to call witnesses at the disciplinary proceeding was established at the time of the hearing and any reasonable person should have known of the right.[58]

---

[55]   Ponte v. Real, 471 U.S. 491 (1985).
[56]   Walker v. Bates, 23 F.3d 652 (2d Cir. 1994).
[57]   *See also* Patterson v. Coughlin, 761 F.2d 886 (2d Cir. 1985), *cert. denied,* 474 U.S. 1100 (1986).
[58]   Johnson v. Coombe, 156 F. Supp. 2d 273 (S.D.N.Y. 2001).

§ 8.3.5 —Administrative Review

Administrative review of the decision resulting from a prison disciplinary hearing is wise administrative policy, although it is not constitutionally required. A suggested procedure states that an inmate "shall be provided and advised of a regular channel of appeal from the finding made or the penalty assessed at any disciplinary hearing."[59] The right to review of a disciplinary decision has not been interpreted as a requirement under constitutional procedural due process, but the presence of an appellate procedure has been an element encouraged by the courts.[60] However, if a statute or prison regulation provides for an appeal, the equal protection clause of the Fourteenth Amendment requires that all those affected be treated alike.

The review must be restricted to the charge made and to the evidence presented. Reviewing the decision based on evidence that is not in the record is not permitted. If an appeal is granted, notice of the right to appeal must be distributed to all inmates. Word-of-mouth notification to inmates of their right to appeal or the procedures for such an appeal cannot be permitted. Because the equal protection clause of the Fourteenth Amendment contemplates uniform treatment, failure to notify certain inmates at the conclusion of the disciplinary procedure of their right to appeal, when other inmates *are* notified, is a violation of inmates' constitutional rights.

Administrative review by a warden, or even an official of the state corrections department, also provides the opportunity to set forth policy to be followed in certain situations. For example, standards can be established for the exercise of discretion in calling witnesses or allowing cross-examination. It should be noted that state statutes dealing with administrative procedures may foreclose "rulemaking" in this manner; nevertheless, the use of administrative review as a check on the arbitrary action of subordinates is a wise policy. Furthermore, judges then feel free to require inmates to follow the administrative appeal process to its end. A system of administrative appeals may keep many cases out of the federal courts as long as the administrative review process is not a rubber stamp for arbitrary decisions made at the institutional level.

There is no requirement of a "stay" pending appeal. However, if the finding of guilt is set aside, the inmate's record should be expunged, and his or her prior status restored.

---

[59] American Correctional Association, Manual of Correctional Standards 410 (1966).

[60] Beishir v. Swenson, 331 F. Supp. 1227 (W.D. Mo. 1971); Morris v. Travisono, 310 F. Supp. 857 (D.R.I. 1970); Burns v. Swenson, 300 F. Supp. 759 (W.D. Mo. 1969); Riner v. Raines, 409 N.E.2d 575 (Ind. 1980); Scott v. DeJarnette, 470 F. Supp. 766 (E.D. Ark. 1979); Adams v. Duckworth, 412 N.E.2d 789 (Ind. 1980); Dawson v. Hearing Committee, 597 P.2d 1353 (Wash. 1979).

§ 8.3.6 —The Record

Wolff v. McDonnell requires that a written statement be made by the fact finders as to the evidence relied upon and reasons for the disciplinary action. This requirement is consistent with the earlier decision in *Morrissey v. Brewer,* dealing with parole revocation.[61] *Wolff* does not require that the inmate receive a copy of the written statement, but this is essential if there is an available means of administrative appeal. No appeal procedure is meaningful if the inmate is not made fully aware of the basis of the original decision. It is also good policy to expand the scope of the written record to include the reasons underlying any exercise of discretion concerning the disciplinary proceeding. This may include why witnesses were denied, why an inmate's request for counsel substitute was not granted, or why a more stringent sanction than usual was imposed for a given offense. Organizing these reasons in a written record of the proceeding will help ensure that decisions are not made arbitrarily, and it can be shown that discretion was not abused. Such a record may be used not only to state the evidence relied upon (which often will be the allegations in a conduct report), but also to summarize the evidence that was rejected. Tape-recording all hearings is expensive, but may prove invaluable to counter inmate allegations of unfairness, to document inmate literacy, or to obtain oral waivers.

In *Walpole v. Hill,* inmates received disciplinary reports charging them with assaulting another inmate. At separate hearings, the disciplinary board heard testimony from a correctional officer and received his written report. The officer testified that he heard a commotion in the prison walkway and, upon investigation, discovered an inmate who had been assaulted. He saw three other inmates fleeing down the walkway. The disciplinary board found the inmates guilty, and revoked their good-time credits. The decision will be upheld if there is any evidence in the record that could support the conclusions reached by the disciplinary board.[62]

§ 8.3.7 —Impartiality

Wolff v. McDonnell requires that the prison disciplinary board be impartial. This is one of the traditional aspects of a "fair hearing" and generally requires that the decisionmaker not be directly involved in the incident in question or the investigation of it. This helps assure that the decision will be based strictly on the facts adduced at the hearing, and not on personal knowledge or impressions that a decisionmaker brings with him or her to the hearing.[63] One court specif-

---

[61] Morrissey v. Brewer, 408 U.S. 471 (1972); Hayes v. Thompson, 637 F.2d 483 (7th Cir. 1980); Rinehard v. Brewer, 483 F. Supp. 165 (S.D. Iowa 1980); State ex rel. Meeks v. Gagnon, 289 N.W.2d 357 (Wis. Ct. App. 1980); Jerry v. Wainwright, 383 So. 2d 1110 (Fla. Dist. Ct. App. 1980); Craig v. Franke, 478 F. Supp. 19 (E.D. Wis. 1979); Jensen v. Satran, 651 F.2d 605 (8th Cir. 1981).

[62] Superintendent, Mass. Corr. Inst. Walpole v. Hill, 472 U.S. 445 (1985).

[63] Landman v. Royster, 333 F. Supp. 621 (E.D. Va. 1971); Langley v. Scurr, 305 N.W.2d 418 (Iowa 1981).

ically held that a disciplinary committee, which included as one of its members a correctional officer involved in the incidents leading to the disciplinary hearing, was not sufficiently impartial to satisfy the due process clause.[64] The court felt that the presence of the "charging party" prevented the board from rationally determining the facts.

The requirement that the decision be based strictly on facts adduced at the hearing also involves the concept of "command influence." This occurs when a warden, or other official, in effect dictates what the decision of the disciplinary committee should be. One court analyzed "command influence" as follows:

> It is not improper for a member of the adjustment committee to discuss with the warden the procedures which should be followed, although it would clearly be improper for the warden to tell a member of the adjustment committee what the decision of the adjustment committee should be or for them to discuss what the decision should be. Nor is it improper for the members of the adjustment committee to discuss among themselves the procedure to be followed, although it would be improper for them to decide the proper disposition of the case before the hearing.

If the prison system has an appeal procedure, it is not necessary to have a different disciplinary board hear the case if the prior decision is reversed and sent back for a "new hearing." In criminal cases, the judge who pronounced sentence, or determined guilt after a nonjury trial, may be the judge at the new trial. Similarly, the judge who presides over a preliminary hearing is not barred from being the judge at the later hearing.

§ 8.3.8 —Prehearing Detention and Emergencies

When an inmate has committed a physical assault, or in other cases in which his or her conduct poses an immediate threat to the security of the institution, pre-hearing detention may be justified, so long as a hearing complying with the requirements of *Wolff v. McDonnell* is held within a reasonable time after the detention begins. Whether to place an inmate in prehearing detention is another area in which the discretion of prison officials comes into play. It is good administrative policy to ensure that the exercise of such discretion is not abused. Thus, standards should be developed by which a hearing officer or another official can determine what factual circumstances trigger pre-hearing detention under administrative guidelines. The practice of imposing prolonged detention prior to disciplinary hearings should be avoided.

---

[64] Crooks v. Warne, 516 F.2d 837 (2d Cir. 1975); *See also* Commonwealth v. Manlin, 441 A.2d 532 (Pa. Super. 1979). (Conviction of deputy warden was upheld for "official oppression" by Superior Court.)

One court approved a policy requiring immediate removal from a mini-mum-security honor farm of any inmate charged by a formal conduct report pending a prompt hearing, even though such inmate must spend a brief peri-od in isolated confinement.[65] This is an example of a court balancing the requirement of *Wolff* against the practical realities of the institutional setting—the honor farm was not equipped to handle disciplinary hearings.

A few courts have also recognized the overriding concerns for security in emergency situations, and have allowed greater flexibility in administering disciplinary cases than would be permissible under normal conditions.[66]

So long as the conditions of confinement do not constitute "punishment," or there is no undue delay, there would appear to be no sound reason to deny prison officials the authority to hold an inmate in isolation for investigation prior to formal charges being made. As in pre-hearing detention after charges have been made, *Wolff* does not specify the maximum delay; *Wolff* requires only a minimum of 24 hours. In any event, the hearing should be held, or the inmate returned to his or her former status, as soon as practicable.

§ 8.3.9 —Double Jeopardy

Frequently, the argument is made that it is double jeopardy for an inmate to receive administrative punishment for conduct that is subject to a criminal prosecution. This argument was rejected in *United States v. Hedges*. "Five hun-dred and forty-three days of good behavior time were administratively forfeit-ed . . . because of an attempted escape."[67] In affirming the conviction in the sub-sequent criminal trial, a federal court of appeals stated: "It is established . . . that administrative punishment does not render a subsequent judicial prosecu-tion violative of the Fifth Amendment prohibition of double jeopardy."[68] The same reasoning applies to proceedings in state prisons.

However, criticism of this view is widespread. The rationale of *Hedges* was rejected in considering a disciplinary proceeding held after an inmate was acquitted of criminal charges arising out of the same conduct in *Barrows v. Hogan*. The court said:

---

[65] Bickham v. Cannon, 516 F.2d 885 (7th Cir. 1975); *See also* Deane v. Coughlin, 439 N.Y.S.2d 792 (N.Y. App. Div. 1981); Collins v. Coughlin, 442 N.Y.S.2d 191 (N.Y. App. Div. 1981); *cf.* United States ex rel. Smith v. Robinson, 495 F. Supp. 696 (E.D. Pa. 1980). (An inmate has a right to freedom from discipli-nary sanctions until proven guilty of a rule violation. An inmate has a constitutional liberty interest in freedom from segregated confinement.)

[66] Morris v. Travisono, 509 F.2d 1358 (1st Cir. 1975); La Batt v. Twomey, 513 F.2d 641 (7th Cir. 1975); Aikens v. Lash, 390 F. Supp. 663 (N.D. Ind. 1975), *modified in* 514 F.2d 55 (7th Cir. 1975); Hayward v. Procunier, 629 F.2d 599 (9th Cir. 1981); Gray v. Levine, 455 F. Supp. 267 (D. Mo. 1978), *aff'd,* 605 F.2d 1202 (4th Cir. 1979); Clifton v. Robinson, 500 F. Supp. 30 (C.D. Pa. 1980).

[67] United States v. Hedges, 458 F.2d 188, 190 (10th Cir. 1972).

[68] *Id.*

The question here is not one of double jeopardy, for the [inmate] does not allege that he has been charged twice for the same offense. The holding of a jury of twelve men and women is a final determination against the government on the question of whether [the inmate] assaulted the officer. In view of the judicial determination that this prisoner is not guilty of the offense charged, it is impermissible for the prison administration to determine otherwise and punish the prisoner for an offense as to which he has been acquitted.[69]

Because *Baxter* carefully distinguished criminal proceedings, to which the double jeopardy clause applies, from disciplinary proceedings, which are civil in nature, the authority of prison officials to proceed independently of the criminal courts should be recognized and approved.

§ 8.3.10 —Evidence

The evidence relied upon in many prison disciplinary proceedings may be limited to the written conduct report of a correctional officer or other staff member. It may include the oral testimony of witnesses for both sides or documents such as letters. It is impossible to quantify the amount of evidence required to make a decision, but it is clear that the criminal trial standard of proof *beyond a reasonable doubt* does not apply to prison disciplinary proceedings. A popular standard is that borrowed from administrative law for purposes of judicial review: *substantial evidence considering the record as a whole.*[70] Thus, after considering the evidence on both sides of the case, if the members of the board feel that there is substantial evidence of guilt, in light of the evidence offered by the inmate, they may validly find an inmate guilty of the offense charged.

A conviction on a disciplinary charge cannot rest solely upon the hearsay report of an unidentified informant whose credibility is unsubstantiated.[71]

Although polygraph examinations are looked upon with disfavor by the courts, the results of a polygraph may be considered as evidence in a prison disciplinary proceeding. However, there must be additional evidence, in addition to the polygraph report, on which a decision is based. The polygraph may be used as corroborative evidence on the issue of guilt.

A difficult problem arises when the traditional criminal law defenses are raised. For example, an officer might come upon a fight in progress and charge the two inmates with "fighting." At the disciplinary hearing, one inmate might assert "self-defense." The general rule of criminal law is that one who is free from fault is privileged to use reasonable and necessary force to defend him- or herself against personal harm threatened by the unlawful act of

---

[69] Barrows v. Hogan, 379 F. Supp. 314 (M.D. Pa. 1974); *cf.* Rusher v. Arnold, 550 F.2d 896 (3d Cir. 1977).
[70] Universal Camera Corp. v. NLRB, 340 U.S. 474 (1951).
[71] Helms v. Hewitt, 655 F.2d 487 (3d Cir. 1981), *rev'd on other grounds,* 459 U.S. 460 (1983); *See* § 8.3.4.

another. The force he or she uses for this purpose must be reasonable under the circumstances. Thus, this defense would raise a number of questions, all of which should be dealt with by the disciplinary board: Which party was the aggressor? Was the inmate who claimed self-defense free from fault? Was the force he or she used reasonable under the circumstances? Did the "defendant" become the aggressor by the use of excessive force in self-defense?

An inmate may assert his or her ignorance of a rule of conduct. However, in response, the familiar phrase "ignorance of the law is no excuse" may be applied. This, however, applies only to offenses that would be crimes outside of the penal setting. Due process requires that inmates be given notice of what rules of conduct govern prison life and it further requires that those rules clearly define what conduct violates those rules. Due process is violated if an inmate is punished for violating a rule that is so vague as to make it impossible to conform his or her conduct to the rule.[72]

In *Moore v. Plaster*, a district court erred in dismissing a claim that disciplinary charges against an inmate were false and filed in retaliation for the exercise of his constitutional rights. The only evidence at the hearing were the conclusory statements of a reporting officer that the inmate was trafficking in controlled substances within the institution. There was no other evidence regarding the underlying facts. The accusations were without sufficient evidence.[73]

§ 8.4 The Inmate's Legal Remedies

A violation of rights afforded to inmates either under state or federal law will give rise to a number of remedial actions. Although they are discussed fully in Chapter 11, it should be noted that the remedies in the federal courts are usually limited to injunctive relief, civil suit under 42 U.S.C. § 1983, and habeas corpus under 28 U.S.C. § 2241.

State courts have shown interest in the conduct of prison disciplinary proceedings. This has ranged from hearing complaints concerning conditions and practices[74] to detailed judicial review of disciplinary board findings.[75]

---

[72] Meyers v. Alldredge, 492 F.2d 296 (3d Cir. 1974); Sagerser v. Oregon State Penitentiary, Corrections Division, 597 P.2d 1257 (Or. Ct. App. 1979); Haller v. Oregon State Penitentiary, Corr. Div., 570 P.2d 983 (Or. Ct. App. 1977).

[73] Moore v. Plaster, 266 F.3d 928 (8th Cir. 2001).

[74] People ex rel. Bright v. Warden, 361 N.Y.S.2d 809 (Trial term SC Bronx County, 1975); McGinnis v. Stevens, 543 P.2d 1221 (Alaska 1975); Wilkerson v. Oregon, 544 P.2d 198 (Or. Ct. App. 1976); Steele v. Gray, 223 N.W.2d 614 (Wis. Sup. Ct. 1974).

[75] Palmer v. Oregon State Penitentiary, 545 P.2d 141 (Or. Ct. App. 1976); Dawson v. Hearing Committee, 597 P.2d 1353 (Wash. 1979); Sandlin v. Oregon Women's Correctional Center, Corrections Division, 559 P.2d 1308 (Or. Ct. App. 1977); Riner v. Raines, 409 N.E.2d 575 (Ind. 1980); Reed v. Parratt, 301 N.W.2d 343 (Neb. 1981).

Whether pursued in state or federal court, one of the results of the reversal of a disciplinary board's action will probably be an order requiring the expungement of any records dealing with or relying on the disciplinary action that is found to have been invalid. One court deemed expungement appropriate to protect the inmate "from future prejudice in obtaining parole, work assignments, and the transfer to a prison nearer his home."[76]

§ 8.5 Conclusion

Federal courts have indicated a willingness to inquire into all aspects of prison administration to ensure that the constitutional rights of inmates are observed. Although the courts have traditionally been extremely hesitant to place restraints on prison authorities in matters of internal prison administration, one court noted that:

> This simple hands-off attitude has been made more complex by Supreme Court cases which have held that prisoners are not stripped of their constitutional rights, including the right to due process, when the prison gate slams shut behind them. Rather, prisoners continue to enjoy the protections of the Due Process Clause subject to restrictions imposed by the practical necessities of prison life and the legitimate aims of the correctional process.[77]

In the context of "due process," it is important to note that long before the requirements of procedural due process were imposed on prison disciplinary proceedings, it was recognized that such proceedings must at least afford substantive due process,[78] in that they must be fair.

Clearly, the courts have gone beyond the era when inmates' constitutional claims were disregarded out-of-hand by statements such as: "A convicted felon . . . has, as a consequence of his crime, not only forfeited his liberty, but all of his personal rights except those which the law in its humanity accords to him. He is for the time being the slave of the State."[79] The contemporary view in the federal courts is that if a constitutionally protected interest can be made out, and if some harm thereto can be shown that is sufficiently grievous and that cannot be justified by the exigencies of incarceration, then a proper case for relief exists.[80] However, *Baxter* makes it clear that the days of federal court tinkering with internal prison management are over. Prison disciplinarians who follow the clear teachings of *Wolff,* and who initiate procedures to prevent the abuse of administrative discretion, need not fear legal liability.

---

[76] Chapman v. Kleindienst, 517 F.2d 1246 (7th Cir. 1974); Powell v. Ward, 487 F. Supp. 917 (S.D.N.Y. 1980); Hurley v. Ward, 402 N.Y.S.2d 870 (N.Y. App. Div. 1976).

[77] United States ex rel. Gereau v. Henderson, 526 F.2d 889 (5th Cir. 1976).

[78] Wilwording v. Swenson, 502 F.2d 844 (8th Cir. 1974).

[79] Ruffin v. Commonwealth, 62 Va. (21 Gratt.) 790, 796 (1871).

[80] Shimabuku v. Britton, 503 F.2d 38 (10th Cir. 1974); Haines v. Kerner, 404 U.S. 519 (1972).

Sandin has severely restricted the type of hearing to which procedural due process rights apply. The decision has had a profound effect on all aspects of institutional life. "Liberty" has been greatly restricted, particularly as it applies to prison discipline.

Parole   9

Chapter Outline

§ 9.1 Introduction

The term *parole* means a procedure by which a duly convicted defendant who has been sentenced to a term of imprisonment is allowed to serve the last portion of his or her sentence outside the prison walls, although he or she remains under supervision. The essence of parole is release from prison before the completion of his or her sentence, on the condition that the parolee abide by certain rules during the balance of the sentence. It applies only to cases in which the convicted and sentenced defendant has served part of the imposed sentence. It is a conditional release from confinement, contingent upon future conduct as set forth in the terms of the parole. The parolee is subject to future confinement for the unserved portion of his or her sentence in the event that he or she violates the provisions of parole.[1]

§ 9.2 Parole Is Not a Right

One of the primary purposes of parole is to aid inmates in reintegrating with society as constructive individuals as soon as they are able, without being confined for the full term of the court-imposed sentence. Another purpose is to alleviate the costs to society of keeping inmates in prison.

In some states, parole is granted automatically after inmates serve an established minimum prison term. In others, parole is granted or withheld by the discretionary action of a parole authority that bases its decision on information about an inmate. In essence, the parole authority makes a prediction as to whether the inmate is ready to return to society.

In *Greenholtz v. Inmates of the Nebraska Penal and Correctional Complex,*[2] the Supreme Court held that there is no protected liberty interest in the possibility of parole before the termination of the sentence. Because there is no entitlement, due process hearings are not required by the state's parole sys-

---

[1] Nibert v. Carroll Trucking Co., 82 S.E.2d 445 (W. Va. 1954); Richmond v. Commonwealth, 402 A.2d 1134 (Pa. Commw. 1979).

[2] 442 U.S. 1 (1979); Board of Pardons v. Alleni, 482 U.S. 369 (1987) (A Montana statute provided that a prisoner eligible for parole "shall" be released when there is a reasonable probability that no detriment will result to him or the community, and specified that parole shall be ordered for the best interests of society, and when the State Board of Pardons believes that the prisoner is able and willing to assume the obligations of a law-abiding citizen. This statute created the same liberty interest that was protected in *Greenholtz*).

tem. States are not constitutionally required to establish a parole system; it is instead a discretionary decision of the state to determine when an inmate is ready for release. The Court explained that the reason for not requiring due process standards is simply that a decision for the granting of parole is not the equivalent of a guilt determination as in a criminal proceeding or in the revocation of parole.

In *Martinez v. California,*[3] a 15-year-old girl was murdered by a parolee with a history of being a sex offender, five months after he had been released from prison. The Supreme Court held that because the parolee was not an agent of the parole board, and the parole board was unaware that the decedent, as distinguished from the public at large, faced any special danger, the death was too remote a consequence of the decision to grant parole to hold the board responsible under the Civil Rights Act.[4]

In *Connecticut Board of Pardons v. Dumschat,*[5] a prisoner applied for commutation of his life sentence. His application was rejected without any explanation being given. Relying upon *Greenholtz,* the Supreme Court held that an inmate has no constitutionally inherent right to commutation of a life sentence. The inmate has nothing more than an expectation, as, for example, the expectation that he will not be transferred to another prison within the system. It is not a constitutional right, but a unilateral hope. It was pointed out that the Connecticut statute at issue referred to the mere existence of a power to commute. There was no limit on what procedure was to be followed, what evidence could be considered, nor what criteria were to be applied, all in contrast to the statute in *Greenholtz,* which created a right to parole under state law. However, this does not mean that the inmate has no constitutional rights in the procedure used in granting or denying parole.

Statutes usually control the time at which specific groups of inmates will become eligible for parole. The right to be considered at a parole hearing and the timing of the parole hearing are frequently within the sole discretion of the parole authority. However, in *Grasso v. Norton,*[6] the court held that a federal prisoner who is sentenced under a statute that permits parole eligibility consideration at any time is entitled to "effective and meaningful" parole consideration at or before the one-third point of the maximum sentence. This was required even though the prisoner was given an initial parole hearing when entering the prison. "Meaningful" consideration for parole was satisfied by a "file review" and did not require a personal interview. However, *Garafola v. Benson*[7] held that a "file review" was not "meaningful" and a full-scale insti-

---

[3]   444 U.S. 277 (1980).

[4]   42 U.S.C. § 1983.

[5]   452 U.S. 458 (1981).

[6]   520 F.2d 27 (2d Cir. 1975); Didousis v. New York State Board of Parole, 391 N.Y.S.2d 222 (1977).

[7]   505 F.2d 1212 (7th Cir. 1974); Walker v. Prisoner Review Board, 694 F.2d 499 (7th Cir. 1982) (The rules governing parole have no exception for withholding documents that are considered by the Parole Board from a candidate for parole. This created a justified expectation of access to his file. A prisoner's civil rights case was remanded to the District Court to determine whether the Board considered papers that it did not permit the prisoner to see.); Dixon v. Hadden, 550 F. Supp. 157 (D. Colo. 1982) (The use of a letter that makes serious accusations without indicating the reliability of sources in making a parole decision violates due process).

tutional hearing was required. In *Franklin v. Shields,*[8] the Fourth Circuit Court of Appeals held that there is no constitutional requirement that each prisoner receive a personal hearing, have access to his or her files, or be entitled to call witnesses in his or her behalf to appear before a parole board. The court believed that such matters were better left to the discretion of the parole authorities. As a general rule, the courts will not interfere with the exercise of discretion in granting or refusing parole to an inmate. This rule of noninterference was used in *Tarlton v. Clark.*[9] An inmate sought an order reviewing the action of the United States Board of Parole in not granting him parole at the time he first became eligible. The petitioner claimed that §§ 4202 and 4203 of Title 18 of the United States Code gave him the right to parole after completing one-third of his total sentence, provided that he had obeyed all the rules of the institution in which he was confined. The court held that:

> By the language of Title 18 U.S.C.A. 4203, the Board of Parole is given absolute discretion in matters of parole. The courts are without power to grant a parole or to determine judicially eligibility for parole. . . . Furthermore, it is not the function of the courts to review the discretion of the Board in the denial of application for parole or to review the credibility of reports and information received by the Board in making its determination.[10]

There is, in light of this and several other cases,[11] no right to be paroled at any specified time, although there may be a "right" to be considered for parole eligibility.[12] Under present case law, the determination as to eligibility for release is vested entirely in the paroling authority.

Similarly, the paroling authority is given wide discretion in determining how the interview or hearing with the inmate will be conducted. *Menechino v. Oswald*[13] summarized the rights of the inmate at a parole hearing.

The petitioner alleged that due process rights had been violated at his parole hearing. He claimed that the Constitution required that he be given: (1) notice; (2) a fair hearing with right to counsel, cross-examination, and presentation of witnesses; and (3) specification of the reasons used by the parole authority in its determination. The court denied that the inmate had any due process rights at his parole hearing. It asserted that many of the essential conditions necessary for the application of due process standards are absent in the context of a parole hearing.

---

[8]   569 F.2d 784 (4th Cir. 1977); *see also* Garafola v. Benson, 505 F.2d 1212 (7th Cir. 1974).
[9]   441 F.2d 384 (5th Cir.), *cert. denied,* 403 U.S. 934 (1971); Schlobohm v. United States Parole Commission, 479 F. Supp. 474 (M.D. Pa. 1979).
[10]   *Id.* at 385.
[11]   *See* United States v. Frederick, 405 F.2d 129 (3d Cir. 1968); State v. Freitas, 602 P.2d 914 (Haw. 1979); Boothe v. Hammock, 605 F.2d 661 (2d Cir. 1979); Smith v. Marchewka, 519 F. Supp. 897 (D.C.N.Y. 1981).
[12]   *See* Stroud v. Weger, 380 F. Supp. 897 (M.D. Pa. 1974); Matter of Bonds, 613 P.2d 1196 (Wash. Ct. App. 1980).
[13]   430 F.2d 403 (2d Cir. 1970).

First, the proceeding is non-adversary in nature. Both parties (the parole authority and the inmate) have the same concern—rehabilitation.

Second, the primary function of the hearing is not fact-finding. On the contrary, the parole authority is making a determination based upon numerous tangible and intangible factors.

Third, the inmate has no present private interest to be protected, as is required before the due process clause is applicable.

The wide discretion given to the paroling authority is limited, however. Written reasons for the denial of parole must be given to the inmate. In *United States ex rel. Johnson v. Chairman, New York State Board of Parole,*[14] the court stated that the due process clause of the Fourteenth Amendment requires the parole board to provide a written statement of reasons to the inmate when parole is denied. This conclusion is consistent with *Menechino,* which held only that an inmate was not entitled to a specification of charges, counsel, and cross-examination.

In federal courts, the requirement to provide an inmate with written reasons for the denial of parole has been based on either statutory or constitutional grounds. First, it is argued that the parole board is an agency under the Federal Administrative Procedure Act, § 555(e), which provides generally for notice of the denial in whole or in part of a written application made in connection with any agency proceeding.[15] Second, it is argued that the parole granting decision results in a "grievous loss" of conditional liberty to the inmate and therefore due process requires that written reasons for denial be provided.[16] The U.S. Parole Commission and Reorganization Act[17] states that a prisoner must be provided with written notice of the Parole Commission's decision after the parole determination proceeding. If parole is denied, the notice must state with particularity the reasons for such denial.[18]

---

[14] 363 F. Supp. 416 (W.D.N.Y. 1973), *aff'd,* 500 F.2d 925 (2d Cir. 1974), *vacated as moot,* Regan v. Johnson, 419 U.S. 1015 (1974).

[15] King v. United States, 492 F.2d 1337 (7th Cir. 1974).

[16] Childs v. United States Board of Parole, 511 F.2d 1270 (D.D.C. 1974); United States ex rel. Harrison v. Pace, 357 F. Supp. 354 (E.D. Pa. 1973); United States ex rel. Richerson v. Wolff, 525 F.2d 797 (7th Cir. 1975), *cert. denied,* 425 U.S. 914 (1976).

[17] Pub. L. No. 94-233, March 15, 1976. *See* Appendix I (includes only portions relevant to this section). §§ 4206, 4218.

[18] Ronning v. United States, 547 F. Supp. 301 (M.D. Pa. 1982) (In order for a District Court to overturn the U.S. Parole Commission's parole determination, a court must find that there was no rational basis in the record for the Commission's decisions.); Campbell v. United States Parole Commission, 704 F.2d 106 (3d Cir. 1983) (a prisoner, with intent to rob a bank, participated in a murder, although his two confederates actually did the killing. This fact was properly considered by the U.S. Parole Commission as an aggravating factor to keep him in prison six years longer than recommended by the guidelines. A District Court's decision to require the Commission to reconsider the prisoner's parole eligibility without reference to the murder was an "unjustified interference" with the Commission's discretion, and was reversed); Artez v. Mulcrone, 673 F.2d 1169 (10th Cir. 1982) (A prisoner's parole category in the most severe category was not denying him any fundamental right. An administrative classification is permissible if it has a rational basis or advances a legitimate government interest).

In *Rowe v. Whyte*,[19] the court held that release on parole is a substantial liberty interest and the procedures by which it is granted or denied must satisfy due process standards. Compare this to the position taken by the Sixth Circuit Court of Appeals, which has stated that a prisoner does not have a sufficient liberty interest in his or her future parole release to be entitled to due process in his or her parole release proceedings.[20]

In *Franklin v. Shields*,[21] it was held that certain other minimum procedures are required at the parole hearing. The statute in effect in Virginia, as interpreted by the court, extended an "expectation of liberty" to its prisoners. Therefore, the procedure to determine eligibility for parole had to be "fundamentally fair," including:

1. Published standards and criteria governing parole determinations that must be made available to the inmates.

2. A personal hearing.

3. Access by the inmate to the information the Parole Board relies upon in making its decision. Although most of the information in the prisoner's files is harmless, certain information may be removed and some reports may be rewritten to protect the author's identity. Reports considered potentially harmful include psychiatric and psychological reports on the inmate and reports by informers or others who made statements in confidence. The board must give an inmate access to the information in his or her file for a reasonable period prior to the parole hearing. Access may be denied to information that would threaten prison security or present a substantial likelihood of harm to the inmate or others.

4. A statement of the reasons for denial. Such reasons are to be as clear and precise as possible but they need only be substantially related to the criteria adopted by the board.

No right exists to call witnesses in the prisoner's behalf or to call and cross-examine persons who have provided adverse information to the board. The inmate has no right to legal counsel.

In addition to case law, the Federal Parole Commission and Reorganization Act should be consulted for the procedure required in the federal correctional system.[22]

The Parole Commission and Reorganization Act was repealed as of 1992 by the Sentencing Reform Act of 1994[23] which, among other things, created the United States Sentencing Commission[24] as an independent body in the

---

[19] 280 S.E.2d 301 (W. Va. 1981); Williams v. Missouri Bd. of Probation and Parole, 661 F.2d 697 (8th Cir. 1981); Bradford v. Weinstein, 519 F.2d 728 (4th Cir. 1976), *vacated as moot,* 423 U.S. 147 (1976). (The prisoner had obtained a full release by that time).

[20] Wagner v. Gilligan, 609 F.2d 866 (6th Cir. 1979); Sharp v. Leonard, 611 F.2d 136 (6th Cir. 1979).

[21] 399 F. Supp. 309 (W.D. Va. 1975). This case must be reevaluated in light of *Sandin v. Conner. See* Chapter 8, Prison Disciplinary Procedures, regarding what is a constitutionally protected liberty interest.

[22] Appendix I §§ 4206, 4207, and 4208.

[23] 28 U.S.C. §§ 991, 994, and 995(a)(1) (1998).

[24] 18 U.S.C. § 3551 et seq. (1982 ed., Supp. IV), and 28 U.S.C. §§ 991-998 (1982 ed., Supp. IV).

Judicial Branch, with power to promulgate binding Sentencing Guidelines establishing a range of determinate sentences for all categories of federal offenses and defendants according to specific and detailed factors. The Sentencing Reform Act was held to be constitutional in *Mistretta v. United States.*[25]

The purpose of requiring written reasons for the denial of parole is to provide the courts with a record upon which to determine whether the actions of the Parole Board have been "arbitrary and capricious"—a standard of judicial review of administrative acts. The reason for denial that has been attacked most often is "release at this time would depreciate the seriousness of the offense." Although many courts still recognize the broad discretion vested in the paroling authority,[26] courts have held that something more than a general reason for the denial of parole is required.[27] Denial of parole based in general language and not specifically addressed to the inmate's personal situation may amount to no reason at all and does not protect the inmate from arbitrary and capricious action by the parole board.

Another limitation was recognized in *Palermo v. Rockefeller,*[28] in which an early release was guaranteed for the petitioners in exchange for a guilty plea. The offer of early release was later withdrawn. The court held that the board had abused its discretionary powers.

Similarly, the courts will not permit a parole authority to exercise power allocated exclusively to the courts. In *Johnson v. Haskins,*[29] the court released an inmate from custody because the parole authority had deliberately circumvented the obvious intent of the sentencing court that the inmate's sentences run concurrently. The court admonished the parole authority by reminding it that the court's judgment as to whether sentences are to be concurrent or consecutive is not subject to modification, directly or indirectly, by the parole authority.

In discussing limitations on the discretion of the parole authority to grant or refuse release, we should note that the above cases are exceptional. The prevailing view is that the discretion of the parole authority in release hearings is broad.

Restrictions on the granting of parole have been challenged under ex post facto analysis. The Eighth Circuit Court of Appeals held that a state parole eligibility statute, enforcing a rehabilitation program applied to an inmate who committed the crime before completion of the program, would violate the ex post facto clause of the Constitution.[30] The state parole eligibility statute required all sex offenders to complete a treatment and rehabilitation program in order to be eligible for parole.

---

[25]   488 U.S. 361 (1989).

[26]   Wiley v. United States Board of Parole, 380 F. Supp. 1194 (M.D. Pa. 1974); Roach v. Board of Pardons and Paroles, Arkansas, 503 F.2d 1367 (8th Cir. 1974); Calabro v. United States Board of Parole, 525 F.2d 660 (5th Cir. 1975); Zannino v. Arnold, 531 F.2d 687 (3d Cir. 1976); Lott v. Dalsheim, 474 F. Supp. 897 (N.Y. 1979); Campbell v. Montana State Board of Pardons, 470 F. Supp. 1301 (D. Mont. 1979).

[27]   Soloway v. Weger, 389 F. Supp. 409 (M.D. Pa. 1974); Candarini v. United States Attorney General, 369 F. Supp. 1132 (E.D.N.Y. 1974); Craft v. United States Attorney General, 379 F. Supp. 538 (M.D. Pa. 1974); *cf.* Young v. Duckworth, 394 N.E.2d 123 (Ind. 1979); Bowles v. Tenant, 613 F.2d 776 (9th Cir. 1980).

[28]   323 F. Supp. 478 (S.D.N.Y. 1971).

[29]   Johnson v. Haskins, 20 Ohio St. 2d 156, 49 Ohio Op. 481, 254 N.E.2d 362 (Ohio 1969); Wilkerson v. United States Board of Parole, 606 F.2d 750 (7th Cir. 1979).

[30]   Armontrout v. Parton, 895 F.2d 1214 (8th Cir.), *cert. denied,* 498 U.S. 879 (1990).

In *California Department of Corrections v. Morales,*[31] a prisoner was sentenced to 15 years to life for the 1980 murder of his wife and became eligible for parole in 1990. As required by California law, the Board of Prison Terms held a hearing in 1989, at which time it found the prisoner unsuitable for parole for numerous reasons, including the fact that he had committed his crime while on parole for an earlier murder. The prisoner would have been entitled to subsequent suitability hearings annually under the law in place when he murdered his wife. The law was amended in 1981, however, to allow the Board to defer subsequent hearings for up to three years for a prisoner convicted of more than one offense involving the taking of a life, if the Board finds that it is not reasonable to expect that parole would be granted at a hearing during the intervening years and states the bases for the finding. Pursuant to this amendment, the Board scheduled the prisoner's next hearing for 1992. The prisoner then filed a federal habeas corpus petition, asserting that as applied to him, the 1981 amendment constituted an ex post facto law barred by the United States Constitution. The United States Supreme Court held that the amendment's application to prisoners who committed their crimes before it was enacted did not violate the ex post facto clause. The amendment did not increase the "punishment" attached to the prisoner's crime. It left untouched his indeterminate sentence and the substantive formula for securing any reductions to the sentencing range. By introducing the possibility that the Board would not have to hold another parole hearing in the year or two after the initial hearing, the amendment simply altered the method to be followed in fixing a parole release date under identical substantive standards.[32]

The argument that the clause would forbid any legislative change that has any conceivable risk of affecting a prisoner's punishment was rejected. In contrast, the Supreme Court has long held that the question of what legislative adjustments are of sufficient moment to transgress the constitutional prohibition must be a matter of degree, and has declined to articulate a single "formula" for making this determination. The Supreme Court felt that there was no need to do so here, either, because the amendment creates only the most speculative and attenuated possibility of increasing the measure of punishment for covered crimes, and such conjectural effects are insufficient under any threshold that might be established under the clause. The amendment applies only to those who have taken more than one life, a class of prisoners for whom the likelihood of release on parole is quite remote. In addition, the amendment affects only the timing of subsequent hearings, and does so only when the Board makes specific findings in the first hearing. Moreover, the Board has the authority to tailor the frequency of subsequent hearings. The prisoner offered no support for his speculation that prisoners might experience an unanticipated change that is sufficiently monumental to alter their suitability for parole, or that such prisoners might be precluded from receiving a subse-

---

[31]   514 U.S. 499 (1995).

[32]   *See* Lindsey v. Washington, 301 U.S. 397 (1937); Miller v. Florida, 482 U.S. 423 (1987); and Weaver v. Graham, 450 U.S. 24 (1981).

quent expedited hearing. Nor was there a reason to think that postponing an expedited hearing would extend any prisoner's actual confinement period. Because a parole release date often comes at least several years after a suitability finding, the Board could consider when a prisoner became "suitable" for parole in setting the actual release date.

The information used during the grant of parole may raise constitutional issues. In *Johnson v. Texas Department of Criminal Justice,*[33] inmates sued the Parole Board of Texas to prohibit them from using furlough history, writ-writing activities, and the Board's receipt of protest letters when making parole determinations. Relief was denied with respect to a consideration of an inmate's furlough history when making parole determinations. However, with respect to the writ-writing activities, the district court noted that historically there has been a bias against inmates considered to be writ-writers by the employees of the Texas Department of Corrections (TDC), and determined that there should be a Board rule that prohibits the consideration of an inmate's legal activities when the Board determines that inmate's candidacy for parole. To do anything less would restrict, at least as a practical matter, an inmate's access to the courts. The state and its officers may not abridge or impair the petitioner's right to apply to a federal court for a writ of habeas corpus. Whether a writ of habeas corpus addressed to a federal court is properly drawn and what allegations it must contain are questions for that court alone to determine. Given inmates' constitutional right of access to the courts, any consideration of writ-writing as a factor in the parole decision is a deprivation of due process and also violates the equal protection clause.[34] Any distinction made between inmates who seek access to the courts and those who do not violates the equal protection clause. Further, prison officials may not retaliate against or harass an inmate for exercising the right of access to the courts.[35]

With respect to the Board's receipt of protest letters when making parole determinations, the Board sends out notification to persons entitled to receive notice under Texas law. Many of the recipients then send protests to the Board in varying forms: some are simply form letters indicating opposition to release, some express opinions that the inmate has not done enough time for the crime, others contain newspaper clippings or first-person narratives describing the original crime. Other letters come from victims and their families describing the effects that the crime has had upon them, while others include information about the inmate, such as his criminal history, unadjudicated offenses, and family circumstances. Motives for sending letters vary widely from a concern for the safety of the general public, personal dislike of an inmate, local political considerations, and a desire to obtain an advantage over an inmate.

---

[33]   910 F. Supp. 1208 (W.D. Tex. 1995).

[34]   City of Cleburne, Texas v. Cleburne Living Center, Inc., 473 U.S. 432 (1985) (equal protection requires that similarly situated persons be treated alike).

[35]   Woods v. Smith, 60 F.3d 1161 (5th Cir. 1995).

Effective September 1, 1995, the Texas Code of Criminal Procedure was amended to allow for victims or their representative to present oral statements to board members. The parole panel is obligated to allow one person to appear before the board members to present a statement of that person's views about the offense, the defendant, and the effect of the offense on the victim.[36]

The court recognized that Texas law does not create a liberty interest in release on parole. Thus, having no constitutionally protected right, an inmate cannot state "a claim for either civil rights or habeas relief by his allegation that he was denied due process when seeking parole because he has no constitutionally protected expectancy of release."[37] An inmate may, however, assert an equal protection claim in a civil rights suit.[38]

The evidence showed that inmates who received protest letters of any kind are treated differently from those who do not. According to the court, an inmate's potential for receiving protest letters is unpredictable; this fact, coupled with the unpredictability of the contents of those letters, leads to disparate results among prisoners eligible and being reviewed for parole. A system has been created that is extremely arbitrary and capricious and violates the equal protection rights of the plaintiff and the plaintiff class, no matter how small the number of parole candidates adversely affected by protest letters.

Consequently, the Court determined that the statutory scheme under which the Board can accept statements, whether written or oral, and then prevent knowledge of said statements' existence and prohibit disclosure of their contents and of the writer's or speaker's identity, violates the equal protection rights of inmates because the Board, as a rule, denies parole to inmates who have received protest statements. The Board's sole function is to determine whether an inmate should be released on parole; its function is not to effectively re-try the case by accepting "testimony" that was inadmissible at trial on evidentiary grounds (or would have been inadmissible had introduction been attempted) or was excluded as part of trial strategy, or by entering findings that the actual jury did not find at the inmate's trial. Evidentiary determinations are made in the trial court. The Board was ordered not to consider unadjudicated offenses or offenses extraneous to the conviction for which the inmate is currently incarcerated, as the Board must be bound by the conviction that the inmate received and must apply the statutory requirements regarding the time to be served on parole for that conviction, without adding ad hoc information that results in additional time being served.

Parole authorities may consider a jailhouse lawyer's activity in considering parole.[39]

---

[36] Tex. Crim. Proc. Code Ann. art. 42.18, § 8(f)(2) (as amended by Act of May 29, 1995, 74th Leg., R.S., ch. 253, § 1, 1995 Tex. Sess. Law Serv. 2179 (Vernon)).

[37] Hilliard v. Board of Pardons and Paroles, 759 F.2d 1190 (5th Cir. 1985).

[38] Hilliard, 759 F.2d at 1193.

[39] Johnson v. Rodriguez, 117 F.3d 1419 (5th Cir. 1997). *See* § 7.6 above.

Rules may not be applied retroactively in most cases. However, any restriction of eligibility for a prison release scheme that is applied to prisoners who committed their crimes under a more permissive regime violates the ex post facto provision of the Constitution.[40]

With regard to sentence reduction, in *Stiver v. Meko* a federal prison regulation that made inmates who had a prior conviction for a violent offense ineligible for the sentence reduction, while a prisoner who completes a drug treatment program was eligible, was held to be valid.[41]

The Prison Litigation Reform Act[42] has an impact on parole decisions. In the Seventh Circuit, a suit complaining that the parole commission's calculation of a prisoner's mandatory release date—all based on post-sentencing events unrelated to the validity of the conviction and sentence—was subject to the restrictions contained in the Prison Litigation Reform Act.[43]

Executive clemency consideration is not the same as parole consideration. After a murder conviction and death sentence were affirmed on direct appeal, the Ohio Adult Parole Authority commenced a clemency investigation in accordance with state law. The prisoner was informed that he could have his voluntary interview with Authority members on a particular date and that his clemency hearing would be held one week later. The prisoner filed a civil rights action, alleging that Ohio's clemency process violated his Fourteenth Amendment due process right and his Fifth Amendment right to remain silent.

Noting that *Connecticut Board of Pardons v. Dumschat*[44] had decisively rejected the argument that federal law created any liberty interest in clemency, the Sixth Circuit held that the prisoner failed to establish a life or liberty interest protected by due process. The court also held, however, that the inmate's "original" pretrial life and liberty interests were protected by a "second strand" of due process analysis, although the amount of process due could be minimal because clemency, while an "integral part" of the adjudicatory system, was far removed from trial. The court remanded the case for the lower court to decide what that process should be. Finally, the Sixth Circuit concluded that Ohio's voluntary interview procedure presented the prisoner with a "Hobson's choice" between asserting his Fifth Amendment privilege against self-incrimination and participating in Ohio's clemency review process, thereby raising the specter of an unconstitutional condition on further appeal. The Supreme Court reversed.[45]

On the Fifth Amendment issue, the Supreme Court unanimously held that giving an inmate the option of voluntarily participating in an interview as part of the clemency process did not violate any Fifth Amendment rights. Even on assumptions most favorable to the prisoner's claim—i.e., that nothing in the

---

[40]   Plyler v. Moore, 129 F.3d 728 (4th Cir. 1997), *cert. denied*, 520 U.S.1277 (1997).
[41]   Stiver v. Meko, 130 F.3d 574 (3d Cir. 1997).
[42]   *See* the section on the Prison Litigation Reform Act below, Chapter 13.
[43]   Newlin v. Helman, 123 F.3d 429 (7th Cir. 1997).
[44]   452 U.S. 458 (1981).
[45]   Ohio Adult Parole Authority v. Woodard, 523 U.S. 272 (1998).

clemency procedure granted applicants immunity for what they might say or makes the interview in any way confidential, and that the Authority would draw adverse inferences from a refusal to answer questions—the testimony at a voluntary interview was not "compelled." A prisoner merely faces a choice similar to those made by a criminal defendant in the course of criminal proceedings, as for example, when a defendant chooses to testify in his or her own defense. He or she abandons the privilege against self-incrimination when the prosecution seeks to cross-examine him or her, and may be impeached by proof of prior convictions. In these situations, the undoubted pressures to testify that are generated by the strength of the case do not constitute "compulsion" for Fifth Amendment purposes. Similarly, at the clemency hearing, a prisoner has the choice of providing information to the Authority—at the risk of damaging his or her case for clemency or for post-conviction relief—or of remaining silent. The pressure to speak did not make the interview "compelled."

On the clemency issue, the Court was split. Four members of the Court[46] concluded that an inmate does not establish a violation of the due process clause in clemency proceedings where the procedures in question do no more than confirm that such decisions are committed, as is the nation's tradition, to the executive's authority. Pardon and commutation decisions are rarely, if ever, appropriate subjects for judicial review. The argument that there was a continuing life interest in clemency that is broader in scope than the "original" life interest adjudicated at trial and sentencing was barred by *Dumschat*. The process that the prisoner sought would be inconsistent with the heart of executive clemency, which is to grant clemency as a matter of grace, thus allowing the executive to consider a wide range of factors not comprehended by earlier judicial proceedings and sentencing determinations. Although the prisoner maintained a residual life interest, e.g., in not being summarily executed by prison guards, he could not use that interest to challenge the clemency determination by requiring the procedural protections he sought. The four Justices also rejected any claim that clemency procedures are entitled to due process protection.

Four justices[47] concluded that because a prisoner under a death sentence has a continuing interest in his or her life, the issue in *Woodard* was what process was constitutionally necessary to protect that interest, recognizing that due process demands are reduced once society has validly convicted an individual of a crime. According to these four justices, some minimal procedural safeguards apply to clemency proceedings. Judicial intervention might, for example, be warranted in the face of a scheme whereby a state official flipped a coin to determine whether to grant clemency, or in a case in which the state arbitrarily denied a prisoner any access to its clemency process.

The ninth member of the Court[48] concurred in part and dissented in part, which emphasized the difficulty in analyzing recent Supreme Court cases for

---

[46]   Justices Rehnquist, Scalia, Kennedy, and Thomas.
[47]   Justices O'Connor, Souter, Ginsburg, and Breyer.
[48]   Justice Stevens.

their precedential value. Justice Stevens felt that when a parole board conducts a hearing to determine whether the state shall actually execute one of its death row inmates—in other words, whether the state shall deprive that person of life—it has an obligation to comply with the due process cause of the Fourteenth Amendment. He specifically dissented from Chief Justice Rehnquist's view that a clemency proceeding could never violate the due process clause. Under the Rehnquist view, according to Justice Stevens, even procedures infected by bribery, personal or political animosity, or the deliberate fabrication of false evidence would be constitutionally acceptable.

Justice Stevens joined in the part of the Court's opinion that concluded that giving an inmate the option of voluntarily participating in an interview as part of the clemency process did not violate his or her Fifth Amendment rights but felt that this case should be remanded to the District Court for a determination of whether Ohio's procedures met the minimum requirements of due process.

It thus remains unclear to what extent due process applies to clemency proceedings, if at all.

§ 9.3 Parole Revocation

Three theories have been advanced in the past to justify the unlimited discretion of a parole authority in revoking the parole once it is granted: the privilege theory, the contract theory, and the continuing custody theory. The present judicial treatment of parole revocation modifies these theories by subjecting parole authorities to the requirements of due process in revoking parole.

The principle of *Morales*[49] was applied to parole revocation proceedings. In *Kellogg v. Shoemaker*,[50] Ohio adopted new "emergency" provisions for parole. Under the older, repealed provisions, which were discretionary, Ohio was required to provide parolees with a "meaningful" hearing prior to revoking their parole. Under these old regulations, a parolee convicted of a subsequent crime in Ohio, while on parole, was conclusively presumed to be in violation of his or her parole. The parolee under the old regulations, however, was entitled to a hearing to present any relevant mitigating circumstances. Although plaintiff parolees seem to concede that they were given a "hearing" under the old regulations, they argued that it did not meet the procedural requirements of *Morrissey v. Brewer*.[51]

The Ohio Adult Parole Authority repealed the old regulations and implemented new ones. The new regulations did away with any type of hearing if the defendant was convicted by an Ohio court for an offense he or she committed while on any release granted by the Adult Parole Authority. There would no longer be a hearing to determine mitigating circumstances sur-

---

[49] *See* note 31.
[50] 46 F.3d 503 (6th Cir. 1995).
[51] 408 U.S. 471 (1972). *See* § 9.4.

rounding the revocation. The only process the parolees would receive would be the parole authority's verification that the sentence was imposed for an offense that occurred while the prisoner was under release status. The APA revised the parole procedures to eliminate any agency discretion in deciding whether to revoke parole.[52]

A parolee has no clearly established right to a parole revocation hearing once a subsequent parole violation conviction has been established and the law gave the parole agency no authority to consider further mitigating factors.[53] According to the Sixth Circuit, the Supreme Court in *Morrissey* clearly instructed that the purpose of a final revocation hearing was to give the parolee an opportunity to present facts challenging the determination that he or she has violated a condition of parole and to present all circumstances surrounding the violation to the parole authority so that it may exercise its discretion in a fully informed manner. When revocation is based on a new conviction, a revocation hearing would serve no such purposes.

Morrissey does not require that a parole authority be given discretion regarding when to revoke a parolee's parole status; rather, it simply requires that when such discretion is given, a revocation hearing is required.[54]

With respect to the ex post facto argument, it was pointed out that the binding regulations that were mandatory after September 1, 1992 eliminated any discretion in the parole agency to consider mitigating circumstances. To establish the claimed ex post facto violation, the prisoners had to establish that the regulation at issue: (1) is retroactive in its application and (2) "must disadvantage the offender affected by it."[55]

The focus in determining whether a new law violates the ex post facto clause is the time the offense was committed.[56] Next, a court must look to whether the new regulations were more onerous than the regulations in effect at the time the subclass committed their initial crime. Although the distinction between substance and procedure might sometimes be elusive, "a change in the law that alters a substantial right can be ex post facto 'even if the statute takes a seemingly procedural form.'"[57] Although the change here involves a procedural matter—the right to a hearing on revocation of parole—it still

---

[52]   *See* Black v. Romano, 471 U.S. 606 (1985), which indicated that the hearing procedures required in *Morrissey* applied only if the parole board exercised discretion in revoking parole. *See also* Sneed v. Donahue, 993 F.2d 1239 (6th Cir. 1993).

[53]   Sneed v. Donahue, 993 F.2d 1239 (6th Cir. 1993).

[54]   *See also* United States v. Cornog, 945 F.2d 1504 (11th Cir. 1991); Pickens v. Butler, 814 F.2d 237 (5th Cir.), *cert. denied,* 484 U.S. 924 (1987).

[55]   Miller v. Florida, 482 U.S. 423 (1987) (quoting Weaver v. Graham, 450 U.S. 24 (1981)). *See also* Dale v. Haeberlin, 878 F.2d 930, 935 (6th Cir. 1989), *cert. denied,* 494 U.S. 1058 (1990).

[56]   Weaver, 450 U.S. at 31. *See also* Persky v. Edwards, 1986 WL 16754 (6th Cir.) (quoting Forman v. McCall, 709 F.2d 852, 859 (3d Cir. 1983)) ("It is a fundamental principle of ex post facto jurisprudence that a court entertaining an ex post facto claim must focus upon the law in effect at the time of the offense for which a person is being punished."); Rodriguez v. United States Parole Comm'n, 594 F.2d 170, 176 (7th Cir. 1979) ("Although parole eligibility is determined as of the date of sentencing for some purposes . . . the ex post facto clause looks to the punishment annexed at the time the crime was committed").

[47]   Miller v. Florida, 482 U.S. at 433.

affects substantive rights attendant to parole revocation. Under the old regulations, parole would be revoked for the full amount of time, unless the inmate could convince the parole authority that mitigating circumstances warranted mercy. Under the new procedures, there is no opportunity to present these mitigating circumstances. This procedural change affects substantive rights. Consequently, the new regulation was unconstitutional to an entire class of prisoners. The new regulations were not deemed to be an ex post facto violation as to the inmates whose paroles were revoked after a hearing under the old regulations, because the new parole regulations were not applied to them. Likewise, the statute is not ex post facto as to those who committed their "initial crime" after the date of enactment (September 1, 1992). To the extent that any prisoner fell into the designated category, he or she is entitled under the old regulations to a meaningful hearing as described in *Morrissey v. Brewer.*

§ 9.3.1 —The Privilege Theory

Most frequently argued is the privilege theory. This theory holds that parole is an act of grace by the state. Because release on parole is granted to the inmate as a matter of privilege, no right attaches to it even after it is given. The release may be given, conditioned, or terminated, according to the theory, at the whim of the granting authority.

There are weaknesses to the use of this particular theory of parole. The system of parole has been an integral part of the American criminal justice process. Prison administrators use it as a rehabilitative tool as well as a stimulus for good behavior of inmates. Furthermore, it is relied upon by the inmates and is frequently the reason inmates behave properly while incarcerated. To allow parole authorities unlimited control over the parolee would appear, in light of the above, to be unwise and unjust. Further, courts have expressed their displeasure with the whole concept of "privilege" as opposed to "right." The Supreme Court, in cases concerning students, welfare recipients, and security clearances, has reviewed the privilege theory and has rejected it as improper in these cases. Most recently, the "privilege" theory of parole was repudiated by the United States Supreme Court in *Morrissey v. Brewer.*[58]

§ 9.3.2 —The Contract Theory

A second theory used as a reason for allowing unreviewable revocation of parole is the contract theory. It is argued that release by the parole authority is contingent upon the parolee's acceptance of the conditions of such release. The acceptance constitutes a contractual obligation on the part of the inmate to live up to the conditions specified. If the conditions are violated, there is a

---

[58]   408 U.S. 471 (1972).

"breach of contract" that justifies revocation. An obvious difficulty in the contract theory is that the parolee has no bargaining power in determining the terms of the contract. Furthermore, any "consent" to the terms of his or her contractual release is coerced by virtue of the fact that no alternative means of obtaining release is available.

§ 9.3.3 —The Continuing Custody Theory

A third theory used in conjunction with parole is that of "continuing custody." It is argued that because the parolee remains in the custody of the granting authority, he or she is still subject to the same restrictions as he or she was prior to his or her release on parole. However, the avowed purpose of the parole system is rehabilitation. An inmate is released so that he or she may readjust to the conditions of society, under supervision. It cannot be denied that his or her situation is substantially distinct from that of an inmate. This theory contends that attempting to apply the standards used in dealing with an inmate to a parolee is inherently irrational.

§ 9.3.4 —The Due Process Theory

The present approach to parole revocation modifies, if not rejects, these three theories. This approach recognizes that one of the chief goals of the correctional system is to impress upon those within the system the belief that the criminal justice process operates fairly for the protection of all society. It is recognized that the arbitrary operation of the parole system can only result in the parolees' loss of respect for a system that claims to encourage responsible action in accordance with established law. Furthermore, it is acknowledged that the interests of the people are best served by proper treatment of the parolee in order to prevent recidivism. If revocation is accomplished through an arbitrary procedure, respect for society will be further diminished. Finally, although it cannot be asserted that the parolee maintains the same rights as a free person, it is recognized that basic constitutionally protected rights apply to the parolee. Consequently, the requirements of due process should apply to parole revocation.

§ 9.4 Parole Revocation Proceedings

In *Morrissey v. Brewer,*[59] the United States Supreme Court held that due process applies to parole revocation proceedings.

---

[59] 408 U.S. 471 (1972).

Prior to *Morrissey,* the leading case dealing with revocation proceeding rights was *Mempa v. Rhay.*[60] However, *Mempa v. Rhay* dealt with probation revocation. In *Mempa,* two defendants had each been convicted of felonies and had been placed on probation. Both had violated the conditions of their probation and consequently were given the maximum sentence at a deferred sentencing, or probation, hearing. The petitioners had not been represented by counsel at these proceedings nor were they offered court-appointed counsel at these proceedings. The Supreme Court held that the "right to counsel is not a right confined to representation during the trial on the merits."[61] On the contrary, "appointment of counsel for an indigent is required at every stage of a criminal proceeding where substantial rights of an accused may be affected."[62] For this reason, the Court found that the failure to provide representation at the probation revocation hearing was reversible error.

As noted, the decision rendered in *Mempa* specifically dealt with probation rather than parole. Furthermore, it was limited to the right to counsel rather than to the full panoply of procedural due process rights.

In *Morrissey*, the Supreme Court distinguished parole from probation. Unlike probation, parole only arises at the end of a criminal prosecution, including the imposition of sentence. Further, in parole, supervision is not directed by the courts, but by an administrative agency. Most significantly, parole revocation deprives an individual not of the absolute liberty to which every citizen is entitled, but only of the conditional liberty that depends on compliance with special parole restrictions.

Nevertheless, the requirements of due process apply to parole revocations. The Supreme Court completely rejected the theory that constitutional rights turn upon whether the government benefit is characterized as a "right" or a "privilege." Rather, the crucial issue is the extent to which the individual will be condemned to suffer "grievous loss."

In *Morrissey*, the Supreme Court held that revocation of parole was a "grievous loss" to the parolee.

> The liberty of a parolee enables him to do a wide range of things open to persons who have never been convicted of any crime. The parolee has been released from prison based on an evaluation that he shows reasonable promise of being able to return to society and function as a responsible, self-reliant person. Subject to the conditions of his parole, he can be gainfully employed and is free to be with family and friends and to form the other enduring attachments of normal life. Though the state properly subjects him to many restrictions not applicable to other citizens, his conditions are very different from that of confinement in a prison. He may have been on parole for a number of years and may be living a relatively normal life at the time he is faced with revocation. The parolee has relied

---

60   398 U.S. 128 (1967).
61   *Id.* at 133.
62   *Id.* at 134.

> on at least an implicit promise that parole will be revoked only if he fails to live up to the parole conditions. In many cases, the parolee faces lengthy incarceration if his parole is revoked.

> We see, therefore, that the liberty of a parolee, although indeterminate, includes many of the core values of unqualified liberty and its termination inflicts a "grievous loss" on the parolee and often on others. It is hardly useful any longer to try to deal with this problem in terms of whether the parolee's liberty is a "right" or a "privilege." By whatever name, the liberty is valuable and must be seen as within the protection of the Fourteenth Amendment. Its termination calls for some orderly process, however informal.[63]

The remaining issue is the extent of the "orderly process." The Supreme Court in *Morrissey* recognized that, given the previous criminal conviction and the proper imposition of parole conditions, the state has an interest in being able to return the parolee to imprisonment without the burden of a new criminal trial on the merits if, in fact, the parolee has failed to live up to the conditions of his or her parole. However, the summary treatment that may be necessary in controlling a large group of potentially disruptive inmates in actual custody, and the argument that revocation is so totally a discretionary matter that some form of hearing would be administratively intolerable, was rejected.

> The parolee is not the only one who has a stake in his conditional liberty. Society has a stake in whatever may be the chance of restoring him to normal and useful life within the law. Society thus has an interest in not having parole revoked because of erroneous information or because of an erroneous evaluation of the need to revoke parole, given the breach of parole conditions. And society has a further interest in treating the parolee with basic fairness: fair treatment in parole revocations will enhance the chance of rehabilitation by avoiding reactions to arbitrariness.[64]

Therefore, what the Supreme Court felt was needed was an informal hearing structured to assure that the findings of a parole violation would be based on verified facts and that the exercise of discretion would be based on accurate knowledge of the parolee's behavior.

Pro forma language and routine phrases will not satisfy the requirement of a written statement of evidence and reasons relied upon.[65]

Article III of the Interstate Agreement on Detainers applies only to criminal charges. A probation violation charge that does not accuse an individual with having committed a criminal offense in the sense of initiating a prosecution does not come within Article III. In one case, a probationer from New Jersey was arrested and convicted on burglary, involuntary deviate sexual inter-

---

[63] Morrissey v. Brewer, 408 U.S. 471 (1972).

[64] *Id.* at 484.

[65] United States v. Martinez, 650 F.2d 744 (5th Cir. 1981).

course, and loitering in Pennsylvania. New Jersey sought to revoke the defendant's probation based upon the criminal conduct in Pennsylvania, and placed a detainer on the prisoner in Pennsylvania.[66]

Oklahoma has a Pre-Parole Conditional Supervision Program that takes effect whenever prisons become overcrowded and that authorizes the conditional release of prisoners before their sentences expire. The Pardon and Parole Board determines who can participate, and an inmate could be placed on pre-parole after serving 15 percent of his or her sentence. Under the program, an inmate could be eligible for full parole after serving one-third of his or her sentence and the Governor, based on the Board's recommendation, decided to grant parole. Program participants and parolees were released subject to similar constraints.

Upon reviewing a prisoner's criminal record and prison conduct, the Board simultaneously recommended him for pre-parole and released him under the program. At that time, he had served 15 years of a life sentence. After he spent five months outside the penitentiary, the Governor denied him parole. He was ordered to, and did, report back to prison.

The Supreme Court held[67] that the program, as it existed when the prisoner was released, was equivalent to parole as understood in *Morrissey*[68] and that due process was required. *Morrissey's* description of the "nature of the interest of the parolee in his continued liberty" could just as easily have applied to pre-parolees. In compliance with state procedures, the prisoner was released from prison before the expiration of his sentence. He kept his own residence. He sought, obtained, and maintained a job and he lived a life generally free of the incidents of imprisonment. He was not permitted to use alcohol, to incur other than educational debt, or to travel outside the county without permission, and he was required to report regularly to a parole officer. The Supreme Court pointed out that similar limits on a parolee's liberty did not render such liberty beyond procedural protection in *Morrissey*.

The state attempted to differentiate the program from the type of parole protected under *Meachum v. Fano,*[69] arguing that pre-parole had the purpose of reducing prison overcrowding, and that a pre-parolee continued to serve his or her sentence and receive earned credits, remained within the custody of the Department of Corrections, and was aware that he or she could have been transferred to a higher security level if the governor denied parole. The Supreme Court felt that these factors failed to distinguish the two programs. Other differences identified by the state—that participation in the program was ordered by the board while the governor conferred parole; that escaped pre-parolees could be prosecuted as though they had escaped from prison, while escaped parolees were subject only to parole revocation; and that a pre-parolee could not leave Oklahoma under any circumstances, while a parolee could leave the state with his or her parole officer's permission—served only

---

[66]   Carchman v. Nash, 473 U.S. 716 (1985).
[67]   Young v. Harper, 520 U.S. 143 (1997).
[68]   408 U.S. 471 (1972).
[69]   427 U.S. 215 (1976).

to set pre-parole apart from the specific terms of parole as it existed in Oklahoma, but not from the more general class of parole identified in *Morrissey*. The program differed from parole in name alone, so a pre-parolee was entitled to constitutional protection.

An inmate's claim against the chairperson of a state parole division was dismissed, even though the inmate believed that his testimony at a parole revocation hearing established exceptional mitigating circumstances that should have been taken into account. Further, the inmate confirmed that he received timely notice of the hearing and pled guilty to numerous parole violations. He only argued that the chairman was involved in violations in his supervisory capacity. Failure to plead personal involvement in the alleged discrimination was fatally defective.[70]

A claim against a parole board chairperson in her individual capacity was dismissed where the claim was based entirely on her question at parole hearing, "Have you been practicing a lot of voodoo and black magic?" The inmate believed that this question ruined his chance for parole. In asking the question, the chairperson was acting in an adjudicatory capacity and within the scope of her official duties. Consequently, she was afforded absolute immunity.[71]

§ 9.4.1 —Arrest and Preliminary Hearing

The first step in the parole revocation process is the arrest of the parolee. This can occur either by arrest on new criminal charges, or at the direction of a parole officer for a breach of the terms of parole. There is usually a substantial period of time between arrest and the eventual determination by the parole authority that parole should be revoked. Further, the parolee is often arrested at a place far distant from the prison to which he or she may be returned prior to the formal action of the parole authority.

Given these circumstances, the United States Supreme Court held in *Morrissey v. Brewer* that:

> [D]ue process would seem to require that some minimal inquiry be conducted at or reasonably near the place of the alleged parole violation or arrest and as promptly as convenient after arrest while information is fresh and sources are available.[72]

The inquiry required is in the nature of a "preliminary hearing," in which it must be determined that there is probable cause or reasonable grounds to believe that the arrested parolee has committed acts that would constitute a violation of the conditions of parole. Therefore, *Morrissey* deals with both the "place" and the "promptness" of the initial inquiry. Of these two, the prompt-

---

[70] Alsaifullah v. Travis, 160 F. Supp. 2d 417 (E.D.N.Y. 2001).
[71] Nicolas v. Rhode Island, 160 F. Supp. 2d 229 (D.R.I. 2001). *See also* §8.1 *supra*.
[72] 408 U.S. 471 at 485. *But see* Moody v. Daggett, 429 U.S. 78 (1976).

ness issue has triggered considerable litigation. In addition, questions have arisen as to what proceedings may serve as a "substitute" for the *Morrissey* preliminary hearing. "Promptness" has been determined by statute in some jurisdictions.[73] Other parole authorities have had "promptness" defined for them by the courts.[74] Nevertheless, the entire revocation process should ideally be completed within two months because *Morrissey* stated that this was not an unreasonable period.

Another problem that has arisen concerning the timing of both the preliminary and the final *Morrissey* revocation hearing occurs when a parolee is held in a different jurisdiction for criminal acts committed while on parole and the paroling authority has issued a detainer against the parolee. The issue is whether the issuance of the detainer triggers the requirement for a "prompt" revocation hearing. *Moody v. Daggett*[75] solved the dilemma by holding that there is no requirement for an immediate hearing. The loss of liberty stems from the new conviction and thus the detainer has no immediate effect. Parole authorities may therefore hold the warrant for either execution or dismissal at the completion of the term of the new sentence. It is at that time that the *Morrissey* standard applies.[76]

The United States Parole Commission and Reorganization Act[77] states that imprisonment cannot be used as an excuse for not issuing a detainer against a parole violator, but when new criminal charges are pending, the issuance may be delayed until disposition of the new charge. When a parolee has been convicted of a crime committed while on parole and is serving a new sentence and a detainer has been placed against him or her, a revocation hearing must be held within 180 days of the placement of the detainer, or upon his or her release, whichever occurs first.

Some courts have determined that preliminary hearings on new criminal charges may serve as the *Morrissey* preliminary hearing.[78] The parolee must, however, receive prior notification that the criminal hearing will serve as a substitute. Other situations have been held sufficient to substitute for the *Morrissey* preliminary hearing. Foremost among these is when the parolee is convicted of a new crime. In *United States v. Tucker,*[79] the court stated that when a probationer was incarcerated pursuant to a final conviction at the time of the attempted probation revocation, there was no requirement that there be a preliminary as well as a final probation revocation hearing. This has been held to

---

[73]   Michigan, M.S.A. § 28.2310 (1).

[74]   Thompson v. McEvoy, 337 N.Y.S.2d 83 (1972); State v. Sylvester, 401 So. 2d 1123 (Fla. Dist. Ct. App. 1981); Commonwealth v. Boykin, 411 A.2d 1244 (Pa. Super. 1979).

[75]   429 U.S. 78 (1976).

[76]   Reese v. United States Board of Parole, 530 F.2d 231 (9th Cir. 1976); Gaddy v. Michael, 519 F.2d 699 (4th Cir. 1975); Small v. Britton, 500 F.2d 299 (10th Cir. 1974); Moody v. Daggett, 429 U.S. 78 (1976).

[77]   Appendix I §§ 4213 and 4214. The Act was subsequently repealed and replaced by the Sentencing Reform Act of 1984.

[78]   Inmates' Councilmatic Voice v. Rogers, 541 F.2d 633 (6th Cir. 1976); In re Law, 513 P.2d 621 (Cal. Sup. Ct. 1973); Battle v. Commonwealth, Pennsylvania Board of Probation and Parole, 403 A.2d 1063 (Pa. Commw. Ct. 1979); Commonwealth v. Del Conte, 419 A.2d 780 (Pa. Super. 1980).

[79]   524 F.2d 77 (5th Cir. 1975).

apply even though the conviction is under appeal. However, if the conviction is reversed, logic would suggest that a prompt hearing be held at that time. In *Wells v. Wise,*[80] however, the court held that even though the fact of a violation has already been conclusively determined either by a conviction or an admission, a hearing must be held.

Where a parole board has relied on criminal proceedings as a substitute for the *Morrissey* preliminary hearing, and the parolee was acquitted of the charge, at least one court[81] has held that the parole board was "collaterally estopped" from revoking parole based on the same set of facts. The court held that such a revocation violated the doctrine of collateral estoppel as contained in the double jeopardy clause of the Fifth Amendment.[82] The court rejected the state's argument that the lesser burden of proof (preponderance of evidence) at the revocation hearing permitted the parole board to revoke parole based on the same facts presented at the criminal trial, in which the burden of proof was "beyond a reasonable doubt."

In contrast, the court in *In re Coughlin*[83] held that a court, at a probation revocation hearing, or the Adult Authority, at a parole revocation hearing, may properly consider evidence indicating that a probationer or parolee has committed another criminal offense during the period of his or her probation or parole, despite the fact that he or she was acquitted of the criminal charge at trial.[84] Further, in *Standlee v. Rhay,*[85] the court of appeals held that the doctrine of collateral estoppel did not prohibit the parole board from finding the parolee guilty of a parole violation even after the accused had been acquitted in a criminal trial on the same charges. Parole revocation proceedings require a lower standard of proof than criminal adjudicatory proceedings. This may result in the revocation of parole even though the accused is found not guilty of the charges at the trial level.

The split in opinion centers around the different burden of proof requirements for a criminal trial and a revocation proceeding, and the nature of the proceeding itself. It has been stated that proof beyond a reasonable doubt of the violation of a condition of probation is not required by statute or the Constitution in a revocation proceeding.[86] In spite of this recognized difference in the burden of proof, some courts have imposed the criminal acquittal as a final

---

[80] 390 F. Supp. 229 (C.D. Cal. 1975).

[81] Standlee v. Rhay, 403 F. Supp. 1247 (E.D. Wash. 1975).

[82] *See also* Barrows v. Hogan, 379 F. Supp. 314 (M.D. Pa. 1974); People v. Grayson, 319 N.E.2d 43 (Ill. 1974), *cert. denied,* 421 U.S. 994 (1975); *cf.* People ex rel. Murray v. New York State Board of Parole, 417 N.Y.S.2d 286 (N.Y. App. Div. 1979) and People ex rel. Froats v. Hammock, 443 N.Y.S.2d 500 (N.Y. App. Div. 1981).

[83] 545 P.2d 249 (Cal. 1976)

[84] United States ex rel. Carrasquillo v. Thomas, 527 F. Supp. 1105 (S.D.N.Y. 1981), *aff'd,* 677 F.2d 225 (2d Cir. 1982). (The fact that an indictment was dismissed with prejudice did not preclude a parole revocation proceeding resting upon the same allegations as those contained in the indictment); *See also* In re Dunham, 545 P.2d 255 (Cal. 1976); Standlee v. Smith, 518 P.2d 721 (Wash. 1974).

[85] 557 F.2d 1303 (9th Cir. 1977).

[86] State v. Rasler, 532 P.2d 1077 (Kan. Sup. Ct. 1975); People ex rel. Walker v. Hammock, 435 N.Y.S.2d 410 (N.Y. App. Div. 1981); Avery v. State, 616 P.2d 872 (Alaska 1980).

decision for the parole board. This appears to be too broad, because a technical violation of parole that occurred in the same factual setting as the criminal charge would be precluded from consideration by the parole board in the revocation hearing. In addition, the United States Supreme Court suggested in *Baxter v. Palmigiano*[87] that a prison disciplinary hearing was not a criminal proceeding, but a civil proceeding, and authorized a prison court to hold a disciplinary hearing while state criminal charges were pending, both of which involved the same facts. Although the law is not clear, it can be argued that the revocation of parole is not a criminal proceeding, that the civil standards for burden of proof (preponderance of the evidence) should apply at the revocation hearing, and the doctrine of double jeopardy should not apply.

The United States Parole Commission and Reorganization Act stated in Section 4214(b)(1) that conviction for a federal, state or local crime committed subsequent to release on parole shall constitute probable cause for the purposes of a preliminary hearing. Furthermore, if a full revocation hearing is held on-site "promptly" after the detainer is filed, there would appear to be no justifiable reason for requiring two hearings.[88] At least one court has held that when a probationer is not "in custody," there is no requirement for a preliminary hearing.[89] Further, pending criminal proceedings justify a delay.[90]

Federal authorities may, pursuant to a general policy, wait until after state sentencing proceedings are completed before instituting federal probation revocation proceedings. Further, a plea agreement between the defendant and state prosecutors, contemplating that the state sentence would run concurrently with the federal sentence for the probation violation, was not binding on the federal court.[91]

Subsequent to the arrest, due process now requires that the determination that reasonable grounds exist for parole revocation be made by someone not directly involved in the case. Although it is recognized that a conscientious supervising parole officer will interview the parolee, confront him or her with the reasons for revocation, and bear no personal hostility toward the parolee, the officer directly involved in making recommendations cannot always have complete objectivity in evaluating the status of the parolee. This contention is not to attribute improper motivation to the officer. "Parole agents are human, and it is possible that friction between the agent and parolee may have influenced the agent's judgment."[92]

---

[87]   425 U.S. 308 (1976).

[88]   People v. Gulley, 238 N.W.2d 421 (Mich. Ct. App. 1975).

[89]   United States v. Scuito, 531 F.2d 842 (7th Cir. 1976); *See also* Pearson v. State, 241 N.W.2d 490 (Minn. Sup. Ct. 1976); People ex rel. Spinks v. Dillon 416 N.Y.S.2d 942 (1979) and Board of Trustees of Youth Correctional Institution Complex v. Smalls, 410 A.2d 691 (N.J. Super. A.D. 1979).

[90]   Hall v. Ohio, 535 F. Supp. 1121 (S.D. Ohio 1982) (An indictment returned by a grand jury eliminated the necessity of conducting a preliminary parole violation hearing until such time as the parolee was acquitted on the criminal charges.); United States v. Bazzano, 712 F.2d 826 (3d Cir. 1982) (Probation proceedings in federal court should await completion of the criminal trial resolving the underlying substantive charges, unless the probationer requests otherwise, or the government shows a compelling contrary need).

[91]   United States v. Sackinger, 704 F.2d 29 (2d Cir. 1983).

[92]   Morrissey v. Brewer, 408 U.S. at 486.

Because the granting and revoking of parole are decisions traditionally made by administrative personnel, the reviewing officer need not be a judicial officer or a lawyer. The only requirement is that the reviewing officer be a person other than the one who initially supervised the parolee or caused his or her arrest.

It will be sufficient, therefore, in the parole revocation context, if an evaluation of whether reasonable cause exists to believe that conditions of parole have been violated is made by someone, such as a parole officer, other than the one who has made the report of parole violations or has recommended revocation.[93]

At the preliminary hearing, the parolee must be given notice that the hearing will take place and that its purpose is to determine whether there is probable cause to believe that he has committed a parole violation. The parole conditions alleged to have been violated must be stated in the notice. At the hearing, the parolee has the right to appear and to speak in his or her own behalf. Further, he or she may bring letters, documents, or witnesses who are able to give relevant information to the hearing officer. If the parolee asks to question in his or her presence persons who have given adverse information upon which the revocation is to be based, the request must be granted, unless the hearing officer determines that the adverse witness or informant would risk harm if his or her identity were disclosed.

Finally, the hearing officer must make a summary of the proceedings, including the responses of the parolee, the substance of the documents or evidence given in support of revocation, and the parolee's position. Based upon such information, the hearing officer must then determine whether there is probable cause to hold the parolee for the parole authority's final decision on revocation. Thereafter, the parolee may lawfully be continued in detention and returned to prison pending the final decision of the parole authority.

§ 9.4.2 —The Revocation Hearing

The *Morrissey* holding requires that the parolee be given the opportunity for a hearing, if he or she so desires, prior to the final decision or revocation by the parole authority.

The revocation hearing must lead to a final evaluation of any contested relevant facts, and must consider whether the facts, as determined, warrant parole revocation.

Minimum due process at the parole revocation hearing now requires that the parolee be given an opportunity to be heard and to show, if he or she is able, that he or she did not violate the conditions of his or her parole, or, if he or she did, the mitigating circumstances that might suggest that the violation does not warrant revocation.

Although the Supreme Court requires the revocation hearing to be made within a reasonable period after the parolee is taken into custody, two months was not deemed unreasonable.

---

[93]   *Id.*

§ 9.4.3 —Procedural Due Process at the Revocation Hearing

To conform with the requirements of due process, the following procedure must be followed in a parole revocation hearing:

1. There must be written notice of the claimed violations of parole;

2. The evidence against the parolee must be disclosed to him or her;

3. The parolee must be given the opportunity to be heard in person and to present witnesses and documentary evidence;

4. The parolee has the right to confront and cross-examine adverse witnesses, unless the parole authority specifically finds good cause for not allowing confrontation, such as a risk of harm to the informant if his or her identity were disclosed;

5. The hearing body, such as a traditional parole board, must be neutral and detached, but need not be judicial officers or lawyers;

6. The parole authority must compose a written statement as to the evidence it relied on and the reasons for revoking the parole.[94]

There was no intent by the Supreme Court to equate the revocation hearing to a formal criminal prosecution. Further, a process flexible enough to consider material that would be inadmissible in an adversary criminal trial, such as letters and affidavits, was sanctioned. Also, the power of the parole authorities over the proceedings was authorized to assure that the delaying tactics and other abuses often present in traditional criminal trials do not occur. In any case, a parolee cannot use the revocation hearing to relitigate issues decided against him or her in other forums, such as when the revocation is based on conviction of another crime.

§ 9.4.4 —The Revocation Hearing— Right to Counsel

In *Morrissey*, the Supreme Court stated: "We do not reach or decide the question whether the parolee is entitled to the assistance of retained counsel or to appointed counsel if he is indigent."[95] The Supreme Court answered that question in *Gagnon v. Scarpelli*.[96]

---

[94] Atkins v. Marshall, 533 F. Supp. 1324 (S.D. Ohio 1982) (A parolee's rights at a revocation hearing were violated when there was a disparity in the notice of reasons for revocation and the parole board's asserted grounds for revocation.); Morishita v. Morris, 702 F.2d 207 (10th Cir. 1983) (Written findings in a probation revocation hearing are constitutionally required only when the record is such that a reviewing court is unable to determine the reasons for revocation. Failure to make written findings does not violate a probationer's due process rights when the revocation is based upon a single ground).

[95] Morrissey v. Brewer, 408 U.S. at 389.

[96] 411 U.S. 778 (1973).

In *Scarpelli,* the United States Supreme Court dealt with the question of whether a previously sentenced probationer was entitled to be represented by state-appointed counsel at a probation revocation hearing. As to parole revocation, the Court relied heavily on *Morrissey v. Brewer,* and stated that it could not perceive any relevant difference between the revocation of parole and the revocation of probation.

The court recognized that despite the informal nature of the proceedings and the absence of technical rules of procedure or evidence, an unskilled or uneducated probationer or parolee might have difficulty presenting his or her version of a disputed set of facts without the aid of a lawyer. This was recognized to be particularly true in cases in which the proceedings required the examining or cross-examining of witnesses, or the offering or dissecting of complex documentary evidence. However, the Court did not mandate that counsel be appointed for every parolee in every case, but held that "the need for counsel must be made on a case-by-case basis in the exercise of a sound discretion by the state authority charged with responsibility for administering the probation and parole system."[97]

The Court set no firm guidelines as to when counsel must be provided, but said that the state should do so where the indigent probationer or parolee may have difficulty presenting his or her version of disputed facts or, if the violation is not disputed, there are substantial reasons in justification or mitigation that make revocation inappropriate. The Court did hold that "in every case in which a request for counsel at a preliminary or final hearing is refused, the grounds for refusal should be stated succinctly in the record."[98]

Courts dealing with the issue of counsel at revocation proceedings have not found *Scarpelli* helpful. The Supreme Court of Indiana, in *Russell v. Douthitt,*[99] stated that the suggestion that appointment of counsel be made on a case-by-case basis serves to "delude and only becloud the issue and create uncertainty as to what the law is."[100] The court finally threw up its hands and held:

> In our opinion, "on a case-by-case basis" means that those involved in parole revocation can take no other course than to appoint counsel in all cases and to have a full-blown trial for every alleged charge of parole violation.[101]

---

[97] *Id.* at 790.
[98] *Id.* at 791.
[99] 304 N.E.2d 793 (Ind. 1973).
[100] *Id.* at 794.
[101] *Id.*

§ 9.4.5   —The Revocation Hearing—
Right to Appointed Counsel

Related to the issue of the right to counsel is the right to appointed counsel for the parolee if he or she cannot afford to hire one with private funds. It is arguable that counsel must be provided in all cases in which retained counsel is permitted. In other words, if the state permits counsel to participate at parole revocation hearings for those who can afford it, it should provide counsel at state expense for those who cannot afford representation.

The majority of cases still find that the question of whether a revocation proceeding involving a particular parolee is one that requires counsel is to be determined in the first instance by the paroling authority. The decision is to be made on a case-by-case basis in the exercise of sound discretion and on the guidelines set forth in *Scarpelli*.[102] In contrast, when a revocation proceeding amounts to a resentencing, appointment of counsel for an indigent person is required under *Mempa v. Rhay* and not under the discretionary standards of *Scarpelli*.[103]

When the facts show that counsel is required, it has been held that lack of authority or funds by a state parole commission to appoint counsel is not a legally sufficient reason for refusing to appoint counsel for a parolee.[104] Some states have provided for counsel under the guidelines of *Scarpelli* by regulation or statute. The right to counsel at the preliminary hearing in New York is the same test as *Scarpelli*, a case-by-case approach, but the New York rule on final revocation proceedings guarantees the right to counsel.[105] In Indiana, the Supreme Court has declared that counsel is required in all cases.[106]

Scarpelli states that access to counsel is a presumptive right only, but *Preston v. Piggman*[107] held that the burden is on the paroling authority to overcome that presumption. A silent record containing no reasons for denying counsel, or not providing counsel, would open the possibility for a reversal of the proceedings. It would appear that the presumptive right to counsel could be overcome when the parolee is made aware of the charges against him or her, and the record shows that he or she understands the nature of the proceedings and is capable of adequately expressing him or herself and explaining the circumstances. Under *Scarpelli*, it is also clear that the presumptive right to counsel applies to both preliminary and final revocation hearings.

---

[102] Cottle v. Wainwright, 493 F.2d 397 (5th Cir. 1974).

[103] United States v. Ross, 503 F.2d 940 (5th Cir. 1974).

[104] Rhodes v. Wainwright, 378 F. Supp. 329 (M.D. Fla. 1974).

[105] People ex rel. Donohoe v. Montanye, 318 N.E.2d 781 (N.Y. 1974).

[106] *Supra* at nn. 61 and 62; *cf.* Passaro v. Commonwealth, Pennsylvania Board of Probation and Parole, 424 A.2d 561 (Pa. Commw. 1981) (The Board has no duty or responsibility to appoint counsel for an indigent appearing before it.); Gates v. DeLorenzo, 544 F.2d 82 (2d Cir. 1976), *cert. denied,* 430 U.S. 941 (1977) (Due process does not require the participation of counsel in parole release hearings).

[107] 496 F.2d 270 (6th Cir. 1974).

§ 9.4.6 —Evidence at the Revocation Hearing

Morrissey provides that at the preliminary hearing, "a parolee may appear and speak in his own behalf; he may bring letters, documents, or individuals who can give relevant information to the hearing officer." The court pointed out that the hearing officer should state the reasons for his or her decision and the evidence upon which he or she relied. Because the preliminary hearing is not a final determination, there is no requirement of "formal findings of fact and conclusions of law" at that stage.

As to the final hearing, *Morrissey* states that the inquiry involved is a narrow one. "The process should be flexible enough to consider evidence including letters, affidavits, and other material that would not be admissible in an adversary criminal trial."[108]

In *Scarpelli,* the court makes a distinction between a criminal trial and the revocation hearing.

> In a criminal trial, the State is represented by a prosecutor; formal rules of evidence are in force; a defendant enjoys a number of procedural rights which may be lost if not timely raised; and, in a jury trial, a defendant must make a presentation understandable to untrained jurors. In short, a criminal trial under our system is an adversary proceeding with its own unique characteristics. In a revocation hearing, on the other hand, the State is represented not by a prosecutor, but by a parole officer . . .; formal procedures and rules of evidence are not employed; and the members of the hearing body are familiar with the problems and practice of probation or parole.[109]

The references in *Morrissey* and *Scarpelli* to a revocation hearing as a proceeding not subject to the formal rules of evidence applicable to a criminal trial have raised the question of whether hearsay evidence will be permitted in evidence at the revocation hearing. In simple terms, hearsay is a statement made by someone outside of the hearing, offered at the hearing to prove the truth of the statement. Hearsay may be a statement, conduct, or a writing. The main objection to hearsay is that the person who made the original statement is not available at the hearing to be questioned or cross-examined. Therefore, hearsay evidence cannot be tested for its truthfulness. However, the courts have recognized that hearsay can be admitted under circumstances that assure truthfulness. There are, therefore, many exceptions to the hearsay rule.[110] Al-

---

[108]   Morrissey v. Brewer, 408 U.S. at 489.

[109]   Gagnon v. Scarpelli, 411 U.S. 778 at 789.

[110]   Federal Rules of Evidence, Appendix II, Rules 803 and 804.

though courts have permitted hearsay to be considered at revocation hearings,[111] there is judicial reluctance to accept hearsay at revocation hearings[112] as the sole basis of the final decision.

The United States Supreme Court held in a 5-4 decision that the federal exclusionary rule does not bar the introduction of evidence seized in violation of parolees' Fourth Amendment rights at parole revocation hearings.[113] The State's use of such evidence did not violate the Constitution.

A person was released on parole on the condition that he could not own or possess any weapons. Suspecting a violation, parole officers entered his home and found firearms, a bow, and arrows. After a hearing, the parolee was recommitted to prison, even though the parole officers obtained the evidence against him from an alleged unlawful search under the Fourth Amendment. The Supreme Court ruled that it would not apply the exclusionary rule even though the search violated the Fourth Amendment.

Taking a restricted view toward the exclusionary rule, the Court held that a violation of the Fourth Amendment is "fully accomplished" by the illegal search or seizure and no exclusion of evidence can cure the invasion of rights a person has already suffered. The exclusionary rule is a judicially created means of deterring illegal searches and seizures. There is no provision in the Constitution prohibiting the introduction of illegally seized evidence in all proceedings or against all persons, but applies only in contexts in which its remedial objectives are thought to be most efficiently served. The rule is prudential rather than constitutionally mandated. It applies only when its deterrence benefits outweigh the substantial social costs inherent in precluding consideration of reliable, probative evidence. Consequently, the Supreme Court has repeatedly declined to extend the exclusionary rule to proceedings other than criminal trials.

The Court commented that the social costs of allowing convicted criminals who violate their parole to remain at large are particularly high and are compounded by the fact that parolees (particularly those who have already committed parole violations) are more likely to commit future crimes than are average citizens. Application of the exclusionary rule would be incompatible with the traditionally flexible, nonadversarial, administrative procedures of parole revocation in that it would require extensive litigation to determine whether particular evidence must be excluded. The exclusionary rule would provide only minimal deterrence benefits in this context. Its application in criminal trials already provides significant deterrence of unconstitutional searches. The Supreme Court has never suggested that the exclusionary rule must apply in every circumstance in which it might provide marginal deter-

---

[111] Commonwealth v. Kates, 305 A.2d 701 (Pa. 1973); Ward v. Parole Board, 192 N.W.2d 537 (Mich. Ct. App. 1971); Zizzo v. United States, 470 F.2d 105 (7th Cir. 1972); United States v. Miller, 514 F.2d 41 (9th Cir. 1975); State v. Marrapese, 409 A.2d 544 (R.I. 1979); cf. In re Diane B., 29 Cr. L. 2040 (D.C. Super. Ct. 1981) (Hearsay evidence may not be used in the D.C. court to revoke a juvenile's probation).

[112] State v. Miller, 42 Ohio St. 2d 102 (1975); Birzon v. King, 469 F.2d 1241 (2d Cir. 1972); People v. Lewis, 329 N.E.2d 390 (Ill. App. Ct. 1975); People ex rel. Wallace v. State, 417 N.Y.S.2d 531 (N.Y. App. Div. 1979); Anaya v. State, 606 P.2d 156 (Nev. 1980).

[113] Pennsylvania Board of Probation and Parole v. Scott, 524 U.S. 357 (1998).

rence. Such a piecemeal approach would add an additional layer of collateral litigation regarding an officer's knowledge of the parolee's status. In any event, any additional deterrence would be minimal, whether the person conducting the search was a police officer or a parole officer.

It is becoming increasingly apparent that the record of the hearing is of utmost importance. If the record clearly shows what evidence was relied on and that the evidence was reasonably related to the decision of a finding of probable cause, or the revocation of parole, then the decision has a much higher chance of survival. When the record does not disclose the reasons and evidence upon which the decision is based, or why hearsay rather than live testimony was used, the courts are more likely to reverse the decision.

It should be noted that rights are subject to waiver. However, courts will not approve a waiver unless it has been a voluntary waiver of a known right. It is important that the record reflect that the person waiving the right understood what he or she was doing.

The Fifth and Fourteenth Amendments do not prohibit the introduction of the admissions of a probationer to his or her probation officer into evidence in a criminal trial. In *Minnesota v. Murphy,* after being convicted of a felony, the defendant was placed on probation. The terms of probation required him to participate in a treatment program, to report to his probation officer periodically, and to be truthful with the officer in all matters. While being interviewed by his probation officer concerning a prior rape and murder, the defendant confessed and was subsequently convicted. The conviction was affirmed. The general obligation to appear before the probation officer and answer questions truthfully did not in itself convert the defendant's otherwise voluntary statements into compelled ones. There was no duty to give *Miranda* warnings. When confronted with questions that the probation officer should reasonably expect to elicit incriminating evidence, the probationer must assert the Fifth Amendment privilege rather than answer if he desires not to incriminate himself. If he chose to answer rather than to assert the privilege, his choice is considered voluntary. He was free to claim the privilege and suffers no penalty as a result of his decision to do so. Because there was no formal arrest or restraint on his freedom of movement associated with formal arrest, the probationer was not "in custody." The probationer's failure to claim the privilege in a timely manner is not excused by the fact that the probation officer could compel the probationer's attendance and truthful answers, and consciously sought incriminating evidence, that the probationer did not expect questions about his prior criminal conduct, could not seek counsel before attending the meeting, and that there were no observers to guard against abuse or trickery. Further, the reasonably perceived threat of revocation of his probation does not deter the probationer from claiming the privilege. The legal compulsion to attend the meeting with the probation officer and to truthfully answer the questions of the officer who anticipated incriminating answers was held to be indistinguishable from that felt by any witness who is required to appear and to give testimony. Fear of revocation is not an impermissible penalty so as to trigger *Miranda.*

The fact that the statements made by a probationer to his or her probation officer could well lead to revocation of probation does not mean that the statements are "compelled." Although it is recognized that a state may not impose substantial penalties because a witness elects to exercise his or her Fifth Amendment rights, the rule does not apply in probation cases in which the questioning concerns violations of the terms and conditions of release. A state may require a probationer to appear and discuss matters that affect his or her probationary status. Such a request alone does not give rise to a self-executing privilege. An example would be when a residential restriction is imposed as a condition of probation. Because a violation of this restriction would not be a criminal act, a claim of refusal to answer on Fifth Amendment grounds would be improper.

> Just as there is no right to a jury trial before probation may be revoked, neither is the privilege against compelled self-incrimination available to a probationer. . . . [A] state may validly insist on answers to even incriminating questions and hence sensibly administer its probation system, as long as it recognizes that the required answers may not be used in a criminal proceeding. . . . [N]othing in the Federal Constitution would prevent a State from revoking probation for a refusal to answer that violated an express condition of probation or from using the probationer's silence as 'one of a number of factors to be considered by a finder of fact' in deciding whether other conditions of probation have been violated.

The result would have been opposite had the questioning related solely to new criminal charges not concerning the terms and conditions of probation, or had the probationer been told that his probation would be revoked if he exercised his valid Fifth Amendment rights concerning the new crimes.[114]

Although as an aside and in the context of a confession case, the United States Supreme Court suggested that drug treatment centers receiving federal funds are covered by federal statutes that provide for the confidentiality of patient records. A counselor may inform a patient's probation officer of incriminating statements made by the patient, but may not relate such statements to the police. It was also suggested that the probation officer could not have made the counselor's information available for use in a criminal prosecution.

The voiding of parole because of the failure of the parolee to voluntarily disclose information regarding a pre-parole conspiracy for which he was convicted, violated his Fifth Amendment right against self-incrimination.[115]

If the District Court decides, or the government insists that probation revocation proceedings be held first, the defendant should be given use immunity to testify in the revocation proceedings. This decision was based on the court's supervisory powers and not on constitutional grounds. The exclusion-

---

[114] Minnesota v. Murphy, 465 U.S. 420 (1984).
[115] Tortora v. Petrovsky, 545 F. Supp. 569 (W.D. Mo. 1982).

ary rules of evidence are not to be applied to probation revocation proceedings because the application of the exclusionary rule would do little to deter constitutional violations.[116]

§ 9.4.7 —Rescission of Parole

"Rescission" of parole raises the question of the due process rights of an inmate who has been given a "future parole date," but subsequently has that date changed or withdrawn. There would appear to be three alternatives. First, to consider the "loss" as a revocation, and apply the standards of *Morrissey-Scarpelli*. Second, to equate the "loss" to a prison disciplinary finding, and apply the standards of *Wolff v. McDonnell*.[117] Third, to treat the "loss" as a denial of parole, and apply the same standards as those applicable to parole hearings in general.

At one time, the grant of parole could be summarily rescinded without notice or a hearing prior to final physical release, unless a statute or regulation provided otherwise. The courts, however, have recognized that although the loss of liberty is more grievous to a parolee out on the street, taking away a future parole date clearly seems to be a grievous loss subject to some minimal due process protections.[118]

In *Jackson v. Wise*,[119] the court analogized the rescission of parole to a prison hearing subject to the requirements of *Wolff v. McDonnell*, and determined that the following were the minimum due process requirements for rescission:

1.   advance written notice of the charge;

2.   written statement by fact finders of the evidence relied on and the reasons for their decision;

3.   right of prisoner to be present;

4.   right of prisoner to present witnesses and documentary evidence on his behalf, if so doing would not be unduly hazardous to institutional safety or correctional goals;

5.   the right, if the prisoner is found to be illiterate or otherwise incompetent to protect his own interests, to have an attorney-substitute; and

6.   adjudication of the charges by a panel sufficiently impartial to satisfy due process requirements. Other decisions have also found that minimum due process must accompany the rescission of parole.[120]

---

[116]   United States v. Bazzano, 712 F.2d 826 (3d Cir. 1982). The *Bazzano* decision was not followed in United States v. Dozier, 707 F.2d 862 (5th Cir. 1982) (Specifically, the probationer had no constitutional right to be granted judicial immunity for any testimony that he might be willing to give at the probation revocation hearing).

[117]   418 U.S. 539, 71 Ohio Op. 2d 336 (1974).

[118]   Lepre v. Butler, 394 F. Supp. 185 (E.D. Pa. 1975).

[119]   390 F. Supp. 19 (C.D. Cal. 1974).

[120]   *Id.* at 21. *See also* Karger v. Sigler, 384 F. Supp. 10 (D. Mass. 1974); Batchelder v. Kenton, 383 F. Supp. 299 (C.D. Cal. 1974).

However, in *Williams v. United States Board of Parole*,[121] the court required the full procedural requirements of *Morrissey* and *Scarpelli*.

There are also decisions that follow the earlier view that a future date of parole may be rescinded summarily without notice, or a hearing, until the time that the inmate has been physically released from custody of the institution.[122] Also, where a prisoner had escaped and was not returned until after his parole release date, a state court held that he was not entitled to a full-scale hearing.[123]

Beginning in 1983, the Florida legislature enacted a series of statutes authorizing the award of early release credits to prison inmates when the state prison population exceeded predetermined levels. In 1986, an inmate received a 22-year prison sentence on a charge of attempted murder. In 1992, he was released, based on the determination that he had accumulated five different types of early release credits totaling 5,668 days, including 1,860 days of "provisional credits" awarded as a result of prison overcrowding. Shortly thereafter, the state attorney general issued an opinion interpreting a 1992 statute as having retroactively canceled all provisional credits awarded to inmates convicted of murder and attempted murder. The inmate was therefore rearrested and returned to custody. He filed a habeas corpus petition alleging that the retroactive cancellation of provisional credits violated the ex post facto clause of the United States Constitution. The United States Supreme Court held that the 1992 statute canceling provisional release credits violated the ex post facto clause.[124]

To fall within the ex post facto prohibition, a law must be retrospective and disadvantage the offender affected by, among other things, increasing the punishment for the crime. The operation of the 1992 statute was clearly retrospective, and it obviously disadvantaged the inmate by increasing his punishment.

The Supreme Court also rejected an argument that the inmate was not entitled to relief because his provisional overcrowding credits were awarded pursuant to statutes enacted after the date of his offense rather than pursuant to the 1983 statute. Although the overcrowding statute in effect at the time of his crime was slightly modified in subsequent years, its basic elements remained the same, and the changes did not affect his core ex post facto claim.

§ 9.5 Probation

Probation is a fundamentally different concept from parole. In general, probation is controlled by the court either at the time of sentencing or post-sentencing while the court still has jurisdiction over the offender. Revocation of

---

[121] 383 F. Supp. 402 (D. Conn. 1974).

[122] Sexton v. Wise, 494 F.2d 1176 (5th Cir. 1974); McIntosh v. Woodward, 514 F.2d 95 (5th Cir. 1975); State ex rel. Van Curen v. Ohio Adult Parole Authority, 45 Ohio St. 2d 298 (1976); Van Curen v. Jago, 454 U.S. 14 (1981) (When a state does not make parole a "right," the rescission of parole without a hearing violates no constitutional rights of the prisoner).

[123] Temple v. Smith, 548 P.2d 1274 (Utah Sup. Ct. 1976).

[124] Lynce v. Mathis, 519 U.S. 433, 117 S. Ct. 891 (1997).

probation is controlled by the court, whereas revocation of parole is controlled by an administrative agency that is part of the executive branch of government.

In federal practice, probation is controlled by statute under the Sentencing Guidelines. The guidelines have caused the federal judiciary much difficulty in their interpretation and application. One example is *United States v. Granderson*.[125]

A mail carrier was sentenced to five years' probation and a fine. However, after he tested positive for cocaine, the court resentenced him under 18 U.S.C. § 3565(a), which provides that if a person serving a sentence of probation possesses illegal drugs, the court shall revoke the sentence of probation and sentence the defendant to not less than one-third of the original sentence. Accepting the government's reading of the statute, a District Court concluded that the phrase "original sentence" referred to the term of probation actually imposed (60 months), rather than the zero to six-month imprisonment range authorized by the Sentencing Guidelines. The United States Supreme Court held that the minimum revocation sentence under § 3565(a)'s drug-possession proviso is one-third the maximum of the originally applicable guidelines range of imprisonment, and the maximum revocation sentence is the guidelines' maximum. The proviso mandates imprisonment, not renewed probation, as the required type of punishment. The contrast in §§ 3565(a)(1) and (2) between "continuing" and "revoking" probation as the alternative punishments for a defendant who violates a probation condition suggests that a revocation sentence must be a sentence of imprisonment, not a continuation of probation. Moreover, the court felt that it would be absurd to punish drug-possessing probationers by revoking their probation and imposing a new term of probation no longer than the original. The "original sentence" that sets the duration of the revocation sentence is the applicable Guidelines sentence of imprisonment, not the revoked term of probation.

The benchmark for the revocation sentence under the proviso is the maximum Guidelines sentence of imprisonment. Therefore, because the probationer's maximum revocation sentence under the proviso was six months, and because he had already served 11 months' imprisonment, the probationer was released.

§ 9.6 Conditions of Release

One of the more difficult issues regarding the legal status of parolees is what rights the individual has while on parole. The conditions attached to the issuance of parole frequently conflict with the retained constitutional rights of the parolee.

The "contract" rationale is frequently used as a justification for revocation of parole after a violation of a particular condition. The acceptance of conditional release is said to prevent the parolee from later claiming that one of the conditions imposed was invalid. This contract theory may be discredited, how-

---

[125] 511 U.S. 39 (1994).

ever, because the consent is *coerced*. However, most challenges to the legality of conditions continue to be dismissed by the courts by virtue of the contract theory.

It would appear that the only conditions that courts are likely to invalidate are those that require illegal, immoral, or impossible actions by the parolee. For example, if the pathological nature of one's alcoholism made it impossible to abstain from alcohol completely, a condition requiring complete abstention from alcohol would be invalidated as unreasonable.[126] Another condition that would usually be invalidated as unreasonable, even though possible of performance, is a condition of banishment.[127]

Requiring participation in psychological counseling as a condition of probation does not violate privacy rights.[128]

Due process is violated by the automatic revocation of probation because of an indigent probationer's failure to meet a condition of probation requiring him or her to pay a fine or make restitution. Absent findings that the probationer willfully refused to make bona fide efforts to pay or that alternate forms of punishment, other than imprisonment, are inadequate to meet the state's interests in punishment and deterrence, imprisonment violates the Fourteenth Amendment.[129]

A California juvenile court suspended a sentence of 15 weekends at a detention facility and placed a juvenile offender on probation, conditioned on his naming others involved in the crime. The order was valid.[130]

§ 9.6.1 —Free Speech and Conditions

It is more difficult to predict the validity of conditions that limit the parolee in areas in which free men enjoy broad constitutional rights. These rights, particularly First Amendment freedoms, are respected above other personal rights and thus the courts generally subject conditions that diminish these freedoms to more intensive review. For example, *Hyland v. Procunier*[131] held that a condition requiring a parolee to secure permission before making any public speech is invalid. Such a condition would have "an unwarranted chilling effect on the exercise by plaintiff of his undisputed rights."[132]

---

[126] Sweeney v. United States, 353 F.2d 10 (7th Cir. 1965); *See also cf.* State v. Cooper (N.C. Ct. App. 1981), 29 Cr. L. 2125 (A credit card defendant's condition of probation that he be forbidden to drive a car between midnight and 5:30 A.M. was held to be reasonably related to his offense and therefore valid).

[127] Bird v. State, 190 A.2d 804 (Md. Ct. App. 1963); *But cf.* State v. Morgan 28 Cr. L. 2260 (La. Sup. Ct. 1980) (A probation condition that required a woman convicted of attempted prostitution to stay out of the French Quarter was valid).

[128] United States v. Stine, 675 F.2d 69 (3d Cir. 1982).

[129] Bearden v. Georgia, 461 U.S. 660 (1983).

[130] People v. John W., 55 Cal. App. 4th 1 (1997).

[131] 311 F. Supp. 749 (N.D. Cal. 1970).

[132] *Id.* at 750; *See also* Barton v. Malley, 626 F.2d 151 (10th Cir. 1980).

A similar decision was handed down in *Sobell v. Reed,*[133] in which the parolee was denied the right to give an anti-war speech. The court found that this denial of First Amendment freedoms was beyond the parole authority. Such freedoms may be restricted only "upon a showing that such prevention or withholding of permission is necessary to safeguard against specific, concretely described and highly likely dangers of misconduct by plaintiff himself."[134]

In re Mannino[135] upheld a condition that prohibited speaking at and participating in public demonstrations because the probationer's offense (kicking a police officer) had occurred during the heat of such events. The reason for the condition was the explosive temperament of the defendant. However, a ban on writing and distributing written materials was held invalid because of a lack of relation to the underlying offense.

Similarly, a condition of probation that stipulated that the defendant not communicate with any of his children, except through the State Department of Welfare, and not have any of his children live with him until they reached 18 years of age, did not violate due process. The defendant had been convicted of aggravated crimes against nature, directed at his children.[136]

In *Commonwealth v. Power,*[137] a woman was placed on probation for 20 years with a special condition that she not profit from the sale of her story to the news media. The woman was placed on probation for her second conviction of armed robbery, an offense punishable by life imprisonment.

The probationer argued that the special condition quoted amounted to a prior restraint on content-based speech in violation of her First Amendment rights. This argument was rejected, although it was agreed that because the condition placed a financial disincentive on the probationer based on the content of her speech, it did implicate her First Amendment rights.[138] The condition in this case allowed the probationer to speak on any subject, including her crimes. The condition merely prohibited the defendant from profiting financially from speech about her crime or her experience as a fugitive.

According to the court, the purpose of the special condition was to deter convicted persons from seeking to profit directly or indirectly from criminality. The moral foundations of society are reinforced by the condition, the probationer (and others like her) are given to understand that the crime committed and her successful, albeit illegal, fugitive status of more than 23 years will bring neither reward, nor benefit, nor profit, and her rehabilitation and understanding of the depth of her criminality are enhanced.[139]

In an Illinois state court,[140] a condition of probation for a woman was that she not engage in any activity with the reasonable potential of causing preg-

---

133   327 F. Supp. 1294 (S.D.N.Y. 1971).
134   *Id.* at 1306.
135   92 Cal. Rptr. 880 (Cal. Ct. App. 1971).
136   State v. Credeur, 328 So. 2d 59 (La. 1976).
137   420 Mass. 410 (1995).
138   Simon & Schuster, Inc. v. New York Crime Victims Board, 502 U.S. 105 (1991).
139   *See also* United States v. Terrigno, 838 F.2d 371 (9th Cir. 1988).
140   Illinois v. Ferrell, No. 4-95-0383 (Ill. Ct. App. 4th Dist. 1995).

nancy. After a court-mandated pregnancy test indicated that the defendant was pregnant, the state filed a petition to revoke her probation. Following a hearing, the trial court determined that the probationer had violated the no-pregnancy condition, and revoked her probation.

The Illinois Supreme Court had earlier recognized that offenders necessarily have a reduced expectation of personal privacy[141] and approved a condition of probation requiring a pregnancy test every two months. This condition involved only a slight physical intrusion.[142] The condition was approved and revocation was proper.

Taylor v. Rhode Island Department of Corrections[143] involved a regulation that imposed a monthly supervision fee on criminal offenders sentenced to probation or parole. It was argued that application of the regulation to offenders who were sentenced to probation prior to the regulation violated the prohibition against *ex post facto* laws under Article I § 10 of the United States Constitution.

With respect to the *ex post facto* argument, the probationers alleged that the supervision fee flowed from the commission of the underlying crime and that the fee was punitive, as an additional requirement or condition of probation. The defendants asserted that the fee was not criminal punishment, but rather a civil surcharge. It was pointed out that *California Department of Corrections v. Morales*[144] did not discuss the question of when an additional fee, which is related to an already-imposed punishment, makes that punishment "more burdensome."

In this case, the probationers faced total supervision fees ranging from $180.00 to $1,620.00, even without any increases in the monthly fee amount. These were not insignificant amounts of money. Furthermore, the fact that the fee could be waived for those who could not afford it did not lessen the certainty of the fee's burden on those who did not meet the waiver criteria. Even those who could afford to have their rights violated were entitled to constitutional protections.

Consequently, the district court held that the nature of the supervision fee led inexorably to the conclusion that it did actually increase the burdens of the punishment. The probationers were placed on probation as a result of convictions for either felonies or misdemeanors. Thus, the probation was part of the punishment for the offense. At the time the probationers were convicted, they received sentences, including probation, which did not include any imposition of a monetary payment. Thus, each punishment was made significantly more burdensome than it was at the time of sentencing as a result of the imposition

---

[141] People v. Adams, 149 Ill. 2d 331 (1992).

[142] *See* Schmerber v. California, 384 U.S. 757, 771 (1966) (in which the Supreme Court approved the use of blood tests to detect the presence of alcohol, because such tests were commonplace in the days of periodic physical examinations and for most people the procedure involves virtually no risk, trauma, or pain); *see also* Adams, 149 Ill. 2d at 347, in which the blood test challenged was a minor, routine laboratory procedure, and it posed no threat to the health or safety of the individual tested.

[143] 908 F. Supp. 92 (D.R.I 1995).

[144] 514 U.S. 499 (1995).

of the fee. The court also held that the supervision fee was a condition of probation different from ordinary probation conditions. It was not merely a change in supervision policies or procedures but rather was a direct imposition of a substantial monetary obligation. This obligation was an additional imposition far beyond the scope of the already existing supervisory and conduct-oriented conditions of probation. It increased the burdens of the punishment in a very direct and concrete way. The ex post facto clause was violated.[145]

United States v. Lorenzini[146] concerned the issue of whether making the repayment of court-appointed attorney's fees a condition of probation violated 18 U.S.C. §3563(b). Because the court had early held that a district court could not make repayment of court-appointed attorney's fees a condition of supervised release,[147] the Ninth Circuit held that it was improper to order repayment of court-appointed attorney's fees as a condition of probation.

This has created a conflict in the Circuit Courts of Appeals that has not been resolved by the United States Supreme Court at the time of this writing. Both the First Circuit and the Seventh Circuit have found repayment to be a valid condition of probation. The First Circuit reasoned that such a condition "might be thought to bear a reasonable relationship to the treatment of the accused and the protection of the public."[148] The Seventh Circuit reasoned that the statute gave "the sentencing judge an exceptional degree of flexibility in determining probation conditions," and thus authorized district court orders for counsel fee reimbursement as a probation condition.[149] The Fifth Circuit and the Ninth Circuit are in accord that reimbursement of court-appointed counsel fees is not permitted as a condition of probation pursuant to 18 U.S.C. § 3651, because it is not among the conditions explicitly set forth in the probation statute.[150]

It should be noted that these federal case conflicts are based on the interpretation of a federal statute and not on constitutional grounds that would apply to state courts.

§ 9.6.2 —Search as a Condition

A difficult question is presented when the parolee's Fourth Amendment rights are involved. The Fourth Amendment protects citizens from unreasonable interference with their privacy by the government and generally requires that a warrant be obtained before a government official may undertake a search. However, there are exceptions. The Fourth Amendment prohibits only *unrea-*

---

[145] *See also* § 12.9, concerning *ex post facto* analysis.
[146] 71 F.3d 1489 (9th Cir. 1995).
[147] United States v. Eyler, 67 F.3d 1386, 1393-1394 (9th Cir. 1995).
[148] United States v. Santarpio, 560 F.2d 448, 455 (1st Cir.), *cert. denied,* 434 U.S. 984 (1977).
[149] United States v. Gurtunca, 836 F.2d 283, 287 (7th Cir. 1987); United States v. Allen, 596 F.2d 227, 232 and n. 6 (7th Cir.), *cert. denied,* 444 U.S. 871 (1979).
[150] United States v. Turner, 628 F.2d 461, 467 (5th Cir. 1980), *cert. denied sub nom.,* White v. United States, 451 U.S. 988 (1981); United States v. Jimenez, 600 F.2d 1172, 1174 (5th Cir.), *cert. denied,* 444 U.S. 903 (1979).

sonable searches. When a person is arrested, a search incident to that arrest may lawfully be made. A search may also be undertaken when reasonable cause exists to believe that the law has been or is being broken and a search warrant cannot be obtained without unreasonable delay. Even without a warrant, a search may be made if a person waives Fourth Amendment protection by consenting to the search. All other searches have been held unconstitutional. The argument is made, of course, that the parolee, as a condition of parole, consents to searches by parole authorities.

In searches of parolees and probationers, the courts have focused on the "reasonableness" of the search, and the admissibility of any evidence found while conducting the search, in later criminal or revocation proceedings. In *Latta v. Fitzharris,*[151] the court held that when a parolee was arrested by his parole officer with a pipe full of marijuana in his hand, a warrantless search of that parolee's home by the parole officer and accompanying police officers was reasonable. The use of evidence obtained by such a search was not limited to parole revocation.

A parole officer's searches and seizures are subject to a less stringent standard than the probable cause required for searches of ordinary citizens. In relationships with their parole officers, parolees are not entitled to the full protection of the Fourth Amendment.

Searches and seizures should be subject to the "reasonable suspicion" standard. The parole officer must be able to point to specific and articulable facts that, taken together with rational inferences, reasonably warrant belief that a condition of parole is being violated. With respect to police, however, the parolee is on the same footing as an ordinary citizen.[152]

The traditional view on searches of parolees is set forth in *People v. Hernandez,*[153] which states that a search by a parole officer of the person, residence, or effects of a parolee is not a violation of the Fourth Amendment, even though it is done without a warrant, without consent, and without probable cause. However, other courts have determined that a condition that requires a parolee to submit to searches at any time is too broad, and that a restriction on Fourth Amendment rights cannot exceed the legitimate needs of the probation or parole process.[154]

A condition of probation that allows for the warrantless search of a probationer's person and property by both his probation supervisors and law enforcement officers does not violate the probationer's Fourth Amendment rights. Using a three-part analysis, the court determined that the condition would: (1) dissuade

151   521 F.2d 246 (9th Cir. 1975).
152   United States v. Scott, 678 F.2d 32 (5th Cir. 1982).
153   40 Cal. Rptr. 100 (1964); State v. Cochran, 620 P.2d 116 (Wash. Ct. App. 1980).
154   United States v. Consuelo-Gonzales, 521 F.2d 259 (9th Cir. 1975); Tamez v. State, 534 S.W.2d 686 (1976); United States v. Dally, 606 F.2d 861 (9th Cir. 1979); Gomez v. Superior Court, 132 Cal. App. 3d 947 (Cal. Ct. App. 1982) (A parolee may not be required as a condition of his or her parole to completely waive his or her Fourth Amendment protection against warrantless searches by police officers. A warrantless search by police officers without the knowledge of the parolee's supervisor and for purposes other than the administration of his parole cannot be justified by such a waiver).

the probationer from again possessing illegal drugs; (2) promote his rehabilitation; and (3) further the legitimate needs of law enforcement. Even though they do have some Fourth Amendment rights, probationers are subject to special limitations and have a diminished expectation of privacy.[155]

However, if the police attempt to avoid the Fourth Amendment by using the parole officer as their agent in making a search when a warrant would otherwise be required, the search becomes unreasonable.[156] The Court in *United States v. Winsett*[157] held that evidence obtained in violation of the Fourth Amendment is admissible in revocation proceedings if, at the time of the search, the law enforcement officers did not know or have reason to believe that the suspect was on probation. This follows the almost unanimous view that the exclusionary rule does not usually apply in probation revocation proceedings.[158]

As pointed out by the court in *United States v. Vandemark,*[159] "the primary purpose of the exclusionary rule is to deter unlawful police conduct." The court held that the illegally seized evidence could be considered in imposing sentence on the probationer.

The reasonable warrantless search of the personal belongings of a halfway house resident has also been upheld.[160]

A case involving the search of a probationer's home by a probation officer is *Griffin v. Wisconsin.*[161] Wisconsin law places probationers in the legal custody of the State Department of Health and Social Services and renders them subject to conditions set by the rules and regulations established by the department. One such regulation permitted any probation officer to search a probationer's home without a warrant, as long as his supervisor approved and as long as there were "reasonable grounds" to believe contraband was present. In determining whether "reasonable grounds" existed, an officer was required to consider a variety of factors, including information provided by an informant, the reliability and specificity of that information, the informant's reliability, the officer's experience with the probationer, and the need to verify compliance with the rules of probation and with the law. Another Wisconsin regulation forbade a probationer to possess a firearm without a probation officer's advance approval.

---

[155] Owens v. Kelley, 681 F.2d 1362 (11th Cir. 1982).

[156] *See* People v. Kanos, 14 Cal. App. 3d 642 (1971); *But cf.* Quigg v. France, 502 F. Supp. 516 (D.C. Mont. 1980) (A parolee may be searched by a parole officer assisted by sheriff's deputies if the search is for a parole purpose).

[157] 518 F.2d 51 (9th Cir. 1975).

[158] United States v. Brown, 488 F.2d 94 (5th Cir. 1973); United States v. Farmer, 512 F.2d 160 (6th Cir. 1975); United States v. Hill, 447 F.2d 817 (7th Cir. 1971); State v. Alfaro, 678 F.2d 382 (2d Cir. 1982); *But see* United States v. Rea, 678 F.2d 826 (3d Cir. 1982) (Probation officers, like police officers, need a search warrant to search a probationer's home, or some recognized exception. Evidence seized without a warrant must be excluded at a subsequent revocation proceeding).

[159] 522 F.2d 1019 (9th Cir. 1975).

[160] United States v. Lewis, 400 F. Supp. 1046 (S.D.N.Y. 1975).

[161] 483 U.S. 868 (1987).

Upon information received from a police detective that there were or might be guns in a probationer's apartment, probation officers searched the apartment and found a handgun. The probationer was tried and convicted of the felony of possession of a firearm by a convicted felon. The trial court denied his motion to suppress the evidence seized during the search. It concluded that no warrant was necessary and that the search was reasonable.

The United States Supreme Court held that the warrantless search of the probationer's residence was "reasonable" within the meaning of the Fourth Amendment because it was conducted pursuant to a regulation that is itself a reasonable response to the "special needs" of a probation system.

The Court recognized that supervision of probationers was a "special need" of the state that justified departures from the usual warrant and probable cause requirements of the Fourth Amendment. Supervision was necessary to ensure that probation restrictions were in fact observed, that the probation served as a genuine rehabilitation period, and that the community was not harmed by the probationer being at large.

In this case, the search regulation was valid because the "special needs" of Wisconsin's probation system made the warrant requirement impracticable and justified replacement of the probable cause standard with the regulation's "reasonable grounds" standard. It was reasonable to dispense with the warrant requirement here, because such a requirement would interfere to an appreciable degree with the probation system by setting up a magistrate rather than the probation officer as the determiner of how closely the probationer must be supervised. It would also make it more difficult for probation officials to respond quickly to evidence of misconduct. It would reduce the deterrent effect that the possibility of expeditious searches would otherwise create. Moreover, unlike a police officer who conducts an ordinary search, a probation officer is required to have the probationer's welfare particularly in mind.

It was felt by the Court that a probable cause requirement would unduly disrupt the probation system by reducing the deterrent effect of the supervisory arrangement and by lessening the range of information the probation officer could consider in deciding whether to search. A probation agency must be able to act based upon a lesser degree of certainty in order to intervene before the probationer damages him- or herself or society. It must be able to proceed on the basis of its entire experience with the probationer and to assess probabilities in the light of its knowledge of his or her life, character, and circumstances. Thus, the Supreme Court held that it was reasonable to permit information provided by a police officer, whether or not on the basis of firsthand knowledge, to support a probationary search. All that was required was that the information provided indicate, as it did here, the likelihood of facts justifying the search.

The conclusion that the regulation in question was constitutional made it unnecessary to consider whether any search of a probationer's home is lawful when there are "reasonable grounds" to believe contraband is present. The Supreme Court deferred this issue to another day.

A California court's order sentencing a defendant to probation for a drug offense included the condition that he submit to search at any time, with or without a search or arrest warrant or reasonable cause, by any probation or law enforcement officer. The Supreme Court in *United States v. Knights*[161] held that the warrantless search of a probationer, supported by reasonable suspicion and authorized by a probation condition, satisfied the Fourth Amendment. Here, the sentencing judge reasonably concluded that the search condition would further the two primary goals of probation—rehabilitation and protecting society from future criminal violations. The probationer was unambiguously informed of the search condition. Thus, the probationer's reasonable expectation of privacy was significantly diminished. The Court recognized that the very assumption of probation is that the probationer is more likely than others to violate the law. The state's interest in apprehending criminal law violators, thereby protecting potential victims, may justifiably focus on probationers in a way that it does not focus on the ordinary citizen. On balance, no more than reasonable suspicion was required to search a probationer's house. The degree of individualized suspicion required is a determination that a sufficiently high probability of criminal conduct makes the intrusion on the individual's privacy interest reasonable. Although the Fourth Amendment ordinarily requires probable cause, a lesser degree satisfies the Constitution when the balance of governmental and private interests makes such a standard reasonable. The same circumstances that lead to the conclusion that reasonable suspicion is constitutionally sufficient also render a warrant requirement unnecessary.

§ 9.7 Conclusion

The decisions of *Morrissey v. Brewer* and *Gagnon v. Scarpelli* have defined the center limits of procedural due process with respect to parole revocation. The requirements for granting and rescinding parole have yet to be fully developed. Another confusing area is the status of inmates on furlough or other work-release programs. Calling them "inmates" or "parolees" does not answer the question of what process is due if their status is changed. Hopefully, the courts will not require the full procedural due process requirements of *Morrissey*. If so, the result could well be a reduction of such release programs, with fewer inmates released into viable community activities.

The administrative decisions of granting, rescinding, revoking, and continuing parole will always be subject to judicial attack by those who are adversely affected. Disenchantment with the parole process has led to movements to abolish indeterminate sentencing, upon which parole is based. Whether the proponents of determinate or indeterminate sentencing ultimately

---

[161] 534 U.S. 112 (2001).

win, the majority of jurisdictions in the foreseeable future will be faced with complying with procedural due process requirements necessary for a "fundamentally fair" parole system.

The federal system of parole was abolished in 1992, and was replaced by the United States Sentencing Commission. Although the new scheme was held to be constitutional in *Mistretta*, the relationship between sentencing and release decisions continues to develop. The exclusionary rule does not apply to parole proceedings and it remains an open question as to what extent procedural due process applies to clemency proceedings.

Right to Rehabilitation Programs, Right to Medical Aid, and Right to Life

10

Chapter Outline

§ 10.1 Introduction

The eight areas of inmate complaints that have been most frequently litigated by the courts in recent years—use of force, visitation and association rights, mail, isolated confinement, religious rights, legal services, disciplinary proceedings, and parole—have been analyzed in Chapters 2 through 9. This chapter will discuss four fact situations that are faced less frequently by the judiciary, but are nevertheless of importance to both inmates and prison administrators. The four areas to be discussed are: (1) an inmate's right to rehabilitation programs; (2) an inmate's right to medical aid; (3) the death row inmate's right to life as enunciated by Supreme Court cases concerning the use of death as a criminal penalty; and (4) an inmate's civil disabilities.

§ 10.2 Right to Rehabilitation Programs

Many state constitutions and statutes encourage rehabilitation of inmates.[1] Such programs are considered essential by virtually all penologists if incarceration is to reduce the incidence of crime. For example, the American Correctional Association has stated that "prison serves most effectively for the protection of society against crime when its major emphasis is on rehabilitation."[2] A commission appointed by President Lyndon Johnson to study the crime problem in the United States concluded that "rehabilitation of offenders to prevent their return to crime is, in general, the most promising way to achieve this end (reduction of crime)."[3]

§ 10.2.1 —Judicial Decisions

Despite the view that rehabilitation programs should be the core of any correctional system, the courts have refused to hold that there is an absolute right to rehabilitation during incarceration.

---

[1] *E.g., see*, R.I. GEN. LAWS ANN. 13-3-1 (1956).

[2] THE AMERICAN CORRECTIONAL ASSOCIATION, MANUAL OF CORRECTIONAL STANDARDS 10 (3d ed. 1966).

[3] THE PRESIDENT'S COMMISSION ON LAW ENFORCEMENT AND ADMINISTRATION OF JUSTICE, TASK FORCE REPORT: CORRECTIONS 16 (1967).

In *Padgett v. Stein*,[4] inmates of a county prison sought enforcement of a consent decree entered into with prison authorities to remedy allegedly unconstitutional conditions of confinement. The inmates contended that convicted inmates have a constitutional right to receive meaningful rehabilitative treatment, and that the failure of the prison authorities to afford inmates rehabilitation programs constituted cruel and unusual punishment. The court rejected the inmates' contentions on the ground that there is no constitutional duty imposed on a governmental entity to rehabilitate prisoners. The court went on to state that:

> . . . whether penal institutions should undertake to rehabilitate prisoners at all—in view of the serious questions which exist with respect to the effectiveness of rehabilitation programs—is a social policy question which should be resolved by the representative branches of government—*i.e.,* the legislative and executive branches—and not by the courts.[5]

Courts have repeatedly stated that inmates possess no constitutional right to rehabilitative treatment.[6] One court has characterized the duty owed to an inmate by prison officials as the duty "to exercise ordinary care for his protection and to keep him safe and free from harm."[7]

In *Holt v. Sarver*,[8] however, a district court did state that when examining the totality of conditions within a penal institution, a federal court should consider the lack of any meaningful rehabilitation programs as a factor "in the overall constitutional equation before the Court."[9] But because that court had previously stated that lack of rehabilitative opportunities was not, by itself, a defect of constitutional magnitude, it was evident that the prison administrators could remove the absence of rehabilitative programs from federal judicial consideration. They could do so by rectifying the other major deficiencies in the institution. The court tacitly recognized this by omitting lack of rehabilitative services from its list of defects that had to be corrected. The court that decided *Holt v. Sarver* has since required that an overall program for treatment and rehabilitation of the inmates be submitted to the court.[10]

---

4   Padgett v. Stein, 406 F. Supp. 287 (M.D. Pa. 1976).
5   *Id.* at 296; Pace v. Fauver, 479 F. Supp. 456 (D.N.J. 1979), *aff'd*, 694 F.2d 860 (4th Cir. 1981); Bresolin v. Morris, 558 P.2d 1350 (Wash. 1977); State v. Damon, 20 Cr. L. 2530 (Wash. Ct. App. 1977).
6   Russell v. Oliver, 392 F. Supp. 470 (W.D. Va. 1975); Lunsford v. Reynolds, 376 F. Supp. 526 (W.D. Va. 1974); Wright v. Rushen, 642 F.2d 1129 (9th Cir. 1981); Rucker v. Meachum, 513 F. Supp. 32 (W.D. Okla. 1980).
7   Wilson v. Kelley, 294 F. Supp. 1005 (N.D. Ga. 1968), *aff'd per curiam*, 393 U.S. 266 (1969); Graham v. Vann, 394 So. 2d 180 (Fla. Dist. Ct. App. 1981); Layne v. Vinzant, 657 F.2d 468 (1st Cir. 1981); Leonardo v. Moran, 611 F.2d 397 (1st Cir. 1979).
8   Holt v. Sarver, 309 F. Supp. 362 (E.D. Ark. 1970), *aff'd*, 442 F.2d 304 (8th Cir. 1971).
9   *Id.* at 379.
10   Finney v. Arkansas Board of Corrections, 505 F.2d 194, 209 (8th Cir. 1974).

Lack of meaningful rehabilitative opportunities is one of the grounds upon which several state prison systems have been declared to be unconstitutional.[11] In *James v. Wallace,*[12] it was noted that courts have not made a positive rehabilitative program a constitutional right. It is clear, however, that a penal system cannot be operated in such a manner that it impedes the ability of inmates to attempt their own rehabilitation, or simply to avoid physical, mental, or social deterioration. The court's opinion in *Alberti v. Sheriff of Harris County, Texas*[13] was more specific when it ordered officials who were responsible for the operation and maintenance of a county jail to provide adequate vocational and educational programs to foster the inmates' rehabilitation. However, an inmate has no constitutional right to participate in community programs, to enroll and attend classes in college outside the prison, nor to visit with relatives outside the prison.[14]

Another aspect of the rehabilitation program is the extent of a state's right to rehabilitate its inmates without the consent of the inmates. Aversion therapy—the so-called "Clockwork Orange" technique—has been held to be cruel and unusual punishment, not rehabilitative treatment, and thus unconstitutional. In *Knecht v. Gillman,*[15] severely nauseating injections were used to produce what the officials called a "Pavlovian" aversion to minor infractions of prison rules. The court prohibited the treatment program, holding such sanctions to be cruel and unusual punishment, in violation of the Eighth Amendment, and not treatment. In such cases, the courts look to the substance of a program, not its name or label. Labeling a program as treatment, rather than punishment, makes no difference in terms of the constitutional requirements that must be met.[16]

Short of aversion therapy, courts have been sympathetic toward state requirements that inmates be enrolled, either voluntarily or involuntarily, in education-oriented rehabilitative programs. In *Rutherford v. Hutto,*[17] a state was held to have a sufficient interest in the elimination of illiteracy among its convicts, including adults, to justify its requirement that illiterate convicts attend classes that were designed to bring them up to at least a fourth grade reading level. More than mere attendance at such classes can be required; meaningful participation can be encouraged by using sanctions for non-participation. In *Jackson v. McLemore,*[18] a disciplinary action that arose from an inmate's refusal to comply with a teacher's instruction to spell in a compulsory educational program class was held not to violate the inmate's constitutional right to be let alone.

---

[11] Miller v. Carson, 401 F. Supp. 835, 900 (M.D. Fla. 1975); Battle v. Anderson, 376 F. Supp. 402 (E.D. Okla. 1974); Inmates of Allegheny County Jail v. Pierce, 612 F.2d 754 (3d Cir. 1979).

[12] 406 F. Supp. 318 (M.D. Ala. 1976); Morris v. Travisono, 499 F. Supp. 149 (D.R.I. 1980).

[13] 406 F. Supp. 649 (S.D. Tex. 1975); Ohlinger v. Watson, 652 F.2d 77 (9th Cir. 1980).

[14] Breedlove v. Cripe, 511 F. Supp. 467 (N.D. Tex. 1981).

[15] 488 F.2d 1136 (8th Cir. 1973).

[16] Clonce v. Richardson, 379 F. Supp. 338 (W.D. Mo. 1974).

[17] 377 F. Supp. 268 (E.D. Ark. 1974).

[18] 523 F.2d 838 (8th Cir. 1975); Mukmuk v. Commissioner, 529 F.2d 272 (2d Cir. 1976).

In conjunction with the discussion of involuntary rehabilitative programs, it should be noted that the basically coercive nature of prison life severely undercuts any notion that an inmate's consent to treatment is motivated primarily by the inmate's desire to be rehabilitated, i.e., is not coerced. In *McGee v. Aaron*,[19] the court recognized implicitly that consent may not always be genuine, but is merely choosing the least of several evils. That case involved the sufficiency of the reasons given for denial of parole. One of the reasons given was the parole board's estimation of the need for the inmate to complete his high school equivalency and to complete a training program that would provide him with a salable skill. The court upheld the decision, thus giving the inmate a concrete goal to work toward; not some ideal form of rehabilitation, but freedom in the form of early parole.

The voluntariness of an inmate's consent to participation in therapeutic medical experimentation and research is also suspect. Modern medical research and drug testing techniques require the participation of large numbers of subjects for substantial periods. Prisons provide an excellent source for such volunteers. However, due to the indigency of most inmates and the emphasis that parole boards place upon cooperative activity by inmates, there is a real question as to whether true consent is ever obtainable from inmates for their participation in sometimes painful or dangerous medical experimentation.[20]

A patient has the right to refuse drug treatment. The right is adequately protected by hospital regulations that provide a series of informal consultations and interviews to determine, from a medical standpoint, whether compelled administration of drugs is necessary. It is not necessary to provide the patient with a due process hearing, a system of "patient advocates," or an independent decisionmaker.[21]

The scope and nature of rehabilitation are left largely to the discretion of prison authorities. In *Sellers v. Ciccone*,[22] which involved rejection of long-term inmates for admission to an X-ray technician training program, the court stated that, absent arbitrariness or caprice, the balance between individual benefit and institutional benefit is for prison officials to determine. The court declined to intervene in order to meet the desires of the individual inmate. However, in certain situations courts will order specific rehabilitative opportunities to be made available to specific individual inmates or classes of inmates. In *Cudnik v. Kreiger*,[23] pretrial detainees were held to be entitled to

---

[19]   523 F.2d 825 (7th Cir. 1975).

[20]   Comment, *Non-Therapeutic Prison Search: An Analysis of Potential Legal Remedies,* 39 ALB. L. REV. 799 (1975); Bailey v. Talley, 481 F. Supp. 203 (D. Md. 1979).

[21]   Rennie v. Klein, 653 F.2d 836 (3d Cir. 1981), *vacated and remanded* in light of Youngberg v. Romeo, 457 U.S. 307 (1982).

[22]   530 F.2d 199 (8th Cir. 1976); Yusaf Asad Madyun v. Thompson, 657 F.2d 868 (7th Cir. 1981) (In order to maintain an action based upon insufficient opportunities for vocational and educational training, it is necessary to show that the prison environment threatens a prisoner's mental and physical well-being).

[23]   392 F. Supp. 305 (N.D. Ohio 1974); Gawreys v. D.C. General Hospital, 480 F. Supp. 853 (D.D.C. 1979); *cf.* Holly v. Rapone, 476 F. Supp. 226 (E.D. Pa. 1979) (There is no constitutional right to receive methadone); United States ex rel. Walker v. Fayette County, Pennsylvania, 599 F.2d 573 (3d Cir. 1979) (State law did not require the establishment of methadone maintenance facilities at correctional institutions—therefore, the county was not obligated to provide methadone to its prisoners).

continue with the methadone treatment program in which they had been involved prior to their detention.

There is no requirement that a specialized treatment program be available prior to the transfer of a state prisoner to a federal institution under 18 U.S.C. § 5003(a).[24]

§ 10.2.2 —Analogy of Right to Treatment in Other Areas

In the past few years, several courts have recognized that certain groups of persons who have been deprived of their liberty have a right to treatment. These cases were based, however, on statutory interpretation and not on any constitutional right. Thus, in *Rouse v. Cameron,*[25] a federal appellate court held that the District of Columbia's Hospitalization of the Mentally Ill Act required treatment programs for persons who were involuntarily committed to a mental health facility after their acquittal by reason of insanity. Minnesota's Hospitalization and Commitment Act has been interpreted to confer a statutory right upon persons who are involuntarily civilly committed to state institutions to receive minimally adequate treatment while so institutionalized.[26] In *New York State Assn. for Retard. Ch., Inc. v. Carey,*[27] an expansion of current notions of the right to treatment of involuntarily civilly committed mental patients occurred when inmates of state mental facilities were held to have a constitutional right to some treatment, regardless of whether their confinement was voluntary or involuntary.

In *O'Connor v. Donaldson,*[28] the United States Supreme Court made specific note of its refusal to decide whether mental patients have a constitutional right to treatment as a consequence of their detention by the state. The Fifth Circuit Court of Appeals had concluded[29] that where a nondangerous patient was involuntarily committed to a state mental hospital under a civil commitment procedure, the only constitutionally permissible purpose of such confinement was to provide treatment, and that such confinement must involve rehabilitative treatment, or minimally adequate habilitation and care where rehabilitation was impossible, in order to justify the confinement. The Court of Appeals made a careful distinction between the rights of those who are civilly committed for an indefinite term and those who are adjudged guilty of

---

24 Howe v. Smith, 452 U.S. 473 (1981).
25 373 F.2d 451 (D.C. Cir. 1966).
26 Welsch v. Likins, 373 F. Supp. 487 (D. Minn. 1974).
27 393 F. Supp. 715 (E.D.N.Y. 1975).
28 422 U.S. 563 (1975); *See* Mills v. Rogers, 457 U.S. 291 (1982) (The United States Supreme Court reversed a lower court decision that mental patients who are involuntarily committed have a federal constitutional right to refuse treatment with antipsychotic drugs. The decision must be reexamined by the lower court in light of an intervening state supreme court decision concerning noninstitutionalized mental patients).
29 Donaldson v. O'Connor, 493 F.2d 507 (5th Cir. 1974), *vacated and remanded,* 422 U.S. 563 (1975).

a specific offense and who are sentenced for a fixed term. The Supreme Court's refusal to affirm even this relatively simple distinction suggests that the Court will not require, at least upon a constitutional basis, rehabilitative treatment for ordinary prisoners in the near future.

The United States Supreme Court held that involuntarily committed mentally retarded persons have, under the Fourteenth Amendment due process clause, constitutionally protected liberty interests in reasonably safe conditions of confinement, freedom from unreasonable bodily restraints, and such minimally adequate training as reasonably may be required by such interests.

The proper standard for determining whether the state has adequately protected such rights is whether professional judgment has been exercised. The judgment of a qualified professional is entitled to a presumption of correctness. Liability may only be imposed when the decision is such a substantial departure from accepted professional judgment as to demonstrate that the decision was not based on professional judgment.[30]

Certain trends in juvenile law may eventually affect the right to rehabilitative treatment in prison. The Juvenile Court Act for the District of Columbia mandates treatment services for juvenile pretrial detainees[31] and for juveniles adjudicated to be delinquent.[32] In *Morales v. Turman*,[33] it was held that an incarcerated juvenile must be involved in a cohesive treatment strategy that has been professionally designed to suit his individual needs and to achieve his rehabilitation and return to the community. Without such a program, the involuntary commitment of the juvenile would amount to an arbitrary exercise of governmental power in violation of due process. In *Long v. Powell*,[34] the United States Supreme Court ruled that a juvenile who has been adjudged not amenable to rehabilitation within the programs regularly conducted by his or her state for that purpose, cannot be committed to such programs without provision for greater protection, security, and rehabilitative treatment.

One of the consequences of conviction under a habitual sex offender statute, which usually carries a sentence of from one day to life, seems to be a right to rehabilitative treatment. In *People v. Feagley*,[35] the California Supreme Court ruled that a statutory scheme that provides for confinement of mentally disordered sex offenders for an indefinite period in prison without treatment violates the cruel and unusual punishment clauses of the state and federal constitutions. However, judicial expansion of the indefinitely sentenced inmate's right to treatment[36] has motivated the New York legislature to alter its habitual sex offender statute so as to eliminate such a right.[37]

---

30   Youngberg v. Romeo, 457 U.S. 307 (1982).

31   Creek v. Stone, 379 F.2d 106 (D.C. Cir. 1967).

32   In re Elmore, 382 F.2d 125 (D.C. Cir. 1967).

33   383 F. Supp. 53 (E.D. Tex. 1974), was reversed. Morales v. Turman, 535 F.2d 864 (5th Cir. 1976). The court of appeals ordered that the case be remanded to the district court because it was reversible error for the district court not to empanel a three-judge court to hear the case as required by 78 U.S.C. § 2281.

34   388 F. Supp. 422 (N.D. Ga. 1975), *jud. vac.*, 423 U.S. 808 (1975) (dismissed as moot).

35   14 Cal. App. 3d 338, 535 P.2d 373 (Cal. 1975).

36   People v. Wilkins, 23 App. Div. 2d 178, 259 N.Y.S.2d 462 (N.Y. App. Div. 1965).

37   People v. Hutchings, 74 Misc. 2d 14, 343 N.Y.S.2d 845 (Cortland County Court 1973).

In *Ohlinger v. Watson,*[38] the court held that the goal of the Oregon statutory scheme for sex offenders is rehabilitation. Consequently, sex offenders in Oregon have a right to individual treatment that will afford them a reasonable opportunity to be cured or to improve their mental condition. Further, such treatment is also required by due process.

As noted, many state statutes and constitutions say that rehabilitation is an objective of their correctional systems.[39] It is, therefore, possible that courts in the future will demand that prison administrators implement, with specific programs, the state's statutory and constitutional requirement of rehabilitation programs. Judge David Bazelon, the author of several right-to-treatment decisions from the Federal Circuit Court of Appeals for the District of Columbia, has written that:

> The rationale for the right to treatment is clear. If society confines a man for the benevolent purpose of helping him . . . then its right to so withhold his freedom depends entirely upon whether help is in fact provided. . . . When the legislature justifies confinement by a promise of treatment, it thereby commits the community to provide the resources necessary to fulfill the promise.[40]

§ 10.2.3 Administrative Review

In a case addressing the involuntary medication of inmates with antipsychotic drugs, the United States Supreme Court held that a state may conclude, with good reason, that a judicial hearing will not be as effective, as continuous, or as probing as administrative review using medical decisionmakers.[41] The Court observed that an inmate has a protected liberty interest in being free from the arbitrary administration of antipsychotic drugs through the state's policy and the Fourteenth Amendment's due process clause. However, the Court applied the test of *Turner v. Safley,*[42] and found that a state's interest in prison safety and security is sufficiently great to justify subordinating the inmate's liberty interest in the proper case. Justice Kennedy, writing for the majority, commented that the *Turner* test applies to all circumstances in which the needs of prison administration implicate constitutional rights.

An administrative hearing was held for inmates who refused to be treated with the medication. The panel was comprised of a psychiatrist, a psychologist, and the associate superintendent of the special unit. The Washington state prison system had a special unit in which felons with severe mental disorders were housed. None of the panel members was involved in the prisoner's treatment or diagnosis at the time of the hearing, in order to assure independence.

---

[38] 652 F.2d 775 (9th Cir. 1980)
[39] *See* n. 1.
[40] Bazelon, *Implementing the Right to Treatment,* 36 U. CHI. L. REV. 742, 748-749 (1969).
[41] Washington v. Harper, 494 U.S. 210 (1990).
[42] Turner v. Safley, 482 U.S. 78 (1987).

Among many other procedures, the inmate had the right to attend, present evidence, cross-examine witnesses, and be assisted by a lay advisor. Further, a decision to medicate involuntarily was subject to periodic review. As with most administrative hearings, the inmate was not afforded a right to counsel, and adherence to evidentiary rules was not required.

§ 10.3 Right to Medical Aid

Inmates in state and federal institutions have sought redress in the federal court system for medical treatment they have received and failed to receive. Complaints about medical treatment have included claims about the adequacy and nature of the medical care received, allegations of a total denial of medical care, improper medical care, inadequate care, and conduct of prison officials attendant to the medical care.

The power of the federal courts to adjudicate an inmate's complaint about medical treatment requires that a federal right be involved in the medical treatment.[43] The inmate must allege the presence of a federally protected right. Several federally protected rights have been named by the federal courts in medical treatment cases:

1. Right to due process of law under the Fifth or Fourteenth Amendments.[44] The due process right has been couched in terms of the inmate's right to be free from an abuse of discretion on the part of prison administrators;[45] protection from unconstitutional administrative action;[46] protection of an inmate's life and health from administrative action.[47]

2. Right to be free from the infliction of cruel and unusual punishments as guaranteed by the Eighth Amendment.[48] Violation of Eighth Amendment rights has been found when there is an intentional denial of needed medical care, or when a prison official's conduct indicates deliberate indifference to the medical needs of inmates.

---

[43] A federal inmate complaining about medical treatment in the institution utilizes the federal habeas corpus procedure. A state inmate may use a Civil Rights Action (42 U.S.C. 1983) or the federal habeas corpus procedure. *See* Chapter 11 for a discussion of the prisoner's remedies.

[44] *See* Chapters 8 and 9 for a discussion of due process of law.

[45] Shannon v. Lester, 519 F.2d 76 (6th Cir. 1975); Derrickson v. Keve, 390 F. Supp. 905 (D. Del. 1975); Nickolson v. Choctaw County, Alabama, 498 F. Supp. 295 (S.D. Ala. 1980); Lareau v. Manson, 507 F. Supp. 1177 (D. Conn. 1980), *modified in*, 651 F.2d 96 (2d Cir. 1981).

[46] Clements v. Turner, 364 F. Supp. 270 (D. Utah 1973).

[47] Hoitt v. Vitek, 497 F.2d 598 (1st Cir. 1974); Runnels v. Rosendale, 499 F.2d 733 (9th Cir. 1974); Johnson v. Harris, 479 F. Supp. 333 (S.D.N.Y. 1979).

[48] Bishop v. Stoneman, 508 F.2d 1224 (2d Cir. 1974); Russell v. Sheffer, 528 F.2d 318 (4th Cir. 1975). *See* Comment, *The Eighth Amendment: Medical Treatment of Prisoners as Cruel and Unusual Punishment*, 1 CAP. U. L. REV. 83 (1972). Estelle v. Gamble, 429 U.S. 97 (1976); Burks v. Teasdale, 492 F. Supp. 650 (W.D. Mo. 1980); Hampton v. Holmesburg Prison Officials, 546 F.2d 1077 (3d Cir. 1976); Kelsey v. Ewing, 652 F.2d 4 (8th Cir. 1981); Inmates of Allegheny County Jail v. Pierce, 612 F.2d 754 (3d Cir. 1979); Duncan v. Duckworth, 644 F.2d 653 (7th Cir. 1981).

Despite the willingness of federal courts to hear cases that involve the federally protected rights of inmates to medical aid, there are limits to what inmates can expect to accomplish through the courts. In *Priest v. Cupp*,[49] the court explained that neither federal nor state constitutional prohibitions of cruel and unusual punishment guarantee any inmate that he or she will be free from or cured of all real or imagined medical disabilities while he or she is in custody. What is required is that the inmate be afforded such medical care, in the form of diagnosis and treatment, as is reasonably available under the circumstances of his or her confinement and medical condition.

Just as prison officials cannot deny all medical aid, inmates cannot expect a flawless medical services system. Consequently, litigation involving the medical rights of inmates has now focused upon the nature of so-called *adequate* or *reasonable* medical care.

What amount of medical aid is adequate depends largely upon the facts of each case. In *Gates v. Collier*,[50] the Fifth Circuit Court of Appeals reviewed the medical treatment that was available at the Mississippi State Penitentiary. With more than 1,800 inmates, the prison administration relied upon one full-time physician, several inmate assistants, and a substandard hospital to provide medical care. The court ruled that the services and facilities were inadequate and ordered the prison administration to: (1) employ such additional medical personnel as necessary so that the prison's medical staff would consist of at least three full-time physicians, one of which must be a psychiatrist and another the prison's chief medical officer,[51] two full-time dentists, two full-time trained physicians' assistants, six full-time registered or licensed practical nurses, one medical records librarian, and two medical clerical personnel, and to obtain the consultant services of a radiologist and a pharmacist; (2) comply with the general standards of the American Correctional Association relating to medical services for prisoners; (3) have the prison hospital and equipment brought into compliance with state licensing requirements for a hospital and infirmary, including adequate treatment for the chronically ill; (4) refrain from punishment of inmates who seek medical aid unless the superintendent makes an express finding that the inmate sought medical care unnecessarily and for malingering purposes; and (5) refrain from the use of inmates to fill any of the above described civilian medical staff, but to encourage the use of trained and competent inmates to supplement the above minimal civilian medical staff.[52] As in most "treatment" cases, the lack of funds has not been recognized as a defense or excuse. However, in *Miller v. Carson*,[53] a federal court approved a Florida county prison's medical services staff, which included one full-time physician, a licensed physician's assistant, and 13 nurses, because their work schedule allowed a crisis intervention desk to be staffed 24 hours per day, with

[49]   Priest v. Cupp, 545 P.2d 917 (Or. Ct. App. 1976).
[50]   501 F.2d 1291 (5th Cir. 1974).
[51]   Gates v. Collier, 390 F. Supp. 482, 488 (N.D. Miss. 1975).
[52]   Gates v. Collier, 501 F.2d 1291, 1303 (5th Cir. 1974).
[53]   401 F. Supp. 835 (M.D. Fla. 1975).

the physician or the licensed physician's assistant on call at the jail 24 hours a day as well. The proximity to the jail of a university hospital for emergency treatment made such a minimal staff feasible. This Florida county prison had a maximum capacity of 432 inmates.[54] Other states have also grappled with this personnel problem. In *Craig v. Hocker*,[55] the court found that medical care was adequate and reasonable based on the presence of a full-time physician and a full-time dentist in the prison, as well as two registered nurses, a psychiatrist, a part-time pharmacist who gave reasonably prompt attention to genuine complaints from inmates, a prison hospital ward to which sick inmates could be removed when so directed by a doctor, and provisions for taking inmates under guard to local hospitals for diagnostic or treatment procedures not available in the prison. The prison contained 854 inmates prior to trial.

Once the courts have assured themselves that adequate or reasonable medical care is available to an inmate, the historic "hands off" doctrine is again evident. What constitutes necessary and proper medical care of an inmate, in the absence of allegations of intentional negligence or mistreatment, must be left to the medical judgment of the prison physician, and cannot form the basis for a civil rights complaint.[56] Inmates cannot be the ultimate judges of what medical treatment is necessary or proper, and courts must place their confidence in the reports of reputable prison physicians.[57] The allegations by inmates that they have received inadequate medical care can be disproved by prison medical records.[58]

An apparent difference of opinion between an inmate and his or her physicians as to what treatment is necessary and proper does not give rise to a legal cause of action against the physician.[59] Medical mistreatment or non-treatment must be capable of characterization as cruel and unusual punishment in order to present a claim under a civil rights statute.[60] The standard for what treatment rises to cruel and unusual punishment was set forth in *Estelle v. Gamble*.[61] In that case, the Supreme Court reasoned that there must be facts and evidence to show a deliberate indifference to serious medical needs. Thus, simple negligence will not be sufficient to obtain a judgment against prison medical or security staff for inadequate treatment as a constitutional violation. The lack of medical treatment must be intentional; an accident or inadvertent failure to provide proper medical care is insufficient to meet the Supreme Court's standard of deliberate indifference to serious medical needs. It should be noted, however, that negligence may be actionable in state courts under state law.

---

[54]   *Id.* at 898; *see also* Brown v. Beck, 481 F. Supp. 723 (S.D. Ga. 1980).
[55]   405 F. Supp. 656 (D. Nev. 1975); *see also* Jackson v. State of Mississippi, 644 F.2d 1142 (5th Cir. 1981).
[56]   United States ex rel. Hyde v. McGinnis, 429 F.2d 864 (2d Cir. 1970).
[57]   Fore v. Godwin, 407 F. Supp. 1145 (E.D. Va. 1976).
[58]   Ross v. Bounds, 373 F. Supp. 450 (E.D.N.C. 1974); Estelle v. Gamble, 429 U.S. 97 (1976).
[59]   Ray v. Parrish, 399 F. Supp. 775 (E.D. Va. 1975); Jackson v. Moore, 471 F. Supp. 1068 (D. Colo. 1979).
[60]   Boyce v. Alizadun, 595 F.2d 948 (4th Cir. 1979); Shepard v. Stidham, 502 F. Supp. 1275 (M.D. Ala., 1980); DiLorenze v. United States, 496 F. Supp. 79 (S.D.N.Y. 1980); Campbell v. Sacred Heart Hospital, 496 F. Supp. 692 (E.D. Pa. 1980); Estelle v. Gamble, 429 U.S. 97 (1976).
[61]   429 U.S. 97 (1976).

The deliberate indifference standard embodies both an objective and a subjective prong. First, the alleged deprivation must be, in objective terms, "sufficiently serious."[62] Second, the charged official must act with a sufficiently culpable state of mind. Deliberate indifference requires more than negligence, but less than conduct undertaken for the very purpose of causing harm.[63] More specifically, a prison official does not act in a deliberately indifferent manner unless that official knows of and disregards an excessive risk to inmate health or safety; the official must be aware of facts from which the inference could be drawn that a substantial risk of serious harm exists, and he or she must also draw the inference.

In *Hathaway v. Coughlin,*[64] the Second Circuit applied these standards and held that a prison doctor was deliberately indifferent to the prisoner's serious medical needs in that he knew of and disregarded an excessive risk to his health. The doctor never informed the prisoner that he had two broken pins in his hip. The prisoner did not learn of his condition for one year after an X-ray. The presence of broken pins in a hip is information that would cause most people to consider surgery. Nonetheless, the doctor never shared this information with the prisoner nor raised the possibility of surgery with him following the discovery of the broken pins.

Deliberate indifference was also present in a delay of more than two years between the discovery of the broken pins and the time the doctor asked that the prisoner be re-evaluated for surgery. Despite requests for further evaluation and additional treatment, and the prisoner's constant complaints, the doctor did not take the prisoner's condition seriously.

In *Ricketts v. Ciccone,*[65] the court held that when a federal inmate was in need of medical treatment due to chronic rhinitis caused by allergic sensitivity to an identified mold, the director of the prison and the Bureau of Prisons were legally required to provide the most suitable medical treatment reasonably available. In determining a claim for lack of medical treatment, the standard is whether needed or essential, as opposed to desirable, medical treatment is being denied. The court held that denial of the request by the inmate, suffering from chronic rhinitis, to be transferred to a federal prison in a relatively dry climate as treatment for his illness, was arbitrary and unreasonable. Such action was held to be a denial to the prisoner of the best reasonably available medical treatment, when at least one federal prison was available in a climate beneficial to the prisoner's illness.

In *Anderson v. Romero,*[66] a prisoner was discovered to be infected with the AIDS virus, HIV (human immunodeficiency virus). The superintendent of the cell house at which the prisoner was placed told a correctional officer, in the

---

62   Wilson v. Seiter, 501 U.S. 294 (1991).
63   *See* Farmer v. Brennan, 511 U.S. 825 (1994).
64   37 F.3d 63 (2d Cir. 1994).
65   371 F. Supp. 1249 (W.D. Mo. 1974); Commissioner of Corrections v. Meyers, 399 N.E.2d 452 (Mass. 1979).
66   72 F.3d 518 (7th Cir. 1995).

presence of another officer, to make sure that he was put in a cell by himself because he was HIV positive. The officer told at least one other officer that the prisoner was HIV positive. Later the officer noticed an inmate sleeping on the floor of the prisoner's cell. The officer told the inmate that the prisoner was a homosexual and a faggot and that the inmate could catch AIDS from him and so had better stay away from him. The officer told an inmate barber not to cut the prisoner's hair because he had AIDS. His yard privileges were denied for several months because he was HIV positive.

The court could not find any cases holding that prisoners have a constitutional right to the confidentiality of their medical records. The closest was *Harris v. Thigpen*,[67] which involved a challenge to the compulsory testing of inmates for HIV and the segregation of those who tested positive. The challenge was based in part on a claimed constitutional right to the confidentiality of one's HIV status. The *Thigpen* court refused to go further than to assume, *arguendo,* that seropositive prisoners enjoy some significant constitutionally protected privacy interest in preventing the nonconsensual disclosure of their HIV-positive diagnosis to other inmates, as well as to their families and other outside visitors to the facilities in question. This was not felt to be a holding that inmates have such a right.

However, it was recognized that certain disclosures of medical information or records would be actionable under the cruel and unusual punishments clause of the Eighth Amendment rather than the due process clause of the Fourteenth Amendment. If prison officials disseminated humiliating but penologically irrelevant details of a prisoner's medical history, their action might conceivably constitute the infliction of cruel and unusual punishment; the fact that the punishment was purely psychological would not excuse it.[68]

The *Anderson* court conceded that the law is not clearly established that a prison cannot, without violating the constitutional rights of its HIV-positive inmates, reveal their condition to other inmates and to officers in order to enable the other inmates and officers to protect themselves from infection.[69] The Seventh Circuit had previously held that the knowing failure to protect an inmate from the danger posed by an HIV-positive cellmate with a propensity to rape violated the inmate's right not to be subjected to cruel and unusual punishments.[70]

---

[67]　941 F.2d 1495 (11th Cir. 1991).

[68]　*See, e.g.,* Thomas v. Farley, 31 F.3d 557 (7th Cir. 1994); Joseph v. Brierton, 739 F.2d 1244 (7th Cir. 1984); Williams v. Boles, 841 F.2d 181 (7th Cir. 1988); Northington v. Jackson, 973 F.2d 1518 (10th Cir. 1992). It was also suggested that branding or tattooing HIV-positive inmates (the branding of persons who are HIV-positive was once seriously proposed as a method of retarding the spread of AIDS), or making them wear a sign around their neck that read "I AM AN AIDS CARRIER!" would constitute cruel and unusual punishment. So, too, if employees of the prison, knowing that an inmate identified as HIV positive was a likely target of violence by other inmates, yet indifferent to his fate, gratuitously revealed his HIV status to other inmates and a violent attack upon him ensued. *Cf.* Bowers v. DeVito, 686 F.2d 616 (7th Cir. 1982).

[69]　*Cf.* Camarillo v. McCarthy, 998 F.2d 638 (9th Cir. 1993).

[70]　Billman v. Indiana Department of Corrections, 56 F.3d 785, 788-789 (7th Cir. 1995).

The Eighth Amendment only forbids cruel and unusual punishments; it does not require the most intelligent, progressive, humane, or efficacious prison administration. The *Anderson* court held that warnings to endangered inmates or staff did not violate the Constitution just because they are *ad hoc*. The duty to protect prisoners from lethal encounters with their fellows is derived from the Eighth Amendment. The officer could not be criticized for having warned the other inmate that the prisoner in whose cell he was seen sleeping was HIV-positive or even for having warned the inmate barber about the prisoner. It was recognized that a barber, especially if he uses a razor, may cut the skin of the person whose hair he is cutting and if the person's blood makes contact with a part of his skin where he has a cut or abrasion, he may become infected.

However, it is one thing to warn other prisoners that an inmate is an HIV carrier; it is another to "punish" him or her for being a carrier by refusing to allow him or her to get a haircut or to exercise in the prison yard. *Anderson* was the first appellate case in which these specific modalities of punishing HIV carriers have been alleged. The Eighth Amendment forbids the state to punish people for a physical condition, as distinct from acts.[71] The equal protection clause forbids the state to treat one group, including a group of prison inmates, arbitrarily worse than another. If the only reason the prison officials denied haircuts and yard privileges to the prisoner was that he was HIV-positive, and there was no conceivable justification for these as AIDS-fighting measures the denial was improper. Toward the end of the 1997-1998 term of the Supreme Court, two important cases were decided that will have a profound effect on the management of prisons. The first applied the Americans with Disabilities Act of 1990 (ADA) to prisons.[72]

A prisoner was sentenced to 18 to 36 months in a Pennsylvania correctional facility, but was recommended for placement in a motivational boot camp for first-time offenders, the successful completion of which would have led to his parole in just six months. He was refused admission because of his medical history of hypertension. He then sued the Pennsylvania Department of Corrections and several officials, alleging that the exclusion violated the Americans with Disabilities Act of 1990 (ADA), Title II of which prohibits a "public entity" from discriminating against a "qualified individual with a disability" on account of that disability.[73]

The Supreme Court unanimously held that state prisons fall squarely within Title II's statutory definition of "public entity," which includes "any . . . instrumentality of a State . . . or local government."[74] The attempt to derive an intent not to cover prisons from the statutory references to the "benefits" of programs, and to "qualified individual" was rejected.

---

[71] *See* Robinson v. California, 370 U.S. 660 (1962); Despears v. Milwaukee County, 63 F.3d 635 (7th Cir. 1995).

[72] Pennsylvania Dept. of Corrections v. Yeskey, 524 U.S. 206 (1998).

[73] 42 U.S.C. § 12132 (1998).

[74] 42 U.S.C. § 12131(1)(B) (1998).

The second made it clear that HIV was a covered disability under the ADA.[75]

Prisoners are entitled to reasonable medical care, and exercise is now regarded in many quarters as an indispensable component of preventive medicine. But cases that purport to recognize a right to outdoor exercise[76] involve special circumstances, such as that the prisoners were confined to their cells almost 24 hours a day and were not offered alternative indoor exercise facilities, or the only alternative offered to the prisoners was exercise in the corridor outside their cells rather than in an indoor exercise facility and the lack of outdoor exercise was merely one of a number of circumstances that in the aggregate constituted the infliction of cruel and unusual punishment.[77]

The right to medical aid also includes the right of refusal. A competent person has a constitutionally protected liberty interest to refuse unwanted medical treatment, as was stated in *Cruzan v. Director, Missouri Dept. of Health.*[78] However, in *North Dakota ex rel. Timothy Schuetzle v. Vogel,*[79] a prisoner was required to submit to diabetes monitoring of his blood sugar and, if ordered by a physician, to forcibly submit to food, insulin, and other medications to prevent deterioration of his health or premature death.

In the case of a prison inmate, the state has an important interest in maintaining the confinement of the prisoner. The integrity of its correctional system must also be considered.[80] Courts will not condone a prisoner's manipulation of his or her medical circumstances to the detriment of a state's interest in prison order, security, and discipline. The "purpose" for refusing unwanted medical treatment is a factor that prison officials may legitimately consider in determining whether the refusal is likely to be a disruptive influence, or otherwise detrimental to the effective administration of the prison system[81] because the state's interest in orderly prison administration is the controlling factor.[82]

In *Singletary v. Costello,*[83] a prisoner fasted to protest his punitive transfer to another institution as well as to protest an allegedly false disciplinary report. According to a doctor, not intervening in such a circumstance would result in suicide. The issue was whether a prisoner has the legal right to refuse medical treatment and intervention when the need for the treatment and inter-

---

75 Bragdon v. Abbott, 524 U.S. 624 (1998). *See also* Onishea v. Hopper, 126 F.3d 1323 (11th Cir. 1997), which held that a district court must consider claims of HIV-positive prisoners that their segregation from virtually all prison programs violated the 1973 Rehabilitation Act. The decision of the Eleventh Circuit was vacated and a rehearing ordered en banc, 113 F.3d 1377 (11th Cir. 1998).

76 Allen v. Sakai, 40 F.3d 1001 (1994), *amended,* 48 F.3d 1082 (9th Cir. 1995).

77 Wilkerson v. Maggio, 703 F.2d 909 (5th Cir. 1983), held that an hour per day of indoor exercise satisfied the constitutional minimum.

78 497 U.S. 261 (1990).

79 537 N.W.2d 358 (N.D. 1995).

80 Washington v. Harper, 494 U.S. 210 (1990). The extent of a prisoner's right under the due process clause to avoid the unwanted administration of antipsychotic drugs must be defined in the context of the inmate's confinement. *See also* Sandin v. Conner, 515 U.S. 472 (1995).

81 Jones v. North Carolina Prisoners' Labor Union, Inc., 433 U.S. 119 (1977).

82 *See* Zant v. Prevatte, 248 Ga. 832, 286 S.E.2d 715 (1982), in which the Supreme Court of Georgia held that a hunger-striking prisoner, who began fasting to obtain transfer out of the Georgia prison system for fear of his safety, had the right to die by refusing food and medical treatment.

83 665 So. 2d 1099 (Fla. Dist. Ct. App. 1996).

vention stems from a self-induced hunger strike. This issue involved the breadth of an individual's right to refuse medical treatment.

The Constitution protects an individual's right to refuse medical care. In *Cruzan v. Director, Missouri Department of Health*,[84] the Supreme Court held that Missouri's clear and convincing evidentiary standard, before the termination of a life support system, did not interfere with a competent person's right to refuse medical treatment. The Supreme Court also concluded that a competent person has a liberty interest under the due process clause in refusing unwarranted medical treatment. Therefore, a competent person has a constitutionally protected right to refuse lifesaving hydration and nutrition.

Accordingly, the *Singletary* court determined that under the Florida Constitution as well as the United States Constitution, a prisoner retained the fundamental right to refuse nonconsensual medical treatment even though he or she was incarcerated. The remaining issue was for the court to delineate and balance the various state interests that might overcome this fundamental right. The state's obligation to assure a person's wishes regarding medical treatment had to be respected and could only be overcome if the state had a compelling interest great enough to override this constitutional right. The state's interest in the preservation of life generally is considered the most significant state interest.[85] It was noted that if the prisoner were successful in evading the prison's control over his or her behavior, it might jeopardize prison discipline and tax prison resources. Prison officials would lose much of their ability to enforce institutional order if any inmate could shield him or herself from the administration's control and authority by announcing that he or she is on a starvation diet. Prisoners are not permitted to live in accordance with their own desires, nor may they be permitted to die on their own terms because this adversely and impermissibly affects the state's legitimate authority over inmates.

Even considering the breadth of Florida's privacy right, the state's interest in the preservation of life, in and of itself, could not overcome the prisoner's fundamental right to forego life-sustaining medical intervention. However, the prisoner testified that he did not want to die. He commenced his hunger strike as a form of protest, with the resolution of his complaints as the desired end. The purpose of the hunger strike was to bring about change, not death. Therefore, the state's interest in the prevention of suicide was not implicated. Also, the interest in the protection of innocent third parties was held to be inapplicable. The refusal of medical treatment would not endanger the public health, nor implicate the emotional or financial welfare of a patient's minor children. The death of a prison inmate serving a life sentence would in no way endanger the public health, according to the *Singletary* court.

---

[84]   497 U.S. 261 (1990).

[85]   *See* In re Caulk, 125 N.H. 226, 480 A.2d 93 (N.H. 1984), in which the Supreme Court of New Hampshire determined that a prison inmate had no constitutional right to starve himself to death, even though the decision to do so was made knowingly and voluntarily. In *Caulk*, the inmate did not make any demands during his hunger strike, but rather his course of conduct was aimed at achieving one goal—death. After noting that the inmate enjoyed a constitutional right to privacy, the New Hampshire court concluded that the state interest in the maintenance of institutional security was implicated.

Singletary held that the prisoner's right to refuse medical intervention had to be balanced against only the state interest in the preservation of life. This interest, in and of itself, was not felt to overcome the fundamental nature of the prisoner's privacy right. Consequently, a prison inmate has the legal right to refuse medical treatment where the need for the treatment stems from a self-induced hunger strike.

In a related case, *Thor v. Superior Court,*[86] a quadriplegic inmate intermittently refused to be fed. A prison doctor petitioned the trial court for an order allowing him to use a gastrojejunostomy or percutaneous gastrostomy tube to feed and medicate the inmate. After thoroughly discussing the right "to be left alone," the California Supreme Court concluded, as a general proposition, that a physician has no duty to treat an individual who declines medical intervention after reasonable disclosure of the available choices with respect to proposed therapy (including non-treatment) and of the dangers inherently and potentially involved in each. A competent adult patient's "informed refusal" supersedes and discharges the obligation to render further treatment. The *Thor* court dismissed the state interest in the prevention of suicide because no state interest was compromised by allowing an individual to experience a dignified death rather than an excruciatingly painful life. The California court also found inapplicable the state interest in the protection of innocent third parties because the inmate was childless. The prisoner, in refusing to consent to further treatment, was exercising his fundamental right of self-determination in medical decisions. Further, unlike *Singletary*, the prisoner offered no evidence that allowing him to do so would undermine prison integrity or endanger the public. In *Thor*, the prisoner had the constitutional right to refuse treatment.

Ordinary and normal health needs are the criteria. The Constitution does not require a state prison system to permit a prisoner to have a sex change operation.[87]

In *Gutierrez v. Peters*, prisoner suffered from a cyst on his back that became infected and caused severe pain and a high fever. His medical needs were "serious." Serious medical needs include not only life-threatening illnesses, but also conditions that when left untreated cause needless pain and suffering. However, the treatment that the prisoner received, although not prompt, was sufficient to preclude a finding of "deliberate indifference" to his medical needs.[88]

Segregated confinement may be used for health needs. A form of confinement called "tuberculin hold" for prisoners who refuse to submit to testing for latent tuberculosis did not amount to cruel and unusual punishment.[89]

Because health care is costly, there is no constitutional problem with requiring prisoners to pay nominal fees for health care.[90]

---

[86] 5 Cal. 4th 725, 855 P.2d 375 (Cal. 1993).
[87] Maggert v. Hanks, 131 F.3d 670 (7th Cir. 1997). *But see* Farmer v. Hawk, 991 F. Supp. 19 (D.D.C. 1998).
[88] Gutierrez v. Peters, 111 F.3d 1364 (7th Cir. 1997).
[89] Word v. Croce, 169 F. Supp. 2d 219 (S.D.N.Y. 2001).
[90] Reynolds v. Wagner, 128 F.3d 166 (3d Cir. 1997).

In *Comstock v. McCrary*, a prison psychologist subjectively perceived a risk of serious harm to an inmate but displayed deliberate indifference to the inmate's serious medical needs. The psychologist took the prisoner off the suicide watch he had placed him on just the day before. He did not make a thorough assessment of the inmate's emotional state, or make a reasoned assessment or evaluation of the inmate's suicide risk. The psychologist knew that the inmate was concerned about possibly being harmed by other inmates.[91]

However, jail officials were not deliberately indifferent to the risk of a decedent's suicide where the jail was in compliance with the state's minimum standards for suicide prevention although the intake officers had only general training in recognizing a suicide risk and the intake form was inadequate. The decedent acted as if he were joking when he spoke of a prior suicide attempt.[92]

A commissioner rejected a prison medical staff's recommended transfer of a disabled inmate to another facility with appropriate accommodations. The failure to maintain the prison in accordance with federal standards of accessibility was contrary to a clearly established requirement that the state not act in deliberate indifference to an inmate's serious medical needs. The commissioner was not entitled to qualified immunity in an inmate's Eighth Amendment claim.[93]

An inmate alleged a series of failures attributable to different county officials on multiple occasions to attend to his medical needs. The continuing failures over a period of several weeks adequately pleaded that county officials had a widespread custom of failing to provide care for his serious medical needs.[94]

A deliberate indifference to serious medical needs claim was shown where an inmate alleged numerous problems and symptoms he suffered without proper glasses in the fluorescent lighting of his cell. Prison officials ignored the orders of two doctors that the inmate be provided with tinted glasses with side shields.[95]

Prison officials were held deliberately indifferent to an inmate's medical needs when his dentures were not given to him. This resulted in an inability to chew or eat properly, as well as bleeding, headaches, and disfigurement. Also, he was not given his heart medication, resulting in heart "fluttering" due to lapse in medication, and severe chest pain.[96]

Deliberate indifference is shown against a dental hygienist where an inmate complained that he suffered from a toothache for the better part of year, and that the hygienist saw him once, examined a lump in his mouth, and remarked "oh, that is kind of bad," and told him she would schedule an appointment.[97]

---

[91]   Comstock v. McCrary, 273 F.3d 693 (6th Cir. 2001).
[92]   Estate of Boncher v. Brown County, 272 F.3d 484 (7th Cir. 2001).
[93]   Navedo v. Maloney 172 F. Supp. 2d 276 (D.C. Mass. 2001).
[94]   Thornton v. United States DOJ, 93 F. Supp. 2d 1057 (D.C. Minn. 2001).
[95]   Shelton v. Angelone, 148 F. Supp. 2d 670 (W.D. Va. 2001).
[96]   Wynn v. Southward, 251 F.3d 588 (7th Cir. 2001).
[97]   Manney v. Monroe, 151 F. Supp. 2d 976 (N.D. Ill. 2001).

However, a deliberate indifference to medical needs claim failed in *Bout v. Bolden*, even though the inmate alleged that he was forcefully held down and subjected to dental work without benefit of anesthesia. The inmate needed tooth repair and the treatment was successful. The decision to drill without anesthesia rather than further delay treatment—given the minor nature of repair and relatively brief period of pain—did not amount to a constitutional violation.[98]

An inmate stated a valid claim where it was shown that a prior gunshot injury to his leg was so severe that he required reconstructive surgery and was unable to walk without the assistance of a cane or crutches. An officer denied him use of the cane and crutches and forced him to walk without assistance, resulting in unnecessary pain and suffering.[99]

Prison officials conditioned hernia surgery on an inmate's release of future liability that might arise after surgery. These actions establish a deliberate indifference to the inmate's Eighth Amendment right to basic medical care.[100]

An inmate experienced frequent, sometimes unbearable, pain in his left hip. He was diagnosed with avascular necrosis of his left femoral head, and was recommended for a bone graft procedure in August 1998. He received no surgery by August 1999, even though at that time, following further X-rays, a decision was made to cancel the surgery. The lengthy delay raised the issue of deliberate indifference to a serious medical need.[101]

Youth detention center employees were entitled to qualified immunity for a sexual assault on a minor while he was in the custody of the center. A four-hour delay in medical attention did not amount to deliberate indifference to serious medical needs where the youth told no one of the assault, the blood stain on his underwear was reasonably assumed to be evidence of gastrointestinal problems for which the youth was already being treated, emergency treatment was not required, and there was no medical evidence indicating that the four-hour delay before he was taken to hospital worsened his medical condition.[102]

Prison officials were entitled to qualified immunity in an inmate's claim that officials violated his right to privacy of medical information regarding his HIV-positive status. The law was not clearly established that the officials' conduct in not keeping the inmate's medical condition confidential violated the inmate's constitutional rights.[103]

Qualified immunity protected jail personnel sued by an inmate who was catheterized against his will. The procedure was ordered by a prison doctor for diagnostic purposes after a scuffle with a guard. It would not have been either

---

[98]   Bout v. Bolden, 22 F. Supp. 2d 646 (E.D. Mich. 1998) , *aff'd*, 225 F.3d 658 (6th Cir. 2000).

[99]   Castellano v. Chicago P.D., 129 F. Supp. 2d 1184 (N.D. Ill. 2001).

[100]   Beck v. Skon, 253 F.3d 330 (8th Cir. 2001).

[101]   Palermo v. Corr. Med. Servs., 133 F. Supp. 2d 1348 (S.D. Fla. 2001).

[102]   Hill v. Dekalb Regional Youth Detention Ctr., 40 F.3d 1176 (11th Cir. 1994), *criticized in* United States v. Lopez-Lukis, 102 F.3d 1164 (11th Cir. 1997), and Lancaster v. Monroe County, 116 F.3d 1419 (11th Cir. 1997).

[103]   Doe v. Delie, 257 F.3d 309 (3d Cir. 2001).

apparent or sufficiently clear to a reasonable official at that time that the forcible catheterizing of a prisoner, for medical purposes only, would constitute an unreasonable search under the Fourth Amendment.[104]

§ 10.4 Right to Life

The Eighth Amendment prohibits cruel and unusual punishments. The language derives from the English Bill of Rights of 1689, which states that "excessive bail ought not to be required, nor excessive fines imposed, nor cruel and unusual punishments inflicted."[105] The proscription of cruel and unusual punishments has been attributed to reaction to barbaric, torturous punishments imposed by the Stuarts,[106] and to illegal punishments (such as defrocking) imposed by the King's Bench. Either way, "there is no doubt whatever that in borrowing the language and including it in the Eighth Amendment, our Founding Fathers intended to outlaw torture and other cruel punishments."[107]

The clause has historically been interpreted to forbid such "punishments of torture" as disembowelment, beheading, quartering, burning at the stake, and breaking at the wheel.[108]

The United States Supreme Court, in its landmark five-to-four decision in *Furman v. Georgia*[109] held, in the cases under review, that the death penalty amounted to cruel and unusual punishment because it was imposed in an arbitrary manner. Only two justices held that the death penalty amounted to cruel and unusual punishment in all cases. Because each member of the Court wrote a separate opinion, the exact effect of the *Furman* decision upon the constitutionality of the death penalty as such was uncertain. The focus of the opinions holding the statute in question unconstitutional was that standardless capital sentencing discretion, whether vested in a judge or a jury, allowed the imposition of this most irrevocable of all legal sanctions to be freakish or discriminatory.

In apparent response to the *Furman* decision, the majority of states enacted modified death penalty statutes. Some of the new statutes attempted to comply with *Furman* by complete elimination of capital sentencing discretion. These statutes specified mandatory death sentences for certain crimes. Other new statutes sought to fulfill *Furman's* requirement of nondiscriminatory, reasoned capital sentencing by stringent specification of standards within which capital sentencing discretion must be exercised.

---

[104] Sauleberry v. Maricopa County, 151 F. Supp. 2d 1109 (D.C. Ariz. 2001).
[105] *See* Furman v. Georgia, 408 U.S. 238, 243-244 (1972) (Douglas, J., concurring).
[106] *See* Furman, 408 U.S. at 253-255 (Douglas, J., concurring).
[107] Furman, 408 U.S. at 319 (Marshall, J., concurring).
[108] Furman, 408 U.S. at 264-265 (Brennan, J., concurring) (quoting Wilkerson v. Utah, 99 U.S. 130, 135 (1878)).
[109] 408 U.S. 238 (1972).

After careful selection of representative capital sentencing statutes, the Supreme Court decided five death penalty cases on July 2, 1976. In *Gregg v. Georgia*,[110] the Court analyzed the perennial argument that the death penalty amounts to cruel and unusual punishment in all cases. Rejecting this argument, Justice Stewart stated that the existence of capital punishment was accepted by the Framers of the Constitution, and that the Supreme Court has recognized for nearly two centuries that capital punishment for the crime of murder is not invalid *per se*. The *Gregg* case involved a double murder during an armed robbery. The Georgia capital sentencing statute requires a two-part trial: a guilt stage and a penalty stage. The Georgia statute provides for jury sentencing, with instructions from the judge. Jury sentencing is considered desirable in capital cases in order to maintain a link between contemporary community values and the penal system—a link without which the determination of punishment could hardly reflect the evolving standards of decency that mark the progress of a maturing society. When it is considering whether to sentence an inmate to life imprisonment or death, a Georgia jury must consider mitigating and aggravating circumstances of the crime and the criminal. The jury's attention is directed to the specific circumstances of the crime.

Was it committed in the course of another capital felony? Was it committed for money? Was it committed upon a peace officer or judicial officer? Was it committed in a particularly heinous way or in a manner that endangered the lives of many people? In addition, the jury's attention is focused on the characteristics of the person who committed the crime: Does he have a record of prior convictions for capital offenses? Are there any special facts about this defendant that mitigate against imposing capital punishment (e.g., youth, the extent of cooperation with the police, emotional state at the time of the crime)?[111]

An automatic review of each death sentence by the Georgia Supreme Court is provided to standardize capital sentencing statewide. Such standardization is to be achieved by a comparison, on a case-by-case basis by the Georgia Supreme Court, of each new death sentence with sentences imposed on similarly situated defendants. The Georgia Supreme Court can reduce such sentences. In *Gregg*, for example, the court vacated a death sentence imposed for the armed robbery alone because the death penalty had rarely been imposed in Georgia for that offense. It should be noted that *Zant v. Stephens*[112] indicates that the state of Georgia may be relaxing the standards used for the imposition of capital punishment as espoused in *Gregg v. Georgia*. In *Zant*, the state court explained that statutory aggravating factors were used in Georgia as merely a threshold to determine the class of cases in which defendants who are convicted of murder may be eligible for the death penalty. Further case law amplification may indicate that such a posture does not satisfy the *Furman v. Georgia* prohibition against standardless sentencing.

---

[110]   428 U.S. 153 (1976).
[111]   *Id.*
[112]   462 U.S. 862 (1983).

The other four death sentence cases that the U.S. Supreme Court decided in July 1976 were *Proffitt v. Florida*,[113] *Jurek v. Texas*,[114] *Woodson v. North Carolina*,[115] and *Roberts v. Louisiana*.[116] These cases presented statutory variations on the theme of the Georgia statute, i.e., elimination of standardless capital sentencing discretion. The Supreme Court affirmed the Florida and Texas cases, and reversed the North Carolina and Louisiana cases.

The Florida capital sentencing statute vests capital sentencing discretion in its trial judges, who are given specific and detailed guidance to assist them in deciding whether to impose the death penalty or life imprisonment.[117] Capital cases are also two-part proceedings in Florida. Juries make advisory sentence recommendations by majority vote in the penalty stage. The trial judge must justify the imposition of the death penalty with written findings. Such written findings encourage the meaningful appellate review mandated by the statute. Trial judges are directed to weigh eight specific aggravating factors against seven justified mitigating factors to determine whether the death penalty will be imposed. This determination requires the trial judge to focus on the circumstances of the crime and the character of the convict.

In *Jurek v. Texas*,[118] a statutory scheme that is somewhat more mechanical than those upheld in *Gregg* and *Proffitt* was also upheld. Texas mandated two-part proceedings, and its juries are the actual sentencing authorities because, depending upon the jury's response to specific statutorily mandated questions, the trial judge imposes the single statutory sanction available. As Texas narrows its capital offense category, it implicitly requires its juries to find the existence of a statutory aggravating circumstance before the death penalty can be imposed. Although mitigating circumstances are not explicitly mentioned in the statute, Texas courts have construed the statute to allow juries to consider such evidence.[119] The Texas capital sentencing statute guides and focuses the jury's objective consideration of the specific circumstances of the individual offender and offense. Thus, it fulfills *Furman's* requirement for guided discretion.

In *Woodson v. North Carolina*[120] and *Roberts v. Louisiana*,[121] the death penalty statutes of North Carolina and Louisiana were declared unconstitutional. Rather than establishing specific standards as Georgia, Florida, and Texas had, North Carolina and Louisiana tried to completely eliminate all capital sentencing discretion. To this end, they adopted mandatory capital sentencing. Historically they were on firm ground because all the states had mandatory death sentences for specified offenses at the time of the adoption

---

[113]   428 U.S. 242 (1976).
[114]   428 U.S. 262 (1976).
[115]   428 U.S. 280 (1976).
[116]   428 U.S. 325 (1976).
[117]   Proffitt v. Florida, 428 U.S. 242 (1976).
[118]   428 U.S. 262 (1976). *Id.* at 265.
[119]   *Id.* at 265.
[120]   428 U.S. 280 (1976).
[121]   428 U.S. 325 (1976).

of the Eighth Amendment in 1791. However, the Supreme Court concluded that the two crucial indicators of evolving standards of decency with respect to the imposition of punishment in our society—jury determinations and legislative enactments—conclusively point to present-day repudiation of automatic death sentences. Additionally, both the North Carolina and Louisiana statutes fall within *Furman's* prohibition against standardless discretion in that each merely pushes unfettered sentencing discretion into the ostensible guilt determination stage of the proceeding. The difference between the North Carolina and Louisiana statutes lies in the somewhat narrower definition of capital murder under Louisiana law.[122] In addition, Louisiana's subsequent attempt to cure the defects found in *Roberts* by narrowing the scope of mandatory capital punishment to include only cases in which the victim is a murdered police officer, was similarly rejected by the Supreme Court.[123]

In *Gregg*, the United States Supreme Court specifically noted that it was not deciding whether states could or could not allow or provide for death sentences in cases that do not involve murder of the victim, i.e., rape, kidnapping, armed robbery, etc. However, since 1976 the Court has begun to address this issue and has demonstrated a general reluctance to uphold the imposition of capital punishment when, although convicted of a serious crime, the defendant has not taken the life of another. By way of example, in *Coker v. Georgia*[124] the Court held that Georgia's death penalty statute was unconstitutional as applied to a defendant who, although guilty of rape, had not killed the victim. This position was modified somewhat in *Enmund v. Florida*.[125] In *Enmund*, the Court refused to permit the death penalty to be imposed on a so-called non-triggerman in a felony-murder conviction. However, the Supreme Court carefully noted that its decision did not establish a requirement that imposition of the death penalty mandates that the defendant be the actual killer; rather, the trial court's reversible error was its refusal during sentencing to consider the defendant's lack of intent that the killings occur.

In 1987, the United States Supreme Court held that although two brothers neither intended to kill the victims nor inflicted the fatal wounds, the record supported a finding that they had the culpable mental state of reckless indifference to human life. Consequently, the Eighth Amendment did not prohibit the death penalty as disproportionate in the case of a defendant whose participation in a felony that results in murder is major and whose mental state is one of reckless indifference. A survey of state felony-murder laws and judicial decisions after *Enmund* indicated societal consensus that a combination of factors may justify the death penalty even without a specific "intent to kill." Reckless disregard for human life also represents a highly culpable mental state that may support a capital sentencing judgment in combination with major participation in the felony resulting in death.[126]

---

[122] Roberts v. Louisiana, 428 U.S. 325 (1976).
[123] Roberts v. Louisiana, 431 U.S. 633 (1977).
[124] 433 U.S. 584 (1977).
[125] 458 U.S. 782 (1982).
[126] Tison v. Arizona, 481 U.S. 137 (1987).

Since 1976, the Supreme Court has spent considerable time attempting to determine the constitutional parameters of mitigating and aggravating circumstances as utilized by the various states in the determination of whether to impose capital punishment in a particular case. In *Lockett v. Ohio*,[127] the Supreme Court held that a statute that provided too limited a range of mitigating circumstances is unconstitutional. The Court established in *Lockett* that only rarely should the sentencing authority be precluded from considering "any" mitigating factors relative to the defendant's character or the circumstances of the offense. In *Eddings v. Oklahoma*,[128] the Supreme Court vacated the death sentence of a convicted murderer by applying the rule established in *Lockett*. In *Eddings*, the Court explicitly noted that a state may not by statute preclude the sentencer from considering any mitigating factor. The United States Supreme Court continues to define "mitigating evidence."

In a capital murder case, the defendant presented as mitigating evidence his own testimony and that of his former wife, his mother, his sister, and his grandmother. He then sought to introduce testimony of two jailers and a "regular visitor" to the effect that he had "made a good adjustment" during the seven and one-half months he had spent in jail between his arrest and trial. The trial court ruled such evidence irrelevant and inadmissible, and the defendant was sentenced to death. The United States Supreme Court reversed, and held that the trial court's exclusion of the testimony of the jailers and the visitor from the sentencing hearing denied the defendant his right to place before the sentencing jury all relevant evidence in mitigation of punishment.[129]

In another capital murder case, the trial judge instructed the advisory jury not to consider, and himself refused to consider, evidence of mitigating circumstances not specifically enumerated in the state's death penalty statute. The United States Supreme Court reversed and held that this procedure was inconsistent with the requirement that the sentencer may neither refuse to consider nor be precluded from considering any relevant mitigating evidence.[130]

While serving a life sentence without the possibility of parole for a first-degree murder conviction, an inmate was sentenced to death for the murder of a fellow prisoner. Under Nevada statute, the death penalty was mandated in these circumstances. The United States Supreme Court held that under the individualized capital sentencing doctrine, it is constitutionally required that the sentencing authority consider, as a mitigating factor, any aspect of the defendant's character or record and any of the circumstances of the particular offense. Consequently, a statute that mandates the death penalty for a prison inmate who is convicted of murder while serving a life sentence without possibility of parole, violates the Eighth and Fourteenth Amendments.[131]

---

[127] 438 U.S. 586 (1978).
[128] 455 U.S. 104 (1982).
[129] Skipper v. South Carolina, 476 U.S. 1 (1986).
[130] Hitchcock v. Dugger, 481 U.S. 393 (1987).
[131] Sumner v. Nevada, 483 U.S. 66 (1987).

Decisions related to aggravating factors tend to focus on the content rather than the presence or absence of statutory provisions. In *Godfrey v. Georgia*,[132] the Supreme Court held that aggravating factors may be so vague that a sentencing authority may have so much discretion as to give rise to a standardless imposition of the death penalty, which the United States Supreme Court specifically rejected as unconstitutional in *Furman v. Georgia*.

Affirmation of the constitutionality of capital punishment by the Supreme Court in *Gregg* and its related cases does not, however, resolve this issue. Two other considerations must be noted. One is the status of capital punishment under state constitutions, and the other is the effect of future community values toward the constitutionality of capital punishment in a federal constitutional sense.

In *Commonwealth v. O'Neal*,[133] the Massachusetts Supreme Judicial Court concluded that a Massachusetts statute that provided for the death penalty for a convicted rapist-murderer was unconstitutional under the Massachusetts state constitution. The major focus of this decision was that the state's imposition of capital punishment is the least compelling means available to attain its legitimate goal of public safety. This argument was specifically rejected by the United States Supreme Court in *Gregg v. Georgia*, but because of the vagaries of our federal system of government, it is not binding upon a state's interpretation of its own constitution. This case points out the basically minimal nature of United States Supreme Court decisions—in many areas the minimum a state must do is mandated through the federal courts. A state is free to adopt standards higher than the federal standard if it wishes. As a result of the *O'Neal* decision, Massachusetts has ended capital punishment, regardless of the latitude that was bestowed upon all the states in the *Gregg* decision.

Another example of higher state standards is *People v. Anderson*.[134] In that case, the California Supreme Court declared its state capital punishment statute to be unconstitutional. The basis of that decision was the existence of the disjunctive "or" rather than the conjunctive "and" in the California constitution's equivalent of the federal constitution's Eighth Amendment prohibition against "cruel and unusual punishment." California's phrase reads "cruel or unusual punishment." The California Supreme Court concluded that infrequent imposition of the death penalty equals unusual punishment, and struck down its use completely. The opinion noted that public acceptance of capital punishment is a relevant, but not controlling, factor in any assessment of whether it is consonant with contemporary standards of decency. However, the California court readily acknowledged the distribution of political clout when it enforced the new capital punishment statute enacted in California following a statewide referendum on whether the death penalty should be used in California.[135]

---

[132]   446 U.S. 420 (1980).
[133]   339 N.E.2d 676 (Mass. 1975).
[134]   6 Cal. 3d 628, 493 P.2d 880, *cert. denied*, 406 U.S. 958 (1976).
[135]   *See* Gregg v. Georgia, 428 U.S. 153 (1976).

The other consideration that should enter into any discussion of capital punishment after *Gregg* is the effect of ethical evolution. One of the primary supports for *Gregg* is the United States Supreme Court's assessment of the level of decency in the states. Several states do not authorize capital punishment under their internal laws. If these states ever become the majority, the U.S. Supreme Court may reconsider the holding of *Gregg* so as to better reflect the needs of a maturing society.

Other issues continue to plague the Court. In *Booth v. Maryland,* the jury's imposition of a death sentence after considering a presentence report that included a victim impact statement violated the Eighth Amendment. The information contained in the victim impact statement was held to be irrelevant to a capital sentencing decision, and its admission creates a constitutionally unacceptable risk that the jury may impose the death penalty in an arbitrary and capricious manner.[136] However, four years later, in *Payne v. Tennessee,*[137] *Booth* was overruled. Victim impact statements may be used.

The prosecutor's closing argument at the sentencing phase in a death penalty case included his reading to the jury at length from a religious tract the victim was carrying and commenting on the personal qualities that the prosecutor inferred from the victim's possession of the religious tract and a voter registration card. The United States Supreme Court held that for purposes of imposing the death penalty, the defendant's punishment must be tailored to his personal responsibility and moral guilt. The prosecutor's comments concerned the victim's personal characteristics, and allowing the jury to rely on this information could result in imposing the death sentence because of factors about which the defendant was unaware, and that were irrelevant to the decision to kill. The content of the religious tract and the voter registration card could not possibly have been relevant to the "circumstances of the crime." Where there was no evidence that the defendant read either the tract or the voter card, the content of the papers the victim was carrying was purely fortuitous and could not provide any information relevant to respondent's moral culpability, notwithstanding that the papers had been admitted in evidence for other purposes. The death penalty was set aside.[138] However, as in *Booth*, *Gathers* was overruled four years later and is no longer valid authority.

Although the Eighth Amendment prohibits a state from inflicting the death penalty on a prisoner who is insane,[139] the Eighth Amendment does not categorically prohibit the execution of mentally retarded capital murderers of diminished reasoning ability nor does it prohibit the execution of youth.[140] The imposition of capital punishment on an individual for a crime committed at 16 or 17 years of age does not constitute cruel and unusual punishment under the Eighth Amendment.[141] However, when a 15-year-old youth actively participat-

---

[136]   Booth v. Maryland, 482 U.S. 496 (1987), *overruled by* Payne v. Tennessee, 501 U.S. 808 (1991).
[137]   501 U.S. 808 (1991).
[138]   South Carolina v. Gathers, 490 U.S. 805 (1989), *overruled by* Payne v. Tennessee, 501 U.S. 808 (1991).
[139]   Ford v. Wainwright, 477 U.S. 399 (1986).
[140]   Penry v. Lynaugh, 492 U.S. 302 (1989).
[141]   Stanford v. Kentucky, 492 U.S. 361 (1989).

ed in a brutal murder and was sentenced to death, a plurality of the United States Supreme Court reversed the death penalty.[142] Four members of the Supreme Court—Justices Stevens, Brennan, Marshall, and Blackmun—concluded that the "cruel and unusual punishment" prohibition of the Eighth Amendment, made applicable to the states by the Fourteenth Amendment, prohibits the execution of a person who was under 16 years of age at the time of his or her offense. To establish the plurality in setting aside the death sentence, Justice O'Connor held that because the available evidence suggested a national consensus forbidding the imposition of capital punishment for crimes committed before the age of 16, the youth and others whose crimes were committed before that age may not be executed pursuant to a capital punishment statute that specifies no minimum age.

The Supreme Court has rarely, however, addressed whether particular *methods* of execution employed in this country are unconstitutionally cruel. Judicial hanging was last directly addressed by the Court in 1878, in *Wilkerson v. Utah*. The Court specifically distinguished between various punishments of torture and hanging, the traditional method of execution at common law.[143]

Decisions construing the Eighth Amendment focus on whether the sentence constitutes "one of 'those modes or acts of punishment that had been considered cruel and unusual at the time that the Bill of Rights was adopted,' "[144] and on whether the punishment is contrary to "the evolving standards of decency that mark the progress of a maturing society."[145]

The Ninth Circuit applied these principles in a hanging case.[146] There was no dispute that execution by hanging was acceptable when the Bill of Rights was adopted.[147] To determine whether hanging is unconstitutionally cruel and unusual, the court looked to objective factors to the maximum extent possible.[148] Among these factors are statutes passed by society's elected representatives,[149] because there is a presumption that a punishment selected by a democratically elected legislature is constitutionally valid.[150]

The court did not consider hanging to be cruel and unusual simply because it causes death, or because there may be some pain associated with death. "Punishments are cruel when they involve torture or a lingering death . . ."[151] As used in the Constitution, "cruel" implies "something inhuman and barbarous, something more than the mere extinguishment of life."[152] "The cruelty against

---

[142]   Thompson v. Oklahoma, 487 U.S. 815 (1988).

[143]   Wilkerson v. Utah, 99 U.S. at 135-137; *see also* In re Kemmler, 136 U.S. 436 (1890) (upholding electrocution as method of execution); Louisiana ex rel. Francis v. Resweber, 329 U.S. 459, 464 (1947) (upholding second attempt at electrocution after first attempt failed to cause death); *but see* Glass v. Louisiana, 471 U.S. 1080 (1985) (Brennan, J., dissenting).

[144]   Stanford v. Kentucky, 492 U.S. 361 (1989) (quoting Ford v. Wainwright, 477 U.S. 399 (1986)).

[145]   Trop v. Dulles, 356 U.S. 86 (1958).

[146]   Campbell v. Wood, 18 F.3d 662 (9th Cir. 1994).

[147]   *See* Wilkerson, 99 U.S. at 133-134.

[148]   Stanford, 492 U.S. at 369 (quoting Coker v. Georgia, 433 U.S. 584 (1977) (plurality opinion)).

[149]   *Id.* at 370 (citing McCleskey v. Kemp, 481 U.S. 279 (1987)).

[150]   Gregg, 428 U.S. at 175.

[151]   In re Kemmler, 136 U.S. 436 (1890).

[152]   *Ibid.*

which the Constitution protects a convicted person is cruelty inherent in the method of punishment, not the necessary suffering involved in any method employed to extinguish life humanely."[153] A prisoner is entitled to an execution free only of "the unnecessary and wanton infliction of pain."[154] It was held that hanging did not involve the unnecessary and wanton infliction of pain.

In 2002, the execution of a mental retarded criminal was held by *Atkins v. Virginia* to be "cruel and unusual punishment" and prohibited by the Eighth Amendment.[155]

In death penalty cases, the Supreme Court in *Jones v. United States*[156] held that the Eighth Amendment does not require that a jury be instructed as to the consequences of their failure to agree. In federal cases, the Federal Death Penalty Act requires judge sentencing when the jury, after retiring for deliberations, reports itself as unable to reach a unanimous verdict. In such a case, the sentencing duty falls upon the district court pursuant to 18 U.S.C. §3594. The Eighth Amendment, however, does not require that a jury be instructed as to the consequences of a breakdown in the deliberative process. Such an instruction has no bearing on the jury's role in the sentencing process. Moreover, the jury system's very object is to secure unanimity, and the government has a strong interest in having the jury express the conscience of the community on the ultimate life or death question. The Supreme Court declined to invoke its supervisory power over the federal courts and require that such an instruction be given in every capital case in these circumstances.

In a death penalty case, so that a jury has full information before it before deciding cases of life or death, a defendant is entitled to a jury instruction that he would be ineligible for parole under a life sentence.[157]

In a death penalty case, the Supreme Court held that *Walton v. Arizona,*[158] and *Apprendi v. New Jersey*[159] are irreconcilable. Accordingly, *Walton* was overruled to the extent that it allows a sentencing judge, sitting without a jury, to find an aggravating circumstance necessary for imposition of the death penalty. Because Arizona's enumerated aggravating factors operate as the functional equivalent of an element of a greater offense, the Sixth Amendment requires that they be found by a jury. In upholding Arizona's capital sentencing scheme against a charge that it violated the Sixth Amendment, the *Walton* Court ruled that aggravating factors were not elements of the offense. They were sentencing considerations guiding the choice between life and death. In *Apprendi,* the sentencing judge's finding that racial animus motivated the petitioner's weapons offense triggered application of a state hate crime enhancement that doubled the maximum authorized sentence. In 2002, the Supreme Court held[160] that the sentence enhancement violated Apprendi's right to a jury

---

[153]   Resweber, 329 U.S. at 464 (1947).
[154]   Gregg v. Georgia, 428 U.S. 153 (1976) (plurality opinion).
[155]   536 U.S. 304 (2002).
[156]   527 U.S. 373 (1999).
[157]   Kelly v. South Carolina, 534 U.S. 246 (2002).
[158]   497 U.S. 639 (1990).
[159]   530 U.S. 466 (2000).
[160]   Ring v. Arizona, 536 U.S. 584 (2002).

determination of whether he was guilty of every element of the crime with which he was charged beyond a reasonable doubt. That right attached not only to Apprendi's weapons offense, but also to the hate crime aggravating circumstance. The dispositive question is one not of form, but of effect. If a state makes an increase in a defendant's authorized punishment contingent on the finding of a fact, that fact—no matter how the state labels it—must be found by a jury beyond a reasonable doubt.

For European reaction to how the United States deals with death penalty issues, *see* Chapter 14.3, Extradition, and Appendix V.

Death penalty cases remain a source of contention among the Justices of the United States Supreme Court. According to a former law clerk, the Court's death penalty cases are inconsistent, irrational, driven by an unprecedented degree of ideology, and the Justices are manipulated by unprincipled law clerks.[161]

§ 10.5   Civil Disabilities

Occasionally, a case that involves the extent to which a prisoner is "civilly dead" or suffers a loss of his or her civil rights upon conviction of a felony reaches the courts. Historically, convicted felons were held to have forfeited all their civil rights; they were considered mere slaves of the state.[162] This extreme view has been modified in recent years.[163]

In *Richardson v. Ramirez,*[164] the United States Supreme Court considered a provision of the California constitution that disenfranchised convicted felons. The Court held that this provision did not violate the equal protection clause of the Fourteenth Amendment, without reaching the general constitutional issue of "civil death."

In *In re Goalen,*[165] an inmate in the Utah State Prison and his girlfriend desired to marry. Both were of legal age and were competent to enter into marriage under state law. However, a section of the Utah Code provided:

> A sentence of imprisonment in the state prison for any term less than for life suspends all civil rights of the person so sentenced during such imprisonment, and forfeits all private trusts and public offices, authority or power.[166]

---

[161]   *See* EDWARD P. LAZARUS, CLOSED CHAMBERS: THE FIRST EYEWITNESS ACCOUNT OF THE EPIC STRUGGLES INSIDE THE SUPREME COURT (1998).

[162]   Ruffin v. Commonwealth, 62 Va. (21 Gratt.) 790, 796 (1871).

[163]   Wolff v. McDonnell, 418 U.S. 539, 555-556 (1974); Chesapeake Utilities Corp. v. Hopkins, 340 A.2d 154 (Del. 1975).

[164]   418 U.S. 24 (1974).

[165]   30 Utah 2d 27, 512 P.2d 1028 (1973), *cert. denied,* 414 U.S. 1148 (1974). *See also* Holden v. Florida Dept. of Corr., 400 So. 2d 142 (Fla. Dist. Ct. App. 1981); Department of Corrections v. Roseman, 390 So. 2d 394 (Fla. Dist. Ct. App. 1980); *cf.* Salisbury v. List, 501 F. Supp. 105 (D. Nev. 1980) (A state prison regulation severely restricting an inmate's right to marry was declared unconstitutional).

[166]   In re Goalen, 414 U.S. at 1149 (dissenting opinion).

In implementation of this statute, the Utah Board of Corrections issued the following policy statement: "It shall be the policy that the warden may, upon recommendation of the treatment team, authorize inmates nearing their release dates to marry."[167] This policy had been interpreted and applied by the state correctional officials to permit marriage by an inmate only when he or she was within six months of release, if the marriage was recommended by the treatment team. Upon application by the prisoner, the warden determined that he was not within the terms of the policy and denied permission for the marriage. The prisoner contended that the freedom to marry was constitutionally protected and that the state could not prohibit the marriage in the absence of some compelling state interest. The interest that the state asserted in support of its policy was that the denial of such civil rights, in conjunction with their gradual return to the convict, "acts as an incentive for the convict to aid in his own rehabilitation."[168] Judicial relief was denied. A prison rule that prohibited prisoners from marrying while incarcerated was a lawful exercise of the prison's administrative power.[169] However, prison restrictions on the right to marry are no longer valid. Inmates in Missouri challenged a regulation permitting an inmate to marry only with the prison superintendent's permission, which could be given only when there were "compelling reasons" to do so. Only a pregnancy or the birth of an illegitimate child would be considered "compelling." This regulation was declared unconstitutional and the United States Supreme Court held that prisoners have a constitutionally protected right to marry.[170]

Although marriages are subject to substantial restrictions as a result of incarceration, sufficient important attributes of marriage remain to form a constitutionally protected relationship. The Missouri regulation was facially invalid under the reasonable relationship test. Although prison officials may regulate the time and circumstances under which a marriage takes place, and may require prior approval by the warden, an almost complete ban on marriages is not reasonably related to legitimate penological objectives. The contention that the regulation served security concerns by preventing "love triangles" that may lead to violent inmate confrontations was held to be without merit, because inmate rivalries were likely to develop with or without a formal marriage ceremony. Moreover, the regulation's broad prohibition was not justified by the security of fellow inmates and prison staff, who were not affected where the inmate made the private decision to marry a civilian. Rather, the regulation represented an exaggerated response to the claimed security objectives, because allowing marriages—unless the warden found a threat to security, order, or the public safety—represented an obvious, easy alternative that would accommodate the right to marry while imposing a *de minimis* burden. Nor was the regulation reasonably related to the articulated rehabilitation goal

---

[167]   *Id.*
[168]   *Id.*
[169]   Bradbury v. Wainwright, 538 F. Supp. 377 (M.D. Fla. 1982).
[170]   Turner v. Safley, 482 U.S. 78 (1987).

of fostering self-reliance by female prisoners. In forbidding all inmates to marry absent a compelling reason, the regulation swept much more broadly than was necessary. Male inmates' marriages had generally caused prison officials no problems and they had no objections to prisoners marrying civilians.

In *Bush v. Reid,*[171] the Alaska Supreme Court held that an Alaska "civil death" statute that barred prisoners and parolees from bringing a civil lawsuit that was unrelated to conviction or confinement was unconstitutional. According to this court, the right to bring a civil suit for damages is a form of property. In this case, denying a parolee the opportunity to convert his claim to a far more valuable money judgment was held to be "taking of property" without due process.

The extent of a convicted felon's civil disability is the focus of substantial litigation. For example, the issue of the liability of ex-felons for possession of firearms was in such confusion that in *Barrett v. United States,*[172] the United States Supreme Court held that the Gun Control Act,[173] which forbids a convicted felon to receive any firearm that has been shipped or transported in interstate commerce, applied to a felon's isolated intrastate purchase of a firearm that had previously traveled in interstate commerce. This is also true when the firearm is issued by a state to a rehabilitated felon for use within the scope of his employment as a state corrections officer.[174]

Convicted felons have unsuccessfully litigated their purported rights to use checking accounts while incarcerated,[175] to rear their children in prison,[176] and to fully exercise their First Amendment rights.[177]

The supremacy clause of the federal Constitution prevents a state from attaching Social Security benefits, as well as other types of pension or retirement benefits, in order to help defray the costs of maintaining its prison system.[178]

The state has a compelling interest in maintaining security and order in its prisons and, to the extent that it furthers that interest in reasonable and nonarbitrary ways, property claims by inmates must give way. A prison's restrictions on possessing currency amount to reasonable attempts to guarantee the individual safety of the prisoner and the security of the prison and therefore the confiscation of an inmate's money does not violate his or her civil rights.[179]

---

[171] 516 P.2d 1215 (Alaska 1973); Thompson v. Bond, 421 F. Supp. 878 (W.D. Mo. 1976).

[172] Barrett v. United States, 423 U.S. 212 (1976).

[173] 18 U.S.C. § 922h.

[174] Hyland v. Fukuda, 580 F.2d 1977 (9th Cir. 1978).

[175] Nix v. Paderick, 407 F. Supp. 844 (E.D. Va. 1976).

[176] Pendergrass v. Toombs, 546 P.2d 1103 (Or. Ct. App. 1976); Wainwright v. Moore, 374 So. 2d 586 (Fla. Dist. Ct. App. 1979); Delaney v. Booth, 400 So. 2d 1268 (Fla. Dist. Ct. App. 1981).

[177] United States v. Huss, 394 F. Supp. 752 (S.D.N.Y. 1975); Secretary, Department of Public Safety and Correctional Services v. Allen, 406 A.2d 104 (Md. 1979); French v. Butterworth, 614 F.2d 23 (1st Cir. 1980); Garland v. Polley, 594 F.2d 1220 (8th Cir. 1979); People v. Coleman, 174 Cal. Rptr. 756 (Cal. Ct. App. 1981).

[178] Bennett v. Arkansas, 485 U.S. 395 (1988).

[179] Harris v. Forsyth, 735 F.2d 1235 (11th Cir. 1984).

§ 10.6   Sex Discrimination

Inmates at the Iowa Correctional Institution for Women argued that they were similarly situated to male inmates with the same security classification at other prisons, but that they received different treatment, programs, and services. One major focus was on inmates classified as *minimum live-out.* They claimed that women were treated unconstitutionally in comparison with their male counterparts: women were classified in a different manner, lived in more confined housing, had fewer furlough and off-ground work opportunities, enjoyed less library time and fewer yard privileges, participated in different substance abuse programs, and saw visitors in more restrictive settings. They also contended that female inmates in other security classification levels did not have the same legal assistance, work release, behavior modification classes, sex offender therapy programs, and yard and library privileges as those available to male inmates with the same classification.

The district court found no evidence of invidious discrimination. It also determined that the programs and services available to female and male inmates as a whole, or according to custody level, were substantially similar to those received by any male inmate given the various institutional needs and circumstances. Any differences were found to be rationally related to legitimate penological interests such as security and rehabilitation. The findings were affirmed by the Eighth Circuit.[180]

§ 10.7   Federal Protective Statutes

Lower courts have taken a restricted view of the application of federal protective statutes. In *Torcasio v. Murray,*[181] an obese inmate filed suit under section 504 of the Rehabilitation Act of 1973 (Rehabilitation Act),[182] and Title II of the Americans with Disabilities Act (ADA).[183] On appeal, the Fourth Circuit concluded that neither the statutes, nor the case law, nor the applicable regulations clearly establish that the ADA or the Rehabilitation Act apply to the obese.

The court felt that there could be little question that application of the ADA and Rehabilitation Act would have serious implications for the management of state prisons, in matters ranging from cell construction and modification to inmate assignment, scheduling, and security procedures. That the acts threaten to intrude so significantly upon the management of state prisons was also recognized by the Ninth Circuit, which observed in *Gates v. Rowland*[184] that the Act was not designed to deal specifically with the prison environment; it was intended for general societal application. There is no indication that

---

[180]   Pargo v. Elliott, 69 F.3d 280 (8th Cir. 1995).
[181]   57 F.3d 1340 (4th Cir. 1995).
[182]   29 U.S.C. § 794.
[183]   42 U.S.C. § 12132.
[184]   39 F.3d 1439 (9th Cir. 1994).

Congress intended the Act to apply to prison facilities, irrespective of the reasonable requirements of effective prison administration. This recognition in fact led the Ninth Circuit to substantially limit an earlier holding that the Rehabilitation Act applies to state prisons.

The Ninth Circuit had earlier held that the Rehabilitation Act applied to prisons in *Bonner v. Lewis.*[185] *Bonner* has been cited by a number of district courts considering Rehabilitation Act claims brought by prison inmates.[186] However, the Ninth Circuit has retreated from its holding in *Bonner.* In *Gates v. Rowland,*[187] the court considered how the Act is to be applied in a prison setting, and observed that the Act was not designed to deal specifically with the prison environment. The Ninth Circuit held that the applicable standard for the review of the Act's statutory rights in a prison setting is equivalent to the standard for the review of constitutional rights in a prison setting. Similarly, in *Williams v. Meese,*[188] the Tenth Circuit held that a federal prisoner could not invoke the Rehabilitation Act because the Federal Bureau of Prisons does not fit the definition of "programs or activities" governed by the Rehabilitation Act.

The issue was settled by the Supreme Court in 1998. In *Pennsylvania Dept. of Corrections v. Yeskey,*[189] a prisoner was sentenced to 18 to 36 months in a Pennsylvania correctional facility, but was recommended for placement in a Motivational Boot Camp for first-time offenders, the successful completion of which would have led to his parole in just six months. He was refused admission because of his medical history of hypertension. He then sued the Pennsylvania's Department of Corrections and several officials, alleging that the exclusion violated the Americans with Disabilities Act of 1990 (ADA), Title II of which prohibits a "public entity" from discriminating against a "qualified individual with a disability" on account of that disability.

The Supreme Court unanimously held that state prisons fall squarely within Title II's statutory definition of "public entity," which includes "any . . . instrumentality of a State . . . or local government."[190] In the Court's view, there was no ambiguous exception that rendered the coverage uncertain. Any attempt to derive an intent not to cover prisons from the statutory references to the "benefits" of programs, and to "qualified individual" was rejected.

The Supreme Court did not address the issue of whether applying the ADA to state prisons is a constitutional exercise of Congress's power under either the commerce clause or the Fourteenth Amendment as it was addressed by the lower courts.

---

[185] Bonner v. Lewis, 857 F.2d 559 (9th Cir. 1988).
[186] *See* Donnell C. v. Illinois State Board of Education, 829 F. Supp. 1016, 1020 (N.D. Ill. 1993) ("Contrary to defendants' assertion, the Act applies to inmates at correctional facilities."). Casey v. Lewis, 834 F. Supp. 1569, 1583-1585 (D. Ariz. 1993) (no claim of non-applicability raised by defendants) (holding that "plaintiffs failed to establish violations of § 504 of the Rehabilitation Act of 1973").
[187] 39 F.3d 1439 (9th Cir. 1994).
[188] 926 F.2d 994 (10th Cir. 1991).
[189] 524 U.S. 206 (1998).
[190] 42 U.S.C. § 12131(1)(B).

During the same term the Supreme Court also held that even though an HIV infection had not progressed to the so-called symptomatic phase, it was a "disability" under the ADA.[191]

Similarly, state prisoners involved in an employment skills development program in prison are not entitled to the minimum wage specified in the Fair Labor Standards Act (FLSA).[192] Most courts have been unwilling to extend the protections of the FLSA to prison inmates.[193] Some of these courts have refused to adopt a per se rule that the FLSA does not apply to prisoners, and have instead employed an "economic reality" test, which in theory permits an inmate to qualify as an employee.[194] However, the fact that some courts have followed this course does not cast doubt on the premise that broadly-worded federal statutes do not presumptively apply to state prisons. However, the FLSA is more plausibly interpreted as applying to state prisons than are the ADA and the Rehabilitation Act, because it contains a list of particular classes of workers who are not entitled to FLSA protections.[195]

§ 10.8 Conclusion

Penologists argue that effective rehabilitation programs are the key to success from any correctional system. Judicial concern for penal reform, coupled with the fact that many state statutes and constitutions specifically make rehabilitation an objective of incarceration, raise the probability that treatment programs may soon be judicially required in penal facilities, although *O'Connor v. Donaldson* and more recently *Sandin v. Conner*, have slowed, if not reversed this trend.

---

[191] Bragdon v. Abbott, 524 U.S. 624 (1998). 42 U.S.C. § 12102(2)(A). A disability is "a physical . . . impairment that substantially limits one or more of [an individual's] major life activities."

[192] Even with a broad reading of the term *employee,* there was no indication that Congress provided FLSA coverage for inmates engaged in prison labor programs. If the FLSA's coverage is to extend within prison walls, Congress must say so, not the courts. *See* Gilbreath v. Cutter Biological, Inc., 931 F.2d 1320, 1325 (9th Cir. 1991) (Opinion of Trott, J.) ("It is equally plausible, if not more so, that in view of the manifest purpose of Congress in enacting the FLSA, it did not cross any member's mind—even for a moment—that felons serving hard time in prison and working in the process would be covered by this economic protection. I reject as almost whimsical the notion that Congress could have intended such a radical result as bringing prisoners within the FLSA without expressly so stating. There are obvious policy considerations in such a result that should be openly addressed by Congress, not the courts").

[193] *See* Harker, 990 F.2d at 135 (citing Vanskike v. Peters, 974 F.2d 806, 808 (7th Cir. 1992); Miller v. Dukakis, 961 F.2d 7, 8 (1st Cir. 1992); Gilbreath, 931 F.2d at 1325-1326, 1328-1331).

[194] *See, e.g.,* Carter v. Dutchess Community College, 735 F.2d 8, 12 (2d Cir. 1984).

[195] *See* 29 U.S.C. § 213(a) (exempting, among others, executives, casual babysitters). This provision supplies some of the specificity lacking from the Rehabilitation Act and ADA, because where Congress has specifically excluded some would-be employees from the scope of a statute, the inference can be drawn that Congress intended the act to cover employees not included in that list. *See, e.g.,* Carter, 735 F.2d at 13 (relying on this *expressio unius* reasoning).

It should be recognized that the main objective to "treatment" or "medical experimentation" is the reality that no "voluntary" program in prison is truly free from coercion. Perhaps innovative techniques, such as the appointment of legal guardians for the inmates concerned, or prior judicial review or approval may answer the problem of "free and voluntary consent" within the prison context.

Judicial intervention in medical treatment cases has increased markedly in recent years. Unfortunately, however, federal courts are divided as to when a complaint alleging inadequate medical treatment is sufficient to state a cause of action for deprivation of a federal right. The Supreme Court has not yet rendered a decision clarifying the law in this area.

The constitutionality of capital punishment for the crime of murder has been firmly underscored. Certain types of capital sentencing statutes are necessary to constitutionally impose the death penalty, but the death penalty is not unconstitutional per se. The furor over death as a sanction will abate for some time, but the problem will not be permanently solved because of continual changes in community and ethical values.

Litigation in the area of the civil disabilities of convicted felons, both incarcerated and released, will continue to increase as the revolution in prison law follows the inmate beyond the prison wall.

It is clear that the Americans with Disabilities Act applies to prisons and that inmates with HIV infections or AIDS are covered by the Act.

Civil and Criminal Liabilities of Prison Officials

11

Chapter Outline

§ 11.1 Introduction

The preceding chapters have described various rights that inmates retain while they are incarcerated. This chapter will set forth, in general terms, the judicial remedies that exist to vindicate past violations and to prevent future deprivations of those rights. Several frequently encountered obstacles to inmate suits will also be discussed.

It is important to note that this chapter will discuss only judicial remedies. Not included in this chapter, therefore, is a discussion of possible "administrative remedies"—that is, methods that have been established within the correctional system itself to investigate, punish, and prevent deprivations of inmate rights.

Two reasons can be given for this exclusion: (1) many correctional systems simply do not have formal administrative remedies; and (2) among the states that do have administrative methods to investigate inmate complaints, there is a lack of uniformity, and thus general statements would be misleading at best. Nevertheless, prison officials should seriously consider developing administrative remedies as a faster and more effective method of dealing with inmate complaints.

§ 11.2 Jurisdiction of Federal Courts

With some exceptions not relevant here, the subject matter jurisdiction of federal courts is limited to cases arising under the Constitution or laws of the United States.[1] Thus, before a federal court can render a valid decision in a case, the plaintiff must show that he or she is being denied a right secured to him or her by either the Constitution or a specific federal statute. If the inmate-plaintiff's allegations do not constitute a violation of a federal right, the case must be dismissed if it is instituted in a federal court.[2] Because the judicial power of federal courts is defined and limited by the Constitution, federal courts are commonly referred to as courts of limited jurisdiction.

---

[1]   U.S. CONST., art. III, § 2.
[2]   United States ex rel. Atterbury v. Ragen, 237 F.2d 953 (7th Cir. 1956).

§ 11.3 Jurisdiction of State Courts

In contrast to federal courts, state courts are courts of general jurisdiction. That is, there is a presumption that they have jurisdiction over a particular controversy unless a contrary showing is made. Thus, the subject matter jurisdiction of state courts is much broader than that of federal courts. In addition to being the exclusive means of judicially enforcing rights created by the state's constitution, statutes, and common law, a state court has concurrent jurisdiction with the federal courts to decide cases based entirely on a federal claim,[3] provided that Congress has not given the federal judiciary exclusive jurisdiction in the matter. Therefore, an inmate who alleges a violation of his or her federal constitutional rights may have a choice of forums in which he or she may bring the action; that is, either state or federal court, at his or her option.

However, state law may prevent a claimant from any recovery. In one case, parole authorities were sued based on the fact that a parolee had committed a murder while on parole.[4] Under California law, both the legislature and the courts have squarely rejected public liability for harm resulting from the failure to properly supervise a parolee. Parole authorities are immunized by § 845.8 of the California Government Code, which provides in relevant part, "Neither a public entity nor a public employee is liable for: [P] (a) Any injury resulting from determining whether to parole or release a prisoner or from determining the terms and conditions of his parole or release or from determining whether to revoke his parole or release." In addition, § 846 of the Government Code states, "Neither a public entity nor a public employee is liable for injury caused by the failure to make an arrest or by the failure to retain an arrested person in custody."

Similarly, in *Brenneman v. State of California*,[5] it was alleged that a child had been molested and murdered by a parolee. The appellate court dismissed a lawsuit, despite allegations of negligent supervision of the parolee and breach of a mandatory duty to conduct a reassessment of his risks and needs, stating that the allegations fit squarely under Government Code § 845.8, subdivision (a).

It was also argued that there was a deprivation of due process rights[6] by the release on parole, and the parole officer's failure to make mandatory home visits and to follow other mandatory provisions of California's parole procedures manual. These failings, however, were held to be insufficient to remove this case from the general rule that members of the public have no constitutional right to recover damages from state employees who fail to protect them from harm inflicted by third parties.[7]

---

[3]   Claflin v. Houseman, 93 U.S. 130 (1976).

[4]   Fleming v. California, 34 Cal. App. 4th 1378 (1995).

[5]   208 Cal. App. 3d 812 (1989).

[6]   42 U.S.C. § 1983.

[7]   DeShaney v. Winnebago County Dept. of Soc. Servs., 489 U.S. 189 (1989) (no liability for failure of social workers to remove child from custody of abusive father).

§ 11.4   Barriers to Inmate Lawsuits—Doctrine of Sovereign Immunity

An inmate attempting to sue his or her keepers faces several serious obstacles, one of which is the doctrine of sovereign immunity. According to this doctrine, a private citizen may not sue a government unit or its agent without its consent. Various reasons advanced in support of the doctrine are: the idea that "the King can do no wrong"; that public funds should not be dissipated to compensate private injuries; and that governmental officials need to be free from the threat of suit in order to function most effectively for the common good. Thus, in a state where sovereign immunity is recognized, the state prison system is immune from a private suit for damages.[8] Similarly, California has held that the operation of a jail by a municipality or a county is a governmental function and therefore an inmate may not sue the political subdivision for injuries received while he or she is incarcerated.[9]

Many states have either totally or partially abrogated the doctrine of sovereign immunity by judicial decision or by constitutional or statutory amendment.[10] Thus, the defense of sovereign immunity in an inmate's suit depends on the law in each state.

Even in states that retain the doctrine of sovereign immunity, an inmate who has been denied his or her constitutional rights may obtain an injunction against the allegedly wrongful conduct of an official in his or her individual capacity. In *Alabama v. Pugh,*[11] the Supreme Court dismissed an injunction sought by inmates of the Alabama prison system against the state and the Alabama Board of Corrections because the Eleventh Amendment prohibits federal courts from entertaining suits against states and their agencies without its consent. The case, which alleged that conditions of the Alabama prisons constituted cruel and unusual punishment, had to proceed against the individual officials responsible for the administration of the prisons, instead of the state government itself. Even though it is a legal fiction, the courts treat such a suit as being against the defendant personally, and not against the state, therefore the defense of sovereign immunity is not available. The courts reason that a governmental official acting unconstitutionally is not acting as an agent of the government.[12]

---

[8]   Moody v. State's Prison, 128 N.C. 12, 38 S.E. 131 (1901); Pharr v. Garibaldi, 252 N.C. 803, 115 S.E.2d 18 (1960); Staley v. Commonwealth, 380 A.2d 515 (Pa. Commw. 1977); McKnight v. Civiletti, 497 F. Supp. 657 (E.D. Pa. 1980); City of Newport v. Fact Concerts, 453 U.S. 247 (1981).

[9]   Grove v. County of San Joaquin, 156 Cal. App. 2d 808, 320 P.2d 161 (1958); Bruce v. Riddle 631 F.2d 272 (4th Cir. 1980); *cf.* Meyer v. City of Oakland, 166 Cal. Rptr. 79 (Cal. App. 1980) (The City of Oakland was held liable in the amount of $35,000 for an assault on an inmate by fellow inmates. The court, while recognizing the doctrine of sovereign immunity, did not apply it to the facts of this case. The court held that a detainee in a drunk tank is not a "prisoner" for purposes of this statute). *See* § 11.3.

[10] Van Alstyne, *Governmental Tort Liability: A Decade of Change,* 1966 U. ILL. L. R. 919.

[11] 438 U.S. 781 (1978).

[12] Ex parte Young, 209 U.S. 123 (1908).

The liability of government officials in monetary damage suits presents a confusing picture. Federal employees on practically every level are given immunity from suit, even if they act maliciously.[13] The rationale of these decisions is that federal officers must be free from fear of monetary liability for their acts in order to accomplish their public duties. However, in many states, government employees can be sued as individuals for committing intentional wrongs. Thus, in *Gullatte v. Potts,*[14] the court held that the state classification officer may be sued for the death of an inmate where the officer could reasonably have expected his action to result in harm to the inmate. The court stated that the action involved in this case was precisely the sort of abuse of governmental power that is necessary to raise an ordinary tort by a government agent to the stature of a constitutional violation. In states adhering to sovereign immunity, the liability of officers for negligence will often depend upon the discretionary or nondiscretionary nature of their acts, as will be more fully discussed later in this chapter.[15] In a case from the Fourth Circuit Court of Appeals,[16] the question of the liability of a probation officer for negligent supervision of a probationer was litigated. The Court held that there is a duty to protect the public from the reasonably foreseeable risk of harm at the hands of a person on probation. The facts giving rise to this suit involved an individual who had been indicted for abducting a young girl. Before his trial he was placed in an institute for psychiatric treatment. The judge, after conferring with the doctor responsible for his evaluation, sentenced the prisoner, based on his guilty plea, to 20 years imprisonment but suspended the sentence based on further treatment and commitment to the psychiatric facility.

When the doctor and probation officer asked the judge to permit the probationer to visit his family, the judge approved. When the probationer informed his probation officer of possible job opportunities out of state, the probation officer granted passes to the probationer to travel to the location to make the necessary arrangements. The probation officer had discussed these trips with the doctor prior to approving the passes. None of the passes was submitted to the judge for approval. Subsequently, the out-of-state probation officer refused to accept the probationer's transfer and the doctor discharged the probationer from the facility. The doctor, after the probation officer instructed the probationer to return, placed the probationer in therapy sessions that met two nights per week. The probationer obtained a job and lived outside the facility to which he had been committed by the judge in the original sentence. The judge was never informed of the changes surrounding the probationer. The probation officer was later promoted and a new probation officer took over; the probationer then killed the plaintiff's daughter.

---

[13] Barr v. Matteo, 360 U.S. 564 (1959) (acting director of Office of Rent Stabilization); Norton v. McShane, 332 F.2d 855 (5th Cir. 1964) (Deputy United States Marshal); Eide v. Timberlake, 497 F. Supp. 1272 (D. Kan. 1980); *cf.* Procunier v. Navarette, 434 U.S. 555 (1978).

[14] 654 F.2d 1007 (5th Cir. 1981); Bogard v. Cook, 586 F.2d 399 (5th Cir. 1978); Fitchette v. Collins, 402 F. Supp. 147 (D. Md. 1975); *see also* Carder v. Steiner, 170 A.2d 220 (1961).

[15] *See* § 11.11.1.

[16] Semler v. Psychiatric Institute of Washington, D.C., 588 F.2d 121 (4th Cir. 1976); Martinez v. California, 444 U.S. 277 (1980).

The court, in finding the doctor and probation officer liable, stated that the decision to release the probationer from a mental facility was not simply a medical judgment. That decision also involved the question of whether release would be in the best interests of the community. The court found liability for negligent supervision in large part because the probation officer and doctor had substituted their judgment for that of the court. Had the court been kept informed, and approved the actions taken, the doctor and probation officer would not have been liable.

In another case involving the supervision of a probationer, an action was brought against state probation officers by the estate of a victim who was murdered by a probationer. The suit alleged that the probation officers acted unreasonably in a grossly negligent manner and with reckless disregard for the safety of persons in the class of the probationer's abuse victims by mismanaging the supervision of the probationer. The essence of the claim was that the probation officer failed to conduct home visits.

The district court dismissed the suit on summary judgment, holding that the state was immune from suit and that the probation officer also shared that immunity insofar as she was sued in her official capacity. However, the suit against the probation officer in her personal capacity was also dismissed. First, there was no causation between the failure of the probation officer to make home visits and the murder. Second, there was no evidence that the probation officer ever knew of a substantial risk of serious harm to any of the probationer's victims. The probationer's compliance with the conditions of probation and the reports that the probation officer received from the experts to whom she had referred him gave her no reason to believe that he was dangerous or that a visit to his home was necessary to verify the absence of any illegality. Third, the probation officer was protected by the doctrine of official immunity because of the discretionary nature of her duties.

The Seventh Circuit affirmed.[17] It is well established that a cause of action alleging a violation of the due process clause can be sustained only where the defendant's actions are "reckless." Reckless or deliberately indifferent conduct is conduct that is criminally reckless—that is, conduct that reflects a complete indifference to risk such that we can infer the actor's knowledge or intent.[18]

On the facts in *Weinberger*, there was insufficient evidence that the probation officer's conduct was reckless. Significant to the court's decision was the fact that the administrative code section governing parole/probation supervision gave parole/probation officers a great deal of discretion and allowed probation officers to establish probation conditions designed to "achieve the goals and objectives" of probation.

---

[17]   Weinberger v. Chester, 105 F.3d 1182 (7th Cir. 1997).

[18]   For example, an inmate injured by slipping on a pillow negligently left on a stairway by a prison official was not deprived of due process of law. Daniels v. Williams, 474 U.S. 327 (1986). The failure of state or local government officials to prevent child abuse by a private actor is not a due process violation. DeShaney v. Winnebago County Dep't of Soc. Servs., 489 U.S. 189 (1989).

It is clear that the defense of sovereign immunity will often deny relief to innocent citizens injured by government officers. On the other hand, it is also clear that immunity for such officers will encourage them to work vigorously for the public good without fear of nuisance lawsuits. One possible solution to this paradox is suggested by Professor Kenneth C. Davis, a leading authority on administrative law in America.

What the law of tort liability of public officers and employees most needs is an expansion of tort liability of government units. If the particular government unit is liable for the tort, so that the loss will be properly allocated, then the courts will be relieved of the need to choose between leaving a deserving plaintiff without a remedy and imposing liability upon the individual officer or employee, who is usually either ill-equipped to bear the loss or is performing the type of function that can be properly performed only if the officer is free from the need to consider his or her own pocketbook. The public interest in fearless administration usually should come first, so that officers are immune from liability even when the plaintiff asserts that the officers have acted maliciously; when this is so, the only proper way to compensate deserving plaintiffs is to impose liability on the government unit. When the public receives the benefit of a program, the public should pay for the torts that may be expected, in order to carry out the program. The only satisfactory solution of many problems regarding liability of officers and employees is to compensate the plaintiff but to hold the officer or employee immune.[19]

A distinction must be made between a public official being sued in his official capacity, in which the "real" defendant is a government unit, and a public official being sued for his or her individual conduct. Personal capacity suits seek to impose personal liability upon a government official for actions taken under color of state law. In official capacity suits, as long as the governmental entity receives notice and an opportunity to respond, the suit is, in all respects other than the name, a suit against the entity. It is not a suit against the official personally, because the real party in interest is the governmental entity. An award of damages against an official in his or her personal capacity can be enforced only against the official's personal assets. A plaintiff seeking to recover on a damages judgment in an official capacity suit must look to the governmental entity itself. To establish liability in a § 1983 suit, it must be shown that the official, acting under color of law, caused the deprivation of a federal right. More is required in an official capacity suit. It must be shown that the governmental entity was a "moving force" behind the deprivations. In an official capacity suit, the entity's "policy or custom" must have played a part in the violation of federal law. As to defenses of liability, an official in a personal capacity suit may, depending on his or her position, be able to assert personal immunity defenses, such as objectively reasonable reliance on existing law. The only immunities that can be claimed in an official capacity action are forms of sovereign immunity that the entity may possess, such as the

---

19   KENNETH C. DAVIS, ADMINISTRATIVE LAW § 26.07 (1959).

Eleventh Amendment. There is no longer any need to bring official capacity suits against officials of local government, because local government may be sued directly for damages and injunctive or declaratory relief. Absent waiver, however, under the Eleventh Amendment, a state cannot be sued directly in its own name, regardless of the relief sought. In this regard, a civil rights suit against a government official in his or her personal capacity cannot lead to imposition of attorney fee liability upon the governmental entity. A plaintiff's victory against a governmental official being sued in his or her individual capacity is a victory against the individual defendant, not against the governmental entity that employs him or her. However, although a state in a § 1983 action may be found liable either because the state was a proper party defendant or because state officials were sued in their official capacity, attorney fees may be awarded to a state under § 1983. Only in an official capacity action is a plaintiff who wins entitled to look for relief, both on the merits and for attorney fees, to the government entity.[20]

Neither a state nor state officials acting in their official capacities are "persons" within meaning of § 1983. A state is not a person under § 1983. This is supported by the statute's language, congressional purpose, and legislative history. In common usage, the term "person" does not include a state. This usage is particularly applicable where it is claimed that Congress has subjected the states to liability to which they had not been subject before. Reading § 1983 to include states would be a decidedly awkward way of expressing such a congressional intent. The statute's language also falls short of satisfying the ordinary rule of statutory construction that Congress must make its intention to alter the constitutional balance between the states and the federal government unmistakably clear in a statute's language. Moreover, the doctrine of sovereign immunity was one of the well-established common law immunities and defenses that Congress did not intend to override in enacting § 1983. The ruling in *Monell*—which held that a municipality is a person under § 1983—is not to the contrary, because states are protected by the Eleventh Amendment, while municipalities are not. Further, a suit against state officials in their official capacities is not a suit against the officials but rather is a suit against the officials' offices and, thus, is no different from a suit against the state itself. Such a suit cannot be predicated on § 1983.[21]

§ 11.4.1 —The *Hands-Off* Doctrine

Courts have traditionally abstained from hearing suits brought by inmates against their keepers. This practice became so prevalent that it acquired its own name—the "hands-off" doctrine. Some courts have explained the doctrine in terms of a lack of subject matter jurisdiction over inmate claims.[22] An

---

[20]   Kentucky v. Graham, 473 U.S. 159 (1985).
[21]   Will v. Michigan Department of State Police, 491 U.S. 58 (1989).
[22]   Garcia v. Steele, 193 F.2d 276 (8th Cir. 1951).

article discussing inmates' complaints recognized three separate reasons relied on by courts to support the doctrine:[23] (1) separation of powers (administration of prisons is an executive function); (2) lack of judicial expertise in penology; and (3) fear that judicial intervention will subvert prison discipline.

The hands-off doctrine has subsided in importance, at least in federal courts. One extremely important step in the doctrine's decline was *Cooper v. Pate*,[24] in which the United States Supreme Court expressly held that a state inmate could bring suit against his or her keepers under the Civil Rights Act.[25] The hands-off doctrine in federal courts today can probably best be described as a reluctance on the part of the judiciary to interfere in prison administration, but a reluctance that it will quickly shed upon allegations of denials of important federal constitutional or statutory rights.[26] The increasing number of inmate suits being heard in federal courts tends to indicate that many courts today will liberally construe inmate complaints as alleging denials of important federal rights.[27]

However, it is important to note that the flood of inmate suits that has ended up in federal courts has created great concern for the federal judiciary system. As stated by then-Chief Justice Burger of the United States Supreme Court in 1976:

> Fully a sixth of the 117,000 cases of the civil docket of federal courts (19,000) are petitions from prisoners, most of which could be handled effectively and fairly within the prison systems. . . . Federal judges should not be dealing with prisoner complaints which, although important to a prisoner, are so minor that any well-run institution should be able to resolve them fairly without resorting to federal judges.[28]

This would indicate that the courts may not be willing to liberally construe inmate complaints unless it appears that there have been denials of important federally protected rights.

§ 11.5 Federal Remedies—Civil Suits Against Federal Prison Officials

A federal inmate who claims that he suffered injuries as a result of negligent conduct by federal prison officials should theoretically be able to sue for damages. However, the doctrine of sovereign immunity[29] precluded such suits

---

23 Goldfarb and Singer, *Redressing Prisoners' Grievances,* 39 Geo. Wash. L. Rev. 175, 181 (1970).

24 378 U.S. 546 (1964).

25 42 U.S.C. § 1983 (1970).

26 Johnson v. Avery, 393 U.S. 483 (1969); Wright v. McMann, 387 F.2d 519 (2d Cir. 1967).

27 For an exhaustive study of judicial treatment of inmate suits, *see* Goldfarb and Singer, *Redressing Prisoners' Grievances,* 39 Geo. Wash. L. Rev. 175 (1976).

28 62 American Bar Association Journal 189 (Feb. 1976).

29 *See* § 11.4.

until Congress, in 1946, passed the Federal Tort Claims Act, in which the federal government consented to be sued in certain situations. In 1963, the Supreme Court held that federal inmates could maintain an action under the Federal Tort Claims Act.[30]

Claims arising from certain specific fact situations are expressly excepted from the act.[31] The most important exception in a prison setting exempts:

> Any claim arising out of assault, battery, false imprisonment, false arrest, malicious prosecution, abuse of process, libel, slander, misrepresentation, deceit, or interference with contract rights.[32]

However, subject to the immunity doctrine,[33] federal officers are now liable for "constitutional torts" to the same extent as state officials under 42 U.S.C § 1983.[34]

In addition, the Federal Bureau of Prisons has put into effect an internal "administrative remedy procedure" that has helped to keep federal inmate complaints out of the federal courts. As pointed out by the late Chief Justice Burger:

> Rather than litigate complaints in overburdened federal courts, inmates may now file them with prison officials. To date, 17 percent of those complaints have been resolved in the inmate's favor by prison wardens. An additional 27 percent of complaints appealed to a regional director were resolved favorably to the inmate. Many of these complaints would otherwise have been presented to federal courts as civil rights or habeas corpus suits.[35]

§ 11.6 Federal Remedies—Civil Rights Act

The federal remedy most frequently used today by state inmates is § 1983 of the Civil Rights Act, which provides:

> Every person who, under color of any statute, ordinance, regulation, custom, or usage, of any State or Territory, subjects, or causes to be subjected, any citizen of the United States or other person within the jurisdiction thereof to the deprivation of any rights, privileges, or

---

[30] United States v. Muniz, 374 U.S. 150 (1963).

[31] *See* § 11.4.

[32] 28 U.S.C. § 2680 (h) (1964).

[33] *See* § 11.6.2.

[34] Bivens v. Six Unknown Fed. Narcotics Agents, 403 U.S. 388 (1971); Butz v. Economou, 438 U.S. 478 (1978). A plaintiff may maintain a *Bivens* action, with trial by jury, even though he or she also has a remedy under the Federal Tort Claims Act. Further, when a defendant's unconstitutional act leads to death, federal common law permits survival of the *Bivens* claim, even though state law would not permit survival. Carlson v. Green, 446 U.S. 14 (1980).

[35] 61 American Bar Association Journal 303 (March 1975).

immunities secured by the Constitution and laws, shall be liable to
the party injured in an action at law, suit in equity, or other proper
proceeding for redress.[36]

In 1964, the United States Supreme Court held that state inmates can bring
suit against their keepers under the Civil Rights Act.[37]

In 1973, the United States Supreme Court held that a § 1983 action was a
proper remedy for a state inmate to make a constitutional challenge to the conditions of his prison life, but not to the fact or length of his custody.[38] If the
fact or length of custody is challenged, habeas corpus must be used.

To be liable under § 1983, a defendant must act under "color of law." Not
every injury is a "federal case." Questions often arise as to whether private
parties who contract with state agencies act under "color of law" in dealing
with prisoners.

A private physician was under contract with North Carolina to provide
orthopedic services at a state prison hospital on a part-time basis. He treated
a prisoner for a leg injury sustained in prison. The prisoner was barred by state
law from employing or electing to see a physician of his own choosing. The
doctor's conduct in treating the prisoner was fairly attributable to the state. The
state has an obligation, under the Eighth Amendment and state law, to provide
adequate medical care to those whom it has incarcerated. The state had delegated that function to physicians and deferred to their professional judgment.
This result was not altered by the fact that the doctor was paid by contract and
was not on the state payroll, nor by the fact that he was not required to work
exclusively for the prison. It was the physician's function within the state system, not the precise terms of his employment, that was determinative.[39]

The liability of a defendant in a civil rights case must be personal. In civil
rights litigation, there is no basis for *respondeat superior* liability.[40] The mas-
ter-servant or employer-employee basis for liability does not apply in these

---

[36]   42 U.S.C. § 1983 (1970).

[37]   Cooper v. Pate, 378 U.S. 546 (1964); Even though the state is exempt from damages under a 42 U.S.C.
       § 1983 action, cities do not have a similar immunity. In *Monell v. Department of Social Services,* 436
       U.S. 658 (1978), the Supreme Court held that cities are not immune from civil rights suits. Under this
       holding, municipalities can now be directly liable for their constitutional deprivations as long as the
       violation stems from official policy and not simply from the actions of an employee or agent. In the lat-
       ter instance, a complaining party would have to seek relief from the individual official and not the city
       itself.

           Monell left open the issue of whether a municipality could cloak itself with the good faith immu-
       nity defense available to its public officers. This issue was decided in the negative in *Owen v. City of
       Independence,* 445 U.S. 622 (1980). Municipalities are not subject to immunity from liability in § 1983
       actions, even though the unconstitutional conduct was undertaken in good faith.

[38]   Preiser v. Rodriguez, 411 U.S. 475 (1973).

[39]   West v. Atkins, 487 U.S. 42 (1988).

[40]   City of Los Angeles v. Heller, 475 U.S. 796 (1986).

federal lawsuits. To be liable under the federal civil rights act, the action of the defendant must have directly caused the injury. Mere negligence is not enough.[41] A sheriff was accused of condoning a deputy's use of excessive force against a county detention center detainee who was not resisting, by failing to immediately terminate the deputy. As the failure to terminate occurred after the fact, the failure to terminate did not cause the deputy's conduct. Therefore, there was no basis for holding the sheriff individually liable.[42]

The due process clause was not implicated by a state official's negligent act that caused unintended loss of or injury to life, liberty, or property. The due process clause was intended to protect individuals from the abuse of power by government officials. Far from an abuse of power, lack of due care, such as from alleged negligence, suggests no more than a failure to measure up to the conduct of a reasonable person. To hold that injury caused by such conduct is a deprivation within the meaning of the due process clause would trivialize the centuries-old principle of due process of law. *Parratt v. Taylor*[43] was overruled to the extent that it stated otherwise.

The Constitution does not purport to supplant traditional tort law in laying down rules of conduct to regulate liability for injuries that attend living together in society. While the due process clause speaks to some facets of the relationship between jailers and inmates, its protections are not triggered by lack of due care by the jailers. Jailers may owe a special duty of care under state tort law to those in their custody, but the due process clause does not embrace such a tort law concept.[44]

In a police brutality case, it was a jury question as to whether police officers used excessive and unreasonable force against a suspect, which resulted in severe injury. Regarding personal liability, it was held that the mere presence of an officer at the beating is sufficient to make him liable under 42 U.S.C. § 1983, when he made no effort to intervene and stop the beating. Under these circumstances, the involvement was personal. An inmate's civil rights claim was dismissed, to the extent it sought damages for a prison door closing on him or for misplaced medical paperwork, because these complaints alleged mere negligence and not violation of constitutional rights.[45]

A city may only be held accountable if the deprivation was the result of a municipal "custom or policy." A city cannot be held liable solely on the basis of the acts of its officers and agents. As a general rule, a city is not responsible for the unauthorized and unlawful acts of its officers, even though done under color of law. It must further appear that the officers were expressly

---

[41] Estelle v. Gamble, 429 U.S. 97 (1976); *see* § 10.3; Stewart v. Love, 696 F.2d 43 (6th Cir. 1982) (An inmate was assaulted by another prisoner. Because the conduct of the prison officials did not constitute gross negligence or deliberate indifference to the inmate's risk of injury, there was no violation of the Eighth Amendment. In the context of prison cases involving assaults on inmates by inmates, mere negligence on the part of prison officials is insufficient to give rise to liability).

[42] Morris v. Crawford County, 173 F. Supp. 2d 870 (W.D. Ark. 2001).

[43] 451 U.S. 527 (1981).

[44] Daniels v. Williams, 474 U.S. 327 (1985).

[45] Breakiron v. Neal, 166 F. Supp. 2d 1110 (W.D. Texas 2001).

authorized to do the acts by the city government, or that the acts were done legitimately pursuant to a general authority to act for the city on the subject to which they related; or that, in either case, the act was adopted and ratified by the city. The word "policy" generally implies a course of action consciously chosen from among various alternatives. The "official policy" requirement of *Monell*[46] intended to distinguish acts of the municipality from acts of the municipality's employees. Municipal liability is limited to actions for which the municipality is actually responsible. *Monell* held that recovery from a municipality is limited to acts that are, properly speaking, "of the municipality"—that is, acts that the municipality has officially sanctioned or ordered. Municipal liability may be imposed for a single decision by municipal policymakers under appropriate circumstances. If the decision to adopt a particular course of action is directed by those who establish government policy, the municipality is equally responsible whether that action is to be taken only once or repeatedly.[47]

Custom

A custom, for purposes of liability, was not established where one inmate was beaten to death by another. Two cell doors were left open by a jail officer, allowing one inmate to attack the other. The official policy of the county was that no two cell doors were to be open simultaneously. Although two doors were sometimes left open and disregard of the policy was tolerated, this was insufficient to create a custom and liability of the county.[48]

A District of Columbia inmate was transferred to a Virginia prison pursuant to the interstate compact. He was then transferred back to the District of Columbia and claimed that the District was responsible for his mistreatment by Virginia officials. There was no liability under either the theory of official municipal policy or as agent for the District. The inmate made no allegation that the District had a policy of sending inmates to Virginia prisons that routinely mistreated inmates.[49]

Alabama sheriffs, when executing their law enforcement duties, represent the State of Alabama, not their counties.[50] Although the sheriff in this case had final policymaking authority in the area of law enforcement, there was a disagreement in the lower court about whether Alabama sheriffs were policymakers for the state or for the county when acting in their law enforcement capacity. In deciding this dispute, the question was not whether Alabama sheriffs act as county or state officials in all of their official actions, but whom they represented in a particular area or on a particular issue. The answer depended on the definition of the official's functions under relevant state law. In other words, Alabama procedural law governed the outcome of the case.

---

[46] Monell v. Department of Social Services, 436 U.S. 658 (1978).
[47] Pembaur v. City of Cincinnati, 475 U.S. 469 (1986).
[48] Gregory v. Shelby County, 220 F.3d 433 (6th Cir. 2000).
[49] Abdus-Shahid M.S. Ali v. District of Columbia, 278 F.3d 1 (D.C. Cir. 2002).
[50] McMillian v. Monroe County, Ala., 520 U.S. 781 (1997).

Here, the Court determined that under Alabama law, the state's constitutional provisions concerning sheriffs, the historical development of those provisions, and the interpretation given them by the State Supreme Court strongly supported the proposition that sheriffs represent the State when acting in their law enforcement capacity. The Supreme Court reasoned that the nation's federal system allows the states wide authority to establish their state and local governments. The Court stressed that local variations can be tolerated under the federal system.

The inadequacy of training may serve as the basis for § 1983 liability only when the failure to train in a relevant respect amounts to deliberate indifference to the constitutional rights of persons with whom the officials come into contact. This "deliberate indifference" standard is most consistent with the rule of *Monell*—that a city is not liable under § 1983 unless a municipal "policy" or "custom" is the moving force behind the constitutional violation. Only when a failure to train reflects a "deliberate" or "conscious" choice by the municipality can the failure be properly thought of as an actionable city "policy." *Monell* cannot be satisfied by a mere allegation that a training program represents a policy for which the city is responsible. Rather, the focus must be on whether the program is adequate to the tasks the particular employees must perform, and if it is not, on whether such inadequate training can justifiably be said to represent "city policy." Moreover, the identified deficiency in the training program must be closely related to the ultimate injury. Thus, the plaintiff must still prove that the deficiency in training actually caused the constitutional violation. To adopt lesser standards of fault and causation would open municipalities to unprecedented liability under § 1983; would result in de facto *respondeat superior* liability, a result rejected in *Monell*; would engage federal courts in an endless exercise of second-guessing municipal employee training programs, a task that they are ill-suited to undertake; and would implicate serious questions of federalism.[51]

A county was held liable where a sheriff, as policymaker, made a conscious decision not to train reserve deputy sheriffs. The need to train reserve deputies was obvious. The failure to train constituted deliberate indifference to the constitutional rights of citizens. The failure to train was the moving force behind severe injuries inflicted on an arrestee who was hurt by a reserve deputy when he used force because the arrestee got out of a car too slowly.[52]

Women who were sexually assaulted by a jailer while they were detained in a jail failed to establish liability on the grounds that the county failed to train jailers or to properly screen jailers before hiring them. The county did not act with deliberate indifference, as the sheriff and commissioners were unaware of any previous incidents involving a sexual assault of inmates by a jailer. The jailer had completed a state certification training program and correctional officer course, and the jailer's background did not indicate that he was highly likely to sexually assault female inmates.[53]

---

[51]   City of Canton v. Harris, 489 U.S. 378 (1989); *see also* Oklahoma City v. Tuttle, 471 U.S. 808 (1985).
[52]   Brown v. Bryan, 219 F.3d 450 (5th Cir. 2000).
[53]   Barney v. Pulsipher, 143 F.3d 1299 (10th Cir. 1998).

As to municipal liability for a failure to train its officers, the United States Supreme Court held that a municipality may, in certain circumstances, be held liable under § 1983 for constitutional violations resulting from its failure to train its employees. The contention that § 1983 liability can be imposed only when the municipal policy in question is itself unconstitutional was rejected. There are circumstances in which a "failure to train" allegation can be the basis for liability.[54]

A sheriff was held not deliberately indifferent to a female inmate's safety when she was assaulted in the county jail by a jail employee. The sheriff was not aware of any substantial risk of danger from the employee, notwithstanding a claim by the inmate that leaving her alone with a male employee for close to two hours in an unmonitored room without an operating voice-activated security device supported a claim of negligent training and supervision of employees.[55]

When there is a basis for § 1983 liability against a municipality, the city is not entitled to a defense of "good faith," as is an individual.[56]

A civil rights action in district court against a county and two municipal corporations based on failure to train police officers was rejected because the complaints failed to meet a "heightened pleading standard," which requires that complaints against municipal corporations in § 1983 cases state with factual detail and particularity the basis for the claim. The United States Supreme Court reversed.[57]

Training

A county was sued for damages caused by a deputy sheriff who used excessive force. The suit was based on the proposition that the sheriff has hired the deputy without adequately reviewing his background. The deputy had pleaded guilty to various driving infractions and other misdemeanors, including assault and battery. The sheriff, who was the department's policymaker, had obtained the deputy's driving and criminal records, but had not closely reviewed either before hiring him. The United States Supreme Court held that a policymaker's single hiring decision could not give rise to § 1983 municipal liability. There was no evidence that the sheriff's decision reflected a conscious disregard of a high risk that the deputy would use excessive force in violation of any federally protected right.[58]

Reaffirming its earlier decisions in *Monell*[59] and *Pembaur*,[60] the Supreme Court held that a municipality may not be held liable under § 1983 solely because it employs a tortfeasor. To recover damages, a plaintiff must identify a municipal "policy" or "custom" that caused the injury. A "policy" giving rise

---

54   Pembaur v. City of Cincinnati, 475 U.S. 469 (1986).

55   Downey v. Denton County, 119 F.3d 381 (5th Cir. 1997).

56   Brandon v. Holt, 469 U.S. 464 (1984).

57   Leatherman v. Tarrant County, 507 U.S. 163 (1993).

58   Board of the County Commissioners of Bryan County, Oklahoma v. Brown, 520 U.S. 397 (1997).

59   Monell v. Department of Social Services, 436 U.S. 658 (1978).

60   Pembaur v. City of Cincinnati, 475 U.S. 469 (1986).

to liability cannot be established merely by identifying a policymaker's conduct that is properly attributable to the municipality. A successful plaintiff must also demonstrate that, through its deliberate conduct, the municipality was the "moving force" behind the injury. A plaintiff must show that the municipal action was taken with the requisite degree of culpability and must demonstrate a direct causal link between the municipal action and the deprivation of federal rights.

Any claim that a policymaker's single facially lawful hiring decision can trigger municipal liability presents difficult problems of proof. In *Pembaur*, the Supreme Court held that a § 1983 cause of action based on a single decision attributable to a municipality will exist only where the municipality had acted and that the plaintiff had suffered a deprivation of federal rights also proved fault and causation. Claims not involving an allegation that the municipal action itself violated federal law or directed or authorized the deprivation of federal rights require application of rigorous culpability and causation standards in order to ensure that the municipality is not held liable solely for its employees' actions.[61]

Predicting the consequences of a single hiring decision, even one based on an inadequate assessment of a record, will impose liability only where adequate scrutiny of the applicant's background would lead a reasonable policymaker to conclude that the plainly obvious consequence of the decision to hire the applicant would be the deprivation of a third party's federally protected right. An official's failure to adequately scrutinize an applicant's background does not constitute "deliberate indifference."

The Court further commented that even assuming without deciding that proof of a single instance of inadequate screening could trigger municipal liability, the sheriff's failure to scrutinize the deputy's record did not constitute "deliberate indifference" to any federally protected right to be free from the use of excessive force. To test the link between the sheriff's action and the injury, a plaintiff must prove that from a full review of the deputy's record, the sheriff should have concluded that the deputy's use of excessive force would be a plainly obvious consequence of his decision to hire the deputy. There were no facts to support this conclusion in *Bryan County*.

Under ordinary principles of tort law, there is no liability for failure to take action unless there is a legal duty to act. A claim against a prison officer for failing to protect an attacked inmate who later died from injuries inflicted by other inmates was denied. The officer did not callously, deliberately, or recklessly disregard the inmate's safety. The inmates were not engaged in any argument that was visible to the officer. The officer's failure to properly inspect the barracks at lights out time demonstrated negligence at most. The officer did

---

[61] In City of Canton v. Harris, 489 U.S. 378 (1989), the Court held that a plaintiff seeking to establish municipal liability on the theory that a facially lawful municipal action—in that case, an allegedly inadequate training program—that led an employee to violate a plaintiff's rights, must demonstrate that the municipal action was not simply negligent, but was taken with "deliberate indifference" as to its known or obvious consequences.

not know something was wrong between the inmates until the fight was over and the attacked inmate was beaten.[62]

A Fifth Circuit case reached similar results where a pretrial detainee was raped by a jailer. The staffing policies at the jail did not reflect deliberate indifference on the part of the municipality. An episodic act or admission does not create a condition of confinement.[63]

A federal court may not apply a "heightened pleading standard"—more stringent than the usual pleading requirements of Federal Rule of Civil Procedure 8(a)—in civil rights cases alleging municipal liability under § 1983. First, the heightened standard cannot be justified on the ground that a more relaxed pleading standard would eviscerate municipalities' immunity from suit by subjecting them to expensive and time-consuming discovery in every § 1983 case. Municipalities, although free from *respondeat superior* liability under § 1983,[64] do not enjoy absolute or qualified immunity from § 1983 suits.[65] Second, it is not possible to reconcile the heightened standard with the liberal system of "notice pleading" set up by the Federal Rules.[66]

Settlement agreements to preclude future litigation may be enforced in certain situations. In *Town of Newbury v. Rumery,* an agreement was negotiated whereby the prosecutor would dismiss the charges against the defendant if he would agree to release any claims that he might have against the town, its officials, or the victim for any harm caused by his arrest. The agreement was enforced when, 10 months later, he filed an action under 42 U.S.C. § 1983, alleging that the town and its officers had violated his constitutional rights by arresting him, defaming him, and imprisoning him falsely. The suit was dismissed on the basis of the assertion by the defendants of the release-dismissal agreement as an affirmative defense. The United States Supreme Court held that such agreements are not invalid *per se*. The question of whether the policies underlying § 1983 may in some circumstances render a waiver of the right to sue thereunder unenforceable is one of federal law, to be resolved by reference to traditional common law principles. The relevant principle is that a promise is unenforceable if the interest in its enforcement is outweighed in the circumstances by a public policy harmed by enforcement of the agreement.[67]

Courts make every effort to summarily dismiss prisoner civil rights actions and avoid protracted pretrial discovery and trial. One court of appeals attempted to accomplish this aim by adopting a "clear and convincing" evidence requirement to deal with civil rights suits against prison officials who allegedly violate a prisoner's constitutional rights. The usual standard of proof

---

[62]   Tucker v. Evans, 276 F.3d 999 (8th Cir. 2002).

[63]   Scott v. Moore, 114 F.3d 51 (5th Cir. 1997).

[64]   *See* Monell v. Department of Social Services, 436 U.S. 658 (1978).

[65]   Owen v. City of Independence, 445 U.S. 622 (1980).

[66]   Federal Rule of Civil Procedure 8(a)(2) requires that a complaint include only "a short and plain statement of the claim showing that the pleader is entitled to relief." And while Rule 9(b) requires greater particularity in pleading certain actions, it does not include among the enumerated actions any reference to complaints alleging municipal liability under § 1983.

[67]   Town of Newton v. Rumery, 480 U.S. 386 (1986).

in civil cases is the lesser "preponderance of the evidence" standard. The Court reasoned that because an official's state of mind was easy to allege and difficult to disprove, insubstantial claims turning on improper intent may be less amenable to summary disposition than other types of claims against government officials.

The Supreme Court reversed,[68] holding that changing the burden of proof for an entire category of claims would stray far from the traditional limits on judicial authority. Nothing in § 1983 or any other federal statute or the Federal Rules of Civil Procedure provide any support for imposing a clear and convincing burden of proof. The lower court's unprecedented change lacked any common law authority and altered the cause of action in a way that undermined § 1983's very purpose—to provide a remedy for the violation of federal rights.

To the extent that the lower court was concerned with preventing excessive discovery, such questions are most frequently and effectively resolved by the rule-making or legislative process, not by the judicial process. In the Supreme Court's view, the lower court's indirect effort to regulate discovery employed a blunt instrument with a high cost that also imposed a heightened standard of proof at trial upon plaintiffs with bona fide constitutional claims.

In order to prevent threats and harassment of prison officials, in 1998 Congress passed a statute limiting an inmate's access to information relating to prison employees.[69] The Act provides that in any civil rights action brought against a federal, state, or local jail, prison, or correctional facility, or any of their employees or former employees, that arises out of an inmate's incarceration, the financial records of any employee cannot be disclosed without the written consent of the employee or pursuant to a court order, unless a verdict of liability has been entered against the employee. Also not subject to disclosure without the written consent of the employee or pursuant to a court order is the home address, home phone number, Social Security number, identity of family members, personal tax returns, and personal banking information of the employee, and any other records or information of a similar nature relating to that person.

Significant to the Supreme Court's ruling was that Congress had already fashioned special rules to discourage inmates' insubstantial suits by means of the Prison Litigation Reform Act.[70] The Act draws no distinction between constitutional claims that require proof of an improper motive and those that do not. According to the Supreme Court, changing the rules is not a judicial act but a legislative decision.

Many civil rights cases are filed by prisoners without the burden of paying filing fees. However, *in forma pauperis* proceedings are personal. A representative association of inmates has no right to proceed *in forma pauperis*

---

[68]   Crawford-El v. Britton, 523 U.S. 574 (1998).

[69]   Act Oct. 21, 1998, P.L. 105-277, Div A, §101(b) [Title I, §127], 112 Stat. 2681-74. The text of the statute is in Appendix II.

[70]   *See* Chapter 13.

under 28 U.S.C. § 1915(a), which permits litigation without prepayment of fees, costs, or security by a person who makes affidavit that he or she is unable to pay. Only a natural person may qualify for treatment *in forma pauperis* under § 1915.[71]

There is a trend to hire private firms to run jails and prisons. According to the Supreme Court, prison guards employed by private firms are not entitled to qualified immunity from suit by prisoners charging a § 1983 violation.[72] While government-employed prison guards may have enjoyed an immunity defense arising out of their status as public employees at common law,[73] correctional functions have never been exclusively public. In the nineteenth century, both private entities and government carried on prison management activities. The Court found no conclusive evidence of a historical tradition of immunity for private parties carrying out these functions.

Further, the governmental immunity doctrine's purposes do not warrant immunity for private prison guards. The mere performance of a governmental function does not support any immunity for a private person, especially one who performs a job without government supervision or direction. There are significant differences between private and public persons with respect to immunity. First, the most important special government immunity-producing concern—protecting the public from unwarranted timidity on the part of public officials—is less likely to be present when a private company subject to competitive market pressures operates a prison. A firm whose guards are too aggressive will face damages that raise costs, thereby threatening its replacement by another contractor, but a firm whose guards are too timid will face replacement by firms with safer and more effective job records. Marketplace pressures were present in *Richardson v. McKnight*. The private firm was systematically organized. It performed independently, was statutorily obligated to carry insurance, and had to renew its first contract after three years. The private firm was provided with incentives to avoid overly timid job performance. Consequently, private employees differ from government employees. Government employees act within a system that is responsible through elected officials to the voters, often characterized by civil service rules providing employee security but limiting the government departments' flexibility to reward or punish individual employees.

Second, privatization helps to meet the immunity-related need to ensure that talented candidates are not deterred from entering public service by the threat of damage suits. Comprehensive insurance coverage that is available to private companies increases the likelihood of employee indemnification and thereby reduces the employment-discouraging fear of unwarranted liability. A private firm is also freed from many civil service restraints. Unlike a government department, a private firm may offset increased employee liability risk

71   Rowland v. California Men's Colony, 506 U.S. 194 (1993); *see* § 3.3. *See* Chapter 13, The Prison Litigation Reform Act.

72   Richardson v. McKnight, 521 U.S. 399 (1997).

73   *See* Procunier v. Navarette, 434 U.S. 555 (1978).

with higher pay or extra benefits. Third, while lawsuits may distract private employees from their duties, the risk of distraction alone cannot be sufficient grounds for immunity.

A private corporation was under contract with the Federal Bureau of Prisons to operate a Community Correctional Center, a facility that housed federal inmates. A federal inmate afflicted with a heart condition that limited his ability to climb stairs was assigned to a bedroom on the fifth floor. The Center instituted a policy requiring inmates residing below the sixth floor to use the stairs rather than the elevator. The inmate was exempted from this policy. But when a Center employee forbade the inmate to use the elevator to reach his bedroom, he climbed the stairs, suffered a heart attack, and fell. A District Court treated the complaint as raising claims under *Bivens* v. *Six Unknown Fed. Narcotics Agents.*[74] *In Bivens,* the Supreme Court recognized for the first time an implied private action for damages against federal officers alleged to have violated a citizen's constitutional rights. In *Correctional Services Corp. v. Malesko,*[75] the Supreme Court held that *Bivens'* limited holding may not be extended to confer a right of action for damages against private entities acting under color of federal law. The Supreme Court's authority to create a new constitutional tort, not expressly authorized by statute, is anchored in its general jurisdiction to decide all cases arising under federal law. The Supreme Court first exercised this authority in *Bivens.* From a discussion of that and subsequent cases, it was clear that the inmate's claim was fundamentally different from anything the Supreme Court had previously recognized. In 30 years of *Bivens* jurisprudence, the Supreme Court had extended its holding only twice, to provide an otherwise nonexistent cause of action against *individual officers* alleged to have acted unconstitutionally, and to provide a cause of action for a plaintiff who lacked *any alternative remedy* for harms caused by an individual officer's unconstitutional conduct. Where such circumstances are not present, the Supreme Court has consistently rejected invitations to extend *Bivens.* The purpose of *Bivens* is to deter individual federal officers, not the agency, from committing constitutional violations. Liability under federal law was denied, leaving the inmate to a state remedy.

Prison officials may constitutionally refuse to allow an inmate to be present at a civil deposition of prison staff members in his or her civil rights case.[76] An expert witness justified the exclusion. Reasons given were: (1) maintaining staff authority, (2) preventing the aggrandizement of inmates, (3) avoiding unnecessary tension, (4) protecting staff morale, and (5) preserving limited resources.

Retaliation claims arising from the exercise of First Amendment rights must be "shocking to the conscience" in order to give rise to a claim for damages under the Civil Rights Act.[77]

---

[74]   403 U.S. 388 (1971).
[75]   534 U.S. 61 (2001).
[76]   In re Wilkinson, 137 F.3d 911 (6th Cir. 1998).
[77]   McLaurin v. Cole, 115 F.3d 408 (6th Cir. 1997).

§ 11.6.1 —Civil Rights Act— Exhaustion of Remedies

Whether exhaustion of available state judicial and administrative remedies is a prerequisite to bringing a lawsuit in federal court under the Civil Rights Act is frequently discussed by lower-level federal courts. Although the Supreme Court has stated that exhaustion of state remedies is not required,[78] it has confused the question by stressing that futility or unavailability of state remedies in a particular case will not require an inmate to perform the act of processing his claim through state agencies. However, several factors indicate that exhaustion is not required if the lawsuit seeks to redress past deprivations of constitutional rights by prison administrators. First, the statute itself does not require such exhaustion. Second, there is no reason to believe that federal courts are any less competent than state courts to punish violations of the federal constitution. Hence, the Supreme Court has held that a state inmate complaining of living conditions at the Missouri State Penitentiary need not exhaust state judicial or administrative remedies.[79] As the great bulk of inmate complaints under the Civil Rights Act complain of past deprivations of constitutional rights, no exhaustion is required.[80]

The exhaustion doctrine was radically changed by the Prison Litigation Reform Act.[81] In two Supreme Court decisions,[82] the courts held that one of the most important provisions of the PLRA is that prisoners, jail inmates, and certain juveniles confined in correctional or detention facilities must exhaustion any available administrative remedies before filing a lawsuit in federal court. This applies even when an inmate seeks only money damages even though the administrative process has no provision for recovery of money damages.

Inmates seeking judicial relief must be mindful of the remedy sought, because there is a vast procedural difference between a civil rights action under 42 U.S.C. § 1983 and a request for habeas corpus under 42 U.S.C. § 2241. Federal habeas corpus requires exhaustion of all state judicial remedies before filing for the writ. Section 1983 contains no judicially imposed exhaustion requirement. Absent some other bar to the suit, a claim either is cognizable under § 1983 and should immediately go forward, or is not cognizable and should be dismissed.[83]

---

[78] McNeese v. Board of Educ., 373 U.S. 668 (1963); Monroe v. Pape, 365 U.S. 167 (1961); Steffel v. Thompson, 415 U.S. 452 (1974); Preiser v. Rodriguez, 411 U.S. 475 (1973); Huffman v. Pursue, Ltd., 420 U.S. 592 (1975).

[79] Wilwording v. Swenson, 404 U.S. 249 (1971); *see also* United States v. Mogavero, 521 F.2d 625 (4th Cir. 1975). *See also* Dickerson v. Warden, Marquette Prison, 298 N.W.2d 841 (Mich. Ct. App. 1980).

[80] *See, e.g.,* Sostre v. McGinnis, 442 F.2d 178 (2d Cir. 1971), *cert. denied,* 405 U.S. 978 (1972); Clutchette v. Procunier, 328 F. Supp. 767 (N.D. Cal. 1971).

[81] *See* Chapter 13.

[82] Booth v. Churner, 532 U.S. 731 (2001); Porter v. Nussle, 534 U.S. 516 (2002).

[83] The Prison Litigation Reform Act of 1996 mandates that no civil action under § 1983 can be brought by a prisoner confined in any jail, prison, or other correctional facility until all administrative remedies that are available have been exhausted. 42 U.S.C. § 1997e(a). *See* Chapter 13.

The distinction was considered in *Edwards v. Balisok.*[84] An inmate was found guilty of prison rule infractions and sentenced, among other things, to the loss of 30 days' good-time credit that he had previously earned toward his release. Alleging that the procedures used in his disciplinary proceeding violated his Fourteenth Amendment due process rights, he filed a suit under § 1983 for a declaration that those procedures were unconstitutional, for compensatory and punitive damages, and for an injunction to prevent future violations.

The District Court held that a state prisoner's claim for damages is not cognizable under § 1983 if a judgment in his favor would "necessarily imply" that his conviction or sentence was invalid, unless he could demonstrate that the conviction or sentence previously had been invalidated by another court action.[85] Although holding that a judgment for the prisoner would necessarily imply the invalidity of his disciplinary hearing and the resulting sanctions, the court did not dismiss the suit, but stayed it, pending filing and resolution of a state court action for restoration of the good-time credits.

On appeal, the Supreme Court held that the inmate's claim for declaratory relief and money damages was not cognizable under § 1983. The Court rejected the argument that a claim seeking damages only for using the wrong procedures, not for reaching the wrong result, is always cognizable under § 1983. This argument disregards the possibility that the nature of the challenge to the procedures implies the invalidity of the judgment. If established, the inmate's allegations of deceit and bias by the hearing officer at his disciplinary proceeding would necessarily imply the invalidity of the deprivation of his good-time credits. Habeas corpus was the proper remedy, and use of this remedy requires exhaustion of all state judicial remedies. Unless the PLRA is involved, exhaustion of state remedies is unnecessary in a § 1983 lawsuit.[86]

§ 11.6.2 —The Immunity Defenses

Sovereign Immunity

It is evident that if sovereign immunity could be asserted by state officials as a defense to a suit based on the Civil Rights Act, the statute would be stripped of its vitality, as it literally applies to persons acting under state law. Thus it is not surprising to find that the Civil Rights Act has been successfully used against prison wardens[87] and prison guards.[88]

---

[84]   520 U.S. 641 (1997).

[85]   *Applying* Heck v. Humphrey, 512 U.S. 477 (1994).

[86]   Morgan v. LaVallee, 526 F.2d 221 at 223 (2d Cir. 1975).

[87]   Sostre v. McGinnis, 442 F.2d 178 (2d Cir. 1971), *cert. denied*, 405 U.S. 978 (1972); Withers v. Levine, 615 F.2d 158 (4th Cir. 1980); Estelle v. Gamble, 429 U.S. 97 (1976).

[88]   Wiltsie v. California Department of Corrections, 406 F.2d 515 (9th Cir. 1968). *See also* Meredith v. Arizona, 523 F.2d 481 (9th Cir. 1975); Harris v. Chancellor, 537 F.2d 204 (5th Cir. 1976); Collins v. Cundy, 603 F.2d 824 (10th Cir. 1979).

There are no reported cases in which money damages have been recovered from a state's chief executive under the Civil Rights Act. However, the Supreme Court has stated that Congress did not intend "to abolish wholesale all common-law immunities"[89] when it passed the Civil Rights Act. Thus, the Court has approved the immunity of state legislators[90] and state judges.[91] In 1909, the Supreme Court had an opportunity to give state governors absolute immunity, but it refused to do so, apparently satisfied with giving governors a qualified immunity when they act in good faith.[92]

In *Scheuer v. Rhodes*,[93] the United States Supreme Court stated: ". . . the Eleventh Amendment[94] provides no shield for a state official confronted by a claim he had deprived another of a federal right under the color of state law."[95] The Court cited the case of *Ex parte Young*,[96] stating that a state official acting under state law in a manner that violates the federal Constitution is ". . . stripped of his official or representative character and is subjected in his person to the consequences of his individual conduct."[97]

Executive Immunity—Absolute Immunity

The idea that government officials are immune from personal liability follows the same rationale that brought us the doctrine of sovereign immunity. The general proposition that has supported this immunity has been that the public has an interest in public officials making decisions and taking action to enforce the laws for the protection of the public, without worrying about facing numerous lawsuits for their actions. This immunity has been the product of constitutional and legislative provisions as well as judicial determination, as pointed out above.

Whenever the issue of official immunity is discussed, a distinction must be made between absolute immunity and qualified immunity. Absolute immunity means just that. If the doctrine applies, it is not possible to maintain a civil action for personal damages against the individual, no matter how extensive the injuries or malicious the intent. If such injury occurs, the remedy is injunctive relief, impeachment, or criminal prosecution. The class of persons pro-

---

89   Pierson v. Ray, 386 U.S. 547, 554 (1967).
90   Tenney v. Brandhove, 341 U.S. 367 (1951).
91   Pierson v. Ray, 386 U.S. 547 (1967); Briscoe v. LaHue, 460 U.S. 325 (1983) (Even though a testifying police officer allegedly committed perjury at a criminal trial, he is immune from a suit for damages under the Civil Rights Act (42 U.S.C. 1983) brought by the former defendant. The common law provides absolute immunity from subsequent damages liability for all persons, governmental or private, who are integral parts of the judicial process).
92   Moyer v. Peabody, 212 U.S. 78 (1909) (state governor not liable for ordering arrest of plaintiff when governor acted in good faith belief that such arrest was necessary to prevent insurrection).
93   416 U.S. 232 (1974).
94   Appendix I.
95   Scheuer v. Rhodes, 416 U.S. at 237; Ex parte Young, 209 U.S. 123 (1908).
96   209 U.S. 123 (1908).
97   *Id.* at 159-160.

tected by absolute immunity is basically limited to judges,[98] prosecutors,[99] and legislators.[100] The United States Supreme Court has held that federal executive officials exercising discretion are entitled to the qualified immunity specified in *Scheuer v. Rhodes*,[101] subject to situations in which the official is performing judicial acts, such as an agency attorney. In those cases, the official is entitled to absolute immunity because it is deemed essential for the conduct of the public business. However, even though there may be no absolute immunity, the government official may still be protected by qualified immunity.

Qualified Immunity

Whether an official has qualified immunity will depend on the functions and responsibilities of the official claiming the immunity, as well as the purposes behind Title 42 U.S.C. § 1983. Section 1983 includes "misuse of power, possessed by virtue of state law and made possible only because the wrongdoer is clothed with the authority of state law."

The Court in *Scheuer* stated:

> In varying scope, a qualified immunity is available to officers of the executive branch of government, the violation being dependent upon the scope of discretion and responsibilities of the office and all the circumstances as they reasonably appeared at the time of the action on which liability is sought to be based. It is the existence of reasonable grounds for the belief formed at the time and in light of all the circumstances, coupled with good-faith belief, that affords a basis for qualified immunity of executive officers for acts performed in the course of official conduct.[102]

---

[98] Pierson v. Ray, 386 U.S. 547, 554 (1967).

[99] Burns v. Reed, 500 U.S. 478 (1981); *see* Hoffman v. Harris, No. 92-6161 (6th Cir. 1994), *cert. denied*, 511 U.S. 1060 (1994) (social workers who file legal actions). The public policy embodied in the doctrine of absolute immunity is not one that the courts have invented recently. According to *Bradley v. Fisher*, 80 U.S. (13 Wall.) 335, 20 L. Ed. 646, the doctrine of absolute immunity for persons performing a judicial function has roots stretching far back into the common law. *See* Pierson v. Ray, 386 U.S. 547, 553-554 (1967); *see* Burns v. Reed, 111 S. Ct. at 1941, quoting the observation of Lord Mansfield in *King v. Skinner*, Lofft 55, 56, 98 A.E.R. 529, 530 (K.B. 1772), that "neither party, witness, counsel, jury, or judge can be put to answer, civilly or criminally, for words spoken in office." The *Burns* Court went on to note that "this immunity extended to 'any hearing before a tribunal which performed a judicial function.' W. Prosser, Law of Torts § 94, pp. 826-827 (1941). The same sort of absolute immunity that applies to judges in the performance of judicial acts applies as well to prosecutors in the performance of their official functions. Yaselli v. Goff, 275 U.S. 503 (1927), *aff'g*, 12 F.2d 396 (2d Cir. 1926); Imbler v. Pachtman, 424 U.S. 409 (1976). *See* Butz v. Economou, 438 U.S. 478 (1978), for a full exposition of the development of the modern absolute immunity doctrine as applied to judges and prosecutors. *See* Watts v. Burkhart, 978 F.2d 269 (6th Cir. 1992); In Salyer v. Patrick, 874 F.2d 374, 378 (6th Cir. 1989), the Sixth Circuit held that "due to their quasi-prosecutorial function in the initiation of child abuse proceedings," social workers are absolutely immune from liability for filing juvenile abuse petitions. However, *see* Antoine v. Byers & Anderson, Inc., 508 U.S. 429 (1993) (denying court reporter absolute immunity in large part because official court reporters did not begin appearing in state courts until the late nineteenth century).

[100] Tenney v. Brandhove, 341 U.S. 367 (1951).

[101] 416 U.S. 232 (1974).

[102] *Id.* at 247.

The issue of qualified immunity arose in the school setting with respect to a working definition of "good faith." The case was *Wood v. Strickland*,[103] and the United States Supreme Court established a two-pronged test based on "subjective" and "objective" good-faith determinations. The Court held:

> Therefore, in the specific context of school discipline, we hold that a school board member is not immune from liability for damages under § 1983 if he knew or reasonably should have known that the action he took within his sphere of official responsibility would violate the constitutional rights of the student affected, or if he took the action with the malicious intention to cause a deprivation of constitutional rights or other injury to the student. That is not to say that school board members are "charged with predicting the future course of constitutional law." A compensatory award will be appropriate with such disregard of the student's clearly established constitutional rights that his action cannot reasonably be characterized as being in good faith.[104]

Under the *Wood* test, the official involved must act sincerely, and with a belief that he or she is doing right. However, an act violating a constitutional right cannot be justified by ignorance or disregard of settled law. In other words, an executive official is held to a standard of conduct based not only on permissible intentions, but also on knowledge of the basic, unquestioned constitutional rights of the individuals for whom the official is responsible.

Wood was a five-to-four decision. The dissenting justices argued, in effect, that it is unsound to hold public officials liable for actions taken, without malice, that violated "unquestioned constitutional rights," when the Supreme Court itself cannot determine unanimously what those rights are. Justice Powell, writing for the dissent, stated:

> The Court states the standard of required knowledge in two cryptic phrases: "settled, indisputable law" and "unquestioned constitutional rights." Presumably these are intended to mean the same thing, although the meaning of neither phrase is likely to be self-evident to constitutional law scholars—much less the average school board member. One need only look to the decisions of this Court—to our reversals, our recognition of evolving concepts, and our five-four splits—to recognize the hazard of even informed prophecy as to what are "unquestioned constitutional rights."[105]

The dilemma facing public officials is highlighted by *O'Connor v. Donaldson*.[106] In *O'Connor*, a mental patient sued the superintendent of the mental institution for depriving the patient of his liberty. The judge and jury

---

[103]   420 U.S. 308 (1975).
[104]   *Id.* at 322.
[105]   *Id.* at 329.
[106]   422 U.S. 563 (1975).

agreed, and the mental patient recovered a judgment of $38,500 against the superintendent personally. The superintendent argued on appeal that he was merely acting pursuant to an Alabama statute, and that he could not reasonably have been expected to know that the state law, as he understood it, was constitutionally invalid. The Court of Appeals was not sympathetic, and affirmed the money judgment. On appeal to the United States Supreme Court, the case was reversed and remanded to the lower courts for reconsideration in light of *Wood v. Strickland.*

The subsequent decision of a federal court of appeals found "bad faith" along more traditional lines. The court found that the state officials had maintained a defense stratagem of delay for delay's sake, as well as an unconscionable—and continued—denial of facts that were well-documented and known to all parties interested in the subject. An award of $52,000 was made.[107]

In *Procunier v. Navarette,*[108] the *Wood* standard was applied to prison officials. The court ruled that, as prison officials, the defendants were not absolutely immune from liability in the § 1983 damage suit and could rely only on qualified immunity as described in *Scheuer* and *Wood.* Using the first standard put forth in *Wood,* the court stated ". . . the immunity defense would be unavailing to [the prison officials] if the constitutional right allegedly infringed by them was clearly established at the time of their challenged conduct, if they knew or should have known of that right, and if they knew or should have known that their conduct violated the constitutional norm."

In *Knell v. Bensinger*[109] the *Wood* standard was also applied to prison officials. In discussing *Wood's* two-pronged test for qualified immunity, the court defined the subjective good-faith requirement as whether, in enforcing the challenged regulation against the plaintiff, the defendant "sincerely and with a belief that he was doing right" carried out the regulation. In defining the objective good faith requirement, the court stated that the prison official would not be immune if he acted "with such disregard of the plaintiff's clearly established constitutional rights that his action cannot reasonably be characterized as being in good faith."

The court then held that in the field of prison administration, officials must be aware of the protections given to inmates through the judicial process. Imposition of personal liability is a shorthand method of informing prison officials that they must be concerned with and informed of legal developments in the rights of the confined, as set forth by the courts, the legislature, and the agency for which the officials work. At the same time, the court recognized the importance of experimentation and discretion in developing correctional policies and disciplinary procedures.

Another case imposing the *Wood* standard on prison officials is *Cruz v. Beto,*[110] in which the former Director of the Texas Department of Corrections was held liable in the amount of approximately $10,000 for violating an

---

[107]   Gates v. Collier, 70 F.R.D. 341 (N.D. Miss. 1976).
[108]   434 U.S. 555 (1978).
[109]   522 F.2d 720 (7th Cir. 1975).
[110]   405 U.S. 319 (1972).

inmate's rights. The violations that were actionable for money damages included: (1) wrongful segregation, humiliation, denial of access to the courts and to the attorney of the inmate's choice, and improper censorship of mail between attorney and client; (2) denial of access to educational materials with a corresponding interference in inmates' efforts to rehabilitate themselves; (3) wrongful deprivation of the opportunity to earn Point Incentive Program merit points solely because of inmate's choice of counsel; and (4) imposition of excessive demands of physical labor upon inmates who were duly categorized by corrections officials as medically unfit to perform such tasks.

Cruz is an example of facts alleged by prison officials to justify their decisions and actions that were not proved in court. The court took note that the witnesses who were to testify regarding the danger to security failed to appear, that no complaints were ever made to the Texas Bar Association about the conduct of the attorney, nor were any criminal charges ever filed. Prison officials must realize that naked allegations are not a sufficient defense. The burden of proving justification for interfering with fundamental constitutional rights is on the prison officials—and this must be proved in court.

The doctrine of qualified immunity was substantially changed in *Harlow v. Fitzgerald*.[111] In *Harlow*, the Supreme Court felt that too many cases were going to the jury or leading to overly extensive pretrial discovery. The Supreme Court also felt that more cases should be disposed of on summary judgment. The Court stated:

> ". . . [B]are allegations of malice should not suffice to subject government officials either to the costs of trial or to the burdens of broad-reaching discovery. . . . [G]overnment officials performing discretionary functions generally are shielded from liability for civil damages insofar as their conduct does not violate clearly established statutory or constitutional rights of which a reasonable person would have known. . . . On summary judgment, the judge appropriately may determine, not only the currently applicable law, but whether that law was clearly established at the time the action occurred. If the law at that time was not clearly established, an official could not reasonably be expected to anticipate subsequent legal developments, nor could he fairly be said to 'know' that the law forbade conduct not previously identified as unlawful. Until this threshold immunity question is resolved, discovery should not be allowed. If the law was clearly established, the immunity defense ordinarily should fail, since a reasonably competent public official should know the law governing his conduct. Nevertheless, if the official pleading the defense claims extraordinary circumstances and can prove that he neither knew nor should have known the relevant legal standard, the defense should be sustained.

---

[111]   457 U.S. 800 (1982).

Other examples of bad faith include *Williams v. Treen*[112] and *Bennett v. Williams.*[113] In *Treen*, it was held that where state prison officials violated clearly established state law, their belief in the lawfulness of their actions was per se unreasonable. They were not entitled to claim immunity based upon the defense of good faith. In other words, a good faith immunity from liability in a civil rights action cannot be asserted by officials whose actions clearly violate established state law. In this case, applicable state fire, safety, and health regulations were violated. Further, state officials are charged with knowledge of their state's own explicit and clearly established regulations.

In *Bennett*—in light of a determination that living conditions in Alabama prisons constituted cruel and unusual punishment in violation of the Eighth Amendment in a prior § 1983 case—prison officials were precluded from invoking qualified immunity because the prior litigation put them on notice of the continuing violations of the prisoner's constitutional rights. A jury instruction suggesting that the state could not be required to pay any part of the judgment against the officials and employees was sufficiently prejudicial to the prisoner that reversal of the favorable judgment for the prison officials was reversed.

Lack of standing may also be asserted as a defense. In *Leeke v. Timmerman*, a lower court decision awarding $3,000 in compensatory damages, $1,000 in punitive damages, and attorney's fees, against the legal advisor to the South Carolina Department of Corrections and the Director of the Department of Corrections, was reversed. The allegation was that the two defendants had attempted to prevent criminal charges from being filed by an inmate against correctional officers after an alleged beating within the prison by intervening with the local prosecutor. The Supreme Court held that a private citizen (in this case the inmate) had no standing in federal court to challenge the discretion of a prosecutor in his determination that criminal charges should or should not be filed. Because a complaining witness has the right to try to persuade a prosecutor to file charges, potential targets also have the right to try to persuade a prosecutor to not file charges.[114]

In *Procunier v. Navarette,*[115] the Court held that a prison official was eligible for qualified immunity because his interference with an inmate's mail was not a firmly established constitutionally protected right at the time that the alleged interference occurred. Thus, unless the constitutional protection of some right is firmly established at the time of the action, the official cannot be held to the knowledge that he has invaded a constitutional right of an inmate.

The defense of qualified immunity is available so long as the official's actions do not violate clearly established statutory or constitutional rights of which a reasonable person would have known. This standard permits an official to carry out his or her duties free from concern for his or her personal lia-

---

[112]   671 F.2d 892 (5th Cir. 1982).
[113]   689 F.2d 1370 (11th Cir. 1983).
[114]   Leeke v. Timmerman, 457 U.S. 496 (1981).
[115]   434 U.S. 555 (1978).

bility. On the other hand, he or she may on occasion have to consider whether a proposed course of action can be squared with the Constitution and laws of the United States. Where an official could be expected to know that his or her conduct would violate statutory or constitutional rights, he or she should hesitate. The essential issue—and problem—of the qualified immunity defense is timing. If the best that a public official-defendant can expect is a favorable jury instruction at the termination of a case, the defense is really unsatisfactory. What is needed is a summary procedure to avoid long and costly pretrial discovery proceedings, and the trial itself.

Harlow v. Fitzgerald refashioned the qualified immunity doctrine in such a way as to permit the resolution of many insubstantial claims on summary judgment and to avoid subjecting government officials either to the costs of trial or to the burdens of broad-reaching discovery in cases in which the legal norms the officials were alleged to have violated were not clearly established at the time. Unless a plaintiff's allegations state a claim of the violation of clearly established law, a defendant pleading qualified immunity is entitled to dismissal before the commencement of discovery. Further, even if the plaintiff's complaint adequately alleges the commission of acts that violate clearly established law, the defendant is entitled to summary judgment if discovery fails to uncover evidence sufficient to create a genuine issue as to whether the defendant in fact committed those acts. There is an entitlement not to stand trial or face the other burdens of litigation, conditioned on the resolution of the essentially legal question of whether the conduct of which the plaintiff complains violated clearly established law. The entitlement is an immunity from suit rather than a mere defense to liability. Consequently, an order denying qualified immunity is an appealable "final decision." An appellate court reviewing the denial of a defendant's claim of immunity need not consider the correctness of the plaintiff's version of the facts, nor even determine whether the plaintiff's allegations actually state a claim. All that is needed is for the appellate court to determine a question of law; whether the legal norms established at the time of the challenged actions or, in cases in which the trial court has denied summary judgment for the defendant on the ground that even under the defendant's version of the facts, the defendant's conduct violated clearly established law, whether the law clearly forbade the actions the defendant claims he or she took.[116]

Under current law,[117] in order to prevail in a §1983 action for civil damages from a government official performing discretionary functions, the qualified immunity defense requires that the official be shown to have violated clearly established statutory or constitutional rights of which a reasonable person would have known.

---

[116] Mitchell v. Forsyth, 472 U.S. 511 (1985).
[117] Conn v. Gabbert, 526 U.S. 286 (1999).

Martinez v. California[118] came to the Supreme Court involving, among other issues, whether parole officials enjoyed quasijudicial immunity under the Civil Rights Act[119] in parole-release decisions. In affirming the decision below on other grounds, it was said in a footnote: "We reserve the question of what immunity, if any, a state parole officer has in a § 1983 action, where a constitutional violation is made out by the allegations."[120]

In *Payton v. United States,*[121] the federal government was not liable for the allegedly negligent parole of a dangerously psychotic prisoner who later killed a woman. The actual decision to grant or deny parole is within the complete discretion of the parole board, and therefore falls under the "discretionary function" exemption of the Federal Tort Claims Act. However, the Bureau of Prisons may be held liable for its failure to supply the parole board with records that would show an inmate to be dangerously psychotic and a menace to society when that inmate, after being paroled, kills a woman. Further, the law places an affirmative nondiscretionary mandate upon the federal government to examine inmates who may be insane. Any negligence on the part of the federal government for failure to examine an inmate and later report their findings to the Attorney General or his designee is actionable.

Members of a disciplinary committee are entitled only to qualified immunity, and not absolute immunity.[122] However, the director of inmate disciplinary programs, as a judge, has absolute immunity for his actions on administrative appeals arising out of determinations of disciplinary hearings held in New York State prisons. He performs a quasi-judicial role as a professional civilian hearing officer.[123]

For personal responsibility for damages to apply, the constitutional right allegedly violated must be well established at the time of the alleged violation.

In *Maxie v. Felix,*[124] a prison guard's unprovoked and unjustified act of throwing a prisoner across a hallway and into a wall, which allegedly caused bruising, soreness, and emotional damage, was found to violate the prisoner's then-existing constitutional rights. The court relied on the 1975 Ninth Circuit Court of Appeals decision in *Meredith v. Arizona,*[125] which held that strong blows for no purpose amounted to excessive force, in violation of the Eighth Amendment. The Court held that such action could reasonably be understood by a guard to violate the prisoner's then-existing constitutional rights and thus a qualified immunity defense would be unavailable to the guard.

---

[118]   444 U.S. 277 (1980).

[119]   42 U.S.C. §1983.

[120]   Martinez, at 285, n. 11.

[121]   679 F.2d 475 (5th Cir. 1982); *see also* Bowers v. DeVito, 686 F.2d 616 (7th Cir. 1982) (The dismissal of a § 1983 action against Illinois state health officials for the release of an allegedly dangerous mental patient who later stabbed a woman to death was upheld. Members of the general public do not have a constitutional right to be protected by the state from attacks by convicts and madmen).

[122]   Cleavinger v. Saxner, 474 U.S. 193 (1985).

[123]   Gaston v. Coughlin, 861 F. Supp. 199 (W.D.N.Y. 1994), *remanded,* 249 F.3d 156 (2d Cir. 2001). *See also* §9.4 *supra.* For the application of absolute immunity in parole-making decisions, *see* 9.4 *supra.*

[124]   Maxie v. Felix, 939 F.2d 699 (9th Cir. 1991), *cert. denied,* 502 U.S. 1093 (1992).

[125]   523 F.2d 481 (9th Cir. 1975).

This decision is in line with *Hudson v. McMillian*,[126] which held that in an excessive force claim, a significant injury is not the basis of the claim, but rather whether the correctional officer acted maliciously.

In *Long v. Norris*,[127] the Sixth Circuit Court of Appeals found that a Tennessee prison regulation created a constitutionally protected liberty interest in visitation. The officials' threats to remove visitation rights in retaliation for visitors' refusal to submit to strip and body cavity searches in the absence of probable cause was contrary to the prison regulation, and therefore the officials were not entitled to qualified immunity.

It should be noted that for purposes of qualified immunity, decisions of courts other than the Supreme Court and Courts of Appeals can clearly establish law for purposes of qualified immunity. However, they must point unmistakably to unconstitutionality of conduct and be so clearly foreshadowed by applicable direct authority as to leave no doubt in the mind of a reasonable officer that his or her conduct was unconstitutional.[128]

Even if a jail policy of releasing sick or injured inmates violated the constitution, the sheriff was entitled to qualified immunity where the law at the time was not clearly established that a reasonable sheriff would know that the policy was unlawful.[129]

Youth detention center employees were entitled to qualified immunity for a sexual assault on a minor while he was in the custody of the Center. A four-hour delay in medical attention did not amount to deliberate indifference to serious medical needs where the youth told no one of the assault, the blood stain on his underwear was reasonably assumed to be evidence of gastrointestinal problems for which he was already being treated, emergency treatment was not required, and there was no medical evidence indicating that the four-hour delay before he was taken to hospital worsened his medical condition.[130]

Prison officials were entitled to qualified immunity in an inmate's claim that officials violated the inmate's right to privacy of medical information regarding his HIV-positive status. The law was not clearly established that the officials' conduct in not keeping the inmate's medical condition confidential violated the inmate's constitutional rights.[131]

Qualified immunity protected jail personnel sued by an inmate who was catheterized against his will. The procedure was ordered by a prison doctor for diagnostic purposes after a scuffle with a guard. It would not have been either apparent or sufficiently clear to a reasonable official at that time that the

---

[126]   503 U.S. 1 (1992). *See* § 2.2.

[127]   929 F.2d 1111 (6th Cir.), *cert. denied*, 502 U.S. 863 (1991). Cases like *Long* must be revisited in light of *Sandin*. *See* § 8.1.

[128]   Strouss v. Mich. Dep't of Corr., 75 F. Supp. 2d 711 (E.D. Mich. 1999), *aff'd*, 250 F.3d 336 (6th Cir. 2001).

[129]   Marsh v. Butler County, 268 F.3d 1014 (11th Cir. 2001).

[130]   Hill v. Dekalb Regional Youth Detention Ctr., 40 F.3d 1176 (11th Cir. 1994), *criticized in* United States v. Lopez-Lukis, 102 F.3d 1164 (11th Cir. 1997), and Lancaster v. Monroe County, 116 F.3d 1419 (11th Cir. 1997).

[131]   Doe v. Delie, 257 F.3d 309 (3d Cir. 2001).

forcible catheterizing of a prisoner for medical purposes only would constitute an unreasonable search under the Fourth Amendment.[132]

An eight-day lockdown and search of two prison blocks did not result in liability where the search followed a rash of assaults and stabbings. The search resulted in the recovery of 88 weapons. Even if any of various inconveniences caused to the inmates during the lockdown rose to the level of an Eighth Amendment violation, no reasonable prison official would have believed his actions violated the law at the time of the lockdown.[133]

County officials were entitled to qualified immunity arising out of the two and one-half year administrative segregation of a detainee after he was suspected of killing another inmate. Any reasonable person in the officials' position would have believed that holding the detainee in segregation did not violate any of his rights, but that it promoted the safety of other inmates and promoted the detainee's safety.[134]

Correctional officials were entitled to qualified immunity in a claim by inmates challenging under the First Amendment the Department of Corrections' policy of prohibiting the receipt of standard rate mail, as applied to subscription nonprofit organization mail. The contours of the publisher's right to send and inmates' right to receive subscriptions from nonprofit organizations were not clearly established, and department officials may have relied on unpublished decisions upholding the departmental regulation at issue.[135]

A prison guard was not entitled to qualified immunity in a civil rights action based on an Eighth Amendment violation resulting from three blows to an inmate's face by the guard. The guard knew his actions were unlawful. He acted with a wanton state of mind, and the law of the circuit made it clear that contemporary standards of decency always are violated when a prison guard wantonly applies force to a prisoner to cause harm regardless of whether significant injury results.[136]

The scope of qualified immunity was narrowed in *Hope v. Pelzer*.[137] Under the *Hope* doctrine, defendants in civil rights cases may be shielded from liability for their constitutionally impermissible conduct if their actions did not violate clearly established statutory or constitutional rights of which a reasonable person would have known. Courts commit error in requiring that the facts of previous cases and an inmate's case be "materially similar." Qualified immunity operates to ensure that before they are subjected to suit, officers are on notice that their conduct is unlawful. Officers sued in a civil rights action have the same fair notice right as do defendants charged under the criminal statutes,[138] which makes it a crime for a state official to act willfully and under

---

[132] Sauleberry v. Maricopa County, 151 F. Supp. 2d 1109 (D.C. Ariz. 2001).

[133] Waring v. Meachum, 175 F. Supp. 2d 230 (D.C. Conn. 2001).

[134] Love v. Cook County, 82 F. Supp. 2d 911 (N.D. Ill. 2000), *dismissed in part*, 156 F. Supp. 2d 749 (N.D. Ill. 2001).

[135] Prison Legal News v. Cook, 238 F.3d 1145 (9th Cir. 2001).

[136] Romaine v. Rawson, 140 F. Supp. 2d 204 (ND.N.Y. 2001).

[137] 536 U.S. 730 (2002).

[138] 18 U.S.C. §242.

color of state law to deprive a person of constitutional rights. Officials can be on notice that their conduct violates established law even in novel fact situations. The Supreme Court expressly rejected a requirement that previous cases be "fundamentally similar." Accordingly, the salient question a court must ask is whether the state of the law gave prison officials fair warning that an inmate's alleged treatment was unconstitutional.

The same analysis for § 1983 lawsuits applies to *Bivens* suits against federal officials.[139] A court evaluating a qualified immunity claim must first determine whether the plaintiff has alleged the deprivation of a constitutional right and, if so, proceed to determine whether that right was clearly established at the time of the violation. "Clearly established" for qualified immunity purposes means that the contours of the right must be sufficiently clear that a reasonable official would understand that what he is doing violates that right. His very action need not previously have been held unlawful, but in the light of preexisting law its unlawfulness must be apparent. When the state of the law is at best undeveloped at the relevant time, and the officers cannot have been expected to predict the future course of constitutional law, qualified immunity applies.

The timing of when the qualified immunity defense is raised is critical to prevent unnecessary lawsuits. Law suits can be terminated early in the litigation by means of summary judgment. This is a procedural device to terminate a lawsuit when there is no factual basis to continue under applicable law. Summary judgments are often decided on the basis of affidavits.

According to the Supreme Court,[140] a qualified immunity defense must be considered in proper sequence. A ruling should be made early in the proceedings so that the cost and expenses of trial are avoided where the defense is dispositive. Such immunity is an entitlement not to stand trial, not a defense from liability. The initial inquiry is whether a constitutional right would have been violated on the facts alleged, for if no right would have been violated, there is no need for further inquiry into immunity. However, if a violation could be made out on a favorable view of the parties' submissions, the next step is to determine whether the right was clearly established. This inquiry must be undertaken in light of the case's specific context, not as a broad general proposition. The relevant, dispositive inquiry is whether it would be clear to a reasonable officer that the conduct was unlawful in the situation he confronted.

§ 11.6.3 —Monetary Damages

A plaintiff who brings an action under the Civil Rights Act is entitled to an award of monetary damages in order to redress deprivations of his or her constitutional rights. A federal court listed three distinct classes of damages that an inmate might recover from prison officials who have violated his or her

---

[139] Wilson v. Lane, 526 U.S. 603 (1999).
[140] Saucier v. Katz, 533 U.S. 194 (2001).

constitutional rights:[141] (1) actual damages to compensate the inmate for out-of-pocket expenses and mental suffering; (2) nominal damages to vindicate the inmate's rights, if no actual damages were sustained; and (3) punitive damages if the wrongful act was done intentionally and maliciously.

In the case of *Sostre v. McGinnis,*[142] a federal appellate court upheld an award of $9,300 in compensatory damages rendered against a prison warden and state commissioner of corrections. The damages were based upon the rate of $25 per day for the 372 days that the plaintiff spent in isolated confinement in deplorable conditions.[143] However, the appellate court reversed an additional award of $3,720 in punitive damages because it found no malice on the part of the defendants.

In *Cruz v. Beto,*[144] the following formula was used by the court in determining monetary damages to the inmates:

1. $1.00 to each inmate-plaintiff for each day the segregation policy was imposed upon him . . .;

2. $25.00 to each inmate-plaintiff for being deprived of PIP (merit) points while segregated;

3. $250.00 to each inmate-plaintiff who was classified as medically unfit and who should not have been required, but was required, to perform field labor while segregated;

4. $250.00 to each inmate-plaintiff who was prohibited from continuing college-level or secondary-level education while segregated. In addition, the court found that the attorney involved in the *Cruz* case was entitled to damages of $1,000.00 for "embarrassment, humiliation, and improper deprivation . . . of the right to practice law through representation of . . . inmates."

Another court held that when an inmate was punished for possession of inflammatory papers, the prison officials were liable, the commissioner and the warden were each personally liable, and a verdict of $1,000.00 was not excessive.[145]

---

[141]   Wilson v. Prasse, 325 F. Supp. 9 (W.D. Pa. 1971).

[142]   442 F.2d 178 (2d Cir. 1971), *rev'g in part,* 312 F. Supp. 863 (S.D.N.Y. 1971), *cert. denied,* 405 U.S. 978 (1972).

[143]   The district court expressly held that the conditions of confinement, such as lack of exercise, restricted diet, sensory deprivation, and deprivation of intellectual stimulation, constituted cruel and unusual punishment, and based its award of compensatory damages on this finding. Sostre v. Rockefeller, 312 F. Supp. 863, 885 (S.D. N.Y. 1970). However, the appellate court overruled this finding, stating that the conditions of segregated confinement did not amount to cruel and unusual punishment. Sostre v. McGinnis, 442 F.2d 178, 190-194 (2d Cir. 1971), *cert. denied,* 405 U.S. 978 (1972). Nevertheless, the appellate court based its affirmation of the compensatory damages upon "the conditions . . . of segregation." *Id.* at 205, n. 52. Thus, exactly what the plaintiff was being compensated for is somewhat unclear, but because the appellate court held that the prison officials placed Sostre in segregated confinement for invalid reasons, it may be presumed that damages were upheld merely because Sostre had been placed in isolation.

[144]   Cruz v. Beto, 453 F. Supp. 905 (S.D. Texas 1976), *aff'd,* 603 F.2d 1178 (5th Cir. 1979). *See also* discussion of this case in § 11.6.2.

[145]   United States ex rel. Larkins v. Oswald, 510 F.2d 583 (2d Cir. 1975).

Punitive damages may be recovered for reckless or callously indifferent deprivations of federal statutory or constitutional rights, as well as for deprivations motivated by actual malicious intent. Punitive damages may be recovered for reckless or callous indifference to federally protected rights even when the standard of liability for compensatory damages is also one of recklessness. In one case, the respondent, while an inmate in a Missouri reformatory for youthful first offenders, was harassed, beaten, and sexually assaulted by his cellmates. He sued an officer at the reformatory, as well as others, alleging that his Eighth Amendment rights had been violated. Damages affirmed were $25,000 compensatory and $5,000 punitive. Smith, the correctional officer, placed the inmate in administrative segregation. He was placed in a cell with another inmate. Smith later placed a third inmate in the cell. The cellmates harassed, beat, and sexually assaulted the inmate-plaintiff. Evidence at trial showed that the inmate-plaintiff had placed himself in protective custody because of prior incidents of violence against him by other inmates. The third prisoner that Smith placed in the cell had been placed in administrative segregation for fighting. Smith made no effort to find out whether another cell was available. In fact, there was another cell in the same dormitory with only one occupant. Further, only a few weeks earlier, another inmate had been beaten to death in the same dormitory during the same shift, while Smith was on duty. It was held that Smith knew or should have known that an assault against the inmate-plaintiff was likely under the circumstances.[146] However, municipalities are immune from punitive damages in civil rights suits under 42 U.S.C. § 1983.[147]

Damages based on the abstract "value" or "importance" of constitutional rights are not a permissible element of compensatory damages in § 1983 cases. The basic purpose of a damage award in a § 1983 case is to compensate for injuries that are caused by the deprivation of constitutional rights. Damages measured by a jury's perception of the abstract "importance" of a constitutional right are not necessary to vindicate the constitutional rights that § 1983 protects, and moreover are an unwieldy tool for ensuring compliance with the Constitution. Because such damages are wholly divorced from any compensatory purpose, they cannot be justified as presumed damages, which are a substitute for ordinary compensatory damages, not a supplement for an award that fully compensates the alleged injury.[148]

§ 11.6.4 —Attorney's Fees

An item of monetary expense that a defendant prison official may be required to pay is the cost of attorney's fees to the inmate-plaintiff. The United States Supreme Court in *Alyeska Pipeline Service Co. v. Wilderness Society*[149]

---

[146] Smith v. Wade, 461 U.S. 302 (1983).
[147] City of Newport v. Fact Concerts, 453 U.S. 247 (1981).
[148] Memphis Community School District v. Stachura, 477 U.S. 299 (1986).
[149] 421 U.S. 240 (1975).

reaffirmed the general rule that, absent a statute or enforceable contract, litigants must pay their own attorney's fees. The Court pointed out, however, that there are recognized exceptions to this general rule. One exception is that a court may assess attorneys' fees for the willful disobedience of a court order, or when the losing party has acted in bad faith, "vexatiously, wantonly, or for oppressive reasons." However, in response to the *Alyeska* decision in 1976, Congress passed a statute that grants attorney's fees in various civil rights actions, including suits against prison officials.[150]

An example of court-awarded attorney's fees is *Gates v. Collier*.[151] The court stated that under the Civil Rights Attorney's Fees Award Act,[152] the court may order that fees be paid out of the state treasury, and to effectuate this, may join the state auditor and treasurer as defendants. The court also held that interest may be awarded on attorney's fees but not on out-of-pocket costs, which are reimbursed under the Act. *Hutto v. Finney*[153] also held that the award of attorney's fees to be paid out of Department of Correction funds is adequately supported by the court's finding that state officials acted in bad faith, and does not violate the Eleventh Amendment. The court further held that 42 U.S.C. § 1988 supports the court's award of additional attorney's fees to offset the cost of appeal."[154] Attorney's fees under 42 U.S.C. § 1988 may be awarded to the appropriate prevailing party in any § 1983 action, even though the action was brought in state court rather than federal court.[155]

A favorable judicial statement of law in the course of litigation that results in a judgment against the plaintiff in civil rights cases is insufficient to render a plaintiff a "prevailing party." Even if the prisoner's nonmonetary claims were not rendered moot by his release from prison, and it could be said that those claims were kept alive by his interest in expunging his misconduct conviction from his prison record, his counsel never took the steps necessary to have a declaratory judgment or expungement order properly entered. The argument that the initial holding of the District Court was a "vindication of rights"—that is, at least the equivalent of declaratory relief—ignored the fact that a judicial decree is not the end of the judicial process, but rather is the means of prompting some action (or cessation of action) by the defendant. In this case, the prisoner obtained nothing from the state. Moreover, equating statements of law (even legal holdings en route to a final judgment for the defendant) with declaratory judgments has the practical effect of depriving a defendant of any valid defenses that a court might take into account in deciding whether to enter a declaratory judgment. Furthermore, the same considerations that influence courts to issue declaratory judgments may not enter into the decision of whether to include statements of law in opinions. However, if they do, the court's decision is not appealable in the same manner as is its entry of a declaratory judgment.[156]

---

[150]   42 U.S.C. § 1988 (1976).
[151]   616 F.2d 1268 (5th Cir. 1980).
[152]   42 U.S.C. § 1988.
[153]   437 U.S. 678 (1978).
[154]   *Id.* at 689.
[155]   Maine v. Thiboutot, 448 U.S. 1 (1980).
[156]   Hewitt v. Helms, 482 U.S. 755 (1987).

There is no entitlement to attorney's fees unless the requesting party prevailed. By the time a District Court entered its judgment in the underlying suit, one of the plaintiffs had died and the other was no longer in custody. Under the circumstances, the plaintiffs were not "prevailing parties" under *Hewitt v. Helms* and were not entitled to attorney's fees.[157]

A prevailing party must be one who has succeeded on any significant claim affording it some of the relief sought, either during litigation or at the conclusion of the litigation. A plaintiff has crossed the threshold to a fee award of some kind if he or she satisfies the "significant issue"-"some benefit" standard. Under that standard, at a minimum, the plaintiff must be able to point to a resolution of the dispute that materially alters the parties' legal relationship in a manner that Congress sought to promote in the fee statute. When the plaintiff's success on a legal claim can be characterized as purely technical or *de minimis*, a district court would be justified in concluding that it is so insignificant as to be insufficient to support prevailing party status. However, when the parties' relationship has been materially changed, the degree of the plaintiff's overall success goes to the reasonableness of the award under *Hensley*, not to the availability of the fee award.[158]

Identifying the prevailing party was the issue in *Hanrahan v. Hampton*[159] and *Maher v. Gagne*.[160] In *Hanrahan*, the court held that a party does not "prevail" merely by obtaining an appellate court order for a new trial. In *Maher*, the court held that fees may be awarded in a consent decree, even though there was no judicial determination that federal rights had been violated.

The extent of a plaintiff's success is a crucial factor in determining the proper amount of such fees. The time spent on unsuccessful claims that are completely distinct from successful claims should be excluded in determining a reasonable fee. However, the fee should not be reduced simply because the court did not adopt each of several related claims. A plaintiff who achieves only limited success with a group of related claims should be awarded only the amount that is reasonably related to the results obtained. In order to recover, the plaintiff must be a prevailing party. Plaintiffs may be considered prevailing parties for attorney's fee purposes if they succeed on any significant issue in litigation that achieves some of the benefit the parties sought in bringing the suit. The starting point is the number of hours reasonably expended on the litigation, multiplied by a reasonable hourly rate. The fee may then be adjusted up or down, depending upon the results obtained. The burden is on the fee applicant to establish entitlement to an award and to document the appropriate hours expended and hourly rates. For appellate review, if a district court has articulated a fair explanation for its fee award in a given case, the court of appeals should not reverse or remand the judgment unless the award is so low as to provide clearly inadequate compensation to the attorneys in the case, or

---

[157]   Rhodes v. Stewart, 488 U.S. 1 (1988).
[158]   Texas State Teachers Association v. Garland, 489 U.S. 782 (1989).
[159]   446 U.S. 754 (1980).
[160]   448 U.S. 122 (1980).

so high as to constitute a windfall. However, in *Hensley v. Eckerhart,* the decision of the district court was reversed because the opinion did not properly consider the relationship between the extent of success and the amount of the fee award. The fee award against Missouri hospital officials at the forensic unit of a Missouri state hospital was in excess of $133,000.[161]

In a controversial decision, two inmates who served as class representatives in a civil rights case arising out of a riot in their place of confinement were entitled to "incentive awards" over and above the damages they were able to claim from the fund established as a result of the litigation.[162]

Attorney's fees awarded under 42 U.S.C. § 1988 are to be calculated according to the prevailing market rates in the relevant community. Fees are not to be calculated according to the actual cost of providing legal services. Policy arguments based on a cost-based standard should be made to Congress and not to the courts. The rule applies to both private and non-profit counsel. An upward adjustment in determining attorney's fees in civil rights cases is permissible. This is calculated by multiplying the reasonable number of hours expended by a reasonable hourly rate. However, in some cases of exceptional success, an enhanced award may be justified. In seeking an enhanced award, the burden is on the attorney. However, once the attorney has carried his or her burden of showing that the claimed rate and number of hours are reasonable, the resulting product is presumed to be the reasonable fee contemplated by 42 U.S.C. § 1988. The record must show the complexity of the litigation, the novelty of the issues, the high-quality representation, and the great benefit to the class represented by the attorney. There is no basis for an award on "riskiness" of the lawsuit.[163]

However, an important factor for consideration in adjusting the figure upward or downward is the "results obtained." Where a plaintiff has obtained excellent results, his or her attorney should recover a fully compensatory fee, and the fee award should not be reduced simply because the plaintiff failed to prevail on every issue raised in the lawsuit.

The "catalyst theory" is not a permissible basis for the award of attorney's fees under the Americans with Disabilities Act of 1990. Under the "American Rule," parties are ordinarily required to bear their own attorney's fees, and courts follow a general practice of not awarding fees to a prevailing party absent explicit statutory authority. Congress has employed the legal term of art "prevailing party" in numerous statutes authorizing awards of attorney's fees. A "prevailing party" is one who has been awarded some relief by a court. The "catalyst theory," however, allows an award where there is no judicially sanctioned change in the parties' legal relationship. A defendant's voluntary change in conduct, although perhaps accomplishing what the plaintiff sought to achieve by the lawsuit, lacks the necessary judicial imprimatur on the change. The legislative history of the ADA is at best ambiguous as to the availability of the "catalyst theory." Particularly in view of the "American Rule,"

---

[161] Hensley v. Eckerhart, 457 U.S. 496 (1983).
[162] In re Southern Ohio Correctional Facility, 175 F.R.D. 270 (S.D. Ohio 1997).
[163] Blum v. Stetson, 465 U.S. 886 (1984).

such history is clearly insufficient to alter the clear meaning of "prevailing party" in the fee-shifting statutes. Attorney's fees were denied in *Buckahonnon v. West Virginia Dept. of Health and Human Resources.*[164]

It is important to note that the PLRA put limits on the amount of attorney's fees recoverable in prisoners' rights lawsuits. *See* Chapter 13.

The lodestar approach is appropriate in civil rights cases in which a plaintiff recovers only monetary damages. Fees in excess of the amount of damages recovered are not necessarily unreasonable. Although the amount of damages recovered is relevant to the amount of attorney's fees to be awarded under § 1988, it is only one of many factors that a court should consider in calculating an award of attorney's fees.

A civil rights action for damages is not merely a private tort suit benefiting only the individual plaintiffs whose rights were violated. Unlike most private tort litigants, a civil rights plaintiff seeks to vindicate important civil and constitutional rights that cannot be valued solely in monetary terms. Because damage awards do not fully reflect the public benefit advanced by civil rights litigation, Congress did not intend for fees in civil rights cases, unlike most private law cases, to depend on obtaining substantial monetary relief, but instead recognized that reasonable attorney's fees under § 1988 are not conditioned upon, and need not be proportionate to, an award of money damages. Consequently, a rule limiting attorney's fees in civil rights cases to a proportion of the damages awarded would seriously undermine Congress's purpose in enacting § 1988. Congress enacted § 1988 specifically because it found that the private market for legal services failed to provide many victims of civil rights violations with effective access to the judicial process. A rule of proportionality would make it difficult, if not impossible, for individuals with meritorious civil rights claims but relatively small potential damages to obtain redress from the courts, and would be totally inconsistent with Congress's purpose of ensuring sufficiently vigorous enforcement of civil rights. In order to ensure that lawyers would be willing to represent persons with legitimate civil rights grievances, Congress determined that it would be necessary to compensate lawyers for all time reasonably expended on a case.[165]

Later during the same term, the Supreme Court held that a trial court erred in increasing the attorney's fee award based on the "superior quality" of counsel's performance. The lodestar figure includes most, if not all, of the relevant factors constituting a "reasonable" attorney's fee, and it is unnecessary to enhance the fee for superior performance in order to serve the statutory purpose of enabling plaintiffs to receive legal assistance.[166]

However, a meritorious civil rights suit that breaks no new legal ground and triggers only a small award of damages may still merit an award of attorneys' fees.[167]

---

[164]   532 U.S. 598 (2001).
[165]   City of Riverside v. Rivera, 477 U.S. 561 (1986).
[166]   Pennsylvania v. Delaware Valley Citizens' Council for Clean Air, 478 U.S. 546 (1986).
[167]   Hyde v. Small, 123 F.3d 583 (7th Cir. 1997).

An attorney's fee allowed under § 1988 is not limited to the amount provided in a plaintiff's contingent fee arrangement with his or her counsel. To hold otherwise would be inconsistent with the statute, which broadly requires all defendants to pay a reasonable fee to all prevailing plaintiffs if ordered to do so by the court acting in its sound judgment and in light of all the circumstances of the case.[168]

Immunity from damages does not prevent an injunction from being issued. In such a case, the defendant may be liable for costs and attorney's fees.[169]

Attorney's fees are payable for work done in optional administrative proceedings involving the prevailing party in a § 1983 action only when a "discrete portion" of the attorney's work in the state proceeding was "useful and of a type ordinarily necessary" to advance the § 1983 litigation.[170] However, they are not awarded solely for legal services performed before state administrative agencies.[171]

The settlement of a § 1983 action may be made contingent upon the waiver of attorney fees under § 1988. Neither the statute nor the legislative history suggests that Congress intended to forbid all waivers of attorney's fees. Congress neither bestowed fee awards upon attorneys nor rendered them nonwaivable or nonnegotiable. It added them to the remedies available to combat civil rights violations—a goal that is consistent with conditioning settlement on the merits on a waiver of statutory attorney's fees. A general prohibition against waiver of attorney's fees in exchange for a settlement on the merits would itself impede vindication of civil rights by reducing the attractiveness of settlement. It is reasonable to assume that parties to a significant number of civil rights cases would refuse to settle if liability for attorney's fees remained open, thereby forcing more cases to trial, unnecessarily burdening the judicial system and deserving civil rights litigants.[172]

A distinction must be made between a public official being sued in his or her official capacity when the "real" defendant is a governmental unit, and when the public official is sued for his or her individual conduct. In official capacity suits, as long as the government entity receives notice and an opportunity to respond, the suit is, in all respects other than the name, a suit against the entity. When a state becomes involved in a § 1983 action either because the state was a proper party defendant or because state officials were sued in their official capacity, attorney's fees may be awarded to the state under § 1988. Only in an official capacity action is a plaintiff who wins entitled to seek relief, both on the merits and for attorney's fees, from the government entity.[173]

---

[168] Blanchard v. Bergeron, 488 U.S. 235 (1989).
[169] Pulliam v. Allen, 466 U.S. 522 (1984).
[170] Webb v. Board of Educ. of Dyer City, Tenn., 471 U.S. 234 (1975).
[171] North Carolina Department of Transportation v. Crest Street Community Council, 479 U.S. 6 (1986).
[172] Evans v. Jeff D., 475 U.S. 717 (1986).
[173] Kentucky v. Graham, 473 U.S. 159 (1985).

A civil rights plaintiff runs the risk of refusing an offer to settle a § 1983 case. If the eventual judgment is less than the amount proposed by the defense, the plaintiff must pay all costs incurred after the offer.[174] Costs include attorney's fees.[175]

Filing law suits *in forma pauperis* can also be costly. In *Olson v. Coleman,*[176] an appeal taken *in forma pauperis* failed to present any reasonable argument that the district court erred in its disposition, and was frivolous. As a sanction, the Court of Appeals assessed double costs[177] and attorney's fees.

§ 11.6.5   —Injunctive Relief

In addition to monetary damages, the Civil Rights Act authorizes equitable remedies, such as injunctions. An injunction is a judicial order that requires the person to whom it is directed to do a particular thing or to refrain from doing it. Injunctive relief is extremely useful in prison litigation, because the successful inmate-plaintiff will usually remain in custody and thus will wish to prevent future deprivations of his or her constitutional rights.

A trend in prison litigation is a judicial examination of the totality of internal conditions at specific detention facilities. In a number of cases, federal courts have declared such conditions to be so intolerable as to amount to the imposition of cruel and unusual punishment.[178] Although some courts in such cases have allowed the prison administrators to submit plans to the court for rectification of the facility's deficiencies,[179] several courts have judicially detailed the changes that must be made,[180] and other courts have offered the state legislature the opportunity to solve the problem before intervening.[181] In the case of *Jones v. Wittenberg,*[182] several months after declaring that the totality of conditions within the Lucas County (Toledo, Ohio) Jail rendered incarceration there cruel and unusual punishment,[183] the federal court issued a lengthy relief decree mandating many specific changes.[184] This remedial relief

---

[174]   Fed. R. Civ. P. 68.

[175]   Marek v. Chesny, 473 U.S. 1 (1985).

[176]   997 F.2d 726 (10th Cir. 1993). *See* Chapter 13, The Prison Litigation Reform Act.

[177]   Pursuant to Fed. R. App. P. 38.

[178]   Jones v. Wittenberg, 328 F. Supp. 93 (N.D. Ohio 1971), *aff'd sub nom.*, Jones v. Metzger, 456 F.2d 854 (6th Cir. 1972); Hamilton v. Schriro, 338 F. Supp. 1016 (E.D. La. 1970); Holt v. Sarver, 309 F. Supp. 362 (E.D. Ark. 1970), *aff'd,* 442 F.2d 304 (8th Cir. 1971); Felciano v. Barcelo, 497 F. Supp. 14 (D.P.R. 1979); Ramos v. Lamm, 520 F. Supp. 1059 (D. Colo. 1981).

[179]   *See, e.g.,* Holt v. Sarver, 309 F. Supp. 362 (E.D. Ark. 1970), *aff'd,* 442 F.2d 304 (8th Cir. 1971).

[180]   Costello v. Wainwright, 397 F. Supp. 20 (M.D. Fla. 1975); Gates v. Collier, 390 F. Supp. 482 (N.D. Miss. 1975); James v. Wallace, 406 F. Supp. 318 (M.D. Ala. 1976).

[181]   McCray v. Sullivan, 399 F. Supp. 271 (S.D. Ala. 1975).

[182]   323 F. Supp. 93 (N.D. Ohio 1971), *aff'd sub nom.*, Jones v. Metzger, 456 F.2d 854 (6th Cir. 1972); Jones v. Wittenberg, 509 F. Supp. 653 (N.D. Ohio 1980) (In the federal supervision of the Lucas County Jail, the court held that the sheriff had complied with most of the rules adopted by the state court, but had not complied with others).

[183]   The declaratory judgment opinion, which sets forth in detail the deplorable conditions of the jail, can be found in *Jones v. Wittenberg,* 323 F. Supp. 93 (N.D. Ohio 1971).

[184]   The relief decree in *Jones v. Wittenberg* is set out in 330 F. Supp. 707 (N.D. Ohio 1971).

covered all aspects of operating the institution, from the required wattage of lightbulbs to work-release programs, and in effect made the federal judge the jailer for Lucas County.

The substandard conditions that exist in many American detention facilities, and the courts' awareness that needed changes are not being initiated by prison administrators or legislators has and will continue to result in judicial orders specifying the required changes to bring the facilities up to constitutional standards. The complaint that money is not available to make the required changes will not be an acceptable excuse for maintaining unconstitutional confinement conditions.[185]

In most instances, judges are immune from liability under the Civil Rights Act. However, immunity from damages does not prevent an injunction from being issued against a judicial officer under some circumstances. In such cases, the judge may be liable for costs and attorney's fees, even though the result may eviscerate the doctrine of judicial immunity. Suit was filed against a magistrate by former county jail inmates, alleging that the practice of imposing bail on persons arrested for nonjailable offenses and incarcerating them if they could not make bail violated the Constitution. The practice was enjoined by a federal judge. Attorney's fees and court costs in the amount of $7,691 were awarded.[186]

§ 11.6.6   —Statute of Limitations

A statute of limitations prevents the litigation of "stale" claims. Section 1983 does not specify the appropriate statute of limitations for civil rights actions. Federal rather than state law governs the characterization of a § 1983 claim for statute of limitations purposes. However, the length of the limitations period, and related questions of tolling and application, are to be governed by state law.[187] In such cases, the claims are to be treated as personal injury actions under state law. For example, in Ohio, the two-year statute of limitations set forth in Revised Code § 2305.10 governs actions brought under § 1983.[188]

A state "notice of claim" statute has the same effect as an abbreviated statute of limitations. These are unconstitutional when applied to 42 U.S.C. § 1983 when litigated in a state court. Application of "notice of claims" statutes to state-court § 1983 actions cannot be approved as a matter of equitable federalism. Just as federal courts are constitutionally obligated to apply state law to

---

[185]   Alberti v. Sheriff of Harris Co. Tex., 406 F. Supp. 649 (S.D. Tex. 1975); Costello v. Wainwright, 525 F.2d 1239 (5th Cir. 1976); Miller v. Carson, 401 F. Supp. 835 (M.D. Fla. 1975); Gates v. Collier, 501 F.2d 1291 (5th Cir. 1974); Smith v. Sullivan, 553 F.2d 373 (5th Cir. 1977); Mitchell v. Untreiner, 421 F. Supp. 886 (N.D. Fla. 1976); Martinez-Rodriguez v. Jiminez, 409 F. Supp. 582 (D.P.R. 1976).

[186]   Pulliam v. Allen, 466 U.S. 522 (1984). *See* § 11.6.4, Attorney Fees.

[187]   Wilson v. Garcia, 471 U.S. 261 (1985).

[188]   LRL Properties v. Portage Metro Housing Auth., 55 F.3d 1097, 1105 (6th Cir. 1995).

state claims, the supremacy clause imposes on state courts a constitutional duty to proceed in such a manner that all the substantial rights of the parties under controlling federal law are protected. A state law that predictably alters the outcome of § 1983 claims depending solely on whether they are brought in state or federal court within the state is obviously inconsistent with the federal interest in intrastate uniformity.[189]

A district court rejected the contention that § 1983 actions were governed by the state's one-year statute of limitations covering assault, battery, false imprisonment, and five other intentional torts, and applied the state's three-year residual statute of limitations for personal injury claims not embraced by specific statutes of limitation. The United States Supreme Court held that when state law provides multiple statutes of limitation for personal injury actions, courts considering § 1983 claims should borrow the state's general or residual personal injury statute of limitations. Although *Wilson v. Garcia* ruled that 42 U.S.C. § 1983 required courts to borrow and apply to all § 1983 claims a state's personal injury statute of limitations, *Wilson* did not indicate which statute of limitations applies in states with multiple personal injury statutes. In light of *Wilson's* practical approach of eliminating uncertainty by providing one simple broad characterization of all § 1983 actions, a rule endorsing the choice of the state statute of limitations for intentional torts would be manifestly inappropriate. Every state has multiple intentional tort limitations provisions. In contrast, every state has one general or residual personal injury statute of limitations that is easily identifiable by language or application. The argument that intentional tort limitations periods should be borrowed because such torts are most analogous to § 1983 claims failed to recognize the enormous practical disadvantages of such a selection in terms of the confusion and unpredictability the selection would cause for potential § 1983 plaintiffs and defendants. Moreover, the analogy between § 1983 claims and state causes of action was felt to be too imprecise to justify such a result, in light of the wide spectrum of claims that § 1983 has come to span, many of which bear little, if any, resemblance to a common law intentional tort.[190]

A tolling statute stops, or tolls, the running of a statute of limitations. A federal court applying a state statute of limitations to an inmate's federal civil rights action should give effect to the state's provision tolling the limitations period for prisoners. Limitations periods in § 1983 suits are to be determined by referring to the appropriate state statute of limitations and the coordinate tolling rules, as long as the state law would not defeat the goals of the federal law at issue. The state tolling statute in this case was consistent with § 1983's remedial purpose, because some inmates may be loath to sue adversaries to whose daily supervision and control they remain subject, and even those who do file suit may not have a fair opportunity to establish the validity of their allegations while they are confined.[191]

---

[189]   Felder v. Casey, 487 U.S. 131 (1988).
[190]   Owens v. Okure, 488 U.S. 235 (1989).
[191]   Hardin v. Straub, 490 U.S. 536 (1989).

The Ninth Circuit Court of Appeals in *Bagley v. CMC Real Estate Corp.*[192] held that the statute of limitations for actions alleging constitutional violations leading to a plaintiff's unconstitutional conviction, brought under 42 U.S.C. § 1983 and the doctrine of *Bivens v. Six Unknown Fed. Narcotics Agents*,[193] began to run from the date the plaintiff first learned of the injury giving rise to the claims, and not at the completion of a habeas corpus proceeding that overturned the conviction.

It should be noted that under the *continuing tort* theory, when wrongful conduct in violation of § 1983 has occurred over a period of time, the violation is considered a *continuing wrong*.[194] The continuing wrong doctrine has been applied by the courts as an equitable remedy to ameliorate the harsh effects that may occur when a date must otherwise be arbitrarily selected to test whether a statute of limitations has expired. Under the continuing wrong doctrine, a cause of action for a continuous tort accrues and the limitations period begins when the tortious conduct ceases.[195]

§ 11.7   Federal Remedies—Declaratory Judgments

In the Anglo-American judicial system, court action is normally based upon past actions of two or more adverse parties. However, it is plain that many situations could arise in which two or more parties are uncertain of their legal relationship and desire a judicial determination of their respective rights and responsibilities prior to committing an act that might result in legal liability. In order to provide such a remedy, Congress passed the Declaratory Judgment Act, which provides in part:

> In a case of actual controversy within its jurisdiction . . . any court
> of the United States, upon the filing of an appropriate pleading, may
> declare the rights and other legal relations of any interested party
> seeking such declaration . . .[196]

The federal law further authorizes federal courts to grant "necessary or proper relief based on a declaratory judgment . . ."[197] This power to grant relief beyond the declaratory judgment is discretionary with the court. Thus, a court that is wary of interfering with internal management of a prison,[198] but that has found a certain rule or regulation or course of conduct by the prison officials to be unconstitutional, may partially avoid interference by issuing a judgment declaring the alleged practice to be unconstitutional, but allowing the administrators to submit plans for remedying the problem to the court.

---

[192]   Bagley v. CMC Real Estate Corp, 923 F.2d 758 (9th Cir. 1991), *cert. denied,* 502 U.S. 1091 (1992).
[193]   403 U.S. 388 (1971).
[194]   *See* United Airlines, Inc. v. Evans, 431 U.S. 553 (1977).
[195]   *See* Pope v. Bond, 641 F. Supp. 489 (D.D.C. 1986).
[196]   28 U.S.C. § 2201 (1970).
[197]   28 U.S.C. § 2202 (1970).
[198]   *See* § 11.4.1.

Thus, in *Holt v. Sarver*,[199] a federal district court, after examining the totality of conditions at Arkansas's two state prison farms, declared incarceration there to be cruel and unusual punishment. The burden of eliminating these constitutional defects, however, was placed upon the state prison administration, whose progress (or lack of progress) would be monitored by the court through submission of reports by the defendants.

§ 11.8   Federal Remedies—Habeas Corpus

Traditionally, the writ of habeas corpus has been used to contest the legality of confinement itself.[200] However, in a 1944 case, a federal appellate court expanded the scope of federal habeas corpus to include suits that contest the conditions of confinement, and not merely the legality of the confinement itself.[201] The court reasoned that:

> A prisoner is entitled to the writ of habeas corpus when, though lawfully in custody, he is deprived of some right to which he is lawfully entitled even in his confinement, the deprivation of which serves to make his imprisonment more burdensome than the law allows or curtails his liberty to a greater extent than the law permits.[202]

The 1963 ruling of the Supreme Court expressly approving the expanded use of habeas corpus[203] is now seriously questioned. Although the doctrine remains valid, over the years there have been serious setbacks regarding federal relief in habeas corpus.

Federal habeas corpus action to rectify an allegedly unconstitutional condition of incarceration presents a serious procedural problem to state inmates. The statute requires them to exhaust state judicial and administrative remedies before they apply for the writ in federal court.[204] In *Preiser v. Rodriguez*,[205] the United States Supreme Court held that federal habeas corpus must be used by an inmate in a state institution to obtain release by challenging the fact or duration of his physical imprisonment, and that he could not avoid the "exhaustion of state remedies" doctrine[206] by using 42 U.S.C. § 1983. Thus, even though § 1983 on its face gives a remedy for every deprivation of federal rights by state law, the writ of habeas corpus is the exclusive federal remedy for state inmates who, on the grounds that they were unconstitutionally deprived of

---

[199] 309 F. Supp. 362 (E.D. Ark. 1970), *aff'd*, 442 F.2d 304 (8th Cir. 1971).

[200] 28 U.S.C. § 2254 (1970) authorizes federal courts to hear applications for writs of habeas corpus from persons who allege that their detention by the state violates a federal right.

[201] Coffin v. Reichard, 143 F.2d 443 (6th Cir. 1944).

[202] *Id.* at 445.

[203] Jones v. Cunningham, 371 U.S. 236 (1963).

[204] 28 U.S.C. § 2254(b) (1970).

[205] 411 U.S. 475 (1973).

[206] *See* § 11.6.1.

good-time credits under prison disciplinary rules, challenge the fact or duration of their confinement, and seek immediate release.

Wolff v. McDonnell[207] considered whether *Preiser* applied to a § 1983 action involving the validity of the procedures for denying good-time credits. The Court held that although *Preiser* prevented the restoration of good-time credits under § 1983, damage claims were properly before the Court. Consequently, the District Court was held to have jurisdiction under the Civil Rights Act to determine the validity of the procedures employed for imposing punishment, including loss of good-time credits, for flagrant or serious misconduct. However, exhaustion of state remedies will not be required if resort to them would obviously be futile.[208] Probably the best example of a futile state remedy that would not have to be pursued by the inmate is a prior adverse decision by the state's highest court on the identical federal question that the inmate seeks to raise.[209]

A prisoner's right to federal habeas corpus review of a state proceeding turns on whether the state court declined to review federal claims in reliance upon a state-recognized procedural bar. If the state court declined review, then these claims generally may not be recognized in subsequent federal habeas corpus proceedings.

The Supreme Court, in a number of separate decisions, has addressed the ambiguities related to federal habeas corpus review of a state court's decision. In its analysis, the Supreme Court is progressively limiting the use of the writ.

Fay v. Noia [210] may have been the broadest decision the Supreme Court has made in the long line of federal habeas corpus review cases. *Fay*, in 1963, held that a petitioner whose conviction rested on adequate and independent state grounds is nevertheless entitled to pursue a constitutional claim on federal habeas corpus that he or she failed to raise in state court, unless he or she deliberately bypassed state procedures.

Since the Supreme Court's 1977 decision in *Wainwright v. Sykes*,[211] there has been a trend to cut back on the availability of federal habeas corpus review afforded to state prisoners. In *Wainwright,* the Court held that a petitioner's procedural default on a constitutional claim in state court bars federal habeas corpus review of that claim unless he or she can demonstrate cause for the default and actual prejudice to him or her. The United States Supreme Court stated in *Caldwell v. Mississippi*[212] that the state court must actually have relied on the procedural bar as an independent basis for its disposition of the case. Further, the ambiguities associated with reliance on state grounds is to be resolved by application of the *Michigan v. Long*[213] standard. In *Long*, the Court adopted a presumption in favor of federal court review when a state

---

[207]   418 U.S. 539 (1974).
[208]   Patton v. North Carolina, 381 F.2d 636 (4th Cir. 1967), *cert. denied*, 390 U.S. 905 (1968).
[209]   *See, e.g.,* Davis v. Sigler, 415 F.2d 1159 (8th Cir. 1969). *See* § 11.6.1.
[210]   372 U.S. 391 (1963).
[211]   433 U.S. 72 (1977).
[212]   472 U.S. 320, 327 (1985).
[213]   463 U.S. 1032 (1983).

court decision fairly appears to rest primarily on federal law, or appears to be interwoven with the federal law, and when the adequacy and independence of any possible state law ground is not clear from the face of the opinion. The presumption is based on the assumption that when the state court's judgment contains no plain statement to the effect that federal cases are being used solely as persuasive authority, and when state law is interwoven with federal law, it can be accepted as the most reasonable explanation that the state court decided the case the way it did because it believed that federal law required it to do so.

In *Harris v. Reed*,[214] the Supreme Court extended *Long*'s "plain statement" rule to federal habeas corpus review. In that case, it declared that a judgment appearing to rest primarily on federal law is conclusively presumed to so rest, unless the state court makes a plain statement to the contrary. The Court reasoned that because, as *Sykes* made clear, the adequate and independent state ground doctrine applies to federal habeas corpus, and, because federal courts on habeas corpus review commonly face the same problem of ambiguity that was resolved by *Long*, the "plain statement" rule is to be adopted for federal habeas corpus cases. A procedural default will not bar consideration of a federal claim on habeas corpus review unless the last state court rendering a judgment in the case clearly and expressly stated that its judgment rested on a state procedural bar.

The Supreme Court limited the reach of the *Harris* presumption. The majority placed great emphasis on the importance of giving deference to state court judgments. The Supreme Court made it clear that a petitioner bears a heavy burden in seeking to prove that an unexplained state court decision rested on federal law rather than independent state grounds and thus is subject to federal habeas corpus review.

In *Coleman v. Thompson*,[215] the petitioner sought federal relief when state habeas corpus relief was denied. The state appellate court refused to consider certain issues on appeal because the time for filing had passed. He petitioned to the state supreme court, which denied relief. The petitioner then sought federal habeas corpus on the same claims. The Fourth Circuit Court of Appeals upheld the state judgment because it was based on an adequate and independent state ground—the procedural default—and the petitioner failed to show "cause" to excuse default.[216]

On appeal to the United States Supreme Court, the petitioner relied on *Harris*, arguing that because the state supreme court's order did not "clearly and expressly" state that it was based on adequate and independent state law, the state's judgment should be presumed to be based on federal law and thus federal review of his claims would be appropriate. The majority of the United States Supreme Court rejected this broad application of *Harris* and held that one predicate to the application of the *Harris* presumption is that the state holding must be fairly susceptible to being read as resting primarily on federal law.

---

[214]   489 U.S. 255 (1989).

[215]   501 U.S. 722 (1991).

[216]   Coleman v. Thompson, 895 F.2d 139 (4th Cir. 1990).

The Supreme Court went further in *Ylst v. Nunnemaker*.[217] There was again an unexplained state order denying habeas corpus relief. Justice Scalia, speaking for the majority, commented that where there has been one reasoned state judgment rejecting a federal claim, later unexplained orders upholding that judgment or rejecting the same claim rest upon the same ground.

In *Preiser v. Rodriguez*,[218] the Supreme Court delineated what constitutes a habeas action as opposed to a 42 U.S.C. § 1983 claim. The prisoner's label cannot control. The essence of habeas corpus is an attack by a person in custody upon the legality of that custody. If a prisoner is not challenging the validity of his or her conviction or the length of his or her detention, such as loss of good-time credits, then a writ of habeas corpus is not the proper remedy. It is the substance of the relief sought that counts. Where a petitioner seeks a writ of habeas corpus and fails to attack the validity of his or her sentence or the length of his or her state custody, the district court lacks the power or subject matter jurisdiction to issue a writ. There are fundamental differences between a civil rights action under 42 U.S.C. § 1983, in which a prisoner might seek money damages or injunctive relief from unlawful treatment, and a habeas action under 28 U.S.C. § 2254. Under a petition for a writ of habeas corpus, a petitioner must exhaust his or her state judicial remedies,[219] whereas under a § 1983 action, exhaustion is not required.[220] Furthermore, a state court judgment is not binding on the petitioner in a habeas corpus action, whereas the doctrines of issue and claim preclusion[221] apply to the issues in a § 1983 case that have been fully litigated in the state court.[222]

Only certain kinds of alleged sentencing errors may be raised in a collateral proceeding under § 2255.[223] These are: (1) a sentence violates the Constitution or the laws of the United States; (2) the district court was without jurisdiction to impose the sentence; (3) the sentence is greater than the statutory maximum; and (4) the sentence "is otherwise subject to collateral attack."[224] The Supreme Court "has narrowly confined the scope and availability of collateral attack for claims that do not allege constitutional or jurisdictional errors."[225] Such claims are properly brought under § 2255 only if the claimed error is a fundamental defect that inherently results in a complete miscarriage of justice or an omission inconsistent with the rudimentary demands of fair procedure. The error must present exceptional circumstances where the need for the remedy afforded by the writ of habeas corpus is apparent.[226]

---

[217] 501 U.S. 797 (1991).

[218] 411 U.S. 475 (1973).

[219] *See* 28 U.S.C. § 2254(b); Heck v. Humphrey, 512 U.S. 477 (1994).

[220] Wilwording v. Swenson, 404 U.S. 249 (1971).

[221] As well as 28 U.S.C. § 1738.

[222] *See* Migra v. Warren City Sch. Dist. Bd. of Educ., 465 U.S. 75 (1984); Kruger v. Erickson, 77 F.3d 1071 (8th Cir. 1996).

[223] *See* Oscar Diaz-Cruz v. United States, 1996 U.S. App. LEXIS 3526 (1st Cir. 1996).

[224] *See* 28 U.S.C. § 2255; Knight v. United States, 37 F.3d 769, 772 (1st Cir. 1994).

[225] Knight, 37 F.3d at 772.

[226] *Id.;* Hill v. United States, 368 U.S. 424 (1962).

§ 11.9   Federal Remedies—Criminal Prosecution

The criminal counterpart of the Civil Rights Act provides in part:

> Whoever, under color of any law, statute, ordinance, regulation, or
> custom, willfully subjects any inhabitant of any State, Territory, or
> District to the deprivation of any rights, privileges, or immunities
> secured or protected by the Constitution or laws of the United States
> shall be fined not more than $1,000 or imprisoned not more than
> one year, or both; and if death results, shall be subject to imprison-
> ment for any term of years or for life.[227]

The elements that must be present for a conviction under this statute, and
the interpretation given these elements by the Supreme Court, are as follows:

1. There must be a deprivation of a right, privilege, or immunity secured by
   the Constitution or by federal law. In refuting the contention that inclusion of Fourteenth Amendment rights of due process and equal protection in the criminal statute would make it void because of vagueness, the
   Supreme Court has stated that the deprivation must be "of a right which
   has been made specific, either by the express terms of the Constitution
   or laws of the United States or by decisions interpreting them."[228]

2. The deprivation must be *willful*. That is, there must be a specific intent
   to deprive the person of his or her constitutional rights.

3. The deprivation must be *under color of state law*. This phrase has been
   interpreted as meaning "[m]isuse of power, possessed by virtue of state
   law and made possible only because the wrongdoer is clothed with the
   authority of state law . . ."[229]

In *United States v. Jackson*,[230] an Arkansas correctional officer was indicted under this statute for allegedly beating an inmate with a club. The district
court dismissed the indictment for failure to state an offense against the United States. In reversing the lower court and in reinstating the indictment, the
court of appeals held that:

> A convicted prisoner remains under the protection of the Fourteenth
> Amendment except as to those rights expressly or by necessary
> implication taken from him by law. He still has his right to be secure
> in his person against unlawful beating done under color of law will-
> fully to deprive him of the right.[231]

---

[227] 18 U.S.C. § 242 (1970).

[228] Screws v. United States, 325 U.S. 91, 104 (1945); *See also* United States v. Senak, 477 F.2d 304 (7th
Cir. 1973).

[229] United States v. Classic, 313 U.S. 299, 326 (1941).

[230] 235 F.2d 925 (8th Cir. 1956).

[231] *Id.* at 929. *See also* United States v. Walker, 216 F.2d 683 (5th Cir. 1954); United States v. Jones, 207
F.2d 785 (5th Cir. 1953).

§ 11.10 Federal Remedies—Contempt

Contempt of court has been defined as "disobedience to the court, by acting in opposition to the authority, justice, and dignity thereof."[232] Because they are responsible for executing sentences imposed by the courts, prison officials are regarded as officers of the courts. Moreover, a state official who is holding an inmate sentenced by a federal court has been held to be an official of the sentencing federal court, in relation to his treatment of the federal inmate.[233] In the case of *In re Birdsong*,[234] a federal judge held a county jailer in contempt for mistreating a federal inmate who was being detained in the local jail.

§ 11.11 State Remedies—Civil Suits

Prison officials have the duty, often imposed by statute,[235] to provide their inmates with the basic necessities of life, such as clothing, food, shelter, and medical care. Failure to provide these items will render the official liable to the inmate in a civil action. Thus, prison officials have been held liable in state courts for failing to provide needed medical services,[236] food,[237] and other necessities such as bedding, clothing, and sanitary conditions.[238]

In addition to their duties to provide the necessities of life, prison officials have a general duty to use reasonable care to prevent injuries to their inmates. Failure to exercise such care is negligence, and a prison official will be liable in damages for the injuries caused by his or her negligence. Thus, a complaint that alleged that the superintendent of a camp for delinquent juveniles used one of his charges to fight a forest fire, without warning the youth of the danger, was held to state a cause of action for the boy's wrongful death.[239]

Similarly, a petition that alleged that a sheriff forced an inmate to use a wobbly ladder when painting, knowing it to be defective, was sufficient to state a cause of action for negligence.[240]

---

[232] 17 C.J.S. *Contempt* § 2 (1963).

[233] Randolph v. Donaldson, 13 U.S. (9 Cranch) 76 (1815).

[234] 39 F. 599 (S.D. Ga. 1889); *see also* United States v. Shipp, 203 U.S. 563 (1906); McCall v. Swain, 510 F.2d 167 (D.C. Cir. 1975).

[235] *See, e.g.,* MASS. GEN. LAWS ANN. 16, 28, 34 (1958) (county detention facilities); N.Y. CORRECTIONAL LAWS 137 (Supp. 1971) (state penal institutions).

[236] Farmer v. State, 224 Miss. 96, 79 So. 2d 528 (1955); State ex rel. Morris v. National Surety Co., 162 Tenn. 547, 39 S.W.2d 581 (1931); State ex rel. Williams v. Davis, 219 S.E.2d 198 (N.C. 1975).

[237] Smith v. Slack, 125 W. Va. 812, 26 S.E.2d 387 (1943); Richardson v. Capwell, 63 Utah 616, 176 P. 205 (1918).

[238] Clark v. Kelly, 101 W. Va. 650, 133 S.E. 365 (1926); Roberts v. Williams, 456 F.2d 819 (5th Cir. 1972).

[239] Collenburg v. County of Los Angeles, 150 Cal. App. 2d 795, 310 P.2d 989 (1957) (sovereign immunity protects the county, but not the individual official).

[240] Moore v. Murphy, 254 Iowa 969, 119 N.W.2d 759 (1963).

A prison official who intentionally injures an inmate will be liable to him or her in a tort action for damages. Assault and battery are the most common intentional tort situations in a prison environment. An inmate, like any other person, has the right to be free from offensive bodily contact that is intentionally inflicted upon him.[241]

§ 11.11.1 —Effect of Sovereign Immunity

An inmate seeking to recover damages against prison officials for neglect, negligence, or intentional injury will often be faced with the defense of sovereign immunity.[242] The courts generally split on the question of liability, depending upon whether the officials' actions are labeled *ministerial* or *discretionary*. A ministerial duty is one that is absolute and certain. It is a duty that involves no freedom of choice on the part of the official. Several states have held that the duty of prison officials to provide their inmates with necessities is ministerial, and so the official is liable to the inmates for failure to fulfill that duty.[243] Other states, however, interpret the officials' duties as "discretionary." That is, the official has a certain freedom of choice in providing necessities to his or her prisoners. He or she is thus free from liability for his or her acts, and he or she should not be discouraged by fear of lawsuit from freely exercising this discretion.[244] However, if the discretion is grossly abused, the result is liability.

In *Martinez v. California*,[245] the Supreme Court considered the constitutionality of a California statute that gave public employees absolute immunity from liability for any injury resulting from parole-release determinations. The statute was upheld as applied to defeat a state tort claim arising from California law.

States and state entities that claim to be "arms of the state" may take an interlocutory appeal from a district court order that denies a claim of Eleventh Amendment immunity from suit in federal court. Although 28 U.S.C. § 1291 requires that appeals be taken from "final decisions of the district courts," a "small class" of judgments that are not complete and final are immediately appealable. First, denials of Eleventh Amendment immunity claims purport to be conclusive determinations that states and their entities have no right not to be sued in federal court. Second, a motion to dismiss on Eleventh Amendment grounds involves a claim to a fundamental constitutional protection whose

---

[241] Fernelius v. Pierce, 22 Cal. 2d 226, 138 P.2d 12 (1943); Farmer v. Rutherford, 136 Kan. 298, 15 P.2d 474 (1932); Bowman v. Hayward, 1 Utah 2d 131, 262 P.2d 957 (1953).

[242] See § 11.4.

[243] Kusah v. McCorkle, 100 Wash. 318, 170 P. 1023 (1918); Smith v. Slack, 125 W. Va. 812, 26 S.E.2d 387 (1943).

[244] Bush v. Babb, 23 Ill. App. 2d 285, 162 N.E.2d 594 (1959); St. Louis ex rel. Forest v. Nickolas, 374 S.W.2d 547 (Mo. Ct. App. 1964); Rose v. Toledo, 1 Ohio C.C.R. (N.S.) 321, 14 Ohio C. Dec. 540 (1903).

[245] 444 U.S. 277 (1980).

resolution generally will have no bearing on the merits of the underlying action. Third, the value to the states of their constitutional immunity—like the benefits conferred by qualified immunity to individual officials[246]—is for the most part lost as litigation proceeds past motion practice, such that the denial order will be effectively unreviewable on appeal from a final judgment. The claim that the Eleventh Amendment does not confer immunity from suit, but is merely a defense to liability, misunderstood the role of the amendment in the American system of federalism and was rejected.[247]

§ 11.12   State Remedies—Declaratory Judgments

Many states[248] have enacted declaratory judgment acts similar in scope to the federal act previously discussed.[249] Although a state declaratory judgment action would be an excellent method of testing the legality of conditions of confinement in state institutions, this state remedy has been totally ignored by inmates and prison officials in the past.

§ 11.13   State Remedies—Habeas Corpus

The availability of state habeas corpus proceedings to contest conditions of state confinement depends on the wording of the state statute and the judicial interpretation of it. For example, Ohio's habeas corpus statute has a section that provides:

> If it appears that a person alleged to be restrained of his liberty is in the custody of an officer under process issued by a court or magistrate, or by virtue of the judgment or order of a court of record, and that the court or magistrate had jurisdiction to issue the process, render the judgment, or make the order, the writ of habeas corpus shall not be allowed . . .[250]

Thus, habeas corpus relief is not available in Ohio unless the court ordering confinement lacked jurisdiction.[251] In other words, Ohio has limited habeas corpus to cases that would result in release from confinement for the petitioner if he were successful in his action.[252] Thus, state habeas corpus is not a proper method of contesting conditions of confinement in Ohio.

---

[246]   *See* Mitchell v. Forsyth, 472 U.S. 511 (1985).

[247]   Puerto Rico Aqueduct and Sewer Authority v. Metcalf & Eddy, Inc., 506 U.S. 139 (1993).

[248]   *See, e.g.,* N.Y. CIVIL. PRAC. LAW AND RULES 3001 (McKinney 1963); OHIO REV. CODE ANN. § 2721.02 (Anderson 1998).

[249]   *See* § 11.7.

[250]   OHIO REV. CODE ANN. § 2725.05 (1976).

[251]   In re Edsall, 26 Ohio St. 2d 145 (1971).

[252]   Ball v. Maxwell, 177 Ohio St. 39 (1964).

Other states, however, have extended the scope of habeas corpus to include cases of alleged unlawful treatment of an inmate lawfully in custody,[253] and follow the federal analogy.

§ 11.14 State Remedies—Criminal Prosecution

Some states have criminal statutes that are specifically aimed at mistreatment of inmates by correctional officers. For example, an Arizona law provides that:

> A public officer who is guilty of willful inhumanity or oppression toward a prisoner under his care or in his custody shall be punished by a fine not exceeding one thousand dollars, by imprisonment in the county jail not to exceed six months, or both.[254]

In the absence of any specific criminal statute directed solely at them, correctional officials are subject to the general criminal statutes of the state, such as assault and battery and the homicide laws. Thus, in *State v. Mincher,*[255] the North Carolina Supreme Court upheld an assault and battery conviction against an inmate-officer who had administered excessive corporal punishment to another inmate.

§ 11.15 State Remedies—Contempt

As stated previously,[256] prison officials are officers of the sentencing court, and can be held in contempt by such a court for mistreating an inmate sentenced to the institution by the court. At least two states have sanctioned the use of contempt to punish mistreatment of inmates. In *Howard v. State,*[257] the Arizona Supreme Court upheld a contempt citation against the superintendent of an adult prison who allegedly mistreated inmates. However, in 1952, the same court dismissed a contempt proceeding against the director of a boys' training school,[258] expressly overruling any holding of the *Howard* case that might lead to an opposite result. Another case seemed to reaffirm the *Howard* decision as it pertained to adult correctional officials. *Dutton v. Eytnan*[259] held

---

253 *See* In re Riddle, 57 Cal. 2d 848, 372 P.2d 304, 22 Cal. Rptr. 472 (1962). *See generally* 155 A.L.R. 145 (1945).
254 Ariz. Rev. Stat. Ann. § 31-127 (1956). *See also* Cal. Penal Code 2650 (West 1970).
255 172 N.C. 895, 90 S.E. 429 (1916).
256 *See* § 11.10.
257 28 Ariz. 433, 237 P. 203 (1925).
258 Ridgway v. Superior Court, 74 Ariz. 117, 245 P.2d 268 (1952).
259 95 Ariz. 95, 387 P.2d 799 (1963).

that state habeas corpus is not a valid method of contesting the conditions of confinement. However, the court cited the *Howard* case with approval as a possible remedy in such a situation.

The Supreme Court of Rhode Island has also held that contempt is a proper method of punishing abuse of prisoners.[260]

§ 11.16   Conclusion

An inmate has a wide variety of remedies to rectify past denials of constitutional rights and to ensure future respect of these rights by prison administrators. The inmate often has the choice of going to either federal or state courts. However, many obstacles, most notably the "hands-off" doctrine, blocked judicial redress of constitutional deprivations in the past. With the decline of this doctrine in recent years, courts are hearing and deciding an increasing number of inmate complaints.

The judicial concern for penal reform has probably abated, and judicial intervention in prison administration will probably decrease as time goes on. Federal and state correctional officials have initiated necessary administrative reforms in many of the areas of constitutional concern.

Prison officials have become increasingly aware of the potential for liability when conducting the operations and forming the policies for the prison system. The Supreme Court decisions make it clear that prison officials are expected to know the constitutional rights of inmates, and this places the burden on prison officials to keep themselves apprised of the current state of the law. Ignorance is not a defense when confronted with a lawsuit for monetary damages.

---

[260]   State v. Brant, 99 R.I. 583, 209 A.2d 455 (1965).

Additional Litigation 12

Chapter Outline

§ 12.1 Introduction

There are numerous different legal issues of constitutional magnitude affecting inmates that do not readily fit into any of the preceding chapters. The topics noted here do not, of course, exhaust the differences between free people and inmates. They do, however, point out the fact that incarceration is much more than merely a change in location. It is a change in constitutional status.

§ 12.2 Classification

Classification is the assessment, for rehabilitative and security purposes, of an inmate's personality, background, and potential, and assignment of the inmate to a specific status or setting that is commensurate with these findings. Classification occurs at numerous times during an inmate's involvement with the criminal justice system; this section, however, is concerned only with the narrow area of classification by prison authorities—that is, administrative classification. That prison authorities have the right and duty to classify inmates has been clearly determined by the courts.[1] The assessment aspect of administrative classification is usually fulfilled by committees of prison officials.[2] Such bodies are frequently called *adjustment committees,* because their initial goal is to enable new inmates to adjust to the rigors of incarceration. Administrative classification committees, however, have a mission beyond intake assessment and assignment. Behavioral changes in inmates, which occur as time is served, demand constant reassessment and reassignment.[3]

In *Meachum v. Fano,*[4] the United States Supreme Court held that the transfer of an inmate from one prison to another, although arguably a "grievous loss," did not require a due process hearing. This decision, by analogy, may also apply to the classification of inmates. However, lower federal courts that have considered the classification issue have determined that some degree of

---

[1] Marchesani v. McCune, 531 F.2d 459 (10th Cir. 1976); McGruder v. Phelps, 608 F.2d 1023 (5th Cir. 1979); Jones v. Diamond, 594 F.2d 997 (5th Cir. 1979); Jennings v. State, 389 N.E.2d 283 (Ind. 1979) (State only needs to show a reasonable basis for the classification).

[2] James v. Wallace, 406 F. Supp. 318 (M.D. Ala. 1976); Zaczek v. Hutto, 642 F.2d 74 (4th Cir. 1981); French v. Hevne, 547 F.2d 994 (7th Cir. 1976).

[3] Fitzgerald v. Procunier, 393 F. Supp. 335 (N.D. Cal. 1975).

[4] 427 U.S. 215 (1976); *cf.* Cuyler v. Adams, 449 U.S. 433 (1981); Vitek v. Jones, 445 U.S. 480 (1980).

procedural due process is applicable to prison classification hearings. In *Kirby v. Blackledge,*[5] an informal hearing procedure that was used to assign inmates to maximum-security cellblocks was found to violate due process. Illiterate or otherwise disadvantaged inmates, for whom the complexity of issues may foreclose the needed capacity to collect and present the evidence necessary for an adequate comprehension of the case, were allowed the assistance of fellow inmates or a designated staff member. Other courts have specified the form of intake classification to be undertaken. In *Alberti v. Sheriff of Harris County, Texas,*[6] the court held that a sufficient number of classification officers should be employed so that at least one is on duty at all times to interview incoming inmates. Inmates are to be classified and segregated on the basis of the danger that they pose to others, based on their prior criminal record, the danger posed to the new inmate by the existing prison population, and the likelihood of successful rehabilitation by proper placement.

The proposed imposition or assignment of certain classifications can trigger a need for more substantial due process safeguards. In *Cardopoli v. Norton,*[7] the court held that inasmuch as classification of an inmate as a special offender hinders or precludes eligibility for social furloughs, work release, transfer to community treatment centers, and the opportunity for early parole, changes in an inmate's status that accompany the designation create a "grievous loss," and may not be imposed in the absence of basic elements of rudimentary due process. When a special offender classification is contemplated, the inmate must be given at least 10 days' notice in writing, specifying the reason or reasons for the proposed designation and providing a description of the evidence to be relied upon. The inmate must be afforded a personal appearance before a neutral decisionmaker and must be permitted to call witnesses and present documentary evidence. If the hearing officer determines that the classification is warranted, he or she must support that decision with written findings submitted within a reasonable time after the hearing.

Beyond the procedural considerations of classification hearings, there exists the problem of the permissibility of certain types of classifications or statuses. In *McDonald v. McCracken,*[8] a court held that if an inmate is placed in lockup status for the protection of other prisoners and prison employees rather than for the imposition of punishment, in this case for 13 months, and such classification is not arbitrary, abusive, or capricious, the hearing requirements of *Wolff v. McDonnell*[9] for rule infraction board proceedings do not

---

[5]   530 F.2d 583 (4th Cir. 1976); In re Westfall, 162 Cal. Rptr. 462 (Cal. Ct. App. 1980); United States v. Swift & Co., 286 U.S. 106 (1932); Cobb v. Aytch, 643 F.2d 946 (3d Cir. 1981) (in which the court distinguishes between the transfer rights of sentenced and pretrial prisoners).

[6]   406 F. Supp. 649 (S.D. Tex. 1975).

[7]   523 F.2d 990 (2d Cir. 1975); *See also* Raia v. Arnold, 405 F. Supp. 766 (M.D. Pa. 1975); People ex rel. Williams v. Ward, 423 N.Y.S.2d 692 (N.Y. App. Div. 1980); Makris v. United States Bureau of Prisons, 606 F.2d 575 (5th Cir. 1979).

[8]   399 F. Supp. 869 (E.D. Okla. 1975); Wojtczak v. Cuyler, 480 F. Supp. 1288 (E.D. Pa. 1979).

[9]   418 U.S. 539 (1974).

apply. Classification based upon a discriminatory basis such as race or religion will usually be held to be unconstitutional. However, classification on the basis of sex or age is permissible.

Under Indiana law, inmates have no right to be assigned to a particular security class. The decision to alter security classifications is solely within the discretion of the Department of Corrections.[10]

The use of the "level system," a mandatory behavior modification system employed by the Kentucky Correctional Institute for Women to govern the access of female prisoners to certain inmate privileges, was declared unconstitutional. The system resulted in grossly unequal treatment of female, as opposed to male, prisoners in the availability of inmate privileges. In addition, the imposition of the system on the prison population as a whole violates the inmates' substantive due process rights. Behavior modification was found to have a unique effect upon each individual. Officials of the Kentucky Correctional Institute for Women were cited by the district court for failing to fulfill their obligation to provide equal programs and facilities for women, especially in the areas of prison industries, institutional jobs, vocational education and training, and community release programs.[11]

Associated with classification is administrative segregation of inmates. The state cannot place a detainee in segregation for no reason,[12] but maintaining jail security comprises an appropriate justification for inflicting restrictions on pretrial detainees. The same principle should apply to convicted prisoners.

In *Zarnes v. Rhodes*,[13] Zarnes, a pretrial detainee, argued with other inmates about the selection of the television channel. The fight did not include any physical contact, but upon hearing from one inmate that Zarnes was to blame, the officer in charge at the time placed Zarnes in "lockdown." He did not give Zarnes any reason for his action. Zarnes remained segregated from the general population for 19 days without receiving any explanation.

The correctional officer was held to have put Zarnes in administrative segregation for her protection and the protection of other inmates, following Zarnes' verbal confrontations with other prisoners. His action was pursuant to the Sheriff's Department's policies and procedures that allow placement in segregation only when housing an inmate in the general population would pose a serious threat to life, property, self, staff, or other inmates, or to secure orderly operations of the facility. The court found that these declarations adequately established that the officer assigned Zarnes to segregation for a legitimate reason, thereby making his conduct constitutional.

In *Anderson v. County of Kern*,[14] prisoners challenged as unconstitutional the use of safety cells for suicidal and mentally disturbed inmates. Safety cells are padded cells that are used to temporarily confine violent or suicidal pris-

---

[10] Kincaid v. Duckworth, 689 F.2d 702 (7th Cir. 1982); Hoptowit v. Ray, 682 F.2d 1237 (9th Cir. 1982) (The misclassification of prisoners is not a violation of the Eighth Amendment).

[11] Carterino v. Wilson, 546 F. Supp. 174 (W.D. Ky. 1982), 562 F. Supp. 106 (W.D. Ky. 1983).

[12] Hawkins v. Poole, 779 F.2d 1267, 1269 (7th Cir. 1985)

[13] Zarnes v. Rhodes, 64 F.3d 285 (7th Cir. 1995).

[14] 45 F.3d 1310 (9th Cir. 1994).

oners so they cannot hurt themselves. The claims were evaluated under the Eighth Amendment, and the pretrial detainees' challenge was evaluated under the Fourteenth Amendment. Under the Eighth Amendment, the pertinent inquiry is whether placement of mentally disturbed or suicidal inmates in safety cells constitutes an infliction of pain or a deprivation of basic human needs, such as adequate food, clothing, shelter, sanitation, and medical care, and if so, whether prison officials acted with the requisite culpable intent such that the infliction of pain is "unnecessary and wanton."[15]

On the basis of testimony, the district court rejected inmates' challenge to the use of safety cells, finding that nothing suggested that the safety cells had been inappropriately used as more than a temporary measure to control violent inmates until they "cooled down" sufficiently to be released from those cells. The experts agreed that the cells could appropriately be used for this purpose. The district court's ruling was affirmed. Safety cells are a very severe environment, but are employed in response to very severe safety concerns.

It was recognized that prison officials must have some means of controlling violent or self-destructive inmates temporarily until the episode passes, and as the plaintiffs' own expert testified, it is difficult to distinguish between violent, mentally healthy inmates and violent, mentally disturbed ones. Similarly, in an emergency, prison officials are not culpable when they put an inmate who imminently threatens or attempts suicide temporarily in a place where he or she cannot hurt him or herself. In light of the safety concerns underlying use of the safety cell, there was no inference that the prison officials were knowingly and unreasonably disregarding an objectively intolerable risk of harm and would continue to do so in the future.

Also at issue in *Anderson* was an order by the district court requiring jail officials to develop a policy allowing prison officials to exercise discretion in determining whether certain prisoners housed in administrative segregation can safely exercise or have day room access together. The law is clear that the transfer of an inmate to less amenable and more restrictive quarters for non-punitive reasons is well within the terms of confinement ordinarily contemplated by a prison sentence.[16] Thus, the hardship associated with administrative segregation, such as loss of recreational and rehabilitative programs or confinement to one's cell for a lengthy period, does not violate the due process clause because there is no liberty interest in remaining in the general population.[17] Administrative segregation, even in a single cell for 23 hours per day, is within the terms of confinement ordinarily contemplated by a sentence. Further, prison officials have a legitimate penological interest in administrative segregation, and they must be given wide-ranging deference in the adoption and execution of policies and practices that in their judgment are needed to preserve internal order and discipline and to maintain institutional security.

---

[15]   *See* Farmer v. Brennan, 511 U.S. 825 (1994).

[16]   Hewitt v. Helms, 459 U.S. 460 (1983).

[17]   Toussaint v. McCarthy, 801 F.2d 1080, 1091-1092 (9th Cir. 1986) (applying Hewitt v. Helms), *cert. denied*, 481 U.S. 1069 (1987).

Here, inmates in administrative segregation retained all inmate privileges such as family visits, telephone access, and exercise. They were all single-celled, however, and had no contact with any other inmate, either for exercise, day room access, or otherwise.

See § 12.6, Conditions of Confinement, and § 5.3.2, Constitutionality of the Conditions of Isolated Confinement.

§ 12.3   Transfer

Incident to all classifications, whether initial or review, is transfer. This topic has generated much litigation. Federal district courts and courts of appeals that have dealt with the need for due process safeguards in conjunction with intraprison and interprison transfers of inmates have specified substantial safeguards. A typical case is *Fano v. Meachum*,[18] in which the First Circuit Court of Appeals held that whether an inmate's transfer is thought of as punishment or as a way of preserving institutional order, its effect on the inmate is the same. The appropriateness of the transfer depends upon the accuracy of the official allegation of misconduct. Under normal circumstances, notice and a hearing must be afforded to an inmate prior to a transfer from a medium-security to a maximum-security prison and, at the very least, must state the time and place of the alleged offense with reasonable accuracy. However, the decision was reversed by the United States Supreme Court. In *Meachum v. Fano*[19] the Court held that, absent a state law or practice that conditions the transfer of inmates between institutions upon proof of serious misconduct or the occurrence of other specified events, the Fourteenth Amendment's due process clause in and of itself does not entitle an inmate to a fact-finding hearing prior to his or her transfer from one penal institution to another, even if the conditions of the recipient institution are substantially less favorable than those in the institution from which he or she was transferred, provided that such conditions are within the sentence imposed upon him or her and do not otherwise violate the Constitution. The Supreme Court further considered inmates' transfer rights in *Montanye v. Haymes*,[20] a companion case to *Meachum*, and held that the Fourteenth Amendment's due process clause does not, on its face, require a hearing prior to the transfer, for whatever reason, of an inmate from one institution to another in the same penal system, provided that the conditions or degree of the confinement to which the inmate is thus subjected are within the sentence imposed upon him or her and do not otherwise violate the Constitution.

A state prisoner has no justifiable expectation that he or she will not be transferred to a prison in another state, where state prison regulations create no constitutionally protected liberty interest against such a transfer. The regulation under review provided for a pretransfer hearing, but left prison admin-

---

[18]   520 F.2d 374 (1st Cir. 1975).
[19]   427 U.S. 215 (1976).
[20]   427 U.S. 236 (1976).

istrators with unfettered discretion over transfers. Confinement in another state is within the normal limits or range of custody that the conviction has authorized the transferring state to impose.[21]

Taken together, *Meachum* and *Montanye* eliminate the constitutional underpinnings of the argument that minimal procedural due process must be provided to inmates before they are transferred. As mentioned in the preceding section, beyond the narrow scope of the inmate transfer issue, these decisions suggest a possible reexamination by the Supreme Court of the constitutional validity of the "grievous loss" argument that has required minimal procedural due process requirements for administrative classification hearings in general.

The statutory right of a prisoner to a hearing under Article IV(d) of the Interstate Agreement on Detainers before he or she is transferred to another jurisdiction was upheld in *Cuyler v. Adams*.[22] However, the involuntary transfer of a convicted felon from a state prison to a mental hospital violates a liberty interest that is protected by the due process clause of the Fourteenth Amendment.[23] The stigmatizing consequences of a transfer to a mental institution for involuntary psychiatric treatment, including mandatory behavior modification, require the following procedure:

1. A written notice to the prisoner that a transfer to a mental institution is being considered;

2. A hearing, sufficiently after the notice to permit the prisoner to prepare, at which disclosure to the prisoner is made aware of the evidence being relied upon for the transfer and at which an opportunity to be heard in person and to present documentary evidence is given;

3. An opportunity at the hearing to present testimony of witnesses by the inmate and to confront and cross-examine witnesses called by the state, except upon a finding, not arbitrarily made, of good cause for not permitting such presentation, confrontation, or cross-examination;

4. An independent decisionmaker;

5. A written statement by the fact finder as to the evidence relied on and the reasons for transferring the inmate;

6. Availability of legal counsel, furnished by the state, if the inmate is financially unable to furnish his or her own; and

7. Effective and timely notice of all the foregoing rights.

---

[21]   Olim v. Wakinekona, 456 U.S. 1005 (1983); Shango v. Jurich, 681 F.2d 1091 (7th Cir. 1982) (A state prison inmate has no liberty interest in remaining in any particular prison that is protected by the United States Constitution).

[22]   449 U.S. 433 (1981).

[23]   Vitek v. Jones, 445 U.S. 480 (1980).

With respect to the appointment of legal counsel, the decision was indecisive. Four of the nine Justices believed:

> The District Court did go beyond the requirements imposed by prior cases by holding that counsel must be made available to inmates facing transfer hearings if they are financially unable to furnish their own. We have not required the automatic appointment of counsel for indigent prisoners facing other deprivations of liberty. *Gagnon v. Scarpelli; Wolff v. McDonnell;* but we have recognized that prisoners who are illiterate and uneducated have a greater need for assistance in exercising their rights. *Gagnon v. Scarpelli; Wolff v. McDonnell.* A prisoner thought to be suffering from a mental disease or defect requiring involuntary treatment probably has an even greater need for legal assistance, for such a prisoner is more likely to be unable to understand or exercise his rights. In these circumstances, it is appropriate that counsel be provided to indigent prisoners whom the State seeks to treat as mentally ill.

Mr. Justice Powell concurred in the decision,[24] except for the provision for legal counsel. He agreed that qualified and independent assistance must be provided, but stated that an inmate need not always be provided with a licensed attorney.

The Interstate Agreement on Detainers creates uniform procedures for lodging and executing a detainer, i.e., a legal order that requires a state to hold a currently imprisoned individual when he has finished serving his sentence so that he may be tried by a different state for a different crime. The Agreement provides that a state that obtains a prisoner for purposes of trial must try him within 120 days of his arrival, and if it returns him to his original place of imprisonment prior to that trial, charges shall be dismissed with prejudice. While an inmate was serving a federal prison sentence in Florida, an Alabama district attorney sought temporary custody of him to arraign him on firearms charges and to appoint counsel. When taken to Alabama, he spent one day in Alabama and was returned to federal prison that evening. About one month later, he was brought back to the county for trial. His counsel moved to dismiss the state charges on the ground that, because he had been returned to the original place of imprisonment, the federal prison, prior to trial on state charges being had, in violation of Article IV(e), the local court had to dismiss the charges with prejudice in light of Article IV(e)'s command as to remedy. The inmate was convicted but the conviction was reversed. The Supreme Court held[25] that the literal language of Article IV(e) bars any further criminal proceedings when a defendant is returned to the original place of imprisonment before trial.

---

[24]   *Id.* at 496, 497.
[25]   Alabama v. Bozeman, 533 U.S. 146 (2001).

The issue of transferring prisoners from state custody to the federal system for service of sentence arose in *Howe v. Smith*.[26] A high-risk Vermont prisoner was transferred to a federal prison because Vermont had closed its only maximum-security prison. It was held that the transfer was authorized and proper, even though no particularized, specialized treatment program was available in the federal system to meet the needs of the prisoner. The plain wording of the statute[27] authorizes transfers not simply for treatment, but also for the custody, care, subsistence, education, and training of state prisoners in federal institutions. However, a prisoner was deprived of an independent decisionmaker guaranteed by Hawaii regulations. The same committee that recommended his transfer to a California prison also initiated the transfer. A valid claim under 42 U.S.C. § 1983 was stated.[28]

Although an inmate has no right to a hearing before being transferred and can be transferred for no reason at all, an inmate may nevertheless establish a civil rights claim if the decision to transfer him was made by reason of his exercise of constitutionally protected First Amendment freedoms.[29]

For example, a corrections officer violated an inmate's rights when he wrote false disciplinary reports against an inmate in retaliation for grievances filed against him. The inmate was transferred 250 miles from his home after he questioned the corrections officer regarding prisoners' rights to legal assistance.[30]

Similarly, an officer made repeated death threats to an inmate resulting in his transfer to worse conditions of confinement. The inmate had a pending civil rights suit against the officer's brother. These allegations state a viable claim of retaliation for filing the lawsuit.[31]

§ 12.3.1 —Extradition

One aspect of prison litigation that occasionally arises is the transfer of prisoners to foreign countries, either to serve their sentences or by extradition.

In a case involving interstate extradition of a parole violator,[32] a parolee was sentenced to a term of 25 years for armed robbery involving drugs and was paroled from the Ohio correctional system in 1992. In 1993, the parolee was told that Ohio planned to revoke his parole status. Before the scheduled date of his meeting with his parole officer, he fled from Ohio to New Mexico.

Ohio sought extradition and the governor of New Mexico issued a warrant directing the extradition of the parolee. He was arrested in October 1994, and later that year sought a writ of habeas corpus from the New Mexico State Dis-

---

26   452 U.S. 473 (1981).
27   18 U.S.C. § 5003(a).
28   Wakinekona v. Olim, 664 F.2d 708 (9th Cir. 1981), *rev'd on other grounds,* 456 U.S. 1005 (1983).
29   McDonald v. Hall, 610 F.2d 16 (1st Cir. 1979), *criticized* in McGrath v. Johnson, 155 F. Supp. 2d 294 (E.D. Pa. 2001).
30   Farver v. Schwartz, 255 F.3d 473 (8th Cir. 2001).
31   Wilson v. Silcox, 151 F. Supp. 2d 1345 (N.D. Fla. 2001).
32   New Mexico ex rel. Ortiz v. Reed, 524 U.S. 151 (1998).

trict Court. He claimed he was not a "fugitive" for purposes of extradition because he fled under duress, believing that Ohio authorities intended to revoke his parole without due process and to cause him physical harm if he were returned to an Ohio prison. The state courts in New Mexico ruled in his favor and ordered his release.

Article IV of the United States Constitution § 2, cl.2. provides:

> A person charged in any State with Treason, Felony, or other Crime, who shall flee from Justice, and be found in another State, shall on Demand of the Executive Authority of the State from which he fled, be delivered up, to be removed to the State having Jurisdiction of the Crime.

The Federal Extradition Act[33] provides the procedures by which this constitutional command is carried out.

According to established case law,[34] once a governor has granted extradition, a court considering release on habeas corpus can do no more than decide: (a) whether the extradition documents on their face are in order; (b) whether the petitioner has been charged with a crime in the demanding state; (c) whether the petitioner is the person named in the request for extradition; and (d) whether the petitioner is a fugitive.

The Supreme Court of New Mexico held that the respondent was not a "fugitive" from justice but rather was a "refugee from injustice,"[35] holding that the parolee fled Ohio because of fear that his parole would be revoked without due process, and that he would be thereafter returned to prison where he faced the threat of bodily injury. According to the New Mexico court, this "duress" negated his status as a fugitive under Article IV.

The United States Supreme Court reversed, citing *Sweeney v. Woodall.*[36] The parolee was extradited to Ohio. *Woodall* held that extradition does not contemplate an appearance by the demanding state in the asylum state to defend against the claimed abuses of its prison system. Ohio did not make an appearance in New Mexico to protest the failure of New Mexico to extradite the parolee.

According to the Supreme Court, claims relating to what actually happened in Ohio, the law of Ohio, and what may be expected to happen in Ohio when the fugitive returns, are issues that must be tried in the courts of Ohio, and not in those of New Mexico.[37]

The Supreme Court's reasoning was based on practical considerations. In a brief filed by 40 states as *amici curiae*, the Court was advised that in 1997, Ohio made 218 extradition requests from its sister states, and returned 209

---

[33]   18 U.S.C. § 3182 (1998).
[34]   Michigan v. Doran, 439 U.S. 282 (1978).
[35]   124 N.M. at 146.
[36]   344 U.S. 86 (1952).
[37]   *See* Drew v. Thaw, 235 U.S. 432 (1914); Sweeney v. Woodall, 344 U.S. 86 (1952); Michigan v. Doran, *supra,* Pacileo v. Walker, 449 U.S. 86 (1980).

prisoners to other states. California in that same year had a total of 685 demands and returns, New York 490, Texas 700, and Pennsylvania 543. The burden on Ohio of producing witnesses and records in the New Mexico, or any other state, to counter allegations such as those of the parolee in New Mexico would make the system virtually unworkable.

In *Marquez-Ramos v. Reno,*[38] a Mexican national imprisoned in Colorado filed a petition with the United States Attorney General, requesting that he be transferred to a Mexican prison pursuant to a treaty.[39] On February 15, 1994, "after considering all appropriate factors," the Attorney General denied the transfer on the basis of the seriousness of the offense and prisoner's significant ties to the United States.

Article IV of the Treaty delineates the procedures for initiating the international transfer of a prisoner. Section (2) states that "if the Authority of the Transferring State finds the transfer of an offender appropriate, and if the offender gives his express consent for his transfer, said Authority shall transmit a request for transfer, through diplomatic channels, to the Authority of the Receiving State." The first clause of this section sets forth a necessary precondition to a prisoner transfer under the Treaty—whether the Attorney General finds a transfer "appropriate." In deciding upon the transfer of an offender, all factors bearing upon the probability that the transfer will contribute to the social rehabilitation of the offender, including the nature and severity of the offense and his or her previous criminal record, if any, his or her medical condition, the strength of his or her connections by residence, presence in the territory, family relations and otherwise to the social life of the transferring state and the receiving state must be taken into consideration.

The Treaty on its face makes the decision to transfer a prisoner a discretionary one, so relief was properly denied in *Marquez-Ramos.*

Similarly, in *Bagguley v. Bush,*[40] an English national asked to be sent home to England to serve his American sentence. In 1985, the United States and the United Kingdom ratified the Convention on the Transfer of Sentenced Persons,[41] which provides for the transfer of foreign prisoners to their home countries. The Transfer of Offenders to and from Foreign Countries Act[42] authorizes the Attorney General to implement the Convention. Relief was denied on the same grounds as in *Marquez-Ramos.*[43]

---

[38]   69 F.3d 477 (10th Cir. 1995).

[39]   Treaty on the Execution of Penal Sentences, November 25, 1976, U.S.-Mexico, T.I.A.S. No. 8718, and its implementing legislation, the Transfer of Offenders to and from Foreign Countries Act, 18 U.S.C. 4100 to 4115.

[40]   953 F.2d 660 (D.C. Cir. 1991).

[41]   T.I.A.S. No. 10824, 22 I.L.M. 530 (1983).

[42]   18 U.S.C. § 4100 *et seq.* (1988).

[43]   *See also* the *Soering* Case, European Court of Human Rights, n. 28, in Chapter 13.

§ 12.4 Search and Seizure

A prison inmate has no reasonable expectation of privacy in his or her prison cell that would entitle him or her to any Fourth Amendment protection against unreasonable searches and seizures. It would be impossible for prison officials to accomplish the objective of preventing the introduction of weapons, drugs, and other contraband into the prison if inmates retained a right of privacy in their cells. The unpredictability that attends random searches of cells renders such searches the most effective weapon of the prison official in the fight against contraband. Further, prison officials must be free to seize from cells any articles that, in their view, undermine legitimate institutional interests.[44]

Pretrial detainees have no due process rights to observe jail officials' random shakedown searches of their cells.[45]

A state's right to incarcerate inmates includes the right to limit or extinguish inmates' constitutional rights that are inconsistent with incarceration. In *Olsen v. Klecker*,[46] the federal Constitution's Fourth Amendment prohibition on unreasonable searches and seizures was held not to restrict warrantless searches of prison cells. The basic point of this case is not that the Fourth Amendment does not apply to inmates, but that the reasonableness of prison searches and seizures is to be assessed in light of the institutional needs of security, order, and rehabilitation. An example of this special measure of reasonableness is evident in the cases that involve body cavity searches. In *Hodges v. Klein*,[47] it was stated that a prison policy that requires inmates to submit to anal searches, not only upon leaving or entering the institution, but following personal contact visits with other prisoners or friends and relatives as well, is constitutional. The state's interest in the prevention of contraband transmission into and within the prison is very strong, and private contact with an individual from outside the prison presents an excellent opportunity for the introduction of all types of contraband into the prison community. Prison officials must be able to completely shut off this port of entry for contraband. To do so, an anal examination, degrading though it is, as part of a strip search, is not, in view of the state's compelling interest, an unreasonable requirement. However, the court held that mandatory anal searches were not permissible as applied to inmates who are entering or leaving solitary confinement. There is no compelling state interest that can justify anal examinations prior to or fol-

---

[44] Hudson v. Palmer, 468 U.S. 517 (1984).

[45] Block v. Rutherford, 468 U.S. 576 (1984).

[46] 642 F.2d 1115 (8th Cir. 1981); Clifton v. Robinson, 500 F. Supp. 30 (E.D. Pa. 1980); Becket v. Powers, 494 F. Supp. 364 (W.D. Wis. 1980); Brown v. Hilton, 492 F. Supp. 771 (D.N.J. 1980); State v. Pietraszewski, 283 N.W.2d 887 (Minn. 1979); Butler v. Bensinger, 377 F. Supp. 870 (N.D. Ill. 1974).

[47] 412 F. Supp. 896 (D.N.J. 1976); *see also* United States v. Lilly, 599 F.2d 619 (5th Cir. 1979); Coleman v. Hutto, 500 F. Supp. 586 (E.D. Va. 1980); Vera v. State, 29 Cr. L. 2409 (Fla. Dist. Ct. App. 1981); Williams v. State, 400 So. 2d 988 (Fla. Dist. Ct. App. 1981); *but cf.* Sims v. Brierton, 500 F. Supp. 813 (N.D. Ill. 1980); Arruda v. Berman, 522 F. Supp. 766 (D. Mass. 1981) (Repeated rectal cavity searches accompanied by abusive and insulting comments and beatings stated a cause of action under the Civil Rights Act).

lowing a segregated inmate's transfer within the segregation area or anywhere in the prison while under escort or observation. The court felt that metal detectors provide the necessary security.[48]

The Supreme Court has approved both body cavity searches and room searches. In *Bell v. Wolfish*,[49] the Court held that body cavity searches are not unreasonable and do not violate the Constitution. Prison officials may conduct them on less than probable cause as long as they are not conducted in an abusive manner. Also, room searches are a reasonable security measure and do not infringe upon a detainee's or prisoner's right to privacy. Further, inmates do not have a protected right to be present or to watch room searches.

There are, however, certain factors that can counterbalance the institutional needs of security, order, and rehabilitation, and that can make the search or seizure unreasonable, and therefore unconstitutional. Clearly established inmate rights, such as the right to possess legal and religious material, can clash with the state's right to search and seize inmate property. For example, in *Bonner v. Coughlin*,[50] an inmate was awarded damages for the seizure by prison guards of his copy of his trial transcript. Also, in *O'Connor v. Keller*,[51] an inmate was awarded punitive damages from a prison official who made an unreasonable seizure of personal property from the inmate's cell. In such cases it is not an inherent right to be free from searches and seizures that allows recovery, but the constitutional protection that surrounds and flows from the property seized.

In a jail setting, a prisoner's personal bag may be "inventoried" without violating the Fourth Amendment. It is reasonable for police to search the personal effects of a person under lawful arrest as part of the routine administrative procedure at a police station incident to the booking and jailing of persons arrested. It is entirely proper for police to remove and list or inventory property found on the person or in the possession of an arrested person who is to be jailed. The justification of the search is not based on probable cause. The absence of a warrant is immaterial to the reasonableness of the search. Reasons justifying the search are considerations of orderly police administration, protection of a suspect's property, deterrence of false claims of theft against the police, security, and identification of the suspect. The fact that the bag could have been secured otherwise does not make the search unreasonable. Even if some less intrusive means existed, it would be unreasonable to expect police officers in the everyday course of business to make subtle distinctions in deciding which containers or items may be searched, and which must be sealed without examination. As a caution, the Court stresses that it is impor-

---

[48]   *Cf.* Lee v. Downs, 641 F.2d 1117 (4th Cir. 1981) (Where a female prisoner was possibly suicidal, it was proper for correctional officers to forcibly remove her clothes in the presence of male officers).

[49]   441 U.S. 520 (1979).

[50]   517 F.2d 1311 (7th Cir. 1975).

[51]   510 F. Supp. 1359 (D. Md. 1981); Steinburg v. Taylor, 500 F. Supp. 477 (D. Conn. 1980); Digiuseppe v. Ward, 514 F. Supp. 503 (S.D.N.Y. 1981); *cf.* Roque v. Warden, Conn. Corrections, 434 A.2d 348 (Conn. 1980).

tant as to whether the suspect was to be incarcerated or released after being booked. If the suspect was to be released, there is arguably no reason to inventory his or her property.[52]

Several cases discuss the problems associated with cross-gender searches. One case also raised the religious issue in cross-gender searches.[53] In support of their claim that the searches violated their First Amendment rights, two female inmates testified that their religion prohibited them from being touched by men who are not their husbands. It was recognized that requiring female employees to perform all searches would have an adverse effect on the institution, and that a single-sex search policy created a number of labor problems and conflicted with the requirements of the collective bargaining agreement. Further, requiring female employees to perform all searches made the "pat" searches more predictable and less effective for controlling the movement of contraband through the facility. Under the facts, it was determined that pulling female employees off their posts to perform searches in other areas of the prison would create additional security problems in terms of leaving that post vacant, and also by creating delays in moving inmates through the facility.

The prisoners also argued that the cross-gender searches were unreasonable and violated the Fourth Amendment. The practice of routine body cavity searches of pretrial detainees was upheld in *Bell v. Wolfish*.[54] The argument that the "pat" searches constituted cruel and unusual punishment was also rejected.

Grummett v. Rushen[55] rejected a constitutional challenge to a prison policy that permitted female guards to perform pat-down searches on clothed male inmates and occasionally view naked inmates. Although the searches included the groin area, they were done briefly and while the inmates were fully clothed. There was no intimate contact with the inmates' bodies.

During a shakedown of his housing unit, two female correctional officers strip-searched an inmate. Ten male officers were nearby while the two female officers conducted the search. It was also alleged that female officers regularly observed male inmates in a variety of settings typically considered private, including while they dressed, showered, defecated, and slept in various states of undress. The Seventh Circuit Court of Appeals[56] held that the right to privacy is firmly ensconced among the individual liberties protected by the Constitution and one of the clearest forms of degradation in western society is to strip a person of his or her clothes. The right to be free from strip searches and degrading body inspections is basic to the concept of privacy. However, some diminution of privacy is to be expected in prison.[57]

---

[52]   Illinois v. Lafayette, 462 U.S. 640 (1983).

[53]   Jordan v. Gardner, 953 F.2d 1137 (9th Cir. 1992); *see also* Chapter 6, Religion in Prison.

[54]   441 U.S. 520 (1979).

[55]   779 F.2d 491 (9th Cir. 1985).

[56]   Canedy v. Boardman, 16 F.3d 183 (7th Cir. 1994).

[57]   *See* Hudson v. Palmer, 468 U.S. 517 (1984), holding that prisoners are entitled to no reasonable expectation of privacy in their prison cells ensuring them of Fourth Amendment protection against unreasonable searches and seizures.

Prisons must be allowed to utilize female correctional officers to the fullest extent possible. But that does not mean that inmates are without constitutional protection against invasion of their privacy by members of the opposite sex.[58] The Court recognized the right of one sex not to be discriminated against in job opportunities within the prison because of gender, but concluded that inmates do have some right to avoid unwanted intrusions by persons of the opposite sex. Where it is reasonable—taking account of a state's interests in prison security and in providing equal employment opportunity for female officers—to respect an inmate's constitutional privacy interests, doing so is not just a palliative to be doled out at the state's indulgence. It is a constitutional mandate.[59]

Canedy v. Boardman was distinguished in *Johnson v. Phelan,*[60] in which female officers at the Cook County Jail were assigned to monitor male prisoners' movements and could see men naked in their cells, the shower, and the toilet. The court stated that there are two justifications for cross-gender searches and monitoring. First, it makes good use of the staff, because it is more expensive for a prison to have a group of officers dedicated to shower and toilet monitoring than to have all officers serving in each role in the prison. If only men can monitor showers, then female officers are less useful to the prison; if female officers cannot perform this task, the prison must have more officers on hand to cover for them. It is a form of featherbedding. Similarly, an interest in efficient deployment of the staff supports cross-sex monitoring.[61] By the same token, the prison may assign homosexual male officers to monitor male prisoners, heterosexual male officers to monitor effeminate male homosexual prisoners, and so on. There are too many permutations to place officers and prisoners into multiple classes by sex and sexual orientation.

Second, cross-sex monitoring reduces the need for prisons to make sex a criterion of employment, and therefore reduces the potential for conflict with Title VII of the Equal Employment Opportunity Act and the equal protection clause. Cells and showers are designed so that guards can see in, to prevent violence and other offenses. Prisoners dress, undress, and bathe under watchful eyes. Guards roaming the corridors are bound to see naked prisoners. A prison could comply with the rule that *Johnson* proposes, and still maintain surveillance, only by relegating women to the administrative wing, limiting their duties or eliminating them from the staff. There was no constitutional infirmity.

For searches of parolees and probationers, *see* § 9.5.2.

---

[58]   *See* Forts v. Ward, 471 F. Supp. 1095 (S.D.N.Y. 1979), *vacated in part*, 621 F.2d 1210 (2d Cir. 1980), in which the court ordered that adjustments be made either in scheduling or in the physical structure of the facilities to protect the women inmates from male surveillance while they were dressing or undressing, showering, using the toilet facilities, or sleeping in the housing units.

[59]   Canedy, at 17.

[60]   69 F.3d 144 (7th Cir. 1995).

[61]   *See* Timm v. Gunter, 917 F.2d 1093 (8th Cir. 1990), which concluded that opposite sex surveillance of male inmates, performed on the same basis as same sex surveillance, is constitutionally permissible.

§ 12.5   Overcrowding

For a variety of reasons, overcrowding is a major problem at almost all penal institutions. Overcrowding has not, in itself, been declared unconstitutional. However, overcrowding has been viewed as a causal factor that, when other conditions are present, may be enough to declare a prison's conditions to be unconstitutional.[62]

Constitutional treatment of human beings who are confined to penal institutions does not depend upon the willingness or the financial ability of the state to provide decent penitentiaries,[63] especially when the legislature has had ample opportunity to provide for the state to meet its constitutional responsibilities.[64]

While overcrowding itself may not be a violation of the Eighth Amendment, overcrowding can, under certain circumstances, cause unsanitary conditions or high levels of violence, which violate the Eighth Amendment.[65]

The Prison Litigation Reform Act has greatly restricted the ability of state courts to remedy conditions of overcrowding.[66]

---

[62] Wichman v. Fisher, 629 P.2d 896 (Utah 1981); Benjamin v. Malcolm, 495 F. Supp. 1357 (S.D.N.Y. 1980). In *Bell v. Wolfish*, the Court held that double bunking does not deprive pretrial detainees of liberty without due process and that a particular restriction is valid if it is reasonably related to a legitimate, nonpunitive government objective. The Court emphasized that regulations or practices must be rationally related to a legitimate, nonpunitive government purpose and must not appear excessive in relation to that purpose. Security and order is a nonpunitive objective that may necessarily infringe upon or cause many restrictions to the rights of inmates or pretrial detainees. Bell v. Wolfish, 441 U.S. 520 (1979).

In *Rhodes v. Chapman*, the Supreme Court held that double-celling at Ohio's maximum-security prison did not amount to cruel and unusual punishment prohibited by the Eighth and Fourteenth Amendments. In order for conditions of confinement to constitute punishment, they must involve the wanton and unnecessary infliction of pain or be grossly disproportionate to the severity of the crime warranting imprisonment. The fact that overcrowding falls below contemporary standards does not make the overcrowding unconstitutional. The Supreme Court recognizes that to the extent that such conditions are restrictive, and even harsh, they are part of the price that criminals must pay for their offenses against society. Ruiz v. Estelle, 679 F.2d 1115 (5th Cir. 1982) (A district court decree requiring single-celling in Texas prisons and at least 60 square feet per inmate in dormitories was set aside. The district court's requirements go beyond that which is necessary for the elimination of unconstitutional prison conditions. Also, the district court acted properly within its discretion in prescribing certain exercise requirements for the Texas Department of Corrections. Although the deprivation of exercise is not per se cruel and unusual punishment, in certain circumstances such a denial may constitute an impairment of health forbidden under the Eighth Amendment); Smith v. Fairman, 690 F.2d 122 (7th Cir. 1982) (A prison practice of housing two inmates in a single cell did not violate the Eighth Amendment. The lower court's ruling was reversed).

[63] Smith v. Sullivan, 611 F.2d 1039 (5th Cir. 1980); Williams v. Edwards, 547 F.2d 1209 (5th Cir. 1977); Gates v. Collier, 407 F. Supp. 1117 (N.D. Miss. 1975).

[64] Clay v. Miller, 626 F.2d 345 (4th Cir. 1980); Battle v. Anderson, 594 F.2d 786 (10th Cir. 1979); James v. Wallace, 406 F. Supp. 318 (M.D. Ala. 1976).

[65] *See* Hoptowit v. Ray, 682 F.2d 1237 (9th Cir. 1982).

[66] *See* Chapter 13.

§ 12.6   Conditions of Confinement

Courts have a duty to protect inmates from unlawful and onerous treatment of a nature that, in itself, adds punitive measures to those legally meted out by a court.[67] While the federal courts continue to recognize the broad discretion that state prison officials require in order to maintain orderly and secure institutions, constitutional deprivations of such a magnitude as to allow the maintenance of facilities that are wholly unfit for human habitation cannot be tolerated. The courts are under a duty to, and will, intervene to protect incarcerated persons from such infringements of their constitutional rights.[68] However, federal courts are limited in their intervention into the operations of institutions to the issue of whether there are constitutional violations. In *Bell v. Wolfish*,[69] the Supreme Court said:

> . . . There was a time not too long ago when the federal judiciary took a completely "hands-off" approach to the problem of prison administration. In recent years, however, these courts largely have discarded this "hands-off" attitude and have waded into this complex arena. The deplorable conditions and draconian restrictions of some of our Nation's prisons are too well known to require recounting here, and the federal courts rightly have condemned these sordid aspects of our prison systems. But many of these same courts have, in the name of the Constitution, become increasingly enmeshed in the minutiae of prison operations. Judges, after all, are human. They, no less than others in our society, have a natural tendency to believe that their individual solutions to often intractable problems are better and more workable than those of the persons who are actually charged with and trained in the running of the particular institution under examination. But under the Constitution, the first question to be answered is not whose plan is best, but in what branch of the Government is lodged the authority to initially devise the plan. This does not mean that constitutional rights are not to be scrupulously observed. It does mean, however, that the inquiry of federal courts into prison management must be limited to the issue of whether a particular system violates any prohibition of the Constitution, or in the case of a federal prison, a statute. The wide range of "judgment calls" that meet constitutional and statutory requirement[s] are confided to officials outside of the Judicial Branch of Government.

Similarly, in *Rhodes v. Chapman*,[70] the Supreme Court reinforced its holding in *Bell v. Wolfish*, and admonished the lower federal courts that in determining whether prison conditions constitute cruel and unusual punishment

---

[67]   Stickney v. List, 519 F. Supp 617 (D. Nev. 1981).
[68]   Jordan v. Arnold, 472 F. Supp. 265 (M.D. Pa. 1979); Taylor v. Sterrett, 600 F.2d 1135 (5th Cir. 1979); Robson v. Biester, 420 A.2d 9 (Pa. Commw. Ct. 1980); James v. Wallace, 406 F. Supp. 318 (M.D. Ala. 1976).
[69]   441 U.S. 520 (1979).
[70]   452 U.S. 337 (1981).

under federal standards, federal courts cannot assume that state legislatures and prison officials are insensitive to the requirements of the Constitution, or to the sociological problems of how best to achieve the goals of the prison in the criminal justice system.

Although federal courts may lack the power to order public or governmental entities, which represent the public, to expend funds to build new facilities, they do have the power to order the release of persons who are being held under conditions that deprive them of rights guaranteed to them by the federal Constitution, unless such conditions are corrected within a reasonable period.[71] Some courts have gone so far with the conditions-of-confinement argument that they have allowed escapee defendants to raise the criminal defenses of necessity and duress to criminal charges of prison escape. Such cases usually involve threats of homosexual rape as the mitigating condition of confinement.

Most aspects of prison life are dictated by the needs of institutionalization. Prison authorities have wide discretion to regulate or prohibit inmates' comforts, including the keeping of pets,[72] permissible clothing,[73] plumbing,[74] and checking accounts.[75]

Inmates who complain of their conditions of confinement, but who are transferred to other facilities before their complaints are adjudicated, may have their complaints dismissed as moot.[76]

As a result of the increase in conditions-of-confinement suits, the United States Supreme Court has added to the obstacles that prisoners face in filing such suits.

In *Wilson v. Seiter,*[77] a civil rights action was filed against an Ohio facility where the prisoner was housed. The complaint alleged overcrowding, mixing of healthy inmates with physically and mentally ill inmates, excessive noise, inadequate heating and cooling, and lack of sanitation.

In such cases, prisoners must prove a culpable mental state on the part of prison officials. Such proof is an essential element in a claim that prison conditions violate the Eighth Amendment's prohibition of cruel and unusual punishment. *Estelle v. Gamble,*[78] *Rhodes v. Chapman,*[79] and *Whitley v. Albers*[80]

---

[71] Clay v. Miller, 626 F.2d 345 (4th Cir. 1980); Battle v. Anderson, 594 F.2d 786 (10th Cir. 1979); James v. Wallace, 406 F. Supp. 318 (M.D. Ala. 1976).

[72] Sparks v. Fuller, 506 F.2d 1238 (1st Cir. 1974).

[73] *Id.* at 1239; *see also,* State v. Rouse, 629 P.2d 167 (Kan. 1981).

[74] Mims v. Shapp, 399 F. Supp. 818 (W.D. Pa. 1975), *was vacated and remanded on appeal.* Mims v. Shapp, 541 F.2d 415 (2d Cir. 1976). The court of appeals held that the inmates' affidavits sufficiently alleged personal bias of the judge and that the district judge erred in denying the inmates' recusal motion; *see also* Freeman v. Trudell, 497 F. Supp. 481 (E.D. Mich. 1980) and Jefferson v. Douglas, 493 F. Supp. 43 (D. Okla. 1979) (Whether a prisoner has a proper diet is a question wholly within the discretion of the prison administration). Herring v. Superintendent, Danville City Jail, 387 F. Supp. 410 (W.D. Va. 1974).

[75] Nix v. Paderick, 407 F. Supp. 844 (E.D. Va. 1976).

[76] Strader v. Blalock, 405 F. Supp. 1155 (W.D. Va. 1975).

[77] 501 U.S. 294 (1991).

[78] 429 U.S. 97 (1976).

[79] 452 U.S. 337 (1981).

[80] 475 U.S. 312 (1986).

were observed by the Supreme Court as showing that a mental element is implicit in the Eighth Amendment's language. The cases require a prisoner to show "deliberate indifference" on the part of the official.

The Supreme Court indicated that there is no distinction between cases involving prison-wide conditions of confinement and cases alleging unconstitutional acts or omissions directed at particular prisoners. The Court remanded the case for reconsideration.[81]

The idea that no distinctions will be made between prison-wide conditions and isolated incidents was again reiterated, but in a different context, in the Federal Magistrates Act.[82] The Act allows suits brought by prisoners to be referred to a magistrate without the consent of the parties. The wording of the Act makes specific reference to petitions challenging conditions of confinement.

In *Rufo v. Inmates of Suffolk County Jail*,[83] state officials sought to modify a consent decree previously entered into, which had resulted from constitutionally deficient conditions at the facility known as the Charles Street Jail. The terms of the program set out in the decree were designed to include 309 single-occupancy rooms. By the time construction began in 1984, the inmate population had outpaced population projections. State officials were then ordered to build a larger jail. The number of cells was later increased to 453 with construction beginning in 1987. In 1989, the sheriff moved to modify the consent decree to allow double-bunking in a portion of the cells to raise the capacity of the new jail to 610 male detainees. The federal district court supervising the consent decree applied the standard of *United States v. Swift & Co.*[84]

> Nothing less than a clear showing of grievous wrong evoked by new
> and unforeseen conditions should lead us to change what was decreed
> after years of litigation with the consent of all concerned.[85]

The district court stated that because a separate cell was an important element of the original relief sought, a more flexible standard would not be available to the sheriff. In moving to modify the decree, the sheriff relied on Federal Rule of Civil Procedure 60(b)(5) and (6), which in part provides that a court may relieve a party from a final judgment, order, or proceeding for the reason that the judgment has been satisfied, or it is no longer equitable that the judgment should have prospective application, or if there is any other reason justifying relief from the operation of the judgment.

The sheriff asserted that modification of the decree would improve conditions by cutting down on transfers of detainees away from the area where their family members and legal counsel were located. Further, in the transfer facilities, the detainees would be double-celled in less desirable conditions. Finally,

---

[81]　This indication by the Court could explain the confusion about the standard to be used in an excessive force claim later raised by *Hudson v. McMillian. See* § 2.2.

[82]　28 U.S.C. § 636(b)(1)(B).

[83]　502 U.S. 367 (1992).

[84]　286 U.S. 106 (1932).

[85]　Inmates of the Suffolk County Jail v. Kearney, 734 F. Supp. 561, 564 (D.C. Mass. 1990).

the public interest would be served by such modification because fewer releases and transfers to halfway houses would be necessary and thus fewer escapes would occur.

On appeal, the Supreme Court held that the *Swift* "grievous wrong" standard does not apply to requests to modify consent decrees that stem from institutional reform litigation. The Court then adopted a much more flexible standard that a party seeking modification of a consent decree must establish. A significant change in facts or law must be present in order to warrant revision and the proposed modification must be suitably tailored to the changed circumstances. The Court further directed the lower court on remand to consider whether the increase in the inmate population was foreseeable.

The above ruling may in fact lead to delay on the part of state officials who are working under consent decrees as a result of prison conditions. The prison system is constantly changing and it could be argued that most of those changes are foreseeable. The lasting effect of consent decrees in conditions-of-confinement cases is yet to be known.

In *Helling v. McKinney*,[86] the Ninth Circuit Court of Appeals held that a non-smoking prisoner's compelled exposure to environmental tobacco smoke can amount to cruel and unusual punishment prohibited by the Eighth Amendment. The Supreme Court vacated and remanded the case.[87]

The Nevada state prisoner claimed that his involuntary exposure to environmental tobacco smoke (ETS) from his cellmate's and other inmates' cigarettes posed an unreasonable risk to his health, thus subjecting him to cruel and unusual punishment in violation of the Eighth Amendment. A federal magistrate granted petitioners' motion for a directed verdict, but the Court of Appeals reversed in part, holding that McKinney should have been permitted to prove that his ETS exposure was sufficient to constitute an unreasonable danger to his future health.

The Supreme Court held that by alleging that the prison officials had, with deliberate indifference, exposed him to ETS levels that posed an unreasonable risk to his future health, the prisoner had stated an Eighth Amendment claim on which relief could be granted. An injunction cannot be denied to inmates who plainly prove an unsafe, life-threatening condition on the ground that nothing yet has happened to them.[88]

However, as the Court could not rule that the prisoner could not possibly prove an Eighth Amendment violation based on ETS exposure, the Court held that it would be premature to base a reversal on the argument that the harm from ETS exposure is speculative, with no risk sufficiently grave to implicate a serious medical need, and that the exposure is not contrary to current standards of decency. The lower court, on remand, was directed to give the prisoner the opportunity to prove his allegations, which would require that he establish both the subjective and objective elements necessary to prove an

---

[86]　924 F.2d 1500 (9th Cir. 1991).
[87]　509 U.S. 25 (1993).
[88]　*See* Hutto v. Finney, 437 U.S. 678 (1978).

Eighth Amendment violation. With respect to the objective factor, it was pointed out that he may have difficulty showing that he is being exposed to unreasonably high ETS levels, because he has been moved to a new prison and no longer has a cellmate who smokes, and because a new state prison policy restricts smoking to certain areas and makes reasonable efforts to respect non-smokers' wishes with regard to double-bunking. He was required to also show that the risk of which he complained is not one that today's society chooses to tolerate. The subjective factor, deliberate indifference, was to be determined in light of the prison authorities' current attitudes and conduct, which, as evidenced by the new smoking policy, might have changed considerably since the Court of Appeals' original judgment. The inquiry into this factor also was deemed to be an appropriate vehicle to consider arguments regarding the realities of prison administration.

In a lower court case subsequent to *Helling*,[89] an inmate was "roomed up" with a heavy smoker. He informed a prison official that he suffered various medical problems—severe headaches, dizziness, nausea, vomiting, and breathing difficulties—when roomed with a smoking inmate. The prisoner's room was designated a "nonsmoking" room. However, his roommate continued to smoke; a "shakedown" revealed that the "smoking conditions were still the same." Although the prisoner personally showed the orders to the prison officials, the officials made no attempts to enforce the orders. The prisoner filed a second grievance, and the Director of Correctional Services responded by reiterating that the room was non-smoking and by indicating that if the prisoner continued to experience problems, he should contact unit management staff for an investigation or a room change. The prisoner did so and asked that either he or his roommate be moved to another room, but no move was forthcoming. Finally, the prisoner asked to see the prison doctor, who ordered that he be switched to a room with a non-smoking roommate immediately. The prison officials complied with the doctor's orders. The prisoner then filed suit.

The district court found that the prisoner, like the prisoner in *Helling*, had alleged that the prison officials were deliberately indifferent to the future health risks posed by his continued exposure to environmental tobacco smoke. However, the Court of Appeals read the complaint differently and found that *Helling* was not on point. In this case, the prisoner did not allege that prison officials showed deliberate indifference to his future health; rather, he alleged deliberate indifference to his *existing* ill health. As portrayed in the complaint, environmental tobacco smoke was the catalyst for his existing health problems. *Helling*, in contrast, did not involve deliberate indifference to existing medical needs. However, the Eighth Circuit concluded that the deliberate indifference to his existing serious medical needs was a violation of a constitutional right.

An asthmatic inmate was awarded $36,500 in compensatory and $18,250 in punitive damages. Prison administrators responsible for assigning prisoners were clearly reckless in their five-year-long disregard of the inmate's serious

---

[89]   Weaver v. Clarke, 45 F.3d 1253 (8th Cir. 1995).

medical need to be placed in a smoke-free environment. Such ignorance of supervisory obligations warranted a punishment designed to deter other officials in like positions from ignoring their responsibilities.[90]

An inmate claimed that his exposure to second-hand smoke violated his rights. He was exposed to second-hand smoke on several occasions while riding a bus to and from work assignments, causing him to gasp for breath, aggravating existing medical conditions, and increasing his cancer risk. This was insufficient to state an Eighth Amendment violation.[91]

However, an inmate with severe chronic asthma stated a valid claim under the Eighth Amendment, in which he alleged that his health deteriorated as a result of his exposure to environmental tobacco smoke, even though the inmate was housed with a nonsmoking cellmate in a nonsmoking unit. Prison officials' deliberate failure to enforce smoking rules contributed to ambient tobacco smoke in prison.[92]

More v. Farrier[93] involved a civil rights action on behalf of three wheelchair-bound inmates to require the prison authorities to install cable television service in their individual cells. It was held that wheelchair-bound inmates are not a class that requires protection under the equal protection clause.

A significant Supreme Court pronouncement on Eighth Amendment claims arising from unconstitutional conditions of confinement is *Farmer v. Brennan,*[94] which involved the rape of an inmate. A preoperative transsexual was transferred from a Federal Correctional Institute to a penitentiary and raped soon after his arrival. He claimed that the wardens and officials in the two prisons acted with deliberate indifference to his safety in violation of the Eighth Amendment because they knew that the penitentiary had a violent environment and a history of inmate assaults and that the plaintiff would be particularly vulnerable to sexual attack if placed in the general inmate population. The Supreme Court held that a prison official cannot be found liable under the Eighth Amendment for denying an inmate humane conditions of confinement unless the official knows of and disregards an excessive risk to inmate health or safety; the official must both be aware of facts from which the inference could be drawn that a substantial risk of serious harm exists, and he or she must also draw the inference.

Sexual assaults are often the basis for litigation. In *Taylor v. Michigan Department of Corrections,*[95] the basis of the prisoner's Eighth Amendment claim was that the warden knew about the risk of sexual assault in the camp program to small, vulnerable-looking prisoners such as Taylor, and neither had a policy to identify and screen out potential transferees who would not be safe in the camp, nor created guidelines for prison staff to follow when screening inmates for transfer. These were questions for a jury.

---

[90] Reilly v. Grayson, 157 F. Supp. 2d 762 (E.D. Mich. 2001).
[91] Richardson v. Spurlock, 260 F.3d 495 (5th Cir. 2001).
[92] Alvarado v. Litscher, 267 F.3d 648 (7th Cir. 2001).
[93] 984 F.2d 269 (8th Cir. 1993).
[94] 511 U.S. 825 (1994).
[95] 69 F.3d 76 (6th Cir. 1995).

The Sixth Circuit pointed out that, in 1910, Winston Churchill coined a phrase and recognized an obvious truth when he said that the "treatment of crime and criminals is one of the most unfailing tests of civilization of any country."[96] In *Farmer*, the Supreme Court applied the same idea to prison rapes, saying that "gratuitously allowing the beating or rape of one prisoner by another serves no 'legitimate penological objective,' any more than it squares with 'evolving standards of decency.'" Prisons are dangerous places because they house dangerous people in congested conditions. But the Eighth Amendment to the Constitution mandates that prison officials maintain humane conditions of confinement and take reasonable measures to guarantee the safety of inmates. Their duty includes protecting prisoners from violence at the hands of other prisoners: "Having stripped [prisoners] of virtually every means of self-protection and foreclosed their access to outside aid, the government and its officials are not free to let the state of nature take its course."[97]

In *Del Raine v. Williford*,[98] a prisoner claimed that in the period following the lockdown he was forced to inhabit a cold cell and was not given adequate clothing or blankets. The prisoner alleged:

> Every few days I'm strip-searched in my cell (notwithstanding the bitter cold resulting from the open window above my cell), cuffed behind my back, pulled backwards from my cell, put in an empty cell while cuffed, from fifteen to thirty minutes, while my cell is ransacked, i.e., personal property is stolen, legal papers mixed up, scattered, walked on, towels and sheets thrown on the floor. This practice continues to the present time. On December 23, 1983 while the chill factor was minus 40 degrees to 50 degrees below zero, according to the radio weather reports, I was strip-searched and placed in an empty cell while my cell was ransacked. No hats, jackets, or gloves were allowed, nor could we put a blanket over our cell bars to warm the cell. Many other days were also bitterly cold. Repeated requests to . . . close the windows and fix broken ones were futile.

Applying *Farmer*,[99] the Seventh Circuit Court of Appeals held that a prison official cannot be found liable under the Eighth Amendment for denying an inmate humane conditions of confinement unless the official knows of and disregards an excessive risk to inmate health or safety; the official must both be aware of facts from which the inference could be drawn that a substantial risk of serious harm exists, and he must also draw the inference. The Eighth Amendment does not outlaw cruel and unusual "conditions"; it outlaws cruel and unusual "punishments." An act or omission unaccompanied by

---

[96]   Addressing the issue of prison reform, Winston Churchill made these remarks before the House of Commons in 1910 while he was Home Secretary.

[97]   Farmer v. Brennan, 511 U.S. 825 (1994).

[98]   32 F.3d 1024 (7th Cir. 1994).

[99]   Farmer v. Brennan, 511 U.S. 825 (1994).

knowledge of a significant risk of harm might well be something society wishes to discourage, and if harm does result, society might well wish to assure compensation. The common law reflects such concerns when it imposes tort liability on a purely objective basis.

The Court concluded that the prisoner was entitled to have the trier of fact determine whether the conditions of his administrative confinement, principally with regard to the cell temperature and the provision of hygiene items, violated the minimal standards required by the Eighth Amendment. However, the Court also concluded that the right of a prisoner not to be confined in a cell at so low a temperature as to cause severe discomfort and in conditions lacking basic sanitation was well established in 1986. The defendants therefore were not entitled to summary judgment on the basis of qualified immunity. Other circuits have recognized the temperature factor in assessing conditions of confinement. The Second Circuit reversed dismissal of a prisoner's complaint of exposure to extreme cold.[100] Subsequently, it affirmed on the merits a finding of cruel and unusual punishment in confining an inmate for 11 days, naked, without soap, towels, or toilet paper, and without bedding of any kind, forcing the inmate to sleep on the floor, the temperature being sufficiently cold to cause extreme discomfort.[101] The Fourth Circuit[102] found two sets of conditions of confinement involving the same prison inmate to violate the Eighth Amendment. In the first, the inmate was confined for two days in a cell where a concrete slab was initially the inmate's bed. A mattress was furnished later during the first night, but no blankets were supplied. Although the record did not disclose the temperature in the cell, it was so cold that the inmate tore open the mattress and nestled inside. The inmate also was denied personal hygiene items. The court held that in the case of an ordinary prisoner, these conditions violated the Eighth Amendment; the only justification would be such mental derangement on the part of the inmate that self-harm was a real danger, in which case immediate contact with a psychologist/psychiatrist was required. The second set of conditions included another two-day confinement in a cell without clothing, blanket, or mattress, where the inmate claimed sleep was impossible and that he had to stand up most of the first night. He was also denied articles of personal hygiene. The court held that these conditions also violated the inmate's Eighth Amendment rights in the absence of mental derangement.

In *Maxwell v. Mason,*[103] the Eighth Circuit affirmed a finding of cruel and unusual punishment in the confinement of an inmate to 14 days in a solitary cell with no clothing except undershorts and no bedding except a mattress. Correctional officers had testified that the temperature would have been at least 70 degrees, but the inmate had testified that he huddled in the corner of his cell to stay warm. The court stated that prisoners in punitive solitary con-

---

[100]   Wright v. McMann, 387 F.2d 519 (2d Cir. 1967).
[101]   Wright v. McMann, 460 F.2d 126 (2d Cir. 1972).
[102]   McCray v. Burrell, 516 F.2d 357 (4th Cir. 1975).
[103]   668 F.2d 361 (8th Cir. 1981).

finement should not be deprived of basic necessities, including light, heat, ventilation, sanitation, clothing, and a proper diet, and affirmed a denial of qualified immunity for two penitentiary officials.

The Seventh Circuit[104] reversed the dismissal of a prisoner's complaint that alleged being placed in solitary confinement for three days without a mattress, bedding, or blankets, and without articles of personal hygiene. It also set aside summary judgment in *Lewis v. Lane,*[105] in which two state prisoners alleged that the heat in their cells was maintained at an unreasonably low temperature during December and January and that the lack of heat was severe enough to produce physical discomfort. Consequently, an allegation of inadequate heating may state an Eighth Amendment violation.[106]

In *Anderson v. County of Kern,*[107] prisoners challenged as unconstitutional the use of safety cells for suicidal and mentally disturbed inmates. Safety cells are padded cells that are used to temporarily confine violent or suicidal prisoners so they cannot hurt themselves. The claims were evaluated under the Eighth Amendment, and the pretrial detainees' challenge was evaluated under the Fourteenth Amendment. Under the Eighth Amendment, the pertinent inquiry is whether placement of mentally disturbed or suicidal inmates in safety cells constitutes an infliction of pain or a deprivation of basic human needs, such as adequate food, clothing, shelter, sanitation, and medical care, and if so, whether prison officials acted with the requisite culpable intent such that the infliction of pain is "unnecessary and wanton."[108] In prison conditions cases, prison officials act with the requisite culpable intent when they act with deliberate indifference to the inmates' suffering.[109] Similarly, the placement of pretrial detainees in safety cells is "punishment" in violation of the Fourteenth Amendment only if prison officials act with deliberate indifference to the inmates' needs.[110]

On the basis of testimony, the district court rejected the inmates' challenge to the use of safety cells, finding that nothing suggested that the safety cells had been inappropriately used as more than a temporary measure to control violent inmates until they "cooled down" sufficiently to be released from those cells. The experts agreed that the cells could appropriately be used for this purpose. The district court's ruling was affirmed. The Ninth Circuit Court of Appeals found that a safety cell is admittedly a severe environment, but it is employed in response to serious safety concerns. There was ample testimony that some prisoners became so violent and such a danger to themselves that temporary placement in a safety cell was needed in order to deprive the pris-

---

[104]   Kimbrough v. O'Neil, 523 F.2d 1057 (7th Cir. 1975).

[105]   816 F.2d 1165 (7th Cir. 1987).

[106]   *See, e.g.,* Ramos v. Lamm, 639 F.2d 559, 568 (10th Cir. 1980) ("a state must provide . . . reasonably adequate ventilation, sanitation, bedding, hygienic materials, and utilities (i.e., hot and cold water, light, heat, plumbing").

[107]   45 F.3d 1310 (9th Cir. 1994).

[108]   *See* Farmer v. Brennan, 511 U.S. 825 (1994).

[109]   *Id.;* Wilson v. Seiter, 501 U.S. 294 (1991); Jordan v. Gardner, 986 F.2d 1521, 1528 (9th Cir. 1993) (en banc).

[110]   Redman, 942 F.2d at 1441-1443; Hallstrom v. Garden City, 991 F.2d 1473, 1485 (9th Cir.) (applying *Redman* to conditions of confinement claim), *cert. denied,* 114 S. Ct. 549 (1993).

oners of all means of harming themselves. The fact that some prisoners who are violent or threaten violence to themselves or others may be mentally disturbed or suicidal does not detract from the need. There was testimony that sinks, stand-up toilets, and beds can be and have been used by prisoners to harm themselves by banging against them or by other means. Deprivation of these articles for short periods during violent episodes was found to be constitutionally justifiable. There was sufficient evidence to support the district court's factual finding that the safety cell was used to control violent inmates, and that the inmates were confined to the safety cell only for short periods.

A county was liable to an inmate who was raped while she was a jail inmate. Rampant sexual misconduct of employees toward female inmates was shown. The director of the jail was the final policymaker for the county and had notice of sexual incidents. In violation of the Eighth Amendment, he failed to investigate incidents or to take disciplinary action. The failure of the director to address sexual misconduct by jail personnel was the moving force behind the violation of the raped inmate's rights.[111]

A suit by female residents of a state detention facility for juveniles who were sexually assaulted by a youth development aide at the facility against the executive director of the facility was dismissed. The claim was that the policies and procedures approved by him created an unreasonably unsafe environment that allowed abuse. The director was not aware of any pattern of known injuries, and was not deliberately indifferent to a great and obvious risk of safety to the residents.[112]

A county was also liable to jail inmates who were beaten by other jail inmates based on deliberate indifference to a substantial risk of serious harm. The county failed to maintain the jail building. Sewage leaked from pipes, sinks and toilets were dilapidated and inoperable, windows could not be closed, shards of broken glass lay on window sills, and vermin entered the jail through windows and wall cracks. The inmates could and did fashion weapons by vandalizing the dilapidated physical structure. Cell locks on the second floor were broken and jailers did not have any surveillance system. The jail was grossly understaffed, and had no system for segregating inmates with mental illness or for other reasons.[113]

Constitutional rights were violated when inmates were held outside while prison officials quelled a disturbance. The inmates were forced to stay in a prone position for most of several days, without proper sanitation facilities, temperatures were alternately extremely hot and below freezing, and the inmates were not afforded blankets or proper drinking water or food.[114]

---

[111]   Ware v. Jackson County, 150 F.3d 873 (8th Cir. 1998).
[112]   Beers-Capitol v. Whetzel, 256 F.3d 120 (3d Cir. 2001).
[113]   Marsh v. Butler County, 225 F.3d 1243 (11th Cir. 2002), *on reh'g remanded*, 268 F.3d 1014 (11th Cir. 2001).
[114]   Johnson v. Lewis, 217 F.3d 726 (9th Cir. 2000).

Prison officials did not violate an inmate's rights by forcing him to perform certain field work despite his asthma, where after receiving a complaint from the inmate, the prison officials contacted medical staff members who informed the officials that the assigned work did not violate the inmate's medical duty status.[115]

Corrections officers were entitled to qualified immunity in a civil rights action by the mother of an inmate who died from heat exhaustion after collapsing while on a work squad in 72 degree weather. The supervisor did not compel inmates to perform physical labor in disregard of known serious medical needs, the inmate displayed no signs of physical difficulties prior to his collapse, and corrections officers promptly responded to the emergency and transported the inmate to the prison infirmary.[116]

Fecal contamination of blankets and clothing used to sop up sewage raises an Eighth Amendment claim. An inmate claimed that improper laundering caused blankets and clothes to continue to smell of sewage after laundering, and that when inmates re-rinsed clothes, the resulting rinse water was brown. However, the inmate did not prove a deliberate indifference by prison officials.[117]

However, an inmate demonstrated a serious condition-of-confinement claim, where he alleged that he was required to live in a feces-covered cell for three days without access to cleaning supplies.[118]

An Eighth Amendment claim is shown where an inmate suffered a six-month deprivation of all out-of-cell exercise due to a lockdown to conduct an extensive shakedown of a prison and to implement new security measures. Reasonable officials should have known that such complete and lengthy deprivation of exercise was constitutionally questionable.[119]

An inmate who was deprived of a lower bunk, subjected to a flooded cell, and deprived of a working toilet did not state a claim under the civil rights act. The claims, although not frivolous, referred to temporary inconveniences and did not demonstrate that conditions fell beneath the minimal civilized measure of life's necessities as measured by a contemporary standard of decency.[120]

Constitutional rights were violated by unsanitary conditions and prolonged cold in cells, where prison employees had actual knowledge of conditions. They made daily rounds and were directly responsible for placing inmates in inhumane conditions.[121]

A pretrial detainee slipped in a shower and injured himself. The defendants failed to repair the shower in his unit for more than nine months even though they were alerted to the conditions in the shower area several times.

---

[115] Lewis v. Lynn 236 F.3d 766 (5th Cir. 2001).
[116] Mays v. Rhodes, 255 F.3d 644 (8th Cir. 2001).
[117] Shannon v. Graves, 257 F.3d 1164 (11th Cir. 2001).
[118] McBride v. Deer, 240 F.3d 1287 (11th Cir. 2001).
[119] Delaney v. DeTella, 123 F. Supp. 2d 429 (N.D. Ill. 2000) , aff'd, remanded, 256 F.3d 679 (7th Cir. 2001).
[120] Dellis v. Correctional Corp. of Am., 257 F.3d 508 (6th Cir. 2001).
[121] Gaston v. Coughlin, 249 F.3d 156 (2d Cir. 2001).

The exposure of the detainee to the unsanitary and hazardous showering area for more than nine months was "sufficiently serious" to meet an objective element of a due process claim based upon conditions of his confinement.[122]

A county's promulgation and implementation of a program requiring pretrial detainees to reimburse the county for confinement costs and booking fees did not violate clearly established statutory or constitutional rights that a reasonable person would have known to be invalid or unconstitutional. Defendants were entitled to qualified immunity.[123]

A claim that radium levels of prison water supply exceeded federal maximums and a failure of prison administration to provide a maximally safe environment completely free of pollution or safety hazards did not violate the Eighth Amendment. Other state water systems had similar problems, and concentration of radium was less than one-half the maximum in a proposed revision of existing standards.[124]

See also § 7.1 and § 13.3.

§ 12.7 Correctional Personnel

There are several unique problems that affect correctional personnel. As free people they are entitled, of course, to the full measure of liberty accorded all other persons. However, two counterforces may circumscribe the exercise of such liberty. First, prison employees who are also police officers are subject to the same occupationally generated need for uniformity and discipline as regular civil police forces. There is a paramilitary aspect to prison employment, and certain sacrifices must be made by the employees so that the police power of the state may be most efficiently used and effectively displayed. In *Kelley v. Johnson*,[125] the United States Supreme Court upheld a county regulation that specified its police officers' hair length. The Court concluded that whether a state or local government's choice to have its police in uniform reflects a desire to make police officers readily recognizable to the public or to foster the esprit de corps that similarity of garb and appearance may inculcate within the police force itself, the justification for the hair length regulation is sufficiently rational to defeat a claim based upon the liberty guarantee of the Fourteenth Amendment.[126]

The second counterforce to the untrammeled exercise of the constitutional liberties of correctional personnel applies equally to uniformed and nonuniformed employees. The institutional needs of security, order, and rehabilitation provide the basis for certain limitations upon such employees' liberties. Limitations upon the right to be free from searches and seizures and upon the exer-

---

[122] Curry v. Kerik, 163 F. Supp. 2d 232 (S.D.N.Y 2001).
[123] Allen v. Leis, 154 F. Supp. 2d 1240 (S.D. Ohio 2001).
[124] Carroll v. DeTella, 255 F.3d 470 (7th Cir. 2001).
[125] 425 U.S. 238 (1976).
[126] *Id.*

cise of the rights to free association are examples of the numerous daily adjustments that correctional personnel must make when they physically cross the barriers between prison society and free society. The smuggling of contraband into prisons is so dangerous to institutional order that its prevention outweighs the probable cause requirement that normally limits searches and seizures in free society. Rehabilitative considerations can dictate that correctional personnel limit or minimize their personal associations with inmates.

Another aspect of corrections work is the standard prohibition against the use of armed trusties, or inmate assistants, as correctional officers. Once quite prevalent, this practice is now limited[127] to areas such as medical services. Medically trained inmate assistants are encouraged in addition to, although not as total fulfillment of, the prison's medical services staff.[128] Some prison systems, however, still use unarmed trusties as corridor bosses.[129]

Employees are also subject to search. A visual body cavity search of a prison employee was constitutionally permissible where the search was within the scope of a warden's authority. The warden had a particularized and individualized tip from an informant that the employee was bringing contraband into the prison hidden in a tampon on a specific occasion.[130]

In *Armstrong v. Newark State Comm. of Corrections*,[131] it was held that there was no justification in subjecting a correctional officer to a body cavity search where there was only a bare assertion that officials had received information that the officer was involved in smuggling contraband, and there were no other articulable facts to support the allegation.

§ 12.8   Rights of Privacy

The right of privacy of female prisoners customarily housed inside cells in a county jail was infringed by the failure to provide toilets sheltered from general vision. Consequently, the failure to provide prisoners with clean bedding, towels, clothing, sanitary mattresses, toilet articles, and sanitary napkins for female prisoners violates constitutional rights.[132] However, female officers may perform frisk searches of male prison inmates. Although it may be humiliating and degrading, it is not offensive to the Constitution.[133]

Searches also involve the right of privacy. *See* §12.4.

---

[127]   Finney v. Arkansas Board of Corrections, 505 F.2d 194 (8th Cir. 1974); Alberti v. Sheriff of Harris Co., Tex., 406 F. Supp. 649 (S.D. Tex. 1975).
[128]   Gates v. Collier, 501 F.2d 1291 (5th Cir. 1974).
[129]   Taylor v. Sterrett, 499 F.2d 367 (5th Cir. 1974).
[130]   Leverette v. Bell, 247 F.3d 160 (4th Cir. 2001).
[131]   545 F. Supp. 728 (N.D.N.Y. 1982).
[132]   Dawson v. Kendrick, 527 F. Supp. 1252 (S.D. W. Va. 1982).
[133]   Smith v. Fairman, 678 F.2d 52 (7th Cir. 1982).

§ 12.9   Ex Post Facto

Inmates often attack laws and regulations that affect them adversely on the ground that the application of the law or regulation to them violates the ex post facto clause of the Constitution. An example is *Dominique v. Weld.*[134] A sentenced inmate was returned to confinement after he had been allowed to participate in a work-release program for almost four years. It was asserted that the administrative action violated the ex post facto clause[135] based on a new state regulation governing the treatment and movement of sex offenders from commitment to release. The regulation became effective in October 1994, at which time the inmate was incarcerated at the medium-security facility to which he had been transferred following his removal from work-release earlier that year. He did not dispute the Commonwealth's contention that under the regulation, he was ineligible to participate in the work-release program. The inmate was an identified sex offender who could not be moved to a minimum-security facility, with associated privileges, unless and until he successfully completed a treatment program, admitted his offense, and otherwise obtained approval for a transfer.

The policy requires identified sex offenders to complete a four-phase treatment program at a medium-security facility as a precondition for transfer. It outlines further transition phases and evaluation processes as well.

According to the Supreme Court, the proper focus of ex post facto inquiry is whether the relevant change "alters the definition of criminal conduct or increases the penalty by which a crime is punishable."[136]

California Department of Corrections v. Morales examined a California statutory amendment that authorized the Board of Prison Terms to defer for up to three years parole suitability hearings for multiple murderers. The Supreme Court found no ex post facto violation, because the amendment created only the most speculative and attenuated possibility of producing the prohibited effect of increasing the measure of punishment for covered crimes. The Supreme Court did not develop a precise formula; rather, it said these judgments must be a matter of "degree." However, a change that simply alters the method to be followed in fixing a parole release date under identical substantive standards, but does not change the applicable sentencing range, was insufficient.[137]

---

[134]   73 F.3d 1156 (1st Cir. 1996).

[135]   The ex post facto clause provides that "No State shall . . . pass any . . . ex post facto law." U.S. CONST., art. I, § 10. Ex post facto laws include "every law that changes the punishment, and inflicts a greater punishment, than the law annexed to the crime, when committed." Miller v. Florida, 482 U.S. 423 (1987) (quoting Calder v. Bull, 3 U.S. (Dall.) 386, 390, 1 L. Ed. 648 (1798)).

[136]   California Department of Corrections v. Morales, 514 U.S. 499 (1995); *see also* Collins v. Youngblood, 497 U.S. 37 (1990).

[137]   *See* Miller v. Florida, 482 U.S. 423 (1987) in which a violation was found when a statutory amendment increased presumptive sentencing ranges for certain sexual offenses and permitted departure only for clear and convincing reasons; Weaver v. Graham, 450 U.S. 24 (1981), in which a violation was found where the statute retroactively reduced "gain time" credits to prisoners, thereby eliminating the lower end of the possible range of prison terms.

In this case, the regulation did not increase the penalty by which the inmate's crime was punishable. The change in the conditions determining the nature of his confinement while serving his sentence was held to be an allowed alteration in the prevailing "legal regime" rather than an "increased penalty" for ex post facto purposes. Further, the change did not affect the length of the inmate's sentence or his parole options.

Another example is *Williams v. Lee.*[138] After the inmate, who was confined at the South Dakota State Penitentiary, violated his parole, the state of South Dakota, acting on the authority of legislation enacted after Williams had committed the offense that resulted in his conviction and sentence, revoked his accumulated good-time credits. The application of the statute to the inmate violated the ex post facto clause.[139]

A state violates the ex post facto clause of the Constitution if it attempts to punish as a crime an act that was not criminal when done, removes a defense that was available when the act was committed, or increases the punishment for a crime after it was committed.[140] For a law to run afoul of this ban, it must be retrospective—that is, it must apply to events that occurred before its enactment, and it must disadvantage the offender affected by it.[141]

§ 12.10   Conclusion

As this chapter has demonstrated, incarceration is much more than merely a change in location or an obstacle to physical mobility. It is a fundamental change in one's constitutional status. There is one final consideration that is relevant in this regard. There is a grain of truth to the oft-repeated aphorism that a society is best judged by its prisons, and the treatment of its outcasts. Certainly the accomplishments of science and the arts are a correct measure of the character of a people. However, a society's ethics, as manifested by its treatment of those who have offended it, may be a more telling characteristic. Beyond considerations such as "there but for the grace of God go I," a society's treatment of its prison inmates can be viewed as the constitutional floor below which society will tolerate no variations in condition. The treatment of prison inmates may be characterized as a society's moral lowest common denominator.

In a pluralistic society such as America, there can be no moral ceiling. This is the essence of our theory and practice—people are and of right ought to be free to realize their potential, to reach their own level. However, given our society's relatively haphazard processes of socialization and values inter-

---

[138]   Williams v. Lee, 33 F.3d 1010 (8th Cir. 1994).

[139]   For an example of ex post facto application to parole, *see* Shabazz v. Gary, 900 F. Supp. 118 (E.D. Mich. 1995); *see also* § 9.2 and § 9.6, regarding ex post facto application to parole and probation.

[140]   Collins v. Youngblood, 497 U.S. 37 (1990).

[141]   Weaver v. Graham, 450 U.S. 24 (1981); *See also* § 9.2, Parole is Not a Right, and in particular *Kellogg v. Shoemaker.*

nalization, failure, though somewhat less prevalent than success, is still rather commonplace. Thus, the need for some externally dictated minimum standard is felt. Our criminal codes fill this need, but create the problem of defining the constitutional status of the resultant inmates. The evolving solution to this problem is that prison inmates retain all the rights of free people except those that are inconsistent with the institutional needs of security, order, and rehabilitation, and of necessity must be withdrawn during incarceration. The determination of which rights are restricted and which are guaranteed is at the root of the explosive increase and frenzied pace of prison-related litigation today. As our society evidences the evolving standards of decency that mark the progress of a maturing society, reassessment of prior determinations will be necessary and, thus, the need for prison-related litigation will be constant.

The Prison Litigation
Reform Act   13

Chapter Outline

§ 13.1 Introduction

During the past 20 years there has been a virtual explosion of lawsuits in the federal courts by prisoners challenging the conditions of their confinement or otherwise alleging violations of their constitutional rights.

During the 1960s, prisoners filed only a few hundred such suits in the federal courts. In 1993, the number rose to more than 33,000, and in 1994 to more than 39,000. These cases absorbed more than 15 percent of the federal caseload and an inordinate amount of judicial time and energy. Judicial orders involved issues ranging from the temperature of food to whether a prisoner's hair could be cut only by a licensed barber. Lawsuits alleged constitutional violations for a prisoner receiving Converse shoes rather than Reebok shoes and claims that prison guards got a prisoner's pinochle cards wet after the prisoner had intentionally flooded his own cell. It has been estimated that more than 70 percent of such lawsuits were without merit and indeed frivolous. In the Ninth Circuit, the figure was more than 99 percent.[1]

From the author's personal experience, the burden on prison administrators in answering pretrial discovery requests and making court appearances is overwhelming and occupies a considerable amount of time.

As many of these lawsuits were filed by prisoners who were indigent, the costs of litigation were in effect paid by the taxpayers. There was no meaningful disincentive to filing lawsuit after lawsuit. If a prisoner were lucky, filing a lawsuit might gain him or her a trip to a federal court and a day out of the routine life of a prison. Perjury or filing false documents was not a disincentive, and it is not uncommon for prisoners to tailor the facts of their complaint to those of a federal court decision granting relief in another case.

Public opinion strongly supported reform. Whether true or not, stories were reported that prisons were nothing less than country clubs, where the prisoners enjoyed a standard of living surpassing many citizens in free society, with luxuries such as cable TV, catered food, and exercise facilities. Federal judicial orders required medical facilities in prisons that sometimes surpassed the facilities available to law-abiding citizens.[2]

---

[1]   *See* the comments of various Senators at 141 Cong. Rec. S14413 (September 27, 1995).

[2]   The medical facilities and conditions at the maximum-security state prison in Lucasville, Ohio, far exceed that of Vinton County with a population of more than 15,000.

The federal judiciary was accused of micro-managing state courts and state prison systems. Dangerous prisoners were being released back into the community by federal judicial mandate, due to chronic overcrowding in jails and prisons. Jail and prison administrators were being ousted from their ability to run the institutions by expensive court-appointed masters who were responsible only to the courts that had appointed them. Considerable expenses were charged back to the local and state governments.

§ 13.2 Congressional Legislation

Prior to 1995, it was relatively easy for prisoners to file federal lawsuits alleging violations of constitutional rights. However, in 1994 Congress restricted the federal courts in cases involving overcrowding of prisons.[3] When such cases were before the federal judiciary, the statute required a prisoner to show that the crowding resulted in cruel and unusual punishment against him or her in violation of the Eighth Amendment.[4] Relief under the statute for this violation could extend no further than was necessary to remove those conditions.[5] The statute also prohibited the imposition of population caps unless the overcrowding was inflicting cruel and unusual punishment on identified prisoners in violation of the Eighth Amendment.[6] One restriction on this provision, however, was to permit judicial intervention to award equitable relief for cruel and unusual conditions other than overcrowding. In other words, the restrictions on the federal judiciary in the statute were limited to cases involving overcrowding.[7]

No federal statute required any particular judicial screening of prisoner lawsuits. However, prisoners without funds were subject to 15 U.S.C. § 1915, dealing with proceedings *in forma pauperis*. Under this statute, indigent prisoners could file a lawsuit without paying the filing fee and other costs normally incurred by litigants. The only requirement was the filing of an affidavit showing indigency. However, the statute did authorize the federal courts to dismiss a case if the allegations of poverty were untrue or if satisfied that the action was frivolous or malicious.[8]

These relaxed standards changed on April 26, 1996, when President Clinton signed into law the Prison Litigation Reform Act. The emphasis and purpose of the new legislation was to limit the ability of prisoners to complain about their conditions of confinement and to limit the jurisdiction of the federal courts to issue orders relieving conditions of confinement that allegedly violated the constitutional rights of the prisoners. The Act was also intended

---

3   18 U.S.C. § 3626 (1998).
4   18 U.S.C. § 3626(a)(1) (1998).
5   18 U.S.C. § 3626(a)(2) (1998).
6   18 U.S.C. § 3626(b)(1) (1998).
7   18 U.S.C. § 3626(b)(2) (1998).
8   28 U.S.C. § 1915(d) (1998).

to give the states more authority to manage their prison systems and to prevent federal judges from micro-managing state and local prison systems. Congress, in effect, mandated a return to "hard time" for prisoners.

The reason that Congress amended the PLRA in 1995—which precluded the bringing of any action with respect to prison conditions under 42 U.S.C. § 1983, or any other federal law, by state prisoners confined in any jail, prison, or other correctional facility until available administrative remedies were exhausted—was to reduce the quantity and improve quality of prisoner suits. In the Act, Congress intended to give corrections officials time and opportunity to address complaints internally before allowing initiation of a federal lawsuit.[9] The Act does not define "prison conditions," and applies to all inmate suits seeking redress for prison circumstances or occurrences, whether suits involved general circumstances or particular episodes, and whether the lawsuit alleges excessive force or some other wrong.[10]

The PLRA limits when courts can award "prospective relief." This is defined as relief "other than compensatory monetary damages," in cases challenging the legality of conditions of confinement in correctional facilities. Further, the PLRA places additional limitations on the issuance of "prisoner release orders," or population caps. The purpose or effect of these court orders is to reduce the size of the inmate population in correctional facilities. The PLRA also restricts the length of time that a preliminary injunction can remain in effect in a prison conditions lawsuit. Unless the court makes certain findings prescribed by the statute, any preliminary injunction automatically expires 90 days after the date on which it was issued.

The PLRA also places restrictions on the remedial relief courts can award in prison conditions cases. Under the PLRA's "Termination of Relief" provision, any prospective relief awarded in a prison conditions case must generally be terminated, on the motion of a defendant or intervenor, unless the relief is ordered with sufficient findings by the court that the relief is needed to remedy a violation of a federal right, extends no further than necessary to correct the violation, is narrowly drawn, and is the least intrusive means of correcting the violation. If the court did not previously make those findings, the prospective relief must be terminated unless the court makes new written findings that the relief is needed to rectify a current and ongoing violation of the federal right, extends no further than necessary to correct the violation, is "narrowly drawn," and is the least intrusive means of remedying the violation.

A stay of the prospective relief awarded in a prison conditions case is mandated if the court fails to rule on a termination motion within 30 days of filing. For "good cause," the court can, however, postpone the operation of the automatic stay for up to 60 additional days.

---

[9]   *See* Booth v. Churner, 532 U.S. 731 (2001) and Porter v. Nussle, 534 U.S. 516 (2002). *See* the full PLRA in Appendix II.

[10]   *Ibid.*

The PLRA places a number of restrictions on the appointment, compensation, and powers of special masters in prison conditions cases. Special masters are forbidden from engaging in any ex parte communications with the parties, or with one party without the presence of the other.

In order to limit the filing of frivolous lawsuits by inmates, there are a number of provisions in the PLRA to accomplish this end. First, inmates who cannot afford to pay the full filing fee when bringing a civil action or appeal usually must still pay an initial partial filing fee. The inmate must then generally make incremental payments each month thereafter until the balance of the filing fee has been paid. Second, under the "three strikes" provision, inmates who have had civil suits or appeals dismissed on three or more occasions because they were frivolous, malicious, or failed to state a claim for which relief can be granted must, in most cases, must pay the full filing fee up front when bringing a lawsuit or appeal in a civil case. Only if an inmate is unable to pay the full fee and is facing an imminent threat of serious physical injury can the inmate with three strikes bring a complaint or appeal *in forma pauperis*.[11] Third, the PLRA mandates a physical injury requirement. Inmates cannot seek monetary damages for mental or emotional injuries sustained while they were in custody unless they also suffered a physical injury. Fourth, federal courts must screen prisoners' civil complaints and dismiss any claims that are frivolous or malicious, fail to state a claim upon which relief can be granted, or seek damages from a defendant with immunity from damages liability. The PLRA authorizes a dismissal on these grounds by the court itself. A motion by the defendant is not necessary.

Further, a federal inmate whom a court finds has brought a claim for malicious reasons or to harass the defendant can lose good-time credits, thereby extending the length of his or her incarceration. Courts can also revoke credits earned by a federal prisoner who testifies falsely or otherwise knowingly presents false evidence to the court.

The PLRA limits the amount of the attorney's fees that the court can award to prevailing prisoners.[12] The fee restrictions include a requirement that the fees be proportionately related to the relief awarded by the court. For example, if an inmate receives an award of damages, a portion of the judgment, not to exceed 25 percent, must be paid toward the attorney's fees awarded against the defendant. If the fee award does not exceed 150 percent of the judgment, the defendant must pay the balance of the fee award. There is also a limitation on the hourly rate that can be used when calculating the fee award. The Act directs that the hourly rate not exceed 150 percent of the hourly rate under the Criminal Justice Act.

One of the most important provisions of the PLRA is that prisoners, jail inmates, and certain juveniles confined in correctional or detention facilities must exhaust any available administrative remedies before filing a lawsuit in

---

[11]   *See* Higgins v. Carpenter, 258 F.3d 797 (8th Cir. 2001).
[12]   42 U.S.C. § 1988.

federal court. This applies even when an inmate seeks only money damages even though the administrative process has no provision for recovery of money damages.[13]

§ 13.2.1 —Remedial Discretion Is Restricted

The Act amended § 18 U.S.C. 3626 in three significant ways:

1. New requirements for prospective judicial relief are required in all civil actions concerning the conditions of confinement in prisons.

In any civil action concerning the conditions of confinement of a prisoner, a federal court cannot grant or approve any prospective relief unless it finds that such relief is narrowly drawn, extends no further than necessary to correct the violation of a federal right, and is the least intrusive means necessary to correct the violation of any federal right.[14] Prospective relief includes all relief other than compensatory monetary damages, including preliminary injunctive relief.[15]

2. The availability of prisoner release orders as a remedial option is limited.

No release order may be entered unless the federal court has already ordered less intrusive relief and that the relief ordered has failed to remedy the deprivation of the federal right sought to be remedied, and that the prison officials have had a reasonable period in which to comply with the earlier relief.[16] Further, only a three-judge panel is authorized to enter a release order and then only after the panel has found by clear and convincing evidence that overcrowding is the primary cause of the violation of a federal right and that no other remedy would remedy the violation of the federal right.[17]

3. Previously granted prospective judicial relief is automatically stayed and potentially terminated, pending a hearing.

The termination provision provides that in any prison conditions case, prospective relief is terminable upon the motion of any party or intervenor two years after the date the court granted or approved the prospective relief; one year after the date the court has entered an order denying termination of prospective relief under the Act; or in the case of an order issued on or before the date of enactment of the Act, two years after such date of enactment.[18]

---

13   *See* Booth v. Churner, 532 U.S. 731 (2001); Porter v. Nussle, 534 U.S. 516 (2002).
14   18 U.S.C. § 3626(a)(1)(A) (1998).
15   18 U.S.C. § 3626(g)(7); 18 U.S.C. § 3626(a)(2) (1998).
16   18 U.S.C. § 3626(a)(3)(A)(i) (1998).
17   18 U.S.C. § 3626(a)(3)(B), (E) (1998).
18   18 U.S.C. § 3626(b)(1) (1998).

Either the prison authorities or an intervener is entitled to the immediate termination of prospective relief if the federal court approved or granted the relief without a finding that it met the initial three requirements for relief listed above. The relief may be continued, however, if the federal court makes written findings that the prospective relief remains necessary to correct a current or ongoing violation of a federal right, extends no further than necessary to correct the violation of the federal right, and that the prospective relief is narrowly drawn and the least intrusive means of correcting the violation.[19] Finally, while the motion for termination is pending, the prospective relief must be stayed automatically on the thirtieth day after the motion was filed.[20]

In 1997, Congress amended the Act's automatic stay provision.[21] Prior to the amendments, the automatic stay provision instituted an automatic stay of all prospective relief on the thirtieth day after the filing of a motion to terminate such relief. The amended provision additionally permits a court to "postpone the effective date of an automatic stay . . . for not more than 60 days for good cause."[22] "Good cause" does not include matters concerning the general congestion of a court's calendar.

Congress also added a subsection providing for interlocutory appeal of "any order staying, suspending, delaying, or barring the operation of the automatic stay," other than an order postponing the stay for up to 60 days pursuant to § 3626(e)(3).[23]

The authority of federal judges to fashion relief for the improvement of prison conditions was significantly restricted, particularly with respect to population caps and prisoner release orders.

§ 13.2.2 —Abusive Litigation Is Restricted and Disincentives to Prisoner Lawsuits Are Provided

The Act provides several amendments to 28 U.S.C. § 1915 to discourage the filing of meritless lawsuits by prisoners.

1. Prisoners are required to file a trust fund account statement when they seek to file a claim or appeal as an indigent. Further, prisoners must make at least partial payment of the filing fees and costs in all civil suits and appeals.[24]

---

[19]   18 U.S.C. § 3626(b)(3) (1998).
[20]   18 U.S.C. § 3626(e)(2) (1998).
[21]   Pub. L. No. 105-119, § 123, 111 Stat. 2440, 2470 (1997).
[22]   § 123(a)(3)(c), 111 Stat. at 2470, amending 18 U.S.C. § 3626(e) (1998).
[23]   § 123(a)(4), 111 Stat. at 2470, amending 18 U.S.C. § 3626(e) (1998).
[24]   28 U.S.C. § 1915(a)(2); (b)(1) (1998).

If a prisoner cannot pay the full amount at the time of filing, the prisoner's account will be attached each month until the fee is paid.[25] There are provisions, however, that permit a truly indigent prisoner to file his or her claim or appeal without financial burden.[26]

>   2. Federal courts may summarily dismiss such a case at any time if they find that the complaint fails to state a claim upon which relief may be granted.[27]

This new disincentive also requires a prisoner to pay the entire filing fee even when a federal court dismisses the case.

>   3. There is a "three strikes" provision that bars indigent prisoners from filing new lawsuits when they have previously filed frivolous or meritless claims unless there is an immediate threat of physical harm.[28]

§ 13.2.3 —Courts May Dismiss Prisoner Suits and Prisoners Must Exhaust All Administrative Remedies Before Filing Suit in a Federal Court; Claims for Mental or Emotional Injuries Are Limited

Section 1997e of Title 42 gives a federal judge the authority to dismiss any action brought by a prisoner with respect to conditions of confinement on the basis of frivolity, maliciousness, failure to state a claim under the Federal Rules of Civil Procedure, or a defendant's immunity.[29] Unlike 42 U.S.C. § 1915, which provides sanctions only against indigent prisoners, § 1997e permits a federal court to dismiss non-indigent filings.

Further, a federal court may now revoke a portion of a prisoner's earned release credit if it determines that the prisoner filed a lawsuit for a malicious purpose, solely to harass the defendants, or if the prisoner knowingly presented false evidence or information to the court.[30] This provision should provide a meaningful disincentive to prisoners who file false affidavits regarding their indigent status.

Section 1997e(a) gives clear deference to state administrative procedures by providing that no action can be filed under § 1983 or any other federal law by a prisoner confined in any jail, prison, or other correctional facility until all available administrative remedies have been exhausted.

---

25   28 U.S.C. § 1915(b)(2) (1998).
26   28 U.S.C. § 1915(b)(4) (1998).
27   28 U.S.C. § 1915(e)(2(b)(ii) (1998).
28   28 U.S.C. § 1915(g) (1998).
29   42 U.S.C. § 1997e(c) (1998).
30   28 U.S.C. § 1932 (1998).

Finally, 42 U.S.C. § 1997e(e) provides that no federal civil action can be brought by a prisoner confined in a jail, prison, or other correctional facility, for mental or emotional injury suffered while in custody without a prior showing of a physical injury.

§ 13.2.4 —Screening of Cases

Under the Act, a federal court is required to review before docketing if feasible, or, in any event, as soon as practicable after docketing, a complaint in any civil action in which a prisoner seeks redress from a governmental entity, or officer or employee of a governmental entity.[31]

Under this procedure, a federal court is required to identify cognizable claims or dismiss the complaint, or any portion of the complaint, if the complaint is frivolous, malicious, or fails to state a claim upon which relief can be granted, or seeks monetary relief from a defendant who is immune from such relief.[32]

This provision applies to any incarcerated or detained person, adult or juvenile, who files a civil suit in federal court, and applies to both indigent and nonindigent prisoners.[33]

§ 13.3 Litigation

§ 13.3.1 —42 U.S.C. § 1915

The Second Circuit held that the fee requirements of the Prison Litigation Reform Act apply to extraordinary writs that seek relief analogous to civil complaints under 42 U.S.C. § 1983, but not to writs directed at judges conducting criminal trials.[34]

Several cases under § 1915 concerned suits that had already been filed by April 26, 1996 and the retroactive effect of the Prison Litigation Reform Act. Courts have held that the Act's provisions apply to cases pending prior to its passage. Further, the filing fee requirements do not violate equal protection guarantees.[35]

With respect to the "three strikes" rule, the Tenth Circuit stated that the Act announced a procedural rule and thus could be applied to prisoner suits that were dismissed prior to the Act's enactment. The Act did not change the merits of the prisoner's underlying action or legal consequences of any prisoner actions that were dismissed prior to enactment.[36]

---

[31]   42 U.S.C. § 1915A(a) (1998).
[32]   42 U.S.C. § 1915A(b) (1998).
[33]   42 U.S.C. § 1915A(c) (1998).
[34]   In re Nagy, 89 F.3d 115 (2d Cir. 1996).
[35]   Mitchell v. Farcass, 112 F.3d 1483 (11th Cir. 1997). *See also* Nicholas v. Tucker, 114 F.3d 17 (2d Cir. 1997).
[36]   Green v. Nottingham, 90 F.3d 415 (10th Cir. 1996).

A prisoner has "three strikes" when he or she has had three prior civil suits dismissed as frivolous, malicious, or for failure to state claim. A case presently before a court should not be counted, given the plain meaning of the Act's use of "prior."[37]

A lawsuit was dismissed under the "three strikes" rule prohibiting inmates from bringing a civil action *in forma pauperis*, where the inmate had previously filed three meritless suits and the inmate was not in imminent danger of any serious physical injury.[38]

However, the "three strikes" rule does not apply to habeas corpus petitions under 28 U.S.C. § 2254, because they are different from traditional civil actions. Its application would be contrary to a long tradition of ready access of prisoners to federal habeas corpus. Further, the nearly contemporaneous enactment of the Antiterrorism and Effective Death Penalty Act, which contains separate procedures for addressing abuses of the habeas corpus process, strongly suggested that Congress did not intend the Act to apply to habeas corpus petitions.[39]

An inmate in the Fifth Circuit had three or more qualifying dismissals under the Act, and thus, except for cases involving imminent danger of serious physical injury, would be barred from proceeding further as an indigent.[40]

A remand was required to determine whether a prisoner's previously dismissed § 1983 petitions were filed when he was a prisoner. It appeared likely that he had at least three dismissals that would trigger § 1915(g).[41]

In light of the fact that a state prisoner had previously filed 33 appeals and original proceedings, most of which were summarily terminated or dismissed and five of which were dismissed as frivolous and with warning of sanctions, a court should direct the clerk not to accept any further filings from the prisoner, except those claiming imminent danger of serious physical injury, without payment of the filing fee.[42]

A dismissal of a prisoner's suit as frivolous counts as a "strike" even if the suit was not brought *in forma pauperis*. The Act does not limit "strikes" to actions brought *in forma pauperis*. A prisoner who had brought three suits or appeals that lacked sufficient merit to go beyond pleadings or were outright an abuse of process was not an appealing candidate for a waiver of the filing fee in the fourth and later cases, even if he paid for the previous suits.[43]

In the Second Circuit, an *in forma pauperis* prisoner was not required to comply with the Act's fee provisions because his appeal was fully briefed, considered by the appellate court, and deemed submitted for decision before the

---

[37] Pigg v. FBI, 106 F.3d 1497 (10th Cir. 1997).

[38] Higgins v. Carpenter, 258 F.3d 797 (8th Cir. 2001).

[39] Smith v. Angelone, 111 F.3d 1126 (4th Cir. 1997); Carson v. Johnson, 112 F.3d 818 (5th Cir. 1997); United States v. Simmonds, 111 F.3d 737 (10th Cir. 1997); Anderson v. Singletary, 111 F.3d 801 (11th Cir. 1997); United States v. Levi, 111 F.3d 955 (D.C. Cir. 1997).

[40] Adepegba v. Hammons, 103 F.3d 383 (5th Cir. 1996).

[41] Arvie v. Lastrapes, 106 F.3d 1230 (5th Cir. 1997).

[42] Schlicher v. Thomas, 111 F.3d 777 (10th Cir. 1997). *See also* Keener v. Pennsylvania Bd. of Probation & Parole, 128 F.3d 143 (3d Cir. 1997).

[43] Duvall v. Miller, 122 F.3d 489 (7th Cir. 1997).

Act became effective. According to the court, requiring him to comply with the Act's fee provisions would not further any congressional purpose of reducing the state's burden of responding to frivolous actions or of deterring frivolous prisoner litigation.[44]

However, the Fifth Circuit held that a prisoner whose appeal was pending on the effective date of the Act would be given 30 days to either pay the filing fee in a civil suit or file an affidavit of assets, including a statement by the custodian of his trust fund account for the six-month period immediately preceding the date of filing the notice of appeal.[45] The Fifth Circuit also stated that the Act applied to cases pending on the date of its enactment, requiring prisoners to meet the Act's procedural mandates. The Act impaired no rights, created no new liability, imposed no new duties, and did not affect the substance of an underlying appeal.[46]

The Second Circuit also held that the Act's fee requirements did not apply to a released prisoner. A literal reading of the Act as applied to released prisoners was not possible. The Act was construed to mean that required partial fee payments are to be made only while a prisoner remains in prison, and upon release his obligation to pay fees is determined, like any nonprisoner, solely by whether he qualifies for *in forma pauperis* status.[47]

The Third Circuit held that the filing fee requirements of the Act do not apply to *in forma pauperis* habeas corpus petitions and appeals because the definition of "civil action" in the Act is not plain. Habeas corpus petitions are hybrid actions whose nature is not adequately captured by the term, certain other federal laws applicable to civil actions are not applicable to habeas corpus actions, and Congress enacted the Act primarily to curtail claims brought by prisoners under 42 U.S.C. § 1983 and the Federal Tort Claims Act, most of which are routinely dismissed as legally frivolous.[48]

However, a petition for a writ of mandamus is a "civil action" for purposes of the Act.[49]

With respect to appeals filed on or after its effective date, the Act applies even if the prisoner was released before the full filing and docket fees had been paid. The prisoner's current status did not alter the fact that he was a prisoner when he filed the appeals. The Act is clear in requiring the prisoner to pay the full amount of the filing fee.[50]

The filing fee provisions of the Act were held constitutional in the Fourth Circuit.[51] Similarly, the Fourth Circuit upheld the Act regarding a challenge that it limits indigent prisoners' access to the courts.[52]

---

[44]   Ramsey v. Coughlin, 94 F.3d 71 (2d Cir. 1996); Duamutef v. O'Keefe, 98 F.3d 22 (2d Cir. 1996).

[45]   Moreno v. Collins, 105 F.3d 955 (5th Cir. 1997).

[46]   Strickland v. Rankin County Correctional Facility, 105 F.3d 972 (5th Cir. 1997).

[47]   McGann v. Commissioner, 96 F.3d 28 (2d Cir. 1996).

[48]   Santana v. United States, 98 F.3d 752 (3d Cir. 1996). The same approach was taken by the Ninth Circuit. Naddi v. Hill, 106 F.3d 275 (9th Cir. 1997) and Kincade v. Sparkman, 117 F.3d 949 (6th Cir. 1997).

[49]   In re Washington, 122 F.3d 1345 (10th Cir. 1997).

[50]   Robbins v. Switzer, 104 F.3d 895 (7th Cir. 1997).

[51]   Roller v. Gunn, 107 F.3d 227 (4th Cir. 1997).

[52]   Norton v. Dimazana, 122 F.3d 286 (5th Cir. 1997).

An inmate was not permitted to proceed with a § 1983 case *in forma pauperis* when the court was unable to consider which of two methods of payment was applicable to his case. The inmate failed to submit a certified copy of his inmate trust fund account statement for the six-month period immediately preceding the filing of the complaint.[53]

It was error for a district court to dismiss a prisoner's § 1983 complaint as frivolous after accepting his partial filing fee, before giving him the opportunity to correct any defects in the pleading.[54]

§ 13.3.2　—42 U.S.C. § 1915A

A § 1983 complaint was held to be plainly frivolous when an inmate alleged that the U.S. Attorney's Office, his court-appointed counsel, the U.S. probation officer, and five judges conspired and "fabricated" a statute with the specific goal of imprisoning him. The claim was "fantastical" and "delusional" and did not describe any cognizable action under color of state law.[55]

A *pro se* prisoner's self-styled federal tort claim was actually an abuse of the writ application process and was dismissed *sua sponte*. The prisoner, following four prior filings for federal habeas corpus relief, accused the U.S. Attorney of using illegally obtained evidence to coerce his guilty plea.[56]

However, a Court is not authorized to engage in the screening contemplated by § 1915A for *in forma pauperis* prisoners, when the prisoner, who had been a prisoner in a county jail, brought a § 1983 action against the county department of corrections and various of its employees, alleging that they beat and robbed him. The prisoner was not a prisoner at time he brought the suit.[57]

§ 13.3.3　—42 U.S.C. § 1997e

In principle, 42 U.S.C. § 1997e is constitutional. It neither nullifies the Eighth Amendment by leaving violations without a remedy nor violates the equal protection clause. The statute is rationally related to the stated purpose of Congress to limit frivolous lawsuits.[58]

The Sixth Circuit held that a District Court properly dismissed an inmate's civil rights complaint for failure to exhaust his administrative remedies. Although the inmate claimed that Michigan's administrative process was inadequate to redress his grievance, he did not allege that he was precluded from exhausting his administrative remedies at this point.[59]

---

[53]　Smith v. Urban, 928 F. Supp. 532 (E.D. Pa. 1996).
[54]　Church v. AG, 125 F.3d 210 (4th Cir. 1997).
[55]　Sandles v. Randa, 945 F. Supp. 169 (E.D. Wis. 1996).
[56]　Casiano v. United States, 953 F. Supp. 158 (S.D. Tex. 1997).
[57]　Kane v. Lancaster County Dep't of Corrections, 960 F. Supp. 219 (D.C. Neb. 1997).
[58]　Zehner v. Trigg, 133 F.3d 459 (7th Cir. 1997).
[59]　White v. McGinnis, 131 F.3d 593 (6th Cir. 1997).

The administrative exhaustion requirement of the amendment to 42 U.S.C. § 1997e(a) does not apply to appeals pending on the enactment date, as the statute expressly governs the bringing of new actions rather than disposition of pending cases.[60]

The Prison Litigation Reform Act requires a prisoner to exhaust "such administrative remedies as are available" before suing over prison conditions. An inmate claimed that corrections officers violated his Eighth Amendment right to be free from cruel and unusual punishment by assaulting him, using excessive force against him, and denying him medical attention to treat ensuing injuries. He sought various forms of injunctive relief and money damages. At the time, Pennsylvania provided an administrative grievance and appeals system that addressed the inmate's complaints but had no provision for recovery of money damages. Before resorting to federal court, the inmate filed an administrative grievance, but did not seek administrative review after the prison authority denied relief. In the lower federal courts, the lawsuit was dismissed because the inmate failed to exhaust his administrative remedies under Pennsylvania law. The Supreme Court affirmed, and held that an inmate seeking only money damages must complete any prison administrative process capable of addressing his or her complaint and providing some form of relief, even if the process does not make specific provision for monetary relief.[61]

The PLRA's exhaustion requirement applies to all inmate suits about prison life, whether they involve general circumstances or particular episodes, and whether they allege excessive force or some other wrong. The current exhaustion provision differs markedly from its predecessor. Once within the district court's discretion, exhaustion in prison condition cases is now mandatory.[62] Unlike the previous provision, which encompassed only § 1983 suits, exhaustion is now required for all actions brought with respect to prison conditions. The PLRA is designed to reduce the quantity and improve the quality of prisoner suits and to give corrections officials an opportunity to address complaints internally before allowing the initiation of a federal case. In some instances, corrective action taken in response to an inmate's grievance might improve prison administration and satisfy the inmate, thereby obviating the need for litigation. In other instances, the internal review might filter out some frivolous claims. And for cases ultimately brought to court, an administrative record clarifying the controversy's contours could facilitate adjudication.[63]

A 42 U.S.C. § 1983 complaint seeking damages for alleged emotional and mental injuries was dismissed without prejudice, when the plaintiffs could not show any physical injuries at the time. The prisoners and former prisoners

---

[60] Wright v. Morris, 111 F.3d 414 (6th Cir. 1997), *cert. denied,* 522 U.S. 906 (1997).

[61] Booth v. Churner, 532 U.S. 731 (2001).

[62] *See id.*

[63] *See* Porter v. Nussle, 534 U.S. 516 (2002).

could not obtain such damages for injuries occurring while in custody without showing "physical injury" within the meaning of 42 U.S.C. § 1997e(e).[64]

Physical touching is not enough to avoid the effects of the statute. An inmate's § 1983 claims for mental and emotional injuries were dismissed with leave to amend. The only alleged physical contact was that he had "bodily fluids thrown on" him. In order to recover for mental or emotional injury, the prisoner must allege a prior physical injury.[65]

§ 13.3.4 —42 U.S.C. § 3626

The Fourth Circuit held that 18 U.S.C. § 3626(b)(2) is constitutional and does not violate the separation of powers doctrine, the Fifth Amendment equal protection principles, or the due process clause of the Fifth Amendment.[66]

However, federal district courts do not easily relinquish their jurisdiction or power. The federal courts have a tendency to protect their "turf" from Congressional efforts to restrict their judicial jurisdiction or authority.

A Michigan district court held that the section was an unconstitutional encroachment by Congress into a court's final order, as it overturned the order until a later date.[67] The district court also held that the automatic stay provision of 18 U.S.C. § 3626(b), which allows the stay of any prospective relief that has been approved or granted beginning 30 days after a motion for termination of relief has been filed, violated the vested right doctrine grounded in the due process clause of the Fifth Amendment by removing prisoners' vested rights in a consent decree, which was a final judgment, without granting due process.[68] As a result, a consent decree reforming a state prison would not be disturbed by the District Court because, in its opinion, the statute violated the separation of powers by retroactively instructing federal courts to reopen final judgments.[69]

In May of 1998, The Sixth Circuit reversed and remanded the case to the District Court.[70] The Court of Appeals construed the Act's automatic stay provision to permit the courts to exercise their inherent equitable powers and thus did not give rise to an unconstitutional incursion by Congress into the powers reserved for the judiciary.

---

[64] Zehner v. Trigg, 952 F. Supp. 1318 (S.D. Ind. 1997). This case was criticized in Hollimon v. DeTella, (N.D. Ill. 1997), U.S. Dist. LEXIS 1083 and Calhoun v. DeTella (N.D. Ill. 1997) 1997 U.S. Dist. LEXIS 1745).

[65] Evans v. Allen, 981 F. Supp. 1102 (N.D. Ill. 1997).

[66] Plyler v. Moore, 100 F.3d 365 (4th Cir. 1996), *cert. denied,* 520 U.S. 1277 (1997).

[67] Hadix v. Johnson, 933 F. Supp. 1360 (E.D. Mich. 1966), *rev'd in,* Hadix v. Johnson, 144 F.3d 925 (6th Cir. 1998).

[68] *Ibid.*, motion gr. *sub nom.* Knop v. Johnson, 1996 U.S. Dist. LEXIS 16719 (W.D. Mich. 1996). *See also* Glover v. Johnson, 957 F. Supp. 110 (E.D. Mich. 1997).

[69] Hadix v. Johnson, 947 F. Supp. 1100 (E.D. Mich. 1996), *request gr.,* 947 F. Supp. 1113 (E.D. Mich. 1996), *rev'd in,* Hadix v. Johnson, 144 F.3d 925 (6th Cir. 1998).

[70] Hadix v. Johnson, 144 F.3d 925 (6th Cir. 1998).

Significant to the Sixth Circuit's ruling, after this case was submitted to the court on appeal, Congress amended the Act's automatic stay provision.[71] Whereas prior to the amendments the automatic stay provision instituted an automatic stay of all prospective relief on the thirtieth day after the filing of a motion to terminate such relief, the amended provision additionally permits a court to "postpone the effective date of an automatic stay . . . for not more than 60 days for good cause."[72] "Good cause" does not include matters concerning the general congestion of a court's calendar.

Although the amended provision enabled a court to extend for good cause the effective date of an automatic stay by 60 days, it still provided that a court-enforced consent decree would automatically be stayed if the court failed to make the findings required by § 3626(b)(3) within the prescribed period. Congress also added a subsection providing for interlocutory appeal of "any order staying, suspending, delaying, or barring the operation of the automatic stay," other than an order postponing the stay for up to 60 days pursuant to § 3626(e)(3).[73] Because the Act as amended implicitly recognizes the lower courts' discretionary power to stay an automatic stay in accordance with principles of equity, Congress did not intend to bar the courts from issuing orders suspending operation of the automatic stay.

The Sixth Circuit's interpretation of the amended statute and its accompanying legislative history indicated a failure of Congress to reveal any clear congressional intent to displace the equitable powers of the federal courts. Consequently, the Sixth Circuit construed the Act's automatic stay provision as preserving the courts' inherent power to suspend the automatic stay in accordance with general equitable principles. Given this construction, the amended automatic stay provision of the Act was held to be constitutional.

An Arizona district court held that a consent decree involving prison conditions would not be terminated, even though 18 U.S.C. § 3626(b)(2) provides for the immediate termination of the 1972 decree. According to this district court, legislative history clearly illustrated a congressional intent to set aside judgments made by "liberal federal judges" based on populist sentiment that courts were mollycoddling prisoners. According to this court, this is precisely the type of legislation that is inimical to separation of powers and is unconstitutional.[74]

One district court avoided the constitutional issue by deciding that for purposes of a motion under 18 U.S.C. § 3626 to terminate consent decrees governing certain conditions in city jails, decrees were not "final judgments"; thus, the statute did not violate the principle that the separation of powers doctrine prevents Congress from requiring courts to reopen final judgments. Rather, consent decrees were "executory judgments" that had prospective effects, and over which the court retained supervisory jurisdiction.[75]

---

[71] Pub. L. No. 105-119, § 123, 111 Stat. 2440, 2470 (1997).

[72] § 123(a)(3)(c), 111 Stat. at 2470, amending 18 U.S.C. § 3626(e) (1998).

[73] § 123(a)(4), 111 Stat. at 2470, amending 18 U.S.C. § 3626(e) (1998).

[74] Taylor v. Arizona, 972 F. Supp. 1239 (D. Ariz. 1997).

[75] Benjamin v. Jacobson, 935 F. Supp. 332 (S.D.N.Y. 1996).

The Act did not apply to a district court's order reinstating nine institutions that had been partially released from the court's supervision under a consent decree governing state prisons, because the court had yet to fashion prospective relief. Thus, the Act's provisions had not yet been triggered.[76]

Another means by which courts have circumvented the provisions of the Act is to label overcrowding as "failure to protect," which focused not on overcrowding, but on the manner of assignment of new prisoners to cells.[77]

Section 3626(b)(2) of Title 18 provides for the termination of prospective relief if relief was granted in the absence of a finding that relief extends no further than necessary to correct a violation of a "federal right." The term does not include rights conferred by consent decrees to the extent that those rights rise above the requirements of federal law.[78]

Prison inmates brought a class action, and the district court issued an injunction to remedy violations of the Eighth Amendment regarding conditions of confinement. Congress subsequently enacted the Prison Litigation Reform Act, which set a standard for the entry and termination of prospective relief in civil actions challenging prison conditions. Specifically, the Act provides that a defendant or intervenor may move to terminate prospective relief under an existing injunction that does not meet that standard. A court may not terminate such relief if it makes certain findings; and a motion to terminate such relief shall operate as a stay of that relief beginning 30 days after the motion is filed and ending when the court rules on the motion.

The Supreme Court held[79] that Congress clearly intended to make operation of the PLRA's automatic stay provision mandatory, precluding courts from exercising their equitable power to enjoin the stay. Under the Act, a stay is automatic once a state defendant has filed an appropriate motion, and the command that it shall operate as a stay during the specified period indicates that it is mandatory throughout that period. The PLRA provides for an appeal from an order *preventing* the automatic stay's operation, not from the *denial* of a motion to enjoin a stay. While construing the PLRA to remove courts' equitable discretion raises constitutional questions, the canon of constitutional doubt permits the Supreme Court to avoid such questions only where the saving construction is not plainly contrary to Congress' intent. Further, the PLRA does not violate separation of powers principles.

On the effective date of the PLRA, the prevailing market rate for attorney's fees was $150 per hour. However, the PLRA limits the size of fees that may be awarded to attorneys who litigate prisoner lawsuits. In Michigan, those fees were capped at a maximum hourly rate of $112.50. The Supreme Court held[80] that the PLRA limits attorney's fees for postjudgment monitoring services performed after the PLRA's effective date, but does not limit fees for monitoring performed before that date.

---

[76] Williams v. Edwards, 87 F.3d 126 (5th Cir. 1996).

[77] Jensen v. Clarke, 94 F.3d 1191 (8th Cir. 1996).

[78] Plyler v. Moore, 100 F.3d 365 (4th Cir. 1996), *cert. denied*, 520 U.S. 1277 (1997).

[79] Miller v. French, 530 U.S. 327 (2000).

[80] Martin v. Hadix, 527 U.S. 343 (1999).

Following a negative jury verdict in his civil trial, costs were imposed against an inmate in the amount of $3,857.35. The inmate first claimed that the PLRA was unconstitutional, as a large financial burden resulting from his unsuccessful litigation denies him access to the courts in violation of the First Amendment. This argument was rejected, as inmates asserting civil claims in federal court have never been guaranteed a "free ride." The court noted that because the payment provisions of the PLRA[81] levy a 20 percent "tax" on his monthly assets above $10, the inmate would not be that heavily affected on a day-to-day basis by the award. In prison, on the PLRA's "extended payment plan" and with his necessities provided for, the inmate's indigency is effectively mitigated.[82]

§ 13.4   Conclusion

The 1996 Prison Litigation Reform Act, as amended in 1997, was intended to have a substantial impact in limiting prisoner litigation and in curtailing the interference of federal judges in state and local correctional systems. Only time will tell how effective the Act will be in curtailing the propensities of federal district judges to exercise their power to remedy what they perceive as gross violations of constitutional rights by correctional administrators.

---

[81]   28 U.S.C. § 1915(b)(2).
[82]   Singleton v. Smith, 241 F.3d 534 (6th Cir. 2001).

Human Rights of Prisoners: A Comparison Study of the European Convention on Human Rights 14

Chapter Outline

§ 14.1 Introduction

In the United States, challenges to the inhumanity of correctional practices focus on the Constitution. Thus, by examining litigation and the criteria that the United States Supreme Court and lower courts have established, it is possible to form a picture of what constitutes the humane treatment of prisoners in the United States. On an international scale, however, how are prisoners' human rights created and protected?

A major instrument concerning human rights, instituted by the Council of Europe,[1] is the European Convention on Human Rights.[2] Although the Council of Europe is a regional institution, as opposed to a world institution, it serves as an example of the realistic implementation of international law into the realm of prisons. The Convention specifically speaks of human rights and fundamental freedoms. It is understood, however, that the Convention does not preempt the existing national standards of each member state, but is designed to complement those standards.

Without explaining in great detail the structure of the Council of Europe, it is important to distinguish between the mandatory and non-mandatory aspects of the Council's governing instruments. Resolutions adopted by the Council of Europe are treated as recommendations, and have no binding effect. However, of great importance is Resolution (73)5 of the Standard Minimum Rules for the Treatment of Prisoners and Resolution (87)3 of the European Prison Rules.[3] Under these resolutions, the Council of Europe's Committee of Ministers set minimum rules (recommendations) to be applied in the member states' legislation.

---

[1] Founded in 1949, with a membership of 45 in May 2003: Albania, Andorra, Armenia, Austria, Azerbaïjan, Belgium, Bosnia and Herzegouina, Bulgaria, Croatia, Cyprus, Czech Republic, Denmark, Estonia, Finland, France, Georgia, Germany, Greece, Hungary, Iceland, Ireland, Italy, Latvia, Liechtenstein, Lithuania, Luxembourg, Macedonia, Malta, Moldova, Netherlands, Norway, Poland, Portugal, Romania, Russian Federation, San Marino, Serbia and Montenegro, Slovak Republic, Slovenia, Spain, Sweden, Switzerland, Turkey, Ukraine, and the United Kingdom. It should be noted that under current policies, it is a precondition to joining the Council of Europe that the applicant state abolish the death penalty.

[2] The first multilateral treaty entered into by the Council of Europe on September 3, 1953, which has been signed and ratified by all the member states (hereinafter the Convention). *See* Appendix I.

[3] Resolution (73)5 was adopted on January 19, 1973. The Resolution reflects the Standard Minimum Rules adopted by the United Nations in 1957. Resolution (87)3 was adopted on February 12, 1987. *See* EUROPEAN LEGAL RULES, Council of Europe Press, Strasbourg, 1987.

There are a total of 100 articles in the European Prison Rules. (See Appendix II. *See also* European Prison Rules, Council of Europe Press, Strasbourg, 1987.) These articles could be and are used to formulate actual prison regulations in the member states under the separate internal laws of the member states.

In December, 1998, the executive branch of the European Union adopted a resolution pertaining to prison conditions in the European Union. The resolution can be found in Appendix IV.

Binding governing instruments in the Council of Europe, as opposed to the resolutions, are conventions. The convention of interest to the prisoners is the European Convention of Human Rights. By signing the European Convention, the member states have obligated themselves to respect the rights and freedoms of their separate states and those of other member states.

Under the Convention, a Commission was set up as a "human rights protection body." The number of members is equal to that of the contracting parties and they are elected for a period of six years.[4] The Commission is competent to deal with "any alleged breach of the provisions of the Convention" by another contracting state, but only at the request of another contracting state.[5] Subject to some restrictions, at the request of an individual, the Commission may investigate any violation by one of the contracting states.

However, Article 26 provides:

> The Commission may only deal with the matter after all domestic remedies have been exhausted, according to the generally recognized rules of international law, and within a period of six months from the date on which the final decision was taken.

Thus, review of claims by the Commission is somewhat limited. Also, by exercising its discretion, the Commission may deny applications if anonymous, or if the issue has been resolved by a prior decision, or if the petition is manifestly ill-founded or an abuse of the right of petition.[6] If an application is accepted, the Commission then acts as an investigating judge and works to bring about a friendly settlement.[7] If a friendly settlement is not reached, a report is sent to the Committee of Ministers and the countries concerned.[8] Article 48 of the European Convention then allows referral of the case to the European Court of Human Rights. There is no provision of the European Convention for individual applicants to refer cases to the Court. Referral may be made by a High Contracting Party (member state) whose national is alleged to be a victim; a High Contracting Party that referred the case to the commission; or by a High Contracting Party against whom the complaint has been made.

---

[4]   *See* Rules 9, 21, and 22 of the Rules of Procedure of the Commission.
[5]   Arts. 25, 28, 31, and 32.
[6]   Art. 27.
[7]   Art. 28.
[8]   Art. 31.

§ 14.2 Cases

Many decisions made by the European Court of Human Rights or the Commission have related to prisons, although the European Convention does not specifically refer to prisoners. The remaining portion of this section addresses several of these decisions. By analyzing the development of comparative law, one can develop a better understanding of one's own law.

Most applications made to the Commission relate to specific measures of discipline and the maintenance of order. Rule 33 of the European Rules provides that "[d]iscipline and order shall be maintained in the interest of safe custody and well-ordered community life."[9]

Article 3 of the Convention states that "no one shall be subject to torture or to inhuman or degrading treatment or punishment." Article 3 is probably the most fundamental provision used in claims dealing with the discipline and order of prisons, as the Eighth Amendment is in the United States.

§ 14.2.1 —Searches, Solitary Confinement, and Conditions of Confinement

Article 3 of the Convention has been used as a basis for claims stating that close body searches are inhuman and degrading.[10]

The Commission has also reasoned that solitary confinement for one month did not cause an inmate great physical or mental suffering, and was not designed to extract confessions.[11] The Commission stated that in solitary confinement cases, particular regard must be made to its strictness, its duration, and the end pursued. The Commission found that not only was the inmate's confinement period short, but he had access to a doctor if necessary, and could have requested relaxation of his confinement with respect to visits by counsel.

Another confinement case brought before the Commission involved an exceptional detention arrangement.[12] The applicants complained that they were subjected, deliberately and without any possible justification, to unduly restrictive conditions of detention, which caused them considerable physical and psychological suffering. The inmates were considered "dangerous prisoners" and were therefore being housed in a maximum-security wing. The Commission denied the application, stating that "[c]omplete sensory isolation coupled with complete social isolation can no doubt ultimately destroy the

---

[9]   *See* Appendix II, European Prison Rules.

[10] The Commission denied admission of any application concerning close body searches that are required before and after visits and transfers, in the presence of prison officials only, and involving no actual physical contact unless the prisoner resists. These were considered permissible and necessary in the interest of security, given the special circumstances of prison. *See* HUMAN RIGHTS IN PRISON, Directorate of Human Rights, Council of Europe Press, Strasbourg, 1986, pp. 61-62.

[11] Application Nos. 8954/77 Decision of July 1978, D.R. No. 12, p. 185 *et seq.*

[12] Decision of 8 July 1978 on the admissibility of Application Nos. 7572/76, 7586/76 and 7587/76. Dr. 14, p. 64 *et seq.*

personality; thus it constitutes a form of inhuman treatment which cannot be justified by the requirements of security, . . ." However, the Commission found no evidence that suggested that the inmates were subjected to sensory isolation of a degree that constituted an Article 3 violation. Thus, the segregation of a prisoner from the prison community does not alone constitute a form of inhuman treatment.

§ 14.2.2 —Use of Special Disciplinary Procedures

The European Court of Human Rights has approved the use of a special disciplinary procedure in the prison context rather than a full hearing, as set out in Article 6 of the Convention.[13] The petition from which this determination was made alleged that the inmates' discipline for "mutiny" and having "struck an officer" were, in substance, criminal charges. The inmate claimed that he was entitled to a hearing that complied with Article 6. The Court stated that inquiry must be made as to whether the alleged offenses fit into criminal law or disciplinary law according to the individual's national legal system.

The prison rules applicable to the inmate stated that the offenses at issue should be "an offence against discipline" and further set out how to discipline the inmate for such violations. The Court set out a standard that should be considered in determining whether the charge is criminal or disciplinary in nature under Article 6, through the application of "the very nature of the offense" test. The more serious the grade that the minimum rules give the offense, and the fact that under the rules the offense could be a criminal offense if committed outside of prison, caused the Court to conclude that such offenses must be treated as "criminal" for purposes of the European Convention. The Court held that the offenses of "mutiny" and the assault on the guard were criminal in nature.

The Court then considered the degree of severity of the penalty that the applicant risked incurring. The inmate here was given 450 and 120 days' loss of good-time credits, with 56 and 35 days' loss of privileges, exclusion from associated work, stoppage of earnings, and isolated confinement, both sentences to run consecutively. The Court determined that the practice of granting good-time credits, unless they have been forfeited in disciplinary proceedings, created a legitimate expectation in the inmate that he would recover his liberty before the end of his term. The Court reasoned that the deprivation of the expectation of liberty was a severe sanction that must be regarded as "criminal" for purposes of Article 6 guarantees in the Convention.

---

[13] Article 6 of the Convention provides certain guarantees in the determination of civil rights and obligations or of any criminal charge. It is somewhat similar to the requirements of "due process" in the United States. *See* Appendix I.

§ 14.2.3 —Degree of Force

Typical European prison legislation directs the staff (in principle) not to resort to force except:

> in self-defense or to protect others; to protect a prisoner against his own actions; in the event of an escape; in the event of violent resistance or physical inertia in response to orders given.[14]

Neither the Court of Human Rights nor the Commission has interpreted Article 3 of the Convention to set any particular degree of force that may be used by prison officials. Applications made by prisoners claiming to have been victims of ill treatment by prison staff are usually declared inadmissible. The European Prison Rules do, however, address the issue of the use of restraints in Rules 39 and 40.[15]

Although applications to the Commission alleging Article 3 violations due to the use of excessive force are many, usually individual country legislation or regulations give redress to prisoners. Further, a settlement of this type of case is usually reached by the parties.

§ 14.2.4 —Right to Treatment

Rule 65 of the European Prison Rules suggests that in order to fully protect society against crime, it is necessary to ensure that the offender, upon returning to society, will be able to lead a law-abiding and self-supporting life. Rule 66 adds that "all the remedial, educational, moral, spiritual, and other resources that are appropriate" should be made available for the treatment of prisoners. The question arises, although various rules have been implemented into the legislation of the member states, whether prisoners have a right to "rehabilitation."

The Commission has rejected the admissibility of an application, stating, among other things, that the Convention does not guarantee certain privileges in the treatment of prisoners.[16] The applicant complained that, unlike the prison from which he was transferred, he had not been afforded certain privileges such as visits and correspondence, vocational training, a personal radio, association with other prisoners, or television. The Commission would not accept the application that the prisoner was being subjected to inhuman treatment according to Article 3.

---

[14]   COUNCIL OF EUROPE PRESS, DIRECTORATE OF HUMAN RIGHTS, HUMAN RIGHTS IN PRISONS 77 (1986).

[15]   *See* Appendix II, EUROPEAN PRISON RULES.

[16]   Application No. 3868/68, Decision of 25 May 1970, Coll. Dec. 34, p. 10.

§ 14.2.5 —Medical Treatment

Rules 26 to 32 contain explicit provisions regarding medical treatment.[17] Rule 100 specifically deals with the treatment of insane and mentally abnormal prisoners. The objective of the medical treatment for prisoners is contained in Rule 64. So far, the Commission has not held that the lack of appropriate medical care constituted inhuman or degrading treatment within the meaning of Article 3 of the Convention.

§ 14.2.6 —Practice of Religion

The Commission has had the opportunity to consider a number of applications by prisoners alleging interference by prison authorities with the exercise of their right to practice their religion. Article 9 of the Convention establishes a right to practice freedom of thought, conscience, and religion.[18] Article 9, however, recognizes that one's religion or beliefs are subject to limitations as prescribed by law "and are necessary in a democratic society in the interests of public safety, for the protection of public order, health or morals, or for the protection of the rights and freedoms of others."[19] Thus, if prison authorities do everything practical in the assistance of the prisoner's religious exercise, the Commission would likely refuse admissibility.[20] The Commission has rejected admissibility of an inmate's complaint that he was not permitted to grow a chin beard as part of his religion.[21] The basis of the decision was that the regulation was necessary in a democratic society for the protection of public order. Overall, the Commission has broadly applied the limitations to the unfettered practice of religion in prisons.[22]

§ 14.2.7 —Contact with the Outside World

An additional concern within European prisons that is affected by the Convention is the contact that the prisoner has with the outside world. Under the European Prison Rules,[23] a prisoner is permitted to communicate with the "outside world" and to receive visits subject to the interests of treatment, security, and order.

Rule 44 deals specifically with foreign nationals, and Rule 45 addresses the availability of the media.

---

[17]   *See* Appendix II, EUROPEAN PRISON RULES.

[18]   *See* Appendix I.

[19]   *See* EUROPEAN PRISON RULES 46 and 47, also Appendix II, EUROPEAN PRISON RULES.

[20]   *See* Application No. 6886/75, decision of May, 1976, D.R. 5, p. 100.

[21]   Application No. 1753/63, partial decision of 15 February 1965, Coll. Dec. 16, p. 20.

[22]   *See* Application No. 6886/75/ decision of 18 May 1976, D.R. 5, p. 100; No. 5947/72, decision of 5 March 1975, D.R. 5, p. 8; No. 5442/72, decision of 20 December 1974, D.R. 1, p. 41; No. 7291/75, decision of 4 October 1977, D.R. 11, p. 55; No. 8317/78, decision of 15 May 1986, D.R.20, p. 44.

[23]   European Prison Rules 43-45; Appendix II, European Prison Rules.

The Convention has frequently been used to obtain or maintain inmates' various contacts with the outside world. The Commission has noted that the monitoring of mail is justified under Article 8, paragraph 2 of the Convention, as necessary for the maintenance of order.[24] Restrictions on visitors have also been approved by the rationale that Article 8, paragraph 2 permits interference with the exercise of the right to respect for private life "as in accordance with the law and is necessary in a democratic society . . . for the prevention of . . . crime . . ."[25] The prison authorities had stopped visitors to an inmate because there was a risk that the inmate was using visitors as contacts for illegal purposes and the restrictions were permitted by the member state's law. The Commission agreed with the prison authorities.

Application was made to the Commission on the lack of availability of the media as a violation of Article 10 of the Convention.[26]

The Commission denied admissibility on the grounds that, because the "interference" with their freedom of expression was "prescribed by law," this loss of privileges might be regarded as a "penalty" for the purpose of maintaining prison order and security.[27] The Commission then justified the interference as being necessary in a democratic society for the prevention of disorder, within the meaning of Article 10, paragraph 2.

§ 14.3   Extradition

Through extradition of prisoners from Europe to the United States, American conditions of confinement are sometimes called into question.

A German national, Jens Soering, was arrested in England and faced extradition to the State of Virginia on a charge of capital murder under the Extradition Treaty of 1972 between the United Kingdom and the United States. Soering filed an application with the Commission on Human Rights, challenging his extradition. Ultimately, the application was accepted and the case was brought before the European Court of Human Rights by the Commission against the United Kingdom.[28] It was alleged that in extraditing Soering, the United Kingdom would violate, among others, Article 3 of the European Convention on Human Rights.

Article 3 of the Convention provides that "No one shall be subjected to torture or to inhuman or degrading treatment or punishment."

The homicides were committed in Virginia. The deaths were the result of multiple and massive stab and slash wounds to the neck, throat, and body. The victims were the parents of Soering's girlfriend.

---

[24]   Application No. 8283/78, decision of 14 October 1980, D.R. 23, p. 127. *See* Appendix I.

[25]   Application No. 1983/63, partial decision of 13 December 1965, Coll. Dec. 18, p. 19 *et seq.*

[26]   Application No. 8317/78 D.R. 20, pp 44-160, lack of media meaning no access to television, radio, or newspaper.

[27]   *Id.*

[28]   *Soering* Case, European Court of Human Rights, 1/1989/161/217 (1989).

During the extradition proceedings, the British government addressed a request to the United States authorities in the following terms:

> Because the death penalty has been abolished in Great Britain, the Embassy has been instructed to seek an assurance, in accordance with the terms of . . . the Extradition Treaty, that, in the event of Mr. Soering being surrendered and being convicted of the crimes for which he has been indicted . . . , the death penalty, if imposed, will not be carried out.

> Should it not be possible on constitutional grounds for the United States Government to give such an assurance, the United Kingdom authorities ask that the United States Government undertake to recommend to the appropriate authorities that the death penalty should not be imposed or, if imposed, should not be executed.

In response, the Virginia prosecutor stated:

> I hereby certify that should Jens Soering be convicted of the offence of capital murder as charged in Bedford County, Virginia . . . a representation will be made in the name of the United Kingdom to the judge at the time of sentencing that it is the wish of the United Kingdom that the death penalty should not be imposed or carried out.

It should be noted that Article IV of the Extradition Treaty provides:

> If the offence for which extradition is requested is punishable by death under the relevant law of the requesting Party, but the relevant law of the requested Party does not provide for the death penalty in a similar case, extradition maybe refused unless the requesting Party gives assurances satisfactory to the requested Party that the death penalty will not be carried out.

Of primary concern to the European Court of Justice were the conditions of Virginia's death row.

At the time of the appeal (1989), there were 40 people under sentence of death in Virginia. The majority were detained in the Mecklenburg Correctional Center. There were uniform operating procedures for the administration, security, control, and delivery of necessary services to death row inmates. In addition, conditions of confinement were governed by the comprehensive consent decree of a federal district court in Richmond in 1985. Both the Virginia Department of Corrections and the American Civil Liberties Union monitored compliance with the terms of the consent decree.

The size of a death row inmate's cell was 8 feet by 10 feet. The inmates had an opportunity for approximately seven and one-half hours of recreation per week in summer and approximately six hours per week, weather permitting, in winter. The death row area had two recreation yards, both of which were equipped with basketball courts and one of which was equipped with weights and weight benches. Inmates were also permitted to leave their cells on other occasions, such as to receive visitors, to use the law library, or to visit the prison infirmary. Death row inmates were also given one hour of out-of-cell time in the morning in a common area. Each death row inmate was eligible for work assignments, such as cleaning duties. When prisoners moved around the prison, they were handcuffed, with special shackles around the waist. When not in their cells, death row inmates were housed in a common area called "the pod." The guards were not in this area but remained in a box outside. In the event of a disturbance or an inter-inmate assault, the guards were not allowed to intervene until instructed to do so by the ranking officer present. There was evidence of extreme stress, psychological deterioration, and risk of homosexual abuse and physical attack on inmates on death row, which was strongly contested by Virginia authorities. Death row inmates received the same medical service as inmates in the general population. An infirmary equipped with adequate supplies, equipment, and staff provided for 24-hour inpatient care, and emergency facilities were provided in each building. Psychological and psychiatric services were also provided to death row inmates. The adequacy of mental health treatment available to death row inmates at the prison was found to be constitutional in 1988.

Death row inmates were allowed noncontact visits in a visiting room on Saturdays, Sundays, and holidays between 8:30 A.M. and 3:30 P.M. Attorneys had access to their clients during normal working hours on request as well as during scheduled visiting hours. The death row inmates who had a record of good behavior were eligible for contact visits with members of their immediate family two days per week. Outgoing correspondence from inmates was picked up daily and all incoming correspondence was delivered each evening. As a security precaution, pursuant to rules applicable to all inmates in the Virginia prison system, routine searches were conducted of the entire institution on a quarterly basis. During such times, called lockdowns, inmates were confined to their cells. They showered, received medical, dental, and psychological services outside their cells as deemed necessary by medical staff and, upon request, they were permitted law library visits, legal visits, and legal telephone calls.

Other services such as meals were provided to the inmates in their cells. During lockdown, privileges and out-of-cell time were gradually increased to return to normal operations. Lockdowns could be ordered from time to time in relation to death row if information was received indicating that certain of its inmates might be planning a disturbance, hostage situation, or escape.

A death row inmate was moved to the death house 15 days before he was due to be executed. The death house was next to the death chamber where the electric chair was situated. While an inmate was in the death house, he was watched 24 hours per day. He was isolated and had no light in his cell. The lights outside were permanently lit. An inmate who utilized the appeals process could be placed in the death house several times. In Soering's application to the European Commission on Human Rights, he argued that notwith-standing the assurance given to the government of the United Kingdom, there was a serious likelihood that he would be sentenced to death if extradited to the United States. He maintained that, under the circumstances, and in particular having regarding the "death row phenomenon," he would be subjected to inhuman and degrading treatment and punishment contrary to Article 3 of the Convention.

"Death row phenomenon" was described as consisting of a combination of circumstances to which Soering would be exposed if, after having been extradited to Virginia to face a capital murder charge, he was sentenced to death.

According to the Court, Article 3 makes no provision for exceptions, and no derogation from it is permissible in time of war or other national emergency. The absolute prohibition of torture and of inhuman or degrading treatment or punishment under the terms of the European Convention enshrines one of the fundamental values of the democratic societies making up the Council of Europe. It is also to be found in similar terms in other international instruments, such as the 1966 International Covenant on Civil and Political Rights and the 1969 American Convention on Human Rights, and is generally recognized as an international standard.[29]

The Court found that a condemned prisoner in Virginia could expect to spend an average of six to eight years on death row before being executed, even though this length of time was largely of the inmate's own making, if he took advantage of all avenues of appeal that were offered to him by law. The consequence is that the condemned inmate has to endure the conditions on death row for many years and the anguish and mounting tension of living in the ever-present apprehension of death.[30]

Significant to the Court was Soering's youth at the time of the offense and his mental state at that time. These factors were taken into consideration as contributing factors tending to bring the treatment on death row within the terms of Article 3.[31]

In finding that the extradition of Soering to Virginia would constitute a breach of Article 3 of the Convention, the Court stated:

> For any prisoner condemned to death, some element of delay between imposition and execution of the sentence and the experience of severe stress in conditions necessary for strict incarceration are inevitable. The democratic character of the Virginia legal system in general and the positive features of Virginia trial, sentencing, and appeal procedures in particular are beyond doubt. The Court agrees with the Commission that the machinery of justice to which the applicant would be subject in the United States is in itself neither arbitrary nor unreasonable, but, rather, respects the rule of law and affords not inconsiderable procedural safeguards to the assistance of inmates, notably through provision of psychological and psychiatric services.

---

[29]   *Id.,* para. 88.
[30]   *Id.,* para. 106.
[31]   *Id.,* para. 109.

However, in the Court's view, regarding the very long period of time spent on death row in such extreme conditions, with the ever-present and mounting anguish of awaiting execution, and to the personal circumstances of the applicant, especially his age and mental state at the time of the offense, the applicant's extradition to the United States would expose him to a real risk of treatment going beyond the threshold set by Article 3.[32]

Thus, it can be seen that emerging and developing international standards for the protection of human rights can have an effect on the treatment of offenders in the United States. It may certainly be argued that the treatment of death row inmates in the United States does in fact fall below internationally recognized standards for the humane treatment of offenders.

The International Court of Justice, sitting in The Hague, Netherlands, held that the United States was in violation of international law with respect to the execution of a German national by the State of Arizona.[33] Germany sought enforcement of an order by the International Court of Justice, on its own motion and with no opportunity for the United States to respond, directing the United States to prevent Arizona's scheduled execution of Walter LaGrand. Germany asserted that LaGrand held German citizenship. Relief was denied by the United States Supreme Court. This action was filed within two hours of a scheduled execution based upon a sentence imposed by Arizona in 1984, about which the Federal Republic of Germany learned in 1992. Given the tardiness of the pleas and the jurisdictional barriers they implicated, the Supreme Court declined to exercise its original jurisdiction. Further, the Supreme Court held that the United States had not waived its sovereign immunity. Additionally, Article III, § 2, clause 2 of the United States Constitution does not provide a means to prevent execution of a German citizen who is not an ambassador or consul. With respect to the action against the State of Arizona, a foreign government's ability to assert a claim against a state is without evident support in the Vienna Convention and is in probable contravention of Eleventh Amendment principles. Relief was denied.

§ 14.4   Conclusion

The internationalization of concerns regarding the treatment of prisoners will surely help in promoting reform among participating countries, regardless of the subject. The European Convention on Human Rights has served as a powerful guide in the reform of prisons in countries that are members of the Council of Europe. Although the Convention is "young," compared to the development of case law on the subject of prisoner's rights in the United States, changes are constant. Because the two institutions are similar, the study of the development of both systems can only serve to help prison officials improve the humane treatment of offenders.

---

[32]   *Id.*, para. 111.

[33]   The decision can be found in Appendix V.

Part II:
Judicial Decisions
Relating To Part I

Part II: Table of Cases

Cases Relating to Chapter 2

Use of Force; Use of Corporal Punishment to Enforce Prison Discipline

WHITLEY

v.

ALBERS

475 U.S. 312; 106 S. Ct. 1078; 89 L. Ed. 2d 251 (1986)

JUSTICE O'CONNOR delivered the opinion of the Court.

This case requires us to decide what standard governs a prison inmate's claim that prison officials subjected him to cruel and unusual punishment by shooting him during the course of their attempt to quell a prison riot.

I

At the time he was injured, respondent Gerald Albers was confined in cellblock "A" of the Oregon State Penitentiary. Cellblock "A" consists of two tiers of barred cells housing some 200 inmates. The two tiers are connected by a stairway that offers the only practical way to move from one tier to another.

At about 8:30 on the evening of June 27, 1980, several inmates were found intoxicated at the prison annex. Prison guards attempted to move the intoxicated prisoners, some of whom resisted, to the penitentiary's isolation and segregation facility. This incident could be seen from the cell windows in cellblock "A," and some of the onlookers became agitated because they thought that the guards were using unnecessary force. Acting on instructions from their superiors, Officers Kemper and Fitts, who were on duty in cellblock "A," ordered the prisoners to return to

their cells. The order was not obeyed. Several inmates confronted the two officers, who were standing in the open area of the lower tier. One inmate, Richard Klenk, jumped from the second tier and assaulted Officer Kemper. Kemper escaped but Officer Fitts was taken hostage. Klenk and other inmates then began breaking furniture and milling about.

Upon being informed of the disturbance, petitioner Harol Whitley, the prison security manager, entered cellblock "A" and spoke with Klenk. Captain Whitley agreed to permit four residents of cellblock "A" to view the inmates who had been taken to segregation earlier. These emissaries reported back that the prisoners in segregation were intoxicated but unharmed. Nonetheless, the disturbance in cellblock "A" continued.

Whitley returned to the cellblock and confirmed that Fitts was not harmed. Shortly thereafter, Fitts was moved from an office on the lower tier to cell 201 on the upper tier, and Klenk demanded that media representatives be brought into the cellblock. In the course of the negotiations, Klenk, who was armed with a homemade knife, informed Whitley that one inmate had already been killed and other deaths would follow. In fact, an inmate had been beaten but not killed by other prisoners.

Captain Whitley left the cellblock to organize an assault squad. When Whitley returned to cellblock "A," he was taken to see Fitts in cell 201. Several inmates assured Whitley that they would protect Fitts from harm, but Klenk threatened to kill the hostage if an attempt was made to lead an assault. Klenk and at least some other inmates were aware that guards had assembled outside the cellblock and that shotguns had been issued. Meanwhile, respondent had left his cell on the upper tier to see if elderly prisoners housed on the lower tier could be moved out of harm's way in the event that tear gas was used. Respondent testified that he asked Whitley for the key to the row of cells housing the elderly prisoners, and Whitley indicated that he would return with the key. Whitley denied that he spoke to respondent at any time during the disturbance.

Whitley next consulted with his superiors, petitioners Cupp, the prison Superintendent, and Kenney, the Assistant Superintendent. They agreed that forceful intervention was necessary to protect the life of the hostage and the safety of the inmates who were not rioting, and ruled out tear gas as an unworkable alternative. Cupp ordered Whitley to take a squad armed with shotguns into cellblock "A."

Whitley gave the final orders to the assault team, which was assembled in the area outside cellblock "A." Petitioner Kennicott and two other officers armed with shotguns were to follow Whitley, who was unarmed, over the barricade the inmates had constructed at the cellblock entrance. A second group of officers, without firearms, would be behind them. Whitley ordered Kennicott to fire a warning shot as he crossed the barricade. He also ordered Kennicott to shoot low at any prisoners climbing the stairs toward cell 201, since they could pose a threat to the safety of the hostage or to Whitley himself, who would be climbing the stairs in an attempt to free the hostage in cell 201.

At about 10:30 P.M., Whitley reappeared just outside the barricade. By this time, about a half hour had elapsed since the earlier breaking of furniture, and the noise level in the cellblock had noticeably diminished. Respondent, who was standing at the bottom of the stairway, asked about the key. Whitley replied "No," clambered over the barricade, yelled "shoot the bastards," and ran toward the stairs after Klenk, who had been standing in the open areaway along with a number of other inmates. Kennicott fired a warning shot into the wall opposite the cellblock entrance as he followed Whitley over the barricade. He then fired a second shot that struck a post near the

stairway. Meanwhile, Whitley chased Klenk up the stairs, and shortly thereafter respondent started up the stairs. Kennicott fired a third shot that struck respondent in the left knee. Another inmate was shot on the stairs and several others on the lower tier were wounded by gunshot. The inmates in cell 201 prevented Klenk from entering, and Whitley subdued Klenk at the cell door, freeing the hostage.

As a result of the incident, respondent sustained severe damage to his left leg and mental and emotional distress. He subsequently commenced this action pursuant to 42 U.S.C. § 1983, alleging that petitioners deprived him of his rights under the Eighth and Fourteenth Amendments and raising pendent state law claims for assault and battery and negligence. Many of the facts were stipulated, but both sides also presented testimony from witnesses to the disturbance and the rescue attempt, as well as from expert witnesses with backgrounds in prison discipline and security. At the conclusion of trial, the District Judge directed a verdict for petitioners. He understood respondent's claim to be based solely on the Eighth Amendment as made applicable to the States by the Fourteenth Amendment. See Robinson v. California, 370 U.S. 660 (1962). The District Judge held:

[Defendants]' use of deadly force was justified under the unique circumstances of this case. Possible alternatives were considered and reasonably rejected by prison officers. The use of shotguns and specifically the order to shoot low anyone following the unarmed Whitley up the stairs were necessary to protect Whitley, secure the safe release of the hostage and to restore order and discipline. Even in hindsight, it cannot be said that defendants' actions were not reasonably necessary. 546 F.Supp. 726, 735 (Ore. 1982).

In the alternative, he held that petitioners were immune from damages liability because the constitutional constraints on the use of force in a prison riot were not clearly established. Finally, the District Judge held that respondent was barred from recovery on his pendent state law claims by virtue of an immunity conferred on public officers by the Oregon Tort Claims Act as to claims arising out of riots or mob actions.

A panel of the Court of Appeals for the Ninth Circuit reversed in part and affirmed in part, with one judge dissenting. 743 F.2d 1372 (1984). The court held that an Eighth Amendment violation would be established "if a prison official deliberately shot Albers under circumstances where the official, with due allowance for the exigency, knew or should have known that it was unnecessary," id., at 1375, or "if the emergency plan was adopted or carried out with 'deliberate indifference' to the right of Albers to be free of cruel [and] unusual punishment." Ibid. The Court of Appeals pointed to evidence that the general disturbance in cellblock "A" was subsiding and to respondent's experts' testimony that the use of deadly force was excessive under the circumstances and should have been preceded by a verbal warning, and concluded that the jury could have found an Eighth Amendment violation. Id., at 1376.

* * *

II

The language of the Eighth Amendment, "[excessive] bail shall not be required, nor excessive fines imposed, nor cruel and unusual punishments inflicted," manifests "an intention to limit the power of those entrusted with the criminal-law function of government." Ingraham v. Wright, 430 U.S. 651, 664 (1977). The Cruel and Unusual Punishments Clause "was designed to protect those convicted of crimes," ibid., and consequently the Clause applies "only after the State has complied with the constitutional guarantees traditionally associated with criminal prosecutions." Id., at 671, n. 40. See also Revere v. Massachusetts General Hospital, 463 U.S. 239, 244 (1983); Bell v. Wolfish, 441 U.S. 520, 535, n. 16 (1979). An express intent to inflict unnecessary pain is not required, Estelle v. Gamble, 429 U.S. 97, 104 (1976) ("deliberate indifference" to a prisoner's serious medical needs is cruel and unusual punishment), and harsh "conditions of confinement" may constitute cruel and unusual punishment unless such conditions "are part of the penalty that criminal offenders pay for their offenses against society.") Rhodes v. Chapman, 452 U.S. 337, 347 (1981).

Not every governmental action affecting the interests or well-being of a prisoner is subject to Eighth Amendment scrutiny, however. "After incarceration, only the 'unnecessary and wanton infliction of pain' . . . constitutes cruel and unusual punishment forbidden by the Eighth Amendment." Ingraham v. Wright, supra, at 670 (quoting Estelle v. Gamble, supra, at 103) (citations omitted). To be cruel and unusual punishment, conduct that does not purport to be punishment at all must involve more than ordinary lack of due care for the prisoner's interests or safety. This reading of the Clause underlies our decision in Estelle v. Gamble, supra, at 105-106, which held that a prison physician's "[negligence] in diagnosing or treating a medical condition" did not suffice to make out a claim of cruel and unusual punishment. It is obduracy and wantonness, not inadvertence or error in good faith, that characterize the conduct prohibited by the Cruel and Unusual Punishments Clause, whether that conduct occurs in connection with establishing conditions of confinement, supplying medical needs, or restoring official control over a tumultuous cellblock. The infliction of pain in the course of a prison security measure, therefore, does not amount to cruel and unusual punishment simply because it may appear in retrospect that the degree of force authorized or applied for security purposes was unreasonable, and hence unnecessary in the strict sense.

The general requirement that an Eighth Amendment claimant allege and prove the unnecessary and wanton infliction of pain should also be applied with due regard for differences in the kind of conduct against which an Eighth Amendment objection is lodged. The deliberate indifference standard articulated in Estelle was appropriate in the context presented in that case because the State's responsibility to attend to the medical needs of prisoners does not ordinarily clash with other equally important governmental responsibilities. Consequently, "deliberate indifference to a prisoner's serious illness or injury," Estelle, supra, at 105, can typically be established or disproved without the necessity of balancing competing institutional concerns for the safety of prison staff or other inmates. But, in making and carrying out decisions involving the use of force to restore order in the face of a prison disturbance, prison officials undoubtedly must take into account the very real threats the unrest presents to inmates and prison officials alike, in addition to the possible harms to inmates against whom force might be used. As we said in Hudson v. Palmer, 468 U.S. 517, 526-527 (1984), prison administrators are charged with the responsibility of ensuring the safety of the prison staff, administrative personnel, and visitors, as well as the "obligation to take reasonable measures to guarantee the safety of the inmates themselves." In this setting, a deliberate indifference standard does not adequately capture the importance of such competing obligations, or convey the appropriate hesitancy to critique in hindsight decisions necessarily made in haste, under pressure, and frequently without the luxury of a second chance.

Where a prison security measure is undertaken to resolve a disturbance, such as occurred in this case, that indisputably poses significant risks to the safety of inmates and prison staff, we think the question whether the measure taken inflicted unnecessary and wanton pain and suffering ultimately turns on "whether force was applied in a good faith effort to maintain or restore discipline or maliciously and sadistically for the very purpose of causing harm." Johnson v. Glick, 481 F.2d 1028, 1033 (CA2) (Friendly, J.), cert. denied sub nom. John v. Johnson, 414 U.S. 1033 (1973). As the District Judge correctly perceived, "such factors as the need for the application of force, the relationship between the need and the amount of force that was used, [and] the extent of injury inflicted," 481 F.2d, at 1033, are relevant to that ultimate determination. See 546 F.Supp., at 733. From such considerations inferences may be drawn as to whether the use of force could plausibly have been thought necessary, or instead evinced such wantonness with respect to the unjustified infliction of harm as is tantamount to a knowing willingness that it occur. See Duckworth v. Franzen, 780 F.2d 645, 652 (CA7 1985) (equating "deliberate indifference," in an Eighth Amendment case involving security risks, with "recklessness in criminal law," which "implies an act so dangerous that the defendant's knowledge of the risk

can be inferred"); cf. Block v. Rutherford, 468 U.S. 576, 584 (1984) (requiring pretrial detainees claiming that they were subjected to "punishment" without due process to prove intent to punish or show that the challenged conduct "is not reasonably related to a legitimate goal," from which an intent to punish may be inferred); Bell v. Wolfish, supra, at 539. But equally relevant are such factors as the extent of the threat to the safety of staff and inmates, as reasonably perceived by the responsible officials on the basis of the facts known to them, and any efforts made to temper the severity of a forceful response.

When the "ever-present potential for violent confrontation and conflagration," Jones v. North Carolina Prisoners' Labor Union, Inc., 433 U.S. 119, 132 (1977), ripens into actual unrest and conflict, the admonition that "a prison's internal security is peculiarly a matter normally left to the discretion of prison administrators," Rhodes v. Chapman, supra, at 349, n. 14, carries special weight. "Prison administrators . . . should be accorded wide-ranging deference in the adoption and execution of policies and practices that in their judgment are needed to preserve internal order and discipline and to maintain institutional security." Bell v. Wolfish, 441 U.S., at 547. That deference extends to a prison security measure taken in response to an actual confrontation with riotous inmates, just as it does to prophylactic or preventive measures intended to reduce the incidence of these or any other breaches of prison discipline. It does not insulate from review actions taken in bad faith and for no legitimate purpose, but it requires that neither judge nor jury freely substitute their judgment for that of officials who have made a considered choice. Accordingly, in ruling on a motion for a directed verdict in a case such as this, courts must determine whether the evidence goes beyond a mere dispute over the reasonableness of a particular use of force or the existence of arguably superior alternatives. Unless it appears that the evidence, viewed in the light most favorable to the plaintiff, will support a reliable inference of wantonness in the infliction of pain under the standard we have described, the case should not go to the jury.

III

... The Court of Appeals believed that testimony that the disturbance was subsiding at the time the assault was made, and the conflicting expert testimony as to whether the force used was excessive, were enough to allow a jury to find that respondent's Eighth Amendment rights were violated. We think the Court of Appeals effectively collapsed the distinction between mere negligence and wanton conduct that we find implicit in the Eighth Amendment. Only if ordinary errors of judgment could make out an Eighth Amendment claim would this evidence create a jury question.

To begin with, although the evidence could be taken to show that the general disturbance had quieted down, a guard was still held hostage, Klenk was armed and threatening, several other inmates were armed with homemade clubs, numerous inmates remained outside their cells, and the cellblock remained in the control of the inmates. The situation remained dangerous and volatile. As respondent concedes, at the time he was shot "an officer's safety was in question and . . . an inmate was armed and dangerous." Brief for Respondent 25. Prison officials had no way of knowing what direction matters would take if they continued to negotiate or did nothing, but they had ample reason to believe that these options presented unacceptable risks.

Respondent's expert testimony is likewise unavailing. One of respondent's experts opined that petitioners gave inadequate consideration to less forceful means of intervention, and that the use of deadly force under the circumstances was not necessary to "prevent imminent danger" to the hostage guard or other inmates. Respondent's second expert testified that prison officials were "possibly a little hasty in using the firepower" on the inmates. Id., at 314. At most, this evidence, which was controverted by petitioners' experts, establishes that prison officials arguably erred in judgment when they decided on a plan that employed potentially deadly force. It falls far short of a showing that there was no plausible basis for the officials' belief that this degree of force was necessary. Indeed, any such conclusion would run counter to common sense, in light of the risks to the life of the hostage and the safety of inmates that demonstrably persisted notwithstanding repeated attempts to defuse the situation. An expert's after-the-fact opinion that danger was not "imminent" in no way establishes that there was no danger, or that a conclusion by the officers that it was imminent would have been wholly unreasonable.

Once the basic design of the plan was in place, moreover, it is apparent why any inmate running up the stairs after Captain Whitley, or interfering with his progress towards the hostage, could reasonably be thought to present a threat to the success of the rescue attempt and to Whitley—particularly after a warning shot was fired. A sizable group of inmates, in defiance of the cell—in order and in apparent support of Klenk, continued to stand in the open area on the lower tier. Respondent testified that this was not "an organized group," id., at 113, and that he saw no inmates armed with clubs in that area. Id., at 114. But the fact remains that the officials had no way of knowing which members of that group of inmates had joined with Klenk in destroying furniture, breaking glass, seizing the hostage, and setting up the barricade, and they certainly had reason to believe that some members of this group might intervene in support of Klenk. It was perhaps also foreseeable that one or more of these inmates would run up the stairs after the shooting started in order to return to their cells. But there would be neither means nor time to inquire into the reasons why each inmate acted as he did. Consequently, the order to shoot, qualified as it was by an instruction to shoot low, falls short of commanding the infliction of pain in a wanton and unnecessary fashion.

As petitioners' own experts conceded, a verbal warning would have been desirable, in addition to a warning shot, if circumstances permitted it to be given without undue risk. See id., at 446, 556. While a jury might conclude that this omission was unreasonable, we think that an inference of wantonness could not properly be drawn. First, some warning was given in the form of the first shot fired by Officer Kennicott. Second, the prison officials could have believed in good faith that such a warning might endanger the success of the security measure because of the risk that it would have allowed one or more inmates to climb the stairs before they could be stopped. The failure to provide for verbal warnings is thus not so insupportable as to be wanton. Accordingly, a jury could not properly find that this omission, coupled with the order to shoot, offended the Eighth Amendment.

To be sure, the plan was not adapted to take into account the appearance of respondent on the scene, and, on the facts as we must take them, Whitley was aware that respondent was present on the first tier for benign reasons. Conceivably, Whitley could have added a proviso exempting respondent from his order to shoot any prisoner climbing the stairs. But such an oversight simply does not rise to the level of an Eighth Amendment violation. Officials cannot realistically be expected to consider every contingency or minimize every risk, and it was far from inevitable that respondent would react as he did. Whitley was about to risk his life in an effort to rescue the hostage, and he was understandably focusing on the orders essential to the success of the plan. His failure to make special provision for respondent may have been unfortunate, but is hardly behavior from which a wanton willingness to inflict unjustified suffering on respondent can be inferred.

Once it is established that the order to shoot low at anyone climbing the stairs after a warning shot was not wanton, respondent's burden in showing that the actual shooting constituted the wanton and unnecessary infliction of pain is an extremely heavy one. Accepting that respondent could not have sought safety in a cell on the lower tier, the fact remains that had respondent thrown himself to the floor he would not have been shot at. Instead, after the warning shot was fired, he attempted to return to his cell by running up the stairs behind Whitley. That is equivocal conduct. While respondent had not been actively involved in the riot and indeed had attempted to help matters, there is no indication that Officer Kennicott knew this, nor any claim that he acted vindictively or in retaliation. Respondent testified that as he started to run up the stairs he "froze" when he looked to his left and saw Kennicott, and that "we locked eyes." Id., at 119. Kennicott testified that he saw several inmates running up the stairs, that he thought they were pursuing Whitley, and that he fired at their legs. Id., at

459. To the extent that this testimony is conflicting, we resolve the conflict in respondent's favor by assuming that Kennicott shot at respondent rather than at the inmates as a group. But this does not establish that Kennicott shot respondent knowing it was unnecessary to do so. Kennicott had some basis for believing that respondent constituted a threat to the hostage and to Whitley, and had at most a few seconds in which to react. He was also under orders to respond to such a perceived threat in precisely the manner he did. Under these circumstances, the actual shooting was part and parcel of a good-faith effort to restore prison security. As such, it did not violate respondent's Eighth Amendment right to be free from cruel and unusual punishments.

IV

As an alternative ground for affirmance, respondent contends that, independently of the Eighth Amendment, the shooting deprived him of a protected liberty interest without due process of law, in violation of the Fourteenth Amendment. Respondent . . . argues that he has maintained throughout this litigation that his "constitutional protection against the use of excessive and unnecessary force, as well as the use of deadly force without meaningful warning," derives from the Due Process Clause as well as the Eighth Amendment.

* * *

We need say little on this score. We think the Eighth Amendment, which is specifically concerned with the unnecessary and wanton infliction of pain in penal institutions, serves as the primary source of substantive protection to convicted prisoners in cases such as this one, where the deliberate use of force is challenged as excessive and unjustified. It would indeed be surprising if, in the context of forceful prison security measures, "conduct that shocks the conscience" or "afford[s] brutality the cloak of law," and so violates the Fourteenth Amendment, Rochin v. California, 342 U.S. 165, 172, 173 (1952), were not also punishment "inconsistent with contemporary standards of decency" and "repugnant to the conscience of mankind," Estelle v. Gamble, 429 U.S., at 103, 106, in violation of the Eighth. We only recently reserved the general question "whether something less than intentional conduct, such as recklessness or 'gross negligence,' is enough to trigger the protections of the Due Process Clause." Daniels v. Williams, 474 U.S. 327, 334, n. 3 (1986). Because this case involves prison inmates rather than pretrial detainees or persons enjoying unrestricted liberty we imply nothing as to the proper answer to that question outside the prison security context by holding, as we do, that in these circumstances the Due Process Clause affords respondent no greater protection than does the Cruel and Unusual Punishments Clause.

* * *

The judgment of the Court of Appeals is Reversed.

JUSTICE MARSHALL, with whom JUSTICE BRENNAN, JUSTICE BLACKMUN, and JUSTICE STEVENS join, dissenting.

I share the majority's concern that prison officials be permitted to respond reasonably to inmate disturbances without unwarranted fear of liability. I agree that the threshold for establishing a constitutional violation under these circumstances is high. I do not agree, however, that the contested existence of a "riot" in the prison lessens the constraints imposed on prison authorities by the Eighth Amendment.

The majority has erred, I believe, both in developing its legal analysis and in employing it. First, the especially onerous standard the Court has devised for determining whether a prisoner injured during a prison disturbance has been subjected to cruel and unusual punishment is incorrect and not justified by precedent. That standard is particularly inappropriate because courts deciding whether to apply it must resolve a preliminary issue of fact that will often be disputed and properly left to the jury. Finally, the Court has applied its test improperly to the facts of this case. For these reasons, I must respectfully dissent.

I

The Court properly begins by acknowledging that, for a prisoner attempting to prove a violation of the Eighth Amendment, "[an] express intent to inflict unnecessary pain is not required, Estelle v. Gamble, 429 U.S. 97, 104 (1976)." Ante, at 319. Rather, our cases have established that the "unnecessary and wanton" infliction of pain on prisoners constitutes cruel and unusual punishment prohibited by the Eighth Amendment, even in the absence of intent to harm. Ibid.; see also Ingraham v. Wright, 430 U.S. 651, 670 (1977); Gregg v. Georgia, 428 U.S. 153, 173 (1976) (joint opinion of Stewart, POWELL, and STEVENS, JJ.). Having correctly articulated the teaching of our cases on this issue, however, the majority inexplicably arrives at the conclusion that a constitutional violation in the context of a prison uprising can be established only if force was used "maliciously and sadistically for the very purpose of causing harm," ante, at 320-321—thus requiring the very "express intent to inflict unnecessary pain" that it had properly disavowed.

The Court imposes its heightened version of the "unnecessary and wanton" standard only when the injury occurred in the course of a "disturbance" that "poses significant risks," ante, at 320. But those very questions—whether a disturbance existed and whether it posed a risk—are likely to be hotly contested. It is inappropriate, to say the least, to condition the choice of a legal standard, the purpose of which is to determine whether to send a constitutional claim to the jury, upon the court's resolution of factual disputes that in many cases should themselves be resolved by the jury.

The correct standard for identifying a violation of the Eighth Amendment under our cases is clearly the "unnecessary and wanton" standard, which establishes a high hurdle to be overcome by a prisoner seeking relief for a constitutional violation. The full circumstances of the plaintiff's injury, including whether it was inflicted during an attempt to quell a riot and whether there was a reasonable apprehension of danger, should be considered by the factfinder in determining whether that standard is satisfied in a particular case. There is simply no justification for creating a distinct and more onerous burden for the plaintiff to meet merely because the judge believes that the injury at issue was caused during a disturbance that "pose[d] significant risks to the safety of inmates and prison staff," ante, at 320. Determination of whether there was such a disturbance or risk, when disputed, should be made by the jury when it resolves disputed facts, not by the court in its role as arbiter of law. See Byrd v. Blue Ridge Cooperative, 356 U.S. 525, 537 (1958).

II

The Court properly begins its application of the law by reciting the principle that the facts must be viewed in the light most favorable to respondent, who won a reversal of a directed verdict below. See Galloway v. United States, 319 U.S. 372, 395 (1943). If, under any reasonable interpretation of the facts, a jury could have found the "unnecessary and wanton" standard to be met, then the directed verdict was improper. The majority opinion, however, resolves factual disputes in the record in petitioners' favor and discounts much of respondent's theory of the case. This it is not entitled to do.

The majority pays short shrift to respondent's significant contention that the disturbance had quieted down by the time the lethal force was employed. Ante, at 322-323. Respondent presented substantial testimony to show that the disturbance had subsided; that only one prisoner, Klenk, remained in any way disruptive, id., at 212; and that even Klenk had calmed down enough at that point to admit that he had "gone too far." Id., at 117. The majority asserts that "a guard was still held hostage, Klenk was armed and threatening, several other inmates were armed with homemade clubs, numerous inmates remained outside their cells, and . . . [t]he situation remained dangerous and volatile." Ante, at 322-323. Respondent's evidence, however, indicated that the guard was not, in fact, in danger. He had been put into a cell by several inmates to prevent Klenk from harming him. Captain Whitley had been to see the guard, and had observed that the

inmates protecting him from Klenk were not armed and had promised to keep Klenk out. Id., at 58 (stipulation), 163. According to respondent's evidence, moreover, no other inmates were assisting Klenk in any way when the riot squad was called in; they were simply "milling around," waiting for Klenk to be taken into custody, or for orders to return to their cells. Id., at 188. Respondent's evidence tended to show not that the "situation remained dangerous and volatile," ante, at 323, but, on the contrary, that it was calm. Although the Court sees fit to emphasize repeatedly "the risks to the life of the hostage and the safety of inmates that demonstrably persisted notwithstanding repeated attempts to defuse the situation," ibid., I can only point out that respondent bitterly disputed that any such risk to guards or inmates had persisted. The Court just does not believe his story.

The Court's treatment of the expert testimony is equally insensitive to its obligation to resolve all disputes in favor of respondent. Respondent's experts testified that the use of deadly force under these circumstances was not justified by any necessity to prevent imminent danger to the officers or the inmates; that the force used was excessive, ibid.; and that even if deadly force had been justified, it would have been unreasonable to unleash such force without a clear warning to allow nonparticipating inmates to return to their cells. Id., at 269. Insofar as expert testimony can ever be useful to show that prison authorities engaged in the "unnecessary and wanton" infliction of pain, even though it will always amount to "after-the-fact opinion" regarding the circumstances of the injury, see ante, at 323, respondent's expert evidence contributed to the creation of a factual issue.

The majority characterizes the petitioners' error in using deadly force where it was not justified as an "oversight." Ante, at 325. This is an endorsement of petitioners' rendition of the facts. As portrayed by respondent's evidence, the "error" was made in cold blood. Respondent's involvement started when, at the request of one of the inmates, he approached petitioner Whitley, who was talking to Klenk, to ask if Whitley would supply a key to a gate so that the elderly and sick patients in so-called "medical cells" near the area of disturbance could be removed before any tear gas was used. Captain Whitley said that he would go and get the key, and left the cellblock. Ibid. In two or three minutes, Whitley returned. Id., at 118. Respondent went to the door of the cellblock, and asked Whitley if he had brought the key. Whitley responded "No," turned his head back and yelled: "Let's go, let's go. Shoot the bastards!" Ibid.

Respondent, afraid, ran from his position by the door and headed for the stairs, the only route back to his cell. Id., at 118-119. He caught some movement out of the corner of his eye, looked in its direction, and saw petitioner Kennicott. According to respondent: "I froze. I looked at him; we locked eyes, then I looked down and seen the shotgun in his hand, then I seen the flash, and the next thing I know I was sitting down, grabbing my leg." Id., at 119. Losing a great deal of blood, respondent crawled up the stairs and fell on his face, trying to get out of range of the shotguns. Ibid. After about 10 minutes, an officer grabbed respondent by the hair and dragged him downstairs. Id., at 194. As he lay there, another officer came and stood over respondent and shoved the barrel of a gun or gas pistol into respondent's face. Id., at 122. Respondent was left lying and bleeding profusely for approximately 10 or 15 more minutes, and was then taken to the prison hospital. Id., at 194. He suffered very severe injury. Meanwhile, Klenk had been subdued with no resistance by Whitley, id., at 164, 234, who was unarmed, id., at 233.

Other testimony showed that, although most of the inmates assembled in the area were clearly not participating in the misconduct, they received no warning, instructions, or opportunity to leave the area and return to their cells before the officers started shooting. Id., at 163. Neither respondent nor any other inmate attempted to impede the officers as they entered the cellblock. Id., at 234. The officers were described as "wild," "agitated, excited," not in full control of their emotions. Id., at 192. One officer, prior to entering cellblock "A," told the others to "shoot their asses off, and if Klenk gets in the way, kill him." Ibid. At the time of this assault, the cellblock was described as "quiet." Id., at 193.

If a jury credited respondent's testimony and that of his witnesses, it would have believed that there was only one inmate who was temporarily out of control, Klenk— "scared," id., at 165, and "high," id., at 117— and ready to give up. The disturbance in the block had lasted only 15 or 20 minutes when it subsided, and there appeared to be no lasting danger to anyone. Respondent was shot while he stood motionless on the stairs, and was left to bleed for a perilously long time before receiving any assistance.

III

* * *

The majority suggests that the existence of more appropriate alternative measures for controlling prison disturbances is irrelevant to the constitutional inquiry, but surely it cannot mean what it appears to say. For if prison officials were to drop a bomb on a cellblock in order to halt a fistfight between two inmates, for example, I feel confident that the Court would have difficulty concluding, as a matter of law, that such an action was not sufficiently wanton to present a jury question, even though concededly taken in an effort to restore order in the prison. Thus, the question of wantonness in the context of prison disorder, as with other claims of mistreatment under the Eighth Amendment, is a matter of degree. And it is precisely in cases like this one, when shading the facts one way or the other can result in different legal conclusions, that a jury should be permitted to do its job. Properly instructed, a jury would take into account the petitioners' legitimate need to protect security, the extent of the danger presented, and the reasonableness of force used, in assessing liability. Moreover, the jury would know that a prisoner's burden is a heavy one, if he is to establish an Eighth Amendment violation under these circumstances. Whether respondent was able to meet that burden here is a question for the jury. From the Court's usurpation of the jury's function, I dissent. I would affirm the judgment of the Court of Appeals.

HUDSON
v.
McMILLIAN

503 U.S. 1; 112 S. Ct. 995; 117 L. Ed. 2d 156 (1992)
[Most citations and footnotes omitted]

JUSTICE O'CONNOR delivered the opinion of the Court.

This case requires us to decide whether the use of excessive physical force against a prisoner may constitute cruel and unusual punishment when the inmate does not suffer serious injury. We answer that question in the affirmative.

I

At the time of the incident that is the subject of this suit, petitioner Keith Hudson was an inmate at the state penitentiary in Angola, Louisiana. Respondents Jack McMillian, Marvin Woods, and Arthur Mezo served as corrections security officers at the Angola facility. During the early morning hours of October 30, 1983, Hudson and McMillian argued. Assisted by Woods, McMillian then placed Hudson in handcuffs and shackles, took the prisoner out of his cell, and walked him toward the penitentiary's "administrative lockdown" area. Hudson testified that, on the way there, McMillian punched Hudson in the mouth, eyes, chest, and stomach while Woods held the inmate in place and kicked and punched him from behind. He further testified that Mezo, the supervisor on duty, watched the beating but merely told the officers "not to have too much fun." . . . As a result of this episode, Hudson suffered minor bruises and swelling of his face, mouth, and lip. The blows also loosened Hudson's teeth and cracked his partial dental plate, rendering it unusable for several months.

Hudson sued the three corrections officers in Federal District Court under 42 U.S.C. § 1983, alleging a violation of the Eighth Amendment's prohibition on cruel and unusual punishments and seeking compensatory damages. The parties consented to disposition of the case before a Magistrate, who found that McMillian and Woods used force when there was no need to do so and that

Mezo expressly condoned their actions. . . . The Magistrate awarded Hudson damages of $800.

The Court of Appeals for the Fifth Circuit reversed. It held that inmates alleging use of excessive force in violation of the Eighth Amendment must prove: (1) significant injury; (2) resulting "directly and only from the use of force that was clearly excessive to the need"; (3) the excessiveness of which was objectively unreasonable; and (4) that the action constituted an unnecessary and wanton infliction of pain. The court determined that respondents' use of force was objectively unreasonable because no force was required. Furthermore, "the conduct of McMillian and Woods qualified as clearly excessive and occasioned unnecessary and wanton infliction of pain." Ibid. However, Hudson could not prevail on his Eighth Amendment claim because his injuries were "minor" and required no medical attention. Ibid.

We granted certiorari to determine whether the "significant injury" requirement applied by the Court of Appeals accords with the Constitution's dictate that cruel and unusual punishment shall not be inflicted.

II

In Whitley v. Albers, the principal question before us was what legal standard should govern the Eighth Amendment claim of an inmate shot by a guard during a prison riot. We based our answer on the settled rule that "the unnecessary and wanton infliction of pain . . . constitutes cruel and unusual punishment forbidden by the Eighth Amendment." What is necessary to establish an "unnecessary and wanton infliction of pain," we said, varies according to the nature of the alleged constitutional violation. For example, the appropriate inquiry when an inmate alleges that prison officials failed to attend to serious medical needs is whether the officials exhibited "deliberate indifference." See Estelle v. Gamble. This standard is appropriate because the State's responsibility to provide inmates with medical care ordinarily does not conflict with competing administrative concerns.

By contrast, officials confronted with a prison disturbance must balance the threat unrest poses to inmates, prison workers, administrators, and visitors against the harm inmates may suffer if guards use force. Despite the weight of these competing concerns, corrections officials must make their decisions "in haste, under pressure, and frequently without the luxury of a second chance." We accordingly concluded in Whitley that application of the deliberate indifference standard is inappropriate when authorities use force to put down a prison disturbance. Instead, "the question whether the measure taken inflicted unnecessary and wanton pain and suffering ultimately turns on whether force was applied in a good faith effort to maintain or restore discipline or maliciously and sadistically for the very purpose of causing harm."

Many of the concerns underlying our holding in Whitley arise whenever guards use force to keep order. Whether the prison disturbance is a riot or a lesser disruption, corrections officers must balance the need "to maintain or restore discipline" through force against the risk of injury to inmates. Both situations may require prison officials to act quickly and decisively. Likewise, both implicate the principle that "prison administrators . . . should be accorded wide-ranging deference in the adoption and execution of policies and practices that in their judgment are needed to preserve internal order and discipline and to maintain institutional security." In recognition of these similarities, we hold that whenever prison officials stand accused of using excessive physical force in violation of the Cruel and Unusual Punishments Clause, the core judicial inquiry is that set out in Whitley: whether force was applied in a good-faith effort to maintain or restore discipline, or maliciously and sadistically to cause harm.

Extending Whitley's application of the "unnecessary and wanton infliction of pain" standard to all allegations of excessive force works no innovation. This Court derived the Whitley test from one articulated by Judge Friendly in Johnson v. Glick, supra, a case arising out of a prisoner's claim to have been beaten and harassed by a guard. Moreover, many Courts of Appeals already apply the Whitley standard to allegations of excessive force outside of the riot situation. . . .

A

Under the Whitley approach, the extent of injury suffered by an inmate is one factor that may suggest "whether the use of force could plausibly have been thought necessary" in a particular situation, "or instead evinced such wantonness with respect to the unjustified infliction of harm as is tantamount to a knowing willingness that it occur." In determining whether the use of force was wanton and unnecessary, it may also be proper to evaluate the need for application of force, the relationship between that need and the amount of force used, the threat "reasonably perceived by the responsible officials," and "any efforts made to temper the severity of a forceful response." Ibid. The absence of serious injury is therefore relevant to the Eighth Amendment inquiry, but does not end it.

Respondents nonetheless assert that a significant injury requirement of the sort imposed by the Fifth Circuit is mandated by what we have termed the "objective component" of Eighth Amendment analysis. Wilson extended the deliberate indifference standard applied to Eighth Amendment claims involving medical care to claims about conditions of confinement. In taking this step, we suggested that the subjective aspect of an Eighth Amendment claim (with which the Court was concerned) can be distinguished from the objective facet of the same claim. Thus, courts considering a prisoner's claim must ask both if "the officials acted with a sufficiently culpable state of mind" and if the alleged wrongdoing was objectively "harmful enough" to establish a constitutional violation.

With respect to the objective component of an Eighth Amendment violation, Wilson announced no new rule. Instead, that decision suggested a relationship between the requirements applicable to different types of Eighth Amendment claims. What is necessary to show sufficient harm for purposes of the Cruel and Unusual Punishments Clause depends upon the claim at issue, for two reasons. First, "the general requirement that an Eighth Amendment claimant allege and prove the unnecessary and wanton infliction of pain should . . . be applied with due regard for differences in the kind of conduct against which an Eighth Amendment objection is lodged." Second, the Eighth Amendment's prohibition of cruel and unusual punishments "draw[s] its meaning from the evolving standards of decency that mark the progress of a maturing society," and so admits of few absolute limitations.

The objective component of an Eighth Amendment claim is therefore contextual and responsive to "contemporary standards of decency." For instance, extreme deprivations are required to make out a conditions-of-confinement claim. Because routine discomfort is "part of the penalty that criminal offenders pay for their offenses against society," "only those deprivations denying the minimal civilized measure of life's necessities are sufficiently grave to form the basis of an Eighth Amendment violation." A similar analysis applies to medical needs. Because society does not expect that prisoners will have unqualified access to health care, deliberate indifference to medical needs amounts to an Eighth Amendment violation only if those needs are "serious."

In the excessive force context, society's expectations are different. When prison officials maliciously and sadistically use force to cause harm, contemporary standards of decency are always violated. This is true whether or not significant injury is evident. Otherwise, the Eighth Amendment would permit any physical punishment, no matter how diabolic or inhuman, inflicting less than some arbitrary quantity of injury. Such a result would have been as unacceptable to the drafters of the Eighth Amendment as it is today. See Estelle (proscribing torture and barbarous punishment was "the primary concern of the drafters" of the Eighth Amendment); Wilkerson v. Utah ("It is safe to affirm that punishments of torture . . . and all others in the same line of unnecessary cruelty, are forbidden by [the Eighth Amendment]").

That is not to say that every malevolent touch by a prison guard gives rise to a federal cause of action. See Johnson v. Glick, 481 F. 2d, at 1033 ("Not every push or shove, even if it may later seem unnecessary in the peace of a judge's chambers, violates a prisoner's constitutional rights"). The Eighth Amendment's prohibition of "cruel and unusual" punishment necessarily excludes from constitutional recognition de minimis

uses of physical force, provided that the use of force is not of a sort "repugnant to the conscience of mankind."

In this case, the Fifth Circuit found Hudson's claim untenable because his injuries were "minor." Yet the blows directed at Hudson, which caused bruises, swelling, loosened teeth, and a cracked dental plate, are not de minimis for Eighth Amendment purposes. The extent of Hudson's injuries thus provides no basis for dismissal of his § 1983 claim.

B

The dissent's theory that Wilson requires an inmate who alleges excessive use of force to show serious injury in addition to the unnecessary and wanton infliction of pain misapplies Wilson and ignores the body of our Eighth Amendment jurisprudence. As we have already suggested, the question before the Court in Wilson was "whether a prisoner claiming that conditions of confinement constitute cruel and unusual punishment must show a culpable state of mind on the part of prison officials and, if so, what state of mind is required." Wilson presented neither an allegation of excessive force nor any issue relating to what was dubbed the "objective component" of an Eighth Amendment claim.

Wilson did touch on these matters in the course of summarizing our prior holdings, beginning with Estelle v. Gamble, supra. Estelle, we noted, first applied the Cruel and Unusual Punishments Clause to deprivations that were not specifically part of the prisoner's sentence. As might be expected from this primacy, Estelle stated the principle underlying the cases discussed in Wilson: punishments "incompatible with the evolving standards of decency that mark the progress of a maturing society" or "involving the unnecessary and wanton infliction of pain" are "repugnant to the Eighth Amendment." This is the same rule the dissent would reject. With respect to the objective component of an Eighth Amendment claim, however, Wilson suggested no departure from Estelle and its progeny.

The dissent's argument that claims based on excessive force and claims based on conditions of confinement are no different in kind, is likewise unfounded. Far from rejecting Whitley's insight that the unnecessary and wanton infliction of pain standard must be applied with regard for the nature of the alleged Eighth Amendment violation, the Wilson Court adopted it. How could it be otherwise when the constitutional touchstone is whether punishment is cruel and unusual? To deny, as the dissent does, the difference between punching a prisoner in the face and serving him unappetizing food is to ignore the "concepts of dignity, civilized standards, humanity, and decency" that animate the Eighth Amendment.

C

Respondents argue that, aside from the significant injury test applied by the Fifth Circuit, their conduct cannot constitute an Eighth Amendment violation because it was "isolated and unauthorized." The beating of Hudson, they contend, arose from "a personal dispute between correctional security officers and a prisoner," and was against prison policy. Ibid. Respondents invoke the reasoning of courts that have held the use of force by prison officers under such circumstances beyond the scope of "punishment" prohibited by the Eighth Amendment. See Johnson v. Glick, supra, at 1032 ("Although a spontaneous attack by a guard is 'cruel' and, we hope, 'unusual,' it does not fit any ordinary concept of punishment"); George v. Evans, 633 F. 2d 413, 416 (CA5 1980) ("[A] single, unauthorized assault by a guard does not constitute cruel and unusual punishment . . ."). But see Duckworth v. Franzen, 780 F. 2d 645, 652 (CA7 1985) ("If a guard decided to supplement a prisoner's official punishment by beating him, this would be punishment . . .")

We take no position on respondents' legal argument because we find it inapposite on this record. The Court of Appeals left intact the Magistrate's determination that the violence at issue in this case was "not an isolated assault." . . . Indeed, there was testimony that McMillian and Woods beat another prisoner shortly after they finished with Hudson. Ibid. To the extent that respondents rely on the unauthorized nature of their acts, they make a claim not addressed by the Fifth Circuit, not presented by the question on which we granted certiorari, and, accordingly, not before this Court. Moreover, respondents

ignore the Magistrate's finding that Lieutenant Mezo, acting as a supervisor, "expressly condoned the use of force in this instance."

* * *

The judgment of the Court of Appeals is reversed.

JUSTICE STEVENS, concurring in part and concurring in the judgment.

In Whitley v. Albers, the Court held that injuries to prisoners do not constitute cruel and unusual punishment when they are inflicted during a prison disturbance "that indisputably poses significant risks to the safety of inmates and prison staff" unless force was applied "maliciously and sadistically for the very purpose of causing harm." The Court's opinion explained that the justification for that particularly high standard of proof was required by the exigencies present during a serious prison disturbance. "When the ever-present potential for violent confrontation and conflagration ripens into actual unrest and conflict," then prison officials must be permitted to "take into account the very real threats the unrest presents to inmates and prison officials alike."

Absent such special circumstances, however, the less demanding standard of "unnecessary and wanton infliction of pain" should be applied. Estelle v. Gamble; see Unwin v. Campbell, 863 F. 2d 124, 135 (CA1 1988) (opinion of Campbell, C. J.) ("where institutional security is not at stake, the officials' license to use force is more limited; to succeed, a plaintiff need not prove malicious and sadistic intent"); see also Wyatt v. Delaney, 818 F. 2d 21, 23 (CA8 1987). This approach is consistent with the Court's admonition in Whitley that the standard to be used is one that gives "due regard for differences in the kind of conduct against which an Eighth Amendment objection is lodged." In this case, because there was no prison disturbance and "no need to use any force since the plaintiff was already in restraints," . . . the prison guards' attack upon petitioner resulted in the infliction of unnecessary and wanton pain.

Although I think that the Court's reliance on the malicious and sadistic standard is misplaced, I agree with the Court that even this more demanding standard was met here. Accordingly, I concur in Parts I, II(A), II(B), and II(C) of the Court's opinion and in its judgment.

JUSTICE BLACKMUN, concurring in the judgment.

The Court today appropriately puts to rest a seriously misguided view that pain inflicted by an excessive use of force is actionable under the Eighth Amendment only when coupled with "significant injury," e.g., injury that requires medical attention or leaves permanent marks. Indeed, were we to hold to the contrary, we might place various kinds of state-sponsored torture and abuse—of the kind ingeniously designed to cause pain but without a telltale "significant injury"— entirely beyond the pale of the Constitution. In other words, the constitutional prohibition of "cruel and unusual punishments" then might not constrain prison officials from lashing prisoners with leather straps, whipping them with rubber hoses, beating them with naked fists, shocking them with electric currents, asphyxiating them short of death, intentionally exposing them to undue heat or cold, or forcibly injecting them with psychosis-inducing drugs. These techniques, commonly thought to be practiced only outside this Nation's borders, are hardly unknown within this Nation's prisons. See, e.g., Campbell v. Grammer, 889 F.2d 797, 802 (CA8 1989) (use of high-powered fire hoses); Jackson v. Bishop, 404 F.2d 571, 574-575 (CA8 1968) (use of the "Tucker Telephone," a hand-cranked device that generated electric shocks to sensitive body parts, and flogging with leather strap).

Because I was in the dissent in Whitley v. Albers, I do not join the Court's extension of Whitley's malicious-and-sadistic standard to all allegations of excessive force, even outside the context of a prison riot. Nevertheless, I otherwise join the Court's solid opinion and judgment that the Eighth Amendment does not require a showing of "significant injury" in the excessive-force context. I write separately to highlight two concerns not addressed by the Court in its opinion.

I

Citing rising caseloads, respondents, represented by the Attorney General of Louisiana, and joined by the States of Texas, Hawaii, Nevada, Wyoming, and Florida as amici curiae, suggest that a "significant injury" requirement is necessary to curb the number of court filings by prison inmates. We are informed that the "significant injury requirement has been very effective in the Fifth Circuit in helping to control its system-wide docket management problems." . . .

This audacious approach to the Eighth Amendment assumes that the interpretation of an explicit constitutional protection is to be guided by pure policy preferences for the paring down of prisoner petitions. Perhaps judicial overload is an appropriate concern in determining whether statutory standing to sue should be conferred upon certain plaintiffs. Since the burden on the courts is presumably worth bearing when a prisoner's suit has merit, the States' "concern" is more aptly termed a "conclusion" that such suits are simply without merit. One's experience on the federal bench teaches the contrary. Moreover, were particular classes of cases to be nominated for exclusion from the federal courthouse, we might look first to cases in which federal law is not sensitively at issue rather than to those in which fundamental constitutional rights are at stake. The right to file for legal redress in the courts is as valuable to a prisoner as to any other citizen. Indeed, for the prisoner it is more valuable. Inasmuch as one convicted of a serious crime and imprisoned usually is divested of the franchise, the right to file a court action stands, in the words of Yick Wo v. Hopkins, 118 U.S. 356, 370 (1886), as his most "fundamental political right, because preservative of all rights."

Today's ruling, in any event, does not open the floodgates for filings by prison inmates. By statute, prisoners—alone among all other § 1983 claimants—are required to exhaust administrative remedies. Moreover, prison officials are entitled to a determination before trial whether they acted in an objectively reasonable manner, thereby entitling them to a qualified immunity defense. Procunier v. Navarette; see also Harlow v. Fitzgerald, (unsubstantiated allegations of malice are insufficient to overcome pretrial qualified immunity). Additionally, a federal district court is authorized to dismiss a prisoner's complaint in forma pauperis "if satisfied that the action is frivolous or malicious." These measures should be adequate to control any docket-management problems that might result from meritless prisoner claims.

II

I do not read anything in the Court's opinion to limit injury cognizable under the Eighth Amendment to physical injury. It is not hard to imagine inflictions of psychological harm—without corresponding physical harm—that might prove to be cruel and unusual punishment. See, e.g., Wisniewski v. Kennard, 901 F.2d 1276, 1277 (CA5) (guard placing a revolver in inmate's mouth and threatening to blow prisoner's head off), cert. denied, U.S. (1990). The issue was not presented here, because Hudson did not allege that he feared that the beating incident would be repeated or that it had caused him anxiety and depression.

As the Court makes clear, the Eighth Amendment prohibits the unnecessary and wanton infliction of "pain," rather than "injury." "Pain" in its ordinary meaning surely includes a notion of psychological harm. I am unaware of any precedent of this Court to the effect that psychological pain is not cognizable for constitutional purposes. If anything, our precedent is to the contrary. See Sierra Club v. Morton (recognizing Article III standing for "aesthetic" injury); Brown v. Board of Education (identifying school children's feelings of psychological inferiority from segregation in the public schools).

To be sure, as the Court's opinion intimates, de minimis or nonmeasurable pain is not actionable under the Eighth Amendment. But psychological pain can be more than de minimis. Psychological pain often may be clinically diagnosed and quantified through well established methods, as in the ordinary tort context where damages for pain and suffering are regularly awarded. I have no doubt that to read a "physical pain" or "physical injury" requirement into the Eighth Amendment would be no less pernicious and without foundation than the "significant injury" requirement we reject today.

JUSTICE THOMAS, with whom JUSTICE SCALIA joins, dissenting.

. . . In my view, a use of force that causes only insignificant harm to a prisoner may be immoral, it may be tortious, it may be criminal, and it may even be remediable under other provisions of the Federal Constitution, but it is not "cruel and unusual punishment." In concluding to the contrary, the Court today goes far beyond our precedents.

A

Until recent years, the Cruel and Unusual Punishment Clause was not deemed to apply at all to deprivations that were not inflicted as part of the sentence for a crime. For generations, judges and commentators regarded the Eighth Amendment as applying only to torturous punishments meted out by statutes or sentencing judges, and not generally to any hardship that might befall a prisoner during incarceration. In Weems v. United States, 217 U.S. 349 (1910), the Court extensively chronicled the background of the amendment, discussing its English antecedents, its adoption by Congress, its construction by this Court, and the interpretation of analogous provisions by state courts. Nowhere does Weems even hint that the Clause might regulate not just criminal sentences but the treatment of prisoners. Scholarly commentary also viewed the Clause as governing punishments that were part of the sentence. See T. Cooley, *Constitutional Limitations* ("It is certainly difficult to determine precisely what is meant by cruel and unusual punishments. Probably any punishment declared by statute for an offence which was punishable in the same way at the common law, could not be regarded as cruel or unusual in the constitutional sense. And probably any new statutory offence may be punished to the extent and in the mode permitted by the common law for offences of similar nature. But those degrading punishments which in any State had become obsolete before its existing constitution was adopted, we think may well be held forbidden by it as cruel and unusual")

Surely prison was not a more congenial place in the early years of the Republic than it is today; nor were our judges and commentators so naive as to be unaware of the often harsh conditions of prison life. Rather, they simply did not conceive of the Eighth Amendment as protecting inmates from harsh treatment. Thus, historically, the lower courts routinely rejected prisoner grievances by explaining that the courts had no role in regulating prison life. "It is well settled that it is not the function of the courts to superintend the treatment and discipline of prisoners in penitentiaries, but only to deliver from imprisonment those who are illegally confined." It was not until 1976—185 years after the Eighth Amendment was adopted—that this Court first applied it to a prisoner's complaint about a deprivation suffered in prison. Estelle v. Gamble.

B

We made clear in Estelle that the Eighth Amendment plays a very limited role in regulating prison administration. The case involved a claim that prison doctors had inadequately attended an inmate's medical needs. We rejected the claim because the inmate failed to allege "acts or omissions sufficiently harmful to evidence deliberate indifference to serious medical needs." From the outset, thus, we specified that the Eighth Amendment does not apply to every deprivation, or even every unnecessary deprivation, suffered by a prisoner, but only that narrow class of deprivations involving "serious" injury inflicted by prison officials acting with a culpable state of mind. We have since described these twin elements as the "objective" and "subjective" components of an Eighth Amendment prison claim.

We have never found a violation of the Eighth Amendment in the prison context when an inmate has failed to establish either of these elements. In Rhodes v. Chapman, for instance, we upheld a practice of placing two inmates in a single cell on the ground that the injury alleged was insufficiently serious. Only where prison conditions deny an inmate "the minimal civilized measure of life's necessities," we said, could they be considered "cruel and unusual punishment." Similarly, in Whitley v. Albers, we held that a guard did not violate the Eighth Amendment when he shot an inmate during a prison riot because he had not acted with a sufficiently culpable state of mind. When an official uses force to quell a riot, we said, he does not violate the Eighth Amendment unless he acts "maliciously and sadistically for the very purpose of causing harm."

We synthesized our Eighth Amendment prison jurisprudence last Term in Wilson, supra. There the inmate alleged that the poor conditions of his confinement per se amounted to cruel and unusual punishment, and argued that he should not be required in addition to establish that officials acted culpably. We rejected that argument, emphasizing that an inmate seeking to establish that a prison deprivation amounts to cruel and unusual punishment always must satisfy both the "objective component . . . (was the deprivation sufficiently serious?)" and the "subjective component (did the officials act with a sufficiently culpable state of mind?)" of the Eighth Amendment. Both are necessary components; neither suffices by itself.

These subjective and objective components, of course, are implicit in the traditional Eighth Amendment jurisprudence, which focuses on penalties meted out by statutes or sentencing judges. Thus, if a State were to pass a statute ordering that convicted felons be broken at the wheel, we would not separately inquire whether the legislature had acted with "deliberate indifference," since a statute, as an intentional act, necessarily satisfies an even higher state-of-mind threshold. Likewise, the inquiry whether the deprivation is objectively serious would be encompassed within our determination whether it was "cruel and unusual."

When we cut the Eighth Amendment loose from its historical moorings and applied it to a broad range of prison deprivations, we found it appropriate to make explicit the limitations described in Estelle, Rhodes, Whitley, and Wilson. "If the pain inflicted is not formally meted out as punishment by the statute or the sentencing judge, some mental element must be attributed to the inflicting officer before it can qualify,"—thus, the subjective component. Similarly, because deprivations of all sorts are the very essence of imprisonment, we made explicit the serious deprivation requirement to ensure that the Eighth Amendment did not transfer wholesale the regulation of prison life from executive officials to judges. That is why, in Wilson, we described the inquiry mandated by the objective component as: "Was the deprivation sufficiently serious?" That formulation plainly reveals our prior assumption that a serious deprivation is always required. Under that analysis, a court's task in any given case was to determine whether the challenged deprivation was "sufficiently" serious. It was not, as the Court's interpretation today would have it, to determine whether a "serious" deprivation is required at all.

C

Given Estelle, Rhodes, Whitley, and Wilson, one might have assumed that the Court would have little difficulty answering the question presented in this case by upholding the Fifth Circuit's "significant injury" requirement. Instead, the Court announces that "the objective component of an Eighth Amendment claim is . . . contextual and responsive to contemporary standards of decency." In the context of claims alleging the excessive use of physical force, the Court then asserts, the serious deprivation requirement is satisfied by no serious deprivation at all. "When prison officials maliciously and sadistically use force to cause harm, contemporary standards of decency are always violated." Ibid. Ascertaining prison officials' state of mind, in other words, is the only relevant inquiry in deciding whether such cases involve "cruel and unusual punishment." In my view, this approach is an unwarranted and unfortunate break with our Eighth Amendment prison jurisprudence.

The Court purports to derive the answer to this case from Whitley. The sum and substance of an Eighth Amendment violation, the Court asserts, is "the unnecessary and wanton infliction of pain." This formulation has the advantage, from the Court's perspective, of eliminating the objective component. As noted above, however, the only dispute in Whitley concerned the subjective component; the prisoner, who had been shot, had self-evidently been subjected to an objectively serious injury. Whitley did not say, as the Court does today, that the objective component is contextual, and that an Eighth Amendment claim may succeed where a prisoner is not seriously injured. Rather, Whitley stands for the proposition that, assuming the existence of an objectively serious deprivation, the culpability of an official's state of mind depends on the context in which he acts. "Whitley teaches that, assuming the conduct is harmful enough to satisfy the objective component of an Eighth Amendment claim, see Rhodes v. Chapman, whether it can be characterized as 'wanton' depends upon the constraints facing the official." Wilson, supra. Whether officials subject a prisoner to the "unnecessary and wanton infliction of pain" is simply one way to describe the state of mind inquiry that was at issue in Whitley itself. As Wilson made clear, that inquiry is necessary but not sufficient when a prisoner seeks to show that he has been subjected to cruel and unusual punishment.

Perhaps to compensate for its elimination of the objective component in excessive force cases, the Court simultaneously makes it harder for prisoners to establish the subjective component. As we explained in Wilson, "deliberate indifference" is the baseline mental state required to establish an Eighth Amendment violation. Departure from this baseline is justified where, as in Whitley, prison officials act in response to an emergency; in such situations their conduct cannot be characterized as "wanton" unless it is taken "maliciously and sadistically for the very purpose of causing harm." The Court today extends the heightened mental state applied in Whitley to all excessive force cases, even where no competing institutional concerns are present. The Court simply asserts that "many of the concerns underlying our holding in Whitley arise whenever guards use force to keep order." I do not agree. Many excessive force cases do not arise from guards' attempts to "keep order." (In this very case, the basis for petitioner's Eighth Amendment claim is that the guards hit him when there was no need for them to use any force at all.) The use of excessive physical force is by no means invariably (in fact, perhaps not even predominantly) accompanied by a "malicious and sadistic" state of mind. I see no justification for applying the extraordinary Whitley standard to all excessive force cases, without regard to the constraints facing prison officials. The Court's unwarranted extension of Whitley, I can only suppose, is driven by the implausibility of saying that minor injuries imposed upon prisoners with anything less than a "malicious and sadistic" state of mind can amount to "cruel and unusual punishment."

D

The Court's attempts to distinguish the cases expressly resting upon the objective component are equally unconvincing. As noted above, we have required an extreme deprivation in cases challenging conditions of confinement, Rhodes v. Chapman. Why should such an objectively serious deprivation be required there and not here? The Court's explanation is that "routine discomfort is part of the penalty that criminal offenders pay for their offenses against society.'" But there is quite a gap between "routine discomfort" and the denial of "the minimal civilized measure of life's necessities" required to establish an Eighth Amendment violation. In the Court's view, then, our society's standards of decency are not violated by anything short of uncivilized conditions of confinement (no matter how malicious the mental state of the officials involved), but are automatically violated by any malicious use of force, regardless of whether it even causes an injury. This is puzzling. I see no reason why our society's standards of decency should be more readily offended when officials, with a culpable state of mind, subject a prisoner to a deprivation on one discrete occasion than when they subject him to continuous deprivations over time. If anything, I would think that a deprivation inflicted continuously over a long period would be of greater concern to society than a deprivation inflicted on one particular occasion.

The Court's attempted distinction of Estelle is also unpersuasive: "Because society does not expect that prisoners will have unqualified access to health care, deliberate indifference to medical needs amounts to an Eighth Amendment violation only if those needs are serious.'" Ante, at 6. In my view, our society similarly has no expectation that prisoners will have "unqualified" freedom from force, since forcibly keeping prisoners in detention is what prisons are all about. Why should the seriousness of injury matter when doctors maliciously decide not to treat an inmate, but not when guards maliciously decide to strike him?

At bottom, of course, there is no conclusive way to refute the Court's assertions about our society's "contemporary notions of decency." That is precisely why this Court has long insisted that determinations of whether punishment is cruel and unusual "should be informed by objective factors to the maximum possible extent." The Court attempts to justify its departure from precedent by saying that if a showing of serious injury were required, "the Eighth Amendment would permit any physical punishment, no matter how diabolic or inhuman, inflicting less than some arbitrary quantity of injury." That statement, in my view, reveals a central flaw in the Court's reasoning. "Diabolic or inhuman" punishments by definition inflict serious injury. That is not to say that the injury must be, or always will be, physical. "Many things—beating with a rubber truncheon, water torture, electric shock, incessant noise, reruns of Space '1999'—may cause agony as they occur yet leave no enduring injury. The state is not free to inflict such pains without cause just so long as it is careful to leave no marks." Williams v. Boles, 841 F. 2d 181, 183 (CA7 1988). Surely a prisoner who alleges that prison officials tortured him with a device like the notorious "Tucker Telephone" described by JUSTICE BLACKMUN, has alleged a serious injury. But petitioner has not alleged a deprivation of this type; the injuries he has alleged are entirely physical and were found below to be "minor."

Furthermore, to characterize the serious injury requirement as "arbitrary" is not to explain why it should be eliminated in this particular context while it remains applicable to all other prison deprivations. To be sure, it will not always be obvious which injuries are "serious." But similarly, it will not always be obvious which medical needs are "serious," or which conditions of confinement deny "the minimal civilized measure of life's necessities." These determinations are, however, required by the Eighth Amendment, which prohibits only those punishments that are "cruel and unusual." As explained above, I think our precedents clearly establish that a prisoner seeking to prove that he has been subjected to "cruel and unusual" punishment must always show that he has suffered a serious deprivation.

If the Court is to be taken at its word that "the unnecessary and wanton infliction of pain" upon a prisoner per se amounts to "cruel and unusual punishment," the implications of today's opinion are sweeping. For this formulation replaces the objective component described in our prior cases with a "necessity" component. Many prison deprivations, however, are not "necessary," at least under any meaningful definition of that word. Thus, under today's analysis, Rhodes was wrongly decided. Surely the "double-celling" of inmates was not "necessary" to fulfill the State's penal mission; in fact, the prison in that case had been designed for individual cells, but was simply overcrowded. We rejected the prisoners' claim in Rhodes not because we determined that double-celling was "necessary," but because the deprivations alleged were not sufficiently serious to state a claim of cruel and unusual punishment. After today, the "necessity" of a deprivation is apparently the only relevant inquiry beyond the wantonness of official conduct. This approach, in my view, extends the Eighth Amendment beyond all reasonable limits.

II

Today's expansion of the Cruel and Unusual Punishment Clause beyond all bounds of history and precedent is, I suspect, yet another manifestation of the pervasive view that the Federal Constitution must address all ills in our society. Abusive behavior by prison guards is deplorable conduct that properly evokes outrage and contempt. But that does not mean that it is invariably unconstitutional. The Eighth Amendment is not, and should not be turned into, a National Code of Prison Regulation. To reject the notion that the infliction of concededly "minor" injuries can be considered either "cruel" or "unusual" "punishment" (much less cruel and unusual punishment) is not to say that it amounts to acceptable conduct. Rather, it is to recognize that primary responsibility for preventing and punishing such conduct rests not with the Federal Constitution but with the laws and regulations of the various States.

Petitioner apparently could have, but did not, seek redress for his injuries under state law. Respondents concede that if available state remedies were not constitutionally adequate, petitioner would have a claim under the Due Process Clause of the Fourteenth Amendment. I agree with respondents that this is the appropriate, and appropriately limited, federal constitutional inquiry in this case.

Because I conclude that, under our precedents, a prisoner seeking to establish that he has been subjected to "cruel and unusual punishment" must always show that he has suffered a serious injury, I would affirm the judgment of the Fifth Circuit.

HOPE
v.
PELZER

536 U.S. 730; 122 S. Ct. 2508 (2002)
(Footnotes and citations omitted)

JUSTICE STEVENS delivered the opinion of the Court.

* * *

I

In 1995, Alabama was the only State that followed the practice of chaining inmates to one another in work squads. It was also the only State that handcuffed prisoners to "hitching posts" if they either refused to work or otherwise disrupted work squads.[1] Hope was handcuffed to a hitching post on two occasions. On May 11, 1995, while Hope was working in a chain gang near an interstate highway, he got into an argument with another inmate. Both men were taken back to the Limestone prison and handcuffed to a hitching post. Hope was released two hours later, after the guard captain determined that the altercation had been caused by the other inmate. During his two hours on the post, Hope was offered drinking water and a bathroom break every 15 minutes, and his responses to these offers were recorded on an activity log. Because he was only slightly

---

[30] Germany v. United States, 526 U.S. 111 (1999). The full decision can be found in Appendix V.

taller than the hitching post, his arms were above shoulder height and grew tired from being handcuffed so high. Whenever he tried moving his arms to improve his circulation, the handcuffs cut into his wrists, causing pain and discomfort.

On June 7, 1995, Hope was punished more severely. He took a nap during the morning bus ride to the chain gang's worksite, and when it arrived he was less than prompt in responding to an order to get off the bus. An exchange of vulgar remarks led to a wrestling match with a guard. Four other guards intervened, subdued Hope, handcuffed him, placed him in leg irons and transported him back to the prison where he was put on the hitching post. The guards made him take off his shirt, and he remained shirtless all day while the sun burned his skin. He remained attached to the post for approximately seven hours. During this 7-hour period, he was given water only once or twice and was given no bathroom breaks. At one point, a guard taunted Hope about his thirst. According to Hope's affidavit: "[The guard] first gave water to some dogs, then brought the water cooler closer to me, removed its lid, and kicked the cooler over, spilling the water onto the ground." * * *

II

* * *

We agree with the Court of Appeals that the attachment of Hope to the hitching post under the circumstances alleged in this case violated the Eighth Amendment.

"'The unnecessary and wanton infliction of pain . . . constitutes cruel and unusual punishment forbidden by the Eighth Amendment.'" * * * We have said that "among 'unnecessary and wanton' inflictions of pain are those that are 'totally without penological justification.'" * * * In making this determination in the context of prison conditions, we must ascertain whether the officials involved acted with "deliberate indifference" to the inmates' health or safety. * * * We may infer the existence of this subjective state of mind

from the fact that the risk of harm is obvious. * * *

As the facts are alleged by Hope, the Eighth Amendment violation is obvious. Any safety concerns had long since abated by the time petitioner was handcuffed to the hitching post because Hope had already been subdued, handcuffed, placed in leg irons, and transported back to the prison. He was separated from his work squad and not given the opportunity to return to work. Despite the clear lack of an emergency situation, the respondents knowingly subjected him to a substantial risk of physical harm, to unnecessary pain caused by the handcuffs and the restricted position of confinement for a 7-hour period, to unnecessary exposure to the heat of the sun, to prolonged thirst and taunting, and to a deprivation of bathroom breaks that created a risk of particular discomfort and humiliation. The use of the hitching post under these circumstances violated the "basic concept underlying the Eighth Amendment [, which] is nothing less than the dignity of man." * * * This punitive treatment amounts to gratuitous infliction of "wanton and unnecessary" pain that our precedent clearly prohibits.

* * *

IV

The use of the hitching post as alleged by Hope "unnecessarily and wantonly inflicted pain," * * * and thus was a clear violation of the Eighth Amendment. * * *. Arguably, the violation was so obvious that our own Eighth Amendment cases gave the respondents fair warning that their conduct violated the Constitution. Regardless, in light of binding Eleventh Circuit precedent, an Alabama Department of Corrections (ADOC) regulation, and a DOJ report informing the ADOC of the constitutional infirmity in its use of the hitching post, we readily conclude that the respondents' conduct violated "clearly established statutory or constitutional rights of which a reasonable person would have known." * * *

Cases Relating to Chapter 3

Prisoner's Rights to Visitation/Association; Searches

PELL
v.
PROCUNIER

417 U.S. 817; 94 S. Ct. 2800; 41 L. Ed. 2d 495 (1974)

MR. JUSTICE STEWART delivered the opinion of the Court.

* * *

I

In No. 73-754, the inmate plaintiffs claim that § 415.071, by prohibiting their participation in face-to-face communication with newsmen and other members of the general public, violates their right of free speech under the First and Fourteenth Amendments. Although the constitutional right of free speech has never been thought to embrace a right to require a journalist or any other citizen to listen to a person's views, let alone a right to require a publisher to publish those views in his newspaper, see Avins v. Rutgers, State University of New Jersey, 385 F.2d 151 (CA3 1967); Chicago Joint Board, Clothing Workers v. Chicago Tribune Co., 435 F.2d 470 (CA7 1970); Associates & Aldrich Co. v. Times Mirror Co., 440 F.2d 133 (CA9 1971), we proceed upon the hypothesis that under some circumstances the right of free speech includes a right to communicate a person's views to any willing listener, including a willing representative of the press for the purpose of publication by a willing publisher.

We start with the familiar proposition that "lawful incarceration brings about the necessary withdrawal or limitation of many privileges and rights, a retraction justified by the considerations underlying our penal system." Price v. Johnston, 334 U.S. 266, 285 (1948). See also Cruz v. Beto, 405 U.S. 319, 321 (1972). In the First Amendment context a corollary of this principle is that a prison inmate retains those First Amendment rights that are not inconsistent with his status as a prisoner or with the legitimate penological objectives of the corrections system. Thus, challenges to prison restrictions that are asserted to inhibit First Amendment interests must be analyzed in terms of the legitimate policies and goals of the corrections system, to whose custody and care the prisoner has been committed in accordance with due process of law.

An important function of the corrections system is the deterrence of crime. The premise is that by confining criminal offenders in a facility where they are isolated from the rest of society, a condition that most people presumably find undesirable, they and others will be deterred from committing additional criminal offenses. This isolation, of course, also serves a protective function by quarantining criminal offenders for a given period of time while, it is hoped, the rehabilitative processes of the corrections system work to correct the offender's demonstrated criminal proclivity. Thus, since most offenders will eventually return to society, another paramount objective of the corrections system is the rehabilitation of those committed to its custody. Finally, central to all other corrections goals is the institutional consideration of internal security within the corrections facilities themselves. It is in the light of these legitimate penal objectives that a court must assess challenges to prison regulations based on asserted constitutional rights of prisoners.

The regulation challenged here clearly restricts one manner of communication between prison inmates and members of the general public beyond the prison walls. But this is merely to state the problem, not to resolve it. For the same could be said of a refusal by corrections authorities to permit an inmate temporarily to leave the prison in order to communicate with persons outside. Yet no one could sensibly contend that the Constitution requires the authorities to give even individualized consideration to such requests. Cf. Zemel v. Rusk, 381 U.S. 1, 16-17 (1965). In order properly to evaluate the constitutionality of § 415.071, we think that the regulation cannot be considered in isolation but must be viewed in the light of the alternative means of communication permitted under the regulations with persons outside the prison. We recognize that there "may be particular qualities inherent in sustained, face-to-face debate, discussion and questioning," and "that [the] existence of other alternatives [does not] extinguis[h] altogether any constitutional interest on the part of the appellees in this particular form of access." Kleindienst v. Mandel, 408 U.S. 753, 765 (1972). But we regard the available "alternative means of [communication as] a relevant factor" in a case such as this where "we [are] called upon to balance First Amendment rights against [legitimate] governmental . . . interests." Ibid.

One such alternative available to California prison inmates is communication by mail. Although prison regulations, until recently, called for the censorship of statements, inter alia, that "unduly complain" or "magnify grievances," that express "inflammatory political, racial, religious or other views," or that were deemed "defamatory" or "otherwise inappropriate," we recently held that "the Department's regulations authorized censorship of prisoner mail far broader than any legitimate interest of penal administration demands," and accordingly affirmed a district court judgment invalidating the regu-

lations. Procunier v. Martinez, 416 U.S. 396, 416 (1974). In addition, we held that "the interest of prisoners and their correspondents in uncensored communication by letter, grounded as it is in the First Amendment, is plainly a 'liberty' interest within the meaning of the Fourteenth Amendment even though qualified of necessity by the circumstance of imprisonment." Accordingly, we concluded that any "decision to censor or withhold delivery of a particular letter must be accompanied by minimal procedural safeguards." Id., at 418, 417. Thus, it is clear that the medium of written correspondence affords inmates an open and substantially unimpeded channel for communication with persons outside the prison, including representatives of the news media.

Moreover, the visitation policy of the California Corrections Department does not seal the inmate off from personal contact with those outside the prison. Inmates are permitted to receive limited visits from members of their families, the clergy, their attorneys, and friends of prior acquaintance.[4] The selection of these categories of visitors is based on the Director's professional judgment that such visits will aid in the rehabilitation of the inmate while not compromising the other legitimate objectives of the corrections system. This is not a case in which the selection is based on the anticipated content of the communication between the inmate and the prospective visitor. If a member of the press fell within any of these categories, there is no suggestion that he would not be permitted to visit with the inmate. More importantly, however, inmates have an unrestricted opportuni-

---

[4] This policy does not appear to be codified or otherwise expressly articulated in any generally applicable rule or regulation. The statement of visiting privileges for San Quentin State Penitentiary indicates that all visitors must be approved by the corrections officials and must be either "members of the family or friends of long standing." It also permits visits by attorneys to their clients. Although nothing is said in this statement about visits by members of the clergy, there is no dispute among the parties that the practice of the Department of Corrections is to permit such visits. There is also no disagreement among the parties that this visitation policy is generally applied by the Department throughout the state corrections system.

ty to communicate with the press or any other member of the public through their families, friends, clergy, or attorneys who are permitted to visit them at the prison. Thus, this provides another alternative avenue of communication between prison inmates and persons outside the prison.

We would find the availability of such alternatives unimpressive if they were submitted as justification for governmental restriction of personal communication among members of the general public. We have recognized, however, that "the relationship of state prisoners and the state officers who supervise their confinement is far more intimate than that of a State and a private citizen," and that the "internal problems of state prisons involve issues . . . peculiarly within state authority and expertise." Preiser v. Rodriguez, 411 U.S. 475, 492 (1973).

In Procunier v. Martinez, supra, we could find no legitimate governmental interest to justify the substantial restrictions that had there been imposed on written communication by inmates. When, however, the question involves the entry of people into the prisons for face-to-face communication with inmates, it is obvious that institutional considerations, such as security and related administrative problems, as well as the accepted and legitimate policy objectives of the corrections system itself, require that some limitation be placed on such visitations. So long as reasonable and effective means of communication remain open and no discrimination in terms of content is involved, we believe that, in drawing such lines, "prison officials must be accorded latitude." Cruz v. Beto, 405 U.S., at 321.

In a number of contexts, we have held "that reasonable 'time, place and manner' regulations [of communicative activity] may be necessary to further significant governmental interests, and are permitted." Grayned v. City of Rockford, 408 U.S. 104, 115 (1972); Cox v. New Hampshire, 312 U.S. 569, 575-576 (1941); Poulos v. New Hampshire, 345 U.S. 395, 398 (1953); Cox v. Louisiana, 379 U.S. 536, 554-555 (1965); Adderley v. Florida, 385 U.S. 39, 46-48

(1966). "The nature of a place, the pattern of its normal activities, dictate the kinds of regulations of time, place, and manner that are reasonable." Grayned, supra, at 116 (internal quotation marks omitted). The "normal activity" to which a prison is committed—the involuntary confinement and isolation of large numbers of people, some of whom have demonstrated a capacity for violence—necessarily requires that considerable attention be devoted to the maintenance of security. Although they would not permit prison officials to prohibit all expression or communication by prison inmates, security considerations are sufficiently paramount in the administration of the prison to justify the imposition of some restrictions on the entry of outsiders into the prison for face-to-face contact with inmates.

In this case the restriction takes the form of limiting visitations to individuals who have either a personal or professional relationship to the inmate—family, friends or prior acquaintance, legal counsel, and clergy. In the judgment of the state corrections officials, this visitation policy will permit inmates to have personal contact with those persons who will aid in their rehabilitation, while keeping visitations at a manageable level that will not compromise institutional security. Such considerations are peculiarly within the province and professional expertise of corrections officials, and, in the absence of substantial evidence in the record to indicate that the officials have exaggerated their response to these considerations, courts should ordinarily defer to their expert judgment in such matters. Courts cannot, of course, abdicate their constitutional responsibility to delineate and protect fundamental liberties. But when the issue involves a regulation limiting one of several means of communication by an inmate, the institutional objectives furthered by that regulation and the measure of judicial deference owed to corrections officials in their attempt to serve those interests are relevant in gauging the validity of the regulation.

Accordingly, in light of the alternative channels of communication that are open to prison inmates,[5] we cannot say on the record in this case that this restriction on one manner in which prisoners can communicate with persons outside of prison is unconstitutional. So long as this restriction operates in a neutral fashion, without regard to the content of the expression, it falls within the "appropriate rules and regulations" to which "prisoners necessarily are subject," Cruz v. Beto, supra, at 321, and does not abridge any First Amendment freedoms retained by prison inmates.[6]

---

[5] It is suggested by the inmate appellees that the use of the mail as an alternative means of communication may not be effective in the case of prisoners who are inarticulate or even illiterate. There is no indication, however, that any of the four inmates before the Court suffer from either of these disabilities. Indeed, the record affirmatively shows that two of the inmates are published writers. Although the complaint was filed as a class action, the plaintiffs never moved the District Court to certify the case as a class action as required by Fed. Rules Civ. Proc. 23 (b)(3) and (c). Thus, the short answer to the inmates' contention is that there is neither a finding by the District Court nor support in the record for a finding that the alternative channels of communication are not an effective means for the inmate appellees to express themselves to persons outside the prison.

Even with respect to inmates who may not be literate or articulate, however, there is no suggestion that the corrections officials would not permit such inmates to seek the aid of fellow inmates or of family and friends who visit them to commit their thoughts to writing for communication to individuals in the general public. Cf. Johnson v. Avery, 393 U.S. 483 (1969). Merely because such inmates may need assistance to utilize one of the alternative channels does not make it an ineffective alternative, unless, of course, the State prohibits the inmate from receiving such assistance.

[6] The inmates argue that restricting their access to press representatives unconstitutionally burdens their First and Fourteenth Amendment right to petition the government for the redress of grievances. Communication with the press, the inmates contend, provides them with their only effective opportunity to communicate their grievances, through the channel of public opinion, to the legislative and executive branches of the government. We think, however, that the alternative means of communication with the

II

In No. 73-918, the media plaintiffs ask us to hold that the limitation on press interviews imposed by § 415.071 violates the freedom of the press guaranteed by the First and Fourteenth Amendments. They contend that, irrespective of what First Amendment liberties may or may not be retained by prison inmates, members of the press have a constitutional right to interview any inmate who is willing to speak with them, in the absence of an individualized determination that the particular interview might create a clear and present danger to prison security or to some other substantial interest served by the corrections system. In this regard, the media plaintiffs do not claim any impairment of their freedom to publish, for California imposes no restrictions on what may be published about its prisons, the prison inmates, or the officers who administer the prisons. Instead, they rely on their right to gather news without governmental interference, which the media plaintiffs assert includes a right of access to the sources of what is regarded as newsworthy information.

---

press that are available to prisoners, together with the substantial access to prisons that California accords the press and other members of the public, see infra, at 830-831, satisfies whatever right the inmates may have to petition the government through the press.

We also note that California accords prison inmates substantial opportunities to petition the executive, legislative, and judicial branches of government directly. Section 2600 of the California Penal Code permits an inmate to correspond confidentially with any public officeholder. And various rules promulgated by the Department of Corrections explicitly permit an inmate to correspond with the Governor, any other elected state or federal official, and any appointed head of a state or federal agency. Similarly, California has acted to assure prisoners the right to petition for judicial relief. See, e.g., In re Jordan, 7 Cal. 3d 930, 500 P. 2d 873 (1972); In re Van Geldern, 5 Cal. 3d 832, 489 P. 2d 578 (1971); In re Harrell, 2 Cal. 3d 675, 470 P. 2d 640 (1970). Section 845.4 of the California Government Code also makes prison officials liable for intentional interference with the right of a prisoner to obtain judicial relief from his confinement.

We note at the outset that this regulation is not part of an attempt by the State to conceal the conditions in its prisons or to frustrate the press' investigation and reporting of those conditions. Indeed, the record demonstrates that, under current corrections policy, both the press and the general public are accorded full opportunities to observe prison conditions.[7] The Department of Corrections regularly conducts public tours through the prisons for the benefit of interested citizens. In addition, newsmen are permitted to visit both the maximum security and minimum security sections of the institutions and to stop and speak about any subject to any inmates whom they might encounter. If security considerations permit, corrections personnel will step aside to permit such interviews to be confidential. Apart from general access to all parts of the institutions, newsmen are also permitted to enter the prisons to interview inmates selected at random by the corrections officials. By the same token, if a newsman wishes to write a story on a particular prison program, he is permitted to sit in on group meetings and to interview the inmate participants. In short, members of the press enjoy access to California prisons that is not available to other members of the public.

The sole limitation on newsgathering in California prisons is the prohibition in § 415.071 of interviews with individual inmates specifically designated by representatives of the press. This restriction is of recent vintage, hav-

ing been imposed in 1971 in response to a violent episode that the Department of Corrections felt was at least partially attributable to the former policy with respect to face-to-face prisoner-press interviews. Prior to the promulgation of § 415.071, every journalist had virtually free access to interview any individual inmate whom he might wish. Only members of the press were accorded this privilege; other members of the general public did not have the benefit of such an unrestricted visitation policy. Thus, the promulgation of § 415.071 did not impose a discrimination against press access, but merely eliminated a special privilege formerly given to representatives of the press vis-a-vis members of the public generally.[8]

In practice, it was found that the policy in effect prior to the promulgation of § 415.071 had resulted in press attention being concentrated on a relatively small number of inmates who, as a result, became virtual "public figures" within the prison society and gained a disproportionate degree of notoriety and influence among their fellow inmates. Because of this notoriety and influence, these inmates often became the source of severe disciplinary problems. For example, extensive press attention to an inmate who espoused a practice of noncooperation with prison regulations encouraged other inmates to follow suit, thus eroding the institutions' ability to deal effectively with the inmates generally. Finally, in the words of the District Court, on August 21, 1971, "during an escape attempt at San Quentin three staff members and two inmates were killed. This was viewed by the officials as the climax of mounting disciplinary problems caused, in

---

[7]   This policy reflects a recognition that the conditions in this Nation's prisons are a matter that is both newsworthy and of great public importance. As THE CHIEF JUSTICE has commented, we cannot "continue . . . to brush under the rug the problems of those who are found guilty and subject to criminal sentence. . . . It is a melancholy truth that it has taken the tragic prison outbreaks of the past three years to focus widespread public attention on this problem." Burger, *Our Options are Limited*, 18 VILL. L. REV. 165, 167 (1972). Along the same lines, THE CHIEF JUSTICE has correctly observed that "if we want prisoners to change, public attitudes toward prisoners and ex-prisoners must change. . . . A visit to most prisons will make you a zealot for prison reform." W. Burger, FOR WHOM THE BELL TOLLS, reprinted at 25 RECORD OF N. Y. C. B. A. (Supp.) 14, 20, 21 (1970).

[8]   It cannot be contended that because California permits family, friends, attorneys, and clergy to visit inmates, it cannot limit visitations by the press. No member of the general public who does not have a personal or professional relationship to the inmate is permitted to enter the prison and name an inmate with whom he would like to engage in face-to-face discourse. Thus, the press is granted the same access in this respect to prison inmates as is accorded any member of the general public. Indeed, as is noted in the text, the aggregate access that the press has to California prisons and their inmates is substantially greater than that of the general public.

part, by its liberal posture with regard to press interviews, and on August 23 § 415.071 was adopted to mitigate the problem." 364 F.Supp., at 198. It is against this background that we consider the media plaintiffs' claims under the First and Fourteenth Amendments.

The constitutional guarantee of a free press "assures the maintenance of our political system and an open society," Time, Inc. v. Hill, 385 U.S. 374, 389 (1967), and secures "the paramount public interest in a free flow of information to the people concerning public officials," Garrison v. Louisiana, 379 U.S. 64, 77 (1964). See also New York Times Co. v. Sullivan, 376 U.S. 254 (1964). By the same token, "any system of prior restraints of expression comes to this Court bearing a heavy presumption against its constitutional validity." New York Times Co. v. United States, 403 U.S. 713, 714 (1971); Organization for a Better Austin v. Keefe, 402 U.S. 415 (1971); Bantam Books, Inc. v. Sullivan, 372 U.S. 58, 70 (1963); Near v. Minnesota ex rel. Olson, 283 U.S. 697 (1931). Correlatively, the First and Fourteenth Amendments also protect the right of the public to receive such information and ideas as are published. Kleindienst v. Mandel, 408 U.S., at 762-763; Stanley v. Georgia, 394 U.S. 557, 564 (1969).

In Branzburg v. Hayes, 408 U.S. 665 (1972), the Court went further and acknowledged that "news gathering is not without its First Amendment protections," id., at 707, for "without some protection for seeking out the news, freedom of the press could be eviscerated," id., at 681. In Branzburg the Court held that the First and Fourteenth Amendments were not abridged by requiring reporters to disclose the identity of their confidential sources to a grand jury when that information was needed in the course of a good-faith criminal investigation. The Court there could "perceive no basis for holding that the public interest in law enforcement and in ensuring effective grand jury proceedings [was] insufficient to override the consequential, but uncertain, burden on news gathering that is said to result from insisting that reporters, like other citizens, respond to relevant questions put to them in the course of a valid grand jury investigation or criminal trial," id., at 690-691.

In this case, the media plaintiffs contend that § 415.071 constitutes governmental inter-

ference with their newsgathering activities that is neither consequential nor uncertain, and that no substantial governmental interest can be shown to justify the denial of press access to specifically designated prison inmates. More particularly, the media plaintiffs assert that, despite the substantial access to California prisons and their inmates accorded representatives of the press—access broader than is accorded members of the public generally—face-to-face interviews with specifically designated inmates is such an effective and superior method of newsgathering that its curtailment amounts to unconstitutional state interference with a free press. We do not agree.

"It has generally been held that the First Amendment does not guarantee the press a constitutional right of special access to information not available to the public generally. . . . Despite the fact that news gathering may be hampered, the press is regularly excluded from grand jury proceedings, our own conferences, the meetings of other official bodies gathering in executive session, and the meetings of private organizations. Newsmen have no constitutional right of access to the scenes of crime or disaster when the general public is excluded." Branzburg v. Hayes, supra, at 684-685. Similarly, newsmen have no constitutional right of access to prisons or their inmates beyond that afforded the general public.

The First and Fourteenth Amendments bar government from interfering in any way with a free press. The Constitution does not, however, require government to accord the press special access to information not shared by members of the public generally.[9] It is one thing to say that a journalist is free to seek out sources of information not available to members of the general public, that he is

---

[9] As Mr. Chief Justice Warren put the matter in writing for the Court in Zemel v. Rusk, 381 U.S. 1, 16-17 (1965), "there are few restrictions on action which could not be clothed by ingenious argument in the garb of decreased data flow. For example, the prohibition of unauthorized entry into the White House diminishes the citizen's opportunities to gather information he might find relevant to his opinion of the way the country is being run, but that does not make entry into the White House a First Amendment right. The right to speak and publish does not carry with it the unrestrained right to gather information."

entitled to some constitutional protection of the confidentiality of such sources, cf. Branzburg v. Hayes, supra, and that government cannot restrain the publication of news emanating from such sources. Cf. New York Times Co. v. United States, supra. It is quite another thing to suggest that the Constitution imposes upon government the affirmative duty to make available to journalists sources of information not available to members of the public generally. That proposition finds no support in the words of the Constitution or in any decision of this Court. Accordingly, since § 415.071 does not deny the press access to sources of information available to members of the general public, we hold that it does not abridge the protections that the First and Fourteenth Amendments guarantee.

For the reasons stated, we reverse the District Court's judgment that § 415.071 infringes the freedom of speech of the prison inmates and affirm its judgment that that regulation does not abridge the constitutional right of a free press. Accordingly, the judgment is vacated, and the cases are remanded to the District Court for further proceedings consistent with this opinion.

It is so ordered.

SAXBE
v.
WASHINGTON POST CO.

417 U.S. 843; 94 S. Ct. 2811; 41 L. Ed. 2d 514 (1974)

MR. JUSTICE STEWART delivered the opinion of the Court.

The respondents, a major metropolitan newspaper and one of its reporters, initiated this litigation to challenge the constitutionality of para. 4b (6) of Policy Statement 1220.1A of the Federal Bureau of Prisons.[1] At the time that the case was in the District Court and the

---

[1] "Press representatives will not be permitted to interview individual inmates. This rule shall apply even where the inmate requests or seeks an interview. However, conversation may be permitted with inmates whose identity is not to be made public, if it is limited to the discussion of institutional facilities, programs and activities."

Court of Appeals, this regulation prohibited any personal interviews between newsmen and individually designated federal prison inmates. The Solicitor General has informed the Court that the regulation was recently amended "to permit press interviews at federal prison institutions that can be characterized as minimum security."[2] The general prohibition of press interviews with inmates remains in effect, however, in three-quarters of the federal prisons, i.e., in all medium security and maximum security institutions, including the two institutions involved in this case.

In March 1972, the respondents requested permission from the petitioners, the officials responsible for administering federal prisons, to conduct several interviews with specific inmates in the prisons at Lewisburg, Pennsylvania, and Danbury, Connecticut. The petitioners denied permission for such interviews on the authority of Policy Statement 1220.1A. The respondents thereupon commenced this suit to challenge these denials and the regulation on which they were predicated. Their essential contention was that the prohibition of all press interviews with prison inmates abridges the protection that the First Amendment accords the newsgathering activity of a free press. The District Court agreed with this contention and held that the Policy Statement, insofar as it totally prohibited all press interviews at the institutions involved, violated the First Amendment. Although the court acknowledged that institutional considerations could justify the prohibition of some press-inmate interviews, the District Court ordered the petitioners to cease enforcing the blanket prohibition of all such interviews and, pending modification of the Policy Statement, to consider interview requests on an individual basis and "to withhold permission to interview . . . only where demonstrable administrative or disciplinary considerations dominate." 357 F. Supp. 770, 775 (DC 1972).

The petitioners appealed the District Court's judgment to the Court of Appeals for the District of Columbia Circuit. We stayed the District Court's order pending the completion of that appeal, sub nom. Kleindienst

---

[2] Letter of Apr. 16, 1974, to Clerk, Supreme Court of the United States, presently on file with the Clerk.

v. Washington Post Co., 406 U.S. 912 (1972).
The first time this case was before it, the
Court of Appeals remanded it to the District
Court for additional findings of fact and particularly for reconsideration in light of this
Court's intervening decision in Branzburg v.
Hayes, 408 U.S. 665 (1972). 155 U.S. App.
D. C. 283, 477 F.2d 1168 (1972). On remand,
the District Court conducted further evidentiary hearings, supplemented its findings of
fact, and reconsidered its conclusions of law
in light of Branzburg and other recent decisions that were urged upon it. In due course,
the court reaffirmed its original decision, 357
F.Supp. 779 (DC 1972), and the petitioners
again appealed to the Court of Appeals.

The Court of Appeals affirmed the judgment of the District Court. It held that press
interviews with prison inmates could not be
totally prohibited as the Policy Statement
purported to do, but may "be denied only
where it is the judgment of the administrator
directly concerned, based on either the
demonstrated behavior of the inmate, or special conditions existing at the institution at
the time the interview is requested, or both,
that the interview presents a serious risk of
administrative or disciplinary problems." 161
U.S. App. D. C. 75, 87-88, 494 F.2d 994,
1006-1007 (1974). Any blanket prohibition
of such face-to-face interviews was held to
abridge the First Amendment's protection of
press freedom. Because of the important constitutional question involved, and because of
an apparent conflict in approach to the question between the District of Columbia Circuit
and the Ninth Circuit,[3] we granted certiorari.
415 U.S. 956 (1974).

The policies of the Federal Bureau of Prisons regarding visitations to prison inmates do
not differ significantly from the California
policies considered in Pell v. Procunier, ante,
p. 817. As the Court of Appeals noted,
"inmates' families, their attorneys, and religious counsel are accorded liberal visitation
privileges. Even friends of inmates are
allowed to visit, although their privileges
appear to be somewhat more limited." 161
U.S. App. D. C., at 78, 494 F.2d, at 997. Other

than members of these limited groups with
personal and professional ties to the inmates,
members of the general public are not permitted under the Bureau's policy to enter the
prisons and interview consenting inmates.
This policy is applied with an even hand to
all prospective visitors, including newsmen,
who, like other members of the public, may
enter the prisons to visit friends or family
members. But, again like members of the
general public, they may not enter the prison
and insist on visiting an inmate with whom
they have no such relationship. There is no
indication on this record that Policy Statement 1220.1A has been interpreted or
applied to prohibit a person, who is otherwise
eligible to visit and interview an inmate,
from doing so merely because he is a member of the press.[4]

Except for the limitation in Policy Statement 1220.1A on face-to-face press-inmate
interviews, members of the press are accorded substantial access to the federal prisons in
order to observe and report the conditions
they find there. Indeed, journalists are given
access to the prisons and to prison inmates
that in significant respects exceeds that
afforded to members of the general public.
For example, Policy Statement 1220.1A permits press representatives to tour the prisons
and to photograph any prison facilities.[5] During such tours a newsman is permitted to
conduct brief interviews with any inmates he
might encounter.[6] In addition, newsmen and
inmates are permitted virtually unlimited
written correspondence with each other.[7]
Outgoing correspondence from inmates to
press representatives is neither censored nor
inspected. Incoming mail from press representatives is inspected only for contraband or

---

[3] See Seattle-Tacoma Newspaper Guild v. Parker,
     480 F.2d 1062, 1066-1067 (1973). See also
     Hillery v. Procunier, 364 F.Supp. 196, 199-200
     (ND Cal. 1973).

---

[4] The Solicitor General's brief represents that
     "members of the press, like the public general-
     ly, may visit the prison to see friends there." Pre-
     sumably, the same is true with respect to family
     members. The respondents have not disputed
     this representation.
[5] Policy Statement 1220.1A paras. 4b (5) and (7).
[6] See id., para. 4b (6) set out in n. 1, supra. The
     newsman is requested not to reveal the identity
     of the inmate, and the conversation is to be lim-
     ited to institutional facilities, programs, and
     activities.
[7] Id., paras. 4b (1) and (2).

statements inciting illegal action. Moreover, prison officials are available to the press and are required by Policy Statement 1220.1A to "give all possible assistance" to press representatives "in providing background and a specific report" concerning any inmate complaints.[8]

The respondents have also conceded in their brief that Policy Statement 1220.1A "has been interpreted by the Bureau to permit a newsman to interview a randomly selected group of inmates." As a result, the reporter respondent in this case was permitted to interview a randomly selected group of inmates at the Lewisburg prison. Finally, in light of the constant turnover in the prison population, it is clear that there is always a large group of recently released prisoners who are available to both the press and the general public as a source of information about conditions in the federal prisons.[9]

Thus, it is clear that Policy Statement 1220.1A is not part of any attempt by the Federal Bureau of Prisons to conceal from the public the conditions prevailing in federal prisons. This limitation on prearranged press interviews with individually designated inmates was motivated by the same disciplinary and administrative considerations that underlie § 115.071 of the California Department of Corrections Manual, which we considered in Pell v. Procunier and Procunier v. Hillery, ante, p. 817. The experience of the Bureau accords with that of the California Department of Corrections and suggests that the interest of the press is often "concentrated on a relatively small number of inmates who, as a result, [become] virtual 'public figures' within the prison society and gai[n] a disproportionate degree of notoriety and influence among their fellow inmates." Pell, ante, at 831-832. As a result those inmates who are conspicuously publicized because of their repeated contacts with the press tend to become the source of substantial disciplinary

problems that can engulf a large portion of the population at a prison.

The District Court and the Court of Appeals sought to meet this problem by decreeing a selective policy whereby prison officials could deny interviews likely to lead to disciplinary problems. In the expert judgment of the petitioners, however, such a selective policy would spawn serious discipline and morale problems of its own by engendering hostility and resentment among inmates who were refused interview privileges granted to their fellows. The Director of the Bureau testified that "one of the very basic tenets of sound correctional administration" is "to treat all inmates incarcerated in [the] institutions, as far as possible, equally." This expert and professional judgment is, of course, entitled to great deference.

In this case, however, it is unnecessary to engage in any delicate balancing of such penal considerations against the legitimate demands of the First Amendment. For it is apparent that the sole limitation imposed on newsgathering by Policy Statement 1220.1A is no more than a particularized application of the general rule that nobody may enter the prison and designate an inmate whom he would like to visit, unless the prospective visitor is a lawyer, clergyman, relative, or friend of that inmate. This limitation on visitations is justified by what the Court of Appeals acknowledged as "the truism that prisons are institutions where public access is generally limited." 161 U.S. App. D. C., at 80, 494 F.2d, at 999. See Adderley v. Florida, 385 U.S. 39, 41 (1966). In this regard, the Bureau of Prisons visitation policy does not place the press in any less advantageous position than the public generally. Indeed, the total access to federal prisons and prison inmates that the Bureau of Prisons accords to the press far surpasses that available to other members of the public.

We find this case constitutionally indistinguishable from Pell v. Procunier, ante, p. 817, and thus fully controlled by the holding in that case. "Newsmen have no constitutional right of access to prisons or their inmates beyond that afforded the general public." Id., at 834. The proposition "that the Constitution imposes upon government the affirmative duty to make available to journalists sources

---

[8] Id., para. 4b (12).

[9] The Solicitor General's brief informs us that "approximately one-half of the prison population on any one day will be released within the following 12 months. The average population is 23,000, of whom approximately 12,000 are released each year."

of information not available to members of the public generally . . . finds no support in the words of the Constitution or in any decision of this Court." Id., at 834-835. Thus, since Policy Statement 1220.1A "does not deny the press access to sources of information available to members of the general public," id., at 835, we hold that it does not abridge the freedom that the First Amendment guarantees. Accordingly, the judgment of the Court of Appeals is reversed and the case is remanded to the District Court for further proceedings consistent with this opinion.

It is so ordered.

JONES
v.
NORTH CAROLINA PRISONERS' LABOR UNION, INC.

433 U.S. 119; 97 S. Ct. 2532; 53 L. Ed. 2d 629 (1977)

MR. JUSTICE REHNQUIST delivered the opinion of the Court.

* * *

I

Appellee, an organization self-denominated as a Prisoners' Labor Union, was incorporated in late 1974, with a stated goal of "the promotion of charitable labor union purposes" and the formation of a "prisoners' labor union at every prison and jail in North Carolina to seek through collective bargaining . . . to improve . . . working . . . conditions. . . ." It also proposed to work toward the alteration or elimination of practices and policies of the Department of Correction which it did not approve of, and to serve as a vehicle for the presentation and resolution of inmate grievances. By early 1975, the Union had attracted some 2,000 inmate "members" in 40 different prison units throughout North Carolina. The State of North Carolina, unhappy with these developments, set out to prevent inmates from forming or operating a "union." While the State tolerated individual "membership," or belief, in the Union, it sought to prohibit inmate solicitation of other inmates, meet-

ings between members of the Union, and bulk mailings concerning the Union from outside sources. Pursuant to a regulation promulgated by the Department of Correction on March 26, 1975, such solicitation and group activity were proscribed.

Suit was filed by the Union in the United States District Court for the Eastern District of North Carolina on March 18, 1975, approximately a week before the date upon which the regulation was to take effect. The Union claimed that its rights, and the rights of its members, to engage in protected free speech, association, and assembly activities were being infringed by the no-solicitation and no-meeting rules. It also alleged a deprivation of equal protection of the laws in that the Jaycees and Alcoholics Anonymous were permitted to have meetings and other organizational rights, such as the distribution of bulk mailing material, that the Union was being denied. A declaratory judgment and injunction against continuation of these restrictive policies were sought, as were substantial damages.

A three-judge District Court, convened pursuant to 28 U.S.C. §§ 2281 and 2284, while dismissing the Union's prayers for damages and attorney's fees, granted it substantial injunctive relief. The court found that appellants "permitted" inmates to join the Union, but "oppose[d] the solicitation of other inmates to join," either by inmate-to-inmate solicitation or by correspondence. 409 F.Supp., at 941. The court noted id., at 942:

[Appellants] sincerely believe that the very existence of the Union will increase the burdens of administration and constitute a threat of essential discipline and control. They are apprehensive that inmates may use the Union to establish a power bloc within the inmate population which could be utilized to cause work slowdowns or stoppages or other undesirable concerted activity.

The District Court concluded, however, that there was "no consensus" among experts on these matters, and that it was "left with no firm conviction that an association of inmates is necessarily good or bad. . . ." Id., at 942-943. The court felt that since appellants countenanced the bare fact of Union membership, it had to allow solicitation activity, whether by inmates or by outsiders:

> We are unable to perceive why it is necessary or essential to security and order in the prisons to forbid solicitation of membership in a union permitted by the authorities. This is not a case of riot. There is not one scintilla of evidence to suggest that the Union has been utilized to disrupt the operation of the penal institutions." Id., at 944.

The other questions, respecting the bulk mailing by the Union of literature into the prisons for distribution and the question of meetings of inmate members, the District Court resolved against appellants "by application of the equal protection clause of the fourteenth amendment." Ibid. Finding that such meetings and bulk mailing privileges had been permitted the Jaycees, Alcoholics Anonymous, and, in one institution, the Boy Scouts, the District Court concluded that appellants "may not pick and choose depending on [their] approval or disapproval of the message or purpose of the group" unless "the activity proscribed is shown to be detrimental to proper penological objectives, subversive to good discipline, or otherwise harmful." Ibid. The court concluded that appellants had failed to meet this burden. Appropriate injunctive relief was thereupon ordered.

II

A

The District Court, we believe, got off on the wrong foot in this case by not giving appropriate deference to the decisions of prison administrators and appropriate recognition to the peculiar and restrictive circumstances of penal confinement. While litigation by prison inmates concerning conditions of confinement, challenged other than under the Eighth Amendment, is of recent vintage, this Court has long recognized that "[l]awful incarceration brings about the necessary withdrawal or limitation of many privileges and rights, a retraction justified by the con-

siderations underlying our penal system." Price v. Johnston, 334 U.S. 266, 285 (1948); see also Pell v. Procunier, 417 U.S. 817, 822 (1974); Wolff v. McDonnell, 418 U.S. 539, 555 (1974). The fact of confinement and the needs of the penal institution impose limitations on constitutional rights, including those derived from the First Amendment, which are implicit in incarceration. We noted in Pell v. Procunier, supra, at 822:

> [A] prison inmate retains those First Amendment rights that are not inconsistent with his status as a prisoner or with the legitimate penological objectives of the corrections system. Thus, challenges to prison restrictions that are asserted to inhibit First Amendment interests must be analyzed in terms of the legitimate policies and goals of the corrections system, to whose custody and care the prisoner has been committed in accordance with due process of law.

Perhaps the most obvious of the First Amendment rights that are necessarily curtailed by confinement are those associational rights that the First Amendment protects outside of prison walls. The concept of incarceration itself entails a restriction on the freedom of inmates to associate with those outside of the penal institution. Equally as obvious, the inmate's "status as a prisoner" and the operational realities of a prison dictate restrictions on the associational rights among inmates.

Because the realities of running a penal institution are complex and difficult, we have also recognized the wide-ranging deference to be accorded the decisions of prison administrators. We noted in Procunier v. Martinez, 416 U.S. 396, 405 (1974):

> [C]ourts are ill equipped to deal with the increasingly urgent problems of prison administration and reform. Judicial recognition of that fact reflects no more than a healthy sense of realism. Moreover, where state penal institutions are involved, federal courts have a further reason for deference to the appropriate prison authorities. (Footnote omitted.)

See also Cruz v. Beto, 405 U.S. 319, 321 (1972). It is in this context that the claims of the Union must be examined.

B

State correctional officials uniformly testified that the concept of a prisoners' labor union was itself fraught with potential dangers, whether or not such a union intended, illegally, to press for collective-bargaining recognition. Appellant Ralph Edwards, the Commissioner of the Department of Correction, stated in his affidavit:

The creation of an inmate union will naturally result in increasing the existing friction between inmates and prison personnel. It can also create friction between union inmates and non-union inmates.

Appellant David Jones, the Secretary of the Department of Correction, stated:

The existence of a union of inmates can create a divisive element within the inmate population. In a time when the units are already seriously over-crowded, such an element could aggravate already tense conditions. The purpose of the union may well be worthwhile projects. But it is evident that the inmate organizers could, if recognized as spokesman for all inmates, make themselves to be power figures among the inmates. If the union is successful, these inmates would be in a position to misuse their influence. After the inmate union has become established, there would probably be nothing this Department could do to terminate its existence, even if its activities became overtly subversive to the functioning of the Department. Work stoppages and mutinies are easily foreseeable. Riots and chaos would almost inevitably result. Thus, even if the purposes of the union are as stated in the complaint, the potential for a dangerous situation exists, a situation which could not be brought under control.

The District Court did not reject these beliefs as fanciful or erroneous. It, instead, noted that they were held "sincerely," and were arguably correct. 409 F.Supp., at 942-943. Without a showing that these beliefs were unreasonable, it was error for the District Court to conclude that appellants needed to show more. In particular, the burden was not on appellants to show affirmatively that the Union would be "detrimental to proper penological objectives" or would constitute a "present danger to security and order." Id., at 944-945. Rather, "[s]uch considerations are peculiarly within the province and professional expertise of corrections officials, and, in the absence of substantial evidence in the record to indicate that the officials have exaggerated their response to these considerations, courts should ordinarily defer to their expert judgment in such matters." Pell v. Procunier, 417 U.S., at 827. The necessary and correct result of our deference to the informed discretion of prison administrators permits them, and not the courts, to make the difficult judgments concerning institutional operations in situations such as this.

The District Court, however, gave particular emphasis to what it viewed as appellants' tolerance of membership by inmates in the Union as undermining appellants' position. It viewed a system which permitted inmate "membership" but prohibited inmate-to-inmate solicitation (as well, it should be noted, as meetings, or other group activities) as bordering "on the irrational," and felt that "[t]he defendants' own hypothesis in this case is that the existence of the Union and membership in it are not dangerous, for otherwise they would surely have undertaken to forbid membership." 409 F.Supp., at 944. This, however, considerably overstates what appellants' concession as to pure membership entails. Appellants permitted membership because of the reasonable assumption that each individual prisoner could believe what he chose to believe, and that outside individuals should be able to communicate ideas and beliefs to individual inmates. Since a member qua member incurs no dues or obligations—a prisoner apparently may become a member simply by considering himself a member—this position simply reflects the concept that thought control, by means of prohibiting beliefs, would not only be undesirable but impossible.

But appellants never acquiesced in, or permitted, group activity of the Union in the nature of a functioning organization of the inmates within the prison, nor did the District Court find that they had. It is clearly not irrational to conclude that individuals may believe what they want, but that concerted group activity, or solicitation therefor, would pose additional and unwarranted problems and frictions in the operation of the State's penal institutions. The ban on inmate solicitation and group meetings, therefore, was rationally related to the reasonable, indeed to the central, objectives of prison administration. Cf. Pell v. Procunier, supra, at 822.

C

The invocation of the First Amendment, whether the asserted rights are speech or associational, does not change this analysis. In a prison context, an inmate does not retain those First Amendment rights that are "inconsistent with his status as a prisoner or with the legitimate penological objectives of the corrections system." Pell v. Procunier, supra, at 822. Prisons, it is obvious, differ in numerous respects from free society. They, to begin with, are populated, involuntarily, by people who have been found to have violated one or more of the criminal laws established by society for its orderly governance. In seeking a "mutual accommodation between institutional needs and objectives [of prisons] and the provisions of the Constitution that are of general application," Wolff v. McDonnell, 418 U.S., at 556, this Court has repeatedly recognized the need for major restrictions on a prisoner's rights. See, e.g., id., at 561-562; Lanza v. New York, 370 U.S. 139, 143 (1962). These restrictions have applied as well where First Amendment values were implicated. See, e.g., Pell v. Procunier, supra; Procunier v. Martinez, 416 U.S. 396 (1974); Meachum v. Fano, 427 U.S. 215 (1976).

An examination of the potential restrictions on speech or association that have been imposed by the regulations under challenge, demonstrates that the restrictions imposed are reasonable, and are consistent with the inmates' status as prisoners and with the legitimate operational considerations of the institution. To begin with, First Amendment speech rights are barely implicated in this case. Mail rights are not themselves implicated; the only question respecting the mail is

that of bulk mailings. The advantages of bulk mailings to inmates by the Union are those of cheaper rates and convenience. While the District Court relied on the cheaper bulk mailing rates in finding an equal protection violation, infra, at 133, it is clear that losing these cost advantages does not fundamentally implicate free speech values. Since other avenues of outside informational flow by the Union remain available, the prohibition on bulk mailing, reasonable in the absence of First Amendment considerations, remains reasonable. Cf. Pell v. Procunier, supra; Saxbe v. Washington Post Co., 417 U.S. 843 (1974).

Nor does the prohibition on inmate-to-inmate solicitation of membership trench untowardly on the inmates' First Amendment speech rights. Solicitation of membership itself involves a good deal more than the simple expression of individual views as to the advantages or disadvantages of a union or its views; it is an invitation to collectively engage in a legitimately prohibited activity. If the prison officials are otherwise entitled to control organized union activity within the prison walls, the prohibition on solicitation for such activity is not then made impermissible on account of First Amendment considerations, for such a prohibition is then not only reasonable but necessary. Pell v. Procunier, 417 U.S., at 822.

First Amendment associational rights, while perhaps more directly implicated by the regulatory prohibitions, likewise must give way to the reasonable considerations of penal management. As already noted, numerous associational rights are necessarily curtailed by the realities of confinement. They may be curtailed whenever the institution's officials, in the exercise of their informed discretion, reasonably conclude that such associations, whether through group meetings or otherwise, possess the likelihood of disruption to prison order or stability, or otherwise interfere with the legitimate penological objectives of the prison environment. As we noted in Pell v. Procunier, supra, at 823, "central to all other corrections goals is the institutional consideration of internal security within the corrections facilities themselves."

Appellant prison officials concluded that the presence, perhaps even the objectives, of a prisoners' labor union would be detrimental to order and security in the prisons, supra, at

127. It is enough to say that they have not been conclusively shown to be wrong in this view. The interest in preserving order and authority in the prisons is self-evident. Prison life, and relations between the inmates themselves and between the inmates and prison officials or staff, contain the ever-present potential for violent confrontation and conflagration. Wolff v. McDonnell, 418 U.S., at 561-562. Responsible prison officials must be permitted to take reasonable steps to forestall such a threat, and they must be permitted to act before the time when they can compile a dossier on the eve of a riot. The case of a prisoners' union, where the focus is on the presentation of grievances to, and encouragement of adversary relations with, institution officials surely would rank high on anyone's list of potential trouble spots. If the appellants' views as to the possible detrimental effects of the organizational activities of the Union are reasonable, as we conclude they are, then the regulations are drafted no more broadly than they need be to meet the perceived threat—which stems directly from group meetings and group organizational activities of the Union. Cf. Procunier v. Martinez, 416 U.S., at 412-416. When weighed against the First Amendment rights asserted, these institutional reasons are sufficiently weighty to prevail.

D

The District Court rested on the Equal Protection Clause of the Fourteenth Amendment to strike down appellants' prohibition against the receipt and distribution of bulk mail from the Union as well as the prohibition of Union meetings among the inmates. It felt that this was a denial of equal protection because bulk mailing and meeting rights had been extended to the Jaycees, Alcoholics Anonymous, and the Boy Scouts. The court felt that just as outside the prison, a "government may not pick and choose depending upon its approval or disapproval of the message or purpose of the group," 409 F.Supp., at 944, so, too, appellants could not choose among groups without first demonstrating that the activity proscribed is "detrimental to proper penological objectives, subversive to good discipline, or otherwise harmful." Ibid.

This analysis is faulty for two reasons. The District Court erroneously treated this case as if the prison environment were essentially a "public forum." We observed last Term in upholding a ban on political meetings at Fort Dix that a Government enclave such as a military base was not a public forum. Greer v. Spock, 424 U.S. 828 (1976). We stated, id., at 838 n. 10:

The fact that other civilian speakers and entertainers had sometimes been invited to appear at Fort Dix did not of itself serve to convert Fort Dix into a public forum or to confer upon political candidates a First or Fifth Amendment right to conduct their campaigns there. The decision of the military authorities that a civilian lecture on drug abuse, a religious service by a visiting preacher at the base chapel, or a rock musical concert would be supportive of the military mission of Fort Dix surely did not leave the authorities powerless thereafter to prevent any civilian from entering Fort Dix to speak on any subject whatever.

A prison may be no more easily converted into a public forum than a military base. Thus appellants need only demonstrate a rational basis for their distinctions between organizational groups. Cf. City of Charlotte v. Firefighters, 426 U.S. 283 (1976). Here, appellants' affidavits indicate exactly why Alcoholics Anonymous and the Jaycees have been allowed to operate within the prison. Both were seen as serving a rehabilitative purpose, working in harmony with the goals and desires of the prison administrators, and both had been determined not to pose any threat to the order or security of the institution. The affidavits indicate that the administrators' view of the Union differed critically in both these respects.

Those conclusions are not unreasonable. Prison administrators may surely conclude that the Jaycees and Alcoholics Anonymous differ in fundamental respects from appellee Union, a group with no past to speak of, and with the avowed intent to pursue an adversary relationship with the prison officials. Indeed, it would be enough to distinguish the Union from Alcoholics Anonymous to note that the chartered purpose of the Union, apparently pursued in the prison, was illegal under North Carolina law.

Since a prison is most emphatically not a "public forum," these reasonable beliefs of appellants are sufficient, cf. Greer v. Spock, supra; City of Charlotte v. Firefighters, supra. The District Court's further requirement of a demonstrable showing that the Union was in fact harmful is inconsistent with the deference federal courts should pay to the informed discretion of prison officials. Procunier v. Martinez, 416 U.S., at 405. It is precisely in matters such as this, the decision as to which of many groups should be allowed to operate within the prison walls, where, confronted with claims based on the Equal Protection Clause, the courts should allow the prison administrators the full latitude of discretion, unless it can be firmly stated that the two groups are so similar that discretion has been abused. That is surely not the case here. There is nothing in the Constitution which requires prison officials to treat all inmate groups alike where differentiation is necessary to avoid an imminent threat of institutional disruption or violence. The regulations of appellants challenged in the District Court offended neither the First nor the Fourteenth Amendment, and the judgment of that court holding to the contrary is

Reversed.

* * *

MR. JUSTICE MARSHALL, with whom MR. JUSTICE BRENNAN joins, dissenting.

There was a time, not so very long ago, when prisoners were regarded as "slave[s] of the State," having "not only forfeited [their] liberty, but all [their] personal rights. . . ." Ruffin v. Commonwealth, 62 Va. 790, 796 (1871). In recent years, however, the courts increasingly have rejected this view, and with it the corollary which holds that courts should keep their "hands off" penal institutions. Today, however, the Court, in apparent fear of a prison reform organization that has the temerity to call itself a "union," takes a giant step backwards toward that discredited conception of prisoners' rights and the role of the courts. I decline to join in what I hope will prove to be a temporary retreat.

I

In Procunier v. Martinez, 416 U.S. 396 (1974), I set forth at some length my understanding of the First Amendment rights of prison inmates. The fundamental tenet I advanced is simply stated: "A prisoner does not shed . . . basic First Amendment rights at the prison gate. Rather, he 'retains all the rights of an ordinary citizen except those expressly, or by necessary implication, taken from him by law.' Coffin v. Reichard, 143 F.2d 443, 445 (CA6 1944)." Id., at 422 (concurring opinion). It follows from this tenet that a restriction on the First Amendment rights of prisoners, like a restriction on the rights of nonprisoners, "can only be justified by a substantial government interest and a showing that the means chosen to effectuate the State's purpose are not unnecessarily restrictive of personal freedoms." Id., at 423. This does not mean that any expressive conduct that would be constitutionally protected outside a prison is necessarily protected inside; as I also stated in Martinez: "[T]he First Amendment must in each context 'be applied "in light of the special characteristics of the . . . environment," Healy v. James, 408 U.S. 169, 180 (1972), and the exigencies of governing persons in prisons are different from and greater than those in governing persons without." Id., at 424. But the basic mode of First Amendment analysis—the requirement that restrictions on speech be supported by "reasons imperatively justifying the particular deprivation," ibid.—should not be altered simply because the First Amendment claimants are incarcerated.

The Court today rejects this analytic framework, at least as it applies to the right of prisoners to associate in something called a prison "union." In testing restrictions on the exercise of that right the Court asks only whether the restrictions are "rationally related to the . . . objectives of prison administration," ante, at 129, and whether the reasons offered in defense of the restrictions have been "conclusively shown to be wrong," ante, at 132. While proclaiming faithfulness to the teaching of Pell v. Procunier, 417 U.S. 817, 822 (1974), that "a prison inmate retains those First Amendment rights that are not inconsistent with his status as a prisoner," ante, at 125, the Court ultimately upholds the challenged regulations on a ground that would apply to any restriction on inmate freedom: they "are consistent with the inmates' status as prisoners," ante, at 130.

Nothing in the Court's opinion justifies its wholesale abandonment of traditional principles of First Amendment analysis. I realize, of course, that "the realities of running a penal institution are complex and difficult," ante, at 126, and that correctional officers possess considerably more "professional expertise," ante, at 128, in prison management than do judges. I do not in any way minimize either the seriousness of the problems or the significance of the expertise. But it does seem to me that "the realities of running" a school or a city are also "complex and difficult," and that those charged with these tasks—principals, college presidents, mayors, councilmen, and law enforcement personnel—also possess special "professional expertise," yet in no First Amendment case of which I am aware has the Court deferred to the judgment of such officials simply because their judgment was "rational." Cf. Healy v. James, 408 U.S. 169 (1972); Tinker v. Des Moines School Dist., 393 U.S. 503 (1969); Cox v. Louisiana, 379 U.S. 536, 544-551 (1965); Edwards v. South Carolina, 372 U.S. 229 (1963). I do not understand why a different rule should apply simply because prisons are involved.

The reason courts cannot blindly defer to the judgment of prison administrators—or any other officials for that matter—is easily understood. Because the prison administrator's business is to maintain order, "there inheres the danger that he may well be less responsive than a court—part of an independent branch of government—to the constitutionally protected interests in free expression." Freedman v. Maryland, 380 U.S. 51, 57-58 (1965). A warden seldom will find himself subject to public criticism or dismissal because he needlessly repressed free speech; indeed, neither the public nor the warden will have any way of knowing when repression was unnecessary. But a warden's job can be jeopardized and public criticism is sure to come should disorder occur. Consequently, prison officials inevitably will err on the side of too little freedom. That this has

occurred in the past is made clear by the recent report of the American Bar Association Joint Committee on the Legal Status of Prisoners:

> All organizations, including correctional organizations, overreact to suggested changes, whether sweeping or merely incremental. . . . [M]any of the fears voiced by prison officials in the 1960s to the growing tide of court determinations invalidating prison regulations have simply not come to pass; indeed, in several instances . . . those groups feared by the prisons in the 1960s have become stablilizing influences in the 1970s.

I do not mean to suggest that the views of correctional officials should be cavalierly disregarded by courts called upon to adjudicate constitutional claims of prisoners. Far from it. The officials' views "constitute a body of experience and informed judgment to which courts . . . may properly resort for guidance. The weight of such a judgment in a particular case will depend upon the thoroughness evident in its consideration, the validity of its reasoning . . . and all those factors which give it power to persuade . . . ," General Electric Co. v. Gilbert, 429 U.S. 125, 142 (1976), quoting Skidmore v. Swift & Co., 323 U.S. 134, 140 (1944). My point is simply that the ultimate responsibility for evaluating the prison officials' testimony, as well as any other expert testimony, must rest with the courts, which are required to reach an independent judgment concerning the constitutionality of any restriction on expressive activity.

The approach I advocate is precisely the one this Court has followed in other cases involving the rights of prisoners. In Johnson v. Avery, 393 U.S. 483 (1969), for example, the Court expressly acknowledged the rationality of the rule at issue which prohibited inmate writ writers from aiding fellow prisoners in preparing legal papers, id., at 488. We nevertheless concluded that the rule was unconstitutional because of its impact on prisoners' right of access to the courts. In Lee v. Washington, 390 U.S. 333 (1968), we did not even inquire whether segregating prisoners by race was rational, although it could be argued that integration in a southern prison would lead to disorder among inmates; we held that in any event segregation was prohibited by the Fourteenth Amendment. And in Bounds v. Smith, 430 U.S. 817 (1977); Wolff v. McDonnell, 418 U.S. 539 (1974); and Cruz v. Beto, 405 U.S. 319 (1972), we followed the approach of Lee. By word and deed, then, we have repeatedly reaffirmed that "a policy of judicial restraint cannot encompass any failure to take cognizance of valid constitutional claims. . . . When a prison regulation or practice offends a fundamental constitutional guarantee, federal courts will discharge their duty to protect constitutional rights." Procunier v. Martinez, 416 U.S., at 405.

II

Once it is established that traditional First Amendment principles are applicable in prisoners'-rights cases, the dispute here is easily resolved. The three-judge court not only found that there was "not one scintilla of evidence to suggest that the Union had been utilized to disrupt the operation of the penal institutions," 409 F.Supp. 937, 944 (EDNC 1976), as the Court acknowledges, ante, at 127 n. 5, it also found no evidence "that the inmates intend to operate [the Union] to hamper and interfere with the proper interests of government," 409 F.Supp., at 944, or that the Union posed a "present danger to security and order," id., at 945. In the face of these findings, it cannot be argued that the restrictions on the Union are "imperatively [justified]."

The regulation barring inmates from soliciting fellow prisoners to join the Union is particularly vulnerable to attack. As the late Judge Craven stated for the court below: "To permit an inmate to join a union and forbid his inviting others to join borders on the irrational." Id., at 943. The irrationality of the regulation is perhaps best demonstrated by the fact that the Court does not defend it; rather, as my Brother STEVENS suggests, ante, at 138-139, the Court defends some hypothetical regulation banning "an invitation to collectively engage in a legitimately prohibited activity.' Ante, at 132"; see also ante, at 129 (discussing ban on "concerted group activity, or solicitation therefor"). Because the actual regulation at issue here needlessly bars solicitation for an

activity—joining the Union—which is not and presumably could not be prohibited, I would hold it unconstitutional.

Once the rule outlawing solicitation is invalidated, the prohibition on bulk mailing by the Union must fall with it. Since North Carolina allows the Union to mail its newsletters to prisoners individually, the State cannot claim that the bulk mail rule serves to keep "subversive material" out of the prison. Rather, the primary purpose of the rule must be to supplement the ban on solicitation; overturning that ban would sap all force from the rationale for excluding bulk mailings. The exclusion would then be left as one that unnecessarily increases the cost to the Union of exercising its First Amendment rights while allowing other inmate groups such as the Jaycees to exercise their rights at a lower price. It would, therefore, be plainly unconstitutional.

The regulation prohibiting the Union from holding meetings within the prison is somewhat more justifiable than the regulations previously considered. Once the Union is permitted to hold meetings it will become operational within the prisons. Appellants' fears that the leaders of an operating union "would be in a position to misuse their influence" and that the Union itself could engage in disruptive, concerted activities or increase tension within the prisons, App. 121, are not entirely fanciful. It is important to note, however, that appellee's two expert witnesses, both correctional officers who had dealt with inmate reform organizations, testified that such groups actually play a constructive role in their prisons, id., at 38, 90-95. The weight of professional opinion seems to favor recognizing such groups. Moreover, the risks appellants fear are inherent in any inmate organization, no matter how innocuous its stated goals; indeed, even without any organizations some inmates inevitably will become leaders capable of "misus[ing] their influence," id., at 84-86, 102-103, and some concerted activity can still occur, id., at 118-119.

But even if the risks posed by the Union were unique to it, and even if appellants' fear of the Union were more widely shared by other professionals, the prohibition on Union meetings still could not survive constitutional attack. The central lesson of over a half century of First Amendment adjudication is that freedom is sometimes a hazardous enterprise, and that the Constitution requires the State to bear certain risks to preserve our liberty. See, e.g., Whitney v. California, 274 U.S. 357, 375-378 (1927) (Brandeis, J., concurring); Terminiello v. Chicago, 337 U.S. 1 (1949); Tinker v. Des Moines School Dist., 393 U.S. 503 (1969). As the ABA Joint Committee, supra, put it: "The doubts and risks raised by creating a humane and open prison must be accepted as a cost of our society; democracy is self-definitionally a risk-taking form of government." To my mind, therefore, the fact that appellants have not acted wholly irrationally in banning Union meetings is not dispositive. Rather, I believe that where, as here, meetings would not pose an immediate and substantial threat to the security or rehabilitative functions of the prisons, the First Amendment guarantees Union members the right to associate freely, and the Fourteenth Amendment guarantees them the right to be treated as favorably as members of other inmate organizations. The State can surely regulate the time, place, and manner of the meetings, and perhaps can monitor them to assure that disruptions are not planned, but the State cannot outlaw such assemblies altogether.

III

If the mode of analysis adopted in today's decision were to be generally followed, prisoners eventually would be stripped of all constitutional rights, and would retain only those privileges that prison officials, in their "informed discretion," deigned to recognize. The sole constitutional constraint on prison officials would be a requirement that they act rationally. Ironically, prisoners would be left with a right of access to the courts, see Bounds v. Smith, 430 U.S. 817 (1977); Johnson v. Avery, 393 U.S. 483 (1969), but no substantive rights to assert once they get there. I cannot believe that the Court that decided Bounds and Johnson—the Court that has stated that "[t]here is no iron curtain drawn between the Constitution and the prisons of this country," Wolff v. McDonnell, 418 U.S., at 555-556, and that "[a] prison inmate retains those First Anmednment rights that are not inconsistent with his status as a prisoner," Pell v. Procunier, 417 U.S., at 822— intends to allow this to happen. I therefore

believe that the tension between today's decision and our prior cases ultimately will be resolved, not by the demise of the earlier cases, but by the recognition that the decision today is an aberration, a manifestation of the extent to which the very phrase "prisoner union" is threatening to those holding traditional conceptions of the nature of penal institutions.

I respectfully dissent.

KENTUCKY
v.
THOMPSON

490 U.S. 454; 109 S. Ct. 1904;
104 L. Ed. 2d 506 (1989)

JUSTICE BLACKMUN delivered the opinion of the Court.

In this case we consider whether Kentucky prison regulations give state inmates, for purposes of the Fourteenth Amendment, a liberty interest in receiving certain visitors.

I

In September 1976, Kentucky inmates brought a federal class action under 42 U.S.C. § 1983 challenging conditions of confinement in the Kentucky State Penitentiary at Eddyville. Other cases, one of them relating to the Kentucky State Reformatory at La Grange, were consolidated with the one concerning the penitentiary. The litigation was settled by a consent decree dated 28 May 1980, and supplemented 22 July 1980, containing provisions governing a broad range of prison conditions. App. 2-44, 45-55. See Kendrick v. Bland, 541 F. Supp. 21, 27-50 (WD Ky. 1981); see also Kendrick v. Bland, 740 F. 2d 432 (CA6 1984). Of sole relevance here, the consent decree provides: "The Bureau of Corrections encourages and agrees to maintain visitation at least at the current level, with minimal restrictions," and to "continue [its] open visiting policy." See 541 F. Supp., at 37.

The Commonwealth in 1981 issued "Corrections Policies and Procedures" governing general prison visitation, including a nonexhaustive list of visitors who may be excluded. Four years later, the reformatory issued its own more detailed "Procedures Memorandum" on the subject of "Visiting Regulations." The memorandum begins with a Statement of Policy and Purpose: "Although administrative staff reserves the right to allow or disallow visits, it is the policy of the Kentucky State Reformatory to respect the right of inmates to have visits in the spirit of the Court decisions and the Consent Decree, while insuring the safety and security of the institution." App. 106. The memorandum then goes on to state that a visitor may be denied entry if his or her presence would constitute a "clear and probable danger to the safety and security of the institution or would interfere with the orderly operation of the institution." para. K(1)(a), App. 133. A nonexhaustive list of nine specific reasons for excluding visitors is set forth. The memorandum also states that the decision whether to exclude a visitor rests with the duty officer, who is to be consulted by any staff member who "feels a visitor should not be allowed admittance." para. K(3), App. 134.

This particular litigation was prompted in large part by two incidents when applicants were denied the opportunity to visit an inmate at the reformatory. The mother of one inmate was denied visitation for six months because she brought to the reformatory a person who had been barred for smuggling contraband. Another inmate's mother and woman friend were denied visitation for a limited time when the inmate was found with contraband after a visit by the two women. In both instances the visitation privileges were suspended without a hearing. The inmates were not prevented from receiving other visitors.

The representatives of the Kendrick-inmate class filed a motion with the United States District Court for the Western District of Kentucky (the court which had issued the consent decree), claiming that the suspension of visitation privileges without a hearing in these two instances violated the decree and the Due Process Clause of the Fourteenth Amendment. By a memorandum dated June 26, 1986, the District Court found that the prison policies did not violate the decree, App. 147, but concluded that the language of the decree was "mandatory in character," id., at 148, and that, under the standards articu-

lated by this Court in Hewitt v. Helms, 459 U.S. 460 (1983), respondents "possess a liberty interest in open visitation." The District Court directed petitioners to develop "minimal due process procedures," including "an informal, nonadversary review in which a prisoner receives notice of and reasons for" any decision to exclude a visitor, as well as an opportunity to respond. App. 148. A formal order was issued accordingly. Id., at 149.

* * *

II

* * *

Respondents do not argue—nor can it seriously be contended, in light of our prior cases—that an inmate's interest in unfettered visitation is guaranteed directly by the Due Process Clause. We have rejected the notion that "any change in the conditions of confinement having a substantial adverse impact on the prisoner involved is sufficient to invoke the protections of the Due Process Clause." (Emphasis in original.) Meachum v. Fano, 427 U.S. 215, 224 (1976). This is not to say that a valid conviction extinguishes every direct due process protection; "consequences visited on the prisoner that are qualitatively different from the punishment characteristically suffered by a person convicted of crime" may invoke the protections of the Due Process Clause even in the absence of a state-created right. Vitek v. Jones, 445 U.S. 480, 493 (1980) (transfer to mental hospital). However, "[a]s long as the conditions or degree of confinement to which the prisoner is subjected is within the sentence imposed upon him and is not otherwise violative of the Constitution, the Due Process Clause does not in itself subject an inmate's treatment by prison authorities to judicial oversight." Montanye v. Haymes, 427 U.S. 236, 242 (1976). The denial of prison access to a particular visitor "is well within the terms of confinement ordinarily contemplated by a prison sentence," Hewitt v. Helms, 459 U.S., at 468, and therefore is not independently protected by the Due Process Clause.

We have held, however, that state law may create enforceable liberty interests in the prison setting. We have found, for example, that certain regulations granted inmates a protected interest in parole, Board of Pardons v. Allen, 482 U.S. 369 (1987); Greenholtz v. Nebraska Penal Inmates, 442 U.S. 1 (1979), in good-time credits, Wolff v. McDonnell, 418 U.S., at 556-572, in freedom from involuntary transfer to a mental hospital, Vitek v. Jones, 445 U.S., at 487-494, and in freedom from more restrictive forms of confinement within the prison, Hewitt v. Helms, supra. In contrast, we have found that certain state statutes and regulations did not create a protected liberty interest in transfer to another prison. Meachum v. Fano, 427 U.S., at 225 (intrastate transfer); Olim v. Wakinekona, supra (interstate transfer). The fact that certain state-created liberty interests have been found to be entitled to due process protection, while others have not, is not the result of this Court's judgment as to what interests are more significant than others; rather, our method of inquiry in these cases always has been to examine closely the language of the relevant statutes and regulations.

Stated simply, "a State creates a protected liberty interest by placing substantive limitations on official discretion." Olim v. Wakinekona, 461 U.S., at 249. A State may do this in a number of ways. Neither the drafting of regulations nor their interpretation can be reduced to an exact science. Our past decisions suggest, however, that the most common manner in which a State creates a liberty interest is by establishing "substantive predicates" to govern official decisionmaking, Hewitt v. Helms, 459 U.S., at 472, and, further, by mandating the outcome to be reached upon a finding that the relevant criteria have been met.

Most of our procedural due process cases in the prison context have turned on the presence or absence of language creating "substantive predicates" to guide discretion. For example, the failure of a Connecticut statute governing commutation of sentences to provide "particularized standards or criteria [to] guide the State's decisionmakers," Connecticut Board of Pardons v. Dumschat, 452 U.S., at 467 (Brennan, J., concurring), defeated an inmate's claim that the State had created a liberty interest. Id., at 465 (majority opinion). See also Olim v. Wakinekona, 461 U.S., at 249-250 (interstate prison transfer left to "completely unfettered" discretion of administrator); Meachum v. Fano, 427 U.S., at 228 (intrastate prison transfer at discretion of officials); Montanye v. Haymes, 427 U.S., at 243 (same). In other instances, we have found that prison regulations or statutes do provide decisionmaking criteria which serve to limit discretion. See, e. g., Hewitt v. Helms, 459 U.S., at 472 (administrative segregation not proper absent particular substantive predicates); Board of Pardons v. Allen, 482 U.S., at 381 (parole granted unless certain standards met, even though the decision is "necessarily subjective . . . and predictive").

We have also articulated a requirement, implicit in our earlier decisions, that the regulations contain "explicitly mandatory language," i.e., specific directives to the decisionmaker that if the regulations' substantive predicates are present, a particular outcome must follow, in order to create a liberty interest. See Hewitt v. Helms, 459 U.S., at 471-472. The regulations at issue in Hewitt mandated that certain procedures be followed, and "that administrative segregation will not occur absent specified substantive predicates." Id., at 472. In Board of Pardons v. Allen, supra, the relevant statute "use[d] mandatory language ('shall') to 'creat[e] a presumption that parole release will be granted' when the designated findings are made," 482 U.S., at 377-378, quoting Greenholtz v. Nebraska Penal Inmates, 442 U.S., at 12. See also id., at 11 (statute providing that board "shall order" release unless one of four specified conditions is found). In sum, the use of "explicitly mandatory language," in connection with the establishment of "specified substantive predicates" to limit discretion, forces a conclusion that the State has created a liberty interest. Hewitt v. Helms, 459 U.S., at 472.

III

The regulations and procedures at issue in this case do provide certain "substantive predicates" to guide the decisionmaker. See nn. 1 and 2, supra. The state procedures provide that a visitor "may be excluded" when, inter alia, officials find reasonable grounds to believe that the "visitor's presence in the institution would constitute a clear and probable danger to the institution's security or interfere with [its] orderly operation." See n.

1, supra. Among the more specific reasons listed for denying visitation are the visitor's connection to the inmate's criminal behavior, the visitor's past disruptive behavior or refusal to submit to a search or show proper identification, and the visitor's being under the influence of alcohol or drugs. Ibid. The reformatory procedures are nearly identical, and include a prohibition on a visit from a former reformatory inmate, without the prior approval of the warden. See n. 2, supra. These regulations and procedures contain standards to be applied by a staff member in determining whether to refer a situation to the duty officer for resolution, and require the staff member to notify the duty officer if the staff member feels that a visitor should not be allowed admittance. Ibid. The same "substantive predicates" undoubtedly are intended to guide the duty officer's discretion in making the ultimate decision.

The regulations at issue here, however, lack the requisite relevant mandatory language. They stop short of requiring that a particular result is to be reached upon a finding that the substantive predicates are met. The Reformatory Procedures Memorandum begins with the caveat that "administrative staff reserves the right to allow or disallow visits," and goes on to note that "it is the policy" of the reformatory "to respect the right of inmates to have visits." App. 106. This language is not mandatory. Visitors may be excluded if they fall within one of the described categories, see n. 1, supra, but they need not be. Nor need visitors fall within one of the described categories in order to be excluded. The overall effect of the regulations is not such that an inmate can reasonably form an objective expectation that a visit would necessarily be allowed absent the occurrence of one of the listed conditions. Or, to state it differently, the regulations are not worded in such a way that an inmate could reasonably expect to enforce them against the prison officials.

Because the regulations at issue here do not establish a liberty interest entitled to the protections of the Due Process Clause, the judgment of the Court of Appeals is reversed.

It is so ordered.

JUSTICE KENNEDY, concurring.

I concur fully in the opinion and judgment of the Court. I write separately to note that this case involves a denial of prison access to particular visitors, not a general ban on all prison visitation. Nothing in the Court's opinion forecloses the claim that a prison regulation permanently forbidding all visits to some or all prisoners implicates the protections of the Due Process Clause in a way that the precise and individualized restrictions at issue here do not.

JUSTICE MARSHALL, with whom JUSTICE BRENNAN and JUSTICE STEVENS join, dissenting.

As a result of today's decision, correctional authorities at the Kentucky State Reformatory are free to deny prisoners visits from parents, spouses, children, clergy members, and close friends for any reason whatsoever, or for no reason at all. Prisoners will not even be entitled to learn the reason, if any, why a visitor has been turned away. In my view, the exercise of such unbridled governmental power over the basic human need to see family members and friends strikes at the heart of the liberty protected by the Due Process Clause of the Fourteenth Amendment. Recognizing a liberty interest in this case would not create a right to "unfettered visitation," ante, at 460, but would merely afford prisoners rudimentary procedural safeguards against retaliatory or arbitrary denials of visits. Because the majority refuses to take this small step, I dissent.

I

The majority begins its analysis by conceding, as it must under our precedents, that prisoners do not shed their constitutional rights at the prison gate, but instead retain a residuum of constitutionally protected liberty independent of any state laws or regulations. See ante, at 459-461. In the balance of its opinion, however, the majority proceeds to prove the emptiness of this initial gesture. In concluding that prison visits implicate no retained liberty interest, the majority applies the following oft-cited test: "As long as the conditions or degree of confinement to which the prisoner is subjected is within the sentence imposed upon him and is not otherwise violative of the Constitution, the Due Process Clause does not in itself subject an inmate's treatment by prison authorities to judicial oversight." Ante, at 460-461, quoting Montanye v. Haymes, 427 U.S. 236, 242 (1976). On its face, the "within the sentence" test knows few rivals for vagueness and pliability, not the least because a typical prison sentence says little more than that the defendant must spend a specified period of time behind bars. As applied, this test offers prisoners scant more protection, for the Justices employing it have rarely scrutinized the actual conditions of confinement faced by the prisoners in the correctional institutions at issue. Under this approach, therefore, "a prisoner crosses into limbo when he enters into penal confinement." Hewitt v. Helms, 459 U.S. 460, 482 (1983) (Stevens, J., dissenting). In theory he retains some minimal interest in liberty protected by the Due Process Clause, but in practice this interest crystallizes only on those infrequent occasions when a majority of the Court happens to say so.

* * *

Prison visits have long been recognized as critically important to inmates as well as to the communities to which the inmates ultimately will return. Without visits, a prisoner "may be entirely cut off from his only contacts with the outside world." Olim, supra, at 253 (Marshall, J., dissenting). Confinement without visitation "brings alienation and the longer the confinement the greater the alienation. There is little, if any, disagreement that the opportunity to be visited by friends and relatives is more beneficial to the confined person than any other form of communication.

* * *

The majority intimates that the actions taken against prisoners Bobbitt and Black were based on good cause, see ante, at 458, but the very essence of these prisoners' factual allegations is that no such cause existed. Id., at 57-58, 61, 66-68, 70-71. If Bobbitt and Black are correct, they may well have suffered a "grievous loss" by being singled out arbitrarily for unjustifiably harsh treatment. No evidence whatsoever indicates that visi-

tors to the reformatory have ever been barred for any reason except those enumerated as legitimate in the Commonwealth Procedures and the institution-specific Reformatory Procedures Memorandum (Reformatory Memorandum). See ante, at 456-458, nn. 1, 2. It is nowhere suggested, furthermore, that these prisoners' sentences contemplated denials of visits for nonenumerated reasons, or that such denials are "well within the terms of confinement ordinarily contemplated" in the reformatory. Ante, at 461, quoting Hewitt, 459 U.S., at 468. Under the majority's disposition, neither prisoner will ever have a right to contest the prison authorities' account. One need hardly be cynical about prison administrators to recognize that the distinct possibility of retaliatory or otherwise groundless deprivations of visits calls for a modicum of procedural protections to guard against such behavior.

II

Even if I believed that visit denials did not implicate a prisoner's retained liberty interest, I would nonetheless find that a liberty interest has been "created" by the Commonwealth's visitation regulations and policies. As the majority notes, "a State creates a protected liberty interest by placing substantive limitations on official discretion." Ante, at 462, quoting Olim, 461 U.S., at 249. I fully agree with the majority that "[t]he regulations and procedures at issue in this case do provide certain 'substantive predicates' to guide the decisionmaker." Ante, at 463. But I cannot agree that Kentucky's prison regulations do not create a liberty interest because they "lack the requisite relevant mandatory language." Ante, at 464.

As an initial matter, I fail to see why mandatory language always is an essential element of a state-created liberty interest. Once it is clear that a State has imposed substantive criteria in statutes or regulations to guide or limit official discretion, there is no reason to assume—as the majority does—that officials applying the statutes or regulations are likely to ignore the criteria if there is not some undefined quantity of the words "shall" or "must." Drafters of statutes or regulations do not ordinarily view the criteria they establish as mere surplusage. Absent concrete evidence that state officials routinely ignore substantive criteria set forth in statutes or regulations (and there is no such evidence here), it is only proper to assume that the criteria are regularly employed in practice, thereby creating legitimate expectations worthy of protection by the Due Process Clause. Common sense suggests that expectations stem from practice as well as from the language of statutes or regulations. Vitek v. Jones, 445 U.S., at 489 (approving lower courts' reliance on "objective expectation, firmly fixed in state law and official Penal Complex practice"). This point escapes the majority, which apparently harbors the "unrealistic [belief] that variations such as the use of 'may' rather than 'shall' could negate the expectations derived from experience with a [prison] system and . . . enumerated criteria . . . ." Greenholtz v. Nebraska Penal Inmates, 442 U.S. 1, 29-30, n. 9 (1979) (Marshall, J., dissenting) (citation omitted).

Even if I thought it proper to rely on the presence or absence of mandatory language, I would still disagree with the majority's determination that the regulations here lack such language. The majority relies primarily on a statement in the Reformatory Memorandum that "administrative staff reserves the right to allow or disallow visits." It is important, however, to put this "caveat," ante, at 464, in proper context. The Reformatory Memorandum's section on visitation occupies 33 pages of the joint appendix. The caveat appears just once in a general, introductory paragraph which also includes the statement that "it is the policy of the Kentucky State Reformatory to respect the right of inmates to have visits." App. 106 (emphasis added). Over the next 20 pages, the Reformatory Memorandum lays out in great detail the mandatory "procedures to be enforced in regard to all types of visits." Ibid. (emphasis added). It states, for example, that "[v]isits will be conducted seven (7) days a week," id., at 107 (emphasis added); that "[a]n inmate is allowed three (3) separate visits . . . per week," id., at 108 (emphasis added); that "[t]here will be no visit list maintained which specifies who may visit an inmate," ibid. (emphasis added); that "[a]n inmate is allowed to have . . . three (3) adult visitors . . . per visit," id., at 108-109 (emphasis added); that visits "will be one and one-half hours," id., at 109 (emphasis added);

and that "[e]ach inmate will be allowed one (1) outdoor visit per week," id., at 125 (emphasis added).

Only then does the Reformatory Memorandum enumerate the very specific reasons for which a visitor may be excluded. Id., at 132-134, quoted ante, at 457-458, n. 2. The duty officer does not have unfettered discretion with respect to visitors. Rather, he "has the responsibility of denying a visit for the above [enumerated] reasons." App. 134 (emphasis added). When a visit is denied, the reasons "will be documented." Ibid. (emphasis added). Presumably this means that the duty officer must keep a record of which of "the above reasons" caused him to exclude the visitor. The Reformatory Memorandum also expressly references the American Correctional Association's visitation standards, which provide that "visits may be limited only by the institution's schedule, space, and personnel constraints, or when there are substantial reasons to justify such limitations." American Correctional Association, Standards for Adult Correctional Institutions, Standard 2-4381 (2d ed. 1981) (emphasis added), cited at App. 106. Nothing in these standards even remotely contemplates the arbitrary exclusion of visitors.

When these mandatory commands are read in conjunction with the detailed rules set forth in the Commonwealth Procedures, it is inconceivable that prisoners in the reformatory would not "reasonably form an objective expectation that a visit would necessarily be allowed absent the occurrence of one of the listed conditions." Ante, at 465. The majority inexplicably ignores nearly all of these commands, despite claiming to have considered the "overall effect of the regulations," ibid., and despite the Commonwealth's striking concession that the regulations "repeatedly use 'will', 'shall', and similar directive or mandatory language" in an effort "to advise inmates and potential visitors what is expected." In light of these mandatory commands, the caveat, as well as any other language that could be taken to suggest that visitors need not "fall within one of the described categories in order to be excluded," ante, at 464, amount to nothing more than mere boilerplate. The Court should reject the view that "state laws which impose substantive limitations and elaborate procedural requirements on official conduct create no liberty interest solely because there remains the possibility that an official will act in an arbitrary manner at the end of the process." Olim, 461 U.S., at 258-259 (Marshall, J., dissenting) (discussing holding in Hewitt); see also 461 U.S., at 259, n. 13 (discussing similar holding in Greenholtz v. Nebraska Penal Inmates, 442 U.S. 1 (1979); cf. Brennan v. Cunningham, 813 F. 2d 1, 8 (CA1 1987).

Finally, the majority's reliance on the fact that both the Commonwealth Procedures and the Reformatory Memorandum provide that a visitor "may" be excluded if he falls within one of the enumerated categories, . . .

III

The prisoners in this case do not seek a right to unfettered visitation. All they ask is that the Court recognize that visitation is suf-ficiently important to warrant procedural protections to ensure that visitors are not arbitrarily denied. The protections need not be extensive, but simply commensurate with the special "needs and exigencies of the institutional environment." Wolff, 418 U.S., at 555. In making the threshold determination that the denial of visits can never implicate a prisoner's liberty interest, the majority thus establishes that when visitors are turned away, no process, not even notice, is constitutionally due. I cannot accept such a parsimonious reading of the Due Process Clause, and therefore dissent.

Cases Relating to Chapter 4

Prisoners' Rights to Use of the Mail and Telephone

PROCUNIER

v.

MARTINEZ

**416 U.S. 396; 94 S. Ct. 1800;
40 L. Ed. 2d 224 (1974)**

MR. JUSTICE POWELL delivered the opinion of the Court.

* * *

I

First we consider the constitutionality of the Director's rules restricting the personal correspondence of prison inmates. Under these regulations, correspondence between inmates of California penal institutions and persons other than licensed attorneys and holders of public office was censored for nonconformity to certain standards. Rule 2401 stated the Department's general premise that personal correspondence by prisoners is "a privilege, not a right. . . ." More detailed regulations implemented the Department's policy. Rule 1201 directed inmates not to write letters in which they "unduly complain" or "magnify grievances." Rule 1205 (d) defined as contraband writings "expressing inflammatory political, racial, religious or other views or beliefs . . . ." Finally, Rule 2402 (8) provided that inmates "may not send or receive letters that pertain to criminal activity; are lewd, obscene, or defamatory; contain foreign matter, or are otherwise inappropriate."

Prison employees screened both incoming and outgoing personal mail for violations of these regulations. No further criteria were provided to help members of the mailroom staff decide whether a particular letter contravened any prison rule or policy. When a prison employee found a letter objectionable, he could take one or more of the following actions: (1) refuse to mail or deliver the letter and return it to the author; (2) submit a disciplinary report, which could lead to suspension of mail privileges or other sanctions; or (3) place a copy of the letter or a summary of its contents in the prisoner's file, where it might be a factor in determining the inmate's work and housing assignments and in setting a date for parole eligibility.

The District Court held that the regulations relating to prisoner mail authorized censorship of protected expression without adequate justification in violation of the First Amendment and that they were void for vagueness. The court also noted that the regulations failed to provide minimum procedural safeguards against error and arbitrariness in the censorship of inmate correspondence. Consequently, it enjoined their continued enforcement.

* * *

A

Traditionally, federal courts have adopted a broad hands-off attitude toward problems of prison administration. In part this policy is the product of various limitations on the scope of federal review of conditions in state penal institutions. More fundamentally, this attitude springs from complementary perceptions about the nature of the problems and the efficacy of judicial intervention. Prison administrators are responsible for maintaining internal order and discipline, for securing their institutions against unauthorized access or escape, and for rehabilitating, to the extent that human nature and inadequate resources allow, the inmates placed in their custody. The Herculean obstacles to effective discharge of these duties are too apparent to warrant explication. Suffice it to say that the problems of prisons in America are complex and intractable, and, more to the point, they are not readily susceptible of resolution by decree. Most require expertise, comprehensive planning, and the commitment of resources, all of which are peculiarly within the province of the legislative and executive branches of government. For all of those reasons, courts are ill equipped to deal with the increasingly urgent problems of prison administration and reform.[9] Judicial recognition of that fact reflects no more than a healthy sense of realism. Moreover, where state penal institutions are involved, federal courts have a further reason for deference to the appropriate prison authorities.

But a policy of judicial restraint cannot encompass any failure to take cognizance of valid constitutional claims whether arising in a federal or state institution. When a prison regulation or practice offends a fundamental constitutional guarantee, federal courts will discharge their duty to protect constitutional rights. Johnson v. Avery, 393 U.S. 483, 486 (1969). This is such a case. Although the District Court found the regulations relating to prisoner mail deficient in several respects, the first and principal basis for its decision was the constitutional command of the First Amendment, as applied to the States by the Fourteenth Amendment.[10]

The issue before us is the appropriate standard of review for prison regulations restricting freedom of speech. This Court has not previously addressed this question, and the tension between the traditional policy of judicial restraint regarding prisoner complaints and the need to protect constitutional rights has led the federal courts to adopt a variety of widely inconsistent approaches to the problem. Some have maintained a hands-off posture in the face of constitutional challenges to censorship of prisoner mail. E. g., McCloskey

v. Maryland, 337 F.2d 72 (CA4 1964); Lee v. Tahash, 352 F.2d 970 (CA8 1965) (except insofar as mail censorship rules are applied to discriminate against a particular racial or religious group); Krupnick v. Crouse, 366 F.2d 851 (CA10 1966); Pope v. Daggett, 350 F.2d 296 (CA10 1965). Another has required only that censorship of personal correspondence not lack support "in any rational and constitutionally acceptable concept of a prison system." Sostre v. McGinnis, 442 F.2d 178, 199 (CA2 1971), cert. denied sub nom. Oswald v. Sostre, 405 U.S. 978 (1972). At the other extreme some courts have been willing to require demonstration of a "compelling state interest" to justify censorship of prisoner mail. E.g., Jackson v. Godwin, 400 F.2d 529 (CA5 1968) (decided on both equal protection and First Amendment grounds); Morales v. Schmidt, 340 F.Supp. 544 (WD Wis. 1972); Fortune Society v. McGinnis, 319 F.Supp. 901 (SDNY 1970). Other courts phrase the standard in similarly demanding terms of "clear and present danger." E.g., Wilkinson v. Skinner, 462 F.2d 670, 672-673 (CA2 1972). And there are various intermediate positions, most notably the view that a "regulation or practice which restricts the right of free expression that a prisoner would have enjoyed if he had not been imprisoned must be related both reasonably and necessarily to the advancement of some justifiable purpose." E.g., Carothers v. Follette, 314 F.Supp. 1014, 1024 (SDNY 1970) (citations omitted). See also Gates v. Collier, 349 F.Supp. 881, 896 (ND Miss. 1972); LeMon v. Zelker, 358 F.Supp. 554 (SDNY 1972).

This array of disparate approaches and the absence of any generally accepted standard for testing the constitutionality of prisoner mail censorship regulations disserve both the competing interests at stake. On the one hand, the First Amendment interests implicated by censorship of inmate correspondence are given only haphazard and inconsistent protection. On the other, the uncertainty of the constitutional standard makes it impossible for correctional officials to anticipate what is required of them and invites repetitive, piecemeal litigation on behalf of inmates. The result has been unnecessarily to perpetuate the involvement of the federal courts in affairs of prison administration. Our task is to formulate a standard of review for prisoner mail censorship that will be responsive to these concerns.

B

We begin our analysis of the proper standard of review for constitutional challenges to censorship of prisoner mail with a somewhat different premise from that taken by the other federal courts that have considered the question. For the most part, these courts have dealt with challenges to censorship of prisoner mail as involving broad questions of "prisoners' rights." This case is no exception. The District Court stated the issue in general terms as "the applicability of First Amendment rights to prison inmates . . . ," 354 F.Supp., at 1096, and the arguments of the parties reflect the assumption that the resolution of this case requires an assessment of the extent to which prisoners may claim First Amendment freedoms. In our view this inquiry is unnecessary. In determining the proper standard of review for prison restrictions on inmate correspondence, we have no occasion to consider the extent to which an individual's right to free speech survives incarceration, for a narrower basis of decision is at hand. In the case of direct personal correspondence between inmates and those who have a particularized interest in communicating with them, mail censorship implicates more than the rights of prisoners.

Communication by letter is not accomplished by the act of writing words on paper. Rather, it is effected only when the letter is read by the addressee. Both parties to the correspondence have an interest in securing that result, and censorship of the communication between them necessarily impinges on the interest of each. Whatever the status of a prisoner's claim to uncensored correspondence with an outsider, it is plain that the latter's interest is grounded in the First Amendment's guarantee of freedom of speech. And this does not depend on whether the nonprisoner correspondent is the author or intended recipient of a particular letter, for the addressee as well as the sender of direct personal correspondence derives from the First and Fourteenth Amendments a protection against unjustified governmental interference with the intended communication. Lamont v. Postmaster General, 381

U.S. 301 (1965); accord, Kleindienst v. Mandel, 408 U.S. 753, 762-765 (1972); Martin v. City of Struthers, 319 U.S. 141, 143 (1943). We do not deal here with difficult questions of the so-called "right to hear" and third-party standing but with a particular means of communication in which the interests of both parties are inextricably meshed. The wife of a prison inmate who is not permitted to read all that her husband wanted to say to her has suffered an abridgment of her interest in communicating with him as plain as that which results from censorship of her letter to him. In either event, censorship of prisoner mail works a consequential restriction on the First and Fourteenth Amendments rights of those who are not prisoners.

Accordingly, we reject any attempt to justify censorship of inmate correspondence merely by reference to certain assumptions about the legal status of prisoners. Into this category of argument falls appellants' contention that "an inmate's rights with reference to social correspondence are something fundamentally different than those enjoyed by his free brother." Brief for Appellants 19. This line of argument and the undemanding standard of review it is intended to support fail to recognize that the First Amendment liberties of free citizens are implicated in censorship of prisoner mail. We therefore turn for guidance, not to cases involving questions of "prisoners' rights," but to decisions of this Court dealing with the general problem of incidental restrictions on First Amendment liberties imposed in furtherance of legitimate governmental activities.

As the Court noted in Tinker v. Des Moines School District, 393 U.S. 503, 506 (1969), First Amendment guarantees must be "applied in light of the special characteristics of the . . . environment." Tinker concerned the interplay between the right to freedom of speech of public high school students and "the need for affirming the comprehensive authority of the States and of school officials, consistent with fundamental constitutional safeguards, to prescribe and control conduct in the schools." Id., at 507. In overruling a school regulation prohibiting the wearing of antiwar armbands, the Court undertook a careful analysis of the legitimate requirements of orderly school administration in order to ensure that the students were afford-ed maximum freedom of speech consistent with those requirements. The same approach was followed in Healy v. James, 408 U.S. 169 (1972), where the Court considered the refusal of a state college to grant official recognition to a group of students who wished to organize a local chapter of the Students for a Democratic Society (SDS), a national student organization noted for polit-ical activism and campus disruption. The Court found that neither the identification of the local student group with the national SDS, nor the purportedly dangerous political philosophy of the local group, nor the college administration's fear of future, unspecified disruptive activities by the students could justify the incursion on the right of free asso-ciation. The Court also found, however, that this right could be limited if necessary to pre-vent campus disruption, id., at 189-190, n. 20, and remanded the case for determination of whether the students had in fact refused to accept reasonable regulations governing stu-dent conduct.

In United States v. O'Brien, 391 U.S. 367 (1968), the Court dealt with incidental restrictions on free speech occasioned by the exercise of the governmental power to con-script men for military service. O'Brien had burned his Selective Service registration cer-tificate on the steps of a courthouse in order to dramatize his opposition to the draft and to our country's involvement in Vietnam. He was convicted of violating a provision of the Selective Service law that had recently been amended to prohibit knowing destruction or mutilation of registration certificates. O'Brien argued that the purpose and effect of the amendment were to abridge free expression and that the statutory provision was therefore unconstitutional, both as enacted and as applied to him. Although O'Brien's activity involved "conduct" rather than pure "speech," the Court did not define away the First Amend-ment concern, and neither did it rule that the presence of a communicative intent necessari-ly rendered O'Brien's actions immune to gov-ernmental regulation. Instead, it enunciated the following four-part test:

[A] government regulation is sufficiently justified if it is within the constitutional power of the Government; if it furthers an

important or substantial governmental interest; if the governmental interest is unrelated to the suppression of free expression; and if the incidental restriction on alleged First Amendment freedoms is no greater than is essential to the further-ance of that interest.

Of course, none of these precedents direct-ly controls the instant case. In O'Brien the Court considered a federal statute which on its face prohibited certain conduct having no nec-essary connection with freedom of speech. This led the Court to differentiate between "speech" and "nonspeech" elements of a sin-gle course of conduct, a distinction that has lit-tle relevance here. Both Tinker and Healy con-cerned First and Fourteenth Amendment liberties in the context of state educational institutions, a circumstance involving rather different governmental interests than are at stake here. In broader terms, however, these precedents involved incidental restrictions on First Amendment liberties by governmental action in furtherance of legitimate and sub-stantial state interest other than suppression of expression. In this sense these cases are generally analogous to our present inquiry.

The case at hand arises in the context of prisons. One of the primary functions of gov-ernment is the preservation of societal order through enforcement of the criminal law, and the maintenance of penal institutions is an essential part of that task. The identifiable governmental interests at stake in this task are the preservation of internal order and dis-cipline, the maintenance of institutional security against escape or unauthorized entry, and the rehabilitation of the prisoners. While the weight of professional opinion seems to be that inmate freedom to corre-spond with outsiders advances rather than retards the goal of rehabilitation, the legiti-mate governmental interest in the order and security of penal institutions justifies the imposition of certain restraints on inmate correspondence. Perhaps the most obvious example of justifiable censorship of prisoner mail would be refusal to send or deliver let-ters concerning escape plans or containing other information concerning proposed crim-inal activity, whether within or without the prison. Similarly, prison officials may prop-erly refuse to transmit encoded messages.

Other less obvious possibilities come to mind, but it is not our purpose to survey the range of circumstances in which particular restrictions on prisoner mail might be warranted by the legitimate demands of prison administration as they exist from time to time in the various kinds of penal institutions found in this country. Our task is to determine the proper standard for deciding whether a particular regulation or practice relating to inmate correspondence constitutes an impermissible restraint of First Amendment liberties.

Applying the teachings of our prior decisions to the instant context, we hold that censorship of prisoner mail is justified if the following criteria are met. First, the regulation or practice in question must further an important or substantial governmental interest unrelated to the suppression of expression. Prison officials may not censor inmate correspondence simply to eliminate unflattering or unwelcome opinions or factually inaccurate statements. Rather, they must show that a regulation authorizing mail censorship furthers one or more of the substantial governmental interests of security, order, and rehabilitation. Second, the limitation of First Amendment freedoms must be no greater than is necessary or essential to the protection of the particular governmental interest involved. Thus a restriction on inmate correspondence that furthers an important or substantial interest of penal administration will nevertheless be invalid if its sweep is unnecessarily broad. This does not mean, of course, that prison administrators may be required to show with certainty that adverse consequences would flow from the failure to censor a particular letter. Some latitude in anticipating the probable consequences of allowing certain speech in a prison environment is essential to the proper discharge of an administrator's duty. But any regulation or practice that restricts inmate correspondence must be generally necessary to protect one or more of the legitimate governmental interests identified above.

C

On the basis of this standard, we affirm the judgment of the District Court. The regulations invalidated by that court authorized, inter alia, censorship of statements that "unduly complain" or "magnify grievances," expression of "inflammatory political, racial, religious or other views," and matter deemed "defamatory" or "otherwise inappropriate." These regulations fairly invited prison officials and employees to apply their own personal prejudices and opinions as standards for prisoner mail censorship. Not surprisingly, some prison officials used the extraordinary latitude for discretion authorized by the regulations to suppress unwelcome criticism. For example, at one institution under the Department's jurisdiction, the checklist used by the mailroom staff authorized rejection of letters "criticizing policy, rules or officials," and the mailroom sergeant stated in a deposition that he would reject as "defamatory" letters "belittling staff or our judicial system or anything connected with Department of Corrections." Correspondence was also censored for "disrespectful comments," "derogatory remarks," and the like.

Appellants have failed to show that these broad restrictions on prisoner mail were in any way necessary to the furtherance of a governmental interest unrelated to the suppression of expression. Indeed, the heart of appellants' position is not that the regulations are justified by a legitimate governmental interest but that they do not need to be. This misconception is not only stated affirmatively; it also underlies appellants' discussion of the particular regulations under attack. For example, appellants' sole defense of the prohibition against matter that is "defamatory" or "otherwise inappropriate" is that it is "within the discretion of the prison administrators." Brief for Appellants 21. Appellants contend that statements that "magnify grievances" or "unduly complain" are censored "as a precaution against flash riots and in the furtherance of inmate rehabilitation." Id., at 22. But they do not suggest how the magnification of grievances or undue complaining, which presumably occurs in outgoing letters, could possibly lead to flash riots, nor do they specify what contribution the suppression of complaints makes to the rehabilitation of criminals. And appellants defend the ban against "inflammatory political, racial, religious or other views" on the ground that "such matter clearly presents a danger to prison security . . . ." Id., at 21. The regulation, however, is not narrowly drawn to reach only material that might be thought to encourage violence nor is its application limited to incoming letters. In short, the Department's regulations authorized censorship of prisoner mail far broader than any legitimate interest of penal administration demands and were properly found invalid by the District Court.

D

We also agree with the District Court that the decision to censor or withhold delivery of a particular letter must be accompanied by minimum procedural safeguards. The interest of prisoners and their correspondents in uncensored communication by letter, grounded as it is in the First Amendment, is plainly a "liberty" interest within the meaning of the Fourteenth Amendment even though qualified of necessity by the circumstance of imprisonment. As such, it is protected from arbitrary governmental invasion. See Board of Regents v. Roth, 408 U.S. 564 (1972); Perry v. Sindermann, 408 U.S. 593 (1972). The District Court required that an inmate be notified of the rejection of a letter written by or addressed to him, that the author of that letter be given a reasonable opportunity to protest that decision, and that complaints be referred to a prison official other than the person who originally disapproved the correspondence. These requirements do not appear to be unduly burdensome, nor do appellants so contend. Accordingly, we affirm the judgment of the District Court with respect to the Department's regulations relating to prisoner mail.

* * *

WOLFF
v.
McDONNELL

**418 U.S. 539; 94 S. Ct. 2963;
41 L. Ed. 2d 935 (1974)**

MR. JUSTICE WHITE delivered the opinion of the Court.

* * *

VII

The issue of the extent to which prison authorities can open and inspect incoming mail from attorneys to inmates, has been considerably narrowed in the course of this litigation. The prison regulation under challenge provided that "[all] incoming and outgoing mail will be read and inspected," and no exception was made for attorney-prisoner mail. The District Court held that incoming mail from attorneys might be opened if normal contraband detection techniques failed to disclose contraband, and if there was a reasonable possibility that contraband would be included in the mail. It further held that if an incoming letter was marked "privileged," thus identifying it as from an attorney, the letter could not be opened except in the presence of the inmate. Prison authorities were not to read the mail from attorneys. The Court of Appeals affirmed the District Court order, but placed additional restrictions on prison authorities. If there was doubt that a letter was actually from an attorney, "a simple telephone call should be enough to settle the matter," 483 F.2d, at 1067, the court thus implying that officials might have to go beyond the face of the envelope, and the "privileged" label, in ascertaining what kind of communication was involved. The court further stated that "the danger that a letter from an attorney, an officer of the court, will contain contraband is ordinarily too remote and too speculative to justify the [petitioners'] regulation permitting the opening and inspection of all legal mail." Ibid. While methods to detect contraband could be employed, a letter was to be opened only "in the appropriate circumstances" in the presence of the inmate.

Petitioners now concede that they cannot open and read mail from attorneys to inmates, but contend that they may open all letters from attorneys as long as it is done in the presence of the prisoners. The narrow issue thus presented is whether letters determined or found to be from attorneys may be opened by prison authorities in the presence of the inmate or whether such mail must be delivered unopened if normal detection techniques fail to indicate contraband.

Respondent asserts that his First, Sixth, and Fourteenth Amendment rights are infringed, under a procedure whereby the State may open mail from his attorney, even though in his presence and even though it may not be read. To begin with, the constitutional status of the rights asserted, as applied in this situation, is far from clear. While First Amendment rights of correspondents with prisoners may protect against the censoring of inmate mail, when not necessary to protect legitimate governmental interests, see Procunier v. Martinez, 416 U.S. 396 (1974), this Court has not yet recognized First Amendment rights of prisoners in this context, cf. Cruz v. Beto, 405 U.S. 319 (1972); Cooper v. Pate, 378 U.S. 546 (1964). Furthermore, freedom from censorship is not equivalent to freedom from inspection or perusal. As to the Sixth Amendment, its reach is only to protect the attorney-client relationship from intrusion in the criminal setting, see Black v. United States, 385 U.S. 26 (1966); O'Brien v. United States, 386 U.S. 345 (1967); see also Coplon v. United States, 89 U.S. App. D. C. 103, 191 F.2d 749 (1951), while the claim here would insulate all mail from inspection, whether related to civil or criminal matters. Finally, the Fourteenth Amendment due process claim based on access to the courts, Ex parte Hull, 312 U.S. 546 (1941); Johnson v. Avery, 393 U.S. 483 (1969); Younger v. Gilmore, 404 U.S. 15 (1971), has not been extended by this Court to apply further than protecting the ability of an inmate to prepare a petition or complaint. Moreover, even if one were to accept the argument that inspection of incoming mail from an attorney placed an obstacle to access to the court, it is far from clear that this burden is a substantial one. We need not decide, however, which, if any, of the asserted rights are operative here, for the question is whether, assuming some constitutional right is implicated, it is infringed by the procedure now found acceptable by the State.

In our view, the approach of the Court of Appeals is unworkable and none of the above rights is infringed by the procedures petitioners now accept. If prison officials had to check in each case whether a communication was from an attorney before opening it for inspection, a near-impossible task of administration would be imposed. We think it entirely appropriate that the State require any such communications to be specially marked as originating from an attorney, with his name and address being given, if they are to receive special treatment. It would also cer-

tainly be permissible that prison authorities require that a lawyer desiring to correspond with a prisoner, first identify himself and his client to the prison officials, to assure that the letters marked privileged are actually from members of the bar. As to the ability to open the mail in the presence of inmates, this could in no way constitute censorship, since the mail would not be read. Neither could it chill such communications, since the inmate's presence insures that prison officials will not read the mail. The possibility that contraband will be enclosed in letters, even those from apparent attorneys, surely warrants prison officials' opening the letters. We disagree with the Court of Appeals that this should only be done in "appropriate circumstances." Since a flexible test, besides being unworkable, serves no arguable purpose in protecting any of the possible constitutional rights enumerated by respondent, we think that petitioners, by acceding to a rule whereby the inmate is present when mail from attorneys is inspected, have done all, and perhaps even more, than the Constitution requires.

* * *

TURNER
v.
SAFLEY

482 U.S. 78; 107 S. Ct. 2254; 96 L. Ed. 2d 64 (1987)

JUSTICE O'CONNOR delivered the opinion of the Court.

This case requires us to determine the constitutionality of regulations promulgated by the Missouri Division of Corrections relating to inmate marriages and inmate-to-inmate correspondence. The Court of Appeals for the Eighth Circuit, applying a strict scrutiny analysis, concluded that the regulations violate respondents' constitutional rights. We hold that a lesser standard of scrutiny is appropriate in determining the constitutionality of the prison rules. Applying that standard, we uphold the validity of the correspondence regulation . . .

I

Respondents brought this class action for injunctive relief and damages in the United States District Court for the Western District of Missouri. The regulations challenged in the complaint were in effect at all prisons within the jurisdiction of the Missouri Division of Corrections. This litigation focused, however, on practices at the Renz Correctional Institution (Renz), located in Cedar City, Missouri. The Renz prison population includes both male and female prisoners of varying security levels. Most of the female prisoners at Renz are classified as medium or maximum security inmates, while most of the male prisoners are classified as minimum security offenders. Renz is used on occasion to provide protective custody for inmates from other prisons in the Missouri system. The facility originally was built as a minimum security prison farm, and it still has a minimum security perimeter without guard towers or walls.

. . . The first of the challenged regulations relates to correspondence between inmates at different institutions. It permits such correspondence "with immediate family members who are inmates in other correctional institutions," and it permits correspondence between inmates "concerning legal matters." Other correspondence between inmates, however, is permitted only if "the classification/treatment team of each inmate deems it in the best interest of the parties involved." App. 34. Trial testimony indicated that as a matter of practice, the determination whether to permit inmates to correspond was based on team members' familiarity with the progress reports, conduct violations, and psychological reports in the inmates' files rather than on individual review of each piece of mail. See 777 F.2d 1307, 1308 (CA8 1985). At Renz, the District Court found that the rule "as practiced is that inmates may not write non-family inmates." 586 F.Supp. 589, 591 (WD Mo. 1984).

The challenged marriage regulation, which was promulgated while this litigation was pending, permits an inmate to marry only with the permission of the superintendent of the prison, and provides that such approval should be given only "when there are compelling reasons to do so." App. 47. The term "compelling" is not defined, but prison officials testified at trial that generally only a pregnancy or the birth of an illegitimate child would be considered a compelling reason. See 586 F.Supp., at 592. Prior to the promulgation of this rule, the applicable regulation did not obligate Missouri Division of Corrections officials to assist an inmate who wanted to get married, but it also did not specifically authorize the superintendent of an institution to prohibit inmates from getting married. Ibid.

The District Court certified respondents as a class pursuant to Federal Rule of Civil Procedure 23. The class certified by the District Court includes "persons who either are or may be confined to the Renz Correctional Center and who desire to correspond with inmates at other Missouri correctional facilities." It also encompasses a broader group of persons "who desire to . . . marry inmates of Missouri correctional institutions and whose rights of . . . marriage have been or will be violated by employees of the Missouri Division of Corrections." See App. 21-22.

The District Court issued a memorandum opinion and order finding both the correspondence and marriage regulations unconstitutional. The court, relying on Procunier v. Martinez, 416 U.S. 396, 413-414 (1974), applied a strict scrutiny standard. It held the marriage regulation to be an unconstitutional infringement upon the fundamental right to marry because it was far more restrictive than was either reasonable or essential for the protection of the State's interests in security and rehabilitation. 586 F.Supp., at 594. The correspondence regulation also was unnecessarily broad, the court concluded, because prison officials could effectively cope with the security problems raised by inmate-to-inmate correspondence through less restrictive means, such as scanning the mail of potentially troublesome inmates. Id., at 596. The District Court also held that the correspondence regulation had been applied in an arbitrary and capricious manner.

* * *

III

* * *

A

... [T]he Missouri correspondence provision was promulgated primarily for security reasons. Prison officials testified that mail between institutions can be used to communicate escape plans and to arrange assaults and other violent acts. Witnesses stated that the Missouri Division of Corrections had a growing problem with prison gangs, and that restricting communications among gang members, both by transferring gang members to different institutions and by restricting their correspondence, was an important element in combating this problem. Officials also testified that the use of Renz as a facility to provide protective custody for certain inmates could be compromised by permitting correspondence between inmates at Renz and inmates at other correctional institutions.

The prohibition on correspondence between institutions is logically connected to these legitimate security concerns. Undoubtedly, communication with other felons is a potential spur to criminal behavior: this sort of contact frequently is prohibited even after an inmate has been released on parole. See, e.g., 28 CFR § 2.40(a)(10) (1986) (federal parole conditioned on nonassociation with known criminals, unless permission is granted by the parole officer). In Missouri prisons, the danger of such coordinated criminal activity is exacerbated by the presence of prison gangs. The Missouri policy of separating and isolating gang members—a strategy that has been frequently used to control gang activity, see G. Camp & C. Camp, U.S. Dept. of Justice, Prison Gangs: Their Extent, Nature and Impact on Prisons 64-65 (1985)—logically is furthered by the restriction on prisoner-to-prisoner correspondence. Moreover, the correspondence regulation does not deprive prisoners of all means of expression. Rather, it bars communication only with a limited class of other people with whom prison officials have particular cause to be concerned—inmates at other institutions within the Missouri prison system.

... Prison officials have stated that in their expert opinion, correspondence between prison institutions facilitates the development of informal organizations that threaten the core functions of prison administration, maintaining safety and internal security. As a result, the correspondence rights asserted by respondents, like the organizational activities at issue in Jones v. North Carolina Prisoners' Union, 433 U.S. 119 (1977), can be exercised only at the cost of significantly less liberty and safety for everyone else, guards and other prisoners alike. Indeed, the potential "ripple effect" is even broader here than in Jones, because exercise of the right affects the inmates and staff of more than one institution. Where exercise of a right requires this kind of tradeoff, we think that the choice made by corrections officials—which is, after all, a judgment "peculiarly within [their] province and professional expertise," Pell v. Procunier, 417 U.S., at 827—should not be lightly set aside by the courts.

Finally, there are no obvious, easy alternatives to the policy adopted by petitioners. Other well-run prison systems, including the Federal Bureau of Prisons, have concluded that substantially similar restrictions on inmate correspondence were necessary to protect institutional order and security. See, e.g., 28 CFR § 540.17 (1986). As petitioners have shown, the only alternative proffered by the claimant prisoners, the monitoring of inmate correspondence, clearly would impose more than a de minimis cost on the pursuit of legitimate corrections goals. Prison officials testified that it would be impossible to read every piece of inmate-to-inmate correspondence, 4 id., at 42-43, and consequently there would be an appreciable risk of missing dangerous messages. In any event, prisoners could easily write in jargon or codes to prevent detection of their real messages. See Camp & Camp, supra, at 130 (noting "frequent" use of coded correspondence by gang members in federal prison); see also Brief for State of Texas as Amicus Curiae 7-9. The risk of missing dangerous communications, taken together with the sheer burden on staff resources required to conduct item-by-item censorship, supports the judgment of prison officials that this alternative is not an adequate alternative to restricting correspondence.

The prohibition on correspondence is reasonably related to valid corrections goals. The rule is content neutral, it logically advances the goals of institutional security and safety identified by Missouri prison officials, and it is not an exaggerated response to those objectives. On that basis, we conclude that the regulation does not unconstitutionally abridge the First Amendment rights of prison inmates.

* * *

THORNBURGH

v.

ABBOTT

**490 U.S. 401; 109 S. Ct. 1874;
104 L. Ed. 2d 459 (1989)**

JUSTICE BLACKMUN delivered the opinion of the Court.

I

Regulations promulgated by the Federal Bureau of Prisons broadly permit federal prisoners to receive publications from the "outside," but authorize prison officials to reject incoming publications found to be detrimental to institutional security. For 15 years, respondents, a class of inmates and certain publishers, have claimed that these regulations violate their First Amendment rights under the standard of review enunciated in Procunier v. Martinez, 416 U.S. 396 (1974). They mount a facial challenge to the regulations as well as a challenge to the regulations as applied to 46 specific publications excluded by the Bureau.

After a 10-day bench trial, the District Court refrained from adopting the Martinez standard. Instead, it favored an approach more deferential to the judgment of prison authorities and upheld the regulations without addressing the propriety of the 46 specific exclusions. The Court of Appeals, on the other hand, utilized the Martinez standard, found the regulations wanting, and remanded the case to the District Court for an individualized determination of the constitutionality of the 46 exclusions. Abbott v. Meese, 263 U.S. App. D. C. 186, 824 F. 2d 1166 (1987).

* * *

We now hold that the District Court correctly anticipated that the proper inquiry in this case is whether the regulations are "reasonably related to legitimate penological interests," Turner v. Safley, 482 U.S. 78, 89 (1987), and we conclude that under this standard the regulations are facially valid. We therefore disagree with the Court of Appeals on the issue of facial validity, but we agree with that court's remand of the case to the District Court for a determination of the validity of the regulations as applied to each of the 46 publications.

II

We are concerned primarily with the regulations set forth at 28 CFR §§ 540.70 and 540.71 (1988), first promulgated in 1979. These generally permit an inmate to subscribe to, or to receive, a publication without prior approval, but authorize the warden to reject a publication in certain circumstances. The warden may reject it "only if it is determined detrimental to the security, good order, or discipline of the institution or if it might facilitate criminal activity." § 540.71(b). The warden, however, may not reject a publication "solely because its content is religious, philosophical, political, social or sexual, or because its content is unpopular or repugnant." Ibid. The regulations contain a nonexhaustive list of criteria which may support rejection of a publication. The warden is prohibited from establishing an excluded list of publications: each issue of a subscription publication is to be reviewed separately. § 540.71(c). The regulatory criteria for rejecting publications have been supplemented by Program Statement No. 5266.5, which provides further guidance on the subject of sexually explicit material.

The regulations provide procedural safeguards for both the recipient and the sender. The warden may designate staff to screen and, where appropriate, to approve incoming publications, but only the warden may reject a publication. § 540.70(b). The warden must advise the inmate promptly in writing of the reasons for the rejection, § 540.71(d), and must provide the publisher or sender with a copy of the rejection letter, § 540.71(e). The notice must refer to "the specific article(s) or material(s) considered objectionable." § 540.71(d). The publisher or sender may obtain an independent review of the warden's rejection decision by a timely writing to the Regional Director of the Bureau. § 540.71(e). An inmate may appeal through the Bureau's Administrative Remedy Procedure. See §§ 542.10 to 542.16. The warden is instructed to permit the inmate to review the rejected material for the purpose of filing an appeal "unless such review may provide the inmate with information of a nature which is deemed to pose a threat or detriment to the security, good order or discipline of the institution or to encourage or instruct in criminal activity." § 540.71(d).

III

There is little doubt that the kind of censorship just described would raise grave First Amendment concerns outside the prison context. It is equally certain that "[p]rison walls do not form a barrier separating prison inmates from the protections of the Constitution," Turner v. Safley, 482 U.S., at 84, nor do they bar free citizens from exercising their own constitutional rights by reaching out to those on the "inside," id., at 94-99; Bell v. Wolfish, 441 U.S. 520 (1979); Jones v. North Carolina Prisoners' Labor Union, Inc., 433 U.S. 119 (1977); Pell v. Procunier, 417 U.S. 817 (1974). We have recognized, however, that these rights must be exercised with due regard for the "inordinately difficult undertaking" that is modern prison administration. Turner v. Safley, 482 U.S., at 85.

In particular, we have been sensitive to the delicate balance that prison administrators must strike between the order and security of the internal prison environment and the legitimate demands of those on the "outside" who seek to enter that environment, in person or through the written word. Many categories of noninmates seek access to prisons. Access is essential to lawyers and legal assistants representing prisoner clients, see Procunier v. Martinez, 416 U.S. 396 (1974), to journalists seeking information about prison conditions, see Pell v. Procunier, supra, and to families and friends of prisoners who seek to sustain relationships with them, see Procunier v. Martinez, supra. All these claims to prison access undoubtedly are legitimate; yet prison officials may well conclude that certain proposed interactions, though seemingly innocu-

ous to laymen, have potentially significant implications for the order and security of the prison. Acknowledging the expertise of these officials and that the judiciary is "ill equipped" to deal with the difficult and delicate problems of prison management, this Court has afforded considerable deference to the determinations of prison administrators who, in the interest of security, regulate the relations between prisoners and the outside world. Id., at 404-405.

In this case, there is no question that publishers who wish to communicate with those who, through subscription, willingly seek their point of view have a legitimate First Amendment interest in access to prisoners. The question here, as it has been in our previous First Amendment cases in this area, is what standard of review this Court should apply to prison regulations limiting that access.

Martinez was our first significant decision regarding First Amendment rights in the prison context. There, the Court struck down California regulations concerning personal correspondence between inmates and noninmates, regulations that provided for censorship of letters that "unduly complain," "magnify grievances," or "expres[s] inflammatory political, racial, religious or other views or beliefs." Id., at 399. We reviewed these regulations under the following standard:

> First, the regulation or practice in question must further an important or substantial governmental interest unrelated to the suppression of expression. Prison officials . . . must show that a regulation authorizing mail censorship furthers one or more of the substantial governmental interests of security, order, and rehabilitation. Second, the limitation of First Amendment freedoms must be no greater than is necessary or essential to the protection of the particular governmental interest involved. Thus a restriction on inmate correspondence that furthers an important or substantial interest of penal administration will nevertheless be invalid if its sweep is unnecessarily broad.

It is clear from this language, however, that we did not deprive prison officials of the degree of discretion necessary to vindicate "the particular governmental interest involved." Accordingly, we said:

> Some latitude in anticipating the probable consequences of allowing certain speech in a prison environment is essential to the proper discharge of an administrator's duty. But any regulation or practice that restricts inmate correspondence must be generally necessary to protect one or more . . . legitimate governmental interests.

The Court's subsequent decisions regarding First Amendment rights in the prison context, however, laid down a different standard of review from that articulated in Martinez. As recently explained in Turner, these later decisions, which we characterized as involving "prisoners' rights," adopted a standard of review that focuses on the reasonableness of prison regulations: the relevant inquiry is whether the actions of prison officials were "reasonably related to legitimate penological interests." 482 U.S., at 89. The Court ruled that "such a standard is necessary if 'prison administrators . . ., and not the courts, [are] to make the difficult judgments concerning institutional operations.'" Ibid., quoting Jones v. North Carolina Prisoners' Labor Union, Inc., 433 U.S., at 128. The Court set forth in Turner the development of this reasonableness standard in the respective decisions in Pell and Jones and in Block v. Rutherford, 468 U.S. 576 (1984), and we need not repeat that discussion here.

The Court's decision to apply a reasonableness standard in these cases rather than Martinez' less deferential approach stemmed from its concern that language in Martinez might be too readily understood as establishing a standard of "strict" or "heightened" scrutiny, and that such a strict standard simply was not appropriate for consideration of regulations that are centrally concerned with the maintenance of order and security within prisons. See Turner v. Safley, 482 U.S., at 81, 87, 89. Specifically, the Court declined to apply the Martinez standard in "prisoners' rights" cases because, as was noted in Turner, Martinez could be (and had been) read to require a strict "least restrictive alternative" analysis, without sufficient sensitivity to the need for discretion in meeting legitimate prison needs. 482 U.S., at 89-90. The Court

expressed concern that "every administrative judgment would be subject to the possibility that some court somewhere would conclude that it had a less restrictive way of solving the problem at hand," id., at 89, and rejected the costs of a "least restrictive alternative" rule as too high. Id., at 90. See also O'Lone v. Estate of Shabazz, 482 U.S. 342, 350 (1987) (refusing to apply a least restrictive alternative standard for regulation of prisoner work rules having an impact on religious observance).

Pell involved the right of representatives of the news media to conduct interviews in the prisons in order to inform the public about prison conditions. The asserted right at issue in Jones was the right of a prisoners' union to send its literature into the prison. In Wolfish, publishers sought to send hardback books into the prison. In all these cases, regulations worked a "consequential restriction on the . . . rights of those who are not prisoners." Martinez, 416 U.S., at 409. But the Court in Turner observed: "In none of these . . . cases did the Court apply a standard of heightened scrutiny, but instead inquired whether a prison regulation that burdens fundamental rights is 'reasonably related' to legitimate penological objectives, or whether it represents an 'exaggerated response' to those concerns." 482 U.S., at 87.

We do not believe that Martinez should, or need, be read as subjecting the decisions of prison officials to a strict "least restrictive means" test. As noted, Martinez required no more than that a challenged regulation be "generally necessary" to a legitimate governmental interest. 416 U.S., at 414. Certainly, Martinez required a close fit between the challenged regulation and the interest it purported to serve. But a careful reading of Martinez suggests that our rejection of the regulation at issue resulted not from a least restrictive means requirement, but from our recognition that the regulated activity centrally at issue in that case—outgoing personal correspondence from prisoners—did not, by its very nature, pose a serious threat to prison order and security. We pointed out in Martinez that outgoing correspondence that magnifies grievances or contains inflammatory racial views cannot reasonably be expected to present a danger to the community inside the prison. Id., at 416. In addition, the implications for security are far more predictable. Dangerous outgoing correspondence is more likely to fall within readily identifiable categories: examples noted in Martinez include escape plans, plans relating to ongoing criminal activity, and threats of blackmail or extortion. Id., at 412-413. Although we were careful in Martinez not to limit unduly the discretion of prison officials to reject even outgoing letters, we concluded that the regulations at issue were broader than "generally necessary" to protect the interests at stake. Id., at 414.

In light of these considerations, it is understandable that the Court in Martinez concluded that the regulations there at issue swept too broadly. Where, as in Martinez, the nature of the asserted governmental interest is such as to require a lesser degree of case-by-case discretion, a closer fit between the regulation and the purpose it serves may safely be required. Categorically different considerations—considerations far more typical of the problems of prison administration—apply to the case presently before this Court.

We deal here with incoming publications, material requested by an individual inmate but targeted to a general audience. Once in the prison, material of this kind reasonably may be expected to circulate among prisoners, with the concomitant potential for coordinated disruptive conduct. Furthermore, prisoners may observe particular material in the possession of a fellow prisoner, draw inferences about their fellow's beliefs, sexual orientation, or gang affiliations from that material, and cause disorder by acting accordingly; see generally Prisoners and the Law 3-14 (I. Robbins ed. 1988) (noting that possession of homosexually explicit material may identify the possessor as homosexual and target him for assault). As the Deputy Solicitor General noted at oral argument: "The problem is not . . . in the individual reading the materials in most cases. The problem is in the material getting into the prison." In the volatile prison environment, it is essential that prison officials be given broad discretion to prevent such disorder.

In Turner, we dealt with incoming personal correspondence from prisoners; the impact of the correspondence on the internal environment of the prison was of great concern. There, we recognized that Martinez was too

readily understood as failing to afford prison officials sufficient discretion to protect prison security. In light of these same concerns, we now hold that regulations affecting the sending of a "publication" (see the regulations' specific definition of this word, n. 4, supra) to a prisoner must be analyzed under the Turner reasonableness standard. Such regulations are "valid if [they are] reasonably related to legitimate penological interests."

Furthermore, we acknowledge today that the logic of our analyses in Martinez and Turner requires that Martinez be limited to regulations concerning outgoing correspondence. As we have observed, outgoing correspondence was the central focus of our opinion in Martinez. The implications of outgoing correspondence for prison security are of a categorically lesser magnitude than the implications of incoming materials. Any attempt to justify a similar categorical distinction between incoming correspondence from prisoners (to which we applied a reasonableness standard in Turner) and incoming correspondence from nonprisoners would likely prove futile, and we do not invite it. To the extent that Martinez itself suggests such a distinction, we today overrule that case; the Court accomplished much of this step when it decided Turner.

In so doing, we recognize that it might have been possible to apply a reasonableness standard to all incoming materials without overruling Martinez: we instead could have made clear that Martinez does not uniformly require the application of a "least restrictive alternative" analysis. We choose not to go that route, however, for we prefer the express flexibility of the Turner reasonableness standard. We adopt the Turner standard in this case with confidence that, as petitioners here have asserted, "a reasonableness standard is not toothless."

IV

The Court in Turner identified several factors that are relevant to, and that serve to channel, the reasonableness inquiry.

The first Turner factor is multifold: we must determine whether the governmental objective underlying the regulations at issue is legitimate and neutral, and that the regulations are rationally related to that objective.

We agree with the District Court that this requirement has been met.

The legitimacy of the Government's purpose in promulgating these regulations is beyond question. The regulations are expressly aimed at protecting prison security, a purpose this Court has said is "central to all other corrections goals." Pell v. Procunier, 417 U.S., at 823.

As to neutrality, "[w]e have found it important to inquire whether prison regulations restricting inmates' First Amendment rights operated in a neutral fashion, without regard to the content of the expression." Turner, 482 U.S., at 90. The ban on all correspondence between certain classes of inmates at issue in Turner clearly met this "neutrality" criterion, as did the restrictions at issue in Pell and Wolfish. The issue, however, in this case is closer.

On their face, the regulations distinguish between rejection of a publication "solely because its content is religious, philosophical, political, social or sexual, or because its content is unpopular or repugnant" (prohibited) and rejection because the publication is detrimental to security (permitted). 28 CFR § 540.71(b)(1988). Both determinations turn, to some extent, on content. But the Court's reference to "neutrality" in Turner was intended to go no further than its requirement in Martinez that "the regulation or practice in question must further an important or substantial governmental interest unrelated to the suppression of expression." 416 U.S., at 413. Where, as here, prison administrators draw distinctions between publications solely on the basis of their potential implications for prison security, the regulations are "neutral" in the technical sense in which we meant and used that term in Turner.

We also conclude that the broad discretion accorded prison wardens by the regulations here at issue is rationally related to security interests. We reach this conclusion for two reasons. The first has to do with the kind of security risk presented by incoming publications. This has been explored above in Part III. The District Court properly found that publications can present a security threat, and that a more closely tailored standard "could result in admission of publications which, even if they did not lead directly to violence, would exacerbate tensions and lead indirectly to disorder." Where the regulations at issue concern the entry of materials into the prison, we agree with the District Court that a regulation which gives prison authorities broad discretion is appropriate.

Second, we are comforted by the individualized nature of the determinations required by the regulation. Under the regulations, no publication may be excluded unless the warden himself makes the determination that it is "detrimental to the security, good order, or discipline of the institution or . . . might facilitate criminal activity." 28 CFR §§ 540.70(b), 540.71(b) (1988). This is the controlling standard. A publication which fits within one of the "criteria" for exclusion may be rejected, but only if it is determined to meet that standard under the conditions prevailing at the institution at the time. Indeed, the regulations expressly reject certain shortcuts that would lead to needless exclusions. See § 540.70(b) (nondelegability of power to reject publications); § 540.71(c) (prohibition against establishing an excluded list of publications). We agree that it is rational for the Bureau to exclude materials that, although not necessarily "likely" to lead to violence, are determined by the warden to create an intolerable risk of disorder under the conditions of a particular prison at a particular time.

A second factor the Court in Turner held to be "relevant in determining the reasonableness of a prison restriction . . . is whether there are alternative means of exercising the right that remain open to prison inmates." 482 U.S., at 90. As has already been made clear in Turner and O'Lone, "the right" in question must be viewed sensibly and expansively. The Court in Turner did not require that prisoners be afforded other means of communicating with inmates at other institutions, 482 U.S., at 92, nor did it in O'Lone require that there be alternative means of attending the Jumu'ah religious ceremony, 482 U.S., at 351. Rather, it held in Turner that it was sufficient if other means of expression (not necessarily other means of communicating with inmates in other prisons) remained available, and in O'Lone if prisoners were permitted to participate in other Muslim religious ceremonies. As the regulations at issue in the present case permit a broad range of publications to be sent, received, and read, this factor is clearly satisfied.

The third factor to be addressed under the Turner analysis is the impact that accommodation of the asserted constitutional right will have on others (guards and inmates) in the prison. 482 U.S., at 90. Here, the class of publications to be excluded is limited to those found potentially detrimental to order and security; the likelihood that such material will circulate within the prison raises the prospect of precisely the kind of "ripple effect" with which the Court in Turner was concerned. Where, as here, the right in question "can be exercised only at the cost of significantly less liberty and safety for everyone else, guards and other prisoners alike," id., at 92, the courts should defer to the "informed discretion of corrections officials," id., at 90.

Finally, Turner held: "[T]he existence of obvious, easy alternatives may be evidence that the regulation is not reasonable, but is an 'exaggerated response' to prison concerns. . . . But if an inmate claimant can point to an alternative that fully accommodates the prisoner's rights at de minimis cost to valid penological interests, a court may consider that as evidence that the regulation does not satisfy the reasonable relationship standard." 482 U.S., at 90-91. We agree with the District Court that these regulations, on their face, are not an "exaggerated response" to the problem at hand: no obvious, easy alternative has been established.

* * *

V

In sum, we hold that Turner's reasonableness standard is to be applied to the regulations at issue in this case, and that those regulations are facially valid under that standard. We agree with the remand for an examination of the validity of the regulations as applied to any of the 46 publications introduced at trial as to which there remains a live controversy. See 263 U.S. App. D. C., at 196, 824 F. 2d, at 1176.

The judgment of the Court of Appeals is vacated, and the case is remanded for further proceedings consistent with this opinion.

It is so ordered.

JUSTICE STEVENS, with whom JUSTICE BRENNAN and JUSTICE MARSHALL join, concurring in part and dissenting in part.

An article in Labyrinth, a magazine published by the Committee for Prisoner Humanity & Justice, began as follows:

In January 1975, William Lowe, a black prisoner at the United States Penitentiary at Terre Haute, Indiana died of asthma. . . . In August 1975, Joseph (Yusef) Jones, Jr., a black prisoner at the U.S. Penitentiary, Terre Haute, IN. died of asthma.

. . . The prison infirmary at that time had only one respirator[,] known to be inoperative in January 1975 when William Lowe died. It was still broken in August 1975 when Joseph Jones needed it.

On the day of his death Jones was suffering an acute asthma attack; he was gasping for breath in the stale, hot, humid air in the cell. He requested medical aid of the guards. After several hours of unheeded pleading, accompanied by complaints to the guards from fellow prisoners in the cell block, Jones became frantic. Each breath was painful; each breath brought him closer to suffocation. Finally, guards called the PA (physician's assistant) . . ., who brought with him the broken respirator. Finding the equipment unusable, the PA gave Jones an injection of the tranquilizer, thorazine, to calm him. Treatment with a tranquilizer was unquestionably contraindicated by Jones' medical condition. Twenty minutes later, Jones was dead.

. . .

Conclusion: Jones, who was convicted of bank robbery and sentenced to 10 years in prison, was in fact, sentenced to death and was murdered by neglect."

The incident described above eventually came to the attention of this Court, which allowed Jones' mother to pursue her civil rights action against prison officials. Carlson v. Green, 446 U.S. 14 (1980). Clearly the

Labyrinth article's report of inadequate medical treatment of federal prisoners raised "a matter that is both newsworthy and of great public importance." Pell v. Procunier, 417 U.S. 817, 830, n. 7 (1974). As the Court concedes, ante, at 407, both publishers and recipients of such criticism ordinarily enjoy the fullest First Amendment protections. See Pell, supra, at 822; Martin v. Struthers, 319 U.S. 141, 146-147 (1943).

Yet Labyrinth's efforts to disseminate the article to its subscribers at Marion Federal Penitentiary met Government resistance. Marion officials, acting within Federal Bureau of Prisons (Bureau) regulations, returned the magazine on the ground that "the article entitled 'Medical Murder' would be detrimental to the good order and discipline of this institution . . . . [T]his type of philosophy could guide inmates in this institution into situations which could cause themselves and other inmates problems with the Medical Staff." J. L. 12. Two years after publication a Marion official testified that he believed the article had posed no threat. App. 104. Nonetheless, the District Court below found the suppression of this and 45 other publications "reasonable," and thus sustained the rejections wholesale. App. to Pet. for Cert. 28a-34a, 47a. This Court holds today that such carte blanche deference was improper and remands for case-by-case review. I agree with this aspect of the Court's decision. I cannot agree, however, with either its holding that another finding of "reasonableness" will justify censorship or its premature approval of the Bureau's regulations. These latter determinations upset precedent in a headlong rush to strip inmates of all but a vestige of free communication with the world beyond the prison gate.

I

This Court first addressed the First Amendment in the prison context in Procunier v. Martinez, 416 U.S. 396 (1974). Prior lower court treatments had varied: some courts had maintained "a hands-off posture," while others had required "demonstration of a 'compelling state interest' to justify censorship of prisoner mail." Id., at 406. With characteristic wisdom Justice Powell, in his opinion for the Court, rejected both extremes. The

difficulties of prison administration, he perceived, make the strict scrutiny that the First Amendment demands in other contexts inappropriate. See, e.g., First National Bank of Boston v. Bellotti, 435 U.S. 765, 786 (1978); Elrod v. Burns, 427 U.S. 347, 362 (1976) (opinion of Brennan, J.); Brandenburg v. Ohio, 395 U.S. 444, 447 (1969) (per curiam). Focusing not on the rights of prisoners, but on the "inextricably meshed" rights of nonprisoners "who have a particularized interest in communicating with them," he wrote that an "undemanding standard of review" could not be squared with the fact "that the First Amendment liberties of free citizens are implicated in censorship of prisoner mail." Martinez, supra, at 408, 409. Thus he chose an "intermediate" means of evaluating speech restrictions, 416 U.S., at 407, allowing censorship if it "further[ed] an important or substantial governmental interest unrelated to the suppression of expression," and "the limitation of First Amendment freedoms [was] no greater than [was] necessary or essential," id., at 413. "Prison officials may not censor inmate correspondence simply to eliminate unflattering or unwelcome opinions or factually inaccurate statements," Justice Powell stressed. Ibid. Censorship might be permitted, however, to ensure "the preservation of internal order and discipline, the maintenance of institutional security against escape or unauthorized entry, and the rehabilitation of the prisoners." Id., at 412 (footnote omitted). Prison administrators did not have "to show with certainty that adverse consequences would flow from the failure to censor a particular letter," but "any regulation or practice that restricts inmate correspondence must be generally necessary to protect one or more of the legitimate governmental interests identified above." Id., at 414.

In the 15 years since Martinez was decided, lower courts routinely have applied its standard to review limitations not only on correspondence between inmates and private citizens, but also on communications—such as the newsletters, magazines, and books at issue—between inmates and publishers. Carefully examining free speech rights and countervailing governmental interests, these courts approved some restrictions and invalidated others. This Court thus correctly recognizes that Martinez's standard of review does not deprive prison officials of the discretion necessary to perform their difficult tasks. Ante, at 409. Inexplicably, it then partially overrules Martinez by limiting its scope to outgoing mail; letters and publications sent to prisoners now are subject only to review for "reasonableness." Ante, at 413-414.

This peculiar bifurcation of the constitutional standard governing communications between inmates and outsiders is unjustified. The decision in Martinez was based on a distinction between prisoners' constitutional rights and the protection the First Amendment affords those who are not prisoners— not between nonprisoners who are senders and those who are receivers. As Justice Powell explained:

Whatever the status of a prisoner's claim to uncensored correspondence with an outsider, it is plain that the latter's interest is grounded in the First Amendment's guarantee of freedom of speech. And this does not depend on whether the nonprisoner correspondent is the author or intended recipient of a particular letter, for the addressee as well as the sender of direct personal correspondence derives from the First and Fourteenth Amendments a protection against unjustified governmental interference with the intended communication. . . . The wife of a prison inmate who is not permitted to read all that her husband wanted to say to her has suffered an abridgment of her interest in communicating with him as plain as that which results from censorship of her letter to him." 416 U.S., at 408-409 (citations omitted). The Court today abandons Martinez's fundamental premise. In my opinion its suggestion that three later opinions applying reasonableness standards warrant this departure, see ante, at 410, n. 9, is disingenuous. Those cases did involve communications between inmates and outsiders; however, as I shall demonstrate, their legal and factual foundations differed critically from those in Martinez or in this case.

In Pell v. Procunier, 417 U.S. 817 (1974), inmates and reporters challenged regulations prohibiting face-to-face media interviews with specific prisoners. Id., at 819. The infringement on prisoners' rights, the Court held, was reasonable because prisoners could write letters to the media—a means of communication less disruptive than the physical entry of reporters into the prison. Id., at 824. The reporters' assertion of a special right of access could not prevail, the Court explained, because the First Amendment does not give the media greater access to public events or institutions—including prisons—than it gives ordinary citizens. Id., at 835. Pell in no way diluted the basic distinction articulated in Martinez.

Inmates in Jones v. North Carolina Prisoners' Labor Union, Inc., 433 U.S. 119 (1977), had maintained that First Amendment associational rights protected their efforts to form a union. The Court concluded that the administrators' grounds for preventing union organizing within the prison—an activity occurring largely among inmates—were reasonable. Id., at 129. It also approved the officials' refusal to deliver bulk packets of union literature to specific inmates for distribution to others. Applying Equal Protection Clause as well as First Amendment standards, the Court held that the restriction was reasonable because it was limited in scope and because the union retained "other avenues of outside informational flow. . . ." Id., at 131; see id., at 133, 136.

In the third case, Bell v. Wolfish, 441 U.S. 520 (1979), the Court upheld a regulation that allowed only publishers, bookstores, and book clubs to mail hardbound books to pretrial detainees. Hardbacks might serve as containers for contraband, jail administrators argued. Since the risk of improper use by publishers and similar sources was low, the jail delivered books from them but not from other outsiders. Id., at 549. The Court found this explanation acceptable and held that the rule did not violate the detainees' First Amendment rights. Id., at 550. Although the Court did not expressly address the rights of nonprisoners, the fact that softcover publications were delivered without restriction, see id., at 552, minimized the abridgment of outsiders' rights. The approval in Wolfish of greater protection for publishers than for individual citizens reinforces Martinez's view that the First Amendment rights of nonprisoners must be carefully weighed and undermines the Court's approach today.

Most recently, Turner v. Safley, 482 U.S. 78 (1987), confirmed the vitality of Martinez for evaluating encroachments on the First Amendment rights of nonprisoners. The Court relied on the three interim "prisoners' rights" cases to establish a reasonableness standard for reviewing inmate-to-inmate correspondence. Id., at 89. But in its unanimous invalidation of a restriction on inmate marriages, the Court acknowledged that "because the regulation may entail a 'consequential restriction on the [constitutional] rights of those who are not prisoners,'" Martinez might posit the correct level of review. 482 U.S., at 97 (quoting Martinez, 416 U.S., at 409). It did not "reach this question, however, because even under the reasonable relationship test, the marriage regulation does not withstand scrutiny." 482 U.S., at 97.

The Turner opinion cited and quoted from Martinez more than 20 times; not once did it disapprove Martinez's holding, its standard, or its recognition of a special interest in protecting the First Amendment rights of those who are not prisoners. Notwithstanding, today the Court abandons the premise on which Martinez was grounded. This casual discarding of "the secure foundation" of considered precedent ill serves the orderly development of the law. See Runyon v. McCrary, 427 U.S. 160, 190-191 (1976) (Stevens, J., concurring) (quoting B. Cardozo, The Nature of the Judicial Process 149 (1921)).

II

In lieu of Martinez's rationale, which properly takes into consideration the effects that prison regulations have on the First Amendment rights of nonprisoners, the Court applies a manipulable "reasonableness" standard to a set of regulations that too easily may be interpreted to authorize arbitrary rejections of literature addressed to inmates. As I pointed out in my partial dissent in Turner, an "open-ended 'reasonableness' standard makes it much too easy to uphold restrictions on prisoners' First Amendment rights on the basis of administrative concerns and speculation about possible security risks rather than on the basis of evidence that the restrictions are needed to further an important governmental interest." 482 U.S., at 101, n. 1.

To be sure, courts must give prison administrators some berth to combat the "Herculean obstacles" blocking their efforts to maintain security and prevent escapes or other criminal conduct, see Martinez, 416 U.S., at 404, and I do not object to those regulations clearly targeted at such interests. Nevertheless, I agree with the Court of Appeals that provisions allowing prison officials to reject a publication if they find its contents are "detrimental" to "security, good order, or discipline" or "might facilitate criminal activity" are impermissibly ambiguous. See Abbott v. Meese, 263 U.S. App. D. C. 186, 193, 824 F. 2d 1166, 1173 (1987). The term "detrimental" invites so many interpretations that it scarcely checks administrators' actions. Similarly, "might facilitate"—in contrast with "encourage" or "advocate"—so attenuates the causal connection between expression and proscribed conduct that the warden has virtually free rein to censor incoming publications.

Despite this vagueness, the Court accepts petitioners' assertion that they need "broad discretion" to prevent internal disorder, and thus holds that all the regulations are facially valid. See ante, at 416. This premature leap of faith creates a presumption that rejections pursuant to these regulations are "reasonable"—a presumption that makes likely far less judicial protection of publishers' rights than I believe the First Amendment requires. As was Justice Blackmun in Block v. Rutherford, 468 U.S. 576, 593 (1984) (concurring in judgment), I am concerned that the Court today too readily "substitute[s] the rhetoric of judicial deference for meaningful scrutiny of constitutional claims in the prison setting." Cf. O'Lone v. Estate of Shabazz, 482 U.S. 342, 358 (1987) (Brennan, J., dissenting); Jones, 433 U.S., at 142-143 (Marshall, J., dissenting).

The feeble protection provided by a "reasonableness" standard applied within the framework of these regulations is apparent in this record. Like the Labyrinth issue, many of the 46 rejected publications criticized prison conditions or otherwise presented viewpoints that prison administrators likely would not welcome. Testimony by one mail clerk and the rote explanations for decisions suggest that rejections were based on personal prejudices or categorical assumptions rather than individual assessments of risk. Cf. Martinez,

416 U.S., at 415. These circumstances belie the Court's interpretation of these regulations as "content-neutral" and its assertion that rejection decisions are made individually. See ante, at 414-417. Some of the rejected publications may represent the sole medium for conveying and receiving a particular unconventional message; thus it is irrelevant that the regulations permit many other publications to be delivered to prisoners. See ante, at 417-418. No evidence supports the Court's assumption that, unlike personal letters, these publications will circulate within the prison and cause ripples of disruption. See ante, at 412, 418. Nor is there any evidence that an incoming publication ever caused a disciplinary or security problem; indeed, some of the rejected publications were delivered to inmates in other prisons without incident. See App. 60, 99, 116-117. In sum, the record convinces me that under either the Martinez standard or the more deferential "reasonableness" standard these regulations are an impermissibly exaggerated response to security concerns. Cf. Turner, 482 U.S., at 89-90.

III

If a prison official deems part of a publication's content—even just one page of a book—to present an intolerable security risk, the Bureau's regulations authorize the official to return the entire issue to the publisher. See 28 CFR § 540.71(e) (1988). In their challenge to this all-or-nothing rule, respondents argue that First Amendment interests easily could be accommodated if administrators omitted the objectionable material and forwarded the rest of the publication to the inmate. The District Court, however, found that "defendants' fears" that "such censorship would create more discontent than the current practice" were "reasonably founded." App. to Pet. for Cert. 34a. To the contrary, the Court of Appeals applied the Martinez standard and held that "rejection of the balance is not 'generally necessary' to protect the legitimate governmental interest involved in the portion properly rejected." 263 U.S. App. D. C., at 193-194, 824 F. 2d, at 1173-1174.

In this Court petitioners argue that on remand the Court of Appeals should conduct "a detailed analysis of the evidence in this case" to determine if the all-or-nothing rule is "reasonable." Brief for Petitioners 31. "The validity of that policy," they continue, "will depend, among other things, on the security and administrative justifications for that policy, the availability of alternative courses of action, and the costs and risks associated with employing those alternatives." Ibid. It is remarkable that after 16 years of litigation petitioners have failed to develop an argument that tells us anything about the assumed security or administrative justification for this rule. Even more remarkable is the Court's conclusion that since it does not apply the Martinez standard, it need not examine the appropriateness of the District Court's finding that the rule was reasonable. See ante, at 419. A review of the record reveals that the Court thus defers to "findings" of a security threat that even prison officials admitted to be nonexistent.

There is no evidence that delivery of only part of a publication would endanger prison security. Rather, the primary justification advanced for the all-or-nothing rule was administrative convenience. See App. 41, 68. The Bureau has objected that a contrary rule "would mean defacing the material and laboriously going over each article in each publication. . . ." 44 Fed. Reg. 38258 (1979). But general speculation that some administrative burden might ensue should not be sufficient to justify a meat-ax abridgment of the First Amendment rights of either a free citizen or a prison inmate. It is difficult even to imagine such a burden in this instance: if, as the regulations' text seems to require, prison officials actually read an article before rejecting it, the incremental burden associated with clipping out the offending matter could not be of constitutional significance. The Bureau's administrative convenience justification thus is insufficient as a matter of law under either the Martinez standard or a "reasonableness" standard. The District Court's contradictory finding simply highlights the likelihood that an attitude of broad judicial deference, coupled with a "reasonableness" standard, will provide inadequate protection for the rights at stake.

For these reasons, I would affirm the judgment of the Court of Appeals.

Cases Relating to Chapter 5

Isolated Confinement—"The Hole" and Administrative Segregation

RHODES

v.

CHAPMAN

**452 U.S. 337; 101 S. Ct. 2392;
69 L. Ed. 2d 59 (1981)**

JUSTICE POWELL delivered the opinion of the Court.

The question presented is whether the housing of two inmates in a single cell at the Southern Ohio Correctional Facility is cruel and unusual punishment prohibited by the Eighth and Fourteenth Amendments.

I

Respondents Kelly Chapman and Richard Jaworski are inmates at the Southern Ohio Correctional Facility (SOCF), a maximum-security state prison in Lucasville, Ohio. They were housed in the same cell when they brought this action in the District Court for the Southern District of Ohio on behalf of themselves and all inmates similarly situated at SOCF. Asserting a cause of action under 42 U.S.C. § 1983, they contended that "double celling" at SOCF violated the Constitution. The gravamen of their complaint was that double celling confined cellmates too closely. It also was blamed for overcrowding at SOCF, said to have overwhelmed the prison's facilities and staff. As relief, respondents sought an injunction barring petitioners, who are Ohio officials responsible for the administration of SOCF, from housing

more than one inmate in a cell, except as a temporary measure.

The District Court made extensive findings of fact about SOCF on the basis of evidence presented at trial and the court's own observations during an inspection that it conducted without advance notice. 434 F.Supp. 1007 (1977). These findings describe the physical plant, inmate population, and effects of double celling. Neither party contends that these findings are erroneous.

SOCF was built in the early 1970's. In addition to 1,620 cells, it has gymnasiums, workshops, schoolrooms, "dayrooms," two chapels, a hospital ward, commissary, barbershop, and library. Outdoors, SOCF has a recreation field, visitation area, and garden. The District Court described this physical plant as "unquestionably a top-flight, first-class facility." Id., at 1009.

Each cell at SOCF measures approximately 63 square feet. Each contains a bed measuring 36 by 80 inches, a cabinet-type night stand, a wall-mounted sink with hot and cold running water, and a toilet that the inmate can flush from inside the cell. Cells housing two inmates have a two-tiered bunk bed. Every cell has a heating and air circulation vent near the ceiling, and 960 of the cells have a window that inmates can open and close. All of the cells have a cabinet, shelf, and radio built into one of the walls, and in all of the cells one wall consists of bars through which the inmates can be seen.

The "dayrooms" are located adjacent to the cellblocks and are open to inmates between 6:30 A.M. and 9:30 P.M. According to the District Court, "[the] dayrooms are in a sense part of the cells and they are designed to furnish that type of recreation or occupation which an ordinary citizen would seek in his living room or den." Id., at 1012. Each dayroom contains a wall-mounted television, card tables, and chairs. Inmates can pass between their cells and the dayrooms during a 10-minute period each hour, on the hour, when the doors to the dayrooms and cells are opened.

As to the inmate population, the District Court found that SOCF began receiving inmates in late 1972 and double celling them in 1975 because of an increase in Ohio's statewide prison population. At the time of trial, SOCF housed 2,300 inmates, 67% of whom were serving life or other long-term sentences for first-degree felonies. Approximately 1,400 inmates were double celled. Of these, about 75% had the choice of spending much of their waking hours outside their cells, in the dayrooms, school, workshops, library, visits, meals, or showers. The other double-celled inmates spent more time locked in their cells because of a restrictive classification.

The remaining findings by the District Court addressed respondents' allegation that overcrowding created by double celling overwhelmed SOCF's facilities and staff. The food was "adequate in every respect," and respondents adduced no evidence "whatsoever that prisoners have been underfed or that the food facilities have been taxed by the prison population." Id., at 1014. The air ventilation system was adequate, the cells were substantially free of offensive odor, the temperature in the cellblocks was well controlled, and the noise in the cellblocks was not excessive. Double celling had not reduced significantly the availability of space in the dayrooms or visitation facilities, nor had it rendered inadequate the resources of the library or schoolrooms. Although there were isolated incidents of failure to provide medical or dental care, there was no evidence of indifference by the SOCF staff to inmates' medical or dental needs. As to violence, the court found that the number of acts of violence at SOCF had increased with the prison population, but only in proportion to the

increase in population. Respondents failed to produce evidence establishing that double celling itself caused greater violence, and the ratio of guards to inmates at SOCF satisfied the standard of acceptability offered by respondents' expert witness. Finally, the court did find that the SOCF administration, faced with more inmates than jobs, had "[watered] down" jobs by assigning more inmates to each job than necessary and by reducing the number of hours that each inmate worked, id., at 1015; it also found that SOCF had not increased its staff of psychiatrists and social workers since double celling had begun.

Despite these generally favorable findings, the District Court concluded that double celling at SOCF was cruel and unusual punishment. The court rested its conclusion on five considerations. One, inmates at SOCF are serving long terms of imprisonment. In the court's view, that fact "can only [accentuate] the problems of close confinement and overcrowding." Id., at 1020. Two, SOCF housed 38% more inmates at the time of trial than its "design capacity." In reference to this the court asserted: "Overcrowding necessarily involves excess limitation of general movement as well as physical and mental injury from long exposure." Ibid. Three, the court accepted as contemporary standards of decency several studies recommending that each person in an institution have at least 50-55 square feet of living quarters. In contrast, double-celled inmates at SOCF share 63 square feet. Four, the court asserted that "[at] the best a prisoner who is double celled will spend most of his time in the cell with his cellmate." Id., at 1021. Five, SOCF has made double celling a practice; it is not a temporary condition.

On appeal to the Court of Appeals for the Sixth Circuit, petitioners argued that the District Court's conclusion must be read, in light of its findings, as holding that double celling is per se unconstitutional. The Court of Appeals disagreed; it viewed the District Court's opinion as holding only that double celling is cruel and unusual punishment under the circumstances at SOCF. It affirmed, without further opinion, on the ground that the District Court's findings were not clearly erroneous, its conclusions of law were "permissible from the findings," and its remedy was a reasonable response to the violations found.

. . . We now reverse.

II

We consider here for the first time the limitation that the Eighth Amendment, which is applicable to the States through the Fourteenth Amendment, Robinson v. California, 370 U.S. 660 (1962), imposes upon the conditions in which a State may confine those convicted of crimes. It is unquestioned that "[confinement] in a prison . . . is a form of punishment subject to scrutiny under the Eighth Amendment standards." Hutto v. Finney, 437 U.S. 678, 685 (1978); see Ingraham v. Wright, 430 U.S. 651, 669 (1977); cf. Bell v. Wolfish, 441 U.S. 520 (1979). But until this case, we have not considered a disputed contention that the conditions of confinement at a particular prison constituted cruel and unusual punishment. Nor have we had an occasion to consider specifically the principles relevant to assessing claims that conditions of confinement violate the Eighth Amendment. We look, first, to the Eighth Amendment precedents for the general principles that are relevant to a State's authority to impose punishment for criminal conduct.

A

The Eighth Amendment, in only three words, imposes the constitutional limitation upon punishments: they cannot be "cruel and unusual." The Court has interpreted these words "in a flexible and dynamic manner," Gregg v. Georgia, 428 U.S. 153, 171 (1976) (joint opinion), and has extended the Amendment's reach beyond the barbarous physical punishments at issue in the Court's earliest cases. See Wilkerson v. Utah, 99 U.S. 130 (1879); In re Kemmler, 136 U.S. 436 (1890). Today the Eighth Amendment prohibits punishments which, although not physically barbarous, "involve the unnecessary and wanton infliction of pain," Gregg v. Georgia, supra, at 173, or are grossly disproportionate to the severity of the crime, Coker v. Georgia, 433 U.S. 584, 592 (1977) (plurality opinion); Weems v. United States,

217 U.S. 349 (1910). Among "unnecessary and wanton" inflictions of pain are those that are "totally without penological justification." Gregg v. Georgia, supra, at 183; Estelle v. Gamble, 429 U.S. 97, 103 (1976).

No static "test" can exist by which courts determine whether conditions of confinement are cruel and unusual, for the Eighth Amendment "must draw its meaning from the evolving standards of decency that mark the progress of a maturing society." Trop v. Dulles, 356 U.S. 86, 101 (1958) (plurality opinion). The Court has held, however, that "Eighth Amendment judgments should neither be nor appear to be merely the subjective views" of judges. Rummel v. Estelle, 445 U.S. 263, 275 (1980). To be sure, "the Constitution contemplates that in the end [a court's] own judgment will be brought to bear on the question of the acceptability" of a given punishment. Coker v. Georgia, supra, at 597 (plurality opinion); Gregg v. Georgia, supra, at 182 (joint opinion). But such "[judgments] should be informed by objective factors to the maximum possible extent." Rummel v. Estelle, supra, at 274-275, quoting Coker v. Georgia, supra, at 592 (plurality opinion). For example, when the question was whether capital punishment for certain crimes violated contemporary values, the Court looked for "objective indicia" derived from history, the action of state legislatures, and the sentencing by juries. Gregg v. Georgia, supra, at 176-187; Coker v. Georgia, supra, at 593-596. Our conclusion in Estelle v. Gamble, supra, that deliberate indifference to an inmate's medical needs is cruel and unusual punishment rested on the fact, recognized by the common law and state legislatures, that "[an] inmate must rely on prison authorities to treat his medical needs; if the authorities fail to do so, those needs will not be met." 429 U.S., at 103.

These principles apply when the conditions of confinement compose the punishment at issue. Conditions must not involve the wanton and unnecessary infliction of pain, nor may they be grossly disproportionate to the severity of the crime warranting imprisonment. In Estelle v. Gamble, supra, we held that the denial of medical care is cruel and unusual because, in the worst case, it can result in physical torture, and, even in less serious cases, it can result in pain without any penological purpose. 429 U.S., at 103. In Hutto v. Finney, supra, the conditions of confinement in two Arkansas prisons constituted cruel and unusual punishment because they resulted in unquestioned and serious deprivations of basic human needs. Conditions other than those in Gamble and Hutto, alone or in combination, may deprive inmates of the minimal civilized measure of life's necessities. Such conditions could be cruel and unusual under the contemporary standard of decency that we recognized in Gamble, supra, at 103-104. But conditions that cannot be said to be cruel and unusual under contemporary standards are not unconstitutional. To the extent that such conditions are restrictive and even harsh, they are part of the penalty that criminal offenders pay for their offenses against society.

B

In view of the District Court's findings of fact, its conclusion that double celling at SOCF constitutes cruel and unusual punishment is insupportable. Virtually every one of the court's findings tends to refute respondents' claim. The double celling made necessary by the unanticipated increase in prison population did not lead to deprivations of essential food, medical care, or sanitation. Nor did it increase violence among inmates or create other conditions intolerable for prison confinement. 434 F.Supp., at 1018. Although job and educational opportunities diminished marginally as a result of double celling, limited work hours and delay before receiving education do not inflict pain, much less unnecessary and wanton pain; deprivations of this kind simply are not punishments. We would have to wrench the Eighth Amendment from its language and history to hold that delay of these desirable aids to rehabilitation violates the Constitution.

The five considerations on which the District Court relied also are insufficient to support its constitutional conclusion. The court relied on the long terms of imprisonment served by inmates at SOCF; the fact that SOCF housed 38% more inmates than its "design capacity"; the recommendation of several studies that each inmate have at least 50-55 square feet of living quarters; the suggestion that double-celled inmates spend most of their time in their cells with their cellmates; and the fact that double celling at SOCF was not a temporary condition. Supra, at 343-344. These general considerations fall far short in themselves of proving cruel and unusual punishment, for there is no evidence that double celling under these circumstances either inflicts unnecessary or wanton pain or is grossly disproportionate to the severity of crimes warranting imprisonment. At most, these considerations amount to a theory that double celling inflicts pain. Perhaps they reflect an aspiration toward an ideal environment for long-term confinement. But the Constitution does not mandate comfortable prisons, and prisons of SOCF's type, which house persons convicted of serious crimes, cannot be free of discomfort. Thus, these considerations properly are weighed by the legislature and prison administration rather than a court. There being no constitutional violation, the District Court had no authority to consider whether double celling in light of these considerations was the best response to the increase in Ohio's statewide prison population.

III

This Court must proceed cautiously in making an Eighth Amendment judgment because, unless we reverse it, "[a] decision that a given punishment is impermissible under the Eighth Amendment cannot be reversed short of a constitutional amendment," and thus "[revisions] cannot be made in the light of further experience." Gregg v. Georgia, 428 U.S., at 176. In assessing claims that conditions of confinement are cruel and unusual, courts must bear in mind that their inquiries "spring from constitutional requirements and that judicial answers to them must reflect that fact rather than a court's idea of how best to operate a detention facility." Bell v. Wolfish, 441 U.S., at 539.

Courts certainly have a responsibility to scrutinize claims of cruel and unusual confinement, and conditions in a number of prisons, especially older ones, have justly been described as "deplorable" and "sordid." Bell v. Wolfish, supra, at 562. When conditions of confinement amount to cruel and unusual punishment, "federal courts will discharge their duty to protect constitutional rights." Procunier v. Martinez, 416 U.S. 396, 405-406 (1974); see Cruz v. Beto, 405 U.S.

319, 321 (1972) (per curiam). In discharging this oversight responsibility, however, courts cannot assume that state legislatures and prison officials are insensitive to the requirements of the Constitution or to the perplexing sociological problems of how best to achieve the goals of the penal function in the criminal justice system: to punish justly, to deter future crime, and to return imprisoned persons to society with an improved chance of being useful, law-abiding citizens.

In this case, the question before us is whether the conditions of confinement at SOCF are cruel and unusual. As we find that they are not, the judgment of the Court of Appeals is reversed.

It is so ordered.

[Concurring and dissenting opinions omitted]

BOAG
v.
MacDOUGALL

454 U.S. 364; 102 S. Ct. 700; 70 L. Ed. 2d 551 (1982)

PER CURIAM

OPINION: Petitioner, who was then an inmate of the Arizona Department of Corrections Reception and Treatment Center, filed a crudely written complaint in the United States District Court for the District of Arizona, in which he alleged, inter alia, that he had been placed in solitary confinement on March 3, 1980, without any notice of charges or any hearing, that he was threatened with violence when he asked what the charges were, and that he was still in "the hole" a week later. The District Court dismissed the complaint on the ground that the case was moot because petitioner had been transferred to another facility.

On appeal, the Court of Appeals did not endorse the District Court's mootness rationale, and rightfully so, since the transfer did not moot the damages claim. Nevertheless, the Court of Appeals affirmed, 642 F.2d 455 (1981), concluding that first, district courts

have "especially broad" discretion to dismiss frivolous actions against prison officials under 28 U.S.C. § 1915(d), and second, petitioner's action is frivolous because it does not state a claim upon which relief can be granted. We need not address the permissible contours of the Court of Appeals' first conclusion, for its second conclusion is erroneous as a matter of law. Construing petitioner's inartful pleading liberally, as Haines v. Kerner, 404 U.S. 519 (1972), instructs the federal courts to do in pro se actions, it states a cause of action. See Wolff v. McDonnell, 418 U.S. 539, 555-572 (1974). On the basis of the record before us, we cannot find a sufficient ground for affirming the dismissal of the complaint.

The motion of petitioner for leave to proceed in forma pauperis and the petition for certiorari are granted, the judgment of the Court of Appeals is reversed, and the case is remanded for further proceedings consistent with this opinion.

It is so ordered.

JUSTICE O'CONNOR, concurring.

I join in the per curiam, but write separately to emphasize two points. First, nothing in the Court's opinion prevents the District Court on remand from dismissing this suit under 28 U.S.C. § 1915(d) if it finds grounds to believe that the complaint is "malicious or frivolous." This Court only requires the District Court to articulate briefly its reasons for dismissal in order to facilitate appellate review. Second, I find merit in JUSTICE REHNQUIST's comments that this Court is not equipped to correct every perceived error coming from the lower federal courts. The effectiveness of this Court rests in part on its practice of deciding cases of broad significance and of declining to expend limited judicial resources on cases, such as the present one, whose significance is limited to the parties. In exercising our discretionary certiorari jurisdiction, we should not be influenced solely by the merits of the petitioner's case.

* * *

HEWITT
v.
HELMS

459 U.S. 460; 103 S. Ct. 864; 74 L. Ed. 2d 675 (1983)

JUSTICE REHNQUIST delivered the opinion of the Court.

Respondent Aaron Helms was serving a term in the State Correctional Institution at Huntingdon, Pa. (SCIH), which was administered by petitioners. He sued in the United States District Court for the Middle District of Pennsylvania, claiming that petitioners' actions confining him to administrative segregation within the prison violated his rights under the Due Process Clause of the Fourteenth Amendment to the United States Constitution. The District Court granted petitioners' motion for summary judgment, but the Court of Appeals for the Third Circuit reversed. 655 F.2d 487 (1981). We granted certiorari, 455 U.S. 999 (1982), to consider what limits the Due Process Clause of the Fourteenth Amendment places on the authority of prison administrators to remove inmates from the general prison population and confine them to a less desirable regimen for administrative reasons.

In the early evening of December 3, 1978, a prisoner in the state penitentiary at Huntingdon, assaulted two guards. The prisoner was subdued with the assistance of other guards, but one guard received a broken nose, and another a broken thumb. Later in the evening, the violence erupted into a riot during which a group of prisoners attempted to seize the institution's "control center." . . .

This uprising was eventually quelled, but only with the assistance of state police units, local law enforcement officers, and off-duty prison guards whose aid was summoned. Several hours after the riot ended, respondent Helms was removed from his cell and the general prison population for questioning by the state police. Following the interview, he was placed in restrictive confinement, and the state police and prison authorities began an investigation into his role in the riot.

On December 4, 1978, Helms was given a "Misconduct Report" charging him with "Assaulting Officers and Conspiracy to Disrupt Normal Institution Routine by Forcefully Taking Over the Control Center." The report briefly described the factual basis for the charge and contained a lengthy recitation of the procedures governing the institution's disciplinary hearing. On December 8, 1978, a "Hearing Committee," consisting of three prison officials charged with adjudicating alleged instances of misconduct by inmates, was convened to dispose of the charges against Helms. Following a review of the misconduct report, the panel summarized its decision as "[no] finding as to guilt reached at this time, due to insufficient information," and ordered that Helms' confinement in restricted housing be continued.

While as a matter of probabilities it seems likely that Helms appeared personally before the December 8 Hearing Committee, we agree with the Court of Appeals that the record does not allow definitive resolution of the issue on summary judgment. Helms signed a copy of the misconduct report stating that "[the] circumstance of the charge has been read and fully explained to me," and that "I have had the opportunity to have my version reported as part of the record." App. 41a. Likewise, he admitted in an affidavit filed during this litigation that he was "informed by an institutional hearing committee" of the disposition of the misconduct charge against him. Id., at 33a. The same affidavit, however, asserted that no "hearing" was conducted on December 8, suggesting that respondent did not appear before the Committee. The State did not file any affidavit controverting Helms' contention.

On December 11, 1978, the Commonwealth of Pennsylvania filed state criminal charges against Helms, charging him with assaulting Correction Officer Rhodes and with riot. On January 2, 1979, SCIH's Program Review Committee, which consisted of three prison officials, was convened. The Committee met to review the status of respondent's confinement in administrative segregation and to make recommendations as to his future confinement. The Committee unanimously concluded that Helms should remain in administrative segregation; affidavits of the Committee members said that the decision was based on several related concerns. Helms was seen as "a danger to staff and to other inmates if released back into general population," id., at 11a; he was to be arraigned the following day on state criminal charges, id., at 24a; and the Committee was awaiting information regarding his role in the riot, id., at 16a. The Superintendent of SCIH personally reviewed the Program Review Committee's determination and concurred in its recommendation. Id., at 15a, 18a.

The preliminary hearing on the state criminal charges against Helms was postponed on January 10, 1979, apparently due to a lack of evidence. On January 19, 1979, a second misconduct report was given to respondent; the report charged Helms with assaulting a second officer during the December 3 riot. On January 22 a Hearing Committee composed of three prison officials heard testimony from one guard and Helms. Based on this, the Committee found Helms guilty of the second misconduct charge and ordered that he be confined to disciplinary segregation for six months, effective December 3, 1978. The Committee also decided to drop the earlier misconduct charge against respondent, without determining guilt. On February 6, 1979, the State dropped criminal charges relating to the prison riot against Helms.

The Court of Appeals, reviewing these facts, concluded that Helms had a protected liberty interest in continuing to reside in the general prison population. While the court seemed to doubt that this interest could be found in the Constitution, it held that Pennsylvania regulations governing the administration of state prisons created such an interest. It then said that Helms could not be deprived of this interest without a hearing, governed by the procedures mandated in Wolff v. McDonnell, 418 U.S. 539 (1974), to determine whether such confinement was proper. Being uncertain whether the hearing conducted on December 8 satisfied the Wolff requirements, see supra, at 464-465, the Court of Appeals remanded the case to the District Court for an evidentiary hearing regarding the character of that proceeding. On these same facts, we agree with the Court of Appeals that the Pennsylvania statutory framework governing the administration of state prisons gave rise to a liberty interest in respondent, but we conclude that the procedures afforded respondent were "due process" under the Fourteenth Amendment.

While no State may "deprive any person of life, liberty, or property, without due process of law," it is well settled that only a limited range of interests fall within this provision. Liberty interests protected by the Fourteenth Amendment may arise from two sources—the Due Process Clause itself and the laws of the States. Meachum v. Fano, 427 U.S. 215, 223-227 (1976). Respondent argues, rather weakly, that the Due Process Clause implicitly creates an interest in being confined to a general population cell, rather than the more austere and restrictive administrative segregation quarters. While there is little question on the record before us that respondent's confinement added to the restraints on his freedom, we think his argument seeks to draw from the Due Process Clause more than it can provide.

We have repeatedly said both that prison officials have broad administrative and discretionary authority over the institutions they manage and that lawfully incarcerated persons retain only a narrow range of protected liberty interests. As to the first point, we have recognized that broad discretionary authority is necessary because the administration of a prison is "at best an extraordinarily difficult undertaking," Wolff v. McDonnell, supra, at 566, and have concluded that "to hold . . . that any substantial deprivation imposed by prison authorities triggers the procedural protections of the Due Process Clause would subject to judicial review a wide spectrum of discretionary actions that traditionally have been the business of prison administrators rather than of the federal courts." Meachum v. Fano, supra, at 225. As to the second point, our decisions have consistently refused to recognize more than the most basic liberty interests in prisoners. "Lawful incarceration brings about the necessary withdrawal or limitation of many privileges and rights, a retraction justified by the considerations underlying our penal system." Price v. Johnston, 334 U.S. 266, 285 (1948). Thus, there is no "constitutional or inherent right" to parole, Greenholtz v. Nebraska Penal Inmates, 442 U.S. 1, 7 (1979), and "the Constitution itself does not guarantee good-time credit for satisfactory behavior while in prison," Wolff v. McDonnell, supra, at 557, despite the undoubted impact of such credits on the freedom of inmates. Finally, in Meachum v. Fano, supra, at 225, the transfer of a prisoner from one institution to another was found unprotected by "the Due Process Clause in and of itself," even though the change of facilities involved a significant modification in conditions of confinement, later characterized by the Court as a "grievous loss." Moody v. Daggett, 429 U.S. 78, 88, n. 9 (1976). As we have held previously, these decisions require that "[as] long as the conditions or degree of confinement to which the prisoner is subjected is within the sentence imposed upon him and is not otherwise violative of the Constitution, the Due Process Clause does not in itself subject an inmate's treatment by prison authorities to judicial oversight." Montanye v. Haymes, 427 U.S. 236, 242 (1976). See also Vitek v. Jones, 445 U.S. 480, 493 (1980).

It is plain that the transfer of an inmate to less amenable and more restrictive quarters for nonpunitive reasons is well within the terms of confinement ordinarily contemplated by a prison sentence. The phrase "administrative segregation," as used by the state authorities here, appears to be something of a catchall: it may be used to protect the prisoner's safety, to protect other inmates from a particular prisoner, to break up potentially disruptive groups of inmates, or simply to await later classification or transfer. See 37 Pa. Code §§ 95.104 and 95.106 (1978), and n. 1, supra. Accordingly, administrative segregation is the sort of confinement that inmates should reasonably anticipate receiving at some point in their incarceration. This conclusion finds ample support in our decisions regarding parole and good-time credits. Both these subjects involve release from institutional life altogether, which is a far more significant change in a prisoner's freedoms than that at issue here, yet in Greenholtz and Wolff we held that neither situation involved an interest independently protected by the Due Process Clause. These decisions compel an identical result here.

Despite this, respondent points out that the Court has held that a State may create a liberty interest protected by the Due Process Clause through its enactment of certain statutory or regulatory measures. Thus, in Wolff, where we rejected any notion of an interest in good-time credits inherent in the Constitution, we also found that Nebraska had created a right to such credits. 418 U.S., at 556-557. See also Greenholtz v. Nebraska Penal Inmates, supra (parole); Vitek v. Jones, supra (transfer to mental institution). Likewise, and more relevant here, was our summary affirmance in Wright v. Enomoto, 462 F.Supp. 397 (ND Cal. 1976), summarily aff'd, 434 U.S. 1052 (1978), where the District Court had concluded that state law created a liberty interest in confinement to any sort of segregated housing within a prison. Hughes v. Rowe, 449 U.S. 5 (1980) (per curiam), while involving facts similar to these in some respects, was essentially a pleading case rather than an exposition of the substantive constitutional issues involved.

Respondent argues that Pennsylvania, in its enactment of regulations governing the administration of state prisons, has created a liberty interest in remaining free from the restraints accompanying confinement in administrative segregation. Except to the extent that our summary affirmance in Wright v. Enomoto, supra, may be to the contrary, we have never held that statutes and regulations governing daily operation of a prison system conferred any liberty interest in and of themselves. Meachum v. Fano, 427 U.S. 215 (1976), and Montanye v. Haymes, supra, held to the contrary; in Wolff, supra, we were dealing with good-time credits which would have actually reduced the period of time which the inmate would have been in the custody of the government; in Greenholtz, supra, we dealt with parole, which would likewise have radically transformed the nature of the custody to which the inmate was subject; and in Vitek, supra, we considered the transfer from a prison to a mental institution.

There are persuasive reasons why we should be loath to transpose all of the reasoning in the cases just cited to the situation where the statute and regulations govern the day-to-day administration of a prison system. The deprivations imposed in the course of the daily operations of an institution are likely to be minor when compared to the release from custody at issue in parole decisions and good-time credits. Moreover, the safe and efficient operation of a prison on a day-to-day basis has traditionally been entrusted to the expertise of prison officials, see Meachum v. Fano, supra, at 225. These facts suggest that regulations

structuring the authority of prison administrators may warrant treatment, for purposes
of creation of entitlements to "liberty," different from statutes and regulations in other
areas. Nonetheless, we conclude in the light
of the Pennsylvania statutes and regulations
here in question, the relevant provisions of
which are set forth in full in the margin, that
respondent did acquire a protected liberty
interest in remaining in the general prison
population.

Respondent seems to suggest that the mere
fact that Pennsylvania has created a careful
procedural structure to regulate the use of
administrative segregation indicates the existence of a protected liberty interest. We cannot agree. The creation of procedural guidelines to channel the decisionmaking of prison
officials is, in the view of many experts in the
field, a salutary development. It would be
ironic to hold that when a State embarks on
such desirable experimentation it thereby
opens the door to scrutiny by the federal
courts, while States that choose not to adopt
such procedural provisions entirely avoid the
strictures of the Due Process Clause. The
adoption of such procedural guidelines, without more, suggests that it is these restrictions
alone, and not those federal courts might also
impose under the Fourteenth Amendment,
that the State chose to require.

Nonetheless, in this case the Commonwealth has gone beyond simple procedural
guidelines. It has used language of an unmistakably mandatory character, requiring that
certain procedures "shall," "will," or "must"
be employed, see n. 6, supra, and that administrative segregation will not occur absent
specified substantive predicates—viz., "the
need for control," or "the threat of a serious
disturbance." . . . We are persuaded that the
repeated use of explicitly mandatory language in connection with requiring specific
substantive predicates demands a conclusion
that the State has created a protected liberty
interest.

That being the case, we must then decide
whether the process afforded respondent satisfied the minimum requirements of the Due
Process Clause. We think that it did. The
requirements imposed by the Clause are, of
course, flexible and variable dependent upon
the particular situation being examined. E.g.,
Greenholtz v. Nebraska Penal Inmates, 442

U.S., at 12; Morrissey v. Brewer, 408 U.S.
471, 481 (1972). In determining what is "due
process" in the prison context, we are
reminded that "one cannot automatically
apply procedural rules designed for free citizens in an open society . . . to the very different situation presented by a disciplinary
proceeding in a state prison." Wolff v.
McDonnell, 418 U.S., at 560. "Prison administrators . . . should be accorded wide-ranging deference in the adoption and execution
of policies and practices that in their judgment are needed to preserve internal order
and discipline and to maintain institutional
security." Bell v. Wolfish, 441 U.S. 520, 547
(1979). These considerations convince us
that petitioners were obligated to engage only
in an informal, non-adversary review of the
information supporting respondent's administrative confinement, including whatever
statement respondent wished to submit, within a reasonable time after confining him to
administrative segregation.

Under Mathews v. Eldridge, 424 U.S. 319,
335 (1976), we consider the private interests
at stake in a governmental decision, the governmental interests involved, and the value of
procedural requirements in determining what
process is due under the Fourteenth Amendment. Respondent's private interest is not one
of great consequence. He was merely transferred from one extremely restricted environment to an even more confined situation.
Unlike disciplinary confinement the stigma
of wrongdoing or misconduct does not attach
to administrative segregation under Pennsylvania's prison regulations. Finally, there is no
indication that administrative segregation
will have any significant effect on parole
opportunities.

Petitioners had two closely related reasons
for confining Helms to administrative segregation prior to conducting a hearing on the
disciplinary charges against him. First, they
concluded that if housed in the general population, Helms would pose a threat to the safety of other inmates and prison officials and to
the security of the institution. Second, the
prison officials believed that it was wiser to
separate respondent from the general population until completion of state and institutional
investigations of his role in the December 3
riot and the hearing on the charges against
him. Plainly, these governmental interests are

of great importance. The safety of the institution's guards and inmates is perhaps the most fundamental responsibility of the prison administration. See Bell v. Wolfish, supra, at 547; Jones v. North Carolina Prisoners' Labor Union, 433 U.S. 119, 132 (1977); Pell v. Procunier, 417 U.S. 817, 823 (1974); Procunier v. Martinez, 416 U.S. 396, 404 (1974). Likewise, the isolation of a prisoner pending investigation of misconduct charges against him serves important institutional interests relating to the insulating of possible witnesses from coercion or harm, see infra, at 476.

Neither of these grounds for confining Helms to administrative segregation involved decisions or judgments that would have been materially assisted by a detailed adversary proceeding. As we said in Rhodes v. Chapman, 452 U.S. 337, 349, n. 14 (1981), "a prison's internal security is peculiarly a matter normally left to the discretion of prison administrators." In assessing the seriousness of a threat to institutional security, prison administrators necessarily draw on more than the specific facts surrounding a particular incident; instead, they must consider the character of the inmates confined in the institution, recent and longstanding relations between prisoners and guards, prisoners inter se, and the like. In the volatile atmosphere of a prison, an inmate easily may constitute an unacceptable threat to the safety of other prisoners and guards even if he himself has committed no misconduct; rumor, reputation, and even more imponderable factors may suffice to spark potentially disastrous incidents. The judgment of prison officials in this context, like that of those making parole decisions, turns largely on "purely subjective evaluations and on predictions of future behavior," Connecticut Board of Pardons v. Dumschat, 452 U.S. 458, 464 (1981); indeed, the administrators must predict not just one inmate's future actions, as in parole, but those of an entire institution. Owing to the central role of these types of intuitive judgments, a decision that an inmate or group of inmates represents a threat to the institution's security would not be appreciably fostered by the trial-type procedural safeguards suggested by respondent. This, and the balance of public and private interests, lead us to conclude that the Due Process Clause requires only an informal nonadversary review of evidence, discussed more fully below, in order to confine an inmate feared to be a threat to institutional security to administrative segregation.

Likewise, confining respondent to administrative segregation pending completion of the investigation of the disciplinary charges against him is not based on an inquiry requiring any elaborate procedural safeguards. . . .

* * *

We think an informal, nonadversary evidentiary review is sufficient both for the decision that an inmate represents a security threat and the decision to confine an inmate to administrative segregation pending completion of an investigation into misconduct charges against him. An inmate must merely receive some notice of the charges against him and an opportunity to present his views to the prison official charged with deciding whether to transfer him to administrative segregation. Ordinarily a written statement by the inmate will accomplish this purpose, although prison administrators may find it more useful to permit oral presentations in cases where they believe a written statement would be ineffective. So long as this occurs, and the decisionmaker reviews the charges and then-available evidence against the prisoner, the Due Process Clause is satisfied. This informal procedure permits a reasonably accurate assessment of probable cause to believe that misconduct occurred, and the "value [of additional 'formalities and safeguards'] would be too slight to justify holding, as a matter of constitutional principle" that they must be adopted, Gerstein v. Pugh, supra, at 122.

Measured against these standards we are satisfied that respondent received all the process that was due after being confined to administrative segregation. . . .

Accordingly, the judgment of the Court of Appeals is reversed.

It is so ordered.

Cases Relating to Chapter 6

Religion in Prison

O'LONE
v.
SHABAZZ

482 U.S. 342; 107 S. Ct. 2400;
96 L. Ed. 2d 282 (1987)

CHIEF JUSTICE REHNQUIST delivered the opinion of the Court.

This case requires us to consider once again the standard of review for prison regulations claimed to inhibit the exercise of constitutional rights. Respondents, members of the Islamic faith, were prisoners in New Jersey's Leesburg State Prison. They challenged policies adopted by prison officials which resulted in their inability to attend Jumu'ah, a weekly Muslim congregational service regularly held in the main prison building and in a separate facility known as "the Farm." Jumu'ah is commanded by the Koran and must be held every Friday after the sun reaches its zenith and before the Asr, or afternoon prayer. See Koran 62:9-10; Brief for Imam Jamil Abdullah Al-Amin et al. as Amici Curiae 18-31. There is no question that respondents' sincerely held religious beliefs compelled attendance at Jumu'ah. We hold that the prison regulations here challenged did not violate respondents' rights under the Free Exercise Clause of the First Amendment to the United States Constitution.

Inmates at Leesburg are placed in one of three custody classifications. Maximum security and "gang minimum" security inmates are housed in the main prison building, and those with the lowest classification—full mini-

mum—live in "the Farm." Both respondents were classified as gang minimum security prisoners when this suit was filed, and respondent Mateen was later classified as full minimum.

Several changes in prison policy prompted this litigation. In April 1983, the New Jersey Department of Corrections issued Standard 853, which provided that inmates could no longer move directly from maximum security to full minimum status, but were instead required to first spend a period of time in the intermediate gang minimum status. App. 147. This change was designed to redress problems that had arisen when inmates were transferred directly from the restrictive maximum security status to full minimum status, with its markedly higher level of freedom. Because of serious overcrowding in the main building, Standard 853 further mandated that gang minimum inmates ordinarily be assigned jobs outside the main building. Ibid. These inmates work in details of 8 to 15 persons, supervised by one guard. Standard 853 also required that full minimum inmates work outside the main institution, whether on or off prison grounds, or in a satellite building such as the Farm. Ibid.

Corrections officials at Leesburg implemented these policies gradually and, as the District Court noted, with some difficulty. Shabazz v. O'Lone, 595 F.Supp. 928, 929 (NJ 1984). In the initial stages of outside work details for gang minimum prisoners, officials apparently allowed some Muslim inmates to work inside the main building on Fridays so that they could attend Jumu'ah. This alternative was eventually eliminated in March 1984, in light of the directive of Standard 853 that all gang minimum inmates work outside the main building.

Significant problems arose with those inmates assigned to outside work details. Some avoided reporting for their assignments, while others found reasons for returning to the main building during the course of the workday (including their desire to attend religious services). Evidence showed that the return of prisoners during the day resulted in security risks and administrative burdens that prison officials found unacceptable. Because details of inmates were supervised by only one guard, the whole detail was forced to return to the main gate when one prisoner desired to return to the facility. The gate was the site of all incoming foot and vehicle traffic during the day, and prison officials viewed it as a high security risk area. When an inmate returned, vehicle traffic was delayed while the inmate was logged in and searched.

In response to these burdens, Leesburg officials took steps to ensure that those assigned to outside details remained there for the whole day. Thus, arrangements were made to have lunch and required medications brought out to the prisoners, and appointments with doctors and social workers were scheduled for the late afternoon. These changes proved insufficient, however, and prison officials began to study alternatives. After consulting with the director of social services, the director of professional services, and the prison's imam and chaplain, prison officials in March 1984 issued a policy memorandum which prohibited inmates assigned to outside work details from returning to the prison during the day except in the case of emergency.

The prohibition of returns prevented Muslims assigned to outside work details from attending Jumu'ah. Respondents filed suit under 42 U.S.C. § 1983, alleging that the prison policies unconstitutionally denied them their Free Exercise rights under the First Amendment, as applied to the States through the Fourteenth Amendment. The District Court, applying the standards announced in an earlier decision of the Court of Appeals for the Third Circuit, concluded that no constitutional violation had occurred. The District Court decided that Standard 853 and the March 1984 prohibition on returns "plausibly advance" the goals of security,

order, and rehabilitation. 595 F.Supp., at 934. It rejected alternative arrangements suggested by respondents, finding that "no less restrictive alternative could be adopted without potentially compromising a legitimate institutional objective." Ibid.

The Court of Appeals, sua sponte hearing the case en banc, decided that its earlier decision relied upon by the District Court was not sufficiently protective of prisoners' free exercise rights, and went on to state that prison policies could be sustained only if:

the state . . . show[s] that the challenged regulations were intended to serve, and do serve, the important penological goal of security, and that no reasonable method exists by which [prisoners'] religious rights can be accommodated without creating bona fide security problems. The expert testimony of prison officials should be given due weight, but such testimony is not dispositive of the issue whether no reasonable adjustment is possible. . . . Where it is found that reasonable methods of accommodation can be adopted without sacrificing either the state's interest in security or the prisoners' interest in freely exercising their religious rights, the state's refusal to allow the observance of a central religious practice cannot be justified and violates the prisoner's first amendment rights.

Shabazz v. O'Lone, 782 F.2d 416, 420 (CA3 1986) (footnotes omitted). In considering whether a potential method of accommodation is reasonable, the court added, relevant factors include cost, the effects of overcrowding, understaffing, and inmates' demonstrated proclivity to unruly conduct. See id., at 420, n. 3. The case was remanded to the District Court for reconsideration under the standards enumerated in the opinion. We granted certiorari to consider the important federal constitutional issues presented by the Court of Appeals' decision, and to resolve apparent confusion among the Courts of Appeals on the proper standards to be applied in considering prisoners' free exercise claims. 479 U.S. 881 (1986).

Several general principles guide our consideration of the issues presented here. First, "convicted prisoners do not forfeit all constitutional protections by reason of their conviction and confinement in prison." Bell v. Wolfish, 441 U.S. 520, 545 (1979). See Turner v. Safley, ante, at 84; Jones v. North Carolina Prisoners' Labor Union, Inc., 433 U.S. 119, 129 (1977). Inmates clearly retain protections afforded by the First Amendment, Pell v. Procunier, 417 U.S. 817, 822 (1974), including its directive that no law shall prohibit the free exercise of religion. See Cruz v. Beto, 405 U.S. 319 (1972) (per curiam). Second, "lawful incarceration brings about the necessary withdrawal or limitation of many privileges and rights, a retraction justified by the considerations underlying our penal system." Price v. Johnston, 334 U.S. 266, 285 (1948). The limitations on the exercise of constitutional rights arise both from the fact of incarceration and from valid penological objectives—including deterrence of crime, rehabilitation of prisoners, and institutional security. Pell v. Procunier, supra, at 822-823; Procunier v. Martinez, 416 U.S. 396, 412 (1974).

In considering the appropriate balance of these factors, we have often said that evaluation of penological objectives is committed to the considered judgment of prison administrators, "who are actually charged with and trained in the running of the particular institution under examination." Bell v. Wolfish, supra, at 562. See Turner v. Safley, ante, at 86-87. To ensure that courts afford appropriate deference to prison officials, we have determined that prison regulations alleged to infringe constitutional rights are judged under a "reasonableness" test less restrictive than that ordinarily applied to alleged infringements of fundamental constitutional rights. See, e.g., Jones v. North Carolina Prisoners' Labor Union, Inc., supra, at 128. We recently restated the proper standard: "When a prison regulation impinges on inmates' constitutional rights, the regulation is valid if it is reasonably related to legitimate penological interests." Turner v. Safley, ante, at 89. This approach ensures the ability of corrections officials "to anticipate security problems and to adopt innovative solutions to the intractable problems of prison administration," ibid., and avoids unnecessary intrusion of the judiciary into problems particularly ill suited to "resolution by decree." Procunier v. Martinez, supra, at 405. See also Turner v.

Safley, ante, at 89; Bell v. Wolfish, supra, at 548.

We think the Court of Appeals decision in this case was wrong when it established a separate burden on prison officials to prove "that no reasonable method exists by which [prisoners'] religious rights can be accommodated without creating bona fide security problems." 782 F.2d, at 420. See also id., at 419 (Prison officials should be required "to produce convincing evidence that they are unable to satisfy their institutional goals in any way that does not infringe inmates' free exercise rights"). Though the availability of accommodations is relevant to the reasonableness inquiry, we have rejected the notion that "prison officials . . . have to set up and then shoot down every conceivable alternative method of accommodating the claimant's constitutional complaint." Turner v. Safley, ante, at 90-91. By placing the burden on prison officials to disprove the availability of alternatives, the approach articulated by the Court of Appeals fails to reflect the respect and deference that the United States Constitution allows for the judgment of prison administrators.

Turning to consideration of the policies challenged in this case, we think the findings of the District Court establish clearly that prison officials have acted in a reasonable manner. Turner v. Safley drew upon our previous decisions to identify several factors relevant to this reasonableness determination. First, a regulation must have a logical connection to legitimate governmental interests invoked to justify it. Ante, at 89-90. The policies at issue here clearly meet that standard. The requirement that full minimum and gang minimum prisoners work outside the main facility was justified by concerns of institutional order and security, for the District Court found that it was "at least in part a response to a critical overcrowding in the state's prisons, and . . . at least in part designed to ease tension and drain on the facilities during that part of the day when the inmates were outside the confines of the main buildings." 595 F.Supp., at 929. We think it beyond doubt that the standard is related to this legitimate concern.

The subsequent policy prohibiting returns to the institution during the day also passes muster under this standard. Prison officials testified that the returns from outside work details generated congestion and delays at the main gate, a high risk area in any event. Return requests also placed pressure on guards supervising outside details, who previously were required to "evaluate each reason possibly justifying a return to the facilities and either accept or reject that reason." Id., at 931. Rehabilitative concerns further supported the policy; corrections officials sought a simulation of working conditions and responsibilities in society. Chief Deputy Ucci testified: "One of the things that society demands or expects is that when you have a job, you show up on time, you put in your eight hours, or whatever hours you are supposed to put in, and you don't get off. . . . If we can show inmates that they're supposed to show up for work and work a full day, then when they get out at least we've done something." These legitimate goals were advanced by the prohibition on returns; it cannot seriously be maintained that "the logical connection between the regulation and the asserted goal is so remote as to render the policy arbitrary or irrational." Turner v. Safley, ante, at 89-90.

Our decision in Turner also found it relevant that "alternative means of exercising the right . . . remain open to prison inmates." Ante, at 90. There are, of course, no alternative means of attending Jumu'ah; respondents' religious beliefs insist that it occur at a particular time. But the very stringent requirements as to the time at which Jumu'ah may be held may make it extraordinarily difficult for prison officials to assure that every Muslim prisoner is able to attend that service. While we in no way minimize the central importance of Jumu'ah to respondents, we are unwilling to hold that prison officials are required by the Constitution to sacrifice legitimate penological objectives to that end. In Turner, we did not look to see whether prisoners had other means of communicating with fellow inmates, but instead examined whether the inmates were deprived of "all means of expression." Ante, at 92. Here, similarly, we think it appropriate to see whether under these regulations respondents retain the ability to participate in other Muslim religious ceremonies. The record establishes that respondents are not deprived of all forms of religious exercise, but instead freely observe a number of their religious obligations. The

right to congregate for prayer or discussion is "virtually unlimited except during working hours," Tr. 182 (testimony of O'Lone), and the state-provided imam has free access to the prison. Muslim prisoners are given different meals whenever pork is served in the prison cafeteria. Special arrangements are also made during the month-long observance of Ramadan, a period of fasting and prayer. During Ramadan, Muslim prisoners are awakened at 4 A.M. for an early breakfast, and receive dinner at 8:30 each evening. We think this ability on the part of respondents to participate in other religious observances of their faith supports the conclusion that the restrictions at issue here were reasonable.

Finally, the case for the validity of these regulations is strengthened by examination of the impact that accommodation of respondents' asserted right would have on other inmates, on prison personnel, and on allocation of prison resources generally. See Turner v. Safley, ante, at 90. Respondents suggest several accommodations of their practices, including placing all Muslim inmates in one or two inside work details or providing weekend labor for Muslim inmates. See Brief for Respondents 52-53. As noted by the District Court, however, each of respondents' suggested accommodations would, in the judgment of prison officials, have adverse effects on the institution. Inside work details for gang minimum inmates would be inconsistent with the legitimate concerns underlying Standard 853, and the District Court found that the extra supervision necessary to establish weekend details for Muslim prisoners "would be a drain on scarce human resources" at the prison. 595 F.Supp., at 932. Prison officials determined that the alternatives would also threaten prison security by allowing "affinity groups" in the prison to flourish. Administrator O'Lone testified that "we have found out and think almost every prison administrator knows that any time you put a group of individuals together with one particular affinity interest . . . you wind up with . . . a leadership role and an organizational structure that will almost invariably challenge the institutional authority." Tr. 179-180. Finally, the officials determined that special arrangements for one group would create problems as "other inmates [see] that a certain segment is escaping a rigorous work detail" and perceive favoritism. Id., at 178-179. These concerns of prison administrators provide adequate support for the conclusion that accommodations of respondents' request to attend Jumu'ah would have undesirable results in the institution. These difficulties also make clear that there are no "obvious, easy alternatives to the policy adopted by petitioners." Turner v. Safley, ante, at 93.

We take this opportunity to reaffirm our refusal, even where claims are made under the First Amendment, to "substitute our judgment on . . . difficult and sensitive matters of institutional administration," Block v. Rutherford, 468 U.S. 576, 588 (1984), for the determinations of those charged with the formidable task of running a prison. Here the District Court decided that the regulations alleged to infringe constitutional rights were reasonably related to legitimate penological objectives. We agree with the District Court, and it necessarily follows that the regulations in question do not offend the Free Exercise Clause of the First Amendment to the United States Constitution. The judgment of the Court of Appeals is therefore

Reversed.

JUSTICE BRENNAN, with whom JUSTICE MARSHALL, JUSTICE BLACKMUN, and JUSTICE STEVENS join, dissenting.

The religious ceremony that these respondents seek to attend is not presumptively dangerous, and the prison has completely foreclosed respondents' participation in it. I therefore would require prison officials to demonstrate that the restrictions they have imposed are necessary to further an important government interest, and that these restrictions are no greater than necessary to achieve prison objectives. See Turner v. Safley, ante, at 101, n. 1 (STEVENS, J., concurring in part and dissenting in part) (citing Abdul Wali v. Coughlin, 754 F.2d 1015 (CA2 1985)). As a result, I would affirm the Court of Appeals' order to remand the case to the District Court, and would require prison officials to make this showing. Even were I to accept the Court's standard of review, however, I would remand the case to the District

Court, since that court has not had the opportunity to review respondents' claim under the new standard established by this Court in Turner. As the record now stands, the reasonableness of foreclosing respondents' participation in Jumu'ah has not been established.

I

Prisoners are persons whom most of us would rather not think about. Banished from everyday sight, they exist in a shadow world that only dimly enters our awareness. They are members of a "total institution" that controls their daily existence in a way that few of us can imagine:

Prison is a complex of physical arrangements and of measures, all wholly governmental, all wholly performed by agents of government, which determine the total existence of certain human beings (except perhaps in the realm of the spirit, and inevitably there as well) from sundown to sundown, sleeping, waking, speaking, silent, working, playing, viewing, eating, voiding, reading, alone, with others. It is not so, with members of the general adult population. State governments have not undertaken to require members of the general adult population to rise at a certain hour, retire at a certain hour, eat at a certain hour, live for periods with no companionship whatever, wear certain clothing, or submit to oral and anal searches after visiting hours, nor have state governments undertaken to prohibit members of the general adult population from speaking to one another, wearing beards, embracing their spouses, or corresponding with their lovers. Morales v. Schmidt, 340 F.Supp. 544, 550 (WD Wis. 1972).

It is thus easy to think of prisoners as members of a separate netherworld, driven by its own demands, ordered by its own customs, ruled by those whose claim to power rests on raw necessity. Nothing can change the fact, however, that the society that these prisoners inhabit is our own. Prisons may exist on the margins of that society, but no act of will can sever them from the body politic. When prisoners emerge from the shadows to press a constitutional claim, they invoke no alien set of principles drawn from a distant culture. Rather, they speak the language of the charter upon which all of us rely to hold official power accountable. They ask us to acknowledge that power exercised in the shadows must be restrained at least as diligently as power that acts in the sunlight.

In reviewing a prisoner's claim of the infringement of a constitutional right, we must therefore begin from the premise that, as members of this society, prisoners retain constitutional rights that limit the exercise of official authority against them. See Bell v. Wolfish, 441 U.S. 520, 545 (1979). At the same time, we must acknowledge that incarceration by its nature changes an individual's status in society. Prison officials have the difficult and often thankless job of preserving security in a potentially explosive setting, as well as of attempting to provide rehabilitation that prepares some inmates for re-entry into the social mainstream. Both these demands require the curtailment and elimination of certain rights.

The challenge for this Court is to determine how best to protect those prisoners' rights that remain. Our objective in selecting a standard of review is therefore not, as the Court declares, "to ensure that courts afford appropriate deference to prison officials." Ante, at 349. The Constitution was not adopted as a means of enhancing the efficiency with which government officials conduct their affairs, nor as a blueprint for ensuring sufficient reliance on administrative expertise. Rather, it was meant to provide a bulwark against infringements that might otherwise be justified as necessary expedients of governing. The practice of Europe, wrote James Madison, was "charters of liberty . . . granted by power"; of America, "charters of power granted by liberty." 6 Writings of James Madison 83 (G. Hunt ed. 1906). While we must give due consideration to the needs of those in power, this Court's role is to ensure that fundamental restraints on that power are enforced.

In my view, adoption of "reasonableness" as a standard of review for all constitutional challenges by inmates is inadequate to this task. Such a standard is categorically deferential, and does not discriminate among degrees of deprivation. From this perspec-tive, restricting use of the prison library to certain hours warrants the same level of scrutiny as preventing inmates from reading at all. Various "factors" may be weighed differently in each situation, but the message to prison officials is clear: merely act "reasonably" and your actions will be upheld. If a directive that officials act "reasonably" were deemed sufficient to check all exercises of power, the Constitution would hardly be necessary. Yet the Court deems this single standard adequate to restrain any type of conduct in which prison officials might engage.

It is true that the degree of deprivation is one of the factors in the Court's reasonableness determination. This by itself does not make the standard of review appropriate, however. If it did, we would need but a single standard for evaluating all constitutional claims, as long as every relevant factor were considered under its rubric. Clearly, we have never followed such an approach. A standard of review frames the terms in which justification may be offered, and thus delineates the boundaries within which argument may take place. The use of differing levels of scrutiny proclaims that on some occasions official power must justify itself in a way that otherwise it need not. A relatively strict standard of review is a signal that a decree prohibiting a political demonstration on the basis of the participants' political beliefs is of more serious concern, and therefore will be scrutinized more closely, than a rule limiting the number of demonstrations that may take place downtown at noon.

Thus, even if the absolute nature of the deprivation may be taken into account in the Court's formulation, it makes a difference that this is merely one factor in determining if official conduct is "reasonable." Once we provide such an elastic and deferential principle of justification, "the principle . . . lies about like a loaded weapon ready for the hand of any authority that can bring forth a plausible claim of an urgent need. Every repetition imbeds that principle more deeply in our law and thinking and expands it to new purposes." Korematsu v. United States, 323 U.S. 214, 246 (1944) (Jackson, J., dissenting). Mere assertions of exigency have a way of providing a colorable defense for governmental deprivation, and we should be especially wary of expansive delegations of power to those who wield it on the margins of society. Prisons are too often shielded from public view; there is no need to make them virtually invisible.

An approach better suited to the sensitive task of protecting the constitutional rights of inmates is laid out by Judge Kaufman in Abdul Wali v. Coughlin, 754 F.2d 1015 (CA2 1985). That approach maintains that the degree of scrutiny of prison regulations should depend on "the nature of the right being asserted by prisoners, the type of activity in which they seek to engage, and whether the challenged restriction works a total deprivation (as opposed to a mere limitation) on the exercise of that right." Id., at 1033. Essentially, if the activity in which inmates seek to engage is presumptively dangerous, or if a regulation merely restricts the time, place, or manner in which prisoners may exercise a right, a prison regulation will be invalidated only if there is no reasonable justification for official action. Ibid. Where exercise of the asserted right is not presumptively dangerous, however, and where the prison has completely deprived an inmate of that right, then prison officials must show that "a particular restriction is necessary to further an important governmental interest, and that the limitations on freedoms occasioned by the restrictions are no greater than necessary to effectuate the governmental objective involved." Ibid.

The court's analytical framework in Abdul Wali recognizes that in many instances it is inappropriate for courts "to substitute our judgments for those of trained professionals with years of firsthand experience." Ibid. It would thus apply a standard of review identical to the Court's "reasonableness" standard in a significant percentage of cases. At the same time, the Abdul Wali approach takes seriously the Constitution's function of requiring that official power be called to account when it completely deprives a person of a right that society regards as basic. In this limited number of cases, it would require more than a demonstration of "reasonableness" to justify such infringement. To the extent that prison is meant to inculcate a respect for social and legal norms, a requirement that prison officials persuasively demonstrate the need for the absolute deprivation of inmate rights is consistent with that

end. Furthermore, prison officials are in control of the evidence that is essential to establish the superiority of such deprivation over other alternatives. It is thus only fair for these officials to be held to a stringent standard of review in such extreme cases.

The prison in this case has completely prevented respondent inmates from attending the central religious service of their Muslim faith. I would therefore hold prison officials to the standard articulated in Abdul Wali, and would find their proffered justifications wanting. The State has neither demonstrated that the restriction is necessary to further an important objective nor proved that less extreme measures may not serve its purpose. Even if I accepted the Court's standard of review, however, I could not conclude on this record that prison officials have proved that it is reasonable to preclude respondents from attending Jumu'ah. Petitioners have provided mere unsubstantiated assertions that the plausible alternatives proposed by respondents are infeasible.

II

In Turner, the Court set forth a framework for reviewing allegations that a constitutional right has been infringed by prison officials. The Court found relevant to that review "whether there are alternative means of exercising the right that remain open to prison inmates." Ante, at 90. The Court in this case acknowledges that "respondents' sincerely held religious beliefs compe[l] attendance at Jumu'ah," ante, at 345, and concedes that there are "no alternative means of attending Jumu'ah." Ante, at 351. Nonetheless, the Court finds that prison policy does not work a complete deprivation of respondents' asserted religious right, because respondents have the opportunity to participate in other religious activities. Ante, at 352. This analysis ignores the fact that, as the District Court found, Jumu'ah is the central religious ceremony of Muslims, "comparable to the Saturday service of the Jewish faith and the Sunday service of the various Christian sects." Shabazz v. O'Lone, 595 F.Supp. 928, 930 (NJ 1984). As with other faiths, this ceremony provides a special time in which Muslims "assert their identity as a community covenanted to God."

Brief for Imam Jamil Abdullah Al-Amin et al. as Amici Curiae 32. As a result:

> unlike other Muslim prayers which are performed individually and can be made up if missed, the Jumu'ah is obligatory, cannot be made up, and must be performed in congregation. The Jumu'ah is therefore regarded as the central service of the Muslim religion, and the obligation to attend is commanded by the Qur'an, the central book of the Muslim religion.

Jumu'ah therefore cannot be regarded as one of several essentially fungible religious practices. The ability to engage in other religious activities cannot obscure the fact that the denial at issue in this case is absolute: respondents are completely foreclosed from participating in the core ceremony that reflects their membership in a particular religious community. If a Catholic prisoner were prevented from attending Mass on Sunday, few would regard that deprivation as anything but absolute, even if the prisoner were afforded other opportunities to pray, to discuss the Catholic faith with others, and even to avoid eating meat on Friday if that were a preference. Prison officials in this case therefore cannot show that "other avenues remain available for the exercise of the asserted right." Turner, ante, at 90 (quoting Jones v. North Carolina Prisoners' Union, 433 U.S. 119, 131 (1977)).

Under the Court's approach, as enunciated in Turner, the availability of other means of exercising the right in question counsels considerable deference to prison officials. Ante, at 90. By the same token, the infliction of an absolute deprivation should require more than mere assertion that such a deprivation is necessary. In particular, "the existence of obvious, easy alternatives may be evidence that the regulation is not reasonable, but is an 'exaggerated response' to prison concerns." Ibid. In this case, petitioners have not established the reasonableness of their policy, because they have provided only bare assertions that the proposals for accommodation offered by respondents are infeasible. As discussed below, the federal policy of permitting inmates in federal prisons to participate in Jumu'ah, as well as Leesburg's own policy of permitting participation for several years, lends plausibility to respon-

dents' suggestion that their religious practice can be accommodated.

In Turner, the Court found that the practices of the Federal Bureau of Prisons were relevant to the availability of reasonable alternatives to the policy under challenge. In upholding a ban on inmate-to-inmate mail, the Court noted that the Bureau had adopted "substantially similar restrictions." Ante, at 93 (citing 28 CFR § 540.17 (1986)). In finding that there were alternatives to a stringent restriction on the ability to marry, the Court observed that marriages by inmates in federal prisons were generally permitted absent a threat to security or public safety. See ante, at 97 (citing 28 CFR § 551.10 (1986)). In the present case, it is therefore worth noting that Federal Bureau of Prisons regulations require the adjustment of work assignments to permit inmate participation in religious ceremonies, absent a threat to "security, safety, and good order." 28 CFR § 548.14 (1986). The Bureau's Directive implementing the regulations on Religious Beliefs and Practices of Committed Offenders, 28 CFR §§ 548.10-548.15 (1986), states that, with respect to scheduling religious observances, "the more central the religious activity is to the tenets of the inmate's religious faith, the greater the presumption is for relieving the inmate from the institution program or assignment." App. to Brief for Respondents 8a. Furthermore, the Chaplain Director of the Bureau has spoken directly to the issue of participation of Muslim inmates in Jumu'ah:

> Provision is made, by policy, in all Bureau facilities for the observance of Jumu-ah by all inmates in general population who wish to keep this faith practice. The service is held each Friday afternoon in the general time frame that corresponds to the requirements of Islamic jurisprudence. . . .

> Subject only to restraints of security and good order in the institution all routine and normal work assignments are suspended for the Islamic inmates to ensure freedom to attend such services. . . .

> In those institutions where the outside work details contain Islamic inmates, they are permitted access to the inside of the institution to attend the Jumu-ah.

That Muslim inmates are able to participate in Jumu'ah throughout the entire federal prison system suggests that the practice is, under normal circumstances, compatible with the demands of prison administration. Indeed, the Leesburg State Prison permitted participation in this ceremony for five years, and experienced no threats to security or safety as a result. In light of both standard federal prison practice and Leesburg's own past practice, a reasonableness test in this case demands at least minimal substantiation by prison officials that alternatives that would permit participation in Jumu'ah are infeasible. Under the standard articulated by the Court in Turner, this does not mean that petitioners are responsible for identifying and discrediting these alternatives; "prison officials do not have to set up and then shoot down every conceivable alternative method of accommodating the claimant's constitutional complaint." Ante, at 90-91. When prisoners themselves present alternatives, however, and when they fairly call into question official claims that these alternatives are infeasible, we must demand at least some evidence beyond mere assertion that the religious practice at issue cannot be accommodated. Examination of the alternatives proposed in this case indicates that prison officials have not provided such substantiation.

III

Respondents' first proposal is that gang minimum prisoners be assigned to an alternative inside work detail on Friday, as they had been before the recent change in policy. Prison officials testified that the alternative work detail is now restricted to maximum security prisoners, and that they did not wish maximum and minimum security prisoners to mingle. Even the District Court had difficulty with this assertion, as it commented that "the defendants did not explain why inmates of different security levels are not mixed on work assignments when otherwise they are mixed." 595 F.Supp., at 932. The court found, nonetheless, that this alternative would be inconsistent with Standard 853's mandate to move gang minimum inmates to outside work details. Ibid. This conclusion, however, neglects the fact that the very issue is whether the prison's policy, of which Standard 853 is a part, should be administered so as to accommodate Muslim inmates. The policy itself cannot serve as a justification for its failure to provide reasonable accommodation. The record as it now stands thus does not establish that the Friday alternative work detail would create a problem for the institution.

Respondents' second proposal is that gang minimum inmates be assigned to work details inside the main building on a regular basis. While admitting that the prison used inside details in the kitchen, bakery, and tailor shop, officials stated that these jobs are reserved for the riskiest gang minimum inmates, for whom an outside job might be unwise. Ibid. Thus, concluded officials, it would be a bad idea to move these inmates outside to make room for Muslim gang minimum inmates. Respondents contend, however, that the prison's own records indicate that there are a significant number of jobs inside the institution that could be performed by inmates posing a lesser security risk. This suggests that it might not be necessary for the riskier gang minimum inmates to be moved outside to make room for the less risky inmates. Officials provided no data on the number of inside jobs available, the number of high-risk gang minimum inmates performing them, the number of Muslim inmates that might seek inside positions, or the number of staff that would be necessary to monitor such an arrangement. Given the plausibility of respondents' claim, prison officials should present at least this information in substantiating their contention that inside assignments are infeasible.

Third, respondents suggested that gang minimum inmates be assigned to Saturday or Sunday work details, which would allow them to make up any time lost by attending Jumu'ah on Friday. While prison officials admitted the existence of weekend work details, they stated that "since prison personnel are needed for other programs on weekends, the creation of additional weekend details would be a drain on scarce human resources." Ibid. The record provides no indication, however, of the number of Muslims that would seek such a work detail, the current number of weekend details, or why it would be infeasible simply to reassign current Saturday or Sunday workers to Friday, rather than create additional details.

The prison is able to arrange work schedules so that Jewish inmates may attend services on Saturday and Christian inmates may attend services on Sunday. Id., at 935. Despite the fact that virtually all inmates are housed in the main building over the weekend, so that the demand on the facility is greater than at any other time, the prison is able to provide sufficient staff coverage to permit Jewish and Christian inmates to participate in their central religious ceremonies. Given the prison's duty to provide Muslims a "reasonable opportunity of pursuing [their] faith comparable to the opportunity afforded fellow prisoners who adhere to conventional religious precepts," Cruz v. Beto, 405 U.S. 319, 322 (1972), prison officials should be required to provide more than mere assertions of the infeasibility of weekend details for Muslim inmates.

Finally, respondents proposed that minimum security inmates living at the Farm be assigned to jobs either in the Farm building or in its immediate vicinity. Since Standard 853 permits such assignments for full minimum inmates, and since such inmates need not return to prison facilities through the main entrance, this would interfere neither with Standard 853 nor the concern underlying the no-return policy. Nonetheless, prison officials stated that such an arrangement might create an "affinity group" of Muslims representing a threat to prison authority. Officials pointed to no such problem in the five years in which Muslim inmates were permitted to assemble for Jumu'ah, and in which the alternative Friday work detail was in existence. Nor could they identify any threat resulting from the fact that during the month of Ramadan all Muslim prisoners participate in both breakfast and dinner at special times. Furthermore, there was no testimony that the concentration of Jewish or Christian inmates on work details or in religious services posed any type of "affinity group" threat. As the record now stands, prison officials have declared that a security risk is created by a grouping of Muslim inmates in the least dangerous security classification, but not by a grouping of maximum security inmates who are concentrated in a work detail inside the main building, and who are the only Muslims assured of participating in Jumu'ah. Surely, prison officials should be required to provide at least some

substantiation for this facially implausible contention.

Petitioners also maintained that the assignment of full minimum Muslim inmates to the Farm or its near vicinity might provoke resentment because of other inmates' perception that Muslims were receiving special treatment. Officials pointed to no such perception during the period in which the alternative Friday detail was in existence, nor to any resentment of the fact that Muslims' dietary preferences are accommodated and that Muslims are permitted to operate on a special schedule during the month of Ramadan. Nor do they identify any such problems created by the accommodation of the religious preferences of inmates of other faiths. Once again, prison officials should be required at a minimum to identify the basis for their assertions.

Despite the plausibility of the alternatives proposed by respondents in light of federal practice and the prison's own past practice, officials have essentially provided mere pronouncements that such alternatives are not workable. If this Court is to take seriously its commitment to the principle that "prison walls do not form a barrier separating prison inmates from the protections of the Constitution," Turner, ante, at 84, it must demand more than this record provides to justify a Muslim inmate's complete foreclosure from participation in the central religious service of the Muslim faith.

IV

That the record in this case contains little more than assertions is not surprising in light of the fact that the District Court proceeded on the basis of the approach set forth in St. Claire v. Cuyler, 634 F.2d 109 (CA3 1980). That case held that mere "sincer[e]" and "arguably correct" testimony by prison officials is sufficient to demonstrate the need to limit prisoners' exercise of constitutional rights. Id., at 114 (quoting Jones, 433 U.S., at 127). This Court in Turner, ante, p. 78, however, set forth a more systematic framework for analyzing challenges to prison regulations. Turner directed attention to two factors of particular relevance to this case: the degree of constitutional deprivation and the availability of reasonable alternatives. The respondents in this case have been absolutely foreclosed from participating in the central religious ceremony of their Muslim faith. At least a colorable claim that such a drastic policy is not necessary can be made in light of the ability of federal prisons to accommodate Muslim inmates, Leesburg's own past practice of doing so, and the plausibility of the alternatives proposed by respondents. If the Court's standard of review is to represent anything more than reflexive deference to prison officials, any finding of reasonableness must rest on firmer ground than the record now presents.

Incarceration by its nature denies a prisoner participation in the larger human community. To deny the opportunity to affirm membership in a spiritual community, however, may extinguish an inmate's last source of hope for dignity and redemption. Such a denial requires more justification than mere assertion that any other course of action is infeasible. While I would prefer that this case be analyzed under the approach set out in Part I, supra, I would at a minimum remand to the District Court for an analysis of respondents' claims in accordance with the standard enunciated by the Court in Turner and in this case.

I therefore dissent.

UNITED STATES
v.
KNIGHTS

534 U.S. 112; 122 S. Ct. 587 (2001)
(Footnotes and citations omitted)

* * *

A California court sentenced respondent Mark James Knights to summary probation for a drug offense. The probation order included the following condition: that Knights would "submit his . . . person, property, place of residence, vehicle, personal effects, to search at anytime, with or without a search warrant, warrant of arrest or reasonable cause by any probation officer or law enforcement officer." Knights signed the probation order, which stated immediately above his signature that "I HAVE RECEIVED A COPY, READ AND UNDERSTAND THE ABOVE TERMS AND CONDITIONS OF PROBATION AND AGREE TO ABIDE BY SAME." * * * In this case, we decide whether a search pursuant to this probation condition, and supported by reasonable suspicion, satisfied the Fourth Amendment.

* * *

The touchstone of the Fourth Amendment is reasonableness, and the reasonableness of a search is determined "by assessing, on the one hand, the degree to which it intrudes upon an individual's privacy and, on the other, the degree to which it is needed for the promotion of legitimate governmental interests." * * * Knights's status as a probationer subject to a search condition informs both sides of that balance. "Probation, like incarceration, is 'a form of criminal sanction imposed by a court upon an offender after verdict, finding, or plea of guilty.'" * * * Probation is "one point . . . on a continuum of possible punishments ranging from solitary confinement in a maximum-security facility to a few hours of mandatory community service." * * * Inherent in the very nature of probation is that probationers "do not enjoy 'the absolute liberty to which every citizen is entitled.'" * * * Just as other punishments for criminal convictions curtail an offender's freedoms, a court granting probation may impose reasonable conditions that deprive the offender of some freedoms enjoyed by law-abiding citizens.

* * *

It was reasonable to conclude that the search condition would further the two primary goals of probation—rehabilitation and protecting society from future criminal violations. The probation order clearly expressed the search condition and Knights was unambiguously informed of it. The probation condition thus significantly diminished Knights's reasonable expectation of privacy.

In assessing the governmental interest side of the balance, it must be remembered that "the very assumption of the institution of probation" is that the probationer "is more likely than the ordinary citizen to violate the law." * * * The recidivism rate of probationers is significantly higher than the general crime rate. * * * And probationers have even more of an incentive to conceal their criminal activities and quickly dispose of incriminating evidence than the ordinary criminal because probationers are aware that they may be subject to supervision and face revocation of probation, and possible incarceration, in proceedings in which the trial rights of a jury and proof beyond a reasonable doubt, among other things, do not apply. * * *

The State has a dual concern with a probationer. On the one hand is the hope that he will successfully complete probation and be integrated back into the community. On the other is the concern, quite justified, that he will be more likely to engage in criminal conduct than an ordinary member of the community. The view of the Court of Appeals in this case would require the State to shut its eyes to the latter concern and concentrate only on the former. But we hold that the Fourth Amendment does not put the State to such a choice. Its interest in apprehending violators of the criminal law, thereby protecting potential victims of criminal enterprise, may therefore justifiably focus on probationers in a way that it does not on the ordinary citizen.

[We hold that the balance of these considerations requires no more than reasonable suspicion to conduct a search of this probationer's house. The degree of individualized suspicion required of a search is a determination of when there is a sufficiently high probability that criminal conduct is occurring to make the intrusion on the individual's privacy interest reasonable.* * * . Although the Fourth Amendment ordinarily requires the degree of probability embodied in the term "probable cause," a lesser degree satisfies the Constitution when the balance of governmental and private interests makes such a standard reasonable. * * * Those interests warrant a lesser than probable-cause standard here. When an officer has reasonable suspicion that a probationer subject to a search condition is engaged in criminal activity, there is enough likelihood that criminal conduct is occurring that an intrusion on the probationer's significantly diminished privacy interests is reasonable.

The same circumstances that lead us to conclude that reasonable suspicion is constitutionally sufficient also render a warrant requirement unnecessary. * * * Because our holding rests on ordinary Fourth Amendment analysis that considers all the circumstances of a search, there is no basis for examining official purpose. With the limited exception of some special needs and administrative search cases, * * * "we have been unwilling to entertain Fourth Amendment challenges based on the actual motivations of individual officers." * * *

The District Court found, and Knights concedes, that the search in this case was supported by reasonable suspicion. We therefore hold that the warrantless search of Knights, supported by reasonable suspicion and authorized by a condition of probation, was reasonable within the meaning of the Fourth Amendment. * * *

Cases Relating to Chapter 7

Legal Services

JOHNSON

v.

AVERY

393 U.S. 483; 89 S. Ct. 747; 21 L. Ed. 2d 718 (1969)

MR. JUSTICE FORTAS delivered the opinion of the Court.

I.

Petitioner is serving a life sentence in the Tennessee State Penitentiary. In February 1965 he was transferred to the maximum security building in the prison for violation of a prison regulation which provides:

No inmate will advise, assist or otherwise contract to aid another, either with or without a fee, to prepare Writs or other legal matters. It is not intended that an innocent man be punished. When a man believes he is unlawfully held or illegally convicted, he should prepare a brief or state his complaint in letter form and address it to his lawyer or a judge. A formal Writ is not necessary to receive a hearing. False charges or untrue complaints may be punished. Inmates are forbidden to set themselves up as practitioners for the purpose of promoting a business of writing Writs.

In July 1965 petitioner filed in the United States District Court for the Middle District of Tennessee a "motion for law books and a typewriter," in which he sought relief from his confinement in the maximum security build-

ing. The District Court treated this motion as a petition for a writ of habeas corpus and, after a hearing, ordered him released from disciplinary confinement and restored to the status of an ordinary prisoner. The District Court held that the regulation was void because it in effect barred illiterate prisoners from access to federal habeas corpus and conflicted with 28 U.S.C. § 2242. 252 F.Supp. 783.

By the time the District Court order was entered, petitioner had been transferred from the maximum security building, but he had been put in a disciplinary cell block in which he was entitled to fewer privileges than were given ordinary prisoners. Only when he promised to refrain from assistance to other inmates was he restored to regular prison conditions and privileges. At a second hearing, held in March 1966, the District Court explored these issues concerning the compliance of the prison officials with its initial order. After the hearing, it reaffirmed its earlier order.

The State appealed. The Court of Appeals for the Sixth Circuit reversed, concluding that the regulation did not unlawfully conflict with the federal right of habeas corpus. According to the Sixth Circuit, the interest of the State in preserving prison discipline and in limiting the practice of law to licensed attorneys justified whatever burden the regulation might place on access to federal habeas corpus. 382 F.2d 353.

II.

This Court has constantly emphasized the fundamental importance of the writ of habeas corpus in our constitutional scheme, and the Congress has demonstrated its solicitude for the vigor of the Great Writ. The Court has steadfastly insisted that "there is no higher duty than to maintain it unimpaired." Bowen v. Johnston, 306 U.S. 19, 26 (1939).

Since the basic purpose of the writ is to enable those unlawfully incarcerated to obtain their freedom, it is fundamental that access of prisoners to the courts for the purpose of presenting their complaints may not be denied or obstructed. For example, the Court has held that a State may not validly make the writ available only to prisoners who could pay a $4 filing fee. Smith v. Bennett, 365 U.S. 708 (1961). And it has insisted that, for the indigent as well as for the affluent prisoner, post-conviction proceedings must be more than a formality. For instance, the State is obligated to furnish prisoners not otherwise able to obtain it, with a transcript or equivalent recordation of prior habeas corpus hearings for use in further proceedings. Long v. District Court, 385 U.S. 192 (1966). Cf. Griffin v. Illinois, 351 U.S. 12 (1956).

Tennessee urges, however, that the contested regulation in this case is justified as a part of the State's disciplinary administration of the prisons. There is no doubt that discipline and administration of state detention facilities are state functions. They are subject to federal authority only where paramount federal constitutional or statutory rights supervene. It is clear, however, that in instances where state regulations applicable to inmates of prison facilities conflict with such rights, the regulations may be invalidated.

For example, in Lee v. Washington, 390 U.S. 333 (1968), the practice of racial segregation of prisoners was justified by the State as necessary to maintain good order and discipline. We held, however, that the practice was constitutionally prohibited, although we were careful to point out that the order of the District Court, which we affirmed, made allowance for "the necessities of prison security and discipline." Id., at 334. And in Ex parte Hull, 312 U.S. 546 (1941), this Court invalidated a state regulation which required that habeas corpus petitions first be submitted to prison authorities and then approved by the "legal investigator" to the parole board as "properly drawn" before being transmitted to the court. Here again, the State urged that the requirement was necessary to maintain prison discipline. But this Court held that the regulation violated the principle that "the state and its officers may not abridge or impair petitioner's right to apply to a federal court for a writ of habeas corpus." 312 U.S., at 549. Cf. Cochran v. Kansas, 316 U.S. 255, 257 (1942).

There can be no doubt that Tennessee could not constitutionally adopt and enforce a rule forbidding illiterate or poorly educated prisoners to file habeas corpus petitions. Here Tennessee has adopted a rule which, in the absence of any other source of assistance for such prisoners, effectively does just that. The District Court concluded that "for all practical purposes, if such prisoners cannot have the assistance of a 'jail-house lawyer,' their possibly valid constitutional claims will never be heard in any court." 252 F.Supp., at 784. The record supports this conclusion.

Jails and penitentiaries include among their inmates a high percentage of persons who are totally or functionally illiterate, whose educational attainments are slight, and whose intelligence is limited. This appears to be equally true of Tennessee's prison facilities.

In most federal courts, it is the practice to appoint counsel in post-conviction proceedings only after a petition for post-conviction relief passes initial judicial evaluation and the court has determined that issues are presented calling for an evidentiary hearing. E.g., Taylor v. Pegelow, 335 F.2d 147 (C. A. 4th Cir. 1964); United States ex rel. Marshall v. Wilkins, 338 F.2d 404 (C. A. 2d Cir. 1964). See 28 U.S.C. § 1915 (d); R. Sokol, A Handbook of Federal Habeas Corpus 71-73 (1965).

It has not been held that there is any general obligation of the courts, state or federal, to appoint counsel for prisoners who indicate, without more, that they wish to seek post-conviction relief. See, e.g., Barker v. Ohio, 330 F.2d 594 (C. A. 6th Cir. 1964). Accordingly, the initial burden of presenting a claim to post-conviction relief usually rests upon the indigent prisoner himself with such help as he can obtain within the prison walls or the prison system. In the case of all except those who are able to help themselves—usually a few old hands or exceptionally gifted prisoners—the prisoner is, in effect, denied access to the courts unless such help is available.

It is indisputable that prison "writ writers" like petitioner are sometimes a menace to prison discipline and that their petitions are often so unskillful as to be a burden on the courts which receive them. But, as this Court held in Ex parte Hull, supra, in declaring invalid a state prison regulation which required that prisoners' legal pleadings be screened by state officials:

The considerations that prompted [the regulation's] formulation are not without merit, but the state and its officers may not abridge or impair petitioner's right to apply to a federal court for a writ of habeas corpus.

Tennessee does not provide an available alternative to the assistance provided by other inmates. The warden of the prison in which petitioner was confined stated that the prison provided free notarization of prisoners' petitions. That obviously meets only a formal requirement. He also indicated that he sometimes allowed prisoners to examine the listing of attorneys in the Nashville telephone directory so they could select one to write to in an effort to interest him in taking the case, and that "on several occasions" he had contacted the public defender at the request of an inmate. There is no contention, however, that there is any regular system of assistance by public defenders. In its brief the State contends that "there is absolutely no reason to believe that prison officials would fail to notify the court should an inmate advise them of a complete inability, either mental or physical, to prepare a habeas application on his own behalf," but there is no contention that they have in fact ever done so.

This is obviously far short of the showing required to demonstrate that, in depriving prisoners of the assistance of fellow inmates, Tennessee has not, in substance, deprived those unable themselves, with reasonable adequacy, to prepare their petitions, of access to the constitutionally and statutorily protected availability of the writ of habeas corpus. By contrast, in several States, the public defender system supplies trained attorneys, paid from public funds, who are available to consult with prisoners regarding their habeas corpus petitions. At least one State employs

senior law students to interview and advise inmates in state prisons. Another State has a voluntary program whereby members of the local bar association make periodic visits to the prison to consult with prisoners concerning their cases. We express no judgment concerning these plans, but their existence indicates that techniques are available to provide alternatives if the State elects to prohibit mutual assistance among inmates.

Even in the absence of such alternatives, the State may impose reasonable restrictions and restraints upon the acknowledged propensity of prisoners to abuse both the giving and the seeking of assistance in the preparation of applications for relief: for example, by limitations on the time and location of such activities and the imposition of punishment for the giving or receipt of consideration in connection with such activities. Cf. Hatfield v. Bailleaux, 290 F.2d 632 (C. A. 9th Cir. 1961) (sustaining as reasonable regulations on the time and location of prisoner work on their own petitions). But unless and until the State provides some reasonable alternative to assist inmates in the preparation of petitions for post-conviction relief, it may not validly enforce a regulation such as that here in issue, barring inmates from furnishing such assistance to other prisoners.

The judgment of the Court of Appeals is reversed and the case is remanded for further proceedings consistent with this opinion.

Reversed and remanded.

CRUZ
v.
BETO

Civil No. 71-H-1371
(S.D. Tex., filed Mar. 18, 1976)

I. FINDINGS OF FACT

A. Introduction

Plaintiffs are an attorney, Mrs. Frances T. Jalet Cruz ("Mrs. Cruz"), and 12 prisoners ("prisoner-plaintiffs") who in 1971 were in the custody of the Texas Department of Corrections ("TDC"). Mrs. Cruz is a citizen of the United States and an attorney admitted to practice in the State of Texas and other states, as well as in the federal courts. All of the prisoner-plaintiffs are citizens of the United States.

Defendant George J. Beto is the former Director of the TDC and was serving as Director during 1971 and 1972. Defendant W.J. Estelle, Jr., is the present Director of the TDC, having succeeded defendant Beto on September 1, 1972. All the actions of both defendants involved in this case were taken under color of state law.

This controversy has arisen in part because of actions taken by defendant Beto against Mrs. Cruz for acts she allegedly committed while representing inmates at the TDC.

B. Background of Mrs. Cruz; Relationship of Mrs. Cruz with the Prisoner-Plaintiffs

Prior to 1971 when the salient events of this lawsuit commenced, Mrs. Cruz had served for several years as an attorney working for legal aid organizations, the Office of Economic Opportunity, or Volunteers in Service to America ("VISTA"), at offices in Texas. Her extensive legal background and experience in poverty law as well as her initial participation as an inmates' attorney have been described previously by this Court. See Dreyer v. Jalet, 349 F.Supp. 453, 468-70 (S.D. Tex. 1972), and per curiam, 479 F.2d 1044 (5th Cir. 1973).

Pursuing a career in poverty law and related areas in 1971, Mrs. Cruz was employed as a VISTA attorney. She provided prisoners with advice and representation in suits seeking post-conviction relief as well as in suits challenging the constitutionality of various prison practices and conditions.

During the latter half of 1971, Mrs. Cruz was providing advice and representation to all of the prisoner-plaintiffs. She assisted them in prosecuting their habeas corpus petitions and/or their "prison" suits under 42 U.S.C. § 1983. She was representing each of the prisoner-plaintiffs as clients in her capacity as an attorney. There is no persuasive evidence in this case, although defendants contend otherwise, that she did not have a proper attorney-client relationship with each of the prisoner-plaintiffs.

In representing these prisoner-plaintiffs or responding to other prisoners who sought her advice or assistance during the years in question, Mrs. Cruz devoted much of her time to prisoners and regularly visited and corresponded with many TDC inmates. The credible evidence in this case supports plaintiffs' position that these many visits were in keeping with Mrs. Cruz's views of her professional responsibility to her clients and the practice of her profession. At all material times, Mrs. Cruz was required to observe, and did observe, all visiting and correspondence regulations promulgated by the TDC. During the years before the occurrence of the events in question, Mrs. Cruz never knowingly violated any rules of the TDC and never was charged with any such violations by TDC authorities.

C. Exclusion of Mrs. Cruz From TDC; Segregation of the Prisoner-Plaintiffs

On October 14, 1971, defendant Beto as Director of the TDC wrote to Mrs. Cruz informing her as follows:

"Your continued and frequent visits to the Department of Corrections as well as your correspondence with inmates make it impossible for me to guarantee tranquility within the institutions and the protection of the inmates.

Accordingly, effective this date, I am requesting all wardens of the Texas Department of Corrections to deny your admission to the institutions under my general supervision and to terminate correspondence between you and any inmate in the Texas Department of Corrections.

The communiqué from defendant Beto to Mrs. Cruz reflected his position that Mrs. Cruz had taken certain actions in coordination with some of the prisoner-plaintiffs to arouse the animosity of the TDC inmate population and to spur the filing of federal civil rights lawsuits by inmates. However, defendant Beto and later defendant Estelle and TDC subordinates never complained to any law enforcement agency that Mrs. Cruz had committed any illegal or improper act or participated in any unethical behavior. Also, defendants never complained of such conduct to the State Bar of Texas or any coordinate grievance committee.

The evidence conclusively demonstrates that Mrs. Cruz did not interfere with the "tranquility" of TDC institutions. Her contact with the TDC was solely initiated in the course of proper and professional representation of TDC prisoners whereby she advised inmates of their federal constitutional rights and represented them in lawsuits as described above.

The October 14, 1971, telegram from defendant Beto to Mrs. Cruz, provoked stringent efforts by several members of the State Bar of Texas and other out-of-state attorneys to object to the exclusion of Mrs. Cruz from the TDC. These letters of protest were accompanied by efforts at negotiation between counsel for Mrs. Cruz and defendant Beto.

As a result of these negotiations, defendant Beto sent a telegram to Mrs. Cruz on November 5, 1971, which stated that he was restoring the communication between Mrs. Cruz and 27 inmates named in the telegram. These included the prisoner-plaintiffs, who had been represented by her and who thus had been deprived of access to any counsel between October 14 and November 5, 1971.

All of the inmates named in the telegram who wished to remain clients of Mrs. Cruz were then transferred by defendant Beto, without notice or any hearing, to one wing of the Wynne Unit of the TDC in November, 1971. They were segregated from other prisoners and deprived of many of the privileges they had formerly enjoyed as members of the general prison population. This wing of the Wynne Unit became known as the "Eight Hoe" Squad.

The segregation policy imposed in November, 1971, lasted for a period of approximately eleven (11) months, until October 25, 1972. With the exception of inmate Cruz, who was discharged from the TDC on March 8, 1972, after 125 days on the Eight Hoe Squad, each prisoner-plaintiff remained on Eight Hoe Squad a total of 356 days, until October 25, 1972. Certain other inmates who were at first assigned to the Eight Hoe Squad were later reclassified and removed to other less restrictive units only when they expressed their intention to relinquish Mrs. Cruz as their attor-

ney. Inmates such as Gomez, Perry and Mills, upon relinquishment of Mrs. Cruz's representation, were transferred immediately from the Wynne Unit. They later were assigned to desirable positions, such as trusty, and had no difficulty in maintaining creditable ratings as prisoners.

The preponderance of the credible evidence demonstrates that during the prisoner-plaintiffs' period of segregation on the Eight Hoe Squad, lower echelon TDC officials under defendant Beto's direction regularly pressured such prisoners to abandon Mrs. Cruz's legal representation. As TDC officials expressed it to the prisoner-plaintiffs, such action would result promptly in their release from the Eight Hoe Squad and a corresponding improvement in their status as prisoners.

D. Deprivations Imposed Upon the
   Prisoner-Plaintiffs

The Point Incentive Program (PIP) is utilized by TDC officials as an equivalent to a "merit/demerit" rating system for prisoners. All privileges and parole consideration are keyed to attaining a certain number of PIP "points," or merits, which are awarded on a quarterly basis under this program. A level of 80-90 points must be earned by an inmate during each quarter for that quarter to be considered in determining parole eligibility.

At the time the segregation policy was imposed, each prisoner-plaintiff's PIP point total was altered uniformly to reflect a total of only 40 PIP points for the fourth quarter of 1971, well below a satisfactory level. No prisoner-plaintiff ever was able to attain a satisfactory level during the existence of the segregation policy. Thus, no remaining prisoner-plaintiff (inmate Cruz having been discharged from TDC on March 8, 1972), could maintain a high rating and remain eligible for privileges and time credited towards parole.

Certain prisoner-plaintiffs were not permitted to pursue the attainment of academic certificates. That is, as members of the Eight Hoe Squad, they were prohibited from enrolling or remaining in courses required in the respective educational programs in which they were enrolled. When the segregation policy was imposed, prisoner-plaintiffs Cruz, Mauricio and Baker were enrolled in college degree programs, and prisoner-plaintiffs Bilton and

Barbosa were participating in the "G.E.D." program, a program offering secondary education level courses.

While on Eight Hoe, most of the prisoner-plaintiffs were required regularly to perform manual field labor. This work schedule was imposed on several Eight Hoe residents despite the fact that they had medical ratings of "Fourth Class." Such a rating denotes a poor medical condition and normally renders an inmate ineligible for any prison work assignment requiring rigorous physical exertion. Prisoner-plaintiffs Montana, Bilton, Zilka, Barbosa and Soto all had medical ratings of Fourth Class.

The segregation policy worked additional deprivations on the prisoner-plaintiffs as set out in the margin.[1]

E. Impact of Interference with Plaintiff's Attorney-Client Relationship

Mrs. Cruz continued to be barred by defendants from communicating with any TDC inmates except those listed in the telegram of November 5, 1971, who remained assigned to the Eight Hoe Squad. There is no evidence that any other attorney has ever been barred from the TDC or so restricted in the exercise of rights conferred by the law license granted by the State Bar of Texas. Inmates represented by other Texas attorneys have not been denied the right to communicate with them. Mrs. Cruz thus could not fulfill her professional obligations to her clients because the prohibition against her prevented her from responding to numerous requests for legal assistance from other TDC inmates.

Inmates who attempted to write to Mrs. Cruz for assistance were prevented from doing so by defendants' agents at the direction of defendant Beto. Such actions impeded inmates' access to the courts in pending cases.

The prisoner-plaintiffs were without funds and unable to pay fees in order to retain another attorney to represent them. Because they were deprived of or penalized for accepting Mrs. Cruz's pro bono legal assistance and being generally poorly educated, they were unable to obtain adequate legal assistance. Yet they were in need of such assistance on various legal problems affecting both their convictions and sentences and their claims of violations of federal constitutional rights as prisoners.

F. Action of Defendant Estelle

Defendant Estelle assumed the Directorship of the TDC on September 1, 1972, and continued the enforcement of the policy of defendant Beto, alleging that it was necessary for the protection of the prisoner-plaintiffs. Having concluded that their safety was no longer in doubt, he terminated the policy on October 25, 1972, and returned the prisoner-plaintiffs to the general prison population.

G. Defendants' Justifications for Barring Mrs. Cruz and for Segregating the Prisoner-Plaintiffs Between November, 1971, and October 25, 1972

Defendants seek to justify the actions which defendant Beto took against Mrs. Cruz and the prisoner-plaintiffs by asserting that these actions were prompted by the alleged existence of inflammatory prison conditions at the TDC in 1971; suggesting that the prisoner-plaintiffs operated a plan of group action designed to endanger other inmates or overturn the prison administration; and alleging that Mrs. Cruz conspired to contribute to unrest by attempting to incite inmate insurrection and stir up prisoner litigation.

---

[1]   Additional deprivations to prisoner-plaintiffs as a result of the segregation in the Eight Hoe Squad fall within the category of "humiliation" and include: (a) denial of mailing privileges to their counsel, Mrs. Cruz; (b) elimination of recreation and time for an exercise period in the gym; (c) separation from all other inmates especially during meal times; (d) minimal availability of hot water for coffee and other amenities; (e) sharp reduction in time available for writ room privileges; (f) reduced available time for recreational television viewing to one television set for two-three hours at night with location of the lone television set in the writ room so as to interfere with use of the room for either writ writing or television recreation; (g) subjection to repeated "shakedowns" disproportionate to those imposed upon the general inmate population; and (h) subjection to repeated disciplinary actions and penalties disproportionate to those imposed on the general inmate population.

However, defendants have failed to demonstrate in any persuasive fashion the existence during the subject period time of any inflammatory prison situation that would require the caliber of action taken in this case. Defendants also have failed to demonstrate by any persuasive, objective evidence in this trial that either Mrs. Cruz or the prisoner-plaintiffs presented any real threat to prison security or inmate security under the circumstances. The evidence conclusively points to the fact that the prisoner-plaintiffs were segregated not because they were violence-prone but because they wished to have Mrs. Cruz represent them.

H. Consistency of the Finding of Lack of Justification in the Instant Case with the Findings in Dreyer v. Jalet

In view of the nature of this case this Court has scrutinized the record with extreme care for some legally justifiable basis for defendant Beto's actions during the period in question. No such basis is evident, and this finding is reinforced when the credibility of the evidence is evaluated. Indeed, the findings in this case are wholly consistent with those made by this Court some four years ago in Dreyer v. Jalet, supra 349 F.Supp. 452,[2] in which no conspiracy was found to exist between Mrs. Cruz (then Mrs. Jalet) and TDC inmates.

---

[2] In the Dreyer case, a consolidated action, three inmates of the TDC filed suits in this Court against Mrs. Cruz (then Mrs. Jalet) seeking injunctive relief to bar her from providing legal assistance to inmates of the TDC. The Dreyer suits were premised fundamentally on the theory that Mrs. Jalet was attempting to organize prisoners incarcerated at the TDC for the purpose of instigating an inmate uprising to the detriment of plaintiffs who would not join in the alleged conspiracy and who wished to serve their time without intimidation or deprivation of inmate privileges. 349 F.Supp. at 456-57.

Trial on the merits in this highly unusual case lasted approximately six weeks. In ruling on the merits, the Court recited preliminarily the antagonisms which previously had characterized the relationship between Mrs. Cruz and defendant Beto; the Court then proceeded to relate the events which culminated in the exclusionary and segregation policies of October and November, 1971, imposed by defendant Beto on Mrs. Jalet and her clients. 349 F.Supp. at 470-71.

In the instant case, which lasted but three days, the evidence forthcoming on conspiracy was even more attenuated.

I. THE REASONABLENESS AND GOOD FAITH OF DEFENDANT BETO'S ACTIONS

Defendants have failed to demonstrate in this record that defendant Beto acted reasonably and in good faith and solely for the purpose of preserving and protecting prison security. There is simply no persuasive evidence which reflects that defendant Beto had any reasonable or good faith grounds on which to base his actions.

The evidence conclusively demonstrates that: Mrs. Cruz engaged in no efforts to disrupt prison security and violated no prison regulations; the prisoner-plaintiffs operated no plan of group action, such as a communications network, designed to endanger other inmates or overturn the prison administration; defendant Beto's actions were prompted by his long-standing antagonism towards Mrs. Cruz's contact with TDC inmates; and they were taken primarily to discourage the prisoner-plaintiffs from exercising certain constitutional rights and to prevent Mrs. Cruz from representing TDC inmates in civil rights litigation. Under the circumstances such actions must be found to have been taken unjustifiably and in bad faith.

II. CONCLUSIONS OF LAW

A. Applicable Legal Principles

Jurisdiction is proper in this Court pursuant to 42 U.S.C. §1983 and 28 U.S.C. §1343.

Access to the courts must be provided to prisoners so that they may challenge unlawful convictions and seek redress for violations of their constitutional rights. Inmates

---

The Court thereafter evaluated the Dreyer plaintiff's allegations regarding the existence of a conspiracy between Mrs. Jalet and TDC inmates and concluded that there was no merit to the allegations. 349 F.Supp. at 472-74. The evidence presented at length in Dreyer demonstrated no illegal activity on the part of Mrs. Jalet and certainly no proof of any conduct on her part that rose to the level of a conspiracy. Id. at 474.

must have a reasonable opportunity to seek and receive the assistance of counsel. Any regulation or practice which unjustifiably obstructs the availability of professional representation or other aspects of the right of access to the courts is invalid. Procunier v. Martinez, 416 U.S. 396, 419 (1974). This principle of federal constitutional guarantee has long and frequently been espoused by the federal courts. See Younger v. Gilmore, 404 U.S. 15 (1971) (per curiam), aff'g, Gilmore v. Lynch, 319 F.Supp. 105 (N.D. Cal. 1970).

A prisoner attempting to gain access to the courts cannot be disciplined in any manner. Andrade v. Hauck, 452 F.2d 1071, 1072 (5th Cir. 1971). Transferring a prisoner and causing him to lose privileges for using the courts is a very serious allegation. Wolff v. McDonnell, 418 U.S. 539 (1974); Hooks v. Kelley, 463 F.2d 1210, 1211 (5th Cir. 1972).

The segregation of these prisoner-plaintiffs under the circumstances in this case was therefore punitive in nature, not merely administrative, compare Carlo v. Gunter, 520 F.2d 1293 (1st Cir. 1975) with Shields v. Hopper, 519 F.2d 1131 (5th Cir. 1975), and presents the extreme circumstances alluded to by the United States Court of Appeals for the Fifth Circuit, see Young v. Wainwright, 449 F.2d 338, 339 (5th Cir. 1971) and cases cited therein, which justify the interference by this Court with prison administration and a finding of liability against defendant Beto. Cf. Woolsey v. Beto, 450 F.2d 321 (5th Cir. 1971).

A prisoner has the right to be represented by an attorney of his choice if the attorney indicates a willingness to represent him. This right is protected by the First and Fourteenth Amendments and may not be limited unreasonably by state officials. Sanders v. Russell, 401 F.2d 241, 245-47 (5th Cir. 1968).

The combination of a prisoner's impoverished financial condition and a prison official's interference with his right to legal representation translates into a denial of the prisoner-litigant's right to equal protection of the laws. See Weintraub v. Adair, 331 F.Supp. 148 (S.D. Fla. 1971).

As the Supreme Court has made clear in Procunier v. Martinez, the exchange of written communications between an attorney and his inmate client calls into play the inmate's First Amendment rights and the First Amendment rights of the attorney, who has a significant interest in receiving or sending such communications. 416 U.S. at 408. The attorney's First Amendment interest is enhanced by his obligation, as an officer of the court, to represent his client's interests adequately and to assist a court in which a client's suit is pending to adjudicate such a suit promptly and justly.

Impeding the access of an attorney to his prisoner clients may be necessary in certain cases based on the reasonable, good faith belief of prison officials that such action is required under the circumstances. E.g., Elie v. Henderson, 340 F.Supp. 958 (E.D. La. 1972). The facts of Elie v. Henderson demonstrate an attorney's overt attempt, under the guise of representing inmate clients, to incite a riot at a prison as well as to participate in other activities which clearly have nothing to do with appropriate legal representation.

However, Elie v. Henderson should be the exception, not the rule, for First Amendment reasons. A prison official may not, by his own actions or through orders to subordinates, see Carter v. Estelle, 519 F.2d 1136 (5th Cir. 1975), impede communication between attorney and client by mail or in person where no immediate threat of disorder exists. Cf. Glasson v. City of Louisville, 518 F.2d 899 (6th Cir. 1975).

Under the Fourteenth Amendment, the arbitrary barring of an attorney from communicating with his proper clients is impermissible because it contravenes the attorney's right to procedural due process. In re Ruffalo, 390 U.S. 544, 43 Ohio Op.2d 459 (1968). Legal aid attorneys have a right to represent prisoner clients. Cf. Weintraub v. Adair, supra, 331 F.Supp. 148.

Thus, when a prison official impedes "attorney access," his actions must be subjected to rigorous scrutiny to afford proper protection to the First Amendment rights of communication of the attorney and his clients.

B. Violation of Plaintiff's Rights

Defendant Beto's actions, including the blanket exclusion of Mrs. Cruz on October 14, 1971, and the segregation thereafter imposed upon her prisoner clients do not survive such rigorous scrutiny on the facts of this case.

Defendant Beto's actions denied the prisoner-plaintiffs their right of access to the courts during the period in question and their right to receive effective legal assistance from the attorney of their choice. Defendant Beto's actions further denied the prisoner-plaintiffs the right to equal protection of the laws and to due process of law by subjecting them to discriminatory treatment and deprivation of normal prison privileges as a consequence of their remaining clients of Mrs. Cruz.

Defendant Beto by his actions denied Mrs. Cruz the right to practice her profession. He also violated her First and Fourteenth Amendment rights by denying her access to her clients and by then attempting thereafter to punish her and her clients for maintaining an appropriate attorney-client relationship.

The segregation policy fashioned and enforced by defendant Beto in the instant case in 1971 denied the prisoner-plaintiffs their right of access to the courts by unjustifiably obstructing such right of access. The implementation of this policy by defendant Beto's subordinates, at his direction, by means of threats, intimidation, coercion or punishment also violates this principle. Campbell v. Beto, 460 F.2d 765, 768 (5th Cir. 1972). Conditioning release from Eight Hoe Squad upon the relinquishment of Mrs. Cruz's representation illustrates the violation by means of unlawful intimidation. Depriving the prisoner-plaintiffs of opportunities to educate and rehabilitate themselves for failure to relinquish Mrs. Cruz's representation illustrates the violation by means of the unlawful punishment exacted in this case.

Defendant Beto's actions in restricting Mrs. Cruz's representation and in making costly the prisoner-plaintiffs' exercise of their choice of her as counsel impeded and infringed unjustifiably her exercise of her First Amendment rights. Plaintiffs have demonstrated that Mrs. Cruz's conduct in no way justified the sanctions imposed upon her by defendants.

On the other hand, defendants have failed to demonstrate: that Mrs. Cruz presented a threat to TDC administration of the prisons; that Mrs. Cruz organized or participated in a con-

spiracy among inmates to challenge TDC administration, cf. Dreyer v. Jalet, 349 F.Supp. 452 (S.D. Tex. 1972); or that the actions of defendant Beto were motivated in good faith or by a genuine concern for prisoner safety or prison security.

Rather, the evidence demonstrates that defendant Beto instituted reprisals against Mrs. Cruz and, by association, those prisoners including the prisoner-plaintiffs who were her clients, for reasons totally unrelated to considerations of proper prison administration. Such actions were taken in violation of Mrs. Cruz's constitutional rights. Defendant Beto did not act with good purpose and with a belief that he was doing right. Wood v. Strickland, 420 U.S. 308, 321 (1975).

C. Relief

Defendant Beto is liable in damages to the prisoner-plaintiffs in the total amount of $9,291.00. Findings of Fact, supra. Additionally, defendant Beto is liable in damages to Mrs. Cruz in the amount of $1,000.00. Defendant Estelle is not liable in damages for any amount.

The plaintiffs are entitled to declaratory and injunctive relief. Defendants are hereby enjoined from arbitrarily restricting the access of inmates to the courts; from restricting the access of any inmate to Mrs. Cruz as an attorney in person or by mail; from restricting Mrs. Cruz's visitation privileges at the TDC in any manner when she journeys to a prison unit to consult with a client in a lawful way; and from arbitrarily imposing upon any prisoner or group of prisoners a policy of segregation prompted solely as a means to punish their choice of legal representative.

In view of the arbitrary reduction by defendant Beto of the PIP point rating of each prisoner-plaintiff during the period in which the segregation policy was imposed, defendants hereafter shall not evaluate any prisoner-plaintiff's PIP record so as to penalize him during such period when evaluating his present and future eligibility for parole. Cf. Novak v. Beto, 453 F.2d 661, 664 (5th Cir. 1971) (restoring lost "good time").

The Court has canvassed available case authority in the Fifth Circuit and the Texas federal courts and concludes that this is the first case in which defendant Beto has ever been held liable in money damages for actions taken as Director of the TDC which violated the constitutional rights of inmates or an attorney. Cf. McManis, Personal Liability of State Officials Under State and Federal Law, 9 Ga.L.Rev. 821, 846 (1975) ("cases in which prisoners [in the Fifth Circuit] have recovery of damages have been few"). This situation is no doubt due in large part to defendant Beto's outstanding record as Director of the TDC, a tenure recognized for its high quality by the Court of Appeals. Novak v. Beto, supra, 453 F.2d at 666.

The plaintiffs have prevailed here because of the extraordinary nature of the facts and circumstances of this case. This Court has noted earlier in this opinion the highly unusual nature of this lawsuit and its counterpart, Dreyer v Jalet. Together these cases represent an unparalleled, indeed aberrant, episode in the administration of the TDC. Against this background, the unique circumstances which prompt the rewarding of money damages in this case should also operate to isolate it sufficiently so as to deprive it of significant precedential value.

CRUZ
v.
BETO

405 U.S. 319; 92 S. Ct. 1079;
31 L. Ed. 2d 263 (1972)

PER CURIAM

OPINION: The complaint, alleging a cause of action under 42 U.S.C. § 1983, states that Cruz is a Buddhist, who is in a Texas prison. While prisoners who are members of other religious sects are allowed to use the prison chapel, Cruz is not. He shared his Buddhist religious material with other prisoners and, according to the allegations, in retaliation was placed in solitary confinement on a diet of bread and water for two weeks, without access to newspapers, magazines, or other sources of news. He also alleged that he was prohibited from corresponding with his religious advisor in the Buddhist sect. Those in the isolation unit spend 22 hours a day in total idleness.

Again, according to the allegations, Texas encourages inmates to participate in other religious programs, providing at state expense chaplains of the Catholic, Jewish, and Protestant faiths; providing also at state expense copies of the Jewish and Christian Bibles, and conducting weekly Sunday school classes and religious services. According to the allegations, points of good merit are given prisoners as a reward for attending orthodox religious services, those points enhancing a prisoner's eligibility for desirable job assignments and early parole consideration. Respondent answered, denying the allegations and moving to dismiss.

The Federal District Court denied relief without a hearing or any findings, saying the complaint was in an area that should be left "to the sound discretion of prison administration." It went on to say, "Valid disciplinary and security reasons not known to this court may prevent the 'equality' of exercise of religious practices in prison." The Court of Appeals affirmed. 445 F.2d 801.

Federal courts sit not to supervise prisons but to enforce the constitutional rights of all "persons," including prisoners. We are not unmindful that prison officials must be accorded latitude in the administration of prison affairs, and that prisoners necessarily are subject to appropriate rules and regulations. But persons in prison, like other individuals, have the right to petition the Government for redress of grievances which, of course, includes "access of prisoners to the courts for the purpose of presenting their complaints." Johnson v. Avery, 393 U.S. 483, 485; Ex parte Hull, 312 U.S. 546, 549. See also Younger v. Gilmore, 404 U.S. 15, aff'g Gilmore v. Lynch, 319 F.Supp. 105 (ND Cal.). Moreover, racial segregation, which is unconstitutional outside prisons, is unconstitutional within prisons, save for "the necessities of prison security and discipline." Lee v. Washington, 390 U.S. 333, 334. Even more closely in point is Cooper v. Pate, 378 U.S. 546, where we reversed a dismissal of a complaint brought under 42 U.S.C. § 1983. We said: "Taking as true the allegations of the complaint, as they must be on a motion to dismiss, the complaint stated a cause of action." Ibid. The allegation made by that petitioner was that solely because of his religious beliefs he was denied permission to purchase certain religious publications and denied other privileges enjoyed by other prisoners.

We said in Conley v. Gibson, 355 U.S. 41, 45-46, that "a complaint should not be dismissed for failure to state a claim unless it appears beyond doubt that the plaintiff can prove no set of facts in support of his claim which would entitle him to relief." If Cruz was a Buddhist and if he was denied a reasonable opportunity of pursuing his faith comparable to the opportunity afforded fellow prisoners who adhere to conventional religious precepts, then there was palpable discrimination by the State against the Buddhist religion, established 600 B.C., long before the Christian era.[1] The First Amendment, applicable to the States by reason of the Fourteenth Amendment, Torcaso v. Watkins, 367 U.S. 488, 492-493, prohibits government from making a law "prohibiting the free exercise" of religion. If the allegations of this complaint are assumed to be true, as they must be on the motion to dismiss, Texas has violated the First and Fourteenth Amendments.

The motion for leave to proceed in forma pauperis is granted. The petition for certiorari is granted, the judgment is vacated, and the cause remanded for a hearing and appropriate findings.

So ordered.

* * *

MR. JUSTICE REHNQUIST, dissenting.

Unlike the Court, I am not persuaded that petitioner's complaint states a claim under the First Amendment, or that if the opinion of the Court of Appeals is vacated the trial court

---

[1] We do not suggest, of course, that every religious sect or group within a prison—however few in number—must have identical facilities or personnel. A special chapel or place of worship need not be provided for every faith regardless of size; nor must a chaplain, priest, or minister be provided without regard to the extent of the demand. But reasonable opportunities must be afforded to all prisoners to exercise the religious freedom guaranteed by the First and Fourteenth Amendments without fear of penalty.

must necessarily conduct a trial upon the complaint.

Under the First Amendment, of course, Texas may neither "establish a religion" nor may it "impair the free exercise" thereof. Petitioner alleges that voluntary services are made available at prison facilities so that Protestants, Catholics, and Jews may attend church services of their choice. None of our prior holdings indicates that such a program on the part of prison officials amounts to the establishment of a religion.

Petitioner is a prisoner serving 15 years for robbery in a Texas penitentiary. He is understandably not as free to practice his religion as if he were outside the prison walls. But there is no intimation in his pleadings that he is being punished for his religious views, as was the case in Cooper v. Pate, 378 U.S. 546 (1964), where a prisoner was denied the receipt of mail about his religion. Cooper presented no question of interference with prison administration of the type that would be involved here in retaining chaplains, scheduling the use of prison facilities, and timing the activities of various prisoners.

None of our holdings under the First Amendment requires that, in addition to being allowed freedom of religious belief, prisoners be allowed freely to evangelize their views among other prisoners. There is no indication in petitioner's complaint that the prison officials have dealt more strictly with his efforts to convert other convicts to Buddhism than with efforts of communicants of other faiths to make similar conversions.

By reason of his status, petitioner is obviously limited in the extent to which he may practice his religion. He is assuredly not free to attend the church of his choice outside the prison walls. But the fact that the Texas prison system offers no Buddhist services at this particular prison does not, under the circumstances pleaded in his complaint, demonstrate that his religious freedom is being impaired. Presumably prison officials are not obligated to provide facilities for any particular denominational services within a prison, although once they undertake to provide them for some they must make only such reasonable distinctions as may survive analysis under the Equal Protection Clause.

What petitioner's basic claim amounts to is that because prison facilities are provided for denominational services for religions with more numerous followers, the failure to provide prison facilities for Buddhist services amounts to a denial of the equal protection of the laws. There is no indication from petitioner's complaint how many practicing Buddhists there are in the particular prison facility in which he is incarcerated, nor is there any indication of the demand upon available facilities for other prisoner activities. Neither the decisions of this Court after full argument, nor those summarily reversing the dismissal of a prisoner's civil rights complaint have ever given full consideration to the proper balance to be struck between prisoners' rights and the extensive administrative discretion that must rest with correction officials. I would apply the rule of deference to administrative discretion that has been overwhelmingly accepted in the courts of appeals. Failing that, I would at least hear argument as to what rule should govern.

A long line of decisions by this Court has recognized that the "equal protection of the laws" guaranteed by the Fourteenth Amendment is not to be applied in a precisely equivalent way in the multitudinous fact situations that may confront the courts. On the one hand, we have held that racial classifications are "invidious" and "suspect." I think it quite consistent with the intent of the framers of the Fourteenth Amendment, many of whom would doubtless be surprised to know that convicts came within its ambit, to treat prisoner claims at the other end of the spectrum from claims of racial discrimination. Absent a complaint alleging facts showing that the difference in treatment between petitioner and his fellow Buddhists and practitioners of denominations with more numerous adherents could not reasonably be justified under any rational hypothesis, I would leave the matter in the hands of the prison officials.

* * *

BOUNDS
v.
SMITH

430 U.S. 817; 97 S. Ct. 1491;
52 L. Ed. 2d 72 (1977)

MR. JUSTICE MARSHALL delivered the opinion of the Court.

The issue in this case is whether States must protect the right of prisoners to access to the courts by providing them with law libraries or alternative sources of legal knowledge. In Younger v. Gilmore, 404 U.S. 15 (1971), we held per curiam that such services are constitutionally mandated. Petitioners, officials of the State of North Carolina, ask us to overrule that recent case, but for reasons explained below, we decline the invitation and reaffirm our previous decision.

I

Respondents are inmates incarcerated in correctional facilities of the Division of Prisons of the North Carolina Department of Correction. They filed three separate actions under 42 U.S.C. § 1983, all eventually consolidated in the District Court for the Eastern District of North Carolina. Respondents alleged, in pertinent part, that they were denied access to the courts in violation of their Fourteenth Amendment rights by the State's failure to provide legal research facilities.

The District Court granted respondents' motion for summary judgment on this claim, finding that the sole prison library in the State was "severely inadequate" and that there was no other legal assistance available to inmates. It held on the basis of Younger v. Gilmore that respondents' rights to access to the courts and equal protection of the laws had been violated because there was "no indication of any assistance at the initial stage of preparation of writs and petitions." The court recognized, however, that determining the "appropriate relief to be ordered . . . presents a difficult problem," in view of North Carolina's decentralized prison system. Rather than attempting "to dictate precisely what course the State should follow," the court "charge[d] the Department of Correction with the task of devising a Constitutionally sound program" to assure inmate access to the courts. It left to the State the choice of what alternative would "most easily and economically" fulfill this duty, suggesting that a program to make available lawyers, law students, or public defenders might serve the purpose at least as well as the provision of law libraries. Supp. App. 12-13. The suggestion that it be consolidated with the other two cases, then still pending in the District Court.

The State responded by proposing the establishment of seven libraries in institutions located across the State chosen so as to serve best all prison units. In addition, the State planned to set up smaller libraries in the Central Prison segregation unit and the Women's Prison. Under the plan, inmates desiring to use a library would request appointments. They would be given transportation and housing, if necessary, for a full day's library work. In addition to its collection of lawbooks, each library would stock legal forms and writing paper and have typewriters and use of copying machines. The State proposed to train inmates as research assistants and typists to aid fellow prisoners. It was estimated that ultimately some 350 inmates per week could use the libraries, although inmates not facing court deadlines might have to wait three or four weeks for their turn at a library. Respondents protested that the plan was totally inadequate and sought establishment of a library at every prison.

The District Court rejected respondents' objections, finding the State's plan "both economically feasible and practicable," and one that, fairly and efficiently run would "insure each inmate the time to prepare his petitions. . . ."

* * *

Both sides appealed from those portions of the District Court orders adverse to them. The Court of Appeals for the Fourth Circuit affirmed in all respects save one. It found that the library plan denied women prisoners

the same access rights as men to research facilities. Since there was no justification for this discrimination, the Court of Appeals ordered it eliminated. The State petitioned for review and we granted certiorari. 425 U.S. 910 (1976). We affirm.

II

A. It is now established beyond doubt that prisoners have a constitutional right of access to the courts. This Court recognized that right more than 35 years ago when it struck down a regulation prohibiting state prisoners from filing petitions for habeas corpus unless they were found "properly drawn" by the "legal investigator" for the parole board. Ex parte Hull, 312 U.S. 546 (1941). We held this violated the principle that "the state and its officers may not abridge or impair petitioner's right to apply to a federal court for a writ of habeas corpus." Id., at 549. See also Cochran v. Kansas, 316 U.S. 255 (1942).

More recent decisions have struck down restrictions and required remedial measures to insure that inmate access to the courts is adequate, effective, and meaningful. Thus, in order to prevent "effectively foreclosed access," indigent prisoners must be allowed to file appeals and habeas corpus petitions without payment of docket fees. Burns v. Ohio, 360 U.S. 252, 257 (1959); Smith v. Bennett, 365 U.S. 708 (1961). Because we recognized that "adequate and effective appellate review" is impossible without a trial transcript or adequate substitute, we held that States must provide trial records to inmates unable to buy them. Griffin v. Illinois, 351 U.S. 12, 20 (1956). Similarly, counsel must be appointed to give indigent inmates "a meaningful appeal" from their convictions. Douglas v. California, 372 U.S. 353, 358 (1963).

Essentially the same standards of access were applied in Johnson v. Avery, 393 U.S. 483 (1969), which struck down a regulation prohibiting prisoners from assisting each other with habeas corpus applications and other legal matters. Since inmates had no alternative form of legal assistance available to them, we reasoned that this ban on jailhouse lawyers effectively prevented prisoners who were "unable themselves, with reasonable adequacy, to prepare their petitions," from challenging the legality of their confinements. Id., at 489. Johnson was unanimously extended to cover assistance in civil rights actions in Wolff v. McDonnell, 418 U.S. 539, 577-580 (1974). And even as it rejected a claim that indigent defendants have a constitutional right to appointed counsel for discretionary appeals, the Court reaffirmed that States must "assure the indigent defendant an adequate opportunity to present his claims fairly." Ross v. Moffitt, 417 U.S., at 616. "[M]eaningful access" to the courts is the touchstone. See id., at 611, 612, 615.

Petitioners contend, however, that this constitutional duty merely obliges States to allow inmate "writ writers" to function. They argue that under Johnson v. Avery, supra, as long as inmate communications on legal problems are not restricted, there is no further obligation to expend state funds to implement affirmatively the right of access. This argument misreads the cases.

* * *

Moreover, our decisions have consistently required States to shoulder affirmative obligations to assure all prisoners meaningful access to the courts. It is indisputable that indigent inmates must be provided at state expense with paper and pen to draft legal documents, with notarial services to authenticate them, and with stamps to mail them. States must forgo collection of docket fees otherwise payable to the treasury and expend funds for transcripts. State expenditures are necessary to pay lawyers for indigent defendants at trial, Gideon v. Wainwright, 372 U.S. 335 (1963); Argersinger v. Hamlin, 407 U.S. 25 (1972), and in appeals as of right, Douglas v. California, supra. This is not to say that economic factors may not be considered, for example, in choosing the methods used to provide meaningful access. But the cost of protecting a constitutional right cannot justify its total denial. Thus, neither the availability of jailhouse lawyers nor the necessity for affirmative state action is dispositive of respondents' claims. The inquiry is rather whether law libraries or other forms of legal assistance are needed to give prisoners a reasonably adequate opportunity to present claimed violations of fundamental constitutional rights to the courts.

* * *

We reject the State's claim that inmates are "ill-equipped to use" "the tools of the trade of the legal profession," making libraries useless in assuring meaningful access. Brief for Petitioners 17. In the first place, the claim is inconsistent with the State's representations on its LEAA grant application, supra, at 821, and with its argument that access is adequately protected by allowing inmates to help each other with legal problems. More importantly, this Court's experience indicates that pro se petitioners are capable of using lawbooks to file cases raising claims that are serious and legitimate even if ultimately unsuccessful. Finally, we note that if petitioners had any doubts about the efficacy of libraries, the District Court's initial decision left them free to choose another means of assuring access.

* * *

We hold, therefore, that the fundamental constitutional right of access to the courts requires prison authorities to assist inmates in the preparation and filing of meaningful legal papers by providing prisoners with adequate law libraries or adequate assistance from persons trained in the law.

* * *

It should be noted that while adequate law libraries are one constitutionally acceptable method to assure meaningful access to the courts, our decision here, as in Gilmore, does not foreclose alternative means to achieve that goal. Nearly half the States and the District of Columbia provide some degree of professional or quasi-professional legal assistance to prisoners. Brief for Respondents, Ex. B. Such programs take many imaginative forms and may have a number of advantages over libraries alone. Among the alternatives are the training of inmates as paralegal assistants to work under lawyers' supervision, the use of paraprofessionals and law students, either as volunteers or in formal clinical programs, the organization of volunteer attorneys through bar associations or other groups, the hiring of lawyers on a part-time consultant basis, and the use of full-time staff attorneys, working either in new prison legal assistance organizations or as part of public defender or legal services offices. Legal services plans not only result in more efficient and skillful handling of prisoner cases, but also avoid the disciplinary problems associated with writ writers, see Johnson v. Avery, 393 U.S., at 488; Procunier v. Martinez, 416 U.S. 396, 421-422 (1974). Independent legal advisors can mediate or resolve administratively many prisoner complaints that would otherwise burden the courts, and can convince inmates that other grievances against the prison or the legal system are ill-founded, thereby facilitating rehabilitation by assuring the inmate that he has not been treated unfairly. It has been estimated that as few as 500 full-time lawyers would be needed to serve the legal needs of the entire national prison population. Nevertheless, a legal access program need not include any particular element we have discussed, and we encourage local experimentation. Any plan, however, must be evaluated as a whole to ascertain its compliance with constitutional standards.

* * *

The judgment is

Affirmed.

MURRAY
v.
GIARRATANO

492 U.S. 1; 109 S. Ct. 2765; 106 L. Ed. 2d 1 (1989)

CHIEF JUSTICE REHNQUIST announced the judgment of the Court and delivered an opinion, in which JUSTICE WHITE, JUSTICE O'CONNOR, and JUSTICE SCALIA join.

Virginia death row inmates brought a civil rights suit against various officials of the Commonwealth of Virginia. The prisoners claimed, based on several theories, that the Constitution required that they be provided with counsel at the Commonwealth's expense for the purpose of pursuing collateral proceedings related to their convictions and sentences. The courts below ruled that appointment of counsel upon request was necessary for the prisoners to enjoy their constitutional right to access to the courts in pursuit of state habeas corpus relief. We think this holding is inconsistent with our decision two Terms ago in Pennsylvania v. Finley, 481 U.S. 551 (1987), and rests on a misreading of our decision in Bounds v. Smith, 430 U.S. 817 (1977).

* * *

In Finley we ruled that neither the Due Process Clause of the Fourteenth Amendment nor the equal protection guarantee of "meaningful access" required the State to appoint counsel for indigent prisoners seeking state postconviction relief. The Sixth and Fourteenth Amendments to the Constitution assure the right of an indigent defendant to counsel at the trial stage of a criminal proceeding, Gideon v. Wainwright, 372 U.S. 335 (1963), and an indigent defendant is similarly entitled as a matter of right to counsel for an initial appeal from the judgment and sentence of the trial court. Douglas v. California, 372 U.S. 353 (1963); Griffin v. Illinois, 351 U.S. 12 (1956). But we held in Ross v. Moffitt, supra, at 610, that the right to counsel at these earlier stages of a criminal procedure did not carry over to a discretionary appeal provided by North Carolina law from the intermediate appellate court to the Supreme Court of North Carolina. We contrasted the trial stage of a criminal proceeding, where the State by presenting witnesses and arguing to a jury attempts to strip from the defendant the presumption of innocence and convict him of a crime, with the appellate stage of such a proceeding, where the defendant needs an attorney "not as a shield to protect him against being 'haled into court' by the State and stripped of his presumption of innocence, but rather as a sword to upset the prior determination of guilt." 417 U.S., at 610-611.

We held in Finley that the logic of Ross v. Moffitt required the conclusion that there was no federal constitutional right to counsel for indigent prisoners seeking state postconviction relief: "Postconviction relief is even further removed from the criminal trial than is discretionary direct review. It is not part of the criminal proceeding itself, and it is in fact considered to be civil in nature. See Fay v. Noia, 372 U.S. 391, 423-424 (1963). . . . States have no obligation to provide this avenue of relief, cf. United States v. MacCollom, 426 U.S. 317, 323 (1976) (plurality opinion), and when they do, the fundamental fairness mandated by the Due Process Clause does not require that the state supply a lawyer as well." 481 U.S., at 556-557.

* * *

The Court of Appeals, . . . relied on what it perceived as a tension between the rule in Finley and the implication of our decision in Bounds v. Smith, 430 U.S. 817 (1977); we find no such tension. Whether the right of access at issue in Bounds is primarily one of due process or equal protection, in either case it rests on a constitutional theory considered in Finley. The Court held in Bounds that a prisoner's "right of access" to the courts required a State to furnish access to adequate law libraries in order that the prisoners might prepare petitions for judicial relief. Bounds, supra, at 828. But it would be a strange jurisprudence that permitted the extension of that holding to partially overrule a subsequently decided case such as Finley which held that prisoners seeking judicial relief from their sentence in state proceedings were not entitled to counsel.

It would be an even stranger jurisprudence to allow, as the dissent would, the "right of access" involved in Bounds v. Smith, supra, to partially overrule Pennsylvania v. Finley, based on "factual" findings of a particular district court regarding matters such as the perceived difficulty of capital sentencing law and the general psychology of death row inmates. Treating such matters as "factual findings," presumably subject only to review under the "clearly-erroneous" standard, would permit a different constitutional rule to apply in a different State if the district judge hearing that claim reached different conclusions. Our cases involving the right to counsel have never taken this tack; they have been categorical holdings as to what the Constitution requires with respect to a particular stage of a criminal proceeding in general. See Powell v. Alabama, 287

U.S. 45 (1932); Griffin v. Illinois, 351 U.S. 12 (1956); Gideon v. Wainwright, 372 U.S. 335 (1963); Douglas v. California, 372 U.S. 353 (1963); Ross v. Moffitt, 417 U.S. 600 (1974); Pennsylvania v. Finley, 481 U.S. 551 (1987). Indeed, as the dissent itself points out, post, at 17, and n. 2, it was the Court's dissatisfaction with the case-by-case approach of Betts v. Brady, 316 U.S. 455 (1942), that led to the adoption of the categorical rule requiring appointed counsel for indigent felony defendants in Gideon.

There is no inconsistency whatever between the holding of Bounds and the holding in Finley; the holding of neither case squarely decides the question presented in this case. For the reasons previously stated in this opinion, we now hold that Finley applies to those inmates under sentence of death as well as to other inmates, and that holding necessarily imposes limits on Bounds.

* * *

The judgment of the Court of Appeals is

Reversed.

JUSTICE O'CONNOR concurring.

I join in The Chief Justice's opinion. As his opinion demonstrates, there is nothing in the Constitution or the precedents of this Court that requires that a State provide counsel in postconviction proceedings. A postconviction proceeding is not part of the criminal process itself, but is instead a civil action designed to overturn a presumptively valid criminal judgment. Nothing in the Constitution requires the States to provide such proceedings, see Pennsylvania v. Finley, 481 U.S. 551 (1987), nor does it seem to me that the Constitution requires the States to follow any particular federal model in those proceedings. I also join in Justice Kennedy's opinion concurring in the judgment, since I do not view it as inconsistent with the principles expressed above. As Justice Kennedy observes, our decision in Bounds v. Smith, 430 U.S. 817 (1977), allows the States considerable discretion in assuring that those imprisoned in their jails obtain meaningful access to the judicial process. Beyond the requirements of Bounds, the matter is one of legislative choice based on difficult policy considerations and the allocation of scarce legal resources. Our decision today rightly leaves these issues to resolution by Congress and the state legislatures.

JUSTICE KENNEDY, with whom JUSTICE O'CONNOR joins, concurring in the judgment.

It cannot be denied that collateral relief proceedings are a central part of the review process for prisoners sentenced to death. As Justice Stevens observes, a substantial proportion of these prisoners succeed in having their death sentences vacated in habeas corpus proceedings. Post, at 23-24, and n. 13. The complexity of our jurisprudence in this area, moreover, makes it unlikely that capital defendants will be able to file successful petitions for collateral relief without the assistance of persons learned in the law.

The requirement of meaningful access can be satisfied in various ways, however. This was made explicit in our decision in Bounds v. Smith, 430 U.S. 817 (1977). The intricacies and range of options are of sufficient complexity that state legislatures and prison administrators must be given "wide discretion" to select appropriate solutions. Id., at 833. Indeed, judicial imposition of a categorical remedy such as that adopted by the court below might pretermit other responsible solutions being considered in Congress and state legislatures. Assessments of the difficulties presented by collateral litigation in capital cases are now being conducted by committees of the American Bar Association and the Judicial Conference of the United States, and Congress has stated its intention to give the matter serious consideration. See 134 Cong. Rec. 33237 (1988) (providing for expedited consideration of proposals of the Judicial Conference committee).

Unlike Congress, this Court lacks the capacity to undertake the searching and comprehensive review called for in this area, for we can decide only the case before us. While Virginia has not adopted procedures for securing representation that are as far reaching and effective as those available in other States, no prisoner on death row in Virginia has been unable to obtain counsel to repre-

sent him in postconviction proceedings, and Virginia's prison system is staffed with institutional lawyers to assist in preparing petitions for postconviction relief. I am not prepared to say that this scheme violates the Constitution.

On the facts and record of this case, I concur in the judgment of the Court.

JUSTICE STEVENS, with whom JUSTICE BRENNAN, JUSTICE MARSHALL, and JUSTICE BLACKMUN join, dissenting.

Two Terms ago this Court reaffirmed that the Fourteenth Amendment to the Federal Constitution obligates a State "to assure the indigent defendant an adequate opportunity to present his claims fairly in the context of the State's appellate process." Pennsylvania v. Finley, 481 U.S. 551, 556 (1987) (quoting Ross v. Moffitt, 417 U.S. 600, 616 (1974)). The narrow question presented is whether that obligation includes appointment of counsel for indigent death row inmates who wish to pursue state postconviction relief. Viewing the facts in light of our precedents, we should answer that question in the affirmative.

I

The parties before us, like the Court of Appeals en banc and the District Court below, have accorded controlling importance to our decision in Bounds v. Smith, 430 U.S. 817 (1977). In that case, inmates had alleged that North Carolina violated the Fourteenth Amendment by failing to provide research facilities to help them prepare habeas corpus petitions and federal civil rights complaints. Stressing "meaningful" access to the courts as a "touchstone," id., at 823, we held:

[T]he fundamental constitutional right of access to the courts requires prison authorities to assist inmates in the preparation and filing of meaningful legal papers by providing prisoners with adequate law libraries or adequate assistance from persons trained in the law.

Far from creating a discrete constitutional right, Bounds constitutes one part of a jurisprudence that encompasses "right-to-counsel" as well as "access-to-courts" cases. Although each case is shaped by its facts, all share a concern, based upon the Fourteenth Amendment, that accused and convicted persons be permitted to seek legal remedies without arbitrary governmental interference.

* * *

I respectfully dissent.

CASEY
v.
LEWIS

518 U.S. 343 (1996)

[Most citations and footnotes omitted]

[The dissenting and concurring opinions of Justices Stevens, Souter, Ginsburg, and Breyer have been deleted]

JUSTICE SCALIA delivered the opinion of the Court.

In Bounds v. Smith, 430 U.S. 817 (1977), we held that "the fundamental constitutional right of access to the courts requires prison authorities to assist inmates in the preparation and filing of meaningful legal papers by providing prisoners with adequate law libraries or adequate assistance from persons trained in the law." Petitioners, who are officials of the Arizona Department of Corrections (ADOC), contend that the United States District Court for the District of Arizona erred in finding them in violation of Bounds, and that the court's remedial order exceeded lawful authority.

I

Respondents are 22 inmates of various prisons operated by ADOC. In January 1990, they filed this class action "on behalf of all adult prisoners who are or will be incarcerated by the State of Arizona Department of Corrections," alleging that petitioners were "depriving [respondents] of their rights of access to the courts and counsel protected by the First, Sixth, and Fourteenth Amendments." Following a 3-month bench trial, the District Court ruled in favor of respondents,

finding that "prisoners have a constitutional right of access to the courts that is adequate, effective and meaningful," and that "[ADOC's] system fails to comply with constitutional standards." The court identified a variety of shortcomings of the ADOC system, in matters ranging from the training of library staff, to the updating of legal materials, to the availability of photocopying services. In addition to these general findings, the court found that two groups of inmates were particularly affected by the system's inadequacies: "lockdown prisoners" (inmates segregated from the general prison population for disciplinary or security reasons), who "are routinely denied physical access to the law library" and "experience severe interference with their access to the courts," and illiterate or non-English-speaking inmates, who do not receive adequate legal assistance.

Having thus found liability, the court appointed a special master "to investigate and report about" the appropriate relief—that is (in the court's view), "how best to accomplish the goal of constitutionally adequate inmate access to the courts." Following eight months of investigation, and some degree of consultation with both parties, the special master lodged with the court a proposed permanent injunction, which the court proceeded to adopt, substantially unchanged. The 25-page injunctive order, mandated sweeping changes designed to ensure that ADOC would "provide meaningful access to the Courts for all present and future prisoners." It specified in minute detail the times that libraries were to be kept open, the number of hours of library use to which each inmate was entitled (10 per week), the minimal educational requirements for prison librarians (a library science degree, law degree or paralegal degree), the content of a videotaped legal-research course for inmates (to be prepared by persons appointed by the special master but funded by ADOC) and similar matters. The injunction addressed the court's concern for lockdown prisoners by ordering that "ADOC prisoners in all housing areas and custody levels shall be provided regular and comparable visits to the law library," except that such visits "may be postponed on an individual basis because of the prisoner's documented inability to use the law library without creating a threat to safety or security, or a physical condition if determined by medical personnel to prevent library use." With respect to illiterate and non-English-speaking inmates, the injunction declared that they were entitled to "direct assistance" from lawyers, paralegals or "a sufficient number of at least minimally trained prisoner Legal Assistants"; it enjoined ADOC that "particular steps must be taken to locate and train bilingual prisoners to be Legal Assistants."

* * *

II

Although petitioners present only one question for review, namely whether the District Court's order "exceeds the constitutional requirements set forth in Bounds," they raise several distinct challenges, including renewed attacks on the court's findings of Bounds violations with respect to illiterate, non-English-speaking and lockdown prisoners, and on the breadth of the injunction. But their most fundamental contention is that the District Court's findings of injury were inadequate to justify the finding of system wide injury and hence the granting of system-wide relief. This argument has two related components. First, petitioners claim that in order to establish a violation of Bounds, an inmate must show that the alleged inadequacies of a prison's library facilities or legal assistance program caused him "actual injury"—that is, "actual prejudice with respect to contemplated or existing litigation, such as the inability to meet a filing deadline or to present a claim." Second, they claim that the District Court did not find enough instances of actual injury to warrant system wide relief. We agree that the success of respondents' systemic challenge was dependent on their ability to show widespread actual injury, and that the court's failure to identify anything more than isolated instances of actual injury renders its finding of a systemic Bounds violation invalid.

A

The requirement that an inmate alleging a violation of Bounds must show actual injury derives ultimately from the doctrine of stand-

ing, a constitutional principle that prevents courts of law from undertaking tasks assigned to the political branches. It is the role of courts to provide relief to claimants, in individual or class actions, who have suffered, or will imminently suffer, actual harm; it is not the role of courts, but that of the political branches, to shape the institutions of government in such fashion as to comply with the laws and the Constitution. In the context of the present case: It is for the courts to remedy past or imminent official interference with individual inmates' presentation of claims to the courts; it is for the political branches of the State and Federal Governments to manage prisons in such fashion that official interference with the presentation of claims will not occur. Of course the two roles briefly and partially coincide when a court, in granting relief against actual harm that has been suffered, or that will imminently be suffered, by a particular individual or class of individuals, orders the alteration of an institutional organization or procedure that causes the harm. But the distinction between the two roles would be obliterated if, to invoke intervention of the courts, no actual or imminent harm were needed, but merely the status of being subject to a governmental institution that was not organized or managed properly. If—to take another example from prison life—a healthy inmate who had suffered no deprivation of needed medical treatment were able to claim violation of his constitutional right to medical care, see *Estelle v. Gamble, 429 U.S. 97 (1976),* simply on the ground that the prison medical facilities were inadequate, the essential distinction between judge and executive would have disappeared: it would have become the function of the courts to assure adequate medical care in prisons.

The foregoing analysis would not be pertinent here if, as respondents seem to assume, the right at issue—the right to which the actual or threatened harm must pertain—were the right to a law library or to legal assistance. But Bounds established no such right, any more than Estelle established a right to a prison hospital. The right that Bounds acknowledged was the (already well-established) right of access to the courts. In the cases to which Bounds traced its roots, we had protected that right by prohibiting

State prison officials from actively interfering with inmates' attempts to prepare legal documents, or file them, and by requiring state courts to waive filing fees, or transcript fees for indigent inmates. Bounds focused on the same entitlement of access to the courts. Although it affirmed a court order requiring North Carolina to make law library facilities available to inmates, it stressed that that was merely "one constitutionally acceptable method to assure meaningful access to the courts," and that "our decision here . . . does not foreclose alternative means to achieve that goal. In other words, prison law libraries and legal assistance programs are not ends in themselves, but only the means for ensuring "a reasonably adequate opportunity to present claimed violations of fundamental constitutional rights to the courts."

Because Bounds did not create an abstract, free-standing right to a law library or legal assistance, an inmate cannot establish relevant actual injury simply by establishing that his prison's law library or legal assistance program is sub-par in some theoretical sense. That would be the precise analogue of the healthy inmate claiming constitutional violation because of the inadequacy of the prison infirmary. Insofar as the right vindicated by Bounds is concerned, "meaningful access to the courts is the touchstone," and the inmate therefore must go one step further and demonstrate that the alleged shortcomings in the library or legal assistance program hindered his efforts to pursue a legal claim. He might show, for example, that a complaint he prepared was dismissed for failure to satisfy some technical requirement which, because of deficiencies in the prison's legal assistance facilities, he could not have known. Or that he had suffered arguably actionable harm that he wished to bring before the courts, but was so stymied by inadequacies of the law library that he was unable even to file a complaint.

Although Bounds itself made no mention of an actual-injury requirement, it can hardly be thought to have eliminated that constitutional prerequisite. And actual injury is apparent on the face of almost all the opinions in the 35-year line of access-to-courts cases on which Bounds relied. Moreover, the assumption of an actual-injury requirement seems to us implicit in the opinion's statement that "we encourage local experimentation" in various methods of assuring access to the courts. One such experiment, for example, might replace libraries with some minimal access to legal advice and a system of court-provided forms such as those that contained the original complaints in two of the more significant inmate-initiated cases in recent years, Sandin v. Conner and Hudson v. McMillian, forms that asked the inmates to provide only the facts and not to attempt any legal analysis. We hardly think that what we meant by "experimenting" with such an alternative was simply announcing it, whereupon suit would immediately lie to declare it theoretically inadequate and bring the experiment to a close. We think we envisioned, instead, that the new program would remain in place at least until some inmate could demonstrate that a non-frivolous legal claim had been frustrated or was being impeded.

It must be acknowledged that several statements in Bounds went beyond the right of access recognized in the earlier cases on which it relied, which was a right to bring to court a grievance that the inmate wished to present. These statements appear to suggest that the State must enable the prisoner to discover grievances, and to litigate effectively once in court. These elaborations upon the right of access to the courts have no antecedent in our pre-Bounds cases, and we now disclaim them. To demand the conferral of such sophisticated legal capabilities upon a mostly uneducated and indeed largely illiterate prison population is effectively to demand permanent provision of counsel, which we do not believe the Constitution requires.

Finally, we must observe that the injury requirement is not satisfied by just any type of frustrated legal claim. Nearly all of the access-to-courts cases in the Bounds line involved attempts by inmates to pursue direct appeals from the convictions for which they were incarcerated, or habeas petitions, we extended this universe of relevant claims only slightly, to "civil rights actions"—i.e., actions under 42 U.S.C. § 1983 to vindicate "basic constitutional rights." Significantly, we felt compelled to justify even this slight extension of the right of access to the courts, stressing that "the demarcation line between civil rights actions and habeas petitions is not always clear," and that "it is futile to contend that the Civil Rights Act of 1871 has less importance in our constitutional scheme than does the Great Writ." The prison law library imposed in Bounds itself was far from an all-subject facility. In rejecting the contention that the State's proposed collection was inadequate, the District Court there said: "This Court does not feel inmates need the entire U.S. Code Annotated. Most of that code deals with federal laws and regulations that would never involve a state prisoner. . . . It is also the opinion of this Court that the cost of N.C. Digest and Modern Federal Practice Digest will surpass the usefulness of these research aids. They cover mostly areas not of concern to inmates."

In other words, Bounds does not guarantee inmates the wherewithal to transform themselves into litigating engines capable of filing everything from shareholder derivative actions to slip-and-fall claims. The tools it requires to be provided are those that the inmates need in order to attack their sentences, directly or collaterally, and in order to challenge the conditions of their confinement. Impairment of any other litigating capacity is simply one of the incidental (and perfectly constitutional) consequences of conviction and incarceration.

B

Here the District Court identified only two instances of actual injury. In describing ADOC's failures with respect to illiterate and non-English-speaking prisoners, it found that "as a result of the inability to receive adequate legal assistance, prisoners who are slow readers have had their cases dismissed with prejudice," and that "other prisoners have been unable to file legal actions." Although the use of the plural suggests that several prisoners sustained these actual harms, the court identified only one prisoner in each instance.

Petitioners contend that "any lack of access experienced by these two inmates is not attributable to unconstitutional State policies," because ADOC "has met its constitutional obligations." The claim appears to be that all inmates, including the illiterate and non-English-speaking, have a right to nothing more than "physical access to excellent libraries, plus help from legal assistants and

law clerks." This misreads Bounds, which as we have said guarantees no particular methodology but rather the conferral of a capability—the capability of bringing contemplated challenges to sentences or conditions of confinement before the courts. When any inmate, even an illiterate or non-English-speaking inmate, shows that an actionable claim of this nature which he desired to bring has been lost or rejected, or that the presentation of such a claim is currently being prevented, because this capability of filing suit has not been provided, he demonstrates that the State has failed to furnish "adequate law libraries or adequate assistance from persons trained in the law." Of course, we leave it to prison officials to determine how best to ensure that inmates with language problems have a reasonably adequate opportunity to file non-frivolous legal claims challenging their convictions or conditions of confinement. But it is that capability, rather than the capability of turning pages in a law library, that is the touchstone.

C

Having rejected petitioners' argument that the injuries suffered by Bartholic and Harris do not count, we turn to the question whether those injuries, and the other findings of the District Court, support the injunction ordered in this case. The actual-injury requirement would hardly serve the purpose we have described above—of preventing courts from undertaking tasks assigned to the political branches—if once a plaintiff demonstrated harm from one particular inadequacy in government administration, the court were authorized to remedy all inadequacies in that administration. The remedy must of course be limited to the inadequacy that produced the injury-in-fact that the plaintiff has established.

This is no less true with respect to class actions than with respect to other suits. "That a suit may be a class action, . . . adds nothing to the question of standing, for even named plaintiffs who represent a class 'must allege and show that they personally have been injured, not that injury has been suffered by other, unidentified members of the class to which they belong and which they purport to represent.' " The general allegations of the complaint in the present case may well have sufficed to claim injury by named plaintiffs, and hence standing to demand remediation, with respect to various alleged inadequacies in the prison system, including failure to provide adequate legal assistance to non-English-speaking inmates and lockdown prisoners. That point is irrelevant now, however, for we are beyond the pleading stage.

* * *

After the trial in this case, the court found actual injury on the part of only one named plaintiff, Bartholic; and the cause of that injury—the inadequacy which the suit empowered the court to remedy—was failure of the prison to provide the special services that Bartholic would have needed, in light of his illiteracy, to avoid dismissal of his case. At the outset, therefore, we can eliminate from the proper scope of this injunction provisions directed at special services or special facilities required by non-English-speakers, by prisoners in lockdown, and by the inmate population at large. If inadequacies of this character exist, they have not been found to have harmed any plaintiff in this lawsuit, and hence were not the proper object of this District Court's remediation.

As to remediation of the inadequacy that caused Bartholic's injury, a further question remains: Was that inadequacy widespread enough to justify system wide relief? The only findings supporting the proposition that, in all of ADOC's facilities, an illiterate inmate wishing to file a claim would be unable to receive the assistance necessary to do so were (1) the finding with respect to Bartholic, at the Florence facility, and (2) the finding that Harris, while incarcerated at Perryville, had once been "unable to file [a] legal action." These two instances were a patently inadequate basis for a conclusion of system wide violation and imposition of system wide relief.

To be sure, the District Court also noted that "the trial testimony . . . indicated that there are prisoners who are unable to research the law because of their functional illiteracy." As we have discussed, however, the Constitution does not require that prisoners (literate or illiterate) be able to conduct generalized research, but only that they be able to present their grievances to the

courts—a more limited capability that can be produced by a much more limited degree of legal assistance. Apart from the dismissal of Bartholic's claim with prejudice, and Harris's inability to file his claim, there is no finding, and as far as we can discern from the record no evidence, that in Arizona prisons illiterate prisoners cannot obtain the minimal help necessary to file particular claims that they wish to bring before the courts. The constitutional violation has not been shown to be system wide, and granting a remedy beyond what was necessary to provide relief to Harris and Bartholic was therefore improper.

III

There are further reasons why the order here cannot stand. We held in *Turner v. Safley,* that a prison regulation impinging on inmates' constitutional rights "is valid if it is reasonably related to legitimate penological interests." Such a deferential standard is necessary, we explained,

> if 'prison administrators . . ., and not the courts, [are] to make the difficult judgments concerning institutional operations.' Subjecting the day-to-day judgments of prison officials to an inflexible strict-scrutiny analysis would seriously hamper their ability to anticipate security problems and to adopt innovative solutions to the intractable problems of prison administration.

These are the same concerns that led us to encourage "local experimentation" in Bounds, and we think it quite obvious that Bounds and Turner must be read in pari materia.

The District Court here failed to accord adequate deference to the judgment of the prison authorities in at least three significant respects. First, in concluding that ADOC's restrictions on lockdown prisoners' access to law libraries were unjustified. Turner's principle of deference has special force with regard to that issue, since the inmates in lockdown include "the most dangerous and violent prisoners in the Arizona prison system," and other inmates presenting special disciplinary and security concerns. The District Court made much of the fact that lockdown prisoners routinely experience delays in receiving legal materials or legal assistance, some as long as 16 days, but so long as they are the product of prison regulations reasonably related to legitimate penological interests, such delays are not of constitutional significance, even where they result in actual injury (which, of course, the District Court did not find here).

Second, the injunction imposed by the District Court was inordinately—indeed, wildly—intrusive. There is no need to belabor this point. One need only read the order, to appreciate that it is the ne plus ultra of what our opinions have lamented as a court's "in the name of the Constitution, becoming . . . enmeshed in the minutiae of prison operations."

Finally, the order was developed through a process that failed to give adequate consideration to the views of state prison authorities. We have said that "the strong considerations of comity that require giving a state court system that has convicted a defendant the first opportunity to correct its own errors . . . also require giving the States the first opportunity to correct errors made in the internal administration of their prisons." *Preiser v. Rodriguez.* For an illustration of the proper procedure in a case such as this, we need look no further than Bounds itself. There, after granting summary judgment for the inmates, the District Court refrained from "dictating precisely what course the State should follow." Rather, recognizing that "determining the 'appropriate relief to be ordered . . . presents a difficult problem,'" the court " 'charged the Department of Correction with the task of devising a Constitutionally sound program' to assure inmate access to the courts." State responded with a proposal, which the District Court ultimately approved with minor changes, after considering objections raised by the inmates. We praised this procedure, observing that the court had "scrupulously respected the limits on [its] role," by "not . . . thrusting itself into prison administration" and instead permitting "prison administrators [to] exercise wide discretion within the bounds of constitutional requirements."

As Bounds was an exemplar of what should be done, this case is a model of what should not. The District Court totally failed to heed the admonition of Preiser. Having found a violation of the right of access to the

courts, it conferred upon its special master, a law professor from Flushing, New York, rather than upon ADOC officials, the responsibility for devising a remedial plan. To make matters worse, it severely limited the remedies that the master could choose. Because, in the court's view, its order in an earlier access-to-courts case (an order that adopted the recommendations of the same special master) had "resolved successfully" most of the issues involved in this litigation, the court instructed that as to those issues it would implement the earlier order statewide, "with any modifications that the parties and Special Master determine are necessary due to the particular circumstances of the prison facility." This will not do. The State was entitled to far more than an opportunity for rebuttal, and on that ground alone this order would have to be set aside.

For the foregoing reasons, we reverse the judgment of the Court of Appeals and remand the case for further proceedings consistent with this opinion. It is so ordered.

JUSTICE THOMAS, concurring.

* * *

I write separately to make clear my doubts about the validity of Bounds and to reiterate my observation in *Missouri v. Jenkins*, 515 U.S. ___ (1995), that the federal judiciary has for the last half-century been exercising "equitable" powers and issuing structural decrees entirely out of line with its constitutional mandate.

I

A

This case is not about a right of "access to the courts." There is no proof that Arizona has prevented even a single inmate from filing a civil rights lawsuit or submitting a petition for a writ of habeas corpus. Instead, this case is about the extent to which the Constitution requires a State to finance or otherwise assist a prisoner's efforts to bring suit against the State and its officials.

In *Bounds v. Smith,* we recognized for the first time a "fundamental constitutional right" of all inmates to have the State "assist [them] in the preparation and filing of meaningful legal papers." We were not explicit as to the forms the State's assistance must take, but we did hold that, at a minimum, States must furnish prisoners "with adequate law libraries or adequate assistance from persons trained in the law." Ibid. Although our cases prior to Bounds occasionally referenced a constitutional right of access to the courts, we had never before recognized a freestanding constitutional right that requires the States to "shoulder affirmative obligations," in order to "insure that inmate access to the courts is adequate, effective, and meaningful."

Recognition of such broad and novel principles of constitutional law are rare enough under our system of law that I would have expected the Bounds Court to explain at length the constitutional basis for the right to state-provided legal materials and legal assistance. But the majority opinion in Bounds failed to identify a single provision of the Constitution to support the right created in that case, a fact that did not go unnoticed in strong dissents by Chief Justice Burger and then-Justice Rehnquist. . . . The dissents' call for an explanation as to which provision of the Constitution guarantees prisoners a right to consult a law library or a legal assistant, however, went unanswered. This is perhaps not surprising: just three years before Bounds was decided we admitted that the "the precise rationale" for many of the "access to the courts" cases on which Bounds relied had "never been explicitly stated," and that no Clause that had thus far been advanced "by itself provides an entirely satisfactory basis for the result reached."

The weakness in the Court's constitutional analysis in Bounds is punctuated by our inability, in the 20 years since, to agree upon the constitutional source of the supposed right. We have described the right articulated in Bounds as a "consequence" of due process, as an "aspect" of equal protection, or as an "equal protection guarantee." In no instance, however, have we engaged in rigorous constitutional analysis of the basis for the asserted right. Thus, even as we endeavor to address the question presented in this case— whether the District Court's order "exceeds the constitutional requirements set forth in Bounds,"—we do so without knowing which

Amendment to the Constitution governs our inquiry.

It goes without saying that we ordinarily require more exactitude when evaluating asserted constitutional rights. "As a general matter, the Court has always been reluctant" to extend constitutional protection to "uncharted areas," where the "guideposts for responsible decision making . . . are scarce and open-ended." It is a bedrock principle of judicial restraint that a right be lodged firmly in the text or tradition of a specific constitutional provision before we will recognize it as fundamental. Strict adherence to this approach is essential if we are to fulfill our constitutionally assigned role of giving full effect to the mandate of the Framers without infusing the constitutional fabric with our own political views.

B

In lieu of constitutional text, history, or tradition, *Bounds* turned primarily to precedent in recognizing the right to state assistance in the researching and filing of prisoner claims. Our cases, however, had never recognized a right of the kind articulated in *Bounds*, and, in my opinion, could not reasonably have been read to support such a right. Prior to Bounds, two lines of cases dominated our so-called "access to the courts" jurisprudence. One of these lines, rooted largely in principles of equal protection, invalidated state filing and transcript fees and imposed limited affirmative obligations on the States to ensure that their criminal procedures did not discriminate on the basis of poverty. These cases recognized a right to equal access, and any affirmative obligations imposed (e.g., a free transcript or counsel on a first appeal as of right) were strictly limited to ensuring equality of access, not access in its own right. In a second line of cases, we invalidated state prison regulations that restricted or effectively prohibited inmates from filing habeas corpus petitions or civil rights lawsuits in federal court to vindicate federally protected rights. While the cases in this line did guarantee a certain amount of access to the federal courts, they imposed no affirmative obligations on the States to facilitate access, and held only that

States may not "abridge or impair" prisoners' efforts to petition a federal court for vindication of federal rights. Without pausing to consider either the reasoning behind, or the constitutional basis for, each of these independent lines of case law, the Court in *Bounds* engaged in a loose and selective reading of our precedents as it created a freestanding and novel right to state-supported legal assistance. Despite the Court's purported reliance on prior cases, *Bounds* in fact represented a major departure both from precedent and historical practice.

* * *

Quite simply, there is no basis in constitutional text, pre-*Bounds* precedent, history, or tradition for the conclusion that the constitutional right of access imposes affirmative obligations on the States to finance and support prisoner litigation.

II

A

Even when compared to the federal judicial overreaching to which we have now become accustomed, this is truly a remarkable case. The District Court's order vividly demonstrates the danger of continuing to afford federal judges the virtually unbridled equitable power that we have for too long sanctioned. We have here yet another example of a federal judge attempting to "direct or manage the reconstruction of entire institutions and bureaucracies, with little regard for the inherent limitations on [his] authority." And we will continue to see cases like this unless we take more serious steps to curtail the use of equitable power by the federal courts.

Principles of federalism and separation of powers impose stringent limitations on the equitable power of federal courts. When these principles are accorded their proper respect, Article III cannot be understood to authorize the federal judiciary to take control of core state institutions like prisons, schools, and hospitals, and assume responsibility for making the difficult policy judgments that state officials are both constitutionally entitled and uniquely qualified to make. Broad

remedial decrees strip state administrators of their authority to set long-term goals for the institutions they manage and of the flexibility necessary to make reasonable judgments on short notice under difficult circumstances. At the state level, such decrees override the "State's discretionary authority over its own program and budgets and force state officials to reallocate state resources and funds to the [district court's] plan at the expense of other citizens, other government programs, and other institutions not represented in court." The federal judiciary is ill-equipped to make these types of judgments, and the Framers never imagined that federal judges would displace state executive officials and state legislatures in charting state policy.

Though we have sometimes closed our eyes to federal judicial overreaching, as in the context of school desegregation, we have been vigilant in opposing sweeping remedial decrees in the context of prison administration. "It is difficult to imagine an activity in which a State has a stronger interest, or one that is more intricately bound up with state laws, regulations, and procedures, than the administration of its prisons." In this area, perhaps more than any other, we have been faithful to the principles of federalism and separation of powers that limit the Federal Judiciary's exercise of its equitable powers in all instances.

* * *

State prisons should be run by the state officials with the expertise and the primary authority for running such institutions. Absent the most "extraordinary circumstances," federal courts should refrain from meddling in such affairs. Prison administrators have a difficult enough job without federal court intervention. An over broad remedial decree can make an already daunting task virtually impossible.

I realize that judges, "no less than others in our society, have a natural tendency to believe that their individual solutions to often intractable problems are better and more workable than those of the persons who are actually charged with and trained in the running of the particular institution under examination." Judges occupy a unique and limited role, one that does not allow them to substitute their views for those in the executive and legislative branches of the various States, who have the constitutional authority and institutional expertise to make these uniquely non-judicial decisions and who are ultimately accountable for these decisions. Though the temptation may be great, we must not succumb. The Constitution is not a license for federal judges to further social policy goals that prison administrators, in their discretion, have declined to advance.

B

The District Court's opinion and order demonstrate little respect for the principles of federalism, separation of powers, and judicial restraint that have traditionally governed federal judicial power in this area. In a striking arrogation of power, the District Court sought to micromanage every aspect of Arizona's "court access program" in all institutions statewide, dictating standard operating procedures and subjecting the state system to ongoing federal supervision. A sweeping remedial order of this nature would be inappropriate in any case. That the violation sought to be remedied was so minimal, to the extent there was any violation at all, makes this case all the more alarming.

The District Court cited only one instance of a prison inmate having a case dismissed due to the State's alleged failure to provide sufficient assistance, and one instance of another inmate who was unable to file an action. All of the other alleged "violations" found by the District Court related not to court access, but to library facilities and legal assistance. Many of the found violations were trivial, such as a missing pocket part to a small number of volumes in just a few institutions. And though every facility in the Arizona system already contained law libraries that greatly exceeded prisoner needs, the District Court found the State to be in violation because some of its prison libraries lacked Pacific Second Reporters. The District Court also struck down regulations that clearly pass muster under *Turner v. Safley,* such as restrictions at some facilities on "browsing the shelves," the physical exclusion from the library of "lockdown" inmates, who are the most dangerous and disobedient prisoners in the prison population,

and the allowance of phone calls only for "legitimate pressing legal issues."

To remedy these and similar "violations," the District Court imposed a sweeping, indiscriminate, and system-wide decree. The microscopically detailed order leaves no stone unturned. It covers everything from training in legal research to the ratio of typewriters to prisoners in each facility. It dictates the hours of operation for all prison libraries statewide, without regard to inmate use, staffing, or cost. It guarantees each prisoner a minimum two-hour visit to the library per trip, and allows the prisoner, not prison officials, to determine which reading room he will use. The order tells ADOC the types of forms it must use to take and respond to prisoner requests for materials. It requires all librarians to have an advanced degree in library science, law, or paralegal studies. If the State wishes to remove a prisoner from the law library for disciplinary reasons, the order requires that the prisoner be provided written notice of the reasons and factual basis for the decision within 48 hours of removal. The order goes so far as to dictate permissible noise levels in law library reading rooms and requires the State to "take all necessary steps, and correct any structural or acoustical problems."

The order also creates a "legal assistance program," imposing rules for the selection and retention of prisoner legal assistants. It requires the State to provide all inmates with a 30-40 hour videotaped legal research course, covering everything from habeas corpus and claims under 42 U.S.C. § 1983 to torts, immigration, and family law. Prisoner legal assistants are required to have an additional 20 hours of live instruction. Prisoners are also entitled to a minimum of three 20-minute phone calls each week to an attorney or legal organization, without regard to the purpose for the call; the order expressly requires Arizona to install extra phones to accommodate the increased use. Of course, legal supplies are covered under the order, which even provides for "ko-rec-type" to correct typographical errors. A Special Master retains ongoing supervisory power to ensure that the order is followed.

The District Court even usurped authority over the prison administrator's core responsibility: institutional security and discipline.

Apparently undeterred by this Court's repeated admonitions that security concerns are to be handled by prison administrators, see, e.g., the District Court decreed that "ADOC prisoners in all . . . custody levels shall be provided regular and comparable visits to the law library." Only if prison administrators can "document" an individual prisoner's "inability to use the law library without creating a threat to safety or security" may a potentially dangerous prisoner be kept out of the library, ibid., and even then the decision must be reported to the Special Master. And since, in the District Court's view, "[a] prisoner cannot adequately use the law library under restraint, including handcuffs and shackles," the State is apparently powerless to take steps to ensure that inmates known to be violent do not injure other inmates or prison guards while in the law library "researching" their claims. This "one free bite" approach conflicts both with our case law, and with basic common sense. The District Court apparently misunderstood that a prison is neither a law firm nor a legal aid bureau. Prisons are inherently dangerous institutions, and decisions concerning safety, order, and discipline must be, and always have been, left to the sound discretion of prison administrators.

Like the remedial decree in Jenkins, the District Court's order suffers from flaws characteristic of overly broad remedial decrees. First "the District Court retained jurisdiction over the implementation and modification of the remedial decree, instead of terminating its involvement after issuing its remedy."Arizona correctional officials must continually report to a Special Master on matters of internal prison administration, and the District Court retained discretion to change the rules of the game if, at some unspecified point in the future, it feels that Arizona has not done enough to facilitate court access. Thus, the District Court has "injected the judiciary into the day-to-day management of institutions and local policies—a function that lies outside of our Article III competence." The District Court also "failed to target its equitable remedies in this case specifically to cure the harm suffered by

the victims" of unconstitutional conduct. We reaffirmed in Jenkins that "the nature of the [equitable] remedy is to be determined by the nature and scope of the constitutional violation." Yet, in this case, when the District Court found the law library at a handful of institutions to be deficient, it subjected the entire system to the requirements of the decree and to ongoing federal supervision. And once it found that lockdown inmates experienced delays in receiving law books in some institutions, the District Court required all facilities statewide to provide physical access to all inmates, regardless of custody level. And again, when it found that some prisoners in some facilities were untrained in legal research, the District Court required the State to provide all inmates in all institutions with a 30-40 hour videotaped course in legal research. The remedy far exceeded the scope of any violation, and the District Court far exceeded the scope of its authority.

The District Court's order cannot stand under any circumstances. It is a stark example of what a district court should not do when it finds that a state institution has violated the Constitution. System wide relief is never appropriate in the absence of a system wide violation, and even then should be no broader and last no longer than necessary to remedy the discrete constitutional violation.

SHAW
v.
MURPHY

532 U.S. 223; 121 S. Ct. 1475; 149 L. Ed. 2d 420 (2001)
(Footnotes and citations omitted)

Under our decision in Turner v. Safley, * * * restrictions on prisoners' communications to other inmates are constitutional if the restrictions are "reasonably related to legitimate penological interests." * * *. In this case, we are asked to decide whether prisoners possess a First Amendment right to provide legal assistance that enhances the protections otherwise available under Turner. We hold that they do not.

I

While respondent Kevin Murphy was incarcerated at the Montana State Prison, he served as an "inmate law clerk," providing legal assistance to fellow prisoners. Upon learning that inmate Pat Tracy had been charged with assaulting Correctional Officer Glen Galle, Murphy decided to assist Tracy with his defense. Prison rules prohibited Murphy's assignment to the case, but he nonetheless investigated the assault. After discovering that other inmates had complained about Officer Galle's conduct, Murphy sent Tracy a letter, which included the following: "I do want to help you with your case against Galle. It wasn't your fault and I know he provoked whatever happened! Don't plead guilty because we can get at least 100 witnesses to testify that Galle is an overzealous guard who has a personal agenda to punish and harrass [sic] inmates. He has made homo-sexual [sic] advances towards certain inmates and that can be brought up into the record. There are petitions against him and I have tried to get the Unit Manager to do something about what he does in Close II, but all that happened is that I received two writeups from him myself as retaliation. So we must pursue this out of the prison system. I am filing a suit with everyone in Close I and II named against him. So you can use that too! Another poiont [sic] is that he grabbed you from behind. You tell your lawyer to get ahold of me on this. Don't take a plea bargain unless it's for no more time."

In accordance with prison policy, prison officials intercepted the letter, and petitioner Robert Shaw, an officer in the maximum-security unit, reviewed it. Based on the accusations against Officer Galle, Shaw cited Murphy for violations of the prison's rules prohibiting insolence, interference with due process hearings, and conduct that disrupts or interferes with the security and orderly operation of the institution. After a hearing, Murphy was found guilty of violating the first two prohibitions. The hearings officer sanctioned him by imposing a suspended sentence of 10 days' detention and issuing demerits that could affect his custody level.

In response, Murphy brought this action, seeking declaratory and injunctive relief under * * * 42 U.S.C. §1983. The case was styled as a class action, brought on behalf of himself, other inmate law clerks, and other prisoners. The complaint alleged that the disciplining of Murphy violated due process, the rights of inmates to access the courts, and, as relevant here, Murphy's First Amendment rights, including the right to provide legal assistance to other inmates.

* * *

II

In this case, we are not asked to decide whether prisoners have *any* First Amendment rights when they send legal correspondence to one another. In Turner, we held that restrictions on inmate-to-inmate communications pass constitutional muster only if the restrictions are reasonably related to legitimate and neutral governmental objectives. * * * We did not limit our holding to nonlegal correspondence, and petitioners do not ask us to construe it that way. Instead, the question presented here simply asks whether Murphy possesses a First Amendment right to provide legal advice that enhances the protections otherwise available under Turner. The effect of such a right, as the Court of Appeals described it, * * * would be that inmate-to-inmate correspondence that includes legal assistance would receive more First Amendment protection than correspondence without any legal assistance. We conclude that there is no such special right.

Traditionally, federal courts did not intervene in the internal affairs of prisons and instead "adopted a broad hands-off attitude toward problems of prison administration." Procunier v. Martinez, * * * Indeed, for much of this country's history, the prevailing view was that a prisoner was a mere "slave of the State," who "not only forfeited his liberty, but all his personal rights except those which the law in its humanity accords him." Jones v. North Carolina Prisoners' Labor Union, Inc. * * * In recent decades, however, this Court has determined that incarceration does not divest prisoners of all constitutional protections. Inmates retain, for example, the right to be free from racial discrimination, Lee v. Washington, * * * the right to due process,

Wolff v. McDonnell, * * * and, as relevant here, certain protections of the First Amendment, Turner * * *

We nonetheless have maintained that the constitutional rights that prisoners possess are more limited in scope than the constitutional rights held by individuals in society at large. In the First Amendment context, for instance, some rights are simply inconsistent with the status of a prisoner or "with the legitimate penological objectives of the corrections system," Pell v. Procunier * * *. We have thus sustained proscriptions of media interviews with individual inmates, * * * prohibitions on the activities of a prisoners' labor union, * * * and restrictions on inmate-to-inmate written correspondence * * *. Moreover, because the "problems of prisons in America are complex and intractable," and because courts are particularly "ill equipped" to deal with these problems, Martinez, * * * we generally have deferred to the judgments of prison officials in upholding these regulations against constitutional challenge.

Reflecting this understanding, in Turner we adopted a unitary, deferential standard for reviewing prisoners' constitutional claims: "When a prison regulation impinges on inmates' constitutional rights, the regulation is valid if it is reasonably related to legitimate penological interests." * * * Under this standard, four factors are relevant. First and foremost, "there must be a 'valid, rational connection' between the prison regulation and the legitimate [and neutral] governmental interest put forward to justify it." * * * If the connection between the regulation and the asserted goal is "arbitrary or irrational," then the regulation fails, irrespective of whether the other factors tilt in favor. * * * In addition, courts should consider three other factors: the existence of "alternative means of exercising the right" available to inmates; "the impact accommodation of the asserted constitutional right will have on guards and other inmates, and on the allocation of prison resources generally;" and "the absence of ready alternatives" available to the prison for achieving the governmental objectives. * * *

Because Turner provides the test for evaluating prisoners' First Amendment challenges, the issue before us is whether Turner permits an increase in constitutional protection whenever a prisoner's communication includes legal advice. We conclude that it does not. To increase the constitutional protection based upon the content of a communication first requires an assessment of the value of that content. But the Turner test, by its terms, simply does not accommodate valuations of content. On the contrary, the Turner factors concern only the relationship between the asserted penological interests and the prison regulation. * * *

Moreover, under Turner and its predecessors, prison officials are to remain the primary arbiters of the problems that arise in prison management. * * * If courts were permitted to enhance constitutional protection based on their assessments of the content of the particular communications, courts would be in a position to assume a greater role in decisions affecting prison administration. Seeking to avoid "'unnecessarily perpetuating the involvement of the federal courts in affairs of prison administration,'" * * * we reject an alteration of the Turner analysis that would entail additional federal-court oversight.

Finally, even if we were to consider giving special protection to particular kinds of speech based upon content, we would not do so for speech that includes legal advice. Augmenting First Amendment protection for inmate legal advice would undermine prison officials' ability to address the "complex and intractable" problems of prison administration. * * * Although supervised inmate legal assistance programs may serve valuable ends, it is "indisputable" that inmate law clerks "are sometimes a menace to prison discipline" and that prisoners have an "acknowledged propensity . . . to abuse both the giving and the seeking of [legal] assistance." * * * Prisoners have used legal correspondence as a means for passing contraband and communicating instructions on how to manufacture drugs or weapons. * * * The legal text also could be an excuse for making clearly inappropriate comments, which "may be expected to circulate among prisoners," * * * despite prison measures to screen individual inmates or officers from the remarks.

We thus decline to cloak the provision of legal assistance with any First Amendment protection above and beyond the protection normally accorded prisoners' speech. Instead, the proper constitutional test is the one we set forth in Turner. Irrespective of whether the correspondence contains legal advice, the constitutional analysis is the same.

III

Under Turner, the question remains whether the prison regulations, as applied to Murphy, are "reasonably related to legitimate penological interests." * * * To prevail, Murphy must overcome the presumption that the prison officials acted within their "broad discretion." * * * Petitioners ask us to answer, rather than remand, the question whether Murphy has satisfied this heavy burden. We decline petitioners' request, however, because we granted certiorari only to decide whether inmates possess a special First Amendment right to provide legal assistance to fellow inmates.

* * *

The judgment of the Court of Appeals is reversed, and the case is remanded for further proceedings consistent with this opinion.

Cases Relating to Chapter 8

Prison Disciplinary Proceedings

BAXTER
v.
PALMIGIANO

425 U.S. 308; 96 S. Ct. 1551;
47 L. Ed. 2d 810 (1976)

MR. JUSTICE WHITE delivered the opinion of the Court.

* * *

II

In Wolff v. McDonnell, supra, drawing comparisons to Gagnon v. Scarpelli, 411 U.S. 778 (1973), we said:

The insertion of counsel into the [prison] disciplinary process would inevitably give the proceedings a more adversary cast and tend to reduce their utility as a means to further correctional goals. There would also be delay and very practical problems in providing counsel in sufficient numbers at the time and place where hearings are to be held. At this stage of the development of these procedures we are not prepared to hold that inmates have a right to either retained or appointed counsel in disciplinary proceedings.

Relying on Miranda v. Arizona, 384 U.S. 436 (1966), and Mathis v. United States, 391 U.S. 1 (1968), both Courts of Appeals in these cases held that prison inmates are entitled to representation at prison disciplinary hearings where the charges involve conduct punishable as a crime under state law, not because of the services that counsel might render in connection with the disciplinary proceedings themselves, but because statements inmates might make at the hearings would perhaps be used in later state-court prosecutions for the same conduct.

Neither Miranda, supra, nor Mathis, supra, has any substantial bearing on the question whether counsel must be provided at "[p]rison disciplinary hearings [which] are not part of a criminal prosecution." Wolff v. McDonnell, supra, at 556. The Court has never held, and we decline to do so now, that the requirements of those cases must be met to render pretrial statements admissible in other than criminal cases.

We see no reason to alter our conclusion so recently made in Wolff that inmates do not "have a right to either retained or appointed counsel in disciplinary hearings." 418 U.S., at 570. Plainly, therefore, state authorities were not in error in failing to advise Palmigiano to the contrary, i.e., that he was entitled to counsel at the hearing and that the State would furnish counsel if he did not have one of his own.

III

Palmigiano was advised that he was not required to testify at his disciplinary hearing and that he could remain silent but that his silence could be used against him. . . .

As the Court has often held, the Fifth Amendment "not only protects the individual against being involuntarily called as a witness against himself in a criminal prosecution but also privileges him not to answer official questions put to him in any other proceeding, civil or criminal, formal or informal, where the answers might incriminate him in future criminal proceedings." Lefkowitz v. Turley, 414 U.S. 70, 77 (1973). Prison disciplinary hearings are not criminal proceedings; but if inmates are compelled in those proceedings to furnish testimonial evidence that might incriminate them in later criminal proceedings, they must be offered "whatever immunity is required to supplant the privilege" and may not be required to "waive such immunity." Id., at 85; Garrity v. New Jersey, 385 U.S. 493 (1967); Gardner v. Broderick, 392 U.S. 273 (1968); Sanitation Men v. Sanitation Comm'r, 392 U.S. 280 (1968). In this line of cases from Garrity to Lefkowitz, the States, pursuant to statute, sought to interrogate individuals about their job performance or about their contractual relations with the State; insisted upon waiver of the Fifth Amendment privilege not to respond or to object to later use of the incriminating statements in criminal prosecutions; and, upon refusal to waive, automatically terminated employment or eligibility to contract with the State. Holding that the State could not constitutionally seek to compel testimony that had not been immunized by threats of serious economic reprisal, we invalidated the challenged statutes.

* * *

The Rhode Island prison rules do not transgress the foregoing principles. No criminal proceedings are or were pending against Palmigiano. The State has not, contrary to Griffin, sought to make evidentiary use of his silence at the disciplinary hearing in any criminal proceeding. Neither has Rhode Island insisted or asked that Palmigiano waive his Fifth Amendment privilege. He was notified that he was privileged to remain silent if he chose. He was also advised that his silence could be used against him, but a prison inmate in Rhode Island electing to remain silent during his disciplinary hearing, as respondent Palmigiano did here, is not in consequence of his silence automatically found guilty of the infraction with which he has been charged. Under Rhode Island law, disciplinary decisions "must be based on substantial evidence

manifested in the record of the disciplinary proceeding." Morris v. Travisono, 310 F. Supp. 857, 873 (RI 1970). It is thus undisputed that an inmate's silence in and of itself is insufficient to support an adverse decision by the Disciplinary Board. In this respect, this case is very different from the circumstances before the Court in the Garrity-Lefkowitz decisions, where refusal to submit to interrogation and to waive the Fifth Amendment privilege, standing alone and without regard to the other evidence, resulted in loss of employment or opportunity to contract with the State. There, failure to respond to interrogation was treated as a final admission of guilt. Here, Palmigiano remained silent at the hearing in the face of evidence that incriminated him; and, as far as this record reveals, his silence was given no more evidentiary value than was warranted by the facts surrounding his case. This does not smack of an invalid attempt by the State to compel testimony without granting immunity or to penalize the exercise of the privilege. The advice given inmates by the decision-makers is merely a realistic reflection of the evidentiary significance of the choice to remain silent.

Had the State desired Palmigiano's testimony over his Fifth Amendment objection, we can but assume that it would have extended whatever use immunity is required by the Federal Constitution. Had this occurred and had Palmigiano nevertheless refused to answer, it surely would not have violated the Fifth Amendment to draw whatever inference from his silence that the circumstances warranted. Insofar as the privilege is concerned, the situation is little different where the State advises the inmate of his right to silence but also plainly notifies him that his silence will be weighed in the balance.

Our conclusion is consistent with the prevailing rule that the Fifth Amendment does not forbid adverse inferences against parties to civil actions when they refuse to testify in response to probative evidence offered against them: the Amendment "does not preclude the inference where the privilege is claimed by a party to a civil cause." 8 J. Wigmore, Evidence 439 (McNaughton rev. 1961). In criminal cases, where the stakes are higher and the State's sole interest is to convict, Griffin prohibits the judge and prosecutor from suggesting to the jury that it may treat the defendant's silence as substantive evidence of guilt. Disciplinary proceedings in state prisons, however, involve the correctional process and important state interests other than conviction for crime. We decline to extend the Griffin rule to this context.

* * *

Although acknowledging the strictures of Wolff with respect to confrontation and cross-examination, the Court of Appeals for the Ninth Circuit, on rehearing in No. 74-1194, went on to require prison authorities to provide reasons in writing to inmates denied the privilege to cross-examine or confront witnesses against them in disciplinary proceedings; absent explanation, failure to set forth reasons related to the prevention of one or more of the four concerns expressly mentioned in Wolff would be deemed prima facie abuse of discretion.

This conclusion is inconsistent with Wolff. We characterized as "useful," but did not require, written reasons for denying inmates the limited right to call witnesses in their defense. We made no such suggestion with respect to confrontation and cross-examination which, as was there pointed out, stand on a different footing because of their inherent danger and the availability of adequate bases of decision without them. See 418 U.S., at 567-568. Mandating confrontation and cross-examination, except where prison officials can justify their denial on one or more grounds that appeal to judges, effectively preempts the area that Wolff left to the sound discretion of prison officials. We add that on the record before us there is no evidence of the abuse of discretion by the state prison officials.

* * *

We said in Wolff v. McDonnell: "As the nature of the prison disciplinary process changes in future years, circumstances may then exist which will require further consideration and reflection of this Court. It is our view, however, that the procedures we have now required in prison disciplinary proceedings represent a reasonable accommodation between the interests of the inmates and the needs of the institution." 418 U.S., at 572. We do not retreat from that view. However, the procedures required by the Courts of Appeals in Nos. 74-1187 and 74-1194 are either inconsistent with the "reasonable accommodation" reached in Wolff, or premature on the bases of the records before us. The judgments in Nos. 74-1187 and 74-1194 accordingly are

Reversed.

* * *

WOLFF
v.
McDONNELL
418 U.S. 539; 94 S. Ct. 2963;
41 L. Ed. 2d 935 (1974)

MR. JUSTICE WHITE delivered the opinion of the Court.

* * *

Petitioners assert that the procedure for disciplining prison inmates for serious misconduct is a matter of policy raising no constitutional issue. If the position implies that prisoners in state institutions are wholly without the protections of the Constitution and the Due Process Clause, it is plainly untenable. Lawful imprisonment necessarily makes unavailable many rights and privileges of the ordinary citizen, a "retraction justified by the considerations underlying our penal system." Price v. Johnston, 334 U.S. 266, 285 (1948). But though his rights may be diminished by the needs and exigencies of the institutional environment, a prisoner is not wholly stripped of constitutional protections when he is imprisoned for crime. There is no iron curtain drawn between the Constitution and the prisons of this country. Prisoners have been held to enjoy substantial religious freedom under the First and Fourteenth Amendments. Cruz v. Beto, 405 U.S. 319 (1972); Cooper v. Pate, 378 U.S. 546 (1964). They retain right of access to the courts. Younger v. Gilmore, 404 U.S. 15 (1971), aff'g Gilmore v. Lynch, 319 F.Supp. 105 (ND

Cal. 1970); Johnson v. Avery, 393 U.S. 483 (1969); Ex parte Hull, 312 U.S. 546 (1941). Prisoners are protected under the Equal Protection Clause of the Fourteenth Amendment from invidious discrimination based on race. Lee v. Washington, 390 U.S. 333 (1968). Prisoners may also claim the protections of the Due Process Clause. They may not be deprived of life, liberty, or property without due process of law. Haines v. Kerner, 404 U.S. 519 (1972); Wilwording v. Swenson, 404 U.S. 249 (1971); Screws v. United States, 325 U.S. 91 (1945).

Of course, as we have indicated, the fact that prisoners retain rights under the Due Process Clause in no way implies that these rights are not subject to restrictions imposed by the nature of the regime to which they have been lawfully committed. Cf. CSC v. Letter Carriers, 413 U.S. 548 (1973); Broadrick v. Oklahoma, 413 U.S. 601 (1973); Parker v. Levy, 417 U.S. 733 (1974). Prison disciplinary proceedings are not part of a criminal prosecution, and the full panoply of rights due a defendant in such proceedings does not apply. Cf. Morrissey v. Brewer, 408 U.S., at 488. In sum, there must be mutual accommodation between institutional needs and objectives and the provisions of the Constitution that are of general application.

We also reject the assertion of the State that whatever may be true of the Due Process Clause in general or of other rights protected by that Clause against state infringement, the interest of prisoners in disciplinary procedures is not included in that "liberty" protected by the Fourteenth Amendment. It is true that the Constitution itself does not guarantee good-time credit for satisfactory behavior while in prison. But here the State itself has not only provided a statutory right to good time but also specifies that it is to be forfeited only for serious misbehavior. Nebraska may have the authority to create, or not, a right to a shortened prison sentence through the accumulation of credits for good behavior, and it is true that the Due Process Clause does not require a hearing "in every conceivable case of government impairment of private interest." Cafeteria Workers v. McElroy, 367 U.S. 886, 894 (1961). But the State having created the right to good time and itself recognizing that its deprivation is a sanction authorized for major misconduct, the prisoner's interest has real

substance and is sufficiently embraced within Fourteenth Amendment "liberty" to entitle him to those minimum procedures appropriate under the circumstances and required by the Due Process Clause to insure that the state-created right is not arbitrarily abrogated. This is the thrust of recent cases in the prison disciplinary context. In Haines v. Kerner, supra, the state prisoner asserted a "denial of due process in the steps leading to [disciplinary] confinement." 404 U.S., at 520. We reversed the dismissal of the § 1983 complaint for failure to state a claim. In Preiser v. Rodriguez, supra, the prisoner complained that he had been deprived of good-time credits without notice or hearing and without due process of law. We considered the claim a proper subject for a federal habeas corpus proceeding.

This analysis as to liberty parallels the accepted due process analysis as to property. The Court has consistently held that some kind of hearing is required at some time before a person is finally deprived of his property interests. Anti-Fascist Committee v. McGrath, 341 U.S. 123, 168 (1951) (Frankfurter, J., concurring). The requirement for some kind of a hearing applies to the taking of private property, Grannis v. Ordean, 234 U.S. 385 (1914), the revocation of licenses, In re Ruffalo, 390 U.S. 544 (1968), the operation of state dispute-settlement mechanisms, when one person seeks to take property from another, or to government-created jobs held, absent "cause" for termination, Board of Regents v. Roth, 408 U.S. 564 (1972); Arnett v. Kennedy, 416 U.S. 134, 164 (1974) (POWELL, J., concurring); id., at 171 (WHITE, J., concurring in part and dissenting in part); id., at 206 (MARSHALL, J., dissenting). Cf. Stanley v. Illinois, 405 U.S. 645, 652-654 (1972); Bell v. Burson, 402 U.S. 535 (1971).

We think a person's liberty is equally protected, even when the liberty itself is a statutory creation of the State. The touchstone of due process is protection of the individual against arbitrary action of government, Dent v. West Virginia, 129 U.S. 114, 123 (1889). Since prisoners in Nebraska can only lose good-time credits if they are guilty of serious misconduct, the determination of whether such behavior has occurred becomes critical, and the minimum requirements of procedural due process appropriate for the circumstances must be observed.

IV

* * *

Morrissey held that due process imposed certain minimum procedural requirements which must be satisfied before parole could finally be revoked. These procedures were:

(a) written notice of the claimed violations of parole; (b) disclosure to the parolee of evidence against him; (c) opportunity to be heard in person and to present witnesses and documentary evidence; (d) the right to confront and cross-examine adverse witnesses (unless the hearing officer specifically finds good cause for not allowing confrontation); (e) a 'neutral and detached' hearing body such as a traditional parole board, members of which need not be judicial officers or lawyers; and (f) a written statement by the factfinders as to the evidence relied on and reasons for revoking parole.

* * *

We have often repeated that "[the] very nature of due process negates any concept of inflexible procedures universally applicable to every imaginable situation." Cafeteria Workers v. McElroy, 367 U.S., at 895. "[Consideration] of what procedures due process may require under any given set of circumstances must begin with a determination of the precise nature of the government function involved as well as of the private interest that has been affected by governmental action." Ibid.; Morrissey, 408 U.S., at 481. Viewed in this light it is immediately apparent that one cannot automatically apply procedural rules designed for free citizens in an open society, or for parolees or probationers under only limited restraints, to the very different situation presented by a disciplinary proceeding in a state prison.

Revocation of parole may deprive the parolee of only conditional liberty, but it nevertheless "inflicts a 'grievous loss' on the parolee and often on others." Id., at 482. Simply put, revocation proceedings determine whether the parolee will be free or in prison, a matter of obvious great moment to him. For the prison inmate, the deprivation of good time is not the same immediate disaster that the revocation of parole is for the parolee. The deprivation, very likely, does not then and there work any change in the conditions of his liberty. It can postpone the date of eligibility for parole and extend the maximum term to be served, but it is not certain to do so, for good time may be restored. Even if not restored, it cannot be said with certainty that the actual date of parole will be affected; and if parole occurs, the extension of the maximum term resulting from loss of good time may affect only the termination of parole, and it may not even do that. The deprivation of good time is unquestionably a matter of considerable importance. The State reserves it as a sanction for serious misconduct, and we should not unrealistically discount its significance. But it is qualitatively and quantitatively different from the revocation of parole or probation.

In striking the balance that the Due Process Clause demands, however, we think the major consideration militating against adopting the full range of procedures suggested by Morrissey for alleged parole violators is the very different stake the State has in the structure and content of the prison disciplinary hearing. That the revocation of parole be justified and based on an accurate assessment of the facts is a critical matter to the State as well as the parolee; but the procedures by which it is determined whether the conditions of parole have been breached do not themselves threaten other important state interests, parole officers, the police, or witnesses—at least no more so than in the case of the ordinary criminal trial. Prison disciplinary proceedings, on the other hand, take place in a closed, tightly controlled environment peopled by those who have chosen to violate the criminal law and who have been lawfully incarcerated for doing so. Some are first offenders, but many are recidivists who have repeatedly employed illegal and often very violent means to attain their ends. They may have little regard for the safety of others or their property or for the rules designed to provide an orderly and reasonably safe prison life. Although there are very many varieties of prisons with different degrees of security, we must realize that in many of them the inmates are closely supervised and their activities controlled around the clock. Guards and inmates co-exist in direct and intimate contact. Tension between them is unremitting. Frustration, resentment, and despair are commonplace. Relationships among the inmates are varied and complex and perhaps subject to the unwritten code that exhorts inmates not to inform on a fellow prisoner.

It is against this background that disciplinary proceedings must be structured by prison authorities; and it is against this background that we must make our constitutional judgments, realizing that we are dealing with the maximum security institution as well as those where security considerations are not paramount. The reality is that disciplinary hearings and the imposition of disagreeable sanctions necessarily involve confrontations between inmates and authority and between inmates who are being disciplined and those who would charge or furnish evidence against them. Retaliation is much more than a theoretical possibility; and the basic and unavoidable task of providing reasonable personal safety for guards and inmates may be at stake, to say nothing of the impact of disciplinary confrontations and the resulting escalation of personal antagonisms on the important aims of the correctional process.

Indeed, it is pressed upon us that the proceedings to ascertain and sanction misconduct themselves play a major role in furthering the institutional goal of modifying the behavior and value systems of prison inmates sufficiently to permit them to live within the law when they are released. Inevitably there is a great range of personality and character among those who have transgressed the criminal law. Some are more amenable to suggestion and persuasion than others. Some may be incorrigible and would merely disrupt and exploit the disciplinary process for their own ends. With some, rehabilitation may be best achieved by simulating procedures of a free society to the maximum possible extent; but with others, it may be essential that discipline be swift and sure. In any event, it is argued, there would be great unwisdom in encasing the disciplinary procedures in an inflexible constitutional straitjacket that would necessarily call for adversary proceedings typical of the criminal trial, very likely raise the level of confrontation between staff and inmate,

and make more difficult the utilization of the disciplinary process as a tool to advance the rehabilitative goals of the institution. This consideration, along with the necessity to maintain an acceptable level of personal security in the institution, must be taken into account as we now examine in more detail the Nebraska procedures that the Court of Appeals found wanting.

V

Two of the procedures that the Court held should be extended to parolees facing revocation proceedings are not, but must be, provided to prisoners in the Nebraska Complex if the minimum requirements of procedural due process are to be satisfied. These are advance written notice of the claimed violation and a written statement of the factfinders as to the evidence relied upon and the reasons for the disciplinary action taken. As described by the Warden in his oral testimony, on the basis of which the District Court made its findings, the inmate is now given oral notice of the charges against him at least as soon as the conference with the Chief Corrections Supervisor and charging party. A written record is there compiled and the report read to the inmate at the hearing before the Adjustment Committee where the charges are discussed and pursued. There is no indication that the inmate is ever given a written statement by the Committee as to the evidence or informed in writing or otherwise as to the reasons for the disciplinary action taken.

Part of the function of notice is to give the charged party a chance to marshal the facts in his defense and to clarify what the charges are, in fact. See In re Gault, 387 U.S. 1, 33-34, and n. 54 (1967). Neither of these functions was performed by the notice described by the Warden. Although the charges are discussed orally with the inmate somewhat in advance of the hearing, the inmate is sometimes brought before the Adjustment Committee shortly after he is orally informed of the charges. Other times, after this initial discussion, further investigation takes place which may reshape the nature of the charges or the evidence relied upon. In those instances, under procedures in effect at the time of trial, it would appear that the inmate first receives notice of the actual charges at the time of the hearing before the Adjustment Committee. We hold that written notice of the charges must be given to the disciplinary-action defendant in order to inform him of the charges and to enable him to marshal the facts and prepare a defense. At least a brief period of time after the notice, no less than 24 hours, should be allowed to the inmate to prepare for the appearance before the Adjustment Committee.

We also hold that there must be a "written statement by the factfinders as to the evidence relied on and reasons" for the disciplinary action. Morrissey, 408 U.S., at 489. Although Nebraska does not seem to provide administrative review of the action taken by the Adjustment Committee, the actions taken at such proceedings may involve review by other bodies. They might furnish the basis of a decision by the Director of Corrections to transfer an inmate to another institution because he is considered "to be incorrigible by reason of frequent intentional breaches of discipline," Neb. Rev. Stat. § 83-185 (4) (Cum. Supp. 1972), and are certainly likely to be considered by the state parole authorities in making parole decisions. Written records of proceedings will thus protect the inmate against collateral consequences based on a misunderstanding of the nature of the original proceeding. Further, as to the disciplinary action itself, the provision for a written record helps to insure that administrators, faced with possible scrutiny by state officials and the public, and perhaps even the courts, where fundamental constitutional rights may have been abridged, will act fairly. Without written records, the inmate will be at a severe disadvantage in propounding his own cause to or defending himself from others. It may be that there will be occasions when personal or institutional safety is so implicated that the statement may properly exclude certain items of evidence, but in that event the statement should indicate the fact of the omission. Otherwise, we perceive no conceivable rehabilitative objective or prospect of prison disruption that can flow from the requirement of these statements.

We are also of the opinion that the inmate facing disciplinary proceedings should be allowed to call witnesses and present documentary evidence in his defense when permitting him to do so will not be unduly hazardous to institutional safety or correctional goals. Ordinarily, the right to present evidence is basic to a fair hearing; but the unrestricted right to call witnesses from the prison population carries obvious potential for disruption and for interference with the swift punishment that in individual cases may be essential to carrying out the correctional program of the institution. We should not be too ready to exercise oversight and put aside the judgment of prison administrators. It may be that an individual threatened with serious sanctions would normally be entitled to present witnesses and relevant documentary evidence; but here we must balance the inmate's interest in avoiding loss of good time against the needs of the prison, and some amount of flexibility and accommodation is required. Prison officials must have the necessary discretion to keep the hearing within reasonable limits and to refuse to call witnesses that may create a risk of reprisal or undermine authority, as well as to limit access to other inmates to collect statements or to compile other documentary evidence. Although we do not prescribe it, it would be useful for the Committee to state its reason for refusing to call a witness, whether it be for irrelevance, lack of necessity, or the hazards presented in individual cases. Any less flexible rule appears untenable as a constitutional matter, at least on the record made in this case. The operation of a correctional institution is at best an extraordinarily difficult undertaking. Many prison officials, on the spot and with the responsibility for the safety of inmates and staff, are reluctant to extend the unqualified right to call witnesses; and in our view, they must have the necessary discretion without being subject to unduly crippling constitutional impediments. There is this much play in the joints of the Due Process Clause, and we stop short of imposing a more demanding rule with respect to witnesses and documents.

Confrontation and cross-examination present greater hazards to institutional interests. If confrontation and cross-examination of those furnishing evidence against the inmate were to be allowed as a matter of course, as in criminal trials, there would be considerable potential for havoc inside the prison walls. Proceedings would inevitably be longer and tend to unmanageability. These procedures are essential in criminal trials where the accused, if found guilty, may be subjected to the most serious deprivations, Pointer v. Texas, 380 U.S. 400 (1965), or where a person may lose his job in society, Greene v. McElroy, 360 U.S. 474, 496-497 (1959). But they are not rights universally applicable to all hearings. See Arnett v. Kennedy, 416 U.S. 134 (1974). Rules of procedure may be shaped by consideration of the risks of error, In re Winship, 397 U.S. 358, 368 (1970) (Harlan, J., concurring); Arnett v. Kennedy, supra, p. 171 (WHITE, J., concurring in part and dissenting in part), and should also be shaped by the consequences which will follow their adoption. Although some States do seem to allow cross-examination in disciplinary hearings, we are not apprised of the conditions under which the procedure may be curtailed; and it does not appear that confrontation and cross-examination are generally required in this context. We think that the Constitution should not be read to impose the procedure at the present time and that adequate bases for decision in prison disciplinary cases can be arrived at without cross-examination.

Perhaps as the problems of penal institutions change and correctional goals are reshaped, the balance of interests involved will require otherwise. But in the current environment, where prison disruption remains a serious concern to administrators, we cannot ignore the desire and effort of many States, including Nebraska, and the Federal Government to avoid situations that may trigger deep emotions and that may scuttle the disciplinary process as a rehabilitation vehicle. To some extent, the American adversary trial presumes contestants who are able to cope with the pressures and aftermath of the battle, and such may not generally be the case of those in the prisons of this country. At least, the Constitution, as we interpret it today, does not require the contrary assumption. Within the limits set forth in this opinion we are content for now to leave the continuing development of measures to review adverse actions affecting inmates to the sound discretion of corrections officials administering the scope of such inquiries.

We recognize that the problems of potential disruption may differ depending on whom the inmate proposes to cross-examine. If he proposes to examine an unknown fellow inmate, the danger may be the greatest, since the disclosure of the identity of the accuser, and the cross-examination which will follow, may pose a high risk of reprisal within the institution. Conversely, the inmate accuser, who might freely tell his story privately to prison officials, may refuse to testify or admit any knowledge of the situation in question. Although the dangers posed by cross-examination of known inmate accusers, or guards, may be less, the resentment which may persist after confrontation may still be substantial. Also, even where the accuser or adverse witness is known, the disclosure of third parties may pose a problem. There may be a class of cases where the facts are closely disputed, and the character of the parties minimizes the dangers involved. However, any constitutional rule tailored to meet these situations would undoubtedly produce great litigation and attendant costs in a much wider range of cases. Further, in the last analysis, even within the narrow range of cases where interest balancing may well dictate cross-examination, courts will be faced with the assessment of prison officials as to the dangers involved, and there would be a limited basis for upsetting such judgments. The better course at this time, in a period where prison practices are diverse and somewhat experimental, is to leave these matters to the sound discretion of the officials of state prisons.

As to the right to counsel, . . .

* * *

The insertion of counsel into the disciplinary process would inevitably give the proceedings a more adversary cast and tend to reduce their utility as a means to further correctional goals. There would also be delay and very practical problems in providing counsel in sufficient numbers at the time and place where hearings are to be held. At this stage of the development of these procedures we are not prepared to hold that inmates have a right to either retained or appointed counsel in disciplinary proceedings.

Where an illiterate inmate is involved, however, or where the complexity of the issue makes it unlikely that the inmate will be able to collect and present the evidence necessary for an adequate comprehension of the case, he should be free to seek the aid of a fellow inmate, or if that is forbidden, to have adequate substitute aid in the form of help from the staff or from a sufficiently competent inmate designated by the staff. We need not pursue the matter further here, however, for there is no claim that respondent, McDonnell, is within the class of inmates entitled to advice or help from others in the course of a prison disciplinary hearing.

Finally, we decline to rule that the Adjustment Committee which conducts the required hearings at the Nebraska Prison Complex and determines whether to revoke good time is not sufficiently impartial to satisfy the Due Process Clause. The Committee is made up of the Associate Warden Custody as chairman, the Correctional Industries Superintendent, and the Reception Center Director. The Chief Corrections Supervisor refers cases to the Committee after investigation and an initial interview with the inmate involved. The Committee is not left at large with unlimited discretion. It is directed to meet daily and to operate within the principles stated in the controlling regulations, among which is the command that "[full] consideration must be given to the causes for the adverse behavior, the setting and circumstances in which it occurred, the man's accountability, and the correctional treatment goals," as well as the direction that "disciplinary measures will be taken only at such times and to such degrees as are necessary to regulate and control a man's behavior within acceptable limits and will never be rendered capriciously or in the nature of retaliation or revenge." We find no warrant in the record presented here for concluding that the Adjustment Committee presents such a hazard of arbitrary decisionmaking that it should be held violative of due process of law.

Our conclusion that some, but not all, of the procedures specified in Morrissey and Scarpelli must accompany the deprivation of good time by state prison authorities is not graven in stone. As the nature of the prison disciplinary process changes in future years, circumstances may then exist which will require further consideration and reflection of this Court. It is our view, however, that the procedures we have now required in prison disciplinary proceedings represent a reason-able accommodation between the interests of the inmates and the needs of the institution.

* * *

SANDIN
v.
CONNER

515 U.S. 472; 115 S. Ct. 2293; 132 L. Ed. 2d 418 (1995)

[Most citations and footnotes omitted]

CHIEF JUSTICE REHNQUIST delivered the opinion of the Court. We granted certiorari to reexamine the circumstances under which state prison regulations afford inmates a liberty interest protected by the Due Process Clause.

I

DeMont Conner was convicted of numerous state crimes, including murder, kidnaping, robbery, and burglary, for which he is currently serving an indeterminate sentence of 30 years to life in a Hawaii prison. He was confined in the Halawa Correctional Facility, a maximum security prison in central Oahu. In August 1987, a prison officer escorted him from his cell to the module program area. The officer subjected Conner to a strip search, complete with an inspection of the rectal area. Conner retorted with angry and foul language directed at the officer. Eleven days later he received notice that he had been charged with disciplinary infractions. The notice charged Conner with "high misconduct" for using physical interference to impair a correctional function, and "low moderate misconduct" for using abusive or obscene language and for harassing employees.

Conner appeared before an adjustment committee on August 28, 1987. The committee refused Conner's request to present witnesses at the hearing, stating that "witnesses were unavailable due to move [sic] to the medium facility and being short staffed on the modules." At the conclusion of proceedings, the committee determined that Conner was guilty of the alleged misconduct. It sentenced him to 30 days disciplinary segregation in the Special Holding Unit for the physical obstruction charge, and four hours segregation for each of the other two charges to be served concurrent with the 30 days. Conner's segregation began August 31, 1987, and ended September 29, 1987.

Conner sought administrative review within 14 days of receiving the committee's decision. Nine months later, the deputy administrator found the high misconduct charge unsupported and expunged Conner's disciplinary record with respect to that charge. But before the Deputy Administrator decided the appeal, Conner had brought this suit against the adjustment committee chair and other prison officials in the United States District Court for the District of Hawaii based on . . . 42 U.S.C. § 1983. His amended complaint prayed for injunctive relief, declaratory relief and damages for, among other things, a deprivation of procedural due process in connection with the disciplinary hearing. The District Court granted summary judgment in favor of the prison officials.

The Court of Appeals for the Ninth Circuit reversed the judgment. It concluded that Conner had a liberty interest in remaining free from disciplinary segregation and that there was a disputed question of fact with respect to whether Conner received all of the process due under this Court's pronouncement in Wolff v. McDonnell. The Court of Appeals based its conclusion on a prison regulation that instructs the committee to find guilt when a charge of misconduct is supported by substantial evidence. The Court of Appeals reasoned from Kentucky Department of Corrections v. Thompson, that the committee's duty to find guilt was nondiscretionary. From the language of the regulation, it drew a negative inference that the committee may not impose segregation if it does not find substantial evidence of misconduct. It viewed this as a state-created liberty interest, and therefore held that respondent was entitled to call witnesses by virtue of our opinion in Wolff, supra. We granted the State's petition for certiorari, and now reverse.

II

Our due process analysis begins with Wolff. There, Nebraska inmates challenged the decision of prison officials to revoke good time credits without adequate procedures. Inmates earned good time credits

under a state statute that bestowed mandatory sentence reductions for good behavior, revocable only for "flagrant or serious misconduct." We held that the Due Process Clause itself does not create a liberty interest in credit for good behavior, but that the statutory provision created a liberty interest in a "shortened prison sentence" which resulted from good time credits, credits which were revocable only if the prisoner was guilty of serious misconduct. The Court characterized this liberty interest as one of "real substance" ibid., and articulated minimum procedures necessary to reach a "mutual accommodation between institutional needs and objectives and the provisions of the Constitution." Id., at 556. Much of Wolff's contribution to the landscape of prisoners' due process derived not from its description of liberty interests, but rather from its intricate balancing of prison management concerns with prisoners' liberty in determining the amount of process due. Its short discussion of the definition of a liberty interest, led to a more thorough treatment of the issue in Meachum v. Fano.

Inmates in Meachum sought injunctive relief, declaratory relief and damages by reason of transfers from a Massachusetts medium security prison to a maximum security facility with substantially less favorable conditions. The transfers were ordered in the aftermath of arson incidents for which the transferred inmates were thought to be responsible, and did not entail a loss of good time credits or any period of disciplinary confinement. The Court began with the proposition that the Due Process Clause does not protect every change in the conditions of confinement having a substantial adverse impact on the prisoner. It then held that the Due Process Clause did not itself create a liberty interest in prisoners to be free from intrastate prison transfers. It reasoned that transfer to a maximum security facility, albeit one with more burdensome conditions, was "within the normal limits or range of custody which the conviction has authorized the State to impose." The Court distinguished Wolff by noting that there the protected liberty interest in good time credit had been created by state law; here no comparable Massachusetts law stripped officials of the discretion to transfer prisoners to alternate facilities "for whatever reason or for no reason at all."

Shortly after Meachum, the Court embarked on a different approach to defining state-created liberty interests. Because dictum in Meachum distinguished Wolff by focusing on whether state action was mandatory or discretionary, the Court in later cases laid ever greater emphasis on this somewhat mechanical dichotomy. Greenholtz v. Inmates of Nebraska Penal and Correctional Complex, foreshadowed the methodology that would come to full fruition in Hewitt v. Helms. The Greenholtz inmates alleged that they had been unconstitutionally denied parole. Their claim centered on a state statute that set the date for discretionary parole at the time the minimum term of imprisonment less good time credits expired. The statute ordered release of a prisoner at that time, unless one of four specific conditions were shown. The Court apparently accepted the inmates' argument that the word "shall" in the statute created a legitimate expectation of release absent the requisite finding that one of the justifications for deferral existed, since the Court concluded that some measure of constitutional protection was due. Nevertheless, the State ultimately prevailed because the minimal process it had awarded the prisoners was deemed sufficient under the Fourteenth Amendment.

The Court made explicit in Hewitt what was implicit in Greenholtz. In evaluating the claims of inmates who had been confined to administrative segregation, it first rejected the inmates' claim of a right to remain in the general population as protected by the Due Process Clause on the authority of Meachum, Montanye, and Vitek. The Due Process Clause standing alone confers no liberty interest in freedom from state action taken "within the sentence imposed." It then concluded that the transfer to less amenable quarters for nonpunitive reasons was "ordinarily contemplated by a prison sentence." Examination of the possibility that the State had created a liberty interest by virtue of its prison regulations followed. Instead of looking to whether the State created an interest of "real substance" comparable to the good time credit scheme of Wolff, the Court asked whether the State had gone beyond issuing mere procedural guidelines and had used "language of an unmistakably mandatory character" such that the incursion on liberty

would not occur "absent specified substantive predicates." Finding such mandatory directives in the regulations before it, the Court decided that the State had created a protected liberty interest. It nevertheless, held, as it had in Greenholtz, that the full panoply of procedures conferred in Wolff were unnecessary to safeguard the inmates' interest and, if imposed, would undermine the prison's management objectives.

As this methodology took hold, no longer did inmates need to rely on a showing that they had suffered a "grievous loss" of liberty retained even after sentenced to terms of imprisonment. For the Court had ceased to examine the "nature" of the interest with respect to interests allegedly created by the State. In a series of cases since Hewitt, the Court has wrestled with the language of intricate, often rather routine prison guidelines to determine whether mandatory language and substantive predicates created an enforceable expectation that the state would produce a particular outcome with respect to the prisoner's conditions of confinement.

In Olim v. Wakinekona, the claimants identified prison regulations that required a particular kind of hearing before the prison administrator could, in his discretion, effect an interstate transfer to another prison. Parsing the language of the regulation led the Court to hold that the discretionary nature of the transfer decision negated any state-created liberty interest. Kentucky Department of Corrections v. Thompson dealt with regulations governing the visitation privileges of inmates. Asserting that a regulation created an absolute right to visitors absent a finding of certain substantive predicates, the inmates sought review of the adequacy of the procedures. As in Wakinekona, the Court determined the regulation left visitor exclusion to the discretion of the officials, and refused to elevate such expectations to the level of a liberty interest.

By shifting the focus of the liberty interest inquiry to one based on the language of a particular regulation, and not the nature of the deprivation, the Court encouraged prisoners to comb regulations in search of mandatory language on which to base entitlements to various state-conferred privileges. Courts have, in response, and not altogether illogically, drawn negative inferences from mandatory language in the text of prison regulations. The Court of Appeals' approach in this case is typical: it inferred from the mandatory directive that a finding of guilt "shall" be imposed under certain conditions the conclusion that the absence of such conditions prevents a finding of guilt.

Such a conclusion may be entirely sensible in the ordinary task of construing a statute defining rights and remedies available to the general public. It is a good deal less sensible in the case of a prison regulation primarily designed to guide correctional officials in the administration of a prison. Not only are such regulations not designed to confer rights on inmates, but the result of the negative implication jurisprudence is not to require the prison officials to follow the negative implication drawn from the regulation, but is instead to attach procedural protections that may be of quite a different nature. Here, for example, the Court of Appeals did not hold that a finding of guilt could not be made in the absence of substantial evidence. Instead, it held that the "liberty interest" created by the regulation entitled the inmate to the procedural protections set forth in Wolff.

Hewitt has produced at least two undesirable effects. First, it creates disincentives for States to codify prison management procedures in the interest of uniform treatment. Prison administrators need be concerned with the safety of the staff and inmate population. Ensuring that welfare often leads prison administrators to curb the discretion of staff on the front line who daily encounter prisoners hostile to the authoritarian structure of the prison environment. Such guidelines are not set forth solely to benefit the prisoner. They also aspire to instruct subordinate employees how to exercise discretion vested by the State in the warden, and to confine the authority of prison personnel in order to avoid widely different treatment of similar incidents. The approach embraced by Hewitt discourages this desirable development: States may avoid creation of "liberty" interests by having scarcely any regulations, or by conferring standardless discretion on correctional personnel.

Second, the Hewitt approach has led to the involvement of federal courts in the day-to-day management of prisons, often squandering judicial resources with little offsetting benefit to anyone. In so doing, it has run counter to the view expressed in several of our cases that federal courts ought to afford appropriate deference and flexibility to state officials trying to manage a volatile environment. Such flexibility is especially warranted in the fine-tuning of the ordinary incidents of prison life, a common subject of prisoner claims since Hewitt. See, e.g., Klos v. Haskell, 48 F.3d 81 (CA2 Feb. 10, 1995) (claiming liberty interest in right to participate in "shock program"—a type of boot camp for inmates); Segal v. Biller (CA9 Oct. 31, 1994) (claiming liberty interest in a waiver of the travel limit imposed on prison furloughs); Burgin v. Nix, 899 F.2d 733, 735 (CA8 1990) (claiming liberty interest in receiving a tray lunch rather than a sack lunch); Spruytte v. Walters, 753 F.2d 498, 506-508 (CA6 1985) (finding liberty interest in receiving a paperback dictionary due to a rule that states a prisoner "may receive any book . . . which does not present a threat to the order or security of the institution") (citation omitted); Lyon v. Farrier, 727 F.2d 766, 768-769 (CA8 1984) (claiming liberty interest in freedom from transfer to a smaller cell without electrical outlets for televisions and liberty interest in a prison job); United States v. Michigan, 680 F. Supp. 270, 277 (WD Mich. 1988) (finding liberty interest in not being placed on food loaf diet).

In light of the above discussion, we believe that the search for a negative implication from mandatory language in prisoner regulations has strayed from the real concerns undergirding the liberty protected by the Due Process Clause. The time has come to return to the due process principles we believe were correctly established and applied in Wolff and Meachum. Following Wolff, we recognize that States may under certain circumstances create liberty interests which are protected by the Due Process Clause. But these interests will be generally limited to freedom from restraint which, while not exceeding the sentence in such an unexpected manner as to give rise to protection by the Due Process Clause of its own force, see, e.g., Vitek, (transfer to mental hospital), and Washington, (involuntary administration of psychotropic drugs), nonetheless imposes atypical and significant hardship on the inmate in relation to the ordinary incidents of prison life.

Conner asserts, incorrectly, that any state action taken for a punitive reason encroaches upon a liberty interest under the Due Process Clause even in the absence of any state regulation. Neither Bell v. Wolfish, nor Ingraham v. Wright, requires such a rule. Bell dealt with the interests of pretrial detainees and not convicted prisoners. See also United States v. Salerno (distinguishing between "impermissible punishment" and "permissible regulation" of pretrial detainees). The Court in Bell correctly noted that a detainee "may not be punished prior to an adjudication of guilt in accordance with due process of law." The Court expressed concern that a State would attempt to punish a detainee for the crime for which he was indicted via preconviction holding conditions. Such a course would improperly extend the legitimate reasons for which such persons are detained—to ensure their presence at trial.

The same distinction applies to Ingraham, which addressed the rights of schoolchildren to remain free from arbitrary corporal punishment. The Court noted that the Due Process Clause historically encompassed the notion that the state could not "physically punish an individual except in accordance with due process of law" and so found schoolchildren sheltered. Although children sent to public school are lawfully confined to the classroom, arbitrary corporal punishment represents an invasion of personal security to which their parents do not consent when entrusting the educational mission to the State.

The punishment of incarcerated prisoners, on the other hand, serves different aims than those found invalid in Bell and Ingraham. The process does not impose retribution in lieu of a valid conviction, nor does it maintain physical control over free citizens forced by law to subject themselves to state control over the educational mission. It effectuates prison management and prisoner rehabilitative goals. Admittedly, prisoners do not shed all constitutional rights at the prison gate, but "lawful incarceration brings about the necessary withdrawal or limitation of many privileges and rights, a retraction justified by the considerations underlying our penal system." Discipline by prison officials in response to a

wide range of misconduct falls within the expected parameters of the sentence imposed by a court of law.

This case, though concededly punitive, does not present a dramatic departure from the basic conditions of Conner's indeterminate sentence. Although Conner points to dicta in cases implying that solitary confinement automatically triggers due process protection, Wolff; Baxter v. Palmigiano (assuming without deciding that freedom from punitive segregation for "serious misconduct" implicates a liberty interest, holding only that the prisoner has no right to counsel), this Court has not had the opportunity to address in an argued case the question whether disciplinary confinement of inmates itself implicates constitutional liberty interests. We hold that Conner's discipline in segregated confinement did not present the type of atypical, significant deprivation in which a state might conceivably create a liberty interest. The record shows that, at the time of Conner's punishment, disciplinary segregation, with insignificant exceptions, mirrored those conditions imposed upon inmates in administrative segregation and protective custody. We note also that the State expunged Conner's disciplinary record with respect to the "high misconduct" charge 9 months after Conner served time in segregation. Thus, Conner's confinement did not exceed similar, but totally discretionary confinement in either duration or degree of restriction. Indeed, the conditions at Halawa involve significant amounts of "lockdown time" even for inmates in the general population. Based on a comparison between inmates inside and outside disciplinary segregation, the State's actions in placing him there for 30 days did not work a major disruption in his environment.

Nor does Conner's situation present a case where the State's action will inevitably affect the duration of his sentence. Nothing in Hawaii's code requires the parole board to deny parole in the face of a misconduct record or to grant parole in its absence, even though misconduct is by regulation a relevant consideration. The decision to release a prisoner rests on a myriad of considerations. And, the prisoner is afforded procedural protection at his parole hearing in order to explain the circumstances behind his misconduct record. The chance that a finding of misconduct will alter the balance is simply too attenuated to invoke the procedural guarantees of the Due Process Clause. The Court rejected a similar claim in Meachum (declining to afford relief on the basis that petitioner's transfer record might affect his future confinement and possibility of parole).

We hold, therefore, that neither the Hawaii prison regulation in question, nor the Due Process Clause itself, afforded Conner a protected liberty interest that would entitle him to the procedural protections set forth in Wolff. The regime to which he was subjected as a result of the misconduct hearing was within the range of confinement to be normally expected for one serving an indeterminate term of 30 years to life.

The judgment of the Court of Appeals is accordingly Reversed.

JUSTICE GINSBURG, with whom JUSTICE STEVENS joins, dissenting.

Respondent DeMont Conner is a prisoner in a maximum-security Hawaii prison. After Conner reacted angrily to a strip search, a misconduct report charged him with obstructing the performance of a correctional officer's duties, using abusive language when talking to a staff member, and harassing a staff member. Conner received notice of the charges and had an opportunity, personally, to answer them. However, the disciplinary committee denied his request to call as witnesses staff members he said would attest to his innocence.

Conner contested the misconduct charges, but, according to the report of the disciplinary committee, he admitted his hesitation to follow orders and his use of profanity during the search. Based on Conner's statement to the committee, and on written statements submitted by the officer who conducted the search and his supervisor, the committee found Conner guilty of all charges. Sentenced to 30 days in the prison's segregation unit, Conner pursued an administrative appeal, which ultimately resulted in reversal of the obstruction conviction.

Unlike the Court, I conclude that Conner had a liberty interest, protected by the Fourteenth Amendment's Due Process Clause, in

avoiding the disciplinary confinement he endured. As JUSTICE BREYER details, Conner's prison punishment effected a severe alteration in the conditions of his incarceration. Disciplinary confinement as punishment for "high misconduct" not only deprives prisoners of privileges for protracted periods; unlike administrative segregation and protective custody, disciplinary confinement also stigmatizes them and diminishes parole prospects. Those immediate and lingering consequences should suffice to qualify such confinement as liberty-depriving for purposes of Due Process Clause protection.

I see the Due Process Clause itself, not Hawaii's prison code, as the wellspring of the protection due Conner. Deriving protected liberty interests from mandatory language in local prison codes would make of the fundamental right something more in certain States, something less in others. Liberty that may vary from Ossining, New York, to San Quentin, California, does not resemble the "Liberty" enshrined among "unalienable Rights" with which all persons are "endowed by their Creator." Declaration of Independence; see Meachum ("The Due Process Clause protects [the unalienable liberty recognized in the Declaration of Independence] rather than the particular rights or privileges conferred by specific laws or regulations.")

Deriving the prisoner's due process right from the code for his prison, moreover, yields this practical anomaly: a State that scarcely attempts to control the behavior of its prison guards may, for that very laxity, escape constitutional accountability; a State that tightly cabins the discretion of its prison workers may, for that attentiveness, become vulnerable to constitutional claims. An incentive for ruleless prison management disserves the State's penological goals and jeopardizes the welfare of prisoners.

To fit the liberty recognized in our fundamental instrument of government, the process due by reason of the Constitution similarly should not depend on the particularities of the local prison's code. Rather, the basic, universal requirements are notice of the acts of misconduct prison officials say the inmate committed, and an opportunity to respond to the charges before a trustworthy decisionmaker. See generally Friendly, "Some Kind of Hearing," 123 U. Pa. L. Rev. 1267, 1278-1281

(1975) (an unbiased tribunal, notice of the proposed government action and the grounds asserted for it, and an opportunity to present reasons why the proposed action should not be taken are fundamental; additional safeguards depend on the importance of the private interest, the utility of the particular safeguards, and the burden of affording them).

For the reasons JUSTICE BREYER cogently presents, a return of this case to the District Court would be unavoidable if it were recognized that Conner was deprived of liberty within the meaning of the Due Process Clause. But upon such a return, a renewed motion for summary judgment would be in order, for the record, as currently composed, does not show that Conner was denied any procedural protection warranted in his case.

In particular, a call for witnesses is properly refused when the projected testimony is not relevant to the matter in controversy. Unless Conner were to demonstrate, in face of the disciplinary committee's stated reliance on his own admissions, that an issue of material fact is genuinely in controversy, his due process claim would fail.

* * *

Because I conclude that Conner was deprived of liberty within the meaning of the Due Process Clause, I dissent from the judgment of the Court. I would return the case for a precisely focused determination whether Conner received the process that was indeed due.

JUSTICE BREYER, with whom JUSTICE SOUTER joins, dissenting. The specific question in this case is whether a particular punishment that, among other things, segregates an inmate from the general prison population for violating a disciplinary rule deprives the inmate of "liberty" within the terms of the Fourteenth Amendment's Due Process Clause. The majority, asking whether that punishment "imposes atypical and significant hardship on the inmate in relation to the ordinary incidents of prison life," concludes that it does not do so. The majority's reasoning, however, particularly when read in light of this Court's precedents, seems to me to lead to the opposite conclusion. And, for that reason, I dissent.

I

The respondent, DeMont Conner, is an inmate at Halawa Correctional Facility, a maximum security prison in Hawaii. In August 1987, as a result of an altercation with a guard, prison authorities charged Conner with violating several prison disciplinary regulations, including one that prohibited "physical interference . . . resulting in the obstruction . . . of the performance of a correctional function. . . ." The prison's "adjustment committee" found Conner "guilty" and imposed a punishment of 30 days of "disciplinary segregation." Eventually, but after Conner had served the 30 days, a review official in the prison set aside the committee's determination, and expunged it from Conner's record.

In the meantime, Conner had brought this "civil rights" action in Federal District Court in Hawaii. He claimed, among other things, that the adjustment committee's failure to let him call certain witnesses had deprived him of his "liberty . . . without due process of law." U.S. Const., Amdt. 14, § 1. The District Court granted summary judgment for the prison officials. But, the Ninth Circuit agreed with Conner that the committee's punishment had deprived him of procedurally protected "liberty." It remanded the case to the District Court to determine whether the refusal to allow Conner to call the particular witnesses denied him of the process he was "due."

The issue before this Court is whether Connner's particular punishment amounted to a deprivation of Conner's "liberty" within the meaning of the Due Process Clause.

II

The Fourteenth Amendment says that a State shall not "deprive any person of life, liberty, or property, without due process of law." U.S. Const., Amdt. 14, § 1. In determining whether state officials have deprived an inmate, such as Conner, of a procedurally protected "liberty," this Court traditionally has looked either (1) to the nature of the deprivation (how severe, in degree or kind) or (2) to the State's rules governing the imposition of that deprivation (whether they, in effect, give the inmate a "right" to avoid it). Thus, this Court has said that certain changes in conditions may be so severe or so different from ordinary conditions of confinement that, whether or not state law gives state authorities broad discretionary power to impose them, the state authorities may not do so "without complying with minimum requirements of due process." Vitek v. Jones, ("involuntary commitment to a mental hospital"); Washington v. Harper ("unwanted administration of antipsychotic drugs"). The Court has also said that deprivations that are less severe or more closely related to the original terms of confinement nonetheless will amount to deprivations of procedurally protected liberty, provided that state law (including prison regulations) narrowly cabins the legal power of authorities to impose the deprivation (thereby giving the inmate a kind of right to avoid it). See Hewitt v. Helms (liberty interest created by regulations "requiring . . . that administrative segregation will not occur absent specified substantive predicates"); Thompson, supra, at 461 ("method of inquiry . . . always has been to examine closely the language of the relevant statutes and regulations"); Board of Pardons v. Allen, (insisting upon "standards that place real limits on decisionmaker discretion"); Olim v. Wakinekona (existence of liberty interest regarding interstate prison transfers depends upon state regulations); Montanye v. Haymes (same for intrastate prison transfers); Meachum v. Fano (same).

If we apply these general pre-existing principles to the relevant facts before us, it seems fairly clear, as the Ninth Circuit found, that the prison punishment here at issue deprived Conner of constitutionally protected "liberty." For one thing, the punishment worked a fairly major change in Conner's conditions. In the absence of the punishment, Conner, like other inmates in Halawa's general prison population would have left his cell and worked, taken classes, or mingled with others for eight hours each day. As a result of disciplinary segregation, however, Conner, for 30 days, had to spend his entire time alone in his cell (with the exception of 50 minutes each day on average for brief exercise and shower periods, during which he nonetheless remained isolated from other inmates and was constrained by leg irons and waist chains). Cf. Hughes v. Rowe (disciplinary "segregation of a prisoner without a prior

hearing may violate due process if the postponement of procedural protections is not justified by apprehended emergency conditions"); Wolff v. McDonnell ("solitary confinement"—i.e., segregation "in the usual 'disciplinary cell'" or a "dry cell"—"represents a major change in the conditions of confinement"); Baxter v. Palmigiano (segregation for "serious misconduct" triggers due process protection) (citation omitted).

Moreover, irrespective of whether this punishment amounts to a deprivation of liberty independent of state law, here the prison's own disciplinary rules severely cabin the authority of prison officials to impose this kind of punishment. They provide (among other things):

(a) that certain specified acts shall constitute "high misconduct";

(b) that misconduct punishable by more than four hours in disciplinary segregation "shall be punished" through a prison "adjustment committee" (composed of three unbiased members);

(c) that, when an inmate is charged with such misconduct, then (after notice and a hearing) "[a] finding of guilt shall be made" if the charged inmate admits guilt or the "charge is supported by substantial evidence"; and

(d) that the "sanctions" for high misconduct that "may be imposed as punishment . . . shall include . . . disciplinary segregation up to thirty days."

The prison rules thus: (1) impose a punishment that is substantial, (2) restrict its imposition as a punishment to instances in which an inmate has committed a defined offense, and (3) prescribe nondiscretionary standards for determining whether or not an inmate committed that offense. Accordingly, under this Court's liberty-defining standards, imposing the punishment would "deprive" Conner of "liberty" within the meaning of the Due Process Clause. Compare Hewitt v. Helms (liberty interest created by regulations "requiring that . . . administrative segregation will not occur absent specified substantive predicates"), with Thompson (no liberty interest created by regulations which gave officials broad discretion to refuse a visit whenever "there are reasonable grounds to believe that," among other things, "the visit will be detrimental to the inmate's rehabilitation"). Thus, under existing law, the Ninth Circuit correctly decided that the punishment deprived Conner of procedurally protected liberty and that the District Court should go on to decide whether or not the prison's procedures provided Conner with the "process" that is "due."

III

The majority, while not disagreeing with this summary of pre-existing law, seeks to change, or to clarify, that law's "liberty" defining standards in one important respect. The majority believes that the Court's present "cabining of discretion" standard reads the Constitution as providing procedural protection for trivial "rights," as, for example, where prison rules set forth specific standards for the content of prison meals. It adds that this approach involves courts too deeply in routine matters of prison administration, all without sufficient justification. Ibid. It therefore imposes a minimum standard, namely that a deprivation falls within the Fourteenth Amendment's definition of "liberty" only if it "imposes atypical and significant hardship on the inmate in relation to the ordinary incidents of prison life."

I am not certain whether or not the Court means this standard to change prior law radically. If so, its generality threatens the law with uncertainty, for some lower courts may read the majority opinion as offering significantly less protection against deprivation of liberty, while others may find in it an extension of protection to certain "atypical" hardships that pre-existing law would not have covered. There is no need, however, for a radical reading of this standard, nor any other signficant change in present law, to achieve the majority's basic objective, namely to read the Constitution's Due Process Clause to protect inmates against deprivations of freedom that are important, not comparatively insignificant. Rather, in my view, this concern simply requires elaborating, and explaining, the Court's present standards (without radical

revision) in order to make clear that courts must apply them in light of the purposes they were meant to serve. As so read, the standards will not create procedurally protected "liberty" interests where only minor matters are at stake.

Three sets of considerations, taken together, support my conclusion that the Court need not (and today's generally phrased minimum standard therefore does not) significantly revise current doctrine by deciding to remove minor prison matters from federal-court scrutiny. First, although this Court has said, and continues to say, that some deprivations of an inmate's freedom are so severe in kind or degree (or so far removed from the original terms of confinement) that they amount to deprivations of liberty, irrespective of whether state law (or prison rules) "cabin discretion," it is not easy to specify just when, or how much of, a loss triggers this protection. There is a broad middle category of imposed restraints or deprivations that, considered by themselves, are neither obviously so serious as to fall within, nor obviously so insignificant as to fall without, the Clause's protection.

Second, the difficult line-drawing task that this middle category implies helps to explain why this Court developed its additional liberty-defining standard, which looks to local law (examining whether that local law creates a "liberty" by significantly limiting the discretion of local authorities to impose a restraint). Despite its similarity to the way in which the Court determines the existence, or nonexistence, of "property" for Due Process Clause purposes, the justification for looking at local law is not the same in the prisoner liberty context. In protecting property, the Due Process Clause often aims to protect reliance, say, reliance upon an "entitlement" that local (i.e., nonconstitutional) law itself has created or helped to define. See Board of Regents of State Colleges v. Roth ("It is a purpose of the ancient institution of property to protect those claims upon which people rely in their daily lives, reliance that must not be arbitrarily undermined"). In protecting liberty, however, the Due Process Clause protects, not this kind of reliance upon a government-conferred benefit, but rather an absence of government restraint, the very absence of restraint that we call freedom.

Nevertheless, there are several other important reasons, in the prison context, to consider the provisions of state law. The fact that a further deprivation of an inmate's freedom takes place under local rules that cabin the authorities' discretionary power to impose the restraint suggests, other things being equal, that the matter is more likely to have played an important role in the life of the inmate. It suggests, other things being equal, that the matter is more likely of a kind to which procedural protections historically have applied, and where they normally prove useful, for such rules often single out an inmate and condition a deprivation upon the existence, or nonexistence, of particular facts. It suggests, other things being equal, that the matter will not involve highly judgmental administrative matters that call for the wise exercise of discretion—matters where courts reasonably should hesitate to second-guess prison administrators. It suggests, other things being equal, that the inmate will have thought that he himself, through control of his own behavior, could have avoided the deprivation, and thereby have believed that (in the absence of his misbehavior) the restraint fell outside the "sentence imposed" upon him. Finally, courts can identify the presence or absence of cabined discretion fairly easily and objectively, at least much of the time. These characteristics of "cabined discretion" mean that courts can use it as a kind of touchstone that can help them, when they consider the broad middle category of prisoner restraints, to separate those kinds of restraints that, in general, are more likely to call for constitutionally guaranteed procedural protection, from those that more likely do not. Given these reasons and the precedent, I believe courts will continue to find this touchstone helpful as they seek to apply the majority's middle category standard.

Third, there is, therefore, no need to apply the "discretion-cabining" approach—the basic purpose of which is to provide a somewhat more objective method for identifying deprivations of protected "liberty" within a broad middle-range of prisoner restraints—where a deprivation is unimportant enough (or so similar in nature to ordinary imprisonment) that it rather clearly falls outside that middle category. Prison, by design, restricts the inmates' freedom. And, one cannot prop-

erly view unimportant matters that happen to be the subject of prison regulations as substantially aggravating a loss that has already occurred. Indeed, a regulation about a minor matter, for example, a regulation that seems to cabin the discretionary power of a prison administrator to deprive an inmate of, say, a certain kind of lunch, may amount simply to an instruction to the administrator about how to do his job, rather than a guarantee to the inmate of a "right" to the status quo. Cf. Colon v. Schneider, 899 F.2d 660, 668 (CA7 1990) (rules governing use of Mace to subdue inmates "directed toward the prison staff, not the inmates"). Thus, this Court has never held that comparatively unimportant prisoner "deprivations" fall within the scope of the Due Process Clause even if local law limits the authority of prison administrators to impose such minor deprivations. See Thompson (leaving question open). And, in my view, it should now simply specify that they do not.

I recognize that, as a consequence, courts must separate the unimportant from the potentially significant, without the help of the more objective "discretion-cabining" test. Yet, making that judicial judgment seems no more difficult than many other judicial tasks. See Goss v. Lopez ("de minimis" line defining property interests under the Due Process Clause). It seems to me possible to separate less significant matters such as television privileges, "sack" versus "tray" lunches, playing the state lottery, attending an ex-stepfather's funeral, or the limits of travel when on prison furlough, from more significant matters, such as the solitary confinement at issue here. Indeed, prison regulations themselves may help in this respect, such as the regulations here which separate (from more serious matters) "low moderate" and "minor" misconduct. Compare, on the one hand, the maximum punishment for "moderate" misconduct of two weeks of disciplinary segregation, with the less severe maximum punishments, on the other hand, for "low moderate" and "minor" misconduct (several hours of disciplinary segregation and "loss of privileges" such as "community recreation; commissary; snacks; cigarettes, smoking; personal visits—no longer than fifteen days; personal correspondence; personal phone calls for not longer than fifteen days";

impounding personal property; extra duty; and reprimand).

The upshot is the following: the problems that the majority identifies suggest that this Court should make explicit the lower definitional limit, in the prison context, of "liberty" under the Due Process Clause—a limit that is already implicit in this Court's precedent. Those problems do not require abandoning that precedent.

IV

The Court today reaffirms that the "liberty" protected by the Fourteenth Amendment includes interests that state law may create. It excludes relatively minor matters from that protection. Ibid. (requiring "atypical and significant hardship on the inmate"). And, it does not question the vast body of case law, including cases from this Court and every Circuit, recognizing that segregation can deprive an inmate of constitutionally-protected "liberty." That being so, it is difficult to see why the Court reverses, rather than affirms, the Court of Appeals in this case.

The majority finds that Conner's "discipline in segregated confinement did not present" an "atypical significant deprivation" because of three special features of his case, taken together. First, the punishment "mirrored" conditions imposed upon inmates in "administrative segregation and protective custody." Second, Hawaii's prison regulations give prison officials broad discretion to impose these other forms of nonpunitive segregation. And, third, the State later "expunged Conner's disciplinary record," thereby erasing any stigma and transforming Conner's segregation for violation of a specific disciplinary rule into the sort of "totally discretionary confinement" that would not have implicated a liberty interest.

I agree with the first two of the majority's assertions. The conditions in administrative and disciplinary segregation are relatively similar in Hawaii. And, the rules governing administrative segregation do, indeed, provide prison officials with broad leeway. But, I disagree with the majority's assertion about the relevance of the expungement. How can a later decision of prison authorities transform Conner's segregation for a violation of a spe-

cific disciplinary rule into a term of segregation under the administrative rules? How can a later expungement restore to Conner the liberty that, in fact, he had already lost? Because Conner was found guilty under prison disciplinary rules, and was sentenced to solitary confinement under those rules, the Court should look to those rules.

In sum, expungement or no, Conner suffered a deprivation that was significant, not insignificant. And, that deprivation took place under disciplinary rules that, as described in Part II, supra, do cabin official discretion sufficiently. I would therefore hold that Conner was deprived of "liberty" within the meaning of the Due Process Clause.

V

Other related legal principles, applicable here, should further alleviate the majority's fear that application of the Due Process Clause to significant prison disciplinary action, see Part III, supra, will lead federal courts to intervene improperly (as the majority sees it) "in the day-to-day management of prisons, often squandering judicial resources with little offsetting benefit to anyone." For one thing, the "process" that is "due" in the context of prison discipline is not the full blown procedure that accompanies criminal trials. Rather, "due process" itself is a flexible concept, which, in the context of a prison, must take account of the legitimate needs of prison administration when deciding what procedural elements basic considerations of fairness require. See, e.g., Goss v. Lopez (the "very nature of due process negates any concept of inflexible procedures universally applicable to every imaginable situation"); Mathews v. Eldridge ("Due process is flexible and calls for such procedural protections as the particular situation demands"); Friendly, "Some Kind of Hearing," 123 U. Pa. L. Rev. 1267, 1278 (1975) ("required degree of procedural safeguards varies"); Wolff (requiring—in addition to notice, some kind of hearing and written reasons for the decision—permission to call witnesses and to present documentary evidence when doing so "will not be unduly hazardous to institutional safety or correctional goals").

More importantly for present purposes, whether or not a particular procedural element normally seems appropriate to a certain kind of proceeding, the Due Process Clause does not require process unless, in the individual case, there is a relevant factual dispute between the parties. Just as courts do not hold hearings when there is no "genuine" and "material" issue of fact in dispute between the parties, so the Due Process Clause does not entitle an inmate to additional disciplinary hearing procedure (such as the calling of a witness) unless there is a factual dispute (relevant to guilt) that the additional procedure might help to resolve.

I mention this latter legal point both because it illustrates a legal protection against the meritless case, and because a review of the record before us indicates that, in this very case, if we were to affirm, it would pose an important obstacle to Conner's eventual success. The record contains the prison adjustment committee's report, which says that its finding of guilt rests upon Conner's own admissions. The com-mittee wrote that it "based" its "decision" upon Conner's "statements" that (when he was strip searched) "he turned around" and "looked at" the officer, he "then 'eyed up'" the officer, he "was hesitant to comply" with the strip-search instructions, he "dislikes" the officer, and he spoke an obscenity during the search process. The record contains no explanation that we have found, either in Conner's affidavits or elsewhere, of how the witnesses he wanted to call (or the other procedures that he sought) could have led to any evidence relevant to the facts at issue.

* * *

Because the Court of Appeals remanded this case to the District Court for consideration of these matters, and because, as explained in Parts II-IV, supra, I believe it correctly decided that Conner was deprived of liberty within the meaning of the Due Process Clause, I would affirm its judgment. For these reasons, I respectfully dissent.

Cases Relating to Chapter 9

Parole

MORRISSEY
v.
BREWER

**408 U.S. 471; 92 S. Ct. 2593;
33 L. Ed. 2d 484 (1972)**

MR. CHIEF JUSTICE BURGER delivered the opinion of the Court.

We granted certiorari in this case to determine whether the Due Process Clause of the Fourteenth Amendment requires that a State afford an individual some opportunity to be heard prior to revoking his parole.

Petitioner Morrissey was convicted of false drawing or uttering of checks in 1967 pursuant to his guilty plea, and was sentenced to not more than seven years' confinement. He was paroled from the Iowa State Penitentiary in June 1968. Seven months later, at the direction of his parole officer, he was arrested in his home town as a parole violator and incarcerated in the county jail. One week later, after review of the parole officer's written report, the Iowa Board of Parole revoked Morrissey's parole, and he was returned to the penitentiary located about 100 miles from his home. Petitioner asserts he received no hearing prior to revocation of his parole.

The parole officer's report on which the Board of Parole acted shows that petitioner's parole was revoked on the basis of information that he had violated the conditions of parole by buying a car under an assumed name and operating it without permission, giving false statements to police concerning his address and insurance company after a minor accident, obtaining credit under an assumed name, and failing to report his place of residence to his parole officer. The report states that the officer interviewed Morrissey, and that he could not explain why he did not contact his parole officer despite his effort to excuse this on the ground that he had been sick. Further, the report asserts that Morrissey admitted buying the car and obtaining credit under an assumed name, and also admitted being involved in the accident. The parole officer recommended that his parole be revoked because of "his continual violating of his parole rules."

The situation as to petitioner Booher is much the same. Pursuant to his guilty plea, Booher was convicted of forgery in 1966 and sentenced to a maximum term of 10 years. He was paroled November 14, 1968. In August 1969, at his parole officer's direction, he was arrested in his home town for a violation of his parole and confined in the county jail several miles away. On September 13, 1969, on the basis of a written report by his parole officer, the Iowa Board of Parole revoked Booher's parole and Booher was recommitted to the state penitentiary, located about 250 miles from his home, to complete service of his sentence. Petitioner asserts he received no hearing prior to revocation of his parole.

The parole officer's report with respect to Booher recommended that his parole be revoked because he had violated the territorial restrictions of his parole without consent, had obtained a driver's license under an assumed name, operated a motor vehicle without permission, and had violated the employment condition of his parole by failing to keep himself in gainful employment. The report stated that the officer had interviewed Booher and that he had acknowledged to the parole officer that he had left the specified territorial limits and had operated the car and had obtained a license under an assumed name "knowing that it was wrong." The report further noted that Booher had stated that he had not found employment because he could not find work that would pay him what he wanted—he stated he would not work for $2.25 to $2.75 per hour—and that he had left the area to get work in another city.

After exhausting state remedies, both petitioners filed habeas corpus petitions in the United States District Court for the Southern District of Iowa alleging that they had been denied due process because their paroles had been revoked without a hearing. The State responded by arguing that no hearing was required. The District Court held on the basis of controlling authority that the State's failure to accord a hearing prior to parole revocation did not violate due process. On appeal, the two cases were consolidated.

The Court of Appeals, dividing 4 to 3, held that due process does not require a hearing. The majority recognized that the traditional view of parole as a privilege rather than a vested right is no longer dispositive as to whether due process is applicable; however, on a balancing of the competing interests involved, it concluded that no hearing is required. The court reasoned that parole is only "a correctional device authorizing service of sentence outside the penitentiary," 443 F.2d 942, 947; the parolee is still "in custody." Accordingly, the Court of Appeals was of the view that prison officials must have large discretion in making revocation determinations, and that courts should retain their traditional reluctance to interfere with disciplinary matters properly under the control of state prison authorities. The majority expressed the view that "non-legal, non-adversary considerations" were often the determinative factors in making a parole revocation decision. It expressed concern that if adversary hearings were required for parole revocation, "with the full panoply of rights accorded in criminal proceedings," the function of the parole board

as "an administrative body acting in the role of parens patriae would be aborted," id., at 949, and the board would be more reluctant to grant parole in the first instance—an apprehension that would not be without some basis if the choice were between a full-scale adversary proceeding or no hearing at all. Additionally, the majority reasoned that the parolee has no statutory right to remain on parole. Iowa law provides that a parolee may be returned to the institution at any time. Our holding in Mempa v. Rhay, 389 U.S. 128 (1967), was distinguished on the ground that it involved deferred sentencing upon probation revocation, and thus involved a stage of the criminal proceeding, whereas parole revocation was not a stage in the criminal proceeding. The Court of Appeals' decision was consistent with many other decisions on parole revocations.

In their brief in this Court, respondents assert for the first time that petitioners were in fact granted hearings after they were returned to the penitentiary. More generally, respondents say that within two months after the Board revokes an individual's parole and orders him returned to the penitentiary, on the basis of the parole officer's written report it grants the individual a hearing before the Board. At that time, the Board goes over "each of the alleged parole violations with the returnee, and he is given an opportunity to orally present his side of the story to the Board." If the returnee denies the report, it is the practice of the Board to conduct a further investigation before making a final determination either affirming the initial revocation, modifying it, or reversing it.[1] Respondents assert that Morrissey, whose parole was revoked on January 31, 1969, was granted a hearing before the Board on February 12, 1969. Booher's parole was revoked on September 13, 1969, and he was granted a hearing on October 14, 1969. At these hearings,

---

[1] The hearing required by due process, as defined herein, must be accorded before the effective decision. See Armstrong v. Manzo, 380 U.S. 545 (1965). Petitioners assert here that only one of the 540 revocations ordered most recently by the Iowa Parole Board was reversed after hearing, Petitioners' Reply Brief 7, suggesting that the hearing may not objectively evaluate the revocation decision.

respondents tell us—in the briefs—both Morrissey and Booher admitted the violations alleged in the parole violation reports.

Nothing in the record supplied to this Court indicates that respondent claimed, either in the District Court or the Court of Appeals, that petitioners had received hearings promptly after their paroles were revoked, or that in such hearing they admitted the violations; that information comes to us only in the respondents' brief here. Further, even the assertions that respondents make here are not based on any public record but on interviews with two of the members of the parole board. In the interview relied on to show that petitioners admitted their violations, the board member did not assert he could remember that both Morrissey and Booher admitted the parole violations with which they were charged. He stated only that, according to his memory, in the previous several years all but three returnees had admitted commission of the parole infractions alleged and that neither of the petitioners was among the three who denied them.

We must therefore treat this case in the posture and on the record respondents elected to rely on in the District Court and the Court of Appeals. If the facts are otherwise, respondents may make a showing in the District Court that petitioners in fact have admitted the violations charged before a neutral officer.

I

Before reaching the issue of whether due process applies to the parole system, it is important to recall the function of parole in the correctional process.

During the past 60 years, the practice of releasing prisoners on parole before the end of their sentences has become an integral part of the penological system. Note, Parole Revocation in the Federal System, 56 Geo. L. J. 705 (1968). Rather than being an ad hoc exercise of clemency, parole is an established variation on imprisonment of convicted criminals. Its purpose is to help individuals reintegrate into society as constructive individuals as soon as they are able, without being confined for the full term of the sentence imposed. It also serves to alleviate the costs to society of keeping an individual in prison.[2] The essence of parole is release from prison, before the completion of sentence, on the condition that the prisoner abide by certain rules during the balance of the sentence. Under some systems, parole is granted automatically after the service of a certain portion of a prison term. Under others, parole is granted by the discretionary action of a board, which evaluates an array of information about a prisoner and makes a prediction whether he is ready to reintegrate into society.

To accomplish the purpose of parole, those who are allowed to leave prison early are subjected to specified conditions for the duration of their terms. These conditions restrict their activities substantially beyond the ordinary restrictions imposed by law on an individual citizen. Typically, parolees are forbidden to use liquor or to have associations or correspondence with certain categories of undesirable persons. Typically, also they must seek permission from their parole officers before engaging in specified activities, such as changing employment or living quarters, marrying, acquiring or operating a motor vehicle, traveling outside the community, and incurring substantial indebtedness. Additionally, parolees must regularly report to the parole officer to whom they are assigned and sometimes they must make periodic written reports of their activities. Arluke, A Summary of Parole Rules—Thirteen Years Later, 15 Crime & Delin. 267, 272-273 (1969).

The parole officers are part of the administrative system designed to assist parolees and to offer them guidance. The conditions of parole serve a dual purpose; they prohibit, either absolutely or conditionally, behavior that is deemed dangerous to the restoration of the individual into normal society. And through the requirement of reporting to the parole officer and seeking guidance and permission before doing many things, the offi-

---

[2] See Warren, Probation in the Federal System of Criminal Justice, 19 Fed. Prob. 3 (Sept. 1955); Annual Report, Ohio Adult Parole Authority 1964/65, pp. 13-14; Note, Parole: A Critique of Its Legal Foundations and Conditions, 38 N. Y. U. L. Rev. 702, 705-707 (1963).

cer is provided with information about the parolee and an opportunity to advise him. The combination puts the parole officer into the position in which he can try to guide the parolee into constructive development.[3]

The enforcement leverage that supports the parole conditions derives from the authority to return the parolee to prison to serve out the balance of his sentence if he fails to abide by the rules. In practice, not every violation of parole conditions automatically leads to revocation. Typically, a parolee will be counseled to abide by the conditions of parole, and the parole officer ordinarily does not take steps to have parole revoked unless he thinks that the violations are serious and continuing so as to indicate that the parolee is not adjusting properly and cannot be counted on to avoid antisocial activity.[4] The broad discretion accorded the parole officer is also inherent in some of the quite vague conditions, such as the typical requirement that the parolee avoid "undesirable" associations or correspondence. Cf. Arciniega v. Freeman, 404 U.S. 4 (1971). Yet revocation of parole is not an unusual phenomenon, affecting only a few parolees. It has been estimated that 35%-45% of all parolees are subjected to revocation and return to prison.[5] Sometimes revocation occurs when the parolee is accused of another crime; it is often preferred to a new prosecution because of the procedural ease of recommitting the individual on the basis of a lesser showing by the State.[6]

Implicit in the system's concern with parole violations is the notion that the parolee is entitled to retain his liberty as long as he substantially abides by the conditions of his parole. The first step in a revocation decision thus involves a wholly retrospective factual question: whether the parolee has in fact acted in violation of one or more conditions of his parole. Only if it is determined that the parolee did violate the conditions does the second question arise: should the parolee be recommitted to prison or should other steps be taken to protect society and improve chances of rehabilitation? The first step is relatively simple; the second is more complex. The second question involves the application of expertise by the parole authority in making a prediction as to the ability of the individual to live in society without committing antisocial acts. This part of the decision, too, depends on facts, and therefore it is important for the board to know not only that some violation was committed but also to know accurately how many and how serious the violations were. Yet this second step, deciding what to do about the violation once it is identified, is not purely factual but also predictive and discretionary.

If a parolee is returned to prison, he usually receives no credit for the time "served" on parole.[7] Thus, the returnee may face a potential of substantial imprisonment.

II

We begin with the proposition that the revocation of parole is not part of a criminal prosecution and thus the full panoply of rights due a defendant in such a proceeding does not apply to parole revocations. Cf. Mempa v. Rhay, 389 U.S. 128 (1967). Parole arises after the end of the criminal prosecution, including imposition of sentence. Supervision is not directly by the court but by an administrative agency, which is sometimes an arm of the court and sometimes of the executive. Revocation deprives an individual, not of the absolute liberty to which every citizen is entitled, but only of the conditional liberty properly dependent on observance of special parole restrictions.

We turn, therefore, to the question whether the requirements of due process in general

---

[3] Note, Observations on the Administration of Parole, 79 Yale L. J. 698, 699-700 (1970).

[4] Ibid.

[5] President's Commission on Law Enforcement and Administration of Justice, Task Force Report: Corrections 62 (1967). The substantial revocation rate indicates that parole administrators often deliberately err on the side of granting parole in borderline cases.

[6] See Morrissey v. Brewer, 443 F.2d 942, at 953-954, n. 5 (CA8 1971) (Lay, J., dissenting); Rose v. Haskins, 388 F.2d 91, 104 (CA6 1968) (Celebrezze, J., dissenting).

[7] Arluke, A Summary of Parole Rules—Thirteen Years Later, 15 Crime and Delinquency 267, 271 (1969); Note, Parole Revocation in the Federal System, 56 Geo. L. J. 705, 733 (1968).

apply to parole revocations. As MR. JUS-
TICE BLACKMUN has written recently,
"this Court now has rejected the concept that
constitutional rights turn upon whether a
governmental benefit is characterized as a
'right' or as a 'privilege.'" Graham v. Richardson, 403 U.S. 365, 374 (1971). Whether any
procedural protections are due depends on
the extent to which an individual will be
"condemned to suffer grievous loss." Joint
Anti-Fascist Refugee Committee v. McGrath,
341 U.S. 123, 168 (1951) (Frankfurter, J.,
concurring), quoted in Goldberg v. Kelly, 397
U.S. 254, 263 (1970). The question is not
merely the "weight" of the individual's interest, but whether the nature of the interest is
one within the contemplation of the "liberty
or property" language of the Fourteenth
Amendment. Fuentes v. Shevin, 407 U.S. 67
(1972). Once it is determined that due
process applies, the question remains what
process is due. It has been said so often by
this Court and others as not to require citation of authority that due process is flexible
and calls for such procedural protections as
the particular situation demands. "Consideration of what procedures due process may
require under any given set of circumstances
must begin with a determination of the precise nature of the government function
involved as well as of the private interest that
has been affected by governmental action."
Cafeteria & Restaurant Workers Union v.
McElroy, 367 U.S. 886, 895 (1961). To say
that the concept of due process is flexible
does not mean that judges are at large to
apply it to any and all relationships. Its flexibility is in its scope once it has been determined that some process is due; it is a recognition that not all situations calling for
procedural safeguards call for the same kind
of procedure.

We turn to an examination of the nature of
the interest of the parolee in his continued
liberty. The liberty of a parolee enables him
to do a wide range of things open to persons
who have never been convicted of any crime.
The parolee has been released from prison
based on an evaluation that he shows reasonable promise of being able to return to society and function as a responsible, self-reliant
person. Subject to the conditions of his
parole, he can be gainfully employed and is

free to be with family and friends and to form
the other enduring attachments of normal
life. Though the State properly subjects him
to many restrictions not applicable to other
citizens, his condition is very different from
that of confinement in a prison.[8] He may
have been on parole for a number of years
and may be living a relatively normal life at
the time he is faced with revocation.[9] The
parolee has relied on at least an implicit
promise that parole will be revoked only if he
fails to live up to the parole conditions. In
many cases, the parolee faces lengthy incarceration if his parole is revoked.

We see, therefore, that the liberty of a
parolee, although indeterminate, includes
many of the core values of unqualified liberty
and its termination inflicts a "grievous loss"
on the parolee and often on others. It is hardly
useful any longer to try to deal with this problem in terms of whether the parolee's liberty is
a "right" or a "privilege." By whatever name,
the liberty is valuable and must be seen as
within the protection of the Fourteenth
Amendment. Its termination calls for some
orderly process, however informal.

Turning to the question what process is
due, we find that the State's interests are several. The State has found the parolee guilty of
a crime against the people. That finding justifies imposing extensive restrictions on the
individual's liberty. Release of the parolee
before the end of his prison sentence is made
with the recognition that with many prisoners
there is a risk that they will not be able to live
in society without committing additional
antisocial acts. Given the previous conviction
and the proper imposition of conditions, the
State has an overwhelming interest in being
able to return the individual to imprisonment
without the burden of a new adversary criminal trial if in fact he has failed to abide by
the conditions of his parole.

---

[8] "It is not sophistic to attach greater importance
    to a person's justifiable reliance in maintaining
    his conditional freedom so long as he abides by
    the conditions of his release, than to his mere
    anticipation or hope of freedom." United States
    ex rel. Bey v. Connecticut Board of Parole, 443
    F.2d 1079, 1086 (CA2 1971).

[9] See, e.g., Murray v. Page, 429 F.2d 1359 (CA10
    1970) (parole revoked after eight years; 15 years
    remaining on original term).

Yet, the State has no interest in revoking parole without some informal procedural guarantees. Although the parolee is often formally described as being "in custody," the argument cannot even be made here that summary treatment is necessary as it may be with respect to controlling a large group of potentially disruptive prisoners in actual custody. Nor are we persuaded by the argument that revocation is so totally a discretionary matter that some form of hearing would be administratively intolerable. A simple factual hearing will not interfere with the exercise of discretion. Serious studies have suggested that fair treatment on parole revocation will not result in fewer grants of parole.[10]

This discretionary aspect of the revocation decision need not be reached unless there is first an appropriate determination that the individual has in fact breached the conditions of parole. The parolee is not the only one who has a stake in his conditional liberty. Society has a stake in whatever may be the chance of restoring him to normal and useful life within the law. Society thus has an interest in not having parole revoked because of erroneous information or because of an erroneous evaluation of the need to revoke parole, given the breach of parole conditions. See People ex rel. Menechino v. Warden, 27 N. Y. 2d 376, 379, and n. 2, 267 N. E. 2d 238, 239, and n. 2 (1971) (parole board had less than full picture of facts). And society has a further interest in treating the parolee with basic fairness: fair treatment in parole revocations will enhance the chance of rehabilitation by avoiding reactions to arbitrariness.[11]

Given these factors, most States have recognized that there is no interest on the part of the State in revoking parole without any pro-

cedural guarantees at all.[12] What is needed is an informal hearing structured to assure that the finding of a parole violation will be based on verified facts and that the exercise of discretion will be informed by an accurate knowledge of the parolee's behavior.

III

We now turn to the nature of the process that is due, bearing in mind that the interest of both State and parolee will be furthered by an effective but informal hearing. In analyzing what is due, we see two important stages in the typical process of parole revocation.

(a) Arrest of Parolee and Preliminary Hearing. The first stage occurs when the parolee is arrested and detained, usually at the direction of his parole officer. The second occurs when parole is formally revoked. There is typically a substantial time lag between the arrest and the eventual determination by the parole board whether parole should be revoked. Additionally, it may be that the parolee is arrested at a place distant from the state institution, to which he may be returned before the final decision is made concerning revocation. Given these factors, due process would seem to require that some minimal inquiry be conducted at or reasonably near the place of the alleged parole violation or arrest and as promptly as convenient after arrest while information is fresh and sources are available. Cf. Hyser v. Reed, 115 U.S. App. D. C. 254, 318 F.2d 225 (1963). Such an inquiry should be seen as in the nature of a "preliminary hearing" to determine whether there is probable cause or reasonable ground to believe that the arrested parolee has committed acts that would constitute a violation of parole conditions. Cf. Goldberg v. Kelly, 397 U.S., at 267-271.

---

[10] Sklar, Law and Practice in Probation and Parole Revocation Hearings, 55 J. Crim. L. C. & P. S. 175, 194 (1964) (no decrease in Michigan, which grants extensive rights); Rose v. Haskins, 388 F.2d 91, 102 n. 16 (CA6 1968) (Celebrezze, J., dissenting) (cost of imprisonment so much greater than parole system that procedural requirements will not change economic motivation).

[11] See President's Commission on Law Enforcement and Administration of Justice, Task Force Report: Corrections 83, 88 (1967).

[12] See n. 15, infra. As one state court has written, "Before such a determination or finding can be made it appears that the principles of fundamental justice and fairness would afford the parolee a reasonable opportunity to explain away the accusation of a parole violation. [The parolee] . . . is entitled to a conditional liberty and possessed of a right which can be forfeited only by reason of a breach of the conditions of the grant." Chase v. Page, 456 P. 2d 590, 594 (Okla. Crim. App. 1969).

In our view, due process requires that after the arrest, the determination that reasonable ground exists for revocation of parole should be made by someone not directly involved in the case. It would be unfair to assume that the supervising parole officer does not conduct an interview with the parolee to confront him with the reasons for revocation before he recommends an arrest. It would also be unfair to assume that the parole officer bears hostility against the parolee that destroys his neutrality; realistically the failure of the parolee is in a sense a failure for his supervising officer.[13] However, we need make no assumptions one way or the other to conclude that there should be an uninvolved person to make this preliminary evaluation of the basis for believing the conditions of parole have been violated. The officer directly involved in making recommendations cannot always have complete objectivity in evaluating them.[14] Goldberg v. Kelly found it unnecessary to impugn the motives of the caseworker to find a need for an independent decisionmaker to examine the initial decision.

This independent officer need not be a judicial officer. The granting and revocation of parole are matters traditionally handled by administrative officers. In Goldberg, the Court pointedly did not require that the hearing on termination of benefits be conducted by a judicial officer or even before the traditional "neutral and detached" officer; it required only that the hearing be conducted by some person other than one initially dealing with the case. It will be sufficient, therefore, in the parole revocation context, if an evaluation of whether reasonable cause exists to believe that conditions of parole have been violated is made by someone such as a parole officer other than the one who has made the

report of parole violations or has recommended revocation. A State could certainly choose some other independent decisionmaker to perform this preliminary function.

With respect to the preliminary hearing before this officer, the parolee should be given notice that the hearing will take place and that its purpose is to determine whether there is probable cause to believe he has committed a parole violation. The notice should state what parole violations have been alleged. At the hearing the parolee may appear and speak in his own behalf; he may bring letters, documents, or individuals who can give relevant information to the hearing officer. On request of the parolee, a person who has given adverse information on which parole revocation is to be based is to be made available for questioning in his presence. However, if the hearing officer determines that an informant would be subjected to risk of harm if his identity were disclosed, he need not be subjected to confrontation and cross-examination.

The hearing officer shall have the duty of making a summary, or digest, of what occurs at the hearing in terms of the responses of the parolee and the substance of the documents or evidence given in support of parole revocation and of the parolee's position. Based on the information before him, the officer should determine whether there is probable cause to hold the parolee for the final decision of the parole board on revocation. Such a determination would be sufficient to warrant the parolee's continued detention and return to the state correctional institution pending the final decision. As in Goldberg, "the decisionmaker should state the reasons for his determination and indicate the evidence he relied on . . ." but it should be remembered that this is not a final determination calling for "formal findings of fact and conclusions of law." 397 U.S., at 271. No interest would be served by formalism in this process; informality will not lessen the utility of this inquiry in reducing the risk of error.

(b) The Revocation Hearing. There must also be an opportunity for a hearing, if it is desired by the parolee, prior to the final decision on revocation by the parole authority. This hearing must be the basis for more than determining probable cause; it must lead to a

---

[13] Note, Observations on the Administration of Parole, 79 Yale L. J. 698, 704-706 (1970) (parole officers in Connecticut adopt role model of social worker rather than an adjunct of police, and exhibit a lack of punitive orientation).

[14] This is not an issue limited to bad motivation. "Parole agents are human, and it is possible that friction between the agent and parolee may have influenced the agent's judgment." 4 Attorney General's Survey on Release Procedures: Parole 246 (1939).

final evaluation of any contested relevant facts and consideration of whether the facts as determined warrant revocation. The parolee must have an opportunity to be heard and to show, if he can, that he did not violate the conditions, or, if he did, that circumstances in mitigation suggest that the violation does not warrant revocation. The revocation hearing must be tendered within a reasonable time after the parolee is taken into custody. A lapse of two months, as respondents suggests occurs in some cases, would not appear to be unreasonable.

We cannot write a code of procedure; that is the responsibility of each State. Most States have done so by legislation, others by judicial decision usually on due process grounds.[15]

Our task is limited to deciding the minimum requirements of due process. They include (a) written notice of the claimed violations of parole; (b) disclosure to the parolee of evidence against him; (c) opportunity to be heard in person and to present witnesses and documentary evidence; (d) the right to confront and cross-examine adverse witnesses (unless the hearing officer specifically finds good cause for not allowing confrontation); (e) a "neutral and detached" hearing body such as a traditional parole board, members of which need not be judicial officers or lawyers; and (f) a written statement by the factfinders as to the evidence relied on and reasons for revoking parole. We emphasize there is no thought to equate this second stage of parole revocation to a criminal prosecution in any sense. It is a narrow inquiry; the process should be flexible enough to consider evidence including letters, affidavits, and other material that would not be admissible in an adversary criminal trial.

We do not reach or decide the question whether the parolee is entitled to the assistance of retained counsel or to appointed counsel if he is indigent.[16]

We have no thought to create an inflexible structure for parole revocation procedures. The few basic requirements set out above, which are applicable to future revocations of parole, should not impose a great burden on any State's parole system. Control over the required proceedings by the hearing officers can assure that delaying tactics and other abuses sometimes present in the traditional adversary trial situation do not occur. Obviously a parolee cannot relitigate issues determined against him in other forums, as in the

---

[15] Very few States provide no hearing at all in parole revocations. Thirty States provide in their statutes that a parolee shall receive some type of hearing. See Ala. Code, Tit. 42, § 12 (1959); Alaska Stat. § 33.15.220 (1962); Ariz. Rev. Stat. Ann. § 31-417 (1956); Ark. Stat. Ann. § 43-2810 (Supp. 1971); Del. Code Ann., Tit. 11, § 4352 (Supp. 1970); Fla. Stat. Ann. § 947.23 (1) (Supp. 1972); Ga. Code Ann. § 77-519 (Supp. 1971); Haw. Rev. Stat. § 353-66 (1968); Idaho Code §§ 20-229, 20-229A (Supp. 1971); Ill. Ann. Stat., c. 108, §§ 204 (e), 207 (Supp. 1972); Ind. Ann. Stat. § 13-1611 (Supp. 1972); Kan. Stat. Ann. § 22-3721 (1971); Ky. Rev. Stat. Ann. § 439.330 (1)(e) (1962); La. Rev. Stat. Ann. § 15:574.9 (Supp. 1972); Me. Rev. Stat. Ann., Tit. 34, § 1675 (Supp. 1970-1971); Md. Ann. Code, Art. 41, § 117 (1971); Mich. Comp. Laws § 791.240a, Mich. Stat. Ann. § 28.2310 (1) (Supp. 1972); Miss. Code Ann. § 4004-13 (1956); Mo. Ann. Stat. § 549.265 (Supp. 1971); Mont. Rev. Codes Ann. §§ 94-9838, 94-9835 (1969); N.H. Rev. Stat. Ann. § 607:46 (1955); N.M. Stat. Ann. § 41-17-28 (1972); N.Y. Correc. Law § 212 subd. 7 (Supp. 1971); N.D. Cent. Code § 12-59-15 (Supp. 1971); Pa. Stat. Ann., Tit. 61, § 331.21a (b) (1964); Tenn. Code Ann. § 40-3619 (1955); Tex. Code Crim. Proc., Art. 42.12, § 22 (1966); Vt. Stat. Ann., Tit. 28, § 1081 (b) (1970); Wash. Rev. Code §§ 9.95.120 through 9.95.126 (Supp. 1971); W. Va. Code Ann. § 62-12-19 (1966). Decisions of state and federal courts have required a number of other States to provide hearings. See Hutchison v. Patterson, 267 F.Supp. 433 (Colo. 1967) (approving parole board regulations); United States ex rel. Bey v. Connecticut State Board of Parole, 443 F.2d 1079 (CA2 1971) (requiring counsel to be appointed for revocation hearings); State v. Holmes, 109 N.J. Super. 180, 262 A. 2d 725

(1970); Chase v. Page, 456 P. 2d 590 (Okla. Crim. App. 1969); Bearden v. South Carolina, 443 F.2d 1090 (CA4 1971); Baine v. Beckstead, 10 Utah 2d 4, 347 P. 2d 554 (1959); Goolsby v. Gagnon, 322 F.Supp. 460 (ED Wis. 1971). A number of States are affected by no legal requirement to grant any kind of hearing.

[16] The Model Penal Code § 305.15 (1) (Proposed Official Draft 1962) provides that "the institutional parole staff shall render reasonable aid to the parolee in preparation for the hearing and he shall be permitted to advise with his own legal counsel."

situation presented when the revocation is based on conviction of another crime.

In the peculiar posture of this case, given the absence of an adequate record, we conclude the ends of justice will be best served by remanding the case to the Court of Appeals for its return of the two consolidated cases to the District Court with directions to make findings on the procedures actually followed by the Parole Board in these two revocations. If it is determined that petitioners admitted parole violations to the Parole Board, as respondents contend, and if those violations are found to be reasonable grounds for revoking parole under state standards, that would end the matter. If the procedures followed by the Parole Board are found to meet the standards laid down in this opinion that, too, would dispose of the due process claims for these cases.

We reverse and remand to the Court of Appeals for further proceedings consistent with this opinion.

Reversed and remanded.

MR. JUSTICE BRENNAN, with whom MR. JUSTICE MARSHALL joins, concurring in the result.

I agree that a parole may not be revoked, consistently with the Due Process Clause, unless the parolee is afforded, first, a preliminary hearing at the time of arrest to determine whether there is probable cause to believe that he has violated his parole conditions and, second, a final hearing within a reasonable time to determine whether he has, in fact, violated those conditions and whether his parole should be revoked. For each hearing the parolee is entitled to notice of the violations alleged and the evidence against him, opportunity to be heard in person and to present witnesses and documentary evidence, and the right to confront and cross-examine adverse witnesses, unless it is specifically found that a witness would thereby be exposed to a significant risk of harm. Moreover, in each case the decisionmaker must be impartial, there must be some record of the proceedings, and the decisionmaker's conclusions must be set forth in written form indicating both the evidence and the reasons

relied upon. Because the Due Process Clause requires these procedures, I agree that the case must be remanded as the Court orders.

The Court, however, states that it does not now decide whether the parolee is also entitled at each hearing to the assistance of retained counsel or of appointed counsel if he is indigent. Goldberg v. Kelly, 397 U.S. 254 (1970), nonetheless plainly dictates that he at least "must be allowed to retain an attorney if he so desires." Id., at 270. As the Court said there, "Counsel can help delineate the issues, present the factual contentions in an orderly manner, conduct cross-examination, and generally safeguard the interests of" his client. Id., at 270-271. The only question open under our precedents is whether counsel must be furnished the parolee if he is indigent.

MR. JUSTICE DOUGLAS, dissenting in part.

Each petitioner was sentenced for a term in an Iowa penitentiary for forgery. Somewhat over a year later each was released on parole. About six months later, each was arrested for a parole violation and confined in a local jail. In about a week, the Iowa Board of Parole revoked their paroles and each was returned to the penitentiary. At no time during any of the proceedings which led to the parole revocations were they granted a hearing or the opportunity to know, question, or challenge any of the facts which formed the basis of their alleged parole violations. Nor were they given an opportunity to present evidence on their own behalf or to confront and cross-examine those on whose testimony their paroles were revoked.

Each challenged the revocation in the state courts and, obtaining no relief, filed the present petitions in the Federal District Court, which denied relief. Their appeals were consolidated in the Court of Appeals which, sitting en banc, in each case affirmed the District Court by a four-to-three vote, 443 F.2d 942. The cases are here on a petition for a writ of certiorari, 404 U.S. 999, which we granted because there is a conflict between the decision below and Hahn v. Burke, 430 F.2d 100, decided by the Court of Appeals for the Seventh Circuit.

Iowa has a board of parole[1] which determines who shall be paroled. Once paroled, a person is under the supervision of the director of the division of corrections of the Department of Social Services, who, in turn, supervises parole agents. Parole agents do not revoke the parole of any person but only recommend that the board of parole revoke it. The Iowa Act provides that each parolee "shall be subject, at any time, to be taken into custody and returned to the institution" from which he was paroled.[2] Thus, Iowa requires no notice or hearing to put a parolee back in prison, Curtis v. Bennett, 256 Iowa 1164, 131 N. W. 2d 1; and it is urged that since parole, like probation, is only a privilege it may be summarily revoked.[3] See Escoe v. Zerbst, 295 U.S. 490, 492-493; Ughbanks v. Armstrong, 208 U.S. 481. But we have long discarded the right-privilege distinction. See, e.g., Graham v. Richardson, 403 U.S. 365, 374; Bell v. Burson, 402 U.S. 535, 539; Pickering v. Board of Education, 391 U.S. 563, 568; cf. Van Alstyne, The Demise of the Right-Privilege Distinction in Constitutional Law, 81 Harv. L. Rev. 1439 (1968).

The Court said in United States v. Wilson, 7 Pet. 150, 161, that a "pardon is a deed." The same can be said of a parole, which when

conferred gives the parolee a degree of liberty which is often associated with property interests.

We held in Goldberg v. Kelly, 397 U.S. 254, that the termination by a State of public assistance payments to a recipient without a prior evidentiary hearing denies him procedural due process in violation of the Fourteenth Amendment. Speaking of the termination of welfare benefits we said:

> Their termination involves state action that adjudicates important rights. The constitutional challenge cannot be answered by an argument that public assistance benefits are a "privilege" and not a "right." Shapiro v. Thompson, 394 U.S. 618, 627 n. 6 (1969). Relevant constitutional restraints apply as much to the withdrawal of public assistance benefits as to disqualification for unemployment compensation, Sherbert v. Verner, 374 U.S. 398 (1963); or to denial of a tax exemption, Speiser v. Randall, 357 U.S. 513 (1958); or to discharge from public employment, Slochower v. Board of Higher Education, 350 U.S. 551 (1956). The extent to which procedural due process must be afforded the recipient is influenced by the extent to which he may be "condemned to suffer grievous loss," Joint Anti-Fascist Refugee Committee v. McGrath, 341 U.S. 123, 168 (1951) (Frankfurter, J., concurring), and depends upon whether the recipient's interest in avoiding that loss outweighs the governmental

---

[1] Iowa Code § 247.5 (1971) provides in part:

"The board of parole shall determine which of the inmates of the state penal institutions qualify and thereafter shall be placed upon parole. Once an inmate is placed on parole he shall be under the supervision of the director of the division of corrections of the department of social services. There shall be a sufficient number of parole agents to insure proper supervision of all persons placed on parole. Parole agents shall not revoke the parole of any person but may recommend that the board of parole revoke such parole."

[2] Id., § 247.9 provides in part:

"All paroled prisoners shall remain, while on parole, in the legal custody of the warden or superintendent and under the control of the chief parole officer, and shall be subject, at any time, to be taken into custody and returned to the institution from which they were paroled."

[3] "A fundamental problem with [the right-privilege] theory is that probation is now the most frequent penal disposition just as release on parole is the most frequent form of release from an institution. They bear little resemblance to

episodic acts of mercy by a forgiving sovereign. A more accurate view of supervised release is that it is now an integral part of the criminal justice process and shows every sign of increasing popularity. Seen in this light, the question becomes whether legal safeguards should be provided for hundreds of thousands of individuals who daily are processed and regulated by governmental agencies. The system has come to depend on probation and parole as much as do those who are enmeshed in the system. Thus, in dealing with claims raised by offenders, we should make decisions based not on an outworn cliche but on the basis of present-day realities." F. Cohen, The Legal Challenge to Corrections: Implications for Manpower and Training 32 (Joint Commission on Correctional Manpower and Training 1969).

interest in summary adjudication. Accordingly, as we said in Cafeteria & Restaurant Workers Union v. McElroy, 367 U.S. 886, 895 (1961), 'consideration of what procedures due process may require under any given set of circumstances must begin with a determination of the precise nature of the government function involved as well as of the private interest that has been affected by governmental action.' See also Hannah v. Larche, 363 U.S. 420, 440, 442 (1960)." 397 U.S., at 262-263.

Under modern concepts of penology, paroling prisoners is part of the rehabilitative aim of the correctional philosophy. The objective is to return a prisoner to a full family and community life. See generally Note, Parole Revocation in the Federal System, 56 Geo. L. J. 705 (1968); Note, Parole: A Critique of Its Legal Foundations and Conditions, 38 N. Y. U. L. Rev. 702 (1963); Comment, 72 Yale L. J. 368 (1962); and see Baine v. Beckstead, 10 Utah 2d 4, 347 P. 2d 554 (1959). The status he enjoys as a parolee is as important a right as those we reviewed in Goldberg v. Kelly. That status is conditioned upon not engaging in certain activities and perhaps in not leaving a certain area or locality. Violations of conditions of parole may be technical, they may be done unknowingly, they may be fleeting and of no consequence.[4] See, e.g., Arciniega v. Freeman, 404 U.S. 4; Cohen, Due Process, Equal Protection and State Parole Revocation Proceedings, 42 U. Colo. L. Rev. 197, 229 (1970). The parolee should, in the concept of fairness implicit in due process, have a chance to explain. Rather, under Iowa's rule, revocation proceeds on the ipse dixit of the parole agent; and on his word alone each of these petitioners has already served three additional years in prison.[5] The charges may or may not be

true. Words of explanation may be adequate to transform into trivia what looms large in the mind of the parole officer.

"There is no place in our system of law for reaching a result of such tremendous consequences without ceremony—without hearing, without effective assistance of counsel, without a statement of reasons." Kent v. United States, 383 U.S. 541, 554 (1966).

Parole,[6] while originally conceived as a judicial function, has become largely an administrative matter. The parole boards have broad discretion in formulating and imposing parole conditions. "Often vague and moralistic, parole conditions may seem oppressive and unfair to the parolee." R. Dawson, Sentencing 306 (1969). They are drawn "to cover any contingency that might occur," id., at 307, and are designed to maximize "control over the parolee by his parole officer." Ibid.

Parole is commonly revoked on mere suspicion that the parolee may have committed a crime. Id., at 366-367. Such great control over the parolee vests in a parole officer a broad discretion in revoking parole and also in counseling the parolee—referring him for psychiatric treatment or obtaining the use of specialized therapy for narcotic addicts or alcoholics. Id., at 321. Treatment of the parolee, rather than revocation of his parole, is a common course. Id., at 322-323. Counseling may include extending help to a parolee in finding a job. Id., at 324 et seq.

A parolee, like a prisoner, is a person entitled to constitutional protection, including procedural due process.[7] At the federal level, the construction of regulations of the Federal Parole Board presents federal questions of which we have taken cognizance. See Arciniega v. Freeman, 404 U.S. 4. At the state

---

[4] The violations alleged in these cases on which revocation was based are listed by the Court of Appeals, 443 F.2d 942, 943-944, nn. 1 and 2.

For a discussion of the British system that dispenses with precise conditions usually employed here see 120 U. Pa. L. Rev. 282, 311-312 (1971). As to conditions limiting constitutional rights see id., at 313-324, 326-339.

[5] As to summary deprivations of individual liberty in Communist nations, see, e. g., Shao-chuan Leng, Justice In Communist China 34 (1967);

1 P. Tang, Communist China Today 271 (2d ed. 1961); J. Hazard, Communists and Their Law 121-126 (1969).

[6] "Parole is used after a sentence has been imposed while probation is usually granted in lieu of a prison term." R. Clegg, Probation and Parole 22 (1964). See Baine v. Beckstead, 10 Utah 2d 4, 9, 347 P. 2d 554, 558; People ex rel. Combs v. LaVallee, 29 App. Div. 2d 128, 131, 286 N. Y. S. 2d 600, 603.

[7] See President's Commission on Law Enforcement and Administration of Justice, Task Force Report: Corrections 83, 84 (1967); 120 U. Pa. L. Rev. 282, 348-358 (1971).

level, the construction of parole statutes and regulations is for the States alone, save as they implicate the Federal Constitution in which event the Supremacy Clause controls.

It is only procedural due process, required by the Fourteenth Amendment, that concerns us in the present cases. Procedural due process requires the following.

If a violation of a condition of parole is involved, rather than the commission of a new offense, there should not be an arrest of the parolee and his return to the prison or to a local jail.[8] Rather, notice of the alleged violation should be given to the parolee and a time set for a hearing.[9] The hearing should not be before the parole officer, as he is the one who is making the charge and "there is inherent danger in combining the functions of judge and advocate." Jones v. Rivers, 338 F.2d 862, 877 (CA4 1964) (Sobeloff, J., con-

curring). Moreover, the parolee should be entitled to counsel.[10] See Hewett v. North Carolina, 415 F.2d 1316, 1322-1325 (CA4 1969); People ex rel. Combs v. LaVallee, 29 App. Div. 2d 128, 286 N. Y. S. 2d 600 (1968); Perry v. Williard, 247 Ore. 145, 427 P. 2d 1020 (1967). As the Supreme Court of Oregon said in Perry v. Williard, "A hearing in which counsel is absent or is present only on behalf of one side is inherently unsatisfactory if not unfair. Counsel can see that relevant facts are brought out, vague and insubstantial allegations discounted, and irrelevancies eliminated." Id., at 148, 427 P. 2d, at 1022. Cf. Mempa v. Rhay, 389 U.S. 128, 135.

The hearing required is not a grant of the full panoply of rights applicable to a criminal trial. But confrontation with the informer may, as Roviaro v. United States, 353 U.S. 53, illus-

---

8   As Judge Skelly Wright said in Hyser v. Reed, 115 U. S. App. D. C. 254, 291, 318 F.2d 225, 262 (1963) (concurring in part and dissenting in part):

"Where serious violations of parole have been committed, the parolee will have been arrested by local or federal authorities on charges stemming from those violations. Where the violation of parole is not serious, no reason appears why he should be incarcerated before hearing. If, of course, the parolee willfully fails to appear for his hearing, this in itself would justify issuance of the warrant." Accord, In re Tucker, 5 Cal. 3d 171, 199-200, 486 P. 2d 657, 676 (1971) (Tobriner, J., concurring and dissenting).

9   As we said in another connection in Greene v. McElroy, 360 U.S. 474, 496-497:

"Certain principles have remained relatively immutable in our jurisprudence. One of these is that where governmental action seriously injures an individual, and the reasonableness of the action depends on fact findings, the evidence used to prove the Government's case must be disclosed to the individual so that he has an opportunity to show that it is untrue. While this is important in the case of documentary evidence, it is even more important where the evidence consists of the testimony of individuals whose memory might be faulty or who, in fact, might be perjurers or persons motivated by malice, vindictiveness, intolerance, prejudice, or jealousy. We have formalized these protections in the requirements of confrontation and cross-examination. They have ancient roots. They find expression in the Sixth

Amendment which provides that in all criminal cases the accused shall enjoy the right 'to be confronted with the witnesses against him.' This Court has been zealous to protect these rights from erosion. It has spoken out not only in criminal cases, but also in all types of cases where administrative and regulatory actions were under scrutiny." (Citations omitted.)

10 American Bar Association Project on Standards for Criminal Justice, Providing Defense Services 43 (Approved Draft 1968); Model Penal Code § 301.4, § 305.15 (1) (Proposed Official Draft 1962); R. Dawson, Sentencing (1969). For the experience of Michigan in giving hearings to parolees see id., at 355. In Michigan, it is estimated that only one out of six parole violators retains counsel. One who cannot afford counsel is said to be protected by the hearing members of the board. Id., at 354. The number who ask for public hearings are typically five or six a year, the largest in a single year being 10. Michigan has had this law since 1937. Id., at 355. But the Michigan experience may not be typical, for a parole violator is picked up and returned at once to the institution from which he was paroled. Id., at 352-353.

By way of contrast, parole revocation hearings in California are secretive affairs conducted behind closed doors and with no written record of the proceedings and in which the parolee is denied the assistance of counsel and the opportunity to present witnesses on his behalf. Van Dyke, Parole Revocation Hearings in California: The Right to Counsel, 59 Calif. L. Rev. 1215 (1971). See also Note, 56 Geo. L. J. 705 (1968) (federal parole revocation procedures).

trates, be necessary for a fair hearing and the ascertainment of the truth. The hearing is to determine the fact of parole violation. The results of the hearing would go to the parole board—or other authorized state agency—for final action, as would cases which involved voluntary admission of violations.

The rule of law is important in the stability of society. Arbitrary actions in the revocation of paroles can only impede and impair the rehabilitative aspects of modern penology. "Notice and opportunity for hearing appropriate to the nature of the case," Boddie v. Connecticut, 401 U.S. 371, 378, are the rudiments of due process which restore faith that our society is run for the many, not the few, and that fair dealing rather than caprice will govern the affairs of men.[11]

I would not prescribe the precise formula for the management of the parole problems. We do not sit as an ombudsman, telling the States the precise procedures they must follow. I would hold that so far as the due process requirements of parole revocation are concerned:[12]

(1) the parole officer—whatever may be his duties under various state statutes—in Iowa appears to be an agent having some of the functions of a prosecutor and of the police: the parole officer is therefore not qualified as a hearing officer;

(2) the parolee is entitled to a due process notice and a due process hearing of the alleged parole violations including, for example, the opportunity to be confronted by his accusers and to present evidence and argument on his own behalf; and

(3) the parolee is entitled to the freedom granted a parolee until the results of the hearing are known and the parole board—or other authorized state agency—acts.[13]

The American Bar Association states at p. 10 of its brief amicus in the present cases that it is "in full agreement with the American Correctional Association in this instance. The position that a hearing is to be afforded on parole revocation is consistent with several sets of criminal justice standards formally approved by the Association through its House of Delegates."

I would reverse the judgments and remand for further consideration in light of this opinion.

---

[11] The Brief of the American Civil Liberties Union, amicus curiae, contains in Appendix A the States that by statute or decision require some form of hearing before parole is revoked and those that do not. All but nine States now hold hearings on revocation of probation and parole, some with trial-type rights including representation by counsel.

[12] We except of course the commission of another offense which from the initial step to the end is governed by the normal rules of criminal procedure.

[13] The American Correctional Association states in its Manual of Correctional Standards 279 (3d ed. 1966) that:

"To an even greater extent than in the case of imprisonment, probation and parole practice is determined by an administrative discretion that is largely uncontrolled by legal standards, protections, or remedies. Until statutory and case law are more fully developed, it is vitally important within all of the correctional fields that there should be established and maintained reasonable norms and remedies against the sorts of abuses that are likely to develop where men have great power over their fellows and where relationships may become both mechanical and arbitrary."

And it provides for parole revocation hearings:

"As soon as practicable after causing an alleged violator [to be] taken into custody on the basis of a parole board warrant, the prisoner should be given an opportunity to appear before the board or its representative. The prisoner should be made fully aware of the reasons for the warrant, and given ample opportunity to refute the charges placed against him or to comment as to extenuating circumstances. The hearing should be the basis for consideration of possible reinstatement to parole supervision on the basis of the findings of fact or of reparole where it appears that further incarceration would serve no useful purpose." Id., at 130.

GAGNON

v.

SCARPELLI

411 U.S. 778; 93 S. Ct. 1756; 36 L. Ed. 2d 656 (1973)

MR. JUSTICE POWELL delivered the opinion of the Court.

This case presents the related questions whether a previously sentenced probationer is entitled to a hearing when his probation is revoked and, if so, whether he is entitled to be represented by appointed counsel at such a hearing.

I

Respondent, Gerald Scarpelli, pleaded guilty in July 1965, to a charge of armed robbery in Wisconsin. The trial judge sentenced him to 15 years' imprisonment, but suspended the sentence and placed him on probation for seven years in the custody of the Wisconsin Department of Public Welfare (the Department). At that time, he signed an agreement specifying the terms of his probation and a "Travel Permit and Agreement to Return" allowing him to reside in Illinois, with supervision there under an interstate compact. On August 5, 1965, he was accepted for supervision by the Adult Probation Department of Cook County, Illinois.

On August 6, respondent was apprehended by Illinois police, who had surprised him and one Fred Kleckner, Jr., in the course of the burglary of a house. After being apprised of his constitutional rights, respondent admitted that he and Kleckner had broken into the house for the purpose of stealing merchandise or money, although he now asserts that his statement was made under duress and is false. Probation was revoked by the Wisconsin Department on September 1, without a hearing. The stated grounds for revocation were that:

1. [Scarpelli] has associated with known criminals, in direct violation of his probation regulations and his supervising agent's instructions;

2. [Scarpelli,] while associating with a known criminal, namely Fred Kleckner, Jr., was involved in, and arrested for, a burglary . . . in Deerfield, Illinois.

On September 4, 1965, he was incarcerated in the Wisconsin State Reformatory at Green Bay to begin serving the 15 years to which he had been sentenced by the trial judge. At no time was he afforded a hearing.

Some three years later, on December 16, 1968, respondent applied for a writ of habeas corpus. After the petition had been filed, but before it had been acted upon, the Department placed respondent on parole.[2] The District Court found that his status as parolee was sufficient custody to confer jurisdiction on the court and that the petition was not moot because the revocation carried "collateral consequences," presumably including the restraints imposed by his parole. On the merits, the District Court held that revocation without a hearing and counsel was a denial of due process. 317 F.Supp. 72 (ED Wis. 1970). The Court of Appeals affirmed sub nom. Gunsolus v. Gagnon, 454 F.2d 416 (CA7 1971), and we granted certiorari. 408 U.S. 921 (1972).

II

Two prior decisions set the bounds of our present inquiry. In Mempa v. Rhay, 389 U.S. 128 (1967), the Court held that a probationer is entitled to be represented by appointed counsel at a combined revocation and sentencing hearing. Reasoning that counsel is required "at every stage of a criminal proceeding where substantial rights of a criminal accused may be affected," id., at 134, and that sentencing is one such stage, the Court concluded that counsel must be provided an indigent at sentencing even when it is accomplished as part of a subsequent probation revocation proceeding. But this line of rea-

---

[2] Respondent was initially paroled to a federal detainer to serve a previously imposed federal sentence arising from another conviction. He was subsequently released from federal custody, but remains a parolee under the supervision of the Department.

soning does not require a hearing or counsel at the time of probation revocation in a case such as the present one, where the probationer was sentenced at the time of trial.

Of greater relevance is our decision last Term in Morrissey v. Brewer, 408 U.S. 471 (1972). There we held that the revocation of parole is not a part of a criminal prosecution.

> Parole arises after the end of the criminal prosecution, including imposition of sentence. . . . Revocation deprives an individual, not of the absolute liberty to which every citizen is entitled, but only of the conditional liberty properly dependent on observance of special parole restrictions.

Even though the revocation of parole is not a part of the criminal prosecution, we held that the loss of liberty entailed is a serious deprivation requiring that the parolee be accorded due process. Specifically, we held that a parolee is entitled to two hearings, one a preliminary hearing at the time of his arrest and detention to determine whether there is probable cause to believe that he has committed a violation of his parole, and the other a somewhat more comprehensive hearing prior to the making of the final revocation decision.

Petitioner does not contend that there is any difference relevant to the guarantee of due process between the revocation of parole and the revocation of probation, nor do we perceive one.[3] Probation revocation, like parole revocation, is not a stage of a criminal prosecution, but does result in a loss of liberty.[4] Accordingly, we hold that a probationer, like a parolee, is entitled to a preliminary and a final revocation hearing, under the conditions specified in Morrissey v. Brewer, supra.[5]

III

The second, and more difficult, question posed by this case is whether an indigent probationer or parolee has a due process right to be represented by appointed counsel at these hearings.[6] In answering that question, we

---

[3] Despite the undoubted minor differences between probation and parole, the commentators have agreed that revocation of probation where sentence has been imposed previously is constitutionally indistinguishable from the revocation of parole. See, e.g., Van Dyke, Parole Revocation Hearings in California: The Right to Counsel, 59 Calif. L. Rev. 1215, 1241-1243 (1971); Sklar, Law and Practice in Probation and Parole Revocation Hearings, 55 J. Crim. L. C. & P. S. 175, 198 n. 182 (1964).

[4] It is clear at least after Morrissey v. Brewer, 408 U.S. 471 (1972), that a probationer can no longer be denied due process, in reliance on the dictum in Escoe v. Zerbst, 295 U.S. 490, 492 (1935), that probation is an "act of grace."

[5] Petitioner argues, in addition, that the Morrissey hearing requirements impose serious practical problems in cases such as the present one in which a probationer or parolee is allowed to leave the convicting State for supervision in another State. Such arrangements are made pursuant to an interstate compact adopted by all of the States, including Wisconsin. Wis. Stat. Ann. § 57.13 (1957). Petitioner's brief asserts that as of June 30, 1972, Wisconsin had a total of 642 parolees and probationers under supervision in other States and that incomplete statistics as of June 30, 1971, indicated a national total of 24,693 persons under out-of-state supervision. Brief for Petitioner 21-22.

Some amount of disruption inevitably attends any new constitutional ruling. We are confident, however, that modification of the interstate compact can remove without undue strain the more serious technical hurdles to compliance with Morrissey. An additional comment is warranted with respect to the rights to present witnesses and to confront and cross-examine adverse witnesses. Petitioner's greatest concern is with the difficulty and expense of procuring witnesses from perhaps thousands of miles away. While in some cases there is simply no adequate alternative to live testimony, we emphasize that we did not in Morrissey intend to prohibit use where appropriate of the conventional substitutes for live testimony, including affidavits, depositions, and documentary evidence. Nor did we intend to foreclose the States from holding both the preliminary and the final hearings at the place of violation or from developing other creative solutions to the practical difficulties of the Morrissey requirements.

[6] In Morrissey v. Brewer, we left open the question "whether the parolee is entitled to the assistance of retained counsel or to appointed counsel if he is indigent." 408 U.S., at 489. Since respondent did not attempt to retain counsel but asked only for appointed counsel, we have no occasion to decide in this case whether a probationer or parolee has a right to be represented at a revocation hearing by retained counsel in situations other than those where the State would be obliged to furnish counsel for an indigent.

draw heavily on the opinion in Morrissey. Our first point of reference is the character of probation or parole. As noted in Morrissey regarding parole, the "purpose is to help individuals reintegrate into society as constructive individuals as soon as they are able . . ." 408 U.S., at 477. The duty and attitude of the probation or parole officer reflect this purpose: "While the parole or probation officer recognizes his double duty to the welfare of his clients and to the safety of the general community, by and large concern for the client dominates his professional attitude. The parole agent ordinarily defines his role as representing his client's best interests as long as these do not constitute a threat to public safety."[7]

Because the probation or parole officer's function is not so much to compel conformance to a strict code of behavior as to supervise a course of rehabilitation, he has been entrusted traditionally with broad discretion to judge the progress of rehabilitation in individual cases, and has been armed with the power to recommend or even to declare revocation.

In Morrissey, we recognized that the revocation decision has two analytically distinct components:

> The first step in a revocation decision thus involves a wholly retrospective factual question: whether the parolee has in fact acted in violation of one or more conditions of his parole. Only if it is determined that the parolee did violate the conditions does the second question arise: should the parolee be recommitted to prison or should other steps be taken to protect society and improve chances of rehabilitation? 408 U.S., at 479-480.[8]

The parole officer's attitude toward these decisions reflects the rehabilitative rather than punitive focus of the probation/parole system:

> Revocation . . . is, if anything, commonly treated as a failure of supervision. While presumably it would be inappropriate for a field agent never to revoke, the whole thrust of the probation-parole movement is to keep men in the community, working with adjustment problems there, and using revocation only as a last resort when treatment has failed or is about to fail.

But an exclusive focus on the benevolent attitudes of those who administer the probation/parole system when it is working successfully obscures the modification in attitude which is likely to take place once the officer has decided to recommend revocation. Even though the officer is not by this recommendation converted into a prosecutor committed to convict, his role as counsellor to the probationer or parolee is then surely compromised.

When the officer's view of the probationer's or parolee's conduct differs in this fundamental way from the latter's own view, due process requires that the difference be resolved before revocation becomes final. Both the probationer or parolee and the State have interests in the accurate finding of fact and the informed use of discretion—the probationer or parolee to insure that his liberty is not unjustifiably taken away and the State to make certain that it is neither unnecessarily interrupting a successful effort at rehabilitation nor imprudently prejudicing the safety of the community.

It was to serve all of these interests that Morrissey mandated preliminary and final

---

[7] F. Remington, D. Newman, E. Kimball, M. Melli & H. Goldstein, Criminal Justice Administration, Materials and Cases 910-911 (1969).

[8] The factors entering into these decisions relate in major part to a professional evaluation, by trained probation or parole officers, as to the overall social readjustment of the offender in the community, and include consideration of such variables as the offender's relationship toward his family, his attitude toward the fulfillment of financial obligations, the extent of his cooperation with the probation or parole officer assigned to his case, his personal associations, and—of course—whether there have been specific and

significant violations of the conditions of the probation or parole. The importance of these considerations, some factual and others entirely judgmental, is illustrated by a Wisconsin empirical study which disclosed that, in the sample studied, probation or parole was revoked in only 34.5% of the cases in which the probationer or parolee violated the terms of his release. S. Hunt, The Revocation Decision: A Study of Probation and Parole Agents' Discretion 10 (unpublished thesis on file at the library of the University of Wisconsin) (1964), cited in Brief for Petitioner, Addendum 106.

revocation hearings. At the preliminary hearing, a probationer or parolee is entitled to notice of the alleged violations of probation or parole, an opportunity to appear and to present evidence in his own behalf, a conditional right to confront adverse witnesses, an independent decisionmaker, and a written report of the hearing. 408 U.S., at 487. The final hearing is a less summary one because the decision under consideration is the ultimate decision to revoke rather than a mere determination of probable cause, but the "minimum requirements of due process" include very similar elements:

(a) written notice of the claimed violations of [probation or] parole; (b) disclosure to the [probationer or] parolee of evidence against him; (c) opportunity to be heard in person and to present witnesses and documentary evidence; (d) the right to confront and cross-examine adverse witnesses (unless the hearing officer specifically finds good cause for not allowing confrontation); (e) a 'neutral and detached' hearing body such as a traditional parole board, members of which need not be judicial officers or lawyers; and (f) a written statement by the factfinders as to the evidence relied on and reasons for revoking [probation or] parole.

These requirements in themselves serve as substantial protection against ill-considered revocation, and petitioner argues that counsel need never be supplied. What this argument overlooks is that the effectiveness of the rights guaranteed by Morrissey may in some circumstances depend on the use of skills which the probationer or parolee is unlikely to possess. Despite the informal nature of the proceedings and the absence of technical rules of procedure or evidence, the unskilled or uneducated probationer or parolee may well have difficulty in presenting his version of a disputed set of facts where the presentation requires the examining or cross-examining of witnesses or the offering or dissecting of complex documentary evidence.

By the same token, we think that the Court of Appeals erred in accepting respondent's contention that the State is under a constitutional duty to provide counsel for indigents in all probation or parole revocation cases. While such a rule has the appeal of simplicity, it would impose direct costs and serious collateral disadvantages without regard to the need or the likelihood in a particular case for a constructive contribution by counsel. In most cases, the probationer or parolee has been convicted of committing another crime or has admitted the charges against him.[10] And while in some cases he may have a justifiable excuse for the violation or a convincing reason why revocation is not the appropriate disposition, mitigating evidence of this kind is often not susceptible of proof or is so simple as not to require either investigation or exposition by counsel.

The introduction of counsel into a revocation proceeding will alter significantly the nature of the proceeding. If counsel is provided for the probationer or parolee, the State in turn will normally provide its own counsel; lawyers, by training and disposition, are advocates and bound by professional duty to present all available evidence and arguments in support of their clients' positions and to contest with vigor all adverse evidence and views. The role of the hearing body itself, aptly described in Morrissey as being "predictive and discretionary" as well as factfinding, may become more akin to that of a judge at a trial, and less attuned to the rehabilitative needs of the individual probationer or parolee. In the greater self-consciousness of its quasi-judicial role, the hearing body may be less tolerant of marginal deviant behavior and feel more pressure to reincarcerate than to continue nonpunitive rehabilitation. Certainly, the decisionmaking process will be prolonged, and the financial cost to the State—for appointed counsel, counsel for the State, a longer record, and the possibility of judicial review—will not be insubstantial.[11]

---

[10] See Sklar, supra, n. 3, at 192 (parole), 193 (probation).

[11] The scope of the practical problem which would be occasioned by a requirement of counsel in all revocation cases is suggested by the fact that in the mid-1960's there was an estimated average of 20,000 adult felony parole revocations and 108,000 adult probation revocations each year. President's Commission on Law Enforcement and Administration of Justice, Task Force Report: The Courts 56 n. 28 (1967).

In some cases, these modifications in the nature of the revocation hearing must be endured and the costs borne because, as we have indicated above, the probationer's or parolee's version of a disputed issue can fairly be represented only by a trained advocate. But due process is not so rigid as to require that the significant interests in informality, flexibility, and economy must always be sacrificed.

In so concluding, we are of course aware that the case-by-case approach to the right to counsel in felony prosecutions adopted in Betts v. Brady, 316 U.S. 455 (1942), was later rejected in favor of a per se rule in Gideon v. Wainwright, 372 U.S. 335 (1963). See also Argersinger v. Hamlin, 407 U.S. 25 (1972). We do not, however, draw from Gideon and Argersinger the conclusion that a case-by-case approach to furnishing counsel is necessarily inadequate to protect constitutional rights asserted in varying types of proceedings: there are critical differences between criminal trials and probation or parole revocation hearings, and both society and the probationer or parolee have stakes in preserving these differences.

In a criminal trial, the State is represented by a prosecutor; formal rules of evidence are in force; a defendant enjoys a number of procedural rights which may be lost if not timely raised; and, in a jury trial, a defendant must make a presentation understandable to untrained jurors. In short, a criminal trial under our system is an adversary proceeding with its own unique characteristics. In a revocation hearing, on the other hand, the State is represented, not by a prosecutor, but by a parole officer with the orientation described above; formal procedures and rules of evidence are not employed; and the members of the hearing body are familiar with the problems and practice of probation or parole. The need for counsel at revocation hearings derives, not from the invariable attributes of those hearings, but rather from the peculiarities of particular cases.

The differences between a criminal trial and a revocation hearing do not dispose altogether of the argument that under a case-by-case approach there may be cases in which a lawyer would be useful but in which none would be appointed because an arguable defense would be uncovered only by a lawyer. Without denying that there is some force in this argument, we think it a sufficient answer that we deal here, not with the right of an accused to counsel in a criminal prosecution, but with the more limited due process right of one who is a probationer or parolee only because he has been convicted of a crime.[12]

We thus find no justification for a new inflexible constitutional rule with respect to the requirement of counsel. We think, rather, that the decision as to the need for counsel must be made on a case-by-case basis in the exercise of a sound discretion by the state authority charged with responsibility for administering the probation and parole system. Although the presence and participation of counsel will probably be both undesirable and constitutionally unnecessary in most revocation hearings, there will remain certain cases in which fundamental fairness—the touchstone of due process—will require that the State provide at its expense counsel for indigent probationers or parolees.

It is neither possible nor prudent to attempt to formulate a precise and detailed set of guidelines to be followed in determining when the providing of counsel is necessary to meet the applicable due process requirements. The facts and circumstances in preliminary and final hearings are susceptible of almost infinite variation, and a considerable discretion must be allowed the responsible agency in making the decision. Presumptively, it may be said that counsel should be provided in cases where, after being informed of his right to request counsel, the probationer or parolee makes such a request, based on a timely and colorable claim (i) that he has not committed the alleged violation of the conditions upon which he is at liberty; or (ii) that, even if the violation is a matter of public

---

[12] Cf. In re Gault, 387 U.S. 1 (1967), establishing a juvenile's right to appointed counsel in a delinquency proceeding which, while denominated civil, was functionally akin to a criminal trial. A juvenile charged with violation of a generally applicable statute is differently situated from an already-convicted probationer or parolee, and is entitled to a higher degree of protection. See In re Winship, 397 U.S. 358 (1970) (the standard of proof in a juvenile delinquency proceeding must be "proof beyond a reasonable doubt").

record or is uncontested, there are substantial reasons which justified or mitigated the violation and make revocation inappropriate, and that the reasons are complex or otherwise difficult to develop or present. In passing on a request for the appointment of counsel, the responsible agency also should consider, especially in doubtful cases, whether the probationer appears to be capable of speaking effectively for himself. In every case in which a request for counsel at a preliminary or final hearing is refused, the grounds for refusal should be stated succinctly in the record.

IV

We return to the facts of the present case. Because respondent was not afforded either a preliminary hearing or a final hearing, the revocation of his probation did not meet the standards of due process prescribed in Morrissey, which we have here held applicable to probation revocations. Accordingly, respondent was entitled to a writ of habeas corpus. On remand, the District Court should allow the State an opportunity to conduct such a hearing. As to whether the State must provide counsel, respondent's admission to having committed another serious crime creates the very sort of situation in which counsel need not ordinarily be provided. But because of respondent's subsequent assertions regarding that admission, see supra, at 780, we conclude that the failure of the Department to provide respondent with the assistance of counsel should be re-examined in light of this opinion. The general guidelines outlined above should be applied in the first instance by those charged with conducting the revocation hearing.

Affirmed in part, reversed in part, and remanded.

MR. JUSTICE DOUGLAS, dissenting in part.

I believe that due process requires the appointment of counsel in this case because of the claim that respondent's confession of the burglary was made under duress. See Morrissey v. Brewer, 408 U.S. 471, 498.

GREENHOLTZ
v.
INMATES OF THE NEBRASKA PENAL AND CORRECTION COMPLEX

442 U.S. 1; 99 S. Ct. 2100; 60 L. Ed. 2d 668 (1979)

MR. CHIEF JUSTICE BURGER delivered the opinion of the Court.

We granted certiorari to decide whether the Due Process Clause of the Fourteenth Amendment applies to discretionary parole-release determinations made by the Nebraska Board of Parole, and, if so, whether the procedures the Board currently provides meet constitutional requirements.

I

Inmates of the Nebraska Penal and Correctional Complex brought a class action under 42 U.S.C. § 1983 claiming that they had been unconstitutionally denied parole by the Board of Parole. The suit was filed against the individual members of the Board. One of the claims of the inmates was that the statutes and the Board's procedures denied them procedural due process.

The statutes provide for both mandatory and discretionary parole. Parole is automatic when an inmate has served his maximum term, less good-time credits. Neb. Rev. Stat. § 83-1,107 (1)(b) (1976). An inmate becomes eligible for discretionary parole when the minimum term, less good-time credits, has been served. § 83-1,110 (1). Only discretionary parole is involved in this case.

The procedures used by the Board to determine whether to grant or deny discretionary parole arise partly from statutory provisions and partly from the Board's practices. Two types of hearings are conducted: initial parole review hearings and final parole hearings. At least once each year initial review hearings must be held for every inmate, regardless of parole eligibility. § 83-192 (9). At the initial review hearing, the Board examines the inmate's entire preconfinement and postconfinement record. Following that examination it provides an informal hearing;

no evidence as such is introduced, but the Board interviews the inmate and considers any letters or statements that he wishes to present in support of a claim for release.

If the Board determines from its examination of the entire record and the personal interview that he is not yet a good risk for release, it denies parole, informs the inmate why release was deferred and makes recommendations designed to help correct any deficiencies observed. It also schedules another initial review hearing to take place within one year.

If the Board determines from the file and the initial review hearing that the inmate is a likely candidate for release, a final hearing is scheduled. The Board then notifies the inmate of the month in which the final hearing will be held; the exact day and time is posted on a bulletin board that is accessible to all inmates on the day of the hearing. At the final parole hearing, the inmate may present evidence, call witnesses and be represented by private counsel of his choice. It is not a traditional adversary hearing since the inmate is not permitted to hear adverse testimony or to cross-examine witnesses who present such evidence. However, a complete tape recording of the hearing is preserved. If parole is denied, the Board furnishes a written statement of the reasons for the denial within 30 days. § 83-1,111 (2).

II

The District Court held that the procedures used by the Parole Board did not satisfy due process. It concluded that the inmate had the same kind of constitutionally protected "conditional liberty" interest, recognized by this Court in Morrissey v. Brewer, 408 U.S. 471 (1972), held that some of the procedures used by the Parole Board fell short of constitutional guarantees, and prescribed several specific requirements.

On appeal, the Court of Appeals for the Eighth Circuit agreed with the District Court that the inmate had a Morrissey-type, conditional liberty interest at stake and also found a statutorily defined, protectible interest in Neb. Rev. Stat. § 83-1,114 (1976). The Court of Appeals, however, 576 F.2d 1274, 1285, modified the procedures required by the District Court as follows:

(a) When eligible for parole each inmate must receive a full formal hearing;

(b) the inmate is to receive written notice of the precise time of the hearing reasonably in advance of the hearing, setting forth the factors which may be considered by the Board in reaching its decision;

(c) subject only to security considerations, the inmate may appear in person before the Board and present documentary evidence in his own behalf. Except in unusual circumstances, however, the inmate has no right to call witnesses in his own behalf;

(d) a record of the proceedings, capable of being reduced to writing, must be maintained; and

(e) within a reasonable time after the hearing, the Board must submit a full explanation, in writing, of the facts relied upon and reasons for the Board's action denying parole.

* * *

III

The Due Process Clause applies when government action deprives a person of liberty or property; accordingly, when there is a claimed denial of due process we have inquired into the nature of the individual's claimed interest.

[To] determine whether due process requirements apply in the first place, we must look not to the 'weight' but to the nature of the interest at stake. Board of Regents v. Roth, 408 U.S. 564, 570-571 (1972).

This has meant that to obtain a protectible right

A person clearly must have more than an abstract need or desire for it. He must have more than a unilateral expectation of it. He must, instead, have a legitimate claim of entitlement to it. Id., at 577.

There is no constitutional or inherent right of a convicted person to be conditionally released before the expiration of a valid sentence. The natural desire of an individual to be released is indistinguishable from the initial resistance to being confined. But the conviction, with all its procedural safeguards, has extinguished that liberty right: "[Given] a valid conviction, the criminal defendant has been constitutionally deprived of his liberty." Meacham v. Fano, 427 U.S. 215, 224, (1976).

Decisions of the Executive Branch, however serious their impact, do not automatically invoke due process protection; there simply is no constitutional guarantee that all executive decisionmaking must comply with standards that assure error-free determinations. See Id., at 225; Montanye v. Haymes, 427 U.S. 236 (1976); Moody v. Daggett, 429 U.S. 78, 88 n. 9 (1976). This is especially true with respect to the sensitive choices presented by the administrative decision to grant parole release.

A state may, as Nebraska has, establish a parole system, but it has no duty to do so. Moreover, to insure that the state-created parole system serves the public-interest purposes of rehabilitation and deterrence, the state may be specific or general in defining the conditions for release and the factors that should be considered by the parole authority. It is thus not surprising that there is no prescribed or defined combination of facts which, if shown, would mandate release on parole. Indeed, the very institution of parole is still in an experimental stage. In parole releases, like its siblings probation release and institutional rehabilitation, few certainties exist. In each case, the decision differs from the traditional mold of judicial decisionmaking in that the choice involves a synthesis of record facts and personal observation filtered through the experience of the decisionmaker and leading to a predictive judgment as to what is best both for the individual inmate and for the community. This latter conclusion requires the Board to assess whether, in light of the nature of the crime, the inmate's release will minimize the gravity of the offense, weaken the deterrent impact on others, and undermine respect for the administration of justice. The entire inquiry is, in a sense, an "equity" type judg-

ment that cannot always be articulated in traditional findings.

IV

Respondents suggest two theories to support their view that they have a constitutionally protected interest in a parole determination which calls for the process mandated by the Court of Appeals. First, they claim that a reasonable entitlement is created whenever a state provides for the possibility of parole. Alternatively, they claim that the language in Nebraska's statute, Neb. Rev. Stat. § 83-1,114 (1) (1976), creates a legitimate expectation of parole, invoking due process protections.

A

In support of their first theory, respondents rely heavily on Morrissey v. Brewer, 408 U.S. 471 (1972), where we held that a parole-revocation determination must meet certain due process standards. See also Gagnon v. Scarpelli, 411 U.S. 778 (1973). They argue that the ultimate interest at stake both in a parole-revocation decision and in a parole determination is conditional liberty and that since the underlying interest is the same the two situations should be accorded the same constitutional protection.

The fallacy in respondents' position is that parole release and parole revocation are quite different. There is a crucial distinction between being deprived of a liberty one has, as in parole, and being denied a conditional liberty that one desires. The parolees in Morrissey (and probationers in Gagnon) were at liberty and as such could "be gainfully employed and [were] free to be with family and friends and to form the other enduring attachments of normal life." 408 U.S., at 482. The inmates here, on the other hand, are confined and thus subject to all of the necessary restraints that inhere in a prison.

A second important difference between discretionary parole release from confinement and termination of parole lies in the nature of the decision that must be made in each case. As we recognized in Morrissey, the parole-revocation determination actually requires two decisions: whether the parolee in fact acted in violation of one or more conditions of parole and whether the parolee should be recommitted either for his or society's benefit. Id., at 479-480. "The first step in a revocation decision thus involves a wholly retrospective factual question." Id., at 479.

The parole-release decision, however, is more subtle and depends on an amalgam of elements, some of which are factual but many of which are purely subjective appraisals by the Board members based upon their experience with the difficult and sensitive task of evaluating the advisability of parole release. Unlike the revocation decision, there is no set of facts which, if shown, mandate a decision favorable to the individual. The parole determination, like a prisoner-transfer decision, may be made

> for a variety of reasons and often [involves] no more than informed predictions as to what would best serve [correctional purposes] or the safety and welfare of the inmate. Meachum v. Fano, 427 U.S., at 225.

The decision turns on a "discretionary assessment of a multiplicity of imponderables, entailing primarily what a man is and what he may become rather than simply what he has done." Kadish, The Advocate and the Expert—Counsel in the Peno-Correctional Process, 45 Minn. L. Rev. 803, 813 (1961).

The differences between an initial grant of parole and the revocation of the conditional liberty of the parolee are well recognized. In United States ex rel. Bey v. Connecticut Board of Parole, 443 F.2d 1079, 1086 (1971), the Second Circuit took note of this critical distinction:

> It is not sophistic to attach greater importance to a person's justifiable reliance in maintaining his conditional freedom so long as he abides by the conditions of his release, than to his mere anticipation or hope of freedom.

Judge Henry Friendly cogently noted that "there is a human difference between losing what one has and not getting what one wants." Friendly, "Some Kind of Hearing," 123 U. Pa. L. Rev. 1267, 1296 (1975). See also Brown v. Lundgren, 528 F.2d, at 1053; Scarpa v. United States Board of Parole, 477

F.2d, at 282; Franklin v. Shields, 569 F.2d, at 799 (Field, J., dissenting); United States ex rel. Johnson v. Chairman, New York State Board of Parole, 500 F.2d 925, 936 (CA2 1974) (Hay, J., dissenting).

That the state holds out the possibility of parole provides no more than a mere hope that the benefit will be obtained. Board of Regents v. Roth, 408 U.S., at 577. To that extent the general interest asserted here is no more substantial than the inmate's hope that he will not be transferred to another prison, a hope which is not protected by due process. Meachum v. Fano, 427 U.S., at 225; Montanye v. Haymes, supra.

B

Respondents' second argument is that the Nebraska statutory language itself creates a protectible expectation of parole. They rely on the section which provides in part:

Whenever the Board of Parole considers the release of a committed offender who is eligible for release on parole, it shall order his release unless it is of the opinion that his release should be deferred because:

(a) There is a substantial risk that he will not conform to the conditions of parole;

(b) His release would depreciate the seriousness of his crime or promote disrespect for law;

(c) His release would have a substantially adverse effect on institutional discipline; or

(d) His continued correctional treatment, medical care, or vocational or other training in the facility will substantially enhance his capacity to lead a law-abiding life when released at a later date. Neb. Rev. Stat. § 83-1,114 (1) (1976).

Respondents emphasize that the structure of the provision together with the use of the word "shall" binds the Board of Parole to release an inmate unless any one of the four specifically designated reasons are found. In their view, the statute creates a presumption that parole release will be granted, and that this in turn creates a legitimate expectation of release absent the requisite finding that one of the justifications for deferral exists.

It is argued that the Nebraska parole-determination provision is similar to the Nebraska statute involved in Wolff v. McDonnell, 418 U.S. 539 (1974), that granted good-time credits to inmates. There we held that due process protected the inmates from the arbitrary loss of the statutory right to credits because they were provided subject only to good behavior. We held that the statute created a liberty interest protected by due process guarantees. The Board argues in response that a presumption would be created only if the statutory conditions for deferral were essentially factual, as in Wolff and Morrissey, rather than predictive.

Since respondents elected to litigate their due process claim in federal court, we are denied the benefit of the Nebraska courts' interpretation of the scope of the interest, if any, the statute was intended to afford to inmates. See Bishop v. Wood, 426 U.S. 341, 345 (1976). We can accept respondents' view that the expectancy of release provided in this statute is entitled to some measure of constitutional protection. However, we emphasize that this statute has unique structure and language and thus whether any other state statute provides a protectible entitlement must be decided on a case-by-case basis. We therefore turn to an examination of the statutory procedures to determine whether they provide the process that is due in these circumstances.

It is axiomatic that due process "is flexible and calls for such procedural protections as the particular situation demands." Morrissey v. Brewer, 408 U.S., at 481; Cafeteria & Restaurant Workers v. McElroy, 367 U.S. 886, 895 (1961); Joint Anti-Fascist Refugee Committee v. McGrath, 341 U.S. 123, 162-163 (1951) (Frankfurter, J., concurring). The function of legal process, as that concept is embodied in the Constitution, and in the realm of factfinding, is to minimize the risk of erroneous decisions. Because of the broad spectrum of concerns to which the term must apply, flexibility is necessary to gear the process to the particular need; the quantum and quality of the process due in a particular situation depend upon the need to serve the

purpose of minimizing the risk of error. Mathews v. Eldridge, 424 U.S. 319, 335 (1976).

Here, as we noted previously, the Parole Board's decision as defined by Nebraska's statute is necessarily subjective in part and predictive in part. Like most parole statutes, it vests very broad discretion in the Board. No ideal, error-free way to make parole-release decisions has been developed; the whole question has been and will continue to be the subject of experimentation involving analysis of psychological factors combined with fact evaluation guided by the practical experience of the actual parole decisionmakers in predicting future behavior. Our system of federalism encourages this state experimentation. If parole determinations are encumbered by procedures that states regard as burdensome and unwarranted, they may abandon or curtail parole. Cf. Me. Rev. Stat. Ann., Tit. 34, §§ 1671-1679 (1964), repealed, 1975 Me. Acts, ch. 499, § 71 (repealing the State's parole system).

It is important that we not overlook the ultimate purpose of parole which is a component of the long-range objective of rehabilitation. The fact that anticipations and hopes for rehabilitation programs have fallen far short of expectations of a generation ago need not lead states to abandon hopes for those objectives; states may adopt a balanced approach in making parole determinations, as in all problems of administering the correctional systems. The objective of rehabilitating convicted persons to be useful, law-abiding members of society can remain a goal no matter how disappointing the progress. But it will not contribute to these desirable objectives to invite or encourage a continuing state of adversary relations between society and the inmate.

Procedures designed to elicit specific facts, such as those required in Morrissey, Gagnon, and Wolff, are not necessarily appropriate to a Nebraska parole determination. See Board of Curators, Univ. of Missouri v. Horowitz, 435 U.S. 78, 90 (1978); Cafeteria & Restaurant Workers v. McElroy, supra, at 895. Merely because a statutory expectation exists cannot mean that in addition to the full panoply of due process required to convict and confine there must also be repeated, adversary hearings in order to continue the confinement. However, since the Nebraska Parole Board provides at least one and often two hearings every year to each eligible inmate, we need only consider whether the additional procedures mandated by the Court of Appeals are required under the standards set out in Mathews v. Eldridge, supra, at 335, and Morrissey v. Brewer, supra, at 481.

Two procedures mandated by the Court of Appeals are particularly challenged by the Board: the requirement that a formal hearing be held for every inmate, and the requirement that every adverse parole decision include a statement of the evidence relied upon by the Board.

The requirement of a hearing as prescribed by the Court of Appeals in all cases would provide at best a negligible decrease in the risk of error. See D. Stanley, Prisoners Among Us 43 (1976). When the Board defers parole after the initial review hearing, it does so because examination of the inmate's file and the personal interview satisfies it that the inmate is not yet ready for conditional release. The parole determination therefore must include consideration of what the entire record shows up to the time of the sentence, including the gravity of the offense in the particular case. The behavior record of an inmate during confinement is critical in the sense that it reflects the degree to which the inmate is prepared to adjust to parole release. At the Board's initial interview hearing, the inmate is permitted to appear before the Board and present letters and statements on his own behalf. He is thereby provided with an effective opportunity first, to insure that the records before the Board are in fact the records relating to his case; and second, to present any special considerations demonstrating why he is an appropriate candidate for parole. Since the decision is one that must be made largely on the basis of the inmate's files, this procedure adequately safeguards against serious risks of error and thus satisfies due process. Cf. Richardson v. Perales, 402 U.S. 389, 408 (1971).

Next, we find nothing in the due process concepts as they have thus far evolved that requires the Parole Board to specify the particular "evidence" in the inmate's file or at his interview on which it rests the discretionary determination that an inmate is not

ready for conditional release. The Board communicates the reason for its denial as a guide to the inmate for his future behavior. See Franklin v. Shields, 569 F.2d, at 800 (en banc). To require the parole authority to provide a summary of the evidence would tend to convert the process into an adversary proceeding and to equate the Board's parole-release determination with a guilt determination. The Nebraska statute contemplates, and experience has shown, that the parole-release decision is, as we noted earlier, essentially an experienced prediction based on a host of variables. See Dawson, The Decision to Grant or Deny Parole: A Study of Parole Criteria in Law and Practice, 1966 Wash. U. L. Q. 243, 299-300. The Board's decision is much like a sentencing judge's choice—provided by many states—to grant or deny probation following a judgment of guilt, a choice never thought to require more than what Nebraska now provides for the parole-release determination. Cf. Dorszynski v. United States, 418 U.S. 424 (1974). The Nebraska procedure affords an opportunity to be heard, and when parole is denied it informs the inmate in what respects he falls short of qualifying for parole; this affords the process that is due under these circumstances. The Constitution does not require more.

Accordingly, the judgment of the Court of Appeals is reversed and the case is remanded for further proceedings consistent with this opinion.

So ordered.

CONNECTICUT BOARD OF PARDONS
v.
DUMSCHAT

452 U.S. 458; 101 S. Ct. 2460; 69 L. Ed. 2d 158 (1981)

CHIEF JUSTICE BURGER delivered the opinion of the Court.

The question presented is whether the fact that the Connecticut Board of Pardons has granted approximately three-fourths of the applications for commutation of life sentences creates a constitutional "liberty interest" or "entitlement" in life-term inmates so as to require that Board to explain its reasons for denial of an application for commutation.

I

In 1964, respondent Dumschat was sentenced to life imprisonment for murder. Under state law, he was not eligible for parole until December 1983. The Connecticut Board of Pardons is empowered to commute the sentences of life inmates by reducing the minimum prison term, and such a commutation accelerates eligibility for parole. The authority of the Board of Pardons derives from Conn. Gen. Stat. § 18-26 (1981), which provides in pertinent part:

(a) Jurisdiction over the granting of, and the authority to grant, commutations of punishment or releases, conditioned or absolute, in the case of any person convicted of any offense against the state and commutations from the penalty of death shall be vested in the board of pardons.

(b) Said board shall have authority to grant pardons, conditioned or absolute, for any offense against the state at any time after the imposition and before or after the service of any sentence.

On several occasions prior to the filing of this suit in February 1976, Dumschat applied for a commutation of his sentence. The Board rejected each application without explanation. Dumschat then sued the Board under 42 U.S.C. § 1983, seeking a declaratory judgment that the Board's failure to provide him with a written statement of reasons for denying commutation violated his rights guaranteed by the Due Process Clause of the Fourteenth Amendment.

After hearing testimony from officials of the Board of Pardons and the Board of Parole, the District Court concluded (a) that Dumschat had a constitutionally protected liberty entitlement in the pardon process, and (b) that his due process rights had been violated when the Board of Pardons failed to give "a written statement of reasons and facts relied on" in denying commutation. 432 F.Supp. 1310, 1315 (1977). The court relied

chiefly on a showing that "at least 75 percent of all lifers received some favorable action from the pardon board prior to completing their minimum sentences" and that virtually all of the pardoned inmates were promptly paroled. Id., at 1314. In response to postjudgment motions, the District Court allowed other life inmates to intervene, certified the suit as a class action, and heard additional evidence. The court held that all prisoners serving life sentences in Connecticut state prisons have a constitutionally protected expectancy of commutation and therefore that they have a right to a statement of reasons when commutation is not granted. The Court of Appeals affirmed. 593 F.2d 165 (CA2 1979). A petition for a writ of certiorari was filed, and we vacated and remanded for reconsideration in light of Greenholtz v. Nebraska Penal Inmates, 442 U.S. 1 (1979). 442 U.S. 926 (1979).

On remand, the Court of Appeals reaffirmed its original decision, 618 F.2d 216 (CA2 1980), stating:

In marked contrast [to the Nebraska statute considered in Greenholtz], Connecticut's pardons statute contains neither a presumption in favor of pardon nor a list of factors to be considered by the Board of Pardons. Instead, the statute grants the board unfettered discretion in the exercise of its power. The statute offers only the 'mere hope' of pardon; it does not create a legitimate expectation of freedom and therefore does not implicate due process. Id., at 219 (citation omitted).

The Court of Appeals also noted that the District Court's holding that the mere possibility of a pardon creates a constitutionally cognizable liberty interest or entitlement was "no longer tenable" in light of Greenholtz. 618 F.2d, at 221; see 442 U.S., at 8-11. However, the Court of Appeals then proceeded to conclude that "[the] overwhelming likelihood that Connecticut life inmates will be pardoned and released before they complete their minimum terms gives them a constitutionally protected liberty interest in pardon proceedings." 618 F.2d, at 220. The Court of Appeals also understood our opinion in Greenholtz to hold that under the Due Process Clause, a brief statement of reasons is "not only constitutionally sufficient but also constitutionally necessary." 618 F.2d, at 222. On that reading of Greenholtz, the case was remanded to the District Court for a determination of "how many years life inmates must serve before the probability of pardon becomes so significant as to give rise to a protected liberty interest."

II

A

A state-created right can, in some circumstances, beget yet other rights to procedures essential to the realization of the parent right. See Meachum v. Fano, 427 U.S. 215, 226 (1976); Wolff v. McDonnell, 418 U.S. 539, 557 (1974). Plainly, however, the underlying right must have come into existence before it can trigger due process protection. See, e.g., Leis v. Flynt, 439 U.S. 438, 442-443 (1979).

In Greenholtz, far from spelling out any judicially divined "entitlement," we did no more than apply the unique Nebraska statute. We rejected the claim that a constitutional entitlement to release from a valid prison sentence exists independently of a right explicitly conferred by the State. Our language in Greenholtz leaves no room for doubt:

> There is no constitutional or inherent right of a convicted person to be conditionally released before the expiration of a valid sentence. The natural desire of an individual to be released is indistinguishable from the initial resistance to being confined. But the conviction, with all its procedural safeguards, has extinguished that liberty right: "[Given] a valid conviction, the criminal defendant has been constitutionally deprived of his liberty. 442 U.S., at 7 (emphasis supplied; citation omitted).

Greenholtz pointedly distinguished parole revocation and probation revocation cases, noting that there is a "critical" difference between denial of a prisoner's request for initial release on parole and revocation of a parolee's conditional liberty. Id., at 9-11, quoting, inter alia, Friendly, "Some Kind of Hearing," 123 U. Pa. L. Rev. 1267, 1296 (1975). Unlike probation, pardon and commutation decisions have not

traditionally been the business of courts; as such, they are rarely, if ever, appropriate subjects for judicial review. Cf. Meachum v. Fano, supra, at 225.

A decision whether to commute a long-term sentence generally depends not simply on objective factfinding, but also on purely subjective evaluations and on predictions of future behavior by those entrusted with the decision. A commutation decision therefore shares some of the characteristics of a decision whether to grant parole. See Greenholtz, 442 U.S., at 9-10. Far from supporting an "entitlement," Greenholtz therefore compels the conclusion that an inmate has "no constitutional or inherent right" to commutation of his sentence.

Respondents nevertheless contend that the Board's consistent practice of granting commutations to most life inmates is sufficient to create a protectible liberty interest. They argue:

> [The] State Board has created an unwritten common law of sentence commutation and parole acceleration for Connecticut life inmates. . . . In effect, there is an unspoken understanding between the State Board and inmates. The terms are simple: If the inmate cooperates with the State, the State will exercise its parole power on the inmate's behalf. Both the State and the inmate recognize those terms. Each expects the other to abide by them. Brief for Respondents 17-18.

This case does not involve parole, and respondents' argument wholly misconceives the nature of a decision by a state to commute the sentence of a convicted felon. The petition in each case is nothing more than an appeal for clemency. See Schick v. Reed, 419 U.S. 256, 260-266 (1974). In terms of the Due Process Clause, a Connecticut felon's expectation that a lawfully imposed sentence will be commuted or that he will be pardoned is no more substantial than an inmate's expectation, for example, that he will not be transferred to another prison; it is simply a unilateral hope. Greenholtz, supra, at 11; see Leis v. Flynt, 439 U.S., at 443-444. A constitutional entitlement cannot "be created—as if by estoppel—merely because a wholly and expressly discretionary state privilege has been granted generously in the past." Id., at 444, n. 5. No matter how frequently a particular form of clemency has been granted, the statistical probabilities standing alone generate no constitutional protections; a contrary conclusion would trivialize the Constitution. The ground for a constitutional claim, if any, must be found in statutes or other rules defining the obligations of the authority charged with exercising clemency.

B

The Court of Appeals correctly recognized that Connecticut has conferred "unfettered discretion" on its Board of Pardons, but—paradoxically—then proceeded to fetter the Board with a halter of constitutional "entitlement." The statute imposes no limit on what procedure is to be followed, what evidence may be considered, or what criteria are to be applied by the Board. Respondents challenge the Board's procedure precisely because of "the absence of any apparent standards." Brief for Respondents 28. We agree that there are no explicit standards by way of statute, regulation, or otherwise.

This contrasts dramatically with the Nebraska statutory procedures in Greenholtz, which expressly mandated that the Nebraska Board of Parole "shall" order the inmate's release "unless" it decided that one of four specified reasons for denial was applicable. 442 U.S., at 11. The Connecticut commutation statute, having no definitions, no criteria, and no mandated "shalls," creates no analogous duty or constitutional entitlement.

It is clear that the requirement for articulating reasons for denial of parole in Greenholtz derived from unique mandates of the Nebraska statutes. Thus, although we noted that under the terms of the Nebraska statute, the inmates' expectancy of parole release "is entitled to some measure of constitutional protection," we emphasized that

this statute has unique structure and language and thus whether any other state statute provides a protectible entitlement must be decided on a case-by-case basis. Id., at 12.

Moreover, from the standpoint of a reasons requirement, there is a vast difference between a denial of parole—particularly on the facts of Greenholtz—and a state's refusal to commute a lawful sentence. When Nebraska statutes directed that inmates who are eligible for parole "shall" be released "unless" a certain finding has been made, the statutes created a right. By contrast, the mere existence of a power to commute a lawfully imposed sentence, and the granting of commutations to many petitioners, create no right or "entitlement." A state cannot be required to explain its reasons for a decision when it is not required to act on prescribed grounds.

We hold that the power vested in the Connecticut Board of Pardons to commute sentences conferred no rights on respondents beyond the right to seek commutation.

Reversed.

MOODY
v.
DAGGETT

429 U.S. 78; 97 S. Ct. 274;
50 L. Ed. 2d 236 (1976)

MR. CHIEF JUSTICE BURGER delivered the opinion of the Court.

We granted certiorari in this case to decide whether a federal parolee imprisoned for a crime committed while on parole is constitutionally entitled to a prompt parole revocation hearing when a parole violator warrant is issued and lodged with the institution of his confinement but not served on him.

(1)

In 1962 petitioner was convicted in the United States District Court for the District of Arizona of the crime of rape on an Indian reservation, in violation of 18 U.S.C. § 1153. There was no appeal, and petitioner received a 10-year prison sentence. He was paroled in 1966 with almost six years remaining to be served. While on parole, petitioner shot and killed two persons on the Fort Apache Indian Reservation. He was convicted on a guilty plea of manslaughter as to one victim and second-degree murder as to the other, for violations of 18 U.S.C. § 1153; he received concurrent 10-year sentences for these two offenses. These crimes constituted obvious violations of the terms of petitioner's 1966 parole. See 18 U.S.C. § 4203(a) (1970 ed. and Supp. V).

Soon after petitioner's incarceration for the two homicides, the United States Board of Parole issued but did not execute a parole violator warrant; this was lodged with prison officials as a "detainer."[2] Petitioner requested the Board to execute the warrant immediately so that any imprisonment imposed for violation of his earlier parole under the rape conviction could run concurrently with his 1971 homicide sentences. The Board replied that it intended to execute the warrant only upon petitioner's release from his second sentence. At its 1974 annual review of petitioner's case, the Board reaffirmed its decision to allow the warrant to remain unexecuted.

Relying on Morrissey v. Brewer, 408 U.S. 471 (1972), petitioner began this federal habeas corpus action in January 1975, seeking dismissal of the parole violator warrant on the ground that he had been denied a prompt hearing at which the pending parole revocation issues could be aired.

The District Court dismissed the petition without awaiting a responsive pleading, stating:

> [A] parole revocation hearing is not required until the parole violator warrant has been executed. The parole board is under no obligation to execute the warrant inasmuch as petitioner has been in custody on his 1971 manslaughter [and murder] [s]entences since the time the warrant was issued and filed as detainer against him.

---

2   A detainer in this context is an internal administrative mechanism to assure that an inmate subject to an unexpired term of confinement will not be released from custody until the jurisdiction asserting a parole violation has had an opportunity to act—in this case by taking the inmate into custody or by making a parole revocation determination. When two autonomous jurisdictions are involved, as for example when a federal detainer is placed against an inmate of a state institution, a detainer is a matter of comity.

The Court of Appeals affirmed, relying on its earlier holding in Small v. Britton, 500 F. 2d 299 (CA10 1974), in which that court had held that an incarcerated parolee is deprived of no liberty interest by the lodging of a detainer against him, and is thus entitled to no due process safeguards unless and until the parole violator warrant is actually executed.

(2)

"The Parole Commission and reorganization Act, Pub. L. 94-233, 90 Stat. 219 et seq., was enacted shortly after we granted certiorari. The Act renamed the Board the Parole Commission and made other changes in federal parole procedures, principally to codify the Board's existing practices. Throughout the progress of this case below, however, parole revocation procedures were controlled by the former statutes, 18 U.S.C. §§ 4205 and 4207. Under them, and the Board's own regulations, 28 CFR § 2.53 (1975), it was the Board's practice to issue a parole violator warrant as a matter of course whenever a federal parolee was convicted of a new offense. Under the former statute and regulations, if the subsequent sentence called for incarceration the warrant was lodged at the institution of confinement as a detainer, for possible later service. A parolee so confined was then notified of the issuance of the unserved warrant and given the opportunity to make a written response. Upon receipt of the response the Board was authorized, in its discretion, to conduct a dispositional interview designed to get the facts relevant to its revocation decision. The parolee could retain counsel for the interview and call witnesses. In lieu of an interview, the Board in its discretion could review the parolee's case based on the record and the written response.

After review—or interview—the Board had three options for disposing of its parole violator warrant:

(a) It could execute the warrant immediately and take the parolee into custody. If parole was revoked at that stage, the remainder of the parolee's original federal sentence, reinstated by the parole revocation, would run concurrently with the subsequent sentence from the time of execution of the warrant. 18 U.S.C. § 4205. Execution of the warrant deprived the parolee of any good-time credits he might have previously earned on his original sentence under 18 U.S.C. § 4161, and of credit for the time spent while on parole. 18 U.S.C. § 4205; 28 CFR § 2.51 (1975).

(b) The Board's second option was to dismiss the warrant and detainer altogether, which operated as a decision not to revoke parole, and under which the parolee retained both his good-time credit and credit for the time spent on parole. Presumably dismissal of the warrant would reflect a Board decision that the violation of conditions of parole was not of such gravity as to justify revocation.

(c) Third, the Board was free to defer a final decision on parole revocation until expiration of the subsequent sentence, as it elected to do in this case; under this third option, the Board was authorized to execute the warrant, take the parolee into custody immediately upon his release, and then conduct a revocation hearing. Deferral of decision while permitting the warrant to stand unexecuted would operate to allow the original sentence to remain in the status it occupied at the time of the asserted parole violation, 18 U.S.C. § 4205; it would not deprive the parolee either of his good time or of the time spent on parole.

Respondent represents that the Board's general practice, before passage of the 1976 Act, was to defer decision in order to have before it the parolee's institutional record during his confinement on the subsequent offense. That record would obviously be highly relevant to the parole revocation decision. Annual reviews of the status of every parolee to whom it had not granted a dispositional interview were conducted under the former statute.

. . . Previously it was general practice to defer execution of the warrant to completion of the subsequent sentence. It is now firm Commission policy that unless "substantial mitigating circumstances" are shown, the parole violator term of a parolee convicted of crime is to run consecutively to the sentence imposed for the subsequent offense. 28 CFR § 2.47(c) (1976).

Petitioner asserts protected liberty interests in both the length and conditions of his confinement. Those interests, he argues, are disregarded in several respects by issuance against him of an unexecuted parole violator warrant, which bars him from serving his 1962 rape conviction sentence concurrently with his 1971 homicide sentences, retards his parole eligibility on the later convictions, and adversely affects his prison classification status. He argues that lack of a prompt hearing risks the loss of evidence in mitigation which might induce the Board not to revoke his parole. Respondent's position is that whatever process may eventually be due petitioner, the mere issuance of a parole violator warrant works no present deprivation of protected liberty sufficient to invoke due process protection.

(3)

In Morrissey, we held that the conditional freedom of a parolee generated by statute is a liberty interest protected by the Due Process Clause of the Fourteenth Amendment which may not be terminated absent appropriate due process safeguards. The revocation hearing mandated by Morrissey[7] is bottomed on the parallel interests of society and the parolee in establishing whether a parole violation has occurred and, if so, whether under all the circumstances the quality of that violation calls for parole revocation. The issue before us here, however, is not whether a Morrissey-type hearing will ever be constitutionally required in the present case, but whether a hearing must be held at the present time, before the parolee is taken into custody as a parole violator. We hold that there is no requirement for an immediate hearing.

---

[7] In the present case, where petitioner has already been convicted of and incarcerated on a subsequent offense, there is no need for the preliminary hearing which Morrissey requires upon arrest for a parole violation. This is so both because the subsequent conviction obviously gives the parole authority "probable cause or reasonable ground to believe that the . . . parolee has committed acts that would constitute a violation of parole conditions," 408 U.S., at 485, and because issuance of the warrant does not immediately deprive the parolee of liberty. The 1976 Act calls for no preliminary hearing in such cases. 18 U.S.C. § 4214(b)(1) (1976 ED.); see 28 CFR § 2.48(f) (1976).

Petitioner's present confinement and consequent liberty loss derive not in any sense from the outstanding parole violator warrant, but from his two 1971 homicide convictions. Issuance of the warrant and notice of that fact to the institution of confinement did no more than express the Board's intent to defer consideration of parole revocation to a later time. Though the gravity of petitioner's subsequent crimes places him under a cloud, issuance of the warrant was not a determination that petitioner's parole under his 1962 rape conviction will be revoked; the time at which the Commission must make that decision has not yet arrived. With only a prospect of future incarceration which is far from certain, we cannot say that the parole violator warrant has any present or inevitable effect upon the liberty interests which Morrissey sought to protect. Indeed, in holding that "[the] revocation hearing must be tendered within a reasonable time after the parolee is taken into custody," Morrissey, 408 U.S., at 488, we established execution of the warrant and custody under that warrant as the operative event triggering any loss of liberty attendant upon parole revocation. This is a functional designation, for the loss of liberty as a parole violator does not occur until the parolee is taken into custody under the warrant. Cf. 18 U.S.C. § 4206; 18 U.S.C. § 4213(d) (1976).

The other injuries petitioner claims to suffer either do not involve a loss of protected liberty or have not occurred by reason of the warrant and detainer. His real complaint is that he desires to serve his sentence for the 1962 rape conviction concurrently with his sentences for two 1971 homicides. But, as we have noted, even after completion of the homicide sentences the Commission retains full discretion to dismiss the warrant or decide, after hearing, that petitioner's parole need not be revoked. If revocation is chosen, the Commission has power to grant, retroactively, the equivalent of concurrent sentences and to provide for unconditional or conditional release upon completion of the subsequent sentence. See 18 U.S.C. §§ 4211, 4214(d) (1976 ED.); 28 CFR §§ 2.21, 2.52(c)(2) (1976). Thus, deferral of the revocation decision does not deprive petitioner of any such opportunity; nothing in the statute or regulations gives him any "right" to force the decision of the Commission at this time.

* * *

Accordingly, and without regard to what process may be due petitioner before his parole may be finally revoked, we hold that he has been deprived of no constitutionally protected rights simply by issuance of a parole violator warrant. The Commission therefore has no constitutional duty to provide petitioner an adversary parole hearing until he is taken into custody as a parole violator by execution of the warrant.

Affirmed.

MR. JUSTICE STEVENS, with whom MR. JUSTICE BRENNAN joins, dissenting.

The Court holds that the lodging of a detainer with an institution in which a parolee is confined does not have the kind of impact on his custodial status that requires a due process hearing. That holding does not answer the question which I regard as critical in this case. For it is clear that sooner or later a parole revocation hearing will be held; the question is whether the timing of that hearing is an element of the procedural fairness to which the parolee is constitutionally entitled. I am persuaded that it is.

I start from the premise that parole revocation is a deprivation of liberty within the meaning of the Fifth and Fourteenth Amendments and therefore must be preceded by due process. The Court so held in Morrissey v. Brewer, 408 U.S. 471, 481-483. In that case the revocation resulted in the return of the parolee to prison whereas in this case the parolee is already incarcerated for a separate offense. But in both situations the revocation affects the length of his confinement and therefore may result in a "grievous loss" of liberty. Accordingly, it is clear—and I do not understand the Court to disagree, see ante, at 85-86, 89—that the parolee's constitutional right to have the revocation hearing conducted fairly is not affected by his custodial status. Moreover, since the parole revocation process begins when the Parole Commission issues the revocation warrant, it plainly follows that the constitutional protections afforded the parolee attach at that time. The question, then, is whether the parolee's right to a fair hearing includes any right to have the hearing conducted with reasonable dispatch.

It is apparently the position of the Parole Commission that it has no obligation to go forward with the revocation hearing until after the parolee has completed the service of his sentence for the second offense. It may therefore wait as long as 10 or 20 years after commencing the revocation process by issuing a warrant. This position, I submit, can be tenable only if one assumes that the constitutional right to a fair hearing includes no right whatsoever to a prompt hearing. Precedent, tradition, and reason require rejection of that assumption.

* * *

This Court has already held that present incarceration for one offense does not deprive an inmate of his right to a prompt trial on a second charge. Smith v. Hooey, 393 U.S. 374; Strunk v. United States, 412 U.S. 434. Moreover, the Court has made it clear that the constitutional protection applies not only to the determination of guilt but also to the discretionary decision on what disposition should be made of the defendant. This point was squarely decided with respect to parole revocation in Morrissey v. Brewer. And in Pollard v. United States, 352 U.S. 354, the Court, though rejecting the particular claim, recognized that a defendant's right to a speedy trial included a right to a prompt sentencing determination. The entire Court subscribed to the view that delay in regard to disposition "must not be purposeful or oppressive." Id., at 361. That view contrasts sharply with the Parole Commission's conscious policy of delaying parole revocation decisions under these circumstances.

Those holdings recognize the defendant's legitimate interest in changing the uncertainty associated with a pending charge into the greater certainty associated with its disposition. In the words of a former director of the Federal Bureau of Prisons that were quoted by the Court in Smith, supra, at 379, the "anxiety and concern" which accompany unresolved charges have as great an impact on the incarcerated as on those at large.

* * *

Petitioner argues that the detainer itself is the source of his grievous loss which mandates a hearing. That is not my view. In my judgment the detainer is comparable to an arrest or an indictment which identifies a time when it is clear that the government has a basis for going forward with appropriate proceedings and from which the right to a speedy determination accrues. Since I believe the right to orderly procedure leading to a reasonably prompt decision is a fundamental attribute of due process, I cannot accept the conclusion that the right is vindicated by simply lodging a detainer and letting it remain outstanding for year after year while the prisoner's interest in knowing where he stands may be entirely ignored.

I therefore respectfully dissent.

JAGO
v.
VAN CUREN

454 U.S. 14; 102 S. Ct. 31;
70 L. Ed. 2d 13 (1981)

PER CURIAM

After pleading guilty to embezzlement and related crimes, respondent was sentenced by an Ohio court to not less than 6 nor more than 100 years in prison. Under existing law respondent would have become eligible for parole in March 1976. On January 1, 1974, however, Ohio enacted a "shock parole" statute which provided for the early parole of first offenders who had served more than six months in prison for nonviolent crimes. Ohio Rev. Code Ann. § 2967.31 (1975).

Pursuant to this statute, respondent was interviewed on April 17, 1974, by a panel representing the Ohio Adult Parole Authority (OAPA). The panel recommended that respondent be paroled "on or after April 23, 1974," and OAPA subsequently approved the panel's recommendation. Respondent was notified of the decision by a parole agreement which stated:

The Members of the Parole Board have agreed that you have earned the opportunity of parole and eventually a final release from your present conviction. The Parole Board is therefore ordering a Parole Release in your case.

Respondent attended and completed prison prerelease classes and was measured for civilian clothes.

At a meeting six days after the panel's interview with respondent, OAPA was informed that respondent had not been entirely truthful in the interview or in the parole plan that he had submitted to his parole officers. Specifically, respondent had told the panel that he had embezzled $1 million when in fact he had embezzled $6 million, and had reported in his parole plan that he would live with his half brother if paroled when in fact he intended to live with his homosexual lover. As a result of these revelations, OAPA rescinded its earlier decision to grant respondent "shock parole" and continued his case to a June 1974 meeting at which parole was formally denied. Neither at this meeting nor at any other time was respondent granted a hearing to explain the false statements he had made during the April interview and in the parole plan which he had submitted.

After denial of his parole, respondent brought a mandamus action against OAPA. The Supreme Court of Ohio held that OAPA was not required to grant respondent a hearing and that it could not be commanded to recall its decision rescinding parole. State ex rel. Van Curen v. Ohio Adult Parole Authority, 45 Ohio St. 2d 298, 345 N.E.2d 75 (1976). We denied respondent's petition for certiorari to review the decision of the Supreme Court of Ohio. 429 U.S. 959 (1976).

Respondent then filed a petition for a writ of habeas corpus in the Federal District Court for the Southern District of Ohio, claiming that the rescission without hearing violated his right to due process of law under the United States Constitution. The District Court denied the writ and the United States Court of Appeals for the Sixth Circuit summarily affirmed the denial. Van Curen v. Jago, 578 F.2d 1382 (1978). We granted certiorari, vacated the judgment of the Court of Appeals, and remanded for further consideration in light of our decision in Greenholtz v.

Nebraska Penal Inmates, 442 U.S. 1 (1979). Jago v. Van Curen, 442 U.S. 926 (1979).

On remand the Court of Appeals in turn remanded to the District Court for further consideration. Applying Greenholtz, the District Court determined that "early release in Ohio is a matter of grace" and that Ohio law "is fairly unambiguous that no protectable interest in early release arises until actual release." App. to Pet. for Cert. 24A-25A. Accordingly, the District Court held that the rescission of respondent's parole without a hearing did not violate due process.

On appeal, the Court of Appeals acknowledged that "[parole] for Ohio prisoners lies wholly within the discretion of the OAPA," and that "[the] statutes which provide for parole do not create a protected liberty interest for due process purposes." 641 F.2d 411, 414 (1981). Nonetheless, the Court of Appeals reversed the decision of the District Court. Relying upon language from our decision in Perry v. Sindermann, 408 U.S. 593 (1972), the Court of Appeals concluded that a liberty interest such as that asserted by respondent can arise from "mutually explicit understandings." See id., at 601. Thus, it held:

> Having been notified that he '[had] been paroled' and that 'the Board is ordering a Parole Release in your case,' [respondent] had a legitimate expectation that his early release would be effected. This expectation was a liberty interest, the deprivation of which would indeed constitute a grievous loss. It was an interest which could not be taken from him without according [him] procedural due process. 641 F.2d, at 416.

We do not doubt that respondent suffered "grievous loss" upon OAPA's rescission of his parole. But we have previously "[rejected] . . . the notion that any grievous loss visited upon a person by the State is sufficient to invoke the procedural protections of the Due Process Clause." Meachum v. Fano, 427 U.S. 215, 224 (1976). In this case, as in our previous cases, "[the] question is not merely the 'weight' of the individual's interest, but whether the nature of the interest is one within the contemplation of the 'liberty or property language of the Fourteenth Amendment." Morrissey v. Brewer, 408 U.S. 471, 481 (1972). We hold that the Court of Appeals erred in finding a constitutionally protected liberty interest by reliance upon the "mutually explicit understandings" language of Perry v. Sindermann, supra.

Our decision in Sindermann was concerned only with the Fourteenth Amendment's protection of "property" interests, and its language, relied upon by the Court of Appeals, was expressly so limited:

* * *

To illustrate the way in which "mutually explicit understandings" operate to create "property" interests, we relied in Sindermann upon two analogous doctrines. First, we compared such understandings to implied contracts:

[The] absence of . . . an explicit contractual provision may not always foreclose the possibility that a teacher has a 'property' interest in re-employment. . . . [The] law of contracts in most, if not all, jurisdictions long has employed a process by which agreements, though not formalized in writing, may be 'implied.' Id., at 601-602.

That the implied-contract aspect of Sindermann "understandings" has been limited to the creation of property interests is illustrated by Bishop v. Wood, 426 U.S. 341 (1976), another property interest case in which we relied upon the "understandings" language of Sindermann to conclude that "[a] property interest in employment can, of course, be created by ordinance, or by an implied contract." 426 U.S., at 344 (footnote omitted).

Principles of contract law naturally serve as useful guides in determining whether or not a constitutionally protected property interest exists. Such principles do not, however, so readily lend themselves to determining the existence of constitutionally protected liberty interests in the setting of prisoner parole. In Meachum v. Fano, supra, we recognized that the administrators of our penal systems need considerable latitude in operating those systems, and that the protected interests of prisoners are necessarily limited:

* * *

We would severely restrict the necessary flexibility of prison administrators and parole authorities were we to hold that any one of their myriad decisions with respect to individual inmates may, as under the general law of contracts, give rise to protected "liberty" interests which could not thereafter be impaired without a constitutionally mandated hearing under the Due Process Clause.

The second analogy relied upon in Sindermann to give content to the notion of "mutually explicit understandings" was the labor law principle that the tradition and history of an industry or plant may add substance to collective-bargaining agreements. See 408 U.S., at 602. Just last Term, however, we rejected an argument that a sort of "industrial common law" could give rise to a liberty interest in the prisoner parole setting. . .

* * *

Thus, this Court has recognized that the "mutually explicit understandings" of Sindermann have a far more useful place in determining protected property interests than in determining those liberty interests protected by the Due Process Clause of the Fourteenth Amendment.

As the majority opinion in the Court of Appeals for the Sixth Circuit observed: "Parole for Ohio prisoners lies wholly within the discretion of the OAPA. The statutes which provide for parole do not create a protected liberty interest for due process purposes." . . .

* * *

Notwithstanding its conclusion that the granting of parole was a purely discretionary matter, the majority of the Court of Appeals in this case concluded that, once the recommendation for "shock parole" had been made, respondent was entitled to a hearing for the purpose of explaining his false statements and representations because the initial recommendation for "shock parole" gave rise to a "mutually explicit understanding." As we have previously stated, however, we deal here not with "property" interests but with "liberty" interests protected by the Fourteenth Amendment. We think that the reasoning of Greenholtz v. Nebraska Penal Inmates, 442

U.S. 1 (1979), Dumschat, supra, and the Court of Appeals' own concession that Ohio law creates no protected "liberty" interest, require reversal of the holding of the Court of Appeals that respondent was entitled to a hearing prior to denial of his parole in June.

The petition for certiorari is granted, the respondent's motion to proceed in forma pauperis is granted, and the judgment of the Court of Appeals for the Sixth Circuit is

Reversed.

* * *

JUSTICE STEVENS, with whom JUSTICE BRENNAN and JUSTICE MARSHALL join, dissenting.

* * *

The Court has fashioned a constitutional distinction between the decision to revoke parole and the decision to grant or to deny parole. Arbitrary revocation is prohibited by Morrissey v. Brewer, 408 U.S. 471, whereas arbitrary denial is permitted by Greenholtz v. Nebraska Penal Inmates, 442 U.S. 1, 9-11. Even if one accepts the validity of that dubious distinction, I believe the Court misapplies it in this case.

In the Court's view, the grant of parole creates a constitutionally protected interest in liberty that previously did not exist. Under that view, a profound change in the status of an individual occurs when he is paroled; he has greater legal rights after parole than before. The question is what event triggers this change in legal status, the act of walking through the exit gates or the State's formal decision, conveyed to the prisoner, to grant him his conditional freedom.

For the ordinary litigant, the entry of judgment by the decisionmaker—not the execution of that judgment by the sheriff—determines his legal rights. In my opinion, the interests in orderly decisionmaking that are protected by the Due Process Clause of the Fourteenth Amendment dictate a similar answer in the context of this case. . . .

* * *

When the Ohio Adult Parole Authority revoked its decision to grant respondent parole, it acted on the basis of ex parte information which respondent had no opportunity to deny or to explain. Even if that information was entirely accurate in this case, and even if it was sufficiently important to justify the changed decision, the effect of the Court's holding today is to allow such decisions to stand even if wrong and wholly arbitrary. I am persuaded that such a holding is erroneous. . . .

BEARDEN
v.
GEORGIA

461 U.S. 660; 103 S. Ct. 2064;
76 L. Ed. 2d 221 (1983)

JUSTICE O'CONNOR delivered the opinion of the Court.

The question in this case is whether the Fourteenth Amendment prohibits a State from revoking an indigent defendant's probation for failure to pay a fine and restitution. Its resolution involves a delicate balance between the acceptability, and indeed wisdom, of considering all relevant factors when determining an appropriate sentence for an individual and the impermissibility of imprisoning a defendant solely because of his lack of financial resources. We conclude that the trial court erred in automatically revoking probation because petitioner could not pay his fine, without determining that petitioner had not made sufficient bona fide efforts to pay or that adequate alternative forms of punishment did not exist. We therefore reverse the judgment of the Georgia Court of Appeals upholding the revocation of probation, and remand for a new sentencing determination.

I

In September 1980, petitioner was indicted for the felonies of burglary and theft by receiving stolen property. He pleaded guilty, and was sentenced on October 8, 1980. Pursuant to the Georgia First Offender's Act, Ga.

Code Ann. § 27-2727 et seq. (current version at § 42-8-60 et seq. (Supp. 1982)), the trial court did not enter a judgment of guilt, but deferred further proceedings and sentenced petitioner to three years on probation for the burglary charge and a concurrent one year on probation for the theft charge. As a condition of probation, the trial court ordered petitioner to pay a $500 fine and $250 in restitution. Petitioner was to pay $100 that day, $100 the next day, and the $550 balance within four months.

Petitioner borrowed money from his parents and paid the first $200. About a month later, however, petitioner was laid off from his job. Petitioner, who has only a ninth-grade education and cannot read, tried repeatedly to find other work but was unable to do so. The record indicates that petitioner had no income or assets during this period.

Shortly before the balance of the fine and restitution came due in February 1981, petitioner notified the probation office he was going to be late with his payment because he could not find a job. In May 1981, the State filed a petition in the trial court to revoke petitioner's probation because he had not paid the balance. After an evidentiary hearing, the trial court revoked probation for failure to pay the balance of the fine and restitution, entered a conviction, and sentenced petitioner to serve the remaining portion of the probationary period in prison. The Georgia Court of Appeals, relying on earlier Georgia Supreme Court cases, rejected petitioner's claim that imprisoning him for inability to pay the fine violated the Equal Protection Clause of the Fourteenth Amendment. The Georgia Supreme Court denied review. Since other courts have held that revoking the probation of indigents for failure to pay fines does violate the Equal Protection Clause, we granted certiorari to resolve this important issue in the administration of criminal justice. 458 U.S. 1105 (1982).

II

This Court has long been sensitive to the treatment of indigents in our criminal justice system. Over a quarter-century ago, Justice Black declared that "[there] can be no equal justice where the kind of trial a man gets depends on the amount of money he has." Griffin v. Illinois, 351 U.S. 12, 19 (1956) (plurality opinion). Griffin's principle of "equal justice," which the Court applied there to strike down a state practice of granting appellate review only to persons able to afford a trial transcript, has been applied in numerous other contexts. See, e.g., Douglas v. California, 372 U.S. 353 (1963) (indigent entitled to counsel on first direct appeal); Roberts v. LaVallee, 389 U.S. 40 (1967) (indigent entitled to free transcript of preliminary hearing for use at trial); Mayer v. Chicago, 404 U.S. 189 (1971) (indigent cannot be denied an adequate record to appeal a conviction under a fine-only statute). Most relevant to the issue here is the holding in Williams v. Illinois, 399 U.S. 235 (1970), that a State cannot subject a certain class of convicted defendants to a period of imprisonment beyond the statutory maximum solely because they are too poor to pay the fine. Williams was followed and extended in Tate v. Short, 401 U.S. 395 (1971), which held that a State cannot convert a fine imposed under a fine-only statute into a jail term solely because the defendant is indigent and cannot immediately pay the fine in full. But the Court has also recognized limits on the principle of protecting indigents in the criminal justice system. For example, in Ross v. Moffitt, 417 U.S. 600 (1974), we held that indigents had no constitutional right to appointed counsel for a discretionary appeal. In United States v. Mac-Collum, 426 U.S. 317 (1976) (plurality opinion), we rejected an equal protection challenge to a federal statute which permits a district court to provide an indigent with a free trial transcript only if the court certifies that the challenge to his conviction is not frivolous and the transcript is necessary to prepare his petition.

Due process and equal protection principles converge in the Court's analysis in these cases. See Griffin v. Illinois, supra, at 17. Most decisions in this area have rested on an equal protection framework, although Justice Harlan in particular has insisted that a due process approach more accurately captures the competing concerns. See, e.g., Griffin v. Illinois, supra, at 29-39 (Harlan, J., dissenting); Williams v. Illinois, supra, at 259-266 (Harlan, J., concurring). As we recognized in Ross v. Moffitt, supra, at 608-609, we generally analyze the fairness of relations between the criminal defendant and the State under the Due Process Clause, while we approach the question whether the State has invidiously denied one class of defendants a substantial benefit available to another class of defendants under the Equal Protection Clause.

The question presented here is whether a sentencing court can revoke a defendant's probation for failure to pay the imposed fine and restitution, absent evidence and findings that the defendant was somehow responsible for the failure or that alternative forms of punishment were inadequate. The parties, following the framework of Williams and Tate, have argued the question primarily in terms of equal protection, and debate vigorously whether strict scrutiny or rational basis is the appropriate standard of review. There is no doubt that the State has treated the petitioner differently from a person who did not fail to pay the imposed fine and therefore did not violate probation. To determine whether this differential treatment violates the Equal Protection Clause, one must determine whether, and under what circumstances, a defendant's indigent status may be considered in the decision whether to revoke probation. This is substantially similar to asking directly the due process question of whether and when it is fundamentally unfair or arbitrary for the State to revoke probation when an indigent is unable to pay the fine. Whether analyzed in terms of equal protection or due process, the issue cannot be resolved by resort to easy slogans or pigeonhole analysis, but rather requires a careful inquiry into such factors as "the nature of the individual interest affected, the extent to which it is affected, the rationality of the connection between legislative means and purpose, [and] the existence of alternative means for effectuating the purpose. . . ." Williams v. Illinois, supra, at 260 (Harlan, J., concurring).

In analyzing this issue, of course, we do not write on a clean slate, for both Williams and Tate analyzed similar situations. The reach and limits of their holdings are vital to a proper resolution of the issue here. In Williams, a defendant was sentenced to the maximum prison term and fine authorized under the statute. Because of his indigency he could not pay the fine. Pursuant to another statute equat-

ing a $5 fine with a day in jail, the defendant was kept in jail for 101 days beyond the maximum prison sentence to "work out" the fine. The Court struck down the practice, holding that "[once] the State has defined the outer limits of incarceration necessary to satisfy its penological interests and policies, it may not then subject a certain class of convicted defendants to a period of imprisonment beyond the statutory maximum solely by reason of their indigency." 399 U.S., at 241-242. In Tate v. Short, 401 U.S. 395 (1971), we faced a similar situation, except that the statutory penalty there permitted only a fine. Quoting from a concurring opinion in Morris v. Schoonfield, 399 U.S. 508, 509 (1970), we reasoned that "the same constitutional defect condemned in Williams also inheres in jailing an indigent for failing to make immediate payment of any fine, whether or not the fine is accompanied by a jail term and whether or not the jail term of the indigent extends beyond the maximum term that may be imposed on a person willing and able to pay a fine." 401 U.S., at 398.

The rule of Williams and Tate, then, is that the State cannot "[impose] a fine as a sentence and then automatically [convert] it into a jail term solely because the defendant is indigent and cannot forthwith pay the fine in full." Tate, supra, at 398. In other words, if the State determines a fine or restitution to be the appropriate and adequate penalty for the crime, it may not thereafter imprison a person solely because he lacked the resources to pay it. Both Williams and Tate carefully distinguished this substantive limitation on the imprisonment of indigents from the situation where a defendant was at fault in failing to pay the fine. As the Court made clear in Williams, "nothing in our decision today precludes imprisonment for willful refusal to pay a fine or court costs." 399 U.S., at 242, n. 19. Likewise in Tate, the Court "[emphasized] that our holding today does not suggest any constitutional infirmity in imprisonment of a defendant with the means to pay a fine who refuses or neglects to do so." 401 U.S., at 400.

This distinction, based on the reasons for nonpayment, is of critical importance here. If the probationer has willfully refused to pay the fine or restitution when he has the means to pay, the State is perfectly justified in using imprisonment as a sanction to enforce collection. See ALI, Model Penal Code § 302.2(1) (Prop. Off. Draft 1962). Similarly, a probationer's failure to make sufficient bona fide efforts to seek employment or borrow money in order to pay the fine or restitution may reflect an insufficient concern for paying the debt he owes to society for his crime. In such a situation, the State is likewise justified in revoking probation and using imprisonment as an appropriate penalty for the offense. But if the probationer has made all reasonable efforts to pay the fine or restitution, and yet cannot do so through no fault of his own, it is fundamentally unfair to revoke probation automatically without considering whether adequate alternative methods of punishing the defendant are available. This lack of fault provides a "substantial [reason] which [justifies] or [mitigates] the violation and [makes] revocation inappropriate." Gagnon v. Scarpelli, 411 U.S. 778, 790 (1973). Cf. Zablocki v. Redhail, 434 U.S. 374, 400 (1978) (POWELL, J., concurring) (distinguishing, under both due process and equal protection analyses, persons who shirk their moral and legal obligation to pay child support from those wholly unable to pay).

* * *

The decision to place the defendant on probation, however, reflects a determination by the sentencing court that the State's penological interests do not require imprisonment. See Williams v. Illinois, supra, at 264 (Harlan, J., concurring); Wood v. Georgia, 450 U.S. 261, 286-287 (1981) (WHITE, J., dissenting). A probationer's failure to make reasonable efforts to repay his debt to society may indicate that this original determination needs reevaluation, and imprisonment may now be required to satisfy the State's interests. But a probationer who has made sufficient bona fide efforts to pay his fine and restitution, and who has complied with the other conditions of probation, has demonstrated a willingness to pay his debt to society and an ability to conform his conduct to social norms. The State nevertheless asserts three reasons why imprisonment is required to further its penal goals.

First, the State argues that revoking probation furthers its interest in ensuring that restitution be paid to the victims of crime. A rule that imprisonment may befall the probationer who fails to make sufficient bona fide efforts to pay restitution may indeed spur probationers to try hard to pay, thereby increasing the number of probationers who make restitution. Such a goal is fully served, however, by revoking probation only for persons who have not made sufficient bona fide efforts to pay. Revoking the probation of someone who through no fault of his own is unable to make restitution will not make restitution suddenly forthcoming. Indeed, such a policy may have the perverse effect of inducing the probationer to use illegal means to acquire funds to pay in order to avoid revocation.

Second, the State asserts that its interest in rehabilitating the probationer and protecting society requires it to remove him from the temptation of committing other crimes. This is no more than a naked assertion that a probationer's poverty by itself indicates he may commit crimes in the future and thus that society needs for him to be incapacitated. We have already indicated that a sentencing court can consider a defendant's employment history and financial resources in setting an initial punishment. Such considerations are a necessary part of evaluating the entire background of the defendant in order to tailor an appropriate sentence for the defendant and crime. But it must be remembered that the State is seeking here to use as the sole justification for imprisonment the poverty of a probationer who, by assumption, has demonstrated sufficient bona fide efforts to find a job and pay the fine and whom the State initially thought it unnecessary to imprison. Given the significant interest of the individual in remaining on probation, see Gagnon v. Scarpelli, supra; Morrissey v. Brewer, 408 U.S. 471 (1972), the State cannot justify incarcerating a probationer who has demonstrated sufficient bona fide efforts to repay his debt to society, solely by lumping him together with other poor persons and thereby classifying him as dangerous. This would be little more than punishing a person for his poverty.

Third, and most plausibly, the State argues that its interests in punishing the lawbreaker and deterring others from criminal behavior require it to revoke probation for failure to pay a fine or restitution. The State clearly has an interest in punishment and deterrence, but this interest can often be served fully by alternative means. As we said in Williams, 399 U.S., at 244, and reiterated in Tate, 401 U.S., at 399, "[the] State is not powerless to enforce judgments against those financially unable to pay a fine." For example, the sentencing court could extend the time for making payments, or reduce the fine, or direct that the probationer perform some form of labor or public service in lieu of the fine. . . . a sentencing court can often establish a reduced fine or alternative public service in lieu of a fine that adequately serves the State's goals of punishment and deterrence, given the defendant's diminished financial resources. Only if the sentencing court determines that alternatives to imprisonment are not adequate in a particular situation to meet the State's interest in punishment and deterrence may the State imprison a probationer who has made sufficient bona fide efforts to pay.

We hold, therefore, that in revocation proceedings for failure to pay a fine or restitution, a sentencing court must inquire into the reasons for the failure to pay. If the probationer willfully refused to pay or failed to make sufficient bona fide efforts legally to acquire the resources to pay, the court may revoke probation and sentence the defendant to imprisonment within the authorized range of its sentencing authority. If the probationer could not pay despite sufficient bona fide efforts to acquire the resources to do so, the court must consider alternative measures of punishment other than imprisonment. Only if alternative measures are not adequate to meet the State's interests in punishment and deterrence may the court imprison a probationer who has made sufficient bona fide efforts to pay. To do otherwise would deprive the probationer of his conditional freedom simply because, through no fault of his own, he cannot pay the fine. Such a deprivation would be contrary to the fundamental fairness required by the Fourteenth Amendment.

* * *

We do not suggest by our analysis of the present record that the State may not place the petitioner in prison. If, upon remand, the Georgia courts determine that petitioner did not make sufficient bona fide efforts to pay his fine, or determine that alternative punish-

ment is not adequate to meet the State's interests in punishment and deterrence, imprisonment would be a permissible sentence. Unless such determinations are made, however, fundamental fairness requires that the petitioner remain on probation.

IV

The judgment is reversed, and the case is remanded for further proceedings not inconsistent with this opinion.

It is so ordered.

MARTINEZ
v.
CALIFORNIA

444 U.S. 277; 100 S. Ct. 553; 62 L. Ed. 2d 481 (1980)

MR. JUSTICE STEVENS delivered the opinion of the Court.

The two federal questions that appellants ask us to decide are (1) whether the Fourteenth Amendment invalidates a California statute granting absolute immunity to public employees who make parole-release determinations, and (2) whether such officials are absolutely immune from liability in an action brought under the federal Civil Rights Act of 1871, 42 U.S.C. § 1983. We agree with the California Court of Appeal that the state statute is valid when applied to claims arising under state law, and we conclude that appellants have not alleged a claim for relief under federal law.

The case arises out of the murder of a 15-year-old girl by a parolee. Her survivors brought this action in a California court claiming that the state officials responsible for the parole-release decision are liable in damages for the harm caused by the parolee.

The complaint alleged that the parolee, one Thomas, was convicted of attempted rape in December 1969. He was first committed to a state mental hospital as a "Mentally Disordered Sex Offender not amenable to treatment" and thereafter sentenced to a term of imprisonment of 1 to 20 years, with a recommendation that he not be paroled.

Nevertheless, five years later, appellees decided to parole Thomas to the care of his mother. They were fully informed about his history, his propensities, and the likelihood that he would commit another violent crime. Moreover, in making their release determination they failed to observe certain "requisite formalities." Five months after his release Thomas tortured and killed appellants' decedent. We assume, as the complaint alleges, that appellees knew, or should have known, that the release of Thomas created a clear and present danger that such an incident would occur. Their action is characterized not only as negligent, but also as reckless, willful, wanton and malicious. Appellants prayed for actual and punitive damages of $2 million.

The trial judge sustained a demurrer to the complaint and his order was upheld on appeal. 85 Cal. App. 3d 430, 149 Cal. Rptr. 519 (1978). After the California Supreme Court denied appellants' petition for a hearing, we noted probable jurisdiction. 441 U.S. 960.

I

Section 845.8 (a) of the Cal. Gov't Code Ann. (West Supp. 1979) provides:

Neither a public entity nor a public employee is liable for:

(a) Any injury resulting from determining whether to parole or release a prisoner or from determining the terms and conditions of his parole or release or from determining whether to revoke his parole or release.

The California courts held that this statute provided appellees with a complete defense to appellants' state-law claims. They considered and rejected the contention that the immunity statute as so construed violates the Due Process Clause of the Fourteenth Amendment to the Federal Constitution.

Like the California courts, we cannot accept the contention that this statute deprived Thomas' victim of her life without due process of law because it condoned a parole decision that led indirectly to her death. The statute neither authorized nor immunized the deliberate killing of any human being. It is not the equivalent of a death penalty statute which expressly authorizes state agents to take a person's life after prescribed procedures have been observed. This statute merely provides a defense to potential state tort-law liability. At most, the availability of such a defense may have encouraged members of the parole board to take somewhat greater risks of recidivism in exercising their authority to release prisoners than they otherwise might. But the basic risk that repeat offenses may occur is always present in any parole system. A legislative decision that has an incremental impact on the probability that death will result in any given situation—such as setting the speed limit at 55-miles-per-hour instead of 45—cannot be characterized as state action depriving a person of life just because it may set in motion a chain of events that ultimately leads to the random death of an innocent bystander.

Nor can the statute be characterized as an invalid deprivation of property. Arguably, the cause of action for wrongful death that the State has created is a species of "property" protected by the Due Process Clause. On that hypothesis, the immunity statute could be viewed as depriving the plaintiffs of that property interest insofar as they seek to assert a claim against parole officials. But even if one characterizes the immunity defense as a statutory deprivation, it would remain true that the State's interest in fashioning its own rules of tort law is paramount to any discernible federal interest, except perhaps an interest in protecting the individual citizen from state action that is wholly arbitrary or irrational.

We have no difficulty in accepting California's conclusion that there "is a rational relationship between the state's purposes and the statute." In fashioning state policy in a "practical and troublesome area" like this, see McGinnis v. Royster, 410 U.S. 263, 270, the California Legislature could reasonably conclude that judicial review of a parole officer's decisions "would inevitably inhibit the exercise of discretion," United States ex rel. Miller v. Twomey, 479 F.2d 701, 721 (CA7 1973), cert. denied, 414 U.S. 1146. That inhibiting effect could impair the State's ability to implement a parole program designed to promote rehabilitation of inmates as well as security within prison walls by holding out a promise of potential rewards. Whether one agrees or disagrees with California's decision to provide absolute immunity for parole officials in a case of this kind, one cannot deny that it rationally furthers a policy that reasonable lawmakers may favor. As federal judges, we have no authority to pass judgment on the wisdom of the underlying policy determination. We therefore find no merit in the contention that the State's immunity statute is unconstitutional when applied to defeat a tort claim arising under state law.

II

We turn then to appellants' § 1983 claim that appellees, by their action in releasing Thomas, subjected appellants' decedent to a deprivation of her life without due process of law. It is clear that the California immunity statute does not control this claim even though the federal cause of action is being asserted in the state courts. We also conclude that it is not necessary for us to decide any question concerning the immunity of state parole officials as a matter of federal law because, as we recently held in Baker v. McCollan, 443 U.S. 137, "[the] first inquiry in any § 1983 suit . . . is whether the plaintiff has been deprived of a right 'secured by the Constitution and laws'" of the United States. The answer to that inquiry disposes of this case.

Appellants contend that the decedent's right to life is protected by the Fourteenth Amendment to the Constitution. But the Fourteenth Amendment protected her only from deprivation by the "State . . . of life . . . without due process of law." Although the decision to release Thomas from prison was action by the State, the action of Thomas five months later cannot be fairly characterized as state action. Regardless of whether, as a matter of state tort law, the parole board could be said either to have had a "duty" to avoid harm to his victim or to have proximately caused her death, see Grimm v. Arizona Bd. of Pardons and Paroles, 115 Ariz. 260, 564 P. 2d 1227 (1977); Palsgraf v. Long Island R. Co., 248 N.Y. 339, 162 N.E. 99 (1928), we hold that, taking these particular allegations as true, appellees did not "deprive" appellants' decedent of life within the meaning of the Fourteenth Amendment.

Her life was taken by the parolee five months after his release. He was in no sense an agent of the parole board. Cf. Scheuer v. Rhodes, 416 U.S. 232. Further, the parole board was not aware that appellants' decedent, as distinguished from the public at large, faced any special danger. We need not and do not decide that a parole officer could never be deemed to "deprive" someone of life by action taken in connection with the release of a prisoner on parole. But we do hold that at least under the particular circumstances of this parole decision, appellants' decedent's death is too remote a consequence of the parole officers' action to hold them responsible under the federal civil rights law. Although a § 1983 claim has been described as "a species of tort liability," Imbler v. Pachtman, 424 U.S. 409, 417, it is perfectly clear that not every injury in which a state official has played some part is actionable under that statute.

The judgment is affirmed.

So ordered.

GRIFFIN
v.
WISCONSIN

483 U.S. 868; 107 S. Ct. 3164;
97 L. Ed. 2d 709 (1987)

JUSTICE SCALIA delivered the opinion of the Court.

Petitioner Joseph Griffin, who was on probation, had his home searched by probation officers acting without a warrant. The officers found a gun that later served as the basis of Griffin's conviction of a state-law weapons offense. We granted certiorari, 479 U.S. 1005 (1986), to consider whether this search violated the Fourth Amendment.

I

On September 4, 1980, Griffin, who had previously been convicted of a felony, was convicted in Wisconsin state court of resisting arrest, disorderly conduct, and obstructing an officer. He was placed on probation.

Wisconsin law puts probationers in the legal custody of the State Department of Health and Social Services and renders them "subject . . . to . . . conditions set by the court and rules and regulations established by the department." Wis. Stat. § 973.10(1) (1985-1986). One of the Department's regulations permits any probation officer to search a probationer's home without a warrant as long as his supervisor approves and as long as there are "reasonable grounds" to believe the presence of contraband—including any item that the probationer cannot possess under the probation conditions. Wis. Admin. Code HSS §§ 328.21(4), 328.16(1) (1981). The rule provides that an officer should consider a variety of factors in determining whether "reasonable grounds" exist, among which are information provided by an informant, the reliability and specificity of that information, the reliability of the informant (including whether the informant has any incentive to supply inaccurate information), the officer's own experience with the probationer, and the "need to verify compliance with rules of supervision and state and federal law." HSS § 328.21(7). Another regulation makes it a violation of the terms of probation to refuse to consent to a home search. HSS § 328.04(3)(k). And still another forbids a probationer to possess a firearm without advance approval from a probation officer. HSS § 328.04(3)(j).

On April 5, 1983, while Griffin was still on probation, Michael Lew, the supervisor of Griffin's probation officer, received information from a detective on the Beloit Police Department that there were or might be guns in Griffin's apartment. Unable to secure the assistance of Griffin's own probation officer, Lew, accompanied by another probation officer and three plainclothes policemen, went to the apartment. When Griffin answered the door, Lew told him who they were and informed him that they were going to search his home. During the subsequent search—carried out entirely by the probation officers under the authority of Wisconsin's probation regulation—they found a handgun.

Griffin was charged with possession of a firearm by a convicted felon, which is itself a felony. Wis. Stat. § 941.29(2) (1985-1986).

He moved to suppress the evidence seized during the search. The trial court denied the motion, concluding that no warrant was necessary and that the search was reasonable. A jury convicted Griffin of the firearms violation, and he was sentenced to two years' imprisonment. The conviction was affirmed by the Wisconsin Court of Appeals, 126 Wis. 2d 183, 376 N. W. 2d 62 (1985).

* * *

II

We think the Wisconsin Supreme Court correctly concluded that this warrantless search did not violate the Fourth Amendment. To reach that result, however, we find it unnecessary to embrace a new principle of law, as the Wisconsin court evidently did, that any search of a probationer's home by a probation officer satisfies the Fourth Amendment as long as the information possessed by the officer satisfies a federal "reasonable grounds" standard. As his sentence for the commission of a crime, Griffin was committed to the legal custody of the Wisconsin State Department of Health and Social Services, and thereby made subject to that Department's rules and regulations. The search of Griffin's home satisfied the demands of the Fourth Amendment because it was carried out pursuant to a regulation that itself satisfies the Fourth Amendment's reasonableness requirement under well-established principles.

A

A probationer's home, like anyone else's, is protected by the Fourth Amendment's requirement that searches be "reasonable." Although we usually require that a search be undertaken only pursuant to a warrant (and thus supported by probable cause, as the Constitution says warrants must be), see, e.g., Payton v. New York, 445 U.S. 573, 586 (1980), we have permitted exceptions when "special needs, beyond the normal need for law enforcement, make the warrant and probable-cause requirement impracticable." New Jersey v. T. L. O., 469 U.S. 325, 351 (1985) (BLACKMUN, J., concurring in judgment).

Thus, we have held that government employers and supervisors may conduct warrantless, work-related searches of employees' desks and offices without probable cause, O'Connor v. Ortega, 480 U.S. 709 (1987), and that school officials may conduct warrantless searches of some student property, also without probable cause, New Jersey v. T. L. O., supra. We have also held, for similar reasons, that in certain circumstances government investigators conducting searches pursuant to a regulatory scheme need not adhere to the usual warrant or probable-cause requirements as long as their searches meet "reasonable legislative or administrative standards." Camara v. Municipal Court, 387 U.S. 523, 538 (1967). See New York v. Burger, 482 U.S. 691, 702-703 (1987); Donovan v. Dewey, 452 U.S. 594, 602 (1981); United States v. Biswell, 406 U.S. 311, 316 (1972).

A State's operation of a probation system, like its operation of a school, government office or prison, or its supervision of a regulated industry, likewise presents "special needs" beyond normal law enforcement that may justify departures from the usual warrant and probable-cause requirements. Probation, like incarceration, is "a form of criminal sanction imposed by a court upon an offender after verdict, finding, or plea of guilty." G. Killinger, H. Kerper, & P. Cromwell, Probation and Parole in the Criminal Justice System 14 (1976); see also 18 U.S.C. § 3651 (1982 ed. and Supp. III) (probation imposed instead of imprisonment); Wis. Stat. § 973.09 (1985-1986) (same). Probation is simply one point (or, more accurately, one set of points) on a continuum of possible punishments ranging from solitary confinement in a maximum-security facility to a few hours of mandatory community service. A number of different options lie between those extremes, including confinement in a medium- or minimum-security facility, work-release programs, "halfway houses," and probation—which can itself be more or less confining depending upon the number and severity of restrictions imposed. See, e.g., 18 U.S.C. § 3563 (1982 ed., Supp. III) (effective Nov. 1, 1987) (probation conditions authorized in federal system include requiring probationers to avoid commission of other crimes; to pursue employment; to avoid certain occupations, places, and peo-

ple; to spend evenings or weekends in prison; and to avoid narcotics or excessive use of alcohol). To a greater or lesser degree, it is always true of probationers (as we have said it to be true of parolees) that they do not enjoy "the absolute liberty to which every citizen is entitled, but only . . . conditional liberty properly dependent on observance of special [probation] restrictions." Morrissey v. Brewer, 408 U.S. 471, 480 (1972).

These restrictions are meant to assure that the probation serves as a period of genuine rehabilitation and that the community is not harmed by the probationer's being at large. See State v. Tarrell, 74 Wis. 2d 647, 652-653, 247 N. W. 2d 696, 700 (1976). These same goals require and justify the exercise of supervision to assure that the restrictions are in fact observed. Recent research suggests that more intensive supervision can reduce recidivism, see Petersilia, Probation and Felony Offenders, 49 Fed. Probation 9 (June 1985), and the importance of supervision has grown as probation has become an increasingly common sentence for those convicted of serious crimes, see id., at 4. Supervision, then, is a "special need" of the State permitting a degree of impingement upon privacy that would not be constitutional if applied to the public at large. That permissible degree is not unlimited, however, so we next turn to whether it has been exceeded here.

B

In determining whether the "special needs" of its probation system justify Wisconsin's search regulation, we must take that regulation as it has been interpreted by state corrections officials and state courts. As already noted, the Wisconsin Supreme Court—the ultimate authority on issues of Wisconsin law—has held that a tip from a police detective that Griffin "had" or "may have had" an illegal weapon at his home constituted the requisite "reasonable grounds." See 131 Wis. 2d, at 64, 388 N. W. 2d, at 544. Whether or not we would choose to interpret a similarly worded federal regulation in that fashion, we are bound by the state court's interpretation, which is relevant to our constitutional analysis only insofar as it fixes the meaning of the regulation. We think it clear that the special needs of Wisconsin's probation system make the warrant requirement impracticable and justify replacement of the standard of probable cause by "reasonable grounds," as defined by the Wisconsin Supreme Court.

A warrant requirement would interfere to an appreciable degree with the probation system, setting up a magistrate rather than the probation officer as the judge of how close a supervision the probationer requires. Moreover, the delay inherent in obtaining a warrant would make it more difficult for probation officials to respond quickly to evidence of misconduct, see New Jersey v. T. L. O., 469 U.S., at 340, and would reduce the deterrent effect that the possibility of expeditious searches would otherwise create, see New York v. Burger, 482 U.S., at 710; United States v. Biswell, 406 U.S., at 316. By way of analogy, one might contemplate how parental custodial authority would be impaired by requiring judicial approval for search of a minor child's room. And on the other side of the equation—the effect of dispensing with a warrant upon the probationer: Although a probation officer is not an impartial magistrate, neither is he the police officer who normally conducts searches against the ordinary citizen. He is an employee of the State Department of Health and Social Services who, while assuredly charged with protecting the public interest, is also supposed to have in mind the welfare of the probationer (who in the regulations is called a "client," HSS § 328.03(5)). The applicable regulations require him, for example, to "provid[e] individualized counseling designed to foster growth and development of the client as necessary," HSS § 328.04(2)(i), and "monito[r] the client's progress where services are provided by another agency and evaluat[e] the need for continuation of the services," HSS § 328.04(2)(o). In such a setting, we think it reasonable to dispense with the warrant requirement.

JUSTICE BLACKMUN's dissent would retain a judicial warrant requirement, though agreeing with our subsequent conclusion that reasonableness of the search does not require probable cause. This, however, is a combination that neither the text of the Constitution nor any of our prior decisions permits. While it is possible to say that Fourth Amendment reasonableness demands probable cause

without a judicial warrant, the reverse runs up against the constitutional provision that "no Warrants shall issue, but upon probable cause." Amdt. 4. The Constitution prescribes, in other words, that where the matter is of such a nature as to require a judicial warrant, it is also of such a nature as to require probable cause. Although we have arguably come to permit an exception to that prescription for administrative search warrants, which may but do not necessarily have to be issued by courts, we have never done so for constitutionally mandated judicial warrants. There it remains true that "if a search warrant be constitutionally required, the requirement cannot be flexibly interpreted to dispense with the rigorous constitutional restrictions for its issue." Frank v. Maryland, 359 U.S. 360, 373 (1959). JUSTICE BLACKMUN neither gives a justification for departure from that principle nor considers its implications for the body of Fourth Amendment law.

We think that the probation regime would also be unduly disrupted by a requirement of probable cause. To take the facts of the present case, it is most unlikely that the unauthenticated tip of a police officer—bearing, as far as the record shows, no indication whether its basis was firsthand knowledge or, if not, whether the firsthand source was reliable, and merely stating that Griffin "had or might have" guns in his residence, not that he certainly had them—would meet the ordinary requirement of probable cause. But this is different from the ordinary case in two related respects: First, even more than the requirement of a warrant, a probable-cause requirement would reduce the deterrent effect of the supervisory arrangement. The probationer would be assured that so long as his illegal (and perhaps socially dangerous) activities were sufficiently concealed as to give rise to no more than reasonable suspicion, they would go undetected and uncorrected. The second difference is well reflected in the regulation specifying what is to be considered "in deciding whether there are reasonable grounds to believe . . . a client's living quarters or property contain contraband," HSS § 328.21(7). The factors include not only the usual elements that a police officer or magistrate would consider, such as the detail and consistency of the information suggesting the presence of contraband and the reliability and motivation to dissemble of the informant, HSS §§ 328.21(7)(c), (d), but also "information provided by the client which is relevant to whether the client possesses contraband," and "the experience of a staff member with that client or in a similar circumstance." HSS §§ 328.21(7)(f), (g). As was true, then, in O'Connor v. Ortega, 480 U.S. 709 (1987), and New Jersey v. T. L. O., 469 U.S. 325 (1985), we deal with a situation in which there is an ongoing supervisory relationship—and one that is not, or at least not entirely, adversarial—between the object of the search and the decisionmaker.

In such circumstances it is both unrealistic and destructive of the whole object of the continuing probation relationship to insist upon the same degree of demonstrable reliability of particular items of supporting data, and upon the same degree of certainty of violation, as is required in other contexts. In some cases—especially those involving drugs or illegal weapons—the probation agency must be able to act based upon a lesser degree of certainty than the Fourth Amendment would otherwise require in order to intervene before a probationer does damage to himself or society. The agency, moreover, must be able to proceed on the basis of its entire experience with the probationer, and to assess probabilities in the light of its knowledge of his life, character, and circumstances.

To allow adequate play for such factors, we think it reasonable to permit information provided by a police officer, whether or not on the basis of firsthand knowledge, to support a probationer search. The same conclusion is suggested by the fact that the police may be unwilling to disclose their confidential sources to probation personnel. For the same reason, and also because it is the very assumption of the institution of probation that the probationer is in need of rehabilitation and is more likely than the ordinary citizen to violate the law, we think it enough if the information provided indicates, as it did here, only the likelihood ("had or might have guns") of facts justifying the search.

The search of Griffin's residence was "reasonable" within the meaning of the Fourth Amendment because it was conducted pursuant to a valid regulation governing probationers. This conclusion makes it unneces-

sary to consider whether, as the court below held and the State urges, any search of a probationer's home by a probation officer is lawful when there are "reasonable grounds" to believe contraband is present. For the foregoing reasons, the judgment of the Wisconsin Supreme Court is

Affirmed.

JUSTICE BLACKMUN, with whom JUSTICE MARSHALL joins and, as to Parts I-B and I-C, JUSTICE BRENNAN joins and, as to Part I-C, JUSTICE STEVENS joins, dissenting.

In ruling that the home of a probationer may be searched by a probation officer without a warrant, the Court today takes another step that diminishes the protection given by the Fourth Amendment to the "right of the people to be secure in their persons, houses, papers, and effects, against unreasonable searches and seizures." In my view, petitioner's probationary status provides no reason to abandon the warrant requirement. The probation system's special law enforcement needs may justify a search by a probation officer on the basis of "reasonable suspicion," but even that standard was not met in this case.

I

The need for supervision in probation presents one of the "exceptional circumstances in which special needs, beyond the normal need for law enforcement," New Jersey v. T. L. O., 469 U.S. 325, 351 (1985) (opinion concurring in judgment), justify an application of the Court's balancing test and an examination of the practicality of the warrant and probable-cause requirements. The Court, however, fails to recognize that this is a threshold determination of special law enforcement needs. The warrant and probable-cause requirements provide the normal standard for "reasonable" searches. "Only when the practical realities of a particular situation suggest that a government official cannot obtain a warrant based upon probable cause without sacrificing the ultimate goals to which a search would contribute, does the Court turn to a 'balancing' test to formulate a standard of reasonableness for this context."

O'Connor v. Ortega, 480 U.S. 709, 741 (1987) (dissenting opinion). The presence of special law enforcement needs justifies resort to the balancing test, but it does not preordain the necessity of recognizing exceptions to the warrant and probable-cause requirements.

My application of the balancing test leads me to conclude that special law enforcement needs justify a search by a probation agent of the home of a probationer on the basis of a reduced level of suspicion. The acknowledged need for supervision, however, does not also justify an exception to the warrant requirement, and I would retain this means of protecting a probationer's privacy. Moreover, the necessity for the neutral check provided by the warrant requirement is demonstrated by this case, in which the search was conducted on the basis of information that did not begin to approach the level of "reasonable grounds."

A

The probation officer is not dealing with an average citizen, but with a person who has been convicted of a crime. This presence of an offender in the community creates the need for special supervision. I therefore agree that a probation agent must have latitude in observing a probationer if the agent is to carry out his supervisory responsibilities effectively. Recidivism among probationers is a major problem, and supervision is one means of combating that threat. See ante, at 875. Supervision also provides a crucial means of advancing rehabilitation by allowing a probation agent to intervene at the first sign of trouble.

One important aspect of supervision is the monitoring of a probationer's compliance with the conditions of his probation. In order to ensure compliance with those conditions, a probation agent may need to search a probationer's home to check for violations. While extensive inquiry may be required to gather the information necessary to establish probable cause that a violation has occurred, a "reasonable grounds" standard allows a probation agent to avoid this delay and to intervene at an earlier stage of suspicion. This standard is thus consistent with the level of supervision necessary to protect the public

and to aid rehabilitation. At the same time, if properly applied, the standard of reasonable suspicion will protect a probationer from unwarranted intrusions into his privacy.

B

I do not think, however, that special law enforcement needs justify a modification of the protection afforded a probationer's privacy by the warrant requirement. The search in this case was conducted in petitioner's home, the place that traditionally has been regarded as the center of a person's private life, the bastion in which one has a legitimate expectation of privacy protected by the Fourth Amendment. . . .

* * *

A probationer usually lives at home, and often, as in this case, with a family. He retains a legitimate privacy interest in the home that must be respected to the degree that it is not incompatible with substantial governmental needs. The Court in New Jersey v. T. L. O. acknowledged that the Fourth Amendment issue needs to be resolved in such a way as to "ensure that the [privacy] interests of students will be invaded no more than is necessary to achieve the legitimate end of preserving order in the schools." 469 U.S., at 343. The privacy interests of probationers should be protected by a similar standard, and invaded no more than is necessary to satisfy probation's dual goals of protecting the public safety and encouraging the rehabilitation of the probationer.

The search in this case was not the result of an ordinary home visit by petitioner's probation agent for which no warrant is required. Cf. Wyman v. James, 400 U.S. 309 (1971). It was a search pursuant to a tip, ostensibly from the police, for the purpose of uncovering evidence of a criminal violation. There is nothing about the status of probation that justifies a special exception to the warrant requirement under these circumstances. If in a particular case there is a compelling need to search the home of a probationer without delay, then it is possible for a search to be conducted immediately under the established exception for exigent circumstances. There is no need to create a separate warrant exception for probationers. The existing exception provides a probation agent with all the flexibility the agent needs.

The circumstances of this case illustrate the fact that the warrant requirement does not create any special impediment to the achievement of the goals of probation. The probation supervisor, Michael T. Lew, waited "two or three hours" after receiving the telephone tip before he proceeded to petitioner's home to conduct the search. App. 16. He testified that he was waiting for the return of petitioner's official agent who was attending a legal proceeding, and that eventually he requested another probation agent to initiate the search. Id., at 16, 51. Mr. Lew thus had plenty of time to obtain a search warrant. If the police themselves had investigated the report of a gun at petitioner's residence, they would have been required to obtain a warrant. There simply was no compelling reason to abandon the safeguards provided by neutral review.

The Court appears to hold the curious assumption that the probationer will benefit by dispensing with the warrant requirement. It notes that a probation officer does not normally conduct searches, as does a police officer, and, moreover, the officer is "supposed to have in mind the welfare of the probationer." Ante, at 876. The implication is that a probation agent will be less likely to initiate an inappropriate search than a law-enforcement officer, and is thus less in need of neutral review. Even if there were data to support this notion, a reduced need for review does not justify a complete removal of the warrant requirement. Furthermore, the benefit that a probationer is supposed to gain from probation is rehabilitation. I fail to see how the role of the probation agent in "foster[ing] growth and development of the client," ante, at 876, quoting Wis. Admin. Code HSS § 328.04 (2)(i) (1981), is enhanced the slightest bit by the ability to conduct a search without the checks provided by prior neutral review. If anything, the power to decide to search will prove a barrier to establishing any degree of trust between agent and "client."

The Court also justifies the exception to the warrant requirement that it would find in the Wisconsin regulations by stressing the need to have a probation agent, rather than a judge, decide how closely supervised a particular probationer should be. See ante, at 876. This argument mistakes the nature of the search at issue. The probation agent retains discretion over the terms of a probationer's supervision—the warrant requirement introduces a judge or a magistrate into the decision only when a full-blown search for evidence of a criminal violation is at stake. The Court's justification for the conclusion that the warrant requirement would interfere with the probation system by way of an analogy to the authority possessed by parents over their children is completely unfounded. The difference between the two situations is too obvious to belabor. Unlike the private nature of a parent's interaction with his or her child, the probation system is a governmental operation, with explicit standards. Experience has shown that a neutral judge can best determine if those standards are met and a search is justified. This case provides an excellent illustration of the need for neutral review of a probation officer's decision to conduct a search, for it is obvious that the search was not justified even by a reduced standard of reasonable suspicion.

C

The Court concludes that the search of petitioner's home satisfied the requirements of the Fourth Amendment "because it was carried out pursuant to a regulation that itself satisfies the Fourth Amendment's reasonableness requirement under well-established principles." Ante, at 873. In the Court's view, it seems that only the single regulation requiring "reasonable grounds" for a search is relevant to its decision. Ante, at 880, n. 8. When faced with the patent failure of the probation agents to comply with the Wisconsin regulations, the Court concludes that it "is irrelevant to the case before us" that the probation agents "may have violated Wisconsin state regulations." Ibid. All of these other regulations, which happen to define the steps necessary to ensure that reasonable grounds are present, can be ignored. This conclusion that the existence of a facial requirement for "reasonable grounds" automatically satisfies the constitutional protection that a search be reasonable can only be termed tautological. The content of a standard is found in its application and, in this case, I cannot discern the application of any standard whatsoever.

The suspicion in this case was based on an unverified tip from an unknown source. With or without the Wisconsin regulation, such information cannot constitutionally justify a search. Mr. Lew testified that he could not recall which police officer called him with the information about the gun, although he thought it "probably" was Officer Pittner. App. 16. Officer Pittner, however, did not remember making any such telephone call. Id., at 39. From all that the record reveals, the call could have been placed by anyone. It is even plausible that the information did not come from the police at all, but from someone impersonating an officer.

Even assuming that a police officer spoke to Mr. Lew, there was little to demonstrate the reliability of the information he received from that unknown officer. The record does not reveal even the precise content of the tip. The unknown officer actually may have reported that petitioner "had" contraband in his possession, id., at 51, or he merely may have suggested that petitioner "may have had guns in his apartment." Id., at 14. Mr. Lew testified to both at different stages of the proceedings. Nor do we know anything about the ultimate source of the information. The unknown officer's belief may have been founded on a hunch, a rumor, or an informant's tip. Without knowing more about the basis of the tip, it is impossible to form a conclusion, let alone a reasonable conclusion, that there were "reasonable grounds" to justify a search.

Mr. Lew failed completely to make the most rudimentary effort to confirm the information he had received or to evaluate whether reasonable suspicion justified a search. Conspicuously absent was any attempt to comply with the Wisconsin regulations that governed the content of the "reasonable grounds" standard. Wis. Admin. Code HSS § 328.21(7) (1981). No observations of a staff member could have been considered, as required by subsection (7)(a), for Mr. Lew did not consult the agent who had personal knowledge of petitioner's case. When information was provided by an informant, subsections (7)(c) and (d) required evaluation of the reliability of the information relied upon and the reliability of the informant.

Mr. Lew proceeded in violation of these basic requirements. Subsection (7)(f) referred to "information provided by the client" and the explanatory notes stated that "the client should be talked to before the search. Sometimes, this will elicit information helpful in determining whether a search should be made." § 328.21 App., p. 250. This requirement, too, was ignored. Nor do any of the other considerations support a finding of reasonable grounds to conduct the search. There is no indication that there had been prior seizures of contraband from petitioner, or that his case presented any special need to verify compliance with the law. See §§ 328.21(7)(h) and (i).

The majority acknowledges that it is "most unlikely" that the suspicion in this case would have met the normal "probable cause" standard. Ante, at 878. It concludes, however, that this is not an "ordinary" case because of the need for supervision and the continuing relationship between the probationer and the probation agency. Ibid. In view of this continuing relationship, the regulations mandated consideration of factors that go beyond those normally considered in determining probable cause to include information provided by the probationer and the experience of the staff member with the probationer. But unless the agency adheres to the regulations, it is sophistic to rely on them as a justification for conducting a search on a lesser degree of suspicion. Mr. Lew drew on no special knowledge of petitioner in deciding to search his house. He had no contact with the agent familiar with petitioner's case before commencing the search. Nor, as discussed above, was there the slightest attempt to obtain information from petitioner. In this case, the continuing relationship between petitioner and the agency did not supply support for any suspicion, reasonable or otherwise, that would justify a search of petitioner's home.

II

There are many probationers in this country, and they have committed crimes that range widely in seriousness. The Court has determined that all of them may be subjected to such searches in the absence of a warrant. Moreover, in authorizing these searches on the basis of a reduced level of suspicion, the Court overlooks the feeble justification for the search in this case.

I respectfully dissent.

JUSTICE STEVENS, with whom JUSTICE MARSHALL joins, dissenting.

Mere speculation by a police officer that a probationer "may have had" contraband in his possession is not a constitutionally sufficient basis for a warrantless, nonconsensual search of a private home. I simply do not understand how five Members of this Court can reach a contrary conclusion. Accordingly, I respectfully dissent.

Cases Relating to Chapter 10

Rights to Rehabilitation Programs, Right to Medical Aid, and Right to Life

COKER

v.

GEORGIA

433 U.S. 584; 97 S. Ct. 2861;
53 L. Ed. 2d 982 (1977)

MR. JUSTICE WHITE announced the judgment of the Court and filed an opinion in which MR. JUSTICE STEWART, MR. JUSTICE BLACKMUN, and MR. JUSTICE STEVENS, joined.

Georgia Code Ann. § 26-2001 (1972) provides that "[a] person convicted of rape shall be punished by death or by imprisonment for life, or by imprisonment for not less than one nor more than 20 years." Punishment is determined by a jury in a separate sentencing proceeding in which at least one of the statutory aggravating circumstances must be found before the death penalty may be imposed. Petitioner Coker was convicted of rape and sentenced to death. Both the conviction and the sentence were affirmed by the Georgia Supreme Court. Coker was granted a writ of certiorari, 429 U.S. 815, limited to the single claim, rejected by the Georgia court, that the punishment of death for rape violates the Eighth Amendment, which proscribes "cruel and unusual punishments" and which must be observed by the States as well as the Federal Government. Robinson v. California, 370 U.S. 660 (1962).

I

While serving various sentences for murder, rape, kidnaping, and aggravated assault, petitioner escaped from the Ware Correctional Institution near Waycross, Ga., on September 2, 1974. At approximately 11 o'clock that night, petitioner entered the house of Allen and Elnita Carver through an unlocked kitchen door. Threatening the couple with a "board," he tied up Mr. Carver in the bathroom, obtained a knife from the kitchen, and took Mr. Carver's money and the keys to the family car. Brandishing the knife and saying "you know what's going to happen to you if you try anything, don't you," Coker then raped Mrs. Carver. Soon thereafter, petitioner drove away in the Carver car, taking Mrs. Carver with him. Mr. Carver, freeing himself, notified the police; and not long thereafter petitioner was apprehended. Mrs. Carver was unharmed.

Petitioner was charged with escape, armed robbery, motor vehicle theft, kidnaping, and rape. Counsel was appointed to represent him. Having been found competent to stand trial, he was tried. The jury returned a verdict of guilty, rejecting his general plea of insanity. A sentencing hearing was then conducted in accordance with the procedures dealt with at length in Gregg v. Georgia, 428 U.S. 153 (1976), where this Court sustained the death penalty for murder when imposed pursuant to the statutory procedures. The jury was instructed that it could consider as aggravating circumstances whether the rape had been committed by a person with a prior record of conviction for a capital felony and whether the rape had been committed in the course of committing another capital felony, namely, the armed robbery of Allen Carver. The court also instructed, pursuant to statute, that even if aggravating circumstances were present, the death penalty need not be imposed if the jury found they were outweighed by mitigating circumstances, that is, circumstances not constituting justification or excuse for the offense in question, "but which, in fairness and mercy, may be considered as extenuating or reducing the degree" of moral culpability or punishment. App. 300. The jury's verdict on the rape count was death by electrocution. Both aggravating circumstances on which the court instructed were found to be present by the jury.

II

. . . It is now settled that the death penalty is not invariably cruel and unusual punishment within the meaning of the Eighth Amendment; it is not inherently barbaric or an unacceptable mode of punishment for crime; neither is it always disproportionate to the crime for which it is imposed. It is also established that imposing capital punishment, at least for murder, in accordance with the procedures provided under the Georgia statutes saves the sentence from the infirmities which led the Court to invalidate the prior Georgia capital punishment statute in Furman v. Georgia, supra.

In sustaining the imposition of the death penalty in Gregg, however, the Court firmly embraced the holdings and dicta from prior cases, Furman v. Georgia, supra; Robinson v. California, 370 U.S. 660 (1962); Trop v. Dulles, 356 U.S. 86 (1958); and Weems v. United States, 217 U.S. 349 (1910), to the effect that the Eighth Amendment bars not only those punishments that are "barbaric" but also those that are "excessive" in relation to the crime committed. Under Gregg, a punishment is "excessive" and unconstitutional if it (1) makes no measurable contribution to acceptable goals of punishment and hence is nothing more than the purposeless and needless imposition of pain and suffering; or (2) is grossly out of proportion to the severity of the crime. A punishment might fail the test on either ground. Furthermore, these Eighth Amendment judgments should not be, or appear to be, merely the subjective views of individual Justices; judgment should be informed by objective factors to the maximum possible extent. To this end, attention must be given to the public attitudes concerning a particular sentence—history and precedent, legislative attitudes, and the response of juries reflected in their sentencing decisions are to be consulted. In Gregg, after giving due regard to such sources, the Court's judgment was that the death penalty for deliberate murder was neither the purposeless imposition of severe punishment nor a punishment grossly disproportionate to the crime. But the Court reserved the question of the constitutionality of the death penalty when imposed for other crimes. 428 U.S., at 187 n. 35.

III

That question, with respect to rape of an adult woman, is now before us. We have concluded that a sentence of death is grossly disproportionate and excessive punishment for the crime of rape and is therefore forbidden by the Eighth Amendment as cruel and unusual punishment.

A

As advised by recent cases, we seek guidance in history and from the objective evidence of the country's present judgment concerning the acceptability of death as a penalty for rape of an adult woman. At no time in the last 50 years have a majority of the States authorized death as a punishment for rape. In 1925, 18 States, the District of Columbia, and the Federal Government authorized capital punishment for the rape of an adult female. By 1971 just prior to the decision in Furman v. Georgia, that number had declined, but not substantially, to 16 States plus the Federal Government. Furman then invalidated most of the capital punishment statutes in this country, including the rape statutes, because, among other reasons, of the manner in which the death penalty was imposed and utilized under those laws.

With their death penalty statutes for the most part invalidated, the States were faced with the choice of enacting modified capital punishment laws in an attempt to satisfy the requirements of Furman or of being satisfied with life imprisonment as the ultimate punishment for any offense. Thirty-five States immediately reinstituted the death penalty for at least limited kinds of crime. Gregg v. Georgia, 428 U.S., at 179 n. 23. This public judgment as to the acceptability of capital punishment, evidenced by the immediate, post-Furman legislative reaction in a large majority of the States, heavily influenced the Court to sustain the death penalty for murder in Gregg v. Georgia, supra, at 179-182.

But if the "most marked indication of society's endorsement of the death penalty for murder is the legislative response to Furman," Gregg v. Georgia, supra, at 179-180, it should also be a telling datum that the public judgment with respect to rape, as reflected in the statutes providing the punishment for that crime, has been dramatically different. . . .

* * *

The current judgment with respect to the death penalty for rape is not wholly unanimous among state legislatures, but it obviously weighs very heavily on the side of rejecting capital punishment as a suitable penalty for raping an adult woman.

B

* * *

. . . the legislative rejection of capital punishment for rape strongly confirms our own judgment, which is that death is indeed a disproportionate penalty for the crime of raping an adult woman.

We do not discount the seriousness of rape as a crime. It is highly reprehensible, both in a moral sense and in its almost total contempt for the personal integrity and autonomy of the female victim and for the latter's privilege of choosing those with whom intimate relationships are to be established. Short of homicide, it is the "ultimate violation of self." It is also a violent crime because it normally involves force, or the threat of force or intimidation, to overcome the will and the capacity of the victim to resist. Rape is very often accompanied by physical injury to the female and can also inflict mental and psychological damage. Because it undermines the community's sense of security, there is public injury as well.

Rape is without doubt deserving of serious punishment; but in terms of moral depravity and of the injury to the person and to the public, it does not compare with murder, which does involve the unjustified taking of human life. Although it may be accompanied by another crime, rape by definition does not include the death of or even the serious injury to another person. The murderer kills; the rapist, if no more than that, does not. Life is over for the victim of the murderer; for the rape victim, life may not be nearly so happy as it was, but it is not over and normally is not beyond repair. We have the abiding conviction that the death penalty, which "is unique in its severity and irrevocability," Gregg v. Georgia, 428 U.S., at 187, is an excessive penalty for the rapist who, as such, does not take human life.

* * *

. . . The judgment of the Georgia Supreme Court upholding the death sentence is reversed, and the case is remanded to that court for further proceedings not inconsistent with this opinion.

So ordered.

* * *

MR. JUSTICE POWELL, concurring in the judgment in part and dissenting in part.

* * *

. . . the plurality draws a bright line between murder and all rapes—regardless of the degree of brutality of the rape or the effect upon the victim. I dissent because I am not persuaded that such a bright line is appropriate. As noted in Snider v. Peyton, 356 F.2d 626, 627 (CA4 1966), "[t]here is extreme variation in the degree of culpability of rapists." The deliberate viciousness of the rapist may be greater than that of the murderer. Rape is never an act committed accidentally. Rarely can it be said to be unpremediated. There also is wide variation in the effect on the victim. The plurality opinion says that "[l]ife is over for the victim of the murderer; for the rape victim, life may not be nearly so happy as it was, but it is not over and normally is not beyond repair." Ante, at 598. But there is indeed "extreme variation" in the crime of rape. Some victims are so grievously injured physically or psychologically that life is beyond repair.

Thus, it may be that the death penalty is not disproportionate punishment for the crime of aggravated rape. Final resolution of the question must await careful inquiry into objective indicators of society's "evolving standards of decency," particularly legislative enactments and the responses of juries in capital cases. See Gregg v. Georgia, supra, at 173-182 (joint opinion of STEWART, POWELL, and STEVENS, JJ.); Woodson v. North Carolina, supra, at 294-295 (plurality opinion); Furman v. Georgia, 408 U.S. 238, 436-443 (1972) (POWELL, J., dissenting). The plurality properly examines these indicia, which do support the conclusion that society finds the death penalty unacceptable for the crime of rape in the absence of excessive brutality or severe injury. But it has not been shown that society finds the penalty disproportionate for all rapes. In a proper case a more discriminating inquiry than the plurality undertakes well might discover that both juries and legislatures have reserved the ultimate penalty for the case of an outrageous rape resulting in serious, lasting harm to the victim. I would not prejudge the issue. To this extent, I respectfully dissent.

MR. CHIEF JUSTICE BURGER, with whom MR. JUSTICE REHNQUIST joins, dissenting.

. . . I accept that the Eighth Amendment's concept of disproportionality bars the death penalty for minor crimes. But rape is not a minor crime; hence the Cruel and Unusual Punishments Clause does not give the Members of this Court license to engraft their conceptions of proper public policy onto the considered legislative judgments of the States. Since I cannot agree that Georgia lacked the constitutional power to impose the penalty of death for rape, I dissent from the Court's judgment.

* * *

. . . A rapist not only violates a victim's privacy and personal integrity, but inevitably causes serious psychological as well as physical harm in the process. The long-range effect upon the victim's life and health is likely to be irreparable; it is impossible to measure the harm which results. Volumes have been written by victims, physicians, and psychiatric specialists on the lasting injury suffered by rape victims. Rape is not a mere physical attack—it is destructive of the human personality. The remainder of the victim's life may be gravely affected, and this in turn may have a serious detrimental effect upon her husband and any children she may have. I therefore wholly agree with MR. JUSTICE WHITE's conclusion as far as it goes—that "[s]hort of homicide, [rape] is the 'ultimate violation of self.' " Ante, at 597. Victims may recover from the physical damage of knife or bullet wounds, or a beating with fists or a club, but recovery from such a gross assault on the human personality is not healed by medicine or surgery. To speak blandly, as the plurality does, of rape victims who are "unharmed," or to classify the human outrage of rape, as does MR. JUSTICE POWELL, in terms of "excessively brutal," ante, at 601, versus " moderately brutal," takes too little account of the profound suffering the crime imposes upon the victims and their loved ones.

* * *

The subjective judgment that the death penalty is simply disproportionate to the crime of rape is even more disturbing than the "objective" analysis discussed supra. The plurality's conclusion on this point is based upon the bare fact that murder necessarily results in the physical death of the victim, while rape does not. Ante, at 598-599, 600. However, no Member of the Court explains why this distinction has relevance, much less constitutional significance. It is, after all, not irrational—nor constitutionally impermissible—for a legislature to make the penalty more severe than the criminal act it punishes in the hope it would deter wrongdoing:

* * *

Rape thus is not a crime "light years" removed from murder in the degree of its heinousness; it certainly poses a serious potential danger to the life and safety of innocent victims—apart from the devastating psychic consequences. It would seem to follow therefore that, affording the States proper leeway under the broad standard of the Eighth Amendment, if murder is properly punishable by death, rape should be also, if that is the considered judgment of the legislators.

* * *

. . . I cannot agree that it is constitutionally impermissible for a state legislature to make the "solemn judgment" to impose such penalty for the crime of rape. Accordingly, I would leave to the States the task of legislating in this area of the law.

LOCKETT
v.
OHIO

438 U.S. 586; 98 S. Ct. 2954; 57 L. Ed. 2d 973 (1978)

MR. CHIEF JUSTICE BURGER delivered the opinion of the Court with respect to the constitutionality of petitioner's conviction (Parts I and II), together with an opinion (Part III), in which MR. JUSTICE STEWART, MR. JUSTICE POWELL, and MR. JUSTICE STEVENS joined, on the constitutionality of the statute under which petitioner was sentenced to death, and announced the judgment of the Court.

We granted certiorari in this case to consider, among other questions, whether Ohio violated the Eighth and Fourteenth Amendments by sentencing Sandra Lockett to death pursuant to a statute that narrowly limits the sentencer's discretion to consider the circumstances of the crime and the record and character of the offender as mitigating factors.

I

Lockett was charged with aggravated murder with the aggravating specifications (1) that the murder was "committed for the purpose of escaping detection, apprehension, trial, or punishment" for aggravated robbery, and (2) that the murder was "committed while . . . committing, attempting to commit, or fleeing immediately after committing or attempting to commit . . . aggravated robbery." That offense was punishable by death in Ohio. See Ohio Rev. Code Ann. §§ 2929.03, 2929.04 (1975). She was also charged with aggravated robbery. The State's case against her depended largely upon the testimony of a coparticipant, one Al Parker, who gave the following account of her participation in the robbery and murder.

Lockett became acquainted with Parker and Nathan Earl Dew while she and a friend, Joanne Baxter, were in New Jersey. Parker and Dew then accompanied Lockett, Baxter, and Lockett's brother back to Akron, Ohio, Lockett's hometown. After they arrived in Akron, Parker and Dew needed money for the trip back to New Jersey. Dew suggested that he pawn his ring. Lockett overheard his suggestion, but felt that the ring was too beautiful to pawn, and suggested instead that they could get some money by robbing a grocery store and a furniture store in the area. She warned that the grocery store's operator was a "big guy" who carried a "45" and that they would have "to get him real quick." She also volunteered to get a gun from her father's basement to aid in carrying out the robberies, but by that time, the two stores had closed and it was too late to proceed with the plan to rob them.

Someone, apparently Lockett's brother, suggested a plan for robbing a pawnshop. He and Dew would enter the shop and pretend to pawn a ring. Next Parker, who had some bullets, would enter the shop, ask to see a gun, load it, and use it to rob the shop. No one planned to kill the pawnshop operator in the course of the robbery. Because she knew the owner, Lockett was not to be among those entering the pawnshop, though she did guide the others to the shop that night.

The next day Parker, Dew, Lockett, and her brother gathered at Baxter's apartment. Lockett's brother asked if they were "still going to do it," and everyone, including Lockett, agreed to proceed. The four then drove by the pawnshop several times and parked the car. Lockett's brother and Dew entered the shop. Parker then left the car and told Lockett to start it again in two minutes. The robbery proceeded according to plan until the pawnbroker grabbed the gun when Parker announced the "stickup." The gun went off with Parker's finger on the trigger, firing a fatal shot into the pawnbroker.

Parker went back to the car where Lockett waited with the engine running. While driving away from the pawnshop, Parker told Lockett what had happened. She took the gun from the pawnshop and put it into her purse. Lockett and Parker drove to Lockett's aunt's house and called a taxicab. Shortly thereafter, while riding away in a taxicab, they were stopped by the police, but by this time Lockett had placed the gun under the front seat. Lockett told the police that Parker rented a room from her mother and lived with her family. After verifying this story with Lockett's parents, the police released Lockett and Parker. Lockett hid Dew and Parker in the attic when the police arrived at the Lockett household later that evening.

Parker was subsequently apprehended and charged with aggravated murder with specifications, an offense punishable by death, and aggravated robbery. Prior to trial, he pleaded guilty to the murder charge and agreed to testify against Lockett, her brother, and Dew. In return, the prosecutor dropped the aggravated robbery charge and the specifications to the murder charge, thereby eliminating the possibility that Parker could receive the death penalty.

Lockett's brother and Dew were later convicted of aggravated murder with specifications. Lockett's brother was sentenced to death, but Dew received a lesser penalty because it was determined that his offense was "primarily the product of mental deficiency," one of the three mitigating circumstances specified in the Ohio death penalty statute.

Two weeks before Lockett's separate trial, the prosecutor offered to permit her to plead guilty to voluntary manslaughter and aggravated robbery (offenses which each carried a maximum penalty of 25 years' imprisonment

and a maximum fine of $10,000, see Ohio Rev. Code Ann. §§ 2903.03, 2911.01, 2929.11 (1975)) if she would cooperate with the State, but she rejected the offer. Just prior to her trial, the prosecutor offered to permit her to plead guilty to aggravated murder without specifications, an offense carrying a mandatory life penalty, with the understanding that the aggravated robbery charge and an outstanding forgery charge would be dismissed. Again she rejected the offer.

At trial, the opening argument of Lockett's defense counsel summarized what appears to have been Lockett's version of the events leading to the killing. He asserted the evidence would show that, as far as Lockett knew, Dew and her brother had planned to pawn Dew's ring for $100 to obtain money for the trip back to New Jersey. Lockett had not waited in the car while the men went into the pawnshop but had gone to a restaurant for lunch and had joined Parker, thinking the ring had been pawned, after she saw him walking back to the car. Lockett's counsel asserted that the evidence would show further that Parker had placed the gun under the seat in the taxicab and that Lockett had voluntarily gone to the police station when she learned that the police were looking for the pawnbroker's killers.

Parker was the State's first witness. His testimony related his version of the robbery and shooting, and he admitted to a prior criminal record of breaking and entering, larceny, and receiving stolen goods, as well as bond jumping. He also acknowledged that his plea to aggravated murder had eliminated the possibility of the death penalty, and that he had agreed to testify against Lockett, her brother, and Dew as part of his plea agreement with the prosecutor. At the end of the major portion of Parker's testimony, the prosecutor renewed his offer to permit Lockett to plead guilty to aggravated murder without specifications and to drop the other charges against her. For the third time Lockett refused the option of pleading guilty to a lesser offense.

Lockett called Dew and her brother as defense witnesses, but they invoked their Fifth Amendment rights and refused to testify. In the course of the defense presentation, Lockett's counsel informed the court, in the presence of the jury, that he believed Lockett was to be the next witness and requested a short recess. After the recess, Lockett's counsel told the judge that Lockett wished to testify but had decided to accept her mother's advice to remain silent, despite her counsel's warning that, if she followed that advice, she would have no defense except the cross-examination of the State's witnesses. Thus, the defense did not introduce any evidence to rebut the prosecutor's case.

* * *

The court instructed the jury that, before it could find Lockett guilty, it had to find that she purposely had killed the pawnbroker while committing or attempting to commit aggravated robbery. The jury was further charged that one

> who purposely aids, helps, associates himself or herself with another for the purpose of committing a crime is regarded as if he or she were the principal offender and is just as guilty as if the person performed every act constituting the offense. . . .

Regarding the intent requirement, the court instructed:

> A person engaged in a common design with others to rob by force and violence an individual or individuals of their property is presumed to acquiesce in whatever may reasonably be necessary to accomplish the object of their enterprise. . . .

> If the conspired robbery and the manner of its accomplishment would be reasonably likely to produce death, each plotter is equally guilty with the principal offender as an aider and abettor in the homicide . . . . An intent to kill by an aider and abettor may be found to exist beyond a reasonable doubt under such circumstances.

The jury found Lockett guilty as charged.

Once a verdict of aggravated murder with specifications had been returned, the Ohio death penalty statute required the trial judge to impose a death sentence unless, after "considering the nature and circumstances of the offense" and Lockett's "history, character, and condition," he found by a preponderance of the evidence that (1) the victim had induced or facilitated the offense, (2) it was unlikely that Lockett would have committed the offense but for the fact that she "was under duress, coercion, or strong provocation," or (3) the offense was "primarily the product of [Lockett's] psychosis or mental deficiency." Ohio Rev. Code §§ 2929.03-2929.04 (B) (1975).

In accord with the Ohio statute, the trial judge requested a presentence report as well as psychiatric and psychological reports. The reports contained detailed information about Lockett's intelligence, character, and background. . . .

* * *

III

Lockett challenges the constitutionality of Ohio's death penalty statute on a number of grounds. We find it necessary to consider only her contention that her death sentence is invalid because the statute under which it was imposed did not permit the sentencing judge to consider, as mitigating factors, her character, prior record, age, lack of specific intent to cause death, and her relatively minor part in the crime. To address her contention from the proper perspective, it is helpful to review the developments in our recent cases where we have applied the Eighth and Fourteenth Amendments to death penalty statutes. We do not write on a "clean slate."

A

Prior to Furman v. Georgia, 408 U.S. 238 (1972), every State that authorized capital punishment had abandoned mandatory death penalties, and instead permitted the jury unguided and unrestrained discretion regarding the imposition of the death penalty in a particular capital case. Mandatory death penalties had proved unsatisfactory, as the plurality noted in Woodson v. North Carolina, 428 U.S. 280, 293 (1976), in part because juries, "with some regularity, disregarded their oaths and refused to convict defendants where a death sentence was the automatic consequence of a guilty verdict."

This Court had never intimated prior to Furman that discretion in sentencing offended the Constitution. See Pennsylvania ex rel. Sullivan v. Ashe, 302 U.S. 51, 55 (1937); Williams v. New York, 337 U.S. 241, 247 (1949); Williams v. Oklahoma, 358 U.S. 576, 585 (1959). As recently as McGautha v. California, 402 U.S. 183 (1971), the Court had specifically rejected the contention that discretion in imposing the death penalty violated the fundamental standards of fairness embodied in Fourteenth Amendment due process, id., at 207-208, and had asserted that States were entitled to assume that "jurors confronted with the truly awesome responsibility of decreeing death for a fellow human [would] act with due regard for the consequences of their decision." Id., at 208.

The constitutional status of discretionary sentencing in capital cases changed abruptly, however, as a result of the separate opinions supporting the judgment in Furman. The question in Furman was whether "the imposition and carrying out of the death penalty [in the cases before the Court] [constituted] cruel and unusual punishment in violation of the Eighth and Fourteenth Amendments." 408 U.S., at 239. Two Justices concluded that the Eighth Amendment prohibited the death penalty altogether and on that ground voted to reverse the judgments sustaining the death penalties. Id., at 305-306 (BRENNAN, J., concurring); id., at 370-371 (MARSHALL, J., concurring). Three Justices were unwilling to hold the death penalty per se unconstitutional under the Eighth and Fourteenth Amendments, but voted to reverse the judgments on other grounds. In separate opinions, the three concluded that discretionary sentencing, unguided by legislatively defined standards, violated the Eighth Amendment because it was "pregnant with discrimination," id., at 257 (Douglas, J., concurring), because it permitted the death penalty to be "wantonly" and "freakishly" imposed, id., at 310 (STEWART, J., concurring), and because it imposed the death penalty with "great infrequency" and afforded "no meaningful basis for distinguishing the few cases in which it [was] imposed from the many cases in which it [was] not," id., at 313 (WHITE, J., concurring). Thus, what had been approved under the Due Process Clause of the Fourteenth Amendment in McGautha became

impermissible under the Eighth and Fourteenth Amendments by virtue of the judgment in Furman. See Gregg v. Georgia, 428 U.S. 153, 195-196, n. 47 (1976) (opinion of STEWART, POWELL, and STEVENS, JJ.).

Predictably, the variety of opinions supporting the judgment in Furman engendered confusion as to what was required in order to impose the death penalty in accord with the Eighth Amendment. Some States responded to what was thought to be the command of Furman by adopting mandatory death penalties for a limited category of specific crimes thus eliminating all discretion from the sentencing process in capital cases. Other States attempted to continue the practice of individually assessing the culpability of each individual defendant convicted of a capital offense and, at the same time, to comply with Furman, by providing standards to guide the sentencing decision.

Four years after Furman, we considered Eighth Amendment issues posed by five of the post-Furman death penalty statutes. Four Justices took the position that all five statutes complied with the Constitution; two Justices took the position that none of them complied. Hence, the disposition of each case varied according to the votes of three Justices who delivered a joint opinion in each of the five cases upholding the constitutionality of the statutes of Georgia, Florida, and Texas, and holding those of North Carolina and Louisiana unconstitutional.

The joint opinion reasoned that, to comply with Furman, sentencing procedures should not create "a substantial risk that the death penalty [will] be inflicted in an arbitrary and capricious manner." Gregg v. Georgia, supra, at 188. In the view of the three Justices, however, Furman did not require that all sentencing discretion be eliminated, but only that it be "directed and limited," 428 U.S., at 189, so that the death penalty would be imposed in a more consistent and rational manner and so that there would be a "meaningful basis for distinguishing the . . . cases in which it is imposed from . . . the many cases in which it is not." Id., at 188. The plurality concluded, in the course of invalidating North Carolina's mandatory death penalty statute, that the sentencing process must permit consideration of the "character and record of the individual offender and the circumstances of the particular offense as a constitutionally indispensable part of the process of inflicting the penalty of death," Woodson v. North Carolina, 428 U.S., at 304, in order to ensure the reliability, under Eighth Amendment standards, of the determination that "death is the appropriate punishment in a specific case." Id., at 305; see Roberts (Harry) v. Louisiana, 431 U.S. 633, 637 (1977); Jurek v. Texas, 428 U.S. 262, 271-272 (1976).

In the last decade, many of the States have been obliged to revise their death penalty statutes in response to the various opinions supporting the judgments in Furman and Gregg and its companion cases. The signals from this Court have not, however, always been easy to decipher. The States now deserve the clearest guidance that the Court can provide; we have an obligation to reconcile previously differing views in order to provide that guidance.

B

With that obligation in mind we turn to Lockett's attack on the Ohio statute. Essentially she contends that the Eighth and Fourteenth Amendments require that the sentencer be given a full opportunity to consider mitigating circumstances in capital cases and that the Ohio statute does not comply with that requirement. She relies, in large part, on the plurality opinions in Woodson, supra, at 303-305, and Roberts (Stanislaus) v. Louisiana, 428 U.S. 325, 333-334 (1976), and the joint opinion in Jurek, supra, at 271-272, but she goes beyond them.

We begin by recognizing that the concept of individualized sentencing in criminal cases generally, although not constitutionally required, has long been accepted in this country. See Williams v. New York, 337 U.S., at 247-248; Pennsylvania ex rel. Sullivan v. Ashe, 302 U.S., at 55. Consistent with that concept, sentencing judges traditionally have taken a wide range of factors into account. That States have authority to make aiders and abettors equally responsible, as a matter of law, with principals, or to enact felony-murder statutes is beyond constitutional challenge. But the definition of crimes generally has not been thought automatically to dictate what should be the proper penalty. See ibid.; Williams v. New York, supra, at 247-248;

Williams v. Oklahoma, 358 U.S., at 585. And where sentencing discretion is granted, it generally has been agreed that the sentencing judge's "possession of the fullest information possible concerning the defendant's life and characteristics" is "[highly] relevant—if not essential—[to the] selection of an appropriate sentence . . ." Williams v. New York, supra, at 247 (emphasis added).

The opinions of this Court going back many years in dealing with sentencing in capital cases have noted the strength of the basis for individualized sentencing. For example, Mr. Justice Black, writing for the Court in Williams v. New York, supra, at 247-248—a capital case—observed that the

> whole country has traveled far from the period in which the death sentence was an automatic and commonplace result of convictions—even for offenses today deemed trivial.

Ten years later, in Williams v. Oklahoma, supra, at 585, another capital case, the Court echoed Mr. Justice Black, stating that

> [in] discharging his duty of imposing a proper sentence, the sentencing judge is authorized, if not required, to consider all of the mitigating and aggravating circumstances involved in the crime.

See also Furman v. Georgia, 408 U.S., at 245-246 (Douglas, J., concurring); id., at 297-298 (BRENNAN, J., concurring); id., at 339 (MARSHALL, J., concurring); id., at 402-403 (BURGER, C. J., dissenting); id., at 413 (BLACKMUN, J., dissenting); McGautha v. California, 402 U.S., at 197-203. Most would agree that "the 19th century movement away from mandatory death sentences marked an enlightened introduction of flexibility into the sentencing process." Furman v. Georgia, supra, at 402 (BURGER, C.J., dissenting).

Although legislatures remain free to decide how much discretion in sentencing should be reposed in the judge or jury in noncapital cases, the plurality opinion in Woodson, after reviewing the historical repudiation of mandatory sentencing in capital cases, 428 U.S., at 289-298, concluded that in capital cases the fundamental respect for humanity underlying the Eighth Amendment . . . requires consideration of the character and record of the individual offender and the circumstances of the particular offense as a constitutionally indispensable part of the process of inflicting the penalty of death. Id., at 304.

That declaration rested "on the predicate that the penalty of death is qualitatively different" from any other sentence. Id., at 305. We are satisfied that this qualitative difference between death and other penalties calls for a greater degree of reliability when the death sentence is imposed. The mandatory death penalty statute in Woodson was held invalid because it permitted no consideration of "relevant facets of the character and record of the individual offender or the circumstances of the particular offense." Id., at 304. The plurality did not attempt to indicate, however, which facets of an offender or his offense it deemed "relevant" in capital sentencing or what degree of consideration of "relevant facets" it would require.

We are now faced with those questions and we conclude that the Eighth and Fourteenth Amendments require that the sentencer, in all but the rarest kind of capital case, not be precluded from considering, as a mitigating factor, any aspect of a defendant's character or record and any of the circumstances of the offense that the defendant proffers as a basis for a sentence less than death. We recognize that, in noncapital cases, the established practice of individualized sentences rests not on constitutional commands, but on public policy enacted into statutes. The considerations that account for the wide acceptance of individualization of sentences in noncapital cases surely cannot be thought less important in capital cases. Given that the imposition of death by public authority is so profoundly different from all other penalties, we cannot avoid the conclusion that an individualized decision is essential in capital cases. The need for treating each defendant in a capital case with that degree of respect due the uniqueness of the individual is far more important than in noncapital cases. A variety of flexible techniques—probation, parole, work furloughs, to name a few—and various postconviction remedies may be available to

modify an initial sentence of confinement in noncapital cases. The nonavailability of corrective or modifying mechanisms with respect to an executed capital sentence underscores the need for individualized consideration as a constitutional requirement in imposing the death sentence.

There is no perfect procedure for deciding in which cases governmental authority should be used to impose death. But a statute that prevents the sentencer in all capital cases from giving independent mitigating weight to aspects of the defendant's character and record and to circumstances of the offense proffered in mitigation creates the risk that the death penalty will be imposed in spite of factors which may call for a less severe penalty. When the choice is between life and death, that risk is unacceptable and incompatible with the commands of the Eighth and Fourteenth Amendments.

C

The Ohio death penalty statute does not permit the type of individualized consideration of mitigating factors we now hold to be required by the Eighth and Fourteenth Amendments in capital cases. Its constitutional infirmities can best be understood by comparing it with the statutes upheld in Gregg, Proffitt, and Jurek.

In upholding the Georgia statute in Gregg, JUSTICES STEWART, POWELL, and STEVENS noted that the statute permitted the jury "to consider any aggravating or mitigating circumstances," see Gregg, 428 U.S., at 206, and that the Georgia Supreme Court had approved "open and far-ranging argument" in presentence hearings, id., at 203. Although the Florida statute approved in Proffitt contained a list of mitigating factors, six Members of this Court assumed, in approving the statute, that the range of mitigating factors listed in the statute was not exclusive. Jurek involved a Texas statute which made no explicit reference to mitigating factors. 428 U.S., at 272. Rather, the jury was required to answer three questions in the sentencing process, the second of which was "whether there is a probability that the defendant would commit criminal acts of violence that would constitute a continuing threat to society." Tex. Code Crim. Proc., Art. 37.071

(b) (Supp. 1975-1976); see 428 U.S., at 269. The statute survived the petitioner's Eighth and Fourteenth Amendment attack because three Justices concluded that the Texas Court of Criminal Appeals had broadly interpreted the second question—despite its facial narrowness—so as to permit the sentencer to consider "whatever mitigating circumstances" the defendant might be able to show. Id., at 272-273 (opinion of STEWART, POWELL, and STEVENS, JJ.), citing and quoting, Jurek v. State, 522 S. W. 2d 934, 939-940 (Tex. Crim. App. 1975). None of the statutes we sustained in Gregg and the companion cases clearly operated at that time to prevent the sentencer from considering any aspect of the defendant's character and record or any circumstances of his offense as an independently mitigating factor.

In this regard the statute now before us is significantly different. Once a defendant is found guilty of aggravated murder with at least one of seven specified aggravating circumstances, the death penalty must be imposed unless, considering "the nature and circumstances of the offense and the history, character, and condition of the offender," the sentencing judge determines that at least one of the following mitigating circumstances is established by a preponderance of the evidence:

(1) The victim of the offense induced or facilitated it.

(2) It is unlikely that the offense would have been committed, but for the fact that the offender was under duress, coercion, or strong provocation.

(3) The offense was primarily the product of the offender's psychosis or mental deficiency, though such condition is insufficient to establish the defense of insanity. Ohio Rev. Code Ann. § 2929.04 (B) (1975).

The Ohio Supreme Court has concluded that there is no constitutional distinction between the statute approved in Proffitt and Ohio's statute, see State v. Bayless, 48 Ohio St. 2d 73, 86-87, 357 N. E. 2d 1035, 1045-1046 (1976), because the mitigating circumstances in Ohio's statute are "liberally construed in favor of the accused," State v. Bell, 48 Ohio St. 2d 270, 281, 358 N. E. 2d 556, 564 (1976); see State v. Bayless, supra, at 86, 357 N. E. 2d, at 1046, and because the sentencing judge or judges may consider factors such as the age and criminal record of the defendant in determining whether any of the mitigating circumstances is established, State v. Bell, supra, at 281, 358 N. E. 2d, at 564. But even under the Ohio court's construction of the statute, only the three factors specified in the statute can be considered in mitigation of the defendant's sentence. See, 48 Ohio St. 2d, at 281-282, 358 N. E. 2d, at 564-565; State v. Bayless, supra, at 87 n. 2, 357 N. E. 2d, at 1046 n. 2. We see, therefore, that once it is determined that the victim did not induce or facilitate the offense, that the defendant did not act under duress or coercion, and that the offense was not primarily the product of the defendant's mental deficiency, the Ohio statute mandates the sentence of death. The absence of direct proof that the defendant intended to cause the death of the victim is relevant for mitigating purposes only if it is determined that it sheds some light on one of the three statutory mitigating factors. Similarly, consideration of a defendant's comparatively minor role in the offense, or age, would generally not be permitted, as such, to affect the sentencing decision.

The limited range of mitigating circumstances which may be considered by the sentencer under the Ohio statute is incompatible with the Eighth and Fourteenth Amendments. To meet constitutional requirements, a death penalty statute must not preclude consideration of relevant mitigating factors.

Accordingly, the judgment under review is reversed to the extent that it sustains the imposition of the death penalty, and the case is remanded for further proceedings.

So ordered.

* * *

GREGG
v.
GEORGIA

**428 U.S. 153; 96 S. Ct. 2909;
49 L. Ed. 2d 859 (1976)**

Judgment of the Court, and opinion of Mr. Justice Stewart, Mr. Justice Powell, and Mr. Justice Stevens, announced by Mr. Justice Stewart.

The issue in this case is whether the imposition of the sentence of death for the crime of murder under the law of Georgia violates the Eighth and Fourteenth Amendments.

I

The petitioner, Troy Gregg, was charged with committing armed robbery and murder. In accordance with Georgia procedure in capital cases, the trial was in two stages, a guilt stage and a sentencing stage. The evidence at the guilt trial established that on November 21, 1973, the petitioner and a traveling companion, Floyd Allen, while hitchhiking north in Florida were picked up by Fred Simmons and Bob Moore. Their car broke down, but they continued north after Simmons purchased another vehicle with some of the cash he was carrying. While still in Florida, they picked up another hitchhiker, Dennis Weaver, who rode with them to Atlanta, where he was let out about 11 P.M. A short time later the four men interrupted their journey for a rest stop along the highway. The next morning the bodies of Simmons and Moore were discovered in a ditch nearby.

On November 23, after reading about the shootings in an Atlanta newspaper, Weaver communicated with the Gwinnett County police and related information concerning the journey with the victims, including a description of the car. The next afternoon, the petitioner and Allen, while in Simmons' car, were arrested in Asheville, N.C. In the search incident to the arrest a .25-caliber pistol, later shown to be that used to kill Simmons and Moore, was found in the petitioner's pocket. After receiving the warnings required by Miranda v. Arizona, 384 U.S. 436 (1966), and signing a written waiver of his rights, the petitioner signed a statement in which he admitted shooting, then robbing Simmons

and Moore. He justified the slayings on grounds of self-defense. The next day, while being transferred to Lawrenceville, Ga., the petitioner and Allen were taken to the scene of the shootings. Upon arriving there, Allen recounted the events leading to the slayings. His version of these events was as follows: After Simmons and Moore left the car, the petitioner stated that he intended to rob them. The petitioner then took his pistol in hand and positioned himself on the car to improve his aim. As Simmons and Moore came up an embankment toward the car, the petitioner fired three shots and the two men fell near a ditch. The petitioner, at close range, then fired a shot into the head of each. He robbed them of valuables and drove away with Allen.

* * *

. . . Although Allen did not testify, a police detective recounted the substance of Allen's statements about the slayings and indicated that directly after Allen had made these statements the petitioner had admitted that Allen's account was accurate. The petitioner testified in his own defense. He confirmed that Allen had made the statements described by the detective, but denied their truth or ever having admitted to their accuracy. He indicated that he had shot Simmons and Moore because of fear and in self-defense, testifying they had attacked Allen and him, one wielding a pipe and the other a knife.

The trial judge submitted the murder charges to the jury on both felony-murder and nonfelony-murder theories. He also instructed on the issue of self-defense but declined to instruct on manslaughter. He submitted the robbery case to the jury on both an armed-robbery theory and on the lesser included offense of robbery by intimidation. The jury found the petitioner guilty of two counts of armed robbery and two counts of murder.

At the penalty stage, which took place before the same jury, neither the prosecutor nor the petitioner's lawyer offered any additional evidence. Both counsel, however, made lengthy arguments dealing generally with the propriety of capital punishment under the circumstances and with the weight of the evidence of guilt. The trial judge instructed the jury that it could recommend either a death sentence or a life prison sentence on each count. The judge further charged the jury that in determining what sentence was appropriate the jury was free to consider the facts and circumstances, if any, presented by the parties in mitigation or aggravation.

Finally, the judge instructed the jury that it "would not be authorized to consider [imposing] the penalty of death" unless it first found beyond a reasonable doubt one of these aggravating circumstances:

"One—That the offense of murder was committed while the offender was engaged in the commission of two other capital felonies, to-wit the armed robbery of [Simmons and Moore].

"Two—That the offender committed the offense of murder for the purpose of receiving money and the automobile described in the indictment.

"Three—The offense of murder was outrageously and wantonly vile, horrible and inhuman, in that they [sic] involved the depravity of [the] mind of the defendant."

Finding the first and second of these circumstances, the jury returned verdicts of death on each count.

The Supreme Court of Georgia affirmed the convictions and the imposition of the death sentences for murder. 233 Ga. 117, 210 S.E. 2d 659 (1974). After reviewing the trial transcript and the record, including the evidence, and comparing the evidence and sentence in similar cases in accordance with the requirements of Georgia law, the court concluded that, considering the nature of the crime and the defendant, the sentences of death had not resulted from prejudice or any other arbitrary factor and were not excessive or disproportionate to the penalty applied in similar cases. The death sentences imposed for armed robbery, however, were vacated on the grounds that the death penalty had rarely been imposed in Georgia for that offense and that the jury improperly considered the murders as aggravating circumstances for the robberies after having considered the armed robberies as aggravating circumstances for the murders. Id., at 127, 210 S.E. 2d, at 667.

We granted the petitioner's application for a writ of certiorari limited to his challenge to the imposition of the death sentences in this case as "cruel and unusual" punishment in violation of the Eighth and the Fourteenth Amendments. 423 U.S. 1082 (1976).

II

Before considering the issues presented it is necessary to understand the Georgia statutory scheme for the imposition of the death penalty. The Georgia statute, as amended after our decision in Furman v. Georgia, 408 U.S. 238 (1972), retains the death penalty for six categories of crime: murder,[4] kidnaping for ransom or where the victim is harmed, armed robbery,[5] rape, treason, and aircraft hijacking.[6] The capital defendant's guilt or innocence is determined in the traditional manner, either by a trial judge or a jury, in the first stage of a bifurcated trial.

---

[4] Georgia Code Ann. § 26-1101 (1972) provides:

"(a) A person commits murder when he unlawfully and with malice aforethought, either express or implied, causes the death of another human being. Express malice is that deliberate intention unlawfully to take away the life of a fellow creature, which is manifested by external circumstances capable of proof. Malice shall be implied where no considerable provocation appears, and where all the circumstances of the killing show an abandoned and malignant heart.

"(b) A person also commits the crime of murder when in the commission of a felony he causes the death of another human being, irrespective of malice.

"(c) A person convicted of murder shall be punished by death or by imprisonment for life."

[5] Section 26-1902 (1972) provides:

"A person commits armed robbery when, with intent to commit theft, he takes property of another from the person or the immediate presence of another by use of an offensive weapon. The offense of robbery by intimidation shall be a lesser included offense in the offense of armed robbery. A person convicted of armed robbery shall be punished by death or imprisonment for life, or by imprisonment for not less than one nor more than 20 years."

[6] These capital felonies currently are defined as they were when *Furman* was decided. The 1973 amendments to the Georgia statute, however, narrowed the class of crimes potentially punishable by death by eliminating capital perjury. Compare § 26-2401 (Supp. 1975) with § 26-2401 (1972).

If trial is by jury, the trial judge is required to charge lesser included offenses when they are supported by any view of the evidence. Sims v. State, 203 Ga. 668, 47 S.E. 2d 862 (1948). See Linder v. State, 132 Ga. App. 624, 625, 208 S.E. 2d 630, 631 (1974). After a verdict, finding, or plea of guilty to a capital crime, a presentence hearing is conducted before whoever made the determination of guilt. The sentencing procedures are essentially the same in both bench and jury trials. At the hearing:

[T]he judge [or jury] shall hear additional evidence in extenuation, mitigation, and aggravation of punishment, including the record of any prior criminal convictions and pleas of guilty or pleas of nolo contendere of the defendant, or the absence of any prior conviction and pleas: Provided, however, that only such evidence in aggravation as the State has made known to the defendant prior to his trial shall be admissible. The judge [or jury] shall also hear argument by the defendant or his counsel and the prosecuting attorney . . . regarding the punishment to be imposed. § 27-2503 (Supp. 1975).

The defendant is accorded substantial latitude as to the types of evidence that he may introduce. See Brown v. State, 235 Ga. 644, 647-650, 220 S.E. 2d 922, 925-926 (1975). Evidence considered during the guilt stage may be considered during the sentencing stage without being resubmitted. Eberheart v. State, 232 Ga. 247, 253, 206 S.E. 2d 12, 17 (1974).

In the assessment of the appropriate sentence to be imposed the judge is also required to consider or to include in his instructions to the jury "any mitigating circumstances or aggravating circumstances otherwise authorized by law and any of [10] statutory aggravating circumstances which may be supported by the evidence. . . ." The scope of the nonstatutory aggravating or mitigating circumstances is not delineated in the statute. Before a convicted defendant may be sentenced to death, however, except in cases of treason or aircraft hijacking, the jury, or the trial judge in cases tried without a jury, must find beyond a reasonable doubt one of the 10 aggravating circumstances specified in the statute. The

sentence of death may be imposed only if the jury (or judge) finds one of the statutory aggravating circumstances and then elects to impose that sentence. If the verdict is death, the jury or judge must specify the aggravating circumstance(s) found. In jury cases, the trial judge is bound by the jury's recommended sentence.

In addition to the conventional appellate process available in all criminal cases, provision is made for special expedited direct review by the Supreme Court of Georgia of the appropriateness of imposing the sentence of death in the particular case. The court is directed to consider "the punishment as well as any errors enumerated by way of appeal," and to determine:

(1) Whether the sentence of death was imposed under the influence of passion, prejudice, or any other arbitrary factor, and

(2) Whether, in cases other than treason or aircraft hijacking, the evidence supports the jury's or judge's finding of a statutory aggravating circumstance as enumerated in section 27.2534.1 (b), and

(3) Whether the sentence of death is excessive or disproportionate to the penalty imposed in similar cases, considering both the crime and the defendant." § 27-2537 (Supp. 1975).

If the court affirms a death sentence, it is required to include in its decision reference to similar cases that it has taken into consideration. § 27-2537 (e) (Supp. 1975).

A transcript and complete record of the trial, as well as a separate report by the trial judge, are transmitted to the court for its use in reviewing the sentence. § 27-2537 (a) (Supp. 1975). The report is in the form of a 6½-page questionnaire, designed to elicit information about the defendant, the crime, and the circumstances of the trial. It requires the trial judge to characterize the trial in several ways designed to test for arbitrariness and disproportionality of sentence. Included in the report are responses to detailed questions concerning the quality of the defendant's representation, whether race played a role in the trial, and, whether, in the trial court's judgment, there was any doubt about the defendant's guilt or the appropriateness of the sentence. A copy of the report is served upon defense counsel. Under its special review authority, the court may either affirm the death sentence or remand the case for resentencing. In cases in which the death sentence is affirmed there remains the possibility of executive clemency.[11]

III

We address initially the basic contention that the punishment of death for the crime of murder is, under all circumstances, "cruel and unusual" in violation of the Eighth and Fourteenth Amendments of the Constitution. In Part IV of this opinion, we will consider the sentence of death imposed under the Georgia statutes at issue in this case.

The Court on a number of occasions has both assumed and asserted the constitutionality of capital punishment. In several cases that assumption provided a necessary foundation for the decision, as the Court was asked to decide whether a particular method of carrying out a capital sentence would be allowed to stand under the Eighth Amendment. But until Furman v. Georgia, 408 U.S. 238 (1972), the Court never confronted squarely the fundamental claim that the punishment of death always, regardless of the enormity of the offense or the procedure followed in imposing the sentence, is cruel and unusual punishment in violation of the Constitution. Although this issue was presented and addressed in Furman, it was not resolved by the Court. Four Justices would have held that capital punishment is not unconstitutional per se; two Justices would have reached the opposite conclusion; and three Justices, while agreeing that the statutes then before the Court were invalid as applied, left open the question whether such punishment may ever be imposed. We now hold that the punishment of death does not invariably violate the Constitution.

---

[11] See Ga. Const., Art. 5, § 1, [*] 12, Ga. Code Ann. § 2-3011 (1973); Ga. Code Ann. §§ 77-501, 77-511, 77-513 (1973 and Supp. 1975) (Board of Pardons and Paroles is authorized to commute sentence of death except in cases where Governor refuses to suspend that sentence).

A

The history of the prohibition of "cruel and unusual" punishment already has been reviewed at length. The phrase first appeared in the English Bill of Rights of 1689, which was drafted by Parliament at the accession of William and Mary. See Granucci, "Nor Cruel and Unusual Punishments Inflicted: The Original Meaning," 57 Calif. L. Rev. 839, 852-853 (1969). The English version appears to have been directed against punishments unauthorized by statute and beyond the jurisdiction of the sentencing court, as well as those disproportionate to the offense involved. Id., at 860. The American draftsmen, who adopted the English phrasing in drafting the Eighth Amendment, were primarily concerned, however, with proscribing "tortures" and other "barbarous" methods of punishment. Id., at 842.

In the earliest cases raising Eighth Amendment claims, the Court focused on particular methods of execution to determine whether they were too cruel to pass constitutional muster. The constitutionality of the sentence of death itself was not at issue, and the criterion used to evaluate the mode of execution was its similarity to "torture" and other "barbarous" methods. . . .

But the Court has not confined the prohibition embodied in the Eighth Amendment to "barbarous" methods that were generally outlawed in the 18th century. Instead, the Amendment has been interpreted in a flexible and dynamic manner. The Court early recognized that "a principle to be vital must be capable of wider application than the mischief which gave it birth." Weems v. United States, 217 U.S. 349, 373 (1910). Thus the Clause forbidding "cruel and unusual" punishments "is not fastened to the obsolete but may acquire meaning as public opinion becomes enlightened by a humane justice." Id., at 378. See also Furman v. Georgia, 408 U.S., at 429-430 (POWELL, J., dissenting); Trop v. Dulles, 356 U.S. 86, 100-101 (1958) (plurality opinion).

In Weems the Court addressed the constitutionality of the Philippine punishment of *cadena temporal* for the crime of falsifying an official document. That punishment included imprisonment for at least 12 years and one day, in chains, at hard and painful labor; the loss of many basic civil rights; and subjection to lifetime surveillance. Although the Court acknowledged the possibility that "the cruelty of pain" may be present in the challenged punishment, 217 U.S., at 366, it did not rely on that factor, for it rejected the proposition that the Eighth Amendment reaches only punishments that are "inhuman and barbarous, torture and the like." Id., at 368. Rather, the Court focused on the lack of proportion between the crime and the offense:

Such penalties for such offenses amaze those who have formed their conception of the relation of a state to even its offending citizens from the practice of the American commonwealths, and believe that it is a precept of justice that punishment for crime should be graduated and proportioned to offense. Id., at 366-367.

Later, in Trop v. Dulles, supra, the Court reviewed the constitutionality of the punishment of denationalization imposed upon a soldier who escaped from an Army stockade and became a deserter for one day. Although the concept of proportionality was not the basis of the holding, the plurality observed in dicta that "[fines], imprisonment and even execution may be imposed depending upon the enormity of the crime." 356 U.S., at 100.

The substantive limits imposed by the Eighth Amendment on what can be made criminal and punished were discussed in Robinson v. California, 370 U.S. 660 (1962). The Court found unconstitutional a state statute that made the status of being addicted to a narcotic drug a criminal offense. It held, in effect, that it is "cruel and unusual" to impose any punishment at all for the mere status of addiction. The cruelty in the abstract of the actual sentence imposed was irrelevant: "Even one day in prison would be a cruel and unusual punishment for the 'crime' of having a common cold." Id., at 667. Most recently, in Furman v. Georgia, supra, three Justices in separate concurring opinions found the Eighth Amendment applicable to procedures employed to select convicted defendants for the sentence of death.

It is clear from the foregoing precedents that the Eighth Amendment has not been regarded as a static concept. As Mr. Chief Justice Warren said, in an often-quoted phrase, "[t]he Amendment must draw its meaning from the evolving standards of decency that mark the progress of a maturing society." Trop v. Dulles, supra, at 101. See also Jackson v. Bishop, 404 F. 2d 571, 579 (CA8 1968). Cf. Robinson v. California, supra, at 666. Thus, an assessment of contemporary values concerning the infliction of a challenged sanction is relevant to the application of the Eighth Amendment. As we develop below more fully, see infra, at 175-176, this assessment does not call for a subjective judgment. It requires, rather, that we look to objective indicia that reflect the public attitude toward a given sanction.

But our cases also make clear that public perceptions of standards of decency with respect to criminal sanctions are not conclusive. A penalty also must accord with "the dignity of man," which is the "basic concept underlying the Eighth Amendment." Trop v. Dulles, supra, at 100 (plurality opinion). This means, at least, that the punishment not be "excessive." When a form of punishment in the abstract (in this case, whether capital punishment may ever be imposed as a sanction for murder) rather than in the particular (the propriety of death as a penalty to be applied to a specific defendant for a specific crime) is under consideration, the inquiry into "excessiveness" has two aspects. First, the punishment must not involve the unnecessary and wanton infliction of pain. Furman v. Georgia, supra, at 392-393 (BURGER, C.J., dissenting). See Wilkerson v. Utah, 99 U.S., at 136; Weems v. United States, supra, at 381. Second, the punishment must not be grossly out of proportion to the severity of the crime. Trop v. Dulles, supra, at 100 (plurality opinion) (dictum); Weems v. United States, supra, at 367.

B

Of course, the requirements of the Eighth Amendment must be applied with an awareness of the limited role to be played by the courts. This does not mean that judges have no role to play, for the Eighth Amendment is a restraint upon the exercise of legislative power.

Judicial review, by definition, often involves a conflict between judicial and legislative judgment as to what the Constitution means or requires. In this respect, Eighth Amendment cases come to us in no different posture. It seems conceded by all that the Amendment imposes some obligations on the judiciary to judge the constitutionality of punishment and that there are punishments that the Amendment would bar whether legislatively approved or not.

But, while we have an obligation to insure that constitutional bounds are not overreached, we may not act as judges as we might as legislators.

Courts are not representative bodies. They are not designed to be a good reflex of a democratic society. Their judgment is best informed, and therefore most dependable, within narrow limits. Their essential quality is detachment, founded on independence. History teaches that the independence of the judiciary is jeopardized when courts become embroiled in the passions of the day and assume primary responsibility in choosing between competing political, economic and social pressures.

Therefore, in assessing a punishment selected by a democratically elected legislature against the constitutional measure, we presume its validity. We may not require the legislature to select the least severe penalty possible so long as the penalty selected is not cruelly inhumane or disproportionate to the crime involved. And a heavy burden rests on those who would attack the judgment of the representatives of the people.

This is true in part because the constitutional test is intertwined with an assessment of contemporary standards and the legislative judgment weighs heavily in ascertaining such standards. "[I]n a democratic society legislatures, not courts, are constituted to respond to the will and consequently the moral values of the people." Furman v. Georgia, supra, at 383 (BURGER, C.J., dissenting). The deference we owe to the decisions of the state legislatures under our federal system, id., at 465-470 (REHNQUIST, J., dissenting), is

enhanced where the specification of punishments is concerned, for "these are peculiarly questions of legislative policy." Gore v. United States, 357 U.S. 386, 393 (1958). Cf. Robinson v. California, 370 U.S., at 664-665; Trop v. Dulles, 356 U.S., at 103 (plurality opinion); In re Kemmler, 136 U.S., at 447. Caution is necessary lest this Court become, "under the aegis of the Cruel and Unusual Punishment Clause, the ultimate arbiter of the standards of criminal responsibility . . . throughout the country." Powell v. Texas, 392 U.S. 514, 533 (1968) (plurality opinion). A decision that a given punishment is impermissible under the Eighth Amendment cannot be reversed short of a constitutional amendment. The ability of the people to express their preference through the normal democratic processes, as well as through ballot referenda, is shut off. Revisions cannot be made in the light of further experience. See Furman v. Georgia, supra, at 461-462 (POWELL, J., dissenting).

C

In the discussion to this point we have sought to identify the principles and considerations that guide a court in addressing an Eighth Amendment claim. We now consider specifically whether the sentence of death for the crime of murder is a per se violation of the Eighth and Fourteenth Amendments to the Constitution. We note first that history and precedent strongly support a negative answer to this question.

The imposition of the death penalty for the crime of murder has a long history of acceptance both in the United States and in England. The common-law rule imposed a mandatory death sentence on all convicted murderers. McGautha v. California, 402 U.S. 183, 197-198 (1971). And the penalty continued to be used into the 20th century by most American States, although the breadth of the common-law rule was diminished, initially by narrowing the class of murders to be punished by death and subsequently by widespread adoption of laws expressly granting juries the discretion to recommend mercy. Id., at 199-200. See Woodson v. North Carolina, post, at 289-292.

It is apparent from the text of the Constitution itself that the existence of capital punishment was accepted by the Framers. At the time the Eighth Amendment was ratified, capital punishment was a common sanction in every State. Indeed, the First Congress of the United States enacted legislation providing death as the penalty for specified crimes. C. 9, 1 Stat. 112 (1790). The Fifth Amendment, adopted at the same time as the Eighth, contemplated the continued existence of the capital sanction by imposing certain limits on the prosecution of capital cases:

No person shall be held to answer for a capital, or otherwise infamous crime, unless on a presentment or indictment of a Grand Jury . . . ; nor shall any person be subject for the same offense to be twice put in jeopardy of life or limb; . . . nor be deprived of life, liberty, or property, without due process of law. . . .

And the Fourteenth Amendment, adopted over three-quarters of a century later, similarly contemplates the existence of the capital sanction in providing that no State shall deprive any person of "life, liberty, or property" without due process of law.

For nearly two centuries, this Court, repeatedly and often expressly, has recognized that capital punishment is not invalid per se. In Wilkerson v. Utah, 99 U.S., at 134-135, where the Court found no constitutional violation in inflicting death by public shooting, it said:

Cruel and unusual punishments are forbidden by the Constitution, but the authorities referred to are quite sufficient to show that the punishment of shooting as a mode of executing the death penalty for the crime of murder in the first degree is not included in that category, within the meaning of the eighth amendment.

Rejecting the contention that death by electrocution was "cruel and unusual," the Court in In re Kemmler, supra, at 447, reiterated:

[T]he punishment of death is not cruel, within the meaning of that word as used in the Constitution. It implies there something inhuman and barbarous, something more than the mere extinguishment of life.

Again, in Louisiana ex rel. Francis v. Resweber, 329 U.S., at 464, the Court remarked: "The cruelty against which the Constitution protects a convicted man is cruelty inherent in the method of punishment, not the necessary suffering involved in any method employed to extinguish life humanely." And in Trop v. Dulles, 356 U.S., at 99, Mr. Chief Justice Warren, for himself and three other Justices, wrote:

Whatever the arguments may be against capital punishment, both on moral grounds and in terms of accomplishing the purposes of punishmet . . . the death penalty has been employed throughout our history, and, in a day when it is still widely accepted, it cannot be said to violate the constitutional concept of cruelty.

Four years ago, the petitioners in Furman and its companion cases predicated their argument primarily upon the asserted proposition that standards of decency had evolved to the point where capital punishment no longer could be tolerated. The petitioners in those cases said, in effect, that the evolutionary process had come to an end, and that standards of decency required that the Eighth Amendment be construed finally as prohibiting capital punishment for any crime regardless of its depravity and impact on society. This view was accepted by two Justices. Three other Justices were unwilling to go so far; focusing on the procedures by which convicted defendants were selected for the death penalty rather than on the actual punishment inflicted, they joined in the conclusion that the statutes before the Court were constitutionally invalid.

The petitioners in the capital cases before the Court today renew the "standards of decency" argument, but developments during the four years since Furman have undercut substantially the assumptions upon which their argument rested. Despite the continuing debate, dating back to the 19th century, over the morality and utility of capital punishment, it is now evident that a large proportion of American society continues to regard it as an appropriate and necessary criminal sanction.

The most marked indication of society's endorsement of the death penalty for murder is the legislative response to Furman. The legislatures of at least 35 States have enacted new statutes that provide for the death penalty for at least some crimes that result in the death of another person. And the Congress of the United States, in 1974, enacted a statute providing the death penalty for aircraft piracy that results in death. These recently adopted statutes have attempted to address the concerns expressed by the Court in Furman primarily (i) by specifying the factors to be weighed and the procedures to be followed in deciding when to impose a capital sentence, or (ii) by making the death penalty mandatory for specified crimes. But all of the post-Furman statutes make clear that capital punishment itself has not been rejected by the elected representatives of the people.

In the only statewide referendum occurring since Furman and brought to our attention, the people of California adopted a constitutional amendment that authorized capital punishment, in effect negating a prior ruling by the Supreme Court of California in People v. Anderson, 6 Cal. 3d 628, 493 P. 2d 880, cert. denied, 406 U.S. 958 (1972), that the death penalty violated the California Constitution.

The jury also is a significant and reliable objective index of contemporary values because it is so directly involved. See Furman v. Georgia, 408 U.S., at 439-440 (POWELL, J., dissenting). See generally Powell, *Jury Trial of Crimes,* 23 Wash. & Lee L. Rev. 1 (1966). The Court has said that "one of the most important functions any jury can perform in making . . . a selection [between life imprisonment and death for a defendant convicted in a capital case] is to maintain a link between contemporary community values and the penal system." Witherspoon v. Illinois, 391 U.S. 510, 519 n. 15 (1968). It may be true that evolving standards have influenced juries in recent decades to be more

discriminating in imposing the sentence of death. But the relative infrequency of jury verdicts imposing the death sentence does not indicate rejection of capital punishment per se. Rather, the reluctance of juries in many cases to impose the sentence may well reflect the humane feeling that this most irrevocable of sanctions should be reserved for a small number of extreme cases. Indeed, the actions of juries in many States since Furman are fully compatible with the legislative judgments, reflected in the new statutes, as to the continued utility and necessity of capital punishment in appropriate cases. At the close of 1974 at least 254 persons had been sentenced to death since Furman, and by the end of March 1976, more than 460 persons were subject to death sentences.

As we have seen, however, the Eighth Amendment demands more than that a challenged punishment be acceptable to contemporary society. The Court also must ask whether it comports with the basic concept of human dignity at the core of the Amendment. Trop v. Dulles, 356 U.S., at 100 plurality opinion. Although we cannot "invalidate a category of penalties because we deem less severe penalties adequate to serve the ends of penology," Furman v. Georgia, supra, at 451 (POWELL, J., dissenting), the sanction imposed cannot be so totally without penological justification that it results in the gratuitous infliction of suffering. Cf. Wilkerson v. Utah, 99 U.S., at 135-136; In re Kemmler, 136 U.S., at 447.

The death penalty is said to serve two principal social purposes: retribution and deterrence of capital crimes by prospective offenders.

In part, capital punishment is an expression of society's moral outrage at particularly offensive conduct. This function may be unappealing to many, but it is essential in an ordered society that asks its citizens to rely on legal processes rather than self-help to vindicate their wrongs.

The instinct for retribution is part of the nature of man, and channeling that instinct in the administration of criminal justice serves an important purpose in promoting the stability of a society governed by law. When people begin to believe that organized society is unwilling or unable to impose upon criminal offenders the punishment they "deserve," then there are sown the seeds of anarchy—of self-help, vigilante justice, and lynch law.

"Retribution is no longer the dominant objective of the criminal law," Williams v. New York, 337 U.S. 241, 248 (1949), but neither is it a forbidden objective nor one inconsistent with our respect for the dignity of men. Indeed, the decision that capital punishment may be the appropriate sanction in extreme cases is an expression of the community's belief that certain crimes are themselves so grievous an affront to humanity that the only adequate response may be the penalty of death.

Statistical attempts to evaluate the worth of the death penalty as a deterrent to crimes by potential offenders have occasioned a great deal of debate. The results simply have been inconclusive. As one opponent of capital punishment has said:

[A]fter all possible inquiry, including the probing of all possible methods of inquiry, we do not know, and for systematic and easily visible reasons cannot know, what the truth about this 'deterrent' effect may be. . . .

The inescapable flaw is . . . that social conditions in any state are not constant through time, and that social conditions are not the same in any two states. If an effect were observed (and the observed effects, one way or another, are not large) then one could not at all tell whether any of this effect is attributable to the presence or absence of capital punishment. A "scientific"—that is to say, a soundly based—conclusion is simply impossible, and no methodological path out of this tangle suggests itself." C. Black, *Capital Punishment: The Inevitability of Caprice and Mistake* 25-26 (1974).

Although some of the studies suggest that the death penalty may not function as a significantly greater deterrent than lesser penalties, there is no convincing empirical evidence either supporting or refuting this view. We may nevertheless assume safely that there are murderers, such as those who act in passion, for whom the threat of death has little or no deterrent effect. But for many others, the death penalty undoubtedly is a significant deterrent. There are carefully contemplated murders, such as murder for hire, where the possible penalty of death may well enter into the cold calculus that precedes the decision to act. And there are some categories of murder, such as murder by a life prisoner, where other sanctions may not be adequate.

The value of capital punishment as a deterrent of crime is a complex factual issue the resolution of which properly rests with the legislatures, which can evaluate the results of statistical studies in terms of their own local conditions and with a flexibility of approach that is not available to the courts. Furman v. Georgia, supra, at 403-405 (BURGER, C.J., dissenting). Indeed, many of the post-Furman statutes reflect just such a responsible effort to define those crimes and those criminals for which capital punishment is most probably an effective deterrent.

In sum, we cannot say that the judgment of the Georgia Legislature that capital punishment may be necessary in some cases is clearly wrong. Considerations of federalism, as well as respect for the ability of a legislature to evaluate, in terms of its particular State, the moral consensus concerning the death penalty and its social utility as a sanction, require us to conclude, in the absence of more convincing evidence, that the infliction of death as a punishment for murder is not without justification and thus is not unconstitutionally severe.

Finally, we must consider whether the punishment of death is disproportionate in relation to the crime for which it is imposed. There is no question that death as a punishment is unique in its severity and irrevocability. When a defendant's life is at stake, the Court has been particularly sensitive to insure that every safeguard is observed. But we are concerned here only with the imposition of capital punishment for the crime of murder, and when a life has been taken deliberately by the offender, we cannot say that the punishment is invariably disproportionate to the crime. It is an extreme sanction, suitable to the most extreme of crimes.

We hold that the death penalty is not a form of punishment that may never be imposed, regardless of the circumstances of the offense, regardless of the character of the offender, and regardless of the procedure followed in reaching the decision to impose it.

IV

We now consider whether Georgia may impose the death penalty on the petitioner in this case.

A

While Furman did not hold that the infliction of the death penalty per se violates the Constitution's ban on cruel and unusual punishments, it did recognize that the penalty of death is different in kind from any other punishment imposed under our system of criminal justice. Because of the uniqueness of the death penalty, Furman held that it could not be imposed under sentencing procedures that created a substantial risk that it would be inflicted in an arbitrary and capricious manner. MR. JUSTICE WHITE concluded that "the death penalty is exacted with great infrequency even for the most atrocious crimes and . . . there is no meaningful basis for distinguishing the few cases in which it is imposed from the many cases in which it is not." 408 U.S., at 313 (concurring). Indeed, the death sentences examined by the Court in Furman were "cruel and unusual in the same way that being struck by lightning is cruel and unusual. For, of all the people convicted of [capital crimes], many just as reprehensible as these, the petitioners [in Furman were] among a capriciously selected random handful upon whom the sentence of death has in fact been imposed . . . . [T]he Eighth and Fourteenth Amendments cannot tolerate the infliction of a sentence of death under legal systems that permit this unique penalty to be so wantonly and so freakishly imposed."

Furman mandates that where discretion is afforded a sentencing body on a matter so grave as the determination of whether a human life should be taken or spared, that discretion must be suitably directed and limited so as to minimize the risk of wholly arbitrary and capricious action.

It is certainly not a novel proposition that discretion in the area of sentencing be exercised in an informed manner. We have long recognized that "[f]or the determination of sentences, justice generally requires . . . that there be taken into account the circumstances of the offense together with the character and propensities of the offender." Otherwise, "the system cannot function in a consistent and a rational manner."

The cited studies assumed that the trial judge would be the sentencing authority. If an experienced trial judge, who daily faces the difficult task of imposing sentences, has a vital need for accurate information about a defendant and the crime he committed in order to be able to impose a rational sentence in the typical criminal case, then accurate sentencing information is an indispensable prerequisite to a reasoned determination of whether a defendant shall live or die by a jury of people who may never before have made a sentencing decision.

Jury sentencing has been considered desirable in capital cases in order "to maintain a link between contemporary community values and the penal system—a link without which the determination of punishment could hardly reflect 'the evolving standards of decency that mark the progress of a maturing society.' " But it creates special problems. Much of the information that is relevant to the sentencing decision may have no relevance to the question of guilt, or may even be extremely prejudicial to a fair determination of that question. This problem, however, is scarcely insurmountable. Those who have studied the question suggest that a bifurcated procedure—one in which the question of sentence is not considered until the determination of guilt has been made—is the best answer. The drafters of the Model Penal Code concluded:

> If a unitary proceeding is used the determination of the punishment must be based on less than all the evidence that has a bearing on that issue, such for example as a previous criminal record of the accused, or evidence must be admitted on the ground that it is relevant to sentence, though it would be excluded as irrelevant or prejudicial with respect to guilt or innocence alone. Trial lawyers understandably have little confidence in a solution that admits the evidence and trusts to an instruction to the jury that it should be

considered only in determining the penalty and disregarded in assessing guilt.

. . . The obvious solution . . . is to bifurcate the proceeding, abiding strictly by the rules of evidence until and unless there is a conviction, but once guilt has been determined opening the record to the further information that is relevant to sentence. This is the analogue of the procedure in the ordinary case when capital punishment is not in issue; the court conducts a separate inquiry before imposing sentence.

When a human life is at stake and when the jury must have information prejudicial to the question of guilt but relevant to the question of penalty in order to impose a rational sentence, a system is more likely to ensure elimination of the constitutional deficiencies identified in Furman.

But the provision of relevant information under fair procedural rules is not alone sufficient to guarantee that the information will be properly used in the imposition of punishment, especially if sentencing is performed by a jury. Since the members of a jury will have had little, if any, previous experience in sentencing, they are unlikely to be skilled in dealing with the information they are given. To the extent that this problem is inherent in jury sentencing, it may not be totally correctable. It seems clear, however, that the problem will be alleviated if the jury is given guidance regarding the factors about the crime and the defendant that the State, representing organized society, deems particularly relevant to the sentencing decision.

The idea that a jury should be given guidance in its decisionmaking is also hardly a novel proposition. Juries are invariably given careful instructions on the law and how to apply it before they are authorized to decide the merits of a lawsuit. It would be virtually unthinkable to follow any other course in a legal system that has traditionally operated by following prior precedents and fixed rules of law. See Gasoline Products Co. v. Champlin Refining Co., 283 U.S. 494, 498 (1931); Fed. Rule Civ. Proc. 51. When erroneous instructions are given, retrial is often required. It is quite simply a hallmark of our legal system that juries be carefully and adequately guided in their deliberations.

While some have suggested that standards to guide a capital jury's sentencing deliberations are impossible to formulate, the fact is that such standards have been developed. When the drafters of the Model Penal Code faced this problem, they concluded "that it is within the realm of possibility to point to the main circumstances of aggravation and of mitigation that should be weighed and weighed against each other when they are presented in a concrete case." ALI, Model Penal Code § 201.6, Comment 3, p. 71 (Tent. Draft No. 9, 1959) (emphasis in original). While such standards are by necessity somewhat general, they do provide guidance to the sentencing authority and thereby reduce the likelihood that it will impose a sentence that fairly can be called capricious or arbitrary. Where the sentencing authority is required to specify the factors it relied upon in reaching its decision, the further safeguard of meaningful appellate review is available to ensure that death sentences are not imposed capriciously or in a freakish manner.

In summary, the concerns expressed in Furman that the penalty of death not be imposed in an arbitrary or capricious manner can be met by a carefully drafted statute that ensures that the sentencing authority is given adequate information and guidance. As a general proposition these concerns are best met by a system that provides for a bifurcated proceeding at which the sentencing authority is apprised of the information relevant to the imposition of sentence and provided with standards to guide its use of the information.

We do not intend to suggest that only the above described procedures would be permissible under Furman or that any sentencing system constructed along these general lines would inevitably satisfy the concerns of Furman, for each distinct system must be examined on an individual basis. Rather, we have embarked upon this general exposition to make clear that it is possible to construct capital-sentencing systems capable of meeting Furman's constitutional concerns.

B

We now turn to consideration of the constitutionality of Georgia's capital-sentencing procedures. In the wake of Furman, Georgia amended its capital punishment statute, but chose not to narrow the scope of its murder provisions. See Part II, supra. Thus, now as before Furman, in Georgia "[a] person commits murder when he unlawfully and with malice aforethought, either express or implied, causes the death of another human being." All persons convicted of murder "shall be punished by death or by imprisonment for life."

Georgia did act, however, to narrow the class of murderers subject to capital punishment by specifying 10 statutory aggravating circumstances, one of which must be found by the jury to exist beyond a reasonable doubt before a death sentence can ever be imposed. In addition, the jury is authorized to consider any other appropriate aggravating or mitigating circumstances. § 27-2534.1 (b) (Supp. 1975). The jury is not required to find any mitigating circumstance in order to make a recommendation of mercy that is binding on the trial court, see § 27-2302 (Supp. 1975), but it must find a statutory aggravating circumstance before recommending a sentence of death.

These procedures require the jury to consider the circumstances of the crime and the criminal before it recommends sentence. No longer can a Georgia jury do as Furman's jury did: reach a finding of the defendant's guilt and then, without guidance or direction, decide whether he should live or die. Instead, the jury's attention is directed to the specific circumstances of the crime: Was it committed in the course of another capital felony? Was it committed for money? Was it committed upon a peace officer or judicial officer? Was it committed in a particularly heinous way or in a manner that endangered the lives of many persons? In addition, the jury's attention is focused on the characteristics of the person who committed the crime: Does he have a record of prior convictions for capital offenses? Are there any special facts about this defendant that mitigate against imposing capital punishment (e.g., his youth, the extent of his cooperation with the police, his emotional state at the time of the crime). As a result, while some jury discretion still exists, "the discretion to be exercised is controlled by clear and objective standards so as to produce non-discriminatory application."

As an important additional safeguard against arbitrariness and caprice, the Georgia statutory scheme provides for automatic appeal of all death sentences to the State's Supreme Court. That court is required by statute to review each sentence of death and determine whether it was imposed under the influence of passion or prejudice, whether the evidence supports the jury's finding of a statutory aggravating circumstance, and whether the sentence is disproportionate compared to those sentences imposed in similar cases.

In short, Georgia's new sentencing procedures require as a prerequisite to the imposition of the death penalty, specific jury findings as to the circumstances of the crime or the character of the defendant. Moreover, to guard further against a situation comparable to that presented in Furman, the Supreme Court of Georgia compares each death sentence with the sentences imposed on similarly situated defendants to ensure that the sentence of death in a particular case is not disproportionate. On their face these procedures seem to satisfy the concerns of Furman. No longer should there be "no meaningful basis for distinguishing the few cases in which [the death penalty] is imposed from the many cases in which it is not." 408 U.S., at 313 (WHITE, J., concurring).

The petitioner contends, however, that the changes in the Georgia sentencing procedures are only cosmetic, that the arbitrariness and capriciousness condemned by Furman continue to exist in Georgia—both in traditional practices that still remain and in the new sentencing procedures adopted in response to Furman.

1

First, the petitioner focuses on the opportunities for discretionary action that are inherent in the processing of any murder case under Georgia law. He notes that the state prosecutor has unfettered authority to select those persons whom he wishes to prosecute for a capital offense and to plea bargain with them. Further, at the trial the jury may choose to convict a defendant of a lesser included offense rather than find him guilty of a crime punishable by death, even if the evidence would support a capital verdict. And finally, a defendant who is convicted and sentenced to die may have his sentence commuted by the Governor of the State and the Georgia Board of Pardons and Paroles.

The existence of these discretionary stages is not determinative of the issues before us. At each of these stages an actor in the criminal justice system makes a decision which may remove a defendant from consideration as a candidate for the death penalty. Furman, in contrast, dealt with the decision to impose the death sentence on a specific individual who had been convicted of a capital offense. Nothing in any of our cases suggests that the decision to afford an individual defendant mercy violates the Constitution. Furman held only that, in order to minimize the risk that the death penalty would be imposed on a capriciously selected group of offenders, the decision to impose it had to be guided by standards so that the sentencing authority would focus on the particularized circumstances of the crime and the defendant.

2

The petitioner further contends that the capital sentencing procedures adopted by Georgia in response to Furman do not eliminate the dangers of arbitrariness and caprice in jury sentencing that were held in Furman to be violative of the Eighth and Fourteenth Amendments. He claims that the statute is so broad and vague as to leave juries free to act as arbitrarily and capriciously as they wish in deciding whether to impose the death penalty. While there is no claim that the jury in this case relied upon a vague or overbroad provision to establish the existence of a statutory aggravating circumstance, the petitioner looks to the sentencing system as a whole (as the Court did in Furman and we do today) and argues that it fails to reduce sufficiently the risk of arbitrary infliction of death sentences. Specifically, Gregg urges that the statutory aggravating circumstances are too broad and too vague, that the sentencing procedure allows for arbitrary grants of mercy, and that the scope of the evidence and argument that can be considered at the presentence hearing is too wide.

The petitioner attacks the seventh statutory aggravating circumstance, which authorizes imposition of the death penalty if the murder was "outrageously or wantonly vile, horrible or inhuman in that it involved torture, depravity of mind, or an aggravated battery to the victim," contending that it is so broad that capital punishment could be imposed in any murder case. It is, of course, arguable that any murder involves depravity of mind or an aggravated battery. But this language need not be construed in this way, and there is no reason to assume that the Supreme Court of Georgia will adopt such an open-ended construction. In only one case has it upheld a jury's decision to sentence a defendant to death when the only statutory aggravating circumstance found was that of the seventh, see McCorquodale v. State, 233 Ga. 369, 211 S.E. 2d 577 (1974), and that homicide was a horrifying torture-murder.

The petitioner also argues that two of the statutory aggravating circumstances are vague and therefore susceptible of widely differing interpretations, thus creating a substantial risk that the death penalty will be arbitrarily inflicted by Georgia juries. In light of the decisions of the Supreme Court of Georgia we must disagree. First, the petitioner attacks that part of § 27-2534.1 (b)(1) that authorizes a jury to consider whether a defendant has a "substantial history of serious assaultive criminal convictions." The Supreme Court of Georgia, however, has demonstrated a concern that the new sentencing procedures provide guidance to juries. It held this provision to be impermissibly vague in Arnold v. State, 236 Ga. 534, 540, 224 S.E. 2d 386, 391 (1976), because it did not provide the jury with "sufficiently 'clear and objective standards.' " Second, the petitioner points to § 27-2534.1 (b)(3) which speaks of creating a "great risk of death to more than one person." While such a phrase might be susceptible of an overly broad interpretation, the Supreme Court of Georgia has not so construed it. The only case in which the court upheld a conviction in reliance on this aggravating circumstance involved a man who stood up in a church and fired a gun indiscriminately into the audience. See Chenault v. State, 234 Ga. 216, 215 S.E. 2d 223 (1975). On the other hand, the court expressly reversed a finding of great risk when the victim was simply kidnapped in a parking lot. See Jarrell v. State, 234 Ga. 410, 424, 216 S.E. 2d 258, 269 (1975).

The petitioner next argues that the requirements of Furman are not met here because the jury has the power to decline to impose the death penalty even if it finds that one or more statutory aggravating circumstances are present in the case. This contention misinterprets Furman. See supra, at 198-199. Moreover, it ignores the role of the Supreme Court of Georgia which reviews each death sentence to determine whether it is proportional to other sentences imposed for similar crimes. Since the proportionality requirement on review is intended to prevent caprice in the decision to inflict the penalty, the isolated decision of a jury to afford mercy does not render unconstitutional death sentences imposed on defendants who were sentenced under a system that does not create a substantial risk of arbitrariness or caprice.

The petitioner objects, finally, to the wide scope of evidence and argument allowed at presentence hearings. We think that the Georgia court wisely has chosen not to impose unnecessary restrictions on the evidence that can be offered at such a hearing and to approve open and far-ranging argument. See, e.g., Brown v. State, 235 Ga. 644, 220 S.E. 2d 922 (1975). So long as the evidence introduced and the arguments made at the presentence hearing do not prejudice a defendant, it is preferable not to impose restrictions. We think it desirable for the jury to have as much information before it as possible when it makes the sentencing decision. See supra, at 189-190.

3

Finally, the Georgia statute has an additional provision designed to assure that the death penalty will not be imposed on a capriciously selected group of convicted defendants. The new sentencing procedures require that the State Supreme Court review every death sentence to determine whether it was imposed under the influence of passion, prejudice, or any other arbitrary factor, whether the evidence supports the findings of a statutory aggravating circumstance, and "[w]hether the sentence of death is excessive or disproportionate to the penalty imposed in similar cases, considering both the crime and the defendant." § 27-2537 (c)(3) (Supp. 1975). In

performing its sentence-review function, the Georgia court has held that "if the death penalty is only rarely imposed for an act or it is substantially out of line with sentences imposed for other acts it will be set aside as excessive." Coley v. State, 231 Ga., at 834, 204 S.E. 2d, at 616. The court on another occasion stated that "we view it to be our duty under the similarity standard to assure that no death sentence is affirmed unless in similar cases throughout the state the death penalty has been imposed generally. . . ." Moore v. State, 233 Ga. 861, 864, 213 S.E. 2d 829, 832 (1975). See also Jarrell v. State, supra, at 425, 216 S.E. 2d, at 270 (standard is whether "juries generally throughout the state have imposed the death penalty"); Smith v. State, 236 Ga. 12, 24, 222 S.E. 2d 308, 318 (1976) (found "a clear pattern" of jury behavior).

It is apparent that the Supreme Court of Georgia has taken its review responsibilities seriously. In Coley, it held that "[the] prior cases indicate that the past practice among juries faced with similar factual situations and like aggravating circumstances has been to impose only the sentence of life imprisonment for the offense of rape, rather than death." 231 Ga., at 835, 204 S.E. 2d, at 617. It thereupon reduced Coley's sentence from death to life imprisonment. Similarly, although armed robbery is a capital offense under Georgia law, § 26-1902 (1972), the Georgia court concluded that the death sentences imposed in this case for that crime were "unusual in that they are rarely imposed for [armed robbery]. Thus, under the test provided by statute, . . . they must be considered to be excessive or disproportionate to the penalties imposed in similar cases." 233 Ga., at 127, 210 S.E. 2d, at 667. The court therefore vacated Gregg's death sentences for armed robbery and has followed a similar course in every other armed robbery death penalty case to come before it. See Floyd v. State, 233 Ga. 280, 285, 210 S.E. 2d 810, 814 (1974); Jarrell v. State, 234 Ga., at 424-425, 216 S.E. 2d, at 270. See Dorsey v. State, 236 Ga. 591, 225 S.E. 2d 418 (1976).

The provision for appellate review in the Georgia capital-sentencing system serves as a check against the random or arbitrary imposition of the death penalty. In particular, the proportionality review substantially eliminates the possibility that a person will be sentenced to die by the action of an aberrant jury. If a time comes when juries generally do not impose the death sentence in a certain kind of murder case, the appellate review procedures assure that no defendant convicted under such circumstances will suffer a sentence of death.

V

The basic concern of Furman centered on those defendants who were being condemned to death capriciously and arbitrarily. Under the procedures before the Court in that case, sentencing authorities were not directed to give attention to the nature or circumstances of the crime committed or to the character or record of the defendant. Left unguided, juries imposed the death sentence in a way that could only be called freakish. The new Georgia sentencing procedures, by contrast, focus the jury's attention on the particularized nature of the crime and the particularized characteristics of the individual defendant. While the jury is permitted to consider any aggravating or mitigating circumstances, it must find and identify at least one statutory aggravating factor before it may impose a penalty of death. In this way the jury's discretion is channeled. No longer can a jury wantonly and freakishly impose the death sentence; it is always circumscribed by the legislative guidelines. In addition, the review function of the Supreme Court of Georgia affords additional assurance that the concerns that prompted our decision in Furman are not present to any significant degree in the Georgia procedure applied here.

For the reasons expressed in this opinion, we hold that the statutory system under which Gregg was sentenced to death does not violate the Constitution. Accordingly, the judgment of the Georgia Supreme Court is affirmed.

It is so ordered.

MR. JUSTICE WHITE, with whom THE CHIEF JUSTICE and MR. JUSTICE REHNQUIST join, concurring in the judgment.

In Furman v. Georgia, 408 U.S. 238 (1972), this Court held the death penalty as then administered in Georgia to be unconstitutional. That same year the Georgia Legislature enacted a new statutory scheme under which the death penalty may be imposed for several offenses, including murder. The issue in this case is whether the death penalty imposed for murder on petitioner Gregg under the new Georgia statutory scheme may constitutionally be carried out. I agree that it may.

I

Under the new Georgia statutory scheme a person convicted of murder may receive a sentence either of death or of life imprisonment. Ga. Code Ann. § 26-1101 (1972). Under Georgia Code Ann. § 26-3102 (Supp. 1975), the sentence will be life imprisonment unless the jury at a separate evidentiary proceeding immediately following the verdict finds unanimously and beyond a reasonable doubt at least one statutorily defined "aggravating circumstance." The aggravating circumstances are:

"(1) The offense of murder, rape, armed robbery, or kidnapping was committed by a person with a prior record of conviction for a capital felony, or the offense of murder was committed by a person who has a substantial history of serious assaultive criminal convictions.

"(2) The offense of murder, rape, armed robbery, or kidnapping was committed while the offender was engaged in the commission of another capital felony or aggravated battery, or the offense of murder was committed while the offender was engaged in the commission of burglary or arson in the first degree.

"(3) The offender by his act of murder, armed robbery, or kidnapping knowingly created a great risk of death to more than one person in a public place by means of a weapon or device which would normally be hazardous to the lives of more than one person.

"(4) The offender committed the offense of murder for himself or another, for the purpose of receiving money or any other thing of monetary value.

"(5) The murder of a judicial officer, former judicial officer, district attorney or solicitor or former district attorney or solicitor during or because of the exercise of his official duty.

"(6) The offender caused or directed another to commit murder or committed murder as an agent or employee of another person.

"(7) The offense of murder, rape, armed robbery, or kidnapping was outrageously or wantonly vile, horrible or inhuman in that it involved torture, depravity of mind, or an aggravated battery to the victim.

"(8) The offense of murder was committed against any peace officer, corrections employee or fireman while engaged in the performance of his official duties.

"(9) The offense of murder was committed by a person in, or who has escaped from, the lawful custody of a peace officer or place of lawful confinement.

"(10) The murder was committed for the purpose of avoiding, interfering with, or preventing a lawful arrest or custody in a place of lawful confinement, of himself or another." § 27-2534.1 (b) (Supp. 1975).

Having found an aggravating circumstance, however, the jury is not required to impose the death penalty. Instead, it is merely authorized to impose it after considering evidence of "any mitigating circumstances or aggravating circumstances otherwise authorized by law and any of the [enumerated] statutory aggravating circumstances. . . ." § 27-2534.1 (b) (Supp. 1975). Unless the jury unanimously determines that the death penalty should be imposed, the defendant will be sentenced to life imprisonment. In the event that the jury does impose the death penalty, it must designate in writing the aggravating circumstance which it found to exist beyond a reasonable doubt.

An important aspect of the new Georgia legislative scheme, however, is its provision for appellate review. Prompt review by the Georgia Supreme Court is provided for in every case in which the death penalty is imposed. To assist it in deciding whether to sustain the death penalty, the Georgia Supreme Court is supplied, in every case, with a report from the trial judge in the form of a standard questionnaire. § 27-2537 (a)

(Supp. 1975). The questionnaire contains, inter alia, six questions designed to disclose whether race played a role in the case and one question asking the trial judge whether the evidence forecloses "all doubt respecting the defendant's guilt." In deciding whether the death penalty is to be sustained in any given case, the court shall determine:

(1) Whether the sentence of death was imposed under the influence of passion, prejudice, or any other arbitrary factor, and

(2) Whether, in cases other than treason or aircraft hijacking, the evidence supports the jury's or judge's finding of a statutory aggravating circumstance as enumerated in section 27-2534.1 (b), and

(3) Whether the sentence of death is excessive or disproportionate to the penalty imposed in similar cases, considering both the crime and the defendant. . . ."

In order that information regarding "similar cases" may be before the court, the post of Assistant to the Supreme Court was created. The Assistant must "accumulate the records of all capital felony cases in which sentence was imposed after January 1, 1970, or such earlier date as the court may deem appropriate." § 27-2537 (f). The court is required to include in its decision a reference to "those similar cases which it took into consideration." § 27-2537 (e).

II

Petitioner Troy Gregg and a 16-year-old companion, Floyd Allen, were hitchhiking from Florida to Asheville, N.C., on November 21, 1973. They were picked up in an automobile driven by Fred Simmons and Bob Moore, both of whom were drunk. The car broke down and Simmons purchased a new one—a 1960 Pontiac—using part of a large roll of cash which he had with him. After picking up another hitchhiker in Florida and dropping him off in Atlanta, the car proceeded north to Gwinnett County, Ga., where it stopped so that Moore and Simmons could urinate. While they were out of the car Simmons was shot in the eye and Moore was shot in the right cheek and in the back of the head. Both died as a result.

On November 24, 1973, at 3 P.M., on the basis of information supplied by the hitch-hiker, petitioner and Allen were arrested in Asheville, N.C. They were then in possession of the car which Simmons had purchased; petitioner was in possession of the gun which had killed Simmons and Moore and $107 which had been taken from them; and in the motel room in which petitioner was staying was a new stereo and a car stereo player.

At about 11 P.M., after the Gwinnett County police had arrived, petitioner made a statement to them admitting that he had killed Moore and Simmons, but asserting that he had killed them in self-defense and in defense of Allen. He also admitted robbing them of $400 and taking their car. A few moments later petitioner was asked why he had shot Moore and Simmons and responded: "By God, I wanted them dead."

At about 1 o'clock the next morning, petitioner and Allen were released to the custody of the Gwinnett County police and were transported in two cars back to Gwinnett County. On the way, at about 5 A.M., the car stopped at the place where Moore and Simmons had been killed. Everyone got out of the car. Allen was asked, in petitioner's presence, how the killing occurred. He said that he had been sitting in the back seat of the 1960 Pontiac and was about half asleep. He woke up when the car stopped. Simmons and Moore got out, and as soon as they did petitioner turned around and told Allen: "Get out, we're going to rob them." Allen said that he got out and walked toward the back of the car, looked around and could see petitioner, with a gun in his hand, leaning up against the car so he could get a good aim. Simmons and Moore had gone down the bank and had relieved themselves and as they were coming up the bank petitioner fired three shots. One of the men fell, the other staggered. Petitioner then circled around the back and approached the two men, both of whom were now lying in the ditch, from behind. He placed the gun to the head of one of them and pulled the trigger. Then he went quickly to the other one and placed the gun to his head and pulled the trigger again. He then took the money, whatever was in their pockets. He told Allen to get in the car and they drove away.

When Allen had finished telling this story, one of the officers asked petitioner if this was the way it had happened. Petitioner hung his head and said that it was. The officer then said: "You mean you shot these men down in cold blooded murder just to rob them," and petitioner said yes. The officer then asked him why and petitioner said he did not know. Petitioner was indicted in two counts for murder and in two counts for robbery.

At trial, petitioner's defense was that he had killed in self-defense. He testified in his own behalf and told a version of the events similar to that which he had originally told to the Gwinnett County police. On cross-examination, he was confronted with a letter to Allen recounting a version of the events similar to that to which he had just testified and instructing Allen to memorize and burn the letter. Petitioner conceded writing the version of the events, but denied writing the portion of the letter which instructed Allen to memorize and burn it. In rebuttal, the State called a handwriting expert who testified that the entire letter was written by the same person.

The jury was instructed on the elements of murder and robbery. The trial judge gave an instruction on self-defense, but refused to submit the lesser included offense of manslaughter to the jury. It returned verdicts of guilty on all counts.

No new evidence was presented at the sentencing proceeding. However, the prosecutor and the attorney for petitioner each made arguments to the jury on the issue of punishment. The prosecutor emphasized the strength of the case against petitioner and the fact that he had murdered in order to eliminate the witnesses to the robbery. The defense attorney emphasized the possibility that a mistake had been made and that petitioner was not guilty. The trial judge instructed the jury on their sentencing function and in so doing submitted to them three statutory aggravating circumstances. He stated:

Now, as to counts one and three, wherein the defendant is charged with the murders of—has been found guilty of the murders of [Simmons and Moore], the following aggravating circumstances are some that you can consider, as I say, you must find that these existed beyond a reasonable doubt before the death penalty can be imposed. "One—That the offense of murder was committed while the offender was engaged in the commission of two other capital felonies, to-wit the armed robbery of [Simmons and Moore]. "Two—That the offender committed the offense of murder for the purpose of receiving money and the automobile described in the indictment. "Three—The offense of murder was outrageously and wantonly vile, horrible and inhuman, in that they involved the depravity of mind of the defendant. "Now, so far as the counts two and four, that is the counts of armed robbery, of which you have found the defendant guilty, then you may find—inquire into these aggravating circumstances. "That the offense of armed robbery was committed while the offender was engaged in the commission of two capital felonies, to-wit the murders of [Simmons and Moore] or that the offender committed the offense of armed robbery for the purpose of receiving money and the automobile set forth in the indictment, or three, that the offense of armed robbery was outrageously and wantonly vile, horrible and inhuman in that they involved the depravity of the mind of the defendant. "Now, if you find that there was one or more of these aggravating circumstances existed beyond a reasonable doubt, then and I refer to each individual count, then you would be authorized to consider imposing the sentence of death. "If you do not find that one of these aggravating circumstances existed beyond a reasonable doubt, in either of these counts, then you would not be authorized to consider the penalty of death. In that event, the sentence as to counts one and three, those are the counts wherein the defendant was found guilty of murder, the sentence could be imprisonment for life."

The jury returned the death penalty on all four counts finding all the aggravating circumstances submitted to it, except that it did not find the crimes to have been "outrageously or wantonly vile," etc.

On appeal the Georgia Supreme Court affirmed the death sentences on the murder counts and vacated the death sentences on

the robbery counts. 233 Ga. 117, 210 S.E.2d 659 (1974). It concluded that the murder sentences were not imposed under the influence of passion, prejudice, or any other arbitrary factor; that the evidence supported the finding of a statutory aggravating factor with respect to the murders; and, citing several cases in which the death penalty had been imposed previously for murders of persons who had witnessed a robbery, held:

After considering both the crimes and the defendant and after comparing the evidence and the sentences in this case with those of previous murder cases, we are also of the opinion that these two sentences of death are not excessive or disproportionate to the penalties imposed in similar cases which are hereto attached. Id., at 127, 210 S.E.2d, at 667.

However, it held with respect to the robbery sentences:

Although there is no indication that these two sentences were imposed under the influence of passion, prejudice or any other arbitrary factor, the sentences imposed here are unusual in that they are rarely imposed for this offense. Thus, under the test provided by statute for comparison (Code Ann. § 27-2537 (c), (3), they must be considered to be excessive or disproportionate to the penalties imposed in similar cases. Ibid.

Accordingly, the sentences on the robbery counts were vacated.

III

The threshold question in this case is whether the death penalty may be carried out for murder under the Georgia legislative scheme consistent with the decision in Furman v. Georgia, supra. In Furman, this Court held that as a result of giving the sentencer unguided discretion to impose or not to impose the death penalty for murder, the penalty was being imposed discriminatorily, wantonly and freakishly, and so infrequently that any given death sentence was cruel and unusual. Petitioner argues that, as in Furman, the jury is still the sentencer; that the statutory criteria to be considered by the jury on the issue of sentence under Georgia's new statutory scheme are vague and do not purport to be all-inclusive; and that, in any event, there are no circumstances under which the jury is required to impose the death penalty. Consequently, the petitioner argues that the death penalty will inexorably be imposed in as discriminatory, standardless, and rare a manner as it was imposed under the scheme declared invalid in Furman.

The argument is considerably overstated. The Georgia Legislature has made an effort to identify those aggravating factors which it considers necessary and relevant to the question whether a defendant convicted of capital murder should be sentenced to death. The jury which imposes sentence is instructed on all statutory aggravating factors which are supported by the evidence, and is told that it may not impose the death penalty unless it unanimously finds at least one of those factors to have been established beyond a reasonable doubt. The Georgia Legislature has plainly made an effort to guide the jury in the exercise of its discretion, while at the same time permitting the jury to dispense mercy on the basis of factors too intangible to write into a statute, and I cannot accept the naked assertion that the effort is bound to fail. As the types of murders for which the death penalty may be imposed become more narrowly defined and are limited to those which are particularly serious or for which the death penalty is peculiarly appropriate as they are in Georgia by reason of the aggravating-circumstance requirement, it becomes reasonable to expect that juries—even given discretion not to impose the death penalty—will impose the death penalty in a substantial portion of the cases so defined. If they do, it can no longer be said that the penalty is being imposed wantonly and freakishly or so infrequently that it loses its usefulness as a sentencing device. There is, therefore, reason to expect that Georgia's current system would escape the infirmities which invalidated its previous system under Furman. However, the Georgia Legislature was not satisfied with a system which might, but also might not, turn out in practice to result in death sentences being imposed with reasonable consistency for certain serious murders. Instead, it gave the Georgia Supreme Court the power and

the obligation to perform precisely the task which three Justices of this Court, whose opinions were necessary to the result, performed in Furman: namely, the task of deciding whether in fact the death penalty was being administered for any given class of crime in a discriminatory, standardless, or rare fashion.

In considering any given death sentence on appeal, the Georgia Supreme Court is to determine whether the sentence imposed was consistent with the relevant statutes—i.e., consistent with the relevant support the finding of an aggravating circumstance. Ga. Code Ann. § 27-2537 (c)(2) (Supp. 1975). However, it must do much more than determine whether the penalty was lawfully imposed. It must go on to decide—after reviewing the penalties imposed in "similar cases"—whether the penalty is "excessive or disproportionate" considering both the crime and the defendant. § 27-2537 (c)(3) (Supp. 1975). The new Assistant to the Supreme Court is to assist the court in collecting the records of "all capital felony cases" in the State of Georgia in which sentence was imposed after January 1, 1970. § 27-2537 (f) (Supp. 1975). The court also has the obligation of determining whether the penalty was "imposed under the influence of passion, prejudice, or any other arbitrary factor." § 27-2537 (c) (1) (Supp. 1975). The Georgia Supreme Court has interpreted the appellate review statute to require it to set aside the death sentence whenever juries across the State impose it only rarely for the type of crime in question; but to require it to affirm death sentences whenever juries across the State generally impose it for the crime in question. Thus, in this case the Georgia Supreme Court concluded that the death penalty was so rarely imposed for the crime of robbery that it set aside the sentences on the robbery counts, and effectively foreclosed that penalty from being imposed for that crime in the future under the legislative scheme now in existence. Similarly, the Georgia Supreme Court has determined that juries impose the death sentence too rarely with respect to certain classes of rape. Compare Coley v. State, 231 Ga. 829, 204 S.E. 2d 612 (1974), with Coker v. State, 234 Ga. 555, 216 S.E.2d 782 (1975). However, it concluded that juries "generally throughout the state" have imposed the death penalty for those who murder witnesses to armed robberies. Jarrell v. State, 234 Ga. 410, 425, 216 S.E. 2d 258, 270 (1975). Consequently, it affirmed the sentences in this case on the murder counts. If the Georgia Supreme Court is correct with respect to this factual judgment, imposition of the death penalty in this and similar cases is consistent with Furman. Indeed, if the Georgia Supreme Court properly performs the task assigned to it under the Georgia statutes, death sentences imposed for discriminatory reasons or wantonly or freakishly for any given category of crime will be set aside. Petitioner has wholly failed to establish, and has not even attempted to establish, that the Georgia Supreme Court failed properly to perform its task in this case or that it is incapable of performing its task adequately in all cases; and this Court should not assume that it did not do so.

Petitioner also argues that decisions made by the prosecutor—either in negotiating a plea to some lesser offense than capital murder or in simply declining to charge capital murder—are standardless and will inexorably result in the wanton and freakish imposition of the penalty condemned by the judgment in Furman. I address this point separately because the cases in which no capital offense is charged escape the view of the Georgia Supreme Court and are not considered by it in determining whether a particular sentence is excessive or disproportionate.

Petitioner's argument that prosecutors behave in a standardless fashion in deciding which cases to try as capital felonies is unsupported by any facts. Petitioner simply asserts that since prosecutors have the power not to charge capital felonies they will exercise that power in a standardless fashion. This is untenable. Absent facts to the contrary, it cannot be assumed that prosecutors will be motivated in their charging decision by factors other than the strength of their case and the likelihood that a jury would impose the death penalty if it convicts. Unless prosecutors are incompetent in their judgments, the standards by which they decide whether to charge a capital felony will be the same as those by which the jury will decide the questions of guilt and sentence. Thus defendants will escape the death penalty through prosecutorial charging decisions

only because the offense is not sufficiently serious; or because the proof is insufficiently strong. This does not cause the system to be standardless any more than the jury's decision to impose life imprisonment on a defendant whose crime is deemed insufficiently serious or its decision to acquit someone who is probably guilty but whose guilt is not established beyond a reasonable doubt. Thus the prosecutor's charging decisions are unlikely to have removed from the sample of cases considered by the Georgia Supreme Court any which are truly "similar." If the cases really were "similar" in relevant respects, it is unlikely that prosecutors would fail to prosecute them as capital cases; and I am unwilling to assume the contrary.

Petitioner's argument that there is an unconstitutional amount of discretion in the system which separates those suspects who receive the death penalty from those who receive life imprisonment, a lesser penalty, or are acquitted or never charged, seems to be in final analysis an indictment of our entire system of justice. Petitioner has argued, in effect, that no matter how effective the death penalty may be as a punishment, government, created and run as it must be by humans, is inevitably incompetent to administer it. This cannot be accepted as a proposition of constitutional law. Imposition of the death penalty is surely an awesome responsibility for any system of justice and those who participate in it. Mistakes will be made and discriminations will occur which will be difficult to explain. However, one of society's most basic tasks is that of protecting the lives of its citizens and one of the most basic ways in which it achieves the task is through criminal laws against murder. I decline to interfere with the manner in which Georgia has chosen to enforce such laws on what is simply an assertion of lack of faith in the ability of the system of justice to operate in a fundamentally fair manner.

IV

For the reasons stated in dissent in Roberts v. Louisiana, post, at 350-356, neither can I agree with the petitioner's other basic argument that the death penalty, however imposed and for whatever crime, is cruel and unusual punishment.

I therefore concur in the judgment of affirmance.

Statement of THE CHIEF JUSTICE and MR. JUSTICE REHNQUIST:

We concur in the judgment and join the opinion of MR. JUSTICE WHITE, agreeing with its analysis that Georgia's system of capital punishment comports with the Court's holding in Furman v. Georgia, 408 U.S. 238 (1972).

MR. JUSTICE BLACKMUN, concurring in the judgment.

I concur in the judgment. See Furman v. Georgia, 408 U.S. 238, 405-414 (1972) (BLACKMUN, J., dissenting), and id., at 375 (BURGER, C.J., dissenting); id., at 414 POWELL, J., dissenting); id., at 465 (REHNQUIST, J., dissenting).

MR. JUSTICE BRENNAN, dissenting.

The Cruel and Unusual Punishments Clause "must draw its meaning from the evolving standards of decency that mark the progress of a maturing society." The opinions of MR. JUSTICE STEWART, MR. JUSTICE POWELL, and MR. JUSTICE STEVENS today hold that "evolving standards of decency" require focus not on the essence of the death penalty itself but primarily upon the procedures employed by the State to single out persons to suffer the penalty of death. Those opinions hold further that, so viewed, the Clause invalidates the mandatory infliction of the death penalty but not its infliction under sentencing procedures that MR. JUSTICE STEWART, MR. JUSTICE POWELL, and MR. JUSTICE STEVENS conclude adequately safeguard against the risk that the death penalty was imposed in an arbitrary and capricious manner.

In Furman v. Georgia, 408 U.S. 238, 257 (1972) (concurring opinion), I read "evolving standards of decency" as requiring focus upon the essence of the death penalty itself and not primarily or solely upon the procedures under which the determination to inflict the penalty upon a particular person was made. I there said:

From the beginning of our Nation, the punishment of death has stirred acute public controversy. Although pragmatic arguments for and against the punishment have been frequently advanced, this long-standing and heated controversy cannot be explained solely as the result of differences over the practical wisdom of a particular government policy. At bottom, the battle has been waged on moral grounds. The country has debated whether a society for which the dignity of the individual is the supreme value can, without a fundamental inconsistency, follow the practice of deliberately putting some of its members to death. In the United States, as in other nations of the western world, "the struggle about this punishment has been one between ancient and deeply rooted beliefs in retribution atonement or vengeance on the one hand, and, on the other, beliefs in the personal value and dignity of the common man that were born of the democratic movement of the eighteenth century, as well as beliefs in the scientific approach to an understanding of the motive forces of human conduct, which are the result of the growth of the sciences of behavior during the nineteenth and twentieth centuries." It is this essentially moral conflict that forms the backdrop for the past changes in and the present operation of our system of imposing death as a punishment for crime. Id., at 296.

That continues to be my view. For the Clause forbidding cruel and unusual punishments under our constitutional system of government embodies in unique degree moral principles restraining the punishments that our civilized society may impose on those persons who transgress its laws. Thus, I too say: "For myself, I do not hesitate to assert the proposition that the only way the law has progressed from the days of the rack, the screw and the wheel is the development of moral concepts, or, as stated by the Supreme Court . . . the application of 'evolving standards of decency' . . ."

This Court inescapably has the duty, as the ultimate arbiter of the meaning of our Constitution, to say whether, when individuals condemned to death stand before our Bar, "moral concepts" require us to hold that the law has progressed to the point where we should declare that the punishment of death, like punishments on the rack, the screw, and the wheel, is no longer morally tolerable in our civilized society. My opinion in Furman v. Georgia concluded that our civilization and the law had progressed to this point and that therefore the punishment of death, for whatever crime and under all circumstances, is "cruel and unusual" in violation of the Eighth and Fourteenth Amendments of the Constitution. I shall not again canvass the reasons that led to that conclusion. I emphasize only that foremost among the "moral concepts" recognized in our cases and inherent in the Clause is the primary moral principle that the State, even as it punishes, must treat its citizens in a manner consistent with their intrinsic worth as human beings—a punishment must not be so severe as to be degrading to human dignity. A judicial determination whether the punishment of death comports with human dignity is therefore not only permitted but compelled by the Clause. 408 U.S., at 270.

I do not understand that the Court disagrees that "[i]n comparison to all other punishments today . . . the deliberate extinguishment of human life by the State is uniquely degrading to human dignity." Id., at 291. For three of my Brethren hold today that mandatory infliction of the death penalty constitutes the penalty cruel and unusual punishment. I perceive no principled basis for this limitation. Death for whatever crime and under all circumstances "is truly an awesome punishment. The calculated killing of a human being by the State involves, by its very nature, a denial of the executed person's humanity. . . . An executed person has indeed 'lost the right to have rights.'" Id., at 290. Death is not only an unusually severe punishment, unusual in its pain, in its finality, and in its enormity, but it serves no penal purpose more effectively than a less severe punishment; therefore the principle inherent in the Clause that prohibits pointless infliction of excessive punishment when less severe punishment can adequately achieve the same purposes invalidates the punishment. Id., at 279.

The fatal constitutional infirmity in the punishment of death is that it treats "members of the human race as nonhumans, as objects to be toyed with and discarded. [It is] thus inconsistent with the fundamental premise of the Clause that even the vilest criminal remains a human being possessed of common human dignity." Id., at 273. As such it is a penalty that "subjects the individual to a fate forbidden by the principle of civilized treatment guaranteed by the [Clause]." I therefore would hold, on that ground alone, that death is today a cruel and unusual punishment prohibited by the Clause. "Justice of this kind is obviously no less shocking than the crime itself, and the new 'official' murder, far from offering redress for the offense committed against society, adds instead a second defilement to the first."

I dissent from the judgments in No. 74-6257, Gregg v. Georgia, No. 75-5706, Proffitt v. Florida, and No. 75-5394, Jurek v. Texas, insofar as each upholds the death sentences challenged in those cases. I would set aside the death sentences imposed in those cases as violative of the Eighth and Fourteenth Amendments.

In Furman v. Georgia, 408 U.S. 238, 314 (1972) (concurring opinion), I set forth at some length my views on the basic issue presented to the Court in these cases. The death penalty, I concluded, is a cruel and unusual punishment prohibited by the Eighth and Fourteenth Amendments. That continues to be my view.

I have no intention of retracing the "long and tedious journey," id., at 370, that led to my conclusion in Furman. My sole purposes here are to consider the suggestion that my conclusion in Furman has been undercut by developments since then, and briefly to evaluate the basis for my Brethren's holding that the extinction of life is a permissible form of punishment under the Cruel and Unusual Punishments Clause.

In Furman I concluded that the death penalty is constitutionally invalid for two reasons. First, the death penalty is excessive. Id., at 331-332; 342-359. And second, the American people, fully informed as to the purposes of the death penalty and its liabilities, would in my view reject it as morally unacceptable. Id., at 360-369.

Since the decision in Furman, the legislatures of 35 States have enacted new statutes authorizing the imposition of the death sentence for certain crimes, and Congress has enacted a law providing the death penalty for air piracy resulting in death. 49 U.S.C. §§ 1472(i), (n) (1970 ed., Supp. IV). I would be less than candid if I did not acknowledge that these developments have a significant bearing on a realistic assessment of the moral acceptability of the death penalty to the American people. But if the constitutionality of the death penalty turns, as I have urged, on the opinion of an informed citizenry, then even the enactment of new death statutes cannot be viewed as conclusive. In Furman, I observed that the American people are largely unaware of the information critical to a judgment on the morality of the death penalty, and concluded that if they were better informed they would consider it shocking, unjust, and unacceptable. 408 U.S., at 360-369. A recent study, conducted after the enactment of the post-Furman statutes, has confirmed that the American people know little about the death penalty, and that the opinions of an informed public would differ significantly from those of a public unaware of the consequences and effects of the death penalty.

Even assuming, however, that the post-Furman enactment of statutes authorizing the death penalty renders the prediction of the views of an informed citizenry an uncertain basis for a constitutional decision, the enactment of those statutes has no bearing whatsoever on the conclusion that the death penalty is unconstitutional because it is excessive. An excessive penalty is invalid under the Cruel and Unusual Punishments Clause "even though popular sentiment may favor" it. Id., at 331; ante, at 173, 182-183 (opinion of STEWART, POWELL, and STEVENS, JJ.); Roberts v. Louisiana, post, at 353-354 (WHITE, J., dissenting). The inquiry here, then, is simply whether the death penalty is necessary to accomplish the legitimate legislative purposes in punishment, or whether a less severe penalty—life imprisonment—would do as well. Furman, supra, at 342 (MARSHALL, J., concurring).

The two purposes that sustain the death penalty as nonexcessive in the Court's view are general deterrence and retribution. In Furman, I canvassed the relevant data on the deterrent effect of capital punishment. 408 U.S., at 347-354. The state of knowledge at that point, after literally centuries of debate,

was summarized as follows by a United Nations Committee:

> It is generally agreed between the retentionists and abolitionists, whatever their opinions about the validity of comparative studies of deterrence, that the data which now exist show no correlation between the existence of capital punishment and lower rates of capital crime.

The available evidence, I concluded in Furman, was convincing that "capital punishment is not necessary as a deterrent to crime in our society." Id., at 353.

The Solicitor General in his amicus brief in these cases relies heavily on a study by Isaac Ehrlich, reported a year after Furman, to support the contention that the death penalty does deter murder. Since the Ehrlich study was not available at the time of Furman and since it is the first scientific study to suggest that the death penalty may have a deterrent effect, I will briefly consider its import.

The Ehrlich study focused on the relationship in the Nation as a whole between the homicide rate and "execution risk"—the fraction of persons convicted of murder who were actually executed. Comparing the differences in homicide rate and execution risk for the years 1933 to 1969, Ehrlich found that increases in execution risk were associated with increases in the homicide rate. But when he employed the statistical technique of multiple regression analysis to control for the influence of other variables posited to have an impact on the homicide rate, Ehrlich found a negative correlation between changes in the homicide rate and changes in execution risk. His tentative conclusion was that for the period from 1933 to 1967 each additional execution in the United States might have saved eight lives.

The methods and conclusions of the Ehrlich study have been severely criticized on a number of grounds. It has been suggested, for example, that the study is defective because it compares execution and homicide rates on a nationwide, rather than a state-by-state, basis. The aggregation of data from all States—including those that have abolished the death penalty—obscures the relationship between murder and execution rates. Under Ehrlich's methodology, a decrease in the execution risk in one State combined with an increase in the murder rate in another State would, all other things being equal, suggest a deterrent effect that quite obviously would not exist. Indeed, a deterrent effect would be suggested if, once again all other things being equal, one State abolished the death penalty and experienced no change in the murder rate, while another State experienced an increase in the murder rate.

The most compelling criticism of the Ehrlich study is that its conclusions are extremely sensitive to the choice of the time period included in the regression analysis. Analysis of Ehrlich's data reveals that all empirical support for the deterrent effect of capital punishment disappears when the five most recent years are removed from his time series—that is to say, whether a decrease in the execution risk corresponds to an increase or a decrease in the murder rate depends on the ending point of the sample period. This finding has cast severe doubts on the reliability of Ehrlich's tentative conclusions. Indeed, a recent regression study, based on Ehrlich's theoretical model but using cross-section state data for the years 1950 and 1960, found no support for the conclusion that executions act as a deterrent.

The Ehrlich study, in short, is of little, if any, assistance in assessing the deterrent impact of the death penalty. Accord, Commonwealth v. O'Neal, ___ Mass. ___, ___, 339 N.E. 2d 676, 684 (1975). The evidence I reviewed in Furman remains convincing, in my view, that "capital punishment is not necessary as a deterrent to crime in our society." 408 U.S., at 353. The justification for the death penalty must be found elsewhere.

The other principal purpose said to be served by the death penalty is retribution. The notion that retribution can serve as a moral justification for the sanction of death finds credence in the opinion of my Brothers STEWART, POWELL, and STEVENS, and that of my Brother WHITE in Roberts v. Louisiana, post, p. 337. See also Furman v. Georgia, 408 U.S., at 394-395 (BURGER, C.J., dissenting). It is this notion that I find to be the most disturbing aspect of today's unfortunate decisions.

The concept of retribution is a multifaceted one, and any discussion of its role in the criminal law must be undertaken with caution. On one level, it can be said that the notion of retribution or reprobation is the basis of our insistence that only those who have broken the law be punished, and in this sense the notion is quite obviously central to a just system of criminal sanctions. But our recognition that retribution plays a crucial role in determining who may be punished by no means requires approval of retribution as a general justification for punishment. It is the question whether retribution can provide a moral justification for punishment—in particular, capital punishment—that we must consider.

My Brothers STEWART, POWELL, and STEVENS offer the following explanation of the retributive justification for capital punishment:

The instinct for retribution is part of the nature of man, and channeling that instinct in the administration of criminal justice serves an important purpose in promoting the stability of a society governed by law. When people begin to believe that organized society is unwilling or unable to impose upon criminal offenders the punishment they "deserve," then there are sown the seeds of anarchy—of self-help, vigilante justice, and lynch law. Ante, at 183, quoting from Furman v. Georgia, supra, at 308 (STEWART, J., concurring).

This statement is wholly inadequate to justify the death penalty. As my Brother BRENNAN stated in Furman, "[t]here is no evidence whatever that utilization of imprisonment rather than death encourages private blood feuds and other disorders." 408 U.S., at 303 (concurring opinion). It simply defies belief to suggest that the death penalty is necessary to prevent the American people from taking the law into their own hands.

In a related vein, it may be suggested that the expression of moral outrage through the imposition of the death penalty serves to reinforce basic moral values—that it marks some crimes as particularly offensive and therefore to be avoided. The argument is akin to a deterrence argument, but differs in that it contemplates the individual's shrinking from antisocial conduct, not because he fears punishment, but because he has been told in the strongest possible way that the conduct is wrong. This contention, like the previous one, provides no support for the death penalty. It is inconceivable that any individual concerned about conforming his conduct to what society says is "right" would fail to realize that murder is "wrong" if the penalty were simply life imprisonment.

The foregoing contentions—that society's expression of moral outrage through the imposition of the death penalty pre-empts the citizenry from taking the law into its own hands and reinforces moral values—are not retributive in the purest sense. They are essentially utilitarian in that they portray the death penalty as valuable because of its beneficial results. These justifications for the death penalty are inadequate because the penalty is, quite clearly I think, not necessary to the accomplishment of those results.

There remains for consideration, however, what might be termed the purely retributive justification for the death penalty—that the death penalty is appropriate, not because of its beneficial effect on society, but because the taking of the murderer's life is itself morally good. Some of the language of the opinion of my Brothers STEWART, POWELL, and STEVENS in No. 74-6257 appears positively to embrace this notion of retribution for its own sake as a justification for capital punishment. They state:

> [The] decision that capital punishment may be the appropriate sanction in extreme cases is an expression of the community's belief that certain crimes are themselves so grievous an affront to humanity that the only adequate response may be the penalty of death. Ante, at 184 (footnote omitted).

They then quote with approval from Lord Justice Denning's remarks before the British Royal Commission on Capital Punishment:

> The truth is that some crimes are so outrageous that society insists on adequate punishment, because the wrong-doer deserves it, irrespective of whether it is a deterrent or not. Ante, at 184 n. 30.

Of course, it may be that these statements are intended as no more than observations as to the popular demands that it is thought must be responded to in order to prevent anarchy. But the implication of the statements appears to me to be quite different— namely, that society's judgment that the murderer "deserves" death must be respected not simply because the preservation of order requires it, but because it is appropriate that society make the judgment and carry it out. It is this latter notion, in particular, that I consider to be fundamentally at odds with the Eighth Amendment. See Furman v. Georgia, 408 U.S., at 343-345 (MARSHALL, J., concurring). The mere fact that the community demands the murderer's life in return for the evil he has done cannot sustain the death penalty, for as Justice Stewart, Powell, and Stevens remind us, "the Eighth Amendment demands more than that a challenged punishment be acceptable to contemporary society." Ante, at 182. To be sustained under the Eighth Amendment, the death penalty must "compor[t] with the basic concept of human dignity at the core of the Amendment," ibid.; the objective in imposing it must be "[consistent] with our respect for the dignity of [other] men." Ante, at 183. See Trop v. Dulles, 356 U.S. 86, 100 (1958) (plurality opinion). Under these standards, the taking of life "because the wrongdoer deserves it" surely must fall, for such a punishment has as its very basis the total denial of the wrongdoer's dignity and worth.

The death penalty, unnecessary to promote the goal of deterrence or to further any legitimate notion of retribution, is an excessive penalty forbidden by the Eighth and Fourteenth Amendments. I respectfully dissent from the Court's judgment upholding the sentences of death imposed upon the petitioners in these cases.

PROFFITT

v.

FLORIDA

428 U.S. 242; 96 S. Ct. 2960; 49 L. Ed. 2d 913 (1976)

Judgment of the Court, and opinion of MR. JUSTICE STEWART, MR. JUSTICE POWELL, and MR. JUSTICE STEVENS, announced by MR. JUSTICE POWELL.

The issue presented by this case is whether the imposition of the sentence of death for the crime of murder under the law of Florida violates the Eighth and Fourteenth Amendments.

I

The petitioner, Charles William Proffitt, was tried, found guilty, and sentenced to death for the first-degree murder of Joel Medgebow. The circumstances surrounding the murder were testified to by the decedent's wife, who was present at the time it was committed. On July 10, 1973, Mrs. Medgebow awakened around 5 A.M. in the bedroom of her apartment to find her husband sitting up in bed, moaning. He was holding what she took to be a ruler. Just then a third person jumped up, hit her several times with his fist, knocked her to the floor, and ran out of the house. It soon appeared that Medgebow had been fatally stabbed with a butcher knife. Mrs. Medgebow was not able to identify the attacker, although she was able to give a description of him.

The petitioner's wife testified that on the night before the murder the petitioner had gone to work dressed in a white shirt and gray pants, and that he had returned at about 5:15 A.M. dressed in the same clothing but without shoes. She said that after a short conversation the petitioner had packed his clothes and departed. A young woman boarder, who overheard parts of the petitioner's conversation with his wife, testified that the petitioner had told his wife that he had stabbed and killed a man with a butcher knife while he was burglarizing a place, and that he had beaten a woman. One of the petitioner's coworkers testified that they had been drink-

ing together until 3:30 or 3:45 on the morning of the murder and that the petitioner had then driven him home. He said that the petitioner at this time was wearing gray pants and a white shirt.

The jury found the defendant guilty as charged. Subsequently, as provided by Florida law, a separate hearing was held to determine whether the petitioner should be sentenced to death or to life imprisonment. Under the state law that decision turned on whether certain statutory aggravating circumstances surrounding the crime outweighed any statutory mitigating circumstances found to exist. At that hearing it was shown that the petitioner had one prior conviction, a 1967 charge of breaking and entering. The State also introduced the testimony of the physician (Dr. Crumbley) at the jail where the petitioner had been held pending trial. He testified that the petitioner had come to him as a physician, and told him that he was concerned that he would harm other people in the future, that he had had an uncontrollable desire to kill that had already resulted in his killing one man, that this desire was building up again, and that he wanted psychiatric help so he would not kill again. Dr. Crumbley also testified that, in his opinion, the petitioner was dangerous and would be a danger to his fellow inmates if imprisoned, but that his condition could be treated successfully.

The jury returned an advisory verdict recommending the sentence of death. The trial judge ordered an independent psychiatric evaluation of the petitioner, the results of which indicated that the petitioner was not, then or at the time of the murder, mentally impaired. The judge then sentenced the petitioner to death. In his written findings supporting the sentence, the judge found as aggravating circumstances that (1) the murder was premeditated and occurred in the course of a felony (burglary); (2) the petitioner has the propensity to commit murder; (3) the murder was especially heinous, atrocious, and cruel; and (4) the petitioner knowingly, through his intentional act, created a great risk of serious bodily harm and death to many persons. The judge also found specifically that none of the statutory mitigating circumstances existed. The Supreme Court of

Florida affirmed. 315 So. 2d 461 (1975). We granted certiorari, 423 U.S. 1082 (1976), to consider whether the imposition of the death sentence in this case constitutes cruel and unusual punishment in violation of the Eighth and Fourteenth Amendments.

II

The petitioner argues that the imposition of the death penalty under any circumstances is cruel and unusual punishment in violation of the Eighth and Fourteenth Amendments. We reject this argument for the reasons stated today in Gregg v. Georgia, ante, at 168-187.

III

A

In response to Furman v. Georgia, 408 U.S. 238 (1972), the Florida Legislature adopted new statutes that authorize the imposition of the death penalty on those convicted of first-degree murder. Fla. Stat. Ann. § 782.04(1) (Supp. 1976-1977). At the same time Florida adopted a new capital-sentencing procedure, patterned in large part on the Model Penal Code. See § 921.141 (Supp. 1976-1977). Under the new statute, if a defendant is found guilty of a capital offense, a separate evidentiary hearing is held before the trial judge and jury to determine his sentence. Evidence may be presented on any matter the judge deems relevant to sentencing and must include matters relating to certain legislatively specified aggravating and mitigating circumstances. Both the prosecution and the defense may present argument on whether the death penalty shall be imposed.

At the conclusion of the hearing the jury is directed to consider "[w]hether sufficient mitigating circumstances exist. . . which outweigh the aggravating circumstances found to exist; and . . . [b]ased on these considerations, whether the defendant should be sentenced to life [imprisonment] or death." §§ 921.141(2)(b) and (c) (Supp. 1976-1977). The jury's verdict is determined by majority vote. It is only advisory; the actual sentence is determined by the trial judge. The Florida Supreme Court has stated, however, that "[i]n

order to sustain a sentence of death following a jury recommendation of life, the facts suggesting a sentence of death should be so clear and convincing that virtually no reasonable person could differ." Tedder v. State, 322 So. 2d 908, 910 (1975). Accord, Thompson v. State, 328 So. 2d 1, 5 (1976). Cf. Spinkellink v. State, 313 So. 2d 666, 671 (1975).

The trial judge is also directed to weigh the statutory aggravating and mitigating circumstances when he determines the sentence to be imposed on a defendant. The statute requires that if the trial court imposes a sentence of death, "it shall set forth in writing its findings upon which the sentence of death is based as to the facts: (a) [t]hat sufficient [statutory] aggravating circumstances exist. . . and (b) [t]hat there are insufficient [statutory] mitigating circumstances . . . to outweigh the aggravating circumstances." § 921.141(3) (Supp. 1976-1977).

The statute provides for automatic review by the Supreme Court of Florida of all cases in which a death sentence has been imposed. § 921.141(4) (Supp. 1976-1977). The law differs from that of Georgia in that it does not require the court to conduct any specific form of review. Since, however, the trial judge must justify the imposition of a death sentence with written findings, meaningful appellate review of each such sentence is made possible, and the Supreme Court of Florida, like its Georgia counterpart, considers its function to be to "[guarantee] that the [aggravating and mitigating] reasons present in one case will reach a similar result to that reached under similar circumstances in another case. . . . If a defendant is sentenced to die, this Court can review that case in light of the other decisions and determine whether or not the punishment is too great." State v. Dixon, 283 So. 2d 1, 10 (1973).

On their face these procedures, like those used in Georgia, appear to meet the constitutional deficiencies identified in Furman. The sentencing authority in Florida, the trial judge, is directed to weigh eight aggravating factors against seven mitigating factors to determine whether the death penalty shall be imposed. This determination requires the trial judge to focus on the circumstances of the crime and the character of the individual defendant. He must, inter alia, consider whether the defendant has a prior criminal record, whether the defendant acted under duress or under the influence of extreme mental or emotional disturbance, whether the defendant's role in the crime was that of a minor accomplice, and whether the defendant's youth argues in favor of a more lenient sentence than might otherwise be imposed. The trial judge must also determine whether the crime was committed in the course of one of several enumerated felonies, whether it was committed for pecuniary gain, whether it was committed to assist in an escape from custody or to prevent a lawful arrest, and whether the crime was especially heinous, atrocious, or cruel. To answer these questions, which are not unlike those considered by a Georgia sentencing jury, see Gregg v. Georgia, ante, at 197, the sentencing judge must focus on the individual circumstances of each homicide and each defendant.

The basic difference between the Florida system and the Georgia system is that in Florida the sentence is determined by the trial judge rather than by the jury. This Court has pointed out that jury sentencing in a capital case can perform an important societal function, Witherspoon v. Illinois, 391 U.S. 510, 519 n. 15 (1968), but it has never suggested that jury sentencing is constitutionally required. And it would appear that judicial sentencing should lead, if anything, to even greater consistency in the imposition at the trial court level of capital punishment, since a trial judge is more experienced in sentencing than a jury, and therefore is better able to impose sentences similar to those imposed in analogous cases.

The Florida capital-sentencing procedures thus seek to assure that the death penalty will not be imposed in an arbitrary or capricious manner. Moreover, to the extent that any risk to the contrary exists, it is minimized by Florida's appellate review system, under which the evidence of the aggravating and mitigating circumstances is reviewed and reweighed by the Supreme Court of Florida "to determine independently whether the imposition of the ultimate penalty is warranted." Songer v. State, 322 So. 2d 481, 484 (1975). See also Sullivan v. State, 303 So. 2d 632, 637 (1974). The Supreme Court of Florida, like that of Georgia, has not hesitated to vacate a death sentence when it has determined that the sentence should not have been imposed. Indeed, it has vacated 8 of the 21 death sentences that it has reviewed to date. See Taylor v. State, 294 So. 2d 648 (1974); Lamadline v. State, 303 So. 2d 17 (1974); Slater v. State, 316 So. 2d 539 (1975); Swan v. State, 322 So. 2d 485 (1975); Tedder v. State, 322 So. 2d 908 (1975); Halliwell v. State, 323 So. 2d 557 (1975); Thompson v. State, 328 So. 2d 1 (1976); Messer v. State, 330 So. 2d 137 (1976).

Under Florida's capital-sentencing procedures, in sum, trial judges are given specific and detailed guidance to assist them in deciding whether to impose a death penalty or imprisonment for life. Moreover, their decisions are reviewed to ensure that they are consistent with other sentences imposed in similar circumstances. Thus, in Florida, as in Georgia, it is no longer true that there is "no meaningful basis for distinguishing the few cases in which [the death penalty] is imposed from the many cases in which it is not." Gregg v. Georgia, ante, at 188, quoting Furman v. Georgia, 408 U.S., at 313 (WHITE, J., concurring). On its face the Florida system thus satisfies the constitutional deficiencies identified in Furman.

B

As in Gregg, the petitioner contends, however, that, while perhaps facially acceptable, the new sentencing procedures in actual effect are merely cosmetic, and that arbitrariness and caprice still pervade the system under which Florida imposes the death penalty.

(1)

The petitioner first argues that arbitrariness is inherent in the Florida criminal justice system because it allows discretion to be exercised at each stage of a criminal proceeding—the prosecutor's decision whether to charge a capital offense in the first place, his decision whether to accept a plea to a lesser offense, the jury's consideration of lesser included offenses, and, after conviction and unsuccessful appeal, the Executive's decision whether to commute a death sentence. As we noted in Gregg, this argument is based on a fundamental misinterpretation of Furman, and we reject it for the reasons expressed in Gregg. See ante, at 199.

(2)

The petitioner next argues that the new Florida sentencing procedures in reality do not eliminate the arbitrary infliction of death that was condemned in Furman. Basically he contends that the statutory aggravating and mitigating circumstances are vague and overbroad, and that the statute gives no guidance as to how the mitigating and aggravating circumstances should be weighed in any specific case.

(a)

Initially the petitioner asserts that the enumerated aggravating and mitigating circumstances are so vague and so broad that virtually "any capital defendant becomes a candidate for the death penalty . . ." In particular, the petitioner attacks the eighth and third statutory aggravating circumstances, which authorize the death penalty to be imposed if the crime is "especially heinous, atrocious, or cruel," or if "[t]he defendant knowingly created a great risk of death to many persons." §§ 921.141 (5)(h), (c) (Supp. 1976-1977). These provisions must be considered as they have been construed by the Supreme Court of Florida.

That court has recognized that while it is arguable "that all killings are atrocious, . . . [s]till, we believe that the Legislature intended something 'especially' heinous, atrocious or cruel when it authorized the death penalty for first degree murder." Tedder v. State, 322 So. 2d, at 910. As a consequence, the court has indicated that the eighth statutory provision is directed only at "the conscienceless or pitiless crime which is unnecessarily torturous to the victim." State v. Dixon, 283 So. 2d, at 9. See also Alford v. State, 307 So. 2d 433, 445 (1975); Halliwell v. State, supra, at 561. We cannot say that the provision, as so construed, provides inadequate guidance to those charged with the duty of recommending or imposing sentences in capital cases. See Gregg v. Georgia, ante, at 200-203.

In the only case, except for the instant case, in which the third aggravating factor— "[t]he defendant knowingly created a great risk of death to many persons"—was found, Alvord v. State, 322 So. 2d 533 (1975), the State Supreme Court held that the defendant created a great risk of death because he "obviously murdered two of the victims in order to avoid a surviving witness to the [first] murder." Id., at 540. As construed by the Supreme Court of Florida these provisions are not impermissibly vague.

(b)

The petitioner next attacks the imprecision of the mitigating circumstances. He argues that whether a defendant acted "under the influence of extreme mental or emotional disturbance," whether a defendant's capacity "to conform his conduct to the requirements of law was substantially impaired," or whether a defendant's participation as an accomplice in a capital felony was "relatively minor," are questions beyond the capacity of a jury or judge to determine. See §§ 921.141 (6)(b), (f), (d) (Supp. 1976-1977).

He also argues that neither a jury nor a judge is capable of deciding how to weigh a defendant's age or determining whether he had a "significant history of prior criminal activity." See §§ 921.141 (6)(g), (a) (Supp. 1976-1977). In a similar vein the petitioner argues that it is not possible to make a rational determination whether there are "sufficient" aggravating circumstances that are not outweighed by the mitigating circumstances, since the state law assigns no specific weight to any of the various circumstances to be considered. See § 921.141 (Supp. 1976-1977).

While these questions and decisions may be hard, they require no more line drawing than is commonly required of a fact-finder in a lawsuit. For example, juries have traditionally evaluated the validity of defenses such as insanity or reduced capacity, both of which involve the same considerations as some of the above-mentioned mitigating circumstances. While the various factors to be considered by the sentencing authorities do not have numerical weights assigned to them, the requirements of Furman are satisfied when the sentencing authority's discretion is guided and channeled by requiring examination of specific factors that argue in favor of or against imposition of the death penalty, thus eliminating total arbitrariness and capriciousness in its imposition.

The directions given to judge and jury by the Florida statute are sufficiently clear and precise to enable the various aggravating circumstances to be weighed against the mitigating ones. As a result, the trial court's sentencing discretion is guided and channeled by a system that focuses on the circumstances of each individual homicide and individual defendant in deciding whether the death penalty is to be imposed.

(c)

Finally, the Florida statute has a provision designed to assure that the death penalty will not be imposed on a capriciously selected group of convicted defendants. The Supreme Court of Florida reviews each death sentence to ensure that similar results are reached in similar cases.

Nonetheless the petitioner attacks the Florida appellate review process because the role of the Supreme Court of Florida in reviewing death sentences is necessarily subjective and unpredictable. While it may be true that that court has not chosen to formulate a rigid objective test as its standard of review for all cases, it does not follow that the appellate review process is ineffective or arbitrary. In fact, it is apparent that the Florida court has undertaken responsibly to perform its function of death sentence review with a maximum of rationality and consistency. For example, it has several times compared the circumstances of a case under review with those of previous cases in which it has assessed the imposition of death sentences. See, e.g., Alford v. State, 307 So. 2d, at 445; Alvord v. State, 322 So. 2d, at 540-541. By following this procedure the Florida court has in effect adopted the type of proportionality review mandated by the Georgia statute. Cf. Gregg v. Georgia, ante, at 204-206. And any suggestion that the Florida court engages in only cursory or rubber-stamp review of death penalty cases is totally controverted by the fact that it has vacated over one-third of the death sentences that have come before it. See supra, at 253.

IV

Florida, like Georgia, has responded to Furman by enacting legislation that passes constitutional muster. That legislation provides that after a person is convicted of first-degree murder, there shall be an informed, focused, guided, and objective inquiry into the question whether he should be sentenced to death. If a death sentence is imposed, the sentencing authority articulates in writing the statutory reasons that led to its decision. Those reasons, and the evidence supporting them, are conscientiously reviewed by a court which, because of its statewide jurisdiction, can assure consistency, fairness, and rationality in the evenhanded operation of the state law. As in Georgia, this system serves to assure that sentences of death will not be "wantonly" or "freakishly" imposed. See Furman v. Georgia, 408 U.S., at 310 (STEWART, J., concurring). Accordingly, the judgment before us is affirmed.

It is so ordered.

MR. JUSTICE WHITE, with whom THE CHIEF JUSTICE and MR. JUSTICE REHNQUIST join, concurring in the judgment.

There is no need to repeat the statement of the facts of this case and of the statutory procedure under which the death penalty was imposed, both of which are described in detail in the opinion of MR. JUSTICE STEWART, MR. JUSTICE POWELL, and MR. JUSTICE STEVENS. I agree with them, see Parts III-B (2)(a) and (b), ante, at 255-258, that although the statutory aggravating and mitigating circumstances are not susceptible of mechanical application, they are by no means so vague and overbroad as to leave the discretion of the sentencing authority unfettered. Under Florida law, the sentencing judge is required to impose the death penalty on all first-degree murderers as to whom the statutory aggravating factors outweigh the mitigating factors. There is good reason to anticipate, then, that as to certain categories of murderers, the penalty will not be imposed freakishly or rarely but will be imposed with regularity; and consequently it cannot be said that the death penalty in Florida as to those categories has ceased "to be a credible deterrent or measurably to contribute to any other end of punishment in the criminal justice system." Furman v. Georgia, 408 U.S. 238, 311 (1972) (WHITE, J., concurring). Accordingly, the Florida statutory scheme for imposing the death penalty does not run afoul of this Court's holding in Furman v. Georgia.

For the reasons set forth in my opinion concurring in the judgments in Gregg v. Georgia, ante, at 224-225, and my dissenting opinion in Roberts v. Louisiana, post, at 348-350, this conclusion is not undercut by the possibility that some murderers may escape the death penalty solely through exercise of prosecutorial discretion or executive clemency. For the reasons set forth in my dissenting opinion in Roberts v. Louisiana, post, at 350-356, I also reject petitioner's argument that under the Eighth Amendment the death penalty may never be imposed under any circumstances.

I concur in the judgment of affirmance.

MR. JUSTICE BLACKMUN, concurring in the judgment.

I concur in the judgment.

MILLS
v.
ROGERS

**457 U.S. 291; 102 S. Ct. 2442;
73 L. Ed. 2d 16 (1982)**

JUSTICE POWELL delivered the opinion of the Court.

The Court granted certiorari in this case to determine whether involuntarily committed mental patients have a constitutional right to refuse treatment with antipsychotic drugs.

I

This litigation began on April 27, 1975, when respondent Rubie Rogers and six other persons filed suit against various officials and staff of the May and Austin Units of the Boston State Hospital. The plaintiffs all were present or former mental patients at the institution. During their period of institutionalization all had been forced to accept unwanted treatment with antipsychotic drugs. Alleging that forcible administration of these drugs violated rights protected by the Constitution

of the United States, the plaintiffs—respondents here—sought compensatory and punitive damages and injunctive relief.

The District Court certified the case as a class action. See Rogers v. Okin, 478 F.Supp. 1342, 1352, n. 1 (Mass. 1979). Although denying relief in damages, the court held that mental patients enjoy constitutionally protected liberty and privacy interests in deciding for themselves whether to submit to drug therapy . . .

The Court of Appeals for the First Circuit affirmed in part and reversed in part. Rogers v. Okin, 634 F.2d 650 (1980). It agreed that mental patients have a constitutionally protected interest in deciding for themselves whether to undergo treatment with antipsychotic drugs . . .

* * *

Because the judgment of the Court of Appeals involved constitutional issues of potentially broad significance, we granted certiorari. Okin v. Rogers, 451 U.S. 906 (1981).

II

A

The principal question on which we granted certiorari is whether an involuntarily committed mental patient has a constitutional right to refuse treatment with antipsychotic drugs. This question has both substantive and procedural aspects. See 634 F.2d, at 656, 661; Rennie v. Klein, 653 F.2d 836, 841 (CA3 1981). The parties agree that the Constitution recognizes a liberty interest in avoiding the unwanted administration of antipsychotic drugs. Assuming that they are correct in this respect, the substantive issue involves a definition of that protected constitutional interest, as well as identification of the conditions under which competing state interests might outweigh it. See Youngberg v. Romeo, post, at 319-320; Bell v. Wolfish, 441 U.S. 520, 560 (1979); Roe v. Wade, 410 U.S. 113, 147-154 (1973); Jacobson v. Massachusetts, 197 U.S. 11, 25-27 (1905). The procedural issue concerns the minimum procedures required by the Constitution for determining that the individual's liberty interest actually is outweighed in a particular instance. See Parham v. J. R., 442 U.S. 584, 606 (1979); Mathews v. Eldridge, 424 U.S. 319, 335 (1976).

As a practical matter both the substantive and procedural issues are intertwined with questions of state law. . . . In theory a court might be able to define the scope of a patient's federally protected liberty interest without reference to state law. . . . For purposes of determining actual rights and obligations, however, questions of state law cannot be avoided. Within our federal system the substantive rights provided by the Federal Constitution define only a minimum. State law may recognize liberty interests more extensive than those independently protected by the Federal Constitution. See Greenholtz v. Nebraska Penal Inmates, 442 U.S. 1, 7, 12 (1979); Oregon v. Hass, 420 U.S. 714, 719 (1975); see also Brennan, State Constitutions and the Protection of Individual Rights, 90 Harv. L. Rev. 489 (1977). If so, the broader state protections would define the actual substantive rights possessed by a person living within that State.

Where a State creates liberty interests broader than those protected directly by the Federal Constitution, the procedures mandated to protect the federal substantive interests also might fail to determine the actual procedural rights and duties of persons within the State. Because state-created liberty interests are entitled to the protection of the federal Due Process Clause, see, e.g., Vitek v. Jones, supra, at 488; Greenholtz v. Nebraska Penal Inmates, supra, at 7, the full scope of a patient's due process rights may depend in part on the substantive liberty interests created by state as well as federal law. Moreover, a State may confer procedural protections of liberty interests that extend beyond those minimally required by the Constitution of the United States. If a State does so, the minimal requirements of the Federal Constitution would not be controlling, and would not need to be identified in order to determine the legal rights and duties of persons within that State.

B

Roughly five months after the Court of Appeals decided this case, and shortly after this Court granted certiorari, the Supreme Judicial Court of Massachusetts announced its decision in Guardianship of Roe, 383 Mass. 415, 421 N. E. 2d 40 (1981) (Roe). Roe involved the right of a noninstitutionalized but mentally incompetent person to refuse treatment with antipsychotic drugs. Expressly resting its decision on the common law of Massachusetts as well as on the Federal Constitution, Massachusetts' highest court held in Roe that a person has a protected liberty interest in "[deciding] for himself whether to submit to the serious and potentially harmful medical treatment that is represented by the administration of antipsychotic drugs." Id., at 433, n. 9, 421 N. E. 2d, at 51, n. 9. The court found—again apparently on the basis of the common law of Massachusetts as well as the Constitution of the United States—that this interest of the individual is of such importance that it can be overcome only by "an overwhelming State interest." Id., at 434, 421 N. E. 2d, at 51. Roe further held that a person does not forfeit his protected liberty interest by virtue of becoming incompetent, but rather remains entitled to have his "substituted judgment" exercised on his behalf. Ibid. Defining this "substituted judgment" as one for which "[no] medical expertise is required," id., at 435, 421 N. E. 2d, at 52, the Massachusetts Supreme Judicial Court required a judicial determination of substituted judgment before drugs could be administered in a particular instance, except possibly in cases of medical emergency.

C

. . . [R]espondents have argued in this Court that Roe may influence the correct disposition of the case at hand. We agree.

Especially in the wake of Roe, it is distinctly possible that Massachusetts recognizes liberty interests of persons adjudged incompetent that are broader than those protected directly by the Constitution of the United States. . . . If the state interest is broader, the substantive protection that the Constitution affords against the involuntary administration of antipsychotic drugs would not determine the actual substantive rights and duties of persons in the State of Massachusetts.

Procedurally, it also is quite possible that a Massachusetts court, as a matter of state law, would require greater protection of relevant liberty interests than the minimum adequate to survive scrutiny under the Due Process Clause. . . . Again on this hypothesis state law would be dispositive of the procedural rights and duties of the parties to this case.

Finally, even if state procedural law itself remains unchanged by Roe, the federally mandated procedures will depend on the nature and weight of the state interests, as well as the individual interests, that are asserted. To identify the nature and scope of state interests that are to be balanced against an individual's liberty interests, this Court may look to state law. See, e.g., Roe v. Wade, 410 U.S., at 148, and n. 42, 151, and nn. 48-50; Ingraham v. Wright, 430 U.S. 651, 661-663 (1977). Here we view the underlying state-law predicate for weighing asserted state interests as being put into doubt, if not altered, by Roe.

D

* * *

Until certain questions have been answered, we think it would be inappropriate for us to attempt to weigh or even to identify relevant liberty interests that might be derived directly from the Constitution, independently of state law. It is this Court's settled policy to avoid unnecessary decisions of constitutional issues. See, e.g., City of Mesquite v. Aladdin's Castle, Inc., 455 U.S. 283, 294 (1982); New York Transit Authority v. Beazer, 440 U.S. 568, 582-583, n. 22 (1979); Poe v. Ullman, 367 U.S. 497, 502-509 (1961); Ashwander v. TVA, 297 U.S. 288, 341, 347-348 (1936) (Brandeis, J., concurring). This policy is supported, although not always required, by the prohibition against advisory opinions. Cf. United States v. Hastings, 296 U.S. 188, 193 (1935) (review of one basis for a decision supported by another basis not subject to examination would represent "an expression of an abstract opinion").

In applying this policy of restraint, we are uncertain here which if any constitutional issues now must be decided to resolve the controversy between the parties. In the wake of Roe, we cannot say with confidence that adjudication based solely on identification of federal constitutional interests would determine the actual rights and duties of the parties before us. And, as an additional cause for hesitation, our reading of the opinion of the Court of Appeals has left us in doubt as to the extent to which state issues were argued below and the degree to which the court's holdings may rest on subsequently altered state-law foundations.

Because of its greater familiarity both with the record and with Massachusetts law, the Court of Appeals is better situated than we to determine how Roe may have changed the law of Massachusetts and how any changes may affect this case. Accordingly, we think it appropriate for the Court of Appeals to determine in the first instance whether Roe requires revision of its holdings or whether it may call for the certification of potentially dispositive state-law questions to the Supreme Judicial Court of Massachusetts, see Bellotti v. Baird, 428 U.S. 132, 150-151 (1976). The Court of Appeals also may consider whether this is a case in which abstention now is appropriate. See generally Colorado River Water Conservation Dist. v. United States, 424 U.S. 800, 813-819 (1976).

The judgment of the Court of Appeals is therefore vacated, and the case is remanded for further proceedings consistent with this opinion.

So ordered.

YOUNGBERG
v.
ROMEO

457 U.S. 307; 102 S. Ct. 2452; 73 L. Ed. 2d 28 (1982)

JUSTICE POWELL delivered the opinion of the Court.

The question presented is whether respondent, involuntarily committed to a state institution for the mentally retarded, has substantive rights under the Due Process Clause of the Fourteenth Amendment to (i) safe conditions of confinement; (ii) freedom from bodily restraints; and (iii) training or "habilitation."

Respondent sued under 42 U.S.C. § 1983 three administrators of the institution, claiming damages for the alleged breach of his constitutional rights.

I

Respondent Nicholas Romeo is profoundly retarded. Although 33 years old, he has the mental capacity of an 18-month-old child, with an I.Q. between 8 and 10. He cannot talk and lacks the most basic self-care skills. Until he was 26, respondent lived with his parents in Philadelphia. But after the death of his father in May 1974, his mother was unable to care for him. Within two weeks of the father's death, respondent's mother sought his temporary admission to a nearby Pennsylvania hospital.

Shortly thereafter, she asked the Philadelphia County Court of Common Pleas to admit Romeo to a state facility on a permanent basis. Her petition to the court explained that she was unable to care for Romeo or control his violence. As part of the commitment process, Romeo was examined by a physician and a psychologist. They both certified that respondent was severely retarded and unable to care for himself. App. 21a-22a and 28a-29a. On June 11, 1974, the Court of Common Pleas committed respondent to the Pennhurst State School and Hospital, pursuant to the applicable involuntary commitment provision of the Pennsylvania Mental Health and Mental Retardation Act, Pa. Stat. Ann., Tit. 50, § 4406(b) (Purdon 1969).

At Pennhurst, Romeo was injured on numerous occasions, both by his own violence and by the reactions of other residents to him. Respondent's mother became concerned about these injuries. After objecting to respondent's treatment several times, she filed this complaint on November 4, 1976, in the United States District Court for the Eastern District of Pennsylvania as his next friend. The complaint alleged that "[during] the period July, 1974 to the present, plaintiff has suffered injuries on at least sixty-three occasions." The complaint originally sought damages and injunctive relief from Pennhurst's director and two supervisors; it alleged that these officials knew, or should have known, that Romeo was suffering

injuries and that they failed to institute appropriate preventive procedures, thus violating his rights under the Eighth and Fourteenth Amendments.

Thereafter, in late 1976, Romeo was transferred from his ward to the hospital for treatment of a broken arm. While in the infirmary, and by order of a doctor, he was physically restrained during portions of each day. These restraints were ordered by Dr. Gabroy, not a defendant here, to protect Romeo and others in the hospital, some of whom were in traction or were being treated intravenously. Although respondent normally would have returned to his ward when his arm healed, the parties to this litigation agreed that he should remain in the hospital due to the pending lawsuit. 5 id., at 248; 6 id., at 57-58 and 137. Nevertheless, in December 1977, a second amended complaint was filed alleging that the defendants were restraining respondent for prolonged periods on a routine basis. The second amended complaint also added a claim for damages to compensate Romeo for the defendants' failure to provide him with appropriate "treatment or programs for his mental retardation." All claims for injunctive relief were dropped prior to trial because respondent is a member of the class seeking such relief in another action.

An 8-day jury trial was held in April 1978. Petitioners introduced evidence that respondent participated in several programs teaching basic self-care skills. A comprehensive behavior-modification program was designed by staff members to reduce Romeo's aggressive behavior, but that program was never implemented because of his mother's objections. Respondent introduced evidence of his injuries and of conditions in his unit.

At the close of the trial, the court instructed the jury that "if any or all of the defendants were aware of and failed to take all reasonable steps to prevent repeated attacks upon Nicholas Romeo," such failure deprived him of constitutional rights. App. 73a. The jury also was instructed that if the defendants shackled Romeo or denied him treatment "as a punishment for filing this lawsuit," his constitutional rights were violated under the Eighth Amendment. Id., at 73a-75a. Finally, the jury was instructed that only if they found the defendants "[deliberately] [indifferent] to the serious medical [and psychological] needs" of Romeo could they find that his Eighth and Fourteenth Amendment rights had been violated. Id., at 74a-75a. The jury returned a verdict for the defendants, on which judgment was entered.

The Court of Appeals for the Third Circuit, sitting en banc, reversed and remanded for a new trial. 644 F.2d 147 (1980). The court held that the Eighth Amendment, prohibiting cruel and unusual punishment of those convicted of crimes, was not an appropriate source for determining the rights of the involuntarily committed. Rather, the Fourteenth Amendment and the liberty interest protected by that Amendment provided the proper constitutional basis for these rights. In applying the Fourteenth Amendment, the court found that the involuntarily committed retain liberty interests in freedom of movement and in personal security. These were "fundamental liberties" that can be limited only by an "overriding, non-punitive" state interest. Id., at 157-158 (footnote omitted). It further found that the involuntarily committed have a liberty interest in habilitation designed to "treat" their mental retardation. Id., at 164-170.

* * *

We granted the petition for certiorari because of the importance of the question presented to the administration of state institutions for the mentally retarded. 451 U.S. 982 (1981).

II

We consider here for the first time the substantive rights of involuntarily committed mentally retarded persons under the Fourteenth Amendment to the Constitution. In this case, respondent has been committed under the laws of Pennsylvania, and he does not challenge the commitment. Rather, he argues that he has a constitutionally protected liberty interest in safety, freedom of movement, and training within the institution; and that petitioners infringed these rights by failing to provide constitutionally required conditions of confinement.

The mere fact that Romeo has been committed under proper procedures does not deprive him of all substantive liberty interests under the Fourteenth Amendment. See, e.g., Vitek v. Jones, 445 U.S. 480, 491-494 (1980). Indeed, the State concedes that respondent has a right to adequate food, shelter, clothing, and medical care. We must decide whether liberty interests also exist in safety, freedom of movement, and training. If such interests do exist, we must further decide whether they have been infringed in this case.

A

Respondent's first two claims involve liberty interests recognized by prior decisions of this Court, interests that involuntary commitment proceedings do not extinguish. The first is a claim to safe conditions. In the past, this Court has noted that the right to personal security constitutes a "historic liberty interest" protected substantively by the Due Process Clause. Ingraham v. Wright, 430 U.S. 651, 673 (1977). And that right is not extinguished by lawful confinement, even for penal purposes. See Hutto v. Finney, 437 U.S. 678 (1978). If it is cruel and unusual punishment to hold convicted criminals in unsafe conditions, it must be unconstitutional to confine the involuntarily committed—who may not be punished at all—in unsafe conditions.

Next, respondent claims a right to freedom from bodily restraint. In other contexts, the existence of such an interest is clear in the prior decisions of this Court. Indeed, "[liberty] from bodily restraint always has been recognized as the core of the liberty protected by the Due Process Clause from arbitrary governmental action." Greenholtz v. Nebraska Penal Inmates, 442 U.S. 1, 18 (1979) (POWELL, J., concurring in part and dissenting in part). This interest survives criminal conviction and incarceration. Similarly, it must also survive involuntary commitment.

B

Respondent's remaining claim is more troubling. In his words, he asserts a "constitutional right to minimally adequate habilitation." Brief for Respondent 8, 23, 45. This is a substantive due process claim that is said to be grounded in the liberty component of the Due Process Clause of the Fourteenth Amendment. The term "habilitation," used in psychiatry, is not defined precisely or consistently in the opinions below or in the briefs of the parties or the amici. As noted previously in n. 1, supra, the term refers to "training and development of needed skills." Respondent emphasizes that the right he asserts is for "minimal" training, see Brief for Respondent 34, and he would leave the type and extent of training to be determined on a case-by-case basis "in light of present medical or other scientific knowledge," id., at 45.

In addressing the asserted right to training, we start from established principles. As a general matter, a State is under no constitutional duty to provide substantive services for those within its border. See Harris v. McRae, 448 U.S. 297, 318 (1980) (publicly funded abortions); Maher v. Roe, 432 U.S. 464, 469 (1977) (medical treatment). When a person is institutionalized—and wholly dependent on the State—it is conceded by petitioners that a duty to provide certain services and care does exist, although even then a State necessarily has considerable discretion in determining the nature and scope of its responsibilities. See Richardson v. Belcher, 404 U.S. 78, 83-84 (1971); Dandridge v. Williams, 397 U.S. 471, 478 (1970). Nor must a State "choose between attacking every aspect of a problem or not attacking the problem at all." Id., at 486-487.

Respondent, in light of the severe character of his retardation, concedes that no amount of training will make possible his release. And he does not argue that if he were still at home, the State would have an obligation to provide training at its expense. The record reveals that respondent's primary needs are bodily safety and a minimum of physical restraint, and respondent clearly claims training related to these needs. As we have recognized that there is a constitutionally protected liberty interest in safety and freedom from restraint, supra, at 315-316, training may be necessary to avoid unconstitutional infringement of those rights. On the basis of the record before us, it is quite uncertain whether respondent seeks any "habilita-

tion" or training unrelated to safety and freedom from bodily restraints. In his brief to this Court, Romeo indicates that even the self-care programs he seeks are needed to reduce his aggressive behavior. See Brief for Respondent 21-22, 50. And in his offer of proof to the trial court, respondent repeatedly indicated that, if allowed to testify, his experts would show that additional training programs, including self-care programs, were needed to reduce his aggressive behavior. App. to Pet. for Cert. 98a-104a. If, as seems the case, respondent seeks only training related to safety and freedom from restraints, this case does not present the difficult question whether a mentally retarded person, involuntarily committed to a state institution, has some general constitutional right to training per se, even when no type or amount of training would lead to freedom.

* * *

. . . [W]e . . . conclude that respondent's liberty interests require the State to provide minimally adequate or reasonable training to ensure safety and freedom from undue restraint. In view of the kinds of treatment sought by respondent and the evidence of record, we need go no further in this case.

III

A

We have established that Romeo retains liberty interests in safety and freedom from bodily restraint. Yet these interests are not absolute; indeed to some extent they are in conflict. In operating an institution such as Pennhurst, there are occasions in which it is necessary for the State to restrain the movement of residents—for example, to protect them as well as others from violence. Similar restraints may also be appropriate in a training program. And an institution cannot protect its residents from all danger of violence if it is to permit them to have any freedom of movement. The question then is not simply whether a liberty interest has been infringed but whether the extent or nature of the restraint or lack of absolute safety is such as to violate due process.

In determining whether a substantive right protected by the Due Process Clause has been violated, it is necessary to balance "the liberty of the individual" and "the demands of an organized society." Poe v. Ullman, 367 U.S. 497, 542 (1961) (Harlan, J., dissenting). In seeking this balance in other cases, the Court has weighed the individual's interest in liberty against the State's asserted reasons for restraining individual liberty. In Bell v. Wolfish, 441 U.S. 520 (1979), for example, we considered a challenge to pretrial detainees' confinement conditions. We agreed that the detainees, not yet convicted of the crime charged, could not be punished. But we upheld those restrictions on liberty that were reasonably related to legitimate government objectives and not tantamount to punishment. See id., at 539. We have taken a similar approach in deciding procedural due process challenges to civil commitment proceedings. In Parham v. J. R., 442 U.S. 584 (1979), for example, we considered a challenge to state procedures for commitment of a minor with parental consent. In determining that procedural due process did not mandate an adversarial hearing, we weighed the liberty interest of the individual against the legitimate interests of the State, including the fiscal and administrative burdens additional procedures would entail. Id., at 599-600.

Accordingly, whether respondent's constitutional rights have been violated must be determined by balancing his liberty interests against the relevant state interests. If there is to be any uniformity in protecting these interests, this balancing cannot be left to the unguided discretion of a judge or jury. We therefore turn to consider the proper standard for determining whether a State adequately has protected the rights of the involuntarily committed mentally retarded.

B

We think the standard articulated by Chief Judge Seitz affords the necessary guidance and reflects the proper balance between the legitimate interests of the State and the rights of the involuntarily committed to reasonable conditions of safety and freedom from unreasonable restraints. He would have held that "the Constitution only requires that the courts make certain that professional judg-

ment in fact was exercised. It is not appropriate for the courts to specify which of several professionally acceptable choices should have been made." 644 F.2d, at 178. Persons who have been involuntarily committed are entitled to more considerate treatment and conditions of confinement than criminals whose conditions of confinement are designed to punish. Cf. Estelle v. Gamble, 429 U.S. 97, 104 (1976). At the same time, this standard is lower than the "compelling" or "substantial" necessity tests the Court of Appeals would require a State to meet to justify use of restraints or conditions of less than absolute safety. We think this requirement would place an undue burden on the administration of institutions such as Pennhurst and also would restrict unnecessarily the exercise of professional judgment as to the needs of residents.

Moreover, we agree that respondent is entitled to minimally adequate training. In this case, the minimally adequate training required by the Constitution is such training as may be reasonable in light of respondent's liberty interests in safety and freedom from unreasonable restraints. In determining what is "reasonable"—in this and in any case presenting a claim for training by a State—we emphasize that courts must show deference to the judgment exercised by a qualified professional. By so limiting judicial review of challenges to conditions in state institutions, interference by the federal judiciary with the internal operations of these institutions should be minimized. Moreover, there certainly is no reason to think judges or juries are better qualified than appropriate professionals in making such decisions. See Parham v. J. R., supra, at 607; Bell v. Wolfish, supra, at 544 (Courts should not "second-guess the expert administrators on matters on which they are better informed"). For these reasons, the decision, if made by a professional, is presumptively valid; liability may be imposed only when the decision by the professional is such a substantial departure from accepted professional judgment, practice, or standards as to demonstrate that the person responsible actually did not base the decision on such a judgment. In an action for damages against a professional in his individual capacity, however, the professional will not be liable if he was unable to satisfy his normal professional standards because of budgetary constraints; in such a situation, good-faith immunity would bar liability. See n. 13, supra.

IV

In deciding this case, we have weighed those postcommitment interests cognizable as liberty interests under the Due Process Clause of the Fourteenth Amendment against legitimate state interests and in light of the constraints under which most state institutions necessarily operate. We repeat that the State concedes a duty to provide adequate food, shelter, clothing, and medical care. These are the essentials of the care that the State must provide. The State also has the unquestioned duty to provide reasonable safety for all residents and personnel within the institution. And it may not restrain residents except when and to the extent professional judgment deems this necessary to assure such safety or to provide needed training. In this case, therefore, the State is under a duty to provide respondent with such training as an appropriate professional would consider reasonable to ensure his safety and to facilitate his ability to function free from bodily restraints. It may well be unreasonable not to provide training when training could significantly reduce the need for restraints or the likelihood of violence.

Respondent thus enjoys constitutionally protected interests in conditions of reasonable care and safety, reasonably nonrestrictive confinement conditions, and such training as may be required by these interests. Such conditions of confinement would comport fully with the purpose of respondent's commitment. Cf. Jackson v. Indiana, 406 U.S. 715, 738 (1972); see n. 27, supra. In determining whether the State has met its obligations in these respects, decisions made by the appropriate professional are entitled to a presumption of correctness. Such a presumption is necessary to enable institutions of this type—often, unfortunately, overcrowded and understaffed—to continue to function. A single professional may have to make decisions with respect to a number of residents with widely varying needs and problems in the course of a normal day. The

administrators, and particularly professional personnel, should not be required to make each decision in the shadow of an action for damages.

In this case, we conclude that the jury was erroneously instructed on the assumption that the proper standard of liability was that of the Eighth Amendment. We vacate the decision of the Court of Appeals and remand for further proceedings consistent with this decision.

So ordered.

TURNER
v.
SAFLEY

482 U.S. 78; 107 S. Ct. 2254;
96 L. Ed. 2d 64 (1987)

JUSTICE O'CONNOR delivered the opinion of the Court.

This case requires us to determine the constitutionality of regulations promulgated by the Missouri Division of Corrections relating to inmate marriages and inmate-to-inmate correspondence. The Court of Appeals for the Eighth Circuit, applying a strict scrutiny analysis, concluded that the regulations violate respondents' constitutional rights. We hold that a lesser standard of scrutiny is appropriate in determining the constitutionality of the prison rules. Applying that standard, we uphold the validity of the correspondence regulation, but we conclude that the marriage restriction cannot be sustained.

I

Respondents brought this class action for injunctive relief and damages in the United States District Court for the Western District of Missouri. The regulations challenged in the complaint were in effect at all prisons within the jurisdiction of the Missouri Division of Corrections. This litigation focused, however, on practices at the Renz Correctional Institution (Renz), located in Cedar City, Missouri. The Renz prison population includes both male and female prisoners of varying security levels. Most of the female prisoners at Renz are classified as medium or maximum security inmates, while most of the male prisoners are classified as minimum security offenders. Renz is used on occasion to provide protective custody for inmates from other prisons in the Missouri system. The facility originally was built as a minimum security prison farm, and it still has a minimum security perimeter without guard towers or walls.

* * *

The challenged marriage regulation, which was promulgated while this litigation was pending, permits an inmate to marry only with the permission of the superintendent of the prison, and provides that such approval should be given only "when there are compelling reasons to do so." App. 47. The term "compelling" is not defined, but prison officials testified at trial that generally only a pregnancy or the birth of an illegitimate child would be considered a compelling reason. See 586 F.Supp., at 592. Prior to the promulgation of this rule, the applicable regulation did not obligate Missouri Division of Corrections officials to assist an inmate who wanted to get married, but it also did not specifically authorize the superintendent of an institution to prohibit inmates from getting married. Ibid.

* * *

The District Court issued a memorandum opinion and order finding . . . the . . . marriage regulations unconstitutional. The court, relying on Procunier v. Martinez, 416 U.S. 396, 413-414 (1974), applied a strict scrutiny standard. It held the marriage regulation to be an unconstitutional infringement upon the fundamental right to marry because it was far more restrictive than was either reasonable or essential for the protection of the State's interests in security and rehabilitation. . . .

* * *

B

* * *

In support of the marriage regulation, petitioners first suggest that the rule does not deprive prisoners of a constitutionally protected right. They concede that the decision to marry is a fundamental right under Zablocki v. Redhail, 434 U.S. 374 (1978), and Loving v. Virginia, 388 U.S. 1 (1967), but they imply that a different rule should obtain "in . . . a prison forum." See Brief for Petitioners 38, n. 6. Petitioners then argue that even if the regulation burdens inmates' constitutional rights, the restriction should be tested under a reasonableness standard. They urge that the restriction is reasonably related to legitimate security and rehabilitation concerns.

We disagree with petitioners that Zablocki does not apply to prison inmates. It is settled that a prison inmate "retains those [constitutional] rights that are not inconsistent with his status as a prisoner or with the legitimate penological objectives of the corrections system." Pell v. Procunier, supra, at 822. The right to marry, like many other rights, is subject to substantial restrictions as a result of incarceration. Many important attributes of marriage remain, however, after taking into account the limitations imposed by prison life. First, inmate marriages, like others, are expressions of emotional support and public commitment. These elements are an important and significant aspect of the marital relationship. In addition, many religions recognize marriage as having spiritual significance; for some inmates and their spouses, therefore, the commitment of marriage may be an exercise of religious faith as well as an expression of personal dedication. Third, most inmates eventually will be released by parole or commutation, and therefore most inmate marriages are formed in the expectation that they ultimately will be fully consummated. Finally, marital status often is a pre-condition to the receipt of government benefits (e.g., Social Security benefits), property rights (e.g., tenancy by the entirety, inheritance rights), and other, less tangible benefits (e.g., legitimation of children born out of wedlock). These incidents of marriage, like the religious and personal aspects of the marriage commitment, are unaffected by the fact of confinement or the pursuit of legitimate corrections goals.

Taken together, we conclude that these remaining elements are sufficient to form a constitutionally protected marital relationship in the prison context. Our decision in Butler v. Wilson, 415 U.S. 953 (1974), summarily affirming Johnson v. Rockefeller, 365 F.Supp. 377 (SDNY 1973), is not to the contrary. That case involved a prohibition on marriage only for inmates sentenced to life imprisonment; and, importantly, denial of the right was part of the punishment for crime. See id., at 381-382 (Lasker, J., concurring in part and dissenting in part) (asserted governmental interest of punishing crime sufficiently important to justify deprivation of right); see generally Mandel v. Bradley, 432 U.S. 173, 176 (1977) ("Because a summary affirmance is an affirmance of the judgment only, the rationale of the affirmance may not be gleaned solely from the opinion below").

The Missouri marriage regulation prohibits inmates from marrying unless the prison superintendent has approved the marriage after finding that there are compelling reasons for doing so. As noted previously, generally only pregnancy or birth of a child is considered a "compelling reason" to approve a marriage. In determining whether this regulation impermissibly burdens the right to marry, we note initially that the regulation prohibits marriages between inmates and civilians, as well as marriages between inmates. See Brief for Petitioners 40. Although not urged by respondents, this implication of the interests of nonprisoners may support application of the Martinez standard, because the regulation may entail a "consequential restriction on the [constitutional] rights of those who are not prisoners." See Procunier v. Martinez, 416 U.S., at 409. We need not reach this question, however, because even under the reasonable relationship test, the marriage regulation does not withstand scrutiny.

Petitioners have identified both security and rehabilitation concerns in support of the marriage prohibition. The security concern emphasized by petitioners is that "love triangles" might lead to violent confrontations between inmates. See Brief for Petitioners 13, 36, 39. With respect to rehabilitation, prison officials testified that female prisoners often were subject to abuse at home or were overly dependent on male figures, and that this dependence or abuse was connected to the crimes they had committed. The superintendent at Renz, petitioner William Turner, testified that in his view, these women prisoners needed to concentrate on developing skills of self-reliance, 1 id., at 80-81, and that the prohibition on marriage furthered this rehabilitative goal. Petitioners emphasize that the prohibition on marriage should be understood in light of Superintendent Turner's experience with several ill-advised marriage requests from female inmates. Brief for Petitioners 32-34.

We conclude that on this record, the Missouri prison regulation, as written, is not reasonably related to these penological interests. No doubt legitimate security concerns may require placing reasonable restrictions upon an inmate's right to marry, and may justify requiring approval of the superintendent. The Missouri regulation, however, represents an exaggerated response to such security objectives. There are obvious, easy alternatives to the Missouri regulation that accommodate the right to marry while imposing a de minimis burden on the pursuit of security objectives. See, e.g., 28 CFR § 551.10 (1986) (marriage by inmates in federal prison generally permitted, but not if warden finds that it presents a threat to security or order of institution, or to public safety). We are aware of no place in the record where prison officials testified that such ready alternatives would not fully satisfy their security concerns. Moreover, with respect to the security concern emphasized in petitioners' brief—the creation of "love triangles"—petitioners have pointed to nothing in the record suggesting that the marriage regulation was viewed as preventing such entanglements. Common sense likewise suggests that there is no logical connection between the marriage restriction and the formation of love triangles: surely in prisons housing both male and female prisoners, inmate rivalries are as likely to develop without a formal marriage ceremony as with one. Finally, this is not an instance where the "ripple effect" on the security of fellow inmates and prison staff justifies a broad restriction on inmates' rights—indeed, where the inmate wishes to marry a civilian, the decision to marry (apart from the logistics of the wedding ceremony) is a completely private one.

Nor, on this record, is the marriage restriction reasonably related to the articulated rehabilitation goal. First, in requiring refusal of permission absent a finding of a compelling reason to allow the marriage, the rule sweeps much more broadly than can be explained by petitioners' penological objectives. Missouri prison officials testified that generally they had experienced no problem with the marriage of male inmates, and the District Court found that such marriages had routinely been allowed as a matter of practice at Missouri correctional institutions prior to adoption of the rule, 586 F.Supp., at 592. The proffered justification thus does not explain the adoption of a rule banning marriages by these inmates. Nor does it account for the prohibition on inmate marriages to civilians. Missouri prison officials testified that generally they had no objection to inmate-civilian marriages, and Superintendent Turner testified that he usually did not object to the marriage of either male or female prisoners to civilians, 2 id., at 141-142. The rehabilitation concern appears from the record to have been centered almost exclusively on female inmates marrying other inmates or ex-felons; it does not account for the ban on inmate-civilian marriages.

Moreover, although not necessary to the disposition of this case, we note that on this record the rehabilitative objective asserted to support the regulation itself is suspect. Of the several female inmates whose marriage requests were discussed by prison officials at trial, only one was refused on the basis of fostering excessive dependency. The District Court found that the Missouri prison system operated on the basis of excessive paternalism in that the proposed marriages of all female inmates were scrutinized carefully even before adoption of the current regulation—only one was approved at Renz in the period from 1979-1983—whereas the marriages of male inmates during the same period were routinely approved. That kind of lop-sided rehabilitation concern cannot provide a justification for the broad Missouri marriage rule.

It is undisputed that Missouri prison officials may regulate the time and circumstances under which the marriage ceremony itself takes place. See Brief for Respondents 5. On this record, however, the almost complete ban on the decision to marry is not reasonably related to legitimate penological objectives. We conclude, therefore, that the Missouri marriage regulation is facially invalid.

* * *

ESTELLE
v.
GAMBLE

429 U.S. 97; 97 S. Ct. 285;
50 L. Ed. 2d 251 (1976)

JUSTICE MARSHALL delivered the opinion of the Court.

Respondent J. W. Gamble, an inmate of the Texas Department of Corrections, was injured on November 9, 1973, while performing a prison work assignment. On February 11, 1974, he instituted this civil rights action under 42 U.S.C. § 1983, complaining of the treatment he received after the injury. Named as defendants were the petitioners, W.J. Estelle, Jr., Director of the Department of Corrections, H.H. Husbands, warden of the prison, and Dr. Ralph Gray, medical director of the Department and chief medical officer of the prison hospital. The District Court, sua sponte, dismissed the complaint for failure to state a claim upon which relief could be granted. The Court of Appeals reversed and remanded with instructions to reinstate the complaint. 516 F. 2d 937 (CA5 1975). We granted certiorari, 424 U.S. 907 (1976).

I

Because the complaint was dismissed for failure to state a claim, we must take as true its handwritten, pro se allegations. Cooper v. Pate, 378 U.S. 546 (1964). According to the complaint, Gamble was injured on November

9, 1973, when a bale of cotton fell on him while he was unloading a truck. He continued to work but after four hours he became stiff and was granted a pass to the unit hospital. At the hospital a medical assistant, "Captain" Blunt, checked him for a hernia and sent him back to his cell. Within two hours the pain became so intense that Gamble returned to the hospital where he was given pain pills by an inmate nurse and then was examined by a doctor. The following day, Gamble saw a Dr. Astone who diagnosed the injury as a lower back strain, prescribed Zactirin (a pain reliever) and Robaxin (a muscle relaxant), and placed respondent on "cell-pass, cell-feed" status for two days, allowing him to remain in his cell at all times except for showers. On November 12, Gamble again saw Dr. Astone who continued the medication and cell-pass, cell-feed for another seven days. He also ordered that respondent be moved from an upper to a lower bunk for one week, but the prison authorities did not comply with that directive. The following week, Gamble returned to Dr. Astone. The doctor continued the muscle relaxant but prescribed a new pain reliever, Febridyne, and placed respondent on cell-pass for seven days, permitting him to remain in his cell except for meals and showers. On November 26, respondent again saw Dr. Astone, who put respondent back on the original pain reliever for five days and continued the cell-pass for another week.

On December 3, despite Gamble's statement that his back hurt as much as it had the first day, Dr. Astone took him off cell-pass, thereby certifying him to be capable of light work. At the same time, Dr. Astone prescribed Febridyne for seven days. Gamble then went to a Major Muddox and told him that he was in too much pain to work. Muddox had respondent moved to "administrative segregation." On December 5, Gamble was taken before the prison disciplinary committee, apparently because of his refusal to work. When the committee heard his complaint of back pain and high blood pressure, it directed that he be seen by another doctor.

On December 6, respondent saw petitioner Gray, who performed a urinalysis, blood test, and blood pressure measurement. Dr. Gray prescribed the drug Ser-Ap-Es for the high blood pressure and more Febridyne for the

back pain. The following week respondent again saw Dr. Gray, who continued the Ser-Ap-Es for an additional 30 days. The prescription was not filled for four days, however, because the staff lost it. Respondent went to the unit hospital twice more in December; both times he was seen by Captain Blunt, who prescribed Tiognolos (described as a muscle relaxant). For all of December, respondent remained in administrative segregation.

In early January, Gamble was told on two occasions that he would be sent to the "farm" if he did not return to work. He refused, nonetheless, claiming to be in too much pain. On January 7, 1974, he requested to go on sick call for his back pain and migraine headaches. After an initial refusal, he saw Captain Blunt who prescribed sodium salicylate (a pain reliever) for seven days and Ser-Ap-Es for 30 days. Respondent returned to Captain Blunt on January 17 and January 25, and received renewals of the pain reliever prescription both times. Throughout the month, respondent was kept in administrative segregation.

On January 31, Gamble was brought before the prison disciplinary committee for his refusal to work in early January. He told the committee that he could not work because of his severe back pain and his high blood pressure. Captain Blunt testified that Gamble was in "first class" medical condition. The committee, with no further medical examination or testimony, placed respondent in solitary confinement.

Four days later, on February 4, at 8 A.M., respondent asked to see a doctor for chest pains and "blank outs." It was not until 7:30 that night that a medical assistant examined him and ordered him hospitalized. The following day a Dr. Heaton performed an electrocardiogram; one day later respondent was placed on Quinidine for treatment of irregular cardiac rhythm and moved to administrative segregation. On February 7, respondent again experienced pain in his chest, left arm, and back and asked to see a doctor. The guards refused. He asked again the next day. The guards again refused. Finally, on February 9, he was allowed to see Dr. Heaton, who ordered the Quinidine continued for three more days. On February 11, he swore out his complaint.

II

The gravamen of respondent's § 1983 complaint is that petitioners have subjected him to cruel and unusual punishment in violation of the Eighth Amendment, made applicable to the States by the Fourteenth. See Robinson v. California, 370 U.S. 660 (1962). We therefore base our evaluation of respondent's complaint on those Amendments and our decisions interpreting them.

The history of the constitutional prohibition of "cruel and unusual punishments" has been recounted at length in prior opinions of the Court and need not be repeated here. See, e.g., Gregg v. Georgia, 428 U.S. 153, 169-173 (1976) (joint opinion of STEWART, POWELL, and STEVENS, JJ. (hereinafter joint opinion)); see also Granucci, Nor Cruel and Unusual Punishment Inflicted: The Original Meaning, 57 Calif. L. Rev. 839 (1969). It suffices to note that the primary concern of the drafters was to proscribe "torture[s]" and other "barbar[ous]" methods of punishment. Id., at 842. Accordingly, this Court first applied the Eighth Amendment by comparing challenged methods of execution to concededly inhuman techniques of punishment. See Wilkerson v. Utah, 99 U.S. 130, 136 (1879) ("[I]t is safe to affirm that punishments of torture . . . and all others in the same line of unnecessary cruelty, are forbidden by that amendment . . ."); In re Kemmler, 136 U.S. 436, 447 (1890) ("Punishments are cruel when they involve torture or a lingering death . . .").

Our more recent cases, however, have held that the Amendment proscribes more than physically barbarous punishments. See, e.g., Gregg v. Georgia, supra, at 171 (joint opinion); Trop v. Dulles, 356 U.S. 86, 100-101 (1958); Weems v. United States, 217 U.S. 349, 373 (1910). The Amendment embodies "broad and idealistic concepts of dignity, civilized standards, humanity, and decency . . . ," Jackson v. Bishop, 404 F. 2d 571, 579 (CA8 1968), against which we must evaluate penal measures. Thus, we have held repugnant to the Eighth Amendment punishments which are incompatible with "the evolving standards of decency that mark the progress of a maturing society," Trop v. Dulles, supra, at 101; see also Gregg v. Georgia, supra, at 172-173 (joint opinion); Weems v. United States,

supra, at 378, or which "involve the unnecessary and wanton infliction of pain," Gregg v. Georgia, supra, at 173 (joint opinion); see also Louisiana ex rel. Francis v. Resweber, 329 U.S. 459, 463 (1947); Wilkerson v. Utah, supra, at 136.

These elementary principles establish the government's obligation to provide medical care for those whom it is punishing by incarceration. An inmate must rely on prison authorities to treat his medical needs; if the authorities fail to do so, those needs will not be met. In the worst cases, such a failure may actually produce physical "torture or a lingering death," In re Kemmler, supra, the evils of most immediate concern to the drafters of the Amendment. In less serious cases, denial of medical care may result in pain and suffering which no one suggests would serve any penological purpose. Cf. Gregg v. Georgia, supra, at 182-183 (joint opinion). The infliction of such unnecessary suffering is inconsistent with contemporary standards of decency as manifested in modern legislation codifying the common law view that "it is but just that the public be required to care for the prisoner, who cannot by reason of the deprivation of his liberty, care for himself."

We therefore conclude that deliberate indifference to serious medical needs of prisoners constitutes the "unnecessary and wanton infliction of pain," Gregg v. Georgia, supra, at 173 (joint opinion), proscribed by the Eighth Amendment. This is true whether the indifference is manifested by prison doctors in their response to the prisoner's needs or by prison guards in intentionally denying or delaying access to medical care or intentionally interfering with the treatment once prescribed. Regardless of how evidenced, deliberate indifference to a prisoner's serious illness or injury states a cause of action under § 1983.

This conclusion does not mean, however, that every claim by a prisoner that he has not received adequate medical treatment states a violation of the Eighth Amendment. An accident, although it may produce added anguish, is not on that basis alone to be characterized as wanton infliction of unnecessary pain. In Louisiana ex rel. Francis v. Resweber, 329 U.S. 459 (1947), for example, the Court concluded that it was not unconstitutional to force a prisoner to undergo a second effort to electrocute him after a mechanical malfunction had thwarted the first attempt. Writing for the plurality, Mr. Justice Reed reasoned that the second execution would not violate the Eighth Amendment because the first attempt was an "unforeseeable accident." Id., at 464. Mr. Justice Frankfurter's concurrence, based solely on the Due Process Clause of the Fourteenth Amendment, concluded that since the first attempt had failed because of "an innocent misadventure," id., at 470, the second would not be "repugnant to the conscience of mankind," id., at 471, quoting Palko v. Connecticut, 302 U.S. 319, 323 (1937).

Similarly, in the medical context, an inadvertent failure to provide adequate medical care cannot be said to constitute "an unnecessary and wanton infliction of pain" or to be "repugnant to the conscience of mankind." Thus, a complaint that a physician has been negligent in diagnosing or treating a medical condition does not state a valid claim of medical mistreatment under the Eighth Amendment. Medical malpractice does not become a constitutional violation merely because the victim is a prisoner. In order to state a cognizable claim, a prisoner must allege acts or omissions sufficiently harmful to evidence deliberate indifference to serious medical needs. It is only such indifference that can offend "evolving standards of decency" in violation of the Eighth Amendment.[14]

---

[14] The Courts of Appeals are in essential agreement with this standard. All agree that mere allegations of malpractice do not state a claim, and, while their terminology regarding what is sufficient varies, their results are not inconsistent with the standard of deliberate indifference. See Page v. Sharpe, 487 F. 2d 567, 569 (CA1 1973); Williams v. Vincent, supra, at 544 (uses the phrase "deliberate indifference"); Gittlemacker v. Prasse, 428 F. 2d 1, 6 (CA3 1970); Russell v. Sheffer, 528 F. 2d 318 (CA4 1975); Newman v. Alabama, 503 F. 2d 1320, 1330 n. 14 (CA5 1974), cert. denied, 421 U.S. 948 (1975) ("callous indifference"); Westlake v. Lucas, supra, at 860 ("deliberate indifference"); Thomas v. Pate, supra, at 158; Wilbron v. Hutto, supra, at 622 ("deliberate indifference"); Tolbert v. Eyman, supra, at 626; Dewell v. Lawson, 489 F. 2d 877, 881-882 (CA10 1974).

III

Against this backdrop, we now consider whether respondent's complaint states a cognizable § 1983 claim. The handwritten pro se document is to be liberally construed. As the Court unanimously held in Haines v. Kerner, 404 U.S. 519 (1972), a pro se complaint, "however inartfully pleaded," must be held to "less stringent standards than formal pleadings drafted by lawyers" and can only be dismissed for failure to state a claim if it appears "beyond doubt that the plaintiff can prove no set of facts in support of his claim which would entitle him to relief." Id., at 520-521, quoting Conley v. Gibson, 355 U.S. 41, 45-46 (1957).

Even applying these liberal standards, however, Gamble's claims against Dr. Gray, both in his capacity as treating physician and as medical director of the Corrections Department, are not cognizable under § 1983. Gamble was seen by medical personnel on 17 occasions spanning a three-month period: by Dr. Astone five times; by Dr. Gray twice; by Dr. Heaton three times; by an unidentified doctor and inmate nurse on the day of the injury; and by medical assistant Blunt six times. They treated his back injury, high blood pressure, and heart problems. Gamble has disclaimed any objection to the treatment provided for his high blood pressure and his heart problem; his complaint is "based solely on the lack of diagnosis and inadequate treatment of his back injury." Response to Pet. for Cert. 4; see also Brief for Respondent 19. The doctors diagnosed his injury as a lower back strain and treated it with bed rest, muscle relaxants, and pain relievers. Respondent contends that more should have been done by way of diagnosis and treatment, and suggests a number of options that were not pursued. Id., at 17, 19. The Court of Appeals agreed, stating: "Certainly an X-ray of [Gamble's] lower back might have been in order and other tests conducted that would have led to appropriate diagnosis and treatment for the daily pain and suffering he was experiencing." 516 F. 2d, at 941. But the question whether an X-ray—or additional diagnostic techniques or forms of treatment—is indicated is a classic example of a matter for medical judgment. A medical decision not to order an X-ray, or like measures, does not represent cruel and unusual punishment. At most it is medical malpractice, and as such the proper forum is the state court under the Texas Tort Claims Act. The Court of Appeals was in error in holding that the alleged insufficiency of the medical treatment required reversal and remand. That portion of the judgment of the District Court should have been affirmed.

The Court of Appeals focused primarily on the alleged actions of the doctors, and did not separately consider whether the allegations against the Director of the Department of Corrections, Estelle, and the warden of the prison, Husbands, stated a cause of action. Although we reverse the judgment as to the medical director, we remand the case to the Court of Appeals to allow it an opportunity to consider, in conformity with this opinion, whether a cause of action has been stated against the other prison officials.

It is so ordered.

HELLING
v.
McKINNEY

509 U.S. 25; 113 S. Ct. 2475;
125 L. Ed. 2d 22 (1993)
[Most citations and footnotes omitted]

JUSTICE WHITE delivered the opinion of the Court.

This case requires us to decide whether the health risk posed by involuntary exposure of a prison inmate to environmental tobacco smoke (ETS) can form the basis of a claim for relief under the Eighth Amendment.

I

Respondent is serving a sentence of imprisonment in the Nevada prison system. . . . The complaint, dated December 18, 1986, alleged that respondent was assigned to a cell with another inmate who smoked five packs of cigarettes a day. The complaint also stated that cigarettes were sold to inmates without properly informing of the health hazards a nonsmoking inmate would encounter by

sharing a room with an inmate who smoked, and that certain cigarettes burned continuously, releasing some type of chemical. Respondent complained of certain health problems allegedly caused by exposure to cigarette smoke. Respondent sought injunctive relief and damages for, inter alia, subjecting him to cruel and unusual punishment by jeopardizing his health.

The parties consented to a jury trial before a magistrate. The magistrate viewed respondent's suit as presenting two issues of law: (1) whether respondent had a constitutional right to be housed in a smoke-free environment, and (2) whether defendants were deliberately indifferent to respondent's serious medical needs. The magistrate, after citing applicable authority, concluded that respondent had no constitutional right to be free from cigarette smoke: while "society may be moving toward an opinion as to the propriety of non-smoking and a smoke-free environment," society cannot yet completely agree "on the resolution of these issues." The magistrate found that respondent nonetheless could state a claim for deliberate indifference to serious medical needs if he could prove the underlying facts, but held that respondent had failed to present evidence showing either medical problems that were traceable to cigarette smoke or deliberate indifference to them. The magistrate therefore granted petitioners' motion for a directed verdict and granted judgment for the defendants.

The Court of Appeals affirmed the magistrate's grant of a directed verdict on the issue of deliberate indifference to respondent's immediate medical symptoms. The Court of Appeals also held that the defendants were immune from liability for damages since there was at the time no clearly established law imposing liability for exposing prisoners to ETS. Although it agreed that respondent did not have a constitutional right to a smoke-free prison environment, the court held that respondent had stated a valid cause of action under the Eighth Amendment by alleging that he had been involuntarily exposed to levels of ETS that posed an unreasonable risk of harm to his future health. In support of this judgment, the court noticed scientific opinion supporting respondent's claim that sufficient exposure to ETS could endanger one's health. The court also concluded that society's attitude had evolved to the point that involuntary exposure to unreasonably dangerous levels of ETS violated current standards of decency. The court therefore held that the magistrate erred by directing a verdict without permitting respondent to prove that his exposure to ETS was sufficient to constitute an unreasonable danger to his future health.

Petitioners sought review in this Court. In the meantime, this Court had decided Wilson v. Seiter, which held that, while the Eighth Amendment applies to conditions of confinement that are not formally imposed as a sentence for a crime, such claims require proof of a subjective component, and that where the claim alleges inhumane conditions of confinement or failure to attend to a prisoner's medical needs, the standard for that state of mind is the "deliberate indifference" standard of Estelle v. Gamble. We granted certiorari in this case, vacated the judgment below, and remanded the case to the Court of Appeals for further consideration in light of Seiter.

On remand, the Court of Appeals noted that Seiter added an additional subjective element that respondent had to prove to make out an Eighth Amendment claim, but did not vitiate its determination that it would be cruel and unusual punishment to house a prisoner in an environment exposing him to levels of ETS that pose an unreasonable risk of harming his health—the objective component of respondent's Eighth Amendment claim. The Court of Appeals therefore reinstated its previous judgment and remanded for proceedings consistent with its prior opinion and with Seiter. Ibid.

Petitioners again sought review in this Court, contending that the decision below was in conflict with the en banc decision of the Court of Appeals for the Tenth Circuit in Clemmons v. Bohannon. We granted certiorari. We affirm.

II

The petition for certiorari which we granted not only challenged the Court of Appeals' holding that respondent had stated a valid Eighth Amendment claim, but also asserted, as did its previous petition, that it was

improper for the Court of Appeals to decide the question at all. Petitioners claim that respondent's complaint rested only on the alleged current effects of exposure to cigarette smoke, not on the possible future effects; that the issues framed for trial were likewise devoid of such an issue; and that such a claim was not presented, briefed or argued on appeal and that the Court of Appeals erred in sua sponte deciding it. The Court of Appeals was apparently of the view that the claimed entitlement to a smoke-free environment subsumed the claim that exposure to ETS could endanger one's future health. From its examination of the record, the court stated that "both before and during trial, McKinney sought to litigate the degree of his exposure to ETS and the actual and potential effects of such exposure on his health"; stated that the magistrate had excluded evidence relating to the potential health effects of exposure to ETS; and noted that two of the issues on appeal addressed whether the magistrate erred in holding as a matter of law that compelled exposure to ETS does not violate a prisoner's rights and whether it was error to refuse to appoint an expert witness to testify about the health effects of such exposure. While the record is ambiguous and the Court of Appeals might well have affirmed the magistrate, we hesitate to dispose of this case on the basis that the court misread the record before it. We passed over the same claim when we vacated the judgment below and remanded when the case was first before us, and the primary question on which certiorari was granted, and the question to which petitioners have devoted the bulk of their briefing and argument, is whether the court below erred in holding that McKinney had stated an Eighth Amendment claim on which relief could be granted by alleging that his compelled exposure to ETS poses an unreasonable risk to his health.

III

It is undisputed that the treatment a prisoner receives in prison and the conditions under which he is confined are subject to scrutiny under the Eighth Amendment. As we said in DeShaney v. Winnebago County Dept. of Social Services:

When the State takes a person into its custody and holds him there against his will, the Constitution imposes upon it a corresponding duty to assume some responsibility for his safety and general well being. . . . The rationale for this principle is simple enough: when the State by the affirmative exercise of its power so restrains an individual's liberty that it renders him unable to care for himself, and at the same time fails to provide for his basic human needs—e.g., food, clothing, shelter, medical care, and reasonable safety—it transgresses the substantive limits on state action set by the Eighth Amendment . . .

Contemporary standards of decency require no less. Estelle v. Gamble. In Estelle, we concluded that although accidental or inadvertent failure to provide adequate medical care to a prisoner would not violate the Eighth Amendment, "deliberate indifference to serious medical needs of prisoners" violates the Amendment because it constitutes the unnecessary and wanton infliction of pain contrary to contemporary standards of decency. Wilson v. Seiter later held that a claim that the conditions of a prisoner's confinement violate the Eighth Amendment requires an inquiry into the prison officials' state of mind. "Whether one characterizes the treatment received by [the prisoner] as inhuman conditions of confinement, failure to attend to his medical needs, or a combination of both, it is appropriate to apply the 'deliberate indifference' standard articulated in Estelle."

Petitioners are well aware of these decisions, but they earnestly submit that unless McKinney can prove that he is currently suffering serious medical problems caused by exposure to ETS, there can be no violation of the Eighth Amendment. That Amendment, it is urged, does not protect against prison conditions that merely threaten to cause health problems in the future, no matter how grave and imminent the threat.

We have great difficulty agreeing that prison authorities may not be deliberately indifferent to an inmate's current health problems but may ignore a condition of confinement that is sure or very likely to cause serious illness and needless suffering the next week or month or year. In Hutto v. Finney, we noted that inmates in punitive isolation were crowded into cells and that some of them had infectious maladies such as hepatitis and venereal disease. This was one of the prison conditions for which the Eighth Amendment required a remedy, even though it was not alleged that the likely harm would occur immediately and even though the possible infection might not affect all of those exposed. We would think that a prison inmate also could successfully complain about demonstrably unsafe drinking water without waiting for an attack of dysentery. Nor can we hold that prison officials may be deliberately indifferent to the exposure of inmates to a serious, communicable disease on the ground that the complaining inmate shows no serious current symptoms.

That the Eighth Amendment protects against future harm to inmates is not a novel proposition. The Amendment, as we have said, requires that inmates be furnished with the basic human needs, one of which is "reasonable safety." DeShaney, supra, at 200. It is "cruel and unusual punishment to hold convicted criminals in unsafe conditions." It would be odd to deny an injunction to inmates who plainly proved an unsafe, life-threatening condition in their prison on the ground that nothing yet had happened to them. The Courts of Appeals have plainly recognized that a remedy for unsafe conditions need not await a tragic event. Two of them were cited with approval in Rhodes v. Chapman. Gates v. Collier, 501 F.2d 1291 (CA5 1974), held that inmates were entitled to relief under the Eighth Amendment when they proved threats to personal safety from exposed electrical wiring, deficient firefighting measures, and the mingling of inmates with serious contagious diseases with other prison inmates. Ramos v. Lamm, 639 F.2d 559, 572 (CA10 1980), stated that a prisoner need not wait until he is actually assaulted before obtaining relief. As respondent points out, the Court of Appeals cases to the effect that the Eighth Amendment protects against sufficiently imminent dangers as well as current unnecessary and wanton infliction of pain and suffering are legion. We thus reject petitioners' central thesis that only deliberate indifference to current serious health problems of inmates is actionable under the Eighth Amendment.

The United States as amicus curiae supporting petitioners does not contend that the Amendment permits "even those conditions of confinement that truly pose a significant risk of proximate and substantial harm to an inmate, so long as the injury has not yet occurred and the inmate does not yet suffer from its effects." Hutto v. Finney, the United States observes, teaches as much. The Government recognizes that there may be situations in which exposure to toxic or similar substances would "present a risk of sufficient likelihood or magnitude—and in which there is a sufficiently broad consensus that exposure of anyone to the substance should therefore be prevented—that" the Amendment's protection would be available even though the effects of exposure might not be manifested for some time. But the United States submits that the harm to any particular individual from exposure to ETS is speculative, that the risk is not sufficiently grave to implicate a "serious medical need," and that exposure to ETS is not contrary to current standards of decency. It would be premature for us, however, as a matter of law to reverse the Court of Appeals on the basis suggested by the United States. The Court of Appeals has ruled that McKinney's claim is that the level of ETS to which he has been involuntarily exposed is such that his future health is unreasonably endangered and has remanded to permit McKinney to attempt to prove his case. In the course of such proof, he must also establish that it is contrary to current standards of decency for anyone to be so exposed against his will and that prison officials are deliberately indifferent to his plight. We cannot rule at this juncture that it will be impossible for McKinney, on remand, to prove an Eighth Amendment violation based on exposure to ETS.

IV

We affirm the holding of the Court of Appeals that McKinney states a cause of action under the Eighth Amendment by alleging that petitioners have, with deliberate indifference, exposed him to levels of ETS that pose an unreasonable risk of serious damage to his future health. We also affirm the remand to the District Court to provide an opportunity for McKinney to prove his allegations, which will require him to prove both the subjective and objective elements necessary to prove an Eighth Amendment violation. The District Court will have the usual authority to control the order of proof, and if there is a failure of proof on the first element that it chooses to consider, it would not be an abuse of discretion to give judgment for petitioners without taking further evidence. McKinney must also prove that he is entitled to the remedy of an injunction.

With respect to the objective factor, McKinney must show that he himself is being exposed to unreasonably high levels of ETS. Plainly relevant to this determination is the fact that McKinney has been moved from Carson City to Ely State Prison and is no longer the cellmate of a five-pack-a-day smoker. While he is subject to being moved back to Carson City and to being placed again in a cell with a heavy smoker, the fact is that at present he is not so exposed. Moreover, the Director of the Nevada State Prisons adopted a formal smoking policy on January 10, 1992. This policy restricts smoking in "program, food preparation/serving, recreational and medical areas" to specifically designated areas. It further provides that Wardens may, contingent on space availability, designate nonsmoking areas in dormitory settings, and that institutional classification committees may make reasonable efforts to respect the wishes of nonsmokers where double bunking obtains. It is possible that the new policy will be administered in a way that will minimize the risk to McKinney and make it impossible for him to prove that he will be exposed to unreasonable risk with respect to his future health or that he is now entitled to an injunction.

Also with respect to the objective factor, determining whether McKinney's conditions of confinement violate the Eighth Amendment requires more than a scientific and statistical inquiry into the seriousness of the potential harm and the likelihood that such injury to health will actually be caused by exposure to ETS. It also requires a court to assess whether society considers the risk that the prisoner complains of to be so grave that it violates contemporary standards of decency to expose anyone unwillingly to such a risk. In other words, the prisoner must show that the risk of which he complains is not one that today's society chooses to tolerate.

On remand, the subjective factor, deliberate indifference, should be determined in light of the prison authorities' current attitudes and conduct, which may have changed considerably since the judgment of the Court of Appeals. Indeed, the adoption of the smoking policy mentioned above will bear heavily on the inquiry into deliberate indifference. In this respect we note that at oral argument McKinney's counsel was of the view that depending on how the new policy was administered, it could be very difficult to demonstrate that prison authorities are ignoring the possible dangers posed by exposure to ETS. The inquiry into this factor also would be an appropriate vehicle to consider arguments regarding the realities of prison administration.

V

The judgment of the Court of Appeals is affirmed and the case is remanded for further proceedings consistent with this opinion.

So ordered.

JUSTICE THOMAS, with whom JUSTICE SCALIA joins, dissenting.

Last Term, in Hudson v. McMillian, the Court held that the Eighth Amendment prohibits the use of force that causes a prisoner only minor injuries. Believing that the Court had expanded the Eighth Amendment "beyond all bounds of history and precedent," I dissented. Today the Court expands the Eighth Amendment in yet another direction, holding that it applies to a prisoner's mere risk of injury. Because I find this holding no more acceptable than the Court's holding in Hudson, I again dissent.

I

The Eighth Amendment provides that "excessive bail shall not be required, nor excessive fines imposed, nor cruel and unusual punishments inflicted." The Court holds that a prisoner states a cause of action under the Cruel and Unusual Punishments

Clause by alleging that prison officials, with deliberate indifference, have exposed him to an unreasonable risk of harm. This decision, like every other "conditions of confinement" case since Estelle v. Gamble, rests on the premise that deprivations suffered by a prisoner constitute "punishment" for Eighth Amendment purposes, even when the deprivations have not been inflicted as part of a criminal sentence. As I suggested in Hudson, I have serious doubts about this premise.

A

At the time the Eighth Amendment was ratified, the word "punishment" referred to the penalty imposed for the commission of a crime. See 2 T. Cunningham, A New and Complete Law Dictionary (1771) ("the penalty of transgressing the laws"); 2 T. Sheridan, A General Dictionary of the English Language (1780) ("any infliction imposed in vengeance of a crime"); J. Walker, A Critical Pronouncing Dictionary (1791) (same); 4 G. Jacob, The Law Dictionary: Explaining the Rise, Progress, and Present State, of the English Law 343 (1811) ("the penalty for transgressing the Law"); 2 N. Webster, American Dictionary of the English Language (1828) ("any pain or suffering inflicted on a person for a crime or offense"). That is also the primary definition of the word today. As a legal term of art, "punishment" has always meant a "fine, penalty, or confinement inflicted upon a person by the authority of the law and the judgment and sentence of a court, for some crime or offense committed by him." Black's Law Dictionary 1234 (6th ed. 1990). And this understanding of the word, of course, does not encompass a prisoner's injuries that bear no relation to his sentence.

Nor, as far as I know, is there any historical evidence indicating that the framers and ratifiers of the Eighth Amendment had anything other than this common understanding of "punishment" in mind. There is "no doubt" that the English Declaration of Rights of 1689 is the "antecedent of our constitutional text," and "the best historical evidence" suggests that the "cruel and unusual Punishments" provision of the Declaration of Rights was a response to sentencing abuses of the King's Bench. Just as there was no suggestion in English constitutional history that harsh prison conditions might constitute cruel and unusual (or otherwise illegal) "punishment," the debates surrounding the framing and ratification of our own Constitution and Bill of Rights were silent regarding this possibility. See 2 J. Elliot, Debates on the Federal Constitution 111 (2d ed. 1854) (Congress should be prevented from "inventing the most cruel and unheard-of punishments, and annexing them to crimes") (emphasis added); 1 Annals of Cong. 753-754 (1789). The same can be said of the early commentaries. See 3 J. Story, Commentaries on the Constitution of the United States 750-751 (1833); T. Cooley, Constitutional Limitations 694 (8th ed. 1927).

To the extent that there is any affirmative historical evidence as to whether injuries sustained in prison might constitute "punishment" for Eighth Amendment purposes, that evidence is consistent with the ordinary meaning of the word. As of 1792, the Delaware Constitution's analogue of the Eighth Amendment provided that "Excessive bail shall not be required, nor excessive fines imposed, nor cruel or unusual punishments inflicted; and in the construction of jails a proper regard shall be had to the health of prisoners." This provision suggests that when members of the founding generation wished to make prison conditions a matter of constitutional guarantee, they knew how to do so.

Judicial interpretations of the Cruel and Unusual Punishments Clause were, until quite recently, consistent with its text and history. As I observed in Hudson, courts routinely rejected "conditions of confinement" claims well into this century, and this Court did not so much as intimate that the Cruel and Unusual Punishments Clause might reach prison conditions for the first 185 years of the provision's existence. It was not until the 1960s that lower courts began applying the Eighth Amendment to prison deprivations, and it was not until 1976, in Estelle v. Gamble, that this Court first did so.

Thus, although the evidence is not overwhelming, I believe that the text and history of the Eighth Amendment, together with the decisions interpreting it, support the view that judges or juries—but not jailers—impose "punishment." At a minimum, I believe that the original meaning of "punish-

ment," the silence in the historical record, and the 185 years of uniform precedent shift the burden of persuasion to those who would apply the Eighth Amendment to prison conditions. In my view, that burden has not yet been discharged. It was certainly not discharged in Estelle v. Gamble.

B

The inmate in Estelle claimed that inadequate treatment of a back injury constituted cruel and unusual punishment. The Court ultimately rejected this claim, but not before recognizing that "deliberate indifference to serious medical needs of prisoners" violates the Eighth Amendment. In essence, however, this extension of the Eighth Amendment to prison conditions rested on little more than an ipse dixit. There was no analysis of the text of the Eighth Amendment in Estelle, and the Court's discussion of the provision's history consisted of the following single sentence: "It suffices to note that the primary concern of the drafters was to proscribe 'tortures' and other 'barbarous' methods of punishment." And although the Court purported to rely upon "our decisions interpreting" the Eighth Amendment, none of the six cases it cited held that the Eighth Amendment applies to prison deprivations—or, for that matter, even addressed a claim that it does. All of those cases involved challenges to a sentence imposed for a criminal offense.

The only authorities cited in Estelle that supported the Court's extension of the Eighth Amendment to prison deprivations were lower court decisions (virtually all of which had been decided within the previous 10 years), and the only one of those decisions upon which the Court placed any substantial reliance was Jackson v. Bishop, 404 F.2d 571 (CA8 1968). But Jackson, like Estelle itself, simply asserted that the Eighth Amendment applies to prison deprivations; the Eighth Circuit's discussion of the problem consisted of a two-sentence paragraph in which the court was content to state the opposing view and then reject it: "Neither do we wish to draw . . . any meaningful distinction between punishment by way of sentence statutorily prescribed and punishment imposed for prison disciplinary purposes. It seems to us that the Eighth Amendment's proscription has application to both." As in Estelle, there was no analysis of the text or history of the Cruel and Unusual Punishments Clause.

II

To state a claim under the Cruel and Unusual Punishments Clause, a party must prove not only that the challenged conduct was both cruel and unusual, but also that it constitutes punishment. The text and history of the Eighth Amendment, together with pre-Estelle precedent, raise substantial doubts in my mind that the Eighth Amendment proscribes a prison deprivation that is not inflicted as part of a sentence. And Estelle itself has not dispelled these doubts. Were the issue squarely presented, therefore, I might vote to overrule Estelle. I need not make that decision today, however, because this case is not a straightforward application of Estelle. It is, instead, an extension.

In Hudson, the Court extended Estelle to cases in which the prisoner has suffered only minor injuries; here, it extends Estelle to cases in which there has been no injury at all. Because I seriously doubt that Estelle was correctly decided, I decline to join the Court's holding. Stare decisis may call for hesitation in overruling a dubious precedent, but it does not demand that such a precedent be expanded to its outer limits. I would draw the line at actual, serious injuries and reject the claim that exposure to the risk of injury can violate the Eighth Amendment. Accordingly, I would reverse the judgment of the Court of Appeals.

Cases Relating to Chapter 11

Civil and Criminal Liabilities of Prison Officials

SCHEUER

v.

RHODES

416 U.S. 232; 94 S. Ct. 1683; 40 L. Ed. 2d 90 (1974)

MR. CHIEF JUSTICE BURGER delivered the opinion of the Court.

We granted certiorari[1] in these cases to resolve whether the District Court correctly dismissed civil damage actions, brought under 42 U.S.C. § 1983, on the ground that these actions were, as a matter of law, against the State of Ohio, and hence barred by the Eleventh Amendment to the Constitution and, alternatively, that the actions were against state officials who were immune from liability for the acts alleged in the complaints. These cases arise out of the same period of alleged civil disorder on the campus of Kent State University in Ohio during May 1970 which was before us, in another context, in Gilligan v. Morgan, 413 U.S. 1 (1973).

In these cases the personal representatives of the estates of three students who died in that episode seek damages against the Governor, the Adjutant General, and his assistant, various named and unnamed officers and enlisted members of the Ohio National Guard, and the president of Kent State University. The com-

plaints in both cases allege a cause of action under the Civil Rights Act of 1871, 17 Stat. 13, now 42 U.S.C. § 1983. Petitioner Scheuer also alleges a cause of action under Ohio law on the theory of pendent jurisdiction. Petitioners Krause and Miller make a similar claim, asserting jurisdiction on the basis of diversity of citizenship.[2]

The District Court dismissed the complaints for lack of jurisdiction over the subject matter on the theory that these actions, although in form against the named individuals, were, in substance and effect, against the State of Ohio and thus barred by the Eleventh Amendment. The Court of Appeals affirmed the action of the District Court, agreeing that the suit was in legal effect one against the State of Ohio and, alternatively, that the common-law doctrine of executive immunity barred action against the state officials who are respondents here. 471 F.2d 430 (1972). We are confronted with the narrow threshold question whether the District Court properly dismissed the complaints. We hold that dismissal was inappropriate at this stage of the litigation and accordingly reverse the judg-

---

[1] 413 U.S. 919 (1973).

[2] The Krause complaint states that the plaintiff is a citizen of Pennsylvania and expressly invokes federal diversity jurisdiction under 28 U. S. C. § 1332. The Miller complaint states that the plaintiff is a citizen of New York. While the complaint does not specifically refer to jurisdiction under 28 U.S.C. § 1332, it alleges facts which clearly support diversity jurisdiction. App. in No. 72-1318, p. 85. See Fed. Rule Civ. Proc. 8 (a)(1).

ments and remand for further proceedings. We intimate no view on the merits of the allegations since there is no evidence before us at this stage.

I

The complaints in these cases are not identical but their thrust is essentially the same. In essence, the defendants are alleged to have "intentionally, recklessly, willfully and wantonly" caused an unnecessary deployment of the Ohio National Guard on the Kent State campus and, in the same manner, ordered the Guard members to perform allegedly illegal actions which resulted in the death of plaintiffs' decedents. Both complaints allege that the action was taken "under color of state law" and that it deprived the decedents of their lives and rights without due process of law. Fairly read, the complaints allege that each of the named defendants, in undertaking such actions, acted either outside the scope of his respective office or, if within the scope, acted in an arbitrary manner, grossly abusing the lawful powers of office.

* * *

II

The Eleventh Amendment to the Constitution of the United States provides: "The Judicial power of the United States shall not be construed to extend to any suit in law or equity, commenced or prosecuted against one of the United States by Citizens of another State . . . ." It is well established that the Amendment bars suits not only against the State when it is the named party but also when it is the party in fact. Edelman v. Jordan, 415 U.S. 651 (1974); Poindexter v. Greenhow, 114 U.S. 270, 287 (1885); Cunningham v. Macon & Brunswick R. Co., 109 U.S. 446 (1883). Its applicability "is to be determined not by the mere names of the titular parties but by the essential nature and effect of the proceeding, as it appears from the entire record." Ex parte New York, 256 U.S. 490, 500 (1921).

However, since Ex parte Young, 209 U.S. 123 (1908), it has been settled that the Eleventh Amendment provides no shield for a state official confronted by a claim that he had deprived another of a federal right under the color of state law. Ex parte Young teaches that when a state officer acts under a state law in a manner violative of the Federal Constitution, he

comes into conflict with the superior authority of that Constitution, and he is in that case stripped of his official or representative character and is subjected in his person to the consequences of his individual conduct. The State has no power to impart to him any immunity from responsibility to the supreme authority of the United States. Id., at 159-160. (Emphasis supplied.)

Ex parte Young, like Sterling v. Constantin, 287 U.S. 378 (1932), involved a question of the federal courts' injunctive power, not, as here, a claim for monetary damages. While it is clear that the doctrine of Ex parte Young is of no aid to a plaintiff seeking damages from the public treasury, Edelman v. Jordan, supra; Kennecott Copper Corp. v. State Tax Comm'n, 327 U.S. 573 (1946); Ford Motor Co. v. Dept. of Treasury, 323 U.S. 459 (1945); Great Northern Life Insurance Co. v. Read, 322 U.S. 47 (1944), damages against individual defendants are a permissible remedy in some circumstances notwithstanding the fact that they hold public office. Myers v. Anderson, 238 U.S. 368 (1915). See generally Monroe v. Pape, 365 U.S. 167 (1961); Moor v. County of Alameda, 411 U.S. 693 (1973). In some situations a damage remedy can be as effective a redress for the infringement of a constitutional right as injunctive relief might be in another.

Analyzing the complaints in light of these precedents, we see that petitioners allege facts that demonstrate they are seeking to impose individual and personal liability on the named defendants for what they claim—but have not yet established by proof—was a deprivation of federal rights by these defendants under color of state law. Whatever the plaintiffs may or may not be able to establish as to the merits of their allegations, their claims, as stated in the complaints, given the favorable reading required by the Federal Rules of Civil Procedure, are not barred by the Eleventh Amendment. Consequently, the District Court erred in dismissing the complaints for lack of jurisdiction.

III

The Court of Appeals relied upon the existence of an absolute "executive immunity" as an alternative ground for sustaining the dismissal of the complaints by the District Court. If the immunity of a member of the executive branch is absolute and comprehensive as to all acts allegedly performed within the scope of official duty, the Court of Appeals was correct; if, on the other hand, the immunity is not absolute but rather one that is qualified or limited, an executive officer may or may not be subject to liability depending on all the circumstances that may be revealed by evidence. The concept of the immunity of government officers from personal liability springs from the same root considerations that generated the doctrine of sovereign immunity. While the latter doctrine—that the "King can do no wrong"—did not protect all government officers from personal liability, the common law soon recognized the necessity of permitting officials to perform their official functions free from the threat of suits for personal liability.[4] This

official immunity apparently rested, in its genesis, on two mutually dependent rationales:[5] (1) the injustice, particularly in the absence of bad faith, of subjecting to liability an officer who is required, by the legal obligations of his position, to exercise discretion; (2) the danger that the threat of such liability would deter his willingness to execute his office with the decisiveness and the judgment required by the public good.

In this country, the development of the law of immunity for public officials has been the product of constitutional provision as well as legislative and judicial processes. The Federal Constitution grants absolute immunity to Members of both Houses of the Congress with respect to any speech, debate, vote, report, or action done in session. Art. I, § 6. See Gravel v. United States, 408 U.S. 606 (1972); United States v. Brewster, 408 U.S. 501 (1972); and Kilbourn v. Thompson, 103 U.S. 168 (1881). This provision was intended

---

[4] In England legislative immunity was secured after a long struggle, by the Bill of Rights of 1689: "That the Freedom of Speech, and Debates or Proceedings in Parliament, ought not to be impeached or questioned in any Court or Place out of Parliament," 1 W. & M., Sess. 2, c. 2. See Stockdale v. Hansard, 9 Ad. & E. 1, 113-114, 112 Eng. Rep. 1112, 1155-1156 (Q. B. 1839). The English experience, of course, guided the drafters of our "Speech or Debate" Clause. See Tenney v. Brandhove, 341 U.S. 367, 372-375 (1951); United States v. Johnson, 383 U.S. 169, 177-178, 181 (1966); United States v. Brewster, 408 U.S. 501 (1972).

In regard to judicial immunity, Holdsworth notes: "In the case of courts of record . . . it was held, certainly as early as Edward III's reign, that a litigant could not go behind the record, in order to make a judge civilly or criminally liable for an abuse of his jurisdiction." 6 W. Holdsworth, A History of English Law 235 (1927). The modern concept owes much to the elaboration and restatement of Coke and other judges of the sixteenth and early seventeenth

centuries. Id., at 234 et seq. See Floyd v. Barker, 12 Co. Rep. 23, 77 Eng. Rep. 1305 (K. B. 1607). The immunity of the Crown has traditionally been of a more limited nature. Officers of the Crown were at first insulated from responsibility since the King could claim the act as his own. This absolute insulation was gradually eroded. Statute of Westminster I, 3 Edw. 1, c. 24 (1275) (repealed); Statute of Westminster II, 13 Edw. 1, c. 13 (1285) (repealed). The development of liability, especially during the times of the Tudors and Stuarts, was slow; see, e.g., Public Officers Protection Act, 7 Jac. 1, c. 5 (1609) (repealed). With the accession of William and Mary, the liability of officers saw what Jaffe has termed "a most remarkable and significant extension" in Ashby v. White, 1 Bro. P. C. 62, 1 Eng. Rep. 417 (H. L. 1704), reversing 6 Mod. 45, 87 Eng. Rep. 808 (Q. B. 1703). Jaffe, Suits Against Governments and Officers: Sovereign Immunity, 77 Harv. L. Rev. 1, 14 (1963); A. Dicey, The Law of the Constitution 193-194 (10th ed. 1959) (footnotes omitted). See generally Barr v. Matteo, 360 U.S. 564 (1959). Good-faith performance of a discretionary duty has remained, it seems, a defense. See Jaffe, Suits Against Governments and Officers: Damage Actions, 77 Harv. L. Rev. 209, 216 (1963). See also Spalding v. Vilas, 161 U.S. 483, 493 et seq. (1896).

[5] Jaffe, Suits Against Governments and Officers: Damage Actions, 77 Harv. L. Rev., at 223.

to secure for the Legislative Branch of the Government the freedom from executive and judicial encroachment which had been secured in England in the Bill of Rights of 1689 and carried to the original Colonies.[6] In United States v. Johnson, 383 U.S. 169, 182 (1966), Mr. Justice Harlan noted:

> There is little doubt that the instigation of criminal charges against critical or disfavored legislators by the executive in a judicial forum was the chief fear prompting the long struggle for parliamentary privilege in England and, in the context of the American system of separation of powers, is the predominate thrust of the Speech or Debate Clause.

Immunity for the other two branches—long a creature of the common law—remained committed to the common law. See, e.g., Spalding v. Vilas, 161 U.S. 483, 498-499 (1896).

Although the development of the general concept of immunity, and the mutations which the underlying rationale has undergone in its application to various positions are not matters of immediate concern here, it is important to note, even at the outset, that one policy consideration seems to pervade the analysis: the public interest requires decisions and action to enforce laws for the protection of the public. Mr. Justice Jackson expressed this general proposition succinctly, stating "it is not a tort for government to govern." Dalehite v. United States, 346 U.S. 15, 57 (1953) (dissenting opinion). Public officials, whether governors, mayors or police, legislators or judges, who fail to make decisions when they are needed or who do not act to implement decisions when they are made

do not fully and faithfully perform the duties of their offices.[7] Implicit in the idea that officials have some immunity—absolute or qualified—for their acts, is a recognition that they may err. The concept of immunity assumes this and goes on to assume that it is better to risk some error and possible injury from such error than not to decide or act at all. In Barr v. Matteo, 360 U.S. 564, 572-573 (1959), the Court observed, in the somewhat parallel context of the privilege of public officers from defamation actions: "The privilege is not a badge or emolument of exalted office, but an expression of a policy designed to aid in the effective functioning of government." See also Spalding v. Vilas, 161 U.S., at 498-499.

For present purposes we need determine only whether there is an absolute immunity, as the Court of Appeals determined, governing the specific allegations of the complaint against the chief executive officer of a State, the senior and subordinate officers and enlisted personnel of that State's National Guard, and the president of a state-controlled university. If the immunity is qualified, not absolute, the scope of that immunity will necessarily be related to facts as yet not established either by affidavits, admissions, or a trial record. Final resolution of this question must take into account the functions and responsibilities of these particular defendants in their capacities as officers of the state gov-

---

[6] Mr. Justice Frankfurter noted in Tenney v. Brandhove, 341 U.S., at 373: "The provision in the United States Constitution was a reflection of political principles already firmly established in the States. Three State Constitutions adopted before the Federal Constitution specifically protected the privilege." See Coffin v. Coffin, 4 Mass. 1, 27 (1808). See also Kilbourn v. Thompson, 103 U.S. 168, 202 (1881).

[7] For example, in Floyd v. Barker, supra, Coke emphasized that judges "are only to make an account to God and the King" since a contrary rule "would tend to the scandal and subversion of all justice. And those who are the most sincere, would not be free from continual calumniations . . . ." 12 Co. Rep., at 25, 77 Eng. Rep., at 1307. See also Yaselli v. Goff, 12 F.2d 396, 399 (CA2 1926), aff'd per curiam, 275 U.S. 503 (1927). In Spalding v. Vilas, 161 U.S., at 498, the Court noted:

"In exercising the functions of his office, the head of an Executive Department, keeping within the limits of his authority, should not be under an apprehension that the motives that control his official conduct may, at any time, become the subject of inquiry in a civil suit for damages. It would seriously cripple the proper and effective administration of public affairs as entrusted to the executive branch of the government, if he were subjected to any such restraint."

ernment, as well as the purposes of 42 U.S.C. § 1983. In neither of these inquiries do we write on a clean slate. It can hardly be argued, at this late date, that under no circumstances can the officers of state government be subject to liability under this statute. In Monroe v. Pape, supra, MR. JUSTICE DOUGLAS, writing for the Court, held that the section in question was meant "to give a remedy to parties deprived of constitutional rights, privileges and immunities by an official's abuse of his position." 365 U.S., at 172. Through the Civil Rights statutes, Congress intended "to enforce provisions of the Fourteenth Amendment against those who carry a badge of authority of a State and represent it in some capacity, whether they act in accordance with their authority or misuse it." Id., at 171-172.

Since the statute relied on thus included within its scope the "misuse of power, possessed by virtue of state law and made possible only because the wrongdoer is clothed with the authority of state law," id., at 184 (quoting United States v. Classic, 313 U.S. 299, 326 (1941)), government officials, as a class, could not be totally exempt, by virtue of some absolute immunity, from liability under its terms. Indeed, as the Court also indicated in Monroe v. Pape, supra, the legislative history indicates that there is no absolute immunity. Soon after Monroe v. Pape, Mr. Chief Justice Warren noted in Pierson v. Ray, 386 U.S. 547 (1967), that the "legislative record [of § 1983] gives no clear indication that Congress meant to abolish wholesale all common-law immunities," id., at 554. The Court had previously recognized that the Civil Rights Act of 1871 does not create civil liability for legislative acts by legislators "in a field where legislators traditionally have power to act." Tenney v. Brandhove, 341 U.S. 367, 379 (1951). Noting that "the privilege of legislators to be free from arrest or civil process for what they do or say in legislative proceedings has taproots in the Parliamentary struggles of the Sixteenth and Seventeenth Centuries," id., at 372, the Court concluded that it was highly improbable that "Congress—itself a staunch advocate of legislative freedom—would impinge on a tradition so well grounded in history and reason by covert inclusion in the general language . . ." of this statute. Id., at 376.

In similar fashion, Pierson v. Ray, supra, examined the scope of judicial immunity under this statute. Noting that the record con-

tained no "proof or specific allegation," 386 U.S., at 553, that the trial judge had "played any role in these arrests and convictions other than to adjudge petitioners guilty when their cases came before his court," ibid., the Court concluded that, had the Congress intended to abolish the common-law "immunity of judges for acts within the judicial role," id., at 554, it would have done so specifically. A judge's

> errors may be corrected on appeal, but he should not have to fear that unsatisfied litigants may hound him with litigation charging malice or corruption. Imposing such a burden on judges would contribute not to principled and fearless decision-making but to intimidation. Ibid.

The Pierson Court was also confronted with whether immunity was available to that segment of the executive branch of a state government that is most frequently and intimately involved in day-to-day contacts with the citizenry and, hence, most frequently exposed to situations which can give rise to claims under § 1983—the local police officer. Mr. Chief Justice Warren, speaking for the Court, noted that the police officers

> did not defend on the theory that they believed in good faith that it was constitutional to arrest the ministers solely for using the ['white only'] waiting room. Rather, they claimed and attempted to prove that . . . [they arrested them] solely for the purpose of preventing violence. They testified, in contradiction to the ministers, that a crowd gathered and that imminent violence was likely. If the jury believed the testimony of the officers and disbelieved that of the ministers, and if the jury found that the officers reasonably believed in good faith that the arrest was constitutional, then a verdict for the officers would follow even though the arrest was in fact [without probable cause and] unconstitutional. Id., at 557.

The Court noted that the "common law has never granted police officers an absolute and unqualified immunity," id., at 555, but that "the prevailing view in this country [is that] a peace officer who arrests someone with probable cause is not liable for false arrest simply because the innocence of the suspect is later proved," ibid.; the Court went on to observe that a "policeman's lot is not so unhappy that he must choose between being charged with dereliction of duty if he does not arrest when he has probable cause, and being mulcted in damages if he does." Ibid. The Court then held that

the defense of good faith and probable cause, which the Court of Appeals found available to the officers in the common-law action for false arrest and imprisonment, is also available to them in the action under § 1983. Id., at 557.

When a court evaluates police conduct relating to an arrest its guideline is "good faith and probable cause." Ibid. In the case of higher officers of the executive branch, however, the inquiry is far more complex since the range of decisions and choices—whether the formulation of policy, of legislation, of budgets, or of day-to-day decisions—is virtually infinite. In common with police officers, however, officials with a broad range of duties and authority must often act swiftly and firmly at the risk that action deferred will be futile or constitute virtual abdication of office. Like legislators and judges, these officers are entitled to rely on traditional sources for the factual information on which they decide and act.[8] When a condition of civil disorder in fact exists, there is obvious need

for prompt action, and decisions must be made in reliance on factual information supplied by others. While both federal and state laws plainly contemplate the use of force when the necessity arises, the decision to invoke military power has traditionally been viewed with suspicion and skepticism since it often involves the temporary suspension of some of our most cherished rights—government by elected civilian leaders, freedom of expression, of assembly, and of association. Decisions in such situations are more likely than not to arise in an atmosphere of confusion, ambiguity, and swiftly moving events and when, by the very existence of some degree of civil disorder, there is often no consensus as to the appropriate remedy. In short, since the options which a chief executive and his principal subordinates must consider are far broader and far more subtle than those made by officials with less responsibility, the range of discretion must be comparably broad. In a context other than a § 1983 suit, Mr. Justice Harlan articulated these considerations in Barr v. Matteo, supra:

To be sure, the occasions upon which the acts of the head of an executive department will be protected by the privilege are doubtless far broader than in the case of an officer with less sweeping functions. But that is because the higher the post, the broader the range of responsibilities and duties, and the wider the scope of discretion, it entails. It is not the title of his office but the duties with which the particular officer sought to be made to respond in damages is entrusted—the relation of the act complained of to "matters committed by law to his control or supervision," Spalding v. Vilas, supra, at 498—which must provide the guide in delineating the scope of the rule which clothes the official acts of the executive officer with immunity from civil defamation suits. 360 U.S., at 573-574.

These considerations suggest that, in varying scope, a qualified immunity is available to officers of the executive branch of government, the variation being dependent upon the scope of discretion and responsibilities of the office and all the circumstances as they reasonably appeared at the time of the action on

---

[8]   In Spalding v. Vilas, 161 U.S., at 498, the Court, after discussing the early principles of judicial immunity in the country, cf. Randall v. Brigham, 7 Wall. 523, 535 (1869), Bradley v. Fisher, 13 Wall. 335 (1872), and Yates v. Lansing, 5 Johns. 282 (N. Y. 1810), noted the similarity in the controlling policy considerations in the case of high-echelon executive officers and judges:

"We are of opinion that the same general considerations of public policy and convenience which demand for judges of courts of superior jurisdiction immunity from civil suits for damages arising from acts done by them in the course of the performance of their judicial functions, apply to a large extent to official communications made by heads of Executive Departments when engaged in the discharge of duties imposed upon them by law. The interests of the people require that due protection be accorded to them in respect of their official acts."

which liability is sought to be based. It is the existence of reasonable grounds for the belief formed at the time and in light of all the circumstances, coupled with good-faith belief, that affords a basis for qualified immunity of executive officers for acts performed in the course of official conduct. Mr. Justice Holmes spoke of this, stating:

No doubt there are cases where the expert on the spot may be called upon to justify his conduct later in court, notwithstanding the fact that he had sole command at the time and acted to the best of his knowledge. That is the position of the captain of a ship. But even in that case great weight is given to his determination and the matter is to be judged on the facts as they appeared then and not merely in the light of the event. Moyer v. Peabody, 212 U.S. 78, 85 (1909). (Citations omitted.)

Under the criteria developed by precedents of this Court, § 1983 would be drained of meaning were we to hold that the acts of a governor or other high executive officer have "the quality of a supreme and unchangeable edict, overriding all conflicting rights of property and unreviewable through the judicial power of the Federal Government." Sterling v. Constantin, 287 U.S., at 397. In Sterling, Mr. Chief Justice Hughes put it in these terms:

If this extreme position could be deemed to be well taken, it is manifest that the fiat of a state Governor, and not the Constitution of the United States, would be the supreme law of the land; that the restrictions of the Federal Constitution upon the exercise of state power would be but impotent phrases, the futility of which the State may at any time disclose by the simple process of transferring powers of legislation to the Governor to be exercised by him, beyond control, upon his assertion of necessity. Under our system of government, such a conclusion is obviously untenable. There is no such avenue of escape from the paramount authority of the Federal Constitution. When there is a substantial showing that the exertion of state power has overridden private rights secured by that Constitution, the subject is

necessarily one for judicial inquiry in an appropriate proceeding directed against the individuals charged with the transgression. Id., at 397-398.

Gilligan v. Morgan, by no means indicates a contrary result. Indeed, there we specifically noted that we neither held nor implied "that the conduct of the National Guard is always beyond judicial review or that there may not be accountability in a judicial forum for violations of law or for specific unlawful conduct by military personnel, whether by way of damages or injunctive relief." 413 U.S., at 11-12. (Footnote omitted.) See generally Laird v. Tatum, 408 U.S. 1, 15-16 (1972); Duncan v. Kahanamoku, 327 U.S. 304 (1946).

IV

These cases, in their present posture, present no occasion for a definitive exploration of the scope of immunity available to state executive officials nor, because of the absence of a factual record, do they permit a determination as to the applicability of the foregoing principles to the respondents here. The District Court acted before answers were filed and without any evidence other than the copies of the proclamations issued by respondent Rhodes and brief affidavits of the Adjutant General and his assistant. In dismissing the complaints, the District Court and the Court of Appeals erroneously accepted as a fact the good faith of the Governor, and took judicial notice that "mob rule existed at Kent State University." There was no opportunity afforded petitioners to contest the facts assumed in that conclusion. There was no evidence before the courts from which such a finding of good faith could be properly made and, in the circumstances of these cases, such a dispositive conclusion could not be judicially noticed. We can readily grant that a declaration of emergency by the chief executive of a State is entitled to great weight but it is not conclusive. Sterling v. Constantin, supra.

The documents properly before the District Court at this early pleading stage specifically placed in issue whether the Governor and his subordinate officers were acting within the scope of their duties under the Constitution and laws of Ohio; whether they acted within the range of discretion permitted the holders of such office under Ohio law and whether they acted in good faith both in proclaiming an emergency and as to the actions taken to cope with the emergency so declared. Similarly, the complaints place directly in issue whether the lesser officers and enlisted personnel of the Guard acted in good-faith obedience to the orders of their superiors. Further proceedings, either by way of summary judgment or by trial on the merits, are required. The complaining parties are entitled to be heard more fully than is possible on a motion to dismiss a complaint.

We intimate no evaluation whatever as to the merits of the petitioners' claims or as to whether it will be possible to support them by proof. We hold only that, on the allegations of their respective complaints, they were entitled to have them judicially resolved.

The judgments of the Court of Appeals are reversed and the cases are remanded for further proceedings consistent with this opinion.

It is so ordered.

MR. JUSTICE DOUGLAS took no part in the decision of these cases.

DANIELS

v.

WILLIAMS

474 U.S. 327; 106 S. Ct. 662; 88 L. Ed. 2d 662 (1986)

JUSTICE REHNQUIST delivered the opinion of the Court.

In Parratt v. Taylor, 451 U.S. 527 (1981), a state prisoner sued under 42 U.S.C. § 1983, claiming that prison officials had negligently deprived him of his property without due process of law. After deciding that § 1983 contains no independent state-of-mind requirement, we concluded that although petitioner had been "deprived" of property within the meaning of the Due Process Clause of the Fourteenth Amendment, the State's postdeprivation tort remedy provided

the process that was due. Petitioner's claim in this case, which also rests on an alleged Fourteenth Amendment "deprivation" caused by the negligent conduct of a prison official, leads us to reconsider our statement in Parratt that "the alleged loss, even though negligently caused, amounted to a deprivation." Id., at 536-537. We conclude that the Due Process Clause is simply not implicated by a negligent act of an official causing unintended loss of or injury to life, liberty, or property.

In this § 1983 action, petitioner seeks to recover damages for back and ankle injuries allegedly sustained when he fell on a prison stairway. He claims that, while an inmate at the city jail in Richmond, Virginia, he slipped on a pillow negligently left on the stairs by respondent, a correctional deputy stationed at the jail. Respondent's negligence, the argument runs, "deprived" petitioner of his "liberty" interest in freedom from bodily injury, see Ingraham v. Wright, 430 U.S. 651, 673 (1977); because respondent maintains that he is entitled to the defense of sovereign immunity in a state tort suit, petitioner is without an "adequate" state remedy, cf. Hudson v. Palmer, 468 U.S. 517, 534-536 (1984). Accordingly, the deprivation of liberty was without "due process of law."

* * *

Because of the inconsistent approaches taken by lower courts in determining when tortious conduct by state officials rises to the level of a constitutional tort, see Jackson v. Joliet, 465 U.S. 1049, 1050 (1984) (WHITE, J., dissenting from denial of certiorari) (collecting cases), and the apparent lack of adequate guidance from this Court, we granted certiorari. 469 U.S. 1207 (1985). We now affirm.

In Parratt v. Taylor, we granted certiorari, as we had twice before, "to decide whether mere negligence will support a claim for relief under § 1983." 451 U.S., at 532. After examining the language, legislative history, and prior interpretations of the statute, we concluded that § 1983, unlike its criminal counterpart, 18 U.S.C. § 242, contains no state-of-mind requirement independent of that necessary to state a violation of the underlying constitutional right. Id., at 534-

535. We adhere to that conclusion. But in any given § 1983 suit, the plaintiff must still prove a violation of the underlying constitutional right; and depending on the right, merely negligent conduct may not be enough to state a claim. See, e.g., Arlington Heights v. Metropolitan Housing Dev. Corp., 429 U.S. 252 (1977) (invidious discriminatory purpose required for claim of racial discrimination under the Equal Protection Clause); Estelle v. Gamble, 429 U.S. 97, 105 (1976) ("deliberate indifference" to prisoner's serious illness or injury sufficient to constitute cruel and unusual punishment under the Eighth Amendment).

In Parratt, before concluding that Nebraska's tort remedy provided all the process that was due, we said that the loss of the prisoner's hobby kit, "even though negligently caused, amounted to a deprivation [under the Due Process Clause]." 451 U.S., at 536-537. JUSTICE POWELL, concurring in the result, criticized the majority for "[passing] over" this important question of the state of mind required to constitute a "deprivation" of property. Id., at 547. He argued that negligent acts by state officials, though causing loss of property, are not actionable under the Due Process Clause. To JUSTICE POWELL, mere negligence could not "[work] a deprivation in the constitutional sense." Id., at 548 (emphasis in original). Not only does the word "deprive" in the Due Process Clause connote more than a negligent act, but we should not "open the federal courts to lawsuits where there has been no affirmative abuse of power." Id., at 548-549; see also id., at 545 (Stewart, J., concurring) ("To hold that this kind of loss is a deprivation of property within the meaning of the Fourteenth Amendment seems not only to trivialize, but grossly to distort the meaning and intent of the Constitution"). Upon reflection, we agree and overrule Parratt to the extent that it states that mere lack of due care by a state official may "deprive" an individual of life, liberty, or property under the Fourteenth Amendment.

The Due Process Clause of the Fourteenth Amendment provides: "[Nor] shall any State deprive any person of life, liberty, or property, without due process of law." Historically, this guarantee of due process has been applied to deliberate decisions of government officials to deprive a person of life, liberty, or property. E.g., Davidson v. New Orleans, 96 U.S. 97 (1878) (assessment of real estate); Rochin v. California, 342 U.S. 165 (1952) (stomach pumping); Bell v. Burson, 402 U.S. 535 (1971) (suspension of driver's license); Ingraham v. Wright, 430 U.S. 651 (1977) (paddling student); Hudson v. Palmer, 468 U.S. 517 (1984) (intentional destruction of inmate's property). No decision of this Court before Parratt supported the view that negligent conduct by a state official, even though causing injury, constitutes a deprivation under the Due Process Clause. This history reflects the traditional and commonsense notion that the Due Process Clause, like its forebear in the Magna Carta, see Corwin, The Doctrine of Due Process of Law Before the Civil War, 24 Harv. L. Rev. 366, 368 (1911), was "intended to secure the individual from the arbitrary exercise of the powers of government," Hurtado v. California, 110 U.S. 516, 527 (1884) (quoting Bank of Columbia v. Okely, 4 Wheat. 235, 244 (1819)). See also Wolff v. McDonnell, 418 U.S. 539, 558 (1974) ("The touchstone of due process is protection of the individual against arbitrary action of government, Dent v. West Virginia, 129 U.S. 114, 123 (1889)"); Parratt, supra, at 549 (POWELL, J., concurring in result). By requiring the government to follow appropriate procedures when its agents decide to "deprive any person of life, liberty, or property," the Due Process Clause promotes fairness in such decisions. And by barring certain government actions regardless of the fairness of the procedures used to implement them, e.g., Rochin, supra, it serves to prevent governmental power from being "used for purposes of oppression," Murray's Lessee v. Hoboken Land & Improvement Co., 18 How. 272, 277 (1856) (discussing Due Process Clause of Fifth Amendment).

We think that the actions of prison custodians in leaving a pillow on the prison stairs, or mislaying an inmate's property, are quite remote from the concerns just discussed. Far from an abuse of power, lack of due care suggests no more than a failure to measure up to the conduct of a reasonable person. To hold that injury caused by such conduct is a deprivation within the meaning of the Fourteenth

Amendment would trivialize the centuries-old principle of due process of law.

The Fourteenth Amendment is a part of a Constitution generally designed to allocate governing authority among the Branches of the Federal Government and between that Government and the States, and to secure certain individual rights against both State and Federal Government. When dealing with a claim that such a document creates a right in prisoners to sue a government official because he negligently created an unsafe condition in the prison, we bear in mind Chief Justice Marshall's admonition that "we must never forget, that it is a constitution we are expounding," McCulloch v. Maryland, 4 Wheat. 316, 407 (1819) (emphasis in original). Our Constitution deals with the large concerns of the governors and the governed, but it does not purport to supplant traditional tort law in laying down rules of conduct to regulate liability for injuries that attend living together in society. We have previously rejected reasoning that "would make of the Fourteenth Amendment a font of tort law to be superimposed upon whatever systems may already be administered by the States," Paul v. Davis, 424 U.S. 693, 701 (1976), quoted in Parratt v. Taylor, 451 U.S., at 544.

The only tie between the facts of this case and anything governmental in nature is the fact that respondent was a sheriff's deputy at the Richmond city jail and petitioner was an inmate confined in that jail. But while the Due Process Clause of the Fourteenth Amendment obviously speaks to some facets of this relationship, see, e.g., Wolff v. McDonnell, supra, we do not believe its protections are triggered by lack of due care by prison officials. . . .

That injuries inflicted by governmental negligence are not addressed by the United States Constitution is not to say that they may not raise significant legal concerns and lead to the creation of protectible legal interests. The enactment of tort claim statutes, for example, reflects the view that injuries caused by such negligence should generally be redressed. It is no reflection on either the breadth of the United States Constitution or the importance of traditional tort law to say that they do not address the same concerns.

In support of his claim that negligent conduct can give rise to a due process "depriva-tion," petitioner makes several arguments, none of which we find persuasive. He states, for example, that "it is almost certain that some negligence claims are within § 1983," and cites as an example the failure of a State to comply with the procedural requirements of Wolff v. McDonnell, supra, before depriving an inmate of good-time credit. We think the relevant action of the prison officials in that situation is their deliberate decision to deprive the inmate of good-time credit, not their hypothetically negligent failure to accord him the procedural protections of the Due Process Clause. But we need not rule out the possibility that there are other constitutional provisions that would be violated by mere lack of care in order to hold, as we do, that such conduct does not implicate the Due Process Clause of the Fourteenth Amendment.

Petitioner also suggests that artful litigants, undeterred by a requirement that they plead more than mere negligence, will often be able to allege sufficient facts to support a claim of intentional deprivation. In the instant case, for example, petitioner notes that he could have alleged that the pillow was left on the stairs with the intention of harming him. This invitation to "artful" pleading, petitioner contends, would engender sticky (and needless) disputes over what is fairly pleaded. What's more, requiring complainants to allege something more than negligence would raise serious questions about what "more" than negligence—intent, recklessness, or "gross negligence"—is required, and indeed about what these elusive terms mean. See Reply Brief for Petitioner 9 ("what terms like willful, wanton, reckless or gross negligence mean" has "left the finest scholars puzzled"). But even if accurate, petitioner's observations do not carry the day. In the first place, many branches of the law abound in nice distinctions that may be troublesome but have been thought nonetheless necessary:

> I do not think we need trouble ourselves with the thought that my view depends upon differences of degree. The whole law does so as soon as it is civilized. LeRoy Fibre Co. v. Chicago, M. & St. P. R. Co., 232 U.S. 340, 354 (1914) (Holmes, J., partially concurring).

More important, the difference between one end of the spectrum—negligence—and the other—intent—is abundantly clear. See O. Holmes, The Common Law 3 (1923). In any event, we decline to trivialize the Due Process Clause in an effort to simplify constitutional litigation.

Finally, citing South v. Maryland, 18 How. 396 (1856), petitioner argues that respondent's conduct, even if merely negligent, breached a sheriff's "special duty of care" for those in his custody. Reply Brief for Petitioner 14. The Due Process Clause, petitioner notes, "was intended to give Americans at least the protection against governmental power that they had enjoyed as Englishmen against the power of the crown." Ingraham v. Wright, 430 U.S., at 672-673. And South v. Maryland suggests that one such protection was the right to recover against a sheriff for breach of his ministerial duty to provide for the safety of prisoners in his custody. 18 How., at 402-403. Due process demands that the State protect those whom it incarcerates by exercising reasonable care to assure their safety and by compensating them for negligently inflicted injury.

We disagree. We read South v. Maryland, supra, an action brought under federal diversity jurisdiction on a Maryland sheriff's bond, as stating no more than what this Court thought to be the principles of common law and Maryland law applicable to that case; it is not cast at all in terms of constitutional law, and indeed could not have been, since at the time it was rendered there was no due process clause applicable to the States. Petitioner's citation to Ingraham v. Wright does not support the notion that all common-law duties owed by government actors were somehow constitutionalized by the Fourteenth Amendment. Jailers may owe a special duty of care to those in their custody under state tort law, see Restatement (Second) of Torts § 314A(4) (1965), but for the reasons previously stated we reject the contention that the Due Process Clause of the Fourteenth Amendment embraces such a tort law concept. Petitioner alleges that he was injured by the negligence of respondent, a custodial official at the city jail. Whatever other provisions of state law or general jurisprudence he may rightly invoke, the Fourteenth Amendment to the United States Constitution does not afford him a remedy.

Affirmed.

CARLSON
v.
GREEN

446 U.S. 14; 100 S. Ct. 1468;
64 L. Ed. 2d 15 (1980)

MR. JUSTICE BRENNAN delivered the opinion of the Court.

Respondent brought this suit in the District Court for the Southern District of Indiana on behalf of the estate of her deceased son, Joseph Jones, Jr., alleging that he suffered personal injuries from which he died because the petitioners, federal prison officials, violated his due process, equal protection, and Eighth Amendment rights. Asserting jurisdiction under 28 U.S.C. § 1331 (a), she claimed compensatory and punitive damages for the constitutional violations. Two questions are presented for decision: (1) Is a remedy available directly under the Constitution, given that respondent's allegations could also support a suit against the United States under the Federal Tort Claims Act? And (2) if so, is survival of the cause of action governed by federal common law or by state statutes?

I

The District Court held that under Estelle v. Gamble, 429 U.S. 97 (1976), the allegations set out in note 1, supra, pleaded a violation of the Eighth Amendment's proscription against infliction of cruel and unusual punishment, giving rise to a cause of action for damages under Bivens v. Six Unknown Fed. Narcotics Agents, 403 U.S. 388 (1971). . . .

II

Bivens established that the victims of a constitutional violation by a federal agent have a right to recover damages against the official in federal court despite the absence of any statute conferring such a right. Such a cause of action may be defeated in a particular case, however, in two situations. The first is when defendants demonstrate "special factors counselling hesitation in the absence of affirmative action by Congress." 403 U.S., at 396; Davis v. Passman, 442 U.S. 228, 245 (1979). The second is when defendants show that Congress has provided an alternative remedy which it explicitly declared to be a substitute for recovery directly under the Constitution and viewed as equally effective. Bivens, supra, at 397; Davis v. Passman, supra, at 245-247.

Neither situation obtains in this case. First, the case involves no special factors counselling hesitation in the absence of affirmative action by Congress. Petitioners do not enjoy such independent status in our constitutional scheme as to suggest that judicially created remedies against them might be inappropriate. Davis v. Passman, supra, at 246. Moreover, even if requiring them to defend respondent's suit might inhibit their efforts to perform their official duties, the qualified immunity accorded them under Butz v. Economou, 438 U.S. 478 (1978), provides adequate protection. See Davis v. Passman, supra, at 246.

Second, we have here no explicit congressional declaration that persons injured by federal officers' violations of the Eighth Amendment may not recover money damages from the agents but must be remitted to another remedy, equally effective in the view of Congress. Petitioners point to nothing in the Federal Tort Claims Act (FTCA) or its legislative history to show that Congress meant to pre-empt a Bivens remedy or to create an equally effective remedy for constitutional violations. FTCA was enacted long before Bivens was decided, but when Congress amended FTCA in 1974 to create a cause of action against the United States for intentional torts committed by federal law enforcement officers, 28 U.S.C. § 2680 (h), the congressional comments accompanying that amendment made it crystal clear that Congress views FTCA and Bivens as parallel, complementary causes of action:

[After] the date of enactment of this measure, innocent individuals who are subjected to raids [like that in Bivens] will have a cause of action against the individual Federal agents and the Federal Government. Furthermore, this provision should be viewed as a counterpart to the Bivens case and its progeny [sic], in that it waives the defense of sovereign immunity so as to make the Government independently liable in damages for the same type of conduct that is alleged to have occurred in Bivens (and for which that case imposes liability upon the individual Government officials involved). S. Rep. No. 93-588, p. 3 (1973) (emphasis supplied).

In the absence of a contrary expression from Congress, § 2680 (h) thus contemplates that victims of the kind of intentional wrongdoing alleged in this complaint shall have an action under FTCA against the United States as well as a Bivens action against the individual officials alleged to have infringed their constitutional rights.

This conclusion is buttressed by the significant fact that Congress follows the practice of explicitly stating when it means to make FTCA an exclusive remedy. See 38 U.S.C. § 4116 (a), 42 U.S.C. § 233 (a), 42 U.S.C. § 2458a, 10 U.S.C. § 1089 (a), and 22 U.S.C. § 817 (a) (malpractice by certain Government health personnel); 28 U.S.C. § 2679 (b) (operation of motor vehicles by federal employees); and 42 U.S.C. § 247b (k) (manufacturers of swine flu vaccine). Furthermore, Congress has not taken action on other bills that would expand the exclusivity of FTCA. See, e.g., S. 695, 96th Cong., 1st Sess. (1979); H. R. 2659, 96th Cong., 1st Sess. (1979); S. 3314, 95th Cong., 2d Sess. (1978).

Four additional factors, each suggesting that the Bivens remedy is more effective than the FTCA remedy, also support our conclusion that Congress did not intend to limit respondent to an FTCA action. First, the Bivens remedy, in addition to compensating victims, serves a deterrent purpose. See Butz v. Economou, supra, at 505. Because the Bivens remedy is recoverable against individuals, it is a more effective deterrent than the FTCA remedy against the United States.

It is almost axiomatic that the threat of damages has a deterrent effect, Imbler v. Pachtman, 424 U.S. 409, 442 (1976) (WHITE, J., concurring in judgment), surely particularly so when the individual official faces personal financial liability.

Petitioners argue that FTCA liability is a more effective deterrent because the individual employees responsible for the Government's liability would risk loss of employment and because the Government would be forced to promulgate corrective policies. That argument suggests, however, that the superiors would not take the same actions when an employee is found personally liable for violation of a citizen's constitutional rights. The more reasonable assumption is that responsible superiors are motivated not only by concern for the public fisc but also by concern for the Government's integrity.

Second, our decisions, although not expressly addressing and deciding the question, indicate that punitive damages may be awarded in a Bivens suit. Punitive damages are "a particular remedial mechanism normally available in the federal courts," Bivens, 403 U.S., at 397, and are especially appropriate to redress the violation by a Government official of a citizen's constitutional rights. Moreover, punitive damages are available in "a proper" § 1983 action, Carey v. Piphus, 435 U.S. 247, 257, n. 11 (1978) (punitive damages not awarded because District Court found defendants "did not act with a malicious intention to deprive respondents of their rights or to do them other injury"), and Butz v. Economou, suggests that the "constitutional design" would be stood on its head if federal officials did not face at least the same liability as state officials guilty of the same constitutional transgression. 438 U.S., at 504. But punitive damages in an FTCA suit are statutorily prohibited. 28 U.S.C. § 2674. Thus FTCA is that much less effective than a Bivens action as a deterrent to unconstitutional acts.

Third, a plaintiff cannot opt for a jury in an FTCA action, 28 U.S.C. § 2402, as he may in a Bivens suit. Petitioners argue that this is an irrelevant difference because juries have been biased against Bivens claimants. Reply Brief for Petitioners 7, and n. 6; Brief for Petitioners 30-31, n. 30. Significantly, however, they do not assert that judges trying the claims as FTCA actions would have been more receptive, and they cannot explain why the plaintiff should not retain the choice.

Fourth, an action under FTCA exists only if the State in which the alleged misconduct occurred would permit a cause of action for that misconduct to go forward. 28 U.S.C. § 1346 (b) (United States liable "in accordance with the law of the place where the act or omission occurred"). Yet it is obvious that the liability of federal officials for violations of citizens' constitutional rights should be governed by uniform rules. See Part III, infra. The question whether respondent's action for violations by federal officials of federal constitutional rights should be left to the vagaries of the laws of the several States admits of only a negative answer in the absence of a contrary congressional resolution.

Plainly FTCA is not a sufficient protector of the citizens' constitutional rights, and without a clear congressional mandate we cannot hold that Congress relegated respondent exclusively to the FTCA remedy.

III

Bivens actions are a creation of federal law and, therefore, the question whether respondent's action survived Jones' death is a question of federal law. See Burks v. Lasker, 441 U.S. 471, 476 (1979). Petitioners, however, would have us fashion a federal rule of survivorship that incorporates the survivorship laws of the forum State, at least where the state law is not inconsistent with federal law. Respondent argues, on the other hand, that only a uniform federal rule of survivorship is compatible with the goal of deterring federal officials from infringing federal constitutional rights in the manner alleged in respondent's complaint. We agree with respondent. Whatever difficulty we might have resolving the question were the federal involvement less clear, we hold that only a uniform federal rule of survivorship will suffice to redress the constitutional deprivation here alleged and to protect against repetition of such conduct.

In short, we agree with and adopt the reasoning of the Court of Appeals, 581 F.2d, at 674-675 (footnote omitted):

The essentiality of the survival of civil rights claims for complete vindication of constitutional rights is buttressed by the need for uniform treatment of those claims, at least when they are against federal officials. As this very case illustrates, uniformity cannot be achieved if courts are limited to applicable state law. Here the relevant Indiana statute would not permit survival of the claim, while in Beard [v. Robinson, 563 F.2d 331 (CA7 1977),] the Illinois statute permitted survival of the Bivens action. The liability of federal agents for violation of constitutional rights should not depend upon where the violation occurred. . . . In sum, we hold that whenever the relevant state survival statute would abate a Bivens-type action brought against defendants whose conduct results in death, the federal common law allows survival of the action.

Robertson v. Wegmann, 436 U.S. 584 (1978), holding that a § 1983 action would abate in accordance with Louisiana survivorship law is not to the contrary. There the plaintiff's death was not caused by the acts of the defendants upon which the suit was based. Moreover, Robertson expressly recognized that to prevent frustrations of the deterrence goals of § 1983 (which in part also underlie Bivens actions, see Part II, supra) "[a] state official contemplating illegal activity must always be prepared to face the prospect of a § 1983 action being filed against him." 436 U.S., at 592. A federal official contemplating unconstitutional conduct similarly must be prepared to face the prospect of a Bivens action. A uniform rule that claims such as respondent's survive the decedent's death is essential if we are not to "frustrate in [an] important way the achievement" of the goals of Bivens actions. Auto Workers v. Hoosier Cardinal Corp., 383 U.S. 696, 702 (1966).

Affirmed.

PATSY
v.
BOARD OF REGENTS OF THE STATE OF FLORIDA

457 U.S. 496; 102 S. Ct. 2557; 73 L. Ed. 2d 172 (1982)

JUSTICE MARSHALL delivered the opinion of the Court.

This case presents the question whether exhaustion of state administrative remedies is a prerequisite to an action under 42 U.S.C. § 1983 (1976 ed., Supp. IV). Petitioner Georgia Patsy filed this action, alleging that her employer, Florida International University (FIU), had denied her employment opportunities solely on the basis of her race and sex. By a divided vote, the United States Court of Appeals for the Fifth Circuit found that petitioner was required to exhaust "adequate and appropriate" administrative remedies, and remanded the case to the District Court to consider the adequacy of the administrative procedures. Patsy v. Florida International University, 634 F.2d 900 (1981) (en banc). We granted certiorari, 454 U.S. 813, and reverse the decision of the Court of Appeals.

I

Petitioner alleges that even though she is well qualified and has received uniformly excellent performance evaluations from her supervisors, she has been rejected for more than 13 positions at FIU. She further claims that FIU has unlawfully filled positions through intentional discrimination on the basis of race and sex. She seeks declaratory and injunctive relief or, in the alternative, damages.

The United States District Court for the Southern District of Florida granted respondent Board of Regents' motion to dismiss because petitioner had not exhausted available administrative remedies. On appeal, a panel of the Court of Appeals reversed, and remanded the case for further proceedings. Patsy v. Florida International University, 612 F.2d 946 (1980). The full court then granted respondent's petition for rehearing and vacated the panel decision.

The Court of Appeals reviewed numerous opinions of this Court holding that exhaustion of administrative remedies was not required, and concluded that these cases did not preclude the application of a "flexible" exhaustion rule. 634 F.2d, at 908. After canvassing the policy arguments in favor of an exhaustion requirement, the Court of Appeals decided that a § 1983 plaintiff could be required to exhaust administrative remedies if the following minimum conditions are met: (1) an orderly system of review or appeal is provided by statute or agency rule; (2) the agency can grant relief more or less commensurate with the claim; (3) relief is available within a reasonable period of time; (4) the procedures are fair, are not unduly burdensome, and are not used to harass or discourage those with legitimate claims; and (5) interim relief is available, in appropriate cases, to prevent irreparable injury and to preserve the plaintiff's rights during the administrative process. Where these minimum standards are met, a court must further consider the particular administrative scheme, the nature of the plaintiff's interest, and the values served by the exhaustion doctrine in order to determine whether exhaustion should be required. Id., at 912-913. The Court of Appeals remanded the case to the District Court to determine whether exhaustion would be appropriate in this case.

II

The question whether exhaustion of administrative remedies should ever be required in a § 1983 action has prompted vigorous debate and disagreement. See, e.g., Turner, *When Prisoners Sue: A Study of Prisoner Section 1983 Cases in the Federal Courts,* 92 Harv. L. Rev. 610 (1979); Note, 8 Ind. L. Rev. 565 (1975); Comment, 41 U. Chi. L. Rev. 537 (1974). Our resolution of this issue, however, is made much easier because we are not writing on a clean slate. This Court has addressed this issue, as well as related issues, on several prior occasions.

Respondent suggests that our prior precedents do not control our decision today, arguing that these cases can be distinguished on their facts or that this Court did not "fully" consider the question whether exhaustion

should be required. This contention need not detain us long. Beginning with McNeese v. Board of Education, 373 U.S. 668, 671-673 (1963), we have on numerous occasions rejected the argument that a § 1983 action should be dismissed where the plaintiff has not exhausted state administrative remedies. See Barry v. Barchi, 443 U.S. 55, 63, n. 10 (1979); Gibson v. Berryhill, 411 U.S. 564, 574 (1973); Carter v. Stanton, 405 U.S. 669, 671 (1972); Wilwording v. Swenson, 404 U.S. 249, 251 (1971); Houghton v. Shafer, 392 U.S. 639, 640 (1968); King v. Smith, 392 U.S. 309, 312, n. 4 (1968); Damico v. California, 389 U.S. 416 (1967). Cf. Steffel v. Thompson, 415 U.S. 452, 472-473 (1974) ("When federal claims are premised on [§ 1983]—as they are here—we have not required exhaustion of state judicial or administrative remedies, recognizing the paramount role Congress has assigned to the federal courts to protect constitutional rights"). Respondent may be correct in arguing that several of these decisions could have been based on traditional exceptions to the exhaustion doctrine. Nevertheless, this Court has stated categorically that exhaustion is not a prerequisite to an action under § 1983, and we have not deviated from that position in the 19 years since McNeese. Therefore, we do not address the question presented in this case as one of first impression.

III

Respondent argues that we should reconsider these decisions and adopt the Court of Appeals' exhaustion rule, which was based on McKart v. United States, 395 U.S. 185 (1969). This Court has never announced a definitive formula for determining whether prior decisions should be overruled or reconsidered. However, in Monell v. New York City Dept. of Social Services, 436 U.S. 658, 695-701 (1978), we articulated four factors that should be considered. Two of these factors—whether the decisions in question misconstrued the meaning of the statute as revealed in its legislative history and whether overruling these decisions would be inconsistent with more recent expressions of congressional intent—are particularly relevant to our decision today. Both concern legislative purpose, which is of paramount importance in the exhaustion context because Congress is vested with the power to prescribe the basic procedural scheme under which claims may be heard in federal courts. Of course, courts play an important role in determining the limits of an exhaustion requirement and may impose such a requirement even where Congress has not expressly so provided. However, the initial question whether exhaustion is required should be answered by reference to congressional intent; and a court should not defer the exercise of jurisdiction under a federal statute unless it is consistent with that intent. Therefore, in deciding whether we should reconsider our prior decisions and require exhaustion of state administrative remedies, we look to congressional intent as reflected in the legislative history of the predecessor to § 1983 and in recent congressional activity in this area.

A

In determining whether our prior decisions misconstrued the meaning of § 1983, we begin with a review of the legislative history to § 1 of the Civil Rights Act of 1871, 17 Stat. 13, the precursor to § 1983. Although we recognize that the 1871 Congress did not expressly contemplate the exhaustion question, we believe that the tenor of the debates over § 1 supports our conclusion that exhaustion of administrative remedies in § 1983 actions should not be judicially imposed.

The Civil Rights Act of 1871, along with the Fourteenth Amendment it was enacted to enforce, were crucial ingredients in the basic alteration of our federal system accomplished during the Reconstruction Era. During that time, the Federal Government was clearly established as a guarantor of the basic federal rights of individuals against incursions by state power. As we recognized in Mitchum v. Foster, 407 U.S. 225, 242 (1972) (quoting Ex parte Virginia, 100 U.S. 339, 346 (1880)), "[the] very purpose of § 1983 was to interpose the federal courts between the States and the people, as guardians of the people's federal rights—to protect the people from unconstitutional action under color of state law, 'whether that action be executive, legislative, or judicial.'"

At least three recurring themes in the debates over § 1 cast serious doubt on the suggestion that requiring exhaustion of state administrative remedies would be consistent with the intent of the 1871 Congress. First, in passing § 1, Congress assigned to the federal courts a paramount role in protecting constitutional rights. . . .

* * *

The 1871 Congress intended § 1 to "throw open the doors of the United States courts" to individuals who were threatened with, or who had suffered, the deprivation of constitutional rights, id., at 376 (remarks of Rep. Lowe), and to provide these individuals immediate access to the federal courts notwithstanding any provision of state law to the contrary. . . .

* * *

A second theme in the debates further suggests that the 1871 Congress would not have wanted to impose an exhaustion requirement. A major factor motivating the expansion of federal jurisdiction through §§ 1 and 2 of the bill was the belief of the 1871 Congress that the state authorities had been unable or unwilling to protect the constitutional rights of individuals or to punish those who violated these rights. See, e.g., Globe 321 (remarks of Rep. Stoughton) ("The State authorities and local courts are unable or unwilling to check the evil or punish the criminals"); id., at 374 (remarks of Rep. Lowe) ("the local administrations have been found inadequate or unwilling to apply the proper corrective"); id., at 459 (remarks of Rep. Coburn); id., at 609 (remarks of Sen. Pool); id., at 687 (remarks of Sen. Shurz); id., at 691 (remarks of Sen. Edmunds); Globe App. 185 (remarks of Rep. Platt). Of primary importance to the exhaustion question was the mistrust that the 1871 Congress held for the factfinding processes of state institutions. See, e.g., Globe 320 (testimony of Hon. Thomas Settle, Justice of the North Carolina Supreme Court, before the House Judiciary Committee) ("The defect lies not so much with the courts as with the juries"); id., at 394 (remarks of Rep. Rainey); Globe App. 311 (remarks of Rep. Maynard). This Congress believed that federal courts would be less susceptible to local prejudice and to the existing defects in the factfinding processes of the state courts. See, e.g., Globe 322 (remarks of Rep. Stoughton); id., at 459 (remarks of Rep. Coburn). This perceived defect in the States' factfinding processes is particularly relevant to the question of exhaustion of administrative remedies: exhaustion rules are often applied in deference to the superior factfinding ability of the relevant administrative agency. See, e.g., McKart v. United States, 395 U.S., at 192-196.

A third feature of the debates relevant to the exhaustion question is the fact that many legislators interpreted the bill to provide dual or concurrent forums in the state and federal system, enabling the plaintiff to choose the forum in which to seek relief. Cf. Monroe v. Pape, 365 U.S. 167, 183 (1961) ("The federal remedy is supplementary to the state remedy, and the latter need not be first sought and refused before the federal one is invoked"). . . .

* * *

This legislative history supports the conclusion that our prior decisions, holding that exhaustion of state administrative remedies is not a prerequisite to an action under § 1983, did not misperceive the statutory intent: it seems fair to infer that the 1871 Congress did not intend that an individual be compelled in every case to exhaust state administrative remedies before filing an action under § 1 of the Civil Rights Act. We recognize, however, that drawing such a conclusion from this history alone is somewhat precarious: the 1871 Congress was not presented with the question of exhaustion of administrative remedies, nor was it aware of the potential role of state administrative agencies. Therefore, we do not rely exclusively on this legislative history in deciding the question presented here. Congress addressed the question of exhaustion under § 1983 when it recently enacted 42 U.S.C. § 1997e (1976 ed., Supp. IV). The legislative history of § 1997e provides strong evidence of congressional intent on this issue.

B

The Civil Rights of Institutionalized Persons Act, 42 U.S.C. § 1997 et seq. (1976 ed.,

Supp. IV), was enacted primarily to ensure that the United States Attorney General has "legal standing to enforce existing constitutional rights and Federal statutory rights of institutionalized persons." H. R. Conf. Rep. No. 96-897, p. 9 (1980) (Conf. Rep.). In § 1997e, Congress also created a specific, limited exhaustion requirement for adult prisoners bringing actions pursuant to § 1983. Section 1997e and its legislative history demonstrate that Congress understood that exhaustion is not generally required in § 1983 actions, and that it decided to carve out only a narrow exception to this rule. A judicially imposed exhaustion requirement would be inconsistent with Congress' decision to adopt § 1997e and would usurp policy judgments that Congress has reserved for itself.

In considering whether an exhaustion requirement should be incorporated into the bill, Congress clearly expressed its belief that a decision to require exhaustion for certain § 1983 actions would work a change in the law. Witnesses testifying before the Subcommittee that drafted the bill discussed the decisions of this Court holding that exhaustion was not required. . . .

* * *

The debates over adopting an exhaustion requirement also reflect this understanding. See, e.g., 124 Cong. Rec. 11988 (1978) (remarks of Rep. Volkmer and Rep. Kastenmeier); id., at 15445 (remarks of Rep. Ertel); id., at 23180 (remarks of Rep. Wiggins) ("it is settled law that an exhaustion of administrative remedies is not required as a precondition of maintaining a 1983 action"); 125 Cong. Rec. 12496 (1979) (remarks of Rep. Butler) ("Under existing law there is no requirement that a complainant first ask the State prison system to help him"). With the understanding that exhaustion generally is not required, Congress decided to adopt the limited exhaustion requirement of § 1997e in order to relieve the burden on the federal courts by diverting certain prisoner petitions back through state and local institutions, and also to encourage the States to develop appropriate grievance procedures. See, e.g., Conf. Rep. 9; 124 Cong. Rec. 11976 (1978) (remarks of Rep. Kastenmeier); id., at 11976, 11983 (remarks of Rep. Railsback); id., at

15442 (remarks of Rep. Kastenmeier); id., at 15445 (remarks of Rep. Ertel); id., at 23176 (remarks of Rep. Kastenmeier); id., at 23179-23180 (remarks of Rep. Butler); id., at 23180 (remarks of Rep. Ertel). Implicit in this decision is Congress' conclusion that the no-exhaustion rule should be left standing with respect to other § 1983 suits.

A judicially imposed exhaustion requirement would also be inconsistent with the extraordinarily detailed exhaustion scheme embodied in § 1997e. Section 1997e carves out a narrow exception to the general no-exhaustion rule to govern certain prisoner claims, and establishes a procedure to ensure that the administrative remedies are adequate and effective. The exhaustion requirement is expressly limited to § 1983 actions brought by an adult convicted of a crime. 42 U.S.C. § 1997e(a)(1) (1976 ed., Supp. IV). Section 1997e(b)(1) instructs the Attorney General to "promulgate minimum standards for the development and implementation of a plain, speedy, and effective system" of administrative remedies, and § 1997e(b)(2) specifies certain minimum standards that must be included. A court may require exhaustion of administrative remedies only if "the Attorney General has certified or the court has determined that such administrative remedies are in substantial compliance with the minimum acceptable standards promulgated under subsection (b)." § 1997e(a)(2). Before exhaustion may be required, the court must further conclude that it "would be appropriate and in the interests of justice." § 1997e(a)(1). Finally, in those § 1983 actions meeting all the statutory requirements for exhaustion, the district court may not dismiss the case, but may only "continue such case for a period of not to exceed ninety days in order to require exhaustion." Ibid. This detailed scheme is inconsistent with discretion to impose, on an ad hoc basis, a judicially developed exhaustion rule in other cases.

Congress hoped that § 1997e would improve prison conditions by stimulating the development of successful grievance mechanisms. See, e.g., Conf. Rep. 9; H. R. Rep. No. 96-80, p. 4 (1979); 1979 Hearings 4 (remarks of Rep. Railsback); 124 Cong. Rec. 11976 (1978) (remarks of Rep. Railsback); 125 Cong. Rec. 12492 (1979) (remarks of Rep. Drinan); 126 Cong. Rec. 10780 (1980)

(remarks of Rep. Kastenmeier). To further this purpose, Congress provided for the deferral of the exercise of federal jurisdiction over certain § 1983 claims only on the condition that the state prisons develop adequate procedures. This purpose would be frustrated by judicial discretion to impose exhaustion generally: the States would have no incentive to adopt grievance procedures capable of certification, because prisoner § 1983 cases could be diverted to state administrative remedies in any event.

In sum, the exhaustion provisions of the Act make sense, and are not superfluous, only if exhaustion could not be required before its enactment and if Congress intended to carve out a narrow exception to this no-exhaustion rule. The legislative history of § 1997e demonstrates that Congress has taken the approach of carving out specific exceptions to the general rule that federal courts cannot require exhaustion under § 1983. It is not our province to alter the balance struck by Congress in establishing the procedural framework for bringing actions under § 1983.

C

Respondent and the Court of Appeals argue that exhaustion of administrative remedies should be required because it would further various policies. They argue that an exhaustion requirement would lessen the perceived burden that § 1983 actions impose on federal courts; would further the goal of comity and improve federal-state relations by postponing federal-court review until after the state administrative agency had passed on the issue; and would enable the agency, which presumably has expertise in the area at issue, to enlighten the federal court's ultimate decision.

As we noted earlier, policy considerations alone cannot justify judicially imposed exhaustion unless exhaustion is consistent with congressional intent. See supra, at 501-502, and n. 4. Furthermore, as the debates over incorporating the exhaustion requirement in § 1997e demonstrate, the relevant policy considerations do not invariably point in one direction, and there is vehement disagreement over the validity of the assumptions underlying many of them. The very difficulty of these policy considerations, and

Congress' superior institutional competence to pursue this debate, suggest that legislative not judicial solutions are preferable. Cf. Diamond v. Chakrabarty, 447 U.S. 303, 317 (1980); Steelworkers v. Bouligny, Inc., 382 U.S. 145, 150, 153 (1965).

Beyond the policy issues that must be resolved in deciding whether to require exhaustion, there are equally difficult questions concerning the design and scope of an exhaustion requirement. These questions include how to define those categories of § 1983 claims in which exhaustion might be desirable; how to unify and centralize the standards for judging the kinds of administrative procedures that should be exhausted; what tolling requirements and time limitations should be adopted; what is the res judicata and collateral estoppel effect of particular administrative determinations; what consequences should attach to the failure to comply with procedural requirements of administrative proceedings; and whether federal courts could grant necessary interim injunctive relief and hold the action pending exhaustion, or proceed to judgment without requiring exhaustion even though exhaustion might otherwise be required, where the relevant administrative agency is either powerless or not inclined to grant such interim relief. These and similar questions might be answered swiftly and surely by legislation, but would create costly, remedy-delaying, and court-burdening litigation if answered incrementally by the judiciary in the context of diverse constitutional claims relating to thousands of different state agencies.

The very variety of claims, claimants, and state agencies involved in § 1983 cases argues for congressional consideration of the myriad of policy considerations, and may explain why Congress, in deciding whether to require exhaustion in certain § 1983 actions brought by adult prisoners, carved out such a narrow, detailed exception to the no-exhaustion rule. After full debate and consideration of the various policy arguments, Congress adopted § 1997e, taking the largest class of § 1983 actions and constructing an exhaustion requirement that differs substantially from the McKart-type standard urged by respondent and adopted by the Court of Appeals. See n. 18, supra. It is not for us to say whether Congress will or should create a sim-

ilar scheme for other categories of § 1983 claims or whether Congress will or should adopt an altogether different exhaustion requirement for nonprisoner § 1983 claims.

IV

Based on the legislative histories of both § 1983 and § 1997e, we conclude that exhaustion of state administrative remedies should not be required as a prerequisite to bringing an action pursuant to § 1983. We decline to overturn our prior decisions holding that such exhaustion is not required. The decision of the Court of Appeals is reversed, and the case is remanded for proceedings consistent with this opinion.

It is so ordered.

HARLOW
v.
FITZGERALD

457 U.S. 800; 102 S. Ct. 2727; 73 L. Ed. 2d 396 (1982)

JUSTICE POWELL delivered the opinion of the Court.

The issue in this case is the scope of the immunity available to the senior aides and advisers of the President of the United States in a suit for damages based upon their official acts.

I

In this suit for civil damages petitioners Bryce Harlow and Alexander Butterfield are alleged to have participated in a conspiracy to violate the constitutional and statutory rights of the respondent A. Ernest Fitzgerald. Respondent avers that petitioners entered the conspiracy in their capacities as senior White House aides to former President Richard M. Nixon. As the alleged conspiracy is the same as that involved in Nixon v. Fitzgerald, ante, p. 731, the facts need not be repeated in detail.

Respondent claims that Harlow joined the conspiracy in his role as the Presidential aide principally responsible for congressional relations. At the conclusion of discovery the supporting evidence remained inferential. . . .

* * *

Together with their codefendant Richard Nixon, petitioners Harlow and Butterfield moved for summary judgment on February 12, 1980. In denying the motion the District Court upheld the legal sufficiency of Fitzgerald's Bivens (Bivens v. Six Unknown Fed. Narcotics Agents, 403 U.S. 388 (1971)) claim under the First Amendment and his "inferred" statutory causes of action under 5 U.S.C. § 7211 (1976 ed., Supp. IV) and 18 U.S.C. § 1505. The court found that genuine issues of disputed fact remained for resolution at trial. It also ruled that petitioners were not entitled to absolute immunity. App. to Pet. for Cert. 1a-3a.

Independently of former President Nixon, petitioners invoked the collateral order doctrine and appealed the denial of their immunity defense to the Court of Appeals for the District of Columbia Circuit. The Court of Appeals dismissed the appeal without opinion. Id., at 11a-12a. Never having determined the immunity available to the senior aides and advisers of the President of the United States, we granted certiorari. 452 U.S. 959 (1981).

II

* * *

Our decisions have recognized immunity defenses of two kinds. For officials whose special functions or constitutional status requires complete protection from suit, we have recognized the defense of "absolute immunity." The absolute immunity of legislators, in their legislative functions, see, e.g., Eastland v. United States Servicemen's Fund, 421 U.S. 491 (1975), and of judges, in their judicial functions, see, e.g., Stump v. Sparkman, 435 U.S. 349 (1978), now is well settled. Our decisions also have extended absolute immunity to certain officials of the Executive Branch. These include prosecutors and similar officials, see Butz v. Economou, 438 U.S. 478, 508-512 (1978), executive officers engaged in adjudicative functions, id., at 513-

517, and the President of the United States, see Nixon v. Fitzgerald, ante, p. 731.

For executive officials in general, however, our cases make plain that qualified immunity represents the norm. In Scheuer v. Rhodes, 416 U.S. 232 (1974), we acknowledged that high officials require greater protection than those with less complex discretionary responsibilities. Nonetheless, we held that a governor and his aides could receive the requisite protection from qualified or good-faith immunity. Id., at 247-248. In Butz v. Economou, supra, we extended the approach of Scheuer to high federal officials of the Executive Branch. . . . the recognition of a qualified immunity defense for high executives reflected an attempt to balance competing values: not only the importance of a damages remedy to protect the rights of citizens, 438 U.S., at 504-505, but also "the need to protect officials who are required to exercise their discretion and the related public interest in encouraging the vigorous exercise of official authority." . . .

* * *

Butz continued to acknowledge that the special functions of some officials might require absolute immunity. But the Court held that "federal officials who seek absolute exemption from personal liability for unconstitutional conduct must bear the burden of showing that public policy requires an exemption of that scope." Id., at 506. This we reaffirmed today in Nixon v. Fitzgerald.

III

A

Petitioners argue that they are entitled to a blanket protection of absolute immunity as an incident of their offices as Presidential aides. . . .

* * *

Having decided in Butz that Members of the Cabinet ordinarily enjoy only qualified immunity from suit, we conclude today that it would be equally untenable to hold absolute immunity an incident of the office of every

Presidential subordinate based in the White House. Members of the Cabinet are direct subordinates of the President, frequently with greater responsibilities, both to the President and to the Nation, than White House staff. The considerations that supported our decision in Butz apply with equal force to this case. It is no disparagement of the offices held by petitioners to hold that Presidential aides, like Members of the Cabinet, generally are entitled only to a qualified immunity.

B

In disputing the controlling authority of Butz, petitioners rely on the principles developed in Gravel v. United States, 408 U.S. 606 (1972). In Gravel we endorsed the view that "it is literally impossible . . . for Members of Congress to perform their legislative tasks without the help of aides and assistants" and that "the day-to-day work of such aides is so critical to the Members' performance that they must be treated as the latter's alter egos . . ." Id., at 616-617. Having done so, we held the Speech and Debate Clause derivatively applicable to the "legislative acts" of a Senator's aide that would have been privileged if performed by the Senator himself. Id., at 621-622.

Petitioners contend that the rationale of Gravel mandates a similar "derivative" immunity for the chief aides of the President of the United States. Emphasizing that the President must delegate a large measure of authority to execute the duties of his office, they argue that recognition of derivative absolute immunity is made essential by all the considerations that support absolute immunity for the President himself.

. . . [I]n general our cases have followed a "functional" approach to immunity law. We have recognized that the judicial, prosecutorial, and legislative functions require absolute immunity. But this protection has extended no further than its justification would warrant. In Gravel, for example, we emphasized that Senators and their aides were absolutely immune only when performing "acts legislative in nature," and not when taking other acts even "in their official capacity." 408 U.S., at 625. See Hutchinson v. Proxmire, 443 U.S. 111, 125-133 (1979). Our cases

involving judges and prosecutors have followed a similar line. The undifferentiated extension of absolute "derivative" immunity to the President's aides therefore could not be reconciled with the "functional" approach that has characterized the immunity decisions of this Court, indeed including Gravel itself.

* * *

IV

. . . [P]etitioners assert that public policy at least mandates an application of the qualified immunity standard that would permit the defeat of insubstantial claims without resort to trial. We agree.

A

The resolution of immunity questions inherently requires a balance between the evils inevitable in any available alternative. In situations of abuse of office, an action for damages may offer the only realistic avenue for vindication of constitutional guarantees. Butz v. Economou, supra, at 506; see Bivens v. Six Unknown Fed. Narcotics Agents, 403 U.S., at 410 ("For people in Bivens' shoes, it is damages or nothing"). It is this recognition that has required the denial of absolute immunity to most public officers. At the same time, however, it cannot be disputed seriously that claims frequently run against the innocent as well as the guilty—at a cost not only to the defendant officials, but to society as a whole. These social costs include the expenses of litigation, the diversion of official energy from pressing public issues, and the deterrence of able citizens from acceptance of public office. Finally, there is the danger that fear of being sued will "dampen the ardor of all but the most resolute, or the most irresponsible [public officials], in the unflinching discharge of their duties." Gregoire v. Biddle, 177 F.2d 579, 581 (CA2 1949), cert. denied, 339 U.S. 949 (1950).

In identifying qualified immunity as the best attainable accommodation of competing values, in Butz, supra, at 507-508, as in Scheuer, 416 U.S., at 245-248, we relied on the assumption that this standard would permit "[insubstantial] lawsuits [to] be quickly terminated." 438 U.S., at 507-508; see Hanrahan v. Hampton, 446 U.S. 754, 765 (1980) (POWELL, J., concurring in part and dissenting in part). Yet petitioners advance persuasive arguments that the dismissal of insubstantial lawsuits without trial—a factor presupposed in the balance of competing interests struck by our prior cases—requires an adjustment of the "good faith" standard established by our decisions.

B

Qualified or "good faith" immunity is an affirmative defense that must be pleaded by a defendant official. Gomez v. Toledo, 446 U.S. 635 (1980). Decisions of this Court have established that the "good faith" defense has both an "objective" and a "subjective" aspect. The objective element involves a presumptive knowledge of and respect for "basic, unquestioned constitutional rights." Wood v. Strickland, 420 U.S. 308, 322 (1975). The subjective component refers to "permissible intentions." Ibid. Characteristically the Court has defined these elements by identifying the circumstances in which qualified immunity would not be available. Referring both to the objective and subjective elements, we have held that qualified immunity would be defeated if an official "knew or reasonably should have known that the action he took within his sphere of official responsibility would violate the constitutional rights of the [plaintiff], or if he took the action with the malicious intention to cause a deprivation of constitutional rights or other injury . . . ." Ibid. (emphasis added).

The subjective element of the good-faith defense frequently has proved incompatible with our admonition in Butz that insubstantial claims should not proceed to trial. Rule 56 of the Federal Rules of Civil Procedure provides that disputed questions of fact ordinarily may not be decided on motions for summary judgment. And an official's subjective good faith has been considered to be a question of fact that some courts have regarded as inherently requiring resolution by a jury.

In the context of Butz' attempted balancing of competing values, it now is clear that substantial costs attend the litigation of the subjective good faith of government offi-

cials. Not only are there the general costs of subjecting officials to the risks of trial—distraction of officials from their governmental duties, inhibition of discretionary action, and deterrence of able people from public service. There are special costs to "subjective" inquiries of this kind. Immunity generally is available only to officials performing discretionary functions. In contrast with the thought processes accompanying "ministerial" tasks, the judgments surrounding discretionary action almost inevitably are influenced by the decisionmaker's experiences, values, and emotions. These variables explain in part why questions of subjective intent so rarely can be decided by summary judgment. Yet they also frame a background in which there often is no clear end to the relevant evidence. Judicial inquiry into subjective motivation therefore may entail broad-ranging discovery and the deposing of numerous persons, including an official's professional colleagues. Inquiries of this kind can be peculiarly disruptive of effective government.

Consistently with the balance at which we aimed in Butz, we conclude today that bare allegations of malice should not suffice to subject government officials either to the costs of trial or to the burdens of broad-reaching discovery. We therefore hold that government officials performing discretionary functions, generally are shielded from liability for civil damages insofar as their conduct does not violate clearly established statutory or constitutional rights of which a reasonable person would have known. See Procunier v. Navarette, 434 U.S. 555, 565 (1978); Wood v. Strickland, 420 U.S., at 322.

Reliance on the objective reasonableness of an official's conduct, as measured by reference to clearly established law, should avoid excessive disruption of government and permit the resolution of many insubstantial claims on summary judgment. On summary judgment, the judge appropriately may determine, not only the currently applicable law, but whether that law was clearly established at the time an action occurred. If the law at that time was not clearly established, an official could not reasonably be expected to anticipate subsequent legal developments, nor could he fairly be said to "know" that the

law forbade conduct not previously identified as unlawful. Until this threshold immunity question is resolved, discovery should
not be allowed. If the law was clearly established, the immunity defense ordinarily
should fail, since a reasonably competent
public official should know the law governing his conduct. Nevertheless, if the official
pleading the defense claims extraordinary
circumstances and can prove that he neither
knew nor should have known of the relevant
legal standard, the defense should be sustained. But again, the defense would turn primarily on objective factors.

By defining the limits of qualified immunity essentially in objective terms, we provide no license to lawless conduct. The public interest in deterrence of unlawful conduct
and in compensation of victims remains protected by a test that focuses on the objective
legal reasonableness of an official's acts.
Where an official could be expected to know
that certain conduct would violate statutory
or constitutional rights, he should be made to
hesitate; and a person who suffers injury
caused by such conduct may have a cause of
action. But where an official's duties legitimately require action in which clearly established rights are not implicated, the public
interest may be better served by action taken
"with independence and without fear of consequences." Pierson v. Ray, 386 U.S. 547, 554
(1967).

C

In this case petitioners have asked us to
hold that the respondent's pretrial showings
were insufficient to survive their motion for
summary judgment. We think it appropriate,
however, to remand the case to the District
Court for its reconsideration of this issue in
light of this opinion. The trial court is more
familiar with the record so far developed and
also is better situated to make any such further findings as may be necessary.

V

The judgment of the Court of Appeals is
vacated, and the case is remanded for further
action consistent with this opinion.

So ordered.

SMITH
v.
WADE

461 U.S. 30; 103 S. Ct. 1625;
75 L. Ed. 2d 632 (1983)

JUSTICE BRENNAN delivered the opinion of the Court.

We granted certiorari in this case, 456 U.S.
924 (1982), to decide whether the District
Court for the Western District of Missouri
applied the correct legal standard in instructing the jury that it might award punitive damages under 42 U.S.C. § 1983 (1976 ed., Supp.
V).[1] The Court of Appeals for the Eighth Circuit sustained the award of punitive damages.
Wade v. Haynes, 663 F.2d 778 (1981). We
affirm.

I

The petitioner, William H. Smith, is a
guard at Algoa Reformatory, a unit of the
Missouri Division of Corrections for youthful first offenders. The respondent, Daniel R.
Wade, was assigned to Algoa as an inmate in
1976. In the summer of 1976 Wade voluntarily checked into Algoa's protective custody
unit. Because of disciplinary violations during his stay in protective custody, Wade was
given a short term in punitive segregation
and then transferred to administrative segregation. On the evening of Wade's first day in
administrative segregation, he was placed in
a cell with another inmate. Later, when Smith
came on duty in Wade's dormitory, he placed
a third inmate in Wade's cell. According to
Wade's testimony, his cellmates harassed,
beat, and sexually assaulted him.

Wade brought suit under 42 U.S.C. § 1983
against Smith and four other guards and correctional officials, alleging that his Eighth
Amendment rights had been violated. At trial
his evidence showed that he had placed himself in protective custody because of prior
incidents of violence against him by other
inmates. The third prisoner whom Smith
added to the cell had been placed in administrative segregation for fighting. Smith had
made no effort to find out whether another
cell was available; in fact there was another
cell in the same dormitory with only one

occupant. Further, only a few weeks earlier, another inmate had been beaten to death in the same dormitory during the same shift, while Smith had been on duty. Wade asserted that Smith and the other defendants knew or should have known that an assault against him was likely under the circumstances.

During trial, the District Judge entered a directed verdict for two of the defendants. He instructed the jury that Wade could make out an Eighth Amendment violation only by showing "physical abuse of such base, inhumane and barbaric proportions as to shock the sensibilities." Further, because of Smith's qualified immunity as a prison guard, see Procunier v. Navarette, 434 U.S. 555 (1978), the judge instructed the jury that Wade could recover only if the defendants were guilty of "gross negligence" (defined as "a callous indifference or a thoughtless disregard for the consequences of one's act or failure to act") or "[egregious] failure to protect" (defined as "a flagrant or remarkably bad failure to protect") Wade. He reiterated that Wade could not recover on a showing of simple negligence. Id., at 644.

The District Judge also charged the jury that it could award punitive damages on a proper showing:

> In addition to actual damages, the law permits the jury, under certain circumstances, to award the injured person punitive and exemplary damages, in order to punish the wrongdoer for some extraordinary misconduct, and to serve as an example or warning to others not to engage in such conduct.

> If you find the issues in favor of the plaintiff, and if the conduct of one or more of the defendants is shown to be a reckless or callous disregard of, or indifference to, the rights or safety of others, then you may assess punitive or exemplary damages in addition to any award of actual damages.

> . . . The amount of punitive or exemplary damages assessed against any defendant may be such sum as you believe will serve to punish that defendant and to deter him and others from like conduct. Id., at 643.

The jury returned verdicts for two of the three remaining defendants. It found Smith liable, however, and awarded $25,000 in compensatory damages and $5,000 in punitive damages. The District Court entered judgment on the verdict, and the Court of Appeals affirmed. Wade v. Haynes, 663 F.2d 778 (1981).

In this Court, Smith attacks only the award of punitive damages. He does not challenge the correctness of the instructions on liability or qualified immunity, nor does he question the adequacy of the evidence to support the verdict of liability for compensatory damages.

II

Section 1983 is derived from § 1 of the Civil Rights Act of 1871, 17 Stat. 13. It was intended to create "a species of tort liability" in favor of persons deprived of federally secured rights. Carey v. Piphus, 435 U.S. 247, 253 (1978); Imbler v. Pachtman, 424 U.S. 409, 417 (1976). We noted in Carey that there was little in the section's legislative history concerning the damages recoverable for this tort liability, 435 U.S., at 255. In the absence of more specific guidance, we looked first to the common law of torts (both modern and as of 1871), with such modification or adaptation as might be necessary to carry out the purpose and policy of the statute. Id., at 253-264. We have done the same in other contexts arising under § 1983, especially the recurring problem of common-law immunities.

Smith correctly concedes that "punitive damages are available in a 'proper' § 1983 action . . . ." Carlson v. Green, 446 U.S. 14, 22 (1980); Brief for Petitioner 8. Although there was debate about the theoretical correctness of the punitive damages doctrine in the latter part of the last century, the doctrine was accepted as settled law by nearly all state and federal courts, including this Court. It was likewise generally established that individual public officers were liable for punitive damages for their misconduct on the same basis as other individual defendants. See also Scott v. Donald, 165 U.S. 58, 77-89 (1897) (punitive damages for constitutional tort).

Further, although the precise issue of the availability of punitive damages under § 1983 has never come squarely before us, we have had occasion more than once to make clear our view that they are available; indeed, we have rested decisions on related questions on the premise of such availability.

Smith argues, nonetheless, that this was not a "proper" case in which to award punitive damages. More particularly, he attacks the instruction that punitive damages could be awarded on a finding of reckless or callous disregard of or indifference to Wade's rights or safety. Instead, he contends that the proper test is one of actual malicious intent— "ill will, spite, or intent to injure." Brief for Petitioner 9. He offers two arguments for this position: first, that actual intent is the proper standard for punitive damages in all cases under § 1983; and second, that even if intent is not always required, it should be required here because the threshold for punitive damages should always be higher than that for liability in the first instance. We address these in turn.

III

Smith does not argue that the common law, either in 1871 or now, required or requires a showing of actual malicious intent for recovery of punitive damages.

Perhaps not surprisingly, there was significant variation (both terminological and substantive) among American jurisdictions in the latter 19th century on the precise standard to be applied in awarding punitive damages—variation that was exacerbated by the ambiguity and slipperiness of such common terms as "malice" and "gross negligence." Most of the confusion, however, seems to have been over the degree of negligence, recklessness, carelessness, or culpable indifference that should be required—not over whether actual intent was essential. On the contrary, the rule in a large majority of jurisdictions was that punitive damages (also called exemplary damages, vindictive damages, or smart money) could be awarded without a showing of actual ill will, spite, or intent to injure.

* * *

The large majority of state and lower federal courts were in agreement that punitive damages awards did not require a showing of actual malicious intent; they permitted punitive awards on variously stated standards of negligence, recklessness, or other culpable conduct short of actual malicious intent.

The same rule applies today. The Restatement (Second) of Torts (1979), for example, states: "Punitive damages may be awarded for conduct that is outrageous, because of the defendant's evil motive or his reckless indifference to the rights of others." § 908(2) (emphasis added); see also id., Comment b. Most cases under state common law, although varying in their precise terminology, have adopted more or less the same rule, recognizing that punitive damages in tort cases may be awarded not only for actual intent to injure or evil motive, but also for recklessness, serious indifference to or disregard for the rights of others, or even gross negligence.

The remaining question is whether the policies and purposes of § 1983 itself require a departure from the rules of tort common law. As a general matter, we discern no reason why a person whose federally guaranteed rights have been violated should be granted a more restrictive remedy than a person asserting an ordinary tort cause of action. Smith offers us no persuasive reason to the contrary.

Smith's argument, which he offers in several forms, is that an actual-intent standard is preferable to a recklessness standard because it is less vague. He points out that punitive damages, by their very nature, are not awarded to compensate the injured party. See Newport v. Fact Concerts, Inc., 453 U.S. 247, 266-267 (1981); Electrical Workers v. Foust, 442 U.S. 42, 48 (1979); Gertz v. Robert Welch, Inc., 418 U.S. 323, 349-350 (1974). He concedes, of course, that deterrence of future egregious conduct is a primary purpose of both § 1983, see Newport, supra, at 268; Owen v. City of Independence, 445 U.S. 622, 651 (1980); Robertson v. Wegmann, 436 U.S. 584, 591 (1978), and of punitive damages, see Newport, supra, at 268; Restatement (Second) of Torts § 908(1) (1979). But deterrence, he contends, cannot be achieved unless the standard of conduct sought to be deterred is stated with sufficient clarity to enable potential defendants to conform to the law and to avoid the proposed sanction. Recklessness or callous indifference, he argues, is too uncertain a standard to achieve deterrence rationally and fairly. A prison guard, for example, can be expected to know whether he is acting with actual ill will or intent to injure, but not whether he is being reckless or callously indifferent.

Smith's argument, if valid, would apply to ordinary tort cases as easily as to § 1983 suits; hence, it hardly presents an argument for adopting a different rule under § 1983. In any event, the argument is unpersuasive. While, arguendo, an intent standard may be easier to understand and apply to particular situations than a recklessness standard, we are not persuaded that a recklessness standard is too vague to be fair or useful. In the Milwaukee case, 91 U.S. 489 (1876), we adopted a recklessness standard rather than a gross negligence standard precisely because recklessness would better serve the need for adequate clarity and fair application. Almost a century later, in the First Amendment context, we held that punitive damages cannot be assessed for defamation in the absence of proof of "knowledge of falsity or reckless disregard for the truth." Gertz, 418 U.S., at 349. Our concern in Gertz was that the threat of punitive damages, if not limited to especially egregious cases, might "inhibit the vigorous exercise of First Amendment freedoms," ibid.—a concern at least as pressing as any urged by Smith in this case. Yet we did not find it necessary to impose an actual-intent standard there. Just as Smith has not shown why § 1983 should give higher protection from punitive damages than ordinary tort law, he has not explained why it gives higher protection than we have demanded under the First Amendment.

More fundamentally, Smith's argument for certainty in the interest of deterrence overlooks the distinction between a standard for punitive damages and a standard of liability in the first instance. Smith seems to assume that prison guards and other state officials look mainly to the standard for punitive damages in shaping their conduct. We question the premise; we assume, and hope, that most officials are guided primarily by the underlying standards of federal substantive law— both out of devotion to duty, and in the inter-est of avoiding liability for compensatory damages. At any rate, the conscientious officer who desires clear guidance on how to do his job and avoid lawsuits can and should look to the standard for actionability in the first instance. The need for exceptional clarity in the standard for punitive damages arises only if one assumes that there are substantial numbers of officers who will not be deterred by compensatory damages; only such officers will seek to guide their conduct by the punitive damages standard. The presence of such officers constitutes a powerful argument against raising the threshold for punitive damages.

In this case, the jury was instructed to apply a high standard of constitutional right ("physical abuse of such base, inhumane and barbaric proportions as to shock the sensibilities"). It was also instructed, under the principle of qualified immunity, that Smith could not be held liable at all unless he was guilty of "a callous indifference or a thoughtless disregard for the consequences of [his] act or failure to act," or of "a flagrant or remarkably bad failure to protect" Wade. These instructions are not challenged in this Court, nor were they challenged on grounds of vagueness in the lower courts. Smith's contention that this recklessness standard is too vague to provide clear guidance and reasonable deterrence might more properly be reserved for a challenge seeking different standards of liability in the first instance. As for punitive damages, however, in the absence of any persuasive argument to the contrary based on the policies of § 1983, we are content to adopt the policy judgment of the common law— that reckless or callous disregard for the plaintiff's rights, as well as intentional violations of federal law, should be sufficient to trigger a jury's consideration of the appropriateness of punitive damages. See Adickes v. S. H. Kress & Co., 398 U.S. 144, 233 (1970) (BRENNAN, J., concurring and dissenting).

IV

Smith contends that even if § 1983 does not ordinarily require a showing of actual malicious intent for an award of punitive damages, such a showing should be required in this case. He argues that the deterrent and punitive purposes of punitive damages are served only if the threshold for punitive damages is higher in every case than the underlying standard for liability in the first instance. In this case, while the District Judge did not use the same precise terms to explain the standards of liability for compensatory and punitive damages, the parties agree that there is no substantial difference between the showings required by the two instructions; both apply a standard of reckless or callous indifference to Wade's rights. Hence, Smith argues, the District Judge erred in not requiring a higher standard for punitive damages, namely, actual malicious intent.

This argument incorrectly assumes that, simply because the instructions specified the same threshold of liability for punitive and compensatory damages, the two forms of damages were equally available to the plaintiff. The argument overlooks a key feature of punitive damages—that they are never awarded as of right, no matter how egregious the defendant's conduct. "If the plaintiff proves sufficiently serious misconduct on the defendant's part, the question whether to award punitive damages is left to the jury, which may or may not make such an award." D. Dobbs, Law of Remedies 204 (1973) (footnote omitted).[14] Compensatory damages, by contrast, are mandatory; once liability is found, the jury is required to award compensatory damages in an amount appropriate to compensate the plaintiff for his loss. Hence, it is not entirely accurate to say that punitive and compensatory damages were awarded in this case on the same standard. To make its punitive award, the jury was required to find not only that Smith's conduct met the recklessness threshold (a question of ultimate fact), but also that his conduct merited a punitive award of $5,000 in addition to the compensatory award (a discretionary moral judgment).

---

[14] See also, e.g., Restatement (Second) of Torts § 908, Comment d (1979); J. Ghiardi & J. Kircher, Punitive Damages Law and Practice § 5.38 (1981); C. McCormick, Law of Damages 296 (1935); W. Prosser, Law of Torts 13 (4th ed. 1971); K. Redden, Punitive Damages § 3.4(A) (1980); Chuy v. Philadelphia Eagles Football Club, 595 F.2d 1265, 1277-1278, n. 15 (CA3 1979) (en banc).

* * *

This common-law rule makes sense in terms of the purposes of punitive damages. Punitive damages are awarded in the jury's discretion "to punish [the defendant] for his outrageous conduct and to deter him and others like him from similar conduct in the future." Restatement (Second) of Torts § 908(1) (1979). The focus is on the character of the tortfeasor's conduct—whether it is of the sort that calls for deterrence and punishment over and above that provided by compensatory awards. If it is of such a character, then it is appropriate to allow a jury to assess punitive damages; and that assessment does not become less appropriate simply because the plaintiff in the case faces a more demanding standard of actionability. To put it differently, society has an interest in deterring and punishing all intentional or reckless invasions of the rights of others, even though it sometimes chooses not to impose any liability for lesser degrees of fault.

As with his first argument, Smith gives us no good reason to depart from the common-law rule in the context of § 1983. He argues that too low a standard of exposure to punitive damages in cases such as this threatens to undermine the policies of his qualified immunity as a prison guard. The same reasoning would apply with at least as much force to, for example, the First Amendment and common-law immunities involved in the defamation cases described above. In any case, Smith overstates the extent of his immunity. Smith is protected from liability for mere negligence because of the need to protect his use of discretion in his day-to-day decisions in the running of a correctional facility. See generally Procunier v. Navarette, 434 U.S. 555 (1978); Wood v. Strickland, 420 U.S. 308 (1975). But the immunity on which Smith relies is coextensive with the interest it protects. The very fact that the privilege is qualified reflects a recognition that there is no societal interest in protecting those uses of a prison guard's discretion that amount to reckless or callous indifference to the rights and safety of the prisoners in his charge. Once the protected sphere of privilege is exceeded, we see no reason why state officers should not be liable for their reckless misconduct on the same basis as private tortfeasors.

V

We hold that a jury may be permitted to assess punitive damages in an action under § 1983 when the defendant's conduct is shown to be motivated by evil motive or intent, or when it involves reckless or callous indifference to the federally protected rights of others. We further hold that this threshold applies even when the underlying standard of liability for compensatory damages is one of recklessness. Because the jury instructions in this case are in accord with this rule, the judgment of the Court of Appeals is

Affirmed.

SAUCIER
v.
KATZ

533 U.S. 194; 121 S. Ct. 2151; 150 L. Ed. 2d 272 (2001)
(Footnotes and citations omitted)

* * *

In this case a citizen alleged excessive force was used to arrest him. The arresting officer asserted the defense of qualified immunity. The matter we address is whether the requisite analysis to determine qualified immunity is so intertwined with the question [of] whether the officer used excessive force in making the arrest that qualified immunity and constitutional violation issues should be treated as one question, to be decided by the trier of fact. * * *

Saucier, represented by the Government of the United States, sought review here, arguing the Court of Appeals erred in its view that the qualified immunity inquiry is the same as the constitutional inquiry and so becomes superfluous or duplicative when excessive force is alleged. We granted certiorari * * *

II

The Court of Appeals ruled first that the right was clearly established; and second that the reasonableness inquiry into excessive force meant that it need not consider aspects of qualified immunity, leaving the whole matter to the jury. * * * This approach cannot be reconciled with Anderson v. Creighton, * * * however, and was in error in two respects. As we shall explain, the first inquiry must be whether a constitutional right would have been violated on the facts alleged; second, assuming the violation is established, the question whether the right was clearly established must be considered on a more specific level than recognized by the Court of Appeals.

In a suit against an officer for an alleged violation of a constitutional right, the requisites of a qualified immunity defense must be considered in proper sequence. Where the defendant seeks qualified immunity, a ruling on that issue should be made early in the proceedings so that the costs and expenses of trial are avoided where the defense is dispositive. Qualified immunity is "an entitlement not to stand trial or face the other burdens of litigation." * * * The privilege is "an *immunity from suit* rather than a mere defense to liability; and like an absolute immunity, it is effectively lost if a case is erroneously permitted to go to trial." * * * As a result, "we repeatedly have stressed the importance of resolving immunity questions at the earliest possible stage in litigation." * * *

A court required to rule upon the qualified immunity issue must consider, then, this threshold question: Taken in the light most favorable to the party asserting the injury, do the facts alleged show the officer's conduct violated a constitutional right? This must be the initial inquiry.* * * In the course of determining whether a constitutional right was violated on the premises alleged, a court might find it necessary to set forth principles which will become the basis for a holding that a right is clearly established. This is the process for the law's elaboration from case to case, and it is one reason for our insisting upon turning to the existence or nonexistence of a constitutional right as the first inquiry. The law might be deprived of this explanation were a court simply to skip ahead to the question [of] whether the law clearly established that the officer's conduct was unlawful in the circumstances of the case.

If no constitutional right would have been violated were the allegations established, there is no necessity for further inquiries concerning qualified immunity. On the other hand, if a violation could be made out on a favorable view of the parties' submissions, the next, sequential step is to ask whether the right was clearly established. This inquiry, it is vital to note, must be undertaken in light of the specific context of the case, not as a broad general proposition; and it too serves to advance understanding of the law and to allow officers to avoid the burden of trial if qualified immunity is applicable.

In this litigation, for instance, there is no doubt that Graham v. Connor, * * * clearly establishes the general proposition that use of force is contrary to the Fourth Amendment if it is excessive under objective standards of reasonableness. Yet that is not enough. Rather, we emphasized in Anderson "that the right the official is alleged to have violated must have been 'clearly established' in a more particularized, and hence more relevant, sense: The contours of the right must be sufficiently clear that a reasonable official would understand that what he is doing violates that right."* * * The relevant, dispositive inquiry in determining whether a right is clearly established is whether it would be clear to a reasonable officer that his conduct was unlawful in the situation he confronted.* * *

The approach the Court of Appeals adopted—to deny summary judgment any time a material issue of fact remains on the excessive force claim—could undermine the goal of qualified immunity to "avoid excessive disruption of government and permit the resolution of many insubstantial claims on summary judgment." Harlow v. Fitzgerald * * *. If the law did not put the officer on notice that his conduct would be clearly unlawful, summary judgment based on qualified immunity is appropriate. * * *

This is not to say that the formulation of a general rule is beside the point, nor is it to insist the courts must have agreed upon the precise formulation of the standard. Assuming, for instance, that various courts have agreed that certain conduct is a constitutional violation under facts not distinguishable in a fair way from the facts presented in the case at hand, the officer would not be entitled to qualified immunity based simply on the argument that courts had not agreed on one verbal formulation of the controlling standard.

The Court of Appeals concluded that qualified immunity is merely duplicative in an excessive force case, eliminating the need for the second step where a constitutional violation could be found based on the allegations. In Anderson, a warrantless search case, we rejected the argument that there is no distinction between the reasonableness standard for warrantless searches and the qualified immunity inquiry. We acknowledged there was some "surface appeal" to the argument that, because the Fourth Amendment's guarantee was a right to be free from "unreasonable" searches and seizures, it would be inconsistent to conclude that an officer who acted unreasonably under the constitutional standard nevertheless was entitled to immunity because he "'reasonably' acted unreasonably." 483 U.S. at 643. This superficial similarity, however, could not overcome either our history of applying qualified immunity analysis to Fourth Amendment claims against officers or the justifications for applying the doctrine in an area where officers perform their duties with considerable uncertainty as to "whether particular [* * *283] searches or seizures comport with the Fourth Amendment." Id., at 644. With respect, moreover, to the argument made in Anderson that an exception should be made for Fourth Amendment cases, we observed "the heavy burden this argument must sustain to be successful," since "the doctrine of qualified immunity reflects a balance that has been struck 'across the board.'" Id., at 642 (quoting Harlow v. Fitzgerald, supra, at 821). We held that qualified immunity applied in the Fourth Amendment context just as it would for any other claim of official misconduct. 483 U.S. at 644.

* * *

The qualified immunity inquiry, on the other hand, has a further dimension. The concern of the immunity inquiry is to acknowledge that reasonable mistakes can be made as to the legal constraints on particular police conduct. It is sometimes difficult for an officer to determine how the relevant legal doctrine, here excessive force, will apply to the factual situation the officer confronts. An officer might correctly perceive all of the relevant facts but have a mistaken understanding as to whether a particular amount of force is legal in those circumstances. If the officer's mistake as to what the law requires is reasonable, however, the officer is entitled to the immunity defense.

* * *

Our instruction to the district courts and courts of appeal to concentrate at the outset on the definition of the constitutional right and to determine whether, on the facts alleged, a constitutional violation could be found is important. As we have said, the procedure permits courts in appropriate cases to elaborate the constitutional right with greater degrees of specificity. Because we granted certiorari only to determine whether qualified immunity was appropriate, however, and because of the limits imposed upon us by the questions on which we granted review, we will assume a constitutional violation could have occurred under the facts alleged based simply on the general rule prohibiting excessive force, then proceed to the question whether this general prohibition against excessive force was the source for clearly established law that was contravened in the circumstances this officer faced. There was no contravention under this standard. Though it is doubtful that the force used was excessive, we need not rest our conclusion on that determination. The question is what the officer reasonably understood his powers and responsibilities to be, when he acted, under clearly established standards.

* * *

CORRECTIONAL SERVICES CORPORATION
v.
MALESKO

534 U.S. 61; 122 S. Ct. 515;
151 L. Ed. 2d 456 (2001)
(Footnotes and citations omitted)

CHIEF JUSTICE REHNQUIST delivered the opinion of the Court.

We decide here whether the implied damages action first recognized in Bivens v. Six Unknown Fed. Narcotics Agents, * * * should be extended to allow recovery against a private corporation operating a halfway house under contract with the Bureau of Prisons. We decline to so extend Bivens.

* * *

In Bivens v. Six Unknown Fed. Narcotics Agents,* * * we recognized for the first time an implied private action for damages against federal officers alleged to have violated a citizen's constitutional rights. Respondent now asks that we extend this limited holding to confer a right of action for damages against private entities acting under color of federal law. * * * We have heretofore refused to imply new substantive liabilities under such circumstances, and we decline to do so here.

Our authority to imply a new constitutional tort, not expressly authorized by statute, is anchored in our general jurisdiction to decide all cases "arising under the Constitution, laws, or treaties of the United States." * * * We first exercised this authority in Bivens, where we held that a victim of a Fourth Amendment violation by federal officers may bring suit for money damages against the officers in federal court. Bivens acknowledged that Congress had never provided for a private right of action against federal officers, and that "the Fourth Amendment does not in so many words provide for its enforcement by award of money damages for the consequences of its violation." * * * Nonetheless, relying largely on earlier decisions implying private damages actions into federal statutes, * * * and finding "no special factors counseling hesitation in the absence of affirmative action by Congress," * * * we found an implied damages remedy available under the Fourth Amendment.

* * *

The purpose of Bivens is to deter individual federal officers from committing constitutional violations. Meyer made clear that the threat of litigation and liability will adequately deter federal officers for Bivens purposes no matter that they may enjoy qualified immunity, * * * are indemnified by the employing agency or entity, * * * or are acting pursuant to an entity's policy,* * * Meyer also made clear that the threat of suit against an individual's employer was not the kind of deterrence contemplated by Bivens. * * * For if a corporate defendant is available for suit, claimants will focus their collection efforts on it, and not the individual directly responsible for the alleged injury. * * * On the logic of Meyer, inferring a constitutional tort remedy against a private entity like CSC is therefore foreclosed.

* * *

DISSENT:

JUSTICE STEVENS, with whom JUSTICE SOUTER, JUSTICE GINSBURG, and JUSTICE BREYER join, dissenting. * * *

HOPE
v.
PELZER

536 U.S. 730; 122 S. Ct. 2508 (2002)
(Footnotes and citations omitted)

JUSTICE STEVENS delivered the opinion of the Court.

* * *

I

In 1995, Alabama was the only State that followed the practice of chaining inmates to one another in work squads. It was also the only State that handcuffed prisoners to "hitching posts" if they either refused to work or otherwise disrupted work squads. Hope was handcuffed to a hitching post on two occasions. On May 11, 1995, while Hope was working in a chain gang near an interstate highway, he got into an argument with another inmate. Both men were taken back to the Limestone prison and handcuffed to a hitching post. Hope was released two hours later, after the guard captain determined that the altercation had been caused by the other inmate. During his two hours on the post, Hope was offered drinking water and a bathroom break every 15 minutes, and his responses to these offers were recorded on an activity log. Because he was only slightly taller than the hitching post, his arms were above shoulder height and grew tired from being handcuffed so high. Whenever he tried moving his arms to improve his circulation, the handcuffs cut into his wrists, causing pain and discomfort.

On June 7, 1995, Hope was punished more severely. He took a nap during the morning bus ride to the chain gang's worksite, and when it arrived he was less than prompt in responding to an order to get off the bus. An exchange of vulgar remarks led to a wrestling match with a guard. Four other guards intervened, subdued Hope, handcuffed him, placed him in leg irons and transported him back to the prison where he was put on the hitching post. The guards made him take off his shirt, and he remained shirtless all day while the sun burned his skin. He remained attached to the post for approximately seven hours. During this 7-hour period, he was given water only once or twice and was given no bathroom breaks. At one point, a guard taunted Hope about his thirst. According to Hope's affidavit: "[The guard] first gave water to some dogs, then brought the water cooler closer to me, removed its lid, and kicked the cooler over, spilling the water onto the ground." * * *

II

The threshold inquiry a court must undertake in a qualified immunity analysis is whether plaintiff's allegations, if true, establish a constitutional violation. Saucier v. Katz * * * The Court of Appeals held that "the policy and practice of cuffing an inmate to a hitching post or similar stationary object for a period of time that surpasses that necessary to quell a threat or restore order is a violation of the Eighth Amendment." * * * The court rejected respondents' submission that Hope could have ended his shackling by offering to return to work, finding instead that the purpose of the practice was punitive, and that the circumstances of his confinement created a substantial risk of harm of which the officers were aware. Moreover, the court relied on Circuit precedent condemning similar practices and the results of a United States Department of Justice (DOJ) report that found Alabama's systematic use of the hitching post to be improper corporal punishment. We agree with the Court of Appeals that the attachment of Hope to the hitching post under the circumstances alleged in this case violated the Eighth Amendment.

* * *

III

Despite their participation in this constitutionally impermissible conduct, the respondents may nevertheless be shielded from liability for civil damages if their actions did not violate "clearly established statutory or constitutional rights of which a reasonable person would have known." Harlow v. Fitzgerald, * * * In assessing whether the Eighth Amendment violation here met the Harlow test, the Court of Appeals required that the facts of previous cases be "'materially similar' to Hope's situation." * * * This rigid gloss on the qualified immunity standard, though supported by Circuit precedent, is not consistent with our cases.

As we have explained, qualified immunity operates "to ensure that before they are subjected to suit, officers are on notice their conduct is unlawful." * * * For a constitutional right to be clearly established, its contours "must be sufficiently clear that a reasonable official would understand that what he is doing violates that right. This is not to say that an official action is protected by qualified immunity unless the very action in question has previously been held unlawful, * * * but it is to say that in the light of pre-existing law the unlawfulness must be apparent." * * *

Officers sued in a civil action for damages under 42 U.S.C. §1983 have the same right to fair notice as do defendants charged with the criminal offense defined in 18 U.S.C. §242. Section 242 makes it a crime for a state official to act "willfully" and under color of law to deprive a person of rights protected by the Constitution. In United States v. Lanier, * * * we held that the defendant was entitled to "fair warning" that his conduct deprived his victim of a constitutional right, and that the standard for determining the adequacy of that warning was the same as the standard for determining whether a constitutional right

was "clearly established" in civil litigation under §1983.

* * *

Our opinion in Lanier thus makes clear that officials can still be on notice that their conduct violates established law even in novel factual circumstances. Indeed, in Lanier, we expressly rejected a requirement that previous cases be "fundamentally similar." Although earlier cases involving "fundamentally similar" facts can provide especially strong support for a conclusion that the law is clearly established, they are not necessary to such a finding. The same is true of cases with "materially similar" facts. Accordingly, pursuant to Lanier, the salient question that the Court of Appeals ought to have asked is whether the state of the law in 1995 gave respondents fair warning that their alleged treatment of Hope was unconstitutional. It is to this question that we now turn.

IV

The use of the hitching post as alleged by Hope "unnecessarily and wantonly inflicted pain," * * * and thus was a clear violation of the Eighth Amendment. * * *. Arguably, the violation was so obvious that our own Eighth Amendment cases gave the respondents fair warning that their conduct violated the Constitution. Regardless, in light of binding Eleventh Circuit precedent, an Alabama Department of Corrections (ADOC) regulation, and a DOJ report informing the ADOC of the constitutional infirmity in its use of the hitching post, we readily conclude that the respondents' conduct violated "clearly established statutory or constitutional rights of which a reasonable person would have known." * * *

* * * The respondents violated clearly established law. Our conclusion that "a reasonable person would have known" Harlow, * * * of the violation is buttressed by the fact that the DOJ specifically advised the ADOC of the unconstitutionality of its practices before the incidents in this case took place. The DOJ had conducted a study in 1994 of Alabama's use of the hitching post. * * * Among other findings, the DOJ report noted that ADOC's officers consistently failed to comply with the policy of immediately releasing any inmate from the hitching post who agrees to return to work. The DOJ concluded that the systematic use of the restraining bar in Alabama constituted improper corporal punishment. Accordingly, the DOJ advised the ADOC to cease use of the hitching post in order to meet constitutional standards. The ADOC replied that it thought the post could permissibly be used "'to preserve prison security and discipline.'" * * * In response, the DOJ informed the ADOC that, "'although an emergency situation may warrant drastic action by corrections staff, our experts found that the "rail" is being used systematically as an improper punishment for relatively trivial offenses. Therefore, we have concluded that the use of the "rail" is without penological justification.'" * * * Although there is nothing in the record indicating that the DOJ's views were communicated to respondents, this exchange lends support to the view that reasonable officials in the ADOC should have realized that the use of the hitching post under the circumstances alleged by Hope violated the Eighth Amendment prohibition against cruel and unusual punishment.

The obvious cruelty inherent in this practice should have provided respondents with some notice that their alleged conduct violated Hope's constitutional protection against cruel and unusual punishment. Hope was treated in a way antithetical to human dignity—he was hitched to a post for an extended period of time in a position that was painful, and under circumstances that were both degrading and dangerous. This wanton treatment was not done of necessity, but as punishment for prior conduct. * * *

V

In response to JUSTICE THOMAS' thoughtful dissent, we make the following three observations. The first is that in granting certiorari to review the summary judgment entered in favor of the officers, we did not take any question about the sufficiency of pleadings and affidavits to raise a genuine possibility that the three named officers were responsible for the punitive acts of shackling alleged. All questions raised by petitioner

(the plaintiff against whom summary judgment was entered) go to the application of the standard that no immunity is available for official acts when "it would be clear to a reasonable officer that his conduct was unlawful in the situation he confronted." Saucier v. Katz, * * * The officers' brief in opposition to certiorari likewise addressed only the legal standard of what is clearly established. The resulting focus in the case was the Eleventh Circuit's position that a violation is not clearly established unless it is the subject of a prior case of liability on facts "'materially similar'" to those charged. * * * We did not take, and do not pass upon, the questions whether or to what extent the three named officers may be held responsible for the acts charged, if proved. Nothing in our decision forecloses any defense other than qualified immunity on the ground relied upon by the Court of Appeals.

Second, we may address the immunity question on the assumption that the act of field discipline charged on each occasion was handcuffing Hope to a hitching post for an extended period apparently to inflict gratuitous pain or discomfort, with no justification in threatened harm or a continuing refusal to work. * * * The Court of Appeals clearly held the act of cuffing petitioner to the hitching post itself to suffice as an unconstitutional act: "We find that cuffing an inmate to a hitching post for a period of time extending past that required to address an immediate danger or threat is a violation of the Eighth Amendment." * * *. Although the court continued that "this violation is exacerbated by the lack of proper clothing, water, or bathroom breaks," * * * this embellishment was not the basis of its decision, and our own decision adequately rests on the same assumption that sufficed for the Court of Appeals.

Third, in applying the objective immunity test of what a reasonable officer would understand, the significance of federal judicial precedent is a function in part of the Judiciary's structure. The unreported District Court opinions cited by the officers are distinguishable on their own terms. But regardless, they would be no match for the Circuit precedents * * * which held that "handcuffing inmates to the fence and to cells for long periods of time," was unconstitutional, and

Ort v. White, * * * which suggested that it would be unconstitutional to inflict gratuitous pain on an inmate (by refusing him water), when punishment was unnecessary to enforce on-the-spot discipline. * * *

It is so ordered.

DISSENT:

JUSTICE THOMAS, with whom THE CHIEF JUSTICE and JUSTICE SCALIA join, dissenting.

The Court today subjects three prison guards to suit based on facts not alleged, law not clearly established, and its own subjective views on appropriate methods of prison discipline. Qualified immunity jurisprudence has been turned on its head.

* * *

It is most unfortunate that the Court holds that Officer McClaran, Sergeant Pelzer, and Lieutenant Gates are not entitled to qualified immunity. It was not at all clear in 1995 that respondents' conduct violated the Eighth Amendment, and they certainly could not have anticipated that this Court or any other would rule against them on the basis of nonexistent allegations or allegations involving the behavior of other prison guards. For the foregoing reasons, I would affirm the judgment of the Court of Appeals. I respectfully dissent.

Cases Relating to Chapter 12

Additional Litigation

MONTANYE
v.
HAYMES

427 U.S. 236; 96 S. Ct. 2543;
49 L. Ed. 2d 466 (1976)

MR. JUSTICE WHITE delivered the opinion of the Court.

On June 7, 1972, respondent Haymes was removed from his assignment as inmate clerk in the law library at the Attica Correctional Facility in the State of New York. That afternoon Haymes was observed circulating among other inmates a document prepared by him and at the time signed by 82 other prisoners. Among other things, each signatory complained that he had been deprived of legal assistance as the result of the removal of Haymes and another inmate from the prison law library. The document, which was addressed to a federal judge but sought no relief, was seized and held by prison authorities. On June 8, Haymes was advised that he would be transferred to Clinton Correctional Facility, which, like Attica, was a maximum-security institution. The transfer was effected the next day. No loss of good time, segregated confinement, loss of privileges, or any other disciplinary measures accompanied the transfer. On August 3, Haymes filed a petition with the United States District Court which was construed by the judge to be an application under 42 U.S.C. § 1983 and 28 U.S.C. § 1343 seeking relief against petitioner Montanye, the then Superintendent at Attica. The petition complained that the seizure

and retention of the document, despite requests for its return, not only violated Administrative Bulletin No. 20, which allegedly made any communication to a court privileged and confidential, but also infringed Haymes' federally guaranteed right to petition the court for redress of grievances. It further asserted that Haymes' removal to Clinton was to prevent him from pursuing his remedies and also was in reprisal for his having rendered legal assistance to various prisoners as well as having, along with others, sought to petition the court for redress.

In response to a show-cause order issued by the court, petitioner Brady, the correctional officer at Attica in charge of the law library, stated in an affidavit that Haymes had been relieved from his assignment as an inmate clerk in the law library "because of his continual disregard for the rules governing inmates and the use of the law library" and that only one of the inmates who had signed the petition being circulated by Haymes had ever made an official request for legal assistance. The affidavit of Harold Smith, Deputy Superintendent of Attica, furnished the court with Paragraph 21 of the Inmate's Rule Book, which prohibited an inmate from furnishing legal assistance to another inmate without official permission and with a copy of a bulletin board notice directing inmates with legal problems to present them to Officer Brady—inmates were in no circumstances to set themselves up as legal counselors and receive pay for their services. The affidavit asserted that the petition taken from Haymes was being circulated "in direct disregard of the above rule forbidding legal assistance except with the approval of the Superintendent" and that Haymes had been cautioned on several occasions about assisting other inmates without the required approval.

Haymes responded by a motion to join Brady as a defendant, which was granted, and with a counteraffidavit denying that there was a rulebook at Attica, reasserting that the document seized was merely a letter to the court not within the scope of the claimed rule and alleging that his removal from the law library, the seizure of his petition, and his transfer to Clinton were acts of reprisal for his having attempted to furnish legal assistance to the other prisoners rather than merely hand out library books to them.

After retained counsel had submitted a memorandum on behalf of Haymes, the District Court dismissed the action. It held that the rule against giving legal assistance without consent was reasonable and that the seizure of Haymes' document was not in violation of the Constitution. The court also ruled that the transfer to Clinton did not violate Haymes' rights: "Although a general allegation is made that punishment was the motive for the transfer, there is no allegation that the facilities at [Clinton] are harsher or substantially different from those afforded to petitioner at Attica. . . . Petitioner's transfer was consistent with the discretion given to prison officials in exercising proper custody of inmates." App. 26a.

The Court of Appeals for the Second Circuit reversed. 505 F. 2d 977 (1974). Because the District Court had considered affidavits outside the pleadings, the dismissal was deemed to have been a summary judgment under Fed. Rule Civ. Proc. 56. The judgment was ruled erroneous because there were two unresolved issues of material fact: whether Haymes' removal to Clinton was punishment for a disobedience of prison rules and if so whether the effects of the transfer were sufficiently burdensome to require a hearing under the Due Process Clause of the Fourteenth Amendment.

The court's legal theory was that Haymes should no more be punished by a transfer having harsh consequences than he should suffer other deprivations which under prison rules could not be imposed without following specified procedures. Disciplinary transfers,

the Court of Appeals thought, were in a different category from "administrative" transfers. "When harsh treatment is meted out to reprimand, deter, or reform an individual, elementary fairness demands that the one punished be given a satisfactory opportunity to establish that he is not deserving of such handling. . . . [T]he specific facts upon which a decision to punish are predicated can most suitably be ascertained at an impartial hearing to review the evidence of the alleged misbehavior, and to assess the effect which transfer will have on the inmate's future incarceration." 505 F. 2d, at 980. The Court of Appeals found it difficult "to look upon the circumstances of the transfer as a mere coincidence," id., at 979; it was also convinced that Haymes might be able to demonstrate sufficiently burdensome consequences attending the transfer to trigger the protections of the Due Process Clause, even though Attica and Clinton were both maximum-security prisons. The case was therefore remanded for further proceedings to the District Court. We granted certiorari, 422 U.S. 1055 (1975), and heard the case with Meachum v. Fano, ante, p. 215. We reverse the judgment of the Court of Appeals.

The Court of Appeals did not hold, as did the Court of Appeals in Meachum v. Fano, that every disadvantageous transfer must be accompanied by appropriate hearings. Administrative transfers, although perhaps having very similar consequences for the prisoner, were exempt from the Court of Appeals ruling. Only disciplinary transfers having substantial adverse impact on the prisoner were to call for procedural formalities. Even so, our decision in Meachum requires a reversal in this case. We held in Meachum v. Fano, that no Due Process Clause liberty interest of a duly convicted prison inmate is infringed when he is transferred from one prison to another within the State, whether with or without a hearing, absent some right or justifiable expectation rooted in state law that he will not be transferred except for misbehavior or upon the occurrence of other specified events. We therefore disagree with the Court of Appeals' general proposition that the Due Process Clause by its own force requires hearings whenever prison authorities transfer a prisoner to another institution because of his breach of prison rules, at least where the transfer may be said to involve substantially burdensome consequences. As long as the conditions or degree of confinement to which the prisoner is subjected is within the sentence imposed upon him and is not otherwise violative of the Constitution, the Due Process Clause does not in itself subject an inmate's treatment by prison authorities to judicial oversight. The Clause does not require hearings in connection with transfers whether or not they are the result of the inmate's misbehavior or may be labeled as disciplinary or punitive.

We also agree with the State of New York that under the law of that State Haymes had no right to remain at any particular prison facility and no justifiable expectation that he would not be transferred unless found guilty of misconduct. Under New York law, adult persons sentenced to imprisonment are not sentenced to particular institutions, but are committed to the custody of the Commissioner of Corrections. He receives adult, male felons at a maximum-security reception center for initial evaluation and then transfers them to specified institutions. N. Y. Correc. Law § 71(1) (McKinney Supp. 1975-1976); 7 N.Y.C.R.R. § 103.10. Thereafter, the Commissioner is empowered by statute to "transfer inmates from one correctional facility to another." N. Y. Correc. Law § 23(1) (McKinney Supp. 1975-1976). The Court of Appeals reasoned that because under the applicable state statutes and regulations, various specified punishments were reserved as sanctions for breach of prison rules and could not therefore be imposed without appropriate hearings, neither could the harsh consequences of a transfer be imposed as punishment for misconduct absent appropriate due process procedures. But under the New York law, the transfer of inmates is not conditional upon or limited to the occurrence of misconduct. The statute imposes no conditions on the discretionary power to transfer, and we are advised by the State that no such requirements have been promulgated. Transfers are not among the punishments which may be imposed only after a prison disciplinary hearing. 7 N.Y.C.R.R. § 253.5. Whatever part an inmate's behavior may play in a decision to transfer, there is no more basis in New York law for invoking the protections of the Due

Process Clause than we found to be the case under the Massachusetts law in the Meachum case.

The judgment of the Court of Appeals is reversed, and the case is remanded to that court for further proceedings consistent with this opinion.

So ordered.

MR. JUSTICE STEVENS, with whom MR. JUSTICE BRENNAN and MR. JUSTICE MARSHALL join, dissenting.

Respondent's complaint, fairly read, alleges two quite different theories of recovery: First, that he was entitled to a hearing before he could be transferred from one facility to another because the transfer deprived him of an interest in liberty; second, that the transfer was a form of punishment for circulating a petition, for communicating with a court, and for rendering legal assistance to other inmates.

Since respondent has not alleged a material difference between the two facilities, I agree with the Court that the transfer did not cause him a grievous loss entitling him to a hearing. In my opinion this conclusion is unaffected by the motivation for the transfer, because I think it is the seriousness of its impact on the inmate's residuum of protected liberty that determines whether a deprivation has occurred.

I am persuaded, however, that the allegations of his complaint are sufficient to require a trial of his claim that the transfer was made in retribution for his exercise of protected rights. On this claim, the reason for the defendants' action is critical and the procedure followed is almost irrelevant. I do not understand the Court to disagree with this analysis, and assume that the Court of Appeals, consistently with this Court's mandate, may direct the District Court to conduct a trial.

The reason for my dissent is that the same result would follow from a simple affirmance. Thus, although the Court has explained why it believes the opinion of the Court of Appeals should be "reversed," it has not explained why that court's judgment was not correct. I would affirm that judgment.

MEACHUM
v.
FANO

427 U.S. 215; 96 S. Ct. 2532;
49 L. Ed. 2d 451 (1976)

MR. JUSTICE WHITE delivered the opinion of the Court.

The question here is whether the Due Process Clause of the Fourteenth Amendment entitles a state prisoner to a hearing when he is transferred to a prison the conditions of which are substantially less favorable to the prisoner, absent a state law or practice conditioning such transfers on proof of serious misconduct or the occurrence of other events. We hold that it does not.

I

During a 2½-month period in 1974, there were nine serious fires at the Massachusetts Correctional Institution at Norfolk—a medium-security institution. Based primarily on reports from informants, the six respondent inmates were removed from the general prison population and placed in the Receiving Building, an administrative detention area used to process new inmates. Proceedings were then had before the Norfolk prison Classification Board with respect to whether respondents were to be transferred to another institution—possibly a maximum-security institution, the living conditions at which are substantially less favorable than those at Norfolk. Each respondent was notified of the classification hearing and was informed that the authorities had information indicating that he had engaged in criminal conduct.

Individual classification hearings were held, each respondent being represented by counsel. Each hearing began by the reading of a prepared statement by the Classification Board. The Board then heard, *in camera* and out of the respondents' presence, the testimony of petitioner Meachum, the Norfolk prison superintendent, who repeated the information that had been received from informants. Each respondent was then told that the evidence supported the allegations contained in the notice but was not then—or ever—given transcripts or summaries of Meachum's testimony before the Board. Each respondent was allowed to present evidence in his own behalf; and each denied involvement in the particular infraction being investigated. Some respondents submitted supportive testimony or written statements from correction officers. A social worker also testified in the presence of each respondent, furnishing the respondent's criminal and custodial record, including prior rule infractions, if any, and other aspects of his performance and "general adjustment" at Norfolk.

The Board recommended that Royce be placed in administrative segregation for 30 days; that Fano, Dussault, and McPhearson be transferred to Walpole, a maximum-security institution where the living conditions are substantially less favorable to the prisoners than those at Norfolk, and that DeBrosky and Hathaway be transferred to Bridgewater which has both maximum-and medium-security facilities. The reasons for its actions were stated in the Board's reports, which, however, were not then available to respondents. Although respondents were aware of the general import of the informants' allegations and were told that the recommendations drew upon informant sources, the details of this information were not revealed to respondents and are not included in the Board's reports which are part of the record before us.

The Board's recommendations were reviewed by the Acting Deputy Commissioner for Classification and Treatment and by the Commissioner of Corrections on the basis of the written report prepared by the Board. They accepted the recommendations of the Board with respect to Fano, Dussault, Hathaway, and McPhearson. DeBrosky and Royce were ordered transferred to Walpole. The transfers were carried out, with two exceptions. No respondent was subjected to disciplinary punishment upon arrival at the transfer prison. None of the transfers ordered entailed loss of good time or disciplinary confinement.

Meanwhile respondents had brought this action under 42 U.S.C. § 1983 against petitioners Meachum, the prison superintendent; Hall, the State Commissioner of Corrections; and Dawber, the Acting Deputy for Classification and Treatment, alleging that respondents were being deprived of liberty without due process of law in that petitioners had ordered them transferred to a less favorable institution without an adequate factfinding hearing. They sought an injunction setting aside the ordered transfer, declaratory relief, and damages.

The District Court understood Wolff v. McDonnell, 418 U.S. 539 (1974), to entitle respondents to notice and hearing and held both constitutionally inadequate in this case. Respondents were ordered returned to the general prison population at Norfolk until transferred after proper notice and hearing. Petitioners were also ordered to promulgate regulations to establish procedures governing future transfer hearings involving informant testimony. A divided panel of the Court of Appeals affirmed, 520 F. 2d 374, holding that the transfers from Norfolk to maximum-security institutions involved "a significant modification of the overall conditions of confinement" and that this change in circumstances was "serious enough to trigger the application of due process protections." Id., at 377-378.

We granted the prison officials' petition for writ of certiorari, 423 U.S. 1013 (1975), in order to determine whether the Constitution required petitioners to conduct a factfinding hearing in connection with the transfers in this case where state law does not condition the authority to transfer on the occurrence of specific acts of misconduct or other events and, if so, whether the hearings granted in this case were adequate. In light of our resolution of the first issue, we do not reach the second.

II

The Fourteenth Amendment prohibits any State from depriving a person of life, liberty, or property without due process of law. The initial inquiry is whether the transfer of respondents from Norfolk to Walpole and Bridgewater infringed or implicated a "liberty" interest of respondents within the meaning of the Due Process Clause. Contrary to the Court of Appeals, we hold that it did not. We reject at the outset the notion that any grievous loss visited upon a person by the State is sufficient to invoke the procedural protections of the Due Process Clause. In

Board of Regents v. Roth, 408 U.S. 564 (1972), a university professor was deprived of his job, a loss which was surely a matter of great substance, but because the professor had no property interest in his position, due process procedures were not required in connection with his dismissal. We there held that the determining factor is the nature of the interest involved rather than its weight. Id., at 570-571.

Similarly, we cannot agree that any change in the conditions of confinement having a substantial adverse impact on the prisoner involved is sufficient to invoke the protections of the Due Process Clause. The Due Process Clause by its own force forbids the State from convicting any person of crime and depriving him of his liberty without complying fully with the requirements of the Clause. But given a valid conviction, the criminal defendant has been constitutionally deprived of his liberty to the extent that the State may confine him and subject him to the rules of its prison system so long as the conditions of confinement do not otherwise violate the Constitution. The Constitution does not require that the State have more than one prison for convicted felons; nor does it guarantee that the convicted prisoner will be placed in any particular prison if, as is likely, the State has more than one correctional institution. The initial decision to assign the convict to a particular institution is not subject to audit under the Due Process Clause, although the degree of confinement in one prison may be quite different from that in another. The conviction has sufficiently extinguished the defendant's liberty interest to empower the State to confine him in any of its prisons.

Neither, in our view, does the Due Process Clause in and of itself protect a duly convicted prisoner against transfer from one institution to another within the state prison system. Confinement in any of the State's institutions is within the normal limits or range of custody which the conviction has authorized the State to impose. That life in one prison is much more disagreeable than in another does not in itself signify that a Fourteenth Amendment liberty interest is implicated when a prisoner is transferred to the institution with the more severe rules.

Our cases hold that the convicted felon does not forfeit all constitutional protections by reason of his conviction and confinement in prison. He retains a variety of important rights that the courts must be alert to protect. See Wolff v. McDonnell, 418 U.S., at 556, and cases there cited. But none of these cases reaches this one; and to hold as we are urged to do that any substantial deprivation imposed by prison authorities triggers the procedural protections of the Due Process Clause would subject to judicial review a wide spectrum of discretionary actions that traditionally have been the business of prison administrators rather than of the federal courts.

Transfers between institutions, for example, are made for a variety of reasons and often involve no more than informed predictions as to what would best serve institutional security or the safety and welfare of the inmate. Yet under the approach urged here, any transfer, for whatever reason, would require a hearing as long as it could be said that the transfer would place the prisoner in substantially more burdensome conditions than he had been experiencing. We are unwilling to go so far.

Wolff v. McDonnell, on which the Court of Appeals heavily relied, is not to the contrary. Under that case, the Due Process Clause entitles a state prisoner to certain procedural protections when he is deprived of good-time credits because of serious misconduct. But the liberty interest there identified did not originate in the Constitution, which "itself does not guarantee good-time credit for satisfactory behavior while in prison." Id., at 557. The State itself, not the Constitution, had "not only provided a statutory right to good time but also specifies that it is to be forfeited only for serious misbehavior." Ibid. We concluded:

> [A] person's liberty is equally protected, even when the liberty itself is a statutory creation of the State. The touchstone of due process is protection of the individual against arbitrary action of government, Dent v. West Virginia, 129 U.S. 114, 123 (1889). Since prisoners in Nebraska can only lose good-time credits if they are guilty of serious misconduct, the determination of whether such behavior has occurred becomes critical, and the mini-

mum requirements of procedural due process appropriate for the circumstances must be observed. Id., at 558.I

The liberty interest protected in Wolff had its roots in state law, and the minimum procedures appropriate under the circumstances were held required by the Due Process Clause "to insure that the state-created right is not arbitrarily abrogated." Id., at 557. This is consistent with our approach in other due process cases such as Goss v. Lopez, 419 U.S. 565 (1975); Board of Regents v. Roth, supra; Perry v. Sindermann, 408 U.S. 593 (1972); Goldberg v. Kelly, 397 U.S. 254 (1970).

Here, Massachusetts law conferred no right on the prisoner to remain in the prison to which he was initially assigned, defeasible only upon proof of specific acts of misconduct. Insofar as we are advised, transfers between Massachusetts prisons are not conditioned upon the occurrence of specified events. On the contrary, transfer in a wide variety of circumstances is vested in prison officials. The predicate for invoking the protection of the Fourteenth Amendment as construed and applied in Wolff v. McDonnell is totally nonexistent in this case.

Even if Massachusetts has not represented that transfers will occur only on the occurrence of certain events, it is argued that charges of serious misbehavior, as in this case, often initiate and heavily influence the transfer decision and that because allegations of misconduct may be erroneous, hearings should be held before transfer to a more confining institution is to be suffered by the prisoner. That an inmate's conduct, in general or in specific instances, may often be a major factor in the decision of prison officials to transfer him is to be expected unless it be assumed that transfers are mindless events. A prisoner's past and anticipated future behavior will very likely be taken into account in selecting a prison in which he will be initially incarcerated or to which he will be transferred to best serve the State's penological goals.

A prisoner's behavior may precipitate a transfer; and absent such behavior, perhaps transfer would not take place at all. But, as we have said, Massachusetts prison officials have the discretion to transfer prisoners for any number of reasons. Their discretion is not limited to instances of serious misconduct. As we understand it no legal interest or right of these respondents under Massachusetts law would have been violated by their transfer whether or not their misconduct had been proved in accordance with procedures that might be required by the Due Process Clause in other circumstances. Whatever expectation the prisoner may have in remaining at a particular prison so long as he behaves himself, it is too ephemeral and insubstantial to trigger procedural due process protections as long as prison officials have discretion to transfer him for whatever reason or for no reason at all.

Holding that arrangements like this are within reach of the procedural protections of the Due Process Clause would place the Clause astride the day-to-day functioning of state prisons and involve the judiciary in issues and discretionary decisions that are not the business of federal judges. We decline to so interpret and apply the Due Process Clause. The federal courts do not sit to supervise state prisons, the administration of which is of acute interest to the States. Preiser v. Rodriguez, 411 U.S. 475, 491-492 (1973); Cruz v. Beto, 405 U.S. 319, 321 (1972); Johnson v. Avery, 393 U.S. 483, 486 (1969). The individual States, of course, are free to follow another course, whether by statute, by rule or regulation, or by interpretation of their own constitutions. They may thus decide that prudent prison administration requires pretransfer hearings. Our holding is that the Due Process Clause does not impose a nationwide rule mandating transfer hearings.

The judgment of the Court of Appeals accordingly is

Reversed.

MR. JUSTICE STEVENS, with whom MR. JUSTICE BRENNAN and MR. JUSTICE MARSHALL join, dissenting.

The Court's rationale is more disturbing than its narrow holding. If the Court had merely held that the transfer of a prisoner from one penal institution to another does not cause a sufficiently grievous loss to amount to a deprivation of liberty within the meaning of the Due Process Clause of the Fourteenth Amendment, I would disagree with the conclusion but not with the constitutional analysis. The Court's holding today, however, appears to rest on a conception of "liberty" which I consider fundamentally incorrect.

The Court indicates that a "liberty interest" may have either of two sources. According to the Court, a liberty interest may "originate in the Constitution," ante, at 226, or it may have "its roots in state law." Ibid. Apart from those two possible origins, the Court is unable to find that a person has a constitutionally protected interest in liberty.

If man were a creature of the State, the analysis would be correct. But neither the Bill of Rights nor the laws of sovereign States create the liberty which the Due Process Clause protects. The relevant constitutional provisions are limitations on the power of the sovereign to infringe on the liberty of the citizen. The relevant state laws either create property rights, or they curtail the freedom of the citizen who must live in an ordered society. Of course, law is essential to the exercise and enjoyment of individual liberty in a complex society. But it is not the source of liberty, and surely not the exclusive source.

I had thought it self-evident that all men were endowed by their Creator with liberty as one of the cardinal unalienable rights. It is that basic freedom which the Due Process Clause protects, rather than the particular rights or privileges conferred by specific laws or regulations.

A correct description of the source of the liberty protected by the Constitution does not, of course, decide this case. For, by hypothesis, we are dealing with persons who may be deprived of their liberty because they have been convicted of criminal conduct after a fair trial. We should therefore first ask whether the deprivation of liberty which follows conviction is total or partial.

At one time the prevailing view was that the deprivation was essentially total. The penitentiary inmate was considered "the slave of the State." See Ruffin v. Commonwealth, 62 Va. 790, 796 (1871). Although the wording of the Thirteenth Amendment provided some support for that point of view, "courts in recent years have moderated the harsh implications of the Thirteenth Amendment."

The moderating trend culminated in this Court's landmark holding that notwithstanding the continuation of legal custody pursuant to a criminal conviction, a parolee has a measure of liberty that is entitled to constitutional protection.

> We see, therefore, that the liberty of a parolee, although indeterminate, includes many of the core values of unqualified liberty and its termination inflicts a 'grievous loss' on the parolee and often on others. It is hardly useful any longer to try to deal with this problem in terms of whether the parolee's liberty is a 'right' or a 'privilege.' By whatever name, the liberty is valuable and must be seen as within the protection of the Fourteenth Amendment. Its termination calls for some orderly process, however informal. Morrissey v. Brewer, 408 U.S. 471, 482.

Although the Court's opinion was narrowly written with careful emphasis on the permission given to the parolee to live outside the prison walls, the Court necessarily held that the individual possesses a residuum of constitutionally protected liberty while in legal custody pursuant to a valid conviction. For release on parole is merely conditional, and it does not interrupt the State's legal custody. I remain convinced that the Court of Appeals for the Seventh Circuit correctly analyzed the true significance of the Morrissey holding, when I wrote for that court in 1973:

> In view of the fact that physical confinement is merely one species of legal custody, we are persuaded that Morrissey actually portends a more basic conceptual holding: liberty protected by the due process clause may—indeed must to some extent—coexist with legal custody pursuant to conviction. The deprivation of liberty following an adjudication of guilt is partial, not total. A residuum of constitutionally protected rights remains.

As we noted in Morales v. Schmidt, the view once held that an inmate is a mere slave is now totally rejected. The restraints and the punishment which a criminal conviction entails do not place the citizen beyond the ethical tradition that accords respect to the dignity and intrinsic worth of every individual. "Liberty" and "custody" are not mutually exclusive concepts.

If the Morrissey decision is not narrowly limited by the distinction between physical confinement and conditional liberty to live at large in society, it requires that due process precede any substantial deprivation of the liberty of persons in custody. We believe a due regard for the interests of the individual inmate, as well as the interests of that substantial segment of our total society represented by inmates, requires that Morrissey be so read. United States ex rel. Miller v. Twomey, 479 F. 2d 701, 712-713.

It demeans the holding in Morrissey—more importantly it demeans the concept of liberty itself—to ascribe to that holding nothing more than a protection of an interest that the State has created through its own prison regulations. For if the inmate's protected liberty interests are no greater than the State chooses to allow, he is really little more than the slave described in the 19th century cases. I think it clear that even the inmate retains an unalienable interest in liberty—at the very minimum the right to be treated with dignity—which the Constitution may never ignore.

This basic premise is not inconsistent with recognition of the obvious fact that the State must have wide latitude in determining the conditions of confinement that will be imposed following conviction of crime. To supervise and control its prison population, the State must retain the power to change the conditions for individuals, or for groups of prisoners, quickly and without judicial review. In many respects the State's problems in governing its inmate population are comparable to those encountered in governing a military force. Prompt and unquestioning obedience by the individual, even to commands he does not understand, may be essential to the preservation of order and discipline. Nevertheless, within the limits imposed by the basic restraints governing the controlled population, each individual retains his dignity and, in time, acquires a status that is entitled to respect.

Imprisonment is intended to accomplish more than the temporary removal of the offender from society in order to prevent him from committing like offenses during the period of his incarceration. While custody denies the inmate the opportunity to offend, it also gives him an opportunity to improve himself and to acquire skills and habits that will help him to participate in an open society after his release. Within the prison community, if my basic hypothesis is correct, he has a protected right to pursue his limited rehabilitative goals, or at the minimum, to maintain whatever attributes of dignity are associated with his status in a tightly controlled society. It is unquestionably within the power of the State to change that status, abruptly and adversely; but if the change is sufficiently grievous, it may not be imposed arbitrarily. In such case due process must be afforded.

That does not mean, of course, that every adversity amounts to a deprivation within the meaning of the Fourteenth Amendment. There must be grievous loss, and that term itself is somewhat flexible. I would certainly not consider every transfer within a prison system, even to more onerous conditions of confinement, such a loss. On the other hand, I am unable to identify a principled basis for differentiating between a transfer from the general prison population to solitary confinement and a transfer involving equally disparate conditions between one physical facility and another.

In view of the Court's basic holding, I merely note that I agree with the Court of Appeals that the transfer involved in this case was sufficiently serious to invoke the protection of the Constitution.

I respectfully dissent.

BELL
v.
WOLFISH

441 U.S. 520; 99 S. Ct. 1861; 60 L. Ed. 2d 447 (1979)

MR. JUSTICE REHNQUIST delivered the opinion of the Court.

Over the past five Terms, this Court has in several decisions considered constitutional challenges to prison conditions or practices by convicted prisoners. This case requires us to examine the constitutional rights of pretrial detainees—those persons who have been charged with a crime but who have not yet been tried on the charge. The parties concede that to ensure their presence at trial, these persons legitimately may be incarcerated by the Government prior to a determination of their guilt or innocence, infra, at 533-535, and n. 15; see 18 U.S.C. §§ 3146, 3148, and it is the scope of their rights during this period of confinement prior to trial that is the primary focus of this case.

This lawsuit was brought as a class action in the United States District Court for the Southern District of New York to challenge numerous conditions of confinement and practices at the Metropolitan Correctional Center (MCC), a federally operated short-term custodial facility in New York City designed primarily to house pretrial detainees. The District Court, in the words of the Court of Appeals for the Second Circuit, "intervened broadly into almost every facet of the institution" and enjoined no fewer than 20 MCC practices on constitutional and statutory grounds. The Court of Appeals largely affirmed the District Court's constitutional rulings and in the process held that under the Due Process Clause of the Fifth Amendment, pretrial detainees may "be subjected to only those 'restrictions and privations' which 'inhere in their confinement itself or which are justified by compelling necessities of jail administration." Wolfish v. Levi, 573 F.2d 118, 124 (1978), quoting Rhem v. Malcolm, 507 F.2d 333, 336 (CA2 1974). We granted certiorari to consider the important constitutional questions raised by these decisions and to resolve an apparent conflict among the Circuits. 439 U.S. 816 (1978). We now reverse.

I

The MCC was constructed in 1975 to replace the converted waterfront garage on West Street that had served as New York City's federal jail since 1928. It is located adjacent to the Foley Square federal courthouse and has as its primary objective the housing of persons who are being detained in custody prior to trial for federal criminal offenses in the United States District Courts for the Southern and Eastern Districts of New York and for the District of New Jersey. Under the Bail Reform Act, 18 U.S.C. § 3146, a person in the federal system is committed to a detention facility only because no other less drastic means can reasonably ensure his presence at trial. In addition to pretrial detainees, the MCC also houses some convicted inmates who are awaiting sentencing or transportation to federal prison or who are serving generally relatively short sentences in a service capacity at the MCC, convicted prisoners who have been lodged at the facility under writs of habeas corpus ad prosequendum or ad testificandum issued to ensure their presence at upcoming trials, witnesses in protective custody, and persons incarcerated for contempt.

The MCC differs markedly from the familiar image of a jail; there are no barred cells, dank, colorless corridors, or clanging steel gates. It was intended to include the most advanced and innovative features of modern design of detention facilities. As the Court of Appeals stated: "[It] represented the architectural embodiment of the best and most progressive penological planning." 573 F.2d, at 121. The key design element of the 12-story structure is the "modular" or "unit" concept, whereby each floor designed to house inmates has one or two largely self-contained residential units that replace the traditional cellblock jail construction. Each unit in turn has several clusters or corridors of private rooms or dormitories radiating from a central 2-story "multipurpose" or common room, to which each inmate has free access approximately 16 hours a day. Because our analysis does not turn on the particulars of the MCC concept or design, we need not discuss them further.

When the MCC opened in August 1975, the planned capacity was 449 inmates, an increase of 50% over the former West Street facility. Id., at 122. Despite some dormitory accommodations, the MCC was designed primarily to house these inmates in 389 rooms, which originally were intended for single occupancy. While the MCC was under construction, however, the number of persons committed to pretrial detention began to rise at an "unprecedented" rate. Ibid. The Bureau of Prisons took several steps to accommodate this unexpected flow of persons assigned to the facility, but despite these efforts, the inmate population at the MCC rose above its planned capacity within a short time after its opening. To provide sleeping space for this increased population, the MCC replaced the single bunks in many of the individual rooms and dormitories with double bunks. Also, each week some newly arrived inmates had to sleep on cots in the common areas until they could be transferred to residential rooms as space became available. See id., at 127-128.

On November 28, 1975, less than four months after the MCC had opened, the named respondents initiated this action by filing in the District Court a petition for a writ of habeas corpus. The District Court certified the case as a class action on behalf of all persons confined at the MCC, pretrial detainees and sentenced prisoners alike. The petition served up a veritable potpourri of complaints that implicated virtually every facet of the institution's conditions and practices. Respondents charged, inter alia, that they had been deprived of their statutory and constitutional rights because of overcrowded conditions, undue length of confinement, improper searches, inadequate recreational, educational, and employment opportunities, insufficient staff, and objectionable restrictions on the purchase and receipt of personal items and books.

In two opinions and a series of orders, the District Court enjoined numerous MCC practices and conditions. With respect to pretrial detainees, the court held that because they are "presumed to be innocent and held only to ensure their presence at trial, 'any deprivation or restriction of . . . rights beyond those which are necessary for confinement alone, must be justified by a compelling necessity." United States ex rel. Wolfish v. Levi, 439 F.Supp. 114, 124 (1977), quoting Detainees of Brooklyn House of Detention v. Malcolm, 520 F.2d 392, 397 (CA2 1975). And while acknowledging that the rights of sentenced inmates are to be measured by the different standard of the Eighth Amendment, the court declared that to house "an inferior minority of persons . . . in ways found unconstitutional for the rest" would amount to cruel and unusual punishment. United States ex rel. Wolfish v. United States, 428 F.Supp. 333, 339 (1977).

Applying these standards on cross-motions for partial summary judgment, the District Court enjoined the practice of housing two inmates in the individual rooms and prohibited enforcement of the so-called "publisher-only" rule, which at the time of the court's ruling prohibited the receipt of all books and magazines mailed from outside the MCC except those sent directly from a publisher or a book club. After a trial on the remaining issues, the District Court enjoined, inter alia, the doubling of capacity in the dormitory areas, the use of the common rooms to provide temporary sleeping accommodations, the prohibition against inmates' receipt of packages containing food and items of personal property, and the practice of requiring inmates to expose their body cavities for visual inspection following contact visits. The court also granted relief in favor of pretrial detainees, but not convicted inmates, with respect to the requirement that detainees remain outside their rooms during routine inspections by MCC officials.

The Court of Appeals largely affirmed the District Court's rulings, although it rejected that court's Eighth Amendment analysis of conditions of confinement for convicted prisoners because the "parameters of judicial intervention into . . . conditions . . . for sentenced prisoners are more restrictive than in the case of pretrial detainees." 573 F.2d, at 125. Accordingly, the court remanded the matter to the District Court for it to determine whether the housing for sentenced inmates at the MCC was constitutionally "adequate." But the Court of Appeals approved the due process standard employed by the District Court in enjoining the conditions of pretrial confinement. It therefore held that the MCC had failed to make a showing of "compelling necessity" sufficient to justify housing two pretrial detainees in the individual rooms. Id., at 126-127. And for purposes of our review (since petitioners challenge only some of the Court of Appeals' rulings), the court affirmed the District Court's granting of relief against the "publisher-only" rule, the practice of conducting body-cavity searches after contact visits, the prohibition against receipt of packages of food and personal items from outside the institution, and the requirement that detainees remain outside their rooms during routine searches of the rooms by MCC officials. Id., at 129-132.

II

As a first step in our decision, we shall address "double-bunking" as it is referred to by the parties, since it is a condition of confinement that is alleged only to deprive pretrial detainees of their liberty without due process of law in contravention of the Fifth Amendment. . . .

A

The Court of Appeals did not dispute that the Government may permissibly incarcerate a person charged with a crime but not yet convicted to ensure his presence at trial. However, reasoning from the "premise that an individual is to be treated as innocent until proven guilty," the court concluded that pretrial detainees retain the "rights afforded unincarcerated individuals," and that therefore it is not sufficient that the conditions of confinement for pretrial detainees "merely comport with contemporary standards of decency prescribed by the cruel and unusual punishment clause of the eighth amendment." 573 F.2d, at 124. Rather, the court held, the Due Process Clause requires that pretrial detainees "be subjected to only those 'restrictions and privations' which 'inhere in their confinement itself or which are justified by compelling necessities of jail administration." Ibid., quoting Rhem v. Malcolm, 507 F.2d, at 336. Under the Court of Appeals' "compelling necessity" standard, "deprivation of the rights of detainees cannot be justified by the cries of fiscal necessity, . . . administrative convenience, . . . or by the cold comfort that conditions in other jails are worse." 573 F.2d, at 124. The court acknowledged, however, that it could not "ignore" our admonition in Procunier v. Martinez, 416 U.S. 396, 405 (1974), that "courts are ill equipped to deal with the increasingly urgent problems of prison administration," and concluded that it would "not [be] wise for [it] to second-guess the expert administrators on matters on which they are better informed." 573 F.2d, at 124.

Our fundamental disagreement with the Court of Appeals is that we fail to find a source in the Constitution for its compelling-necessity standard. Both the Court of Appeals and the District Court seem to have relied on the "presumption of innocence" as the source of the detainee's substantive right to be free from conditions of confinement that are not justified by compelling necessity. 573 F.2d, at 124; 439 F.Supp., at 124; accord, Campbell v. McGruder, 188 U.S. App. D. C. 258, 266, 580 F.2d 521, 529 (1978); Detainees of Brooklyn House of Detention v. Malcolm, 520 F.2d 392, 397 (CA2 1975); Rhem v. Malcolm, supra, at 336. But see Feeley v. Sampson, 570 F.2d 364, 369 n. 4 (CA1 1978); Hampton v. Holmesburg Prison Officials, 546 F.2d 1077, 1080 n. 1 (CA3 1976). But the presumption of innocence provides no support for such a rule.

The presumption of innocence is a doctrine that allocates the burden of proof in criminal trials; it also may serve as an admonishment to the jury to judge an accused's guilt or innocence solely on the evidence adduced at trial and not on the basis of suspicions that may arise from the fact of his arrest, indictment, or custody, or from other matters not introduced as proof at trial. Taylor v. Kentucky, 436 U.S. 478, 485 (1978); see Estelle v. Williams, 425 U.S. 501 (1976); In re Winship, 397 U.S. 358 (1970); 9 J. Wigmore, Evidence § 2511 (3d ed. 1940). It is "an inaccurate, shorthand

description of the right of the accused to 'remain inactive and secure, until the prosecution has taken up its burden and produced evidence and effected persuasion; . . .' an 'assumption' that is indulged in the absence of contrary evidence." Taylor v. Kentucky, supra, at 484 n. 12. Without question, the presumption of innocence plays an important role in our criminal justice system. "The principle that there is a presumption of innocence in favor of the accused is the undoubted law, axiomatic and elementary, and its enforcement lies at the foundation of the administration of our criminal law." Coffin v. United States, 156 U.S. 432, 453 (1895). But it has no application to a determination of the rights of a pretrial detainee during confinement before his trial has even begun.

The Court of Appeals also relied on what it termed the "indisputable rudiments of due process" in fashioning its compelling-necessity test. We do not doubt that the Due Process Clause protects a detainee from certain conditions and restrictions of pretrial detainment. See infra, at 535-540. Nonetheless, that Clause provides no basis for application of a compelling-necessity standard to conditions of pretrial confinement that are not alleged to infringe any other, more specific guarantee of the Constitution.

It is important to focus on what is at issue here. We are not concerned with the initial decision to detain an accused and the curtailment of liberty that such a decision necessarily entails. See Gerstein v. Pugh, 420 U.S. 103, 114 (1975); United States v. Marion, 404 U.S. 307, 320 (1971). Neither respondents nor the courts below question that the Government may permissibly detain a person suspected of committing a crime prior to a formal adjudication of guilt. See Gerstein v. Pugh, supra, at 111-114. Nor do they doubt that the Government has a substantial interest in ensuring that persons accused of crimes are available for trials and, ultimately, for service of their sentences, or that confinement of such persons pending trial is a legitimate means of furthering that interest. Tr. of Oral Arg. 27; see Stack v. Boyle, 342 U.S. 1, 4 (1951). Instead, what is at issue when an aspect of pretrial detention that is not alleged to violate any express guarantee of the Constitution is challenged, is the detainee's right to be free from punishment, see infra, at 535-

537, and his understandable desire to be as comfortable as possible during his confinement, both of which may conceivably coalesce at some point. It seems clear that the Court of Appeals did not rely on the detainee's right to be free from punishment, but even if it had that right does not warrant adoption of that court's compelling-necessity test. See infra, at 535-540. And to the extent the court relied on the detainee's desire to be free from discomfort, it suffices to say that this desire simply does not rise to the level of those fundamental liberty interests . . .

B

In evaluating the constitutionality of conditions or restrictions of pretrial detention that implicate only the protection against deprivation of liberty without due process of law, we think that the proper inquiry is whether those conditions amount to punishment of the detainee. For under the Due Process Clause, a detainee may not be punished prior to an adjudication of guilt in accordance with due process of law. See Ingraham v. Wright, 430 U.S. 651, 671-672 n. 40, 674 (1977); Kennedy v. Mendoza-Martinez, 372 U.S. 144, 165-167, 186 (1963); Wong Wing v. United States, 163 U.S. 228, 237 (1896). A person lawfully committed to pretrial detention has not been adjudged guilty of any crime. He has had only a "judicial determination of probable cause as a prerequisite to [the] extended restraint of [his] liberty following arrest." Gerstein v. Pugh, supra, at 114; see Virginia v. Paul, 148 U.S. 107, 119 (1893). And, if he is detained for a suspected violation of a federal law, he also has had a bail hearing. See 18 U.S.C. §§ 3146, 3148. Under such circumstances, the Government concededly may detain him to ensure his presence at trial and may subject him to the restrictions and conditions of the detention facility so long as those conditions and restrictions do not amount to punishment, or otherwise violate the Constitution.

Not every disability imposed during pretrial detention amounts to "punishment" in the constitutional sense, however. Once the Government has exercised its conceded authority to detain a person pending trial, it obviously is entitled to employ devices that are calculated to effectuate this detention. Traditionally, this has meant confinement in a facility which, no matter how modern or how antiquated, results in restricting the movement of a detainee in a manner in which he would not be restricted if he simply were free to walk the streets pending trial. Whether it be called a jail, a prison, or a custodial center, the purpose of the facility is to detain. Loss of freedom of choice and privacy are inherent incidents of confinement in such a facility. And the fact that such detention interferes with the detainee's understandable desire to live as comfortably as possible and with as little restraint as possible during confinement does not convert the conditions or restrictions of detention into "punishment."

This Court has recognized a distinction between punitive measures that may not constitutionally be imposed prior to a determination of guilt and regulatory restraints that may. . . .

The factors identified in Mendoza-Martinez provide useful guideposts in determining whether particular restrictions and conditions accompanying pretrial detention amount to punishment in the constitutional sense of that word. A court must decide whether the disability is imposed for the purpose of punishment or whether it is but an incident of some other legitimate governmental purpose. See Flemming v. Nestor, supra, at 613-617. Absent a showing of an expressed intent to punish on the part of detention facility officials, that determination generally will turn on "whether an alternative purpose to which [the restriction] may rationally be connected is assignable for it, and whether it appears excessive in relation to the alternative purpose assigned [to it]." Kennedy v. Mendoza-Martinez, supra, at 168-169; see Flemming v. Nestor, supra, at 617. Thus, if a particular condition or restriction of pretrial detention is reasonably related to a legitimate governmental objective, it does not, without more, amount to "punishment." Conversely, if a restriction or condition is not reasonably related to a legitimate goal—if it is arbitrary or purposeless—a court permissibly may infer that the purpose of the governmental action is punishment that may not constitutionally be inflicted upon detainees qua detainees. See ibid.

Courts must be mindful that these inquiries spring from constitutional requirements and that judicial answers to them must reflect that fact rather than a court's idea of how best to operate a detention facility. Cf. United States v. Lovasco, 431 U.S. 783, 790 (1977); United States v. Russell, 411 U.S. 423, 435 (1973).

One further point requires discussion. The petitioners assert, and respondents concede, that the "essential objective of pretrial confinement is to insure the detainees' presence at trial." Brief for Petitioners 43; see Brief for Respondents 33. While this interest undoubtedly justifies the original decision to confine an individual in some manner, we do not accept respondents' argument that the Government's interest in ensuring a detainee's presence at trial is the only objective that may justify restraints and conditions once the decision is lawfully made to confine a person. "If the government could confine or otherwise infringe the liberty of detainees only to the extent necessary to ensure their presence at trial, house arrest would in the end be the only constitutionally justified form of detention." Campbell v. McGruder, 188 U.S. App. D. C., at 266, 580 F.2d, at 529. The Government also has legitimate interests that stem from its need to manage the facility in which the individual is detained. These legitimate operational concerns may require administrative measures that go beyond those that are, strictly speaking, necessary to ensure that the detainee shows up at trial. For example, the Government must be able to take steps to maintain security and order at the institution and make certain no weapons or illicit drugs reach detainees. Restraints that are reasonably related to the institution's interest in maintaining jail security do not, without more, constitute unconstitutional punishment, even if they are discomforting and are restrictions that the detainee would not have experienced had he been released while awaiting trial. We need not here attempt to detail the precise extent of the legitimate governmental interests that may justify conditions or restrictions of pretrial detention. It is enough simply to recognize that in addition to ensuring the detainees' presence at trial, the effective management of the detention facility once the individual is confined is a valid objective that may justify imposition of conditions and restrictions of pretrial detention and dispel any inference that such restrictions are intended as punishment.

C

Judged by this analysis, respondents' claim that "double-bunking" violated their due process rights fails. Neither the District Court nor the Court of Appeals intimated that it considered "double-bunking" to constitute punishment; instead, they found that it contravened the compelling-necessity test, which today we reject. On this record, we are convinced as a matter of law that "double-bunking" as practiced at the MCC did not amount to punishment and did not, therefore, violate respondents' rights under the Due Process Clause of the Fifth Amendment.

Each of the rooms at the MCC that house pretrial detainees has a total floor space of approximately 75 square feet. Each of them designated for "double-bunking," see n. 4, supra, contains a double bunkbed, certain other items of furniture, a wash basin, and an uncovered toilet. Inmates generally are locked into their rooms from 11 p.m. to 6:30 a.m. and for brief periods during the afternoon and evening head counts. During the rest of the day, they may move about freely between their rooms and the common areas.

Based on affidavits and a personal visit to the facility, the District Court concluded that the practice of "double-bunking" was unconstitutional. The court relied on two factors for its conclusion: (1) the fact that the rooms were designed to house only one inmate, 428 F.Supp., at 336-337; and (2) its judgment that confining two persons in one room or cell of this size constituted a "fundamental [denial] of decency, privacy, personal security, and, simply, civilized humanity. . . ." Id., at 339. The Court of Appeals agreed with the District Court. In response to petitioners' arguments that the rooms at the MCC were larger and more pleasant than the cells involved in the cases relied on by the District Court, the Court of Appeals stated:

[We] find the lack of privacy inherent in double-celling in rooms intended for one individual a far more compelling consideration than a comparison of square footage or the substitution of doors for bars, carpet for concrete, or windows for walls. The government has simply failed to show any substantial justification for double-celling. 573 F.2d, at 127.

We disagree with both the District Court and the Court of Appeals that there is some sort of "one man, one cell" principle lurking in the Due Process Clause of the Fifth Amendment. While confining a given number of people in a given amount of space in such a manner as to cause them to endure genuine privations and hardship over an extended period of time might raise serious questions under the Due Process Clause as to whether those conditions amounted to punishment, nothing even approaching such hardship is shown by this record.

Detainees are required to spend only seven or eight hours each day in their rooms, during most or all of which they presumably are sleeping. The rooms provide more than adequate space for sleeping. During the remainder of the time, the detainees are free to move between their rooms and the common area. While "double-bunking" may have taxed some of the equipment or particular facilities in certain of the common areas, United States ex rel. Wolfish v. United States, 428 F.Supp., at 337, this does not mean that the conditions at the MCC failed to meet the standards required by the Constitution. Our conclusion in this regard is further buttressed by the detainees' length of stay at the MCC. See Hutto v. Finney, 437 U.S. 678, 686-687 (1978). Nearly all of the detainees are released within 60 days. See n. 3, supra. We simply do not believe that requiring a detainee to share toilet facilities and this admittedly rather small sleeping place with another person for generally a maximum period of 60 days violates the Constitution.

III

Respondents also challenged certain MCC restrictions and practices that were designed to promote security and order at the facility on the ground that these restrictions violated the Due Process Clause of the Fifth Amendment, and certain other constitutional guarantees, such as the First and Fourth Amendments. The Court of Appeals seemed to approach the challenges to security restrictions in a fashion different from the other contested conditions and restrictions. It stated that "once it has been determined that the mere fact of confinement of the detainee justifies the restrictions, the institution must be permitted to use reasonable means to insure that its legitimate interests in security are safeguarded." 573 F.2d, at 124. The court might disagree with the choice of means to effectuate those interests, but it should not "second-guess the expert administrators on matters on which they are better informed . . . . Concern with minutiae of prison administration can only distract the court from detached consideration of the one overriding question presented to it: does the practice or condition violate the Constitution?" Id., at 124-125. Nonetheless, the court affirmed the District Court's injunction against several security restrictions. The court rejected the arguments of petitioners that these practices served the MCC's interest in security and order and held that the practices were unjustified interferences with the retained constitutional rights of both detainees and convicted inmates. Id., at 129-132. In our view, the Court of Appeals failed to heed its own admonition not to "second-guess" prison administrators.

Our cases have established several general principles that inform our evaluation of the constitutionality of the restrictions at issue. First, we have held that convicted prisoners do not forfeit all constitutional protections by reason of their conviction and confinement in prison. See Jones v. North Carolina Prisoners' Labor Union, 433 U.S. 119, 129 (1977); Meachum v. Fano, 427 U.S. 215, 225 (1976); Wolff v. McDonnell, 418 U.S. 539, 555-556 (1974); Pell v. Procunier, 417 U.S. 817, 822 (1974). "There is no iron curtain drawn between the Constitution and the prisons of this country." Wolff v. McDonnell, supra, at 555-556. So, for example, our cases have held that sentenced prisoners enjoy freedom of speech and religion under the First and Fourteenth Amendments, see Pell v. Procunier, supra; Cruz v. Beto, 405 U.S. 319 (1972); Cooper v. Pate, 378 U.S. 546 (1964); that they are protected against invidious discrimination on the basis of race under the Equal Protection Clause of the Fourteenth Amendment, see Lee v. Washington, 390

U.S. 333 (1968); and that they may claim the protection of the Due Process Clause to prevent additional deprivation of life, liberty, or property without due process of law, . . . A fortiori, pretrial detainees, who have not been convicted of any crimes, retain at least those constitutional rights that we have held are enjoyed by convicted prisoners.

But our cases also have insisted on a second proposition: simply because prison inmates retain certain constitutional rights does not mean that these rights are not subject to restrictions and limitations. "Lawful incarceration brings about the necessary withdrawal or limitation of many privileges and rights, a retraction justified by the considerations underlying our penal system." Price v. Johnston, 334 U.S. 266, 285 (1948); see Jones v. North Carolina Prisoners' Labor Union, supra, at 125; Wolff v. McDonnell, supra, at 555; Pell v. Procunier, supra, at 822. The fact of confinement as well as the legitimate goals and policies of the penal institution limits these retained constitutional rights. Jones v. North Carolina Prisoners' Labor Union, supra, at 125; Pell v. Procunier, supra, at 822. There must be a "mutual accommodation between institutional needs and objectives and the provisions of the Constitution that are of general application." Wolff v. McDonnell, supra, at 556. This principle applies equally to pretrial detainees and convicted prisoners. A detainee simply does not possess the full range of freedoms of an unincarcerated individual.

Third, maintaining institutional security and preserving internal order and discipline are essential goals that may require limitation or retraction of the retained constitutional rights of both convicted prisoners and pretrial detainees. "[Central] to all other corrections goals is the institutional consideration of internal security within the corrections facilities themselves." Pell v. Procunier, supra, at 823; see Jones v. North Carolina Prisoners' Labor Union, supra, at 129; Procunier v. Martinez, 416 U.S. 396, 412 (1974). Prison officials must be free to take appropriate action to ensure the safety of inmates and corrections personnel and to prevent escape or unauthorized entry. Accordingly, we have held that even when an institutional restriction infringes a specific constitutional guarantee, such as the First Amendment, the practice must be evaluated in the light of the central objective of prison administration, safeguarding institutional security. Jones v. North Carolina Prisoners' Labor Union, supra, at 129; Pell v. Procunier, supra, at 822, 826; Procunier v. Martinez, supra, at 412-414.

Finally, as the Court of Appeals correctly acknowledged, the problems that arise in the day-to-day operation of a corrections facility are not susceptible of easy solutions. Prison administrators therefore should be accorded wide-ranging deference in the adoption and execution of policies and practices that in their judgment are needed to preserve internal order and discipline and to maintain institutional security. Jones v. North Carolina Prisoners' Labor Union, supra, at 128; Procunier v. Martinez, supra, at 404-405; Cruz v. Beto, supra, at 321; see Meachum v. Fano, 427 U.S., at 228-229. "Such considerations are peculiarly within the province and professional expertise of corrections officials, and, in the absence of substantial evidence in the record to indicate that the officials have exaggerated their response to these considerations, courts should ordinarily defer to their expert judgment in such matters." Pell v. Procunier, 417 U.S., at 827. We further observe that, on occasion, prison administrators may be "experts" only by Act of Congress or of a state legislature. But judicial deference is accorded not merely because the administrator ordinarily will, as a matter of fact in a particular case, have a better grasp of his domain than the reviewing judge, but also because the operation of our correctional facilities is peculiarly the province of the Legislative and Executive Branches of our Government, not the Judicial. Procunier v. Martinez, supra, at 405; cf. Meachum v. Fano, supra, at 229. With these teachings of our cases in mind, we turn to an examination of the MCC security practices that are alleged to violate the Constitution.

A

At the time of the lower courts' decisions, the Bureau of Prisons' "publisher-only" rule, which applies to all Bureau facilities, permitted inmates to receive books and magazines from outside the institution only if the materials were mailed directly from the publisher or a book club. 573 F.2d, at 129-130. The warden of the MCC stated in an affidavit that "serious" security and administrative problems were caused when bound items were received by inmates from unidentified sources outside the facility. App. 24. He noted that in order to make a "proper and thorough" inspection of such items, prison officials would have to remove the covers of hardback books and to leaf through every page of all books and magazines to ensure that drugs, money, weapons, or other contraband were not secreted in the material. "This search process would take a substantial and inordinate amount of available staff time." Ibid. However, "there is relatively little risk that material received directly from a publisher or book club would contain contraband, and therefore, the security problems are significantly reduced without a drastic drain on staff resources." Ibid.

The Court of Appeals rejected these security and administrative justifications and affirmed the District Court's order enjoining enforcement of the "publisher-only" rule at the MCC. The Court of Appeals held that the rule "severely and impermissibly restricts the reading material available to inmates" and therefore violates their First Amendment and due process rights. 573 F.2d, at 130.

It is desirable at this point to place in focus the precise question that now is before this Court. Subsequent to the decision of the Court of Appeals, the Bureau of Prisons amended its "publisher-only" rule to permit the receipt of books and magazines from bookstores as well as publishers and book clubs. 43 Fed. Reg. 30576 (1978) (to be codified in 28 CFR § 540.71). In addition, petitioners have informed the Court that the Bureau proposes to amend the rule further to allow receipt of paperback books, magazines, and other soft-covered materials from any source. Brief for Petitioners 66 n. 49, 69, and n. 51. The Bureau regards hardback books as the "more dangerous source of risk to institutional security," however, and intends to retain the prohibition against receipt of hardback books unless they are mailed directly from publishers, book clubs, or bookstores. Id., at 69 n. 51. Accordingly, petitioners request this Court to review the District Court's injunction only to the extent it enjoins petitioners from prohibiting receipt of hard-cover books that are not mailed

directly from publishers, book clubs, or bookstores. Id., at 69.

We conclude that a prohibition against receipt of hardback books unless mailed directly from publishers, book clubs, or bookstores does not violate the First Amendment rights of MCC inmates. That limited restriction is a rational response by prison officials to an obvious security problem. It hardly needs to be emphasized that hardback books are especially serviceable for smuggling contraband into an institution; money, drugs, and weapons easily may be secreted in the bindings. E.g., Woods v. Daggett, 541 F.2d 237 (CA10 1976). They also are difficult to search effectively. There is simply no evidence in the record to indicate that MCC officials have exaggerated their response to this security problem and to the administrative difficulties posed by the necessity of carefully inspecting each book mailed from unidentified sources. Therefore, the considered judgment of these experts must control in the absence of prohibitions far more sweeping than those involved here. See Jones v. North Carolina Prisoners' Labor Union, 433 U.S., at 128; Pell v. Procunier, 417 U.S., at 827.

Our conclusion that this limited restriction on receipt of hardback books does not infringe the First Amendment rights of MCC inmates is influenced by several other factors. The rule operates in a neutral fashion, without regard to the content of the expression. Id., at 828. And there are alternative means of obtaining reading material that have not been shown to be burdensome or insufficient. "[We] regard the available 'alternative means of [communication as] a relevant factor' in a case such as this where 'we [are] called upon to balance First Amendment rights against [legitimate] governmental . . . interests." Id., at 824, quoting Kleindienst v. Mandel, 408 U.S. 753, 765 (1972); see Cruz v. Beto, 405 U.S., at 321, 322 n. 2. The restriction, as it is now before us, allows soft-bound books and magazines to be received from any source and hardback books to be received from publishers, bookstores, and book clubs. In addition, the MCC has a "relatively large" library for use by inmates. United States ex rel. Wolfish v. United States, 428 F.Supp., at 340. To the limited extent the rule might possibly increase the cost of obtaining published materials, this Court has held that where "other avenues" remain available for the receipt of materials by inmates, the loss of "cost advantages does not fundamentally implicate free speech values." See Jones v. North Carolina Prisoners' Labor Union, supra, at 130-131. We are also influenced in our decision by the fact that the rule's impact on pretrial detainees is limited to a maximum period of approximately 60 days. See n. 3, supra. In sum, considering all the circumstances, we view the rule, as we now find it, to be a "reasonable 'time, place and manner' [regulation that is] necessary to further significant governmental interests . . . ." Grayned v. City of Rockford, 408 U.S. 104, 115 (1972); see Cox v. New Hampshire, 312 U.S. 569, 575-576 (1941); Cox v. Louisiana, 379 U.S. 536, 554-555 (1965); Adderley v. Florida, 385 U.S. 39, 46-48 (1966).

B

Inmates at the MCC were not permitted to receive packages from outside the facility containing items of food or personal property, except for one package of food at Christmas. This rule was justified by MCC officials on three grounds. First, officials testified to "serious" security problems that arise from the introduction of such packages into the institution, the "traditional file in the cake kind of situation" as well as the concealment of drugs "in heels of shoes [and] seams of clothing." App. 80; see id., at 24, 84-85. As in the case of the "publisher-only" rule, the warden testified that if such packages were allowed, the inspection process necessary to ensure the security of the institution would require a "substantial and inordinate amount of available staff time." Id., at 24. Second, officials were concerned that the introduction of personal property into the facility would increase the risk of thefts, gambling, and inmate conflicts, the "age-old problem of you have it and I don't." Id., at 80; see id., at 85. Finally, they noted storage and sanitary problems that would result from inmates' receipt of food packages. Id., at 67, 80. Inmates are permitted, however, to purchase certain items of food and personal property from the MCC commissary.

The District Court dismissed these justifications as "dire predictions." It was unconvinced by the asserted security problems because other institutions allow greater ownership of personal property and receipt of packages than does the MCC. And because the MCC permitted inmates to purchase items in the commissary, the court could not accept official fears of increased theft, gambling, or conflicts if packages were allowed. Finally, it believed that sanitation could be assured by proper housekeeping regulations. Accordingly, it ordered the MCC to promulgate regulations to permit receipt of at least items of the kind that are available in the commissary. 439 F.Supp., at 152-153. The Court of Appeals accepted the District Court's analysis and affirmed, although it noted that the MCC could place a ceiling on the permissible dollar value of goods received and restrict the number of packages. 573 F.2d, at 132.

Neither the District Court nor the Court of Appeals identified which provision of the Constitution was violated by this MCC restriction. We assume, for present purposes, that their decisions were based on the Due Process Clause of the Fifth Amendment, which provides protection for convicted prisoners and pretrial detainees alike against the deprivation of their property without due process of law. See supra, at 545. But as we have stated, these due process rights of prisoners and pretrial detainees are not absolute; they are subject to reasonable limitation or retraction in light of the legitimate security concerns of the institution.

We think that the District Court and the Court of Appeals have trenched too cavalierly into areas that are properly the concern of MCC officials. It is plain from their opinions that the lower courts simply disagreed with the judgment of MCC officials about the extent of the security interests affected and the means required to further those interests. But our decisions have time and again emphasized that this sort of unguided substitution of judicial judgment for that of the expert prison administrators on matters such as this is inappropriate. See Jones v. North Carolina Prisoners' Labor Union; Pell v. Procunier; Procunier v. Martinez. We do not doubt that the rule devised by the District Court and modified by the Court of Appeals may be a reasonable way of coping with the problems of security, order, and sanitation. It simply is not, however, the only constitutionally permissible approach to these problems. Certainly, the Due Process Clause does not mandate a "lowest common denominator" security standard, whereby a practice permitted at one penal institution must be permitted at all institutions.

Corrections officials concluded that permitting the introduction of packages of personal property and food would increase the risks of gambling, theft, and inmate fights over that which the institution already experienced by permitting certain items to be purchased from its commissary. "It is enough to say that they have not been conclusively shown to be wrong in this view." Jones v. North Carolina Prisoners' Labor Union, 433 U.S., at 132. It is also all too obvious that such packages are handy devices for the smuggling of contraband. There simply is no basis in this record for concluding that MCC officials have exaggerated their response to these serious problems or that this restriction is irrational. It does not therefore deprive the convicted inmates or pretrial detainees of the MCC of their property without due process of law in contravention of the Fifth Amendment.

C

The MCC staff conducts unannounced searches of inmate living areas at irregular intervals. These searches generally are formal unit "shakedowns" during which all inmates are cleared of the residential units, and a team of guards searches each room. Prior to the District Court's order, inmates were not permitted to watch the searches. Officials testified that permitting inmates to observe room inspections would lead to friction between the inmates and security guards and would allow the inmates to attempt to frustrate the search by distracting personnel and moving contraband from one room to another ahead of the search team.

The District Court held that this procedure could not stand as applied to pretrial detainees because MCC officials had not shown that the restriction was justified by "compelling necessity." The court stated that "[at] least until or unless [petitioners] can show a pattern of violence or other disrup-

tions taxing the powers of control—a kind of showing not remotely approached by the Warden's expressions—the security argument for banishing inmates while their rooms are searched must be rejected." 439 F.Supp., at 149. It also noted that in many instances inmates suspected guards of thievery. Id., at 148-149. The Court of Appeals agreed with the District Court. It saw "no reason whatsoever not to permit a detainee to observe the search of his room and belongings from a reasonable distance," although the court permitted the removal of any detainee who became "obstructive." 573 F.2d, at 132.

The Court of Appeals did not identify the constitutional provision on which it relied in invalidating the room-search rule. The District Court stated that the rule infringed the detainee's interest in privacy and indicated that this interest in privacy was founded on the Fourth Amendment. 439 F.Supp., at 149-150. It may well be argued that a person confined in a detention facility has no reasonable expectation of privacy with respect to his room or cell and that therefore the Fourth Amendment provides no protection for such a person. Cf. Lanza v. New York, 370 U.S. 139, 143-144 (1962). In any case, given the realities of institutional confinement, any reasonable expectation of privacy that a detainee retained necessarily would be of a diminished scope. Id., at 143. Assuming, arguendo, that a pretrial detainee retains such a diminished expectation of privacy after commitment to a custodial facility, we nonetheless find that the room-search rule does not violate the Fourth Amendment.

It is difficult to see how the detainee's interest in privacy is infringed by the room-search rule. No one can rationally doubt that room searches represent an appropriate security measure and neither the District Court nor the Court of Appeals prohibited such searches. And even the most zealous advocate of prisoners' rights would not suggest that a warrant is required to conduct such a search. Detainees' drawers, beds, and personal items may be searched, even after the lower courts' rulings. Permitting detainees to observe the searches does not lessen the invasion of their privacy; its only conceivable beneficial effect would be to prevent theft or misuse by those conducting the search. The room-search rule simply facilitates the safe and effective performance of the search which all concede may be conducted. The rule itself, then, does not render the searches "unreasonable" within the meaning of the Fourth Amendment.

D

Inmates at all Bureau of Prisons facilities, including the MCC, are required to expose their body cavities for visual inspection as a part of a strip search conducted after every contact visit with a person from outside the institution. Corrections officials testified that visual cavity searches were necessary not only to discover but also to deter the smuggling of weapons, drugs, and other contraband into the institution. App. 70-72, 83-84. The District Court upheld the strip-search procedure but prohibited the body-cavity searches, absent probable cause to believe that the inmate is concealing contraband. 439 F.Supp., at 147-148. Because petitioners proved only one instance in the MCC's short history where contraband was found during a body-cavity search, the Court of Appeals affirmed. In its view, the "gross violation of personal privacy inherent in such a search cannot be outweighed by the government's security interest in maintaining a practice of so little actual utility." 573 F.2d, at 131.

Admittedly, this practice instinctively gives us the most pause. However, assuming for present purposes that inmates, both convicted prisoners and pretrial detainees, retain some Fourth Amendment rights upon commitment to a corrections facility, see Lanza v. New York, supra; Stroud v. United States, 251 U.S. 15, 21 (1919), we nonetheless conclude that these searches do not violate that Amendment. The Fourth Amendment prohibits only unreasonable searches, Carroll v. United States, 267 U.S. 132, 147 (1925), and under the circumstances, we do not believe that these searches are unreasonable.

The test of reasonableness under the Fourth Amendment is not capable of precise definition or mechanical application. In each case it requires a balancing of the need for the particular search against the invasion of personal rights that the search entails. Courts must consider the scope of the particular intrusion, the manner in which it is conducted, the justification for initiating it, and the place in which it is conducted. E.g., United States v. Ramsey, 431 U.S. 606 (1977); United States v. Martinez-Fuerte, 428 U.S. 543 (1976); United States v. Brignoni-Ponce, 422 U.S. 873 (1975); Terry v. Ohio, 392 U.S. 1 (1968); Katz v. United States, 389 U.S. 347 (1967); Schmerber v. California, 384 U.S. 757 (1966). A detention facility is a unique place fraught with serious security dangers. Smuggling of money, drugs, weapons, and other contraband is all too common an occurrence. And inmate attempts to secrete these items into the facility by concealing them in body cavities are documented in this record, App. 71-76, and in other cases. E.g., Ferraro v. United States, 590 F.2d 335 (CA6 1978); United States v. Park, 521 F.2d 1381, 1382 (CA9 1975). That there has been only one instance where an MCC inmate was discovered attempting to smuggle contraband into the institution on his person may be more a testament to the effectiveness of this search technique as a deterrent than to any lack of interest on the part of the inmates to secrete and import such items when the opportunity arises.

We do not underestimate the degree to which these searches may invade the personal privacy of inmates. Nor do we doubt, as the District Court noted, that on occasion a security guard may conduct the search in an abusive fashion. 439 F.Supp., at 147. Such abuse cannot be condoned. The searches must be conducted in a reasonable manner. Schmerber v. California, supra, at 771-772. But we deal here with the question whether visual body-cavity inspections as contemplated by the MCC rules can ever be conducted on less than probable cause. Balancing the significant and legitimate security interests of the institution against the privacy interests of the inmates, we conclude that they can.

IV

Nor do we think that the four MCC security restrictions and practices described in Part III, supra, constitute "punishment" in violation of the rights of pretrial detainees under the Due Process Clause of the Fifth Amendment. Neither the District Court nor the Court of Appeals suggested that these restrictions and practices were employed by MCC officials with an intent to punish the pretrial detainees housed there. Respondents do not even make such a suggestion; they simply argue that the restrictions were greater than necessary to satisfy petitioners' legitimate interest in maintaining security. Brief for Respondents 51-53. Therefore, the determination whether these restrictions and practices constitute punishment in the constitutional sense depends on whether they are rationally related to a legitimate nonpunitive governmental purpose and whether they appear excessive in relation to that purpose. See supra, at 538-539. Ensuring security and order at the institution is a permissible nonpunitive objective, whether the facility houses pretrial detainees, convicted inmates, or both. Supra, at 539-540; see supra, at 546-547, and n. 28. For the reasons set forth in Part III, supra, we think that these particular restrictions and practices were reasonable responses by MCC officials to legitimate security concerns. Respondents simply have not met their heavy burden of showing that these officials have exaggerated their response to the genuine security considerations that actuated these restrictions and practices. See n. 23, supra. And as might be expected of restrictions applicable to pretrial detainees, these restrictions were of only limited duration so far as the MCC pretrial detainees were concerned. See n. 3, supra.

V

There was a time not too long ago when the federal judiciary took a completely "hands-off" approach to the problem of prison administration. In recent years, however, these courts largely have discarded this "hands-off" attitude and have waded into this complex arena. The deplorable conditions and Draconian restrictions of some of our Nation's prisons are too well known to require recounting here, and the federal courts rightly have condemned these sordid aspects of our prison systems. But many of these same courts have, in the name of the Constitution, become increasingly enmeshed in the minutiae of prison operations. Judges, after all, are human. They, no less than others in our society, have a natural tendency to believe that their individual solutions to often intractable problems are better and more

workable than those of the persons who are actually charged with and trained in the running of the particular institution under examination. But under the Constitution, the first question to be answered is not whose plan is best, but in what branch of the Government is lodged the authority to initially devise the plan. This does not mean that constitutional rights are not to be scrupulously observed. It does mean, however, that the inquiry of federal courts into prison management must be limited to the issue of whether a particular system violates any prohibition of the Constitution or, in the case of a federal prison, a statute. The wide range of "judgment calls" that meet constitutional and statutory requirements are confided to officials outside of the Judicial Branch of Government.

The judgment of the Court of Appeals is, accordingly, reversed, and the case is remanded for proceedings consistent with this opinion.

It is so ordered.

MR. JUSTICE POWELL, concurring in part and dissenting in part.

I join the opinion of the Court except the discussion and holding with respect to body-cavity searches. In view of the serious intrusion on one's privacy occasioned by such a search, I think at least some level of cause, such as a reasonable suspicion, should be required to justify the anal and genital searches described in this case. I therefore dissent on this issue.

MR. JUSTICE MARSHALL, dissenting.

* * *

III

D

In my view, the body-cavity searches of MCC inmates represent one of the most grievous offenses against personal dignity and common decency. After every contact visit with someone from outside the facility, including defense attorneys, an inmate must remove all of his or her clothing, bend over, spread the buttocks, and display the anal cavity for inspection by a correctional officer.

Women inmates must assume a suitable posture for vaginal inspection, while men must raise their genitals. And, as the Court neglects to note, because of time pressures, this humiliating spectacle is frequently conducted in the presence of other inmates. App. 77.

The District Court found that the stripping was "unpleasant, embarrassing, and humiliating." 439 F.Supp., at 146. A psychiatrist testified that the practice placed inmates in the most degrading position possible, App. 48, a conclusion amply corroborated by the testimony of the inmates themselves. Id., at 36-37, 41. There was evidence, moreover, that these searches engendered among detainees fears of sexual assault, id., at 49, were the occasion for actual threats of physical abuse by guards, and caused some inmates to forgo personal visits. 439 F.Supp., at 147.

Not surprisingly, the Government asserts a security justification for such inspections. These searches are necessary, it argues, to prevent inmates from smuggling contraband into the facility. In crediting this justification despite the contrary findings of the two courts below, the Court overlooks the critical facts. As respondents point out, inmates are required to wear one-piece jumpsuits with zippers in the front. To insert an object into the vaginal or anal cavity, an inmate would have to remove the jumpsuit, at least from the upper torso. App. 45; Joint App. in Nos. 77-2035, 77-2135 (CA2), p. 925 (hereinafter Joint App.). Since contact visits occur in a glass-enclosed room and are continuously monitored by corrections officers, see 439 F.Supp., at 140, 147; Joint App. 144, 1208-1209, such a feat would seem extraordinarily difficult. There was medical testimony, moreover, that inserting an object into the rectum is painful and "would require time and opportunity which is not available in the visiting areas," App. 49-50, and that visual inspection would probably not detect an object once inserted. Id., at 50. Additionally, before entering the visiting room, visitors and their packages are searched thoroughly by a metal detector, fluoroscope, and by hand. Id., at 93; Joint App. 601, 1077. Correction officers may require that visitors leave packages or handbags with guards until the visit is over. Joint App. 1077-1078. Only by blinding itself to the facts presented on this record can the Court accept the Government's security rationale.

Without question, these searches are an imposition of sufficient gravity to invoke the compelling-necessity standard. It is equally indisputable that they cannot meet that standard. Indeed, the procedure is so unnecessarily degrading that it "shocks the conscience." Rochin v. California, 342 U.S. 165, 172 (1952). Even in Rochin, the police had reason to believe that the petitioner had swallowed contraband. Here, the searches are employed absent any suspicion of wrongdoing. It was this aspect of the MCC practice that the Court of Appeals redressed, requiring that searches be conducted only when there is probable cause to believe that the inmate is concealing contraband. The Due Process Clause, on any principled reading, dictates no less.

That the Court can uphold these indiscriminate searches highlights the bankruptcy of its basic analysis. Under the test adopted today, the rights of detainees apparently extend only so far as detention officials decide that cost and security will permit. Such unthinking deference to administrative convenience cannot be justified where the interests at stake are those of presumptively innocent individuals, many of whose only proven offense is the inability to afford bail. I dissent.

MR. JUSTICE STEVENS, with whom MR. JUSTICE BRENNAN joins, dissenting.

This is not an equal protection case. An empirical judgment that most persons formally accused of criminal conduct are probably guilty would provide a rational basis for a set of rules that treat them like convicts until they establish their innocence. No matter how rational such an approach might be— no matter how acceptable in a community where equality of status is the dominant goal—it is obnoxious to the concept of individual freedom protected by the Due Process Clause. If ever accepted in this country, it would work a fundamental change in the character of our free society.

Nor is this an Eighth Amendment case. That provision of the Constitution protects individuals convicted of crimes from punishment that is cruel and unusual. The pretrial detainees whose rights are at stake in this case, however, are innocent men and women who have been convicted of no crimes. Their claim is not that they have been subjected to cruel and unusual punishment in violation of the Eighth Amendment, but that to subject them to any form of punishment at all is an unconstitutional deprivation of their liberty.

This is a due process case. The most significant—and I venture to suggest the most enduring—part of the Court's opinion today is its recognition of this initial constitutional premise. The Court squarely holds that "under the Due Process Clause, a detainee may not be punished prior to an adjudication of guilt in accordance with due process of law." Ante, at 535.

This right to be free of punishment is not expressly embodied in any provision in the Bill of Rights. Nor is the source of this right found in any statute. The source of this fundamental freedom is the word "liberty" itself as used in the Due Process Clause, and as informed by "history, reason, the past course of decisions," and the judgment and experience of "those whom the Constitution entrusted" with interpreting that word. Anti-Fascist Committee v. McGrath, 341 U.S. 123, 162-163 (Frankfurter, J., concurring). See Leis v. Flynt, 439 U.S. 438, 457 (STEVENS, J., dissenting).

In my opinion, this latter proposition is obvious and indisputable. Nonetheless, it is worthy of emphasis because the Court has now accepted it in principle. Ante, at 535. In recent years, the Court has mistakenly implied that the concept of liberty encompasses only those rights that are either created by statute or regulation or are protected by an express provision of the Bill of Rights. Today, however, without the help of any statute, regulation, or express provision of the Constitution, the Court has derived the innocent person's right not to be punished from the Due Process Clause itself. It has accordingly abandoned its parsimonious definition of the "liberty" protected by the majestic words of the Clause. I concur in that abandonment. It is with regard to the scope of this fundamental right that we part company.

I

* * *

Prior to conviction every individual is entitled to the benefit of a presumption both that he is innocent of prior criminal conduct and that he has no present intention to commit any offense in the immediate future. That presumption does not imply that he may not be detained or otherwise subjected to restraints on the basis of an individual showing of probable cause that he poses relevant risks to the community. For our system of justice has always and quite properly functioned on the assumption that probable cause to believe (1) that a person has committed a crime, and (2) that absent the posting of bail he poses at least some risk of flight, justifies pretrial detention to ensure his presence at trial.

The fact that an individual may be unable to pay for a bail bond, however, is an insufficient reason for subjecting him to indignities that would be appropriate punishment for convicted felons. Nor can he be subject on that basis to onerous restraints that might properly be considered regulatory with respect to particularly obstreperous or dangerous arrestees. An innocent man who has no propensity toward immediate violence, escape, or subversion may not be dumped into a pool of second-class citizens and subjected to restraints designed to regulate others who have. For him, such treatment amounts to punishment. And because the due process guarantee is individual and personal, it mandates that an innocent person be treated as an individual human being and be free of treatment which, as to him, is punishment.

It is not always easy to determine whether a particular restraint serves the legitimate, regulatory goal of ensuring a detainee's presence at trial and his safety and security in the meantime, or the unlawful end of punishment. But the courts have performed that task in the past, and can and should continue to perform it in the future. Having recognized the constitutional right to be free of punishment, the Court may not point to the difficulty of the task as a justification for confining the scope of the punishment concept so narrowly that it effectively abdicates to correction officials the judicial responsibility to enforce the guarantees of due process.

In addressing the constitutionality of the rules at issue in this case, the Court seems to say that as long as the correction officers are not motivated by "an expressed intent to punish" their wards, ante, at 538, and as long as their rules are not "arbitrary or purposeless," ante, at 539, these rules are an acceptable form of regulation and not punishment. Lest that test be too exacting, the Court abjectly defers to the prison administrator unless his conclusions are "conclusively shown to be wrong." Ante, at 555, quoting Jones v. North Carolina Prisoners' Labor Union, 433 U.S. 119, 132.

Applying this test, the Court concludes that enforcement of the challenged restrictions does not constitute punishment because there is no showing of a subjective intent to punish and there is a rational basis for each of the challenged rules. In my view, the Court has reached an untenable conclusion because its test for punishment is unduly permissive.

The requirement that restraints have a rational basis provides an individual with virtually no protection against punishment. Any restriction that may reduce the cost of the facility's warehousing function could not be characterized as "arbitrary or purposeless" and could not be "conclusively shown" to have no reasonable relation to the Government's mission. This is true even of a restraint so severe that it might be cruel and unusual.

Nor does the Court's intent test ensure the individual the protection that the Constitution guarantees. For the Court seems to use the term "intent" to mean the subjective intent of the jail administrator. This emphasis can only "encourage hypocrisy and unconscious self-deception." While a subjective intent may provide a sufficient reason for finding that punishment has been inflicted, such an intent is clearly not a necessary nor even the most common element of a punitive sanction.

In short, a careful reading of the Court's opinion reveals that it has attenuated the detainee's constitutional protection against punishment into nothing more than a prohibition against irrational classifications or barbaric treatment. Having recognized in theory that the source of that protection is the Due Process Clause, the Court has in practice defined its scope in the far more permissive terms of equal protection and Eighth Amendment analysis.

* * *

VITEK
v.
JONES

445 U.S. 480; 100 S. Ct. 1254; 63 L. Ed. 2d 552 (1980)

MR. JUSTICE WHITE delivered the opinion of the Court, except as to Part IV-B.

The question in this case is whether the Due Process Clause of the Fourteenth Amendment entitles a prisoner convicted and incarcerated in the State of Nebraska to certain procedural protections, including notice, an adversary hearing, and provision of counsel, before he is transferred involuntarily to a state mental hospital for treatment of a mental disease or defect.

I

Nebraska Rev. Stat. § 83-176 (2) (1976) authorizes the Director of Correctional Services to designate any available, suitable, and appropriate residence facility or institution as a place of confinement for any state prisoner and to transfer a prisoner from one place of confinement to another. Section 83-180 (1), however, provides that when a designated physician or psychologist finds that a prisoner "suffers from a mental disease or defect" and "cannot be given proper treatment in that facility," the director may transfer him for examination, study, and treatment to another institution within or without the Department of Correctional Services. Any prisoner so transferred to a mental hospital is to be returned to the Department if, prior to the expiration of his sentence, treatment is no longer necessary. Upon expiration of sentence, if the State desires to retain the prisoner in a mental hospital, civil commitment proceedings must be promptly commenced. § 83-180 (3).

On May 31, 1974, Jones was convicted of robbery and sentenced to a term of three to nine years in state prison. He was transferred to the penitentiary hospital in January 1975. Two days later he was placed in solitary confinement, where he set his mattress on fire, burning himself severely. He was treated in the burn unit of a private hospital. Upon his release and based on findings required by § 83-180 that he was suffering from a mental illness or defect and could not receive proper treatment in the penal complex, he was transferred to the security unit of the Lincoln Regional Center, a state mental hospital under the jurisdiction of the Department of Public Institutions.

Jones then intervened in this case, which was brought by other prisoners against the appropriate state officials (the State) challenging on procedural due process grounds the adequacy of the procedures by which the Nebraska statutes permit transfers from the prison complex to a mental hospital. On August 17, 1976, a three-judge District Court, convened pursuant to 28 U.S.C. § 2281 (1970 ed.), denied the State's motion for summary judgment and trial ensued. On September 12, 1977, the District Court declared § 83-180 unconstitutional as applied to Jones, holding that transferring Jones to a mental hospital without adequate notice and opportunity for a hearing deprived him of liberty without due process of law contrary to the Fourteenth Amendment and that such transfers must be accompanied by adequate notice, an adversary hearing before an independent decision-maker, a written statement by the factfinder of the evidence relied on and the reasons for the decision, and the availability of appointed counsel for indigent prisoners. Miller v. Vitek, 437 F.Supp. 569 (Neb. 1977). Counsel was requested to suggest appropriate relief.

In response to this request, Jones revealed that on May 27, 1977, prior to the District Court's decision, he had been transferred from Lincoln Regional Center to the psychiatric ward of the penal complex but prayed for an injunction against further transfer to Lincoln Regional Center. The State conceded that an injunction should enter if the District Court was firm in its belief that the section was unconstitutional. The District Court then entered its judgment declaring § 83-180

unconstitutional as applied to Jones and permanently enjoining the State from transferring Jones to Lincoln Regional Center without following the procedures prescribed in its judgment.

We noted probable jurisdiction 434 U.S. 1060 (1978). Meanwhile, Jones had been paroled, but only on condition that he accept psychiatric treatment at a Veterans' Administration Hospital. We vacated the judgment of the District Court and remanded the case to that court for consideration of the question of mootness. Vitek v. Jones, 436 U.S. 407 (1978). Both the State and Jones at this juncture insisted that the case was not moot. The State represented that because "Jones' history of mental illness indicates a serious threat to his own safety, as well as to that of others . . . there is a very real expectation" that he would again be transferred if the injunction was removed. App. to Juris. Statement 24. Jones insisted that he was receiving treatment for mental illness against his will and that he was continuing to suffer from the stigmatizing consequences of the previous determination that he was mentally ill. On these representations, the District Court found that the case was not moot because Jones "is subject to and is in fact under threat of being transferred to the state mental hospital under § 83-180." Ibid. The District Court reinstated its original judgment. We postponed consideration of jurisdiction to a hearing on the merits. 441 U.S. 922 (1979). Meanwhile, Jones had violated his parole, his parole had been revoked, and he had been reincarcerated in the penal complex.

II

We agree with the parties in this case that a live controversy exists and that the case is not moot. Jones was declared to be mentally ill pursuant to § 83-180 and was transferred to a mental hospital and treated. He was later paroled but only on condition that he accept mental treatment. He violated that parole and has been returned to the penal complex. On our remand to consider mootness, the District Court, relying on Jones' history of mental illness and the State's representation that he represented a serious threat to his own safety as well as to that of others, found that

Jones "is in fact under threat of being transferred to the state mental hospital under § 83-180." We see no reason to disagree with the District Court's assessment at that time, and the reality of the controversy between Jones and the State has not been lessened by the cancellation of his parole and his return to the state prison, where he is protected from further transfer by the outstanding judgment and injunction of the District Court. The State, believing that the case is not moot, wants the injunction removed by the reversal of the District Court's judgment. Jones, on the other hand, insists that the judgment of the District Court be sustained and the protection against transfer to a mental hospital, except in accordance with the specified procedures, be retained.

Against this background, it is not "absolutely clear," absent the injunction, "that the allegedly wrongful behavior could not reasonably be expected to recur." United States v. Phosphate Export Assn., 393 U.S. 199, 203 (1968); County of Los Angeles v. Davis, 440 U.S. 625, 631 (1979); United States v. W. T. Grant Co., 345 U.S. 629, 633 (1953). Furthermore, as the matter now stands, the § 83-180 determination that Jones suffered from mental illness has been declared infirm by the District Court. Vacating the District Court's judgment as moot would not only vacate the injunction against transfer but also the declaration that the procedures employed by the State afforded an inadequate basis for declaring Jones to be mentally ill. In the posture of the case, it is not moot.

III

On the merits, the threshold question in this case is whether the involuntary transfer of a Nebraska state prisoner to a mental hospital implicates a liberty interest that is protected by the Due Process Clause. The District Court held that it did and offered two related reasons for its conclusion. The District Court first identified a liberty interest rooted in § 83-180 (1), under which a prisoner could reasonably expect that he would not be transferred to a mental hospital without a finding that he was suffering from a mental illness for which he could not secure adequate treatment in the correctional facility. Second, the District Court was convinced

that characterizing Jones as a mentally ill patient and transferring him to the Lincoln Regional Center had "some stigmatizing" consequences which, together with the mandatory behavior modification treatment to which Jones would be subject at the Lincoln Center, constituted a major change in the conditions of confinement amounting to a "grievous loss" that should not be imposed without the opportunity for notice and an adequate hearing. We agree with the District Court in both respects.

A

We have repeatedly held that state statutes may create liberty interests that are entitled to the procedural protections of the Due Process Clause of the Fourteenth Amendment. There is no "constitutional or inherent right" to parole, Greenholtz v. Nebraska Penal Inmates, 442 U.S. 1, 7 (1979), but once a State grants a prisoner the conditional liberty properly dependent on the observance of special parole restrictions, due process protections attach to the decision to revoke parole. Morrissey v. Brewer, 408 U.S. 471 (1972). The same is true of the revocation of probation. Gagnon v. Scarpelli, 411 U.S. 778 (1973). In Wolff v. McDonnell, 418 U.S. 539 (1974), we held that a state-created right to good-time credits, which could be forfeited only for serious misbehavior, constituted a liberty interest protected by the Due Process Clause. We also noted that the same reasoning could justify extension of due process protections to a decision to impose "solitary" confinement because "[it] represents a major change in the conditions of confinement and is normally imposed only when it is claimed and proved that there has been a major act of misconduct." Id., at 571-572, n. 19. Once a State has granted prisoners a liberty interest, we held that due process protections are necessary "to insure that the state-created right is not arbitrarily abrogated." Id., at 557.

In Meachum v. Fano, 427 U.S. 215 (1976), and Montanye v. Haymes, 427 U.S. 236 (1976), we held that the transfer of a prisoner from one prison to another does not infringe a protected liberty interest. But in those cases transfers were discretionary with the prison authorities, and in neither case did the prisoner possess any right or justifiable expectation that he would not be transferred except for misbehavior or upon the occurrence of other specified events. Hence, "the predicate for invoking the protection of the Fourteenth Amendment as construed and applied in Wolff v. McDonnell [was] totally nonexistent." Meachum v. Fano, supra, at 226-227.

Following Meachum v. Fano and Montanye v. Haymes, we continued to recognize that state statutes may grant prisoners liberty interests that invoke due process protections when prisoners are transferred to solitary confinement for disciplinary or administrative reasons. Enomoto v. Wright, 434 U.S. 1052 (1978), summarily aff'd 462 F.Supp. 397 (ND Cal. 1976). Similarly, in Greenholtz v. Nebraska Penal Inmates, supra, we held that state law granted petitioners a sufficient expectancy of parole to entitle them to some measure of constitutional protection with respect to parole decisions.

We think the District Court properly understood and applied these decisions. Section 83-180 (1) provides that if a designated physician finds that a prisoner "suffers from a mental disease or defect" that "cannot be given proper treatment" in prison, the Director of Correctional Services may transfer a prisoner to a mental hospital. The District Court also found that in practice prisoners are transferred to a mental hospital only if it is determined that they suffer from a mental disease or defect that cannot adequately be treated within the penal complex. This "objective expectation, firmly fixed in state law and official Penal Complex practice," that a prisoner would not be transferred unless he suffered from a mental disease or defect that could not be adequately treated in the prison, gave Jones a liberty interest that entitled him to the benefits of appropriate procedures in connection with determining the conditions that warranted his transfer to a mental hospital. Under our cases, this conclusion of the District Court is unexceptionable.

Appellants maintain that any state-created liberty interest that Jones had was completely satisfied once a physician or psychologist designated by the director made the findings required by § 83-180 (1) and that Jones was not entitled to any procedural protections. But if the State grants a prisoner a right or expectation that adverse action will not be taken against him except upon the occurrence of specified behavior, "the determination of whether such behavior has occurred becomes critical, and the minimum requirements of procedural due process appropriate for the circumstances must be observed." Wolff v. McDonnell, 418 U.S., at 558. These minimum requirements being a matter of federal law, they are not diminished by the fact that the State may have specified its own procedures that it may deem adequate for determining the preconditions to adverse official action. In Morrissey, Gagnon, and Wolff, the States had adopted their own procedures for determining whether conditions warranting revocation of parole, probation, or good-time credits had occurred; yet we held that those procedures were constitutionally inadequate. In like manner, Nebraska's reliance on the opinion of a designated physician or psychologist for determining whether the conditions warranting a transfer exist neither removes the prisoner's interest from due process protection nor answers the question of what process is due under the Constitution.

B

The District Court was also correct in holding that independently of § 83-180 (1), the transfer of a prisoner from a prison to a mental hospital must be accompanied by appropriate procedural protections. The issue is whether after a conviction for robbery, Jones retained a residuum of liberty that would be infringed by a transfer to a mental hospital without complying with minimum requirements of due process.

We have recognized that for the ordinary citizen, commitment to a mental hospital produces "a massive curtailment of liberty," Humphrey v. Cady, 405 U.S. 504, 509 (1972), and in consequence "requires due process protection." Addington v. Texas, 441 U.S. 418, 425 (1979); O'Connor v. Donaldson, 422 U.S. 563, 580 (1975) (BURGER, C. J., concurring). The loss of liberty produced by an involuntary commitment is more than a loss of freedom from confinement. It is indisputable that commitment to a mental hospital "can engender adverse social consequences to the individual" and that "[whether] we label this phenomena 'stigma' or choose to call it something else . . . we recognize that it can occur and that it can have a very significant impact on the individual." Addington v. Texas, supra, at 425-426. See also Parham v. J. R., 442 U.S. 584, 600 (1979). Also, "[among] the historic liberties" protected by the Due Process Clause is the "right to be free from, and to obtain judicial relief for, unjustified intrusions on personal security." Ingraham v. Wright, 430 U.S. 651, 673 (1977). Compelled treatment in the form of mandatory behavior modification programs, to which the District Court found Jones was exposed in this case, was a proper factor to be weighed by the District Court. Cf. Addington v. Texas, supra, at 427.

The District Court, in its findings, was sensitive to these concerns:

[The] fact of greater limitations on freedom of action at the Lincoln Regional Center, the fact that a transfer to the Lincoln Regional Center has some stigmatizing consequences, and the fact that additional mandatory behavior modification systems are used at the Lincoln Regional Center combine to make the transfer a "major change in the conditions of confinement" amounting to a "grievous loss" to the inmate. Miller v. Vitek, 437 F.Supp., at 573.

Were an ordinary citizen to be subjected involuntarily to these consequences, it is undeniable that protected liberty interests would be unconstitutionally infringed absent compliance with the procedures required by the Due Process Clause. We conclude that a convicted felon also is entitled to the benefit of procedures appropriate in the circumstances before he is found to have a mental disease and transferred to a mental hospital.

Undoubtedly, a valid criminal conviction and prison sentence extinguish a defendant's right to freedom from confinement. Greenholtz v. Nebraska Penal Inmates, 442 U.S., at 7. Such a conviction and sentence sufficiently extinguish a defendant's liberty "to empower the State to confine him in any of its prisons." Meachum v. Fano, 427 U.S., at 224 (emphasis deleted). It is also true that changes in the conditions of confinement having a substantial adverse impact on the prisoner are not

alone sufficient to invoke the protections of the Due Process Clause "[as] long as the conditions or degree of confinement to which the prisoner is subjected is within the sentence imposed upon him." Montanye v. Haymes, 427 U.S., at 242.

Appellants maintain that the transfer of a prisoner to a mental hospital is within the range of confinement justified by imposition of a prison sentence, at least after certification by a qualified person that a prisoner suffers from a mental disease or defect. We cannot agree. None of our decisions holds that conviction for a crime entitles a State not only to confine the convicted person but also to determine that he has a mental illness and to subject him involuntarily to institutional care in a mental hospital. Such consequences visited on the prisoner are qualitatively different from the punishment characteristically suffered by a person convicted of crime. Our cases recognize as much and reflect an understanding that involuntary commitment to a mental hospital is not within the range of conditions of confinement to which a prison sentence subjects an individual. Baxstrom v. Herold, 383 U.S. 107 (1966); Specht v. Patterson, 386 U.S. 605 (1967); Humphrey v. Cady, 405 U.S. 504 (1972); Jackson v. Indiana, 406 U.S. 715, 724-725 (1972). A criminal conviction and sentence of imprisonment extinguish an individual's right to freedom from confinement for the term of his sentence, but they do not authorize the State to classify him as mentally ill and to subject him to involuntary psychiatric treatment without affording him additional due process protections.

In light of the findings made by the District Court, Jones' involuntary transfer to the Lincoln Regional Center pursuant to § 83-180, for the purpose of psychiatric treatment, implicated a liberty interest protected by the Due Process Clause. Many of the restrictions on the prisoner's freedom of action at the Lincoln Regional Center by themselves might not constitute the deprivation of a liberty interest retained by a prisoner, see Wolff v. McDonnell, 418 U.S., at 572, n. 19; cf. Baxter v. Palmigiano, 425 U.S. 308, 323 (1976). But here, the stigmatizing consequences of a transfer to a mental hospital for involuntary psychiatric treatment, coupled with the subjection of the prisoner to mandatory behavior modification as a treatment for mental illness, constitute the kind of deprivations of liberty that requires procedural protections.

IV

The District Court held that to afford sufficient protection to the liberty interest it had identified, the State was required to observe the following minimum procedures before transferring a prisoner to a mental hospital:

A. Written notice to the prisoner that a transfer to a mental hospital is being considered;

B. A hearing, sufficiently after the notice to permit the prisoner to prepare, at which disclosure to the prisoner is made of the evidence being relied upon for the transfer and at which an opportunity to be heard in person and to present documentary evidence is given;

C. An opportunity at the hearing to present testimony of witnesses by the defense and to confront and cross-examine witnesses called by the state, except upon a finding, not arbitrarily made, of good cause for not permitting such presentation, confrontation, or cross-examination;

D. An independent decisionmaker;

E. A written statement by the factfinder as to the evidence relied on and the reasons for transferring the inmate;

F. Availability of legal counsel, furnished by the state, if the inmate is financially unable to furnish his own; and

G. Effective and timely notice of all the foregoing rights. 437 F.Supp., at 575.

A

We think the District Court properly identified and weighed the relevant factors in arriving at its judgment. Concededly the interest of the State in segregating and treating mentally ill patients is strong. The interest of the prisoner in not being arbitrarily classified as mentally ill and subjected to unwelcome treatment is also powerful, however; and as the District Court found, the risk of error in making the determinations required by § 83-180 is substantial enough to warrant appropriate procedural safeguards against error.

We recognize that the inquiry involved in determining whether or not to transfer an inmate to a mental hospital for treatment involves a question that is essentially medical. The question whether an individual is mentally ill and cannot be treated in prison "turns on the meaning of the facts which must be interpreted by expert psychiatrists and psychologists." Addington v. Texas, 441 U.S., at 429. The medical nature of the inquiry, however, does not justify dispensing with due process requirements. It is precisely "[the] subtleties and nuances of psychiatric diagnoses" that justify the requirement of adversary hearings. Id., at 430.

Because prisoners facing involuntary transfer to a mental hospital are threatened with immediate deprivation of liberty interests they are currently enjoying and because of the inherent risk of a mistaken transfer, the District Court properly determined that procedures similar to those required by the Court in Morrissey v. Brewer, 408 U.S. 471 (1972), were appropriate in the circumstances present here.

The notice requirement imposed by the District Court no more than recognizes that notice is essential to afford the prisoner an opportunity to challenge the contemplated action and to understand the nature of what is happening to him. Wolff v. McDonnell, supra, at 564. Furthermore, in view of the nature of the determinations that must accompany the transfer to a mental hospital, we think each of the elements of the hearing specified by the District Court was appropriate. The interests of the State in avoiding disruption was recognized by limiting in appropriate circumstances the prisoner's right to call witnesses, to confront and cross examine. The District Court also avoided unnecessary intrusion into either medical or correctional judgments by providing that the independent decisionmaker conducting the transfer hearing need not come from outside the prison or hospital administration. 437 F.Supp., at 574.

B

The District Court did go beyond the requirements imposed by prior cases by holding that counsel must be made available to inmates facing transfer hearings if they are financially unable to furnish their own. We have not required the automatic appointment of counsel for indigent prisoners facing other deprivations of liberty, Gagnon v. Scarpelli, 411 U.S., at 790; Wolff v. McDonnell, supra, at 569-570; but we have recognized that prisoners who are illiterate and uneducated have a greater need for assistance in exercising their rights. Gagnon v. Scarpelli, supra, at 786-787; Wolff v. McDonnell, supra, at 570. A prisoner thought to be suffering from a mental disease or defect requiring involuntary treatment probably has an even greater need for legal assistance, for such a prisoner is more likely to be unable to understand or exercise his rights. In these circumstances, it is appropriate that counsel be provided to indigent prisoners whom the State seeks to treat as mentally ill.

V

Because MR. JUSTICE POWELL, while believing that Jones was entitled to competent help at the hearing, would not require the State to furnish a licensed attorney to aid him, the judgment below is affirmed as modified to conform with the separate opinion filed by MR. JUSTICE POWELL.

So ordered.

MR. JUSTICE POWELL, concurring in part.

I join the opinion of the Court except for Part IV-B. I agree with Part IV-B insofar as the Court holds that qualified and independent assistance must be provided to an inmate who is threatened with involuntary transfer to a state mental hospital. I do not agree, however, that the requirement of independent assistance demands that a licensed attorney be provided.

I

In Gagnon v. Scarpelli, 411 U.S. 778 (1973), my opinion for the Court held that counsel is not necessarily required at a probation revocation hearing. In reaching this decision the Court recognized both the effects of providing counsel to each probationer and the likely benefits to be derived from the assistance of counsel. "The introduction of counsel into a revocation proceeding [would] alter significantly the nature of the proceeding," id., at 787, because the hearing would inevitably become more adversary. We noted that probationers would not always need counsel because in most hearings the essential facts are undisputed. In lieu of a per se rule we held that the necessity of providing counsel should be determined on a case-by-case basis. In particular, we stressed that factors governing the decision to provide counsel include (i) the existence of factual disputes or issues which are "complex or otherwise difficult to develop or present," and (ii) "whether the probationer appears to be capable of speaking effectively for himself." Id., at 790, 791.

Consideration of these factors, and particularly the capability of the inmate, persuades me that the Court is correct that independent assistance must be provided to an inmate before he may be transferred involuntarily to a mental hospital. The essence of the issue in an involuntary commitment proceeding will be the mental health of the inmate. The resolution of factual disputes will be less important than the ability to understand and analyze expert psychiatric testimony that is often expressed in language relatively incomprehensible to laymen. It is unlikely that an inmate threatened with involuntary transfer to mental hospitals will possess the competence or training to protect adequately his own interest in these state-initiated proceedings. And the circumstances of being imprisoned without normal access to others who may assist him places an additional handicap upon an inmate's ability to represent himself. I therefore agree that due process requires the provision of assistance to an inmate threatened with involuntary transfer to a mental hospital.

II

I do not believe, however, that an inmate must always be supplied with a licensed attorney. "[Due] Process is flexible and calls for such procedural protections as the particular situation demands." Morrissey v. Brewer, 408 U.S. 471, 481 (1972). See Mathews v. Eldridge, 424 U.S. 319, 334-335 (1976). Our decisions defining the necessary qualifications for an impartial decisionmaker demonstrate that the requirements of due process turn on the nature of the determination which must be made. "Due Process has never been thought to require that the neutral and detached trier of fact be law trained or a judicial or administrative officer." Parham v. J.R., 442 U.S. 584, 607 (1979). In that case, we held that due process is satisfied when a staff physician determines whether a child may be voluntarily committed to a state mental institution by his parents. That holding was based upon recognition that the issues of civil commitment "are essentially medical in nature," and that "neither judges nor administrative hearing officers are better qualified than psychiatrists to render psychiatric judgments." Id., at 607, 609, quoting In re Roger S., 19 Cal. 3d 921, 942, 569 P. 2d 1286, 1299 (1977) (Clark, J., dissenting). See also Morrissey v. Brewer, supra, at 489; Goldberg v. Kelly, 397 U.S. 254, 271 (1970).

In my view, the principle that due process does not always require a law-trained decisionmaker supports the ancillary conclusion that due process may be satisfied by the provision of a qualified and independent adviser who is not a lawyer. As in Parham v. J. R., the issue here is essentially medical. Under state law, a prisoner may be transferred only if he "suffers from a mental disease or defect" and "cannot be given proper treatment" in the prison complex. Neb. Rev. Stat. § 83-180 (1) (1976). The opinion of the Court allows a nonlawyer to act as the impartial decisionmaker in the transfer proceeding. Ante, at 496.

The essence of procedural due process is a fair hearing. I do not think that the fairness of an informal hearing designed to determine a medical issue requires participation by lawyers. Due process merely requires that the State provide an inmate with qualified and independent assistance. Such assistance may be provided by a licensed psychiatrist or other mental health professional. Indeed, in view of the nature of the issue involved in the transfer hearing, a person possessing such professional qualifications normally would be preferred. As the Court notes, "[the] question whether an individual is mentally ill and cannot be treated in prison 'turns on the meaning of the facts which must be interpreted by expert psychiatrists and psychologists.'" Ante, at 495, quoting Addington v. Texas, 441 U.S. 418, 429 (1979). I would not exclude, however, the possibility that the required assistance may be rendered by competent laymen in some cases. The essential requirements are that the person provided by the State be competent and independent, and that he be free to act solely in the inmate's best interest.

In sum, although the State is free to appoint a licensed attorney to represent an inmate, it is not constitutionally required to do so. Due process will be satisfied so long as an inmate facing involuntary transfer to a mental hospital is provided qualified and independent assistance.

CUYLER
v.
ADAMS

**449 U.S. 433; 101 S. Ct. 703;
66 L. Ed. 2d 641 (1981)**

JUSTICE BRENNAN delivered the opinion of the Court.

This case requires us to decide a recurring question concerning the relationship between the Interstate Agreement on Detainers and the Uniform Criminal Extradition Act. The specific issue presented is whether a prisoner incarcerated in a jurisdiction that has adopted the Extradition Act is entitled to the procedural protections of that Act—particularly the right to a pretransfer hearing—before being transferred to another jurisdiction pursuant to Art. IV of the Detainer Agreement. The Court of Appeals for the Third Circuit held as a matter of statutory construction that a prisoner is entitled to such protections. 592 F.2d 720 (1979). The Courts of Appeals and state courts are divided upon the question, and we granted certiorari to resolve the conflict. 444 U.S. 1069 (1980).

I

In April 1976, respondent John Adams was convicted in Pennsylvania state court of robbery and was sentenced to 30 years in the State Correctional Institution at Graterford, Pa. The Camden County (New Jersey) prosecutor's office subsequently lodged a detainer against respondent and in May 1977 filed a "Request for Temporary Custody" pursuant to Art. IV of the Detainer Agreement in order to bring him to Camden for trial on charges of armed robbery and other offenses.

In an effort to prevent his transfer, respondent filed a pro se class-action complaint in June 1977 in the United States District Court for the Eastern District of Pennsylvania. He sought declaratory, injunctive, and monetary relief under 42 U.S.C. §§ 1981 and 1983, alleging (1) that petitioners had violated the Due Process and Equal Protection Clauses by failing to grant him the pretransfer hearing that would have been available had he been transferred pursuant to the Extradition Act; and (2) that petitioners had violated the Due Process Clause by failing to inform him of his right pursuant to Art. IV (a) of the Detainer Agreement to petition Pennsylvania's Governor to disapprove New Jersey's request for custody. Respondent contended, inter alia, that had he been granted a hearing or advised of his right to petition the Governor, he would have been able to convince Pennsylvania authorities to deny the custody request.

The District Court, without reaching the class certification issue, dismissed respondent's complaint in October 1977 for failure to state a claim upon which relief could be granted. 441 F.Supp. 556. Respondent was then transferred to New Jersey, where he was convicted, sentenced to a 9½-year prison term (to be served concurrently with his Pennsylvania sentence), and returned to Pennsylvania.

The Court of Appeals for the Third Circuit vacated the District Court judgment and remanded for further proceedings. 592 F.2d 720 (1979). Finding no need to reach respondent's constitutional claims, see Hagans v. Lavine, 415 U.S. 528, 543 (1974), it concluded as a matter of statutory construction that respondent had a right under Art. IV (d) of the Detainer Agreement to the procedural safeguards, including a pretransfer "hearing," prescribed by § 10 of the Extradition Act. It made no finding with respect to respondent's argument that he was entitled to notification of his right to petition the Governor.

II

While this case was on appeal, a Pennsylvania state court held that state prisoners transferred under Art. IV of the Detainer Agreement have no constitutional right to a pretransfer hearing. Commonwealth ex rel. Coleman v. Cuyler, 261 Pa. Super. 274, 396 A. 2d 394 (1978). Although the Court of Appeals did not reach this constitutional issue, it held that it was not bound by the state court's result because the Detainer Agreement is an interstate compact approved by Congress and is thus a federal law subject to federal rather than state construction. Before reaching the merits of the Third Circuit's decision, we must determine whether that conclusion was correct. We hold that it was.

The Compact Clause of the United States Constitution, Art. I, § 10, cl. 3, provides that "No State shall, without the Consent of the Congress, . . . enter into any Agreement or Compact with another State . . . ." Because congressional consent transforms an interstate compact within this Clause into a law of the United States, we have held that the construction of an interstate agreement sanctioned by Congress under the Compact Clause presents a federal question. See Petty v. Tennessee-Missouri Bridge Comm'n, 359 U.S. 275, 278 (1959); West Virginia ex rel. Dyer v. Sims, 341 U.S. 22, 28 (1951); Delaware River Joint Toll Bridge Comm'n v. Colburn, 310 U.S. 419, 427 (1940). It thus remains to be determined whether the Detainer Agreement is a congressionally sanctioned interstate compact within Art. I, § 10, of the Constitution.

The requirement of congressional consent is at the heart of the Compact Clause. By vesting in Congress the power to grant or withhold consent, or to condition consent on the States' compliance with specified conditions, the Framers sought to ensure that Congress would maintain ultimate supervisory power over cooperative state action that might otherwise interfere with the full and free exercise of federal authority. See Frankfurter & Landis, The Compact Clause of the Constitution—A Study in Interstate Adjustments, 34 Yale L. J. 685, 694-695 (1925).

Congressional consent is not required for interstate agreements that fall outside the scope of the Compact Clause. Where an agreement is not "directed to the formation of any combination tending to the increase of political power in the States, which may encroach upon or interfere with the just supremacy of the United States," it does not fall within the scope of the Clause and will not be invalidated for lack of congressional consent. See, e.g., United States Steel Corp. v. Multistate Tax Comm'n, 434 U.S. 452, 468 (1978), quoting Virginia v. Tennessee, 148 U.S. 503, 519 (1893); New Hampshire v. Maine, 426 U.S. 363, 369-370 (1976). But where Congress has authorized the States to enter into a cooperative agreement, and where the subject matter of that agreement is an appropriate subject for congressional legislation, the consent of Congress transforms the States' agreement into federal law under the Compact Clause.

Congress may consent to an interstate compact by authorizing joint state action in advance or by giving expressed or implied approval to an agreement the States have already joined. Virginia v. Tennessee, supra, at 521; Green v. Biddle, 8 Wheat. 1, 85-87 (1823). In the case of the Detainer Agreement, Congress gave its consent in advance by enacting the Crime Control Consent Act of 1934, 48 Stat. 909, as amended. In pertinent part, this Act provides:

> The consent of Congress is hereby given to any two or more States to enter into agreements or compacts for cooperative effort and mutual assistance in the prevention of crime and in the enforcement of their respective criminal laws and policies . . . 4 U.S.C. § 112 (a).

Because this Act was intended to be a grant of consent under the Compact Clause, and because the subject matter of the Act is an appropriate subject for congressional leg-

islation, we conclude that the Detainer Agreement is a congressionally sanctioned interstate compact the interpretation of which presents a question of federal law. We therefore turn to the merits of the Court of Appeals' holding that as a matter of statutory construction Art. IV (d) of the Detainer Agreement is to be read as incorporating the procedural safeguards provided by § 10 of the Extradition Act.

III

The Detainer Agreement and the Extradition Act both establish procedures for the transfer of a prisoner in one jurisdiction to the temporary custody of another jurisdiction. A prisoner transferred under the Extradition Act is explicitly granted a right to a pretransfer "hearing" at which he is informed of the receiving State's request for custody, his right to counsel, and his right to apply for a writ of habeas corpus challenging the custody request. He is also permitted "a reasonable time" in which to apply for the writ. However, no similar explicit provision is to be found in the Detainer Agreement.

The Detainer Agreement establishes two procedures under which the prisoner against whom a detainer has been lodged may be transferred to the temporary custody of the receiving State. One of these procedures may be invoked by the prisoner; the other by the prosecuting attorney of the receiving State.

Article III of the Agreement provides the prisoner-initiated procedure. It requires the warden to notify the prisoner of all outstanding detainers and then to inform him of his right to request final disposition of the criminal charges underlying those detainers. If the prisoner initiates the transfer by demanding disposition (which under the Agreement automatically extends to all pending charges in the receiving State), the authorities in the receiving State must bring him to trial within 180 days or the charges will be dismissed with prejudice, absent good cause shown.

Article IV of the Agreement provides the procedure by which the prosecutor in the receiving State may initiate the transfer. First, the prosecutor must file with the authorities in the sending State written notice of the custody request, approved by a court having jurisdiction to hear the underlying charges. For the next 30 days, the prisoner and prosecutor must wait while the Governor of the sending State, on his own motion or that of the prisoner, decides whether to disapprove the request. If the Governor does not disapprove, the prisoner is transferred to the temporary custody of the receiving State where he must be brought to trial on the charges underlying the detainer within 120 days of his arrival. Again, if the prisoner is not brought to trial within the time period, the charges will be dismissed with prejudice, absent good cause shown.

Although nothing in the Detainer Agreement explicitly provides for a pretransfer hearing, respondent contends that prisoners who are involuntarily transferred under Art. IV are entitled to greater procedural protections than those who initiate the transfer procedure under Art. III. He argues that a prisoner who initiates his own transfer to the receiving State receives a significant benefit under the Agreement and may thus be required to waive any right he might have to contest his transfer; but that a prisoner transferred against his will to the receiving State under Art. IV does not benefit from the Agreement and is thus entitled to assert any right he might have had under the Extradition Act (or any other state law applicable to interstate transfer of prisoners) to challenge his transfer.

Respondent's argument has substantial support in the language of the Detainer Agreement. Article III (e) provides that "[any] request for final disposition made by a prisoner [under this Article] shall also be deemed to be a waiver of extradition with respect to any charge or proceeding contemplated thereby . . . ." (Emphasis added.) The reference to "waiver of extradition" can reasonably be interpreted to mean "waiver of those rights the sending state affords persons being extradited." Since Pennsylvania has adopted the Uniform Criminal Extradition Act, those rights would include the rights provided by § 10 of that Act.

The language of Art. IV supports respondent's further contention that a prisoner's extradition rights are meant to be preserved when the receiving State seeks disposition of an outstanding detainer. Article IV (d) provides:

Nothing contained in this Article shall be construed to deprive any prisoner of any right which he may have to contest the legality of his delivery as provided in paragraph (a) hereof, but such delivery may not be opposed or denied on the ground that the executive authority of the sending state has not affirmatively consented to or ordered such delivery.

Petitioners argue that the phrase "as provided in paragraph (a) hereof" modifies "right," not "delivery," and that paragraph (d) does no more than protect the right paragraph (a) gives the prisoner to petition the Governor to disapprove the custody request. The Court of Appeals rejected this interpretation, concluding that the phrase "as provided in paragraph (a) hereof" modifies "delivery," not "right." Since the major thrust of paragraph (a) is to describe the means by which the receiving State may obtain temporary custody of the prisoner, the Court of Appeals held that paragraph (d) must have been intended as the vehicle for incorporating all rights a prisoner would have under state or other laws to contest his transfer, except that the prisoner must forfeit his right, otherwise available under § 7 of the Extradition Act, to oppose such transfer on the ground that the Governor had not explicitly approved the custody request.

There are three textual reasons why we find this interpretation convincing. First, if paragraph (d) protects only the right provided by paragraph (a) to petition the Governor, as petitioners claim, it is difficult to understand what purpose paragraph (d) serves in the Agreement. Why would the drafters add a second provision to protect a right already explicitly provided? Common sense requires paragraph (d) to be construed as securing something more.

Second, the one ground for contesting a transfer that paragraph (d) explicitly withholds from the prisoner—that the transfer has not been affirmatively approved by the Governor—is a ground that the Extradition Act expressly reserves to the prisoner. It is surely reasonable to conclude from the elimination of this ground in the Detainer Agreement that the drafters meant the Detainer Agreement to be read as not affecting any rights given prisoners by the Extradition Act that are not expressly withheld by the Detainer Agreement. As the Court of Appeals concluded, "the fact that Article IV (d) does specifically refer to one minor procedural feature of the extradition process which is to be affected suggests forcefully that the other aspects, particularly those furnishing safeguards to the prisoner, are to continue in effect." 592 F.2d, at 724.

Finally, paragraph (d) refers to "any right [the prisoner] may have" (emphasis added) to challenge the legality of his transfer. This suggests that more than one right is involved, a suggestion that is consistent with respondent's contention that all pre-existing rights are preserved. If petitioners' contention were correct—that the only right preserved is the right provided in paragraph (a) to petition the Governor—it is much more likely that paragraph (d) would have referred narrowly to "the right the prisoner does have" to challenge the legality of his transfer.

The legislative history of the Detainer Agreement, contained in the comments on the draft Agreement made by the Council of State Governments at its 1956 conference and circulated to all the adopting States, further supports the Court of Appeals' reading. In discussing the different degrees of protection to which a prisoner is entitled under Arts. III and IV of the Agreement, the drafters stated:

> Article IV (d) safeguards certain of the prisoner's rights. Normally, the only way to get a prisoner from one jurisdiction to another for purposes of trial on an indictment, information or complaint is through resort to extradition or waiver thereof. If the prisoner waives, there is no problem. However, if he does not waive extradition, it is not appropriate to attempt to force him to give up the safeguards of the extradition process, even if this could be done constitutionally. Council of State Governments, Suggested State Legislation, Program for 1957, pp. 78-79 (1956).

The suggestion, of course, is that a prisoner transferred against his will under Art. IV should be entitled to whatever "safeguards of the extradition process" he might otherwise have enjoyed. Those safeguards include the

procedural protections of the Extradition Act (in those States that have adopted it), as well as any other procedural protections the sending State guarantees persons being extradited from within its borders.

That this is what the drafters intended is further suggested by the distinction they make between Art. III and Art. IV procedures:

> The situation contemplated by this portion of the agreement [Article IV] is different than that dealt with in Article III. [Article III] relates to proceedings initiated at the request of the prisoner. Accordingly, in such instances it is fitting that the prisoner be required to waive extradition. In Article IV the prosecutor initiates the proceeding. Consequently, it probably would be improper to require the prisoner to waive those features of the extradition process which are designed for the protection of his rights. Id., at 79.

These statements strongly support respondent's contention that prisoners were meant to be treated differently depending on which Article was being invoked, and that the general body of procedural rights available in the extradition context was meant to be preserved when the transfer was effected pursuant to Art. IV.

Article IX of the Detainer Agreement states that the Agreement "shall be liberally construed so as to effectuate its purpose." The legislative history of the Agreement, including the comments of the Council of State Governments and the congressional Reports and debates preceding the adoption of the Agreement on behalf of the District of Columbia and the Federal Government, emphasizes that a primary purpose of the Agreement is to protect prisoners against whom detainers are outstanding. As stated in the House and Senate Reports:

> [A] prisoner who has had a detainer lodged against him is seriously disadvantaged by such action. He is in custody and therefore in no position to seek witnesses or to preserve his defense. He must often be kept in close custody and is ineligible for desirable work assignments. What is more, when detainers are filed against a prisoner

he sometimes loses interest in institutional opportunities because he must serve his sentence without knowing what additional sentences may lie before him, or when, if ever, he will be in a position to employ the education and skills he may be developing. H. R. Rep. No. 91-1018, p. 3 (1970); S. Rep. No. 91-1356, p. 3 (1970).

The remedial purpose of the Agreement supports an interpretation that gives prisoners the right to a judicial hearing in which they can bring a limited challenge to the receiving State's custody request. In light of the purpose of the Detainer Agreement, as reflected in the structure of the Agreement, [its language, and its legislative history, we conclude as a matter of federal law that prisoners transferred pursuant to the provisions of the Agreement are not required to forfeit any pre-existing rights they may have under state or federal law to challenge their transfer to the receiving State. Respondent Adams has therefore stated a claim for relief under 42 U.S.C. § 1983 for the asserted violation by state officials of the terms of the Detainer Agreement. See Maine v. Thiboutot, 448 U.S. 1 (1980).

Affirmed.

HOWE
v.
SMITH

452 U.S. 473; 101 S. Ct. 2468; 69 L. Ed. 2d 171 (1981)

CHIEF JUSTICE BURGER delivered the opinion of the Court.

The question presented by this case is whether a State may transfer a prisoner to federal custody pursuant to 18 U.S.C. § 5003 in the absence of a prior determination that the prisoner who is being transferred has a need for specialized treatment available in the federal prison system.

I

In December 1974, the Commissioner of Corrections for the State of Vermont an-nounced that he would soon close the 187-year-old Windsor prison, the State's only maximum-security facility, because Windsor had become inadequate in several respects. Rebideau v. Stoneman, 398 F.Supp. 805, 808, n. 7 (Vt. 1975). In anticipation of that closing, the United States and Vermont entered into an agreement pursuant to 18 U.S.C. § 5003 (a) by which the United States agreed to house in federal prisons up to 40 prisoners originally committed to the prisons of Vermont. The contract recited that the Director of the United States Bureau of Prisons had certified that facilities were available at federal institutions to accommodate 40 Vermont prisoners.

In 1975, when Windsor was finally closed, Vermont was left with several minimum-security community correctional centers and the Vermont Correction and Diagnostic Treatment Facility at St. Albans, Vt. St. Albans has the capacity for short-term incarceration of inmates with high security needs, but it is not designed for long-term incarceration of inmates classified as high security risks.

II

The petitioner, Robert Howe, was convicted in a Vermont court of first-degree murder arising out of the rape and strangulation of an elderly female neighbor. He was sentenced to life imprisonment and assigned to the St. Albans facility to begin serving his sentence. Because of the nature of his offense and the length of his term, however, the Classification Committee of the Vermont Department of Corrections determined that he should be kept in a maximum-security facility and recommended that he be transferred to a federal prison. Accordingly, the Vermont Department of Corrections held a hearing to decide whether he should be transferred to a federal institution. Howe was afforded advance notice of the hearing and of the reasons for the proposed transfer; he was present at the hearing; and he was represented by a law adviser from the facility's staff, who submitted various items of evidence in opposition to the proposed transfer.

The hearing officer recommended that the petitioner be transferred to a federal institution on the ground that "no treatment programs exist in the State of Vermont, which could provide both treatment and long term maximum security supervision" for him. App. 25. The hearing officer found that Howe was dangerous and could not be integrated into a community-based program. The State relied on a psychiatric report describing Howe as a "dangerous person who could well repeat the same pattern of assaultive behavior toward women at any time in the future." Id., at 26. The hearing officer also found that Howe would be "highly resistant to treatment" and that he was an escape risk. Indeed, Howe had escaped from the maximum-security wing of St. Albans while detained there prior to his trial.

On March 9, 1977, Vermont's Acting Commissioner of Corrections approved Howe's transfer to the federal prison system. Under the terms of the contract between the United States and Vermont, he was incarcerated initially in the federal penitentiary at Atlanta, Ga., and later was transferred to the federal penitentiary at Terre Haute, Ind.

As an inmate in the federal maximum-security penitentiaries, Howe enjoyed the same complete freedom of movement within the institution as other prisoners. By contrast, at St. Albans, he had not been given this freedom of movement, but had been generally confined to the maximum-security wing. The programs at St. Albans were substantially the same as those at the federal prisons, although Howe had less opportunity to take advantage of them because of the restrictions on his mobility at the state facility. The only two programs in which he actually participated at St. Albans were psychiatric counseling and educational courses. At Terre Haute, he ran a sewing machine until he had a heart attack. His principal activities now are knitting and crocheting.

On December 5, 1978, the petitioner filed this civil action in the United States District Court for the District of Vermont, naming as defendants the Attorney General of the United States and the Director of the Federal Bureau of Prisons. Respondent William Ciuros, Vermont's Commissioner of Corrections, intervened. Relying on Lono v. Fenton, 581 F.2d 645 (CA7 1978) (en banc), the petitioner challenged his transfer to the federal prison system on the ground that the federal officials lacked statutory authority to accept custody. It was the petitioner's position that the sole statutory authority for transfers of state inmates, § 5003, requires federal authorities to make an individual determination that each state prisoner so transferred needs a particular specialized treatment program available in the federal prison system. The petitioner argued that no such individual determination had been made in his case, and that the transfer had not been effected for special treatment needs but for general penological reasons, that is, maximum-security incarceration.

Following a hearing, the District Court denied the petitioner's request for relief, holding:

> [The] [Act] plainly and unambiguously requires no showing of specialized treatment needs or facilities before a Vermont state prisoner may be transferred to the federal prison system in accordance with the contract under which [the petitioner] was so transferred. . . . 18 U.S.C. 5003 (a) requires nothing more of the Director of the Bureau of Prisons than a certification that facilities exist within the federal system in which state prisoners may be accommodated. That requirement has been met in the case at hand. 480 F.Supp. 111, 115 (1978).

The Court of Appeals for the Second Circuit affirmed. 625 F.2d 454 (1980). The court observed that 18 U.S.C. § 5003 authorizes states to contract not simply for "treatment" but for the "custody, care, subsistence, education, treatment, and training of persons convicted." It reasoned that nothing in the language of the statute gives "treatment" primacy or provides a basis for concluding that, whatever other services are provided, "treatment" must always be furnished to prisoners transferred under the statute. While acknowledging that there was a modicum of support in the legislative history for the petitioner's argument, the Court of Appeals rejected it because it "has no basis in the language of the statute." 625 F.2d, at 457.

* * *

III

The challenge here is not to the action of the State of Vermont in seeking to transfer the petitioner, but to the authority of the Federal Government, in the official person of the Attorney General, to receive and to hold him in a federal penitentiary. Under 18 U.S.C. § 4001 (a) "no citizen shall be imprisoned or otherwise detained by the United States except pursuant to an Act of Congress." The petitioner avers that he is being held by the federal authorities illegally because neither § 5003 nor any other provision authorizes his detention. In particular, he argues that § 5003 has a narrow and limited thrust, that is, that a state prisoner may not be transferred to a federal institution except for an identified specialized treatment and that, before any such transfer may be made, the Federal Government must conduct an inquiry and make an individualized determination that the transferee needs, and the federal facility can provide, that treatment. On the other hand, the respondents contend that § 5003 is not so limited, and that the petitioner's detention is clearly authorized by the plain language of that provision.

Because § 5003 obviously authorizes federal detention of state prisoners under some circumstances, our task is to determine the precise nature of those circumstances and whether appropriate circumstances are present in this case.

A

As in every case involving the interpretation of a statute, analysis must begin with the language employed by Congress. Rubin v. United States, 449 U.S. 424, 430 (1981); Reiter v. Sonotone Corp., 442 U.S. 330, 337 (1979). By its terms, § 5003 (a) authorizes the Attorney General to contract with a state or territory "for the custody, care, subsistence, education, treatment, and training of persons convicted of criminal offenses in the courts of [that] State or Territory." On its face, the authority furnished by this language encompasses much more than a limited authority to provide for the specialized treatment needs of state prisoners. "Treatment" is, after all, only one of several services cataloged; the focus of the statute, is upon care,

custody, subsistence, education, and training as well as upon treatment. Nothing in the construction of the provision supports the view that "treatment" is more important than any of the other listed categories, and nothing in the passage can be fairly read as requiring that some kind of "treatment" must be furnished to every state prisoner transferred to a federal facility pursuant to a contract authorized by § 5003 (a).

The petitioner does not contest the breadth of the charter granted by the language just quoted. Rather, he focuses on the requirement that the Director of the Federal Bureau of Prisons certify the availability of "proper and adequate treatment facilities and personnel." The petitioner reads this requirement as imposing a substantive limitation or restriction on the purposes for which prisoners may be transferred: to wit, a prisoner may be transferred only for treatment.

The petitioner's reading of the statute strains the plain meaning of its language. The act of certification by the Director is nothing more than the starting point in the process of contractual negotiation envisioned by § 5003 (a). Absent surplus capacity in the federal system, discussions between federal and state authorities regarding the transfer of state prisoners to federal facilities would be pointless. Once the Director certifies that a surplus capacity exists—that is, that there is room for more inmates—the transfer becomes a possibility. The certification clause cannot be read as requiring any more than that federal facilities and personnel must be available to handle whatever prisoners are received.

There is no special significance to the fact that the Director certifies the existence of "treatment facilities," as opposed to prison facilities generally. First, the term "treatment facilities" is an appropriate general reference to the existing federal prison facilities. It is true, of course, that other terms may be used—and, in fact, are used—to describe the federal prisons; that, however, does not belie the appropriateness of the term "treatment facilities" as a general reference to the federal penal system.

Second, if, as the petitioner advocates, the phrase "treatment facilities" is read as a substantive restriction upon the purposes for which a prisoner may be transferred, § 5003 is rendered internally inconsistent. According to the petitioner, by virtue of § 5003 (a), a state prisoner may be transferred to a federal prison only if that facility affords him specialized treatment found to be needed. However, § 5003 (c) provides, with certain exceptions not applicable to this case, that all state prisoners in federal custody are subject to the same statutory and regulatory scheme that governs federal prisoners. And that statutory and regulatory scheme contains provisions that would undermine § 5003 (a) as that section is read by the petitioner. For example, by statute, federal prisoners may be transferred from one facility to another at the discretion of the Attorney General, 18 U.S.C. § 4082 (b), and federal officials have discretion to decide which inmates have access to rehabilitation programs, Moody v. Daggett, 429 U.S. 78, 88, n. 9 (1976). It makes no sense to interpret § 5003 as forcing federal authorities to accept only a state prisoner who is in need of treatment at a particular facility when those same officials are free to transfer that same prisoner from the facility, thereby denying him access to the treatment program.

In sum, the plain language of § 5003 (a) authorizes contracts not simply for treatment, but also for the custody, care, subsistence, education, and training of state prisoners in federal facilities. The certification requirement is simply a housekeeping measure designed to ensure that the federal system has the capacity to absorb the state prisoners. Nothing in the language of § 5003 (a) restricts or limits the use of federal prison facilities to those state prisoners who are in need of some particular treatment.

B

When the terms of a statute are unambiguous, our inquiry comes to an end, except "in 'rare and exceptional circumstances.' " TVA v. Hill, 437 U.S. 153, 187, n. 33 (1978) (quoting Crooks v. Harrelson, 282 U.S. 55, 60 (1930)). No rare and exceptional circumstances are present here; our reading of the statute is fully supported by the legislative history of § 5003.

The petitioner disagrees. He notes that, when asked on the Senate floor to explain § 5003 (a), Senator McCarran answered that,

whereas 18 U.S.C. § 4002 allows the Federal Government to contract with state officials for the confinement of federal prisoners,

[this] bill would authorize a more or less reciprocal arrangement whereby, under certain conditions in a limited category of cases . . . the Attorney General may contract with State officials for the custody of persons convicted and sentenced under State laws. 97 Cong. Rec. 13543 (1951).

The petitioner finds significance in the Senator's use of the words "under certain conditions" and "in a limited category of cases."

Read as a whole, the legislative record reveals that § 5003 was enacted to provide a practical solution to a simple problem, that is, to permit the states to transfer their prisoners to federal custody in the same way that the Federal Government for years had been placing prisoners in state custody pursuant to 18 U.S.C. § 4002. Until this century, there was no federal prison system to speak of; instead, federal prisoners were housed in state prisons. By 1952, however, a sufficient number of federal prisons had been built that Congress could respond to requests from the states that the Federal Bureau of Prisons provide facilities in cases where state facilities were inadequate in some way. Section 5003 was the congressional response to this evolving situation.

A desire to help states with insufficient facilities, a sentiment that permeates the legislative history of § 5003, may be detected even in the remarks of Senator McCarran quoted by the petitioner. The Senator described the new section as a "reciprocal" of § 4002, one authorizing the Attorney General to extend to the states the same type of service he was authorized to receive from them under § 4002. Because federal officials exercise broad authority under § 4002, the "reciprocal" authority purportedly extended under § 5003 (a) likely was understood by Congress to be equally broad.

In addition to Senator McCarran's remarks, the petitioner relies heavily upon a passage in the Report of the House Judiciary Committee on the bill that was to become § 5003. The Committee stated:

The proposed legislation restricts or limits the use of Federal prison facilities to those convicted State offenders who are in need of treatment. The term "treatment" as used in this bill, in addition to its ordinary meaning of providing medical care, is also meant to include corrective and preventive guidance and training as defined in the Youth Corrections Act. H. R. Rep. No. 1663, 82d Cong., 2d Sess., 2 (1952).

The petitioner's reliance upon this passage is understandable, but a single sentence—especially one taken from a Report issued five months after one chamber, the Senate, had passed § 5003—cannot obscure the unmistakable intent of Congress to create by § 5003 broad authority in federal officials to accept custody of state prisoners in the federal prisons. Indeed, nowhere is this intent clearer than in another passage from the very same page:

> State prisons for many years housed and cared for Federal prisoners—until the Federal Government built its own institutions. Today, by [virtue of § 4002], the Attorney General is authorized to contract for the care and custody of our Federal prisoners. . . . The committee sees no reason why Federal facilities and personnel should not, in turn, be made available for State offenders, provided, of course, the Federal Government is reimbursed for any expenses involved. Ibid.

The legislative history of § 5003 reveals that Congress perceived a need to respond to state requests for the federal prison system to undertake "custody, treatment, and training" of state prisoners where the states lacked an institutional capacity to do so themselves. S. Rep. No. 978, 82d Cong., 1st Sess., 2 (1951). It is clear that § 5003 was a broad response to this perceived need. Nothing in the legislative history of § 5003 makes this case one of the "rare and exceptional cases" requiring a departure from the plain language of the statute.

C

Because the Attorney General, and through him the Bureau of Prisons, are charged with

the administration of § 5003, their view of the meaning of the statute is entitled to considerable deference. NLRB v. Bell Aerospace Co., 416 U.S. 267, 274-275 (1974); Udall v. Tallman, 380 U.S. 1, 16 (1965). Moreover, in this case, the Bureau's interpretation of the statute merits greater than normal weight because it was the Bureau that drafted the legislation and steered it through Congress with little debate.

The contract between the United States and Vermont that served as the basis for the petitioner's transfer to federal custody is just one indication that the Federal Bureau of Prisons has construed § 5003 as broadly authorizing it to accept whatever prisoners are referred to it by state officials. In nearly 30 years of administering this statute, several Attorneys General have interpreted the statute consistently as a grant of plenary authority to contract with the states, limited only by certification that space and personnel were available.

Furthermore, Congress has had ample opportunity to express whatever dissatisfaction it might have regarding this administrative interpretation of § 5003. As early as 1952, in its Annual Report, the Bureau of Prisons advised Congress of its view of the statute:

> [Section 5003] [authorizes] the Attorney General, when adequate facilities and personnel are available, to contract with State officials for the care and custody of State prisoners. . . .

> The confinement of Federal prisoners in State institutions has been authorized since 1776. . . . The present act affords an opportunity for reciprocity which had not hitherto existed. While it is not anticipated that the new statute will be used widely, States may on occasion wish to request Federal care for particular prisoners who need facilities available in the Federal prison system but not in their own. For example, a State may wish to transfer a vicious intractable offender who cannot be handled readily in its own institutions, or a female prisoner for whom appropriate facilities are not available, or a prisoner needing special medical or psychiatric care. U.S. Dept. of Justice,

Annual Report of the Bureau of Prisons 16-17 (1952) (emphasis added).

Congress indicated no reservation or objection to this interpretation of § 5003 in 1952, or in any year thereafter. Furthermore, in 1965, when Congress added § 5003 (d) so as to include the Canal Zone within the purview of § 5003, the Senate Report expressly described § 5003 (a) as broadly permitting the transfer of persons convicted in the Canal Zone to federal prisons. S. Rep. No. 799, 89th Cong., 1st Sess., 2 (1965).

The contemporaneous and uniform construction of § 5003 (a) by the agency that proposed its enactment and is charged with its enforcement has been that the statute authorizes contracts based upon a broad range of purposes, including the transfer shown by this record. In the absence of any evidence of congressional objection, the agency's interpretation must be given great weight.

IV

The plain language, the legislative history, and the longstanding administrative interpretation of § 5003 (a) clearly demonstrate that the provision is a broad charter authorizing the transfer of state prisoners to federal custody. There is no basis in § 5003 (a) for the petitioner's challenge to his transfer to federal custody. Given our disposition of this issue, it is unnecessary to address the other arguments made by the petitioner.

Accordingly, the judgment of the Court of Appeals is

Affirmed.

* * *

OLIM
v.
WAKINEKONA

**461 U.S. 238; 103 S. Ct. 1741;
75 L. Ed. 2d 813 (1983)**

JUSTICE BLACKMUN delivered the opinion of the Court.

The issue in this case is whether the transfer of a prisoner from a state prison in Hawaii to one in California implicates a liberty interest within the meaning of the Due Process Clause of the Fourteenth Amendment.

I

A

Respondent Delbert Kaahanui Wakinekona is serving a sentence of life imprisonment without the possibility of parole as a result of his murder conviction in a Hawaii state court. He also is serving sentences for various other crimes, including rape, robbery, and escape. At the Hawaii State Prison outside Honolulu, respondent was classified as a maximum security risk and placed in the maximum control unit.

Petitioner Antone Olim is the Administrator of the Hawaii State Prison. The other petitioners constituted a prison "Program Committee." On August 2, 1976, the Committee held hearings to determine the reasons for a breakdown in discipline and the failure of certain programs within the prison's maximum control unit. Inmates of the unit appeared at these hearings. The Committee singled out respondent and another inmate as troublemakers. On August 5, respondent received notice that the Committee, at a hearing to be held on August 10, would review his correctional program to determine whether his classification within the system should be changed and whether he should be transferred to another Hawaii facility or to a mainland institution.

The August 10 hearing was conducted by the same persons who had presided over the hearings on August 2. Respondent retained counsel to represent him. The Committee recommended that respondent's classification as a maximum security risk be continued and that he be transferred to a prison on the mainland. He received the following explanation from the Committee:

> The Program Committee, having reviewed your entire file, your testimony and arguments by your counsel, concluded that your control classification remains at Maximum. You are still considered a security risk in view of your escapes and subsequent convictions for serious felonies. The Committee noted the progress you made in vocational training and your expressed desire to continue in this endeavor. However your relationship with staff, who reported that you threaten and intimidate them, raises grave concerns regarding your potential for further disruptive and violent behavior. Since there is no other Maximum security prison in Hawaii which can offer you the correctional programs you require and you cannot remain at [the maximum control unit] because of impending construction of a new facility, the Program Committee recommends your transfer to an institution on the mainland. App. 7-8.

Petitioner Olim, as Administrator, accepted the Committee's recommendation, and a few days later respondent was transferred to Folsom State Prison in California.

B

Rule IV of the Supplementary Rules and Regulations of the Corrections Division, Department of Social Services and Housing, State of Hawaii, approved in June 1976, recites that the inmate classification process is not concerned with punishment. Rather, it is intended to promote the best interests of the inmate, the State, and the prison community. Paragraph 3 of Rule IV requires a hearing prior to a prison transfer involving "a grievous loss to the inmate," which the Rule defines "generally" as "a serious loss to a reasonable man." App. 21. The Administrator, under para. 2 of the Rule, is required to establish "an impartial Program Committee" to conduct such a hearing, the Committee to be "composed of at least three members who were not actively involved in the process by which the inmate . . . was brought before the Committee." App. 20. Under para. 3, the Committee must give the inmate written notice of the hearing, permit him, with certain stated exceptions, to confront and cross-examine witnesses, afford him an opportunity to be heard, and apprise him of the Committee's findings. App. 21-24.

The Committee is directed to make a recommendation to the Administrator, who then decides what action to take:

* * *

C

Respondent filed suit under 42 U.S.C. § 1983 against petitioners as the state officials who caused his transfer. He alleged that he had been denied procedural due process because the Committee that recommended his transfer consisted of the same persons who had initiated the hearing, this being in specific violation of Rule IV, para. 2, and because the Committee was biased against him. The United States District Court for the District of Hawaii dismissed the complaint, holding that the Hawaii regulations governing prison transfers do not create a substantive liberty interest protected by the Due Process Clause. 459 F.Supp. 473 (1978).

The United States Court of Appeals for the Ninth Circuit, by a divided vote, reversed. 664 F.2d 708 (1981). It held that Hawaii had created a constitutionally protected liberty interest by promulgating Rule IV. In so doing, the court declined to follow cases from other Courts of Appeals holding that certain procedures mandated by prison transfer regulations do not create a liberty interest. See, e.g., Cofone v. Manson, 594 F.2d 934 (CA2 1979); Lombardo v. Meachum, 548 F.2d 13 (CA1 1977). The court reasoned that Rule IV gives Hawaii prisoners a justifiable expectation that they will not be transferred to the mainland absent a hearing, before an impartial committee, concerning the facts alleged in the prehearing notice. Because the Court of Appeals' decision created a conflict among the Circuits, and because the case presents the further question whether the Due Process Clause in and of itself protects against interstate prison transfers, we granted certiorari. 456 U.S. 1005 (1982).

II

In Meachum v. Fano, 427 U.S. 215 (1976), and Montanye v. Haymes, 427 U.S. 236 (1976), this Court held that an intrastate prison transfer does not directly implicate the Due Process Clause of the Fourteenth Amendment . . .

* * *

. . . Just as an inmate has no justifiable expectation that he will be incarcerated in any particular prison within a State, he has no justifiable expectation that he will be incarcerated in any particular State. Often, confinement in the inmate's home State will not be possible. A person convicted of a federal crime in a State without a federal correctional facility usually will serve his sentence in another State. Overcrowding and the need to separate particular prisoners may necessitate interstate transfers. For any number of reasons, a State may lack prison facilities capable of providing appropriate correctional programs for all offenders.

Statutes and interstate agreements recognize that, from time to time, it is necessary to transfer inmates to prisons in other States. On the federal level, 18 U.S.C. § 5003(a) authorizes the Attorney General to contract with a State for the transfer of a state prisoner to a federal prison, whether in that State or another. See Howe v. Smith, 452 U.S. 473 (1981). Title 18 U.S.C. § 4002 (1976 ed. and Supp. V) permits the Attorney General to contract with any State for the placement of a federal prisoner in state custody for up to three years. Neither statute requires that the prisoner remain in the State in which he was convicted and sentenced.

On the state level, many States have statutes providing for the transfer of a state prisoner to a federal prison, e.g., Haw. Rev. Stat. § 353-18 (1976), or another State's prison, e.g., Alaska Stat. Ann. § 33.30.100 (1982). Corrections compacts between States, implemented by statutes, authorize incarceration of a prisoner of one State in another State's prison. See, e.g., Cal. Penal Code Ann. § 11189 (West 1982) (codifying Interstate Corrections Compact); § 11190 (codifying Western Interstate Corrections Compact); Conn. Gen. Stat. § 18-102 (1981) (codifying New England Interstate Corrections Compact); § 18-106 (codifying Interstate Corrections Compact); Haw. Rev. Stat. § 355-1 (1976) (codifying Western Interstate Corrections Compact); Idaho Code § 20-701 (1979) (codifying Interstate Corrections Compact); Ky. Rev. Stat. § 196.610 (1982) (same). And prison regulations such as Hawaii's Rule IV anticipate that inmates sometimes will be transferred to prisons in other States.

In short, it is neither unreasonable nor unusual for an inmate to serve practically his entire sentence in a State other than the one in which he was convicted and sentenced, or to be transferred to an out-of-state prison after serving a portion of his sentence in his home State. Confinement in another State, unlike confinement in a mental institution, is "within the normal limits or range of custody which the conviction has authorized the State to impose." Meachum, 427 U.S., at 225. Even when, as here, the transfer involves long distances and an ocean crossing, the confinement remains within constitutional limits. The difference between such a transfer and an intrastate or interstate transfer of shorter distance is a matter of degree, not of kind, and Meachum instructs that "the determining factor is the nature of the interest involved rather than its weight." 427 U.S., at 224. The reasoning of Meachum and Montanye compels the conclusion that an interstate prison transfer, including one from Hawaii to California, does not deprive an inmate of any liberty interest protected by the Due Process Clause in and of itself.

III

The Court of Appeals held that Hawaii's prison regulations create a constitutionally protected liberty interest. In Meachum, however, the State had "conferred no right on the prisoner to remain in the prison to which he was initially assigned, defeasible only upon proof of specific acts of misconduct," 427 U.S., at 226, and "[had] not represented that transfers [would] occur only on the occurrence of certain events," id., at 228. Because the State had retained "discretion to transfer [the prisoner] for whatever reason or for no reason at all," ibid., the Court found that the State had not created a constitutionally protected liberty interest. Similarly, because the state law at issue in Montanye "[imposed] no conditions on the discretionary power to transfer," 427 U.S., at 243, there was no basis for invoking the protections of the Due Process Clause.

These cases demonstrate that a State creates a protected liberty interest by placing substantive limitations on official discretion. An inmate must show "that particularized standards or criteria guide the State's decisionmakers." Connecticut Board of Pardons v. Dumschat, 452 U.S. 458, 467 (1981) (BRENNAN, J., concurring). If the decisionmaker is not "required to base its decisions on objective and defined criteria," but instead "can deny the requested relief for any constitutionally permissible reason or for no reason at all," ibid., the State has not created a constitutionally protected liberty interest. See id., at 466-467 (opinion of the Court); see also Vitek v. Jones, 445 U.S., at 488-491 (summarizing cases).

Hawaii's prison regulations place no substantive limitations on official discretion and thus create no liberty interest entitled to protection under the Due Process Clause. As Rule IV itself makes clear, and as the Supreme Court of Hawaii has held in Lono v. Ariyoshi, 63 Haw., at 144-145, 621 P. 2d, at 980-981, the prison Administrator's discretion to transfer an inmate is completely unfettered. No standards govern or restrict the Administrator's determination. . . .

The Court of Appeals thus erred in attributing significance to the fact that the prison regulations require a particular kind of hearing before the Administrator can exercise his unfettered discretion. As the United States Court of Appeals for the Seventh Circuit recently stated in Shango v. Jurich, 681 F.2d 1091, 1100-1101 (1982), "[a] liberty interest is of course a substantive interest of an individual; it cannot be the right to demand needless formality." Process is not an end in itself. Its constitutional purpose is to protect a substantive interest to which the individual has a legitimate claim of entitlement. See generally Simon, Liberty and Property in the Supreme Court: A Defense of Roth and Perry, 71 Calif. L. Rev. 146, 186 (1983). If officials may transfer a prisoner "for whatever reason or for no reason at all," Meachum, 427 U.S., at 228, there is no such

interest for process to protect. The State may choose to require procedures for reasons other than protection against deprivation of substantive rights, of course, but in making that choice the State does not create an independent substantive right. See Hewitt v. Helms, 459 U.S. 460, 471 (1983).

IV

In sum, we hold that the transfer of respondent from Hawaii to California did not implicate the Due Process Clause directly, and that Hawaii's prison regulations do not create a protected liberty interest. Accordingly, the judgment of the Court of Appeals is

Reversed.

HUDSON
v.
PALMER

468 U.S. 517; 104 S. Ct. 3194;
82 L. Ed. 2d 393 (1984)

CHIEF JUSTICE BURGER delivered the opinion of the Court.

We granted certiorari . . . to decide whether a prison inmate has a reasonable expectation of privacy in his prison cell entitling him to the protection of the Fourth Amendment against unreasonable searches and seizures. . . .

I

The facts underlying this dispute are relatively simple. Respondent Palmer is an inmate at the Bland Correctional Center in Bland, Va., serving sentences for forgery, uttering, grand larceny, and bank robbery convictions. On September 16, 1981, petitioner Hudson, an officer at the Correctional Center, with a fellow officer, conducted a "shakedown" search of respondent's prison locker and cell for contraband. During the "shakedown," the officers discovered a ripped pillowcase in a trash can near respondent's cell bunk. Charges against Palmer were instituted under the prison disciplinary procedures for destroying state property.

After a hearing, Palmer was found guilty on the charge and was ordered to reimburse the State for the cost of the material destroyed; in addition, a reprimand was entered on his prison record.

Palmer subsequently brought this pro se action in United States District Court under 42 U.S.C. § 1983. Respondent claimed that Hudson had conducted the shakedown search of his cell and had brought a false charge against him solely to harass him, and that, in violation of his Fourteenth Amendment right not to be deprived of property without due process of law, Hudson had intentionally destroyed certain of his noncontraband personal property during the September 16 search. Hudson denied each allegation; he moved for and was granted summary judgment. The District Court accepted respondent's allegations as true but held nonetheless, relying on Parratt v. Taylor, supra, that the alleged destruction of respondent's property, even if intentional, did not violate the Fourteenth Amendment because there were state tort remedies available to redress the deprivation, App. 31 and that the alleged harassment did not "rise to the level of a constitutional deprivation," id., at 32.

The Court of Appeals affirmed in part, reversed in part, and remanded for further proceedings. 697 F.2d 1220 (CA4 1983). The court affirmed the District Court's holding that respondent was not deprived of his property without due process. The court acknowledged that we considered only a claim of negligent property deprivation in Parratt v. Taylor, supra. It agreed with the District Court, however, that the logic of Parratt applies equally to unauthorized intentional deprivations of property by state officials: "[Once] it is assumed that a postdeprivation remedy can cure an unintentional but negligent act causing injury, inflicted by a state agent which is unamendable to prior review, then that principle applies as well to random and unauthorized intentional acts." . . .

The Court of Appeals reversed the summary judgment on respondent's claim that the shakedown search was unreasonable. The court recognized that Bell v. Wolfish, 441 U.S. 520, 555-557 (1979), authorized irregular unannounced shakedown searches of prison cells. But the court held that an individual prisoner has a "limited privacy right" in his cell entitling him to protection against searches conducted solely to harass or to humiliate. 697 F.2d, at 1225. The shakedown of a single prisoner's property, said the court, is permissible only if "done pursuant to an established program of conducting random searches of single cells or groups of cells reasonably designed to deter or discover the possession of contraband" or upon reasonable belief that the particular prisoner possessed contraband. Id., at 1224. Because the Court of Appeals concluded that the record reflected a factual dispute over whether the search of respondent's cell was routine or conducted to harass respondent, it held that summary judgment was inappropriate, and that a remand was necessary to determine the purpose of the cell search.

. . . We affirm in part and reverse in part.

II

A

The first question we address is whether respondent has a right of privacy in his prison cell entitling him to the protection of the Fourth Amendment against unreasonable searches. As we have noted, the Court of Appeals held that the District Court's summary judgment in petitioner's favor was premature because respondent had a "limited privacy right" in his cell that might have been breached. The court concluded that, to protect this privacy right, shakedown searches of an individual's cell should be performed only "pursuant to an established program of conducting random searches . . . reasonably designed to deter or discover the possession of contraband" or upon reasonable belief that the prisoner possesses contraband. Petitioner contends that the Court of Appeals erred in holding that respondent had even a limited privacy right in his cell, and urges that we adopt the "bright line" rule that prisoners have no legitimate expectation of privacy in their individual cells that would entitle them to Fourth Amendment protection.

* * *

. . . [W]hile persons imprisoned for crime enjoy many protections of the Constitution, it is also clear that imprisonment carries with it the circumscription or loss of many significant rights. See Bell v. Wolfish, 441 U.S., at 545. These constraints on inmates, and in some cases the complete withdrawal of certain rights, are "justified by the considerations underlying our penal system." Price v. Johnston, 334 U.S. 266, 285 (1948); see also Bell v. Wolfish, supra, at 545-546 and cases cited; Wolff v. McDonnell, supra, at 555. The curtailment of certain rights is necessary, as a practical matter, to accommodate a myriad of "institutional needs and objectives" of prison facilities, Wolff v. McDonnell, supra, at 555, chief among which is internal security, see Pell v. Procunier, supra, at 823. Of course, these restrictions or retractions also serve, incidentally, as reminders that, under our system of justice, deterrence and retribution are factors in addition to correction.

We have not before been called upon to decide the specific question whether the Fourth Amendment applies within a prison cell, but the nature of our inquiry is well defined. We must determine here, as in other Fourth Amendment contexts, if a "justifiable" expectation of privacy is at stake. Katz v. United States, 389 U.S. 347 (1967). The applicability of the Fourth Amendment turns on whether "the person invoking its protection can claim a 'justifiable,' a 'reasonable,' or a 'legitimate expectation of privacy' that has been invaded by government action." Smith v. Maryland, 442 U.S. 735, 740 (1979), and cases cited. We must decide, in Justice Harlan's words, whether a prisoner's expectation of privacy in his prison cell is the kind of expectation that "society is prepared to recognize as 'reasonable.'" Katz, supra, at 360, 361 (concurring opinion).

Notwithstanding our caution in approaching claims that the Fourth Amendment is inapplicable in a given context, we hold that society is not prepared to recognize as legitimate any subjective expectation of privacy that a prisoner might have in his prison cell and that, accordingly, the Fourth Amendment proscription against unreasonable searches does not apply within the confines of the prison cell. The recognition of privacy rights for prisoners in their individual cells simply cannot be reconciled with the concept of incarceration and the needs and objectives of penal institutions.

Prisons, by definition, are places of involuntary confinement of persons who have a demonstrated proclivity for anti-social criminal, and often violent, conduct. Inmates have necessarily shown a lapse in ability to control and conform their behavior to the legitimate standards of society by the normal impulses of self-restraint; they have shown an inability to regulate their conduct in a way that reflects either a respect for law or an appreciation of the rights of others. Even a partial survey of the statistics on violent crime in our Nation's prisons illustrates the magnitude of the problem. During 1981 and the first half of 1982, there were over 120 prisoners murdered by fellow inmates in state and federal prisons. A number of prison personnel were murdered by prisoners during this period. Over 29 riots or similar disturbances were reported in these facilities for the same time frame. And there were over 125 suicides in these institutions. See Prison Violence, 7 Corrections Compendium (Mar. 1983). Additionally, informal statistics from the United States Bureau of Prisons show that in the federal system during 1983, there were 11 inmate homicides, 359 inmate assaults on other inmates, 227 inmate assaults on prison staff, and 10 suicides. There were in the same system in 1981 and 1982 over 750 inmate assaults on other inmates and over 570 inmate assaults on prison personnel.

Within this volatile "community," prison administrators are to take all necessary steps to ensure the safety of not only the prison staffs and administrative personnel, but also visitors. They are under an obligation to take reasonable measures to guarantee the safety of the inmates themselves. They must be ever alert to attempts to introduce drugs and other contraband into the premises which, we can judicially notice, is one of the most perplexing problems of prisons today; they must prevent, so far as possible, the flow of illicit weapons into the prison; they must be vigilant to detect escape plots, in which drugs or weapons may be involved, before the schemes materialize. In addition to these monumental tasks, it is incumbent upon these officials at the same time to maintain as sanitary an environment for the inmates as feasible, given the difficulties of the circumstances.

The administration of a prison, we have said, is "at best an extraordinarily difficult undertaking." Wolff v. McDonnell, 418 U.S., at 566; Hewitt v. Helms, 459 U.S. 460, 467 (1983). But it would be literally impossible to accomplish the prison objectives identified above if inmates retained a right of privacy in their cells. Virtually the only place inmates can conceal weapons, drugs, and other contraband is in their cells. Unfettered access to these cells by prison officials, thus, is imperative if drugs and contraband are to be ferreted out and sanitary surroundings are to be maintained.

Determining whether an expectation of privacy is "legitimate" or "reasonable" necessarily entails a balancing of interests. The two interests here are the interest of society in the security of its penal institutions and the interest of the prisoner in privacy within his cell. The latter interest, of course, is already limited by the exigencies of the circumstances: A prison "shares none of the attributes of privacy of a home, an automobile, an office, or a hotel room." Lanza v. New York, 370 U.S. 139, 143-144 (1962). We strike the balance in favor of institutional security, which we have noted is "central to all other corrections goals," Pell v. Procunier, 417 U.S., at 823. A right of privacy in traditional Fourth Amendment terms is fundamentally incompatible with the close and continual surveillance of inmates and their cells required to ensure institutional security and internal order. We are satisfied that society would insist that the prisoner's expectation of privacy always yield to what must be considered the paramount interest in institutional security. We believe that it is accepted by our society that "[loss] of freedom of choice and privacy are inherent incidents of confinement." Bell v. Wolfish, 441 U.S., at 537.

The Court of Appeals was troubled by the possibility of searches conducted solely to harass inmates; it reasoned that a requirement that searches be conducted only pursuant to an established policy or upon reasonable suspicion would prevent such searches to the maximum extent possible. Of course, there is a risk of maliciously motivated searches, and of course, intentional harassment of even the most hardened criminals cannot be tolerated by a civilized society. However, we disagree with the court's proposed solution. The uncertainty that attends random searches of cells renders these searches perhaps the most effective weapon of the prison administrator in the constant fight against the proliferation of knives and guns, illicit drugs, and other contraband. The Court of Appeals candidly acknowledged that "the device [of random cell searches] is of . . . obvious utility in achieving the goal of prison security." 697 F.2d, at 1224.

A requirement that even random searches be conducted pursuant to an established plan would seriously undermine the effectiveness of this weapon. It is simply naive to believe that prisoners would not eventually decipher any plan officials might devise for "planned random searches," and thus be able routinely to anticipate searches. The Supreme Court of Virginia identified the shortcomings of an approach such as that adopted by the Court of Appeals and the necessity of allowing prison administrators flexibility:

For one to advocate that prison searches must be conducted only pursuant to an enunciated general policy or when suspicion is directed at a particular inmate is to ignore the realities of prison operation. Random searches of inmates, individually or collectively, and their cells and lockers are valid and necessary to ensure the security of the institution and the safety of inmates and all others within its boundaries. This type of search allows prison officers flexibility and prevents inmates from anticipating, and thereby thwarting, a search for contraband. Marrero v. Commonwealth, 222 Va. 754, 757, 284 S. E. 2d 809, 811 (1981).

We share the concerns so well expressed by the Supreme Court and its view that wholly random searches are essential to the effective security of penal institutions. We, therefore, cannot accept even the concededly limited holding of the Court of Appeals.

Respondent acknowledges that routine shakedowns of prison cells are essential to the effective administration of prisons. Brief for Respondent and Cross-Petitioner 7, n. 5. He contends, however, that he is constitutionally entitled not to be subjected to searches conducted only to harass. The crux of his claim is that "because searches and seizures to harass are unreasonable, a prisoner has a reasonable expectation of privacy not to have his cell, locker, personal effects, person invaded for such a purpose." Id., at 24. This argument, which assumes the answer to the predicate question whether a prisoner has a legitimate expectation of privacy in his prison cell at all, is merely a challenge to the reasonableness of the particular search of respondent's cell. Because we conclude that prisoners have no legitimate expectation of privacy and that the Fourth Amendment's prohibition on unreasonable searches does not apply in prison cells, we need not address this issue.

Our holding that respondent does not have a reasonable expectation of privacy enabling him to invoke the protections of the Fourth Amendment does not mean that he is without a remedy for calculated harassment unrelated to prison needs. Nor does it mean that prison attendants can ride roughshod over inmates' property rights with impunity. The Eighth Amendment always stands as a protection against "cruel and unusual punishments." By the same token, there are adequate state tort and common-law remedies available to respondent to redress the alleged destruction of his personal property.

* * *

WILSON

v.

SEITER

**501 U.S. 294; 111 S. Ct. 2321;
115 L. Ed. 2d 271 (1991)**
[Most citations and footnotes omitted]

JUSTICE SCALIA delivered the opinion of the Court.

This case presents the questions whether a prisoner claiming that conditions of confinement constitute cruel and unusual punishment must show a culpable state of mind on the part of prison officials and, if so, what state of mind is required.

Petitioner Pearly L. Wilson is a felon incarcerated at the Hocking Correctional Facility (HCF) in Nelsonville, Ohio. Alleging that a number of the conditions of his confinement constituted cruel and unusual punishment in violation of the Eighth and Fourteenth Amendments, he brought this action under 42 U.S.C. § 1983 against respondents Richard P. Seiter, then Director of the Ohio Department of Rehabilitation and Correction, and Carl Humphreys, then warden of HCF. The complaint alleged overcrowding, excessive noise, insufficient locker storage space, inadequate heating and cooling, improper ventilation, unclean and inadequate restrooms, unsanitary dining facilities and food preparation, and housing with mentally and physically ill inmates. Petitioner sought declaratory and injunctive relief, as well as $900,000 in compensatory and punitive damages.

The parties filed cross-motions for summary judgment with supporting affidavits. Petitioner's affidavits described the challenged conditions and charged that the authorities, after notification, had failed to take remedial action. Respondents' affidavits denied that some of the alleged conditions existed, and described efforts by prison officials to improve the others. The District Court granted summary judgment for respondents. The Court of Appeals for the Sixth Circuit affirmed, and we granted certiorari. . . .

I

The Eighth Amendment, which applies to the States through the Due Process Clause of the Fourteenth Amendment, Robinson v. California, prohibits the infliction of "cruel and unusual punishments" on those convicted of crimes. In Estelle v. Gamble, we first acknowledged that the provision could be applied to some deprivations that were not specifically part of the sentence but were suffered during imprisonment. We rejected, however, the inmate's claim in that case that prison doctors had inflicted cruel and unusual punishment by inadequately attending to his medical needs—because he had failed to establish that they possessed a sufficiently culpable state of mind. Since, we said, only the "'unnecessary and wanton infliction of pain'" implicates the Eighth Amendment, a prisoner advancing such a claim must, at a minimum, allege "deliberate indifference" to his "serious" medical needs. "It is only such indifference" that can violate the Eighth Amendment, ibid. (emphasis added); allegations of "inadvertent failure to provide adequate medical care," or of a "negligent . . . diagnosis," simply fail to establish the requisite culpable state of mind.

Estelle relied in large measure on an earlier case, Louisiana ex rel. Francis v. Resweber, which involved not a prison deprivation but an effort to subject a prisoner to a second electrocution after the first attempt failed by reason of a malfunction in the electric chair. There Justice Reed, writing for a plurality of the Court, emphasized that the Eighth Amendment prohibited "the wanton infliction of pain," Because the first attempt had been thwarted by an "unforeseeable accident," the officials lacked the culpable state of mind necessary for the punishment to be regarded as "cruel," regardless of the actual suffering inflicted. "The situation of the unfortunate victim of this accident is just as though he had suffered the identical amount of mental anguish and physical pain in any other occurrence, such as, for example, a fire in the cell block." Justice Frankfurter, concurring solely on the basis of the Due Process Clause of the Fourteenth Amendment, emphasized that the first attempt had failed because of "an innocent misadventure," and suggested that he might reach a different conclusion in "a hypothetical situation, which assumes a series of abortive attempts at electrocution or even a single, cruelly willful attempt,". . . .

After Estelle, we next confronted an Eighth Amendment challenge to a prison deprivation in Rhodes v. Chapman. In that case, inmates at the Southern Ohio Correctional Facility contended that the lodging of two inmates in a single cell ("double celling") constituted cruel and unusual punishment. We rejected that contention, concluding that it amounts "at most . . . to a theory that double celling inflicts pain," but not that it constitutes the "unnecessary and wanton infliction of pain" that violates the Eighth Amendment. The Constitution, we said, "does not mandate comfortable prisons," and only those deprivations denying "the minimal civilized measure of life's necessities," are sufficiently grave to form the basis of an Eighth Amendment violation.

Our holding in Rhodes turned on the objective component of an Eighth Amendment prison claim (was the deprivation sufficiently serious?), and we did not consider the subjective component (did the officials act with a sufficiently culpable state of mind?). That Rhodes had not eliminated the subjective component was made clear by our next relevant case, Whitley v. Albers. There an inmate shot by a guard during an attempt to quell a prison disturbance contended that he had been subjected to cruel and unusual punishment. We stated: "After incarceration, only the unnecessary and wanton infliction of pain . . . constitutes cruel and unusual punishment forbidden by the Eighth Amendment. To be cruel and unusual punishment, conduct that does not purport to be punishment at all must involve more than ordinary lack of due care for the prisoner's interests or safety. . . . It is obduracy and wantonness, not inadvertence or error in good faith, that characterize the conduct prohibited by the Cruel and Unusual Punishments Clause, whether that conduct occurs in connection with establishing conditions of confinement, supplying medical needs, or restoring official control over a tumultuous cellblock." These cases mandate inquiry into a prison official's state of mind when it is claimed that the official has inflicted cruel and unusual punishment. Petitioner concedes that this is so with respect to some claims of cruel and unusual prison conditions. He acknowledges, for instance, that if a prison boiler malfunctions accidentally during a cold winter, an inmate would have no basis for an Eighth Amendment claim, even if he suffers objectively significant harm. Petitioner, and the United States as amicus curiae in support of petitioner, suggests that we should draw a distinction between "short-term" or "one-time" conditions (in which a state of mind requirement would apply) and "continuing" or "systemic" conditions (where official state of mind would be irrelevant). We perceive neither a logical nor a practical basis for that distinction. The source of the intent requirement is not the predilections of this Court, but the Eighth Amendment itself, which bans only cruel and unusual punishment. If the pain inflicted is not formally meted out as punishment by the statute or the sentencing judge, some mental element must be attributed to the inflicting officer before it can qualify. As Judge Posner has observed: "The infliction of punishment is a deliberate act intended to chastise or deter. This is what the word means today; it is what it meant in the eighteenth century . . . . If [a] guard accidentally stepped on [a] prisoner's toe and broke it, this would not be punishment in anything remotely like the accepted meaning of the word, whether we consult the usage of 1791, or 1868, or 1985."

The long duration of a cruel prison condition may make it easier to establish knowledge and hence some form of intent ; but there is no logical reason why it should cause the requirement of intent to evaporate. The proposed short-term/long-term distinction also defies rational implementation. Apart from the difficulty of determining the day or hour that divides the two categories (is it the same for all conditions?) the violations alleged in specific cases often consist of composite conditions that do not lend themselves to such pigeonholing.

The United States suggests that a state-of-mind inquiry might allow officials to interpose the defense that, despite good-faith efforts to obtain funding, fiscal constraints beyond their control prevent the elimination of inhumane conditions. Even if that were so, it is hard to understand how it could control the meaning of "cruel and unusual punishment" in the Eighth Amendment. An intent requirement is either implicit in the word "punishment" or is not; it cannot be alternately required and ignored as policy considerations might dictate. At any rate, the validity of a "cost" defense as negating the requisite intent is not at issue in this case, since respondents have never advanced it. Nor, we might note, is there any indication that other officials have sought to use such a defense to avoid the holding of Estelle v. Gamble.

II

Having determined that Eighth Amendment claims based on official conduct that does not purport to be the penalty formally imposed for a crime require inquiry into state of mind, it remains for us to consider what state of mind applies in cases challenging prison conditions. As described above, our

cases say that the offending conduct must be wanton. Whitley makes clear, however, that in this context wantonness does not have a fixed meaning but must be determined with "due regard for differences in the kind of conduct against which an Eighth Amendment objection is lodged." Where (as in Whitley) officials act in response to a prison disturbance, their actions are necessarily taken "in haste, under pressure," and balanced against "competing institutional concerns for the safety of prison staff or other inmates." Ibid. In such an emergency situation, we found that wantonness consisted of acting "'maliciously and sadistically for the very purpose of causing harm.'" In contrast, "the State's responsibility to attend to the medical needs of prisoners does not ordinarily clash with other equally important governmental responsibilities," so that in that context, as Estelle held, "deliberate indifference" would constitute wantonness.

The parties agree . . . that the very high state of mind prescribed by Whitley does not apply to prison conditions cases. Petitioner argues that, to the extent officials' state of mind is relevant at all, there is no justification for a standard more demanding than Estelle's "deliberate indifference." Respondents counter that "deliberate indifference" is appropriate only in "cases involving personal injury of a physical nature," and that a malice standard should be applied in cases such as this, which "do not involve . . . detriment to bodily integrity, pain, injury, or loss of life."

We do not agree with respondents' suggestion that the "wantonness" of conduct depends upon its effect upon the prisoner. Whitley teaches that, assuming the conduct is harmful enough to satisfy the objective component of an Eighth Amendment claim, see Rhodes v. Chapman, whether it can be characterized as "wanton" depends upon the constraints facing the official. From that standpoint, we see no significant distinction between claims alleging inadequate medical care and those alleging inadequate "conditions of confinement." Indeed, the medical care a prisoner receives is just as much a "condition" of his confinement as the food he is fed, the clothes he is issued, the temperature he is subjected to in his cell, and the protection he is afforded against other inmates. There is no indication that, as a general matter, the actions of prison officials with respect to these nonmedical conditions are taken under materially different constraints than their actions with respect to medical conditions. Thus, as retired Justice Powell has concluded: "Whether one characterizes the treatment received by [the prisoner] as inhumane conditions of confinement, failure to attend to his medical needs, or a combination of both, it is appropriate to apply the 'deliberate indifference' standard articulated in Estelle."

III

We now consider whether, in light of the foregoing analysis, the Sixth Circuit erred in affirming the District Court's grant of summary judgment in respondents' favor. As a preliminary matter, we must address petitioner's contention that the Court of Appeals erred in dismissing, before it reached the state-of-mind issue, a number of claims (inadequate cooling, housing with mentally ill inmates, and overcrowding) on the ground that, even if proved, they did not involve the serious deprivation required by Rhodes. A court cannot dismiss any challenged condition, petitioner contends, as long as other conditions remain in dispute, for each condition must be "considered as part of the overall conditions challenged. . . ." Petitioner bases this contention upon our observation in Rhodes that conditions of confinement, "alone or in combination," may deprive prisoners of the minimal civilized measure of life's necessities.

As other courts besides the Court of Appeals here have understood, our statement in Rhodes was not meant to establish the broad proposition that petitioner asserts. Some conditions of confinement may establish an Eighth Amendment violation "in combination" when each would not do so alone, but only when they have a mutually enforcing effect that produces the deprivation of a single, identifiable human need such as food, warmth, or exercise—for example, a low cell temperature at night combined with a failure to issue blankets. Compare Spain v. Procunier, (CA9 1979) (outdoor exercise required when prisoners otherwise confined in small cells almost 24 hours per day) with Clay v. Miller, (CA4 1980) (outdoor exercise

not required when prisoners otherwise had access to day room 18 hours per day). To say that some prison conditions may interact in this fashion is a far cry from saying that all prison conditions are a seamless web for Eighth Amendment purposes. Nothing so amorphous as "overall conditions" can rise to the level of cruel and unusual punishment when no specific deprivation of a single human need exists. While we express no opinion on the relative gravity of the various claims that the Sixth Circuit found to pass and fail the threshold test of serious deprivation, we reject the contention made here that no claim can be found to fail that test in isolation. After disposing of the three claims on the basis of Rhodes, the Court of Appeals proceeded to uphold the District Court's dismissal of petitioner's remaining claims on the ground that his affidavits failed to a establish the requisite culpable state of mind. The critical portion of its opinion reads as follows:

> The Whitley standard of obduracy and wantonness requires behavior marked by persistent malicious cruelty. The record before us simply fails to assert facts suggesting such behavior. At best, appellants' claim evidences negligence on appellees' parts in implementing standards for maintaining conditions. Negligence, clearly, is inadequate to support an eighth amendment claim.

It appears from this, and from the consistent reference to "the Whitley standard" elsewhere in the opinion, that the court believed that the criterion of liability was whether the respondents acted "maliciously and sadistically for the very purpose of causing harm," Whitley. To be sure, mere negligence would satisfy neither that nor the more lenient "deliberate indifference" standard, so that any error on the point may have been harmless. Conceivably, however, the court would have given further thought to its finding of "at best . . . negligence" if it realized that that was not merely an argument a fortiori, but a determination almost essential to the judgment. Out of an abundance of caution, we vacate the judgment of the Sixth Circuit and remand the case for reconsideration under the appropriate standard.

It is so ordered.

JUSTICE WHITE, with whom JUSTICE MARSHALL, JUSTICE BLACKMUN, and JUSTICE STEVENS join, concurring in the judgment.

The majority holds that prisoners challenging the conditions of their confinement under the Eighth Amendment must show "deliberate indifference" by the responsible officials. Because that requirement is inconsistent with our prior decisions, I concur only in the judgment.

It is well established, and the majority does not dispute, that pain or other suffering that is part of the punishment imposed on convicted criminals is subject to Eighth Amendment scrutiny without regard to an intent requirement. The linchpin of the majority's analysis therefore is its assertion that "if the pain inflicted is not formally meted out as punishment by the statute or the sentencing judge, some mental element must be attributed to the inflicting officer before it can qualify." Ante, at 5 (emphasis added). That reasoning disregards our prior decisions that have involved challenges to conditions of confinement, where we have made it clear that the conditions are themselves part of the punishment, even though not specifically "meted out" by a statute or judge.

We first considered the relationship between the Eighth Amendment and conditions of confinement in Hutto v. Finney. . . . There, the District Court had entered a series of remedial orders after determining that the conditions in the Arkansas prison system violated the Eighth Amendment. The prison officials, while conceding that the conditions were cruel and unusual, challenged two aspects of the District Court's relief: (1) an order limiting punitive isolation to 30 days; and (2) an award of attorney's fees. In upholding the District Court's limitation on punitive isolation, we first made clear that the conditions of confinement are part of the punishment that is subject to Eighth Amendment scrutiny:

> The Eighth Amendment's ban on inflicting cruel and unusual punishments, made applicable to the States by the Fourteenth Amendment, "proscribes more than physi-

cally barbarous punishments." Estelle v. Gamble. It prohibits penalties that are grossly disproportionate to the offense, Weems v. United States, as well as those that transgress today's "'broad and idealistic concepts of dignity, civilized standards, humanity, and decency." Estelle v. Gamble. Confinement in a prison or in an isolation cell is a form of punishment subject to scrutiny under Eighth Amendment standards.

Focusing only on the objective conditions of confinement, we then explained that we found "no error in the [district] court's conclusion that, taken as a whole, conditions in the isolation cells continued to violate the prohibition against cruel and unusual punishment."

In Rhodes v. Chapman, we addressed for the first time a disputed contention that the conditions of confinement at a particular prison constituted cruel and unusual punishment. There, prisoners challenged the "double celling" of inmates at an Ohio prison. In addressing that claim, we began by reiterating the various bases for an Eighth Amendment challenge:

> Today the Eighth Amendment prohibits punishments which, although not physically barbarous, "involve the unnecessary and wanton infliction of pain," Gregg v. Georgia, or are grossly disproportionate to the severity of the crime, Coker v. Georgia. Among "unnecessary and wanton" inflictions of pain are those that are "totally without penological justification." Gregg v. Georgia; Estelle v. Gamble.

> No static "test" can exist by which courts determine whether conditions of confinement are cruel and unusual, for the Eighth Amendment "must draw its meaning from the evolving standards of decency that mark the progress of a maturing society." Trop v. Dulles. We then explained how those principles operate in the context of a challenge to conditions of confinement:

> These principles apply when the conditions of confinement compose the punishment at issue. Conditions must not involve the wanton and unnecessary infliction of pain, nor may they be grossly dispropor-

tionate to the severity of the crime warranting imprisonment. In Estelle v. Gamble, we held that the denial of medical care is cruel and unusual because, in the worst case, it can result in physical torture, and, even in less serious cases, it can result in pain without any penological purpose. In Hutto v. Finney, the conditions of confinement in two Arkansas prisons constituted cruel and unusual punishment because they resulted in unquestioned and serious deprivations of basic human needs. Conditions other than those in Gamble and Hutto, alone or in combination, may deprive inmates of the minimal civilized measure of life's necessities. Such conditions could be cruel and unusual under the contemporary standard of decency that we recognized in Gamble.

Finally, we applied those principles to the conditions at issue, and found that "there is no evidence that double celling under these circumstances either inflicts unnecessary or wanton pain or is grossly disproportionate to the severity of crimes warranting imprisonment." Id., at 348. Rhodes makes it crystal clear, therefore, that Eighth Amendment challenges to conditions of confinement are to be treated like Eighth Amendment challenges to punishment that is "formally meted out as punishment by the statute or the sentencing judge," ante, at 5—we examine only the objective severity, not the subjective intent of government officials.

The majority relies upon our decisions in Louisiana ex rel. Francis v. Resweber; Estelle v. Gamble, ; and Whitley v. Albers, but none of those cases involved a challenge to conditions of confinement. Instead, they involved challenges to specific acts or omissions directed at individual prisoners. In Gamble, for example, the challenge was not to a general lack of access to medical care at the prison, but to the allegedly inadequate delivery of that treatment to the plaintiff. Similarly, in Whitley the challenge was to the action of a prison guard in shooting the plaintiff during a riot, not to any condition in the prison. The distinction is crucial because "unlike 'conduct that does not purport to be punishment at all' as was involved in Gamble and Whitley, the Court has not made intent

an element of a cause of action alleging unconstitutional conditions of confinement."

Moreover, Whitley expressly supports an objective standard for challenges to conditions of confinement. There, in discussing the Eighth Amendment, we stated: "An express intent to inflict unnecessary pain is not required, Estelle v. Gamble, ('deliberate indifference' to a prisoner's serious medical needs is cruel and unusual punishment), and harsh 'conditions of confinement' may constitute cruel and unusual punishment unless such conditions "are part of the penalty that criminal offenders pay for their offenses against society."

The majority places great weight on the subsequent dictum in Whitley that "it is obduracy and wantonness, not inadvertence or error in good faith, that characterize the conduct prohibited by the Cruel and Unusual Punishments Clause, whether that conduct occurs in connection with establishing conditions of confinement, supplying medical needs, or restoring official control over a tumultuous cellblock." The word "conduct" in that statement, however, is referring to "conduct that does not purport to be punishment at all," rather than to the "harsh 'conditions of confinement'" referred to earlier in the opinion.

Not only is the majority's intent requirement a departure from precedent, it likely will prove impossible to apply in many cases. Inhumane prison conditions often are the result of cumulative actions and inactions by numerous officials inside and outside a prison, sometimes over a long period of time. In those circumstances, it is far from clear whose intent should be examined, and the majority offers no real guidance on this issue. In truth, intent simply is not very meaningful when considering a challenge to an institution, such as a prison system.

The majority's approach also is unwise. It leaves open the possibility, for example, that prison officials will be able to defeat a § 1983 action challenging inhumane prison conditions simply by showing that the conditions are caused by insufficient funding from the state legislature rather than by any deliberate indifference on the part of the prison officials. In my view, having chosen to use imprisonment as a form of punishment, a state must ensure that the conditions in its prisons comport with the "contemporary standard of decency" required by the Eighth Amendment. As the United States argues: "Seriously inhumane, pervasive conditions should not be insulated from constitutional challenge because the officials managing the institution have exhibited a conscientious concern for ameliorating its problems, and have made efforts (albeit unsuccessful) to that end." The ultimate result of today's decision, I fear, is that "serious deprivations of basic human needs," will go unredressed due to an unnecessary and meaningless search for "deliberate indifference."

FARMER
v.
BRENNAN

**511 U.S. 825; 114 S. Ct. 1970;
128 L. Ed. 2d 811 (1994)**
[Most citations and footnotes omitted]

JUSTICE SOUTER delivered the opinion of the Court.

A prison official's "deliberate indifference" to a substantial risk of serious harm to an inmate violates the Eighth Amendment. This case requires us to define the term "deliberate indifference," as we do by requiring a showing that the official was subjectively aware of the risk.

I

The dispute before us stems from a civil suit brought by petitioner, Dee Farmer, alleging that respondents, federal prison officials, violated the Eighth Amendment by their deliberate indifference to petitioner's safety. Petitioner, who is serving a federal sentence for credit card fraud, has been diagnosed by medical personnel of the Bureau of Prisons as a transsexual, one who has "[a] rare psychiatric disorder in which a person feels persistently uncomfortable about his or her anatomical sex," and who typically seeks medical treatment, including hormonal therapy and surgery, to bring about a permanent sex change. American Medical Association,

Encyclopedia of Medicine 1006 (1989); see also American Psychiatric Association, Diagnostic and Statistical Manual of Mental Disorders 74-75 (3d rev. ed. 1987). For several years before being convicted and sentenced in 1986 at the age of 18, petitioner, who is biologically male, wore women's clothing (as petitioner did at the 1986 trial), underwent estrogen therapy, received silicone breast implants, and submitted to unsuccessful "black market" testicle-removal surgery. Petitioner's precise appearance in prison is unclear from the record before us, but petitioner claims to have continued hormonal treatment while incarcerated by using drugs smuggled into prison, and apparently wears clothing in a feminine manner, as by displaying a shirt "off one shoulder," The parties agree that petitioner "projects feminine characteristics."

The practice of federal prison authorities is to incarcerate preoperative transsexuals with prisoners of like biological sex, and over time authorities housed petitioner in several federal facilities, sometimes in the general male prison population but more often in segregation. While there is no dispute that petitioner was segregated at least several times because of violations of prison rules, neither is it disputed that in at least one penitentiary petitioner was segregated because of safety concerns. March 9, 1989, petitioner was transferred for disciplinary reasons from the Federal Correctional Institute in Oxford, Wisconsin (FCI-Oxford), to the United States Penitentiary in Terre Haute, Indiana (USP-Terre Haute). Though the record before us is unclear about the security designations of the two prisons in 1989, penitentiaries are typically higher security facilities that house more troublesome prisoners than federal correctional institutes. See generally Federal Bureau of Prisons, Facilities 1990. After an initial stay in administrative segregation, petitioner was placed in the USP-Terre Haute general population. Petitioner voiced no objection to any prison official about the transfer to the penitentiary or to placement in its general population. Within two weeks, according to petitioner's allegations, petitioner was beaten and raped by another inmate in petitioner's cell. Several days later, after petitioner claims to have reported the incident, officials returned petitioner to segregation to await, according to respondents, a hearing about petitioner's HIV-positive status.

Acting without counsel, petitioner then filed a Bivens complaint, alleging a violation of the Eighth Amendment. As defendants, petitioner named respondents: the warden of USP-Terre Haute and the Director of the Bureau of Prisons (sued only in their official capacities); the warden of FCI-Oxford and a case manager there; and the director of the Bureau of Prisons North Central Region Office and an official in that office (sued in their official and personal capacities). As later amended, the complaint alleged that respondents either transferred petitioner to USP-Terre Haute or placed petitioner in its general population despite knowledge that the penitentiary had a violent environment and a history of inmate assaults, and despite knowledge that petitioner, as a transsexual who "projects feminine characteristics," would be particularly vulnerable to sexual attack by some USP-Terre Haute inmates. This allegedly amounted to a deliberately indifferent failure to protect petitioner's safety, and thus to a violation of petitioner's Eighth Amendment rights. Petitioner sought compensatory and punitive damages, and an injunction barring future confinement in any penitentiary, including USP-Terre Haute.

* * *

Without ruling on respondents' request to stay discovery, the District Court denied petitioner's *** motion and granted summary judgment to respondents, concluding that there had been no deliberate indifference to petitioner's safety. The failure of prison officials to prevent inmate assaults violates the Eighth Amendment, the court stated, only if prison officials were "reckless in a criminal sense," meaning that they had "actual knowledge" of a potential danger. App. 124. Respondents, however, lacked the requisite knowledge, the court found. "[Petitioner] never expressed any concern for his safety to any of [respondents]. Since [respondents] had no knowledge of any potential danger to [petitioner], they were not deliberately indifferent to his safety." Ibid.

The United States Court of Appeals for the Seventh Circuit summarily affirmed without opinion. We granted certiorari, because Courts of Appeals had adopted inconsistent tests for "deliberate indifference." Compare, for example, McGill v. Duckworth, 944 F.2d 344, 348 (CA7 1991) (holding that "deliberate indifference" requires a "subjective standard of recklessness"), cert. denied, 503 U.S. (1992), with Young v. Quinlan, 960 F.2d 351, 360-361 (CA3 1992) ("[A] prison official is deliberately indifferent when he knows or should have known of a sufficiently serious danger to an inmate").

II

A

The Constitution "does not mandate comfortable prisons," Rhodes v. Chapman, but neither does it permit inhumane ones, and it is now settled that "the treatment a prisoner receives in prison and the conditions under which he is confined are subject to scrutiny under the Eighth Amendment." In its prohibition of "cruel and unusual punishments," the Eighth Amendment places restraints on prison officials, who may not, for example, use excessive physical force against prisoners. The Amendment also imposes duties on these officials, who must provide humane conditions of confinement; prison officials must ensure that inmates receive adequate food, clothing, shelter and medical care, and must "take reasonable measures to guarantee the safety of the inmates."

In particular, as the lower courts have uniformly held, and as we have assumed, "prison officials have a duty . . . to protect prisoners from violence at the hands of other prisoners." Cortes-Quinones v. Jimenez-Nettleship, (CA1), cert. denied, 488 U.S. 823 (1988); see also Wilson v. Seiter, (describing "the protection [an inmate] is afforded against other inmates" as a "condition of confinement" subject to the strictures of the Eighth Amendment). Having incarcerated "persons [with] demonstrated proclivities for antisocial criminal, and often violent, conduct," Hudson v. Palmer, having stripped them of virtually every means of self-protection and foreclosed their access to outside aid, the government and its officials are not free to let the state of nature take its course. Prison conditions may be "restrictive and even harsh," Rhodes, but gratuitously allowing the beating or rape of one prisoner by another serves no "legitimate penological objective," any more than it squares with "evolving standards of decency." Being violently assaulted in prison is simply not "part of the penalty that criminal offenders pay for their offenses against society."

It is not, however, every injury suffered by one prisoner at the hands of another that translates into constitutional liability for prison officials responsible for the victim's safety. Our cases have held that a prison official violates the Eighth Amendment only when two requirements are met. First, the deprivation alleged must be, objectively, "sufficiently serious,"; a prison official's act or omission must result in the denial of "the minimal civilized measure of life's necessities," Rhodes. For a claim (like the one here) based on a failure to prevent harm, the inmate must show that he is incarcerated under conditions posing a substantial risk of serious harm.

The second requirement follows from the principle that "only the unnecessary and wanton infliction of pain implicates the Eighth Amendment." To violate the Cruel and Unusual Punishments Clause, a prison official must have a "sufficiently culpable state of mind." In prison-conditions cases that state of mind is one of "deliberate indifference" to inmate health or safety, a standard the parties agree governs the claim in this case. The parties disagree, however, on the proper test for deliberate indifference, which we must therefore undertake to define.

B

1

Although we have never paused to explain the meaning of the term "deliberate indifference," the case law is instructive. The term first appeared in the United States Reports in Estelle v. Gamble, and its use there shows that deliberate indifference describes a state of mind more blameworthy than negligence. In considering the inmate's claim in Estelle

that inadequate prison medical care violated the Cruel and Unusual Punishments Clause, we distinguished "deliberate indifference to serious medical needs of prisoners," from "negligence in diagnosing or treating a medical condition," holding that only the former violates the Clause. We have since read Estelle for the proposition that Eighth Amendment liability requires "more than ordinary lack of due care for the prisoner's interests or safety."

While Estelle establishes that deliberate indifference entails something more than mere negligence, the cases are also clear that it is satisfied by something less than acts or omissions for the very purpose of causing harm or with knowledge that harm will result. That point underlies the ruling that "application of the deliberate indifference standard is inappropriate" in one class of prison cases: when "officials stand accused of using excessive physical force." In such situations, where the decisions of prison officials are typically made "in haste, under pressure, and frequently without the luxury of a second chance," an Eighth Amendment claimant must show more than "indifference," deliberate or otherwise. The claimant must show that officials applied force "maliciously and sadistically for the very purpose of causing harm," or, as the Court also put it, that officials used force with "a knowing willingness that [harm] occur." This standard of purposeful or knowing conduct is not, however, necessary to satisfy the mens rea requirement of deliberate indifference for claims challenging conditions of confinement; "the very high state of mind prescribed by Whitley does not apply to prison conditions cases."

With deliberate indifference lying somewhere between the poles of negligence at one end and purpose or knowledge at the other, the Courts of Appeals have routinely equated deliberate indifference with recklessness. It is, indeed, fair to say that acting or failing to act with deliberate indifference to a substantial risk of serious harm to a prisoner is the equivalent of recklessly disregarding that risk.

That does not, however, fully answer the pending question about the level of culpability deliberate indifference entails, for the term recklessness is not self-defining. The civil law generally calls a person reckless who acts or (if the person has a duty to act) fails to act in the face of an unjustifiably high risk of harm that is either known or so obvious that it should be known. The criminal law, however, generally permits a finding of recklessness only when a person disregards a risk of harm of which he is aware. See R. Perkins & R. Boyce, Criminal Law 850-851 (3d ed. 1982); J. Hall, General Principles of Criminal Law 115-116, 120, 128 (2d ed. 1960) (hereinafter Hall); American Law Institute, Model Penal Code § 2.02(2)(c), and Comment 3 (1985); but see Commonwealth v. Pierce, 138 Mass. 165, 175-178 (1884) (Holmes, J.) (adopting an objective approach to criminal recklessness). The standards proposed by the parties in this case track the two approaches (though the parties do not put it that way): petitioner asks us to define deliberate indifference as what we have called civil-law recklessness, and respondents urge us to adopt an approach consistent with recklessness in the criminal law.

We reject petitioner's invitation to adopt an objective test for deliberate indifference. We hold instead that a prison official cannot be found liable under the Eighth Amendment for denying an inmate humane conditions of confinement unless the official knows of and disregards an excessive risk to inmate health or safety; the official must both be aware of facts from which the inference could be drawn that a substantial risk of serious harm exists, and he must also draw the inference. This approach comports best with the text of the Amendment as our cases have interpreted it. The Eighth Amendment does not outlaw cruel and unusual "conditions"; it outlaws cruel and unusual "punishments." An act or omission unaccompanied by knowledge of a significant risk of harm might well be something society wishes to discourage, and if harm does result society might well wish to assure compensation. The common law reflects such concerns when it imposes tort liability on a purely objective basis. But an official's failure to alleviate a significant risk that he should have perceived but did not, while no cause for commendation, cannot under our cases be condemned as the infliction of punishment.

In Wilson v. Seiter, we rejected a reading of the Eighth Amendment that would allow liability to be imposed on prison officials solely because of the presence of objectively inhumane prison conditions. As we explained there, our "cases mandate inquiry into a prison official's state of mind when it is claimed that the official has inflicted cruel and unusual punishment." Although "state of mind," like "intent," is an ambiguous term that can encompass objectively defined levels of blameworthiness, it was no accident that we said in Wilson and repeated in later cases that Eighth Amendment suits against prison officials must satisfy a "subjective" requirement. It is true, as petitioner points out, that Wilson cited with approval Court of Appeals decisions applying an objective test for deliberate indifference to claims based on prison officials' failure to prevent inmate assaults. But Wilson cited those cases for the proposition that the deliberate-indifference standard applies to all prison-conditions claims, not to undo its holding that the Eighth Amendment has a "subjective component." Petitioner's purely objective test for deliberate indifference is simply incompatible with Wilson's holding.

To be sure, the reasons for focussing on what a defendant's mental attitude actually was (or is), rather than what it should have been (or should be), differ in the Eighth Amendment context from that of the criminal law. Here, a subjective approach isolates those who inflict punishment; there, it isolates those against whom punishment should be inflicted. But the result is the same: to act recklessly in either setting a person must "consciously disregard" a substantial risk of serious harm.

At oral argument, the Deputy Solicitor General advised against frank adoption of a criminal-law mens rea requirement, contending that it could encourage triers of fact to find Eighth Amendment liability only if they concluded that prison officials acted like criminals. We think this concern is misdirected. Bivens actions against federal prison officials (and their § 1983 counterparts against state officials) are civil in character, and a court should no more allude to the criminal law when enforcing the Cruel and Unusual Punishments Clause than when applying the Free Speech and Press Clauses, where we have also adopted a subjective approach to recklessness. See Harte-Hanks Communications, Inc. v. Connaughton, (holding that the standard for "reckless disregard" for the truth in a defamation action by a public figure "is a subjective one," requiring that "the defendant in fact entertained serious doubts as to the truth of his publication," or that "the defendant actually had a high degree of awareness of . . . probable falsity") (internal quotation marks and citations omitted). That said, subjective recklessness as used in the criminal law is a familiar and workable standard that is consistent with the Cruel and Unusual Punishments Clause as interpreted in our cases, and we adopt it as the test for "deliberate indifference" under the Eighth Amendment.

2

Our decision that Eighth Amendment liability requires consciousness of a risk is thus based on the Constitution and our cases, not merely on a parsing of the phrase "deliberate indifference." And we do not reject petitioner's arguments for a thoroughly objective approach to deliberate indifference without recognizing that on the crucial point (whether a prison official must know of a risk, or whether it suffices that he should know) the term does not speak with certainty. Use of "deliberate," for example, arguably requires nothing more than an act (or omission) of indifference to a serious risk that is voluntary, not accidental. Cf. Estelle, (distinguishing "deliberate indifference" from "accident" or "inadvertence"). And even if "deliberate" is better read as implying knowledge of a risk, the concept of constructive knowledge is familiar enough that the term "deliberate indifference" would not, of its own force, preclude a scheme that conclusively presumed awareness from a risk's obviousness.

Because "deliberate indifference" is a judicial gloss, appearing neither in the Constitution nor in a statute, we could not accept petitioner's argument that the test for "deliberate indifference" described in Canton v. Harris, must necessarily govern here. In Canton, interpreting 42 U.S.C. § 1983, we held that a municipality can be liable for failure to train its employees when the municipality's failure shows "a deliberate indifference to the rights of its inhabitants." In speaking to the meaning of the term, we said that "it may

happen that in light of the duties assigned to specific officers or employees the need for more or different training is so obvious, and the inadequacy so likely to result in the violation of constitutional rights, that the policymakers of the city can reasonably be said to have been deliberately indifferent to the need." . . . It would be hard to describe the Canton understanding of deliberate indifference, permitting liability to be premised on obviousness or constructive notice, as anything but objective.

Canton's objective standard, however, is not an appropriate test for determining the liability of prison officials under the Eighth Amendment as interpreted in our cases. Section 1983, which merely provides a cause of action, "contains no state-of-mind requirement independent of that necessary to state a violation of the underlying constitutional right." And while deliberate indifference serves under the Eighth Amendment to ensure that only inflictions of punishment carry liability, the "term was used in the Canton case for the quite different purpose of identifying the threshold for holding a city responsible for the constitutional torts committed by its inadequately trained agents," a purpose the Canton Court found satisfied by a test permitting liability when a municipality disregards "obvious" needs. Needless to say, moreover, considerable conceptual difficulty would attend any search for the subjective state of mind of a governmental entity, as distinct from that of a governmental official. For these reasons, we cannot accept petitioner's argument that Canton compels the conclusion here that a prison official who was unaware of a substantial risk of harm to an inmate may nevertheless be held liable under the Eighth Amendment if the risk was obvious and a reasonable prison official would have noticed it. We are no more persuaded by petitioner's argument that, without an objective test for deliberate indifference, prison officials will be free to ignore obvious dangers to inmates. Under the test we adopt today, an Eighth Amendment claimant need not show that a prison official acted or failed to act believing that harm actually would befall an inmate; it is enough that the official acted or failed to act despite his knowledge of a substantial risk of serious harm. We doubt that a subjective approach will present prison officials with any serious motivation "to take refuge in the zone between 'ignorance of obvious risks' and 'actual knowledge of risks.'" Whether a prison official had the requisite knowledge of a substantial risk is a question of fact subject to demonstration in the usual ways, including inference from circumstantial evidence, cf. Hall 118 (cautioning against "confusing a mental state with the proof of its existence"), and a factfinder may conclude that a prison official knew of a substantial risk from the very fact that the risk was obvious. Cf. LaFave & Scott § 3.7, p. 335 ("If the risk is obvious, so that a reasonable man would realize it, we might well infer that [the defendant] did in fact realize it; but the inference cannot be conclusive, for we know that people are not always conscious of what reasonable people would be conscious of"). For example, if an Eighth Amendment plaintiff presents evidence showing that a substantial risk of inmate attacks was "longstanding, pervasive, well-documented, or expressly noted by prison officials in the past, and the circumstances suggest that the defendant-official being sued had been exposed to information concerning the risk and thus 'must have known' about it, then such evidence could be sufficient to permit a trier of fact to find that the defendant-official had actual knowledge of the risk."

Nor may a prison official escape liability for deliberate indifference by showing that, while he was aware of an obvious, substantial risk to inmate safety, he did not know that the complainant was especially likely to be assaulted by the specific prisoner who eventually committed the assault. The question under the Eighth Amendment is whether prison officials, acting with deliberate indifference, exposed a prisoner to a sufficiently substantial "risk of serious damage to his future health," and it does not matter whether the risk comes from a single source or multiple sources, any more than it matters whether a prisoner faces an risk of attack for reasons personal to him or because all prisoners in his situation face such a risk. See Brief for Respondents 15 (stating that a prisoner can establish exposure to a sufficiently serious risk of harm "by showing that he belongs to an identifiable group of prisoners who are frequently singled out for violent attack by

other inmates"). If, for example, prison officials were aware that inmate "rape was so common and uncontrolled that some potential victims dared not sleep [but] instead . . . would leave their beds and spend the night clinging to the bars nearest the guards' station," it would obviously be irrelevant to liability that the officials could not guess beforehand precisely who would attack whom. Cf. Helling, (observing that the Eighth Amendment requires a remedy for exposure of inmates to "infectious maladies" such as hepatitis and venereal disease "even though the possible infection might not affect all of those exposed"); Commonwealth v. Welansky, 316 Mass. 383, 55 N.E.2d 902 (1944) (affirming conviction for manslaughter under a law requiring reckless or wanton conduct of a nightclub owner who failed to protect patrons from a fire, even though the owner did not know in advance who would light the match that ignited the fire or which patrons would lose their lives); State v. Julius, 185 W. Va. 422, 431-432, 408 S.E.2d 1, 10-11 (1991) (holding that a defendant may be held criminally liable for injury to an unanticipated victim).

Because, however, prison officials who lacked knowledge of a risk cannot be said to have inflicted punishment, it remains open to the officials to prove that they were unaware even of an obvious risk to inmate health or safety. That a trier of fact may infer knowledge from the obvious, in other words, does not mean that it must do so. Prison officials charged with deliberate indifference might show, for example, that they did not know of the underlying facts indicating a sufficiently substantial danger and that they were therefore unaware of a danger, or that they knew the underlying facts but believed (albeit unsoundly) that the risk to which the facts gave rise was insubstantial or nonexistent.

In addition, prison officials who actually knew of a substantial risk to inmate health or safety may be found free from liability if they responded reasonably to the risk, even if the harm ultimately was not averted. A prison official's duty under the Eighth Amendment is to ensure "reasonable safety," a standard that incorporates due regard for prison officials' "unenviable task of keeping dangerous men in safe custody under humane conditions." Whether one puts it in terms of duty or deliberate indifference, prison officials who act reasonably cannot be found liable under the Cruel and Unusual Punishments Clause.

We address, finally, petitioner's argument that a subjective deliberate indifference test will unjustly require prisoners to suffer physical injury before obtaining court-ordered correction of objectively inhumane prison conditions. "It would," indeed, "be odd to deny an injunction to inmates who plainly proved an unsafe, life-threatening condition in their prison on the ground that nothing yet had happened to them." But nothing in the test we adopt today clashes with that common sense.

Petitioner's argument is flawed for the simple reason that "one does not have to await the consummation of threatened injury to obtain preventive relief." Consistently with this principle, a subjective approach to deliberate indifference does not require a prisoner seeking "a remedy for unsafe conditions [to] await a tragic event [such as an] actual assault before obtaining relief."

In a suit such as petitioner's, insofar as it seeks injunctive relief to prevent a substantial risk of serious injury from ripening into actual harm, "the subjective factor, deliberate indifference, should be determined in light of the prison authorities' current attitudes and conduct,": their attitudes and conduct at the time suit is brought and persisting thereafter. An inmate seeking an injunction on the ground that there is "a contemporary violation of a nature likely to continue," United States v. Oregon Medical Society, must adequately plead such a violation; to survive summary judgment, he must come forward with evidence from which it can be inferred that the defendant-officials were at the time suit was filed, and are at the time of summary judgment, knowingly and unreasonably disregarding an objectively intolerable risk of harm, and that they will continue to do so; and finally to establish eligibility for an injunction, the inmate must demonstrate the continuance of that disregard during the remainder of the litigation and into the future. In so doing, the inmate may rely, in the district court's discretion, on developments that postdate the pleadings and pretrial motions, as the defendants may rely on such developments to establish

that the inmate is not entitled to an injunction. If the court finds the Eighth Amendment's subjective and objective requirements satisfied, it may grant appropriate injunctive relief. See Hutto v. Finney, (upholding order designed to halt "an ongoing violation" in prison conditions that included extreme overcrowding, rampant violence, insufficient food, and unsanitary conditions). Of course, a district court should approach issuance of injunctive orders with the usual caution, see Bell v. Wolfish, (warning courts against becoming "enmeshed in the minutiae of prison conditions"), and may, for example, exercise its discretion if appropriate by giving prison officials time to rectify the situation before issuing an injunction.

That prison officials' "current attitudes and conduct," must be assessed in an action for injunctive relief does not mean, of course, that inmates are free to bypass adequate internal prison procedures and bring their health and safety concerns directly to court. "An appeal to the equity jurisdiction conferred on federal district courts is an appeal to the sound discretion which guides the determinations of courts of equity," any litigant making such an appeal must show that the intervention of equity is required. When a prison inmate seeks injunctive relief, a court need not ignore the inmate's failure to take advantage of adequate prison procedures, and an inmate who needlessly bypasses such procedures may properly be compelled to pursue them. Cf. 42 U.S.C. § 1997e (authorizing district courts in § 1983 actions to require inmates to exhaust "such plain, speedy, and effective administrative remedies as are available"). Even apart from the demands of equity, an inmate would be well advised to take advantage of internal prison procedures for resolving inmate grievances. When those procedures produce results, they will typically do so faster than judicial processes can. And even when they do not bring constitutionally required changes, the inmate's task in court will obviously be much easier.

Accordingly, we reject petitioner's arguments and hold that a prison official may be held liable under the Eighth Amendment for denying humane conditions of confinement only if he knows that inmates face a substantial risk of serious harm and disregards that risk by failing to take reasonable measures to abate it.

III

A

Against this backdrop, we consider whether the District Court's disposition of petitioner's complaint, summarily affirmed without briefing by the Court of Appeals for the Seventh Circuit, comports with Eighth Amendment principles. We conclude that the appropriate course is to remand.

In granting summary judgment to respondents on the ground that petitioner had failed to satisfy the Eighth Amendment's subjective requirement, the District Court may have placed decisive weight on petitioner's failure to notify respondents of a risk of harm. That petitioner "never expressed any concern for his safety to any of [respondents],"was the only evidence the District Court cited for its conclusion that there was no genuine dispute about respondents' assertion that they "had no knowledge of any potential danger to [petitioner]," ibid. But with respect to each of petitioner's claims, for damages and for injunctive relief, the failure to give advance notice is not dispositive. Petitioner may establish respondents' awareness by reliance on any relevant evidence.

The summary judgment record does not so clearly establish respondent's entitlement to judgment as a matter of law on the issue of subjective knowledge that we can simply assume the absence of error below. For example, in papers filed in opposition to respondents' summary-judgment motion, petitioner pointed to respondents' admission that petitioner is a "non-violent" transsexual who, because of petitioner's "youth and feminine appearance" is "likely to experience a great deal of sexual pressure" in prison. And petitioner recounted a statement by one of the respondents, then warden of the penitentiary in Lewisburg, Pennsylvania, who told petitioner that there was "a high probability that [petitioner] could not safely function at USP-Lewisburg," an incident confirmed in a published District Court opinion. See Farmer v. Carlson, 685 F. Supp., at 1342; ("Clearly, plac-

ing plaintiff, a twenty-one year old transsexual, into the general population at [USP-]Lewisburg, a [high-]security institution, could pose a significant threat to internal security in general and to plaintiff in particular").

* * *

B

Responents urge us to affirm for reasons not relied on below, but neither of their contentions is so clearly correct as to justify affirmance.

With respect to petitioner's damages claim, respondents argue that the officials sued in their individual capacities (officials at FCI-Oxford and the Bureau of Prisons North Central Region office), were alleged to be liable only for their transfer of petitioner from FCI-Oxford to USP-Terre Haute, whereas petitioner "nowhere alleges any reason for believing that these officials, who had no direct responsibility for administering the Terre Haute institution, would have had knowledge of conditions within that institution regarding danger to transsexual inmates." But petitioner's Rule 56(f) motion alleged just that. Though respondents suggest here that petitioner offered no factual basis for that assertion, that is not a ground on which they chose to oppose petitioner's Rule 56(f) motion below and, in any event, is a matter for the exercise of the District Court's judgment, not ours. Finally, to the extent respondents seek affirmance here on the ground that officials at FCI-Oxford and the Bureau of Prisons regional office had no power to control prisoner placement at Terre Haute, the record gives at least a suggestion to the contrary; the affidavit of one respondent, the warden of USP-Terre Haute, states that after having been at USP-Terre Haute for about a month petitioner was placed in administrative segregation "pursuant to directive from the North Central Regional Office" and a "request . . . by staff at FCI-Oxford." Accordingly, though we do not reject respondents' arguments about petitioner's claim for damages, the record does not permit us to accept them as a basis for affirmance when they were not relied upon below.

Respondents are free to develop this line of argument on remand.

With respect to petitioner's claim for injunctive relief, respondents argued in their merits brief that the claim was "foreclosed by [petitioner's] assignment to administrative detention status because of his high-risk HIV-positive condition, . . . as well as by the absence of any allegation . . . that administrative detention status poses any continuing threat of physical injury to him." At oral argument, however, the Deputy Solicitor General informed us that petitioner was no longer in administrative detention, having been placed in the general prison population of a medium-security prison. He suggested that affirmance was nevertheless proper because "there is no present threat" that petitioner will be placed in a setting where he would face a "continuing threat of physical injury," but this argument turns on facts about the likelihood of a transfer that the District Court is far better placed to evaluate than we are. We leave it to respondents to present this point on remand.

IV

The judgment of the Court of Appeals is vacated, and the case is remanded for further proceedings consistent with this opinion.

JUSTICE BLACKMUN, concurring.

I agree with Justice Stevens that inhumane prison conditions violate the Eighth Amendment even if no prison official has an improper, subjective state of mind. This Court's holding in Wilson v. Seiter, to the effect that barbaric prison conditions may be beyond the reach of the Eighth Amendment if no prison official can be deemed individually culpable, in my view is insupportable in principle and is inconsistent with our precedents interpreting the Cruel and Unusual Punishments Clause. Whether the Constitution has been violated "should turn on the character of the punishment rather than the motivation of the individual who inflicted it." Wilson v. Seiter should be overruled.

Although I do not go along with the Court's reliance on Wilson in defining the "deliberate indifference" standard, I join the Court's opinion, because it creates no new obstacles for prison inmates to overcome, and it sends a clear message to prison officials that their affirmative duty under the Constitution to provide for the safety of inmates is not to be taken lightly. Under the Court's decision today, prison officials may be held liable for failure to remedy a risk so obvious and substantial that the officials must have known about it, see ante, at 16, and prisoners need not "await a tragic event [such as an] actual assault before obtaining relief."

Petitioner is a transsexual who is currently serving a 20-year sentence in an all-male federal prison for credit-card fraud. Although a biological male, petitioner has undergone treatment for silicone breast implants and unsuccessful surgery to have his testicles removed. Despite his overtly feminine characteristics, and his previous segregation at a different federal prison because of safety concerns, prison officials at the United States Penitentiary in Terre Haute, Indiana, housed him in the general population of that maximum-security prison. Less than two weeks later, petitioner was brutally beaten and raped by another inmate in petitioner's cell.

Homosexual rape or other violence among prison inmates serves absolutely no penological purpose. "Such brutality is the equivalent of torture, and is offensive to any modern standard of human dignity." The horrors experienced by many young inmates, particularly those who, like petitioner, are convicted of nonviolent offenses, border on the unimaginable. Prison rape not only threatens the lives of those who fall prey to their aggressors, but is potentially devastating to the human spirit. Shame, depression, and a shattering loss of self-esteem, accompany the perpetual terror the victim thereafter must endure. See Note, Rape in Prison and AIDS: A Challenge for the Eighth Amendment Framework of Wilson v. Seiter, 44 Stan. L. Rev. 1541, 1545 (1992). Unable to fend for himself without the protection of prison officials, the victim finds himself at the mercy of larger, stronger, and ruthless inmates. Although formally sentenced to a term of incarceration, many inmates discover that their punishment, even for nonviolent offenses like credit-card fraud or tax evasion, degenerates into a reign of terror unmitigated by the protection supposedly afforded by prison officials.

The fact that our prisons are badly over-crowded and understaffed may well explain many of the shortcomings of our penal systems. But our Constitution sets minimal standards governing the administration of punishment in this country, and thus it is no answer to the complaints of the brutalized inmate that the resources are unavailable to protect him from what, in reality, is nothing less than torture. I stated in dissent in United States v. Bailey:

It is society's responsibility to protect the life and health of its prisoners. "When a sheriff or a marshall [sic] takes a man from the courthouse in a prison van and transports him to confinement for two or three or ten years, this is our act. We have tolled the bell for him. And whether we like it or not, we have made him our collective responsibility. We are free to do something about him; he is not."

The Court in Wilson v. Seiter, held that any pain and suffering endured by a prisoner which is not formally a part of his sentence—no matter how severe or unnecessary—will not be held violative of the Cruel and Unusual Punishments Clause unless the prisoner establishes that some prison official intended the harm. The Court justified this remarkable conclusion by asserting that only pain that is intended by a state actor to be punishment is punishment. See Wilson, ("The source of the intent requirement is not the predilections of this Court, but the Eighth Amendment itself, which bans only cruel and unusual punishment. If the pain inflicted is not formally meted out as punishment by the statute or the sentencing judge, some mental element must be attributed to the inflicting officer before it can qualify").

The Court's analysis is fundamentally misguided; indeed it defies common sense. "Punishment" does not necessarily imply a culpable state of mind on the part of an identifiable punisher. A prisoner may experience punishment when he suffers "severe, rough, or disastrous treatment," see, e.g., Webster's Third New International Dictionary 1843 (1961), regardless of whether a state actor

intended the cruel treatment to chastise or deter. See also Webster's New International Dictionary of the English Language 1736 (1923) (defining punishment as "any pain, suffering, or loss inflicted on or suffered by a person because of a crime or evil-doing") (emphasis supplied); cf. Wilson, 501 U.S., at 300, quoting Duckworth v. Franzen, 780 F.2d 645, 652 (CA7 1985), cert. denied, 479 U.S. 816, 93 L. Ed. 2d 28, 107 S. Ct. 71 (1986) ("The infliction of punishment is a deliberate act intended to chastise or deter").

The Court's unduly narrow definition of punishment blinds it to the reality of prison life. Consider, for example, a situation in which one individual is sentenced to a period of confinement at a relatively safe, well-managed prison, complete with tennis courts and cable television, while another is sentenced to a prison characterized by rampant violence and terror. Under such circumstances, it is natural to say that the latter individual was subjected to a more extreme punishment. It matters little that the sentencing judge did not specify to which prison the individuals would be sent; nor is it relevant that the prison officials did not intend either individual to suffer any attack. The conditions of confinement, whatever the reason for them, resulted in differing punishment for the two convicts.

Wilson's myopic focus on the intentions of prison officials is also mistaken. Where a legislature refuses to fund a prison adequately, the resulting barbaric conditions should not be immune from constitutional scrutiny simply because no prison official acted culpably. Wilson failed to recognize that "state-sanctioned punishment consists not so much of specific acts attributable to individual state officials, but more of a cumulative agglomeration of action (and inaction) on an institutional level." The responsibility for subminimal conditions in any prison inevitably is diffuse, and often borne, at least in part, by the legislature. Yet, regardless of what state actor or institution caused the harm and with what intent, the experience of the inmate is the same. A punishment is simply no less cruel or unusual because its harm is unintended. In view of this obvious fact, there is no reason to believe that, in adopting the Eighth Amendment, the Framers intended to prohibit cruel and unusual punishments only when they were inflicted intentionally. As Judge Noonan has observed:

> The Framers were familiar from their wartime experience of British prisons with the kind of cruel punishment administered by a warden with the mentality of a Captain Bligh. But they were also familiar with the cruelty that came from bureaucratic indifference to the conditions of confinement. The Framers understood that cruel and unusual punishment can be administered by the failure of those in charge to give heed to the impact of their actions on those within their care.

Before Wilson, it was assumed, if not established, that the conditions of confinement are themselves part of the punishment, even if not specifically "meted out" by a statute or judge. We examined only the objective severity of the conditions of confinement in the pre-Wilson cases, not the subjective intent of government officials, as we found that "an express intent to inflict unnecessary pain is not required. . . . Harsh 'conditions of confinement' may constitute cruel and unusual punishment unless such conditions 'are part of the penalty that criminal offenders pay for their offenses against society.'" This initial approach, which employed an objective standard to chart the boundaries of the Eighth Amendment, reflected the practical reality that "intent simply is not very meaningful when considering a challenge to an institution, such as a prison system." It also, however, demonstrated a commitment to the principles underlying the Eighth Amendment. The Cruel and Unusual Punishments Clause was not adopted to protect prison officials with arguably benign intentions from lawsuits. The Eighth Amendment guarantees each prisoner that reasonable measures will be taken to ensure his safety. Where a prisoner can prove that no such reasonable steps were taken and, as a result, he experienced severe pain or suffering without any penological justification, the Eighth Amendment is violated regardless of whether there is an easily identifiable wrongdoer with poor intentions.

II

Though I believe Wilson v. Seiter should be overruled, and disagree with the Court's reliance upon that case in defining the "deliberate indifference" standard, I nonetheless join the Court's opinion. Petitioner never challenged this Court's holding in Wilson or sought reconsideration of the theory upon which that decision is based. More importantly, the Court's opinion does not extend Wilson beyond its ill-conceived boundaries or erect any new obstacles for prison inmates to overcome in seeking to remedy cruel and unusual conditions of confinement. The Court specifically recognizes that "having incarcerated people with demonstrated proclivities for criminally antisocial and, in many cases, violent conduct, [and] having stripped them of virtually every means of self-protection and foreclosed their access to outside aid, the government and its officials are not free to let the state of nature take its course." The Court further acknowledges that prison rape is not constitutionally tolerable, see ibid. ("being violently assaulted in prison is simply not 'part of the penalty that criminal offenders pay for their offenses against society'"), and it clearly states that prisoners can obtain relief before being victimized, ("a subjective approach to deliberate indifference does not require a prisoner seeking 'a remedy for unsafe conditions [to] await a tragic event [such as an] actual assault before obtaining relief'"). Finally, under the Court's holding, prison officials may be held liable for failure to remedy a risk of harm so obvious and substantial that the prison officials must have known about it. The opinion's clear message is that prison officials must fulfill their affirmative duty under the Constitution to prevent inmate assault, including prison rape, or otherwise face a serious risk of being held liable for damages, or being required by a court to rectify the hazardous conditions. As much as is possible within the constraints of Wilson v. Seiter, the Court seeks to ensure that the conditions in our Nation's prisons in fact comport with the "contemporary standard of decency" required by the Eighth Amendment short of overruling Wilson v. Seiter, the Court could do no better.

* * *

JUSTICE THOMAS, concurring in the judgment.

Prisons are necessarily dangerous places; they house society's most antisocial and violent people in close proximity with one another. Regrettably, "some level of brutality and sexual aggression among [prisoners] is inevitable no matter what the guards do . . . unless all prisoners are locked in their cells 24 hours a day and sedated." Today, in an attempt to rectify such unfortunate conditions, the Court further refines the "National Code of Prison Regulation," otherwise known as the Cruel and Unusual Punishments Clause.

I adhere to my belief, expressed in Hudson and Helling v. McKinney, that "judges or juries—but not jailers—impose 'punishment.'" "Punishment," from the time of the Founding through the present day, "has always meant a 'fine, penalty, or confinement inflicted upon a person by the authority of the law and the judgment and sentence of a court, for some crime or offense committed by him.'" Conditions of confinement are not punishment in any recognized sense of the term, unless imposed as part of a sentence. As an original matter, therefore, this case would be an easy one for me: because the unfortunate attack that befell petitioner was not part of his sentence, it did not constitute "punishment" under the Eighth Amendment.

When approaching this case, however, we do not write on a clean slate. Beginning with Estelle v. Gamble, the Court's prison condition jurisprudence has been guided, not by the text of the Constitution, but rather by "evolving standards of decency that mark the progress of a maturing society." I continue to doubt the legitimacy of that mode of constitutional decisionmaking, the logical result of which, in this context, is to transform federal judges into superintendents of prison conditions nationwide. Although Estelle loosed the Eighth Amendment from its historical moorings, the Court is now unwilling to accept the full consequences of its decision and therefore resorts to the "subjective" (state of mind) component of post-Estelle Eighth Amendment analysis in an attempt to contain what might otherwise be unbounded liability for prison officials under the Cruel and Unusual Punishments Clause.

Although I disagree with the constitutional predicate of the Court's analysis, I share the Court's view that petitioner's theory of liability—that a prison official can be held liable for risks to prisoner safety of which he was ignorant but should have known—fails under even "a straightforward application of Estelle." In adopting the "deliberate indifference" standard for challenges to prison conditions, Estelle held that mere "inadvertence" or "negligence" does not violate the Eighth Amendment. "From the outset, thus, we specified that the Eighth Amendment does not apply to every deprivation, or even every unnecessary deprivation, suffered by a prisoner, but only that narrow class of deprivations involving 'serious' injury inflicted by prison officials acting with a culpable state of mind." We reiterated this understanding in Wilson v. Seiter, holding that "mere negligence" does not constitute deliberate indifference under Estelle. Petitioner's suggested "should have known" standard is nothing but a negligence standard, as the Court's discussion implicitly assumes. Thus, even under Estelle, petitioner's theory of liability necessarily fails.

The question remains, however, what state of mind is sufficient to constitute deliberate indifference under Estelle. Given my serious doubts concerning the correctness of Estelle in extending the Eighth Amendment to cover challenges to conditions of confinement, I believe the scope of the Estelle "right" should be confined as narrowly as possible. In Wilson, the Court has already held that the highest subjective standard known to our Eighth Amendment jurisprudence—"malicious and sadistic" action "for the very purpose of causing harm,"—"does not apply to prison conditions cases." The Court today adopts the next highest level of subjective intent, actual knowledge of the type sufficient to constitute recklessness in the criminal law, noting that "due regard" is appropriate "for prison officials' 'unenviable task of keeping dangerous men in safe custody under humane conditions.'"

Even though the Court takes a step in the right direction by adopting a restrictive definition of deliberate indifference, I cannot join the Court's opinion. For the reasons expressed more fully in my dissenting opinions in Hudson and Helling, I remain unwilling to subscribe to the view, adopted by ipse dixit in Estelle, that the Eighth Amendment regulates prison conditions not imposed as part of a sentence. Indeed, "were the issue squarely presented, . . . I might vote to overrule Estelle." Nonetheless, the issue is not squarely presented in this case. Respondents have not asked us to revisit Estelle, and no one has briefed or argued the question. In addition to these prudential concerns, stare decisis counsels hesitation in overruling dubious precedents. See ibid. For these reasons, I concur in the Court's judgment. In doing so, however, I remain hopeful that in a proper case the Court will reconsider Estelle in light of the constitutional text and history.

Cases Relating to Chapter 13

The Prison Litigation Reform Act

BOOTH
v.
CHURNER

**532 U.S. 731; 121 S. Ct. 1819;
149 L. Ed. 2d 958 (2001)**
(Footnotes and citations omitted)

JUSTICE SOUTER delivered the opinion of the Court.

The Prison Litigation Reform Act of 1995 amended 42 U.S.C. §1997e(a), which now requires a prisoner to exhaust "such administrative remedies as are available" before suing over prison conditions. The question is whether an inmate seeking only money damages must complete a prison administrative process that could provide some sort of relief on the complaint stated, but no money. We hold that he must.

* * *

The meaning of the phrase "administrative remedies . . . available" is the crux of the case, and up to a point the parties approach it with agreement. Neither of them denies that some redress for a wrong is presupposed by the statute's requirement of an "available" "remed[y]"; neither argues that exhaustion is required where the relevant administrative procedure lacks authority to provide any relief or to take any action whatsoever in response to a complaint. The dispute here, then, comes down to whether or not a remedial scheme is "available" where, as in Pennsylvania, the administrative process has authority to take some action in response to a complaint, but not the remedial action an inmate demands to the exclusion of all other forms of redress.

In seeking the congressional intent, the parties urge us to give weight to practical considerations, among others, and at first glance Booth's position holds some intuitive appeal. Although requiring an inmate to exhaust prison grievance procedures will probably obviate some litigation when the administrative tribunal can award at least some of the relief sought, Booth argues that when the prison's process simply cannot satisfy the inmate's sole demand, the odds of keeping the matter out of court are slim. * * * . The prisoner would be clearly burdened, while the government would obtain little or no value in return. The respondents, however, also have something to say. They argue that requiring exhaustion in these circumstances would produce administrative results that would satisfy at least some inmates who start out asking for nothing but money, since the very fact of being heard and prompting administrative change can mollify passions even when nothing ends up in the pocket. And one may suppose that the administrative process itself would filter out some frivolous claims and foster better-prepared litigation once a dispute did move to the courtroom, even absent formal factfinding. Although we have not accorded much weight to these possibilities in the past, * * * Congress, as we explain below, may well have thought we were shortsighted. * * * In any event, the practical arguments for exhaustion at least suffice to refute Booth's claim that no policy considerations justify respondents' position. The upshot is that pragmatism is inconclusive.

Each of the parties also says that the plain meaning of the words "remedies" and "available" in the phrase "such administrative remedies . . . available" is controlling. But as it turns out both of them quote some of the same dictionary definitions of "available" "remedies," and neither comes up with anything conclusive. Booth says the term "remedy" means a procedure that provides redress for wrong or enforcement of a right, and "available" means having sufficient power to achieve an end sought. * * * So far so good, but Booth then claims to be able to infer with particularity that when a prisoner demands money damages as the sole means to compensate his injuries, a grievance system without that relief offers no "available" "remed[y]." The general definitions, however, just do not entail such a specific conclusion.

It strikes us that the same definitions get the respondent corrections officers and their *amicus* the United States closer to firm ground for their assertion that the phrase "such administrative remedies as are available" naturally requires a prisoner to exhaust the grievance procedures offered, whether or not the possible responses cover the specific relief the prisoner demands. * * *. The United States tracks Booth in citing Webster's Third New International Dictionary to define "remedy" as "the legal means to recover a right or to prevent or obtain redress for a wrong" and "available" as "capable of use for the accomplishment of a purpose." * * * But this exercise in isolated definition is ultimately inconclusive, for, depending on where one looks, "remedy" can mean either specific relief obtainable at the end of a process of seeking redress, or the process itself, the procedural avenue leading to some relief. * * *

We find clearer pointers toward the congressional objective in two considerations, the first being the broader statutory context in which "available" "remedies" are mentioned. The entire modifying clause in which the words occur is this: "until such administrative remedies as are available have been exhausted." The "available" "remed[y]" must be "exhausted" before a complaint under §1983 may be entertained. While the modifier "available" requires the possibility of some relief for the action complained of (as

the parties agree), the word "exhausted" has a decidedly procedural emphasis. It makes sense only in referring to the procedural means, not the particular relief ordered. It would, for example, be very strange usage to say that a prisoner must "exhaust" an administrative order reassigning an abusive guard before a prisoner could go to court and ask for something else; or to say (in States that award money damages administratively) that a prisoner must "exhaust" his damages award before going to court for more. How would he "exhaust" a transfer of personnel? Would he have to spend the money to "exhaust" the monetary relief given him? It makes no sense to demand that someone exhaust "such administrative [redress]" as is available; one "exhausts" processes, not forms of relief, and the statute provides that one must.

A second consideration, statutory history, confirms the suggestion that Congress meant to require procedural exhaustion regardless of the fit between a prisoner's prayer for relief and the administrative remedies possible. Before §1997e(a) was amended by the Act of 1995, a court had discretion (though no obligation) to require a state inmate to exhaust "such . . . remedies as are available," but only if those remedies were "plain, speedy, and effective." * * * That scheme, however, is now a thing of the past, for the amendments eliminated both the discretion to dispense with administrative exhaustion and the condition that the remedy be "plain, speedy, and effective" before exhaustion could be required.

* * *

When Congress replaced the text of the statute as construed in McCarthy with the exhaustion requirement at issue today, it presumably understood that under McCarthy the term "effective" in the former §1997e(a) eliminated the possibility of requiring exhaustion of administrative remedies when an inmate sought only monetary relief and the administrative process offered none. It has to be significant that Congress removed the very term we had previously emphasized in reaching the result Booth now seeks, and the fair inference to be drawn is that Congress meant to preclude the McCarthy result. Congress's imposition of an obviously broader exhaustion requirement makes it highly implausible that it meant to give prisoners a strong inducement to skip the administrative process simply by limiting prayers for relief to money damages not offered through administrative grievance mechanisms.

Thus, we think that Congress has mandated exhaustion clearly enough, regardless of the relief offered through administrative procedures.

It is so ordered.

PORTER
v.
NUSSLE
534 U.S. 516; 122 S. Ct. 983;
152 L. Ed. 2d 12 (2002)
(Footnotes and citations omitted)

* * *

This case concerns the obligation of prisoners who claim denial of their federal rights while incarcerated to exhaust prison grievance procedures before seeking judicial relief. Plaintiff-respondent Ronald Nussle, an inmate in a Connecticut prison, brought directly to court, without filing an inmate grievance, a complaint charging that corrections officers singled him out for a severe beating, in violation of the Eighth Amendment's ban on "cruel and unusual punishments." Nussle bypassed the grievance procedure despite a provision of the Prison Litigation Reform Act [PLRA] of 1995 * * * that directs: "No action shall be brought with respect to prison conditions under section 1983 of this title, or any other Federal law, by a prisoner confined in any jail, prison, or other correctional facility until such administrative remedies as are available are exhausted."

* * *

Ordinarily, plaintiffs pursuing civil rights claims under 42 U.S.C. §1983 need not exhaust administrative remedies before filing suit in court. * * * Prisoner suits alleging constitutional deprivations while incarcerated once fell within this general rule. * * *

In 1980, however, Congress introduced an exhaustion prescription for suits initiated by state prisoners. See Civil Rights of Institutionalized Persons Act, 94 Stat. 352, as amended, 42 U.S.C. § 1997e (1994 ed.). This measure authorized district courts to stay a state prisoner's §1983 action "for a period not to exceed 180 days" while the prisoner exhausted available "plain, speedy, and effective administrative remedies." §1997e(a)(1). Exhaustion under the 1980 prescription was in large part discretionary; it could be ordered only if the State's prison grievance system met specified federal standards, and even then, only if, in the particular case, the court believed the requirement "appropriate and in the interests of justice." §§1997e(a) and (b). We described this provision as a "limited exhaustion requirement" in McCarthy v. Madigan, * * * and thought it inapplicable to prisoner suits for damages when monetary relief was unavailable through the prison grievance system.

In 1995, as part of the PLRA, Congress invigorated the exhaustion prescription. The revised exhaustion provision, titled "Suits by prisoners," states: "No action shall be brought with respect to prison conditions under section 1983 of this title, or any other Federal law, by a prisoner confined in any jail, prison, or other correctional facility until such administrative remedies as are available are exhausted." * * *

The current exhaustion provision differs markedly from its predecessor. Once within the discretion of the district court, exhaustion in cases covered by § 1997e(a) is now mandatory. * * * All "available" remedies must now be exhausted; those remedies need not meet federal standards, nor must they be "plain, speedy, and effective." * * * Even when the prisoner seeks relief not available in grievance proceedings, notably money damages, exhaustion is a prerequisite to suit. * * * And unlike the previous provision, which encompassed only §1983 suits, exhaustion is now required for all "actions . . . brought with respect to prison conditions," whether under §1983 or "any other Federal law." * * * Thus federal prisoners suing under Bivens v. Six Unknown Fed. Narcotics Agents, * * * must first exhaust inmate grievance procedures just as state prisoners must exhaust administrative processes prior to instituting a §1983 suit.

Beyond doubt, Congress enacted §1997e(a) to reduce the quantity and improve the quality of prisoner suits; to this purpose, Congress afforded corrections officials time and opportunity to address complaints internally before allowing the initiation of a federal case. In some instances, corrective action taken in response to an inmate's grievance might improve prison administration and satisfy the inmate, thereby obviating the need for litigation. * * * In other instances, the internal review might "filter out some frivolous claims." * * * And for cases ultimately brought to court, adjudication could be facilitated by an administrative record that clarifies the contours of the controversy. * * *.

Congress described the cases covered by §1997e(a)'s exhaustion requirement as "actions . . . brought with respect to prison conditions." Nussle's case requires us to determine what the §1997e(a) term "prison conditions" means, given Congress' failure to define the term in the text of the exhaustion provision. * * * We are guided in this endeavor by the PLRA's text and context, and by our prior decisions relating to "suits by prisoners," §1997e.* * *

We did not "quarrel with" the prisoner's assertion in McCarthy that "the most natural reading of the phrase 'challenging conditions of confinement,' when viewed in isolation, would not include suits seeking relief from isolated episodes of unconstitutional conduct." * * * We nonetheless concluded that the petitioner's argument failed upon reading the phrase "in its proper context." * * * We found no suggestion in §636(b)(1)(B) that Congress meant to divide prisoner petitions "into subcategories." * * * "On the contrary," we observed, "when the relevant section is read in its entirety, it suggests that Congress intended to authorize the nonconsensual reference of *all* prisoner petitions to a magistrate." * * * The Federal Magistrates Act, we noted, covers actions of two kinds: challenges to "conditions of confinement"; and "applica-

tions for habeas corpus relief." * * * Congress, we concluded, "intended to include in their entirety those two primary categories of suits brought by prisoners." * * *

"Just three years before [§636(b)(1)(B)] was drafted," we explained in McCarthy, "our opinion in Preiser v. Rodriguez, * * * had described [the] two broad categories of prisoner petitions: (1) those challenging the fact or duration of confinement itself; and (2) those challenging the conditions of confinement." * * * Preiser v. Rodriguez,* * * left no doubt, we further stated in McCarthy, that "the latter category unambiguously embraced the kind of single episode cases that petitioner's construction would exclude." * * *

As in McCarthy, we here read the term "prison conditions" not in isolation, but "in its proper context." * * * The PLRA exhaustion provision is captioned "Suits by prisoners," * * *; this unqualified heading scarcely aids the argument that Congress meant to bisect the universe of prisoner suits. * * *

This Court generally "presumes that Congress expects its statutes to be read in conformity with the Court's precedents." * * * That presumption, and the PLRA's dominant concern to promote administrative redress, filter out groundless claims, and foster better prepared litigation of claims aired in court, * * * persuade us that §1997e(a)'s key words "prison conditions" are properly read through the lens of McCarthy and Preiser. Those decisions tug strongly away from classifying suits about prison guards' use of excessive force, one or many times, as anything other than actions "with respect to prison conditions."

* * *

For the reasons stated, we hold that the PLRA's exhaustion requirement applies to all inmate suits about prison life, whether they involve general circumstances or particular episodes, and whether they allege excessive force or some other wrong. * * *

Cases Relating to Chapter 14

Human Rights of Prisoners

SOERING

v.

UNITED KINGDOM EUROPEAN COURT OF HUMAN RIGHTS

11 EHRR 439 (1989)
[Most citations and footnotes omitted]

FACTS:

* * *

11. The applicant, Mr. Jens Soering, was born on 1 August 1966 and is a German national. He is currently detained in prison in England pending extradition to the United States of America to face charges of murder in the Commonwealth of Virginia.

12. The homicides in question were committed in Bedford County, Virginia, in March 1985. The victims, William Reginald Haysom (aged 72) and Nancy Astor Haysom (aged 53), were the parents of the applicant's girlfriend, Elizabeth Haysom, who is a Canadian national. Death in each case was the result of multiple and massive stab and slash wounds to the neck, throat and body. At the time the applicant and Elizabeth Haysom, aged 18 and 20 respectively, were students at the University of Virginia. They disappeared together from Virginia in October 1985, but were arrested in England in April 1986 in connection with cheque fraud.

13. The applicant was interviewed in England between 5 and 8 June 1986 by a police investigator from the Sheriff's Department of Bedford County. In a sworn affidavit dated 24 July 1986 the investigator recorded the applicant as having admitted the killings in his presence and in that of two United Kingdom police officers. The applicant had stated that he was in love with Miss Haysom but that her parents were opposed to the relationship. He and Miss Haysom had therefore planned to kill them. They rented a car in Charlottesville and travelled to Washington where they set up an alibi. The applicant then went to the parents' house, discussed the relationship with them and, when they told him they would do anything to prevent it, a row developed during which he killed them with a knife.

On 13 June 1986 a grand jury of the Circuit Court of Bedford County indicted him on charges of murdering the Haysom parents. The charges alleged capital murder of both of them and the separate non-capital murders of each.

14. On 11 August 1986 the Government of the United States of America requested the applicant's and Miss Haysom's extradition under the terms of the Extradition Treaty of 1972 between the United States and the United Kingdom. On 12 September a Magistrate at Bow Street Magistrates' Court was required by the Secretary of State for Home Affairs to issue a warrant for the applicant's arrest under the provisions of section 8 of the Extradition Act 1870. The applicant was subsequently arrested on 30 December at HM Prison Chelmsford after serving a prison sentence for cheque fraud.

15. On 29 October 1986 the British Embassy in Washington addressed a request to the United States' authorities in the following terms:

'Because the death penalty has been abolished in Great Britain, the Embassy has been instructed to seek an assurance, in accordance with the terms of . . . the Extradition Treaty, that, in the event of Mr. Soering being surrendered and being convicted of the crimes for which he has been indicted . . . , the death penalty, if imposed, will not be carried out.

Should it not be possible on constitutional grounds for the United States Government to give such an assurance, the United Kingdom authorities ask that the United States Government undertake to recommend to the appropriate authorities that the death penalty should not be imposed or, if imposed, should not be executed.'

16. On 30 December 1986 the applicant was interviewed in prison by a German prosecutor (Staatsanwalt) from Bonn. In a sworn witness statement the prosecutor recorded the applicant as having said, inter alia, that 'he had never had the intention of killing Mr. and Mrs. Haysom and . . . he could only remember having inflicted wounds at the neck on Mr. and Mrs. Haysom which must have had something to do with their dying later'; and that in the immediately preceding days 'there had been no talk whatsoever [between him and Elizabeth Haysom] about killing Elizabeth's parents.' The prosecutor also referred to documents which had been put at his disposal, for example the statements made by the applicant to the American police investigagor, the autopsy reports and two psychiatric reports on the applicant.

On 11 February 1987 the local court in Bonn issued a warrant for the applicant's arrest in respect of the alleged murders. On 11 March the Government of the Federal Republic of Germany requested his extradition to the Federal Republic under the Extradition Treaty of 1872 between the Federal Republic and the United Kingdom. The Secretary of State was then advised by the Director of Public Prosecutions that, although the German request contained proof that German courts had jurisdiction to try the applicant, the evidence submitted, since it consisted solely of the admissions made by the appli-

cant to the Bonn prosecutor in the absence of a caution, did not amount to a prima facie case against him and that a magistrate would not be able under the Extradition Act 1870 to commit him to await extradition to Germany on the strength of admissions obtained in such circumstances.

17. In a letter dated 20 April 1987 to the Director of the Office of International Affairs, Criminal Division, United States Department of Justice, the Attorney for Bedford County, Virginia (Mr. James W. Updike Jr.) stated that, on the assumption that the applicant could not be tried in Germany on the basis of admissions alone, there was no means of compelling witnesses from the United States to appear in a criminal court in Germany. On 23 April the United States, by diplomatic note, requested the applicant's extradition to the United States in preference to the Federal Republic of Germany.

18. On 8 May 1987 Elizabeth Haysom was surrendered for extradition to the United States. After pleading guilty on 22 August as an accessory to the murder of her parents, she was sentenced on 6 October to 90 years' imprisonment (45 years on each count of murder).

19. On 20 May 1987 the Government of the United Kingdom informed the Federal Republic of Germany that the United States had earlier 'submitted a request, supported by prima facie evidence, for the extradition of Mr. Soering.' The United Kingdom Government notified the Federal Republic that it had 'concluded that, having regard to all the circumstances of the case, the court should continue to consider in the normal way the United States' request.' It further indicated that it had sought an assurance from the United States' authorities on the question of the death penalty and that 'in the event that the court commits Mr. Soering, his surrender to the United States' authorities would be subject to the receipt of satisfactory assurances on this matter.'

20. On 1 June 1987 Mr. Updike swore an affidavit in his capacity as Attorney for Bedford County, in which he certified as follows:

I hereby certify that should Jens Soering be convicted of the offence of capital murder as charged in Bedford County, Virginia . . . a representation will be made in the name of the United Kingdom to the judge at the time of sentencing that it is the wish of the United Kingdom that the death penalty should not be imposed or carried out.

This assurance was transmitted to the United Kingdom Government under cover of a diplomatic note on 8 June. It was repeated in the same terms in a further affidavit from Mr. Updike sworn on 16 February 1988 and forwarded to the United Kingdom by diplomatic note on 17 May 1988. In the same note the Federal Government of the United States undertook to ensure that the commitment of the appropriate authorities of the Commonwealth of Virginia to make representations on behalf of the United Kingdom would be honoured.

During the course of the present proceedings the Virginia authorities have informed the United Kingdom Government that Mr. Updike was not planning to provide any further assurances and intended to seek the death penalty in Mr. Soering's case because the evidence, in his determination, supported such action.

21. On 16 June 1987 at the Bow Street Magistrates' Court committal proceedings took place before the Chief Stipendiary Magistrate.

The Government of the United States adduced evidence that on the night of 30 March 1985 the applicant killed William and Nancy Haysom at their home in Bedford County, Virginia. In particular, evidence was given of the applicant's own admissions as recorded in the affidavit of the Bedford County police investigator.

On behalf of the applicant psychiatric evidence was adduced from a consultant forensic psychiatrist (report dated 15 December 1986 by Dr. Henrietta Bullard) that he was immature and inexperienced and had lost his personal identity in a symbiotic relationship with his girlfriend—a powerful, persuasive and disturbed young woman. The psychiatric report concluded:

There existed between Miss Haysom and Soering a "folie a deux," in which the most disturbed partner was Miss Haysom. . . .

At the time of the offence, it is my opinion that Jens Soering was suffering from [such] an abnormality of mind due to inherent caus-

es as substantially impaired his mental responsibility for his acts. The psychiatric syndrome referred to as "folie a deux" is a well-recognised state of mind where one partner is suggestible to the extent that he or she believes in the psychotic delusions of the other. The degree of disturbance of Miss Haysom borders on the psychotic and, over the course of many months, she was able to persuade Soering that he might have to kill her parents for she and him to survive as a couple. . . . Miss Haysom had a stupefying and mesmeric effect on Soering which led to an abnormal psychological state in which he became unable to think rationally or question the absurdities in Miss Haysom's view of her life and the influence of her parents. . . .

In conclusion, it is my opinion that, at the time of the offences, Soering was suffering from an abnormality of mind which, in this country, would constitute a defence of "not guilty to murder but guilty of manslaughter."

Dr. Bullard's conclusions were substantially the same as those contained in an earlier psychiatric report (dated 11 December 1986 by Dr. John R. Hamilton, Medical Director of Broadmoor Hospital), which was not however put before the Magistrates' Court.

The Chief Magistrate found that the evidence of Dr. Bullard was not relevant to any issue that he had to decide and committed the applicant to await the Secretary of State's order for his return to the United States.

22. On 29 June 1987 Mr. Soering applied to the Divisional Court for a writ of habeas corpus in respect of his committal and for leave to apply for judicial review. On 11 December both applications were refused by the Divisional Court (Lloyd LJ and Macpherson J).

In support of his application for leave to apply for judicial review, Mr. Soering had submitted that the assurance received from the United States' authorities was so worthless that no reasonable Secretary of State could regard it as satisfactory under Article IV of the Extradition Treaty between the United Kingdom and the United States. In his judgment Lloyd LJ agreed that the assurance leaves something to be desired:

Article IV of the Treaty contemplates an assurance that the death penalty will not be carried out. That must presumably mean an assurance by or on behalf of the Executive Branch of Government, which in this case would be the Governor of the Commonwealth of Virginia. The certificate sworn by Mr. Updike, far from being an assurance on behalf of the Executive, is nothing more than an undertaking to make representations on behalf of the United Kingdom to the judge. I cannot believe that this is what was intended when the Treaty was signed. But I can understand that there may well be difficulties in obtaining more by way of assurance in view of the federal nature of the United States Constitution.

Leave to apply for judicial review was refused because the claim was premature. Lloyd LJ stated:

The Secretary of State has not yet decided whether to accept the assurance as satisfactory and he has certainly not yet decided whether or not to issue a warrant for Soering's surrender. Other factors may well intervene between now and then. This court will never allow itself to be put in the position of reviewing an administrative decision before the decision has been made.

As a supplementary reason, he added:

Secondly, even if a decision to regard the assurance as satisfactory had already been made by the Secretary of State, then on the evidence currently before us I am far from being persuaded that such a decision would have been irrational in the WEDNESBURY sense. (As to "irrationality in the WEDNESBURY sense," see para 35 below.)

23. On 30 June 1988 the House of Lords rejected the applicant's petition for leave to appeal against the decision of the Divisional Court.

24. On 14 July 1988 the applicant petitioned the Secretary of State, requesting him to exercise his discretion not to make an order for the applicant's surrender under section 11 of the Extradition Act 1870.

This request was rejected, and on 3 August 1988 the Secretary of State signed a warrant ordering the applicant's surrender to the United States' authorities. However, the applicant has not been transferred to the United States by virtue of the interim measures indicated in the present proceedings firstly by the European Commission and then by the European Court.

25. On 5 August 1988 the applicant was transferred to a prison hospital where he remained until early November 1988 under the special regime applied to suicide-risk prisoners.

According to psychiatric evidence adduced on behalf of the applicant (report dated 16 March 1989 of Dr. D. Somekh), the applicant's dread of extreme physical violence and homosexual abuse from other inmates in death row in Virginia is in particular having a profound psychiatric effect on him. The psychiatrist's report records a mounting desperation in the applicant, together with objective fears that he may seek to take his own life.

26. By a declaration dated 20 March 1989 submitted to this Court, the applicant stated that should the United Kingdom Government require that he be deported to the Federal Republic of Germany he would consent to such requirement and would present no factual or legal opposition against the making or execution of an order to that effect.

II. Relevant domestic law and practice in the United Kingdom

A. Criminal law

27. In England murder is defined as the unlawful killing of a human being with malice aforethought. The penalty is life imprisonment. The death penalty cannot be imposed for murder. (Murder (Abolition of the Death Penalty) Act 1965, § 1.) Section 2 of the Homicide Act 1957 provides that where a person kills another, he shall not be convicted of murder if he was suffering from such abnormality of mind (whether arising from a condition of arrested development of mind or any inherent causes or induced by disease or injury) as substantially impaired his mental responsibility for his acts in doing the killing. A person who but for the section would be

liable to be convicted of murder shall be liable to be convicted of manslaughter.

28. English courts do not exercise criminal jurisdiction in respect of acts of foreigners abroad except in certain cases immaterial to the present proceedings. Consequently, neither the applicant, as a German citizen, nor Elizabeth Haysom, a Canadian citizen, was or is amenable to criminal trial in the United Kingdom.

B. Extradition

29. The relevant general law on extradition is contained in the Extradition Acts 1870-1935.

30. The extradition arrangements between the United Kingdom and the United States of America are governed by the Extradition Treaty signed by the two Governments on 8 June 1972, a Supplementary Treaty signed on 25 June 1982, and an Exchange of Notes dated 19 and 20 August 1986 amending the Supplementary Treaty. These arrangements have been incorporated into the law of the United Kingdom by Orders in Council. (The United States of America (Extradition) Order 1976, SI 1976/2144 and the United States of America (Extradition) (Amendment) Order 1986, SI 1986/2020.

By virtue of Article I of the Extradition Treaty, "each Contracting Party undertakes to extradite to the other, in the circumstances and subject to the conditions specified in this Treaty, any person found in its territory who has been accused or convicted of any offence [specified in the Treaty and including murder], committed within the jurisdiction of the other party."

31. Extradition between the United Kingdom and the Federal Republic of Germany is governed by the Treaty of 14 May 1872 between the United Kingdom and Germany for the Mutual Surrender of Fugitive Criminals, as reapplied with amendments by an agreement signed at Bonn on 23 February 1960 and as further amended by an Exchange of Notes dated 25 and 27 September 1978. These agreements have been incorporated into the law of the United Kingdom by Orders in Council. (The Federal Republic of Germany (Extradition) Order 1960, SI 1960/1375 and the Federal Republic of Ger-

many (Extradition) (Amendment) Order 1978, SI 1978/1403.)

32. After receipt of an extradition request, the Secretary of State may, by order, require a magistrate to issue a warrant for the arrest of the fugitive criminal. (Extradition Act 1870, §§ 7 and 8.)

Extradition proceedings in the United Kingdom consist of an extradition hearing before a magistrate. Section 10 of the Extradition Act 1870 provides that if 'such evidence is produced as (subject to the provisions of this Act) would, according to the law of England, justify the committal for trial of the prisoner if the crime of which he is accused had been committed in England . . . the . . . magistrate shall commit him to prison but otherwise he shall order him to be dischrged.' A magistrate must be satisfied that there is sufficient evidence to put the accused on trial; before committing him a prima facie case must be made out against him. 'The test is whether, if the evidence before the magistrate stood alone at the trial, a reasonable jury properly directed could accept it and find a verdict of guilty. (SCHTRAKS V. GOVERNMENT OF ISRAEL [1964] AC 556.)

33. Section 11 of the Extradition Act 1870 provides that decisions taken in committal proceedings may be challenged by way of application for habeas corpus. In practice, such application is made to a Divisional Court and, with leave, to the House of Lords. Habeas corpus proceedings are primarily concerned with checking that the magistrate had jurisdiction to hear the case; that there was evidence before him which could justify the committal; that the offence is an extradition crime which is not of a political character; and that there is no bar on other grounds to surrender. Section 12 of the 1870 Act provides for the release of a prisoner, if not surrendered, at the conclusion of such proceedings or within two months of committal unless sufficient cause is shown to the contrary.

34. Furthermore, under section 11 of the 1870 Act the Secretary of State enjoys a discretion not to sign the surrender warrant. (ATKINSON V. UNITED STATES [1971] AC 197.) This discretion may override a decision of the courts that a fugitive should be surrendered, and it is open to every prisoner who has exhausted his remedies by way of appli-

cation for habeas corpus to petition the Secretary of State for that purpose. In considering whether to order the fugitive's surrender, the Secretary of State is bound to take account of fresh evidence which had not been before the magistrate. (SCHTRAKS V. GOVERNMENT OF ISRAEL, loc cit.)

35. In addition, it is open to the prisoner to challenge both the decision of the Secretary of State rejecting his petition and the decision to sign the warrant in judicial review proceedings. In such proceedings the court may review the exercise of the Secretary of State's discretion on the basis that it is tainted with illegality, irrationality or procedural impropriety. (COUNCIL OF CIVIL SERVICE UNIONS AND OTHERS V. MINISTER FOR THE CIVIL SERVICE [1984] 3 All ER 935.)

Irrationality is determined on the basis of the administrative law principles set out in ASSOCIATED PROVINCIAL PICTURE HOUSES LTD V. WEDNESBURY CORPORATION [1948] 1 KB 223 (the so-called 'WEDNESBURY principles' of reasonableness). The test in an extradition case would be that no reasonable Secretary of State could have been made an order for return in the circumstances. As the judgment of Lloyd LJ in the Divisional Court in the present case shows, the reliance placed by the Secretary of State on any assurance given by the requesting State may be tested to determine whether such reliance is within the confines of 'reasonableness.' According to the United Kingdom Government, on the same principle a court would have jurisdiction to quash a challenged decision to send a fugitive to a country where it was established that there was a serious risk of inhuman or degrading treatment, on the ground that in all the circumstances of the case the decision was one which no reasonable Secretary of State could take.

In R V. HOME SECRETARY, ex parte BUGDAYCAY [1987] 1 All ER 840 at 952, a House of Lords case concerning a refusal to grant asylum, Lord Bridge, while acknowledging the limitations of the WEDNESBURY principles, explained that the courts will apply them extremely strictly against the Secretary of State in a case in which the life of the applicant is at risk:

Within those limitations the court must, I think, be entitled to subject an administrative decision to the most rigorous examination, to ensure that it is in no way flawed, according to the gravity of the issue which the decision determines. The most fundamental of all human rights is the individual's right to life and, when an administrative decision under challenge is said to be one which may put the applicant's life at risk, the basis of the decision must surely call for the most anxious scrutiny.

In my opinion where the result of a flawed decision may imperil life or liberty a special responsibility lies on the court in the examination of the decision-making process.

However, the courts will not review any decision of the Secretary of State by reason of the fact only that he failed to consider whether or not there was a breach of the European Convention on Human Rights. (R V. SECRETARY OF STATE, ex parte KIRKWOOD [1984] 1 WLR 913.)

In addition, the courts have no jurisdiction to issue interim injunctions against the Crown in judicial review proceedings. (KIRKWOOD, ibid and R V. SECRETARY OF STATE FOR TRANSPORT, ex parte FACTORTAME LTD AND OTHERS, [1989] 2 CMLR 353.

36. There is no provision in the Extradition Acts relating to the death penalty, but Article IV of the United Kingdom-United States Treaty provides:

If the offence for which extradition is requested is punishable by death under the relevant law of the requesting Party, but the relevant law of the requested Party does not provide for the death penalty in a similar case, extradition may be refused unless the requesting Party gives assurances satisfactory to the requested party that the death penalty will not be carried out.

37. In the case of a fugitive requested by the United States who faces a charge carrying the death penalty, it is the Secretary of State's practice, pursuant to Article IV of the United Kingdom-United States Extradition

Treaty, to accept an assurance from the prosecuting authorities of the relevant State that a representation will be made to the judge at the time of sentencing that it is the wish of the United Kingdom that the death penalty should be neither imposed nor carried out. This practice has been described by Mr. David Mellor, then Minister of State at the Home Office, in the following terms:

The written undertakings about the death penalty that the Secretary of State obtains from the federal authorities amount to an undertaking that the views of the United Kingdom will be represented to the judge. At the time of sentencing he will be informed that the United Kingdom does not wish the death penalty to be imposed or carried out. That means that the United Kingdom authorities render up a fugitive or are prepared to send a citizen to face an American court on the clear understanding that the death penalty will not be carried out—it never has been carried out in such cases. It would be a fundamental blow to the extradition arrangements between our two countries if the death penalty were carried out on an individual who had been returned under those circumstances. (Hansard, 10 March 1987, col 955.)

There has, however, never been a case in which the effectiveness of such an understanding has been tested.

38. Concurrent requests for extradition in respect of the same crime from two different States are not a common occurrence. If both requests are received at the same time, the Secretary of State decides which request is to be proceeded with, having regard to all the facts of the case, including the nationality of the fugitive and the place of commission of the offence.

In this respect Article X of the Extradition Treaty between the United Kingdom and the United States provides as follows:

If the extradition of a person is requested concurrently by one of the contracting parties and by another State or States, either for the same offence or for different offences, the requested Party shall make its decision, in so far as its law allows, hav-

ing regard to all the circumstances, including the provisions in this regard in any Agreements in force between the requested party and the requesting State, the relative seriousness and place of commission of the offences, the respective dates of the requests, the nationality of the person sought and the possibility of subsequent extradition to another State.

III. Relevant domestic law in the Commonwealth of Virginia

A. The law relating to murder

39. The relevant definition and classification of murder and sentencing for murder are governed by the Code of Virginia of 1950, as amended, and the decided cases in the State and Federal courts.

40. Section 18.2-31 of the Virginia Code provides that eight types of homicide constitute capital murder, punishable as a Class 1 felony, including 'the wilful, deliberate and premeditated killing of more than one person as part of the same act or transaction.'(Subs (g).) The punishment for a Class 1 felony is 'death or imprisonment for life.' (Virginia Code, § 18.2-10(a).) Except in the case of murder for hire, only the 'triggerman,' that is the actual perpetrator of the killing, may be charged with capital murder. (JOHNSTON V. COMMONWEALTH, 220 VA 146, 255 SE 2d 525 (1979).)

Murder other than capital murder is classified as murder in the first degree or murder in the second degree and is punishable by varying terms of imprisonment. (Virginia Code, §§ 18.2-10(b)(c) and 18.2-32.)

41. In most felony trials, including trials for capital murder, the defendant is guaranteed trial by jury. The defendant may waive this right but does not often do so.

B. Sentencing procedure

42. The sentencing procedure in a capital murder case in Virginia is a separate proceeding from the determination of guilt. Following a determination of guilt of capital murder, the same jury, or judge sitting with-

out a jury, will forthwith proceed to hear evidence regarding punishment. All relevant evidence concerning the offence and the defendant is admissible. Evidence in mitigation is subject to almost no limitation, while evidence of aggravation is restricted by statute. (Virginia Code, § 19.2-264.4.)

43. Unless the prosecution proves beyond a reasonable doubt the existence of at least one of two statutory aggravating circumstances—future dangerousness or vileness—the sentencer may not return a death sentence.

'Future dangerousness' exists where there is a probability that the defendant would commit 'criminal acts of violence' in the future such as would constitute a continuing serious threat to society. (Virginia Code, § 19.2-264.2.)

'Vileness' exists when the crime was 'outrageously or wantonly vile, horrible or inhuman in that it involved torture, depravity of mind or an aggravated battery to the victim'. (Virginia Code, ibid.) The words 'depravity of mind' mean 'a degree of moral turpitude and physical debasement surpassing that inherent in the definition of ordinary legal malice and premeditation.' The words 'aggravated battery' mean a battery which 'qualitatively and quantitatively, is more culpable than the minimum necessary to accomplish an act of murder.' (SMITH V. COMMON-WEALTH, 219 Va 455, 248 SE 2d 135 (1978), certiorari denied, 441 US 967 (1979). Proof of multiple wounds sustained by the victim, particularly a neck wound, which even considered alone, constituted an aggravated battery in the light of the savage, methodical manner in which it was inflicted, leaving the victim to suffer an interval of agony awaiting death, has been held to satisfy the test of 'vileness' under the section. (EDMONDS V. COMMONWEALTH, 229 Va 303, 329 SE 2d 807, certiorari denied, 106 S Ct 339, 88 L Ed 2d 324 (1985).)

44. The imposition of the death penalty on a young person who has reached the age of majority—which is 18 years (Virginia Code, § 1.13.42)—is not precluded under Virginia law. Age is a fact to be weighed by the jury. (PETERSON V. COMMONWEALTH, 225 Va 289, 302 SE 2d 520, certiorari denied, 464 US 865, 104 S Ct 202, 78 L Ed 2d 176 (1983).

45. Facts in mitigation are specified by statute as including but not being limited to the following:

(i) the defendant has no significant history of prior criminal activity, or (ii) the capital felony was committed while the defendant was under the influence of extreme mental or emotional disturbance, or (iii) the victim was a participant in the defendant's conduct or consented to the act, or (iv) at the time of the commission of the capital felony, the capacity of the defendant to appreciate the criminality of his conduct or to conform his conduct ot the requirements of law was significantly impaired, or (v) the age of the defendant at the time of the commission of the capital offence. (Virginia Code, § 19.2.264.4B.)

46. In a case of trial by jury, the jury in a capital murder case has the duty to consider all evidence relevant to sentencing, both favourable and unfavourable, before fixing punishment. In particular, a jury may sentence a defendant to death only after having considered the evidence in mitigation of the offence. (WATKINS V. COMMONWEALTH, 229 Va 469, 331 SE 2d 422 (1985), certiorari denied 475 US 1099, 106 S Ct 1503, 89 L Ed 2d 903 (1986).) Furthermore, unless the jury is unanimous the sentence cannot be death but must be life imprisonment. (Virginia Code, § 19.2-264.4.) Even if one or more of the statutory aggravating circumstances are shown the sentencer still remains at liberty to fix a life sentence instead of death in the light of the mitigating circumstances and even for no reason other than mercy. (SMITH V. COMMONWEALTH, loc cit.)

47. Following a sentence of death, the trial judge must order the preparation of an investigative report detailing the defendant's history and 'any and all other relevant facts, to the end that the court may be fully advised as to whether the penalty of death is appropriate and just'; after consideration of the report, and upon good cause shown, the judge may set aside the sentence of death and impose a life sentence. (Virginia Code, § 19.2-264.5.)

48. Following a moratorium consequent upon a decision of the United States Supreme Court (FURMAN V. GEORGIA, 92 S Ct 2726 (1972)), imposition of the death penalty was

resumed in Virginia in 1977, since which date seven persons have been executed. The means of execution used is electrocution.

The Virginia death penalty statutory scheme, including the provision on mandatory review of sentence, has been judicially determined to be constitutional. It was considered to prevent the arbitrary or capricious imposition of the death penalty and narrowly to channel the sentencer's discretion. (SMITH V. COMMONWEALTH, loc cit, TURNER V. BASS, 753 F 2d 342 (4th Circuit, 1985); BRILEY V. BASS, 750 F 2d 1238 (4th Circuit, 1984).) The death penalty under the Virginia capital murder statute has also been held not to constitute cruel and unusual punishment or to deny a defendant due process or equal protection. (STAMPER V. COMMONWEALTH, 220 Va 260, 257 SE 2d 808 (1979), certiorari denied, 445 US 972, 100 S Ct 1666, 64 L Ed 2d 249 (1980).) The Supreme Court of Virginia rejected the submission that death by electrocution would cause the needless imposition of pain before death and emotional suffering while awaiting execution of sentence.

C. Insanity, mental disorders and diminished responsibility

49. The law of Virginia generally does not recognise a defence of diminished capacity. (STAMPER V. COMMONWEALTH, 228 Va 707, 324 SE 2d 682 (1985).)

50. A plea of insanity at the time of the offence is recognised as a defence in Virginia and, if successful, is a bar to conviction. Such a plea will apply where the defendant knows that the act is wrong but is driven by an irresistible impulse, induced by some mental disease affecting the volitive powers, to commit it (THOMPSON V. COMMONWEALTH, 193 Va 704, 70 SE 2d 284 (1952) and GODLEY V. COMMONWEALTH, 2 Va App 249 (1986)) or where he does not understand the nature, character and consequences of his act or is unable to distinguish right from wrong. (PRICE V. COMMONWEALTH, 228 Va 452, 323 S Ct 2d 106 (1984).) Where no insanity defence is interposed, the defendant's mental condition is only relevant at the guilt stage insofar as it might be probative of a fact in issue, for example premeditation at

the time of the killing. (LE VASSEUR V. COMMONWEALTH, 225 Va 564, 304 SE 2d 644 (1983), certiorari denied, 464 US 1063, 104 S Ct 744, 79 L Ed 2d 202 (1984).)

51. In a capital murder trial, the defendant's mental condition at the time of the offence, including any level of mental illness, may be pleaded as a mitigating factor at the sentencing stage. Evidence on this may include, but is not limited to, showing that the defendant was under the influence of extreme mental or emotional disturbance or that at the time of the offence his capacity to appreciate the criminality of his conduct was significantly impaired. (Virginia Code, § 19.2-264.4B—see para 45 above.)

Additionally, indigent capital murder defendants are entitled by statute to the appointment of a qualified mental health expert to assist in the preparation and presentation of information concerning their history, character and mental condition with a view to establishing factors in mitigation. (Virginia Code, § 19.2-264, 3:1.)

Upon presentation of evidence of the defendant's mental state the sentencer may elect to impose life imprisonment rather than the death penalty.

D. Appeals in capital cases

52. The Supreme Court of Virginia reviews automatically every case in which a capital sentence has been passed, regardless of the plea entered by the defendant at his trial. In addition to consideration of "any errors in the trial" alleged by the defendant on appeal, the Supreme Court reviews the death sentence to determine whether it was imposed 'under the influence of passion, prejudice or any other arbitrary factor' and whether it is excessive or disporprotionate 'to the penalty imposed in similar cases.' (Virginia Code, § 17-110.1.)

This automatic direct appeal is governed by the Rules of the Supreme Court of Virginia and encompasses various time limits for the filing of briefs. In addition, precedence is given to the review of sentences of death before any other cases. (Rule 5:23; see also Virginia Code, § 17-110.2.)

Normally the time taken by this appeal does not exceed six months.

After this appeal process is completed, the sentence of death will be executed unless a stay of execution is entered. As a practical matter, a stay will be entered when the prisoner initiates further proceedings.

There has apparently been only one case since 1977 where the Virginia Supreme Court has itself reduced a death sentence to life imprisonment.

53. The prisoner may apply to the United States Supreme Court for certiorari review of the decision of the Supreme Court of Virginia. If unsuccessful, he may begin collateral attacks upon the conviction and sentence in habeas corpus proceedings in both State and Federal courts.

The prisoner may file a habeas corpus petition either in the Supreme Court of Virginia or in the trial court, with appeal to the Supreme Court of Virginia. Thereafter he may once more apply to the United States Supreme Court for certiorari review of the State's habeas corpus decision.

He may then file a petition for a writ of habeas corpus in the Federal District Court. The decision of the District Court may be appealed to the Federal Circuit Court of Appeals, followed, if no relief is obtained, by a petition for certiorari review in the United States Supreme Court.

At each stage of his collateral attacks, the prisoner may seek a stay of execution pending final determination of his applications.

54. The Virginia and Federal Statutes and rules of court set time limits for the presentation of appeals following conviction or appeals against the decisions in habeas corpus proceedings. There are, however, no time limits for filing the initial State and Federal habeas corpus petitions.

55. The grounds which may be presented and argued on appeal and in habeas corpus proceedings are restricted by the 'contemporaneous objections rule' to those which have been raised in the course of the trial. (See Rule 5.25 of the Rules of the Supreme Court of Virginia.) The rule is based on the principle that the trial itself is the 'main event,' so that the real issues between the parties should be canvassed and determined at the trial and not on appeal or in any subsequent review proceedings. It was adopted to prevent the setting of traps for trial courts (KEENEY V. COMMONWEALTH, 147 Va 678, 137 SE

478 (1927)), and so that the trial judge will be given the opportunity to rule upon the issues intelligently and unnecessary appeals, reversals and mistrials will be avoided. (WOODSON V. COMMONWEALTH, 211 Va 285, 176 SE 2d 818 (1970), certiorari denied, 401 US 958 (1971).) The rule applies equally in capital cases and is recognised by the Federal courts. (BRILEY V. BASS, 584 F Supp 807 (Eastern District Virginia), aff'd, 742, F 2d 155 (4th Circuit, 1984).)

By way of exception to the rule, errors to which no objections were made at the trial may be objected to on appeal where this is necessary to attain the ends of justice or where good cause is shown. This exception has been applied by the Supreme Court of Virginia to overturn a capital murder conviction. (BALL V. COMMONWEALTH, 221 Va 754, 273 SE 2d 790 (1981).) In death penalty cases, the proportionality of the sentence and the issue of whether the sentence was imposed under the influence of passion, prejudice or other arbitrary factor is reviewed without regard to whether objection was made at trial. (See BRILEY V. BASS, loc cit.)

56. The average time between trial and execution in Virginia, calculated on the basis of the seven executions which have taken place since 1977, is six to eight years. The delays are primarily due to a strategy by convicted prisoners to prolong the appeal proceedings as much as possible. The United States Supreme Court has not as yet considered or rules on the 'death row phenomenon' and in particular whether it falls foul of the prohibition of 'cruel and unusual punishment' under the Eighth Amendment to the constitution of the United States.

E. Legal assistance for appeals

57. All prisoners who have been sentenced to death have individual lawyers to represent them, whether privately recruited or court-appointed. On the other hand, there is no statutory provision expressly mandating legal assistance to be made available to the indigent prisoner to file habeas corpus petitions. However, it has recently been affirmed by a United States Court of Appeal that the Commonwealth of Virginia is required to provide indigent prisoners who have been sentenced

to death with the assistance of lawyers to pursue challenges to their death sentences in State habeas corpus actions. (GIARRATANO V. MURRAY, 847 F 2d 1118 (4th Circuit 1988) (en banc)—case currently pending before the United States Supreme Court.) In Federal habeas corpus and certiorari proceedings case law does not impose the same obligations (Ibid p 1122, column 1), for the reason that the Federal courts would have available the appellate briefs, a transcript and State court opinion (in certiorari proceedings) and the briefs of counsel, a transcript and opinion (in habeas corpus proceedings).

Virginia inmates also have access to legal information and assistance in the form of law libraries and institutional attorneys. The institutional attorneys are available to assist inmates in 'any legal matter relating to their incarceration' (Virginia code § 53.1-40) including the drafting of habeas corpus petitions and motions for appointment of counsel for the inmates to file.

A prisoner is not obliged to proceed with counsel, and he may litigate in both State and Federal courts pro se. However, no Virginia prisoner under sentence of death in contemporary times has ever been unrepresented during his trial, appeal or habeas corpus proceedings. Nor has any such prisoner faced execution without counsel.

F. Authorities involved in the death penalty procedure

58. A Commonwealth's Attorney for each county in Virginia is elected every four years. (Art VII(4) of the Constitution of Virginia.) His primary duty is the prosecution of all criminal cases within his locality. (See Virginia Code, § 15.1-18.1.) He has discretion as to what degree of murder to present for indictment, but that discretion is limited by considerations of prosecutorial ethics and his legal duty under the general law and to the public to present the indictment for the crime which is best supported by the evidence. He is independent in the discharge of his duty, not being subject to direction in any relevant way, whether as to charging offences, seeking sentences or giving related assurances, by the Attorney General of Virginia (See Virginia Code, § 2.1-124), the Governor of Vir-

ginia or anyone else. It is open to the Commonwealth's Attorney to engage in plea negotiations, but the court is not bound to accept any resultant agreement. (Rule 3A.8 of the Rules of the Supreme Court of Virginia.)

59. Judges of the district and higher courts of the State of Virginia are not elected but are appointed to the bench. Their conduct is governed by published Canons of Judicial Conduct, which have been adopted by the Supreme Court of Virginia as Rules of the Supreme Court. Observance of high standards of conduct so as to preserve the integrity and independence of the judiciary is included as part of the first Canon.

60. The Governor of the Commonwealth of Virginia has an unrestricted power 'to commute capital punishment'. (Art V, § 12 of the Constitution of Virginia.) As a matter of policy, the Governor does not promise, before a conviction and sentence, that he will later exercise his commutation power. Since 1977 there has been no case in which the Governor has commuted a death sentence.

G. Prison conditions in Mecklenburg Correctional Center

61. There are currently 40 people under sentence of death in Virginia. The majority are detained in Mecklenburg Correctional Center, which is a modern maximum security institution with a total capacity of 335 inmates. Institutional Operating Procedures (IOP 821.1) establish uniform operating procedures for the administration, security, control and delivery of necessary services to death row inmates in Mecklenburg. In addition conditions of confinement are governed by a comprehensive consent decree handed down by the United States District Court in Richmond in the case of ALAN BROWN et al v. ALLYN R SIELAFF (5 April 1985). Both the Virginia Department of Corrections, and the American Civil Liberties Union monitor compliance with the terms of the consent decree. The United States District Court also retains jurisdiction to enforce compliance with the decree.

62. The channels by which grievances may be ventilated and, if well-founded, remedied include (1) the use of a Federal Court approved Inmate Grievance Procedure of the Virginia

Department of Corrections, involving the Warden, the Regional Administrator and the Director of Prisons, and the Regional Ombudsman, (2) formal or informal contact between inmates' counsel and the prison staff, (3) complaint to the courts for breach of the consent decree, and (4) the institution of legal proceedings under Federal or State tort laws.

63. The size of a death row inmate's cell is 3m x 2.2m. Prisoners have an opportunity for approximately 7½ hours recreation per week in summer and approximately 6 hours per week, weather permitting, in winter. The death row area has two recreation yards, both of which are equipped with basketball courts and one of which is equipped with weights and weight benches. Inmates are also permitted to leave their cells on other occasions, such as to receive visits, to visit the law library or to attend the prison infirmary. In addition, death row inmates are given one hour out-of-cell time in the morning in a common area. Each death row inmate is eligible for work assignments, such as cleaning duties. When prisoners move around the prison they are handcuffed with special shackles around the waist.

When not in their cells, death row inmates are housed in a common area called 'the pod.' The guards are not within this area and remain in a box outside. In the event of disturbance or interinmate assault, the guards are not allowed to intervene until instructed to do so by the ranking officer present.

64. The applicant adduced much evidence of extreme stress, psychological deterioration and risk of homosexual abuse and physical attack undergone by prisoners on death row, including Mecklenburg Correctional Center. This evidence was strongly contested by the United Kingdom Government on the basis of affidavits sworn by administrators from the Virginia Department of Corrections.

65. Death row inmates receive the same medical service as inmates in the general population. An infirmary equipped with adequate supplies, equipment and staff provides for 24-hour in-patient care, and emergency facilities are provided in each building. Mecklenburg also provides psychological and psychiatric services to death row inmates. The United States District Court (Eastern District of Virginia) has recently upheld the adequacy of mental health treatment avail-

able to death row inmates in Mecklenburg. (STAMPER et al v. BLAIR et al decision of 14 July 1988.)

66. Inmates are allowed non-contact visits in a visiting room on Saturdays, Sundays and holidays between 8.30 am and 3.30 pm. Attorneys have access to their clients during normal working hours on request as well as during the scheduled visiting hours. Death row inmates who have a record of good behaviour are eligible for contact visits with members of their immediate family two days per week. Outgoing correspondence from inmates is picked up daily and all incoming correspondence is delivered each evening.

67. As a security precaution, pursuant to rules applicable to all institutions in Virginia, routine searches are conducted of the entire institution on a quarterly basis. These searches may last for approximately a week. During such times, called lockdowns, inmates are confined to their cells; they are showered, receive medical, dental and psychological services outside their cells as deemed necessary by medical staff, and upon request may visit the law library, and are alowed legal visits and legal telephone calls. Other services such as meals are provided to the inmates in their cells. During the lockdown, privileges and out-of-cell time are gradually increased to return to normal operations.

Lockdowns may also be ordered from time to time in relation to death row if information is received indicating that certain of its inmates may be planning a disturbance, hostage situation or escape.

68. A death row prisoner is moved to the death house 15 days before he is due to be executed. The death house is next to the death chamber where the electric chair is situated. Whilst a prisoner is in the death house he is watched 24 hours a day. He is isolated and has no light in his cell. The lights outside are permanently lit. A prisoner who utilises the appeals process can be placed in the death house several times.

H. The giving and effect of assurances in relation to the death penalty

69. Relations between the United Kingdom and the United States of America on matters concerning extradition are conducted by and with the Federal and not the State

authorities. However, in respect of offences against State laws the Federal authorities have no legally binding power to provide, in an appropriate extradition case, an assurance that the death penalty will not be imposed or carried out. In such cases the power rests with the State. If a State does decide to give a promise in relation to the death penalty, the United States Government would have the power to give an assurance to the extraditing Government that the State's promise will be honoured.

According to evidence from the Virginia authorities, Virginia's capital sentencing procedure and notably the provision on post-sentencing reports would allow the sentencing judge to consider the representation to be made on behalf of the United Kingdom Government pursuant to the assurance given by the Attorney for Bedford County. In addition, it would be open to the Governor to take into account the wishes of the United Kingdom Government in any application for clemency.

I. Mutual assistance in criminal matters

70. There is no way of compelling American witnesses to give evidence at a trial in the Federal Republic of Germany. However, such witnesses would normally, unless imprisoned, be free to appear voluntarily before a German court and the German authorities would pay their expenses. Furthermore, a United States Federal Court may, pursuant to a letter rogatory or a request from a foreign tribunal, order a person to give testimony or a statement or to produce a document or other thing for use in a proceeding in a foreign tribunal. (28 United States Code, § 1782.) In addition, public documents, for example the transcript of a criminal trial, are available to foreign prosecuting authorities.

IV. Relevant law and practice of the Federal Republic of Germany

71. German criminal law applies to acts committed abroad by a German national if the act is liable to punishment at the place where the offence is committed. (Criminal Code, § 7(2).)

72. Murder is defined as follows in section 211(2) of the Criminal Code:

'He is deemed a murderer who because of murderous lust, to satisfy his sexual instinct, for reasons of covetousness or for otherwise base motives, insidiously or cruelly or by means constituting a public danger or in order to render another crime possible or to conceal another crime kills a person.'

Murder is punishable with life imprisonment (Criminal Code, § 211(1)), the death penalty having been abolished under the constitution. (Art 102 of the Constitution, 1949.)

73. Under the terms of the Juvenile Court Act (1953) as amended, if a young adult— defined as a person who is 18 but not yet 21 years of age at the time of the criminal act (§ 1(3)) commits an offence, the judge will apply the provisions applicable to a juvenile—defined as a person who is at least 14 but not yet 18 years of age—if, inter alia, 'the overall assessment of the offender's personality, having regard also to the circumstances of his environment, reveals that, according to his moral and mental development, he was still equal to a juvenile at the time of committing the offence. (§ 105(1).) The sentence for young adults who come within this section is youth imprisonment of 6 months to 10 years or, under certain conditions, of indeterminate duration. (§§ 18, 19 and 105(3).) Where, on the other hand, the young adult offender's personal development corresponds to his age, the general criminal law applies but the judge may pass a sentence of 10 to 15 years' imprisonment instead of a life sentence. (§ 106(1).)

74. Where an offender at the time of commission of the offence, was incapable of appreciating the wrongfulness of the offence or of acting in accordance with such appreciation by reason of a morbid mental or emotional disturbance, by reason of a profound disturbance of consciousness or by reason of mental deficiency or some other serious mental or emotional abnoromality, there can be no culpability on his part and he may not be punished. (Criminal Code, § 20.) In such a case, however, it is possible for an order to be made placing the offender in a psychiatric hospital indefinitely. (Criminal Code, § 63.)

In a case of diminished responsibility, namely where there is substantial impairment of the offender's ability to appreciate the wrongfulness of the offence or to act in accordance with such appreciation at the time of commission of the offence for one of the reasons set out in section 20, (Criminal Code § 21) punishment may be reduced and, in particular, in homicide cases imprisonment of not less than 3 years shall be substituted for life imprisonment. (Criminal Code, § 49(1)(2).) Alternatively, the court may order placement in a psychiatric hospital.

75. Where a death sentence is risked, the Federal Government will grant extradition only if there is an unequivocal assurance by the requesting State that the death penalty will not be imposed or that it will not be carried out. The German-United States Extradition Treaty of 20 June 1978, in force since 29 August 1980, contains a provision (Art 12) corresponding, in its essentials, to Article IV of the United Kingdom—United States Extradition Treaty. The Government of the Federal Republic of Germany stated in evidence that it would not have deemed an assurance of the kind given by the United States Government in the present case to be adequate and would have refused extradition. In accordance with recent judicial decisions, the question whether an adequate assurance has been given is subject to examination in proceedings before the higher regional court.

PROCEEDINGS BEFORE THE COMMISSION

76. Mr. Soering's application (no 14038/88) was lodged with the Commission on 8 July 1988. In his application Mr. Soering stated his belief that, notwithstanding the assurance given to the United Kingdom Government, there was a serious likelihood that he would be sentenced to death if extradited to the United States of America. He maintained that in the circumstances and, in particular, having regard to the 'death row phenomenon' he would thereby be subjected to inhuman and degrading treatment and punishment contrary to Article 3 of the Convention. In his further submission his extradition to the United States would constitute a violation of Article 6(3)(c) because of the absence of legal aid in the State of Virginia to pursue various appeals. Finally, he claimed that, in breach of Article 13, he had no effective remedy under United Kingdom law in respect of his complaint under Article 3.

77. On 11 August 1988 the President of the Commission indicated to the United Kingdom Government, in accordance with Rule 36 of the Commission's Rules of Procedure, that it was desirable, in the interests of the parties and the proper conduct of the proceedings, not to extradite the applicant to the United States until the Commission had had an opportunity to examine the application. This indication was subsequently prolonged by the Commission on several occasions until the reference of the case to the Court.

78. The Commission declared the application admissible on 10 November 1988.

In its report adopted on 19 January 1989 (Article 31) the Commission expressed the opinion that there had been a breach of Article 13 (seven votes to four) but no breach of either Article 3 (six votes to five) or Article 6(3)(c) (unanimously).

* * *

FINAL SUBMISSIONS TO THE COURT BY THE UNITED KINGDOM GOVERNMENT

79. At the public hearing on 24 April 1989 the United Kingdom Government maintained the concluding submissions set out in its memorial, whereby it requested the Court to hold

1. that neither the extradition of the applicant nor any act or decision of the United Kingdom Government in relation thereto constitutes a breach of Article 3 of the Convention;

2. that neither the extradition of the applicant nor any act or decision of the United Kingdom Government in relation thereto constitutes a breach of Article 6(3)(c) of the convention;

3. that there has been no violation of Article 13 of the convention;

4. that no issues arise under Article 50 of the Convention which call for consideration by the Court.

It also submitted that further complaints under Article 6 made by the applicant before the court were not within the scope of the case as declared admissible by the Commission.

DECISION:

I. Alleged breach of Article 3

80. The applicant alleged that the decision by the Secretary of State for the Home Department to surrender him to the authorities of the United States of America would, if implemented, give rise to a breach by the United Kingdom of Article 3 of the Convention, which provides:

No one shall be subjected to torture or to inhuman or degrading treatment or punishment.

A. Applicability of Article 3 in cases of extradition

81. The alleged breach derives from the applicant's exposure to the so-called 'death row phenomenon.' This phenomenon may be described as consisting in a combination of circumstances to which the applicant would be exposed if, after having been extradited to Virginia to face a capital murder charge, he were sentenced to death.

82. In its report (at paragraph 94) the Commission reaffirmed 'its case law that a person's deportation or extradition may give rise to an issue under Article 3 of the Convention where there are serious reasons to believe that the individual will be subjected, in the receiving State, to treatment contrary to that Article.'

The Government of the Federal Republic of Germany supported the approach of the Commission, pointing to a similar approach in the case law of the German courts.

The applicant likewise submitted that Article 3 not only prohibits the Contracting States from causing inhuman or degrading treatment or punishment to occur within their jurisdiction but also embodies an associated obligation not to put a person in a position where he will or may suffer such treatment or punishment at the hands of other States. For the applicant, at least as far as Article 3 is concerned, an individual may not be surrendered out of the protective zone of the Convention without the certainty that the safeguards which he would enjoy are as effective as the Convention standard.

83. The United Kingdom Government, on the other hand, contended that Article 3 should not be interpreted so as to impose responsibility on a Contracting State for acts which occur outside its jurisdiction. In particular, in its submission, extradition does not involve the responsibility of the extraditing State for inhuman or degrading treatment or punishment which the extradited person may suffer outside the State's jurisdiction. To begin with, it maintained, it would be straining the language of Article 3 intolerably to hold that by surrendering a fugitive criminal the extraditing State has 'subjected' him to any treatment or punishment that he will receive following conviction and sentence in the receiving State. Further arguments advanced against the approach of the Commission were that it interferes with international treaty rights; it leads to a conflict with the norms of international judicial process, in that it in effect involves adjudication on the internal affairs of Foreign States not Parties to the Convention or to the proceedings before the Convention institutions; it entails grave difficulties of evaluation and proof in requiring the examination of alien systems of law and of conditions in foreign States; the practice of national courts and the international community cannot reasonably be invoked to support it; it causes a serious risk of harm in the contracting State which is obliged to harbour the protected person, and leaves criminals untried, at large and unpunished.

In the alternative, the United Kingdom Government submitted that the application of Article 3 in extradition cases should be limited to those occasions in which the treatment or punishment abroad is certain, imminent and serious. In its view, the fact that by definition the matters complained of are only anticipated, together with the common and legitimate interest of all States in bringing fugitive criminals to justice, requires a very high degree of risk, proved beyond reasonable doubt, that ill-treatment will actually occur.

84. The Court will approach the matter on the basis of the following considerations.

85. As results from Article 5(1)(f), which permits 'the lawful . . . detention of a person

against whom action is being taken with a view to . . . extradition,' no right not to be extradited is as such protected by the Convention. Nevertheless, in so far as a measure of extradition has consequences adversely affecting the enjoyment of a Convention right, it may, assuming that the consequences are not too remote, attract the obligations of a contracting State under the relevant Convention guarantee. (See, mutatis mutandis, ABDULAZIZ, CABALES AND BALKAN-DALI V. UNITED KINGDOM (1985) 7 EHRR 471, paras 59-60—in relation to rights in the field of immigration.) What is at issue in the present case is whether Article 3 can be applicable when the adverse consequences of extradition are, or may be, suffered outside the jurisdiction of the extraditing State as a result of treatment or punishment administered in the receiving State.

86. Article 1 of the Convention, which provides that 'the High Contracting parties shall secure to everyone within their jurisdiction the rights and freedoms defined in Section I,' sets a limit, notably territorial, on the reach of the Convention. In particular, the engagement undertaken by a Contracting State is confined to 'securing' ('reconnaitre' in the French text) the listed rights and freedoms to persons within its own 'jurisdiction.' Further, the Convention does not govern the actions of States not parties to it, nor does it purport to be a means of requiring the Contracting States to impose Convention standards on other States. Article 1 cannot be read as justifying a general principle to the effect that, notwithstanding its extradition obligations, a Contracting State may not surrender an individual unless satisfied that the conditions awaiting him in the country of destination are in full accord with each of the safeguards of the Convention. Indeed, as the United Kingdom Government stressed, the beneficial purpose of extradition in preventing fugitive offenders from evading justice cannot be ignored in determining the scope of application of the Convention and of Article 3 in particular.

In the instant case it is common ground that the United Kingdom has no power over the practices and arrangements of the Virginia authorities which are the subject of the applicant's complaints. It is also true that in other international instruments cited by the United Kingdom Government—for example the 1951 United Nations Convention relating to the Status of Refugees (Art 33), the 1957 European Convention on Extradition (Art 11) and the 1984 United Nations Convention against Torture and Other Cruel, Inhuman and Degrading Treatment or Punishment (Art 3)—the problems of removing a person to another jurisdiction where unwanted consequences may follow are addressed expressly and specifically. These considerations cannot, however, absolve the Contracting Parties from responsibility under Article 3 for all and any foreseeable consequences of extradition suffered outside their jurisdiction.

87. In interpreting the Convention regard must be had to its special character as a treaty for the collective enforcement of human rights and fundamental freedoms. (See IRELAND V. UNITED KINGDOM 2 EHRR 25, para 239.) Thus, the object and purpose of the convention as an instrument for the protection of individual human beings require that its provisions be interpreted and applied so as to make its safeguards practical and effective. (See, inter alia ARTICO V. ITALY 3 EHRR 1, para 33.) In addition, any interpretation of the rights and freedoms guaranteed has to be consistent with 'the general spirit of the Convention, an instrument designed to maintain and promote the ideals and values of a democratic society.' (See KJELDSEN, BUSK MADSEN AND PEDERSEN V. DENMARK 1 EHRR 711, para 53.)

88. Article 3 makes no provision for exceptions and no derogation from it is permissible under Article 15 in time of war or other national emergency. (See Article 15(2) ECHR) This absolute prohibition on torture and on inhuman or degrading treatment or punishment under the terms of the Convention shows that Article 3 enshrines one of the fundamental values of the democratic societies making up the Council of Europe. It is also to be found in similar terms in other international instruments such as the 1966 International Covenant on Civil and Political rights and the 1969 American Convention on Human Rights and is generally recognised as an internationally accepted standard.

The question remains whether the extradition of a fugitive to another State where he would be subjected or be likely to be subjected to torture or to inhuman or degrading treatment or punishment would itself engage the responsibility of a Contracting State under Article 3. That the abhorrence of torture has such implications is recognised in Article 3 of the United Nations Convention Against Torture and Other Cruel, Inhuman or Degrading Treatment or Punishment, which provides that 'no State Party shall . . . extradite a person where there are substantial grounds for beliving that he would be in danger of being subjected to torture.' The fact that a specialised treaty should spell out in detail a specific obligation attaching to the prohibition of torture does not mean that an essentially similar obligation is not already inherent in the general terms of Article 3 of the European Convention. It would hardly be compatible with the underlying values of the Convention, that 'common heritage of political traditions, ideals, freedom and the rule of law' to which the Preamble refers, were a Contracting State knowingly to surrender a fugitive to another State where there were substantial grounds for believing that he would be in danger of being subjected to torture, however heinous the crime allegedly committed. Extradition in such circumstances, while not explicitly referred to in the brief and general wording of Article 3, would plainly be contrary to the spirit and intendment of the Article, and in the Court's view this inherent obligation not to extradite also extends to cases in which the fugitive would be faced in the receiving State by a real risk of exposure to inhuman or degrading treatment or punishment proscribed by that Article.

89. What amounts to 'inhuman or degrading treatment or punishment' depends on all the circumstances of the case. Furthermore, inherent in the whole of the convention is a search for a fair balance between the demands of the general interest of the community and the requirements of the protection of the individual's fundamental rights. As movement about the world becomes easier and crime takes on a larger international dimension, it is increasingly in the interest of all nations that suspected offenders who flee abroad should be brought to justice. Conversely, the establishment of safe havens for fugitives would not only result in danger for the State obliged to harbour the protected person but also tend to undermine the foundations of extradition. These considerations must also be included among the factors to be taken into account in the interpretation and application of the notions of inhuman and degrading treatment or punishment in extradition cases.

90. It is not normally for the Convention institutions to pronounce on the existence or otherwise of potential violations of the Convention. However, where an applicant claims that a decision to extradite him would, if implemented, be contrary to Article 3 by reason of its foreseeable consequences in the requesting country, a departure from this principle is necessary, in view of the serious and irreparable nature of the alleged suffering risked, in order to ensure the effectiveness of the safeguard provided by that Article.

91. In sum, the decision by a Contracting State to extradite a fugitive may give rise to an issue under Article 3, and hence engage the responsibility of that State under the Convention, where substantial grounds have been shown for believing that the person concerned, if extradited, faces a real risk of being subjected to torture or to inhuman or degrading treatment or punishment in the requesting country. The establishment of such responsibility inevitably involves an assessment of conditions in the requesting country against the standards of Article 3 of the Convention. Nonetheless, there is no question of adjudicating on or establishing the responsibility of the receiving country, whether under general international law, under the Convention or otherwise insofar as any liability under the Convention is or may be incurred, if is liability incurred by the extraditing Contracting State by reason of its having taken action which has a direct consequence the exposure of an individual to proscribed ill-treatment.

B. Application of Article 3 in the particular circumstances of the present case

92. The extradition procedure against the applicant in the United Kingdom has been completed, the Secretary of State having signed a warrant ordering his surrender to the United States' authorities, this decision, albeit as yet not implemented, directly affects him. It therefore has to be determined on the

above principles whether the foreseeable consequences of Mr. Soering's return to the United States are such as to attract the application of Article 3. This inquiry must concentrate firstly on whether Mr. Soering runs a real risk of being sentenced to death in Virginia, since the source of the alleged inhuman and degrading treatment or punishment, namely the 'death row phenomenon,' lies in the imposition of the death penalty. Only in the event of an affirmative answer to this question need the court examine whether exposure to the 'death row phenomenon' in the circumstances of the applicant's case would involve treatment or punishment incompatible with Article 3.

1. Whether the applicant runs a real risk of a death sentence and hence of exposure to the 'death row phenomenon'

93. The United Kingdom Government, contrary to the Government of the Federal Republic of Germany, the Commission and the applicant, did not accept that the risk of a death sentence attains a sufficient level of likelihood to bring Article 3 into play. Their reasons were fourfold.

Firstly, as illustrated by his interview with the German prosecutor where he appeared to deny any intention to kill, the applicant has not acknowledged his guilt of capital murder as such.

Secondly, only a prima facie case has so far been made out against him. In particular, in the United Kingdom Government's view the psychiatric evidence is equivocal as to whether Mr. Soering was suffering from a disease of the mind sufficient to amount to a defence of insanity under Virginia law.

Thirdly, even if Mr. Soering is convicted of capital murder, it cannot be assumed that in the general exercise of their discretion the jury will recommend, the judge will confirm and the Supreme Court of Virginia will uphold the imposition of the death penalty. The United Kingdom Government referred to the presence of important mitigating factors, such as the applicant's age and mental condition at the time of commission of the offence and his lack of previous criminal activity, which would have to be taken into account by the jury and then by the judge in the separate sentencing proceedings.

Fourthly, the assurance received from the United States must at the very least significantly reduce the risk of a capital sentence either being imposed or carried out.

At the public hearing the Attorney General nevertheless made clear his Government's understanding that if Mr. Soering were extradited to the United States there was 'some risk,' which was 'more than merely negligible,' that the death penalty would be imposed.

94. As the applicant himself pointed out, he has made to American and British police officers and to two psychiatrists admissions of his participation in the killings of the Haysom parents, although he appeared to retract those admissions somewhat when questioned by the German prosecutor. It is not for the European court to usurp the function of the Virginia courts by ruling that a defence of insanity would or would not be available on the psychiatric evidence as it stands. The United Kingdom Government is justified in its assertion that no assumption can be made that Mr. Soering would certainly or even probably be convicted of capital murder as charged. Nevertheless, as the Attorney General conceded on its behalf at the public hearing, there is 'a significant risk' that the applicant would be so convicted.

95. Under Virginia law, before a death sentence can be returned the prosecution must prove beyond reasonable doubt the existence of at least one of the two statutory aggravating circumstances, namely future dangerousness or vileness. In this connection, the horrible and brutal circumstances of the killings would presumably tell against the applicant, regarding being had to the case law on the grounds for establishing the 'vileness' of the crime.

Admittedly, taken on their own the mitigating factors do reduce the likelihood of the death sentence being imposed. No less than four of the five facts in mitigation expressly mentioned in the Code of Virginia could arguably apply to Mr. Soering's case. These are a defendant's lack of any previous criminal history, the fact that the offence was committed while a defendant was under extreme mental or emotional disturbance, the fact that at the time of commission of the offence the capacity of a defendant to appreciate the criminality of his conduct or to conform his conduct to the requirements of the law was significantly diminished, and the defendant's age.

96. These various elements arguing for or against the imposition of a death sentence have to be viewed in the light of the attitude of the prosecuting authorities.

97. The Commonwealth's Attorney for Bedford County, Mr. Updike, who is responsible for conducting the prosecution against the applicant, has certified that 'should Jens Soering be convicted of the offence of capital murder as charged . . . a representation will be made in the name of the United Kingdom to the judge at the time of sentencing that it is the wish of the United Kingdom that the death penalty should not be imposed or carried out'. The Court notes, like Lloyd LJ in the Divisional Court, that this undertaking is far from reflecting the wording of Article IV of the 1972 Extradition Treaty between the United Kingdom and the United States, which speaks of 'assurances satisfactory to the requested Party that the death penalty will not be carried out'. However, the offence charged, being a State and not a Federal offence, comes within the jurisdiction of the Commonwealth of Virginia; it appears as a consequence that no direction could or can be given to the Commonwealth's Attorney by any State or Federal authority to promise more; the Virginia courts as judicial bodies cannot bind themselves in advance as to what decisions they may arrive at on the evidence; and the Governor of Virginia does not, as a matter of policy, promise that he will later exercise his executive power to commute a death penalty.

This being so, Mr. Updike's undertaking may well have been the best 'assurance' that the United Kingdom could hve obtained from the United States Federal Government in the particular circumstances. According to the statement made to Parliament in 1987 by a Home Office Minister, acceptance of undertakings in such terms 'means that the United Kingdom authorities render up a fugitive or are prepared to send a citizen to face an American court on the clear understanding that the death penalty will not be carried out . . . It would be a fundamental blow to the extradition arrangements between our two countries if the death penalty were carried out on an individual who had been returned

under those circumstances'. Nonetheless, the effectiveness of such an undertaking has not yet been put to the test.

98. The applicant contended that representations concerning the wishes of a foreign government would not be admissible as a matter of law under the Virginia Code or, if admissible, of any influence on the sentencing judge.

Whatever the position under Virginia law and practice, and notwithstanding the diplomatic context of the extradition relations between the United Kingdom and the United States, objectively it cannot be said that the undertaking to inform the judge at the sentencing stage of the wishes of the United Kingdom eliminates the risk of the death penalty being imposed. In the independent exercise of his discretion the Commonwealth's Attorney has himself decided to seek and to persist in seeking the death penalty because the evidence, in his determination, supports such action. If the national authority with responsibility for prosecuting the offence takes such a firm stance, it is hardly open to the Court to hold that there are no substantial grounds for believing that the applicant faces a real risk of being sentenced to death and hence experiencing the 'death row phenomenon.'

99. The Court's conclusion is therefore that the likelihood of the feared exposure of the applicant to the 'death row phenomenon' has been shown to be such as to bring Article 3 into play.

2. Whether in the circumstances the risk of exposure to the 'death row phenomenon' would make extradition a breach of Article 3

(a) General considerations

100. As is established in the court's case law, ill-treatment, including punishment, must attain a minimum level of severity if it is to fall within the scope of Article 3. The assessment of this minimum is, in the nature of things, relative; it depends on all the circumstances of the case, such as the nature and context of the treatment or punishment, the manner and method if its execution, it duration, its physical or mental effects and, in some instances, the sex, age and state of health of the victim. (See

IRELAND V. UNITED KINGDOM 2 EHRR 25, para 162; and TYRER V. UNITED KINGDOM 2 EHRR 1, paras 29 and 80.) Treatment has been held by the Court to be both 'inhuman' because it was premeditated, was applied for hours at a stretch and 'caused, if not actual bodily injury, at least intense physical and mental suffering.' and also 'degrading' because it was 'such as to arouse in [its] victims feelings of fear, anguish and inferiority capable of humiliating and debasing them and possibly breaking their physical or moral resistance'. (See IRELAND V. UNITED KINGDOM, para 167.) In order for a punishment or treatment associated with it to be 'inhuman' or 'degrading,' the suffering or humiliation involved must in any event go beyond that inevitable element of suffering or humiliation connected with a given form of legitimate punishment. (See TYRER V. UNITED KINGDOM, loc cit.) In this connection, account is to be taken not only of the physical pain experienced but also, where there is a considerable delay before execution of the punishment, of the sentenced person's mental anguish of anticipating the violence he is to have inflicted on him.

101. Capital punishment is permitted under certain conditions by Article 2(1) of the convention, which reads:

> Everyone's right to life shall be protected by law. No one shall be deprived of his life intentionally save in the execution of a sentence of a court following his conviction of a crime for which this penalty is provided by law.

In view of this wording, the applicant did not suggest that the death penalty per se violated Article 3. He, like the two Government Parties, agreed with the Commission that the extradition of a person to a country where he risks the death penalty does not in itself raise an issue under either Article 2 or Article 3. On the other hand, Amnesty International in their written comments argued that the evolving standards in Western Europe regarding the existence and use of the death penalty required that the death penalty should now be considered as an inhuman and degrading punishment within the meaning of Article 3.

102. Certainly, 'the Convention is a living instrument which . . . must be interpreted in the light of present-day conditions'; and, in assessing whether a given treatment or punishment is to be regarded as inhuman or degrading for the purposes of Article 3, 'the Court cannot but be influenced by the developments and commonly accepted standards in the penal policy of the member States of the Council of Europe in this field. (See TYRER V. UNITED KINGDOM 2 EHRR 1, para 31.) De facto the death penalty no longer exists in time of peace in the contracting States to the Convention. In the few Contracting States which retain the death penalty in law for some peacetime offences, death sentences, if ever imposed, are nowadays not carried out. This 'virtual consensus in Western European legal systems that the death penalty is, under current circumstances, no longer consistent with regional standards of justice,' to use the words of Amnesty International, is reflected in Protocol No. 6 to the Convention, which provides for the abolition of the death penalty in time of peace. Protocol No. 6 was opened for signature in April 1983, which in the practice of the Council of Europe indicates the absence of objection on the part of any of the Member States of the Organisation; it came into force in March 1985 and to date has been ratified by 13 Contracting States to the Convention, not however including the United Kingdom.

Whether these marked changes have the effect of bringing the death penalty per se within the prohibition of ill-treatment under Article 3 must be determined on the principles governing the interpretation of the Convention.

103. The Convention is to be read as a whole and Article 3 should therefore be construed in harmony with the provisions of Article 2. (See, mutatis mutandis, KLASS V. GERMANY 2 EHRR 214, 214, para 68.) On this basis Article 3 evidently cannot have been intended by the drafters of the Convention to include a general prohibition of the death penalty since that would nullify the clear wording of Article 2(1).

Subsequent practice in national penal policy, in the form of a generalised abolition of capital punishment, could be taken as establishing the agreement of the Contracting States to abrogate the exception provided for under Article 2(1) and hence to remove a textual limit on the scope for evolutive interpretation of Article 3. However, Protocol No. 6, as a subsequent written agreement, shows that the intention of the Contracting Parties as recently as 1983 was to adopt the normal method of amendment of the text in order to introduce a new obligation to abolish capital punishment in time of peace and, what is more, to do so by an optional instrument allowing each State to choose the moment when to undertake such an engagement. In these conditions, notwithstanding the special character of the Convention, Article 3 cannot be interpreted as generally prohibiting the death penalty.

104. That does not mean however that circumstances relating to a death sentence can never give rise to an issue under Article 3. The manner in which it is imposed or executed, the personal circumstances of the condemned person and a disproportionality to the gravity of the crime committed, as well as the conditions of detention awaiting execution, are examples of factors capable of bringing the treatment or punishment received by the condemned person with the proscription under Article 3. Present-day attitudes in the contracting States to capital punishment are relevant for the assessment whether the acceptable threshold of suffering or degradation has been exceeded.

(b) The particular circumstances

105. The applicant submitted that the circumstances to which he would be exposed as a consequence of the implementation of the Secretary of State's decision to return him to the United States, namely the 'death row phenomenon,' cumulatively constitute such serious treatment that his extradition would be contrary to Article 3. He cited in particular the delays in the appeal and review procedures following a death sentence, during which time he would be subject to increasing tension and psychological trauma; the fact, so he said, that the judge or jury in determining sentence is not obliged to take into account the defendant's age and mental state at the time of the offence; the extreme conditions of his future detention in 'death row' in Mecklenburg Correctional Center, where he expects to be the victim of violence and sexual abuse because of his age, colour and nationality; and the constant spectre of the execution itself, including the ritual of execution. He also relied on the possibility of extradition or deportation, which he would not oppose, to the Federal Republic of Germany as accentuating the disproportionality of the Secretary of State's decision.

The Government of the Federal Republic of Germany took the view that, taking all the circumstances together, the treatment awaiting the applicant in Virginia would go so far beyond treatment inevitably connected with the imposition and execution of a death penalty as to be 'inhuman' within the meaning of Article 3.

On the other hand, the conclusion expressed by the Commission was that the degree of severity contemplated by Article 3 would not be attained.

The United Kingdom Government shared this opinion. In particular, it disputed many of the applicant's factual allegations as to the conditions on death row in Mecklenburg and his expected fate there.

(i) Length of detention prior to execution
106. The period that a condemned prisoner can expect to spend on death row in Virginia before being executed is on average six to eight years. This length of time awaiting death, is, as the commission and the United Kingdom Government noted, in a sense largely of the prisoner's own making in that he takes advantage of all avenues of appeal which are offered to him by Virginia law. The automatic appeal to the Supreme Court of Virginia normally takes no more than six months. The remaining time is accounted for by collateral attacks mounted by the prisoner himself in habeas corpus proceedings before both the State and Federal courts and in applications to the Supreme Court of the United States for certiorari review, the prisoner at each stage being able to seek a stay of execution. The remedies available under Virginia law serve the purpose of ensuring that the ultimate sanction of death is not unlawfully or arbitrarily imposed.

Nevertheless, just as some lapse of time between sentence and execution is inevitable if appeal safeguards are to be provided to the condemned person, so it is equally part of human nature that the person will cling to life by exploiting those safeguards to the full. However well-intentioned and even potentially beneficial is the provision of the complex of post-sentence procedures in Virginia, the consequence is that the condemned prisoner has to endure for many years the conditions on death row and the anguish and mounting tension of living in the ever-present shadow of death.

(ii) Conditions on death row 107. As to conditions in Mecklenburg Correctional Center, where the applicant could expect to be held if sentenced to death, the court bases itself on the facts which were uncontested by the United Kingdom Government, without finding it necessary to determine the reliability of the additional evidence adduced by the applicant, notably as to the risk of homosexual abuse and physical attack undergone by prisoners on death row.

The stringency of the custodial regime in Mecklenburg, as well as the services (medical, legal and social) and the controls (legislative, judicial and administrative) provided for inmates, are described in some detail above. In this connection, the United Kingdom Government drew attention to the necessary requirement of extra security for the safe custody of prisoners condemned to death for murder. Whilst it might thus well be justifiable in principle, the severity of a special regime such as that operated on death row in Mecklenburg is compounded by the fact of inmates being subject to it for a protracted period lasting on average six to eight years.

(iii) The applicant's age and mental state 108. At the time of the killings, the applicant was only 18 years old and there is some psychiatric evidence, which was not contested as such, that he 'was suffering from [such] an abnormality of mind . . . as substantially impaired his mental responsibility for his acts'.

Unlike Article 2 of the Convention, Article 6 of the 1966 International Covenant on Civil and Political Rights and Article 4 of the 1969 American Convention on Human Rights expressly prohibit the death penalty from being imposed on persons aged less than 18 at the time of commission of the offence. Whether or not such a prohibition be inherent in the brief and general language of Article 2 of the European Convention, its explicit enunciation in other, later international instruments, the former of which has been ratified by a large number of States parties to the European Convention, at the very least indicates that as a general principle the youth of the person concerned is a circumstance which is liable, with others, to put in question the compatibility with Article 3 of measures connected with a death sentence. It is in line with the Court's case law to treat disturbed mental health as having the same effect for the application of Article 3.

109. Virginia law, as the United Kingdom Government and the Commission emphasised, certainly does not ignore these two factors. Under the Virginia Code account has to be taken of mental disturbance in a defendant, either as an absolute bar to conviction it if is judged to be sufficient to amount to insanity or, like age, as a fact in mitigation at the sentencing stage. Additionally, indigent capital murder defendants are entitled to the appointment of a qualified mental health expert to assist in the preparation of their submissions at the separate sentencing proceedings. These provisions in the Virginia Code undoubtedly serve, as the American courts have stated, to prevent the arbitrary or capricious imposition of the death penalty and narrowly to channel the sentencer's discretion. They do not however remove the relevance of age and mental condition in relation to the acceptability, under Article 3, of the 'death row phenomenon' for a given individual once condemned to death.

Although it is not for this Court to prejudge issues of criminal responsibility and appropriate sentence, the applicant's youth at the time of the offence and his then mental state, on the psychiatric evidence as it stands, are therefore to be taken into consideration as contributory factors tending, in his case, to bring the treatment on death row within the terms of Article 3.

(iv) Possibility of extradition to the Federal Republic of Germany 110. For the United Kingdom Government and the majority of the Commission, the possibility of extraditing or deporting the applicant to face trial in the Federal Republic of Germany, where the death penalty has been abolished under the Constitution, is not material for the present purposes. Any other approach, the United Kingdom Government submitted, would lead to a 'dual standard' affording the protection of the Convention to extraditable persons fortunate enough to have such an alternative destination available but refusing it to others not so fortunate.

This argument is not without weight. Furthermore the Court cannot overlook either the horrible nature of the murders with which Mr. Soering is charged or the legitimate and beneficial role of extradition arrangements in combating crime. The purpose for which his removal to the United States was sought, in accordance with the Extradition Treaty between the United Kingdom and the United States, is undoubtedly a legitimate one. However, sending Mr. Soering to be tried in his own country would remove the danger of a fugitive criminal going unpunished as well as the risk of intense and protracted suffering on death row. It is therefore a circumstance of relevance for the overall assessment under Article 3 in that it goes to the search for the requisite fair balance of interests and to the proportionality of the contested extradition decision in the particular case.

(c) Conclusion

111. For any prisoner condemned to death, some element of delay, between imposition and execution of the sentence and the experience of severe stress in conditions necessary for strict incarceration are inevitable. The democratic character of the Virginia legal system in general and the positive features of Virginia trial, sentencing and appeal procedures in particular are beyond doubt. The Court agrees with the Commission that the machinery of justice to which the applicant would be subject in the United States is in itself neither arbitrary nor unreasonable, but, rather, respects the rule of law and affords not inconsiderable procedural safeguards to the defendant in a capital trial. Facilities are available on death row for the assistance of inmates, notably through provision of psychological and psychiatric services.

However, in the Court's view, having regard to the very long period of time spent on death row in such extreme conditions, with the ever-present and mounting anguish of awaiting execution of the death penalty, and to the personal circumstances of the applicant, especially his age and mental state at the time of the offence, the applicant's extradition to the United States would expose him to a real risk of treatment going beyond the threshold set by Article 3. A further consideration of relevance is that in the particular instance the legitimate purpose of extradition could be achieved by another means which would not involve suffering of such exceptional intensity or duration. Accordingly, the Secretary of State's decision to extradite the applicant to the United States would, if implemented, give rise to a breach of Article 3.

This finding in no way puts in question the good faith of the United Kingdom Government, which has from the outset of the present proceedings demonstrated it's desire to abide by its Convention obligations, firstly by staying the applicant's surrender to the United States authorities in accord with the interim measures indicated by the Convention institutions and secondly by itself referring the case to the court for a judicial ruling.

II. Alleged breach of Article 6

A. The United States criminal proceedings

112. The applicant submitted that, because of the absence of legal aid in Virginia to fund collateral challenges before the Federal courts, on his return to the United States he would not be able to secure his legal representation as required by Article 6(3)(c), which reads:

Everyone charged with a criminal offence has the following minimum rights:

. . .

(c) to defend himself in person or through legal assistance of his own choosing or, if he had not sufficient means to pay for legal assistance, to be given it free when the interests of justice so require; . . .

The Commission expressed the opinion that the proposed extradition of the applicant could not give rise to the responsibility of the United Kingdom Government under Article 6(3)(c). The United Kingdom Government concurred with this analysis and, in the alternative, submitted that the applicant's allegations were ill-founded.

113. The right to a fair trial in criminal proceedings, as embodied in Article 6, holds a prominent place in a democratic society.

(See, inter alia, COLOZZA V. ITALY (1985) 7 EHRR 516.) The Court does not exclude that an issue might exceptionally be raised under Article 6 by an extradition decision in circumstances where the fugitive has suffered or risks suffering a flagrant denial of a fair trial in the requesting country. However, the facts of the present case do not disclose such a risk.

Accordingly, no issue arises under Article 6(3)(c) in this respect.

B. The extradition proceedings in England

114. The applicant further contended that the refusal of the Magistrates' Court in the extradition proceedings to consider evidence as to his psychiatric condition violated paragraphs (1) and (3)(d) of Article 6, which respectively provide:

1. In the determination . . . of any criminal charge against him, everyone is entitled to a fair . . . hearing . . .

3. Everyone charged with a criminal offence has the following minimum rights:

. . .

(d) to examine or have examined witnesses against him and to obtain the attendance and examination of witnesses on his behalf under the same conditions as witnesses against him; . . .

115. As the Delegate of the Commission pointed out, this complaint was not pleaded before the Commission. Such claims as the applicant then made of a failure to take proper account of the psychiatric evidence were in relation to Article 3 and limited to the Secretary of State's ultimate decision to extradite him to the United States. He did not formulate any grievances, whether under Article 6, Article 3 or Article 13, regarding the scope or conduct of the Magistrates' Court proceedings as such. This being so, the new allegation of a breach of Article 6 constitutes not merely a further legal submission or argument but a fresh and separate complaint falling outside the compass of the case, which is delimited by the Commission's decision on admissibility. (See, inter alia, SCHIESSER V. SWITZER-LAND 2 EHRR 417, para 41 and JOHNSTON V. IRELAND (1987) 9 EHRR 203.)

Accordingly, the Court has no jurisdiction to entertain the matter.

III. Alleged breach of Article 13

116. Finally, the applicant alleged a breach of Article 13, which provides:

Everyone whose rights and freedoms as set forth in [the] Convention are violated shall have an effective remedy before a national authority notwithstanding that the violation has been committed by persons acting in an official capacity.

In his submission, he had no effective remedy in the United Kingdom in respect of his complaint under Article 3. The majority of the Commission arrived at the same conclusion. The United Kingdom Government however disagreed, arguing that Article 13 had no application in the circumstances of the present case or, in the alternative, that the aggregate of remedies provided for under domestic law was adequate.

117. In view of the Court's finding regarding Article 3, the applicant's claim under that Article cannot be regarded either as incompatible with the provisions of the Convention or as not 'arguable' on its merits. (See, inter alia, BOYLE AND RICE V. UNITED KINGDOM (1980) 10 EHRR 425, para 52.)

The United Kingdom Government contended, however, that Article 13 can have no application in the circumstances of the case, because the challenge is in effect to the terms of a treaty between the United Kingdom and the United States and also because the alleged violation of the substantive provision is of an anticipatory nature.

The Court does not consider it necessary to rule specifically on these two objections to applicability since it has come to the conclusion that in any event the requirements of Article 13 were not violated.

118. The United Kingdom Government relied on the aggregate of remedies provided by the Magistrates' Court proceedings, an application for habeas corpus and an application for judicial review.

119. The Court will commence its examination with judicial review proceedings since

they constitute the principal means for challenging a decision to extradite once it has been taken.

Both the applicant and the Commission were of the opinion that the scope of judicial review was too narrow to allow the courts to consider the subject matter of the complaint which the applicant has made in the context of Article 3. The applicant further contended that the courts' lack of jurisdiction to issue interim injunctions against the Crown was an additional reason rendering judicial review an ineffective remedy.

120. Article 13 guarantees the availability of a remedy at national level to enforce the substance of the Convention rights and freedoms in whatever form they may happen to be secured in the domestic legal order. (See BOYLE AND RICE V. UNITED KINGDOM (1988) 10 EHRR 425, para 52.) The effect of Article 13 is thus to require the provision of domestic remedy allowing the competent 'national atuhority' both to deal with the substance of the relevant Convention complaint and to grant appropriate relief. (See, inter alia, SILVER V. UNITED KINGDOM (1983) 5 EHRR 347, para 113(a).)

121. In judicial review proceedings the court may rule the exercise of executive discretion unlawful on the ground that it is tainted with illegality, irrationality or procedural impropriety. In an extradition case the test of 'irrationality,' on the basis of the so-called 'WEDNESBURY principles,' would be that no reasonable Secretary of State could have made an order for surrender in the circumstances. According to the United Kingdom Government, a court would have jurisdiction to quash a challenged decision to send a fugitive to a country where it was established that there was a serious risk of inhuman or degrading treatment, on the ground that in all the circumstances of the case the decision was one that no reasonable Secretary of State could take. Although the Convention is not considered to be part of United Kingdom law, the Court is satisfied that the English courts can review the 'reasonableness' of an extradition decision in the light of the kind of factors relied on by Mr. Soering before the Convention institutions in the context of Article 3.

122. Mr. Soering did admittedly make an application for judicial review together with

his application for habeas corpus and was met with an unfavourable response from Lloyd LJ on the issue of 'irrationality'. However, as Lloyd LJ explained, the claim failed because it was premature, the courts only having jurisdiction once the Minister has actually taken his decision. Furthermore, the arguments adduced by Mr. Soering were by no means the same as those relied on when justifying his complaint under Article 3 before the Convention institutions. His counsel before the Divisional Court limited himself to submitting that the assurance by the United States' authorities was so worthless that no reasonable Secretary of State could regard it as satisfactory under the Treaty. This is an argument going to the likelihood of the death penalty being imposed but says nothing about the quality of the treatment awaiting Mr. Soering after sentence to death, this being the substance of his allegation of inhuman and degrading treatment.

There was nothing to have stopped Mr. Soering bringing an application for judicial review at the appropriate moment and arguing 'WEDNESBURY unreasonableness' on the basis of much the same material that he adduced before the Convention institutions in relation to the death row phenomenon. Such a claim would have been given 'the most anxious scrutiny' in view of the fundamental nature of the human right at stake. The effectiveness of the remedy, for the purposes of Article 13, does not depend on the certainty of a favourable outcome for Mr. Soering (See SWEDISH ENGINE DRIVERS' UNION V. SWEDEN 1 EHRR 617, para 50), and in any event it is not for this Court to speculate as to what would have been the decision of the English courts.

123. The English courts' lack of jurisdiction to grant interim injunctions against the Crown does not, in the Court's opinion, detract from the effectiveness of judicial review in the present connection, since there is no suggestion that in practice a fugitive would ever be surrendered before his application to the Divisional Court and any eventual appeal therefrom had been determined.

124. The Court concludes that Mr. Soering did have available to him under English law an effective remedy in relation to his complaint under Article 3. This being so, there is no need to inquire into the other two reme-

dies referred to by the United Kingdom Government.

There is accordingly no breach of Article 13.

IV. Application of Article 50

125. Under the terms of Article 50,

If the Court finds that a decision or a measure taken by a legal authority or any other authority of a High Contracting Party is completely or partially in conflict with the obligations arising from the . . . Convention, and if the internal law of the said party allows only partial reparation to be made for the consequences of this decision or measure, the decision of the Court shall, if necessary, afford just satisfaction to the injured party.

Mr. Soering stated that, since the object of his application was to secure the enjoyment of his rights guaranteed by the Convention, just satisfaction of his claims would be achieved by effective enforcement of the Court's ruling. He invited the Court to assist the State parties to the case and himself by giving directions in relation to the operation of its judgment.

In addition, he claimed the costs and expenses of his representation in the proceedings arising from the request to the United Kingdom Government by the authorities of the United States of America for his extradition. He quantified these costs and expenses at L1,500 and L21,000 for lawyers' fees in respect of the domestic and Strasbourg proceedings respectively, L2,067 and 4,885.60 FF for his lawyers' travel and accommodation expenses when appearing before the Convention institutions, and L2,185.80 and 145 FF for sundry out-of-pocket expenses, making an overall total of L26,752.80 and 5,030.60 FF.

126. No breach of Article 3 has as yet occurred. Nevertheless, the Court having found that the Secretary of State's decision to extradite to the United States of America would, if implemented, give rise to a breach of Article 3, Article 50 must be taken as applying to the facts of the present case.

127. The Court considers that its finding regarding Article 3 of itself amounts to adequate just satisfaction for the purposes of Article 50. The Court is not empowered under the Convention to make accessory directions of the kind requested by the applicant. (See, mutatis mutandis, DUDGEON V. UNITED KINGDOM (1983) 5 EHRR 573, para 15.) By virtue of Article 54, the responsibility for supervising execution of the Court's judgment rests with the Committee of Ministers of the Council of Europe.

128. The United Kingdom Government did not in principle contest the claim for reimbursement of costs and expenses, but suggested that, in the event that the Court should find one or more of the applicant's complaints of violation of the Convention to be unfounded, it would be appropriate for the Court, deciding on an equitable basis as required by Article 50, to reduce the amount awarded accordingly. (See LE COMPTE, VAN LEUVEN AND DE MEYERE V BELGIUM (1983) 5 EHRR 183.)

The applicant's essential concern, and the bulk of the argument on all sides, focused on the complaint under Article 3, and on that issue the applicant has been successful. The Court therefore considers that in equity the applicant should recover his costs and expenses in full.

Appendices

APPENDIX I

Articles in addition to, and amendment of, the Constitution of the United States of America, proposed by Congress, and ratified by the legislatures of the several states, pursuant to the Fifth Article of the original Constitution

AMENDMENT I

Congress shall make no law respecting an establishment of religion, or prohibiting the free exercise thereof; or abridging the freedom of speech, or of the press; or the right of the people peaceably to assemble, and to petition the Government for a redress of grievances.

AMENDMENT II

A well regulated Militia, being necessary to the security of a free State, the right of the people to keep and bear Arms, shall not be infringed.

AMENDMENT III

No Soldier shall, in time of peace be quartered in any house, without the consent of the Owner, nor in time of war, but in a manner to be prescribed by law.

AMENDMENT IV

The right of the people to be secure in their persons, houses, papers, and effects, against unreasonable searches and seizures, shall not be violated, and no Warrants shall issue, but upon probable cause, supported by Oath or affirmation, and particularly describing the place to be searched, and the persons or things to be seized.

AMENDMENT V

No person shall be held to answer for a capital, or otherwise infamous crime, unless on a presentment or indictment of a Grand Jury, except in cases arising in the land or naval forces, or in the Militia, when in actual service in time of War or public danger; nor shall any person be subject for the same offence to be twice put in jeopardy of life or limb; nor shall be compelled in any criminal case to be a witness against himself, nor be deprived of life, liberty, or property, without due process of law; nor shall private property be taken for public use, without just compensation.

AMENDMENT VI

In all criminal prosecutions, the accused shall enjoy the right to a speedy and public trial, by an impartial jury of the State and district wherein the crime shall have been committed, which district shall have been previously ascertained by law, and to be informed of the nature and cause of the accusation; to be confronted with the witnesses against him; to have compulsory process for obtaining witnesses in his favor, and to have the Assistance of Counsel for his defence.

AMENDMENT VII

In Suits at common law, where the value in controversy shall exceed twenty dollars, the right of trial by jury shall be preserved, and no fact tried by a jury, shall be otherwise re-examined in any Court of the United States, than according to the rules of the common law.

AMENDMENT VIII

Excessive bail shall not be required, nor excessive fines imposed, nor cruel and unusual punishments inflicted.

AMENDMENT IX

The enumeration in the Constitution, of certain rights, shall not be construed to deny or disparage others retained by the people.

AMENDMENT X

The powers not delegated to the United States by the Constitution, nor prohibited by it to the States, are reserved to the States respectively, or to the people.

AMENDMENT XI

The Judicial power of the United States shall not be construed to extend to any suit in law or equity, commenced or prosecuted against one of the United States by Citizens of another State, or by Citizens or Subjects of any Foreign State.

AMENDMENT XII

The Electors shall meet in their respective states and vote by ballot for President and Vice-President, one of whom, at least, shall not be an inhabitant of the same state with themselves; they shall name in their ballots the person voted for as President, and in distinct ballots the person voted for as Vice-President, and they shall make distinct lists of all persons voted for as President, and of all persons voted for as Vice-President, and of the number of votes for each, which lists they shall sign and certify, and transmit sealed to the seat of the government of the United States, directed to the President of the Senate;—The President of the Senate shall, in the presence of the Senate and House of Representatives, open all the certificates and the votes shall then be counted;—The person having the greatest Number of votes for President, shall be the President, if such number be a majority of the whole number of Electors appointed; and if no person have such majority, then from the persons having the highest numbers not exceeding three on the list of those voted for as President, the House of Representatives shall choose immediately, by ballot, the President. But in choosing the President, the votes shall be taken by states, the representation from each state having one vote; a quorum for this purpose shall consist of a member or members from two-thirds of the states, and a majority of all the states shall be necessary to a choice. And if the

House of Representatives shall not choose a President whenever the right of choice shall devolve upon them, before the fourth day of March next following, then the Vice-President shall act as President, as in the case of the death or other constitutional disability of the President.—The person having the greatest number of votes as Vice-President, shall be the Vice-President, if such number be a majority of the whole number of Electors appointed, and if no person have a majority, then from the two highest numbers on the list, the Senate shall choose the Vice-President; a quorum for the purpose shall consist of two-thirds of the whole number of Senators, and a majority of the whole number shall be necessary to a choice. But no person constitutionally ineligible to the office of President shall be eligible to that of Vice-President of the United States.

AMENDMENT XIII

SECTION 1. Neither slavery nor involuntary servitude, except as a punishment for crime whereof the party shall have been duly convicted, shall exist within the United States, or any place subject to their jurisdiction.

SECTION 2. Congress shall have power to enforce this article by appropriate legislation.

AMENDMENT XIV

SECTION 1. All persons born or naturalized in the United States and subject to the jurisdiction thereof, are citizens of the United States and of the State wherein they reside. No State shall make or enforce any law which shall abridge the privileges or immunities of citizens of the United States; nor shall any State deprive any person of life, liberty, or property, without due process of law; nor deny to any person within its jurisdiction the equal protection of the laws.

SECTION 2. Representatives shall be apportioned among the several States according to their respective numbers, counting the whole number of persons in each State, excluding Indians not taxed. But when the right to vote at any election for the choice of electors for President and Vice President of the United States, Representatives in Congress, the Executive and Judicial officers of a State, or the members of the Legislature thereof, is denied to any of the male inhabitants of such

State, being twenty-one years of age, and citizens of the United States, or in any way abridged, except for participation in rebellion, or other crime, the basis of representation therein shall be reduced in the proportion which the number of such male citizens shall bear to the whole number of male citizens twenty-one years of age in such State.

SECTION 3. No person shall be a Senator or Representative in Congress, or elector of President and Vice President, or hold any office, civil or military, under the United States, or under any State, who, having previously taken an oath, as a member of Congress, or as an officer of the United States, or as a member of any State legislature, or as an executive or judicial officer of any State, to support the Constitution of the United States, shall have engaged in insurrection or rebellion against the same, or given aid or comfort to the enemies thereof. But Congress may by a vote of two-thirds of each House, remove such disability.

SECTION 4. The validity of the public debt of the United States, authorized by law, including debts incurred for payment of pensions and bounties for services in suppressing insurrection or rebellion, shall not be questioned. But neither the United States nor any State shall assume or pay any debt or obligation incurred in aid of insurrection or rebellion against the United States, or any claim for the loss or emancipation of any slave; but all such debts, obligations and claims shall be held illegal and void.

SECTION 5. The Congress shall have power to enforce, by appropriate legislation, the provisions of this article.

AMENDMENT XV

SECTION 1. The right of citizens of the United States to vote shall not be denied or abridged by the United States or by any State on account of race, color, or previous condition of servitude.

SECTION 2. The Congress shall have power to enforce this article by appropriate legislation.

AMENDMENT XVI

The Congress shall have power to lay and collect taxes on incomes, from whatever source derived, without apportionment among the several States, and without regard to any census or enumeration.

AMENDMENT XVII

The Senate of the United States shall be composed of two Senators from each State, elected by the people thereof, for six years; and each Senator shall have one vote. The electors in each State shall have the qualifications requisite for electors of the most numerous branch of the State legislatures.

When vacancies happen in the representation of any State in the Senate, the executive authority of such State shall issue writs of election to fill such vacancies: *Provided*, That the legislature of any State may empower the executive thereof to make temporary appointments until the people fill the vacancies by election as the legislature may direct.

This amendment shall not be so construed as to affect the election or term of any Senator chosen before it becomes valid as part of the Constitution.

AMENDMENT XVIII

SECTION 1. After one year from the ratification of this article the manufacture, sale, or transportation of intoxicating liquors within, the importation thereof into, or the exportation thereof from the United States and all territory subject to the jurisdiction thereof for beverage purposes is hereby prohibited.

SECTION 2. The Congress and the several States shall have concurrent power to enforce this article by appropriate legislation.

SECTION 3. This article shall be inoperative unless it shall have been ratified as an amendment to the Constitution by the legislatures of the several States, as provided in the Constitution, within seven years from the date of the submission hereof to the States by the Congress.

AMENDMENT XIX

The right of citizens of the United States to vote shall not be denied or abridged by the United States or by any State on account of sex.

Congress shall have power to enforce this article by appropriate legislation.

AMENDMENT XX

SECTION 1. The terms of the President and Vice President shall end at noon on the 20th day of January, and the terms of Senators and Representatives at noon on the 3d day of January, of the years in which such terms would have ended if this article had not been ratified; and the terms of their successors shall then begin.

SECTION 2. The Congress shall assemble at least once in every year, and such meeting shall begin at noon on the 3d day of January, unless they shall by law appoint a different day.

SECTION 3. If, at the time fixed for the beginning of the term of the President, the President elect shall have died, the Vice President elect shall become President. If a President shall not have been chosen before the time fixed for the beginning of his term, or if the President elect shall have failed to qualify, then the Vice President elect shall act as President until a President shall have qualified; and the Congress may by law provide for the case wherein neither a President elect nor a Vice President shall have qualified, declaring who shall then act as President, or the manner in which one who is to act shall be selected, and such person shall act accordingly until a President or Vice President shall have qualified.

SECTION 4. The Congress may by law provide for the case of the death of any of the persons from whom the House of Representatives may choose a President whenever the right of choice shall have devolved upon them, and for the case of the death of any of the persons from whom the Senate may choose a Vice President whenever the right of choice shall have devolved upon them.

SECTION 5. Sections 1 and 2 shall take effect on the 15th day of October following the ratification of this article.

SECTION 6. This article shall be inoperative unless it shall have been ratified as an amendment to the Constitution by the legislatures of three-fourths of the several States within seven years from the date of its submission.

AMENDMENT XXI

SECTION 1. The eighteenth article of amendment to the Constitution of the United States is hereby repealed.

SECTION 2. The transportation or importation into any State, Territory, or Possession of the United States for delivery or use therein of intoxicating liquors, in violation of the laws thereof, is hereby prohibited.

SECTION 3. This article shall be inoperative unless it shall have been ratified as an amendment to the Constitution by conventions in the several States, as provided in the Constitution, within seven years from the date of the submission hereof to the States by the Congress.

AMENDMENT XXII

SECTION 1. No person shall be elected to the office of the President more than twice, and no person who has held the office of President, or acted as President, for more than two years of a term to which some other person was elected President shall be elected to the office of the President more than once. But this Article shall not apply to any person holding the office of President, when this Article was proposed by the Congress, and shall not prevent any person who may be holding the office of President, or acting as President, during the term within which this Article becomes operative from holding the office of President or acting as President during the remainder of such term.

SECTION 2. This article shall be inoperative unless it shall have been ratified as an amendment to the Constitution by the legislatures of three-fourths of the several States within seven years from the date of its submission to the States by the Congress.

AMENDMENT XXIII

SECTION 1. The District constituting the seat of Government of the United States shall appoint in such manner as Congress may direct:

A number of electors of President and Vice President equal to the whole number of Senators and Representatives in Congress to which the District would be entitled if it were a State, but in no event more than the least populous State; they shall be in addition to those appointed by the States, but they shall be considered, for the purposes of the election of President and Vice President, to be electors appointed by a State; and they shall meet in the District and perform such duties as provided by the twelfth article of amendment.

SECTION 2. The Congress shall have power to enforce this article by appropriate legislation.

AMENDMENT XXIV

SECTION 1. The right of citizens of the United States to vote in any primary or other election for President or Vice President, for electors for President or Vice President, or for Senator or Representative in Congress, shall not be denied or abridged by the United States or any State by reason of failure to pay any poll tax or other tax.

SECTION 2. The Congress shall have power to enforce this article by appropriate legislation.

AMENDMENT XXV

SECTION 1. In case of the removal of the President from office or of his death or resignation, the Vice President shall become President.

SECTION 2. Whenever there is a vacancy in the office of the Vice President, the President shall nominate a Vice President who shall take office upon confirmation by a majority vote of both Houses of Congress.

SECTION 3. Whenever the President transmits to the President pro tempore of the Senate and the Speaker of the House of Representatives his written declaration that he is unable to discharge the powers and duties of his office, and until he transmits to them a written declaration to the contrary, such powers and duties shall be discharged by the Vice President as Acting President.

SECTION 4. Whenever the Vice President and a majority of either the principal officers of the executive departments or of such other body as Congress may by law provide, transmit to the President pro tempore of the Senate and the Speaker of the House of Representatives their written declaration that the President is unable to discharge the powers and duties of his office, the Vice President shall immediately assume the powers and duties of the office as Acting President.

Thereafter, when the President transmits to the President pro tempore of the Senate and the Speaker of the House of Representatives has written declaration that no inability exists, he shall resume the powers and duties of his office unless the Vice President and a majority of either the principal officers of the executive department or of such other body as Congress may by law provide, transmit within four days to the President pro tempore of the Senate and the Speaker of the House of Representatives their written declaration that the President is unable to discharge the powers and duties of his office. Thereupon Congress shall decide the issue, assembling within forty-eight hours for that purpose if not in session. If the Congress, within twenty-one days after receipt of the latter written declaration, or, if Congress is not in session, within twenty-one days after Congress is required to assemble, determines by two-thirds vote of both Houses that the President is unable to discharge the powers and duties of his office, the Vice President shall continue to discharge the same as Acting President; otherwise, the President shall resume the powers and duties of his office.

AMENDMENT XXVI

SECTION 1. The right of citizens of the United States, who are eighteen years of age or older, to vote shall not be denied or abridged by the United States or by any State on account of age.

SECTION 2. The Congress shall have power to enforce this article by appropriate legislation.

AMENDMENT XXVII

No law, varying the compensation for the services of the Senators and Representatives, shall take effect, until an election of Representatives shall have intervened.

APPENDIX II

§ 1983. CIVIL ACTION FOR DEPRIVATION OF RIGHTS

Every person who, under color of any statute, ordinance, regulation, custom, or usage, of any State or Territory, subjects, or causes to be subjected, any citizen of the United States or other person within the jurisdiction thereof to the deprivation of any rights, privileges, or immunities secured by the Constitution and laws, shall be liable to the party injured in an action at law, suit in equity, or other proper proceeding for redress.
R.S. § 1979.

28 U.S.C. § 1915. PROCEEDINGS *IN FORMA PAUPERIS*

(a) (1) Subject to subsection (b), any court of the United States may authorize the commencement, prosecution or defense of any suit, action or proceeding, civil or criminal, or appeal therein, without prepayment of fees or security therefor, by a person who submits an affidavit that includes a statement of all assets such [person] prisoner possesses that the person is unable to pay such fees or give security therefor. Such affidavit shall state the nature of the action, defense or appeal and affiant's belief that the person is entitled to redress.

(2) A prisoner seeking to bring a civil action or appeal a judgment in a civil action or proceeding without prepayment of fees or security therefor, in addition to filing the affidavit filed under paragraph (1), shall submit a certified copy of the trust fund account statement (or institutional equivalent) for the prisoner for the 6-month period immediately preceding the filing of the complaint or notice of appeal, obtained from the appropriate official of each prison at which the prisoner is or was confined.

(3) An appeal may not be taken *in forma pauperis* if the trial court certifies in writing that it is not taken in good faith.

(b) (1) Notwithstanding subsection (a), if a prisoner brings a civil action or files an appeal *in forma pauperis*, the prisoner shall be required to pay the full amount of a filing fee. The court shall assess and, when funds exist, collect, as a partial payment of any court fees required by law, an initial partial filing fee of 20 percent of the greater of—

(A) the average monthly deposits to the prisoner's account; or

(B) the average monthly balance in the prisoner's account for the 6-month period immediately preceding the filing of the complaint or notice of appeal.

(2) After payment of the initial partial filing fee, the prisoner shall be required to make monthly payments of 20 percent of the preceding month's income credited to the prisoner's account. The agency having custody of the prisoner shall forward payments from the prisoner's account to the clerk of the court each time the amount in the account exceeds $10 until the filing fees are paid.

(3) In no event shall the filing fee collected exceed the amount of fees permitted by statute for the commencement of a civil action or an appeal of a civil action or criminal judgment.

(4) In no event shall a prisoner be prohibited from bringing a civil action or appealing a civil or criminal judgment for the reason that the prisoner has no assets and no means by which to pay the initial partial filing fee.

(c) Upon the filing of an affidavit in accordance with subsections (a) and (b) and the prepayment of any partial filing fee as may be required under subsection (b), the court may direct payment by the United States of the expenses of (1) printing the record on appeal in any civil or criminal case, if such printing is required by the appellate court; (2) preparing a transcript of proceedings before a United States magistrate in any civil or criminal case, if such transcript is required by the district court, in the case of proceedings conducted under section 636(b) of this title or under section 3401(b) of title 18, United States Code; and (3) printing the record on appeal if such printing is required by the appellate court, in the case of proceedings conducted pursuant to section 636(c) of this title. Such expenses shall be paid when authorized by the Director of the Administrative Office of the United States Courts.

(d) The officers of the court shall issue and serve all process, and perform all duties in such cases. Witnesses shall attend as in other cases, and the same remedies shall be available as are provided for by law in other cases.

(e) (1) The court may request an attorney to represent any person unable to afford counsel.

(2) Notwithstanding any filing fee, or any portion thereof, that may have been paid, the court shall dismiss the case at any time if the court determines that—

(A) the allegation of poverty is untrue; or

(B) the action or appeal—

(i) is frivolous or malicious;

(ii) fails to state a claim on which relief may be granted; or

(iii) seeks monetary relief against a defendant who is immune from such relief.

(f) (1) Judgment may be rendered for costs at the conclusion of the suit or action as in other proceedings, but the United States shall not be liable for any of the costs thus incurred. If the United States has paid the cost of a stenographic transcript or printed record for the prevailing party, the same shall be taxed in favor of the United States.

(2) (A) If the judgment against a prisoner includes the payment of costs under this subsection, the prisoner shall be required to pay the full amount of the costs ordered.

(B) The prisoner shall be required to make payments for costs under this subsection in the same manner as is provided for filing fees under subsection (a)(2).

(C) In no event shall the costs collected exceed the amount of the costs ordered by the court.

(g) In no event shall a prisoner bring a civil action or appeal a judgment in a civil action or proceeding under this section if the prisoner has, on 3 or more prior occasions, while incarcerated or detained in any facility, brought an action or appeal in a court of the United States that was dismissed on the grounds that it is frivolous, malicious, or fails to state a claim upon which relief may be granted, unless the prisoner is under imminent danger of serious physical injury.

(h) As used in this section, the term "prisoner" means any person incarcerated or detained in any facility who is accused of, convicted of, sentenced for, or adjudicated delinquent for, violations of criminal law or the terms and conditions of parole, probation, pretrial release, or diversionary program.

28 USCS § 1915A SCREENING

(a) Screening. The court shall review, before docketing, if feasible or, in any event, as soon as practicable after docketing, a complaint in a civil action in which a prisoner seeks redress from a governmental entity or officer or employee of a governmental entity.

(b) Grounds for dismissal. On review, the court shall identify cognizable claims or dismiss the complaint, or any portion of the complaint, if the complaint—

(1) is frivolous, malicious, or fails to state a claim upon which relief may be granted; or

(2) seeks monetary relief from a defendant who is immune from such relief.

(c) Definition. As used in this section, the term "prisoner" means any person incarcerated or detained in any facility who is accused of, convicted of, sentenced for, or adjudicated delinquent for, violations of criminal law or the terms and conditions of parole, probation, pretrial release, or diversionary program.

42 U.S.C. § 1997 CIVIL RIGHTS OF INSTITUTIONALIZED PERSONS

§ 1997. Definitions

As used in this Act—

(1) The term "institution" means any facility or institution—

(A) which is owned, operated, or managed by, or provides services on behalf of any State or political subdivision of a State; and

(B) which is—

(i) for persons who are mentally ill, disabled, or retarded, or chronically ill or handicapped;

(ii) a jail, prison, or other correctional facility;

(iii) a pretrial detention facility;

(iv) for juveniles—

(I) held awaiting trial;

(II) residing in such facility or institution for purposes of receiving care or treatment; or

(III) residing for any State purpose in such facility or institution (other than a residential facility providing only elementary or secondary education that is not an institution in which reside juveniles who are adjudicated delinquent, in need of supervision, neglected, placed in State custody, mentally ill or disabled, mentally retarded, or chronically ill or handicapped); or

(v) providing skilled nursing, intermediate or long-term care, or custodial or residential care.

(2) Privately owned and operated facilities shall not be deemed "institutions" under this Act if—

(A) the licensing of such facility by the State constitutes the sole nexus between such facility and such State;

(B) the receipt by such facility, on behalf of persons residing in such facility, of payments under title XVI, XVIII, or under a State plan approved under title XIX, of the Social Security Act [42 USCS §§ 1381 et seq., §§ 1395 et seq., or §§ 1396 et seq.], constitutes the sole nexus between such facility and such State; or

(C) the licensing of such facility by the State, and the receipt by such facility, on behalf of persons residing in such facility, of payments under title XVI, XVIII, or under a State plan approved under title XIX, of the Social Security Act [42 USCS §§ 381 et seq., §§ 1395 et seq., §§ 1396 et seq.], constitutes the sole nexus between such facility and such State;

(3) The term "person" means an individual, a trust or estate, a partnership, an association, or a corporation;

(4) The term "State" means any of the several States, the District of Columbia, the Commonwealth of Puerto Rico, or any of the territories and possessions of the United States;

(5) The term "legislative days" means any calendar day on which either House of Congress is in session.

§ 1997a. Initiation of civil actions

(a) Discretionary authority of Attorney General; preconditions. Whenever the Attorney General has reasonable cause to believe that any State or political subdivision of a State, official, employee, or agent thereof, or other person acting on behalf of a State or political subdivision of a State is subjecting persons residing in or confined to an institution, as defined in section 2 [42 USCS § 1997], to egregious or flagrant conditions which deprive such persons of any rights, privileges, or immunities secured or protected by the Constitution or laws of the United States causing such persons to suffer grievous harm, and that such deprivation is pursuant to a pattern or practice of resistance to the full enjoyment of such rights, privileges, or immunities, the Attorney General, for or in the name of the United States, may institute a civil action in any appropriate United States district court against such party for such equitable relief as may be appropriate to insure the minimum corrective measures necessary to insure the full enjoyment of such rights, privileges, or immunities, except that such equitable relief shall be available under this Act to persons residing in or confined to an institution as defined in section 2(1)(B)(ii) [42 USCS § 1997(1)(B)(ii)] only insofar as such persons are subjected to conditions which deprive them of rights, privileges, or immunities secured or protected by the Constitution of the United States.

(b) Discretionary award of attorney fees. In any action commenced under this section, the court may allow the prevailing party, other than the United States, a reasonable attorney's fee against the United States as part of the costs.

(c) Attorney General to personally sign complaint. The Attorney General shall personally sign any complaint filed pursuant to this section.

§ 1997b. Certification requirements; Attorney General to personally sign certification

(a) At the time of the commencement of an action under section 3 [42 USCS § 1997a] the Attorney General shall certify to the court—

(1) that at least 49 calendar days previously the Attorney General has notified in writing the Governor or chief executive officer and attorney general or chief legal officer of the appropriate State or political subdivision and the director of the institution of—

(A) the alleged conditions which deprive rights, privileges, or immunities secured or protected by the Constitution or laws of the United States and the alleged pattern or practice of resistance to the full enjoyment of such rights, privileges, or immunities;

(B) the supporting facts giving rise to the alleged conditions and the alleged pattern or practice, including the dates or time period during which the alleged conditions and pattern or practice of resistance occurred; and when feasible, the identity of all persons reasonably suspected of being involved in causing the alleged conditions and pattern or practice at the time of the certification, and the date on which the alleged conditions and pattern or practice were first brought to the attention of the Attorney General; and

(C) the minimum measures which the Attorney General believes may remedy the alleged conditions and the alleged pattern or practice of resistance;

(2) that the Attorney General has notified in writing the Governor or chief executive officer and attorney general or chief legal officer of the appropriate State or political subdivision and the director of the institution of the Attorney General's intention to commence an investigation of such institution, that such notice was delivered at least seven days prior to the commencement of such investigation and that between the time of such notice and the commencement of an action under section 3 of this Act [42 USCS § 1997a]—

(A) the Attorney General has made a reasonable good faith effort to consult with the Governor or chief executive officer and attorney general or chief legal officer of the appropriate State or political subdivision and the director of the institution, or their designees, regarding financial, technical, or other assistance which may be available from the United States and which the Attorney General believes may assist in the correction of such conditions and pattern or practice of resistance;

(B) the Attorney General has encouraged the appropriate officials to correct the alleged conditions and pattern or practice of resistance through informal methods of conference, conciliation and persuasion, including, to the extent feasible, discussion of the possible costs and fiscal impacts of alternative minimum corrective measures, and it is the Attorney General's opinion that reasonable efforts at voluntary correction have not succeeded; and

(C) the Attorney General is satisfied that the appropriate officials have had a reasonable time to take appropriate action to correct such conditions and pattern or practice, taking into consideration the time required to remodel or make necessary changes in physical facilities or relocate residents, reasonable legal or procedural requirements, the urgency of the need to correct such conditions, and other circumstances involved in correcting such conditions; and

(3) that the Attorney General believes that such an action by the United States is of general public importance and will materially further the vindication of rights, privileges, or immunities secured or protected by the Constitution or laws of the United States.

(b) The Attorney General shall personally sign any certification made pursuant to this section.

§ 1997c. Intervention in actions

(a) Discretionary authority of Attorney General; preconditions; time period.

(1) Whenever an action has been commenced in any court of the United States seeking relief from egregious or flagrant conditions which deprive persons residing in institutions of any rights, privileges, or immunities secured or protected by the Constitution or laws of the United States causing them to suffer grievous harm and the Attorney General has reasonable cause to believe that such deprivation is pursuant to a pattern or practice of resistance to the full enjoyment of such rights, privileges, or immunities, the Attorney General, for or in the name of the United States, may intervene in such action upon motion by the Attorney General.

(2) The Attorney General shall not file a motion to intervene under paragraph (1) before 90 days after the commencement of the action, except that if the court determines it would be in the interests of justice, the court may shorten or waive the time period.

(b) Certification requirements by Attorney General.

(1) The Attorney General shall certify to the court in the motion to intervene filed under subsection (a)—

(A) that the Attorney General has notified in writing, at least fifteen days previously, the Governor or chief executive officer, attorney general or chief legal officer of the appropriate State or political subdivision, and the director of the institution—

(i) the alleged conditions which deprive rights, privileges, or immunities secured or protected by the Constitution or laws of the United States and the alleged pattern or practice of resistance to the full enjoyment of such rights, privileges, or immunities;

(ii) the supporting facts giving rise to the alleged conditions, including the dates and time period during which the alleged conditions and pattern or practice of resistance occurred; and

(iii) to the extent feasible and consistent with the interests of other plaintiffs, the minimum measures which he believes may remedy the alleged conditions and the alleged pattern or practice of resistance; and

(B) that the Attorney General believes that such intervention by the United States is of general public importance and will materially further the vindication of rights, privileges, or immunities secured or protected by the Constitution or laws of the United States.

(2) The Attorney General shall personally sign any certification made pursuant to this section.

(c) Attorney General to personally sign motion to intervene. The Attorney General shall personally sign any motion to intervene made pursuant to this section.

(d) Discretionary award of attorney fees; other award provisions unaffected. In any action in which the United States joins as an intervenor under this section, the court may allow the prevailing party, other than the United States, a reasonable attorney's fee against the United States as part of the costs. Nothing in this subsection precludes the award of attorney's fees available under any other provisions of the United States Code.

§ 1997d. Prohibition of retaliation

No person reporting conditions which may constitute a violation under this Act shall be subjected to retaliation in any manner for so reporting.

§ 1997e. Suits by prisoners

(a) Applicability of administrative remedies. No action shall be brought with respect to prison conditions under section 1979 of the Revised Statutes of the United States (42 U.S.C. § 1983), or any other Federal law, by a prisoner confined in any jail, prison, or other correctional facility until such administrative remedies as are available are exhausted.

(b) Failure of State to adopt or adhere to administrative grievance procedure. The failure of a State to adopt or adhere to an administrative grievance procedure shall not constitute the basis for an action under section 3 or 5 of this Act [42 USCS § 1997a or 1997c].

(c) Dismissal.

(1) The court shall on its own motion or on the motion of a party dismiss any action brought with respect to prison conditions under section 1979 of the Revised Statutes of the United States {2 U.S.C. § 1983), or any other Federal law, by a prisoner confined in any jail, prison, or other correctional facility

if the court is satisfied that the action is frivolous, malicious, fails to state a claim upon which relief can be granted, or seeks monetary relief from a defendant who is immune from such relief.

(2) In the event that a claim is, on its face, frivolous, malicious, fails to state a claim upon which relief can be granted, or seeks monetary relief from a defendant who is immune from such relief, the court may dismiss the underlying claim without first requiring the exhaustion of administrative remedies.

(d) Attorney's fees.

(1) In any action brought by a prisoner who is confined to any jail, prison, or other correctional facility, in which attorney's fees are authorized under section 2 of the Revised Statutes of the United States (42 U.S.C. § 1988), such fees shall not be awarded, except to the extent that—

(A) the fee was directly and reasonably incurred in proving an actual violation of the plaintiff's rights protected by a statute pursuant to which a fee may be awarded under section 2 of the Revised Statutes; and

(B)

(i) the amount of the fee is proportionately related to the court ordered relief for the violation; or

(ii) the fee was directly and reasonably incurred in enforcing the relief ordered for the violation.

(2) Whenever a monetary judgment is awarded in an action described in paragraph (1), a portion of the judgment (not to exceed 25 percent) shall be applied to satisfy the amount of attorney's fees awarded against the defendant. If the award of attorney's fees is not greater than 150 percent of the judgment, the excess shall be paid by the defendant.

(3) No award of attorney's fees in an action described in paragraph (1) shall be based on an hourly rate greater than 150 percent of the hourly rate established under section 3006A of title 18, United States Code, for payment of court-appointed counsel.

(4) Nothing in this subsection shall prohibit a prisoner from entering into an agreement to pay an attorney's fee in an amount

greater than the amount authorized under this subsection, if the fee is paid by the individual rather than by the defendant pursuant to section 2 of the Revised Statutes of the United States (42 U.S.C. § 1988).

(e) Limitation on recovery. No Federal civil action may be brought by a prisoner confined in a jail, prison, or other correctional facility, for mental or emotional injury suffered while in custody without a prior showing of physical injury.

(f) Hearings.

(1) To the extent practicable, in any action brought with respect to prison conditions in Federal court pursuant to section 1979 of the Revised Statutes of the United States (42 U.S.C. § 1983), or any other Federal law, by a prisoner confined in any jail, prison, or other correctional facility, pretrial proceedings in which the prisoner's participation is required or permitted shall be conducted by telephone, video conference, or other telecommunications technology without removing the prisoner from the facility in which the prisoner is confined.

(2) Subject to the agreement of the official of the Federal, State, or local unit of government with custody over the prisoner, hearings may be conducted at the facility in which the prisoner is confined. To the extent practicable, the court shall allow counsel to participate by telephone, video conference, or other communications technology in any hearing held at the facility.

(g) Waiver of reply.

(1) Any defendant may waive the right to reply to any action brought by a prisoner confined in any jail, prison, or other correctional facility under section 1979 of the Revised Statutes of the United States (42 U.S.C. § 1983) or any other Federal law. Notwithstanding any other law or rule of procedure, such waiver shall not constitute an admission of the allegations contained in the complaint. No relief shall be granted to the plaintiff unless a reply has been filed.

(2) The court may require any defendant to reply to a complaint brought under this section if it finds that the plaintiff has a reasonable opportunity to prevail on the merits.

(h) Definition. As used in this section, the term "prisoner" means any person incarcerated or detained in any facility who is accused of, convicted of, sentenced for, or adjudicated delinquent for, violations of criminal law or the terms and conditions of parole, probation, pretrial release, or diversionary program.

§ 1997f. Report to Congress

The Attorney General shall include in the report to Congress on the business of the Department of Justice prepared pursuant to section 522 of title 28, United States Code—

(1) a statement of the number, variety, and outcome of all actions instituted pursuant to this Act including the history of, precise reasons for, and procedures followed in initiation or intervention in each case in which action was commenced;

(2) a detailed explanation of the procedures by which the Department has received, reviewed and evaluated petitions or complaints regarding conditions in institutions;

(3) an analysis of the impact of actions instituted pursuant to this Act including, when feasible, an estimate of the costs incurred by States and other political subdivisions;

(4) a statement of the financial, technical, or other assistance which has been made available from the United States to the State in order to assist in the correction of the conditions which are alleged to have deprived a person of rights, privileges, or immunities secured or protected by the Constitution or laws of the United States; and

(5) the progress made in each Federal institution toward meeting existing promulgated standards for such institutions or constitutionally guaranteed minima.

§ 1997g. Priorities for use of funds

[(a)] It is the intent of Congress that deplorable conditions in institutions covered by this Act amounting to deprivations of rights protected by the Constitution or laws of the United States be corrected, not only by litigation as contemplated in this Act, but also by the voluntary good faith efforts of agencies of Federal, State, and local governments. It is the further intention of Congress that where Federal funds are available for use in improving such institutions, priority should be given to the correction or elimination of such uncon-stitutional or illegal conditions which may exist. It is not the intent of this provision to require the redirection of funds from one pro-gram to another or from one State to another.

§ 1997h. Notice to Federal departments

At the time of notification of the com-mencement of an investigation of an institu-tion under section 3 [42 USCS § 997a] or of the notification of an intention to file a motion to intervene under section 5 of this Act [42 USCS § 997c], and if the relevant institution receives Federal financial assis-tance from the Department of Health and Human Services or the Department of Edu-cation, the Attorney General shall notify the appropriate Secretary of the action and the reasons for such action and shall consult with such officials. Following such consultation, the Attorney General may proceed with an action under this Act if the Attorney General is satisfied that such action is consistent with the policies and goals of the executive branch.

§ 1997i. Disclaimer respecting standards of care

Provisions of this Act shall not authorize promulgation of regulations defining stan-dards of care.

§ 1997j. Disclaimer respecting private litigation

The provisions of this Act shall in no way expand or restrict the authority of parties other than the United States to enforce the legal rights which they may have pursuant to existing law with regard to institutionalized persons. In this regard, the fact that the Attor-ney General may be conducting an investiga-tion or contemplating litigation pursuant to this Act shall not be grounds for delay of or prejudice to any litigation on behalf of par-ties other than the United States.

18 U.S.C. § 3626 (1997) APPROPRIATE REMEDIES WITH RESPECT TO PRISON CONDITIONS

(a) Requirements for relief.

(1) Prospective relief.

(A) Prospective relief in any civil action with respect to prison conditions shall extend no further than necessary to correct the violation of the Federal right of a par-ticular plaintiff or plaintiffs. The court shall not grant or approve any prospective relief unless the court finds that such relief is narrowly drawn, extends no further than necessary to correct the violation of the Federal right, and is the least intrusive means necessary to correct the violation of the Federal right. The court shall give sub-stantial weight to any adverse impact on public safety or the operation of a criminal justice system caused by the relief.

(B) The court shall not order any prospective relief that requires or permits a government official to exceed his or her authority under State or local law or other-wise violates State or local law, unless—

(i) Federal law requires such relief to be ordered in violation of State or local law;

(ii) the relief is necessary to correct the violation of a Federal right; and

(iii) no other relief will correct the violation of the Federal right.

(C) Nothing in this section shall be con-strued to authorize the courts, in exercis-ing their remedial powers, to order the construction of prisons or the raising of taxes, or to repeal or detract from other-wise applicable limitations on the remedi-al powers of the courts.

(2) Preliminary injunctive relief. In any civil action with respect to prison conditions, to the extent otherwise authorized by law, the court may enter a temporary restraining order

or an order for preliminary injunctive relief. Preliminary injunctive relief must be narrowly drawn, extend no further than necessary to correct the harm the court finds requires preliminary relief, and be the least intrusive means necessary to correct that harm. The court shall give substantial weight to any adverse impact on public safety or the operation of a criminal justice system caused by the preliminary relief and shall respect the principles of comity set out in paragraph (1)(B) in tailoring any preliminary relief. Preliminary injunctive relief shall automatically expire on the date that is 90 days after its entry, unless the court makes the findings required under subsection (a)(1) for the entry of prospective relief and makes the order final before the expiration of the 90-day period.

(3) Prisoner release order.

(A) In any civil action with respect to prison conditions, no court shall enter a prisoner release order unless—

(i) a court has previously entered an order for less intrusive relief that has failed to remedy the deprivation of the Federal right sought to be remedied through the prisoner release order; and

(ii) the defendant has had a reasonable amount of time to comply with the previous court orders.

(B) In any civil action in Federal court with respect to prison conditions, a prisoner release order shall be entered only by a three-judge court in accordance with section 2284 of title 28, if the requirements of subparagraph (E) have been met.

(C) A party seeking a prisoner release order in Federal court shall file with any request for such relief, a request for a three-judge court and materials sufficient to demonstrate that the requirements of subparagraph (A) have been met.

(D) If the requirements under subparagraph (A) have been met, a Federal judge before whom a civil action with respect to prison conditions is pending who believes that a prison release order should be considered may sua sponte request the convening of a three-judge court to determine whether a prisoner release order should be entered.

(E) The three-judge court shall enter a prisoner release order only if the court finds by clear and convincing evidence that—

(i) crowding is the primary cause of the violation of a Federal right; and

(ii) no other relief will remedy the violation of the Federal right.

(F) Any State or local official including a legislator or unit of government whose jurisdiction or function includes the appropriation of funds for the construction, operation, or maintenance of prison facilities, or the prosecution or custody of persons who may be released from, or not admitted to, a prison as a result of a prisoner release order shall have standing to oppose the imposition or continuation in effect of such relief and to seek termination of such relief, and shall have the right to intervene in any proceeding relating to such relief.

(b) Termination of relief.

(1) Termination of prospective relief.

(A) In any civil action with respect to prison conditions in which prospective relief is ordered, such relief shall be terminable upon the motion of any party or intervener—

(i) 2 years after the date the court granted or approved the prospective relief;

(ii) 1 year after the date the court has entered an order denying termination of prospective relief under this paragraph; or

(iii) in the case of an order issued on or before the date of enactment of the Prison Litigation Reform Act [enacted April 26, 1996], 2 years after such date of enactment.

(B) Nothing in this section shall prevent the parties from agreeing to terminate or modify relief before the relief is terminated under subparagraph (A).

(2) Immediate termination of prospective relief. In any civil action with respect to prison conditions, a defendant or intervener shall be entitled to the immediate termination of any prospective relief if the relief was

approved or granted in the absence of a finding by the court that the relief is narrowly drawn, extends no further than necessary to correct the violation of the Federal right, and is the least intrusive means necessary to correct the violation of the Federal right.

(3) Limitation. Prospective relief shall not terminate if the court makes written findings based on the record that prospective relief remains necessary to correct a current and ongoing violation of the Federal right, extends no further than necessary to correct the violation of the Federal right, and that the prospective relief is narrowly drawn and the least intrusive means to correct the violation.

(4) Termination or modification of relief. Nothing in this section shall prevent any party or intervener from seeking modification or termination before the relief is terminable under paragraph (1) or (2), to the extent that modification or termination would otherwise be legally permissible.

(c) Settlements.

(1) Consent decrees. In any civil action with respect to prison conditions, the court shall not enter or approve a consent decree unless it complies with the limitations on relief set forth in subsection (a).

(2) Private settlement agreements.

(A) Nothing in this section shall preclude parties from entering into a private settlement agreement that does not comply with the limitations on relief set forth in subsection (a), if the terms of that agreement are not subject to court enforcement other than the reinstatement of the civil proceeding that the agreement settled.

(B) Nothing in this section shall preclude any party claiming that a private settlement agreement has been breached from seeking in State court any remedy available under State law.

(d) State law remedies. The limitations on remedies in this section shall not apply to relief entered by a State court based solely upon claims arising under State law.

(e) Procedure for motions affecting prospective relief.

(1) Generally. The court shall promptly rule on any motion to modify or terminate prospective relief in a civil action with respect to prison conditions. Mandamus shall lie to remedy any failure to issue a prompt ruling on such a motion.

(2) Automatic stay. Any motion to modify or terminate prospective relief made under subsection (b) shall operate as a stay during the period—

(A) (i) beginning on the 30th day after such motion is filed, in the case of a motion made under paragraph (1) or (2) of subsection (b); or

(ii) beginning on the 180th day after such motion is filed, in the case of a motion made under any other law; and

(B) ending on the date the court enters a final order ruling on the motion.

(3) Postponement of automatic stay. The court may postpone the effective date of an automatic stay specified in subsection (e)(2)(A) for not more than 60 days for good cause. No postponement shall be permissible because of general congestion of the court's calendar.

(4) Order blocking the automatic stay. Any order staying, suspending, delaying, or barring the operation of the automatic stay described in paragraph (2) (other than an order to postpone the effective date of the automatic stay under paragraph (3)) shall be treated as an order refusing to dissolve or modify an injunction and shall be appealable pursuant to section 1292(a)(1) of title 28, United States Code, regardless of how the order is styled or whether the order is termed a preliminary or a final ruling.

(f) Special masters.

(1) In general.

(A) In any civil action in a Federal court with respect to prison conditions, the court may appoint a special master who shall be disinterested and objective and who will give due regard to the public safety, to conduct hearings on the record and prepare proposed findings of fact.

(B) The court shall appoint a special master under this subsection during the remedial phase of the action only upon a finding that the remedial phase will be sufficiently complex to warrant the appointment.

(2) Appointment.

(A) If the court determines that the appointment of a special master is necessary, the court shall request that the defendant institution and the plaintiff each submit a list of not more than 5 persons to serve as a special master.

(B) Each party shall have the opportunity to remove up to 3 persons from the opposing party's list.

(C) The court shall select the master from the persons remaining on the list after the operation of subparagraph (B).

(3) Interlocutory appeal. Any party shall have the right to an interlocutory appeal of the judge's selection of the special master under this subsection, on the ground of partiality.

(4) Compensation. The compensation to be allowed to a special master under this section shall be based on an hourly rate not greater than the hourly rate established under section 3006A for payment of court-appointed counsel, plus costs reasonably incurred by the special master. Such compensation and costs shall be paid with funds appropriated to the Judiciary.

(5) Regular review of appointment. In any civil action with respect to prison conditions in which a special master is appointed under this subsection, the court shall review the appointment of the special master every 6 months to determine whether the services of the special master continue to be required under paragraph (1). In no event shall the appointment of a special master extend beyond the termination of the relief.

(6) Limitations on powers and duties. A special master appointed under this subsection—

(A) may be authorized by a court to conduct hearings and prepare proposed findings of fact, which shall be made on the record;

(B) shall not make any findings or communications ex parte;

(C) may be authorized by a court to assist in the development of remedial plans; and

(D) may be removed at any time, but shall be relieved of the appointment upon the termination of relief.

(g) Definitions. As used in this section—

(1) the term "consent decree" means any relief entered by the court that is based in whole or in part upon the consent or acquiescence of the parties but does not include private settlements;

(2) the term "civil action with respect to prison conditions" means any civil proceeding arising under Federal law with respect to the conditions of confinement or the effects of actions by government officials on the lives of persons confined in prison, but does not include habeas corpus proceedings challenging the fact or duration of confinement in prison;

(3) the term "prisoner" means any person subject to incarceration, detention, or admission to any facility who is accused of, convicted of, sentenced for, or adjudicated delinquent for, violations of criminal law or the terms and conditions of parole, probation, pretrial release, or diversionary program;

(4) the term "prisoner release order" includes any order, including a temporary restraining order or preliminary injunctive relief, that has the purpose or effect of reducing or limiting the prison population, or that directs the release from or nonadmission of prisoners to a prison;

(5) the term "prison" means any Federal, State, or local facility that incarcerates or detains juveniles or adults accused of, convicted of, sentenced for, or adjudicated delinquent for, violations of criminal law;

(6) the term "private settlement agreement" means an agreement entered into among the parties that is not subject to judicial enforcement other than the reinstatement of the civil proceeding that the agreement settled;

(7) the term "prospective relief" means all relief other than compensatory monetary damages;

(8) the term "special master" means any person appointed by a Federal court pursuant to Rule 53 of the Federal Rules of Civil Procedure or pursuant to any inherent power of the court to exercise the powers of a master, regardless of the title or description given by the court; and

(9) the term "relief" means all relief in any form that may be granted or approved by the court, and includes consent decrees but does not include private settlement agreements.42 U.S. §2000cc

42 U.S.C. § 2000cc RELIGIOUS LAND USE AND INSTITUTIONALIZED PERSONS ACT

(a) Substantial burdens.

(1) General rule. No government shall impose or implement a land use regulation in a manner that imposes a substantial burden on the religious exercise of a person, including a religious assembly or institution, unless the government demonstrates that imposition of the burden on that person, assembly, or institution—

(A) is in furtherance of a compelling governmental interest; and

(B) is the least restrictive means of furthering that compelling governmental interest.

(2) Scope of application. This subsection applies in any case in which—

(A) the substantial burden is imposed in a program or activity that receives Federal financial assistance, even if the burden results from a rule of general applicability;

(B) the substantial burden affects, or removal of that substantial burden would affect, commerce with foreign nations, among the several States, or with Indian tribes, even if the burden results from a rule of general applicability; or

(C) the substantial burden is imposed in the implementation of a land use regulation or system of land use regulations, under which a government makes, or has in place formal or informal procedures or practices that permit the government to make, individualized assessments of the proposed uses for the property involved.

(b) Discrimination and exclusion.

(1) Equal terms. No government shall impose or implement a land use regulation in a manner that treats a religious assembly or institution on less than equal terms with a nonreligious assembly or institution.

(2) Nondiscrimination. No government shall impose or implement a land use regulation that discriminates against any assembly or institution on the basis of religion or religious denomination.

(3) Exclusions and limits. No government shall impose or implement a land use regulation that—

(A) totally excludes religious assemblies from a jurisdiction; or

(B) unreasonably limits religious assemblies, institutions, or structures within a jurisdiction.

P.L. 105-277, Div A, § 101(b) [Title I, § 127], 112 Stat. 2681-74, Oct. 21, 1998, NON-DISCLOSURE OF INFORMATION RELATING TO PRISON EMPLOYEES ACT.

Notwithstanding any other provision of law, in any action brought by a prisoner under section 1979 of the Revised Statutes (42 U.S.C. 1983) against a Federal, State, or local jail, prison, or correctional facility, or any employee or former employee thereof, arising out of the incarceration of that prisoner—

(1) the financial records of a person employed or formerly employed by the Federal, State, or local jail, prison, or correctional facility, shall not be subject to disclosure without the written consent of that person or pursuant to a court order, unless a verdict of liability has been entered against that person; and

(2) the home address, home phone number, social security number, identity of family members, personal tax returns, and personal banking information of a person described in paragraph (1), and any other records or information of a similar nature relating to that person, shall not be subject to disclosure without the written consent of that person, or pursuant to a court order.

APPENDIX III

EUROPEAN CONVENTION ON HUMAN RIGHTS
(Selected Provisions)
(September 3, 1953)

Article 1.

The High Contracting Parties shall secure to everyone within their jurisdiction the rights and freedoms defined in Section 1 of this Convention.

Article 2.

1. Everyone's right to life shall be protected by law. No one shall be deprived of his life intentionally save in the execution of a sentence of a court following his conviction of a crime for which the penalty is provided by law.

2. Deprivation of life shall not be inflicted in contravention of this Article when it results from the use of force which is more than absolutely necessary:

    a. in defence of any person from unlawful violence;

    b. in order to effect a lawful arrest or to prevent the escape of a person lawfully detained;

    c. in action lawfully taken for the purpose of quelling a riot or insurrection.

Protocol No. 6 (Substantive Articles):

1. The death penalty shall be abolished. No one shall be condemned to such penalty or executed.

2. A State may make provision in its law for the death penalty in respect of acts committed in time of war or of imminent threat of war; such penalty shall be applied only in the instances laid down in the law and in accordance with its provisions. The State shall communicate to the Secretary General of the Council of Europe the relevant provisions of that law.

3. No derogation from the provisions of this Protocol shall be made under Article 15 of the Convention.

4. No reservation may be made under Article 64 of the Convention in respect of the provisions of this Protocol.

Article 3.

No one shall be subjected to torture or to inhuman or degrading treatment or punishment.

Article 4.

1. No one shall be held in slavery or servitude.

2. No one shall be required to perform forced or compulsory labor.

3. For purposes of this Article, the term "forced or compulsory labor" shall not include:

    a. Any work required to be done in the ordinary course of detention imposed according to the provisions of Article 5 of this Convention or during conditional release from such detention.

Article 5.

1. Everyone has the right to liberty and security of person. No one shall be deprived of his liberty save in the following cases and in accordance with a procedure prescribed by law:

    a. the lawful detention of a person after conviction by a competent court;

    b. the lawful arrest or detention of a person for non-compliance with the lawful order of a court or in order to secure the fulfillment of any obligation prescribed by law;

* * *

2. Everyone who is arrested shall be informed promptly, in a language which he understands, of the reasons for his arrest and of any charge against him.

* * *

5. Everyone who has been the victim of arrest or detention in contravention of the provisions of this Article shall have an enforceable right to compensation.

Article 6.

1. In the determination of his civil rights and obligations or of any criminal charge against him, everyone is entitled to a fair and public hearing within a reasonable time by an independent and impartial tribunal established by law. Judgment shall be pronounced publicly but the press and public may be excluded in the interests of morals, public order or national security in a democratic society, where the interests of juveniles or the protection of the private life of the parties so require, or to the extent strictly necessary in the opinion of the court in special circumstances where publicity would prejudice the interests of justice.

2. Everyone charged with a criminal offence shall be presumed innocent until proved guilty according to law.

3. Everyone charged with a criminal offense has the following minimum rights:

    a. to be informed promptly, in a language which he understands and in detail, of the nature and cause of the accusation against him;

    b. to have adequate time and facilities for the preparation of his defense;

    c. to defend himself in person or through legal assistance of his own choosing or, if he has not sufficient means to pay for legal assistance, to be given it free when the interests of justice so require;

    d.   to examine or have examined witnesses against him and to obtain the attendance and examination of witnesses on his behalf under the same conditions as witnesses against him.

    e.   to have the free assistance of an interpreter if he cannot understand or speak the language used in court.

Protocol No. 7

Protocol: Article 2.

1. Everyone convicted of a criminal offense by a tribunal shall have the right to have his conviction or sentence reviewed by a higher tribunal. The exercise of this right, including the grounds on which it may be exercised, shall be governed by law.

2. This right may be subject to exceptions in regard to offenses of a minor character, as prescribed by law, or in cases in which the person convicted was tried in the first instance by the highest tribunal or was convicted following an appeal against acquittal.

Protocol: Article 3.

When a person has by a final decision been convicted of a criminal offense and when subsequently his conviction has been reversed, or he has been pardoned, on the ground that a new or newly discovered fact shows conclusively that there has been a miscarriage of justice, the person who has suffered punishment as a result of such conviction shall be compensated according to the law or the practice of the State concerned, unless it is proved that the non-disclosure of the unknown fact in time is wholly or partly attributed to him.

Protocol: Article 4.

1. No one shall be liable to be tried or punished again in criminal proceedings under the jurisdiction of the same State for an offense of which he has already been finally acquitted or convicted in accordance with the law and penal procedure of that State.

2. The provisions of the preceding paragraph shall not prevent the reopening of the case in accordance with the law and penal procedure of the State concerned, if there is evidence of new or newly discovered facts, or if there has been a fundamental defect in the previous proceedings, which could affect the outcome of the case.

3. No derogation from this Article shall be made under Article 15 of the Convention.

* * *

Article 8.

1. Everyone has the right to respect for his private and family life, his home and his correspondence.

2. There shall be no interference by a public authority with the exercise of this right except such as is in accordance with the law and is necessary in a democratic society in the interests of national security, public safety or the economic well-being of the country, for the prevention of disorder or crime, for the protection of health or morals, or for the protection of the rights and freedoms of others.

Article 9.

1. Everyone has the right to freedom of thought, conscience and religion; this right includes freedom to change his religion or belief and freedom, either alone or in community with others and in public or in private, to manifest his religion or belief, in worship, teaching practice and observance.

2. Freedom to manifest one's religion or beliefs shall be subject only to such limitations as are prescribed by law and are necessary in a democratic society in the interests of public safety, for the protection of public order, health or morals, or for the protection of the rights and freedoms of others.

Article 10.

1. Everyone has the right to freedom of expression. This right shall include freedom to hold opinions and to receive and impart information and ideas without interference by public authority and regardless of frontiers. This Article shall not prevent States from requiring the licensing of broadcasting, television or cinema enterprises.

2. The exercise of these freedoms, since it carries with it duties and responsibilities, may be subject to such formalities, conditions, restrictions or penalties as are prescribed by law and are necessary in a democratic society, in the interests of national security, territorial integrity or public safety, for the prevention of disorder or crime, for the protection of health or morals, for the protection of the reputation or rights of others, for preventing the disclosure of information received in confidence, or for maintaining the authority and impartiality of the judiciary.

* * *

Article 13.

Everyone whose rights and freedoms as set forth in this Convention are violated shall have an effective remedy before a national authority notwithstanding that the violation has been committed by persons acting in an official capacity.

APPENDIX IV

EUROPEAN PRISON RULES

I. RECOMMENDATION NO. R (87) 3 OF THE COMMITTEE OF MINISTERS TO MEMBER STATES ON THE EUROPEAN PRISON RULES

The Committee of Ministers under the terms of Article 15.b of the Statute of the Council of Europe,

Considering the importance of establishing common principles regarding penal policy among the member states of the Council of Europe;

Noting that, although considerable progress has been made in developing non-custodial alternatives for dealing with offenders, the deprivation of liberty remains a necessary sanction in criminal justice systems;

Considering the important role of international rules in the practice and philosophy of prison treatment and management;

Noting, however, that significant social trends and changes in regard to prison treatment and management have made it desirable to reformulate the Standard Minimum Rules for the Treatment of Prisoners of the Council of Europe (Resolution (73)(5) so as to support and encourage the best of these developments and offer scope for future progress,

Recommends that the governments of member states be guided in their internal legislation and practice by the principles set out in the rest of the European Prison Rules, appended to the present Recommendation, with a view to their progressive implementation with special emphasis on the purposes set out in the preamble and the rules of basic principle in Part I, and to give the widest possible circulation to this text. Appendix to Recommendation No. R (87) 3

The European Prison Rules
Revised European Version
of the Standard Minimum Rules for the Treatment of Prisoners

PREAMBLE

The purposes of these rules are:

a.   to establish a range of minimum standards for all those aspects of prison administration that are essential to human conditions and positive treatment in modern and progressive systems;

b.   To serve as a stimulus to prison administrations to develop policies and management style and practice based on good contemporary principles of purpose and equity;

c.   to encourage in prison staffs professional attitudes that reflect the important social and moral qualities of their work and to create conditions in which they can optimize their own performance to the benefit of society in general, the prisoners in their care and their own vocational satisfaction;

d.   to provide realistic basic criteria against which prison administrations and those responsible for inspecting the conditions and management of prisons can make valid judgments of performance and measure progress towards higher standards.

It is emphasized that the rules do not constitute a model system and that, in practice, many European prison services are already operating well above many of the standards set out in the rules and that others are striving, and will continue to strive, to do so. Wherever there are difficulties or practical problems to be overcome in the application of the rules, the Council of Europe has the machinery and the expertise available to assist with advice and the fruits of the experience of the various prison administrations within its sphere.

In these rules, renewed emphasis has been placed on the precepts of human dignity, the commitment of prison administrations to humane and positive treatment, the importance of staff roles and effective modern management approaches. They are set out to provide ready reference, encouragement and guidance to those who are working at all levels of prison administration. The explanatory memorandum that accompanies the rules is intended to ensure the understanding, acceptance and flexibility that are necessary to achieve the highest realistic level of implementation beyond the basic standards.

PART I
The Basic Principles

1.   The deprivation of liberty shall be effected in material and moral conditions which ensure respect for human dignity and are in conformity with these rules.

2.   The rules shall be applied impartially. There shall be no discrimination on grounds of race, color, sex, language, religion, political or other opinion, national or social origin, birth, economic or other status. The religious beliefs and moral precepts of the group to which a prisoner belongs shall be respected.

3.   The purposes of the treatment of persons in custody shall be such as to sustain their health and self-respect and, so far as the length of sentence permits, to develop their sense of responsibility and encourage those attitudes and skills that will assist them to return to society with the best chance of leading law-abiding and self-supporting lives after their release.

4.   There shall be regular inspections of penal institutions and services by qualified and experienced inspectors appointed by a competent authority. Their task shall be, in particular, to monitor whether and to what extent these institutions are administered in accordance with existing laws and regulations, the objectives of the prison services and the requirements of these rules.

5.   The protection of the individual rights of prisoners with special regard to the legality of the execution of detention measures shall be secured by means of a control carried out, according to national rules, by a judicial authority or other

duly constituted body authorized to visit the prisoners and not belong to the prison administration.

6.   1.   These rules shall be made readily available to staff in the national languages:

      2.   They shall also be available to prisoners in the same languages and in other languages so far as is reasonable and practicable.

PART II
The Management of Prison Systems

Reception and Registration

7.   1.   No person shall be received in an institution without a valid commitment order.

      2.   The essential details of the commitment and reception shall immediately be recorded.

8.   In every place where persons are imprisoned a complete and secure record of the following information shall be kept concerning each prisoner received:

    a.   information concerning the identity of the prisoner;

    b.   the reasons for commitment and the authority therefor;

    c.   the day and hour of admission and release.

9.   Reception arrangements shall conform with the basic principles of the rules and shall assist prisoners to resolve their urgent personal problems.

10.   1.   As soon as possible after reception, full reports and relevant information about the personal situation and training program of each prisoner with a sentence of suitable length in preparation for ultimate release shall be drawn up and submitted to the director for information or approval as appropriate.

      2.   Such reports shall always include reports by a medical officer and the personnel in direct charge of the prisoner concerned.

      3.   The reports and information concerning prisoners shall be maintained with due regard to confidentiality on an individual basis, regularly kept up to date and only accessible to authorized persons.

The Allocation and Classification of Prisoners

11.   1.   In allocating prisoners to different institutions or regimes, due account shall be taken of their judicial and legal situation (untried or convicted prisoner, first offender or habitual offender, short sentence or long sentence), of the special requirements of their treatment, of their medical needs, their sex and age.

      2.   Males and females shall in principle be detained separately, although they may participate together in organized activities as part of an established treatment program.

3. In principle, untried prisoners shall be detained separately from convicted prisoners unless they consent to being accommodated or involved together in organized activities beneficial to them.

4. Young prisoners shall be detained under conditions which as far as possible protect them from harmful influences and which take account of the needs peculiar to their age.

12. The purposes of classification or re-classification of prisoners shall be:

   a. to separate from others those prisoners who, by reasons of their criminal records or their personality, are likely to benefit from that or who may exercise a bad influence; and

   b. to assist in allocating prisoners to facilitate their treatment and social resettlement taking into account the management and security requirements.

13. So far as possible separate institutions or separate sections of an institution shall be used to facilitate the management of different treatment regimes or the allocation of specific categories of prisoners.

Accommodation

14. 1. Prisoners shall normally be lodged during the night in individual cells except in cases where it is considered that there are advantages in sharing accommodation with other prisoners.

   2. Where accommodation is shared it shall be occupied by prisoners suitable to associate with others in those conditions. There shall be supervision by night, in keeping with the nature of the institution.

15. The accommodation provided for prisoners, and in particular all sleeping accommodation, shall meet the requirements of health and hygiene, due regard being paid to climatic conditions and especially the cubic content of air, a reasonable amount of space, lighting, heating and ventilation.

16. In all places where prisoners are required to live or work:

   a. the windows shall be large enough to enable the prisoners, inter alia, to read or work by natural light in normal conditions. They shall be so constructed that they can allow the entrance of fresh air except where there is an adequate air conditioning system. Moreover, the windows shall, with due regard to security requirements, present in their size, location and construction as normal an appearance as possible;

   b. artificial light shall satisfy recognized technical standards.

17. The sanitary installations and arrangements for access shall be adequate to enable every prisoner to comply with the needs of nature when necessary and in clean and decent conditions.

18. Adequate bathing and showering installations shall be provided so that every prisoner may be enabled and required to have a bath or shower, at a temperature suitable to the climate, as frequently as necessary for general hygiene according to season and geographical region, but at least once a week. Wherever possible there should be free access at all reasonable times.

19.   All parts of an institution shall be properly maintained and kept clean at all times.

Personal Hygiene

20.   Prisoners shall be required to keep their persons clean, and to this end they shall be provided with water and with such toilet articles as are necessary for health and cleanliness.

21.   For reasons of health and in order that prisoners may maintain a good appearance and preserve their self-respect, facilities shall be provided for the proper care of the hair and beard, and men shall be enabled to shave regularly.

Clothing and Bedding

22.   1.   Prisoners who are not allowed to wear their own clothing shall be provided with an outfit of clothing suitable for the climate and adequate to keep them in good health. Such clothing shall in no manner be degrading or humiliating.

      2.   All clothing shall be clean and kept in proper condition. Underclothing shall be changed and washed as often as necessary for the maintenance of hygiene.

      3.   On the admission of prisoners to an institution, adequate arrangements shall be made to ensure that their personal clothing is kept in good condition and fit for use.

24.   Every prisoner shall be provided with a separate bed and separate and appropriate bedding which shall be kept in good order and changed often enough to ensure its cleanliness.

Food

25.   1.   In accordance with the standards laid down by the health authorities, the administration shall provide the prisoners at the normal times with food which is suitably prepared and presented, and which satisfies in quality and quantity the standards of dietetics and modern hygiene and takes into account their age, health, the nature of their work, and so far as possible, religious or cultural requirements.

      2.   Drinking water shall be available to every prisoner.

Medical Services

26.   1.   At every institution there shall be available the services of at least one qualified general practitioner.

      2.   Sick prisoners who require specialist treatment shall be transferred to specialized institutions or to civil hospitals. Where hospital facilities are provided in an institution, their equipment, furnishings and pharmaceutical supplies shall be suitable for the medical care and treatment of sick prisoners, and there shall be a staff of suitably trained officers.

      3.   The services of a qualified dental officer shall be available to every prisoner.

27. Prisoners may not be submitted to any experiments which may result in physical or moral injury.

28. 1. Arrangements shall be made wherever practicable for children to be born in a hospital outside the institution. However, unless special arrangements are made, there shall in penal institutions be the necessary staff and accommodation for the confinement and post-natal care of pregnant women. If a child is born in prison, this fact shall not be mentioned in the birth certificate.

     2. Where infants are allowed to remain in the institution with their mothers, special provision shall be made for a nursery staffed by qualified persons, where the infants shall be placed when they are not in the care of their mothers.

29. The medical officer shall see and examine every prisoner as soon as possible after admission and thereafter as necessary, with a view particularly to the discovery of physical or mental illness and the taking of all measures necessary for medical treatment; the segregation of prisoners suspected of infectious or contagious conditions; the noting of physical or mental defects which might impede resettlement after release, and the determination of the fitness of every prisoner to work.

30. 1. The medical officer shall have the care of the physical and mental health of the prisoners and shall see, under the conditions and with a frequency consistent with hospital standards, all sick prisoners, all who report illness or injury and any prisoner to whom attention is specially directed.

     2. The medical officer shall report to the director whenever it is considered that a prisoner's physical or mental health has been or will be adversely affected by continued imprisonment or by any condition of imprisonment.

31. 1. The medical officer or a competent authority shall regularly inspect and advise the director upon:

         a. the quantity, quality, preparation and serving of food and water;

         b. the hygiene and cleanliness of the institution and prisoners;

         c. the sanitation, heating, lighting and ventilation of the institution;

         d. the suitability and cleanliness of the prisoners' clothing and bedding.

     2. The director shall consider the reports and advice that the medical officer submits according to Rules 30, paragraph 2, and 31, paragraph 1, and, when in concurrence with the recommendations made, shall take immediate steps to give effect to those recommendations; if they are not within the director's competence or if the director does not concur with them, the director shall immediately submit a personal report and the advice of the medical officer to higher authority.

32. The medical services of the institution shall seek to detect and shall treat any physical or mental illnesses or defects which may impede a prisoner's resettlement after release. All necessary medical, surgical and psychiatric services including those available in the community shall be provided to the prisoner to that end.

Discipline and Punishment

33. Discipline and order shall be maintained in the interest of safe custody, ordered community life and the treatment objectives of the institution.

34. 1. No prisoner shall be employed, in the service of the institution, in any disciplinary capacity.

    2. This rule shall not, however, impede the proper functioning of arrangements under which specified social, educational or sports activities or responsibilities are entrusted under supervision to prisoners who are formed into groups for the purposes of their participation in regime programs.

35. The following shall be provided for and determined by the law or by the regulation of the competent authority:

    a. conduct constituting a disciplinary offence;

    b. the types and duration of punishment which may be imposed;

    c. the authority competent to impose such punishment;

    d. access to, and the authority of, the appellate process.

36. 1. No prisoner shall be punished except in accordance with the terms of such law or regulation, and never twice for the same act.

    2. Reports of misconduct shall be presented promptly to the competent authority who shall decide on them without undue delay.

    3. No prisoner shall be punished unless informed of the alleged offence and given a proper opportunity of presenting a defence.

    4. Where necessary and practicable prisoners shall be allowed to make their defence through an interpreter.

37. Collective punishments, corporal punishment, punishment by placing in a dark cell, and all cruel, inhuman or degrading punishment shall be completely prohibited as punishments for disciplinary offenses.

38. 1. Punishment by disciplinary confinement and any other punishment which might have an adverse effect on the physical or mental health of the prisoner shall only be imposed if the medical officer, after examination, certifies in writing that the prisoner is fit to sustain it.

    2. In no case may such punishment be contrary to, or depart from, the principles stated in Rule 37.

    3. The medical officer shall visit daily prisoners undergoing such punishment and shall advise the director if the termination or alteration of the punishment is considered necessary on grounds of physical or mental health.

Instruments of Restraint

39. The use of chains and irons shall be prohibited. Handcuffs, restraint`jackets and other body restraints shall never be applied as a punishment. They shall not be used except in the following circumstances:

a.   If necessary, as a precaution against escape during a transfer, provided that they shall be removed when the prisoner appears before a judicial or administrative authority unless that authority decides otherwise;

b.   on medical grounds by direction and under the supervision of the medical officer;

c.   by order of the director, if other methods of control fail, in order to protect a prisoner from self-injury, injury to others or to prevent serious damage to property; in such instances the director shall at once consult the medical officer and report to the higher administrative authority.

40. The patterns and manner of use of the instruments of restraint authorized in the preceding paragraph shall be decided by law or regulation. Such instruments must not be applied for any longer time than is strictly necessary.

Information to, and Complaints by, Prisoners

41. 1.   Every prisoner shall on admission be provided with written information about the regulations governing the treatment of prisoners of the relevant category, the disciplinary requirements of the institution, the authorized methods of seeking information and making complaints, and all such other matters as are necessary to understand the rights and obligations of prisoners and to adapt to the life of the institution.

    2.   If a prisoner cannot understand the written information provided, this information shall be explained orally.

42. 1.   Every prisoner shall have the opportunity every day of making requests or complaints to the director of the institution or the officer authorized to act in that capacity.

    2.   A prisoner shall have the opportunity to talk to, or to make requests or complaints to an inspector of prisons or to any other duly constituted authority entitled to visit the prison without the director or other members of the staff being present. However, appeals against formal decisions may be restricted to the authorized procedures.

    3.   Every prisoner shall be allowed to make a request or complaint, under confidential cover, to the central prison administration, the judicial authority or other proper authorities.

    4.   Every request or complaint addressed or referred to a prison authority shall be promptly dealt with and replied to by this authority without undue delay.

Contact with the Outside World

43. 1.   Prisoners shall be allowed to communicate with their families and, subject to the needs of treatment, security and good order, persons or representatives of outside organizations and to receive visits from these persons as often as possible.

    2.   To encourage contact with the outside world there shall be a system of prison leave consistent with the treatment objectives in Part IV of these rules.

44. 1. Prisoners who are foreign nationals should be informed, without delay, of their right to request contact and be allowed reasonable facilities to communicate with the diplomatic or consular representative of the state to which they belong. The prison administration should cooperate fully with such representatives in the interests of foreign nationals in prison who may have special needs.

    2. Prisoners who are nationals of states without diplomatic or consular representation in the country and refugees or stateless persons shall be allowed similar facilities to communicate with the diplomatic representative of the state which takes charge of the interests of such persons.

45. Prisoners shall be allowed to keep themselves informed regularly of the news by reading newspapers, periodicals and other publications, by radio or television transmissions, by lectures or by any similar means as authorized or controlled by the administration. Special arrangements should be made to meet the needs of foreign nationals with linguistic difficulties.

Religious and Moral Assistance

46. So far as practicable, every prisoner shall be allowed to satisfy the needs of his religious, spiritual and moral life by attending the services or meetings provided in the institution and having in his possession any necessary books or literature.

47. 1. If the institution contains a sufficient number of prisoners of the same religion, a qualified representative of that religion shall be appointed and approved. If the number of prisoners justifies it and conditions permit, the arrangement should be on a full-time basis.

    2. A qualified representative appointed or approved under paragraph 1 shall be allowed to hold regular services and activities and to pay pastoral visits in private to prisoners of his religion at proper times.

    3. Access to a qualified representative of any religion shall not be refused to any prisoner. If any prisoner should object to a visit of any religious representative, the prisoner shall be allowed to refuse it.

Retention of Prisoners' Property

48. 1. All money, valuables, and other effects belonging to prisoners which under the regulations of the institution they are not allowed to retain shall on admission to the institution be placed in safe custody. An inventory thereof shall be signed by the prisoner. Steps shall be taken to keep them in good condition. If it has been found necessary to destroy any article, this shall be recorded and the prisoner informed.

    2. On the release of the prisoner, all such articles and money shall be returned except insofar as there have been authorized withdrawals of money or the authorized sending of any such property out of the institution, or it has been found necessary on hygienic grounds to destroy any article. The prisoner shall sign a receipt for the articles and money returned.

    3. As far as practicable, any money or effects received for a prisoner from outside shall be treated in the same way unless they are intended for and permitted for use during imprisonment.

4.   If a prisoner brings in any medicines, the medical officer shall decide what use shall be made of them.

Notification of Death, Illness, Transfer, etc.

49. 1.   Upon the death or serious illness of or serious injury to a prisoner, or removal to an institution of the treatment of mental illness or abnormalities, the director shall at once inform the spouse, if the prisoner is married, or the nearest relative and shall in any event inform any other person previously designated by the prisoner.

2.   A prisoner shall be informed at once of the death or serious illness of any near relative. In these cases and whenever circumstances allow, the prisoner should be authorized to visit this sick relative or see the deceased either under escort or alone.

3.   All prisoners shall have the right to inform at once their families of imprisonment or transfer to another institution.

Removal of Prisoners

50. 1.   When prisoners are being removed to or from an institution, they shall be exposed to public view as little as possible, and proper safeguards shall be adopted to protect them from insult, curiosity and publicity in any form.

2.   The transport of prisoners in conveyances with inadequate ventilation or light, or in any way which would subject them to unnecessary physical hardship or indignity shall be prohibited.

3.   The transport of prisoners shall be carried out at the expense of the administration and in accordance with duly authorized regulations.

PART III
Personnel

51. In view of the fundamental importance of the prison staffs to the proper management of the institutions and the pursuit of their organizational and treatment objectives, prison administrations shall give high priority to the fulfillment of the rules concerning personnel.

52. Prison staff shall be continually encouraged through training, consultative procedures and a positive management style to aspire to humane standards, higher efficiency and a committed approach to their duties.

53. The prison administration shall regard it as an important task continually to inform public opinion of the roles of the prison system and the work of the staff, so as to encourage public understanding of the importance of their contribution to society.

54. 1.   The prison administration shall provide for the careful selection on recruitment or in subsequent appointments of all personnel. Special emphasis shall be given to their integrity, humanity, professional capacity and personal suitability for the work.

2. Personnel shall normally be appointed on a permanent basis as professional prison staff and have civil service status with security of tenure subject only to good conduct, efficiency, good physical and mental health and an adequate standard of education. Salaries shall be adequate to attract and retain suitable men and women; employment benefits and conditions of service shall be favorable in view of the exacting nature of the work.

3. Whenever it is necessary to employ part-time staff, these criteria should apply to them as far as that is appropriate.

55. 1. On recruitment or after an appropriate period of practical experience, the personnel shall be given a course of training in their general and specific duties and be required to pass theoretical and practical tests unless their professional qualifications make that unnecessary.

2. During their career, all personnel shall maintain and improve their knowledge and professional capacity by attending courses of in-service training to be organized by the administration at suitable intervals.

3. Arrangement should be made for wider experience and training for personnel whose professional capacity would be improved by this.

4. The training of all personnel should include instruction in the requirements and application of the European Prison Rules and the European Convention on Human Rights.

56. All members of the personnel shall be expected at all times so to conduct themselves and perform their duties as to influence the prisoners for good by their example and to command their respect.

57. 1. So far as possible the personnel shall include a sufficient number of specialists such as psychiatrists, psychologists, social workers, teachers, trade, physical education and sports instructors.

2. These and other specialist staff shall normally be employed on a permanent basis. This shall not preclude part-time or voluntary workers when that is appropriate and beneficial to the level of support and training they can provide.

58. 1. The prison administration shall ensure that every institution is at all times in the full charge of the director, the deputy director or other authorized official.

2. The director of an institution should be adequately qualified for that post by character, administrative ability, suitable professional training and experience.

3. The director shall be appointed on a full-time basis and be available or accessible as required by the prison administration in its management instructions.

4. When two or more institutions are under the authority of one director, each shall be visited at frequent intervals. A responsible official shall be in charge of each of these institutions.

59. The administration shall introduce forms of organization and management systems to facilitate communication between the different categories of staff in an institution with a view to ensuring cooperation between the various services, in particular, with respect to the treatment and re-socialization of prisoners.

60. 1. The director, deputy, and the majority of the other personnel of the institution shall be able to speak the language of the greatest number of prisoners, or a language understood by the greatest number of them.

     2. Whenever necessary and practicable the services of an interpreter shall be used.

61. 1. Arrangements shall be made to ensure at all times that a qualified and approved medical practitioner is able to attend without delay in cases of urgency.

     2. In institutions not staffed by one or more full-time medical officers, a part-time medical officer or authorized staff of a health service shall visit regularly.

     62. The appointment of staff in institutions or parts of institutions housing prisoners of the opposite sex is to be encouraged.

63. 1. Staff of the institutions shall not use force against prisoners except in self-defence or in cases of attempted escape or active or passive physical resistance to an order based on law or regulations. Staff who have recourse to force must use no more than is strictly necessary and must report the incident immediately to the director of the institution.

     2. Staff shall as appropriate be given special technical training to enable them to restrain aggressive prisoners.

     3. Except in special circumstances, staff performing duties which bring them into direct contact with prisoners should not be armed. Furthermore, staff should in no circumstances be provided with arms unless they have been fully trained in their use.

PART IV
Treatment Objectives and Regimes

64. Imprisonment is by the deprivation of liberty a punishment in itself. The conditions of imprisonment and the prison regimes shall not, therefore, except as incidental to justifiable segregation or the maintenance of discipline, aggravate the suffering inherent in this.

65. Every effort shall be made to ensure that the regimes of the institutions are designed and managed so as:

     a. to ensure that the conditions of life are compatible with human dignity and acceptable standards in the community;

     b. to minimize the detrimental effects of imprisonment and the difference between prison life and life at liberty which tend to diminish the self-respect or sense of personal responsibility of prisoners;

c. to sustain and strengthen those links with relatives and the outside community that will promote the best interests of prisoners and their families;

d. to provide opportunities for prisoners to develop skills and aptitudes that will improve their prospects of successful resettlement after release.

66. To these ends all the remedial, educational, moral, spiritual and other resources that are appropriate should be made available and utilized in accordance with the individual treatment needs of prisoners. Thus the regimes should include:

a. spiritual support and guidance and opportunities for relevant work, vocational guidance, and training, education, physical education, the development of social skills, counselling, group and recreational activities;

b. arrangements to ensure that these activities are organized, so far as possible, to increase contacts with and opportunities within the outside community so as to enhance the prospects for social resettlement after release;

c. procedures for establishing and reviewing individual treatment and training programs for prisoners after full consultations among the relevant staff and with individual prisoners who should be involved in these as far as is practicable;

d. communications systems and a management style that will encourage appropriate and positive relationships between staff and prisoners that will improve the prospects for effective and supportive regimes and treatment programs.

67. 1. Since the fulfillment of these objectives requires individualization of treatment and, for this purpose, a flexible system of allocation, prisoners should be placed in separate institutions or units where each can receive the appropriate treatment and training.

2. The type, size, organization and capacity of these institutions or units should be determined essentially by the nature of the treatment to be provided.

3. It is necessary to ensure that prisoners are located with due regard to security and control but such measures should be the minimum compatible with safety and comprehend the special needs of the prisoner. Every effort should be made to place prisoners in institutions that are open in character or provide ample opportunities for contacts with the outside community. In the case of foreign nationals, links with people of their own nationality in the outside community are to be regarded as especially important.

68. As soon as possible after admission and after a study of the personality of each prisoner with a sentence of a suitable length, a program of treatment in a suitable institution shall be prepared in the light of the knowledge obtained about individual needs, capacities and dispositions, especially proximity to relatives.

69. 1. Within the regimes, prisoners shall be given the opportunity to participate in activities of the institution likely to develop their sense of responsibility, self-reliance and to stimulate interest in their own treatment.

2. Efforts should be made to develop methods of encouraging cooperation with and the participation of the prisoners in their treatment. To this end prisoners shall be encouraged to assume, within the limits specified in Rule 34, responsibilities in certain sectors of the institution's activity.

70. 1. The preparation of prisoners for release should begin as soon as possible after reception in a penal institution. Thus, the treatment of prisoners should emphasize not their exclusion from the community but their continuing part in it. Community agencies and social workers should, therefore, be enlisted wherever possible to assist the staff of the institution in the task of social rehabilitation of the prisoners particularly maintaining and improving the relationships with their families, with other persons and with the social agencies. Steps should be taken to safeguard, to the maximum extent compatible with the law and the sentence, the rights relating to civil interests, social security rights and other social benefits of prisoners.

     2. Treatment programs should include provision for prison leave which should also be granted to the greatest extent possible on medical, educational, occupational, family and other social grounds.

     3. Foreign nationals should not be excluded from arrangements for prison leave solely on account of their nationality. Furthermore, every effort should be made to enable them to participate in regime activities together so as to alleviate their feelings of isolation.

Work

71. 1. Prison work should be seen as a positive element in treatment, training and institutional management.

     2. Prisoners under sentence may be required to work, subject to their physical and mental fitness as determined by the medical officer.

     3. Sufficient work of a useful nature, or if appropriate other purposeful activities shall be provided to keep prisoners actively employed for a normal working day.

     4. So far as possible the work provided shall be such as will maintain or increase the prisoner's ability to earn a normal living after release.

     5. Vocational training in useful trades shall be provided for prisoners able to profit thereby and especially for young prisoners.

     6. Within the limits compatible with proper vocational selection and with the requirements of institutional administration and discipline, the prisoners shall be able to choose the type of employment in which they wish to participate.

72. 1. The organization and methods of work in the institutions shall resemble as closely as possible those of similar work in the community so as to prepare prisoners for the conditions of normal occupational life. It should thus be relevant to contemporary working standards and techniques and organized to function within modern management systems and production processes.

     2. Although the pursuit of financial profit from industries in the institutions can be valuable in raising standards and improving the quality and relevance of training, the interests of the prisoners and of their treatment must not be subordinated to that purpose.

73. 1. Work for prisoners shall be assured by the prison administration:

a.   either on its own premises, workshops and farms; or

b.   in cooperation with private contractors inside or outside the institution in which case the full normal wages for such shall be paid by the persons to whom the labor is supplied, account being taken of the output of the prisoners.

74. 1.   Safety and health precautions for prisoners shall be similar to those that apply to workers outside.

     2.   Provision shall be made to indemnify prisoners against industrial injury, including occupational disease, on terms not less favorable than those extended by law to workers outside.

75. 1.   The maximum daily and weekly working hours of the prisoners shall be fixed in conformity with local rules or custom in regard to the employment of free workmen.

     2.   Prisoners should have at least one rest`day a week and sufficient time for education and other activities required as part of their treatment and training for social resettlement.

76. 1.   There shall be a system of equitable remuneration of the work of prisoners.

     2.   Under the system prisoners shall be allowed to spend at least a part of their earnings on approved articles for their own use and to allocate a part of their earnings to their family or for other approved purposes.

     3.   The system may also provide that a part of the earnings be set aside by the administration so as to constitute a savings fund to be handed over to the prisoner on release.

Education

77. A comprehensive education program shall be arranged in every institution to provide opportunities for all prisoners to pursue at least some of their individual needs and aspirations. Such programs should have as their objectives the improvement of the prospects for successful social resettlement, the morale and attitudes of prisoners and their self-respect.

78. Education should be regarded as a regime activity that attracts the same status and basic remuneration within the regime as work, provided that it takes place in normal working hours and is part of an authorized individual treatment program.

79. Special attention should be given by prison administration to the education of young prisoners, those of foreign origin or with particular cultural or ethnic needs.

80. Specific programs of remedial education should be arranged for prisoners with special problems such as illiteracy or innumeracy.

81. So far as practicable, the education of prisoners shall:

a.   be integrated with the educational system of the country so that after their release they may continue their education without difficulty;

b.   take place in outside educational institutions.

82. Every institution shall have a library for the use of all categories of prisoners, adequately stocked with a wide range of both recreational and instructional books, and prisoners shall be encouraged to make full use of it Wherever possible the prison library should be organized in cooperation with community library services.

Physical Education, Exercise, Sport and Recreation

83. The prison regimes shall recognize the importance to physical and mental health of properly organized activities to ensure physical fitness, adequate exercise and recreational opportunities.

84. Thus a properly organized program of physical education, sport and other recreational activity should be arranged within the framework and objectives of the treatment and training regime. To this end, space, installations, and equipment should be provided.

85. Prison administrations should ensure that prisoners who participate in these programs are physically fit to do so. Special arrangements should be made, under medical direction, for remedial physical education and therapy for those prisoners who need it.

86. Every prisoner who is not employed in outdoor work, or located in an open institution, shall be allowed, if the weather permits, at least one hour of walking or suitable exercise in the open air daily, as far as possible, sheltered from inclement weather.

Pre-release Preparation

87. All prisoners should have the benefit of arrangements designed to assist them in returning to society, family life and employment after release. Procedures and special courses should be devised to this end.

88. In the case of those prisoners with longer sentences, steps should be taken to ensure a gradual return to life in society. This aim may be achieved, in particular, by a pre-release regime organized in the same institution or in another appropriate institution, or by conditional release under some kind of supervision combined with effective social support.

89. 1. Prison administrations should work closely with the social services and agencies that assist released prisoners to re-establish themselves in society, in particular with regard to family life and employment.

     2. Steps must be taken to ensure that on release prisoners are provided, as necessary, with appropriate documents and identification papers, and assisted in finding suitable homes and work to go to. They should also be provided with immediate means of subsistence, be suitably and adequately clothed having regard to the climate and season, and have sufficient means to reach their destination.

     3. The approved representatives of the social agencies or services should be afforded all necessary access to the institution and to prisoners with a view to making a full contribution to the preparation for release and after-care program of the prisoner.

PART V
Additional Rules for Special Categories

90. Prison administrations should be guided by the provisions of the rules as a whole so far as they can appropriately and in practice be applied for the benefit of those special categories of prisoners for which additional rules are provided hereafter.

91. Prison administrations should be guided by the provisions of the rules as a whole so far as they can appropriately and in practice be applied for the benefit of those special categories of prisoners for which additional rules are provided hereafter.

Untried Prisoners

91. Without prejudice to legal rules for the protection of individual liberty or prescribing the procedure to be observed in respect of untried prisoners, these prisoners, who are presumed to be innocent until they are found guilty, shall be afforded the benefits that may derive from Rule 90 and treated without restrictions other than those necessary for the penal procedure and the security of the institution.

92. 1. Untried prisoners shall be allowed to inform their families of their detention immediately and given all reasonable facilities for communication with family and friends and persons with whom it is in their legitimate interest to enter into contact.

    2. They shall also be allowed to receive visits from them under humane conditions subject only to such restrictions and supervision as are necessary in the interests of the administration of justice and of the security and good order of the institution.

    3. If an untried prisoner does not wish to inform any of these persons, the prison administration should not do so on its own initiative unless there are good overriding reasons as, for instance, the age, state of mind or any other incapacity of the prisoner.

93. Untried prisoners shall be entitled, as soon as imprisoned, to choose a legal representative, or shall be allowed to apply for free legal aid where such aid is available and to receive visits from that legal adviser with a view to their defence and to prepare and hand to the legal adviser, and to receive, confidential instructions. On request, they shall be given all necessary facilities for this purpose. In particular, they shall be given the free assistance of an interpreter for all essential contacts with the administration and for their defence. Interviews between prisoners and their legal advisers may be within sight but not within hearing, either direct or indirect, of the police or institution staff. The allocation of untried prisoners shall be in conformity with the provisions of Rule 11, paragraph 3.

94. Except where there are circumstances that make it undesirable, untried prisoners shall be given the opportunity of having separate rooms.

95. 1. Untried prisoners shall be given the opportunity of wearing their own clothing if it is clean and suitable.

    2. Prisoners who do not avail themselves of this opportunity, shall be supplied with suitable dress.

3.　If they have no suitable clothing of their own, untried prisoners shall be provided with civilian clothing in good condition in which to appear in court or on authorized outings.

96.　Untried prisoners shall, whenever possible, be offered the opportunity to work but shall not be required to work. Those who choose to work shall be paid as other prisoners. If educational or trade training is available, untried prisoners shall be encouraged to avail themselves of these opportunities.

97.　Untried prisoners shall be allowed to procure at their own expense or at the expense of a third party such books, newspapers, writing materials and other means of occupation as are compatible with the interests of the administration of justice and the security and good order of the institution.

98.　Untried prisoners shall be given the opportunity of being visited and treated by their own doctor or dentist if there is reasonable ground for the application. Reasons should be given if the application is refused. Such costs as are incurred shall not be the responsibility of the prison administration.

Civil Prisoners

99.　In countries where the law permits imprisonment by order of a court under any non-criminal process, persons so imprisoned shall not be subjected to any greater restriction or severity than is necessary to ensure safe custody and good order. Their treatment shall not be less favorable than that of untried prisoners, with the reservation, however, that they may be required to work.

Insane and Mentally Abnormal Prisoners

100. 1.　Persons who are found to be insane should not be detained in prisons and arrangements shall be made to remove them to appropriate establishments for the mentally ill as soon as possible.

2.　Specialized institutions or sections under medical management should be available for the observation and treatment of prisoners suffering gravely from other mental disease or abnormality.

3.　The medical or psychiatric service of the penal institutions shall provide for the psychiatric treatment of all prisoners who are in need of such treatment.

4.　Action should be taken, by arrangement with the appropriate community agencies, to ensure where necessary the continuation of psychiatric treatment after release and the provision of social psychiatric after-care.

COMMISSION OF THE EUROPEAN COMMUNITIES
Official Journal C 098 , 09/04/1999 p. 0299; 1999 OJ C 98
(December 17, 1998)

TITLE: Resolution on prison conditions in the European Union: improvements and alternative penalties

Resolution on prison conditions in the European Union: improvements and alternative penalties

The European Parliament,

—having regard to the Treaty establishing the European Union,

—having regard to the draft Amsterdam Treaty,

—having regard to the Universal Declaration of Human Rights and the related case law,

—having regard to the European Convention for the Protection of Human Rights and Fundamental Freedoms and the protocols thereto,

—having regard to the case law of the European Court of Human Rights,

—having regard to the standard minimum rules for the treatment of prisoners adopted by the Council of Europe in 1973,

—having regard to the resolutions and recommendations of the Council of Europe on custody pending trial (R(80)11), prison leave ((R(82)16), custody and treatment of dangerous prisoners (R(82)17), foreign prisoners (R(84)12), and on the European rules on community sanctions and measures (R(92)16),

—having regard to the European Convention on the Transfer of Sentenced Persons of 1983,

—having regard to the European Convention for the Prevention of Torture and Inhuman or Degrading Treatment or Punishment of 1987,

—having regard to Recommendation No R(87)3 adopted by the Committee of Ministers of the Council of Europe on 12 February 1987, on the European prison rules,

—having regard to the report of 14 May 1998 by the European Committee for the Prevention of Torture and Inhuman or Degrading Treatment or Punishment (CPT) of the Council of Europe,

—having regard to its resolution of 12 April 1989 adopting the Declaration of fundamental rights and freedoms ((OJ C 120, 16.5.1989, p. 51.)),

—having regard to its resolutions of 17 September 1996 ((OJ C 320, 28.10.1996, p. 36.)), 8 April 1997 ((OJ C 132, 28.4.1997, p. 31.)) and 17 February 1998 ((OJ C 80, 16.3.1998, p. 43.)) on respect for human rights in the European Union,

—having regard to its resolution of 18 January 1996 on poor conditions in prisons in the European Union ((OJ C 32, 5.2.1996, p. 102.)),

—having regard to the motion for a resolution tabled by Mr Vandemeulebroucke and Mrs Aelvoet on visiting rights with regard to detainees, in particular in Great Britain (B4-1022/97),

—having regard to Rule 148 of its Rules of Procedure,

—having regard to the report of the Committee on Civil Liberties and Internal Affairs (A4-0369/98),

A.   whereas, in addition to serving as a punishment for crimes, imprisonment should help to re-establish a more harmonious society by protecting property and effectively safeguarding the rights of persons and to make those serving prison sentences aware of their responsibilities and reintegrate them into society,

B.   taking great account of the rights of victims and wishing to promote the principle that those found guilty should make amends for the harm caused to victims,

C.   whereas there are major differences between the judicial and prison systems in use in the EU Member States, particularly as regards the use of alternative measures to prison and alternative penalties to short sentences,

D.   whereas imprisonment often ends up being the only penal sanction for which provision is made and whereas alternative measures to prison or alternative penalties are likely to remain marginal or poorly understood by public opinion,

E.   regretting that little use is made of alternative penalties, which are particularly appropriate in the case of sentences of less than one year, which are by far the most common sentences handed down in almost all EU countries,

F.   welcoming the increased use of alternative measures to imprisonment and alternative penalties in the various systems for the flexibility they offer in enforcing sentences,

G.   aware of the need for a systematic comparison of the way in which different legal and prison systems are developing, including the use of alternative measures and alternative penalties to short sentences and the need to achieve convergence between the different ways in which justice is practised in the Member States, despite the difficulties involved,

H.   expressing concern at the extremely unfavourable conditions still to be found in many European prisons, in particular because there is no respect for the elementary human rights provided for in the international conventions and the constitutions of the Member States, a fact which seriously undermines the subsequent reintegration of prisoners into society,

I.   expressing its full support for the objectives laid down by the Council of Europe, with particular regard to minimising the adverse effects of detention and the need to humanise sentences,

J.   encouraged by the efforts being made by several Member States to improve the effectiveness of their prison systems to make them fairer and more human as regards prison conditions, the rehabilitation of prisoners and the construction of modern establishments,

K.   concerned in particular by overcrowding in prisons in several Member States, which greatly reduces the likelihood of rehabilitation owing to its impact on the physical and mental health of prisoners and which undermines the working conditions of staff and the scope for work, educational, cultural and sporting activities,

L. whereas a large number of prisoners are addicted to illicit substances and are a danger to themselves and their fellow prisoners and, in general, increase the likelihood of malfunctions occurring in prisons (bribery attempts, etc.),

M. alarmed by the recent increase in the number of prison suicides in several European countries,

N. concerned by the frequency with which people are remanded in custody and the length of time they spend there, and firmly underlining the general principle that a defendant in a criminal trial is entitled to freedom and full enjoyment of rights; whereas the use of detention on remand involves not only anticipation of the outcome of a possible conviction and undeniable harm to the individual, but also a denial of the basic right to the presumption of innocence; whereas, therefore, it is only legitimate when absolutely necessary, justified and consistent with the need for precautionary protection of the interests, rights and values referred to in the relevant penal provisions,

1. Calls on the Member States to apply fully the Council of Europe's prison rules with particular regard to the rules on minimum health requirements covering the fitting-out of cells, food, clothing, heating and hygiene and access to health facilities, work, education and training and social and educational, cultural and sporting activities, all of which contribute to the dignity and social rehabilitation of prisoners; calls furthermore on the Member States to comply scrupulously with the recommendations of the European Committee for the Prevention of Torture and Inhuman or Degrading Treatment or Punishment and to implement the recommendations addressed to them;

2. Firmly believes that prisoners' families in particular should be taken into account, unless there are specific and justified grounds for not doing so (possible involvement in crime, mafia links, particular kinds of terrorism, etc.), by ensuring that wherever possible prisoners are held in a place close to the homes of their families and by encouraging family and conjugal visits with special areas set aside for this purpose, given that spouses and children always play an extremely positive role in helping prisoners to change their ways, become more responsible and re-establish themselves in society; requests furthermore that, where both spouses are deprived of their freedom, unless the treatment they require or security considerations make it inadvisable, steps should be taken to allow them to live together, with special mixed sections set up for this purpose;

3. Points out that depriving someone of their freedom of movement does not mean depriving them of all fundamental freedoms, whence the imperative need for due respect to be shown for freedom of thought, opinion, expression and political or religious beliefs, civil rights, and in particular the right to administer one's own property, unless that right has been explicitly withdrawn by the court;

4. Requests that all Member States of the European Union should set to work on drafting a fundamental prison law laying down a legal framework which regulates the internal (substantive) legal position, the external legal position, the right of complaint and the obligations of prisoners and provides for an independent supervisory body to which prisoners can turn in the event of violation of their rights;

5. Takes the view that special security regimes within prisons should be allowable only in exceptional circumstances on the basis of laws which lay down the conditions under which such regimes can be imposed and the maximum duration thereof and specify the rights of defence and the right of appeal of prisoners;

6. Deplores all racial, ethnic, national or religious discrimination inside prisons and calls in particular for vulnerable groups to be protected against hostile behaviour on the part of fellow prisoners or members of the prison staff;

7. Stresses that any application with regard to prison sentences, particularly for a sentence to be reduced or for the conditions under which it is being served to be changed, should be examined by a specialist legal body different from that which handed down the sentence;

8. Calls on the authorities to make provision within prisons for the greatest possible range of opportunities for work and for cultural education and sports training, which are vital for efficient and effective preparation of prisoners for a return to society;

9. Emphasises that, where cell-sharing cannot be avoided, a careful attribution is needed;

10. Calls on the Member States to take all appropriate measures to solve the problem of threats and acts of aggression against staff and prisoners;

11. Points out that all medical services provided in prisons should offer prisoners the same standards of treatment as that provided to the general public in the country and in particular that prisoners should have immediate access to a doctor on night duty;

12. Calls for a proper medical examination for every prisoner on commencement of sentence, and calls for health education and an understanding of how the body works; also stresses the importance of a medical follow-up on release from prison;

13. Draws attention to the specific case of internees and calls for them to be placed in suitable detention conditions with appropriate psychiatric supervision;

14. Calls on the Member States to ensure the strict application of the World Health Organisation directive laying down principles on which to base measures to combat HIV infection and AIDS in prisons;

15. Urges the Member States to introduce legal provisions which, on humanitarian grounds and in the interests of personal dignity, will allow prisoners suffering from serious illness and incurable diseases to spend the final period of their lives with their families and, where their families are not in a position to take them in, that the prison authorities should establish the necessary relations for this purpose with associations and NGOs involved in the care of patients of this kind;

16. Draws attention to the specific needs of women prisoners, particularly during pregnancy, childbirth and infancy; calls for childcare facilities to be provided on the spot for children of women prisoners, at least until they reach

two years of age; points out that, with a view also to eliminating any discrimination in the family and school life of children who are required to stay with their mother and provided that the latter's conditions of imprisonment so allow, efforts should be made to place both mother and child in special units located outside prison premises;

17. Takes the view that minors do not belong in prisons; calls for the introduction of constructive, humane laws on penalties for young offenders in the Member States, geared to the responsibility and skills of young people and providing alternative solutions to locking young people up in prisons and for measures aimed, as far as possible, at remedying the emotional and educational deficiencies which are often the cause of delinquency;

18. Recommends that prisoners who are drug addicts should have access to specialised services within prisons or provided to them by special arrangement and should be able to join external voluntary rehabilitation programmes, subject to strict conditions;

19. Is concerned at the large number of prisoners who are addicted to illicit drugs and calls for anti-drugs and anti-smuggling policies to be introduced in all prisons;

20. Points out that detention on remand must continue to be reserved for exceptional cases, and that it should under no circumstances be used to extract confessions;

21. Notes that frequently the application of alternative measures is hampered by the inadequacy of the resources available to the courts responsible for supervising offenders, by overbureaucratic and inflexible pre-trial procedures and by inadequate knowledge of how these measures work;

22. Considers that an assessment should be made of alternative measures and alternative penalties to short sentences to evaluate their effectiveness, the level of recidivism, and the role played by society;

23. Believes that all social reintegration projects, as well as alternative measures and alternative penalties to imprisonment should be the subject of close cooperation between the various professions involved in the prison and legal services and voluntary organisations;

24. Emphasises the importance of speeding up criminal inquiries, particularly in cases where the accused is already being held on remand;

25. Draws attention to the need to give priority to personalising sentences such that the implementation of the sentence imposed by the judicial authority and the prison authority takes into consideration any statements made by the person condemned; stresses that an alternative penalty or a prison sentence must provide the offender with an opportunity to make good the damaged inflicted on the victim of his offence;

26. Stresses that remission of sentence, amnesties or pardons of whatever kind must be meaningful and must be understood by those concerned and by the general public, and should thus be tailored to the personal circumstances of those for whom they are intended;

27. Stresses that alternative penalties to detention should be used in all cases where they would not jeopardise the safety of persons and property;

28. Calls on the public authorities to make use of semi-custodial arrangements or open regimes based on specific rules and to cultivate conditions under which these regimes can be used in a way which ensures public safety and responsible behaviour on the part of prisoners;

29. Urges the Member State authorities to grant prisoners parole in preparation for their release or to deal with important personal or family matters, provided there is no risk of them breaking parole or committing further crimes;

30. Recommends that short sentences be replaced by alternative penalties, particularly those which have demonstrated their effectiveness in some EU countries, such as community service orders, day fines in Germany and electronic tagging in Sweden; points out in this connection that this form of electronic surveillance should not be used in place of pre-trial detention, probation, valid alternative penalties or suspended sentences, but should be reserved for prisoners on parole;

31. Emphasises the importance of making the general public aware of the aims and methods of the penal system with a view to ensuring that efforts to rehabilitate prisoners receive the support of the population as a whole;

32. Calls on public institutions in the European Union and in particular the governments of the Member States to introduce specific policies to encourage the reintegration into the workforce of former prisoners, and to end the all too frequent discrimination which in practice gives them no chance of finding employment in the broad sector covered by public companies and the civil service;

33. Recognises that the working conditions of prison warders are difficult and emphasises the importance of providing them with basic and continuing training and of improving their working conditions and supports the creation of networks to facilitate exchanges of experience;

34. Takes the view that prisoners should have an opportunity to do worthwhile, properly paid work;

35. Calls on the States and Governments of the Union to step up their efforts to recruit, train and deploy social and educational support staff for prisons, open regimes and post-release follow-up activities;

36. Takes the view that alternative forms of penalties other than prison sentences should be applied to drug addicts in order to reduce overcrowding in prisons while at the same time helping drug addicts to tackle their addiction;

37. Points to the need for governments to retain full responsibility for the organisation of, and living conditions in, prisons and stresses the danger of delegating responsibility for everything concerning the serving of sentences and discipline and security within prisons;

38. Draws the attention of the public authorities to the importance of the work carried out by associations and NGOs operating in and around the prison system, which play a vital role in providing support for and helping to rehabilitate prisoners, and calls for them to be given greater assistance with such activities;

39. Calls on the Member States to take all necessary measures with regard to holding centres and areas to ensure that the persons detained are duly informed about their rights and in a position to exercise them;

40. Calls on the Commission to monitor the development of legal and prison systems and, when drawing up the annual report on human rights, to assess the degree of compliance with the prison standards laid down by the Council of Europe and by this resolution, as well as measures to approximate the various laws in force;

41. Calls for Members of the European Parliament to have the right to visit and inspect prisons and detention centres for refugees on the territory of the European Union;

42. Instructs its President to forward this resolution to the Commission, the Council and the governments and parliaments of the Member States.

APPENDIX V

THE FEDERAL REPUBLIC OF GERMANY v. UNITED STATES
526 U.S. 111; 119 S. Ct. 1016; 143 L. Ed. 2d 192 (1999)

OPINION:

ON APPLICATION FOR TEMPORARY RESTRAINING ORDER OR PRELIMINARY INJUNCTION AND ON MOTION FOR LEAVE TO FILE A BILL OF COMPLAINT

Per Curiam.

The motion of the Federal Republic of Germany, et al. (plaintiffs) for leave to file a bill of complaint and the motion for preliminary injunction against the United States of America and Jane Dee Hull, Governor of the State of Arizona, both raised under this Court's original jurisdiction, are denied. Plaintiffs' motion to dispense with printing requirements is granted. Plaintiffs seek, among other relief, enforcement of an order issued this afternoon by the International Court of Justice, on its own motion and with no opportunity for the United States to respond, directing the United States to prevent Arizona's scheduled execution of Walter LaGrand. Plaintiffs assert that LaGrand holds German citizenship. With regard to the action against the United States, which relies on the *ex parte* order of the International Court of Justice, there are imposing threshold barriers. First, it appears that the United States has not waived its sovereign immunity. Second, it is doubtful that Art. III, §2. cl. 2 provides an anchor for an action to prevent execution of a German citizen who is not an ambassador or consul. With respect to the action against the State of Arizona, as in Breard v. Greene, 523 U.S. 371, 118 S. Ct. 1352, 1356, 140 L. Ed. 2d 529 (1998), a foreign government's ability here to assert a claim against a State is without evident support in the Vienna Convention and in probable contravention of Eleventh Amendment principles. This action was filed within only two hours of a scheduled execution that was ordered on January 15, 1999, based upon a sentence imposed by Arizona in 1984, about which the Federal Republic of Germany learned in 1992. Given the tardiness of the pleas and the jurisdictional barriers they implicate, we decline to exercise our original jurisdiction.

* * *

DISSENT:

JUSTICE BREYER, with whom JUSTICE STEVENS joins, dissenting.

The Federal Republic of Germany has filed a motion for leave to file a complaint, seeking as relief an injunction prohibiting the execution of Walter LaGrand pending final resolution of Germany's case against the United States in the International Court of Justice (ICJ)—a case in which Germany claims that Arizona's execution of LaGrand violates the Vienna Convention. The Federal Republic also seeks a stay of that execution "pending the Court's disposition of the motion to file an original bill of complaint after a normal course of briefing and deliberation on that motion." The International Court of Justice has issued an order "indicating" that the "United States should take all measures at its disposal to ensure that Walter LaGrand is not executed pending the final decision in these [ICJ] proceedings."

The Solicitor General has filed a letter in which he opposes any stay. In his view, the "Vienna Convention does not furnish a basis

817

for this Court to grant a stay of execution," and "an order of the International Court of Justice indicating provisional measures is not binding and does not furnish a basis for judicial relief." The Solicitor General adds, however, that he has "not had time to read the materials thoroughly or to digest the contents."

Germany's filings come at what is literally the eleventh hour. Nonetheless, Germany explains that it did not file its case in the International Court of Justice until it learned that the State of Arizona had admitted that it was aware, when LaGrand was arrested, that he was a German national. That admission came only eight days ago, and the ICJ issued its preliminary ruling only today. Regardless, in light of the fact that both the International Court of Justice and a sovereign nation have asked that we stay this case, or "indicated" that we should do so, I would grant the preliminary stay that Germany requests. That stay would give us time to consider, after briefing from all interested parties, the juris-

dictional and international legal issues involved, including further views of the Solicitor General, after time for study and appropriate consultation.

The Court has made Germany's motion for a preliminary stay moot by denying its motion to file its complaint and "declining to exercise" its original jurisdiction in light of the "tardiness of the pleas and the jurisdictional barriers they implicate." It is at least arguable that Germany's reasons for filing so late are valid, and the jurisdictional matters are arguable. Indeed, the Court says that it is merely *"doubtful* that Art. III, §2, cl. 2 provides an anchor" for the suit and that a foreign government's ability to assert a claim against a State is "without *evident* support in the Vienna convention and in *probable* contravention of Eleventh Amendment principles" (emphasis added). The words "doubtful" and "probable," in my view, suggest a need for fuller briefing. For these reasons I would grant a preliminary stay.

INTERNATIONAL COURT OF JUSTICE
LaGrand Case (June 27, 2001; General List No. 104)
GERMANY v. UNITED STATES OF AMERICA
JUDGMENT

* * *

13. Walter LaGrand and Karl LaGrand were born in Germany in 1962 and 1963 respectively, and were German nationals. In 1967, when they were still young children, they moved with their mother to take up permanent residence in the United States. They returned to Germany only once, for a period of about six months in 1974. Although they lived in the United States for most of their lives, and became the adoptive children of a United States national, they remained at all times German nationals, and never acquired the nationality of the United States. However, the United States has emphasized that both had the demeanour and speech of Americans rather than Germans, that neither was known to have spoken German, and that they appeared in all respects to be native citizens of the United States.

14. On 7 January 1982, Karl LaGrand and Walter LaGrand were arrested in the United States by law enforcement officers on suspicion of having been involved earlier the same day in an attempted armed bank robbery in Marana, Arizona, in the course of which the bank manager was murdered and another bank employee seriously injured. They were subsequently tried before the Superior Court of Pima County, Arizona, which, on 17 February 1984, convicted them both of murder in the first degree, attempted murder in the first degree, attempted armed robbery and two counts of kidnapping. On 14 December 1984, each was sentenced to death for first degree murder and to concurrent sentences of imprisonment for the other charges.

15. At all material times, Germany as well as the United States were parties to both the Vienna Convention on Consular Relations and the Optional Protocol to that Convention.

Article 36, paragraph 1 *(b)*, of the Vienna Convention provides that:

"if he so requests, the competent authorities of the receiving State shall, without delay, inform the consular post of the sending State if, within its consular district, a national of that State is arrested or committed to prison or to custody pending trial or is detained in any other manner. Any communication addressed to the consular post by the person arrested, in prison, custody or detention shall be forwarded by the said authorities without delay. The said authorities shall inform the person concerned without delay of his rights under this subparagraph."

It is not disputed that at the time the LaGrands were convicted and sentenced, the competent United States authorities had failed to provide the LaGrands with the information required by this provision of the Vienna Convention, and had not informed the relevant German consular post of the LaGrands' arrest. The United States concedes that the competent authorities failed to do so, even after becoming aware that the LaGrands were German nationals and not United States nationals, and admits that the United States has therefore violated its obligations under this provision of the Vienna Convention.

16. However, there is some dispute between the Parties as to the time at which the competent authorities in the United States became aware of the fact that the LaGrands were German nationals. Germany argues that the authorities of Arizona were aware of this from the very beginning, and in particular that probation officers knew by April 1982. The United States argues that at the time of their arrest, neither of the LaGrands identified himself to the arresting authorities as a German national, and that Walter LaGrand affirmatively stated that he was a United States citizen. The United States position is that its "competent authorities" for the purposes of Article 36, paragraph 1 *(b)*, of the Vienna Convention were the arresting and detaining authorities, and that these became aware of the German nationality of the LaGrands by late 1984, and possibly by mid-

1983 or earlier, but in any event not at the time of their arrest in 1982. Although other authorities, such as immigration authorities or probation officers, may have known this even earlier, the United States argues that these were not "competent authorities" for the purposes of this provision of the Vienna Convention. The United States has also suggested that at the time of their arrest, the LaGrands may themselves have been unaware that they were not nationals of the United States.

17. At their trial, the LaGrands were represented by counsel assigned by the court, as they were unable to afford legal counsel of their own choice. Their counsel at trial did not raise the issue of non-compliance with the Vienna Convention, and did not themselves contact the German consular authorities.

18. The convictions and sentences pronounced by the Superior Court of Pima County, Arizona, were subsequently challenged by the LaGrands in three principal sets of legal proceedings.

19. The first set of proceedings consisted of appeals against the convictions and sentences to the Supreme Court of Arizona, which were rejected by that court on 30 January 1987. The United States Supreme Court, in the exercise of its discretion, denied applications by the LaGrands for further review of these judgments on 5 October 1987.

20. The second set of proceedings involved petitions by the LaGrands for post-conviction relief, which were denied by an Arizona state court in 1989. Review of this decision was denied by the Supreme Court of Arizona in 1990, and by the United States Supreme Court in 1991.

21. At the time of these two sets of proceedings, the LaGrands had still not been informed by the competent United States authorities of their rights under Article 36, paragraph 1 *(b)*, of the Vienna Convention, and the German consular post had still not been informed of their arrest. The issue of the lack of consular notification, which had not been raised at trial, was also not raised in these two sets of proceedings.

22. The relevant German consular post was only made aware of the case in June 1992 by the LaGrands themselves, who had

learned of their rights from other sources, and not from the Arizona authorities. In December 1992, and on a number of subsequent occasions between then and February 1999, an official of the Consulate-General of Germany in Los Angeles visited the LaGrands in prison. Germany claims that it subsequently helped the LaGrands' attorneys to investigate the LaGrands' childhood in Germany, and to raise the issue of the omission of consular advice in further proceedings before the federal courts.

23. The LaGrands commenced a third set of legal proceedings by filing applications for writs of *habeas corpus* in the United States District Court for the District of Arizona, seeking to have their convictions—or at least their death sentences—set aside. In these proceedings they raised a number of different claims, which were rejected by that court in orders dated 24 January 1995 and 16 February 1995. One of these claims was that the United States authorities had failed to notify the German consulate of their arrest, as required by the Vienna Convention. This claim was rejected on the basis of the "procedural default" rule. According to the United States, this rule:

"is a federal rule that, before a state criminal defendant can obtain relief in federal court, the claim must be presented to a state court. If a state defendant attempts to raise a new issue in a federal *habeas corpus* proceeding, the defendant can only do so by showing cause and prejudice. Cause is an external impediment that prevents a defendant from raising a claim and prejudice must be obvious on its face. One important purpose of this rule is to ensure that the state courts have an opportunity to address issues going to the validity of state convictions before the federal courts intervene."

The United States District Court held that the LaGrands had not shown an objective external factor that prevented them from raising the issue of the lack of consular notification earlier. On 16 January 1998, this judgment was affirmed on appeal by the United States Court of Appeals, Ninth Circuit, which also held that the LaGrands' claim relating to the Vienna Convention was "procedurally defaulted", as it had not been raised in any of

the earlier proceedings in state courts. On 2 November 1998, the United States Supreme Court denied further review of this judgment.

24. On 21 December 1998, the LaGrands were formally notified by the United States authorities of their right to consular access.

25. On 15 January 1999, the Supreme Court of Arizona decided that Karl LaGrand was to be executed on 24 February 1999, and that Walter LaGrand was to be executed on 3 March 1999. Germany claims that the German Consulate learned of these dates on 19 January 1999.

26. In January and early February 1999, various interventions were made by Germany seeking to prevent the execution of the LaGrands. In particular, the German Foreign Minister and German Minister of Justice wrote to their respective United States counterparts on 27 January 1999; the German Foreign Minister wrote to the Governor of Arizona on the same day; the German Chancellor wrote to the President of the United States and to the Governor of Arizona on 2 February 1999; and the President of the Federal Republic of Germany wrote to the President of the United States on 5 February 1999. These letters referred to German opposition to capital punishment generally, but did not raise the issue of the absence of consular notification in the case of the LaGrands. The latter issue was, however, raised in a further letter, dated 22 February 1999, two days before the scheduled date of execution of Karl LaGrand, from the German Foreign Minister to the United States Secretary of State.

27. On 23 February 1999, the Arizona Board of Executive Clemency rejected an appeal for clemency by Karl LaGrand. Under the law of Arizona, this meant that the Governor of Arizona was prevented from granting clemency.

28. On the same day, the Arizona Superior Court in Pima County rejected a further petition by Walter LaGrand, based *inter alia* on the absence of consular notification, on the ground that these claims were "procedurally precluded".

29. On 24 February 1999, certain last-minute federal court proceedings brought by Karl LaGrand ultimately proved to be unsuccessful. In the course of these proceedings the United States Court of Appeals, Ninth

Circuit, again held the issue of failure of consular notification to be procedurally defaulted. Karl LaGrand was executed later that same day.

30. On 2 March 1999, the day before the scheduled date of execution of Walter LaGrand, at 7.30 p.m. (The Hague time), Germany filed in the Registry of this Court the Application instituting the present proceedings against the United States (see paragraph 1 above), accompanied by a request for the following provisional measures:

"The United States should take all measures at its disposal to ensure that Walter LaGrand is not executed pending the final decision in these proceedings, and should inform the Court of all the measures which it has taken in implementation of that Order."

By a letter of the same date, the German Foreign Minister requested the Secretary of State of the United States "to urge [the] Governor [of Arizona] for a suspension of Walter LaGrand's execution pending a ruling by the International Court of Justice".

31. On the same day, the Arizona Board of Executive Clemency met to consider the case of Walter LaGrand. It recommended against a commutation of his death sentence, but recommended that the Governor of Arizona grant a 60-day reprieve having regard to the Application filed by Germany in the International Court of Justice. Nevertheless, the Governor of Arizona decided, "in the interest of justice and with the victims in mind", to allow the execution of Walter LaGrand to go forward as scheduled.

32. In an Order of 3 March 1999, this Court found that the circumstances required it to indicate, as a matter of the greatest urgency and without any other proceedings, provisional measures in accordance with Article 41 of its Statute and with Article 75, paragraph 1, of its Rules (*I.C.J. Reports 1999*, p. 9, para. 26); it indicated provisional measures in the following terms:

"*(a)* The United States of America should take all measures at its disposal to ensure that Walter LaGrand is not executed pending the final decision in these proceedings,

and should inform the Court of all the measures which it has taken in implementation of this Order;

(b) The Government of the United States of America should transmit this Order to the Governor of the State of Arizona."

33. On the same day, proceedings were brought by Germany in the United States Supreme Court against the United States and the Governor of Arizona, seeking *inter alia* to enforce compliance with this Court's Order indicating provisional measures. In the course of these proceedings, the United States Solicitor-General as counsel of record took the position, *inter alia*, that "an order of the International Court of Justice indicating provisional measures is not binding and does not furnish a basis for judicial relief". On the same date, the United States Supreme Court dismissed the motion by Germany, on the ground of the tardiness of Germany's application and of jurisdictional barriers under United States domestic law.

34. On that same day, proceedings were also instituted in the United States Supreme Court by Walter LaGrand. These proceedings were decided against him. Later that day, Walter LaGrand was executed.

*

35. The Court must as a preliminary matter deal with certain issues, which were raised by the Parties in these proceedings, concerning the jurisdiction of the Court in relation to Germany's Application, and the admissibility of its submissions.

* *

36. In relation to the jurisdiction of the Court, the United States, without having raised preliminary objections under Article 79 of the Rules of Court, nevertheless presented certain objections thereto.

Germany bases the jurisdiction of the Court on Article I of the Optional Protocol, which reads as follows:

"Disputes arising out of the interpretation or application of the Convention shall lie within the compulsory jurisdiction of the International Court of Justice and may accordingly be brought before the Court by an application made by any party to the dispute being a Party to the present Protocol."

Germany contends that the

"proceedings instituted by [it] in the present case raise questions of the interpretation and application of the Vienna Convention on Consular Relations and of the legal consequences arising from the non-observance on the part of the United States of certain of its provisions vis-à-vis Germany and two of its nationals".

Accordingly, Germany states that all four of its submissions

"are covered by one and the same jurisdictional basis, namely Art. I of the Optional Protocol to the Vienna Convention on Consular Relations concerning the Compulsory Settlement of Disputes of 24 April 1963".

*

37. The Court will first examine the question of its jurisdiction with respect to the first submission of Germany. Germany relies on paragraph 1 of Article 36 of the Vienna Convention, which provides:

"With a view to facilitating the exercise of consular functions relating to nationals of the sending State:

(a) consular officers shall be free to communicate with nationals of the sending State and to have access to them. Nationals of the sending State shall have the same freedom with respect to communication with and access to consular officers of the sending State;

(b) if he so requests, the competent authorities of the receiving State shall, without delay, inform the consular post of the sending State if, within its consular district, a national of that State is arrested or committed to prison or to custody pending trial or is detained in any other manner.

Any communication addressed to the consular post by the person arrested, in prison, custody or detention shall be forwarded by the said authorities without delay. The said authorities shall inform the person concerned without delay of his rights under this subparagraph;

(c) consular officers shall have the right to visit a national of the sending State who is in prison, custody or detention, to converse and correspond with him and to arrange for his legal representation. They shall also have the right to visit any national of the sending State who is in prison, custody or detention in their district in pursuance of a judgment. Nevertheless, consular officers shall refrain from taking action on behalf of a national who is in prison, custody or detention if he expressly opposes such action."

38. Germany alleges that the failure of the United States to inform the LaGrand brothers of their right to contact the German authorities "prevented Germany from exercising its rights under Art. 36 (1) (a) and (c) of the Convention" and violated "the various rights conferred upon the sending State *vis-à-vis* its nationals in prison, custody or detention as provided for in Art. 36 (1) (b) of the Convention". Germany further alleges that by breaching its obligations to inform, the United States also violated individual rights conferred on the detainees by Article 36, paragraph 1 *(a)*, second sentence, and by Article 36, paragraph 1 *(b)*. Germany accordingly claims that it "was injured in the person of its two nationals", a claim which Germany raises "as a matter of diplomatic protection on behalf of Walter and Karl LaGrand".

39. The United States acknowledges that "there was a breach of the U.S. obligation . . . to inform the LaGrand brothers that they could ask that a German consular post be notified of their arrest and detention". It does not deny that this violation of Article 36, paragraph 1 *(b)*, has given rise to a dispute between the two States and recognizes that the Court has jurisdiction under the Optional Protocol to hear this dispute in so far as it concerns Germany's own rights.

40. Concerning Germany's claims of violation of Article 36, paragraph 1 *(a)* and *(c)*,

the United States however calls these claims "particularly misplaced" on the grounds that the "underlying conduct complained of is the same" as the claim of the violation of Article 36, paragraph 1 *(b)*. It contends, moreover, that "to the extent that this claim by Germany is based on the general law of diplomatic protection, it is not within the Court's jurisdiction" under the Optional Protocol because it "does not concern the interpretation or application of the Vienna Convention". The United States points to the distinction between jurisdiction over treaties and jurisdiction over customary law and observes that "[e]ven if a treaty norm and a customary norm were to have exactly the same content," each would have its "separate applicability". It contests the German assertion that diplomatic protection "enters through the intermediary of the Vienna Convention" and submits:

"the Vienna Convention deals with consular assistance . . . it does not deal with diplomatic protection. Legally, a world of difference exists between the right of the consul to assist an incarcerated national of his country, and the wholly different question whether the State can espouse the claims of its national through diplomatic protection. The former is within the jurisdiction of the Court under the Optional Protocol; the latter is not . . . Germany based its right of diplomatic protection on customary law . . . [T]his case comes before this Court not under Article 36, paragraph 2 of its Statute, but under Article 36, paragraph 1. Is it not obvious . . . that whatever rights Germany has under customary law, they do not fall within the jurisdiction of this Court under the Optional Protocol?"

41. Germany responds that the breach of paragraph 1 *(a)* and *(c)* of Article 36 must be distinguished from that of paragraph 1 *(b)*, and that as a result, the Court should not only rule on the latter breach, but also on the violation of paragraph 1 *(a)* and *(c)*. Germany further asserts "that 'application of the Convention' in the sense of the Optional Protocol very well encompasses the consequences of a violation of individual rights under the Convention, including the espousal of respective claims by the State of nationality".

42. The Court cannot accept the United States' objections. The dispute between the Parties as to whether Article 36, paragraph 1 *(a)* and *(c)*, of the Vienna Convention have been violated in this case in consequence of the breach of paragraph 1 *(b)* does relate to the interpretation and application of the Convention. This is also true of the dispute as to whether paragraph 1 *(b)* creates individual rights and whether Germany has standing to assert those rights on behalf of its nationals. These are consequently disputes within the meaning of Article I of the Optional Protocol. Moreover, the Court cannot accept the contention of the United States that Germany's claim based on the individual rights of the LaGrand brothers is beyond the Court's jurisdiction because diplomatic protection is a concept of customary international law. This fact does not prevent a State party to a treaty, which creates individual rights, from taking up the case of one of its nationals and instituting international judicial proceedings on behalf of that national, on the basis of a general jurisdictional clause in such a treaty. Therefore the Court concludes that it has jurisdiction with respect to the whole of Germany's first submission.

*

43. The United States does not challenge the Court's jurisdiction in regard to Germany's second submission. Nor does it as such address the issue of the jurisdiction of the Court over the third submission concerning the binding nature of the Order of the Court of 3 March 1999 indicating provisional measures. It argues, however, that this submission is inadmissible (see paragraphs 50 and 53-55 below), and that the Court can fully and adequately dispose of the merits of this case without having to rule on the submission.

44. Germany asserts that the Court's Order of 3 March 1999 was intended to "enforce" the rights enjoyed by Germany under the Vienna Convention and "preserve those rights pending its decision on the merits". Germany claims that a dispute as to "whether the United States were obliged to comply and did comply with the Order" necessarily arises out of the interpretation or application of the Convention and thus falls within the

jurisdiction of the Court. Germany argues further that questions "relating to the non-compliance with a decision of the Court under Article 41 para. 1 of the Statute, *e.g.* Provisional Measures, are an integral component of the entire original dispute between the parties". Moreover, Germany contends that its third submission also implicates "in an auxiliary and subsidiary manner . . . the inherent jurisdiction of the Court for claims as closely interrelated with each other as the ones before the Court in the present case".

45. The third submission of Germany concerns issues that arise directly out of the dispute between the Parties before the Court over which the Court has already held that it has jurisdiction (see paragraph 42 above), and which are thus covered by Article I of the Optional Protocol. The Court reaffirms, in this connection, what it said in its Judgment in the *Fisheries Jurisdiction* case, where it declared that in order to consider the dispute in all its aspects, it may also deal with a submission that "is one based on facts subsequent to the filing of the Application, but arising directly out of the question which is the subject-matter of that Application. As such it falls within the scope of the Court's jurisdiction . . ." * * * Where the Court has jurisdiction to decide a case, it also has jurisdiction to deal with submissions requesting it to determine that an order indicating measures which seeks to preserve the rights of the Parties to this dispute has not been complied with.

*

46. The United States objects to the jurisdiction of the Court over the fourth submission in so far as it concerns a request for assurances and guarantees of non-repetition. The United States submits that its "jurisdictional argument [does] not apply to jurisdiction to order cessation of a breach or to order reparation, but is limited to the question of assurances and guarantees . . . [which] are conceptually distinct from reparation". It contends that Germany's fourth submission

"goes beyond any remedy that the Court can or should grant, and should be rejected. The Court's power to decide cases . . . does not extend to the power to order a

State to provide any 'guarantee' intended to confer additional legal rights on the Applicant State . . . The United States does not believe that it can be the role of the Court . . . to impose any obligations that are additional to or that differ in character from those to which the United States consented when it ratified the Vienna Convention".

47. Germany counters this argument by asserting that

"a dispute whether or not the violation of a provision of the Vienna Convention gives rise to a certain remedy is a dispute concerning 'the application and interpretation' of the aforesaid Convention, and thus falls within the scope of Art. I of the Optional Protocol".

Germany notes in this regard that the Court, in its Order of 9 April 1998 in the case concerning the Vienna Convention on Consular Relations (Paraguay v. United States of America), held that

"there exists a dispute as to whether the relief sought by Paraguay is a remedy available under the Vienna Convention, in particular in relation to Articles 5 and 36 thereof; and . . . this is a dispute arising out of the application of the Convention within the meaning of Article I of the Optional Protocol concerning the Compulsory Settlement of Disputes of 24 April 1963" (*I.C.J. Reports 1998*, p. 256, para. 31).

Germany asserts also that its fourth submission arises under principles of State responsibility, according to which Germany is entitled to a "whole range of remedies" as a consequence of the particular violations alleged in this case and that these questions of State responsibility "are clearly within the ambit of the Optional Protocol".

48. The Court considers that a dispute regarding the appropriate remedies for the violation of the Convention alleged by Germany is a dispute that arises out of the interpretation or application of the Convention and thus is within the Court's jurisdiction. Where jurisdiction exists over a dispute on a particular matter, no separate basis for jurisdiction is required by the Court to consider

the remedies a party has requested for the breach of the obligation (*Factory at Chorzów, P.C.I.J., Series A, No. 9*, p. 22). Consequently, the Court has jurisdiction in the present case with respect to the fourth submission of Germany.

* *

49. The United States has argued that the submissions of Germany are inadmissible on various grounds. The Court will consider these objections in the order presented by the United States.

*

50. The United States objects first to Germany's second, third and fourth submissions. According to the United States, these submissions are inadmissible because Germany seeks to have this Court "play the role of ultimate court of appeal in national criminal proceedings", a role which it is not empowered to perform. The United States maintains that many of Germany's arguments, in particular those regarding the rule of "procedural default", ask the Court "to address and correct . . . asserted violations of U.S. law and errors of judgment by U.S. judges" in criminal proceedings in national courts.

51. Germany denies that it requests the Court to act as an appellate criminal court, or that Germany's requests are in any way aimed at interfering with the administration of justice within the United States judicial system. It maintains that it is merely asking the Court to adjudge and declare that the conduct of the United States was inconsistent with its international legal obligations towards Germany under the Vienna Convention, and to draw from this failure certain legal consequences provided for in the international law of State responsibility.

52. The Court does not agree with these arguments of the United States concerning the admissibility of the second, third and fourth German submissions. In the second submission, Germany asks the Court to interpret the scope of Article 36, paragraph 2, of the Vienna Convention; the third submission seeks a finding that the United States violated an Order issued by this Court pursuant to

Article 41 of its Statute; and in Germany's fourth submission, the Court is asked to determine the applicable remedies for the alleged violations of the Convention. Although Germany deals extensively with the practice of American courts as it bears on the application of the Convention, all three submissions seek to require the Court to do no more than apply the relevant rules of international law to the issues in dispute between the Parties to this case. The exercise of this function, expressly mandated by Article 38 of its Statute, does not convert this Court into a court of appeal of national criminal proceedings.

*

53. The United States also argues that Germany's third submission is inadmissible because of the manner in which these proceedings were brought before the Court by Germany. It notes that German consular officials became aware of the LaGrands' cases in 1992, but that the German Government did not express concern or protest to the United States authorities for some six and a half years. It maintains that the issue of the absence of consular notification was not raised by Germany until 22 February 1999, two days before the date scheduled for Karl LaGrand's execution, in a letter from the German Foreign Minister to the Secretary of State of the United States (see paragraph 26 above). Germany then filed the Application instituting these proceedings, together with a request for provisional measures, after normal business hours in the Registry in the evening of 2 March 1999, some 27 hours before the execution of Walter LaGrand (see paragraph 30 above).

54. The United States rejects the contention that Germany found out only seven days before the filing of its Application that the authorities of Arizona knew as early as 1982 that the LaGrands were German nationals; according to the United States, their German nationality was referred to in pre-sentence reports prepared in 1984, which should have been familiar to German consular officers much earlier than 1999, given Germany's claims regarding the vigour and effectiveness of its consular assistance.

55. According to the United States, Germany's late filing compelled the Court to respond to its request for provisional measures by acting *ex parte*, without full information. The United States claims that the procedure followed was inconsistent with the principles of "equality of the Parties" and of giving each Party a sufficient opportunity to be heard, and that this would justify the Court in not addressing Germany's third submission which is predicated wholly upon the Order of 3 March 1999.

56. Germany acknowledges that delay on the part of a claimant State may render an application inadmissible, but maintains that international law does not lay down any specific time-limit in that regard. It contends that it was only seven days before it filed its Application that it became aware of all the relevant facts underlying its claim, in particular, the fact that the authorities of Arizona knew of the German nationality of the LaGrands since 1982. According to Germany, it cannot be accused of negligence in failing to obtain the 1984 pre-sentence reports earlier. It also maintains that in the period between 1992, when it learned of the LaGrands' cases, and the filing of its Application, it engaged in a variety of activities at the diplomatic and consular level. It adds that it had been confident for much of this period that the United States would ultimately rectify the violations of international law involved.

57. The Court recognizes that Germany may be criticized for the manner in which these proceedings were filed and for their timing. The Court recalls, however, that notwithstanding its awareness of the consequences of Germany's filing at such a late date, it nevertheless considered it appropriate to enter the Order of 3 March 1999, given that an irreparable prejudice appeared to be imminent. In view of these considerations, the Court considers that Germany is now entitled to challenge the alleged failure of the United States to comply with the Order. Accordingly, the Court finds that Germany's third submission is admissible.

*

58. The United States argues further that Germany's first submission, as far as it concerns its right to exercise diplomatic protection with respect to its nationals, is inadmissible on the ground that the LaGrands did not exhaust local remedies. The United States maintains that the alleged breach concerned the duty to inform the LaGrands of their right to consular access, and that such a breach could have been remedied at the trial stage, provided it was raised in a timely fashion. The United States contends that when a person fails, for example, to sue in a national court before a statute of limitations has expired, the claim is both procedurally barred in national courts and inadmissible in international tribunals for failure to exhaust local remedies. It adds that the failure of counsel for the LaGrands to raise the breach of the Vienna Convention at the appropriate stage and time of the proceedings does not excuse the non-exhaustion of local remedies. According to the United States, this failure of counsel is imputable to their clients because the law treats defendants and their lawyers as a single entity in terms of their legal positions. Moreover, the State is not accountable for the errors or mistaken strategy by lawyers.

59. Germany responds that international law requires the exhaustion of only those remedies which are legally and practically available. Germany claims that in this case there was no remedy which the LaGrands failed to invoke that would have been available in the specific context of their case. This is so because, prior to 1992, the LaGrands could not resort to the available remedies, since they were unaware of their rights due to failure of the United States authorities to comply with the requirements of the Vienna Convention; thereafter, the "procedural default" rule prevented them from seeking any remedy.

60. The Court notes that it is not disputed that the LaGrands sought to plead the Vienna Convention in United States courts after they learned in 1992 of their rights under the Convention; it is also not disputed that by that date the procedural default rule barred the LaGrands from obtaining any remedy in respect of the violation of those rights. Counsel assigned to the LaGrands failed to raise this point earlier in a timely fashion. However, the United States may not now rely before this Court on this fact in order to preclude the

admissibility of Germany's first submission, as it was the United States itself which had failed to carry our its obligation under the Convention to inform the LaGrand brothers.

*

61. The United States also contends that Germany's submissions are inadmissible on the ground that Germany seeks to have a standard applied to the United States that is different from its own practice. According to the United States, Germany has not shown that its system of criminal justice requires the annulment of criminal convictions where there has been a breach of the duty of consular notification; and that the practice of Germany in similar cases has been to do no more than offer an apology. The United States maintains that it would be contrary to basic principles of administration of justice and equality of the Parties to apply against the United States alleged rules that Germany appears not to accept for itself.

62. Germany denies that it is asking the United States to adhere to standards which Germany itself does not abide by; it maintains that its law and practice is fully in compliance with the standards which it invokes. In this regard, it explains that the German Code of Criminal Procedure provides a ground of appeal where a legal norm, including a norm of international law, is not applied or incorrectly applied and where there is a possibility that the decision was impaired by this fact.

63. The Court need not decide whether this argument of the United States, if true, would result in the inadmissibility of Germany's submissions. Here the evidence adduced by the United States does not justify the conclusion that Germany's own practice fails to conform to the standards it demands from the United States in this litigation. The United States relies on certain German cases to demonstrate that Germany has itself proffered only an apology for violating Article 36 of the Vienna Convention, and that State practice shows that this is the appropriate remedy for such a violation. But the cases concerned entailed relatively light criminal penalties and are not evidence as to German practice where an arrested person, who has

not been informed without delay of his or her rights, is facing a severe penalty as in the present case. It is no doubt the case, as the United States points out, that Article 36 of the Vienna Convention imposes identical obligations on States, irrespective of the gravity of the offence a person may be charged with and of the penalties that may be imposed. However, it does not follow therefrom that the remedies for a violation of this Article must be identical in all situations. While an apology may be an appropriate remedy in some cases, it may in others be insufficient. The Court accordingly finds that this claim of inadmissibility must be rejected.

*

* *

64. Having determined that the Court has jurisdiction, and that the submissions of Germany are admissible, the Court now turns to the merits of each of these four submissions.

* *

65. Germany's first submission requests the Court to adjudge and declare:

"that the United States, by not informing Karl and Walter LaGrand without delay following their arrest of their rights under Article 36 subparagraph 1 *(b)* of the Vienna Convention on Consular Relations, and by depriving Germany of the possibility of rendering consular assistance, which ultimately resulted in the execution of Karl and Walter LaGrand, violated its international legal obligations to Germany, in its own right and in its right of diplomatic protection of its nationals, under Articles 5 and 36 paragraph 1 of the said Convention".

66. Germany claims that the United States violated its obligation under Article 36, paragraph 1 *(b)* to "inform a national of the sending state without delay of his or her right to inform the consular post of his home State of his arrest or detention". Specifically, Germany maintains that the United States violated its international legal obligation to Germany under Article 36, paragraph 1 *(b)*, by

failing to inform the German nationals Karl and Walter LaGrand "without delay" of their rights under that subparagraph.

67. The United States acknowledges, and does not contest Germany's basic claim, that there was a breach of its obligation under Article 36, paragraph 1 *(b)*, of the Convention "promptly to inform the LaGrand brothers that they could ask that a German consular post be notified of their arrest and detention".

68. Germany also claims that the violation by the United States of Article 36, paragraph 1 *(b)*, led to consequential violations of Article 36, paragraph 1 *(a)* and *(c)*. It points out that, when the obligation to inform the arrested person without delay of his or her right to contact the consulate is disregarded, "the other rights contained in Article 36, paragraph 1, become in practice irrelevant, indeed meaningless." Germany maintains that, "[b]y informing the LaGrand brothers of their right to inform the consulate more than 16 years after their arrest, the United States . . . clearly failed to meet the standard of Article 36 [1 *(c)*]". It concludes that, by not preventing the execution of Karl and Walter LaGrand, and by "making irreversible its earlier breaches of Art. 5 and 36 (1) and (2) and causing irreparable harm, the United States violated its obligations under international law".

69. The United States argues that the underlying conduct complained of by Germany is one and the same, namely, the failure to inform the LaGrand brothers as required by Article 36, paragraph 1 *(b)*. Therefore, it disputes any other basis for Germany's claims that other provisions, such as subparagraphs *(a)* and *(c)* of Article 36, paragraph 1, of the Convention, were also violated. The United States asserts that Germany's claims regarding Article 36, paragraph 1 *(a)* and *(c)*, are "particularly misplaced" in that the LaGrands were able to and did communicate freely with consular officials after 1992. There was, in the view of the United States, "no deprivation of Germany's right to provide consular assistance, under Article 5 or Article 36, to Karl or Walter LaGrand" and "Germany's attempt to transform a breach of one obligation into an additional breach of a wholly separate and distinct obligation should be rejected by the Court."

70. In response, Germany asserts that it is "commonplace that one and the same conduct may result in several violations of distinct obligations". Hence, when a detainee's right to notification without delay is violated, he or she cannot establish contact with the consulate, receive visits from consular officers, nor be supported by adequate counsel. "Therefore, violation of this right is bound to imply violation of the other rights . . . [and] later observance of the rights of Article 36, paragraph 1 *(a)* and *(c)*, could not remedy the previous violation of those provisions."

71. Germany further contends that there is a causal relationship between the breach of Article 36 and the ultimate execution of the LaGrand brothers. Germany's inability to render prompt assistance was, in its view, a "direct result of the United States' breach of its Vienna Convention obligations". It is claimed that, had Germany been properly afforded its rights under the Vienna Convention, it would have been able to intervene in time and present a "persuasive mitigation case" which "likely would have saved" the lives of the brothers. Germany believes that, "[h]ad proper notification been given under the Vienna Convention, competent trial counsel certainly would have looked to Germany for assistance in developing this line of mitigating evidence". Moreover, Germany argues that, due to the doctrine of procedural default and the high post-conviction threshold for proving ineffective counsel under United States law, Germany's intervention at a stage later than the trial phase could not "remedy the extreme prejudice created by the counsel appointed to represent the LaGrands".

72. The United States terms these arguments as "suppositions about what might have occurred had the LaGrand brothers been properly informed of the possibility of consular notification". It calls into question Germany's assumption that German consular officials from Los Angeles would rapidly have given extensive assistance to the LaGrands' defence counsel before the 1984 sentencing, and contests that such consular assistance would have affected the outcome of the sentencing proceedings. According to the United States, these arguments "rest on speculation" and do not withstand analysis. Finally, the United States finds it extremely doubtful that the early childhood "mitigating

evidence" mentioned by Germany, if introduced at the trial, would have persuaded the sentencing judge to be lenient, as the brothers' subsequent 17 years of experiences in the United States would have been given at least equal weight. The United States points out, moreover, that such evidence was in fact presented at trial.

73. The Court will first examine the submission Germany advances in its own right. The Court observes, in this connection, that the United States does not deny that it violated paragraph 1 *(b)* in relation to Germany. The Court also notes that as a result of this breach, Germany did not learn until 1992 of the detention, trial and sentencing of the La Grand brothers. The Court concludes therefrom that on the facts of this case, the breach of the United States had the consequence of depriving Germany of the exercise of the rights accorded it under Article 36, paragraph 1 *(a)* and paragraph 1 *(c)*, and thus violated these provisions of the Convention. Although the violation of paragraph 1 *(b)* of Article 36 will not necessarily always result in the breach of the other provisions of this Article, the Court finds that the circumstances of this case compel the opposite conclusion, for the reasons indicated below. In view of this finding, it is not necessary for the Court to deal with Germany's further claim under Article 5 of the Convention.

74. Article 36, paragraph 1, establishes an interrelated régime designed to facilitate the implementation of the system of consular protection. It begins with the basic principle governing consular protection: the right of communication and access (Art. 36, para. 1 *(a)*). This clause is followed by the provision which spells out the modalities of consular notification (Art. 36, para. 1 *(b)*). Finally Article 36, paragraph 1 *(c)*, sets out the measures consular officers may take in rendering consular assistance to their nationals in the custody of the receiving State. It follows that when the sending State is unaware of the detention of its nationals due to the failure of the receiving State to provide the requisite consular notification without delay, which was true in the present case during the period between 1982 and 1992, the sending State has been prevented for all practical purposes from exercising its rights under Article 36,

paragraph 1. It is immaterial for the purposes of the present case whether the LaGrands would have sought consular assistance from Germany, whether Germany would have rendered such assistance, or whether a different verdict would have been rendered. It is sufficient that the Convention conferred these rights, and that Germany and the LaGrands were in effect prevented by the breach of the United States from exercising them, had they so chosen.

*

75. Germany further contends that "the breach of Article 36 by the United States did not only infringe upon the rights of Germany as a State party to the [Vienna] Convention but also entailed a violation of the individual rights of the LaGrand brothers". Invoking its right of diplomatic protection, Germany also seeks relief against the United States on this ground.

Germany maintains that the right to be informed of the rights under Article 36, paragraph 1 *(b)*, of the Vienna Convention, is an individual right of every national of a State party to the Convention who enters the territory of another State party. It submits that this view is supported by the ordinary meaning of the terms of Article 36, paragraph 1 *(b)*, of the Vienna Convention, since the last sentence of that provision speaks of the "rights" under this subparagraph of "the person concerned", i.e., of the foreign national arrested or detained. Germany adds that the provision in Article 36, paragraph 1 *(b)*, according to which it is for the arrested person to decide whether consular notification is to be provided, has the effect of conferring an individual right upon the foreign national concerned. In its view, the context of Article 36 supports this conclusion since it relates to both the concerns of the sending and receiving States and to those of individuals. According to Germany, the *travaux préparatoires* of the Vienna Convention lend further support to this interpretation. In addition, Germany submits that the "United Nations Declaration on the human rights of individuals who are not nationals of the country in which they live," adopted by General Assembly resolution 40/144 on 13 December 1985, confirms the view that the right of access to the consulate of the home State, as well as the information on this right, constitute individual rights of foreign nationals and are to be regarded as human rights of aliens.

76. The United States questions what this additional claim of diplomatic protection contributes to the case and argues that there are no parallels between the present case and cases of diplomatic protection involving the espousal by a State of economic claims of its nationals. The United States maintains that the right of a State to provide consular assistance to nationals detained in another country, and the right of a State to espouse the claims of its nationals through diplomatic protection, are legally different concepts.

The United States contends, furthermore, that rights of consular notification and access under the Vienna Convention are rights of States, and not of individuals, even though these rights may benefit individuals by permitting States to offer them consular assistance. It maintains that the treatment due to individuals under the Convention is inextricably linked to and derived from the right of the State, acting through its consular officer, to communicate with its nationals, and does not constitute a fundamental right or a human right. The United States argues that the fact that Article 36 by its terms recognizes the rights of individuals does not determine the nature of those rights or the remedies required under the Vienna Convention for breaches of that Article. It points out that Article 36 begins with the words "[w]ith a view to facilitating the exercise of consular functions relating to nationals of the sending State," and that this wording gives no support to the notion that the rights and obligations enumerated in paragraph 1 of that Article are intended to ensure that nationals of the sending State have any particular rights or treatment in the context of a criminal prosecution. The *travaux préparatoires* of the Vienna Convention according to the United States, do not reflect a consensus that Article 36 was addressing immutable individual rights, as opposed to individual rights derivative of the rights of States.

77. The Court notes that Article 36, paragraph 1 *(b)*, spells out the obligations the receiving State has towards the detained person and the sending State. It provides that, at the request of the detained person, the receiving State must inform the consular post of the sending State of the individual's detention "without delay". It provides further that any communication by the detained person addressed to the consular post of the sending State must be forwarded to it by authorities of the receiving State "without delay". Significantly, this subparagraph ends with the following language: "The said authorities shall inform the person concerned without delay of *his rights* under this subparagraph" (emphasis added). Moreover, under Article 36, paragraph 1 *(c)*, the sending State's right to provide consular assistance to the detained person may not be exercised "if he expressly opposes such action". The clarity of these provisions, viewed in their context, admits of no doubt. It follows, as has been held on a number of occasions, that the Court must apply these as they stand . * * * Based on the text of these provisions, the Court concludes that Article 36, paragraph 1, creates individual rights, which, by virtue of Article I of the Optional Protocol, may be invoked in this Court by the national State of the detained person. These rights were violated in the present case.

78. At the hearings, Germany further contended that the right of the individual to be informed without delay under Article 36, paragraph 1, of the Vienna Convention was not only an individual right, but has today assumed the character of a human right. In consequence, Germany added, "the character of the right under Article 36 as a human right renders the effectiveness of this provision even more imperative". The Court having found that the United States violated the rights accorded by Article 36, paragraph 1, to the LaGrand brothers, it does not appear necessary to it to consider the additional argument developed by Germany in this regard.

* *

79. The Court will now consider Germany's second submission, in which it asks the Court to adjudge and declare:

"that the United States, by applying rules of its domestic law, in particular the doctrine of procedural default, which barred Karl and Walter LaGrand from raising their claims under the Vienna Convention on Consular Relations, and by ultimately executing them, violated its international legal obligation to Germany under Article 36, paragraph 2, of the Vienna Convention to give full effect to the purposes for which the rights accorded under Article 36 of the said Convention are intended".

80. Germany argues that, under Article 36, paragraph 2, of the Vienna Convention

"the United States is under an obligation to ensure that its municipal 'laws and regulations . . . enable full effect to be given to the purposes for which the rights accorded under this article are intended' [and that it] is in breach of this obligation by upholding rules of domestic law which make it impossible to successfully raise a violation of the right to consular notification in proceedings subsequent to a conviction of a defendant by a jury".

81. Germany points out that the "procedural default" rule is among the rules of United States domestic law whose application make it impossible to invoke a breach of the notification requirement. According to Germany, this rule "is closely connected with the division of labour between federal and state jurisdiction in the United States . . . [where] [c]riminal jurisdiction belongs to the States except in cases provided for in the Constitution". This rule, Germany explains, requires "exhaustion of remedies at the State level before a *habeas corpus* motion can be filed with federal Courts".

Germany emphasizes that it is not the "procedural default" rule as such that is at issue in the present proceedings, but the manner in which it was applied in that it "deprived the brothers of the possibility to raise the violations of their right to consular notification in U.S. criminal proceedings".

82. Furthermore, having examined the relevant United States jurisprudence, Germany contends that the procedural default rule had "made it impossible for the LaGrand brothers to effectively raise the issue of the lack of consular notification after they had at last learned of their rights and established contact with the German consulate in Los Angeles in 1992".

83. Finally, Germany states that it seeks

"[n]othing . . . more than compliance, or, at least, a system in place which does not automatically reproduce violation after violation of the Vienna Convention, only interrupted by the apologies of the United States Government."

84. The United States objects to Germany's second submission, since it considers that "Germany's position goes far beyond the wording of the Convention, the intentions of the parties when it was negotiated, and the practice of States, including Germany's practice".

85. In the view of the United States:

"[t]he Vienna Convention does not require States Party to create a national law remedy permitting individuals to assert claims involving the Convention in criminal proceedings. If there is no such requirement, it cannot violate the Convention to require that efforts to assert such claims be presented to the first court capable of adjudicating them".

According to the United States,

"[i]f there is no obligation under the Convention to create such individual remedies in criminal proceedings, the rule of procedural default—requiring that claims seeking such remedies be asserted at an appropriately early stage—cannot violate the Convention".

86. The United States believes that Article 36, paragraph 2, "has a very clear meaning" and

"means, as it says, that the rights referred to in paragraph 1 shall be exercised in conformity with the laws and regulations of the receiving State, subject to the proviso that said laws and regulations must enable full effect to be given to the purposes for which the rights accorded under the Article are intended".

In the view of the United States,

"[i]n the context of a foreign national in detention, the relevant laws and regulations contemplated by Article 36 (2) are those that may affect the exercise of specific rights under Article 36 (1), such as those addressing the timing of communications, visiting hours, and security in a detention facility. There is no suggestion in the text of Article 36 (2) that the rules of criminal law and procedure under which a defendant would be tried or have his conviction and sentence reviewed by appellate courts are also within the scope of this provision."

87. The United States concludes that Germany's second submission must be rejected "because it is premised on a misinterpretation of Article 36, paragraph 2, which reads the context of the provision—the exercise of a right under paragraph 1—out of existence".

88. Article 36, paragraph 2, of the Vienna Convention reads as follows:

"The rights referred to in paragraph 1 of this article shall be exercised in conformity with the laws and regulations of the receiving State, subject to the proviso, however, that the said laws and regulations must enable full effect to be given to the purposes for which the rights accorded under this article are intended."

89. The Court cannot accept the argument of the United States which proceeds, in part, on the assumption that paragraph 2 of Article 36 applies only to the rights of the sending State and not also to those of the detained individual. The Court has already determined that Article 36, paragraph 1, creates individual rights for the detained person in addition to the rights accorded the sending State, and that consequently the reference to "rights" in paragraph 2 must be read as applying not only to the rights of the sending State, but also to the rights of the detained individual (see paragraph 77 above).

90. Turning now to the "procedural default" rule, the application of which in the present case Germany alleges violated Article 36, paragraph 2, the Court emphasizes that a distinction must be drawn between that rule as such and its specific application in the present case. In itself, the rule does not violate Article 36 of the Vienna Convention. The problem arises when the procedural default rule does not allow the detained individual to challenge a conviction and sentence by claiming, in reliance on Article 36, paragraph 1, of the Convention, that the competent national authorities failed to comply with their obligation to provide the requisite consular information "without delay", thus preventing the person from seeking and obtaining consular assistance from the sending State.

91. In this case, Germany had the right at the request of the LaGrands "to arrange for [their] legal representation" and was eventually able to provide some assistance to that effect. By that time, however, because of the failure of the American authorities to comply with their obligation under Article 36, paragraph 1 *(b)*, the procedural default rule prevented counsel for the LaGrands to effectively challenge their convictions and sentences other than on United States constitutional grounds. As a result, although United States courts could and did examine the professional competence of counsel assigned to the indigent LaGrands by reference to United States constitutional standards, the procedural default rule prevented them from attaching any legal significance to the fact, *inter alia*, that the violation of the rights set forth in Article 36, paragraph 1, prevented Germany, in a timely fashion, from retaining private counsel for them and otherwise assisting in their defence as provided for by the Convention. Under these circumstances, the procedural default rule had the effect of preventing "full effect [from being] given to the purposes for which the rights accorded under this article are intended", and thus violated paragraph 2 of Article 36.

* *

92. The Court will now consider Germany's third submission, in which it asks the Court to adjudge and declare:

"that the United States, by failing to take all measures at its disposal to ensure that Walter LaGrand was not executed pending the final decision of the International Court of Justice on the matter, violated its international legal obligation to comply with the Order on Provisional Measures issued by the Court on 3 March 1999, and to refrain from any action which might interfere with the subject matter of a dispute while judicial proceedings are pending".

93. In its Memorial, Germany contended that "[p]rovisional [m]easures indicated by the International Court of Justice [were] binding by virtue of the law of the United Nations Charter and the Statute of the Court". In support of its position, Germany developed a number of arguments in which it referred to the "principle of effectiveness", to the "procedural prerequisites" for the adoption of provisional measures, to the binding nature of provisional measures as a "necessary consequence of the bindingness of the final decision", to "Article 94 (1), of the United Nations Charter", to "Article 41 (1), of the Statute of the Court" and to the "practice of the Court".

Referring to the duty of the "parties to a dispute before the Court . . . to preserve its subject-matter", Germany added that:

"[a]part from having violated its duties under Art. 94 (1) of the United Nations Charter and Art. 41 (1) of the Statute, the United States has also violated the obligation to refrain from any action which might interfere with the subject-matter of a dispute while judicial proceedings are pending".

At the hearings, Germany further stated the following:

"A judgment by the Court on jurisdiction or merits cannot be treated on exactly the same footing as a provisional measure . . . Article 59 and Article 60 [of the Statute] do not apply to provisional measures or, to be more exact, apply to them only by implication; that is to say, to the extent that such measures, being both incidental and provisional, contribute to the exercise of a judicial function whose end-result is, by definition, the delivery of a judicial decision. There is here an inherent logic in the judicial procedure, and to disregard it would be tantamount, as far as the Parties are concerned, to deviating from the principle of good faith and from what the Ger-

man pleadings call 'the principle of institutional effectiveness' . . . [P]rovisional measures . . . are indeed legal decisions, but they are decisions of procedure . . . Since their decisional nature is, however, implied by the logic of urgency and by the need to safeguard the effectiveness of the proceedings, they accordingly create genuine legal obligations on the part of those to whom they are addressed."

94. Germany claims that the United States committed a threefold violation of the Court's Order of 3 March 1999:

"(1) Immediately after the International Court of Justice had rendered its Order on Provisional Measures, Germany appealed to the U.S. Supreme Court in order to reach a stay of the execution of Walter LaGrand, in accordance with the International Court's Order to the same effect. In the course of these proceedings—and in full knowledge of the Order of the International Court—the Office of the Solicitor General, a section of the U.S. Department of Justice—in a letter to the Supreme Court argued once again that: 'an order of the International Court of Justice indicating provisional measures is not binding and does not furnish a basis for judicial relief'.

This statement of a high-ranking official of the Federal Government . . . had a direct influence on the decision of the Supreme Court. * * *

(2) In the following, the U.S. Supreme Court—an agency of the United States—refused by a majority vote to order that the execution be stayed. In doing so, it rejected the German arguments based essentially on the Order of the International Court of Justice on Provisional Measures . . .

(3) Finally, the Governor of Arizona did not order a stay of the execution of Walter LaGrand although she was vested with the right to do so by the laws of the State of Arizona. Moreover, in the present case, the Arizona Executive Board of Clemency— for the first time in the history of this insti-

tution—had issued a recommendation for a temporary stay, not least in light of the international legal issues involved in the case . . ."

95. The United States argues that it "did what was called for by the Court's 3 March Order, given the extraordinary and unprecedented circumstances in which it was forced to act". It points out in this connection that the United States Government "immediately transmitt[ed] the Order to the Governor of Arizona", that "the United States placed the Order in the hands of the one official who, at that stage, might have had legal authority to stop the execution" and that by a letter from the Legal Counsellor of the United States Embassy in The Hague dated 8 March 1999, it informed the International Court of Justice of all the measures which had been taken in implementation of the Order.

The United States further states that:

"[t]wo central factors constrained the United States ability to act. The first was the extraordinarily short time between issuance of the Court's Order and the time set for the execution of Walter LaGrand . . .

The second constraining factor was the character of the United States of America as a federal republic of divided powers."

96. The United States also alleges that the "terms of the Court's 3 March Order did not create legal obligations binding on [it]". It argues in this respect that "[t]he language used by the Court in the key portions of its Order is not the language used to create binding legal obligations" and that

"the Court does not need here to decide the difficult and controversial legal question of whether its orders indicating provisional measures would be capable of creating international legal obligations if worded in mandatory . . . terms".

It nevertheless maintains that those orders cannot have such effects and, in support of that view, develops arguments concerning "the language and history of Article 41 (1) of the Court's Statute and Article 94 of the Charter of the United Nations", the "Court's

and State practice under these provisions", and the "weight of publicists' commentary".

Concerning Germany's argument based on the "principle of effectiveness", the United States contends that

"[i]n an arena where the concerns and sensitivities of States, and not abstract logic, have informed the drafting of the Court's constitutive documents, it is perfectly understandable that the Court might have the power to issue binding final judgments, but a more circumscribed authority with respect to provisional measures".

Referring to Germany's argument that the United States "violated the obligation to refrain from any action which might interfere with the subject matter of a dispute while judicial proceedings are pending", the United States further asserts that:

"The implications of the rule as presented by Germany are potentially quite dramatic, however. Germany appears to contend that by merely filing a case with the Court, an Applicant can force a Respondent to refrain from continuing any action that the Applicant deems to affect the subject of the dispute. If the law were as Germany contends, the entirety of the Court's rules and practices relating to provisional measures would be surplussage. This is not the law, and this is not how States or this Court have acted in practice."

97. Lastly, the United States states that in any case, "[b]ecause of the press of time stemming from Germany's last-minute filing of the case, basic principles fundamental to the judicial process were not observed in connection with the Court's 3 March Order" and that

"[t]hus, whatever one might conclude regarding a general rule for provisional measures, it would be anomalous—to say the least—for the Court to construe this Order as a source of binding legal obligations".

98. Neither the Permanent Court of International Justice, nor the present Court to date, has been called upon to determine the legal effects of orders made under Article 41

of the Statute. As Germany's third submission refers expressly to an international legal obligation "to comply with the Order on Provisional Measures issued by the Court on 3 March 1999", and as the United States disputes the existence of such an obligation, the Court is now called upon to rule expressly on this question.

99. The dispute which exists between the Parties with regard to this point essentially concerns the interpretation of Article 41, which is worded in identical terms in the Statute of each Court (apart from the respective references to the Council of the League of Nations and the Security Council). This interpretation has been the subject of extensive controversy in the literature. The Court will therefore now proceed to the interpretation of Article 41 of the Statute. It will do so in accordance with customary international law, reflected in Article 31 of the 1969 Vienna Convention on the Law of Treaties. According to paragraph 1 of Article 31, a treaty must be interpreted in good faith in accordance with the ordinary meaning to be given to its terms in their context and in the light of the treaty's object and purpose.

100. The French text of Article 41 reads as follows:

"1. La Cour a le pouvoir *d'indiquer*, si elle estime que les circonstances l'exigent, quelles mesures conservatoires due droit de chacun *doivent* être prises à titre provisoire.

2. En attendant l'arrêt définitif, *l'indication* de ces mesures est immédiatement notifiée aux parties et au Conseil de sécurité." (Emphasis added.)

In this text, the terms "indiquer" and "l'indication" may be deemed to be neutral as to the mandatory character of the measure concerned; by contrast the words "doivent être prises" have an imperative character.

For its part, the English version of Article 41 reads as follows:

"1. The Court shall have the power to *indicate*, if it considers that circumstances so require, any provisional measures which *ought* to be taken to preserve the respective rights of either party.

2. Pending the final decision, notice of the measures *suggested* shall forthwith be given to the parties and to the Security Council." (Emphasis added.)

According to the United States, the use in the English version of "indicate" instead of "order", of "ought" instead of "must" or "shall", and of "suggested" instead of "ordered", is to be understood as implying that decisions under Article 41 lack mandatory effect. It might however be argued, having regard to the fact that in 1920 the French text was the original version, that such terms as "indicate" and "ought" have a meaning equivalent to "order" and "must" or "shall".

101. Finding itself faced with two texts which are not in total harmony, the Court will first of all note that according to Article 92 of the Charter, the Statute "forms an integral part of the present Charter". Under Article 111 of the Charter, the French and English texts of the latter are "equally authentic". The same is equally true of the Statute.

In cases of divergence between the equally authentic versions of the Statute, neither it nor the Charter indicates how to proceed. In the absence of agreement between the parties in this respect, it is appropriate to refer to paragraph 4 of Article 33 of the Vienna Convention on the Law of Treaties, which in the view of the Court again reflects customary international law. This provision reads "when a comparison of the authentic texts discloses a difference of meaning which the application of Articles 31 and 32 does not remove the meaning which best reconciles the texts, having regard to the object and purpose of the treaty, shall be adopted".

The Court will therefore now consider the object and purpose of the Statute together with the context of Article 41.

102. The object and purpose of the Statute is to enable the Court to fulfill the functions provided for therein, and in particular, the basic function of judicial settlement of international disputes by binding decisions in accordance with Article 59 of the Statute. The context in which Article 41 has to be seen within the Statute is to prevent the Court from being hampered in the exercise of its functions because the respective rights of the parties to a dispute before the Court are not preserved. It follows from the object and pur-

pose of the Statute, as well as from the terms of Article 41 when read in their context, that the power to indicate provisional measures entails that such measures should be binding, inasmuch as the power in question is based on the necessity, when the circumstances call for it, to safeguard, and to avoid prejudice to, the rights of the parties as determined by the final judgment of the Court. The contention that provisional measures indicated under Article 41 might not be binding would be contrary to the object and purpose of that Article.

103. A related reason which points to the binding character of orders made under Article 41 and to which the Court attaches importance, is the existence of a principle which has already been recognized by the Permanent Court of International Justice when it spoke of

"the principle universally accepted by international tribunals and likewise laid down in many conventions . . . to the effect that the parties to a case must abstain from any measure capable of exercising a prejudicial effect in regard to the execution of the decision to be given, and, in general, not allow any step of any kind to be taken which might aggravate or extend the dispute" (*Electricity Company of Sofia and Bulgaria, Order of 5 December 1939, P.C.I.J, Series A/B, No. 79*, p. 199).

Furthermore, measures designed to avoid aggravating or extending disputes have frequently been indicated by the Court. They were indicated with the purpose of being implemented. * * *

104. Given the conclusions reached by the Court above in interpreting the text of Article 41 of the Statute in the light of its object and purpose, it does not consider it necessary to resort to the preparatory work in order to determine the meaning of that Article. The Court would nevertheless point out that the preparatory work of the Statute does not preclude the conclusion that orders under Article 41 have binding force.

105. The initial preliminary draft of the Statute of the Permanent Court of International Justice, as prepared by the Committee of Jurists established by the Council of the League of Nations, made no mention of provi-

sional measures. A provision to this effect was inserted only at a later stage in the draft prepared by the Committee, following a proposal from the Brazilian jurist Raul Fernandes.

Basing himself on the Bryan Treaty of 13 October 1914 between the United States and Sweden, Raul Fernandes had submitted the following text:

"Dans le cas où la cause due différend consiste en actes déterminés déjà effectués ou sur le point de l'être, la Cour pourra ordonner, dans le plus bref délai, à titre provisoire, des mesures conservatoires adéquates, en attendant le jugement définitif." (Comité consultatif de juristes, *Procès-verbaux des séances due comité*, 16 juin-24 juillet 1920 (avec annexes), La Haye, 1920, p. 609.)

In its English translation this text read as follows:

"In case the cause of the dispute should consist of certain acts already committed or about to be committed, the Court may, provisionally and with the least possible delay, order adequate protective measures to be taken, pending the final judgment of the Court." (Advisory Committee of Jurists, *Procès-verbaux of the Proceedings of the Committee*, 16 June-24 July 1920 (with Annexes), The Hague, 1920, p. 609.)

The Drafting Committee prepared a new version of this text, to which two main amendments were made: on the one hand, the words "la Cour pourra ordonner" ("the Court may . . . order") were replaced by "la Cour a le pouvoir d'indiquer" ("the Court shall have the power to suggest"), while, on the other, a second paragraph was added providing for notice to be given to the parties and to the Council of the "measures suggested" by the Court. The draft Article 2*bis* as submitted by the Drafting Committee thus read as follows:

"Dans le cas où la cause due différend consiste en un acte effectué ou sur le point de l'être, la Cour a le pouvoir d'indiquer, si elle estime que les circonstances l'exigent, quelles mesures conservatoires due droit de chacun doivent être prises à titre provisoire.

"En attendant son arrêt, cette suggestion de la Cour est immédiatement transmise aux parties et au Conseil." (Comité consultatif de juristes, *Procès-verbaux des séances due comité*, 16 juin-24 juillet 1920 (avec annexes), La Haye, 1920, p. 567-568.)

The English version read:

"If the dispute arises out of an act which has already taken place or which is imminent, the Court shall have the power to suggest, if it considers that circumstances so require, the provisional measures that should be taken to preserve the respective rights of either party.

Pending the final decision, notice of the measures suggested shall forthwith be given to the parties and the Council." (Advisory Committee of Jurists, *Procès-verbaux of the Proceedings of the Committee*, 16 June-24 July 1920 (with Annexes), The Hague, 1920, pp. 567-568.)

The Committee of Jurists eventually adopted a draft Article 39, which amended the former Article 2*bis* only in its French version: in the second paragraph, the words "*cette suggestion*" were replaced in French by the words "*l'indication*".

106. When the draft Article 39 was examined by the Sub-Committee of the Third Committee of the first Assembly of the League of Nations, a number of amendments were considered. Raul Fernandes suggested again to use the word "ordonner" in the French version. The Sub-Committee decided to stay with the word "indiquer", the Chairman of the Sub-Committee observing that the Court lacked the means to execute its decisions. The language of the first paragraph of the English version was then made to conform to the French text: thus the word "suggest" was replaced by "indicate", and "should" by "ought to". However, in the second paragraph of the English version, the phrase "measures suggested" remained unchanged.

The provision thus amended in French and in English by the Sub-Committee was adopted as Article 41 of the Statute of the Perma-

nent Court of International Justice. It passed as such into the Statute of the present Court without any discussion in 1945.

107. The preparatory work of Article 41 shows that the preference given in the French text to "*indiquer*" over "*ordonner*" was motivated by the consideration that the Court did not have the means to assure the execution of its decisions. However, the lack of means of execution and the lack of binding force are two different matters. Hence, the fact that the Court does not itself have the means to ensure the execution of orders made pursuant to Article 41 is not an argument against the binding nature of such orders.

108. The Court finally needs to consider whether Article 94 of the United Nations Charter precludes attributing binding effect to orders indicating provisional measures. That Article reads as follows:

"1. Each Member of the United Nations undertakes to comply with the decision of the International Court of Justice in any case to which it is a party.

2. If any party to a case fails to perform the obligations incumbent upon it under a judgment rendered by the Court, the other party may have recourse to the Security Council, which may, if it deems necessary, make recommendations or decide upon measures to be taken to give effect to the judgment."

The question arises as to the meaning to be attributed to the words "the decision of the International Court of Justice" in paragraph 1 of this Article. This wording could be understood as referring not merely to the Court's judgments but to any decision rendered by it, thus including orders indicating provisional measures. It could also be interpreted to mean only judgments rendered by the Court as provided in paragraph 2 of Article 94. In this regard, the fact that in Articles 56 to 60 of the Court's Statute, both the word "decision" and the word "judgment" are used does little to clarify the matter.

Under the first interpretation of paragraph 1 of Article 94, the text of the paragraph would confirm the binding nature of provisional measures; whereas the second interpretation would in no way preclude their being accorded binding force under Article 41 of the Statute. The Court accordingly concludes that Article 94 of the Charter does not prevent orders made under Article 41 from having a binding character.

109. In short, it is clear that none of the sources of interpretation referred to in the relevant Articles of the Vienna Convention on the Law of Treaties, including the preparatory work, contradict the conclusions drawn from the terms of Article 41 read in their context and in the light of the object and purpose of the Statute. Thus, the Court has reached the conclusion that orders on provisional measures under Article 41 have binding effect.

*

110. The Court will now consider the Order of 3 March 1999. This Order was not a mere exhortation. It had been adopted pursuant to Article 41 of the Statute. This Order was consequently binding in character and created a legal obligation for the United States.

*

111. As regards the question whether the United States has complied with the obligation incumbent upon it as a result of the Order of 3 March 1999, the Court observes that the Order indicated two provisional measures, the first of which states that

"[t]he United States of America should take all measures at its disposal to ensure that Walter LaGrand is not executed pending the final decision in these proceedings, and should inform the Court of all the measures which it has taken in implementation of this Order".

The second measure required the Government of the United States to "transmit this Order to the Governor of the State of Arizona". The information required on the measures taken in implementation of this Order was given to the Court by a letter of 8 March 1999 from the Legal Counsellor of the United States Embassy at The Hague. According to this letter, on 3 March 1999 the State Department had transmitted to the Governor of Arizona a copy of the Court's Order. "In view of the extremely late hour of the receipt of the Court's Order", the letter of 8 March went on to say, "no further steps were feasible".

The United States authorities have thus limited themselves to the mere transmission of the text of the Order to the Governor of Arizona. This certainly met the requirement of the second of the two measures indicated. As to the first measure, the Court notes that it did not create an obligation of result, but that the United States was asked to "take all measures at its disposal to ensure that Walter LaGrand is not executed pending the final decision in these proceedings". The Court agrees that due to the extremely late presentation of the request for provisional measures, there was certainly very little time for the United States authorities to act.

112. The Court observes, nevertheless, that the mere transmission of its Order to the Governor of Arizona without any comment, particularly without even so much as a plea for a temporary stay and an explanation that there is no general agreement on the position of the United States that orders of the International Court of Justice on provisional measures are non-binding, was certainly less than could have been done even in the short time available. The same is true of the United States Solicitor General's categorical statement in his brief letter to the United States Supreme Court that "an order of the International Court of Justice indicating provisional measures is not binding and does not furnish a basis for judicial relief" (see paragraph 33 above). This statement went substantially further than the amicus brief referred to in a mere footnote in his letter, which was filed on behalf of the United States in earlier proceedings before the United States Supreme Court in the case of Angel Francisco Breard (see *Breard* v. *Greene*, United States Supreme Court, 14 April 1998, *International Legal Materials*, Vol. 37 (1988), p. 824; Memorial of Germany, Ann. 34). In that amicus brief, the same Solicitor General had declared less than a year earlier that "there is substantial disagreement among jurists as to whether an ICJ order indicating provisional measures is binding . . . The better reasoned position is that such an order is not binding."

113. It is also noteworthy that the Governor of Arizona, to whom the Court's Order had been transmitted, decided not to give effect to it, even though the Arizona Clemency Board had recommended a stay of execution for Walter LaGrand.

114. Finally, the United States Supreme Court rejected a separate application by Germany for a stay of execution, "[g]iven the tardiness of the pleas and the jurisdictional barriers they implicate". Yet it would have been open to the Supreme Court, as one of its members urged, to grant a preliminary stay, which would have given it "time to consider, after briefing from all interested parties, the jurisdictional and international legal issues involved . . ." (*Federal Republic of Germany et al.* v. *United States et al.*, United States Supreme Court, 3 March 1999).

115. The review of the above steps taken by the authorities of the United States with regard to the Order of the International Court of Justice of 3 March 1999 indicates that the various competent United States authorities failed to take all the steps they could have taken to give effect to the Court's Order. The Order did not require the United States to exercise powers it did not have; but it did impose the obligation to "take all measures at its disposal to ensure that Walter LaGrand is not executed pending the final decision in these proceedings . . .". The Court finds that the United States did not discharge this obligation.

Under these circumstances the Court concludes that the United States has not complied with the Order of 3 March 1999.

116. The Court observes finally that in the third submission Germany requests the Court to adjudge and declare only that the United States violated its international legal obligation to comply with the Order of 3 March 1999; it contains no other request regarding that violation. Moreover, the Court points out that the United States was under great time pressure in this case, due to the circumstances in which Germany had instituted the proceedings. The Court notes moreover that at the time when the United States authorities took their decision the question of the binding character of orders indicating provisional measures had been extensively discussed in the literature, but had not been settled by its jurisprudence. The Court would have taken these factors into consideration had Germany's submission included a claim for indemnification.

* *

117. Finally, the Court will consider Germany's fourth submission, in which it asks the Court to adjudge and declare

"that the United States shall provide Germany an assurance that it will not repeat its unlawful acts and that, in any future cases of detention of or criminal proceedings against German nationals, the United States will ensure in law and practice the effective exercise of the rights under Article 36 of the Vienna Convention on Consular Relations. In particular in cases involving the death penalty, this requires the United States to provide effective review of and remedies for criminal convictions impaired by a violation of the rights under Article 36."

118. Germany states that:

"[c]oncerning the requested assurances and guarantees of non-repetition of the United States, they are appropriate because of the existence of a real risk of repetition and the seriousness of the injury suffered by Germany. Further, the choice of means by which full conformity of the future conduct of the United States with Article 36 of the Vienna Convention is to be ensured, may be left to the United States."

Germany explains that:

"the effective exercise of the right to consular notification embodied in [Article 36,] paragraph 2, requires that, where it cannot be excluded that the judgment was impaired by the violation of the right to consular notification, appellate proceedings allow for a reversal of the judgment and for either a retrial or a re-sentencing".

Finally, Germany points out that its fourth submission has been so worded "as to . . .

leave the choice of means by which to implement the remedy [it seeks] to the United States".

119. In reply, the United States argues as follows:

"Germany's fourth submission is clearly of a wholly different nature than its first three submissions. Each of the first three submissions seeks a judgment and declaration by the Court that a violation of a stated international legal obligation has occurred. Such judgments are at the core of the Court's function, as an aspect of reparation. * * *

In contrast, however, to the character of the relief sought in the first three submissions, the requirement of assurances of non-repetition sought in the fourth submission has no precedent in the jurisprudence of this Court and would exceed the Court's jurisdiction and authority in this case. It is exceptional even as a non-legal undertaking in State practice, and it would be entirely inappropriate for the Court to require such assurances with respect to the duty to inform undertaken in the Consular Convention in the circumstances of this case."

It points out that "U.S. authorities are working energetically to strengthen the regime of consular notification at the state and local level throughout the United States, in order to reduce the chances of cases such as this recurring" and adds that:

"the German request for an assurance as to the duty to inform foreign nationals without delay of their right to consular notification . . . seeks to have the Court require the United States to assure that it will never again fail to inform a German foreign national of his or her right to consular notification",

and that "the Court is aware that the United States is not in a position to provide such an assurance". The United States further contends that it "has already provided appropriate assurances to Germany on this point".

Finally, the United States recalls that:

"[w]ith respect to the alleged breach of Article 36, paragraph 2, . . . Germany seeks an assurance that, 'in any future cases of detention of or criminal proceedings against German nationals, the United States will ensure in law and practice the effective exercise of the rights under Article 36'".

According to the United States,

"[such an assurance] is again absolute in character . . . [and] seeks to create obligations on the United States that exceed those that are contained in the Vienna Convention. For example, the requirement of consular notification under Article 36, paragraph 1 (b), of the Convention applies when a foreign national is arrested, committed to prison or to custody pending trial or detained in any other manner. It does not apply, as the submission would have it, to any future criminal proceedings. That is a new obligation, and it does not arise out of the Vienna Convention."

The United States further observes that:

"[e]ven if this Court were to agree that, as a result of the application of procedural default with respect to the claims of the LaGrands, the United States committed a second internationally wrongful act, it should limit that judgment to the application of that law in the particular case of the LaGrands. It should resist the invitation to require an absolute assurance as to the application of U.S. domestic law in all such future cases. The imposition of such an additional obligation on the United States would . . . be unprecedented in international jurisprudence and would exceed the Court's authority and jurisdiction."

120. The Court observes that in its fourth submission Germany seeks several assurances. First it seeks a straightforward assurance that the United States will not repeat its unlawful acts. This request does not specify the means by which non-repetition is to be assured.

Additionally, Germany seeks from the United States that

"in any future cases of detention of or criminal proceedings against German nationals, the United States will ensure in law and practice the effective exercise of the rights under Article 36 of the Vienna Convention on Consular Relations".

This request goes further, for, by referring to the law of the United States, it appears to require specific measures as a means of preventing recurrence.

Germany finally requests that

"[i]n particular in cases involving the death penalty, this requires the United States to provide effective review of and remedies for criminal convictions impaired by a violation of the rights under Article 36".

This request goes even further, since it is directed entirely towards securing specific measures in cases involving the death penalty.

121. Turning first to the general demand for an assurance of non-repetition, the Court observes that it has been informed by the United States of the "substantial measures [which it is taking] aimed at preventing any recurrence" of the breach of Article 36, paragraph 1 (b). Throughout these proceedings, oral as well as written, the United States has insisted that it "keenly appreciates the importance of the Vienna Convention's consular notification obligation for foreign citizens in the United States as well as for United States citizens travelling and living abroad"; that "effective compliance with the consular notification requirements of Article 36 of the Vienna Convention requires constant effort and attention"; and that

"the Department of State is working intensively to improve understanding of and compliance with consular notification and access requirements throughout the United States, so as to guard against future violations of these requirements".

The United States points out that

"[t]his effort has included the January 1998 publication of a booklet entitled 'Consular Notification and Access: Instructions for Federal, State and Local Law Enforcement and Other Officials Regarding Foreign Nationals in the United States and the Rights of Consular Officials to Assist Them', and development of a small reference card designed to be carried by individual arresting officers."

According to the United States, it is estimated that until now over 60,000 copies of the brochure as well as over 400,000 copies of the pocket card have been distributed to federal, state and local law enforcement and judicial officials throughout the United States. The United States is also conducting training programmes reaching out to all levels of government. In the Department of State a permanent office to focus on United States and foreign compliance with consular notification and access requirements has been created.

122. Germany has stated that it "does not consider the so-called 'assurances' offered by the Respondent as adequate". It says

"[v]iolations of Article 36 followed by death sentences and executions cannot be remedied by apologies or the distribution of leaflets. An effective remedy requires certain changes in U.S. law and practice".

In order to illustrate its point, Germany has presented to the Court a "[l]ist of German nationals detained after January 1, 1998, who claim not to have been informed of their consular rights". The United States has criticized this list as misleading and inaccurate.

123. The Court notes that the United States has acknowledged that, in the case of the LaGrand brothers, it did not comply with its obligations to give consular notification. The United States has presented an apology to Germany for this breach. The Court considers however that an apology is not sufficient in this case, as it would not be in other cases where foreign nationals have not been

advised without delay of their rights under Article 36, paragraph 1, of the Vienna Convention and have been subjected to prolonged detention or sentenced to severe penalties.

In this respect, the Court has taken note of the fact that the United States repeated in all phases of these proceedings that it is carrying out a vast and detailed programme in order to ensure compliance by its competent authorities at the federal as well as at the state and local levels with its obligation under Article 36 of the Vienna Convention.

124. The United States has provided the Court with information, which it considers important, on its programme. If a State, in proceedings before this Court, repeatedly refers to substantial activities which it is carrying out in order to achieve compliance with certain obligations under a treaty, then this expresses a commitment to follow through with the efforts in this regard. The programme in question certainly cannot provide an assurance that there will never again be a failure by the United States to observe the obligation of notification under Article 36 of the Vienna Convention. But no State could give such a guarantee and Germany does not seek it. The Court considers that the commitment expressed by the United States to ensure implementation of the specific measures adopted in performance of its obligations under Article 36, paragraph 1 *(b)*, must be regarded as meeting Germany's request for a general assurance of non-repetition.

125. The Court will now examine the other assurances sought by Germany in its fourth submission. The Court observes in this regard that it can determine the existence of a violation of an international obligation. If necessary, it can also hold that a domestic law has been the cause of this violation. In the present case the Court has made its findings of violations of the obligations under Article 36 of the Vienna Convention when it dealt with the first and the second submission of Germany. But it has not found that a United States law, whether substantive or procedural in character, is inherently inconsistent with the obligations undertaken by the United States in the Vienna Convention. In the present case the violation of Article 36,

paragraph 2, was caused by the circumstances in which the procedural default rule was applied, and not by the rule as such.

In the present proceedings the United States has apologized to Germany for the breach of Article 36, paragraph 1, and Germany has not requested material reparation for this injury to itself and to the LaGrand brothers. It does, however, seek assurances:

"that, in any future cases of detention or of criminal proceedings against German nationals, the United States will ensure in law and practice the effective exercise of the rights under Article 36 of the Vienna Convention on Consular Relations",

and that

"[i]n particular in cases involving the death penalty, this requires the United States to provide effective review of and remedies for criminal convictions impaired by the violation of the rights under Article 36".

The Court considers in this respect that if the United States, notwithstanding its commitment referred to in paragraph 124 above, should fail in its obligation of consular notification to the detriment of German nationals, an apology would not suffice in cases where the individuals concerned have been subjected to prolonged detention or convicted and sentenced to severe penalties. In the case of such a conviction and sentence, it would be incumbent upon the United States to allow the review and reconsideration of the conviction and sentence by taking account of the violation of the rights set forth in the Convention. This obligation can be carried out in various ways. The choice of means must be left to the United States.

126. Given the foregoing ruling by the Court regarding the obligation of the United States under certain circumstances to review and reconsider convictions and sentences, the Court need not examine Germany's further argument which seeks to found a like obligation on the contention that the right of a detained person to be informed without delay pursuant to Article 36, paragraph 1, of the

Vienna Convention is not only an individual right but has today assumed the character of a human right.

127. In reply to the fourth submission of Germany, the Court will therefore limit itself to taking note of the commitment undertaken by the United States to ensure implementation of the specific measures adopted in performance of its obligations under Article 36, paragraph 1 *(b)*, of the Vienna Convention, as well as the aforementioned duty of the United States to address violations of that Convention should they still occur in spite of its efforts to achieve compliance.

* * *

128. For these reasons,

THE COURT,

(1) By fourteen votes to one,

Finds that it has jurisdiction, on the basis of Article I of the Optional Protocol concerning the Compulsory Settlement of Disputes to the Vienna Convention on Consular Relations of 24 April 1963, to entertain the Application filed by the Federal Republic of Germany on 2 March 1999; * * *

(2) *(a)* By thirteen votes to two,

Finds that the first submission of the Federal Republic of Germany is admissible; * * *

(b) By fourteen votes to one,

Finds that the second submission of the Federal Republic of Germany is admissible; * * *

(c) By twelve votes to three,

Finds that the third submission of the Federal Republic of Germany is admissible; * * *

(d) By fourteen votes to one,

Finds that the fourth submission of the Federal Republic of Germany is admissible; * * *

(3) By fourteen votes to one,

Finds that, by not informing Karl and Walter LaGrand without delay following their arrest of their rights under Article 36, paragraph 1 *(b)*, of the Convention, and by thereby depriving the Federal Republic of Ger-

many of the possibility, in a timely fashion, to render the assistance provided for by the Convention to the individuals concerned, the United States of America breached its obligations to the Federal Republic of Germany and to the LaGrand brothers under Article 36, paragraph 1; * * *

(4) By fourteen votes to one,

Finds that, by not permitting the review and reconsideration, in the light of the rights set forth in the Convention, of the convictions and sentences of the LaGrand brothers after the violations referred to in paragraph (3) above had been established, the United States of America breached its obligation to the Federal Republic of Germany and to the LaGrand brothers under Article 36, paragraph 2, of the Convention; * * *

(5) By thirteen votes to two,

Finds that, by failing to take all measures at its disposal to ensure that Walter LaGrand was not executed pending the final decision of the International Court of Justice in the case, the United States of America breached the obligation incumbent upon it under the Order indicating provisional measures issued by the Court on 3 March 1999; * * *

(6) Unanimously,

Takes note of the commitment undertaken by the United States of America to ensure implementation of the specific measures adopted in performance of its obligations under Article 36, paragraph 1 *(b)*, of the Convention; and *finds* that this commitment must be regarded as meeting the Federal Republic of Germany's request for a general assurance of non-repetition;

(7) By fourteen votes to one,

Finds that should nationals of the Federal Republic of Germany nonetheless be sentenced to severe penalties, without their rights under Article 36, paragraph 1 *(b)*, of the Convention having been respected, the United States of America, by means of its own choosing, shall allow the review and reconsideration of the conviction and sentence by taking account of the violation of the rights set forth in that Convention. * * *

Table of Cases

Entries appearing in bold type also appear in Part II: Judicial Decisions Relating to Part I.
See page 387 for the Table of Cases for Part II.

Index